Lecture Notes in Computer Science   13662

More information about this series at https://link.springer.com/bookseries/558

Shai Avidan · Gabriel Brostow ·
Moustapha Cissé · Giovanni Maria Farinella ·
Tal Hassner (Eds.)

Computer Vision – ECCV 2022

17th European Conference
Tel Aviv, Israel, October 23–27, 2022
Proceedings, Part II

 Springer

Editors
Shai Avidan
Tel Aviv University
Tel Aviv, Israel

Gabriel Brostow 🆔
University College London
London, UK

Moustapha Cissé
Google AI
Accra, Ghana

Giovanni Maria Farinella 🆔
University of Catania
Catania, Italy

Tal Hassner 🆔
Facebook (United States)
Menlo Park, CA, USA

ISSN 0302-9743   ISSN 1611-3349 (electronic)
Lecture Notes in Computer Science
ISBN 978-3-031-20085-4   ISBN 978-3-031-20086-1 (eBook)
https://doi.org/10.1007/978-3-031-20086-1

This Springer imprint is published by the registered company Springer Nature Switzerland AG
The registered company address is: Gewerbestrasse 11, 6330 Cham, Switzerland

Foreword

Organizing the European Conference on Computer Vision (ECCV 2022) in Tel-Aviv during a global pandemic was no easy feat. The uncertainty level was extremely high, and decisions had to be postponed to the last minute. Still, we managed to plan things just in time for ECCV 2022 to be held in person. Participation in physical events is crucial to stimulating collaborations and nurturing the culture of the Computer Vision community.

There were many people who worked hard to ensure attendees enjoyed the best science at the 16th edition of ECCV. We are grateful to the Program Chairs Gabriel Brostow and Tal Hassner, who went above and beyond to ensure the ECCV reviewing process ran smoothly. The scientific program includes dozens of workshops and tutorials in addition to the main conference and we would like to thank Leonid Karlinsky and Tomer Michaeli for their hard work. Finally, special thanks to the web chairs Lorenzo Baraldi and Kosta Derpanis, who put in extra hours to transfer information fast and efficiently to the ECCV community.

We would like to express gratitude to our generous sponsors and the Industry Chairs, Dimosthenis Karatzas and Chen Sagiv, who oversaw industry relations and proposed new ways for academia-industry collaboration and technology transfer. It's great to see so much industrial interest in what we're doing!

Authors' draft versions of the papers appeared online with open access on both the Computer Vision Foundation (CVF) and the European Computer Vision Association (ECVA) websites as with previous ECCVs. Springer, the publisher of the proceedings, has arranged for archival publication. The final version of the papers is hosted by SpringerLink, with active references and supplementary materials. It benefits all potential readers that we offer both a free and citeable version for all researchers, as well as an authoritative, citeable version for SpringerLink readers. Our thanks go to Ronan Nugent from Springer, who helped us negotiate this agreement. Last but not least, we wish to thank Eric Mortensen, our publication chair, whose expertise made the process smooth.

October 2022

Rita Cucchiara
Jiří Matas
Amnon Shashua
Lihi Zelnik-Manor

Preface

Welcome to the proceedings of the European Conference on Computer Vision (ECCV 2022). This was a hybrid edition of ECCV as we made our way out of the COVID-19 pandemic. The conference received 5804 valid paper submissions, compared to 5150 submissions to ECCV 2020 (a 12.7% increase) and 2439 in ECCV 2018. 1645 submissions were accepted for publication (28%) and, of those, 157 (2.7% overall) as orals.

846 of the submissions were desk-rejected for various reasons. Many of them because they revealed author identity, thus violating the double-blind policy. This violation came in many forms: some had author names with the title, others added acknowledgments to specific grants, yet others had links to their github account where their name was visible. Tampering with the LaTeX template was another reason for automatic desk rejection.

ECCV 2022 used the traditional CMT system to manage the entire double-blind reviewing process. Authors did not know the names of the reviewers and vice versa. Each paper received at least 3 reviews (except 6 papers that received only 2 reviews), totalling more than 15,000 reviews.

Handling the review process at this scale was a significant challenge. To ensure that each submission received as fair and high-quality reviews as possible, we recruited more than 4719 reviewers (in the end, 4719 reviewers did at least one review). Similarly we recruited more than 276 area chairs (eventually, only 276 area chairs handled a batch of papers). The area chairs were selected based on their technical expertise and reputation, largely among people who served as area chairs in previous top computer vision and machine learning conferences (ECCV, ICCV, CVPR, NeurIPS, etc.).

Reviewers were similarly invited from previous conferences, and also from the pool of authors. We also encouraged experienced area chairs to suggest additional chairs and reviewers in the initial phase of recruiting. The median reviewer load was five papers per reviewer, while the average load was about four papers, because of the emergency reviewers. The area chair load was 35 papers, on average.

Conflicts of interest between authors, area chairs, and reviewers were handled largely automatically by the CMT platform, with some manual help from the Program Chairs. Reviewers were allowed to describe themselves as senior reviewer (load of 8 papers to review) or junior reviewers (load of 4 papers). Papers were matched to area chairs based on a subject-area affinity score computed in CMT and an affinity score computed by the Toronto Paper Matching System (TPMS). TPMS is based on the paper's full text. An area chair handling each submission would bid for preferred expert reviewers, and we balanced load and prevented conflicts.

The assignment of submissions to area chairs was relatively smooth, as was the assignment of submissions to reviewers. A small percentage of reviewers were not happy with their assignments in terms of subjects and self-reported expertise. This is an area for improvement, although it's interesting that many of these cases were reviewers hand-picked by AC's. We made a later round of reviewer recruiting, targeted at the list of authors of papers submitted to the conference, and had an excellent response which helped provide enough emergency reviewers. In the end, all but six papers received at least 3 reviews.

The challenges of the reviewing process are in line with past experiences at ECCV 2020. As the community grows, and the number of submissions increases, it becomes ever more challenging to recruit enough reviewers and ensure a high enough quality of reviews. Enlisting authors by default as reviewers might be one step to address this challenge.

Authors were given a week to rebut the initial reviews, and address reviewers' concerns. Each rebuttal was limited to a single pdf page with a fixed template.

The Area Chairs then led discussions with the reviewers on the merits of each submission. The goal was to reach consensus, but, ultimately, it was up to the Area Chair to make a decision. The decision was then discussed with a buddy Area Chair to make sure decisions were fair and informative. The entire process was conducted virtually with no in-person meetings taking place.

The Program Chairs were informed in cases where the Area Chairs overturned a decisive consensus reached by the reviewers, and pushed for the meta-reviews to contain details that explained the reasoning for such decisions. Obviously these were the most contentious cases, where reviewer inexperience was the most common reported factor.

Once the list of accepted papers was finalized and released, we went through the laborious process of plagiarism (including self-plagiarism) detection. A total of 4 accepted papers were rejected because of that.

Finally, we would like to thank our Technical Program Chair, Pavel Lifshits, who did tremendous work behind the scenes, and we thank the tireless CMT team.

October 2022

Gabriel Brostow
Giovanni Maria Farinella
Moustapha Cissé
Shai Avidan
Tal Hassner

Organization

General Chairs

Rita Cucchiara   University of Modena and Reggio Emilia, Italy
Jiří Matas   Czech Technical University in Prague, Czech
                                   Republic
Amnon Shashua   Hebrew University of Jerusalem, Israel
Lihi Zelnik-Manor   Technion – Israel Institute of Technology, Israel

Program Chairs

Shai Avidan   Tel-Aviv University, Israel
Gabriel Brostow   University College London, UK
Moustapha Cissé   Google AI, Ghana
Giovanni Maria Farinella   University of Catania, Italy
Tal Hassner   Facebook AI, USA

Program Technical Chair

Pavel Lifshits   Technion – Israel Institute of Technology, Israel

Workshops Chairs

Leonid Karlinsky   IBM Research, Israel
Tomer Michaeli   Technion – Israel Institute of Technology, Israel
Ko Nishino   Kyoto University, Japan

Tutorial Chairs

Thomas Pock   Graz University of Technology, Austria
Natalia Neverova   Facebook AI Research, UK

Demo Chair

Bohyung Han   Seoul National University, Korea

Social and Student Activities Chairs

Tatiana Tommasi   Italian Institute of Technology, Italy
Sagie Benaim   University of Copenhagen, Denmark

Diversity and Inclusion Chairs

Xi Yin   Facebook AI Research, USA
Bryan Russell   Adobe, USA

Communications Chairs

Lorenzo Baraldi   University of Modena and Reggio Emilia, Italy
Kosta Derpanis   York University & Samsung AI Centre Toronto,
                               Canada

Industrial Liaison Chairs

Dimosthenis Karatzas   Universitat Autònoma de Barcelona, Spain
Chen Sagiv   SagivTech, Israel

Finance Chair

Gerard Medioni   University of Southern California & Amazon,
                               USA

Publication Chair

Eric Mortensen   MiCROTEC, USA

Area Chairs

Lourdes Agapito   University College London, UK
Zeynep Akata   University of Tübingen, Germany
Naveed Akhtar   University of Western Australia, Australia
Karteek Alahari   Inria Grenoble Rhône-Alpes, France
Alexandre Alahi   École polytechnique fédérale de Lausanne,
                               Switzerland
Pablo Arbelaez   Universidad de Los Andes, Columbia
Antonis A. Argyros   University of Crete & Foundation for Research
                               and Technology-Hellas, Crete
Yuki M. Asano   University of Amsterdam, The Netherlands
Kalle Åström   Lund University, Sweden
Hadar Averbuch-Elor   Cornell University, USA

Hossein Azizpour	KTH Royal Institute of Technology, Sweden
Vineeth N. Balasubramanian	Indian Institute of Technology, Hyderabad, India
Lamberto Ballan	University of Padova, Italy
Adrien Bartoli	Université Clermont Auvergne, France
Horst Bischof	Graz University of Technology, Austria
Matthew B. Blaschko	KU Leuven, Belgium
Federica Bogo	Meta Reality Labs Research, Switzerland
Katherine Bouman	California Institute of Technology, USA
Edmond Boyer	Inria Grenoble Rhône-Alpes, France
Michael S. Brown	York University, Canada
Vittorio Caggiano	Meta AI Research, USA
Neill Campbell	University of Bath, UK
Octavia Camps	Northeastern University, USA
Duygu Ceylan	Adobe Research, USA
Ayan Chakrabarti	Google Research, USA
Tat-Jen Cham	Nanyang Technological University, Singapore
Antoni Chan	City University of Hong Kong, Hong Kong, China
Manmohan Chandraker	NEC Labs America, USA
Xinlei Chen	Facebook AI Research, USA
Xilin Chen	Institute of Computing Technology, Chinese Academy of Sciences, China
Dongdong Chen	Microsoft Cloud AI, USA
Chen Chen	University of Central Florida, USA
Ondrej Chum	Vision Recognition Group, Czech Technical University in Prague, Czech Republic
John Collomosse	Adobe Research & University of Surrey, UK
Camille Couprie	Facebook, France
David Crandall	Indiana University, USA
Daniel Cremers	Technical University of Munich, Germany
Marco Cristani	University of Verona, Italy
Canton Cristian	Facebook AI Research, USA
Dengxin Dai	ETH Zurich, Switzerland
Dima Damen	University of Bristol, UK
Kostas Daniilidis	University of Pennsylvania, USA
Trevor Darrell	University of California, Berkeley, USA
Andrew Davison	Imperial College London, UK
Tali Dekel	Weizmann Institute of Science, Israel
Alessio Del Bue	Istituto Italiano di Tecnologia, Italy
Weihong Deng	Beijing University of Posts and Telecommunications, China
Konstantinos Derpanis	Ryerson University, Canada
Carl Doersch	DeepMind, UK

Matthijs Douze	Facebook AI Research, USA
Mohamed Elhoseiny	King Abdullah University of Science and Technology, Saudi Arabia
Sergio Escalera	University of Barcelona, Spain
Yi Fang	New York University, USA
Ryan Farrell	Brigham Young University, USA
Alireza Fathi	Google, USA
Christoph Feichtenhofer	Facebook AI Research, USA
Basura Fernando	Agency for Science, Technology and Research (A*STAR), Singapore
Vittorio Ferrari	Google Research, Switzerland
Andrew W. Fitzgibbon	Graphcore, UK
David J. Fleet	University of Toronto, Canada
David Forsyth	University of Illinois at Urbana-Champaign, USA
David Fouhey	University of Michigan, USA
Katerina Fragkiadaki	Carnegie Mellon University, USA
Friedrich Fraundorfer	Graz University of Technology, Austria
Oren Freifeld	Ben-Gurion University, Israel
Thomas Funkhouser	Google Research & Princeton University, USA
Yasutaka Furukawa	Simon Fraser University, Canada
Fabio Galasso	Sapienza University of Rome, Italy
Jürgen Gall	University of Bonn, Germany
Chuang Gan	Massachusetts Institute of Technology, USA
Zhe Gan	Microsoft, USA
Animesh Garg	University of Toronto, Vector Institute, Nvidia, Canada
Efstratios Gavves	University of Amsterdam, The Netherlands
Peter Gehler	Amazon, Germany
Theo Gevers	University of Amsterdam, The Netherlands
Bernard Ghanem	King Abdullah University of Science and Technology, Saudi Arabia
Ross B. Girshick	Facebook AI Research, USA
Georgia Gkioxari	Facebook AI Research, USA
Albert Gordo	Facebook, USA
Stephen Gould	Australian National University, Australia
Venu Madhav Govindu	Indian Institute of Science, India
Kristen Grauman	Facebook AI Research & UT Austin, USA
Abhinav Gupta	Carnegie Mellon University & Facebook AI Research, USA
Mohit Gupta	University of Wisconsin-Madison, USA
Hu Han	Institute of Computing Technology, Chinese Academy of Sciences, China

Bohyung Han	Seoul National University, Korea
Tian Han	Stevens Institute of Technology, USA
Emily Hand	University of Nevada, Reno, USA
Bharath Hariharan	Cornell University, USA
Ran He	Institute of Automation, Chinese Academy of Sciences, China
Otmar Hilliges	ETH Zurich, Switzerland
Adrian Hilton	University of Surrey, UK
Minh Hoai	Stony Brook University, USA
Yedid Hoshen	Hebrew University of Jerusalem, Israel
Timothy Hospedales	University of Edinburgh, UK
Gang Hua	Wormpex AI Research, USA
Di Huang	Beihang University, China
Jing Huang	Facebook, USA
Jia-Bin Huang	Facebook, USA
Nathan Jacobs	Washington University in St. Louis, USA
C. V. Jawahar	International Institute of Information Technology, Hyderabad, India
Herve Jegou	Facebook AI Research, France
Neel Joshi	Microsoft Research, USA
Armand Joulin	Facebook AI Research, France
Frederic Jurie	University of Caen Normandie, France
Fredrik Kahl	Chalmers University of Technology, Sweden
Yannis Kalantidis	NAVER LABS Europe, France
Evangelos Kalogerakis	University of Massachusetts, Amherst, USA
Sing Bing Kang	Zillow Group, USA
Yosi Keller	Bar Ilan University, Israel
Margret Keuper	University of Mannheim, Germany
Tae-Kyun Kim	Imperial College London, UK
Benjamin Kimia	Brown University, USA
Alexander Kirillov	Facebook AI Research, USA
Kris Kitani	Carnegie Mellon University, USA
Iasonas Kokkinos	Snap Inc. & University College London, UK
Vladlen Koltun	Apple, USA
Nikos Komodakis	University of Crete, Crete
Piotr Koniusz	Australian National University, Australia
Philipp Kraehenbuehl	University of Texas at Austin, USA
Dilip Krishnan	Google, USA
Ajay Kumar	Hong Kong Polytechnic University, Hong Kong, China
Junseok Kwon	Chung-Ang University, Korea
Jean-Francois Lalonde	Université Laval, Canada

Ivan Laptev	Inria Paris, France
Laura Leal-Taixé	Technical University of Munich, Germany
Erik Learned-Miller	University of Massachusetts, Amherst, USA
Gim Hee Lee	National University of Singapore, Singapore
Seungyong Lee	Pohang University of Science and Technology, Korea
Zhen Lei	Institute of Automation, Chinese Academy of Sciences, China
Bastian Leibe	RWTH Aachen University, Germany
Hongdong Li	Australian National University, Australia
Fuxin Li	Oregon State University, USA
Bo Li	University of Illinois at Urbana-Champaign, USA
Yin Li	University of Wisconsin-Madison, USA
Ser-Nam Lim	Meta AI Research, USA
Joseph Lim	University of Southern California, USA
Stephen Lin	Microsoft Research Asia, China
Dahua Lin	The Chinese University of Hong Kong, Hong Kong, China
Si Liu	Beihang University, China
Xiaoming Liu	Michigan State University, USA
Ce Liu	Microsoft, USA
Zicheng Liu	Microsoft, USA
Yanxi Liu	Pennsylvania State University, USA
Feng Liu	Portland State University, USA
Yebin Liu	Tsinghua University, China
Chen Change Loy	Nanyang Technological University, Singapore
Huchuan Lu	Dalian University of Technology, China
Cewu Lu	Shanghai Jiao Tong University, China
Oisin Mac Aodha	University of Edinburgh, UK
Dhruv Mahajan	Facebook, USA
Subhransu Maji	University of Massachusetts, Amherst, USA
Atsuto Maki	KTH Royal Institute of Technology, Sweden
Arun Mallya	NVIDIA, USA
R. Manmatha	Amazon, USA
Iacopo Masi	Sapienza University of Rome, Italy
Dimitris N. Metaxas	Rutgers University, USA
Ajmal Mian	University of Western Australia, Australia
Christian Micheloni	University of Udine, Italy
Krystian Mikolajczyk	Imperial College London, UK
Anurag Mittal	Indian Institute of Technology, Madras, India
Philippos Mordohai	Stevens Institute of Technology, USA
Greg Mori	Simon Fraser University & Borealis AI, Canada

Vittorio Murino	Istituto Italiano di Tecnologia, Italy
P. J. Narayanan	International Institute of Information Technology, Hyderabad, India
Ram Nevatia	University of Southern California, USA
Natalia Neverova	Facebook AI Research, UK
Richard Newcombe	Facebook, USA
Cuong V. Nguyen	Florida International University, USA
Bingbing Ni	Shanghai Jiao Tong University, China
Juan Carlos Niebles	Salesforce & Stanford University, USA
Ko Nishino	Kyoto University, Japan
Jean-Marc Odobez	Idiap Research Institute, École polytechnique fédérale de Lausanne, Switzerland
Francesca Odone	University of Genova, Italy
Takayuki Okatani	Tohoku University & RIKEN Center for Advanced Intelligence Project, Japan
Manohar Paluri	Facebook, USA
Guan Pang	Facebook, USA
Maja Pantic	Imperial College London, UK
Sylvain Paris	Adobe Research, USA
Jaesik Park	Pohang University of Science and Technology, Korea
Hyun Soo Park	The University of Minnesota, USA
Omkar M. Parkhi	Facebook, USA
Deepak Pathak	Carnegie Mellon University, USA
Georgios Pavlakos	University of California, Berkeley, USA
Marcello Pelillo	University of Venice, Italy
Marc Pollefeys	ETH Zurich & Microsoft, Switzerland
Jean Ponce	Inria, France
Gerard Pons-Moll	University of Tübingen, Germany
Fatih Porikli	Qualcomm, USA
Victor Adrian Prisacariu	University of Oxford, UK
Petia Radeva	University of Barcelona, Spain
Ravi Ramamoorthi	University of California, San Diego, USA
Deva Ramanan	Carnegie Mellon University, USA
Vignesh Ramanathan	Facebook, USA
Nalini Ratha	State University of New York at Buffalo, USA
Tammy Riklin Raviv	Ben-Gurion University, Israel
Tobias Ritschel	University College London, UK
Emanuele Rodola	Sapienza University of Rome, Italy
Amit K. Roy-Chowdhury	University of California, Riverside, USA
Michael Rubinstein	Google, USA
Olga Russakovsky	Princeton University, USA

Mathieu Salzmann	École polytechnique fédérale de Lausanne, Switzerland
Dimitris Samaras	Stony Brook University, USA
Aswin Sankaranarayanan	Carnegie Mellon University, USA
Imari Sato	National Institute of Informatics, Japan
Yoichi Sato	University of Tokyo, Japan
Shin'ichi Satoh	National Institute of Informatics, Japan
Walter Scheirer	University of Notre Dame, USA
Bernt Schiele	Max Planck Institute for Informatics, Germany
Konrad Schindler	ETH Zurich, Switzerland
Cordelia Schmid	Inria & Google, France
Alexander Schwing	University of Illinois at Urbana-Champaign, USA
Nicu Sebe	University of Trento, Italy
Greg Shakhnarovich	Toyota Technological Institute at Chicago, USA
Eli Shechtman	Adobe Research, USA
Humphrey Shi	University of Oregon & University of Illinois at Urbana-Champaign & Picsart AI Research, USA
Jianbo Shi	University of Pennsylvania, USA
Roy Shilkrot	Massachusetts Institute of Technology, USA
Mike Zheng Shou	National University of Singapore, Singapore
Kaleem Siddiqi	McGill University, Canada
Richa Singh	Indian Institute of Technology Jodhpur, India
Greg Slabaugh	Queen Mary University of London, UK
Cees Snoek	University of Amsterdam, The Netherlands
Yale Song	Facebook AI Research, USA
Yi-Zhe Song	University of Surrey, UK
Bjorn Stenger	Rakuten Institute of Technology
Abby Stylianou	Saint Louis University, USA
Akihiro Sugimoto	National Institute of Informatics, Japan
Chen Sun	Brown University, USA
Deqing Sun	Google, USA
Kalyan Sunkavalli	Adobe Research, USA
Ying Tai	Tencent YouTu Lab, China
Ayellet Tal	Technion – Israel Institute of Technology, Israel
Ping Tan	Simon Fraser University, Canada
Siyu Tang	ETH Zurich, Switzerland
Chi-Keung Tang	Hong Kong University of Science and Technology, Hong Kong, China
Radu Timofte	University of Würzburg, Germany & ETH Zurich, Switzerland
Federico Tombari	Google, Switzerland & Technical University of Munich, Germany

James Tompkin   Brown University, USA
Lorenzo Torresani   Dartmouth College, USA
Alexander Toshev   Apple, USA
Du Tran   Facebook AI Research, USA
Anh T. Tran   VinAI, Vietnam
Zhuowen Tu   University of California, San Diego, USA
Georgios Tzimiropoulos   Queen Mary University of London, UK
Jasper Uijlings   Google Research, Switzerland
Jan C. van Gemert   Delft University of Technology, The Netherlands
Gul Varol   Ecole des Ponts ParisTech, France
Nuno Vasconcelos   University of California, San Diego, USA
Mayank Vatsa   Indian Institute of Technology Jodhpur, India
Ashok Veeraraghavan   Rice University, USA
Jakob Verbeek   Facebook AI Research, France
Carl Vondrick   Columbia University, USA
Ruiping Wang   Institute of Computing Technology, Chinese
                               Academy of Sciences, China
Xinchao Wang   National University of Singapore, Singapore
Liwei Wang   The Chinese University of Hong Kong,
                               Hong Kong, China
Chaohui Wang   Université Paris-Est, France
Xiaolong Wang   University of California, San Diego, USA
Christian Wolf   NAVER LABS Europe, France
Tao Xiang   University of Surrey, UK
Saining Xie   Facebook AI Research, USA
Cihang Xie   University of California, Santa Cruz, USA
Zeki Yalniz   Facebook, USA
Ming-Hsuan Yang   University of California, Merced, USA
Angela Yao   National University of Singapore, Singapore
Shaodi You   University of Amsterdam, The Netherlands
Stella X. Yu   University of California, Berkeley, USA
Junsong Yuan   State University of New York at Buffalo, USA
Stefanos Zafeiriou   Imperial College London, UK
Amir Zamir   École polytechnique fédérale de Lausanne,
                               Switzerland
Lei Zhang   Alibaba & Hong Kong Polytechnic University,
                               Hong Kong, China
Lei Zhang   International Digital Economy Academy (IDEA),
                               China
Pengchuan Zhang   Meta AI, USA
Bolei Zhou   University of California, Los Angeles, USA
Yuke Zhu   University of Texas at Austin, USA

Todd Zickler   Harvard University, USA
Wangmeng Zuo   Harbin Institute of Technology, China

Technical Program Committee

Davide Abati
Soroush Abbasi
  Koohpayegani
Amos L. Abbott
Rameen Abdal
Rabab Abdelfattah
Sahar Abdelnabi
Hassan Abu Alhaija
Abulikemu Abuduweili
Ron Abutbul
Hanno Ackermann
Aikaterini Adam
Kamil Adamczewski
Ehsan Adeli
Vida Adeli
Donald Adjeroh
Arman Afrasiyabi
Akshay Agarwal
Sameer Agarwal
Abhinav Agarwalla
Vaibhav Aggarwal
Sara Aghajanzadeh
Susmit Agrawal
Antonio Agudo
Touqeer Ahmad
Sk Miraj Ahmed
Chaitanya Ahuja
Nilesh A. Ahuja
Abhishek Aich
Shubhra Aich
Noam Aigerman
Arash Akbarinia
Peri Akiva
Derya Akkaynak
Emre Aksan
Arjun R. Akula
Yuval Alaluf
Stephan Alaniz
Paul Albert
Cenek Albl

Filippo Aleotti
Konstantinos P.
  Alexandridis
Motasem Alfarra
Mohsen Ali
Thiemo Alldieck
Hadi Alzayer
Liang An
Shan An
Yi An
Zhulin An
Dongsheng An
Jie An
Xiang An
Saket Anand
Cosmin Ancuti
Juan Andrade-Cetto
Alexander Andreopoulos
Bjoern Andres
Jerone T. A. Andrews
Shivangi Aneja
Anelia Angelova
Dragomir Anguelov
Rushil Anirudh
Oron Anschel
Rao Muhammad Anwer
Djamila Aouada
Evlampios Apostolidis
Srikar Appalaraju
Nikita Araslanov
Andre Araujo
Eric Arazo
Dawit Mureja Argaw
Anurag Arnab
Aditya Arora
Chetan Arora
Sunpreet S. Arora
Alexey Artemov
Muhammad Asad
Kumar Ashutosh

Sinem Aslan
Vishal Asnani
Mahmoud Assran
Amir Atapour-Abarghouei
Nikos Athanasiou
Ali Athar
ShahRukh Athar
Sara Atito
Souhaib Attaiki
Matan Atzmon
Mathieu Aubry
Nicolas Audebert
Tristan T.
  Aumentado-Armstrong
Melinos Averkiou
Yannis Avrithis
Stephane Ayache
Mehmet Aygün
Seyed Mehdi
  Ayyoubzadeh
Hossein Azizpour
George Azzopardi
Mallikarjun B. R.
Yunhao Ba
Abhishek Badki
Seung-Hwan Bae
Seung-Hwan Baek
Seungryul Baek
Piyush Nitin Bagad
Shai Bagon
Gaetan Bahl
Shikhar Bahl
Sherwin Bahmani
Haoran Bai
Lei Bai
Jiawang Bai
Haoyue Bai
Jinbin Bai
Xiang Bai
Xuyang Bai

Yang Bai
Yuanchao Bai
Ziqian Bai
Sungyong Baik
Kevin Bailly
Max Bain
Federico Baldassarre
Wele Gedara Chaminda
    Bandara
Biplab Banerjee
Pratyay Banerjee
Sandipan Banerjee
Jihwan Bang
Antyanta Bangunharcana
Aayush Bansal
Ankan Bansal
Siddhant Bansal
Wentao Bao
Zhipeng Bao
Amir Bar
Manel Baradad Jurjo
Lorenzo Baraldi
Danny Barash
Daniel Barath
Connelly Barnes
Ioan Andrei Bârsan
Steven Basart
Dina Bashkirova
Chaim Baskin
Peyman Bateni
Anil Batra
Sebastiano Battiato
Ardhendu Behera
Harkirat Behl
Jens Behley
Vasileios Belagiannis
Boulbaba Ben Amor
Emanuel Ben Baruch
Abdessamad Ben Hamza
Gil Ben-Artzi
Assia Benbihi
Fabian Benitez-Quiroz
Guy Ben-Yosef
Philipp Benz
Alexander W. Bergman

Urs Bergmann
Jesus Bermudez-Cameo
Stefano Berretti
Gedas Bertasius
Zachary Bessinger
Petra Bevandić
Matthew Beveridge
Lucas Beyer
Yash Bhalgat
Suvaansh Bhambri
Samarth Bharadwaj
Gaurav Bharaj
Aparna Bharati
Bharat Lal Bhatnagar
Uttaran Bhattacharya
Apratim Bhattacharyya
Brojeshwar Bhowmick
Ankan Kumar Bhunia
Ayan Kumar Bhunia
Qi Bi
Sai Bi
Michael Bi Mi
Gui-Bin Bian
Jia-Wang Bian
Shaojun Bian
Pia Bideau
Mario Bijelic
Hakan Bilen
Guillaume-Alexandre
    Bilodeau
Alexander Binder
Tolga Birdal
Vighnesh N. Birodkar
Sandika Biswas
Andreas Blattmann
Janusz Bobulski
Giuseppe Boccignone
Vishnu Boddeti
Navaneeth Bodla
Moritz Böhle
Aleksei Bokhovkin
Sam Bond-Taylor
Vivek Boominathan
Shubhankar Borse
Mark Boss

Andrea Bottino
Adnane Boukhayma
Fadi Boutros
Nicolas C. Boutry
Richard S. Bowen
Ivaylo Boyadzhiev
Aidan Boyd
Yuri Boykov
Aljaz Bozic
Behzad Bozorgtabar
Eric Brachmann
Samarth Brahmbhatt
Gustav Bredell
Francois Bremond
Joel Brogan
Andrew Brown
Thomas Brox
Marcus A. Brubaker
Robert-Jan Bruintjes
Yuqi Bu
Anders G. Buch
Himanshu Buckchash
Mateusz Buda
Ignas Budvytis
José M. Buenaposada
Marcel C. Bühler
Tu Bui
Adrian Bulat
Hannah Bull
Evgeny Burnaev
Andrei Bursuc
Benjamin Busam
Sergey N. Buzykanov
Wonmin Byeon
Fabian Caba
Martin Cadik
Guanyu Cai
Minjie Cai
Qing Cai
Zhongang Cai
Qi Cai
Yancheng Cai
Shen Cai
Han Cai
Jiarui Cai

Bowen Cai
Mu Cai
Qin Cai
Ruojin Cai
Weidong Cai
Weiwei Cai
Yi Cai
Yujun Cai
Zhiping Cai
Akin Caliskan
Lilian Calvet
Baris Can Cam
Necati Cihan Camgoz
Tommaso Campari
Dylan Campbell
Ziang Cao
Ang Cao
Xu Cao
Zhiwen Cao
Shengcao Cao
Song Cao
Weipeng Cao
Xiangyong Cao
Xiaochun Cao
Yue Cao
Yunhao Cao
Zhangjie Cao
Jiale Cao
Yang Cao
Jiajiong Cao
Jie Cao
Jinkun Cao
Lele Cao
Yulong Cao
Zhiguo Cao
Chen Cao
Razvan Caramalau
Marlène Careil
Gustavo Carneiro
Joao Carreira
Dan Casas
Paola Cascante-Bonilla
Angela Castillo
Francisco M. Castro
Pedro Castro

Luca Cavalli
George J. Cazenavette
Oya Celiktutan
Hakan Cevikalp
Sri Harsha C. H.
Sungmin Cha
Geonho Cha
Menglei Chai
Lucy Chai
Yuning Chai
Zenghao Chai
Anirban Chakraborty
Deep Chakraborty
Rudrasis Chakraborty
Souradeep Chakraborty
Kelvin C. K. Chan
Chee Seng Chan
Paramanand Chandramouli
Arjun Chandrasekaran
Kenneth Chaney
Dongliang Chang
Huiwen Chang
Peng Chang
Xiaojun Chang
Jia-Ren Chang
Hyung Jin Chang
Hyun Sung Chang
Ju Yong Chang
Li-Jen Chang
Qi Chang
Wei-Yi Chang
Yi Chang
Nadine Chang
Hanqing Chao
Pradyumna Chari
Dibyadip Chatterjee
Chiranjoy Chattopadhyay
Siddhartha Chaudhuri
Zhengping Che
Gal Chechik
Lianggangxu Chen
Qi Alfred Chen
Brian Chen
Bor-Chun Chen
Bo-Hao Chen

Bohong Chen
Bin Chen
Ziliang Chen
Cheng Chen
Chen Chen
Chaofeng Chen
Xi Chen
Haoyu Chen
Xuanhong Chen
Wei Chen
Qiang Chen
Shi Chen
Xianyu Chen
Chang Chen
Changhuai Chen
Hao Chen
Jie Chen
Jianbo Chen
Jingjing Chen
Jun Chen
Kejiang Chen
Mingcai Chen
Nenglun Chen
Qifeng Chen
Ruoyu Chen
Shu-Yu Chen
Weidong Chen
Weijie Chen
Weikai Chen
Xiang Chen
Xiuyi Chen
Xingyu Chen
Yaofo Chen
Yueting Chen
Yu Chen
Yunjin Chen
Yuntao Chen
Yun Chen
Zhenfang Chen
Zhuangzhuang Chen
Chu-Song Chen
Xiangyu Chen
Zhuo Chen
Chaoqi Chen
Shizhe Chen

Xiaotong Chen
Xiaozhi Chen
Dian Chen
Defang Chen
Dingfan Chen
Ding-Jie Chen
Ee Heng Chen
Tao Chen
Yixin Chen
Wei-Ting Chen
Lin Chen
Guang Chen
Guangyi Chen
Guanying Chen
Guangyao Chen
Hwann-Tzong Chen
Junwen Chen
Jiacheng Chen
Jianxu Chen
Hui Chen
Kai Chen
Kan Chen
Kevin Chen
Kuan-Wen Chen
Weihua Chen
Zhang Chen
Liang-Chieh Chen
Lele Chen
Liang Chen
Fanglin Chen
Zehui Chen
Minghui Chen
Minghao Chen
Xiaokang Chen
Qian Chen
Jun-Cheng Chen
Qi Chen
Qingcai Chen
Richard J. Chen
Runnan Chen
Rui Chen
Shuo Chen
Sentao Chen
Shaoyu Chen
Shixing Chen

Shuai Chen
Shuya Chen
Sizhe Chen
Simin Chen
Shaoxiang Chen
Zitian Chen
Tianlong Chen
Tianshui Chen
Min-Hung Chen
Xiangning Chen
Xin Chen
Xinghao Chen
Xuejin Chen
Xu Chen
Xuxi Chen
Yunlu Chen
Yanbei Chen
Yuxiao Chen
Yun-Chun Chen
Yi-Ting Chen
Yi-Wen Chen
Yinbo Chen
Yiran Chen
Yuanhong Chen
Yubei Chen
Yuefeng Chen
Yuhua Chen
Yukang Chen
Zerui Chen
Zhaoyu Chen
Zhen Chen
Zhenyu Chen
Zhi Chen
Zhiwei Chen
Zhixiang Chen
Long Chen
Bowen Cheng
Jun Cheng
Yi Cheng
Jingchun Cheng
Lechao Cheng
Xi Cheng
Yuan Cheng
Ho Kei Cheng
Kevin Ho Man Cheng

Jiacheng Cheng
Kelvin B. Cheng
Li Cheng
Mengjun Cheng
Zhen Cheng
Qingrong Cheng
Tianheng Cheng
Harry Cheng
Yihua Cheng
Yu Cheng
Ziheng Cheng
Soon Yau Cheong
Anoop Cherian
Manuela Chessa
Zhixiang Chi
Naoki Chiba
Julian Chibane
Kashyap Chitta
Tai-Yin Chiu
Hsu-kuang Chiu
Wei-Chen Chiu
Sungmin Cho
Donghyeon Cho
Hyeon Cho
Yooshin Cho
Gyusang Cho
Jang Hyun Cho
Seungju Cho
Nam Ik Cho
Sunghyun Cho
Hanbyel Cho
Jaesung Choe
Jooyoung Choi
Chiho Choi
Changwoon Choi
Jongwon Choi
Myungsub Choi
Dooseop Choi
Jonghyun Choi
Jinwoo Choi
Jun Won Choi
Min-Kook Choi
Hongsuk Choi
Janghoon Choi
Yoon-Ho Choi

Yukyung Choi
Jaegul Choo
Ayush Chopra
Siddharth Choudhary
Subhabrata Choudhury
Vasileios Choutas
Ka-Ho Chow
Pinaki Nath Chowdhury
Sammy Christen
Anders Christensen
Grigorios Chrysos
Hang Chu
Wen-Hsuan Chu
Peng Chu
Qi Chu
Ruihang Chu
Wei-Ta Chu
Yung-Yu Chuang
Sanghyuk Chun
Se Young Chun
Antonio Cinà
Ramazan Gokberk Cinbis
Javier Civera
Albert Clapés
Ronald Clark
Brian S. Clipp
Felipe Codevilla
Daniel Coelho de Castro
Niv Cohen
Forrester Cole
Maxwell D. Collins
Robert T. Collins
Marc Comino Trinidad
Runmin Cong
Wenyan Cong
Maxime Cordy
Marcella Cornia
Enric Corona
Huseyin Coskun
Luca Cosmo
Dragos Costea
Davide Cozzolino
Arun C. S. Kumar
Aiyu Cui
Qiongjie Cui

Quan Cui
Shuhao Cui
Yiming Cui
Ying Cui
Zijun Cui
Jiali Cui
Jiequan Cui
Yawen Cui
Zhen Cui
Zhaopeng Cui
Jack Culpepper
Xiaodong Cun
Ross Cutler
Adam Czajka
Ali Dabouei
Konstantinos M. Dafnis
Manuel Dahnert
Tao Dai
Yuchao Dai
Bo Dai
Mengyu Dai
Hang Dai
Haixing Dai
Peng Dai
Pingyang Dai
Qi Dai
Qiyu Dai
Yutong Dai
Naser Damer
Zhiyuan Dang
Mohamed Daoudi
Ayan Das
Abir Das
Debasmit Das
Deepayan Das
Partha Das
Sagnik Das
Soumi Das
Srijan Das
Swagatam Das
Avijit Dasgupta
Jim Davis
Adrian K. Davison
Homa Davoudi
Laura Daza

Matthias De Lange
Shalini De Mello
Marco De Nadai
Christophe De
    Vleeschouwer
Alp Dener
Boyang Deng
Congyue Deng
Bailin Deng
Yong Deng
Ye Deng
Zhuo Deng
Zhijie Deng
Xiaoming Deng
Jiankang Deng
Jinhong Deng
Jingjing Deng
Liang-Jian Deng
Siqi Deng
Xiang Deng
Xueqing Deng
Zhongying Deng
Karan Desai
Jean-Emmanuel Deschaud
Aniket Anand Deshmukh
Neel Dey
Helisa Dhamo
Prithviraj Dhar
Amaya Dharmasiri
Yan Di
Xing Di
Ousmane A. Dia
Haiwen Diao
Xiaolei Diao
Gonçalo José Dias Pais
Abdallah Dib
Anastasios Dimou
Changxing Ding
Henghui Ding
Guodong Ding
Yaqing Ding
Shuangrui Ding
Yuhang Ding
Yikang Ding
Shouhong Ding

Haisong Ding
Hui Ding
Jiahao Ding
Jian Ding
Jian-Jiun Ding
Shuxiao Ding
Tianyu Ding
Wenhao Ding
Yuqi Ding
Yi Ding
Yuzhen Ding
Zhengming Ding
Tan Minh Dinh
Vu Dinh
Christos Diou
Mandar Dixit
Bao Gia Doan
Khoa D. Doan
Dzung Anh Doan
Debi Prosad Dogra
Nehal Doiphode
Chengdong Dong
Bowen Dong
Zhenxing Dong
Hang Dong
Xiaoyi Dong
Haoye Dong
Jiangxin Dong
Shichao Dong
Xuan Dong
Zhen Dong
Shuting Dong
Jing Dong
Li Dong
Ming Dong
Nanqing Dong
Qiulei Dong
Runpei Dong
Siyan Dong
Tian Dong
Wei Dong
Xiaomeng Dong
Xin Dong
Xingbo Dong
Yuan Dong

Samuel Dooley
Gianfranco Doretto
Michael Dorkenwald
Keval Doshi
Zhaopeng Dou
Xiaotian Dou
Hazel Doughty
Ahmad Droby
Iddo Drori
Jie Du
Yong Du
Dawei Du
Dong Du
Ruoyi Du
Yuntao Du
Xuefeng Du
Yilun Du
Yuming Du
Radhika Dua
Haodong Duan
Jiafei Duan
Kaiwen Duan
Peiqi Duan
Ye Duan
Haoran Duan
Jiali Duan
Amanda Duarte
Abhimanyu Dubey
Shiv Ram Dubey
Florian Dubost
Lukasz Dudziak
Shivam Duggal
Justin M. Dulay
Matteo Dunnhofer
Chi Nhan Duong
Thibaut Durand
Mihai Dusmanu
Ujjal Kr Dutta
Debidatta Dwibedi
Isht Dwivedi
Sai Kumar Dwivedi
Takeharu Eda
Mark Edmonds
Alexei A. Efros
Thibaud Ehret

Max Ehrlich
Mahsa Ehsanpour
Iván Eichhardt
Farshad Einabadi
Marvin Eisenberger
Hazim Kemal Ekenel
Mohamed El Banani
Ismail Elezi
Moshe Eliasof
Alaa El-Nouby
Ian Endres
Francis Engelmann
Deniz Engin
Chanho Eom
Dave Epstein
Maria C. Escobar
Victor A. Escorcia
Carlos Esteves
Sungmin Eum
Bernard J. E. Evans
Ivan Evtimov
Fevziye Irem Eyiokur
    Yaman
Matteo Fabbri
Sébastien Fabbro
Gabriele Facciolo
Masud Fahim
Bin Fan
Hehe Fan
Deng-Ping Fan
Aoxiang Fan
Chen-Chen Fan
Qi Fan
Zhaoxin Fan
Haoqi Fan
Heng Fan
Hongyi Fan
Linxi Fan
Baojie Fan
Jiayuan Fan
Lei Fan
Quanfu Fan
Yonghui Fan
Yingruo Fan
Zhiwen Fan

Zicong Fan
Sean Fanello
Jiansheng Fang
Chaowei Fang
Yuming Fang
Jianwu Fang
Jin Fang
Qi Fang
Shancheng Fang
Tian Fang
Xianyong Fang
Gongfan Fang
Zhen Fang
Hui Fang
Jiemin Fang
Le Fang
Pengfei Fang
Xiaolin Fang
Yuxin Fang
Zhaoyuan Fang
Ammarah Farooq
Azade Farshad
Zhengcong Fei
Michael Felsberg
Wei Feng
Chen Feng
Fan Feng
Andrew Feng
Xin Feng
Zheyun Feng
Ruicheng Feng
Mingtao Feng
Qianyu Feng
Shangbin Feng
Chun-Mei Feng
Zunlei Feng
Zhiyong Feng
Martin Fergie
Mustansar Fiaz
Marco Fiorucci
Michael Firman
Hamed Firooz
Volker Fischer
Corneliu O. Florea
Georgios Floros

Wolfgang Foerstner
Gianni Franchi
Jean-Sebastien Franco
Simone Frintrop
Anna Fruehstueck
Changhong Fu
Chaoyou Fu
Cheng-Yang Fu
Chi-Wing Fu
Deqing Fu
Huan Fu
Jun Fu
Kexue Fu
Ying Fu
Jianlong Fu
Jingjing Fu
Qichen Fu
Tsu-Jui Fu
Xueyang Fu
Yang Fu
Yanwei Fu
Yonggan Fu
Wolfgang Fuhl
Yasuhisa Fujii
Kent Fujiwara
Marco Fumero
Takuya Funatomi
Isabel Funke
Dario Fuoli
Antonino Furnari
Matheus A. Gadelha
Akshay Gadi Patil
Adrian Galdran
Guillermo Gallego
Silvano Galliani
Orazio Gallo
Leonardo Galteri
Matteo Gamba
Yiming Gan
Sujoy Ganguly
Harald Ganster
Boyan Gao
Changxin Gao
Daiheng Gao
Difei Gao

Chen Gao
Fei Gao
Lin Gao
Wei Gao
Yiming Gao
Junyu Gao
Guangyu Ryan Gao
Haichang Gao
Hongchang Gao
Jialin Gao
Jin Gao
Jun Gao
Katelyn Gao
Mingchen Gao
Mingfei Gao
Pan Gao
Shangqian Gao
Shanghua Gao
Xitong Gao
Yunhe Gao
Zhanning Gao
Elena Garces
Nuno Cruz Garcia
Noa Garcia
Guillermo
   Garcia-Hernando
Isha Garg
Rahul Garg
Sourav Garg
Quentin Garrido
Stefano Gasperini
Kent Gauen
Chandan Gautam
Shivam Gautam
Paul Gay
Chunjiang Ge
Shiming Ge
Wenhang Ge
Yanhao Ge
Zheng Ge
Songwei Ge
Weifeng Ge
Yixiao Ge
Yuying Ge
Shijie Geng

Zhengyang Geng
Kyle A. Genova
Georgios Georgakis
Markos Georgopoulos
Marcel Geppert
Shabnam Ghadar
Mina Ghadimi Atigh
Deepti Ghadiyaram
Maani Ghaffari Jadidi
Sedigh Ghamari
Zahra Gharaee
Michaël Gharbi
Golnaz Ghiasi
Reza Ghoddoosian
Soumya Suvra Ghosal
Adhiraj Ghosh
Arthita Ghosh
Pallabi Ghosh
Soumyadeep Ghosh
Andrew Gilbert
Igor Gilitschenski
Jhony H. Giraldo
Andreu Girbau Xalabarder
Rohit Girdhar
Sharath Girish
Xavier Giro-i-Nieto
Raja Giryes
Thomas Gittings
Nikolaos Gkanatsios
Ioannis Gkioulekas
Abhiram
    Gnanasambandam
Aurele T. Gnanha
Clement L. J. C. Godard
Arushi Goel
Vidit Goel
Shubham Goel
Zan Gojcic
Aaron K. Gokaslan
Tejas Gokhale
S. Alireza Golestaneh
Thiago L. Gomes
Nuno Goncalves
Boqing Gong
Chen Gong

Yuanhao Gong
Guoqiang Gong
Jingyu Gong
Rui Gong
Yu Gong
Mingming Gong
Neil Zhenqiang Gong
Xun Gong
Yunye Gong
Yihong Gong
Cristina I. González
Nithin Gopalakrishnan
    Nair
Gaurav Goswami
Jianping Gou
Shreyank N. Gowda
Ankit Goyal
Helmut Grabner
Patrick L. Grady
Ben Graham
Eric Granger
Douglas R. Gray
Matej Grcić
David Griffiths
Jinjin Gu
Yun Gu
Shuyang Gu
Jianyang Gu
Fuqiang Gu
Jiatao Gu
Jindong Gu
Jiaqi Gu
Jinwei Gu
Jiaxin Gu
Geonmo Gu
Xiao Gu
Xinqian Gu
Xiuye Gu
Yuming Gu
Zhangxuan Gu
Dayan Guan
Junfeng Guan
Qingji Guan
Tianrui Guan
Shanyan Guan

Denis A. Gudovskiy
Ricardo Guerrero
Pierre-Louis Guhur
Jie Gui
Liangyan Gui
Liangke Gui
Benoit Guillard
Erhan Gundogdu
Manuel Günther
Jingcai Guo
Yuanfang Guo
Junfeng Guo
Chenqi Guo
Dan Guo
Hongji Guo
Jia Guo
Jie Guo
Minghao Guo
Shi Guo
Yanhui Guo
Yangyang Guo
Yuan-Chen Guo
Yilu Guo
Yiluan Guo
Yong Guo
Guangyu Guo
Haiyun Guo
Jinyang Guo
Jianyuan Guo
Pengsheng Guo
Pengfei Guo
Shuxuan Guo
Song Guo
Tianyu Guo
Qing Guo
Qiushan Guo
Wen Guo
Xiefan Guo
Xiaohu Guo
Xiaoqing Guo
Yufei Guo
Yuhui Guo
Yuliang Guo
Yunhui Guo
Yanwen Guo

Akshita Gupta
Ankush Gupta
Kamal Gupta
Kartik Gupta
Ritwik Gupta
Rohit Gupta
Siddharth Gururani
Fredrik K. Gustafsson
Abner Guzman Rivera
Vladimir Guzov
Matthew A. Gwilliam
Jung-Woo Ha
Marc Habermann
Isma Hadji
Christian Haene
Martin Hahner
Levente Hajder
Alexandros Haliassos
Emanuela Haller
Bumsub Ham
Abdullah J. Hamdi
Shreyas Hampali
Dongyoon Han
Chunrui Han
Dong-Jun Han
Dong-Sig Han
Guangxing Han
Zhizhong Han
Ruize Han
Jiaming Han
Jin Han
Ligong Han
Xian-Hua Han
Xiaoguang Han
Yizeng Han
Zhi Han
Zhenjun Han
Zhongyi Han
Jungong Han
Junlin Han
Kai Han
Kun Han
Sungwon Han
Songfang Han
Wei Han

Xiao Han
Xintong Han
Xinzhe Han
Yahong Han
Yan Han
Zongbo Han
Nicolai Hani
Rana Hanocka
Niklas Hanselmann
Nicklas A. Hansen
Hong Hanyu
Fusheng Hao
Yanbin Hao
Shijie Hao
Udith Haputhanthri
Mehrtash Harandi
Josh Harguess
Adam Harley
David M. Hart
Atsushi Hashimoto
Ali Hassani
Mohammed Hassanin
Yana Hasson
Joakim Bruslund Haurum
Bo He
Kun He
Chen He
Xin He
Fazhi He
Gaoqi He
Hao He
Haoyu He
Jiangpeng He
Hongliang He
Qian He
Xiangteng He
Xuming He
Yannan He
Yuhang He
Yang He
Xiangyu He
Nanjun He
Pan He
Sen He
Shengfeng He

Songtao He
Tao He
Tong He
Wei He
Xuehai He
Xiaoxiao He
Ying He
Yisheng He
Ziwen He
Peter Hedman
Felix Heide
Yacov Hel-Or
Paul Henderson
Philipp Henzler
Byeongho Heo
Jae-Pil Heo
Miran Heo
Sachini A. Herath
Stephane Herbin
Pedro Hermosilla Casajus
Monica Hernandez
Charles Herrmann
Roei Herzig
Mauricio Hess-Flores
Carlos Hinojosa
Tobias Hinz
Tsubasa Hirakawa
Chih-Hui Ho
Lam Si Tung Ho
Jennifer Hobbs
Derek Hoiem
Yannick Hold-Geoffroy
Aleksander Holynski
Cheeun Hong
Fa-Ting Hong
Hanbin Hong
Guan Zhe Hong
Danfeng Hong
Lanqing Hong
Xiaopeng Hong
Xin Hong
Jie Hong
Seungbum Hong
Cheng-Yao Hong
Seunghoon Hong

Yi Hong
Yuan Hong
Yuchen Hong
Anthony Hoogs
Maxwell C. Horton
Kazuhiro Hotta
Qibin Hou
Tingbo Hou
Junhui Hou
Ji Hou
Qiqi Hou
Rui Hou
Ruibing Hou
Zhi Hou
Henry Howard-Jenkins
Lukas Hoyer
Wei-Lin Hsiao
Chiou-Ting Hsu
Anthony Hu
Brian Hu
Yusong Hu
Hexiang Hu
Haoji Hu
Di Hu
Hengtong Hu
Haigen Hu
Lianyu Hu
Hanzhe Hu
Jie Hu
Junlin Hu
Shizhe Hu
Jian Hu
Zhiming Hu
Juhua Hu
Peng Hu
Ping Hu
Ronghang Hu
MengShun Hu
Tao Hu
Vincent Tao Hu
Xiaoling Hu
Xinting Hu
Xiaolin Hu
Xuefeng Hu
Xiaowei Hu

Yang Hu
Yueyu Hu
Zeyu Hu
Zhongyun Hu
Binh-Son Hua
Guoliang Hua
Yi Hua
Linzhi Huang
Qiusheng Huang
Bo Huang
Chen Huang
Hsin-Ping Huang
Ye Huang
Shuangping Huang
Zeng Huang
Buzhen Huang
Cong Huang
Heng Huang
Hao Huang
Qidong Huang
Huaibo Huang
Chaoqin Huang
Feihu Huang
Jiahui Huang
Jingjia Huang
Kun Huang
Lei Huang
Sheng Huang
Shuaiyi Huang
Siyu Huang
Xiaoshui Huang
Xiaoyang Huang
Yan Huang
Yihao Huang
Ying Huang
Ziling Huang
Xiaoke Huang
Yifei Huang
Haiyang Huang
Zhewei Huang
Jin Huang
Haibin Huang
Jiaxing Huang
Junjie Huang
Keli Huang

Lang Huang
Lin Huang
Luojie Huang
Mingzhen Huang
Shijia Huang
Shengyu Huang
Siyuan Huang
He Huang
Xiuyu Huang
Lianghua Huang
Yue Huang
Yaping Huang
Yuge Huang
Zehao Huang
Zeyi Huang
Zhiqi Huang
Zhongzhan Huang
Zilong Huang
Ziyuan Huang
Tianrui Hui
Zhuo Hui
Le Hui
Jing Huo
Junhwa Hur
Shehzeen S. Hussain
Chuong Minh Huynh
Seunghyun Hwang
Jaehui Hwang
Jyh-Jing Hwang
Sukjun Hwang
Soonmin Hwang
Wonjun Hwang
Rakib Hyder
Sangeek Hyun
Sarah Ibrahimi
Tomoki Ichikawa
Yerlan Idelbayev
A. S. M. Iftekhar
Masaaki Iiyama
Satoshi Ikehata
Sunghoon Im
Atul N. Ingle
Eldar Insafutdinov
Yani A. Ioannou
Radu Tudor Ionescu

Umar Iqbal
Go Irie
Muhammad Zubair Irshad
Ahmet Iscen
Berivan Isik
Ashraful Islam
Md Amirul Islam
Syed Islam
Mariko Isogawa
Vamsi Krishna K. Ithapu
Boris Ivanovic
Darshan Iyer
Sarah Jabbour
Ayush Jain
Nishant Jain
Samyak Jain
Vidit Jain
Vineet Jain
Priyank Jaini
Tomas Jakab
Mohammad A. A. K.
    Jalwana
Muhammad Abdullah
    Jamal
Hadi Jamali-Rad
Stuart James
Varun Jampani
Young Kyun Jang
YeongJun Jang
Yunseok Jang
Ronnachai Jaroensri
Bhavan Jasani
Krishna Murthy
    Jatavallabhula
Mojan Javaheripi
Syed A. Javed
Guillaume Jeanneret
Pranav Jeevan
Herve Jegou
Rohit Jena
Tomas Jenicek
Porter Jenkins
Simon Jenni
Hae-Gon Jeon
Sangryul Jeon

Boseung Jeong
Yoonwoo Jeong
Seong-Gyun Jeong
Jisoo Jeong
Allan D. Jepson
Ankit Jha
Sumit K. Jha
I-Hong Jhuo
Ge-Peng Ji
Chaonan Ji
Deyi Ji
Jingwei Ji
Wei Ji
Zhong Ji
Jiayi Ji
Pengliang Ji
Hui Ji
Mingi Ji
Xiaopeng Ji
Yuzhu Ji
Baoxiong Jia
Songhao Jia
Dan Jia
Shan Jia
Xiaojun Jia
Xiuyi Jia
Xu Jia
Menglin Jia
Wenqi Jia
Boyuan Jiang
Wenhao Jiang
Huaizu Jiang
Hanwen Jiang
Haiyong Jiang
Hao Jiang
Huajie Jiang
Huiqin Jiang
Haojun Jiang
Haobo Jiang
Junjun Jiang
Xingyu Jiang
Yangbangyan Jiang
Yu Jiang
Jianmin Jiang
Jiaxi Jiang

Jing Jiang
Kui Jiang
Li Jiang
Liming Jiang
Chiyu Jiang
Meirui Jiang
Chen Jiang
Peng Jiang
Tai-Xiang Jiang
Wen Jiang
Xinyang Jiang
Yifan Jiang
Yuming Jiang
Yingying Jiang
Zeren Jiang
ZhengKai Jiang
Zhenyu Jiang
Shuming Jiao
Jianbo Jiao
Licheng Jiao
Dongkwon Jin
Yeying Jin
Cheng Jin
Linyi Jin
Qing Jin
Taisong Jin
Xiao Jin
Xin Jin
Sheng Jin
Kyong Hwan Jin
Ruibing Jin
SouYoung Jin
Yueming Jin
Chenchen Jing
Longlong Jing
Taotao Jing
Yongcheng Jing
Younghyun Jo
Joakim Johnander
Jeff Johnson
Michael J. Jones
R. Kenny Jones
Rico Jonschkowski
Ameya Joshi
Sunghun Joung

Felix Juefei-Xu
Claudio R. Jung
Steffen Jung
Hari Chandana K.
Rahul Vigneswaran K.
Prajwal K. R.
Abhishek Kadian
Jhony Kaesemodel Pontes
Kumara Kahatapitiya
Anmol Kalia
Sinan Kalkan
Tarun Kalluri
Jaewon Kam
Sandesh Kamath
Meina Kan
Menelaos Kanakis
Takuhiro Kaneko
Di Kang
Guoliang Kang
Hao Kang
Jaeyeon Kang
Kyoungkook Kang
Li-Wei Kang
MinGuk Kang
Suk-Ju Kang
Zhao Kang
Yash Mukund Kant
Yueying Kao
Aupendu Kar
Konstantinos Karantzalos
Sezer Karaoglu
Navid Kardan
Sanjay Kariyappa
Leonid Karlinsky
Animesh Karnewar
Shyamgopal Karthik
Hirak J. Kashyap
Marc A. Kastner
Hirokatsu Kataoka
Angelos Katharopoulos
Hiroharu Kato
Kai Katsumata
Manuel Kaufmann
Chaitanya Kaul
Prakhar Kaushik

Yuki Kawana
Lei Ke
Lipeng Ke
Tsung-Wei Ke
Wei Ke
Petr Kellnhofer
Aniruddha Kembhavi
John Kender
Corentin Kervadec
Leonid Keselman
Daniel Keysers
Nima Khademi Kalantari
Taras Khakhulin
Samir Khaki
Muhammad Haris Khan
Qadeer Khan
Salman Khan
Subash Khanal
Vaishnavi M. Khindkar
Rawal Khirodkar
Saeed Khorram
Pirazh Khorramshahi
Kourosh Khoshelham
Ansh Khurana
Benjamin Kiefer
Jae Myung Kim
Junho Kim
Boah Kim
Hyeonseong Kim
Dong-Jin Kim
Dongwan Kim
Donghyun Kim
Doyeon Kim
Yonghyun Kim
Hyung-Il Kim
Hyunwoo Kim
Hyeongwoo Kim
Hyo Jin Kim
Hyunwoo J. Kim
Taehoon Kim
Jaeha Kim
Jiwon Kim
Jung Uk Kim
Kangyeol Kim
Eunji Kim

Daeha Kim
Dongwon Kim
Kunhee Kim
Kyungmin Kim
Junsik Kim
Min H. Kim
Namil Kim
Kookhoi Kim
Sanghyun Kim
Seongyeop Kim
Seungryong Kim
Saehoon Kim
Euyoung Kim
Guisik Kim
Sungyeon Kim
Sunnie S. Y. Kim
Taehun Kim
Tae Oh Kim
Won Hwa Kim
Seungwook Kim
YoungBin Kim
Youngeun Kim
Akisato Kimura
Furkan Osman Kınlı
Zsolt Kira
Hedvig Kjellström
Florian Kleber
Jan P. Klopp
Florian Kluger
Laurent Kneip
Byungsoo Ko
Muhammed Kocabas
A. Sophia Koepke
Kevin Koeser
Nick Kolkin
Nikos Kolotouros
Wai-Kin Adams Kong
Deying Kong
Caihua Kong
Youyong Kong
Shuyu Kong
Shu Kong
Tao Kong
Yajing Kong
Yu Kong

Zishang Kong
Theodora Kontogianni
Anton S. Konushin
Julian F. P. Kooij
Bruno Korbar
Giorgos Kordopatis-Zilos
Jari Korhonen
Adam Kortylewski
Denis Korzhenkov
Divya Kothandaraman
Suraj Kothawade
Iuliia Kotseruba
Satwik Kottur
Shashank Kotyan
Alexandros Kouris
Petros Koutras
Anna Kreshuk
Ranjay Krishna
Dilip Krishnan
Andrey Kuehlkamp
Hilde Kuehne
Jason Kuen
David Kügler
Arjan Kuijper
Anna Kukleva
Sumith Kulal
Viveka Kulharia
Akshay R. Kulkarni
Nilesh Kulkarni
Dominik Kulon
Abhinav Kumar
Akash Kumar
Suryansh Kumar
B. V. K. Vijaya Kumar
Pulkit Kumar
Ratnesh Kumar
Sateesh Kumar
Satish Kumar
Vijay Kumar B. G.
Nupur Kumari
Sudhakar Kumawat
Jogendra Nath Kundu
Hsien-Kai Kuo
Meng-Yu Jennifer Kuo
Vinod Kumar Kurmi

Yusuke Kurose
Keerthy Kusumam
Alina Kuznetsova
Henry Kvinge
Ho Man Kwan
Hyeokjun Kweon
Heeseung Kwon
Gihyun Kwon
Myung-Joon Kwon
Taesung Kwon
YoungJoong Kwon
Christos Kyrkou
Jorma Laaksonen
Yann Labbe
Zorah Laehner
Florent Lafarge
Hamid Laga
Manuel Lagunas
Shenqi Lai
Jian-Huang Lai
Zihang Lai
Mohamed I. Lakhal
Mohit Lamba
Meng Lan
Loic Landrieu
Zhiqiang Lang
Natalie Lang
Dong Lao
Yizhen Lao
Yingjie Lao
Issam Hadj Laradji
Gustav Larsson
Viktor Larsson
Zakaria Laskar
Stéphane Lathuilière
Chun Pong Lau
Rynson W. H. Lau
Hei Law
Justin Lazarow
Verica Lazova
Eric-Tuan Le
Hieu Le
Trung-Nghia Le
Mathias Lechner
Byeong-Uk Lee

Chen-Yu Lee
Che-Rung Lee
Chul Lee
Hong Joo Lee
Dongsoo Lee
Jiyoung Lee
Eugene Eu Tzuan Lee
Daeun Lee
Saehyung Lee
Jewook Lee
Hyungtae Lee
Hyunmin Lee
Jungbeom Lee
Joon-Young Lee
Jong-Seok Lee
Joonseok Lee
Junha Lee
Kibok Lee
Byung-Kwan Lee
Jangwon Lee
Jinho Lee
Jongmin Lee
Seunghyun Lee
Sohyun Lee
Minsik Lee
Dogyoon Lee
Seungmin Lee
Min Jun Lee
Sangho Lee
Sangmin Lee
Seungeun Lee
Seon-Ho Lee
Sungmin Lee
Sungho Lee
Sangyoun Lee
Vincent C. S. S. Lee
Jaeseong Lee
Yong Jae Lee
Chenyang Lei
Chenyi Lei
Jiahui Lei
Xinyu Lei
Yinjie Lei
Jiaxu Leng
Luziwei Leng

Jan E. Lenssen
Vincent Lepetit
Thomas Leung
María Leyva-Vallina
Xin Li
Yikang Li
Baoxin Li
Bin Li
Bing Li
Bowen Li
Changlin Li
Chao Li
Chongyi Li
Guanyue Li
Shuai Li
Jin Li
Dingquan Li
Dongxu Li
Yiting Li
Gang Li
Dian Li
Guohao Li
Haoang Li
Haoliang Li
Haoran Li
Hengduo Li
Huafeng Li
Xiaoming Li
Hanao Li
Hongwei Li
Ziqiang Li
Jisheng Li
Jiacheng Li
Jia Li
Jiachen Li
Jiahao Li
Jianwei Li
Jiazhi Li
Jie Li
Jing Li
Jingjing Li
Jingtao Li
Jun Li
Junxuan Li
Kai Li

Kailin Li
Kenneth Li
Kun Li
Kunpeng Li
Aoxue Li
Chenglong Li
Chenglin Li
Changsheng Li
Zhichao Li
Qiang Li
Yanyu Li
Zuoyue Li
Xiang Li
Xuelong Li
Fangda Li
Ailin Li
Liang Li
Chun-Guang Li
Daiqing Li
Dong Li
Guanbin Li
Guorong Li
Haifeng Li
Jianan Li
Jianing Li
Jiaxin Li
Ke Li
Lei Li
Lincheng Li
Liulei Li
Lujun Li
Linjie Li
Lin Li
Pengyu Li
Ping Li
Qiufu Li
Qingyong Li
Rui Li
Siyuan Li
Wei Li
Wenbin Li
Xiangyang Li
Xinyu Li
Xiujun Li
Xiu Li

Xu Li
Ya-Li Li
Yao Li
Yongjie Li
Yijun Li
Yiming Li
Yuezun Li
Yu Li
Yunheng Li
Yuqi Li
Zhe Li
Zeming Li
Zhen Li
Zhengqin Li
Zhimin Li
Jiefeng Li
Jinpeng Li
Chengze Li
Jianwu Li
Lerenhan Li
Shan Li
Suichan Li
Xiangtai Li
Yanjie Li
Yandong Li
Zhuoling Li
Zhenqiang Li
Manyi Li
Maosen Li
Ji Li
Minjun Li
Mingrui Li
Mengtian Li
Junyi Li
Nianyi Li
Bo Li
Xiao Li
Peihua Li
Peike Li
Peizhao Li
Peiliang Li
Qi Li
Ren Li
Runze Li
Shile Li

Sheng Li
Shigang Li
Shiyu Li
Shuang Li
Shasha Li
Shichao Li
Tianye Li
Yuexiang Li
Wei-Hong Li
Wanhua Li
Weihao Li
Weiming Li
Weixin Li
Wenbo Li
Wenshuo Li
Weijian Li
Yunan Li
Xirong Li
Xianhang Li
Xiaoyu Li
Xueqian Li
Xuanlin Li
Xianzhi Li
Yunqiang Li
Yanjing Li
Yansheng Li
Yawei Li
Yi Li
Yong Li
Yong-Lu Li
Yuhang Li
Yu-Jhe Li
Yuxi Li
Yunsheng Li
Yanwei Li
Zechao Li
Zejian Li
Zeju Li
Zekun Li
Zhaowen Li
Zheng Li
Zhenyu Li
Zhiheng Li
Zhi Li
Zhong Li

Zhuowei Li
Zhuowan Li
Zhuohang Li
Zizhang Li
Chen Li
Yuan-Fang Li
Dongze Lian
Xiaochen Lian
Zhouhui Lian
Long Lian
Qing Lian
Jin Lianbao
Jinxiu S. Liang
Dingkang Liang
Jiahao Liang
Jianming Liang
Jingyun Liang
Kevin J. Liang
Kaizhao Liang
Chen Liang
Jie Liang
Senwei Liang
Ding Liang
Jiajun Liang
Jian Liang
Kongming Liang
Siyuan Liang
Yuanzhi Liang
Zhengfa Liang
Mingfu Liang
Xiaodan Liang
Xuefeng Liang
Yuxuan Liang
Kang Liao
Liang Liao
Hong-Yuan Mark Liao
Wentong Liao
Haofu Liao
Yue Liao
Minghui Liao
Shengcai Liao
Ting-Hsuan Liao
Xin Liao
Yinghong Liao
Teck Yian Lim

Che-Tsung Lin
Chung-Ching Lin
Chen-Hsuan Lin
Cheng Lin
Chuming Lin
Chunyu Lin
Dahua Lin
Wei Lin
Zheng Lin
Huaijia Lin
Jason Lin
Jierui Lin
Jiaying Lin
Jie Lin
Kai-En Lin
Kevin Lin
Guangfeng Lin
Jiehong Lin
Feng Lin
Hang Lin
Kwan-Yee Lin
Ke Lin
Luojun Lin
Qinghong Lin
Xiangbo Lin
Yi Lin
Zudi Lin
Shijie Lin
Yiqun Lin
Tzu-Heng Lin
Ming Lin
Shaohui Lin
SongNan Lin
Ji Lin
Tsung-Yu Lin
Xudong Lin
Yancong Lin
Yen-Chen Lin
Yiming Lin
Yuewei Lin
Zhiqiu Lin
Zinan Lin
Zhe Lin
David B. Lindell
Zhixin Ling

Zhan Ling
Alexander Liniger
Venice Erin B. Liong
Joey Litalien
Or Litany
Roee Litman
Ron Litman
Jim Little
Dor Litvak
Shaoteng Liu
Shuaicheng Liu
Andrew Liu
Xian Liu
Shaohui Liu
Bei Liu
Bo Liu
Yong Liu
Ming Liu
Yanbin Liu
Chenxi Liu
Daqi Liu
Di Liu
Difan Liu
Dong Liu
Dongfang Liu
Daizong Liu
Xiao Liu
Fangyi Liu
Fengbei Liu
Fenglin Liu
Bin Liu
Yuang Liu
Ao Liu
Hong Liu
Hongfu Liu
Huidong Liu
Ziyi Liu
Feng Liu
Hao Liu
Jie Liu
Jialun Liu
Jiang Liu
Jing Liu
Jingya Liu
Jiaming Liu

Jun Liu
Juncheng Liu
Jiawei Liu
Hongyu Liu
Chuanbin Liu
Haotian Liu
Lingqiao Liu
Chang Liu
Han Liu
Liu Liu
Min Liu
Yingqi Liu
Aishan Liu
Bingyu Liu
Benlin Liu
Boxiao Liu
Chenchen Liu
Chuanjian Liu
Daqing Liu
Huan Liu
Haozhe Liu
Jiaheng Liu
Wei Liu
Jingzhou Liu
Jiyuan Liu
Lingbo Liu
Nian Liu
Peiye Liu
Qiankun Liu
Shenglan Liu
Shilong Liu
Wen Liu
Wenyu Liu
Weifeng Liu
Wu Liu
Xiaolong Liu
Yang Liu
Yanwei Liu
Yingcheng Liu
Yongfei Liu
Yihao Liu
Yu Liu
Yunze Liu
Ze Liu
Zhenhua Liu

Zhenguang Liu
Lin Liu
Lihao Liu
Pengju Liu
Xinhai Liu
Yunfei Liu
Meng Liu
Minghua Liu
Mingyuan Liu
Miao Liu
Peirong Liu
Ping Liu
Qingjie Liu
Ruoshi Liu
Risheng Liu
Songtao Liu
Xing Liu
Shikun Liu
Shuming Liu
Sheng Liu
Songhua Liu
Tongliang Liu
Weibo Liu
Weide Liu
Weizhe Liu
Wenxi Liu
Weiyang Liu
Xin Liu
Xiaobin Liu
Xudong Liu
Xiaoyi Liu
Xihui Liu
Xinchen Liu
Xingtong Liu
Xinpeng Liu
Xinyu Liu
Xianpeng Liu
Xu Liu
Xingyu Liu
Yongtuo Liu
Yahui Liu
Yangxin Liu
Yaoyao Liu
Yaojie Liu
Yuliang Liu

Yongcheng Liu
Yuan Liu
Yufan Liu
Yu-Lun Liu
Yun Liu
Yunfan Liu
Yuanzhong Liu
Zhuoran Liu
Zhen Liu
Zheng Liu
Zhijian Liu
Zhisong Liu
Ziquan Liu
Ziyu Liu
Zhihua Liu
Zechun Liu
Zhaoyang Liu
Zhengzhe Liu
Stephan Liwicki
Shao-Yuan Lo
Sylvain Lobry
Suhas Lohit
Vishnu Suresh Lokhande
Vincenzo Lomonaco
Chengjiang Long
Guodong Long
Fuchen Long
Shangbang Long
Yang Long
Zijun Long
Vasco Lopes
Antonio M. Lopez
Roberto Javier
   Lopez-Sastre
Tobias Lorenz
Javier Lorenzo-Navarro
Yujing Lou
Qian Lou
Xiankai Lu
Changsheng Lu
Huimin Lu
Yongxi Lu
Hao Lu
Hong Lu
Jiasen Lu

Juwei Lu
Fan Lu
Guangming Lu
Jiwen Lu
Shun Lu
Tao Lu
Xiaonan Lu
Yang Lu
Yao Lu
Yongchun Lu
Zhiwu Lu
Cheng Lu
Liying Lu
Guo Lu
Xuequan Lu
Yanye Lu
Yantao Lu
Yuhang Lu
Fujun Luan
Jonathon Luiten
Jovita Lukasik
Alan Lukezic
Jonathan Samuel Lumentut
Mayank Lunayach
Ao Luo
Canjie Luo
Chong Luo
Xu Luo
Grace Luo
Jun Luo
Katie Z. Luo
Tao Luo
Cheng Luo
Fangzhou Luo
Gen Luo
Lei Luo
Sihui Luo
Weixin Luo
Yan Luo
Xiaoyan Luo
Yong Luo
Yadan Luo
Hao Luo
Ruotian Luo
Mi Luo

Tiange Luo
Wenjie Luo
Wenhan Luo
Xiao Luo
Zhiming Luo
Zhipeng Luo
Zhengyi Luo
Diogo C. Luvizon
Zhaoyang Lv
Gengyu Lyu
Lingjuan Lyu
Jun Lyu
Yuanyuan Lyu
Youwei Lyu
Yueming Lyu
Bingpeng Ma
Chao Ma
Chongyang Ma
Congbo Ma
Chih-Yao Ma
Fan Ma
Lin Ma
Haoyu Ma
Hengbo Ma
Jianqi Ma
Jiawei Ma
Jiayi Ma
Kede Ma
Kai Ma
Lingni Ma
Lei Ma
Xu Ma
Ning Ma
Benteng Ma
Cheng Ma
Andy J. Ma
Long Ma
Zhanyu Ma
Zhiheng Ma
Qianli Ma
Shiqiang Ma
Sizhuo Ma
Shiqing Ma
Xiaolong Ma
Xinzhu Ma

Gautam B. Machiraju
Spandan Madan
Mathew Magimai-Doss
Luca Magri
Behrooz Mahasseni
Upal Mahbub
Siddharth Mahendran
Paridhi Maheshwari
Rishabh Maheshwary
Mohammed Mahmoud
Shishira R. R. Maiya
Sylwia Majchrowska
Arjun Majumdar
Puspita Majumdar
Orchid Majumder
Sagnik Majumder
Ilya Makarov
Farkhod F.
  Makhmudkhujaev
Yasushi Makihara
Ankur Mali
Mateusz Malinowski
Utkarsh Mall
Srikanth Malla
Clement Mallet
Dimitrios Mallis
Yunze Man
Dipu Manandhar
Massimiliano Mancini
Murari Mandal
Raunak Manekar
Karttikeya Mangalam
Puneet Mangla
Fabian Manhardt
Sivabalan Manivasagam
Fahim Mannan
Chengzhi Mao
Hanzi Mao
Jiayuan Mao
Junhua Mao
Zhiyuan Mao
Jiageng Mao
Yunyao Mao
Zhendong Mao
Alberto Marchisio

Diego Marcos
Riccardo Marin
Aram Markosyan
Renaud Marlet
Ricardo Marques
Miquel Martí i Rabadán
Diego Martin Arroyo
Niki Martinel
Brais Martinez
Julieta Martinez
Marc Masana
Tomohiro Mashita
Timothée Masquelier
Minesh Mathew
Tetsu Matsukawa
Marwan Mattar
Bruce A. Maxwell
Christoph Mayer
Mantas Mazeika
Pratik Mazumder
Scott McCloskey
Steven McDonagh
Ishit Mehta
Jie Mei
Kangfu Mei
Jieru Mei
Xiaoguang Mei
Givi Meishvili
Luke Melas-Kyriazi
Iaroslav Melekhov
Andres Mendez-Vazquez
Heydi Mendez-Vazquez
Matias Mendieta
Ricardo A. Mendoza-León
Chenlin Meng
Depu Meng
Rang Meng
Zibo Meng
Qingjie Meng
Qier Meng
Yanda Meng
Zihang Meng
Thomas Mensink
Fabian Mentzer
Christopher Metzler

Gregory P. Meyer
Vasileios Mezaris
Liang Mi
Lu Mi
Bo Miao
Changtao Miao
Zichen Miao
Qiguang Miao
Xin Miao
Zhongqi Miao
Frank Michel
Simone Milani
Ben Mildenhall
Roy V. Miles
Juhong Min
Kyle Min
Hyun-Seok Min
Weiqing Min
Yuecong Min
Zhixiang Min
Qi Ming
David Minnen
Aymen Mir
Deepak Mishra
Anand Mishra
Shlok K. Mishra
Niluthpol Mithun
Gaurav Mittal
Trisha Mittal
Daisuke Miyazaki
Kaichun Mo
Hong Mo
Zhipeng Mo
Davide Modolo
Abduallah A. Mohamed
Mohamed Afham
  Mohamed Aflal
Ron Mokady
Pavlo Molchanov
Davide Moltisanti
Liliane Momeni
Gianluca Monaci
Pascal Monasse
Ajoy Mondal
Tom Monnier

Aron Monszpart
Gyeongsik Moon
Suhong Moon
Taesup Moon
Sean Moran
Daniel Moreira
Pietro Morerio
Alexandre Morgand
Lia Morra
Ali Mosleh
Inbar Mosseri
Sayed Mohammad
    Mostafavi Isfahani
Saman Motamed
Ramy A. Mounir
Fangzhou Mu
Jiteng Mu
Norman Mu
Yasuhiro Mukaigawa
Ryan Mukherjee
Tanmoy Mukherjee
Yusuke Mukuta
Ravi Teja Mullapudi
Lea Müller
Matthias Müller
Martin Mundt
Nils Murrugarra-Llerena
Damien Muselet
Armin Mustafa
Muhammad Ferjad Naeem
Sauradip Nag
Hajime Nagahara
Pravin Nagar
Rajendra Nagar
Naveen Shankar Nagaraja
Varun Nagaraja
Tushar Nagarajan
Seungjun Nah
Gaku Nakano
Yuta Nakashima
Giljoo Nam
Seonghyeon Nam
Liangliang Nan
Yuesong Nan
Yeshwanth Napolean

Dinesh Reddy
    Narapureddy
Medhini Narasimhan
Supreeth
    Narasimhaswamy
Sriram Narayanan
Erickson R. Nascimento
Varun Nasery
K. L. Navaneet
Pablo Navarrete Michelini
Shant Navasardyan
Shah Nawaz
Nihal Nayak
Farhood Negin
Lukáš Neumann
Alejandro Newell
Evonne Ng
Kam Woh Ng
Tony Ng
Anh Nguyen
Tuan Anh Nguyen
Cuong Cao Nguyen
Ngoc Cuong Nguyen
Thanh Nguyen
Khoi Nguyen
Phi Le Nguyen
Phong Ha Nguyen
Tam Nguyen
Truong Nguyen
Anh Tuan Nguyen
Rang Nguyen
Thao Thi Phuong Nguyen
Van Nguyen Nguyen
Zhen-Liang Ni
Yao Ni
Shijie Nie
Xuecheng Nie
Yongwei Nie
Weizhi Nie
Ying Nie
Yinyu Nie
Kshitij N. Nikhal
Simon Niklaus
Xuefei Ning
Jifeng Ning

Yotam Nitzan
Di Niu
Shuaicheng Niu
Li Niu
Wei Niu
Yulei Niu
Zhenxing Niu
Albert No
Shohei Nobuhara
Nicoletta Noceti
Junhyug Noh
Sotiris Nousias
Slawomir Nowaczyk
Ewa M. Nowara
Valsamis Ntouskos
Gilberto Ochoa-Ruiz
Ferda Ofli
Jihyong Oh
Sangyun Oh
Youngtaek Oh
Hiroki Ohashi
Takahiro Okabe
Kemal Oksuz
Fumio Okura
Daniel Olmeda Reino
Matthew Olson
Carl Olsson
Roy Or-El
Alessandro Ortis
Guillermo Ortiz-Jimenez
Magnus Oskarsson
Ahmed A. A. Osman
Martin R. Oswald
Mayu Otani
Naima Otberdout
Cheng Ouyang
Jiahong Ouyang
Wanli Ouyang
Andrew Owens
Poojan B. Oza
Mete Ozay
A. Cengiz Oztireli
Gautam Pai
Tomas Pajdla
Umapada Pal

Simone Palazzo
Luca Palmieri
Bowen Pan
Hao Pan
Lili Pan
Tai-Yu Pan
Liang Pan
Chengwei Pan
Yingwei Pan
Xuran Pan
Jinshan Pan
Xinyu Pan
Liyuan Pan
Xingang Pan
Xingjia Pan
Zhihong Pan
Zizheng Pan
Priyadarshini Panda
Rameswar Panda
Rohit Pandey
Kaiyue Pang
Bo Pang
Guansong Pang
Jiangmiao Pang
Meng Pang
Tianyu Pang
Ziqi Pang
Omiros Pantazis
Andreas Panteli
Maja Pantic
Marina Paolanti
Joao P. Papa
Samuele Papa
Mike Papadakis
Dim P. Papadopoulos
George Papandreou
Constantin Pape
Toufiq Parag
Chethan Parameshwara
Shaifali Parashar
Alejandro Pardo
Rishubh Parihar
Sarah Parisot
JaeYoo Park
Gyeong-Moon Park

Hyojin Park
Hyoungseob Park
Jongchan Park
Jae Sung Park
Kiru Park
Chunghyun Park
Kwanyong Park
Sunghyun Park
Sungrae Park
Seongsik Park
Sanghyun Park
Sungjune Park
Taesung Park
Gaurav Parmar
Paritosh Parmar
Alvaro Parra
Despoina Paschalidou
Or Patashnik
Shivansh Patel
Pushpak Pati
Prashant W. Patil
Vaishakh Patil
Suvam Patra
Jay Patravali
Badri Narayana Patro
Angshuman Paul
Sudipta Paul
Rémi Pautrat
Nick E. Pears
Adithya Pediredla
Wenjie Pei
Shmuel Peleg
Latha Pemula
Bo Peng
Houwen Peng
Yue Peng
Liangzu Peng
Baoyun Peng
Jun Peng
Pai Peng
Sida Peng
Xi Peng
Yuxin Peng
Songyou Peng
Wei Peng

Weiqi Peng
Wen-Hsiao Peng
Pramuditha Perera
Juan C. Perez
Eduardo Pérez Pellitero
Juan-Manuel Perez-Rua
Federico Pernici
Marco Pesavento
Stavros Petridis
Ilya A. Petrov
Vladan Petrovic
Mathis Petrovich
Suzanne Petryk
Hieu Pham
Quang Pham
Khoi Pham
Tung Pham
Huy Phan
Stephen Phillips
Cheng Perng Phoo
David Picard
Marco Piccirilli
Georg Pichler
A. J. Piergiovanni
Vipin Pillai
Silvia L. Pintea
Giovanni Pintore
Robinson Piramuthu
Fiora Pirri
Theodoros Pissas
Fabio Pizzati
Benjamin Planche
Bryan Plummer
Matteo Poggi
Ashwini Pokle
Georgy E. Ponimatkin
Adrian Popescu
Stefan Popov
Nikola Popović
Ronald Poppe
Angelo Porrello
Michael Potter
Charalambos Poullis
Hadi Pouransari
Omid Poursaeed

Shraman Pramanick
Mantini Pranav
Dilip K. Prasad
Meghshyam Prasad
B. H. Pawan Prasad
Shitala Prasad
Prateek Prasanna
Ekta Prashnani
Derek S. Prijatelj
Luke Y. Prince
Véronique Prinet
Victor Adrian Prisacariu
James Pritts
Thomas Probst
Sergey Prokudin
Rita Pucci
Chi-Man Pun
Matthew Purri
Haozhi Qi
Lu Qi
Lei Qi
Xianbiao Qi
Yonggang Qi
Yuankai Qi
Siyuan Qi
Guocheng Qian
Hangwei Qian
Qi Qian
Deheng Qian
Shengsheng Qian
Wen Qian
Rui Qian
Yiming Qian
Shengju Qian
Shengyi Qian
Xuelin Qian
Zhenxing Qian
Nan Qiao
Xiaotian Qiao
Jing Qin
Can Qin
Siyang Qin
Hongwei Qin
Jie Qin
Minghai Qin

Yipeng Qin
Yongqiang Qin
Wenda Qin
Xuebin Qin
Yuzhe Qin
Yao Qin
Zhenyue Qin
Zhiwu Qing
Heqian Qiu
Jiayan Qiu
Jielin Qiu
Yue Qiu
Jiaxiong Qiu
Zhongxi Qiu
Shi Qiu
Zhaofan Qiu
Zhongnan Qu
Yanyun Qu
Kha Gia Quach
Yuhui Quan
Ruijie Quan
Mike Rabbat
Rahul Shekhar Rade
Filip Radenovic
Gorjan Radevski
Bogdan Raducanu
Francesco Ragusa
Shafin Rahman
Md Mahfuzur Rahman
    Siddiquee
Hossein Rahmani
Kiran Raja
Sivaramakrishnan
    Rajaraman
Jathushan Rajasegaran
Adnan Siraj Rakin
Michaël Ramamonjisoa
Chirag A. Raman
Shanmuganathan Raman
Vignesh Ramanathan
Vasili Ramanishka
Vikram V. Ramaswamy
Merey Ramazanova
Jason Rambach
Sai Saketh Rambhatla

Clément Rambour
Ashwin Ramesh Babu
Adín Ramírez Rivera
Arianna Rampini
Haoxi Ran
Aakanksha Rana
Aayush Jung Bahadur
    Rana
Kanchana N. Ranasinghe
Aneesh Rangnekar
Samrudhdhi B. Rangrej
Harsh Rangwani
Viresh Ranjan
Anyi Rao
Yongming Rao
Carolina Raposo
Michalis Raptis
Amir Rasouli
Vivek Rathod
Adepu Ravi Sankar
Avinash Ravichandran
Bharadwaj Ravichandran
Dripta S. Raychaudhuri
Adria Recasens
Simon Reiß
Davis Rempe
Daxuan Ren
Jiawei Ren
Jimmy Ren
Sucheng Ren
Dayong Ren
Zhile Ren
Dongwei Ren
Qibing Ren
Pengfei Ren
Zhenwen Ren
Xuqian Ren
Yixuan Ren
Zhongzheng Ren
Ambareesh Revanur
Hamed Rezazadegan
    Tavakoli
Rafael S. Rezende
Wonjong Rhee
Alexander Richard

Christian Richardt
Stephan R. Richter
Benjamin Riggan
Dominik Rivoir
Mamshad Nayeem Rizve
Joshua D. Robinson
Joseph Robinson
Chris Rockwell
Ranga Rodrigo
Andres C. Rodriguez
Carlos Rodriguez-Pardo
Marcus Rohrbach
Gemma Roig
Yu Rong
David A. Ross
Mohammad Rostami
Edward Rosten
Karsten Roth
Anirban Roy
Debaditya Roy
Shuvendu Roy
Ahana Roy Choudhury
Aruni Roy Chowdhury
Denys Rozumnyi
Shulan Ruan
Wenjie Ruan
Patrick Ruhkamp
Danila Rukhovich
Anian Ruoss
Chris Russell
Dan Ruta
Dawid Damian Rymarczyk
DongHun Ryu
Hyeonggon Ryu
Kwonyoung Ryu
Balasubramanian S.
Alexandre Sablayrolles
Mohammad Sabokrou
Arka Sadhu
Aniruddha Saha
Oindrila Saha
Pritish Sahu
Aneeshan Sain
Nirat Saini
Saurabh Saini

Takeshi Saitoh
Christos Sakaridis
Fumihiko Sakaue
Dimitrios Sakkos
Ken Sakurada
Parikshit V. Sakurikar
Rohit Saluja
Nermin Samet
Leo Sampaio Ferraz
    Ribeiro
Jorge Sanchez
Enrique Sanchez
Shengtian Sang
Anush Sankaran
Soubhik Sanyal
Nikolaos Sarafianos
Vishwanath Saragadam
István Sárándi
Saquib Sarfraz
Mert Bulent Sariyildiz
Anindya Sarkar
Pritam Sarkar
Paul-Edouard Sarlin
Hiroshi Sasaki
Takami Sato
Torsten Sattler
Ravi Kumar Satzoda
Axel Sauer
Stefano Savian
Artem Savkin
Manolis Savva
Gerald Schaefer
Simone Schaub-Meyer
Yoni Schirris
Samuel Schulter
Katja Schwarz
Jesse Scott
Sinisa Segvic
Constantin Marc Seibold
Lorenzo Seidenari
Matan Sela
Fadime Sener
Paul Hongsuck Seo
Kwanggyoon Seo
Hongje Seong

Dario Serez
Francesco Setti
Bryan Seybold
Mohamad Shahbazi
Shima Shahfar
Xinxin Shan
Caifeng Shan
Dandan Shan
Shawn Shan
Wei Shang
Jinghuan Shang
Jiaxiang Shang
Lei Shang
Sukrit Shankar
Ken Shao
Rui Shao
Jie Shao
Mingwen Shao
Aashish Sharma
Gaurav Sharma
Vivek Sharma
Abhishek Sharma
Yoli Shavit
Shashank Shekhar
Sumit Shekhar
Zhijie Shen
Fengyi Shen
Furao Shen
Jialie Shen
Jingjing Shen
Ziyi Shen
Linlin Shen
Guangyu Shen
Biluo Shen
Falong Shen
Jiajun Shen
Qiu Shen
Qiuhong Shen
Shuai Shen
Wang Shen
Yiqing Shen
Yunhang Shen
Siqi Shen
Bin Shen
Tianwei Shen

Xi Shen
Yilin Shen
Yuming Shen
Yucong Shen
Zhiqiang Shen
Lu Sheng
Yichen Sheng
Shivanand Venkanna
    Sheshappanavar
Shelly Sheynin
Baifeng Shi
Ruoxi Shi
Botian Shi
Hailin Shi
Jia Shi
Jing Shi
Shaoshuai Shi
Baoguang Shi
Boxin Shi
Hengcan Shi
Tianyang Shi
Xiaodan Shi
Yongjie Shi
Zhensheng Shi
Yinghuan Shi
Weiqi Shi
Wu Shi
Xuepeng Shi
Xiaoshuang Shi
Yujiao Shi
Zenglin Shi
Zhenmei Shi
Takashi Shibata
Meng-Li Shih
Yichang Shih
Hyunjung Shim
Dongseok Shim
Soshi Shimada
Inkyu Shin
Jinwoo Shin
Seungjoo Shin
Seungjae Shin
Koichi Shinoda
Suprosanna Shit

Palaiahnakote
    Shivakumara
Eli Shlizerman
Gaurav Shrivastava
Xiao Shu
Xiangbo Shu
Xiujun Shu
Yang Shu
Tianmin Shu
Jun Shu
Zhixin Shu
Bing Shuai
Maria Shugrina
Ivan Shugurov
Satya Narayan Shukla
Pranjay Shyam
Jianlou Si
Yawar Siddiqui
Alberto Signoroni
Pedro Silva
Jae-Young Sim
Oriane Siméoni
Martin Simon
Andrea Simonelli
Abhishek Singh
Ashish Singh
Dinesh Singh
Gurkirt Singh
Krishna Kumar Singh
Mannat Singh
Pravendra Singh
Rajat Vikram Singh
Utkarsh Singhal
Dipika Singhania
Vasu Singla
Harsh Sinha
Sudipta Sinha
Josef Sivic
Elena Sizikova
Geri Skenderi
Ivan Skorokhodov
Dmitriy Smirnov
Cameron Y. Smith
James S. Smith
Patrick Snape

Mattia Soldan
Hyeongseok Son
Sanghyun Son
Chuanbiao Song
Chen Song
Chunfeng Song
Dan Song
Dongjin Song
Hwanjun Song
Guoxian Song
Jiaming Song
Jie Song
Liangchen Song
Ran Song
Luchuan Song
Xibin Song
Li Song
Fenglong Song
Guoli Song
Guanglu Song
Zhenbo Song
Lin Song
Xinhang Song
Yang Song
Yibing Song
Rajiv Soundararajan
Hossein Souri
Cristovao Sousa
Riccardo Spezialetti
Leonidas Spinoulas
Michael W. Spratling
Deepak Sridhar
Srinath Sridhar
Gaurang Sriramanan
Vinkle Kumar Srivastav
Themos Stafylakis
Serban Stan
Anastasis Stathopoulos
Markus Steinberger
Jan Steinbrener
Sinisa Stekovic
Alexandros Stergiou
Gleb Sterkin
Rainer Stiefelhagen
Pierre Stock

Ombretta Strafforello
Julian Straub
Yannick Strümpler
Joerg Stueckler
Hang Su
Weijie Su
Jong-Chyi Su
Bing Su
Haisheng Su
Jinming Su
Yiyang Su
Yukun Su
Yuxin Su
Zhuo Su
Zhaoqi Su
Xiu Su
Yu-Chuan Su
Zhixun Su
Arulkumar Subramaniam
Akshayvarun Subramanya
A. Subramanyam
Swathikiran Sudhakaran
Yusuke Sugano
Masanori Suganuma
Yumin Suh
Yang Sui
Baochen Sun
Cheng Sun
Long Sun
Guolei Sun
Haoliang Sun
Haomiao Sun
He Sun
Hanqing Sun
Hao Sun
Lichao Sun
Jiachen Sun
Jiaming Sun
Jian Sun
Jin Sun
Jennifer J. Sun
Tiancheng Sun
Libo Sun
Peize Sun
Qianru Sun

Shanlin Sun
Yu Sun
Zhun Sun
Che Sun
Lin Sun
Tao Sun
Yiyou Sun
Chunyi Sun
Chong Sun
Weiwei Sun
Weixuan Sun
Xiuyu Sun
Yanan Sun
Zeren Sun
Zhaodong Sun
Zhiqing Sun
Minhyuk Sung
Jinli Suo
Simon Suo
Abhijit Suprem
Anshuman Suri
Saksham Suri
Joshua M. Susskind
Roman Suvorov
Gurumurthy Swaminathan
Robin Swanson
Paul Swoboda
Tabish A. Syed
Richard Szeliski
Fariborz Taherkhani
Yu-Wing Tai
Keita Takahashi
Walter Talbott
Gary Tam
Masato Tamura
Feitong Tan
Fuwen Tan
Shuhan Tan
Andong Tan
Bin Tan
Cheng Tan
Jianchao Tan
Lei Tan
Mingxing Tan
Xin Tan

Zichang Tan
Zhentao Tan
Kenichiro Tanaka
Masayuki Tanaka
Yushun Tang
Hao Tang
Jingqun Tang
Jinhui Tang
Kaihua Tang
Luming Tang
Lv Tang
Sheyang Tang
Shitao Tang
Siliang Tang
Shixiang Tang
Yansong Tang
Keke Tang
Chang Tang
Chenwei Tang
Jie Tang
Junshu Tang
Ming Tang
Peng Tang
Xu Tang
Yao Tang
Chen Tang
Fan Tang
Haoran Tang
Shengeng Tang
Yehui Tang
Zhipeng Tang
Ugo Tanielian
Chaofan Tao
Jiale Tao
Junli Tao
Renshuai Tao
An Tao
Guanhong Tao
Zhiqiang Tao
Makarand Tapaswi
Jean-Philippe G. Tarel
Juan J. Tarrio
Enzo Tartaglione
Keisuke Tateno
Zachary Teed

Jun Wan
Xiaoyue Wan
Fang Wan
Guowei Wan
Renjie Wan
Zhiqiang Wan
Ziyu Wan
Bastian Wandt
Dongdong Wang
Limin Wang
Haiyang Wang
Xiaobing Wang
Angtian Wang
Angelina Wang
Bing Wang
Bo Wang
Boyu Wang
Binghui Wang
Chen Wang
Chien-Yi Wang
Congli Wang
Qi Wang
Chengrui Wang
Rui Wang
Yiqun Wang
Cong Wang
Wenjing Wang
Dongkai Wang
Di Wang
Xiaogang Wang
Kai Wang
Zhizhong Wang
Fangjinhua Wang
Feng Wang
Hang Wang
Gaoang Wang
Guoqing Wang
Guangcong Wang
Guangzhi Wang
Hanqing Wang
Hao Wang
Haohan Wang
Haoran Wang
Hong Wang
Haotao Wang

Hu Wang
Huan Wang
Hua Wang
Hui-Po Wang
Hengli Wang
Hanyu Wang
Hongxing Wang
Jingwen Wang
Jialiang Wang
Jian Wang
Jianyi Wang
Jiashun Wang
Jiahao Wang
Tsun-Hsuan Wang
Xiaoqian Wang
Jinqiao Wang
Jun Wang
Jianzong Wang
Kaihong Wang
Ke Wang
Lei Wang
Lingjing Wang
Linnan Wang
Lin Wang
Liansheng Wang
Mengjiao Wang
Manning Wang
Nannan Wang
Peihao Wang
Jiayun Wang
Pu Wang
Qiang Wang
Qiufeng Wang
Qilong Wang
Qiangchang Wang
Qin Wang
Qing Wang
Ruocheng Wang
Ruibin Wang
Ruisheng Wang
Ruizhe Wang
Runqi Wang
Runzhong Wang
Wenxuan Wang
Sen Wang

Shangfei Wang
Shaofei Wang
Shijie Wang
Shiqi Wang
Zhibo Wang
Song Wang
Xinjiang Wang
Tai Wang
Tao Wang
Teng Wang
Xiang Wang
Tianren Wang
Tiantian Wang
Tianyi Wang
Fengjiao Wang
Wei Wang
Miaohui Wang
Suchen Wang
Siyue Wang
Yaoming Wang
Xiao Wang
Ze Wang
Biao Wang
Chaofei Wang
Dong Wang
Gu Wang
Guangrun Wang
Guangming Wang
Guo-Hua Wang
Haoqing Wang
Hesheng Wang
Huafeng Wang
Jinghua Wang
Jingdong Wang
Jingjing Wang
Jingya Wang
Jingkang Wang
Jiakai Wang
Junke Wang
Kuo Wang
Lichen Wang
Lizhi Wang
Longguang Wang
Mang Wang
Mei Wang

Min Wang
Peng-Shuai Wang
Run Wang
Shaoru Wang
Shuhui Wang
Tan Wang
Tiancai Wang
Tianqi Wang
Wenhai Wang
Wenzhe Wang
Xiaobo Wang
Xiudong Wang
Xu Wang
Yajie Wang
Yan Wang
Yuan-Gen Wang
Yingqian Wang
Yizhi Wang
Yulin Wang
Yu Wang
Yujie Wang
Yunhe Wang
Yuxi Wang
Yaowei Wang
Yiwei Wang
Zezheng Wang
Hongzhi Wang
Zhiqiang Wang
Ziteng Wang
Ziwei Wang
Zheng Wang
Zhenyu Wang
Binglu Wang
Zhongdao Wang
Ce Wang
Weining Wang
Weiyao Wang
Wenbin Wang
Wenguan Wang
Guangting Wang
Haolin Wang
Haiyan Wang
Huiyu Wang
Naiyan Wang
Jingbo Wang

Jinpeng Wang
Jiaqi Wang
Liyuan Wang
Lizhen Wang
Ning Wang
Wenqian Wang
Sheng-Yu Wang
Weimin Wang
Xiaohan Wang
Yifan Wang
Yi Wang
Yongtao Wang
Yizhou Wang
Zhuo Wang
Zhe Wang
Xudong Wang
Xiaofang Wang
Xinggang Wang
Xiaosen Wang
Xiaosong Wang
Xiaoyang Wang
Lijun Wang
Xinlong Wang
Xuan Wang
Xue Wang
Yangang Wang
Yaohui Wang
Yu-Chiang Frank Wang
Yida Wang
Yilin Wang
Yi Ru Wang
Yali Wang
Yinglong Wang
Yufu Wang
Yujiang Wang
Yuwang Wang
Yuting Wang
Yang Wang
Yu-Xiong Wang
Yixu Wang
Ziqi Wang
Zhicheng Wang
Zeyu Wang
Zhaowen Wang
Zhenyi Wang

Zhenzhi Wang
Zhijie Wang
Zhiyong Wang
Zhongling Wang
Zhuowei Wang
Zian Wang
Zifu Wang
Zihao Wang
Zirui Wang
Ziyan Wang
Wenxiao Wang
Zhen Wang
Zhepeng Wang
Zi Wang
Zihao W. Wang
Steven L. Waslander
Olivia Watkins
Daniel Watson
Silvan Weder
Dongyoon Wee
Dongming Wei
Tianyi Wei
Jia Wei
Dong Wei
Fangyun Wei
Longhui Wei
Mingqiang Wei
Xinyue Wei
Chen Wei
Donglai Wei
Pengxu Wei
Xing Wei
Xiu-Shen Wei
Wenqi Wei
Guoqiang Wei
Wei Wei
XingKui Wei
Xian Wei
Xingxing Wei
Yake Wei
Yuxiang Wei
Yi Wei
Luca Weihs
Michael Weinmann
Martin Weinmann

Congcong Wen
Chuan Wen
Jie Wen
Sijia Wen
Song Wen
Chao Wen
Xiang Wen
Zeyi Wen
Xin Wen
Yilin Wen
Yijia Weng
Shuchen Weng
Junwu Weng
Wenming Weng
Renliang Weng
Zhenyu Weng
Xinshuo Weng
Nicholas J. Westlake
Gordon Wetzstein
Lena M. Widin Klasén
Rick Wildes
Bryan M. Williams
Williem Williem
Ole Winther
Scott Wisdom
Alex Wong
Chau-Wai Wong
Kwan-Yee K. Wong
Yongkang Wong
Scott Workman
Marcel Worring
Michael Wray
Safwan Wshah
Xiang Wu
Aming Wu
Chongruo Wu
Cho-Ying Wu
Chunpeng Wu
Chenyan Wu
Ziyi Wu
Fuxiang Wu
Gang Wu
Haiping Wu
Huisi Wu
Jane Wu

Jialian Wu
Jing Wu
Jinjian Wu
Jianlong Wu
Xian Wu
Lifang Wu
Lifan Wu
Minye Wu
Qianyi Wu
Rongliang Wu
Rui Wu
Shiqian Wu
Shuzhe Wu
Shangzhe Wu
Tsung-Han Wu
Tz-Ying Wu
Ting-Wei Wu
Jiannan Wu
Zhiliang Wu
Yu Wu
Chenyun Wu
Dayan Wu
Dongxian Wu
Fei Wu
Hefeng Wu
Jianxin Wu
Weibin Wu
Wenxuan Wu
Wenhao Wu
Xiao Wu
Yicheng Wu
Yuanwei Wu
Yu-Huan Wu
Zhenxin Wu
Zhenyu Wu
Wei Wu
Peng Wu
Xiaohe Wu
Xindi Wu
Xinxing Wu
Xinyi Wu
Xingjiao Wu
Xiongwei Wu
Yangzheng Wu
Yanzhao Wu

Yawen Wu
Yong Wu
Yi Wu
Ying Nian Wu
Zhenyao Wu
Zhonghua Wu
Zongze Wu
Zuxuan Wu
Stefanie Wuhrer
Teng Xi
Jianing Xi
Fei Xia
Haifeng Xia
Menghan Xia
Yuanqing Xia
Zhihua Xia
Xiaobo Xia
Weihao Xia
Shihong Xia
Yan Xia
Yong Xia
Zhaoyang Xia
Zhihao Xia
Chuhua Xian
Yongqin Xian
Wangmeng Xiang
Fanbo Xiang
Tiange Xiang
Tao Xiang
Liuyu Xiang
Xiaoyu Xiang
Zhiyu Xiang
Aoran Xiao
Chunxia Xiao
Fanyi Xiao
Jimin Xiao
Jun Xiao
Taihong Xiao
Anqi Xiao
Junfei Xiao
Jing Xiao
Liang Xiao
Yang Xiao
Yuting Xiao
Yijun Xiao

Yao Xiao
Zeyu Xiao
Zhisheng Xiao
Zihao Xiao
Binhui Xie
Christopher Xie
Haozhe Xie
Jin Xie
Guo-Sen Xie
Hongtao Xie
Ming-Kun Xie
Tingting Xie
Chaohao Xie
Weicheng Xie
Xudong Xie
Jiyang Xie
Xiaohua Xie
Yuan Xie
Zhenyu Xie
Ning Xie
Xianghui Xie
Xiufeng Xie
You Xie
Yutong Xie
Fuyong Xing
Yifan Xing
Zhen Xing
Yuanjun Xiong
Jinhui Xiong
Weihua Xiong
Hongkai Xiong
Zhitong Xiong
Yuanhao Xiong
Yunyang Xiong
Yuwen Xiong
Zhiwei Xiong
Yuliang Xiu
An Xu
Chang Xu
Chenliang Xu
Chengming Xu
Chenshu Xu
Xiang Xu
Huijuan Xu
Zhe Xu

Jie Xu
Jingyi Xu
Jiarui Xu
Yinghao Xu
Kele Xu
Ke Xu
Li Xu
Linchuan Xu
Linning Xu
Mengde Xu
Mengmeng Frost Xu
Min Xu
Mingye Xu
Jun Xu
Ning Xu
Peng Xu
Runsheng Xu
Sheng Xu
Wenqiang Xu
Xiaogang Xu
Renzhe Xu
Kaidi Xu
Yi Xu
Chi Xu
Qiuling Xu
Baobei Xu
Feng Xu
Haohang Xu
Haofei Xu
Lan Xu
Mingze Xu
Songcen Xu
Weipeng Xu
Wenjia Xu
Wenju Xu
Xiangyu Xu
Xin Xu
Yinshuang Xu
Yixing Xu
Yuting Xu
Yanyu Xu
Zhenbo Xu
Zhiliang Xu
Zhiyuan Xu
Xiaohao Xu

Yanwu Xu
Yan Xu
Yiran Xu
Yifan Xu
Yufei Xu
Yong Xu
Zichuan Xu
Zenglin Xu
Zexiang Xu
Zhan Xu
Zheng Xu
Zhiwei Xu
Ziyue Xu
Shiyu Xuan
Hanyu Xuan
Fei Xue
Jianru Xue
Mingfu Xue
Qinghan Xue
Tianfan Xue
Chao Xue
Chuhui Xue
Nan Xue
Zhou Xue
Xiangyang Xue
Yuan Xue
Abhay Yadav
Ravindra Yadav
Kota Yamaguchi
Toshihiko Yamasaki
Kohei Yamashita
Chaochao Yan
Feng Yan
Kun Yan
Qingsen Yan
Qixin Yan
Rui Yan
Siming Yan
Xinchen Yan
Yaping Yan
Bin Yan
Qingan Yan
Shen Yan
Shipeng Yan
Xu Yan

Yan Yan
Yichao Yan
Zhaoyi Yan
Zike Yan
Zhiqiang Yan
Hongliang Yan
Zizheng Yan
Jiewen Yang
Anqi Joyce Yang
Shan Yang
Anqi Yang
Antoine Yang
Bo Yang
Baoyao Yang
Chenhongyi Yang
Dingkang Yang
De-Nian Yang
Dong Yang
David Yang
Fan Yang
Fengyu Yang
Fengting Yang
Fei Yang
Gengshan Yang
Heng Yang
Han Yang
Huan Yang
Yibo Yang
Jiancheng Yang
Jihan Yang
Jiawei Yang
Jiayu Yang
Jie Yang
Jinfa Yang
Jingkang Yang
Jinyu Yang
Cheng-Fu Yang
Ji Yang
Jianyu Yang
Kailun Yang
Tian Yang
Luyu Yang
Liang Yang
Li Yang
Michael Ying Yang

Yang Yang
Muli Yang
Le Yang
Qiushi Yang
Ren Yang
Ruihan Yang
Shuang Yang
Siyuan Yang
Su Yang
Shiqi Yang
Taojiannan Yang
Tianyu Yang
Lei Yang
Wanzhao Yang
Shuai Yang
William Yang
Wei Yang
Xiaofeng Yang
Xiaoshan Yang
Xin Yang
Xuan Yang
Xu Yang
Xingyi Yang
Xitong Yang
Jing Yang
Yanchao Yang
Wenming Yang
Yujiu Yang
Herb Yang
Jianfei Yang
Jinhui Yang
Chuanguang Yang
Guanglei Yang
Haitao Yang
Kewei Yang
Linlin Yang
Lijin Yang
Longrong Yang
Meng Yang
MingKun Yang
Sibei Yang
Shicai Yang
Tong Yang
Wen Yang
Xi Yang

Xiaolong Yang
Xue Yang
Yubin Yang
Ze Yang
Ziyi Yang
Yi Yang
Linjie Yang
Yuzhe Yang
Yiding Yang
Zhenpei Yang
Zhaohui Yang
Zhengyuan Yang
Zhibo Yang
Zongxin Yang
Hantao Yao
Mingde Yao
Rui Yao
Taiping Yao
Ting Yao
Cong Yao
Qingsong Yao
Quanming Yao
Xu Yao
Yuan Yao
Yao Yao
Yazhou Yao
Jiawen Yao
Shunyu Yao
Pew-Thian Yap
Sudhir Yarram
Rajeev Yasarla
Peng Ye
Botao Ye
Mao Ye
Fei Ye
Hanrong Ye
Jingwen Ye
Jinwei Ye
Jiarong Ye
Mang Ye
Meng Ye
Qi Ye
Qian Ye
Qixiang Ye
Junjie Ye

Yiming Zeng
Tieyong Zeng
Huanqiang Zeng
Dan Zeng
Yu Zeng
Wei Zhai
Yuanhao Zhai
Fangneng Zhan
Kun Zhan
Xiong Zhang
Jingdong Zhang
Jiangning Zhang
Zhilu Zhang
Gengwei Zhang
Dongsu Zhang
Hui Zhang
Binjie Zhang
Bo Zhang
Tianhao Zhang
Cecilia Zhang
Jing Zhang
Chaoning Zhang
Chenxu Zhang
Chi Zhang
Chris Zhang
Yabin Zhang
Zhao Zhang
Rufeng Zhang
Chaoyi Zhang
Zheng Zhang
Da Zhang
Yi Zhang
Edward Zhang
Xin Zhang
Feifei Zhang
Feilong Zhang
Yuqi Zhang
GuiXuan Zhang
Hanlin Zhang
Hanwang Zhang
Hanzhen Zhang
Haotian Zhang
He Zhang
Haokui Zhang
Hongyuan Zhang

Hengrui Zhang
Hongming Zhang
Mingfang Zhang
Jianpeng Zhang
Jiaming Zhang
Jichao Zhang
Jie Zhang
Jingfeng Zhang
Jingyi Zhang
Jinnian Zhang
David Junhao Zhang
Junjie Zhang
Junzhe Zhang
Jiawan Zhang
Jingyang Zhang
Kai Zhang
Lei Zhang
Lihua Zhang
Lu Zhang
Miao Zhang
Minjia Zhang
Mingjin Zhang
Qi Zhang
Qian Zhang
Qilong Zhang
Qiming Zhang
Qiang Zhang
Richard Zhang
Ruimao Zhang
Ruisi Zhang
Ruixin Zhang
Runze Zhang
Qilin Zhang
Shan Zhang
Shanshan Zhang
Xi Sheryl Zhang
Song-Hai Zhang
Chongyang Zhang
Kaihao Zhang
Songyang Zhang
Shu Zhang
Siwei Zhang
Shujian Zhang
Tianyun Zhang
Tong Zhang

Tao Zhang
Wenwei Zhang
Wenqiang Zhang
Wen Zhang
Xiaolin Zhang
Xingchen Zhang
Xingxuan Zhang
Xiuming Zhang
Xiaoshuai Zhang
Xuanmeng Zhang
Xuanyang Zhang
Xucong Zhang
Xingxing Zhang
Xikun Zhang
Xiaohan Zhang
Yahui Zhang
Yunhua Zhang
Yan Zhang
Yanghao Zhang
Yifei Zhang
Yifan Zhang
Yi-Fan Zhang
Yihao Zhang
Yingliang Zhang
Youshan Zhang
Yulun Zhang
Yushu Zhang
Yixiao Zhang
Yide Zhang
Zhongwen Zhang
Bowen Zhang
Chen-Lin Zhang
Zehua Zhang
Zekun Zhang
Zeyu Zhang
Xiaowei Zhang
Yifeng Zhang
Cheng Zhang
Hongguang Zhang
Yuexi Zhang
Fa Zhang
Guofeng Zhang
Hao Zhang
Haofeng Zhang
Hongwen Zhang

Hua Zhang

Jiaxin Zhang

Zhenyu Zhang

Jian Zhang

Jianfeng Zhang

Jiao Zhang

Jiakai Zhang

Lefei Zhang

Le Zhang

Mi Zhang

Min Zhang

Ning Zhang

Pan Zhang

Pu Zhang

Qing Zhang

Renrui Zhang

Shifeng Zhang

Shuo Zhang

Shaoxiong Zhang

Weizhong Zhang

Xi Zhang

Xiaomei Zhang

Xinyu Zhang

Yin Zhang

Zicheng Zhang

Zihao Zhang

Ziqi Zhang

Zhaoxiang Zhang

Zhen Zhang

Zhipeng Zhang

Zhixing Zhang

Zhizheng Zhang

Jiawei Zhang

Zhong Zhang

Pingping Zhang

Yixin Zhang

Kui Zhang

Lingzhi Zhang

Huaiwen Zhang

Quanshi Zhang

Zhoutong Zhang

Yuhang Zhang

Yuting Zhang

Zhang Zhang

Ziming Zhang

Zhizhong Zhang

Qilong Zhangli

Bingyin Zhao

Bin Zhao

Chenglong Zhao

Lei Zhao

Feng Zhao

Gangming Zhao

Haiyan Zhao

Hao Zhao

Handong Zhao

Hengshuang Zhao

Yinan Zhao

Jiaojiao Zhao

Jiaqi Zhao

Jing Zhao

Kaili Zhao

Haojie Zhao

Yucheng Zhao

Longjiao Zhao

Long Zhao

Qingsong Zhao

Qingyu Zhao

Rui Zhao

Rui-Wei Zhao

Sicheng Zhao

Shuang Zhao

Siyan Zhao

Zelin Zhao

Shiyu Zhao

Wang Zhao

Tiesong Zhao

Qian Zhao

Wangbo Zhao

Xi-Le Zhao

Xu Zhao

Yajie Zhao

Yang Zhao

Ying Zhao

Yin Zhao

Yizhou Zhao

Yunhan Zhao

Yuyang Zhao

Yue Zhao

Yuzhi Zhao

Bowen Zhao

Pu Zhao

Bingchen Zhao

Borui Zhao

Fuqiang Zhao

Hanbin Zhao

Jian Zhao

Mingyang Zhao

Na Zhao

Rongchang Zhao

Ruiqi Zhao

Shuai Zhao

Wenda Zhao

Wenliang Zhao

Xiangyun Zhao

Yifan Zhao

Yaping Zhao

Zhou Zhao

He Zhao

Jie Zhao

Xibin Zhao

Xiaoqi Zhao

Zhengyu Zhao

Jin Zhe

Chuanxia Zheng

Huan Zheng

Hao Zheng

Jia Zheng

Jian-Qing Zheng

Shuai Zheng

Meng Zheng

Mingkai Zheng

Qian Zheng

Qi Zheng

Wu Zheng

Yinqiang Zheng

Yufeng Zheng

Yutong Zheng

Yalin Zheng

Yu Zheng

Feng Zheng

Zhaoheng Zheng

Haitian Zheng

Kang Zheng

Bolun Zheng

Haiyong Zheng
Mingwu Zheng
Sipeng Zheng
Tu Zheng
Wenzhao Zheng
Xiawu Zheng
Yinglin Zheng
Zhuo Zheng
Zilong Zheng
Kecheng Zheng
Zerong Zheng
Shuaifeng Zhi
Tiancheng Zhi
Jia-Xing Zhong
Yiwu Zhong
Fangwei Zhong
Zhihang Zhong
Yaoyao Zhong
Yiran Zhong
Zhun Zhong
Zichun Zhong
Bo Zhou
Boyao Zhou
Brady Zhou
Mo Zhou
Chunluan Zhou
Dingfu Zhou
Fan Zhou
Jingkai Zhou
Honglu Zhou
Jiaming Zhou
Jiahuan Zhou
Jun Zhou
Kaiyang Zhou
Keyang Zhou
Kuangqi Zhou
Lei Zhou
Lihua Zhou
Man Zhou
Mingyi Zhou
Mingyuan Zhou
Ning Zhou
Peng Zhou
Penghao Zhou
Qianyi Zhou

Shuigeng Zhou
Shangchen Zhou
Huayi Zhou
Zhize Zhou
Sanping Zhou
Qin Zhou
Tao Zhou
Wenbo Zhou
Xiangdong Zhou
Xiao-Yun Zhou
Xiao Zhou
Yang Zhou
Yipin Zhou
Zhenyu Zhou
Hao Zhou
Chu Zhou
Daquan Zhou
Da-Wei Zhou
Hang Zhou
Kang Zhou
Qianyu Zhou
Sheng Zhou
Wenhui Zhou
Xingyi Zhou
Yan-Jie Zhou
Yiyi Zhou
Yu Zhou
Yuan Zhou
Yuqian Zhou
Yuxuan Zhou
Zixiang Zhou
Wengang Zhou
Shuchang Zhou
Tianfei Zhou
Yichao Zhou
Alex Zhu
Chenchen Zhu
Deyao Zhu
Xiatian Zhu
Guibo Zhu
Haidong Zhu
Hao Zhu
Hongzi Zhu
Rui Zhu
Jing Zhu

Jianke Zhu
Junchen Zhu
Lei Zhu
Lingyu Zhu
Luyang Zhu
Menglong Zhu
Peihao Zhu
Hui Zhu
Xiaofeng Zhu
Tyler (Lixuan) Zhu
Wentao Zhu
Xiangyu Zhu
Xinqi Zhu
Xinxin Zhu
Xinliang Zhu
Yangguang Zhu
Yichen Zhu
Yixin Zhu
Yanjun Zhu
Yousong Zhu
Yuhao Zhu
Ye Zhu
Feng Zhu
Zhen Zhu
Fangrui Zhu
Jinjing Zhu
Linchao Zhu
Pengfei Zhu
Sijie Zhu
Xiaobin Zhu
Xiaoguang Zhu
Zezhou Zhu
Zhenyao Zhu
Kai Zhu
Pengkai Zhu
Bingbing Zhuang
Chengyuan Zhuang
Liansheng Zhuang
Peiye Zhuang
Yixin Zhuang
Yihong Zhuang
Junbao Zhuo
Andrea Ziani
Bartosz Zieliński
Primo Zingaretti

Contents – Part II

MHR-Net: Multiple-Hypothesis Reconstruction of Non-Rigid Shapes from 2D Views

Haitian Zeng[1,2], Xin Yu[1], Jiaxu Miao[3], and Yi Yang[3(✉)]

[1] University of Technology Sydney, Sydney, Australia
haitian.zeng@student.uts.edu.au, xin.yu@uts.edu.au
[2] Baidu Research, Beijing, China
[3] Zhejiang University, Hangzhou, China
jiaxu.miao@yahoo.com, yangyics@zju.edu.cn

Abstract. We propose MHR-Net, a novel method for recovering Non-Rigid Shapes from Motion (NRSfM). MHR-Net aims to find a set of reasonable reconstructions for a 2D view, and it also selects the most likely reconstruction from the set. To deal with the challenging unsupervised generation of non-rigid shapes, we develop a new Deterministic Basis and Stochastic Deformation scheme in MHR-Net. The non-rigid shape is first expressed as the sum of a coarse shape basis and a flexible shape deformation, then multiple hypotheses are generated with uncertainty modeling of the deformation part. MHR-Net is optimized with reprojection loss on the basis and the best hypothesis. Furthermore, we design a new Procrustean Residual Loss, which reduces the rigid rotations between similar shapes and further improves the performance. Experiments show that MHR-Net achieves state-of-the-art reconstruction accuracy on Human3.6M, SURREAL and 300-VW datasets.

Keywords: NRSfM · Multiple-hypothesis

1 Introduction

Recovering 3D structures from multiple 2D views is a classic and important task in computer vision. Non-Rigid Structure-from-Motion (NRSfM), which aims at reconstructing deformable shapes, is a challenging task and has been studied for decades.

The major difficulty of NRSfM is the ambiguity of solutions due to arbitrary deformation of shapes. Most of the NRSfM methods are based on the assumption of Bregler et al. [9] where the deformable shape is a linear combination of a small number of atom shapes. This assumption greatly reduces the degree of freedom in NRSfM, yet it is still not enough for researchers to reach a deterministic and

---

Supplementary Information The online version contains supplementary material available at https://doi.org/10.1007/978-3-031-20086-1_1.

S. Avidan et al. (Eds.): ECCV 2022, LNCS 13662, pp. 1–17, 2022.
https://doi.org/10.1007/978-3-031-20086-1_1

closed-form solution. Prior work of Akhter et al. [25] reveals that the local minimas grows exponentially with the basis number, and the reconstructed shapes from most of local minimas deviate significantly from ground truth. And Dai et al. [16, 18] demonstrate that the rank minimization method also leads to multiple minimas in perspective cases. These reveal that there are usually multiple solutions that all minimize the cost function of a "prior-free" NRSfM, but it is generally intractable to find all those solutions due to the inherent complexity of NRSfM ambiguity.

Nevertheless, in most cases we only need to obtain several most reasonable hypotheses since they are valuable in practical scenarios, while searching for all ambiguous solutions exhaustively is not necessary. This leads us to focus on finding multiple high-quality hypotheses for the NRSfM problem.

Multiple hypotheses are usually modeled with uncertainty or generative models like CVAE [59], MDN [36] or CGAN [37]. However, these conventional modeling methods are supervised by 3D ground-truth, which is not available for a NRSfM problem. Moreover, in NRSfM, a naive ensemble of independent models is prone to decomposition ambiguity [18], and a variational autoencoder is also found hard to train [66].

To overcome the above challenges, we propose a novel MHR-Net for Multiple-Hypothesis Reconstruction of non-rigid shapes. Different from a standard model which outputs one reconstruction for a single input, MHR-Net is capable to produce multiple reasonable solutions and one best solution. We develop several critical designs for the successful generation of multiple hypotheses. Firstly, one non-rigid shape is expressed as the sum of a *basis* and a *deformation*. The basis is the coarse and shared structure among all shapes, while the deformation accounts for the diverse and flexible parts of shapes. This shape expression enhances the representation capability of MHR-Net when trained with an intermediate reprojection loss on the basis. Based on this expression, we further propose a novel Deterministic Basis and Stochastic Deformation (DBSD) scheme for multiple hypotheses generation. Specifically, MHR-Net estimates one basis in a standard deterministic manner and multiple deformations in a stochastic way. Then the multiple reconstructions are obtained by adding the basis and deformations. To optimize MHR-Net, we adopt a pseudo "hindsight" loss which is to select a hypothesis with the minimal reprojection error and calculates the standard loss function on the selected hypothesis. In inference, the model produces the best hypothesis in the same way. The DBSD scheme not only enables MHR-Net to produce multiple high-quality solutions of NRSfM, but also further enhances the accuracy of the reconstruction.

Moreover, we develop a new Procrustean Residual Loss to regularize the reconstruction and reduce undesirable rigid rotations in a differentiable and efficient way. Experiments on Human3.6M, 300-VW and SURREAL datasets demonstrate state-of-the-art reconstruction accuracy of MHR-Net. Finally, we show that MHR-Net is capable to produce multiple possible solutions of 3D human poses and largely-deforming regions of dense human body meshes.

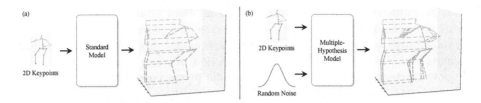

Fig. 1. (a) A standard function-based NRSfM model maps the 2D input to a single 3D output. (b) The proposed MHR-Net is aware of the uncertainty of 2D-to-3D mapping. Given an extra noise vector, MHR-Net is capable to output multiple reasonable reconstructions of the 2D input.

We summarize our contributions as follows:

- We propose the novel MHR-Net for NRSfM. To the best of our knowledge, it is the first method that produces multiple high-quality hypotheses for non-rigid shape reconstruction in one model.
- We introduce a deterministic basis and stochastic deformation scheme together with a intermediate loss and a pseudo hindsight loss. These designs are effective for the challenging unsupervised uncertainty modeling of multiple 3D shapes.
- We develop a novel Procrustean Residual Loss for NRSfM regularization, and it further improves the shape recovery accuracy of MHR-Net.

2   Related Works

NRSfM. Recovering the deforming 3D shape from multiple 2D views is known as the Non-Rigid Structure-from-Motion problem (NRSfM), which is firstly put forward by Bregler et al. [9]. NRSfM is a highly ambiguous problem, and therefore enforcing correct constraints is key to solving this problem. Previous works propose various effective approaches to the non-rigid shape reconstruction, including rank minimization [17,41], smooth trajectories [7,10,20,21], manifold [22,31], metric projection [42], sparsity-based methods [28], energy minimization [52,57], inextensibility [15,64], isometry [43], deep models [28,40,47,69], procrustean normal distribution [34], consensus [13], hierarchical priors [61], force-based and physic-based methods [3,6], union of subspaces [1,4,5,33,70], piecewise methods [19,60], and many other breaking-through methods [2,11,24,32,44,49,50,53].

Much attention has been paid to the uniqueness and determinacy of NRSfM. Xiao et al. [68] show that selecting a set of frames as the basis can lead to a unique closed-form solution. Akhter et al. [25] argue that the orthogonal constraints of rotations is indeed sufficient for a unique solution except for a rigid rotation and the major difficulty lies in the optimization. Dai et al. [17] propose a block-matrix rank-minimizing method and analyze whether their method leads to a unique solution or multiple solutions. Park et al. [45] provide a geometric analysis showing that the quality of sequential reconstruction is affected by the relative motion of a point and the camera, and propose a novel measure reconstructability to indicate the reconstruction quality. Valmadre et al. [62] propose a deterministic approach to 3D human pose recovery by using the rigid sub-structure of human body.

Multiple-Hypothesis 3D Pose Estimation. The ambiguity of monocular 3D human pose estimation has been noticed early [58]. Li et al. [36] use a mixture density network or a Conditional GAN [37] to output a set of plausible 3D poses from a 2D input. Sharma et al. [55] propose to solve the ill-posed 2D-to-3D lifting problem with CVAE [59] and Ordinal Ranking. Wehrbein et al. [67] use Normalizing Flows to model the deterministic 3D-2D projection and solve the ambiguous inverse 2D-3D lifting problem. The major difference between our work and multiple-hypotheses 3D pose estimation is that our model is trained without 3D ground truth.

3   Preliminary

In the classic non-rigid structure-from-motion problem, given N_f frames 2D observations $\{W_i\}_{i=1}^{N_f}$ of a deformable object as input, we are interested in factorizing $W_i \in \mathbb{R}^{2 \times N_p}$ into a camera matrix $M_i \in \mathbb{R}^{2 \times 3}$ and a shape matrix $S_i \in \mathbb{R}^{3 \times N_p}$ such that:

$$W_i = M_i S_i. \tag{1}$$

Here, we suppose that S_i is centered at zero such that the translation term is cancelled, and N_p stands for the number of points. M_i is the composition of a projection matrix $\Pi \in \mathbb{R}^{2 \times 3}$ and a rotation matrix $R_i \in SO(3)$ so that $M_i = \Pi R_i$. For orthographic projection, Π is simply $[I_2 \ 0]$. In this work, we suppose that the camera projection Π is known, allowing us to focus on the estimation of rotation R_i.

In the recent progress of NRSfM [28,40,47], M_i and S_i are modeled as functions of the input W_i. One typical paradigm [14,40] is to first extract features from W_i using a backbone network $\mathcal{H}(W_i)$ like [39], and then to estimate the M_i and S_i with different network branches $\mathcal{F}_0$ and $\mathcal{G}$ subsequent to $\mathcal{H}$:

$$S_i = \mathcal{F}_0(\mathcal{H}(W_i)), \quad M_i = \mathcal{G}(\mathcal{H}(W_i)). \tag{2}$$

Modeling the factorization as a function enables NRSfM methods to be optimized on large-scale datasets, and allows models to directly perform reconstruction on unseen data. To train such models, the cost function usually contains a data term and a regularization term, represented as:

$$\mathcal{L} = \sum_{i=1}^{N_f} \mathcal{L}_{\text{data}}(W_i, M_i, S_i) + \mathcal{L}_{\text{reg}}(M_i, S_i), \tag{3}$$

where the data term $\mathcal{L}_{\text{data}}$ is usually the reprojection error $\|W_i - M_i S_i\|$ and the regularization term is versatile.

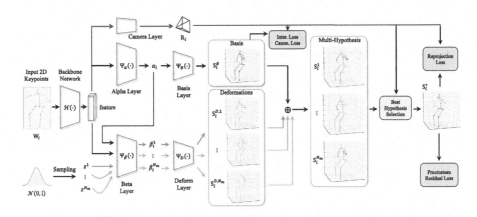

Fig. 2. An overview of the proposed MHR-Net. MHR-Net uses a backbone network $\mathcal{H}$ to extract features from the 2D input W_i. The camera rotation R_i is estimated by the rotation layer. Next, the basis shape S_i^B and its coefficients α_i are estimated by Ψ_B and Ψ_α respectively. To generate multiple hypotheses, beta layer Ψ_β takes α_i, $\mathcal{H}(W_i)$ and random noise $\{z^1, \cdots, z^{N_m}\}$ as inputs, and outputs a set of deformation coefficients $\{\beta_i^1, \cdots, \beta_i^{N_m}\}$. Then the deformation coefficients are passed to the deformation layer Ψ_D to produce deformations $\{S_i^{D,1}, \cdots, S_i^{D,N_m}\}$. By adding each deformation to S_i^B, multiple hypotheses $\{S_i^1, \cdots, S_i^{N_m}\}$ are obtained. Then, the hypothesis with the smallest reprojection error is selected as the best hypothesis S_i^*. Loss functions are calculated on S_i^B and S_i^*.

4 Proposed Method

4.1 Multiple Hypothesis Reconstruction Network - Overview

We aim to develop a prediction function $\mathcal{F}$ that can output N_m reconstructions for a single input W_i:

$$\mathcal{F}(W_i) = \{S_i^1, S_i^2, \cdots, S_i^{N_m}\}, \tag{4}$$

and each of these reconstructions is supposed to minimize the cost function in Eq. 3. As the inherent ambiguity of NRSfM is complex and there exists a large number of poor ambiguous solutions [25], we also expect the hypotheses to be as accurate as possible among all solutions.

However, generating multi-hypothesis reconstruction for NRSfM is challenging for several reasons: (1) Without 3D ground-truth as supervision, the ambiguous 2D-to-3D mappings cannot be learned using standard generative models like CVAE [59], Conditional GAN [37] or Normalizing Flow [67]. (2) Multiple hypotheses easily suffer from the decomposition ambiguity of NRSfM [18], i.e. multiple solutions are trivial if they are related by a certain rotation G inserted in the decomposition $W_i = M_i G G^{-1} S_i$.

We introduce a novel Multiple Hypothesis Reconstruction Network (MHR-Net), which takes a step towards a multiple-hypothesis NRSfM model. MHR-Net overcomes the above difficulties in a simple and effective way, and is capable to produce multiple accurate reconstructions and one best hypothesis. Next, we describe the hypothesis generation scheme in Sect. 4.2, the optimization in Sect. 4.3 and the regularization in Sect. 4.4.

4.2 Deterministic Basis and Stochastic Deformation for Hypothesis Generation

Traditionally, the 3D shape S_i is represented as a linear combination of K_b atom shapes $B_k \in \mathbb{R}^{3 \times N_P}$:

$$S_i = \sum_{k=1}^{K_b} (\alpha_{i,k} \otimes I_3) B_k, \tag{5}$$

where $\alpha_{i,k}$ is the weight of k-th atom shapes in S_i, and $\otimes$ is the Kronecker product. This widely-accepted representation implicitly assumes the low-rankness of all estimated 3D shapes, and it is one of keys to successful recovery of non-rigid shapes. However, the capacity of this shape representation is limited when applied to modern large-scale datasets since they usually contain millions of frames or thousands of keypoints. A naive way is to enlarge the capacity by increasing the dimension K_b, but it also bring undesirable degrees of freedom to the full shape, leading to a regularization-flexibility dillema.

Inspired by previous works [1,8,57], we develop a new shape representation for MHR-Net. We posit that the deformable shape is comprised of a *basis* S_i^B and a *deformation* S_i^D, written as:

$$S_i = \underbrace{\sum_{k=1}^{K_b} (\alpha_{i,k} \otimes I_3) B_k}_{S_i^B} + \underbrace{\sum_{l=1}^{K_d} (\beta_{i,l} \otimes I_3) D_l}_{S_i^D}, \tag{6}$$

where $D_l \in \mathbb{R}^{3 \times N_P}$ denotes the l-th atom deformation, $\beta_{i,l}$ is the weight of D_l in S_i, and $K_b < K_d$. Note that the mean shape for short sequences in [57] is a special case of Eq. 6 with $K_b = 1, \alpha_i = 1$. This basis-deformation modeling enhances the shape representation capability of MHR-Net with hierarchical flexibility. Intuitively, S_i^B is used to capture the low-rank common part of the 3D shapes, while S_i^D fits the diverse small deformations with higher flexibility.

Based on the basis-deformation expression of shapes, we now introduce a novel Deterministic Basis and Stochastic Deformation (DBSD), which is the core scheme for multiple hypothesis generation in MHR-Net. We assume that the variation of N_m accurate hypotheses appears only in S_i^D. While Wang et al. [66] find that introducing randomness to the estimation of full 3D shapes with VAE [27] is not viable, the proposed partial uncertainty in S_i^D makes MHR-Net overcome the training difficulty. More importantly, we find that DBSD can lead to an even better recovery accuracy with the training strategy in Sect. 4.3.

Specifically, MHR-Net generates multiple reconstructions by estimating one basis in the standard deterministic way and multiple deformations with stochastic variations. For the deterministic part, coefficients $\alpha_i = [\alpha_{i,1} \cdots \alpha_{i,K_b}]^T$ are estimated with a convolutional layer Ψ_α:

$$\alpha_i = \Psi_\alpha(\mathcal{H}(W_i)). \tag{7}$$

For the stochastic deformation part, the coefficients $\beta_i = [\beta_{i,1} \cdots \beta_{i,K_d}]^T$ are calculated by a convolutional layer Ψ_β which takes features $\mathcal{H}(W_i)$, coefficients α_i and a noise vector $z \sim N(0, I)$ as inputs:

$$\beta_i = \Psi_\beta(\mathcal{H}(W_i), \alpha_i, z). \tag{8}$$

By sampling N_m noise vectors $\{z^1, \cdots, z^{N_m}\}$ from the isotropic Gaussian with dimension dim_z and passing them to Ψ_β, we have a collection $\{\beta_i^1, \cdots, \beta_i^{N_m}\}$. Next, the basis and multiple deformations are produced by two following convolutional layers Ψ_B and Ψ_D:

$$S_i^B = \Psi_B(\alpha_i), \quad S_i^{D,m} = \Psi_D(\beta_i^m). \tag{9}$$

Note that the atoms B_k and D_l are learned as the parameters of Ψ_B and Ψ_D. Finally, the multiple hypothesis reconstructions $\{S_i^1, \cdots, S_i^{N_m}\}$ are generated by:

$$S_i^m = S_i^B + S_i^{D,m}, \tag{10}$$

where $m = 1 \cdots N_m$.

For camera R_i estimation, we avoid the decomposition ambiguity by simply estimating one rotation matrix for all hypothesis. We follow [40] to predict the rotation matrix using Rodrigues' Rotation Formula, which is parameterized by a 3 dimensional output of a convolutional layer built upon the extracted features. Given Π, we obtain $M_i = \Pi R_i$.

4.3   Optimizing with Intermediate Loss and Best Hypothesis Selection

We introduce two effective methods for optimizing MHR-Net on the data term $\mathcal{L}_{data}$.

Intermediate Loss. First, we consider the optimization of a single hypothesis S_i^m produced by MHR-Net from W_i. The proposed basis-deformation expression of shapes in Eq. 6 is the summation of two linear subspaces. In practice, MHR-Net is prone to using only one flexible subspace S_i^D for shape expression if we adopt the standard reprojection loss $\|W_i - M_i S_i^m\|$. To make the basis-deformation expression work as expected, we propose to add an extra reprojection loss to the intermediate results of reconstruction, i.e. the basis S_i^B. This enforces MHR-Net to produce a low-rank and coarse prediction S_i^B of the 3D shape, thus letting S_i^D focus on the small and diverse residuals. The extra intermediate loss is written as $\|W_i - M_i S_i^B\|$.

Best Hypothesis Selection. Now we consider the optimization of all hypotheses. There are several approaches to train a model with multiple predictions, including minimizing losses of all predictions, selecting one hypothesis with mixture density [36], *etc.* In MHR-Net, we choose to use a pseudo "hindsight" loss [35,51]. The original "hindsight" loss choose a prediction that is the closest to the ground truth and then calculate the standard single-prediction loss. As in NRSfM we do not have any 3D ground truth, we heuristically use the reprojection error as the criterion to select the best hypothesis among our predictions. Together with the intermediate loss, $\mathcal{L}_{\text{data}}$ is written as:

$$\mathcal{L}_{\text{data}} = \lambda_B \left\| W_i - M_i S_i^B \right\| + \lambda_F \min_m \left\| W_i - M_i S_i^m \right\|, \tag{11}$$

where λ_B, λ_F are balancing factors and $\lambda_B + \lambda_F = 1$. Compared to other multi-prediction training approaches, we find that the proposed strategy brings a better reconstruction accuracy to all hypotheses. Moreover, when inferring a single best reconstruction S_i^* of the input, S_i^* is naturally obtained with the same best hypothesis strategy.

Discussion. (1) The insight of successful hypothesis generation in MHR-Net is to constrain the norm of the flexible deformation subspace. Although the proposed shape representation (Eq. 6) has a large degree of freedom (S_i^D could cause a maximum of 2^{9K_d} local minimas [25]), Eq. 11 implicitly constrains the norm of S_i^D to be relatively small compared to S_i^B when the balancing factors are chosen as $\lambda_B = 0.8, \lambda_F = 0.2$. On the other hand, one can choose a smaller λ_B and adding a diversity loss as in [37] for generating more diverse hypotheses. (2) Moreover, we found that the model with DBSD has a slightly higher $\mathcal{L}_{data}$ and a lower $\mathcal{L}_{reg}$ compared to the deterministic model, which indicates that DBSD leads to a better regularized model. The diverse hypotheses reduce overfitting of MHR-Net and enhance the generalization capability.

4.4   Procrustean Residual Loss for Regularization

In this section, we introduce a novel Procrustean Residual Loss for regularizing the non-rigid shape reconstruction.

Motivation. Reducing the rigid motions between reconstructed shapes is one of the keys to successful NRSfM. In the previous work of Novotny et al. [40], the Transversal property is proposed to characterize a space where a shape is enforced to appears in a canonical view, such that the effects of rigid motions between same shapes are removed. Implemented with an auxiliary neural network, the Transversal property is effective in performing non-rigid reconstructions.

However, the Transversal property is still restricted to aligning only identical shapes. That means shapes with small differences are not guaranteed to be aligned in a Transversal set. In other words, the effect of a rigid motion is not removed for similar (but not identical) shapes. As regularization on similar shapes is shown to be useful in a recent work [69], we are motivated to reduce the rigid motion between similar shapes.

To achieve this objective, we first define two distance measures:

Definition 1. *Given two non-degenerated shapes $S_i, S_j \in \mathbb{R}^{3 \times N_p}$ and the optimal rotation R^* aligning S_i to S_j, the Original distance δ_{ori} is $\|S_i - S_j\|_F$, and the Procrustean distance δ_{pro} is $\|R^* S_i - S_j\|_F$.*

Here, a shape is non-degenerated if $\text{rank}(S_i) = 3$, $\|\cdot\|_F$ denotes the Frobenius norm, and the optimal rotation R^* is obtained with the orthogonal Procrustes [54].

Next, we use the two defined distances to: (1) test whether S_i and S_j are similar or not; (2) if S_i, S_j are similar, measure the effect of rigid motions. In step (1), S_i, S_j are considered to be similar if $\delta_{pro} < \epsilon$, where ϵ is a hyperparameter of similarity threshold. We use the Procrustean distance in this step since it is agnostic of rigid rotations. In step (2), we propose to measure the effect of rigid motions with the *Procrustean Residual* δ_{res}, calculated as:

$$\delta_{res} = \delta_{ori} - \delta_{pro}. \tag{12}$$

The Procrustean Residual indicates how much the Original distance can be reduced with rigid motions, and δ_{res} reaches zero if and only if S_i and S_j are already optimally aligned (i.e. $R^* = I$). Therefore, the undesirable rigid motion between S_i, S_j is reduced when we minimize δ_{res}.

Loss Design. We now introduce the Procrustean Residual Loss for NRSfM regularization. This loss function realizes the minimization[1] of δ_{res} and is developed in a differentiable way.

Given two shapes S_i, S_j randomly sampled from the network prediction batch, the optimal rotation that aligns S_i to S_j is calculated with the orthogonal Procrustes [54]:

$$R_{i,j}^* = VU^T, \quad S_i S_j^T = U\Sigma V^T, \tag{13}$$

where $U\Sigma V^T$ is the singular value decomposition of $S_i S_j^T$.

Next, we calculate the (normalized) Procrustean distance and the Procrustean Residual as follows:

$$\bar{\delta}_{pro} = \frac{\|R_{i,j}^* S_i - S_j\|_F}{\|S_j\|_F}, \quad \bar{\delta}_{res} = \frac{\|S_i - S_j\|_F}{\|S_j\|_F} - \bar{\delta}_{pro}. \tag{14}$$

We normalize the differences with $\|S_j\|_F$ to make the loss numerically stable. The Procrustean Residual Loss is:

$$\mathcal{L}_{res}(S_i, S_j) = \rho(\bar{\delta}_{pro}, \epsilon) \cdot \bar{\delta}_{res}, \tag{15}$$

where $\rho(\bar{\delta}_{pro}, \epsilon) = 1$ if $\bar{\delta}_{pro} < \epsilon$, else $\rho = 0$.

The practical problem of the proposed loss function is that $\mathcal{L}_{res}$ contains a non-differentiable operation SVD in Eq. 13. To make $\mathcal{L}_{res}$ differentiable, one effective way is to use the Lagrange multiplier method on Lie Group [46,47] for a closed-form partial derivative, and another way is to leverage modern auto-grad

---

[1] Note that in general δ_{res} cannot be reduce to exactly zero for all pairs simultaneously.

libraries where the numeric computation of SVD is differentiable [28,66,69]. In this paper, we choose to use a simple alternative approach by detaching $R^*_{i,j}$ from the computation graph, namely $R^*_{i,j}$ is viewed as a constant matrix. In such way, $\mathcal{L}_{\text{res}}$ only involves standard differentiable operations of inputs S_i, S_j, which frees us from the calculation of SVD gradient and keeps the model computationally efficient.

For the regularization term $\mathcal{L}_{\text{reg}}$ of MHR-Net, we apply a canonicalization loss $\mathcal{L}_{\text{cano}}{}^2$ [40] to the deterministic basis S^B_i and $\mathcal{L}_{\text{res}}$ to S^*_i, leading to:

$$\mathcal{L}_{\text{reg}} = \mathcal{L}_{\text{cano}} + \lambda_{\text{res}}\mathcal{L}_{\text{res}}, \tag{16}$$

where λ_{res} is the weight of Procrustean Residual Loss. Although only including $\mathcal{L}_{\text{res}}$ in $\mathcal{L}_{\text{reg}}$ is possible and produces good results, we empirically find that using two losses jointly leads to a better performance.

5   Experiments

We evaluate the proposed MHR-Net in two aspects: (1) The reconstruction accuracy of the best hypothesis. (2) The multiple hypothesis reconstructions. We also make an in-depth analysis of proposed components.

5.1   Datasets and Experimental Setups

Human3.6M [26]. It is the largest 3D human pose dataset with a total of 3.6 million frames. It contains 15 different activities performed by 7 professional actors and captured by four cameras. We follow the common protocols to use five subjects (S1, S5-8) as the training set and two subjects (S9 and S11) as the testing set. We adopt the widely-used pre-processing from Pavllo et al. [48].

300VW [56]. The 300VW is a large-scale facial landmark dataset. It has a total of 114 sequences with 2D annotations of 68 landmarks. Following [47], we use the subset of 64 sequences from 300VW, and divide them into a training set and a testing set of 32 sequences respectively. As 3D ground-truth is not provided, we follow [47] to adopt the results from [12] as 3D ground-truths.

SURREAL [63]. The SURREAL dataset contains 6 million synthetic human images with large variations in shape, view-point and pose. The 6,890 dense 3D points are obtained by fitting SMPL [38] to CMU MOCAP dataset. Following [47,66], the training and testing sets include 5,000 and 2,401 frames selected from the full dataset, respectively.

Metrics. We adopt the following two metrics:
(1) MPJPE: It stands for the mean per joint error, which is calculated as $\frac{1}{N_p}\left\|S_i - S^{\text{gt}}_i\right\|_1$. To address the reflection ambiguity, we follow [40,47,66] to report the minimal error with ground-truth between original and flipped shapes.
(2) Normalized Error (NE): It reflects the relative estimation error and is computed by: $\frac{\left\|S_i - S^{\text{gt}}_i\right\|_F}{\left\|S_{\text{gt}}\right\|_F}$.

---

[2] Please refer to the supplementary material or [40] for details.

Table 1. Quantitative results on Human3.6M dataset.

Methods (Ortho.)	Direct.	Discuss	Eating	Greet	Phone	Pose	Purch.	Sitting	SittingD.	Smoke	Photo	Wait	Walk	WalkD.	WalkT.	Mean
CSF2 [23]	87.2	90.1	96.1	95.9	102.9	92.1	99.3	129.8	136.7	99.5	120.1	95.2	90.8	102.4	89.2	101.6
SPM [18]	65.3	68.7	82.0	70.1	95.3	65.1	71.9	117.0	136.0	84.3	88.9	71.2	59.5	73.3	68.3	82.3
C3DPO [40]	**56.1**	55.6	62.2	**66.4**	63.2	**62.0**	62.9	76.3	85.8	**59.9**	88.7	63.3	71.1	70.7	72.3	67.8
PRN [47]	65.3	58.2	60.5	73.8	**60.7**	71.5	64.6	79.8	90.2	60.3	**81.2**	67.1	**54.4**	**61.2**	**65.6**	66.7
MHR-Net (Ours)	60.3	**54.3**	**55.5**	67.9	67.7	69.5	**61.3**	**69.7**	**83.2**	67.6	85.3	**61.7**	61.9	63.4	68.2	**65.8**
Methods (Persp.)	Direct.	Discuss	Eating	Greet	Phone	Pose	Purch.	Sitting	SittingD.	Smoke	Photo	Wait	Walk	WalkD.	WalkT.	Mean
PoseGAN [30]	–	–	–	–	–	–	–	–	–	–	–	–	–	–	–	130.9
SFC [29]	–	–	–	–	–	–	-	–	–	–	–	–	–	–	–	218.0
Consensus [13]	–	–	–	–	–	–	–	–	–	–	–	–	–	–	–	120.1
DNRSFM [28]	–	–	–	–	–	–	–	–	–	–	–	–	–	–	–	101.6
Wang et al. [65]	–	–	–	–	–	–	–	–	–	–	–	–	–	–	–	86.2
C3DPO [40]	96.8	85.7	85.8	107.1	86.0	96.8	93.9	94.9	96.7	86.0	124.3	90.7	95.2	93.4	101.3	95.6
PRN [47]	93.1	83.3	76.2	98.6	78.8	91.7	81.4	87.4	91.6	78.2	104.3	89.6	83.0	80.5	95.3	86.4
PAUL [66]	–	–	–	–	–	–	–	–	–	–	–	–	–	–	–	88.3
PoseDict [14]	74.6	82.9	77.0	86.7	80.0	79.2	94.2	88.4	124.0	77.1	103.8	80.8	78.8	94.2	78.3	85.6
ITES [14]	77.6	77.3	77.1	77.3	77.3	77.4	77.3	77.2	**77.3**	77.1	**77.1**	77.5	77.3	**77.2**	77.5	77.2
MHR-Net (Ours)	**62.8**	**68.3**	62.2	**73.9**	**73.7**	**67.0**	**70.2**	76.7	100.0	**71.5**	90.0	**72.3**	**68.8**	80.2	**71.0**	**72.6**

5.2   Main Results

In this subsection and Sect. 5.3, we treating MHR-Net as a single-prediction model by using the best hypothesis S_i^*. We report the standard NRSfM evaluation results of MHR-Net on three datasets.

For Human3.6M, we test the performance of MHR-Net under two settings: orthographic camera and perspective camera. The major competitors of MHR-Net are state-of-the-art deep NRSfM models, including C3DPO [40], DNRSFM [28], PRN [47], PAUL [66], ITES [14]. In Table 1, we report the MPJPE of all frames and 15 individual activities on the test set. We also includes classic methods like Consensus [13], SFC [29] for comparison. As shown in Table 1, MHR-Net outperforms all competing methods overall in both orthographic and perspective experiments. These results on the challenging Human3.6M dataset verify the effectiveness of MHR-Net on reconstructing highly-flexible human poses.

For 300VW dataset and SURREAL dataset, we compare MHR-NET with C3DPO [40], PRN [47], PR [46] and PAUL [66]. The Normalized Error results are shown in Table 3 and Table 2 respectively. These outcomes validate that MHR-Net is capable to perform accurate reconstruction of both facial landmarks and dense meshes. It is worth noting that MHR-Net recovers the dense point clouds of SURREAL dataset without splitting it into several subsets, unlike [47]. This is achieved by avoiding the burdensome SVD of matrices whose scales are related to N_p. With the differentiable design, MHR-Net shares the same level of scalability as SVD-free methods while achieving better performance.

5.3   Ablation Study

We show the effectiveness of the important designs in MHR-Net. We conduct the experiments on perspective Human 3.6M dataset. BD and IL in Table 4 are short for Basis-Deformation (Eq. 6) and Intermediate Loss (Sect. 4.3).

Table 2. Results on SURREAL.

Model	NE
C3DPO [40]	0.3509
PRN [47]	0.1377
PAUL [66]	0.1236
MHR-Net (w/o $\mathcal{L}_{res}$)	0.1388
MHR-Net	**0.1192**

Table 3. Results on 300VW.

Model	NE
CSF2 [23]	0.2751
PR [46]	0.2730
C3DPO [40]	0.1715
PRN [47]	0.1512
MHR-Net	**0.1007**

Table 4. Ablation study results.

No.	BD	IL	DBSD	Optim.	$\mathcal{L}_{res}$	MPJPE
1	✗	✗	✗	✗	✗	83.5
2	✓					198.3
3	✓	✓				75.5
4	✓	✓	✓	Best		73.7
5	✓	✓	✓	Worst		78.4
6	✓	✓	✓	MD		77.9
7	✓	✓	✓	Worst	✓	76.2
8	✓	✓	✓	MD	✓	77.3
9	✓	✓	✓	Best	✓	72.6

Basis-Deformation and Intermediate Loss. We setup several ablated models: (1) Baseline: We use a modified PoseDict [14] as baseline. We replace the invariance loss of PoseDict with the canonicalization loss [40], and it works slightly better than PoseDict. In Baseline, only the basis and camera are estimated. (2) Baseline with Basis-Deformation. The deformation here is implemented deterministically. (3) Baseline with Basis-Deformation and Intermediate Loss. Comparing the results of (1) and (2) in Table 4, we observe the degradation of performance. This implies that a naive extension of the deformation subspace will harm the regularization of low-rankness and lead to the failure of non-rigid reconstruction. By adding an intermediate loss in (3), the MPJPE is greatly reduced from 83.5 to 75.5, which is already better than the MPJPE (77.2) of the most competitive method ITES.

Stochastic Deformation and Hypothesis Optimization Strategy. We now use the deterministic basis and stochastic deformation with best hypothesis selection strategy, indicated by (4) in Table 4. We compare the proposed design with two alternatives: (5) Worst Hypothesis. In this strategy, we choose to optimize the hypothesis with the largest re-projection error, which is the opposite of the best hypothesis strategy. The intuition of Worst Hypothesis is that it tries to minimize the upper bound of errors. (6) Mixture Density (MD) [36], where a hypothesis is selected by sampling from a learned mixture density. As we do not have ground-truth labels for training, we use the uniform categorical distribu-

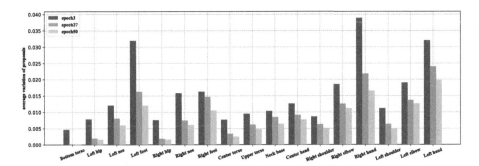

Fig. 3. Point-wise variation of deformations.

tion instead of a learned distribution. The results in Table 4 demonstrates that the combination of DBSD and the Best Hypothesis strategy produce the best performance.

Procrustean Residual Loss. We show the effectiveness of the Procrustean Residual Loss $\mathcal{L}_{res}$. As reported in Table 4, the full model (9) has a better MPJPE of 72.6. Despite the fact that the previous state-of-the-art method ITES uses two networks and the prior knowledge of human pose, MHR-Net outperforms ITES by 4.6 MPJPE. By adding $\mathcal{L}_{res}$ to models with alternative MD and Worst Hypothesis, these two models (7) and (8) also outperform the corresponding models (5) and (6) without $\mathcal{L}_{res}$. Moreover, the improvement by using $\mathcal{L}_{res}$ is also significant on the dense mesh dataset SURREAL, as indicated in Table 2.

5.4   Analysis of Stochastic Deformation

Point-Wise Variation of Deformations. We measure the variation of stochastic deformations of point j as $\frac{1}{N_f} \sum_{i=1}^{N_f} \max_{m,n} \left\| S_{i,j}^{D,m} - S_{i,j}^{D,n} \right\|_F$, where the subscript j denotes the j-th point. As shown in Fig. 3, the variation of deformations decreases as the training processes. One tentative interpretation is that MHR-Net searches solutions with a more diverse set of hypotheses in the early stage of training, and produces less diverse (or more confident) hypotheses after convergence. Moreover, the variation also differs between points. We observe the largest variations at `Left/Right Hand/Elbow/Foot`, which is consistent with the common sense that these are most flexible parts of body.

Accuracy of Other Hypotheses. To verify the accuracy of non-best hypotheses, we evaluate the MPJPE of the worst (largest reprojection error) hypothesis on Human3.6M. Compared to the best hypothesis, the results of worst hypothesis show a decline of –0.5 and –0.1 MPJPE at epoch 10 and epoch 50 with $N_m = 50$. This verifies that other hypotheses from MHR-Net are also accurate.

Visualizing Largely-Deformed Regions of Meshes. Another advantage of MHR-Net is that we can use $\left\| S_i^D \right\|$ as an indicator of the degree of deformations. We visualize the largely-deformed regions of reconstructed dense point clouds

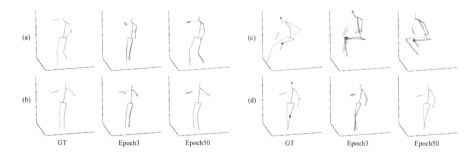

Fig. 4. Visualization of hypotheses ($N_m = 3$) on Human3.6M test set.

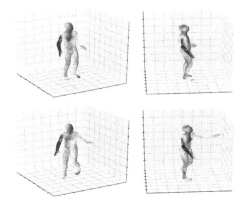

Fig. 5. Visualization of reconstructions on SURREAL. Points with large deformations are marked in red. Best viewed in color. (Color figure online)

from SURREAL dataset, as shown in Fig. 5. The visualization clearly illustrates the largely deformed parts of the body, which is helpful for better understanding of non-rigid reconstruction.

6   Conclusion

We propose MHR-Net, a novel approach for reconstructing non-rigid shapes from 2D observations. To the best of our knowledge, MHR-Net is the first method produces multiple high-quality hypotheses for NRSfM. With the proposed DBSD scheme and optimization strategy, MHR-Net is capable to generate multiple reconstructions and achieves state-of-the-art shape recovery accuracy. Furthermore, we introduce a Procrustean Residual Loss for enhancing performance.

Acknowledgement. This work was partially done when Haitian Zeng interned at Baidu Research. This work was partially supported by ARC DP200100938. We thank Dr. Sungheon Park for sharing the SURREAL dataset. We thank all reviewers and area chairs for their valuable feedback.

References

1. Agudo, A.: Unsupervised 3d reconstruction and grouping of rigid and non-rigid categories. IEEE TPAMI (2020)
2. Agudo, A., Agapito, L., Calvo, B., Montiel, J.M.M.: Good vibrations: a modal analysis approach for sequential non-rigid structure from motion. In: CVPR (2014)
3. Agudo, A., Moreno-Noguer, F.: Learning shape, motion and elastic models in force space. In: ICCV (2015)
4. Agudo, A., Moreno-Noguer, F.: Recovering pose and 3d deformable shape from multi-instance image ensembles. In: ACCV (2016)
5. Agudo, A., Moreno-Noguer, F.: DUST: dual union of spatio-temporal subspaces for monocular multiple object 3d reconstruction. In: CVPR, pp. 1513–1521 (2017)
6. Agudo, A., Moreno-Noguer, F., Calvo, B., Montiel, J.M.M.: Sequential non-rigid structure from motion using physical priors. IEEE TPAMI (2016)
7. Akhter, I., Sheikh, Y., Khan, S., Kanade, T.: Trajectory space: a dual representation for nonrigid structure from motion. IEEE TPAMI $33(7)$, 1442–1456 (2011)
8. Bartoli, A., Gay-Bellile, V., Castellani, U., Peyras, J., Olsen, S.I., Sayd, P.: Coarse-to-fine low-rank structure-from-motion. In: CVPR (2008)
9. Bregler, C., Hertzmann, A., Biermann, H.: Recovering non-rigid 3d shape from image streams. In: CVPR, pp. 2690–2696 (2000)
10. Bue, A.D.: Adaptive non-rigid registration and structure from motion from image trajectories. IJCV $103(2)$, 226–239 (2013)
11. Bue, A.D., Smeraldi, F., Agapito, L.: Non-rigid structure from motion using ranklet-based tracking and non-linear optimization. Image Vis. Comput. $25(3)$, 297–310 (2007)
12. Bulat, A., Tzimiropoulos, G.: How far are we from solving the 2d & 3d face alignment problem? (and a dataset of 230, 000 3d facial landmarks). In: ICCV (2017)
13. Cha, G., Lee, M., Oh, S.: Reconstruct as far as you can: consensus of non-rigid reconstruction from feasible regions. IEEE TPAMI, pp. 1–1 (2019)
14. Chenxin, X., Siheng, C., Maosen, L., Ya, Z.: Invariant teacher and equivariant student for unsupervised 3d human pose estimation. In: AAAI, pp. 3013–3021 (2021)
15. Chhatkuli, A., Pizarro, D., Collins, T., Bartoli, A.: Inextensible non-rigid shape-from-motion by second-order cone programming. In: CVPR, pp. 1719–1727 (2016)
16. Dai, Y., Li, H.: Rank minimization or nuclear-norm minimization: are we solving the right problem? In: International Conference on Digital Image Computing: Techniques and Applications (2014)
17. Dai, Y., Li, H., He, M.: A simple prior-free method for non-rigid structure-from-motion factorization. In: CVPR (2012)
18. Dai, Y., Li, H., He, M.: A simple prior-free method for non-rigid structure-from-motion factorization. IJCV $107(2)$, 101–122 (2014)
19. Fayad, J., Agapito, L., Bue, A.D.: Piecewise quadratic reconstruction of non-rigid surfaces from monocular sequences. In: ECCV, pp. 297–310 (2010)
20. Fragkiadaki, K., Salas, M., Arbeláez, P.A., Malik, J.: Grouping-based low-rank trajectory completion and 3d reconstruction. In: NeurIPS, pp. 55–63 (2014)
21. Gotardo, P.F.U., Martinez, A.M.: Computing smooth time trajectories for camera and deformable shape in structure from motion with occlusion. IEEE TPAMI $33(10)$, 2051–2065 (2011)
22. Gotardo, P.F.U., Martinez, A.M.: Kernel non-rigid structure from motion. In: ICCV, pp. 802–809 (2011)

23. Gotardo, P.F.U., Martínez, A.M.: Non-rigid structure from motion with complementary rank-3 spaces. In: CVPR (2011)
24. Iglesias, J.P., Olsson, C., Örnhag, M.V.: Accurate optimization of weighted nuclear norm for non-rigid structure from motion. In: CVPR (2020)
25. Ijaz, A., Yaser, S., Sohaib, K.: In defense of orthonormality constraints for nonrigid structure from motion. In: CVPR (2009)
26. Ionescu, C., Papava, D., Olaru, V., Sminchisescu, C.: Human3.6m: large scale datasets and predictive methods for 3d human sensing in natural environments. IEEE TPAMI **36**(7), 1325–1339 (2014)
27. Kingma, D.P., Welling, M.: Auto-encoding variational bayes. In: ICLR (2014)
28. Kong, C., Lucey, S.: Deep non-rigid structure from motion with missing data. IEEE TPAMI, pp. 1–1 (2020)
29. Kong, C., Zhu, R., Kiani, H., Lucey, S.: Structure from category: a generic and prior-less approach. In: 3DV, pp. 296–304 (2016)
30. Kudo, Y., Ogaki, K., Matsui, Y., Odagiri, Y.: Unsupervised adversarial learning of 3d human pose from 2d joint locations. CoRR abs/1803.08244 (2018)
31. Kumar, S.: Jumping manifolds: Geometry aware dense non-rigid structure from motion. In: CVPR, pp. 5346–5355 (2019)
32. Kumar, S., Cherian, A., Dai, Y., Li, H.: Scalable dense non-rigid structure-from-motion: a grassmannian perspective. In: CVPR, pp. 254–263 (2018)
33. Kumar, S., Dai, Y., Li, H.: Spatio-temporal union of subspaces for multi-body non-rigid structure-from-motion. Pattern Recogn. **71**, 428–443 (2017)
34. Lee, M., Cho, J., Choi, C.H., Oh, S.: Procrustean normal distribution for non-rigid structure from motion. IEEE TPAMI **39**(7), 1388–1400 (2017)
35. Lee, S., Purushwalkam, S., Cogswell, M., Ranjan, V., Crandall, D.J., Batra, D.: Stochastic multiple choice learning for training diverse deep ensembles. In: NeurIPS (2016)
36. Li, C., Lee, G.H.: Generating multiple hypotheses for 3d human pose estimation with mixture density network. In: CVPR (2019)
37. Li, C., Lee, G.H.: Weakly supervised generative network for multiple 3d human pose hypotheses. In: BMVC (2020)
38. Loper, M., Mahmood, N., Romero, J., Pons-Moll, G., Black, M.J.: SMPL: a skinned multi-person linear model. ACM TOG **34**(6), 248:1–248:16 (2015)
39. Martinez, J., Hossain, R., Romero, J., Little, J.J.: A simple yet effective baseline for 3d human pose estimation. In: ICCV (2017)
40. Novotny, D., Ravi, N., Graham, B., Neverova, N., Vedaldi, A.: C3DPO: canonical 3d pose networks for non-rigid structure from motion. In: ICCV (2019)
41. Paladini, M., Bartoli, A., Agapito, L.: Sequential non-rigid structure-from-motion with the 3d-implicit low-rank shape model. In: ECCV (2010)
42. Paladini, M., Bue, A.D., Stosic, M., Dodig, M., Xavier, J., Agapito, L.: Factorization for non-rigid and articulated structure using metric projections. In: CVPR (2009)
43. Parashar, S., Pizarro, D., Bartoli, A.: Isometric non-rigid shape-from-motion with riemannian geometry solved in linear time. IEEE TPAMI **40**(10), 2442–2454 (2018)
44. Parashar, S., Salzmann, M., Fua, P.: Local non-rigid structure-from-motion from diffeomorphic mappings. In: CVPR (2020)
45. Park, H.S., Shiratori, T., Matthews, I.A., Sheikh, Y.: 3d reconstruction of a moving point from a series of 2d projections. In: ECCV (2010)
46. Park, S., Lee, M., Kwak, N.: Procrustean regression: a flexible alignment-based framework for nonrigid structure estimation. IEEE TIP **27**(1), 249–264 (2018)

47. Park, S., Lee, M., Kwak, N.: Procrustean regression networks: learning 3d structure of non-rigid objects from 2d annotations. In: ECCV, pp. 1–18 (2020)
48. Pavllo, D., Feichtenhofer, C., Grangier, D., Auli, M.: 3d human pose estimation in video with temporal convolutions and semi-supervised training. In: CVPR (2019)
49. Probst, T., Paudel, D.P., Chhatkuli, A., Gool, L.V.: Incremental non-rigid structure-from-motion with unknown focal length. In: ECCV (2018)
50. Rabaud, V.C., Belongie, S.J.: Re-thinking non-rigid structure from motion. In: CVPR (2008)
51. Rupprecht, C., Laina, I., DiPietro, R.S., Baust, M.: Learning in an uncertain world: representing ambiguity through multiple hypotheses. In: ICCV (2017)
52. Russell, C., Fayad, J., Agapito, L.: Energy based multiple model fitting for non-rigid structure from motion. In: CVPR (2011)
53. Salzmann, M., Pilet, J., Ilic, S., Fua, P.: Surface deformation models for nonrigid 3d shape recovery. IEEE TPAMI 29(8), 1481–1487 (2007)
54. Schonemann, P.H.: A generalized solution of the orthogonal procrustes problem. Psychometrika (1966)
55. Sharma, S., Varigonda, P.T., Bindal, P., Sharma, A., Jain, A.: Monocular 3d human pose estimation by generation and ordinal ranking. In: ICCV (2019)
56. Shen, J., Zafeiriou, S., Chrysos, G.G., Kossaifi, J., Tzimiropoulos, G., Pantic, M.: The first facial landmark tracking in-the-wild challenge: benchmark and results. In: ICCVW (2015)
57. Sidhu, V., Tretschk, E., Golyanik, V., Agudo, A., Theobalt, C.: Neural dense non-rigid structure from motion with latent space constraints. In: ECCV, pp. 204–222 (2020)
58. Sminchisescu, C., Triggs, B.: Covariance scaled sampling for monocular 3d body tracking. In: CVPR (2001)
59. Sohn, K., Lee, H., Yan, X.: Learning structured output representation using deep conditional generative models. In: NeurIPS (2015)
60. Taylor, J., Jepson, A.D., Kutulakos, K.N.: Non-rigid structure from locally-rigid motion. In: CVPR, pp. 2761–2768 (2010)
61. Torresani, L., Hertzmann, A., Bregler, C.: Nonrigid structure-from-motion: estimating shape and motion with hierarchical priors. IEEE TPAMI 30(5), 878–892 (2008)
62. Valmadre, J., Lucey, S.: Deterministic 3d human pose estimation using rigid structure. In: ECCV (2010)
63. Varol, G., et al.: Learning from synthetic humans. In: CVPR (2017)
64. Vicente, S., Agapito, L.: Soft inextensibility constraints for template-free non-rigid reconstruction. In: ECCV, pp. 426–440 (2012)
65. Wang, C., Kong, C., Lucey, S.: Distill knowledge from NRSFM for weakly supervised 3d pose learning. In: ICCV (2019)
66. Wang, C., Lucey, S.: PAUL: procrustean autoencoder for unsupervised lifting. In: CVPR (2021)
67. Wehrbein, T., Rudolph, M., Rosenhahn, B., Wandt, B.: Probabilistic monocular 3d human pose estimation with normalizing flows. In: ICCV (2021)
68. Xiao, J., Chai, J., Kanade, T.: A closed-form solution to non-rigid shape and motion recovery. IJCV 67(2), 233–246 (2006)
69. Zeng, H., Dai, Y., Yu, X., Wang, X., Yang, Y.: PR-RRN: pairwise-regularized residual-recursive networks for non-rigid structure-from-motion. In: ICCV (2021)
70. Zhu, Y., Huang, D., Torre, F.D.L., Lucey, S.: Complex non-rigid motion 3d reconstruction by union of subspaces. In: CVPR, pp. 1542–1549 (2014)

Depth Map Decomposition for Monocular Depth Estimation

Jinyoung Jun[1], Jae-Han Lee[2], Chul Lee[3], and Chang-Su Kim[1]([✉])

[1] School of Electrical Engineering, Korea University, Seoul, Korea
jyjun@mcl.korea.ac.kr, changsukim@korea.ac.kr
[2] Gauss Labs Inc., Seoul, Korea
jaehan.lee@gausslabs.ai
[3] Department of Multimedia Engineering, Dongguk University, Seoul, Korea
chullee@dongguk.edu

Abstract. We propose a novel algorithm for monocular depth estimation that decomposes a metric depth map into a normalized depth map and scale features. The proposed network is composed of a shared encoder and three decoders, called G-Net, N-Net, and M-Net, which estimate gradient maps, a normalized depth map, and a metric depth map, respectively. M-Net learns to estimate metric depths more accurately using relative depth features extracted by G-Net and N-Net. The proposed algorithm has the advantage that it can use datasets without metric depth labels to improve the performance of metric depth estimation. Experimental results on various datasets demonstrate that the proposed algorithm not only provides competitive performance to state-of-the-art algorithms but also yields acceptable results even when only a small amount of metric depth data is available for its training.

Keywords: Monocular depth estimation · Relative depth estimation · Depth map decomposition

1 Introduction

Monocular depth estimation is a task to predict a pixel-wise depth map from a single image to understand the 3D geometry of a scene. The distance from a scene point to the camera provides essential information in various applications, including 2D-to-3D image/video conversion [52], augmented reality [35], autonomous driving [8], surveillance [22], and 3D CAD model generation [20]. Since only a single camera is available in many applications, monocular depth estimation, which infers the 3D information of a scene without additional equipment, has become an important research topic.

Supplementary Information The online version contains supplementary material available at https://doi.org/10.1007/978-3-031-20086-1_2.

Fig. 1. Metric depth maps and their normalized depth maps.

Recently, learning-based monocular depth estimators using convolutional neural networks (CNNs) have shown significant performance improvements, overcoming the intrinsic ill-posedness of monocular depth estimation by exploiting a huge amount of training data [1,3,6,7,14,25,28,54,56]. Existing learning-based monocular depth estimators can be classified into two categories according to the properties of estimated depth maps: relative depth estimation and metric depth estimation. Relative depth estimation predicts the relative depth order among pixels [2,34,51,58]. Metric depth estimation, on the other hand, predicts the absolute distance of each scene point from the camera [3,6,14,25,54], which is a pixel-wise regression problem.

To estimate a metric depth map, a network should learn both the 3D geometry of the scene and the camera parameters. This implies that a metric depth estimator should be trained with a dataset obtained by a specific camera. In contrast, a relative depth estimator can be trained with heterogeneous datasets, *e.g.*, disparity maps from stereo image pairs or even manually labeled pixel pairs. Thus, relative depth estimation is an easier task than metric depth estimation is. Moreover, note that the geometry of a scene can be easily estimated when extra cues are available. For example, depth completion [38,39,55], which recovers a dense depth map from sparse depth measurements, can be performed more accurately and more reliably than monocular depth estimation is. Based on these observations, metric depth estimation algorithms using relative depths as extra cues have been developed via fitting [34,43] or fine-tuning [42].

In this paper, we propose a monocular metric depth estimator that decomposes a metric depth map into a normalized depth map and scale features. As illustrated in Fig. 1, a normalized depth map contains relative depth information, and it is less sensitive to scale variations or camera parameters than a metric depth map is. The proposed algorithm consists of a single shared encoder and three decoders, G-Net, N-Net, and M-Net, which estimate gradient maps, a normalized depth map, and a metric depth map, respectively. M-Net learns to estimate metric depth maps using relative depth features extracted by G-Net and N-Net. To this end, we progressively transfer features from G-Net to N-Net and then from N-Net to M-Net. In addition, we develop the mean depth residual (MDR) block for M-Net to utilize N-Net features more effectively. Because the proposed algorithm learns to estimate metric depths by exploiting gradient maps and relative depths, additional datasets containing only relative depths can be used to improve the metric depth estimation performance further. Experimental results show that the proposed algorithm is competitive with state-of-the-art metric depth estimators, even when it is trained with a smaller metric depth dataset.

This paper has the following contributions:

- We propose a novel monocular depth estimator, which decomposes a metric depth map into a normalized depth map and relative depth features and then exploits those relative features to improve the metric depth estimation performance.
- The proposed algorithm can be adapted to a new camera efficiently since it can be trained with a small metric depth dataset together with camera-independent relative depth datasets.
- The proposed algorithm provides competitive performance to conventional state-of-the-art metric depth estimators and can improve the performance further through joint training using multiple datasets.

2   Related Work

2.1   Monocular Metric Depth Estimation

The objective of monocular metric depth estimation is to predict pixel-wise absolute distances of a scene from a camera using a single image. Since different 3D scenes can be projected onto the same 2D image, monocular depth estimation is ill-posed. Nevertheless, active research has been conducted due to its practical importance. To infer depths, early approaches made prior assumptions on scenes, *e.g.* box blocks [9], planar regions [44], or particular layout of objects [10]. However, they may provide implausible results, especially in regions with ambiguous colors or small objects.

With recent advances in deep learning, CNN techniques for monocular depth estimation have been developed, yielding excellent performance. Many attempts have been made to find better network architecture [3,6,14,25,54] or to design more effective loss functions [2,5,16,25]. It has been also demonstrated that the depth estimation performance can be improved by predicting quantized depths through ordinal regression [7], by employing Fourier domain analysis [26], by enforcing geometric constraints of virtual normals [56], or by reweighting multiple loss functions [28]. Recently, the vision transformer [4] was employed for monocular depth estimation [1], improving the performance significantly.

2.2   Relative Depth Estimation

The objective of relative depth estimation is to learn the pairwise depth order [58] or the rank of pixels [2,51] in an image. Recently, listwise ranking, instead of pairwise ranking, was considered for relative depth estimation [34]. Also, scale-invariant loss [6] and its variants [32,33,43,48] have been used to alleviate the scale ambiguity of depths, thereby improving the performance of relative depth estimation.

Unlike metric depths, relative depth information—or depth order information—is invariant to camera parameters. Therefore, even though a training set is composed of images captured by different cameras, it does not affect the performance of relative depth estimation adversely. Therefore, heterogeneous training data, such as disparity maps from stereo image pairs [48,50,51] or videos [43], structure-from-motion reconstruction [32,33], and ordinal labels [2], have been used to train relative depth estimators.

2.3 Relative vs. Metric Depths

A metric depth map contains relative depth information, whereas relative depth information is not sufficient for reconstructing a metric depth map. However, relative-to-metric depth conversion has been attempted by fitting relative depths to metric depths [34,43] or by fine-tuning a relative depth estimator for metric depth estimation [42].

On the other hand, relative and metric depths can be jointly estimated to exploit their correlation and to eventually improve the performance of metric depth estimation. To this end, ordinal labels are used with a ranking loss in [2]. Also, in [27], relative and metric depth maps at various scales are first estimated and then optimally combined to yield a final metric depth map.

The proposed algorithm also estimates relative depth information, in addition to metric depths, to improve the performance of metric depth estimation. However, differently from [2,27], the proposed algorithm better exploits the correlation between relative and metric depths by decomposing a metric depth map. Furthermore, the proposed algorithm can provide promising results even with a small metric depth dataset by exploiting a relative depth dataset additionally.

3 Proposed Algorithm

Figure 2 is an overview of the proposed algorithm, which consists of a shared encoder and three decoders—G-Net, N-Net, and M-Net. The shared encoder extracts common features that are fed into the three decoders. Then, G-Net predicts horizontal and vertical gradients of depths, while N-Net and M-Net estimate a normalized depth map and a metric depth map, respectively. Note that features extracted by G-Net are fed into N-Net to convey edge information, and those by N-Net are, in turn, fed into M-Net to provide relative depth features. Finally, via the MDR block, M-Net exploits the relative depth features to estimate a metric depth map more accurately.

3.1 Metric Depth Decomposition

Given an RGB image $I \in \mathbb{R}^{h \times w \times 3}$, the objective is to estimate a metric depth map $M \in \mathbb{R}^{h \times w}$. However, this is ill-posed because different scenes with different

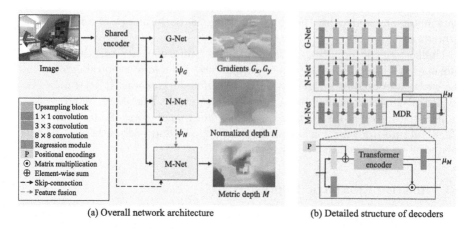

(a) Overall network architecture   (b) Detailed structure of decoders

Fig. 2. (a) Overall network architecture of the proposed algorithm and (b) detailed structure of decoders. The proposed algorithm consists of a shared encoder and three decoders: G-Net, N-Net, and M-Net. G-Net predicts horizontal and vertical gradient maps, while N-Net and M-Net estimate normalized and metric depth maps, respectively. Note that G-Net features are fed into N-Net, and N-Net features are fed into M-Net.

metric depths can be projected onto the same image. Moreover, scale features of depths are hard to estimate from the color information only since they also depend on the camera parameters. To address this issue, we decompose a metric depth map M into a normalized depth map N and scale parameters. The normalized depth map N contains relative depth information, so it is less sensitive to scale variations or camera parameters than the metric depth map M is.

There are several design choices for normalizing a metric depth map, including min-max normalization or ranking-based normalization [11]. However, the min-max normalization is sensitive to outliers, and the ranking-based normalization is unreliable in areas with homogeneous depths, such as walls and floors. Instead, we normalize a metric depth map using the z-score normalization. Given a metric depth map M, we obtain the normalized depth map N by

$$N = \frac{M - \mu_M U}{\sigma_M} \tag{1}$$

where μ_M and σ_M, respectively, denote the mean and standard deviation of metric depths in M. Also, U is the unit matrix whose all elements are 1.

N-Net, denoted by f_N, estimates this normalized depth map, and its estimate is denoted by $\hat{N}$. When the scale parameters μ_M and σ_M are known, the metric depth map M can be reconstructed by

$$\hat{M}_{\text{direct}} = \sigma_M \hat{N} + \mu_M U. \tag{2}$$

In practice, μ_M and σ_M are unknown. Conventional methods in [34,42,43] obtain fixed σ_M and μ_M for all images based on the least-squares criterion. In such a case, the accuracy of $\hat{M}_{\text{direct}}$ in (2) greatly depends on the accuracy of σ_M and μ_M. In this work, instead of the direct conversion in (2), we estimate the metric depth map by employing the features $\psi_N(I)$, which are extracted by the proposed M-Net, f_N, during the estimation of $\hat{N}$. In other words, the proposed M-Net, f_M, estimates the metric depth map by

$$\hat{M} = f_M(I, \psi_N(I)). \tag{3}$$

For metric depth estimation, structural data (*e.g.* surface normals or segmentation maps) have been adopted as additional cues [5,29,37,40], or relative depth features have been used indirectly via loss functions (*e.g.* pairwise ranking loss [2] or scale-invariant loss [1,6,30]). In contrast, we convert a metric depth map to a normalized depth map. Then, the proposed N-Net estimates the normalized depth map to extract the features ψ_N, containing relative depth information. Then, the proposed M-Net uses ψ_N for effective metric depth estimation.

Similarly, we further decompose the normalized depth map N into more elementary data: horizontal and vertical gradients. The horizontal gradient map G_x is given by

$$G_x = \nabla_x N \tag{4}$$

where ∇_x is the partial derivative operator computing the differences between horizontally adjacent pixels. The vertical gradient map G_y is obtained similarly. The proposed G-Net is trained to estimate these gradient maps G_x and G_y. Hence, G-Net learns edge information in a scene, and its features ψ_G are useful for inferring the normalized depth map. Therefore, similar to (3), N-Net estimates the normalized depth map via

$$\hat{N} = f_N(I, \psi_G(I)) \tag{5}$$

using the gradient features $\psi_G(I)$.

3.2 Network Architecture

For the shared encoder in Fig. 2, we adopt EfficientNet-B5 [47] as the backbone network. G-Net and N-Net have an identical structure, consisting of five upsampling blocks. However, G-Net outputs two channels for two gradient maps G_x and G_y, while N-Net yields a single channel for a normalized depth map N. M-Net also has a similar structure, except for the MDR block, which will be detailed in Sect. 3.3. MDR predicts the mean μ_M of M separately, which is added back at the end of M-Net.

The encoder features are fed into the three decoders via skip-connections [13], as shown in Fig. 2(a). To differentiate the encoder features for the different decoders, we apply 1×1 convolution to the encoder features before feeding them to each decoder. Also, we apply the channel attention [15] before each skip-connection to each decoder.

We transfer features unidirectionally from G-Net to N-Net and also from N-Net to M-Net to exploit low-level features for the estimation of high-level

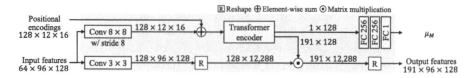

Fig. 3. Detailed structure of the MDR block.

data. To this end, we fuse features through element-wise addition before each of the first four upsampling blocks in N-Net and M-Net, as shown in Fig. 2(b). Specifically, let ψ_G^{out} and ψ_N^{out} denote the output features of G-Net and N-Net, respectively. Then, the input feature ψ_N^{in} to the next layer of N-Net is given by

$$\psi_N^{\text{in}} = \omega_G \psi_G^{\text{out}} + \omega_N \psi_N^{\text{out}} \tag{6}$$

where ω_G and ω_N are pre-defined weights for ψ_G^{out} and ψ_N^{out} to control the relative contributions of the two features. For M-Net, the features from N-Net are added similarly. In order to fuse features, we use addition, instead of multiplication or concatenation, for computational efficiency.

3.3   MDR Block

We design the MDR block to utilize the features ψ_N of N-Net more effectively for the metric depth estimation in M-Net. Figure 3 shows the structure of the MDR block, which applies patchwise attention to an input feature map and estimates the mean μ_M of M separately using the transformer encoder [4]. Note that the transformer architecture enables us to use one of the patchwise-attended feature vectors to regress μ_M.

Specifically, MDR first processes input features using an 8×8 convolution layer with a stride of 8 and a 3×3 convolution layer, respectively. The patchwise output of the 8×8 convolution is added to the positional encodings and then input to the transformer encoder [4]. The positional encodings are learnable parameters, randomly initialized at training. Then, the transformer encoder generates 192 patchwise-attended feature vectors of 128 dimensions. We adopt the mini-ViT architecture [1] for the transformer encoder. The first vector is fed to the regression module, composed of three fully-connected layers, to yield μ_M. The rest 191 vectors form a matrix, which is multiplied with the output of the 3×3 convolution layer to generate $191 \times 96 \times 128$ output features through reshaping. Finally, those output features are fed to the next upsampling block of M-Net. Also, the estimated μ_M is added back at the end of M-Net in Fig. 2(b), which makes the remaining parts of M-Net focus on the estimation of the mean-removed depth map $M - \mu_M U$ by exploiting the N-Net features ψ_N.

3.4   Loss Functions

Let us describe the loss functions for training the three decoders. For G-Net, we use the ℓ_1 loss

$$\mathcal{L}_G = \frac{1}{T}(\|\hat{G}_x - G_x\|_1 + \|\hat{G}_y - G_y\|_1) \tag{7}$$

where $\hat{G}_x$ and $\hat{G}_y$ are predictions of the ground-truth gradient maps G_x and G_y, respectively. Also, T denotes the number of valid pixels in the ground-truth.

For N-Net, we use two loss terms: the ℓ_1 loss and the gradient loss. The ℓ_1 loss is defined as

$$\mathcal{L}_N = \frac{1}{T}\|\hat{N} - N\|_1 \tag{8}$$

where $\hat{N}$ and N are predicted and ground-truth normalized depth maps. Note that scale-invariant terms are often adopted to train monocular depth estimators [1,30,42]. However, we do not use such scale-invariant losses since normalized depth maps are already scale-invariant. Next, the gradient losses [16,33,51] for N in the horizontal direction are defined as

$$\mathcal{L}_{Nx} = \frac{1}{T \cdot s^2}\|\nabla_x \hat{N}_s - \nabla_x N_s\|_1 \tag{9}$$

where $\hat{N}_s$ and N_s are the bilinearly scaled $\hat{N}$ and N with a scaling factor s. We compute the gradient losses at various scales, as in [33,51], by setting s to 0.5, 0.25, and 0.125. The losses L_{Ny} in the vertical direction are also used.

Similarly, for M-Net, we use the loss terms $\mathcal{L}_M$, $\mathcal{L}_{Mx}$, and $\mathcal{L}_{My}$. In addition, we use two more loss terms. First, $\mathcal{L}_{\mu_M}$ is defined to train the MDR block, which is given by

$$\mathcal{L}_{\mu_M} = \|\mu(\hat{M}) - \mu_M\|_1 \tag{10}$$

where $\mu(\hat{M})$ denotes the mean of depth values in $\hat{M}$. Second, we define the logarithmic ℓ_1 loss,

$$\mathcal{L}_{\log M} = \frac{1}{T}\|\log \hat{M} - \log M\|_1. \tag{11}$$

In this work, we adopt inverse depth representation of metric depths to match the depth order with a relative depth dataset [51]. In this case, theoretically, a metric depth can have a value in the range $[0, \infty)$. Thus, when a metric depth is near zero, its inverted value becomes too large, which interferes with training. We overcome this problem through a simple modification. Given an original metric depth m_o, its inverted metric depth m is defined as

$$m = 1/(m_o + 1). \tag{12}$$

In this way, inverted metric depth values are within the range of $(0, 1]$ and also are more evenly distributed.

However, using the ℓ_1 loss $\mathcal{L}_M$ on inverse depths has a disadvantage in learning distant depths. Suppose that $\hat{\chi}$ and χ are predicted and ground-truth metric depth values for a pixel, respectively. Then, the ℓ_1 error E is given by

$$E = \left|\frac{1}{\hat{\chi}} - \frac{1}{\chi}\right|. \tag{13}$$

As χ gets larger, E becomes smaller for the same $|\hat{\chi} - \chi|$. This means that the network is trained less effectively for distant regions. This problem is alleviated by employing $\mathcal{L}_{\log M}$ in (11).

4   Experimental Results

4.1   Datasets

We use four depth datasets: one for relative depths [51] and three for metric depths [23,45,46]. When relative depth data are used in training, losses are generated from the loss terms for N-Net and G-Net only because the loss terms for M-Net cannot be computed.

HR-WSI [51]: It consists of 20,378 training and 400 test images. The ground-truth disparity maps are generated by FlowNet 2.0 [19]. We use only the training data of HR-WSI. We normalize the disparity maps by (1) and regard them as normalized depth maps.

NYUv2 [45]: It contains 120K video frames for training and 654 frames for test, together with the depth maps captured by a Kinect v1 camera. We use the NYUv2 dataset for both training and evaluation. We construct three training datasets of 51K, 17K, and 795 sizes. Specifically, we extract the 51K and 17K images by sampling video frames uniformly. For the 795 images, we use the official training split of NYUv2. We fill in missing depths using the colorization scheme [31], as in [45].

DIML-Indoor [23]: It consists of 1,609 training images and 503 test images, captured by a Kinect v2 camera.

SUN RGB-D [46]: It consists 5,285 training images and 5,050 test images, obtained by four different cameras: Kinect v1, Kinect v2, RealSense, and Xtion.

4.2   Evaluation Metrics

Metric Depths: We adopt the four evaluation metrics in [6], listed below. Here, M_i and $\hat{M}_i$ denote the ground-truth and predicted depths of pixel i, respectively. $|\cdot|$ denotes the number of valid pixels in a depth map. For the NYUv2 dataset, we adopt the center crop protocol [6].

$$\text{RMSE} : \frac{1}{|M|}\Big(\sum_i(\hat{M}_i - M_i)^2\Big)^{0.5}$$

$$\text{REL} : \frac{1}{|M|}\sum_i|\hat{M}_i - M_i|/M_i$$

$$\log 10 : \frac{1}{|M|}\sum_i|\log_{10}(\hat{M}_i) - \log_{10}(M_i)|$$

$$\delta_k : \% \text{ of } M_i \text{ that satisfies } \max\left(\frac{\hat{M}_i}{M_i}, \frac{M_i}{\hat{M}_i}\right) < 1.25^k, \quad k \in \{1,2,3\}$$

Table 1. Comparison of depth estimation results on the NYUv2 dataset. '#' is the number of training images, and † means that additional data is used for training. The best results are **boldfaced**. Lower RMSE, REL, and log 10 indicate better results, while higher δ_k values are better ones.

	#	Encoder backbone	RMSE	REL	log 10	δ_1	δ_2	δ_3
Eigen et al. [6]	120K	–	0.641	0.158	–	0.769	0.950	0.988
Laina et al. [25]	12K	ResNet-50 [13]	0.573	0.127	0.055	0.811	0.953	0.988
Hao et al. [12]	13K	ResNet-101 [13]	0.555	0.127	0.053	0.841	0.966	0.991
Fu et al. [7]	120K	ResNet-101 [13]	0.509	0.115	0.051	0.828	0.965	0.992
Hu et al. [16]	50K	SENet-154 [15]	0.530	0.115	0.050	0.866	0.975	0.993
Chen et al. [3]	50K	SENet-154 [15]	0.514	0.111	0.048	0.878	0.977	0.994
Yin et al. [56]	29K	ResNeXt-101 [53]	0.416	0.108	0.048	0.875	0.976	0.994
Lee et al. [30]	24K	DenseNet-161 [17]	0.392	0.110	0.047	0.885	0.978	0.994
Hyunh et al. [18]	50K	DRN-D-22 [57]	0.412	0.108	–	0.882	0.980	0.996
Lee and Kim [28]	58K	PNASNet-5 [36]	0.430	0.119	0.050	0.870	0.974	0.993
Bhat et al. [1]	50K	EfficientNet-B5 [47]	0.364	0.103	0.044	0.903	0.984	**0.997**
Proposed	51K	EfficientNet-B5 [47]	**0.362**	**0.100**	**0.043**	**0.907**	**0.986**	**0.997**
Wang et al. [49]†	200K	–	0.745	0.220	0.094	0.605	0.890	0.970
Ramam. and Lepetit [41]†	400K	ResNet-50 [13]	0.502	0.139	0.047	0.836	0.966	0.993
Ranftl et al. [42]†	1.4M	ViT-Hybrid [4]	0.357	0.110	0.045	0.904	**0.988**	**0.998**
Proposed†	71K	EfficientNet-B5 [47]	**0.355**	**0.098**	**0.042**	**0.913**	0.987	**0.998**

Relative Depths: we use two metrics for relative depths. First, WHDR (weighted human disagreement rate) [2,43,51] measures the ordinal consistency between point pairs. We follow the evaluation protocol of [51] to randomly sample 50,000 pairs in each depth map. However, WHDR is an unstable protocol, under which the performance fluctuates with each measurement. We hence use Kendall's τ [21] additionally, which considers the ordering relations of all pixel pairs. Given a ground-truth normalized depth map D and its prediction $\hat{D}$, Kendall's τ is defined as

$$\tau(\hat{D}, D) = \frac{\alpha(\hat{D}, D) - \beta(\hat{D}, D)}{\binom{|D|}{2}} \quad (14)$$

where $\alpha(\hat{D}, D)$ and $\beta(\hat{D}, D)$ are the numbers of concordant pairs and discordant pairs between D and $\hat{D}$, respectively. Note that Kendall's τ can measure the quality of a metric depth map, as well as that of a relative one.

4.3 Implementation Details

Network Architecture: We employ EfficientNet-B5 [47] as the encoder backbone. The encoder takes an 512×384 RGB image and generates a 16×12 feature with 2,048 channels. The output feature is used as the input to the three decoders. G-Net and N-Net consist of 5 upsampling blocks, each of which is composed of a bilinear interpolation layer and two 3×3 convolution layers with the

Ground-truth   Eigen *et al.*   Fu *et al.*   Chen *et al.*   Lee *et al.*   Bhat *et al.*   Ranftl *et al.*   Proposed

Fig. 4. Qualitative comparison of the proposed algorithm with the conventional algorithms. For each depth map, the error map is also provided, in which brighter pixels correspond to larger errors.

ReLU activation. Also, in addition to the 5 upsampling blocks, M-Net includes the MDR block, located between the fourth and fifth upsampling blocks. For feature fusion in (6), $\omega_G = \omega_N = 1$.

Training: We train the proposed algorithm in two phases. First, we train the network, after removing M-Net, for 20 epochs with an initial learning rate of 10^{-4}. The learning rate is decreased by a factor of 0.1 at every fifth epoch. Second, we train the entire network, including all three decoders, jointly for 15 epochs with an initial learning rate of 10^{-4}, which is decreased by a factor of 0.1 at every third epoch. We use the Adam optimizer [24] with a weight decay of 10^{-4}. If a relative depth is used in the second phase, losses are calculated from the loss terms for N-Net and G-Net only.

4.4   Performance Comparison

Table 1 compares the proposed algorithm with conventional ones on NYUv2 dataset. Some of the conventional algorithms use only NYUv2 training data

Table 2. Comparison of depth estimation results on various datasets. '#' is the size of metric depth dataset, and † means that 20K HR-WSI data are additionally used for training. A lower Kendall's τ indicates a better result.

	#	Setting	RMSE	REL	log 10	δ_1	δ_2	δ_3	Kendall's τ
NYUv2	795	Baseline	0.487	0.147	0.061	0.809	0.963	0.991	0.738
		Proposed	0.468	0.142	0.059	0.824	0.969	0.992	0.762
		Proposed†	**0.417**	**0.122**	**0.052**	**0.868**	**0.977**	**0.995**	**0.800**
	17K	Baseline	0.400	0.113	0.048	0.880	0.981	0.996	0.803
		Proposed	0.370	0.103	0.045	0.903	0.986	**0.997**	0.829
		Proposed†	**0.362**	**0.100**	**0.043**	**0.909**	**0.987**	**0.997**	**0.835**
	51K	Baseline	0.386	0.109	0.047	0.888	0.980	0.995	0.813
		Proposed	0.362	0.100	0.043	0.907	0.986	0.997	0.837
		Proposed†	**0.355**	**0.098**	**0.042**	**0.913**	**0.987**	**0.998**	**0.840**
DIML-Indoor	1.6K	Baseline	0.589	0.247	0.099	0.701	0.879	0.968	0.492
		Proposed	0.537	0.180	0.075	0.719	0.943	0.986	0.696
		Proposed†	**0.517**	**0.171**	**0.072**	**0.742**	**0.949**	**0.989**	**0.742**
SUN RGB-D	5.3K	Baseline	0.306	0.132	0.055	0.847	0.971	0.992	0.761
		Proposed	0.303	0.129	0.055	0.850	**0.973**	**0.993**	0.776
		Proposed†	**0.301**	**0.127**	**0.054**	**0.853**	**0.973**	0.992	**0.784**

795 NYUv2   DIML-Indoor   SUN RGB-D

Fig. 5. Qualitative comparison of the proposed algorithm with the baseline using the NYUv2 (795), DIML-Indoor, and SUN RGB-D datasets.

[1,3,6,7,12,15,18,25,28,30,56], while the others use extra data [41,42,49]. For fair comparisons, we train the proposed algorithm in both ways: 'Proposed' uses NYUv2 only, while 'Proposed†' uses both HR-WSI and NYUv2. The following observations can be made from Table 1.

– 'Proposed' outperforms all conventional algorithms in all metrics with no exception. For example, 'Proposed' provides a REL score of 0.100, which is 0.003 better than that of the second-best algorithm, Bhat *et al.* [1]. Note that both algorithms use the same encoder backbone of EfficientNet-B5 [47].

Table 3. Ablation studies of the proposed algorithm using the NYUv2 (17K) dataset.

M	N	G	MDR*	MDR	†	RMSE	REL	log 10	δ_1	δ_2	δ_3	Kendall's τ	WHDR(%)
✓	–	–	–	–	–	0.400	0.113	0.048	0.880	0.981	0.996	0.803	14.95
✓	✓	–	–	–	–	0.389	0.111	0.047	0.888	0.982	0.996	0.814	14.19
✓	✓	✓	–	–	–	0.387	0.109	0.047	0.888	0.982	**0.997**	0.817	14.01
✓	✓	✓	✓	–	–	0.381	0.108	0.046	0.894	0.984	**0.997**	0.824	13.54
✓	✓	✓	–	✓	–	0.370	0.103	0.045	0.903	0.986	**0.997**	0.829	13.18
✓	✓	✓	–	✓	✓	**0.362**	**0.100**	**0.043**	**0.909**	**0.987**	**0.997**	**0.835**	**12.72**

- 'Proposed†' provides the best results in five out of six metrics. For δ_2, the proposed algorithm yields the second-best score after Ranftl *et al.* [42]. It is worth pointing out that Ranftl *et al.* uses about 20 times more training data than the proposed algorithm does.

Figure 4 compares the proposed algorithm with the conventional algorithms [1,3,6,7,30,42] qualitatively. We see that the proposed algorithm estimates the depth maps more faithfully with smaller errors.

4.5 Various Datasets

Table 2 verifies the effectiveness of the proposed algorithm on various datasets. The first two columns in Table 2 indicate the metric depth dataset and its size. 'Baseline' is a bare encoder-decoder for monocular depth estimation. Specifically, we remove G-Net and N-Net, as well as the MDR block in M-Net, from the proposed algorithm in Fig. 2 to construct 'Baseline.' For its training, only three loss terms $\mathcal{L}_M$, $\mathcal{L}_{Mx}$, and $\mathcal{L}_{My}$ are used. 'Proposed' means the proposed algorithm without employing the 20K HR-WSI training data, while 'Proposed†' means using the HR-WSI data additionally. The following observations can be made from Table 2.

- By comparing 'Proposed' with 'Baseline,' we see that G-Net and N-Net help M-Net improve the performance of metric depth estimation by transferring edge information and relative depth information. Also, 'Proposed†' meaningfully outperforms 'Proposed' by leveraging relative depth training data in HR-WSI, which contain no metric depth labels.
- Even when only the 795 NYUv2 images are used, the proposed algorithm provides acceptable results. For example, the RMSE score of 0.417 is similar to that of the Hyunh *et al.*'s estimator [18] in Table 1, which uses 50K metric depth map data. In contrast, the proposed algorithm uses the 795 metric depth maps only.
- The proposed algorithm also exhibits similar trends in the DIML-Indoor and SUN RGB-D datasets, which are collected using different cameras: the proposed algorithm can be trained effectively even with a small number of metric depth images. This is advantageous in practical applications in which an algorithm should be adapted for various cameras.

Table 4. Effectiveness of the two-phase training scheme.

Setting	RMSE	REL	log 10	δ_1	δ_2	δ_3	Kendall's τ	WHDR(%)
Single-phase	0.386	0.107	0.046	0.892	0.984	**0.997**	0.820	13.74
Proposed	**0.362**	**0.100**	**0.043**	**0.909**	**0.987**	**0.997**	**0.835**	**12.72**

Table 5. Complexity comparison.

	Ranftl et al.[42]	Proposed
# Params	130M	102M
Speed (fps)	13.4	34.7

Table 6. Complexity of each component.

	Encoder	G	N	M	MDR
# Params	55M	15M	15M	15M	1.7M
Speed (fps)	50.9	475	534	474	447

Figure 5 compares 'Baseline' and 'Proposed†' qualitatively using the 795 NYUv2, DIML-Indoor, and SUN RGB-D datasets. For all datasets, 'Proposed†' provides more accurate and more detailed depth maps, especially around chairs, tables, and desks, than 'Baseline' does.

4.6 Analysis

Ablation Studies: We conduct ablation studies that add the proposed components one by one in Table 3. Here, the 17K images from NYUv2 are used for training. M, N, and G denote the three decoders. MDR* is the MDR block with μ_M deactivated. † indicates the use of relative depth data. We see that all components lead to performance improvements, especially in terms of the two relative depth metrics Kendall's τ and WHDR.

Table 4 shows the effectiveness of the two-phase training scheme of the proposed algorithm. The proposed algorithm, which trains G-Net and N-Net first, shows better results than the single-phase scheme, which trains the entire network at once.

Complexities and Inference Speeds: Table 5 compares the complexities of the proposed algorithm and the Ranftl et al.'s algorithm [42]. The proposed algorithm performs faster with a smaller number of parameters than the Ranftl et al.'s algorithm [42] does. This indicates that the performance gain of the proposed algorithm is not from the increase in complexity but from the effective use of relative depth features. Table 6 lists the complexity of each component of the proposed algorithm. The encoder spends most of the inference time, while the three decoders are relatively fast.

5 Conclusions

We proposed a monocular depth estimator that decomposes a metric depth map into a normalized depth map and scale features. The proposed algorithm is composed of a shared encoder with three decoders, G-Net, N-Net, and M-Net, which estimate gradient maps, a normalized depth map, and a metric depth map, respectively. G-Net features are used in N-Net, and N-Net features are used in M-Net. Moreover, we developed the MDR block for M-Net to utilize N-Net features and improve the metric depth estimation performance. Extensive experiments demonstrated that the proposed algorithm provides competitive performance and yields acceptable results even with a small metric depth dataset.

Acknowledgements. This work was supported by the National Research Foundation of Korea (NRF) grants funded by the Korea government (MSIT) (No. NRF-2021R1A4A1031864 and No. NRF-2022R1A2B5B03002310).

References

1. Bhat, S.F., Alhashim, I., Wonka, P.: AdaBins: depth estimation using adaptive bins. In: CVPR, pp. 4009–4018 (2021)
2. Chen, W., Fu, Z., Yang, D., Deng, J.: Single-image depth perception in the wild. In: NIPS, pp. 730–738 (2016)
3. Chen, X., Chen, X., Zha, Z.J.: Structure-aware residual pyramid network for monocular depth estimation. In: IJCAI, pp. 694–700 (2019)
4. Dosovitskiy, A., et al.: An image is worth 16 x 16 words: transformers for image recognition at scale. In: ICLR (2021)
5. Eigen, D., Fergus, R.: Predicting depth, surface normals and semantic labels with a common multi-scale convolutional architecture. In: ICCV, pp. 2650–2658 (2015)
6. Eigen, D., Puhrsch, C., Fergus, R.: Depth map prediction from a single image using a multi-scale deep network. In: NIPS, pp. 2366–2374 (2014)
7. Fu, H., Gong, M., Wang, C., Batmanghelich, K., Tao, D.: Deep ordinal regression network for monocular depth estimation. In: CVPR, pp. 2002–2011 (2018)
8. Godard, C., Aodha, O.M., Brostow, G.J.: Unsupervised monocular depth estimation with left-right consistency. In: CVPR, pp. 270–279 (2017)
9. Gupta, A., Efros, A.A., Hebert, M.: Blocks world revisited: image understanding using qualitative geometry and mechanics. In: ECCV, pp. 482–496 (2010)
10. Gupta, A., Hebert, M., Kanade, T., Blei, D.: Estimating spatial layout of rooms using volumetric reasoning about objects and surfaces. In: NIPS (2010)
11. Han, J., Pei, J., Kamber, M.: Data Mining: Concepts and Techniques. Elsevier (2011)
12. Hao, Z., Li, Y., You, S., Lu, F.: Detail preserving depth estimation from a single image using attention guided networks. In: 3DV, pp. 304–313 (2018)
13. He, K., Zhang, X., Ren, S., Sun, J.: Deep residual learning for image recognition. In: CVPR, pp. 770–778 (2016)
14. Heo, M., Lee, J., Kim, K.R., Kim, H.U., Kim, C.S.: Monocular depth estimation using whole strip masking and reliability-based refinement. In: ECCV, pp. 36–51 (2018)
15. Hu, J., Shen, L., Sun, G.: Squeeze-and-excitation networks. In: CVPR, pp. 7132–7141 (2018)
16. Hu, J., Ozay, M., Zhang, Y., Okatani, T.: Revisiting single image depth estimation: toward higher resolution maps with accurate object boundaries. In: WACV, pp. 1043–1051 (2019)
17. Huang, G., Liu, Z., Van Der Maaten, L., Weinberger, K.Q.: Densely connected convolutional networks. In: CVPR, pp. 4700–4708 (2017)

18. Huynh, L., Nguyen-Ha, P., Matas, J., Rahtu, E., Heikkilä, J.: Guiding monocular depth estimation using depth-attention volume. In: ECCV, pp. 581–597 (2020)
19. Ilg, E., Mayer, N., Saikia, T., Keuper, M., Dosovitskiy, A., Brox, T.: FlowNet 2.0: evolution of optical flow estimation with deep networks. In: CVPR, pp. 2462–2470 (2017)
20. Izadinia, H., Shan, Q., Seitz, S.M.: IM2CAD. In: CVPR, pp. 5134–5143 (2017)
21. Kendall, M.G.: A new measure of rank correlation. Biometrika **30**(1/2), 81–93 (1938)
22. Kim, H., et al.: Weighted joint-based human behavior recognition algorithm using only depth information for low-cost intelligent video-surveillance system. Expert Syst. Appl. **45**, 131–141 (2016)
23. Kim, Y., Jung, H., Min, D., Sohn, K.: Deep monocular depth estimation via integration of global and local predictions. IEEE Trans. Image Process. **27**(8), 4131–4144 (2018)
24. Kingma, D.P., Ba, J.: Adam: a method for stochastic optimization. In: ICLR (2015)
25. Laina, I., Rupprecht, C., Belagiannis, V., Tombari, F., Navab, N.: Deeper depth prediction with fully convolutional residual networks. In: 3DV, pp. 239–248 (2016)
26. Lee, J.H., Heo, M., Kim, K.R., Kim, C.S.: Single-image depth estimation based on Fourier domain analysis. In: CVPR, pp. 330–339 (2018)
27. Lee, J.H., Kim, C.S.: Monocular depth estimation using relative depth maps. In: CVPR, pp. 9729–9738 (2019)
28. Lee, J.H., Kim, C.S.: Multi-loss rebalancing algorithm for monocular depth estimation. In: ECCV, pp. 785–801 (2020)
29. Lee, J.H., Lee, C., Kim, C.S.: Learning multiple pixelwise tasks based on loss scale balancing. In: ICCV, pp. 5107–5116 (2021)
30. Lee, J.H., Han, M.K., Ko, D.W., Suh, I.H.: From big to small: Multi-scale local planar guidance for monocular depth estimation. arXiv preprint arXiv:1907.10326 (2019)
31. Levin, A., Lischinski, D., Weiss, Y.: Colorization using optimization. ACM Trans. Graph. **23**(3), 689–694 (2004)
32. Li, Z., et al.: Learning the depths of moving people by watching frozen people. In: CVPR, pp. 4521–4530 (2019)
33. Li, Z., Snavely, N.: MegaDepth: learning single-view depth prediction from internet photos. In: CVPR, pp. 2041–2050 (2018)
34. Lienen, J., Hullermeier, E., Ewerth, R., Nommensen, N.: Monocular depth estimation via listwise ranking using the Plackett-Luce model. In: CVPR, pp. 14595–14604 (2021)
35. Liu, C., Yang, J., Ceylan, D., Yumer, E., Furukawa, Y.: PlaneNet: piece-wise planar reconstruction from a single RGB image. In: CVPR, pp. 2579–2588 (2018)
36. Liu, C., et al.: Progressive neural architecture search. In: ECCV, pp. 19–34 (2018)
37. Liu, S., Johns, E., Davison, A.J.: End-to-end multi-task learning with attention. In: CVPR, pp. 1871–1880 (2019)
38. Ma, F., Karaman, S.: Sparse-to-dense: depth prediction from sparse depth samples and a single image. In: ICRA, pp. 4796–4803 (2018)
39. Park, J., Joo, K., Hu, Z., Liu, C.K., So Kweon, I.: Non-local spatial propagation network for depth completion. In: ECCV, pp. 120–136 (2020)
40. Qi, X., Liao, R., Liu, Z., Urtasun, R., Jia, J.: GeoNet: geometric neural network for joint depth and surface normal estimation. In: CVPR, pp. 283–291 (2018)
41. Ramamonjisoa, M., Lepetit, V.: SharpNet: Fast and accurate recovery of occluding contours in monocular depth estimation. In: ICCVW (2019)

42. Ranftl, R., Bochkovskiy, A., Koltun, V.: Vision transformers for dense prediction. In: ICCV, pp. 12179–12188 (2021)
43. Ranftl, R., Lasinger, K., Hafner, D., Schindler, K., Koltun, V.: Towards robust monocular depth estimation: mixing datasets for zero-shot cross-dataset transfer. IEEE Trans. Pattern Anal. Mach. Intell. (2020)
44. Saxena, A., Sun, M., Ng, A.Y.: Make3D: learning 3D scene structure from a single still image. IEEE Trans. Pattern Anal. Mach. Intell. **31**(5), 824–840 (2008)
45. Silberman, N., Hoiem, D., Kohli, P., Fergus, R.: Indoor segmentation and support inference from RGBD images. In: ECCV, pp. 746–760 (2012)
46. Song, S., Lichtenberg, S.P., Xiao, J.: SUN RGB-D: a RGB-D scene understanding benchmark suite. In: CVPR, pp. 567–576 (2015)
47. Tan, M., Le, Q.: EfficientNet: rethinking model scaling for convolutional neural networks. In: ICML, pp. 6105–6114 (2019)
48. Wang, C., Lucey, S., Perazzi, F., Wang, O.: Web stereo video supervision for depth prediction from dynamic scenes. In: 3DV, pp. 348–357. IEEE (2019)
49. Wang, P., Shen, X., Lin, Z., Cohen, S., Price, B., Yuille, A.L.: Towards unified depth and semantic prediction from a single image. In: CVPR, pp. 2800–2809 (2015)
50. Xian, K., et al.: Monocular relative depth perception with web stereo data supervision. In: CVPR, pp. 311–320 (2018)
51. Xian, K., Zhang, J., Wang, O., Mai, L., Lin, Z., Cao, Z.: Structure-guided ranking loss for single image depth prediction. In: CVPR, pp. 611–620 (2020)
52. Xie, J., Girshick, R., Farhadi, A.: Deep3D: fully automatic 2D-to-3D video conversion with deep convolutional neural networks. In: ECCV, pp. 842–857 (2016)
53. Xie, S., Girshick, R., Dollár, P., Tu, Z., He, K.: Aggregated residual transformations for deep neural networks. In: CVPR, pp. 1492–1500 (2017)
54. Xu, D., Ricci, E., Ouyang, W., Wang, X., Sebe, N.: Multi-scale continuous CRFs as sequential deep networks for monocular depth estimation. In: CVPR, pp. 5354–5362 (2017)
55. Xu, Y., Zhu, X., Shi, J., Zhang, G., Bao, H., Li, H.: Depth completion from sparse LiDAR data with depth-normal constraints. In: ICCV, pp. 2811–2820 (2019)
56. Yin, W., Liu, Y., Shen, C., Yan, Y.: Enforcing geometric constraints of virtual normal for depth prediction. In: ICCV, pp. 5684–5693 (2019)
57. Yu, F., Koltun, V., Funkhouser, T.: Dilated residual networks. In: CVPR, pp. 472–480 (2017)
58. Zoran, D., Isola, P., Krishnan, D., Freeman, W.T.: Learning ordinal relationships for mid-level vision. In: ICCV, pp. 388–396 (2015)

Monitored Distillation for Positive Congruent Depth Completion

Tian Yu Liu[1]([✉]) [ID], Parth Agrawal[1] [ID], Allison Chen[1] [ID], Byung-Woo Hong[2] [ID],
and Alex Wong[3] [ID]

[1] UCLA Vision Lab, Los Angeles, CA 90095, USA
{tianyu139,parthagrawal24,allisonchen2}@ucla.edu
[2] Chung-Ang University, Heukseok-Dong, Dongjak-Gu, Seoul 06973, Korea
hong@cau.ac.kr
[3] Yale University, New Haven, CT 06511, USA
alex.wong@yale.edu

Abstract. We propose a method to infer a dense depth map from a single image, its calibration, and the associated sparse point cloud. In order to leverage existing models (teachers) that produce putative depth maps, we propose an adaptive knowledge distillation approach that yields a positive congruent training process, wherein a student model avoids learning the error modes of the teachers. In the absence of ground truth for model selection and training, our method, termed *Monitored Distillation*, allows a student to exploit a blind ensemble of teachers by selectively learning from predictions that best minimize the reconstruction error for a given image. Monitored Distillation yields a distilled depth map and a confidence map, or "monitor", for how well a prediction from a particular teacher fits the observed image. The monitor adaptively weights the distilled depth where if all of the teachers exhibit high residuals, the standard unsupervised image reconstruction loss takes over as the supervisory signal. On indoor scenes (VOID), we outperform blind ensembling baselines by 17.53% and unsupervised methods by 24.25%; we boast a 79% model size reduction while maintaining comparable performance to the best supervised method. For outdoors (KITTI), we tie for 5th overall on the benchmark despite not using ground truth. Code available at: https://github.com/alexklwong/mondi-python.

Keywords: Depth completion · Blind ensemble · Knowledge distillation

---

T. Y. Liu, P. Agrawal and A. Chen—denotes equal contribution.

Supplementary Information The online version contains supplementary material available at https://doi.org/10.1007/978-3-031-20086-1_3.

S. Avidan et al. (Eds.): ECCV 2022, LNCS 13662, pp. 35–53, 2022.
https://doi.org/10.1007/978-3-031-20086-1_3

1   Introduction

Interaction with physical space requires a representation of the 3-dimensional (3D) geometry of the surrounding environment. Most mobile platforms include at least one camera and some means of estimating range at a sparse set of points i.e. a point cloud. These could be from a dedicated range sensor such as a LiDAR or radar, or by processing the images using a visual odometry module. Depth completion consists of inferring a dense depth map, with a range value corresponding to every pixel, from an image and a sparse point cloud. Inherently, depth completion is an ill-posed inverse problem, so priors need to be imposed in the form of generic regularization or learned inductive biases.

Natural scenes exhibit regularities that can be captured by a trained model, for instance a deep neural network (DNN), using a dataset of images and corresponding sparse depths. While we wish to avoid any form of manual or ground truth supervision, we also strive to exploit the availability of differing types of pretrained models, whether from synthetic data or other supervised or unsupervised methods. We refer to these pretrained models as "teachers", each providing a hypothesis of depth map for a given image and sparse point cloud. This leads to a blind ensemble setting where ground truth is not available (e.g. transferring models trained on a specific task to new datasets with no ground truth) for the explicit evaluation of pretrained models i.e. model selection. The key question, then, is how to make use of a heterogeneous collection of teachers, along with other variational principles such as minimization of the photometric reprojection error and generic regularizers such as structural similarity.

In general, different teachers will behave differently not only across images, but even across regions within a given image. The incongruency of different models trained on the same tasks has been observed in the context of classification model versioning [61]. Particularly, the same architecture trained with the same data, but starting from different initial conditions can yield models that *differ on a significant portion of the samples* while achieving the same average error rate. Thus, a naive ensembling of a handful of teachers yields the union of the failure modes, only modestly mitigated by the averaging.

Instead, we propose Monitored Distillation for selecting which teacher to emulate in each image at each pixel. The selection is guided by a "monitor", based on the residual between the observations (e.g. image, sparse point cloud) and their reconstructions generated by each teacher. This yields a spatially-varying confidence map that weights the contribution of the selected teachers as well as the structural and photometric reprojection errors i.e. unsupervised losses, customary in structure-from-motion. In doing so, our method is robust even when poor performing teachers are introduced into the ensemble – discarding their hypotheses in favor of the ones that better reconstruct the scene. In the extreme case where every teacher produces erroneous outputs, our method would still learn a valid depth estimate because of our unsupervised fall-back loss.

Our contributions are as follows: **(i)** We propose an adaptive method to combine the predictions of a blind ensemble of teachers based on their compatibility with the observed data; to the best of our knowledge, we are the first to propose knowledge distillation from a blind ensemble for depth completion. **(ii)** The adaptive mechanism yields a spatially varying confidence map or "monitor" that modulates the contributions of each teacher based on their residuals, leading to a training method that is positive congruent. **(iii)** Even when all members of the ensemble fail, our model automatically reverts to the unsupervised learning criteria and generic regularization, allowing us to avoid distilling erroneous knowledge from teachers. **(iv)** Our method outperforms distillation and unsupervised methods by 17.53% and 24.25% respectively on indoors scenes; we are comparable to top supervised methods with a 79% model size reduction. On the KITTI benchmark, we tie for 5th overall despite not using ground truth.

2 Related Works

Depth completion is a form of imputation and thus requires regularization, which may come from generic assumptions or learned from data. The question is: How to best combine different sources of regularization, adaptively [17,18,57], in a way that leverages their strengths, while addressing their weaknesses?

Supervised depth completion is trained by minimizing a loss with respect to ground truth. Early methods posed the task as learning morphological operators [10] and compressive sensing [8]. Recent works focus on network operations [12,22] and design [5,35,49,62] to effectively deal with the sparse inputs. For example, [29] used a cascade hourglass network, [24,62] used separate image and depth encoders and fused their representations, and [22] proposed an upsampling layer and joint concatenation and convolution. Whereas, [11,12,43,44] learned uncertainty of estimates, [50] leveraged confidence maps to fuse predictions from different modalities, and [42,60,63] used surface normals for guidance. [6,39] use convolutional spatial propagation networks, [21] used separate image and depth networks and fused them with spatial propagation. While supervised methods currently hold the top ranks on benchmark datasets i.e. KITTI [49] and VOID [56], they inevitably require ground truth for supervision, which is typically unavailable. Furthermore, these architectures are often complex and require many parameters (e.g. 132M for [21], 53.4M for [42], and 25.8M for [39]), making them computationally prohibitive to train and impractical to deploy [37].

Unsupervised depth completion assumes that additional data (stereo or monocular videos) is available during training. Both stereo [46,62] and monocular [35,54–56] paradigms focus largely on designing losses that minimize (i) the photometric error between the input image and its reconstructions from other views, and (ii) the difference between the prediction and sparse depth input (sparse depth reconstruction). Architecture-wise, [58] proposed a calibrated backprojection network. However, all of these methods rely on *generic* regularization i.e. local smoothness that is not informed by the data. Attempts to leverage learned priors mainly focused on synthetic data. [34] applied image translation to obtain ground truth in the real domain; whereas [56,62] used synthetic data to learn a prior on the shapes populating a scene. We also employ an unsupervised loss, but unlike them, we distill regularities from a blind ensemble of pretrained models that can be trained on synthetic or real data, supervised or unsupervised.

Knowledge Distillation uses a simpler student model to approximate the function learned by a larger, more complex teacher model by training it to learn the soft target distribution [16]. There exists many works on knowledge distillation, including image classification [33,45,59], object detection [2–4], semantic segmentation [31,38,40], depth estimation [20,32,52], and more recently, depth completion [23]. [9,31,32] utilize pairwise and holistic distillation to capture structural relationships and [38] distills latent representations to guide learning. [52] leverages knowledge distillation for monocular depth estimation on mobile devices, and [41] uses cyclic inconsistency and knowledge distillation for unsupervised depth estimation, where the student network is a sub-network of the teacher. In depth completion, [23] uses knowledge distillation for joint training of both teacher and student models. Unlike ours, this method uses ground truth.

Ensemble learning addresses the limitations of a single teacher by distilling information from multiple teachers [14]. If done effectively, the student will learn to extract the most relevant information from each teacher. This has been explored in classification [26,28,51], but fewer works utilize it in dense prediction tasks. [1] uses it for domain adaptation in semantic segmentation and [15] in selecting lidar points for depth completion. We further assume the blind ensemble setting [48] where we lack ground truth for evaluation of the ensemble.

Positive congruent training [61] observed sample-wise inconsistencies in classification versioning, where new models wrongly predict for samples that were previously classified correctly by an older, reference model on the same task and dataset. To address this, they propose to emulate the reference model (teacher) only when its predictions are correct; otherwise, they minimize a loss with respect to ground truth – yielding reduced error rates and inconsistencies. Monitored distillation is inspired by positive-congruency, but unlike [61], we do not require ground truth and are applicable towards geometric tasks.

3   Method Formulation

We wish to recover the 3D scene from a calibrated RGB image $I : \Omega \subset \mathbb{R}^2 \mapsto \mathbb{R}^3_+$ and its associated sparse point cloud projected onto the image plane $z : \Omega_z \subset \Omega \mapsto \mathbb{R}_+$. To do so, we propose learning a function f_θ that takes as input I, z, and camera intrinsics K and outputs a dense depth map $\hat{d} := f_\theta(I, z, K) \in \mathbb{R}^{H \times W}_+$.

We assume that for each synchronized pair of image and sparse depth map (I_t, z_t) captured at a viewpoint t, we have access to a set of spatially and/or temporally adjacent alternate views T and the corresponding set of images I_T. Additionally, we assume access to a set of M models or "teachers" $\{h_i\}_{i=1}^M$ (e.g. publicly available pretrained models). Figure 2 shows that each teacher has unique failure modes. As we operate in the blind ensemble setting, we lack ground truth to evaluate teacher performance for model selection. To address this, we propose Monitored Distillation, an adaptive knowledge distillation framework

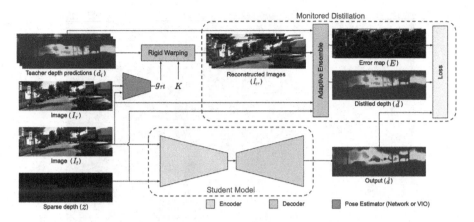

Fig. 1. Monitored distillation. Our method measures the reconstruction residual of predictions from each teacher and constructs the distilled depth $\bar{d}$ based on a pixel-wise selection of predictions that best minimize the reconstruction error E. We derive a monitor function Q from E, which adaptively balances the trade-offs between the distilling from the ensemble and the unsupervised losses.

for ensemble learning that results in positive congruent training: We only learn from a teacher if its predictions are compatible with the observed scene.

To this end, we leverage geometric constraints between I_t and $I_\tau \in I_T$ and validate the correctness of predictions $d_i := h_i(I_t, z_t)$ produced by each teacher through averaging their photometric reprojection residuals from different views I_T and weighting them based on deviations from z. From the error, we derive a confidence map that determines the compatibility of each teacher to the observed image I_t. We then construct distilled depth $\bar{d} \in \mathbb{R}_+^{H \times W}$ via pixel-wise selection from the ensemble that yields the highest confidence. The resulting spatially varying confidence map acts as a "monitor" to balance the trade-off between "trusting" the ensemble and falling back onto unsupervised geometric consistency as a supervisory signal (i.e. when all teachers yield high residuals).

Monitored Distillation. Given $M \in \mathbb{Z}^+$ teachers and their predicted depth maps d_i, for $i \in \{1, \cdots, M\}$, we construct a distilled depth map $\bar{d}$ by adaptively selecting predictions from the teacher ensemble that best minimize reconstruction error of the observed point cloud and image. To this end, we reconstruct the observed image I_t via reprojection from an adjacent view $I_\tau, \tau \in T$:

$$\hat{I}_{t\tau}(x, d) = I_\tau(\pi g_{\tau t} K^{-1} \bar{x} d(x)), \tag{1}$$

where d denotes the depth values for $x \in \Omega$, $\bar{x} = [x^\top \ 1]^\top$ is the homogeneous coordinate of x, $g_{\tau t} \in SE(3)$ is the relative pose of the camera from view t to τ, K is the camera intrinsics, and π is the perspective projection. In practice, $g_{\tau t}$ can be derived from camera baseline if I_t and I_τ are stereo pairs, directly estimated by a visual inertial odometry (VIO) system, or learned from a pose network if the views are taken from a video.

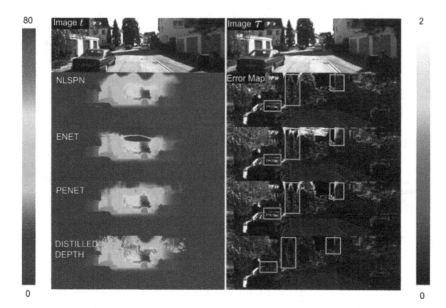

Fig. 2. Error modes of teacher models on KITTI. Row 1 shows the input image I_t (left) and an image taken from another view I_τ (right). Rows 2–4 shows the predicted depth maps (left) and error maps (right) for each teacher, where each has different error modes. Row 5 shows the distilled depth that our method adaptively constructs from the teacher models. The error for each region in the distilled depth lower bounds the reprojection error of the individual teachers.

For each teacher h_i, we measure the photometric reprojection error P_i via the mean SSIM [53] between I_t and each reconstruction $\hat{I}_{t\tau}(x, d_i), \tau \in T$:

$$P_i(x) = \frac{1}{|T|} \sum_{\tau \in T} \left(1 - \phi(\hat{I}_{t\tau}(x, d_i), I_t(x))\right) \tag{2}$$

For ease of notation, we denote SSIM as $\phi(\cdot)$.

As photometric reprojection alone does not afford scale, we additionally measure the local deviation of teacher predictions from the observed sparse point cloud within a $k \times k$ neighborhood of x, denoted by $\mathcal{N}(x)$:

$$Z_i = \frac{1}{k^2 |z_t|} \sum_{x \in \Omega} \sum_{y \in \mathcal{N}(x)} \mathbb{1}_{z_t(x)} \cdot |d_i(y) - z_t(x)| \tag{3}$$

When used as a weight, $\beta_i := 1 - \exp(-\alpha Z_i)$ serves to resolve the scale ambiguity between different teachers, where α is a temperature parameter. We can then define E_i, the weighted reconstruction residual from the i-th teacher, as:

$$E_i(x) = \beta_i P_i(x). \tag{4}$$

To construct the distilled depth, we selectively choose the depth prediction for each pixel $x \in \Omega$ that minimizes the overall residual error E_i across all teachers:

$$\bar{d}(x) = \sum_{i=1}^{M} \mathbb{1}_i(x)d_i(x), \tag{5}$$

where $\mathbb{1}_i$ is a binary weight map of the i-th teacher is given by

$$\mathbb{1}_i(x) = \begin{cases} 1 & E_i(x) < E_j(x) \ \forall \ j \neq i \\ 0 & \text{otherwise.} \end{cases} \tag{6}$$

In other words, $\mathbb{1}_i(x) = 1$ when $d_i(x)$ yields the lowest photometric residual. Figure 1 shows an overview of our method, where teacher predictions are ensembled into distilled depth for supervision. Figure 3 shows the distribution of teachers chosen for constructing the distilled depth. As observed, different teachers perform well in different regions across different depth ranges. Our method selects points from each teacher with the lowest error (i.e. highest confidence) to yield an adaptive ensemble (see Fig. 2).

Despite being trained on ground truth, each teacher can only *approximate* the true distribution of depths in the scene. While selectively ensembling based on the reprojection residual will address *some* error modes of the teachers, it is still possible for all teachers to yield high reconstruction residuals. Hence, we do not trust the ensemble fully, and instead further adaptively weight the ensemble supervision with a monitor Q based on the error of the distilled depth $\bar{d}$. As we have already constructed the error maps E_i for each teacher, we can similarly aggregate the error for each pixel $E(x) = \min_i E_i(x)$ for $x \in \Omega$. The final monitor $Q \in [0, 1]^{H \times W}$ is a spatially adaptive per-pixel confidence map:

$$Q(x) = \exp(-\lambda E(x)), \tag{7}$$

where λ is a temperature parameter (see Supp. Mat.). Q naturally assigns higher confidence to points in the distilled depth that are compatible with the observed image I_t as measured by reconstruction error, and is used to weight the supervision signal. Our monitored knowledge distillation objective reads:

$$\ell_{md} = \frac{1}{|\Omega|} \sum_{x \in \Omega} Q(x) \cdot |\hat{d}(x) - \bar{d}(x)|. \tag{8}$$

Typically, a student learns the error modes of its teacher. But by distilling from the adaptive ensemble of teachers that is positive congruent, our student model learns not to make the same mistake as any individual teacher. We refer to this process as *Monitored Distillation*, in which our monitor function Q gives higher weight to the teachers in regions of lower reconstruction error. For regions where all of the teachers within the ensemble yield high residuals, we default to unsupervised loss to avoid learning the common error modes of any teacher.

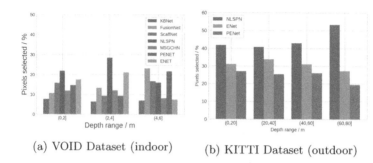

(a) VOID Dataset (indoor)   (b) KITTI Dataset (outdoor)

Fig. 3. Teacher selection distribution. The plots show the proportion of pixels selected from each teacher model. Note: error modes vary across different depth ranges as different teachers dominate the selection at different distances.

Unsupervised Objective. For regions with high reconstruction error, the monitoring function Q allows us to fall back onto standard unsupervised photometric reprojection error, i.e. color and structural consistencies, as the training signal:

$$\ell_{co} = \frac{1}{|\Omega|}\frac{1}{|T|}\sum_{x\in\Omega}\sum_{\tau\in T}(1 - Q(x))\big(|\hat{I}_{t\tau}(x,\hat{d}) - I_t(x)|\big) \tag{9}$$

$$\ell_{st} = \frac{1}{|\Omega|}\frac{1}{|T|}\sum_{x\in\Omega}\sum_{\tau\in T}(1 - Q(x))\big(1 - \phi(\hat{I}_{t\tau}(x,\hat{d}), I_t(x))\big) \tag{10}$$

We weight the relative contributions of these losses with the complement of our adaptive monitor function $(1-Q)$. As a result, our framework naturally allows us to search for the correct correspondences (and in turn better depth estimation) in regions where the ensemble failed. In other words, regions which the monitor deems as high confidence are more heavily influenced by ℓ_{md} as supervision, while lower confidence regions will minimize unsupervised losses instead.

Because the ensemble is informed by large amounts of data, their predictions have regularities of our physical world, e.g. roads are flat and surfaces are locally connected, "baked into" them. This presents an advantage: The student will learn priors, often too complex to be modeled by generic assumptions, from the ensemble. However, these priors may backfire when all the teachers yield high residuals. Luckily, Q naturally limits the influence of the ensemble in such cases, but this in turn reduces the amount of regularization that is needed for ill-posed problems like 3D reconstruction. Hence, for these cases, we default to generic assumptions i.e. a local smoothness regularizer:

$$\ell_{sm} = \frac{1}{|\Omega|}\sum_{x\in\Omega}(1 - Q(x))\big(\lambda_X(x)|\partial_X\hat{d}(x)| + \lambda_Y(x)|\partial_Y\hat{d}(x)|\big) \tag{11}$$

where ∂_X, ∂_Y are gradients along the x and y directions, weighted by $\lambda_X := e^{-|\partial_X I_t(x)|}$ and $\lambda_Y := e^{-|\partial_Y I_t(x)|}$ respectively.

Thus, we have the following overall loss function

$$\mathcal{L} = w_{md}\ell_{md} + w_{ph}\ell_{ph} + w_{st}\ell_{st} + w_{sm}\ell_{sm} \tag{12}$$

where $w_{(.)}$ denotes the respective weights for each loss term (see Supp. Mat.).

Student Model Architecture. Through monitored distillation from an ensemble of teachers, a simpler student model can be trained on the output distribution of more complex teacher models to achieve comparable performance. Therefore, we compress KBNet [58] by replacing the final two layers in the encoder with depth-wise separable convolutions [19] to yield a 23.2% reduction in the number of model parameters. Compared to the best supervised teacher models that require 25.84M (NLSPN [39]), 131.7M (ENet [21]), 132M (PENet [21]), and 6.9M (the original KBNet) parameters, our student model only requires 5.3M.

4   Experiments

We evaluate our method on public benchmarks – VOID [56] for indoor and outdoor scenes and KITTI [49] for outdoor driving settings. We describe evaluation metrics, implementation details, hyper-parameters and learning schedule in the Supp. Mat. [30]. All experiments are performed under the blind ensemble setting where we do not have ground truth for model selection nor training.

VOID dataset [56] contains synchronized 640×480 RGB images and sparse depth maps of indoor (laboratories, classrooms) and outdoor (gardens) scenes. The associated sparse depth maps contain $\approx$1500 sparse depth points with a density of $\approx$0.5%. They are obtained by a set of features tracked by XIVO [13], a VIO system. The dense ground-truth depth maps are acquired by active stereo. As opposed to static scenes in KITTI, the VOID dataset contains 56 sequences with challenging motion. Of the 56 sequences, 48 sequences ($\approx$45,000 frames) are designated for training and 8 for testing (800 frames). We follow the evaluation protocol of [56] and cap the depths between 0.2 and 5.0 m.

KITTI dataset [49] depth completion benchmark contains $\approx$86,000 raw 1242×375 image frames (43K stereo pairs) and synchronized sparse depth maps. The sparse depth is obtained using a Velodyne lidar sensor and, when projected, covers $\approx$5% of the image space. The ground truth depths are semi-dense, which we use only for evaluation purposes. We use the designated 1,000 samples for validation and evaluate test-time accuracy on KITTI's online testing server.

Table 1. Blind ensemble distillation. We compare Monitored Distillation against naive ensembling methods for training a student model.

Ensemble type	Distillation method	MAE	RMSE	iMAE	iRMSE
None	Unsupervised loss only	55.67	117.21	28.68	58.31
Supervised	Mean w/o unsupervised loss	34.27	91.72	17.63	41.39
	Mean	34.04	89.19	17.30	40.43
	Median	34.64	89.80	17.46	39.77
	Random	35.18	92.30	18.41	42.95
	Ours w/o β	32.86	85.53	16.44	39.14
	Ours	**30.88**	**87.48**	**15.31**	**38.33**
Unsupervised	Mean w/o unsupervised loss	44.73	96.56	24.08	49.55
	Mean	41.96	94.47	23.80	50.37
	Median	43.86	99.46	23.62	50.85
	Random	39.38	92.14	20.62	46.04
	Ours w/o β	38.78	90.72	20.53	45.91
	Ours	**36.42**	**87.78**	**19.18**	**43.83**
Heterogeneous	Mean w/o unsupervised loss	44.53	100.59	23.33	48.36
	Mean	35.79	84.78	18.65	42.90
	Median	33.89	85.25	17.31	40.40
	Random	43.64	94.38	24.74	50.27
	Ours w/o β	32.09	80.20	16.15	38.86
	Ours	**29.67**	**79.78**	**14.84**	**37.88**

Teacher Ensembles: We use the following ensembles for VOID (Table 1, 2, 3): (i) supervised ensemble of NLSPN [39], MSG-CHN [29], ENet, and PENet [21], (ii) unsupervised ensemble of FusionNet [54], KBNet [58], and ScaffNet [54] (trained on SceneNet [36]), and (iii) heterogeneous ensemble of all seven methods. For KITTI (Table 4, 5), we used NLSPN [39], ENet, and PENet [21].

VOID Depth Completion Benchmark. We present qualitative and quantitative experiments on VOID against blind ensemble distillation baselines, and top supervised and unsupervised methods. Note that while we evaluate our method and baselines across different ensemble compositions, Monitored Distillationand baselines have no knowledge regarding any individual teacher in the ensemble. For comparison purposes, scores for each teacher can be found in Table 3.

Comparisons Against Baselines: As we are the first to propose knowledge distillation for blind ensembles (Table 1), we begin by presenting several baselines: (1) mean, and (2) median of teachers, and (3) randomly selecting a teacher for each sample per iteration. All baselines are trained with distillation and unsupervised loss, unless specified otherwise, for fair comparisons against our method – which also consistently improves results for all ensemble types.

Table 2. Different teacher ensembles. We apply Monitored Distillation to various combinations of teachers trained on different datasets. Using an ensemble trained only on NYUv2($\ddagger$) and SceneNet($\dagger$) still benefits a student on VOID($\diamond$).

Teachers	Teachers trained on	MAE	RMSE	iMAE	iRMSE
None (unsupervised loss only)	–	55.67	117.21	28.68	58.31
FusionNet$^\diamond$, ScaffNet†	VOID, SceneNet	48.72	102.44	26.94	56.32
FusionNet$^\diamond$, KBNet$^\diamond$	VOID	40.10	92.03	22.16	46.86
KBNet$^\diamond$, ScaffNet†	VOID, SceneNet	38.87	91.76	20.50	46.67
FusionNet$^\diamond$, KBNet$^\diamond$, ScaffNet†	VOID, SceneNet	36.42	87.78	19.18	43.83
FusionNet‡, KBNet‡, ScaffNet†	NYUv2, SceneNet	46.66	104.05	26.13	54.96

Table 3. VOID benchmark. We compare against unsupervised (U) and supervised (S) methods. By distilling from blind ensemble (BE), we outperform all existing works except for [39] which has 5× more parameters. Using our method with an unsupervised ensemble also yields 1st among unsupervised methods.

Method	Type	# Param	Time	MAE	RMSE	iMAE	iRMSE
SS-S2D [35]	U	27.8M	59 ms	178.85	243.84	80.12	107.69
DDP [62]	U	18.8M	54 ms	151.86	222.36	74.59	112.36
VOICED [56]	U	9.7M	29 ms	85.05	169.79	48.92	104.02
ScaffNet [54]	U	7.8M	25 ms	59.53	119.14	35.72	68.36
ENet [21]	S	131.7M	75 ms	46.90	94.35	26.78	52.58
MSG-CHN [29]	S	364K	36 ms	43.57	109.94	23.44	52.09
KBNet [58]	U	6.9M	13 ms	39.80	95.86	21.16	49.72
Ours (Unsupervised)	**BE**	**5.3M**	**13 ms**	**36.42**	**87.78**	**19.18**	**43.83**
PENet [21]	S	132M	226 ms	34.61	82.01	18.89	40.36
Ours (Supervised)	**BE**	**5.3M**	**13 ms**	**30.88**	**87.48**	**15.31**	**38.33**
Ours (Heterogeneous)	**BE**	**5.3M**	**13 ms**	**29.67**	**79.78**	**14.84**	**37.88**
NLSPN [39]	*S*	*25.8M*	*122 ms*	*26.74*	*79.12*	*12.70*	*33.88*

Table 1 row 1 shows the baseline performance of the student network trained only on unsupervised losses. Compared to the KBNet [58] in Table 3 row 7, our compressed KBNet (student) has a 23.2% sharp drop in performance due to a decrease in capacity. While all distillation methods improves its performance, Monitored Distillationbeats all baselines by an average of 8.53% when using an ensemble of supervised teachers. This improvement grows to 11.50% when using an unsupervised ensemble (Table 1, rows 8–13), where the variance in teacher performance is considerably higher than supervised ones. Nonetheless, distilling an unsupervised ensemble improves over the best unsupervised method KBNet by an average of 9.53% – showing that we can indeed leverage the strengths of "weaker" methods to address the weakness of even the best method.

When using our method to distill from a heterogeneous ensemble, we observe the same trend where adding more teachers produces a stronger overall ensemble – improving over both supervised and unsupervised ones alone. This is unlike naive distillation baselines, where "polluting" the ensemble with weaker teachers results in a drop in performance (Table 1, rows 14–19). In fact, naive distillation

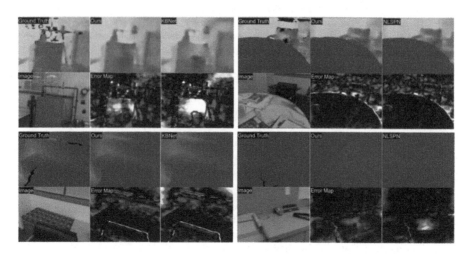

Fig. 4. Monitored Distillationvs. unsupervised (left) and supervised (right) teachers. While KBNet [58] is the best performer among unsupervised methods, by ensembling it with weaker methods, we addressed its error modes on lab equipment (top left). Similarly, we address the failure modes in the top supervised method NLSPN [39] by distilling from a heterogeneous ensemble

of heterogeneous ensemble is only marginally better than distilling unsupervised ensemble and considerably worse than a supervised one. In contrast, our method improves over baselines across all metrics by average of 17.53% and by 4.60% and 16.28% over our method with supervised and unsupervised ensembles, respectively. We also show an ablation study for β (Eq. 4) by removing sparse depth error from our validation criterion, where we observe an average drop of 4.32% without β across all ensemble types due to the inherent ambiguity in scale when using monocular images for reconstruction. β allows us to choose not only predictions that yield high fidelity reconstructions, but also metric scale.

Different Teacher Ensembles: Table 2 shows the effect of having different teacher combinations within the ensemble. In general, the more teachers the better, and the better the teachers, the better the student. For example, combinations of any two teachers from the unsupervised ensemble yields less a performant student than the full ensemble of FusionNet, KBNet and ScaffNet – including that adding an underperforming method like ScaffNet to the ensemble (rows 3, 5). Finally, we show in row 6 that distilling from an ensemble trained on completely different datasets than the target test dataset (i.e. KBNet and FusionNet are trained on NYU v2 [47] and Scaffnet on SceneNet [36]) still improves over unsupervised loss with generic regularizers like local smoothness (row 1).

Benchmark Comparisons: Table 3 shows comparisons on the VOID benchmark. In an indoor setting, scene layouts are very complex with point clouds typically in orders of hundreds to several thousand points. As such, there are many suitable dense representations that can complete a given point cloud. Hence, the accuracy

Table 4. KITTI unsupervised depth completion benchmark. Our method outperforms all unsupervised methods across all metrics on the KITTI leaderboard. * denotes methods that use additional synthetic data for training.

Method	# Param	Time	MAE	RMSE	iMAE	iRMSE
SS-S2D [35]	27.8M	80 ms	350.32	1299.85	1.57	4.07
IP-Basic [27]	0	11 ms	302.60	1288.46	1.29	3.78
DFuseNet [46]	n/a	80 ms	429.93	1206.66	1.79	3.62
DDP* [62]	18.8M	80 ms	343.46	1263.19	1.32	3.58
VOICED [56]	9.7M	44 ms	299.41	1169.97	1.20	3.56
AdaFrame [55]	6.4M	40 ms	291.62	1125.67	1.16	3.32
SynthProj* [34]	2.6M	60 ms	280.42	1095.26	1.19	3.53
ScaffNet* [54]	7.8M	32 ms	280.76	1121.93	1.15	3.30
KBNet [58]	6.9M	16 ms	256.76	1069.47	1.02	2.95
Ours	**5.3M**	**16 ms**	**218.60**	**785.06**	**0.92**	**2.11**

of the model hinges on the regularization as most of the scene does not allow for establishing unique correspondences due to largely homogeneous regions, occlusions and the aperture problem.

Unlike generic regularizers (e.g. piecewise-smoothness), Monitored Distillationis informed by the statistics of many other scenes. Hence, even when distilling from an unsupervised ensemble (row 8), we still beat the best unsupervised method, KBNet [58], by an average of 9.53% over all metrics while using a 23.2% smaller model. This highlights the benefit of our positive congruent training, where our distillation objective can address the error modes of individual teachers. This is shown in Fig. 4 (top left), where we fixed the erroneous predictions in the lab equipment, and reduced errors in homogeneous regions.

Furthermore, distilling from a heterogeneous ensemble yields a student that ranks 2nd on the benchmark, achieving comparable performance to the top method NLSPN [39] while boosting a 79% model size reduction. Note: we do not outperform NLSPN despite it being included in the ensemble. This is likely due to distillation loss from the large size reduction. Figure 4 shows that our model distills complex priors from the teacher ensemble regarding the topology of indoor surfaces, e.g. cabinets and tables are flat. The bottom right of Fig. 4 shows that we can even produce a more accurate depth estimate than NLSPN.

KITTI Depth Completion Benchmark. We provide quantitative comparisons against unsupervised and supervised methods on the KITTI test set. We also provide qualitative comparisons in Supp. Mat.

Comparison with Unsupervised Methods: Table 4 shows that despite having fewer parameters than most unsupervised models (e.g. 23.2% fewer than KBNet [58], 73.0% fewer than DDP [62]), our method outperforms the state of the art [58] across all metrics by an average of 19.93%, and by as much as 28.47% in iRMSE while boasting a 16ms inference time. Compared to methods that use synthetic ground truth to obtain a learned prior (marked with * in Table 4), our method leverages learned priors from pretrained models and improves over [34,54] by an average of 28.32% and 27.06%. We posit that this is largely due to the sim2real domain gap that [34,54,62] have to overcome i.e. covariate shift due to image translation error during training.

Comparison with Distilled and Supervised Methods: We compare our method (having at best *indirect* access to ground truth) against supervised and distilled methods that have *direct* access to ground truth in training. Table 5 shows that we rank 4th in iMAE and iRMSE, and tie for 5th overall. Note: We beat knowledge distillation method Self-Distill [23] by 12.6% despite (i) they use ground truth and (ii) we apply our method in the blind ensemble setting. We achieve comparable performance to the teacher models ENet [21] (131.7M params), PENet [21] (132M params), and NLSPN [39] (25.8M params) across all metrics despite only requiring 5.3M parameters.

Table 5. KITTI supervised depth completion benchmark. We compare against distilled (D) and supervised (S) methods. Despite operating in the blind ensemble (BE) distillation regime, our method beats many supervised methods. Our iMAE (0.92) and iRMSE (2.11) scores rank 4th, and we tie for 5th overall. Note: a method outranks another if it performs better on more than two metrics.

Rank	Method	Type	MAE	RMSE	iMAE	iRMSE
13	CSPN [7]	S	279.46	1019.64	1.15	2.93
12	SS-S2D [35]	S	249.95	814.73	1.21	2.80
9	Self-Distill [23]	D	248.22	949.85	0.98	2.48
9	DeepLiDAR [42]	S	226.50	758.38	1.15	2.56
9	PwP [60]	S	235.73	785.57	1.07	2.52
8	UberATG-FuseNet [5]	S	221.19	752.88	1.14	2.34
5	**Ours**	**BE**	**218.60**	**785.06**	**0.92**	**2.11**
5	RGB_guide&certainty [50]	S	215.02	772.87	0.93	2.19
5	ENet [21]	S	216.26	741.30	0.95	2.14
4	PENet [21]	S	210.55	730.08	0.94	2.17
2	DDP [62]	S	203.96	832.94	0.85	2.10
2	CSPN++ [6]	S	209.28	743.69	0.90	2.07
1	*NLSPN [39]*	*S*	*199.59*	*741.68*	*0.84*	*1.99*

5   Discussion

We propose Monitored Distillationfor blind ensemble learning and knowledge distillation on depth completion tasks. Our method is capable of shrinking model size by 79% compared to the best teacher model, while still attaining comparable performance, enabling lightweight and deployable models.

However, we note that there exists several *risks and limitations*. (i) Our method relies on the composition of teachers and their error modes; if all teachers perform poorly on certain regions, our performance in these regions will not improve beyond training with unsupervised losses. (ii) Our method relies on structure-from-motion. If there is insufficient parallax between the stereo or monocular images, then photometric reprojection is uninformative regarding the depth of the scene. (iii) Reprojection error is limited when Lambertian assumptions are violated. However, the domain coverage of specularities and translucency is sparse due to the sparsity of primary illuminants [25] (rank of the reflectance tensor is deficient and typically small). So, explicitly modeling deviations from diffuse Lambertian reflection is likely to yield modest returns.

Admittedly the scope of this work is limited to depth completion, but we foresee this method being applied to general geometric problems (e.g. optical flow, stereo). Our method is the first attempt in blind ensemble distillation to produce positive congruent students, and we hope it lays the groundwork for approaches aiming to ensemble the abundance of existing pretrained models.

Acknowledgements. This work was supported by ARO W911NF-17-1-0304, ONR N00014-22-1-2252, NIH-NEI 1R01EY030595, and IITP-2021-0-01341 (AIGS-CAU). We thank Stefano Soatto for his continued support.

References

1. Chao, C.H., Cheng, B.W., Lee, C.Y.: Rethinking ensemble-distillation for semantic segmentation based unsupervised domain adaption. In: Proceedings of the IEEE/CVF Conference on Computer Vision and Pattern Recognition, pp. 2610–2620 (2021)
2. Chawla, A., Yin, H., Molchanov, P., Alvarez, J.: Data-free knowledge distillation for object detection. In: Proceedings of the IEEE/CVF Winter Conference on Applications of Computer Vision, pp. 3289–3298 (2021)
3. Chen, G., Choi, W., Yu, X., Han, T., Chandraker, M.: Learning efficient object detection models with knowledge distillation. In: Advances in neural information processing systems, vol. 30 (2017)
4. Chen, L., Yu, C., Chen, L.: A new knowledge distillation for incremental object detection. In: 2019 International Joint Conference on Neural Networks (IJCNN), pp. 1–7. IEEE (2019)
5. Chen, Y., Yang, B., Liang, M., Urtasun, R.: Learning joint 2D-3D representations for depth completion. In: Proceedings of the IEEE International Conference on Computer Vision, pp. 10023–10032 (2019)

6. Cheng, X., Wang, P., Guan, C., Yang, R.: CSPN++: learning context and resource aware convolutional spatial propagation networks for depth completion. In: Proceedings of the AAAI Conference on Artificial Intelligence, vol. 34, pp. 10615–10622 (2020)
7. Cheng, X., Wang, P., Yang, R.: Depth estimation via affinity learned with convolutional spatial propagation network. In: Proceedings of the European Conference on Computer Vision (ECCV), pp. 103–119 (2018)
8. Chodosh, N., Wang, C., Lucey, S.: Deep convolutional compressed sensing for LiDAR depth completion. In: Jawahar, C.V., Li, H., Mori, G., Schindler, K. (eds.) ACCV 2018. LNCS, vol. 11361, pp. 499–513. Springer, Cham (2019). https://doi.org/10.1007/978-3-030-20887-5_31
9. Choi, K., Jeong, S., Kim, Y., Sohn, K.: Stereo-augmented depth completion from a single RGB-LiDAR image. In: 2021 IEEE International Conference on Robotics and Automation (ICRA), pp. 13641–13647. IEEE (2021)
10. Dimitrievski, M., Veelaert, P., Philips, W.: Learning morphological operators for depth completion. In: Blanc-Talon, J., Helbert, D., Philips, W., Popescu, D., Scheunders, P. (eds.) ACIVS 2018. LNCS, vol. 11182, pp. 450–461. Springer, Cham (2018). https://doi.org/10.1007/978-3-030-01449-0_38
11. Eldesokey, A., Felsberg, M., Holmquist, K., Persson, M.: Uncertainty-aware CNNs for depth completion: Uncertainty from beginning to end. In: Proceedings of the IEEE/CVF Conference on Computer Vision and Pattern Recognition, pp. 12014–12023 (2020)
12. Eldesokey, A., Felsberg, M., Khan, F.S.: Propagating confidences through CNNs for sparse data regression. In: Proceedings of British Machine Vision Conference (BMVC) (2018)
13. Fei, X., Wong, A., Soatto, S.: Geo-supervised visual depth prediction. IEEE Robot. Autom. Lett. **4**(2), 1661–1668 (2019)
14. Fukuda, T., Suzuki, M., Kurata, G., Thomas, S., Cui, J., Ramabhadran, B.: Efficient knowledge distillation from an ensemble of teachers. In: Interspeech, pp. 3697–3701 (2017)
15. Gofer, E., Praisler, S., Gilboa, G.: Adaptive LiDAR sampling and depth completion using ensemble variance. IEEE Trans. Image Process. **30**, 8900–8912 (2021)
16. Hinton, G., Vinyals, O., Dean, J.: Distilling the knowledge in a neural network. arXiv preprint arXiv:1503.02531 (2015)
17. Hong, B.-W., Koo, J.-K., Dirks, H., Burger, M.: Adaptive regularization in convex composite optimization for variational imaging problems. In: Roth, V., Vetter, T. (eds.) GCPR 2017. LNCS, vol. 10496, pp. 268–280. Springer, Cham (2017). https://doi.org/10.1007/978-3-319-66709-6_22
18. Hong, B.W., Koo, J., Burger, M., Soatto, S.: Adaptive regularization of some inverse problems in image analysis. IEEE Trans. Image Process. **29**, 2507–2521 (2019)
19. Howard, A.G., et al.: MobileNets: efficient convolutional neural networks for mobile vision applications. arXiv preprint arXiv:1704.04861 (2017)
20. Hu, J., et al.: Boosting light-weight depth estimation via knowledge distillation. arXiv preprint arXiv:2105.06143 (2021)
21. Hu, M., Wang, S., Li, B., Ning, S., Fan, L., Gong, X.: PENet: towards precise and efficient image guided depth completion. arXiv preprint arXiv:2103.00783 (2021)
22. Huang, Z., Fan, J., Cheng, S., Yi, S., Wang, X., Li, H.: HMS-net: hierarchical multi-scale sparsity-invariant network for sparse depth completion. IEEE Trans. Image Process. **29**, 3429–3441 (2019)

23. Hwang, S., Lee, J., Kim, W.J., Woo, S., Lee, K., Lee, S.: LiDAR depth completion using color-embedded information via knowledge distillation. IEEE Trans. Intell. Transp. Syst. (2021)

24. Jaritz, M., De Charette, R., Wirbel, E., Perrotton, X., Nashashibi, F.: Sparse and dense data with CNNs: depth completion and semantic segmentation. In: 2018 International Conference on 3D Vision (3DV), pp. 52–60. IEEE (2018)

25. Jin, H., Soatto, S., Yezzi, A.J.: Multi-view stereo beyond lambert. In: 2003 Proceedings of the IEEE Computer Society Conference on Computer Vision and Pattern Recognition, vol. 1, p. I. IEEE (2003)

26. Kang, J., Gwak, J.: Ensemble learning of lightweight deep learning models using knowledge distillation for image classification. Mathematics 8(10), 1652 (2020)

27. Ku, J., Harakeh, A., Waslander, S.L.: In defense of classical image processing: Fast depth completion on the CPU. In: 2018 15th Conference on Computer and Robot Vision (CRV), pp. 16–22. IEEE (2018)

28. Lan, X., Zhu, X., Gong, S.: Knowledge distillation by on-the-fly native ensemble. arXiv preprint arXiv:1806.04606 (2018)

29. Li, A., Yuan, Z., Ling, Y., Chi, W., Zhang, C., et al.: A multi-scale guided cascade hourglass network for depth completion. In: Proceedings of the IEEE/CVF Winter Conference on Applications of Computer Vision, pp. 32–40 (2020)

30. Liu, T.Y., Agrawal, P., Chen, A., Hong, B.W., Wong, A.: Monitored distillation for positive congruent depth completion. arXiv preprint arXiv:2203.16034 (2022)

31. Liu, Y., Chen, K., Liu, C., Qin, Z., Luo, Z., Wang, J.: Structured knowledge distillation for semantic segmentation. In: Proceedings of the IEEE/CVF Conference on Computer Vision and Pattern Recognition, pp. 2604–2613 (2019)

32. Liu, Y., Shu, C., Wang, J., Shen, C.: Structured knowledge distillation for dense prediction. IEEE Trans. Pattern Anal. Mach. Intell. (2020)

33. Liu, Y., Sheng, L., Shao, J., Yan, J., Xiang, S., Pan, C.: Multi-label image classification via knowledge distillation from weakly-supervised detection. In: Proceedings of the 26th ACM International Conference on Multimedia, pp. 700–708 (2018)

34. Lopez-Rodriguez, A., Busam, B., Mikolajczyk, K.: Project to adapt: domain adaptation for depth completion from noisy and sparse sensor data. In: Proceedings of the Asian Conference on Computer Vision (2020)

35. Ma, F., Cavalheiro, G.V., Karaman, S.: Self-supervised sparse-to-dense: self-supervised depth completion from lidar and monocular camera. In: International Conference on Robotics and Automation (ICRA), pp. 3288–3295. IEEE (2019)

36. McCormac, J., Handa, A., Leutenegger, S., Davison, A.J.: SceneNet RGB-D: can 5m synthetic images beat generic ImageNet pre-training on indoor segmentation? In: Proceedings of the IEEE International Conference on Computer Vision, pp. 2678–2687 (2017)

37. Merrill, N., Geneva, P., Huang, G.: Robust monocular visual-inertial depth completion for embedded systems. In: International Conference on Robotics and Automation (ICRA). IEEE (2021)

38. Michieli, U., Zanuttigh, P.: Knowledge distillation for incremental learning in semantic segmentation. Comput. Vis. Image Underst. 205, 103167 (2021)

39. Park, J., Joo, K., Hu, Z., Liu, C.-K., So Kweon, I.: Non-local spatial propagation network for depth completion. In: Vedaldi, A., Bischof, H., Brox, T., Frahm, J.-M. (eds.) ECCV 2020. LNCS, vol. 12358, pp. 120–136. Springer, Cham (2020). https://doi.org/10.1007/978-3-030-58601-0_8

40. Park, S., Heo, Y.S.: Knowledge distillation for semantic segmentation using channel and spatial correlations and adaptive cross entropy. Sensors 20(16), 4616 (2020)

41. Pilzer, A., Lathuiliere, S., Sebe, N., Ricci, E.: Refine and distill: exploiting cycle-inconsistency and knowledge distillation for unsupervised monocular depth estimation. In: Proceedings of the IEEE/CVF Conference on Computer Vision and Pattern Recognition, pp. 9768–9777 (2019)

42. Qiu, J., et al.: DeepLiDAR: deep surface normal guided depth prediction for outdoor scene from sparse lidar data and single color image. In: Proceedings of the IEEE Conference on Computer Vision and Pattern Recognition, pp. 3313–3322 (2019)

43. Qu, C., Liu, W., Taylor, C.J.: Bayesian deep basis fitting for depth completion with uncertainty. arXiv preprint arXiv:2103.15254 (2021)

44. Qu, C., Nguyen, T., Taylor, C.: Depth completion via deep basis fitting. In: Proceedings of the IEEE/CVF Winter Conference on Applications of Computer Vision, pp. 71–80 (2020)

45. Romero, A., Ballas, N., Kahou, S.E., Chassang, A., Gatta, C., Bengio, Y.: FitNets: hints for thin deep nets. arXiv preprint arXiv:1412.6550 (2014)

46. Shivakumar, S.S., Nguyen, T., Miller, I.D., Chen, S.W., Kumar, V., Taylor, C.J.: DfuseNet: deep fusion of RGB and sparse depth information for image guided dense depth completion. In: 2019 IEEE Intelligent Transportation Systems Conference (ITSC), pp. 13–20. IEEE (2019)

47. Silberman, N., Hoiem, D., Kohli, P., Fergus, R.: Indoor segmentation and support inference from RGBD images. In: Fitzgibbon, A., Lazebnik, S., Perona, P., Sato, Y., Schmid, C. (eds.) ECCV 2012. LNCS, vol. 7576, pp. 746–760. Springer, Heidelberg (2012). https://doi.org/10.1007/978-3-642-33715-4_54

48. Traganitis, P.A., Giannakis, G.B.: Blind multi-class ensemble learning with dependent classifiers. In: 2018 26th European Signal Processing Conference (EUSIPCO), pp. 2025–2029. IEEE (2018)

49. Uhrig, J., Schneider, N., Schneider, L., Franke, U., Brox, T., Geiger, A.: Sparsity invariant CNNs. In: 2017 International Conference on 3D Vision (3DV), pp. 11–20. IEEE (2017)

50. Van Gansbeke, W., Neven, D., De Brabandere, B., Van Gool, L.: Sparse and noisy lidar completion with RGB guidance and uncertainty. In: 2019 16th International Conference on Machine Vision Applications (MVA), pp. 1–6. IEEE (2019)

51. Walawalkar, D., Shen, Z., Savvides, M.: Online ensemble model compression using knowledge distillation. In: Vedaldi, A., Bischof, H., Brox, T., Frahm, J.-M. (eds.) ECCV 2020. LNCS, vol. 12364, pp. 18–35. Springer, Cham (2020). https://doi.org/10.1007/978-3-030-58529-7_2

52. Wang, Y., Li, X., Shi, M., Xian, K., Cao, Z.: Knowledge distillation for fast and accurate monocular depth estimation on mobile devices. In: Proceedings of the IEEE/CVF Conference on Computer Vision and Pattern Recognition, pp. 2457–2465 (2021)

53. Wang, Z., Bovik, A.C., Sheikh, H.R., Simoncelli, E.P.: Image quality assessment: from error visibility to structural similarity. IEEE Trans. Image Process. 13(4), 600–612 (2004)

54. Wong, A., Cicek, S., Soatto, S.: Learning topology from synthetic data for unsupervised depth completion. IEEE Robot. Autom. Lett. 6(2), 1495–1502 (2021)

55. Wong, A., Fei, X., Hong, B.W., Soatto, S.: An adaptive framework for learning unsupervised depth completion. IEEE Robot. Autom. Lett. 6(2), 3120–3127 (2021)

56. Wong, A., Fei, X., Tsuei, S., Soatto, S.: Unsupervised depth completion from visual inertial odometry. IEEE Robot. Autom. Lett. 5, 1899–1906 (2020)

57. Wong, A., Soatto, S.: Bilateral cyclic constraint and adaptive regularization for unsupervised monocular depth prediction. In: Proceedings of the IEEE/CVF Conference on Computer Vision and Pattern Recognition, pp. 5644–5653 (2019)

58. Wong, A., Soatto, S.: Unsupervised depth completion with calibrated backprojection layers. In: Proceedings of the IEEE/CVF International Conference on Computer Vision, pp. 12747–12756 (2021)

59. Xiang, L., Ding, G., Han, J.: Learning from multiple experts: self-paced knowledge distillation for long-tailed classification. In: Vedaldi, A., Bischof, H., Brox, T., Frahm, J.-M. (eds.) ECCV 2020. LNCS, vol. 12350, pp. 247–263. Springer, Cham (2020). https://doi.org/10.1007/978-3-030-58558-7_15

60. Xu, Y., Zhu, X., Shi, J., Zhang, G., Bao, H., Li, H.: Depth completion from sparse LiDAR data with depth-normal constraints. In: Proceedings of the IEEE International Conference on Computer Vision, pp. 2811–2820 (2019)

61. Yan, S., et al.: Positive-congruent training: Towards regression-free model updates. In: Proceedings of the IEEE/CVF Conference on Computer Vision and Pattern Recognition, pp. 14299–14308 (2021)

62. Yang, Y., Wong, A., Soatto, S.: Dense depth posterior (DDP) from single image and sparse range. In: Proceedings of the IEEE/CVF Conference on Computer Vision and Pattern Recognition, pp. 3353–3362 (2019)

63. Zhang, Y., Funkhouser, T.: Deep depth completion of a single RGB-D image. In: Proceedings of the IEEE Conference on Computer Vision and Pattern Recognition, pp. 175–185 (2018)

Resolution-Free Point Cloud Sampling Network with Data Distillation

Tianxin Huang[1], Jiangning Zhang[1,2], Jun Chen[1], Yuang Liu[1], and Yong Liu[1,3(✉)]

[1] APRIL Lab, Zhejiang University, Hangzhou, China
yongliu@iipc.zju.edu.cn
[2] Tencent Youtu Laboratory, Shanghai, China
[3] Huzhou Institute of Zhejiang University, Huzhou, China

Abstract. Down-sampling algorithms are adopted to simplify the point clouds and save the computation cost on subsequent tasks. Existing learning-based sampling methods often need to train a big sampling network to support sampling under different resolutions, which must generate sampled points with the costly maximum resolution even if only low-resolution points need to be sampled. In this work, we propose a novel resolution-free point clouds sampling network to directly sample the original point cloud to different resolutions, which is conducted by optimizing non-learning-based initial sampled points to better positions. Besides, we introduce data distillation to assist the training process by considering the differences between task network outputs from original point clouds and sampled points. Experiments on point cloud reconstruction and recognition tasks demonstrate that our method can achieve SOTA performances with lower time and memory cost than existing learning-based sampling strategies. Codes are available at https://github.com/Tianxinhuang/PCDNet.

Keywords: 3D point clouds · Down sampling · Resolution-free

1 Introduction

With the rapid development of 3D tasks such as SLAM [3] and recognition [23,24,28], point cloud has attracted more and more attentions in computer vision and robots. However, large point clouds limit the efficiency of related algorithms and bring up higher device requirements. Sampling original point clouds to lower resolutions might be an alternative solution to reduce the computational cost on subsequent tasks. Existing works [13,14,18,22,24,33] use random sampling or Farthest Point Sampling (FPS) to down sample the point clouds. However, non-learning-based sampling strategies are lack of relevance to down-stream tasks, which blocks their further improvements on task-oriented performances.

In this condition, some researchers [8,16] propose learning-based sampling methods to improve the task-oriented performances through optimization. S-Net [8] generates initial sampled points directly by fully-connected networks and project them back

---

T. Huang and J. Zhang—Indicates equal contributions.

S. Avidan et al. (Eds.): ECCV 2022, LNCS 13662, pp. 54–70, 2022.
https://doi.org/10.1007/978-3-031-20086-1_4

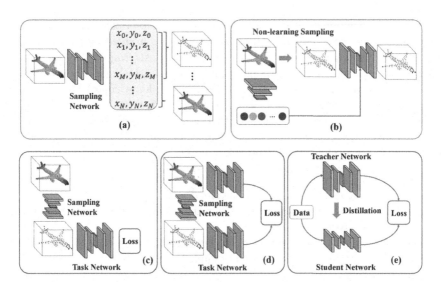

Fig. 1. (a) and (b) show differences between progressive implements of existing sampling networks and our resolution-free network, while (c), (d) and (e) show the architecture of former sampling networks, Ours and knowledge distillation. N and M denote the number of original and sampled points, respectively.

to their nearest neighbors in original point clouds. Sampled points of [8] has relatively weak relevance with the original points because the projection process from generated sampled points to original point clouds is independent from training, while SamNet [16] gets over this problem by designing a differentiable approximation for projection during training. To support different resolutions with a single network, [8, 16] propose progressive implements by generating candidate points with the same number of input point clouds and directly select sampled points from all candidates in order, as illustrated in Fig. 1-(a). Points of multiple sampling resolutions are fed into the task network together to provide constraints for different resolutions. The progress implement always needs to generate sampled points of maximum resolutions even if only low-resolution points are sampled, which introduces extra computational cost. Besides, both S-Net [8] and Sam-Net [16] only use pre-trained task networks to transfer gradients from task-oriented losses in a straightforward process as shown in Fig. 1-(c), which ignore learned distributions of the task network on original point clouds. In other words, they do not make use of the learned knowledge included in pre-trained networks.

In this work, we propose a simple but effective resolution-free Point Cloud sampling network with data Distillation (PCDNet). As presented in Fig. 1-(b), by driving existing initial sampled points from non-learning-based sampling strategies to better positions instead of generating points directly, PCDNet can get over the limitation of fully-connected networks and acquire sampled points of any resolution directly, which avoids the extra computational cost and improves sampling efficiency.

During the training process of PCDNet, we propose a dynamic resolution selection strategy to choose the optimized resolution in each iteration by considering the convergence on each sampling resolution. Resolutions whose task-oriented losses vary larger will acquire higher selection probabilities to help them converge steadily. Besides, we propose data distillation to assist the optimization by considering differences between task network outputs from original and sampled points, which actually takes advantage of the knowledge in pre-trained task networks as knowledge distillation methods [12,25]. As indicated in Fig. 1-(d) and (e), knowledge distillation constrains different networks based on same data, while data distillation constrains different data with same task networks. With the help of data distillation, our sampling network can converge to better results than straightforward training.

Our contributions can be summarized as follows:

- We propose a novel resolution-free point cloud sampling network to sample original point clouds to any resolution directly, where a dynamic resolution selection strategy is proposed to assist the optimization;
- We introduce data distillation by considering differences between the task network outputs from original point clouds and sampled points to supervise the training of sampling network;
- Experiments on reconstruction and recognition tasks demonstrate that PCDNet can outperform former point cloud sampling methods on task-oriented performances with lower time and memory cost than existing learning-based sampling networks.

2 Related Works

2.1 Point Cloud Sampling

Random sampling and farthest point sampling (FPS) [13,22,24,32] are two widely used point cloud sampling strategies. FPS keeps a sampled point set and cyclically adds the point farthest from the sampled set in the remained parts to the sampled set, while random sampling directly down-samples the points by random selection. Since the development of deep learning based methods on point clouds [17,20,26,28], some learning-based works [8,16] have also been released to enhance the performances of sampled points for specified tasks such as recognition [19,23,24,27,29] and reconstruction [1,9,31], which can greatly outperform non-learning sampling strategies. However, the learning-based works are still quite limited by the network designations based on fully-connected networks. Both of [8] and [16] require the progressive implement to get a single sampling network for all resolutions in one training process, it actually trains a big sampling network contains all possible resolutions, which always generates sampled points of maximum resolutions even if only low-resolution points are sampled and introduces extra computational cost.

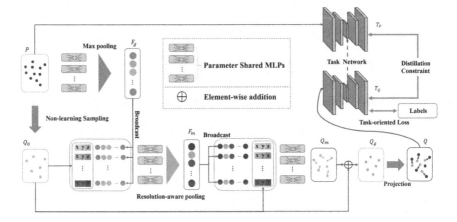

Fig. 2. The whole pipeline of PCDNet. Initial seeds Q_0 are sampled from input set P with a non-learning-based sampling strategy, which is farthest point sampling in this work. Global features F_g is extracted from P and merged with Q_0 to construct merged features F_m, which is further used to predict a displacement field Q_m including an offset for each point in Q_0 and drive them to better positions Q_g. Q_g is projected back to P to get final sampled points Q.

2.2 Knowledge Distillation

Knowledge Distillation includes a series of methods aiming to train a small student network with the help of a big teacher network. Hinton et al. [12] first propose the vanilla knowledge distillation by introducing extra constraints between the outputs of teacher network and student network, which acquires surprising performances on MNIST classification and Automatic Speech recognition. Later works [2,11,15,25,34] further take advantage of the relations between intermediate features to train deeper and thinner student networks. [5] propose an available distillation framework for object detection, which is a common regression problem. [6,10,21] propose data-free methods to reduce the reliance on original training data and improve distillation performances by introducing generated synthetic data. In this work, we propose data distillation to assist the point cloud sampling process based on knowledge distillation methods.

3 Methodology

3.1 Resolution-Free Sampling Network

Network Structure. The whole pipeline of our work is presented in Fig. 2. Input points are sampled with non-learning-based sampling strategies such as FPS [24] to produce initial sampled points, named seeds. Then we aggregate global features from the input points with a set of parameter-shared multilevel perceptions (MLPs) and pooling following [23]. The global features would contain information of original models, which would be concatenated with initial seeds and combined into merged features including information from both initial seeds and original models with MLPs and pooling. The initial seeds will be concatenated again with merged features and fed into MLPs to predict a displacement field including an offset for each initial seed. By moving initial seeds with predicted displacement field, we can acquire generated sampled points of any resolution easily. Finally, we follow [16] to project the generated sampled points back to original point clouds and get final sampled points.

Resolution-Aware Pooling. Specially, to design a network which can easily adapt to different sampling resolutions, we propose resolution-aware pooling to aggregate point features. Common pooling operations such as max pooling or average pooling are not sensitive to the point cloud resolution. In other words, point clouds with different resolutions may have same features when they have identical shapes, which is not distinguishable to sample multiple resolution point clouds. In this condition, we propose resolution-aware pooling to aggregate resolution-related features. Let N be the number of points in the original point cloud, M be current sampling resolution, F_i be i-th point feature need to be aggregated. The resolution-aware pooling is defined as

$$F_o = \frac{\sum_1^M F_i}{N},\tag{1}$$

where F_o is the aggregated feature. We can see that aggregated features will have relatively smaller values when the resolution is low, larger otherwise. The resolution information is then simply introduced to the network, which can improve its adaptability to different sampling resolutions.

3.2 Dynamic Resolution Selection Strategy

During the training process of PCDNet, a certain resolution is chosen in each iteration. To help resolution-free sampling network adapt to different sampling resolutions, we propose a dynamic resolution selection strategy to help decide the training resolution in each iteration. The algorithm is presented in Algorithm 1. In details, given the resolution updating interval n, we evaluate and record errors of the sampling network under different resolutions every $n/2$ iterations, while adjusting selection probabilities each n iterations according to the two recorded errors. Resolutions whose errors vary larger will get higher selection probabilities to help them converge steadily. With the Dynamic resolution selection strategy, PCDNet can get good and balanced convergence under multiple resolutions.

3.3 Data Distillation

Existing learning-based sampling networks feed the sampling results to pre-trained task networks and get optimized in a straightforward process. They do not make full use of the knowledge included in the pre-trained task networks. In this condition, as shown in Fig. 2, we introduce knowledge distillation constraints between task network outputs from original data and sampled results to "distillate" point clouds, which we named data distillation. Data distillation guides to simplify the data based on networks, while knowledge distillation teaches to simplify the network based on the data. In other words, data distillation helps keep task performances during data simplification.

For point cloud reconstruction, a commonly used task-oriented constraint Chamfer Distance(CD) [9] is adopted, which is defined as

$$\mathcal{L}_{CD}(S_1, S_2) = \frac{1}{2}(\frac{1}{|S_1|} \sum_{x \in S_1} \min_{y \in S_2} \|x - y\|_2 + \frac{1}{|S_2|} \sum_{x \in S_2} \min_{y \in S_1} \|x - y\|_2), \quad (2)$$

where S_1 and S_2 are two point sets. CD is actually the average distance from points in one set to their nearest neighbors in another set. Let P and Q be the original point clouds and sampled results, following [7], we can define the data distillation constraint for point cloud reconstruction as

$$\mathcal{L}_{DD}(P, Q, T_P, T_Q) = \begin{cases} \mathcal{L}_{CD}(P, T_Q), if \ \mathcal{L}_{CD}(P, T_Q) + m > \mathcal{L}_{CD}(P, T_P) \\ 0, \ otherwise, \end{cases} \quad (3)$$

where T_P and T_Q are reconstructed point clouds by task networks from P and Q, respectively. m is a margin to adjust the distillation degree. In details, the data distillation for reconstruction means to pay more attention to sampled results with relatively poor reconstruction performances against original point clouds. if m is bigger, more sampled results will be constrained. we set $m = 0.001$ in this work.

For point cloud classification, the task-oriented loss is cross-entropy defined as

$$\mathcal{L}_{CE}(z_S, q_S) = - \sum q_S \cdot log(softmax(z_S)), \quad (4)$$

where q_S and z_S are the label and predicted result of point cloud S, respectively. Let P and Q be the original point clouds and sampled point clouds, following [12], the data distillation constraint for classification can be defined as

$$\mathcal{L}_{DD}(T_P, T_Q) = - \sum softmax(\frac{T_P}{T}) log(softmax(\frac{T_Q}{T})), \quad (5)$$

where T_P, T_Q is the predicted outputs of target networks from original point clouds P and sampled results Q, respectively. The data distillation constraint for point cloud classification works by narrowing the distance between predicted distributions from point clouds before and after sampling. T is the temperature parameter to adjust the distribution of distillation constraint. we set $T = 1.0$ in this work.

Algorithm 1. Training with Dynamic resolution selection

Input: data X, the number of iterations $iter$,
Updating interval n, the number of resolutions m,
Initialize Error lists:
$errlist_1, errlist_2, \cdots, errlist_m = [\,], [\,], \cdots, [\,];$
Initialize Probabilities:
$prob_1, prob_2, \cdots, prob_m = \frac{1}{m}, \frac{1}{m}, \cdots, \frac{1}{m};$
for $i = 1$ **to** $iter$ **do**
    Train the sampling network with resolution selected according to $prob_1, \cdots, prob_m$;
    if i%($\frac{n}{2}$)==0 **then**
        for $j = 1$ **to** m **do**
            $errlist_j$.insert($\mathcal{L}_{task}(X_i)$)
        end for
    end if
    if i%($n + 1$)==0 **then**
        for $j = 1$ **to** m **do**
            error $nerr_j = \frac{max(errlist_j) - min(errlist_j)}{max(errlist_j)}$
        end for
        for $j = 1$ **to** m **do**
            $prob_j = \frac{\exp^{nerr_j}}{\sum_1^m \exp^{nerr_j}}$
            $errlist_j \rightarrow [\,]$
        end for
    end if
end for

3.4 Simplification and Projection

Simplification and Projection. In this work, we follow [16] to project generated sampled points to original point clouds. The projection constraint is defined as

$$\mathcal{L}_{proj} = t^2, \tag{6}$$

where t is a trainable parameter in the projection process. The simplification constraint [8,16] is used to encourage the sampled points to be near from the original point clouds. Distances from points sets S_1 to S_2 can be defined as

$$\mathcal{L}_a(X, Y) = \frac{1}{|X|} \sum_{x \in X} \min_{y \in Y} \|x - y\|_2^2, \tag{7}$$

$$\mathcal{L}_m(X, Y) = \max_{x \in X} \min_{y \in Y} \|x - y\|_2^2. \tag{8}$$

Let Q, P be the sampled points and original point clouds, respectively. The simplification constraint can be defined as

$$\mathcal{L}_{sim}(Q, P) = \mathcal{L}_a(Q, P) + \beta \mathcal{L}_m(Q, P) + (\gamma + \delta |Q| \mathcal{L}_a(P, Q)) \tag{9}$$

Here, we follow the same setting for β, γ and δ as [16].

Move Constraint. Our network acquires sampled points by driving initial seeds to new positions. The Move constraint can be presented as

$$\mathcal{L}_{mc} = \frac{1}{N} \sum \|Q_m\|_2, \tag{10}$$

where N and Q_m denote the sampling resolution and predicted displacement field as claimed in Sect. 3.1.

3.5 Loss Function

Given all just defined components, the final training loss can be defined as

$$\mathcal{L}_{final} = \mathcal{L}_{task} + \lambda_1 * \mathcal{L}_{DD} + \lambda_2 * \mathcal{L}_{sim} + \lambda_3 * \mathcal{L}_{proj} + \lambda_4 * \mathcal{L}_{mc}. \tag{11}$$

In this work, we set $\lambda_1 \sim \lambda_4$ as 0.5, 1.0, 10^{-5}, and 10^{-3}.

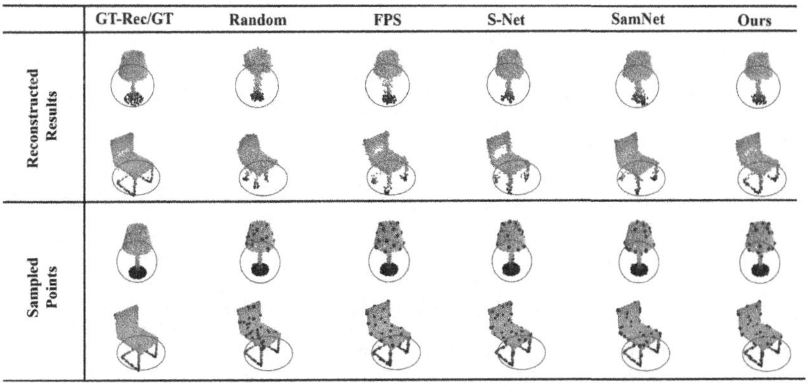

Fig. 3. Qualitative Comparisons between different sampling strategies under 32 sampled points. Sampled points are marked in blue. We can see that our method performs better on the circled thin and small regions by driving more sampled points to these areas. (Color figure online)

4 Experiments

4.1 Dataset and Implmentation Details

In this work, we evaluate the sampling performances based on point cloud reconstruction and recognition. Three datasets: ShapeNet [4], ModelNet10 (MN10) and Model-Net40 (MN40) [30] are adopted for the training and evaluation processes. ShapeNet contains 12288 models in the train split and 2874 models in the test split from 16 categories following [31]. MN10 and MN40 are subsets of ModelNet, which contain 10 categories and 40 categories of CAD models, respectively. All point clouds are composed of 2048 uniformly sampled points from mesh models.

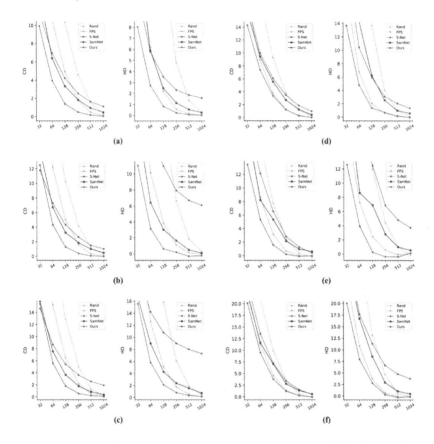

Fig. 4. Comparisons between sampling strategies. (a), (b) and (c) denote results on ShapeNet, MN10 and MN40 based on AE [1], while (d), (e) and (f) are results on ShapeNet, MN10 and MN40 based on FoldingNet [31]. All metrics are multiplied with 10^3.

For point clouds reconstruction, two commonly used baseline models AE [1] and FoldingNet [31] are introduced as task networks. Task networks and sampling networks are both trained on the train split of ShapeNet. As for point cloud recognition, we train and evaluate the network performances on MN10 and MN40 [30] based on the task network PointNet [23] following [8,16]. To make a fair comparison, S-Net [8] and SamNet [16] are trained with progressive implements [8] to train a model for all resolutions.

4.2   Experiments on Reconstruction Baselines

In this section, we evaluate the sampling performances on commonly-used reconstruction networks AE [1] and FoldingNet [31] pre-trained on train split of ShapeNet, while measuring reconstruction errors on the test split of ShapeNet, MN10 and MN40. The quantitative results are presented in Fig. 4. We evaluate sampling performances by increments of reconstruction errors compared to original point clouds, while the reconstruction errors are measured with Chamfer Distance (CD) [9] and Hausdorff Distance (HD) defined as

$$HD(S_1, S_2) = \frac{1}{2}(\underset{x\in S_1}{max}\ \underset{y\in S_2}{min}\ \|x - y\|_2 + \underset{x\in S_2}{max}\ \underset{y\in S_1}{min}\ \|x - y\|_2), \qquad (12)$$

where S_1 and S_2 are two point clouds to be compared. CD and HD focus on the average and worst performances, respectively. We can see that our method can achieve lower reconstruction errors than existing sampling strategies on most adopted networks and datasets under different resolutions, which confirms that it is quite effective. To intuitively compare the performances of different sampling strategies, we also present a qualitative comparison in Fig. 3. Reconstruction results from original point clouds and sampled points are presented in top 2 lines, while original point clouds and sampled results are presented in 2 lines below. Sampled points are marked in blue. We can see that existing methods pay little attention to some thin and small structures in original models as circled in Fig. 3, while our method can drive more sampled points to the error-prone regions and improve reconstruction performances.

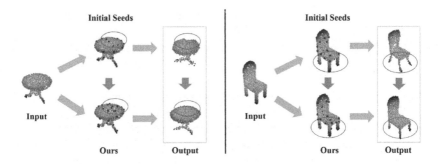

Fig. 5. Visualization of the way PCDNet works. Initial seeds from non-learning-based sampling strategies and final sampled points from our PCDNet are marked in blue. We feed them to a same AE [1] to observe their reconstructed outputs. (Color figure online)

4.3   Experiments on Recognition Baselines

For point clouds recognition, we train the learning-based sampling algorithms on MN10 and MN40 based on PointNet [23] following [8, 16]. The performances under different sampling resolutions are compared in Fig. 6. We can see that our method can achieve higher classification accuracy than other sampling algorithms on both MN10 and MN40. An interesting condition is that our method can even exceed the classification accuracy of original point clouds on MN40, while all learning-based sampling networks get higher accuracy than original point clouds on MN10 under the resolution of 512 points. It reveals the superiority of differentiable sampling networks. Sampling can be regarded as a filtering process to remove noises from original points clouds. There is an trade-off between the sampling resolution and noises. Sampled points are less affected by noises under a lower resolution, while the structural features are also limited by less points. As the resolution increases, impacts from original noises and structural features contained in sampled points are both increased.

In this condition, sampled points under a certain resolution may overstep original point clouds on specific task network with an end-to-end optimization. Higher resolution will instead reduce the performances, as shown in Fig. 6-(a). Note that our method in Fig. 6-(b) has 86.32% accuracy at 512 points and 86.28% accuracy at 1024 points, which is also consistent with our analysis.

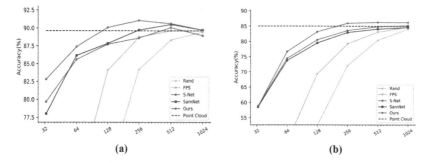

Fig. 6. Comparisons on recognition. (a) and (b) denote results on MN10 and MN40, respectively.

4.4   How Does PCDNet Work?

PCDNet actually works by driving original sampled points to more appropriate positions. We visualize the points before and after the movements to see how PCDNet works. The results are presented in Fig. 5. We can see that initial seeds from FPS may create defective regions as the circled areas. PCDNet can learn to drive more sampled points to the failed areas, which can introduce more structural details from these areas.

4.5   Analysis of the Data Distillation

To observe behaviors of data distillation, we present its improvements on reconstruction and recognition tasks under different resolutions. The results are presented in Fig. 7. We can see that the data distillation brings more improvements on low resolutions. The reason is that the data distillation is based on differences between task performances of sampled points and original point clouds. It can provide stronger supervision when performances of sampled points are quite different with original point clouds.

4.6   Sensitivity to the Non-learning Sampling

In this work, we use FPS to generate initial sampled points. To explore the sensitivity of our method to the initial non-learning sampling strategy, we conduct a group of comparisons on AE [1] between our methods based on a few commonly-used sampling strategies including random sampling, FPS, Voxel sampling, and Sphere filtering. The

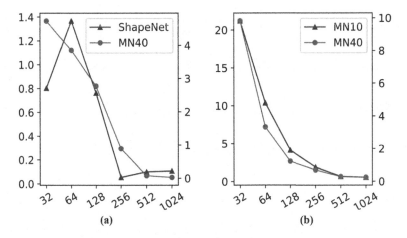

Fig. 7. Improvements from data distillation, i.e. the 0.0 denotes results of PCDNet trained without data distillation. (a) and (b) are measured on reconstruction and recognition tasks, respectively. left and right vertical axises denote metrics measured on datasets marked in blue and red. (Color figure online)

Table 1. Efficiency comparison evaluated on a Nvidia 2080ti GPU with a 2.9Ghz i5-9400 CPU.

Methods	S-Net	SamNet	Ours
Time (ms)	9	17	**7**
Memory (MB)	842	1156	**797**
Parameter (M)	1.77	1.77	**0.28**

results of original Random sampling, FPS and SamNet [16] are also introduced for comparisons. The results are presented in Fig. 8.

We can see that the performances of out methods based on FPS, Voxel sampling, and Sphere filtering are quite close, which confirms that our framework is robust when the initial sampled points have relatively uniform spatial distribution. The performances based on random sampling has relatively obvious decline compared to other strategies due to its randomness. Intuitively speaking, the randomly sampled results may be quite non-uniform to cover the whole shapes, which makes it hard to drive them to well-performed positions. However, our method based on random sampling still has slightly better performances on MN40 than SamNet, while our methods based on FPS and Random sampling both achieve much better performances than the original FPS and Random sampling methods without learning. It confirms that our framework indeed works to improve the performances beyond adopted non-learning sampling strategies.

4.7 Comparisons of Sampling Efficiency

In this section, we compare the inference time and memory cost between different learning-based sampling strategies on AE [1]. The inference time and memory cost

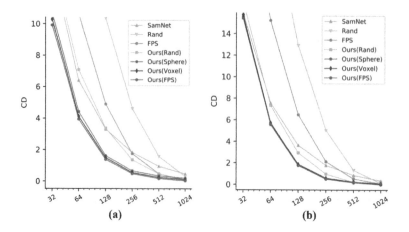

Fig. 8. Comparisons between initial sampling strategies. (a) and (b) denote reconstruction errors measured on ShapeNet and MN40. Ours (Rand), Ours (Sphere), Ours (Voxel) and Ours (FPS) denote our methods based on random sampling, Sphere filtering, Voxel sampling and FPS.

Table 2. Ablation study for components. All metrics are average values under different resolutions, which are multiplied with 10^3.

Base	Reso	dist	dyna	move	CD	HD	CD*
✓					3.70	3.31	12.45
✓	✓				2.99	2.50	10.74
✓	✓	✓			2.89	2.12	10.36
✓	✓	✓	✓		2.74	2.01	10.05
✓	✓	✓	✓	✓	**2.67**	**1.97**	**9.91**

are measured by the average time and memory cost under different resolutions between 32–1024. The results are presented in Table 1. We can see that our method has lower time cost, less memory cost and smaller parameter than existing learning-based sampling strategies S-Net [8] and SamNet [16].

4.8   Ablation Study

Influence of Components in PCDNet. To clarify the influence of each component in PCDNet, we conduct ablation experiments in this section. Dyna, Reso, Move and Dist are Dynamic resolution selection, Resolution-aware pooling, Move constraint and Data distillation, respectively. Base denotes the sampling network without Resolution-aware pooling, which is trained with task-oriented loss, simplification constraint and projection operation following [16]. CD* denotes CD metric measured under 32 sampled points, while CD and HD are average metrics under different resolutions. We can see each module makes sense. Removing any module will reduce the performances (Table 2).

Influence of Resolution Updating Interval. The number of dynamic resolution updating interval n mentioned in Sect. 3.2 has influence on the final performance. In this section, we conduct a series of experiments to observe the influences of different resolution updating intervals as presented in Fig. 9. We can see that too small or big intervals both increases the errors. A smaller interval will lead the network to change resolutions frequently, which may introduce more randomness. Though a big interval can reduce the randomness when evaluating the training errors, the selection frequency may be not high enough to train all resolutions well.

Influence of Distillation Hyper-parameters. Data distillation is an interesting component proposed to improve the network performances by introducing extra supervision from original network outputs. Hyper-parameters such as m for reconstruction networks and T for recognition networks defined in Sect. 3.3 are used to adjust the influence of original outputs. To figure out the influences of these hyper-parameters, we present the ablation experiments performances in Fig. 10. we can see that too big or small distillation parameters also both have negative influences on the performances. It may come from the trade-off from pre-trained task networks. Smaller T, e.g., will increase the impacts of both existing knowledge and mis-classified noises for recognition networks.

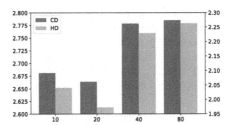

Fig. 9. Ablation study for the resolution updating interval. left and right vertical axises denote CD and HD multiplied by 10^3.

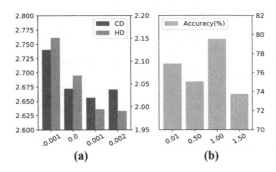

Fig. 10. Ablation study for the distillation hyper-parameters. (a) and (b) denote results measured on reconstruction and recognition tasks, respectively. left and right vertical axises in (a) measure CD and HD multiplied by 10^3.

5   Conclusion

In this work, we propose a new resolution-free point cloud sampling network to deal with different resolutions with a same architecture. By driving initial seeds sampled with non-learning-based sampling strategies such as FPS, we can directly sample original point clouds to any resolution by adjusting the resolution of initial seeds. Besides, we introduce data distillation to assist the optimization by considering differences between task network outputs from sampled points and original point clouds based on knowledge distillation constraints. Experiments on reconstruction and recognition demonstrate that our method achieves better task-oriented performances with lower time and memory cost than existing learning-based sampling networks.

Acknowledgement. We thank all authors, reviewers and the chair for the excellent contributions. This work is supported by the National Science Foundation 62088101.

References

1. Achlioptas, P., Diamanti, O., Mitliagkas, I., Guibas, L.: Learning representations and generative models for 3D point clouds. In: International Conference on Machine Learning, pp. 40–49. PMLR (2018)
2. Ahn, S., Hu, S.X., Damianou, A., Lawrence, N.D., Dai, Z.: Variational information distillation for knowledge transfer. In: Proceedings of the IEEE/CVF Conference on Computer Vision and Pattern Recognition, pp. 9163–9171 (2019)
3. Cadena, C., et al.: Past, present, and future of simultaneous localization and mapping: toward the robust-perception age. IEEE Trans. Rob. **32**(6), 1309–1332 (2016)
4. Chang, A.X., et al.: ShapeNet: an information-rich 3D model repository. arXiv preprint arXiv:1512.03012 (2015)
5. Chen, G., Choi, W., Yu, X., Han, T., Chandraker, M.: Learning efficient object detection models with knowledge distillation. In: Advances in Neural Information Processing Systems, vol. 30 (2017)
6. Chen, H., et al.: Data-free learning of student networks. In: Proceedings of the IEEE/CVF International Conference on Computer Vision, pp. 3514–3522 (2019)
7. Chen, L.C., Papandreou, G., Kokkinos, I., Murphy, K., Yuille, A.L.: DeepLab: semantic image segmentation with deep convolutional nets, Atrous convolution, and fully connected CRFs. IEEE Trans. Pattern Anal. Mach. Intell. **40**(4), 834–848 (2017)
8. Dovrat, O., Lang, I., Avidan, S.: Learning to sample. In: Proceedings of the IEEE/CVF Conference on Computer Vision and Pattern Recognition, pp. 2760–2769 (2019)
9. Fan, H., Su, H., Guibas, L.J.: A point set generation network for 3D object reconstruction from a single image. In: Proceedings of the IEEE Conference on Computer Vision and Pattern Recognition, pp. 605–613 (2017)
10. Fang, G., Song, J., Shen, C., Wang, X., Chen, D., Song, M.: Data-free adversarial distillation. arXiv preprint arXiv:1912.11006 (2019)
11. Heo, B., Lee, M., Yun, S., Choi, J.Y.: Knowledge transfer via distillation of activation boundaries formed by hidden neurons. In: Proceedings of the AAAI Conference on Artificial Intelligence, vol. 33, pp. 3779–3787 (2019)
12. Hinton, G., Vinyals, O., Dean, J.: Distilling the knowledge in a neural network. arXiv preprint arXiv:1503.02531 (2015)

13. Hu, Q., et al.: RandLA-Net: efficient semantic segmentation of large-scale point clouds. In: Proceedings of the IEEE/CVF Conference on Computer Vision and Pattern Recognition, pp. 11108–11117 (2020)

14. Huang, T., et al.: RFNet: recurrent forward network for dense point cloud completion. In: Proceedings of the IEEE/CVF International Conference on Computer Vision, pp. 12508–12517 (2021)

15. Huang, Z., Wang, N.: Like what you like: knowledge distill via neuron selectivity transfer. arXiv preprint arXiv:1707.01219 (2017)

16. Lang, I., Manor, A., Avidan, S.: SampleNet: differentiable point cloud sampling. In: Proceedings of the IEEE/CVF Conference on Computer Vision and Pattern Recognition, pp. 7578–7588 (2020)

17. Li, J., Chen, B.M., Lee, G.H.: SO-Net: self-organizing network for point cloud analysis. In: Proceedings of the IEEE Conference on Computer Vision and Pattern Recognition, pp. 9397–9406 (2018)

18. Li, R., Li, X., Fu, C.W., Cohen-Or, D., Heng, P.A.: PU-GAN: a point cloud upsampling adversarial network. In: Proceedings of the IEEE International Conference on Computer Vision, pp. 7203–7212 (2019)

19. Li, Y., Bu, R., Sun, M., Wu, W., Di, X., Chen, B.: PointCNN: convolution on x-transformed points. Adv. Neural. Inf. Process. Syst. **31**, 820–830 (2018)

20. Liu, Y., Fan, B., Xiang, S., Pan, C.: Relation-shape convolutional neural network for point cloud analysis. In: Proceedings of the IEEE/CVF Conference on Computer Vision and Pattern Recognition, pp. 8895–8904 (2019)

21. Lopes, R.G., Fenu, S., Starner, T.: Data-free knowledge distillation for deep neural networks. arXiv preprint arXiv:1710.07535 (2017)

22. Qi, C.R., Litany, O., He, K., Guibas, L.J.: Deep hough voting for 3D object detection in point clouds. In: Proceedings of the IEEE/CVF International Conference on Computer Vision, pp. 9277–9286 (2019)

23. Qi, C.R., Su, H., Mo, K., Guibas, L.J.: PointNet: deep learning on point sets for 3D classification and segmentation. In: Proceedings of the IEEE Conference on Computer Vision and Pattern Recognition, pp. 652–660 (2017)

24. Qi, C.R., Yi, L., Su, H., Guibas, L.J.: PointNet++: deep hierarchical feature learning on point sets in a metric space. In: Advances in Neural Information Processing Systems, pp. 5099–5108 (2017)

25. Romero, A., Ballas, N., Kahou, S.E., Chassang, A., Gatta, C., Bengio, Y.: FitNets: hints for thin deep nets. arXiv preprint arXiv:1412.6550 (2014)

26. Su, H., et al.: SPLATNet: sparse lattice networks for point cloud processing. In: Proceedings of the IEEE Conference on Computer Vision and Pattern Recognition, pp. 2530–2539 (2018)

27. Thomas, H., Qi, C.R., Deschaud, J.E., Marcotegui, B., Goulette, F., Guibas, L.J.: KPConv: flexible and deformable convolution for point clouds. In: Proceedings of the IEEE/CVF International Conference on Computer Vision, pp. 6411–6420 (2019)

28. Wang, Y., Sun, Y., Liu, Z., Sarma, S.E., Bronstein, M.M., Solomon, J.M.: Dynamic graph CNN for learning on point clouds. ACM Trans. Graph. (TOG) **38**(5), 1–12 (2019)

29. Wu, W., Qi, Z., Fuxin, L.: PointConv: deep convolutional networks on 3D point clouds. In: Proceedings of the IEEE/CVF Conference on Computer Vision and Pattern Recognition, pp. 9621–9630 (2019)

30. Wu, Z., et al.: 3D ShapeNets: a deep representation for volumetric shapes. In: Proceedings of the IEEE Conference on Computer Vision and Pattern Recognition, pp. 1912–1920 (2015)

31. Yang, Y., Feng, C., Shen, Y., Tian, D.: FoldingNet: point cloud auto-encoder via deep grid deformation. In: Proceedings of the IEEE Conference on Computer Vision and Pattern Recognition, pp. 206–215 (2018)

32. Yin, K., Chen, Z., Huang, H., Cohen-Or, D., Zhang, H.: LOGAN: unpaired shape transform in latent overcomplete space. ACM Trans. Graph. (TOG) **38**(6), 1–13 (2019)
33. Yu, L., Li, X., Fu, C.W., Cohen-Or, D., Heng, P.A.: PU-Net: point cloud upsampling network. In: Proceedings of the IEEE Conference on Computer Vision and Pattern Recognition, pp. 2790–2799 (2018)
34. Zagoruyko, S., Komodakis, N.: Paying more attention to attention: improving the performance of convolutional neural networks via attention transfer. arXiv preprint arXiv:1612.03928 (2016)

Organic Priors in Non-rigid Structure from Motion

Suryansh Kumar[1](✉) and Luc Van Gool[1,2]

[1] ETH Zürich Switzerland, Zurich, Switzerland
{sukumar,vangool}@vision.ee.ethz.ch
[2] KU Leuven Belgium, Leuven, Belgium

Abstract. This paper advocates the use of organic priors in classical non-rigid structure from motion (NRSfM). By organic priors, we mean invaluable intermediate prior information intrinsic to the NRSfM matrix factorization theory. It is shown that such priors reside in the factorized matrices, and quite surprisingly, existing methods generally disregard them. The paper's main contribution is to put forward a simple, methodical, and practical method that can effectively exploit such organic priors to solve NRSfM. The proposed method does not make assumptions other than the popular one on the low-rank shape and offers a reliable solution to NRSfM under orthographic projection. Our work reveals that the accessibility of organic priors is independent of the camera motion and shape deformation type. Besides that, the paper provides insights into the NRSfM factorization—both in terms of shape and motion—and is the first approach to show the benefit of single rotation averaging for NRSfM. Furthermore, we outline how to effectively recover motion and non-rigid 3D shape using the proposed organic prior based approach and demonstrate results that outperform prior-free NRSfM performance by a significant margin. Finally, we present the benefits of our method via extensive experiments and evaluations on several benchmark datasets.

Keywords: Organic priors · Non-rigid structure from motion · Rank minimization · Rotation averaging · Matrix factorization

1 Introduction

Non-rigid structure from motion (NRSfM) factorization is a classical problem in geometric computer vision [9,27]. The problem's primary objective is to recover 3D shape of a deforming object from a given set of image key-points tracked across multiple images. As a result, it is sometimes referred as solving an inverse graphics problem [46]. An effective solution to NRSfM is of significant importance to many computer vision and geometry processing applications [10,39].

It is now widely accepted that the NRSfM problem is challenging to work out if the shape deforms arbitrarily across images, as it becomes equivalent to

---

Supplementary Information The online version contains supplementary material available at https://doi.org/10.1007/978-3-031-20086-1_5.

S. Avidan et al. (Eds.): ECCV 2022, LNCS 13662, pp. 71–88, 2022.
https://doi.org/10.1007/978-3-031-20086-1_5

a non-rigid shape recovery problem using a single image at a time, which is ill-posed. Accordingly, several assumptions and priors are often used to make the problem solvable and computationally tractable. For instance, the deforming shape spans a low-rank space [13], smooth temporal shape deformation [1,6], shape or trajectory lies in the union of linear subspace [26,29–31,35,54] and the local surface deformation is rigid or near rigid [14,37,45,48]. Other favored prior assumptions include smooth camera motion [28,43], a piece-wise planar deformation model [14,32–34], a Gaussian shape prior distribution [51], the availability of a 3D shape template [46], and shapes across frames must align [36]. Despite that, NRSfM remains a challenging and active research problem.

Meanwhile, there exist several popular methods to solve NRSfM [3,9,13,36, 51]. Here, we will concern ourselves with the theory of matrix factorization for NRSfM elaborated in 1999–2000 by Bregler *et al.* [9][1]. It is a simple yet an effective approach to solve NRSfM. In the context of matrix factorization, one of the commonly used prior assumptions is that the non-rigid shape spans a low-rank space *i.e.*, the shape at each instance can be represented as a linear combination of a small set of basis shapes [9]. This paper adheres to such an assumption and shows that other important prior information resides within the *intermediate* factorized matrices —termed as organic priors. Surprisingly, most existing methods, if not all, ignore them. We used the word «organic» because they come naturally by properly conceiving the algebraic and geometric construction of NRSfM factorization [9,13,49]. Furthermore, this paper contends that the use of external priors and assumptions not only restricts the practical use of NRSfM methods, but also constrains the understanding and broader use of the well-known theory [13]. Yet, unlike [13], we advocate the use of organic priors, which is predicated on the proposition put forward by Kumar [28]. In this paper, we will show how to procure organic priors and exploit them effectively.

One of the critical innovations in NRSfM factorization that disputed the use of extraneous priors was introduced in [12,13]. The algorithm proposed in that paper does not use any prior other than the low-rank shape assumption. Nevertheless, despite its theoretical elegance and challenging argument, it fails to perform well on benchmark datasets [3,15,25,50]. Recently, Kumar [28] highlighted the possible reasons and exploited its missing pieces to gain performance. It was shown that a better rotation and shape could be estimated using the prior-free method's theory [12,13]. Still, [28] based his work on a smooth camera motion assumption that requires a brute force, heuristic search in the rotation space. In contrast, this paper puts forward a systematic method for NRSfM factorization that encourages the use of organic priors extracted from the factorized matrices. Experiments on synthetic and real benchmarks show that our approach consistently provides excellent 3D reconstruction results. This indicates the strength of matrix factorization theory for NRSfM. In summary, our contributions are

- A methodical approach for solving NRSfM that provides outstanding results using simple matrix factorization idea under the low-rank shape assumption.

---

[1] See, however, *C. Tomasi and T. Kanade*, **pp. 137–154**, IJCV (1992) for the original matrix factorization theory for shape and motion estimation, although devoted to the rigid SfM problem [49].

- An approach that endorses the use of organic priors rather than extraneous priors or assumptions. Our method introduce single rotation averaging to estimate better rotation while being free from smooth camera motion heuristics.
- A different setup for low-rank shape optimization is proposed. We present a blend of partial sum minimization of singular values theory and weighted nuclear norm optimization for shape recovery. We observed that the proposed optimization better exploits the organic shape priors and yields shape reconstructions superior to other popular NRSfM factorization methods [13, 24, 28].

Further, we proffer the benefits of L_1 single rotation averaging for NRSfM factorization, which is excellent at providing robust rotation solutions. Although most of NRSfM factorization focuses on sparse key-point sets, our method is equally effective for dense feature points and compares favorably with well crafted state-of-the-art dense NRSfM methods such as [15, 26, 29].

2 Overview and Key Strategy

General Definition and Classical Setup. In NRSfM, a measurement matrix $\mathbf{W} \in \mathbb{R}^{2F \times P}$ is defined as a matrix containing the image coordinates ($\mathbf{w}_{f,p} \in \mathbb{R}^{2 \times 1}$) of P feature points tracked across F image frames. $\mathbf{W}$ is generally mean-centered and given as an input to the factorization method [9]. Under an orthographic camera model assumption, the NRSfM factorization theory proposes to decompose the $\mathbf{W}$ into a product of a rotation matrix $\mathbf{R} \in \mathbb{R}^{2F \times 3F}$ and a non-rigid shape matrix $\mathbf{X} \in \mathbb{R}^{3F \times P}$ such that $\mathbf{W} \approx \mathbf{RX}$.

A practical method for NRSfM factorization was initially proposed by Bregler *et al.* [9]. Using the linear model proposition, a non-rigid shape $\mathbf{X}_i \in \mathbb{R}^{3 \times P}$ for i^{th} frame was represented as a linear combination of K basis shapes $\mathbf{B}_k \in \mathbb{R}^{3 \times P}$ *i.e.*, $\mathbf{X}_i = \sum_{k=1}^{K} c_{ik} \mathbf{B}_k$, where c_{ik} denotes the shape coefficients. Using such a shape representation, the $\mathbf{W}$ matrix is decomposed as follows:

$$\mathbf{W} = \begin{bmatrix} \mathbf{w}_{11} \dots \mathbf{w}_{1P} \\ \dots \\ \mathbf{w}_{F1} \dots \mathbf{w}_{FP} \end{bmatrix} = \begin{bmatrix} \mathbf{R}_1 \mathbf{X}_1 \\ .. \\ \mathbf{R}_F \mathbf{X}_F \end{bmatrix} = \begin{bmatrix} c_{11}\mathbf{R}_1 \dots c_{1\,K}\mathbf{R}_1 \\ \dots \\ c_{F1}\mathbf{R}_F \dots c_{FK}\mathbf{R}_F \end{bmatrix} \begin{bmatrix} \mathbf{B}_1 \\ .. \\ \mathbf{B}_K \end{bmatrix} \quad (1)$$

$$\Rightarrow \mathbf{W} = \mathbf{R}(\mathbf{C} \otimes \mathbf{I}_3)\mathbf{B} = \mathbf{MB}$$

where, $\mathbf{R}_i \in \mathbb{R}^{2 \times 3}$ denotes the ith frame rotation matrix, and $\otimes$ the Kronecker product. $\mathbf{M} \in \mathbb{R}^{2F \times 3K}$, $\mathbf{B} \in \mathbb{R}^{3K \times P}$ and $\mathbf{I}_3$ is the 3×3 identity matrix. It is easy to infer from the above construction that $\texttt{rank}(\mathbf{W}) \leq 3K$.

Since there is no general way to solve for $\mathbf{R}, \mathbf{C}$, and $\mathbf{B}$ directly, rank $3K$ factorization of $\mathbf{W}$ via its Singular Value Decomposition (svd) gives a natural way to solve the problem under the orthonormality constraint of the rotation space [3,9,13]. As it is well-known that factorization of $\mathbf{W}$ via svd is not unique [9,49], there must exist a corrective matrix $\mathbf{G} \in \mathbb{R}^{3K \times 3K}$ such that $\mathbf{W} = (\mathbf{MG})(\mathbf{G}^{-1}\hat{\mathbf{B}}) = \mathbf{MB}$. And therefore, once the svd of $\mathbf{W}$ is computed, a general rule of thumb in NRSfM factorization is to first solve for the $\mathbf{G}$ matrix, followed by the estimation of $\mathbf{R}$ and $\mathbf{X}$, respectively [3,13].

(a) **Background on Corrective and Rotation Matrix Estimation.** To solve for $\mathbf{G}$, orthonormality constraints are enforced [2,9]. Few works proposed in the past solve for the full $\mathbf{G} \in \mathbb{R}^{3K \times 3K}$ matrix (*i.e.*, for all its matrix entries) to estimate the rotation matrix [2,8,52,53]. In contrast, Dai *et al.* [13] argued that rather than solving for the full $\mathbf{G}$, simply solve for $\mathbf{G}^1 \in \mathbb{R}^{3K \times 3}$ (first 3 columns or first corrective triplet) leveraging Akhter *et al.* 's [2] theory. Yet, there exist K such triplets (see Fig. 1). Even if we don't deviate from [2] theory, the question that still remains with the use of [13] rotation estimation theory is: *Q1. Do we utilize all possible rotations that can be recovered from [13] rotation estimation theory?* The answer is no, as recently argued by Kumar [28]. He proposed to inspect all K column triplets in the corrective matrix ($\mathbf{G}$), and recover K possible rotation solutions $\mathbf{R}^k \in \mathbb{R}^{2F \times 3}$, where $k \in \{1, 2, \ldots, K\}$. He then selected the one $\mathbf{R}^k$ that provides a smooth camera motion trajectory. Yet, this solution is heuristic in nature and requires a qualitative inspection of all the K rotations. The point to note is that, similar to Dai *et al.* [13], Kumar's [28] solution at the end does not fully utilize all the K rotation priors and eventually ends up aborting the rest of the near smooth or non-smooth $(K-1)$ solutions. We call those $(K-1)$ rotation solutions «`organic priors in the rotation space`». Our proposed method utilizes all those organic rotation priors to estimate a better and more informed rotation matrix.

(b) **Background on the Shape Matrix Estimation.** After solving for the rotation, the goal is to estimate the shape with the rank K constraint. Generally, an initial solution to the shape can be estimated in a closed form using $\mathbf{X}_{init} = \mathbf{pinv}(\mathbf{R})\mathbf{W}^2$. Yet, this may produce a planar solution as outlined in [52]. In spite of that, $\mathbf{X}_{init}$ provides useful information about the true shape and can be used as a shape variable ($\mathbf{X}$) initialization in the following rank-optimization problem:

$$\underset{\mathbf{X}^\sharp}{\text{minimize}} \frac{1}{2} \sum_{i=1}^{F} \sum_{j=1}^{P} \| \mathbf{w}_{ij} - \mathbf{R}_i \mathbf{x}_{ij} \|^2, \text{ s.t. } \text{rank}(\mathbf{X}^\sharp) \leq K \tag{2}$$

where, $\mathbf{x}_{ij}$ denote the 3D point j in the ith view, and $\mathbf{w}_{ij}$ is its corresponding projection. $\mathbf{X}^\sharp \in \mathbb{R}^{F \times 3P}$ is the reshape of the shape matrix ($\mathbf{X}$) for K shape basis constraint [4,13].

There exist several approaches to solve the Eq. (2) optimization [4,13,20,42]. Among them, relaxed rank-minimization via appropriate matrix-norm minimization is widely used to recover a low-rank shape matrix providing favorable accuracy and robust results [13,15,24,28,52]. In this paper, we exploit the singular values of the $\mathbf{X}_{init}$, which we call «`organic priors in the shape space`» to recover better solution than the recent state-of-the-art [24,41]. Although Kumar [28] work is the first to propose and utilize such priors for better shape reconstructions, in this paper we show that we can do better[3]. This brings us to the next question:

---

[2] `pinv()` symbolizes Moore-Penrose inverse of a matrix, also known as pseudoinverse.
[3] Familiarity with [13,28] gives a good insight on our paper's novelty.

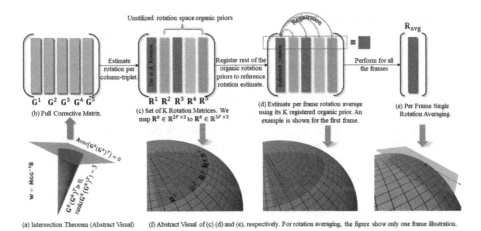

(a) Intersection Theorem (Abstract Visual)   (f) Abstract Visual of (c) (d) and (e), respectively. For rotation averaging, the figure show only one frame illustration.

Fig. 1. A visual illustration of our rotation estimation approach for $K = 5$. (a)–(b) Use the [13] intersection theorem to recover all $\mathbf{G}^k$s'. (b)–(c) Recover $\mathbf{R}^k \in \mathbb{R}^{2F \times 3}$ corresponding to each column triplet. (c) Map per frame 2×3 rotation to $SO(3)$ via a cross product, taking care of the determinant sign. (d) Register $(K - 1)$ rotation to the reference rotation (e) Perform per frame single rotation averaging to recover $\mathbf{R}_{\text{avg}}$.

Q2. Can we make better use of the organic shape prior to solve for the shape matrix? We will show that we can. When solving the relaxed rank minimization optimization problem of the shape matrix [13], it is not beneficial to equally penalize all the singular values of the shape matrix. Hence, for effective shape recovery, one can use the $\mathbf{X}_{init}$ singular values prior to regularize the shape matrix rank-optimization [28]. In particular, perform a weighted nuclear norm (WNN) minimization of the shape matrix, and assign the weights to the shape variable that is inversely proportional to the $\mathbf{X}_{init}$ singular values magnitude [28]. In this paper, we go a step further. We propose to preserve the first component of the shape during its WNN minimization, *i.e.*, to not penalize the first singular value shape prior from $\mathbf{X}_{init}$. We empirically observed that the first singular value of $\mathbf{X}_{init}$, more often than not, does contain rich information about the true shape. Penalizing the first singular value during WNN minimization of the shape matrix may needlessly hurts the overall results. Consequently, we introduce a mix of partial sum minimization of singular values [40] and WNN minimization [28] to recover a better shape matrix estimate.

3 Proposed Approach

First, we provide details of our approach to solve for the rotation matrix, followed by the shape matrix estimation.

3.1 Rotation Estimation

To put our work in context, we highlight some previous efforts that took a similar direction towards enhancing the rotation estimate for NRSfM.

Relation to Previous Methods. As mentioned before, there exist K corrective column triplets in the $\mathbf{G}$ matrix (Fig. 1(b)). Brand [8] and Akhter *et al.* [2] solves for all corrective triplets jointly. Xiao *et al.* [53] proposed to independently solve for each corrective triplet ($\mathbf{G}^k$) and align $\mathbf{G}^k$'s using the Procrustes method up to sign [43]. Lee *et al.* [36] proposed an additional constraint on the rotation by posing NRS*f*M as a shape alignment problem. By comparison, the Dai *et al.* [13] method is a simple and effective way to compute rotation. It estimates only the 1st column-triplet of $\mathbf{G}$ *i.e.*, $\mathbf{G}^1$ to recover $\mathbf{R}$ (see Fig. 1).

On the contrary, we propose to first compute all the column-triplets *i.e.*, $\mathbf{G}^k \ \forall \ k \in \{1, 2, \ldots, K\}$ and their corresponding rotation matrices $\mathbf{R}^k \in \mathbb{R}^{2F \times 3}$, using Dai *et al.* [13]. Later, we use all K rotation estimates per frame to estimate a better rotation matrix $\mathbf{R} \in \mathbb{R}^{2F \times 3F}$ via the theory of single rotation averaging [23]. Rather than aligning $\mathbf{G}^k$s as in [2,53], we register the rotations. Our approach consists of the following steps applied in sequel:

- Recover $\mathbf{G}^k$ and its corresponding $\mathbf{R}^k \in \mathbb{R}^{2F \times 3}$ using [13], $\forall \ k \in \{1, \ldots, K\}$.
- Map $\mathbf{R}^k \in \mathbb{R}^{2F \times 3} \mapsto \mathbf{R}^k \in \mathbb{R}^{3F \times 3}$ via the cross product of per frame 2×3 orthographic rotation estimates, while correcting for the sign of the determinant, if applicable.
- Take the rotation due to the first column-triplet *i.e.*, $\mathbf{R}^1 \in \mathbb{R}^{3F \times 3}$ as the reference rotation matrix and register the other $(K-1)$ *i.e.*, $\mathbf{R}^2$ to $\mathbf{R}^K$ rotation estimates to it. After registration, filter the rotation sample if the distance w.r.t its reference rotation sample is greater than δ [23] (see below for details).
- Perform per frame single rotation averaging of all the aligned rotation priors to recover $\mathbf{R}_{avg} \in \mathbb{R}^{3F \times 3}$. Later, convert $\mathbf{R}_{avg}$ per frame to orthographic form and place it in the block diagonal structure to construct $\mathbf{R} \in \mathbb{R}^{2F \times 3F}$.

Before performing single rotation averaging, we align all rotation priors due to the global ambiguity (see Fig. 1(b)-Fig. 1(c) visual). We align the other $(K-1)$ rotations to $\mathbf{R}^1$ using the following optimization.

$$\underset{R_{\text{reg}}^k}{\text{minimize}} \sum_{f=1}^{F} \|\mathbf{R}_f^1 - \mathbf{R}_f^k (\mathbf{R}_{\text{reg}}^k)^T\|_{\mathcal{F}}^2; \ \text{s.t.} \ \mathbf{R}_{\text{reg}}^k \in SO(3), \ \forall \ k \in \{2, \ldots, K\}$$

$$(3)$$

where, $k \in \mathbb{Z}$. In the paper, $\|.\|_{\mathcal{F}}$ denotes the Frobenius norm. Using Eq. (3) optimization, we recover $(K-1)$ $\mathbf{R}_{\text{reg}}^k \in \mathbb{R}^{3 \times 3}$ to register the organic rotation priors for averaging. Next, we perform single rotation averaging per frame.

Single Rotation Averaging. Given a set of $n \geq 1$ rotations $\{R_1, R_2, \ldots, R_n\} \subset SO(3)$, the goal of single rotation averaging (SRA) is to find the average of a set of rotations [23]. It can also be conceived as finding a rotation sample on the $SO(3)$ manifold that minimizes the following cost function

$$\underset{R \in SO(3)}{\text{argmin}} \sum_{i=1}^{n} d^p(R_i, R)$$

$$(4)$$

$d()$ denotes a suitable metric function. We use $p = 1$ for its robustness and accuracy as compared to $p = 2$ [22]. For our problem, we have K rotation samples for each frame (see Fig. 1(c)). Accordingly, we modify Eq. (4) as:

$$\underset{\mathbf{R}_f \in SO(3)}{\operatorname{argmin}} \sum_{k=1}^{K} d^1(\tilde{\mathbf{R}}_f^k, \mathbf{R}_f) \tag{5}$$

Here, $\tilde{\mathbf{R}}_f^k$ is the kth registered rotation for the fth frame, i.e., averaging across rows after registration (Fig. 1(c)). We solve Eq. (5) for all the frames using the Weiszfeld algorithm for L_1 rotation averaging [22]. The average is computed in the local tangent space of $SO(3)$ centered at the current estimate and then back-projected onto $SO(3)$ using the exponential map (Fig. 1(d)-Fig. 1(e)). Yet, instead of initializing using the chordal L_2 mean, we use the starting point using the following equation proposed recently by Lee and Civera [38].

$$\mathbf{S}_o = \underset{\mathbf{S} \in \mathbb{R}^{3 \times 3}}{\operatorname{argmin}} \sum_{i=1}^{K} \sum_{j=1}^{3} \sum_{k=1}^{3} |(\mathbf{R}_i - \mathbf{S})_{jk}|_1 \tag{6}$$

Equation (6) is an element-wise L_1 norm matrix entries, minimizing the sum of absolute differences from the $\mathbf{R}_i$ at (j, k) value i.e., $(\mathbf{S}_o)_{jk} = $ median $(\{\mathbf{R}_i\}_{i=1}^{K}) \; \forall \; j, k \in \{1, 2, 3\}$. After median computation, its equivalent rotation representation is obtained by projecting $\mathbf{S}_o$ onto $SO(3)$ using Υ operator. For $\Psi \in \mathbb{R}^{3 \times 3}$ matrix, we define $\Upsilon_{SO(3)}(\Psi) = \mathbf{UDV}^T$, where $\mathbf{UDV}^T$ is svd of Ψ and $\mathbf{D} = \texttt{diag}(1, 1, -1)$ if $\det(\mathbf{UV}^T) < 0$ or $\mathbf{I}_{3 \times 3}$ otherwise.

Algorithm 1 provide our implementation for single rotation averaging. Empirically, after registration and minor filtering of the rotation samples[4], we observed per frame rotation samples are reasonably close, which is good for convergence [23]. Averaging per frame rotation priors, we recover $\mathbf{R}_{\text{avg}} \in \mathbb{R}^{3F \times 3}$. For more details on single rotation averaging and its convergence analysis refer [23, 38].

To compute $\mathbf{R} \in \mathbb{R}^{2F \times 3F}$ from $\mathbf{R}_{\text{avg}} \in \mathbb{R}^{3F \times 3}$, we take $\mathbf{R}_{\text{avg}}$'s per frame 3×3 matrix, drop its 3rd row and place it to the diagonal of $\mathbf{R}$, and perform this step for all frame[5].

Algorithm 1: L_1 Single Rotation Avg.

Data: Set of rotation $\{\mathbf{R}_i\}_{i=1}^{K}$, $\epsilon_t = 1e^{-3}$
Result: L_1 mean i.e., median rotation
Set $\mathbf{S}_o := \text{median}(\{\mathbf{R}_i\}_{i=1}^{K})$;
/*Project median on $SO(3)$*/
Set $\mathbf{R}_o := \Upsilon_{SO(3)}(\mathbf{S}_o)$; Set $\mathbf{R}_{\text{avg}} := \mathbf{R}_o$;
while do
    $\mathbf{v}_i := \log(\mathbf{R}_i \mathbf{R}_{\text{avg}}^T) \; \forall \; i = 1, 2.., K$;
    $\Delta \mathbf{v} := \frac{\sum_{i=1}^{K} \mathbf{v}_i / \|\mathbf{v}_i\|}{\sum_{i=1}^{K} 1/\|\mathbf{v}_i\|}$;/*Weiszfeld step*/
    $\mathbf{R}_{\text{avg}} := \exp(\Delta \mathbf{v}) \mathbf{R}_{\text{avg}}$
    if $\|\Delta \mathbf{v}\| < \epsilon_t$ **then**
    | **break**;
    end
end
return $\mathbf{R}_{\text{avg}}$;

---

[4] filter if sample is too far to the reference rotation after registration.

[5] After registration, if samples are filtered out due to its distance from the reference rotation (more than δ), then per frame rotations is less than K.

Table 1. Pseudo inverse (PI) shape results comparison with BMM [13] via e_{3d} metric. Compared to [13], our approach dramatically improves PI shape accuracy, showing the benefit of using rotation organic prior. e_{3d} definition is provided in Sect. 4

Dataset	Drink	Pickup	Yoga	Stretch	Dance	Face	Walking	Shark
BMM-PI [13]	0.4449	0.5989	0.6523	0.4784	0.5764	0.4848	0.5100	0.8784
Ours-PI	**0.2195**	**0.2985**	**0.2740**	**0.2238**	**0.3014**	**0.2995**	**0.2702**	**0.3053**

3.2   Shape Estimation

Once we estimated the rotation matrix, our goal is to recover the shape matrix. An easy way to compute shape is $\mathbf{X}_{init} = \mathtt{pinv}(\mathbf{R})\mathbf{W}$, which is consistent with the assumption of low rank shape matrix and it minimizes the re-projection error. To show the merit of our rotation estimation, we tabulate the pseudo inverse shape reconstruction result using our rotation compared to BMM [13] in Table 1. Clearly, our rotation improves the $\mathbf{X}_{init}$, *i.e.*, the initial shape solution, by a large margin. However, $\mathbf{X}_{init}$ may be a 3D reconstruction co-planar in every frame and "the catch is that there are in fact many solutions which minimize the rank" [52]. Therefore, further optimization of the shape matrix is recommended. Let's review Dai *et al.* 's [13] relaxed rank-minimization and recent improvement over it to better place our approach.

Relation to Previous Methods. Given rotation matrix $\mathbf{R} \in \mathbb{R}^{2F \times 3F}$, Dai *et al.* [13] perform the following optimization for low-rank shape matrix estimation.

$$\underset{\mathbf{X}^{\sharp},\mathbf{X}}{\text{minimize}} \; \frac{1}{2}\|\mathbf{W} - \mathbf{R}\mathbf{X}\|_{\mathcal{F}}^2 + \mu\|\mathbf{X}^{\sharp}\|_*; \text{subject to: } \mathbf{X}^{\sharp} = \mathbf{\Phi}(\mathbf{X}) \qquad (7)$$

Here, $\mathbf{\Phi}(.)$ is a function that maps $\mathbf{X} \in \mathbb{R}^{3F \times P}$ to $\mathbf{X}^{\sharp} \in \mathbb{R}^{F \times 3P}$. μ is a scalar constant and $\|.\|_*$ denotes the nuclear norm of the matrix, which is a convex bound of the matrix rank and can give a good solution to rank minimization problems under restricted isometry property constraints [44]. Equation (7) can be solved efficiently using the ADMM optimization strategy [7]. [13] optimizes Eq. (7) by penalizing each singular value of $\mathbf{X}^{\sharp}$ equally. Yet, we have an initial shape prior $\mathbf{X}_{init}$ that we can exploit to recover a better shape. In the same vein, Kumar [28] introduced WNN minimization to Eq. (7), which shows highly effective results with the use of $\mathbf{X}_{init}$ singular values as prior. [28] suggested the following changes

$$\underset{\mathbf{X}^{\sharp},\mathbf{X}}{\text{minimize}} \; \frac{1}{2}\|\mathbf{W} - \mathbf{R}\mathbf{X}\|_{\mathcal{F}}^2 + \mu\|\mathbf{X}^{\sharp}\|_{*,\theta}; \text{subject to: } \mathbf{X}^{\sharp} = \mathbf{\Phi}(\mathbf{X}) \qquad (8)$$

Here, θ is the weight assigned to $\mathbf{X}^{\sharp}$ based on the $\mathbf{X}_{init}^{\sharp}$ singular values. It is known that for a low-rank shape matrix, a few top singular values contain most of the shape information. Thus, when optimizing Eq. (8) the first singular value should be penalized the least and vice-versa, using the following relation

$$\theta_i = \xi\big(\sigma_i(\mathbf{X}_{init}^{\sharp}) + \gamma\big)^{-1} \qquad (9)$$

where, ξ and γ are small positive scalars, $\sigma_i(\mathbf{X}^{\sharp}_{init})$ denotes the ith singular value of $\mathbf{X}^{\sharp}_{init}$ and θ_i denotes its weight. It is observed and empirically tested that such a strategy provides significantly better minima after optimization [28].

Nevertheless, for shape estimation, contrary to Kumar [28], we propose the mixed use of partial sum minimization of singular values and weighted nuclear norm optimization of $\mathbf{X}^{\sharp}$. Based on our extensive empirical study over several non-rigid shapes, we found that the first singular value of $\mathbf{X}^{\sharp}_{init}$ contains useful information. Thus, penalizing it during WNN minimization may hurt performance unnecessarily. Therefore, we propose to preserve the first singular value of the shape during optimization, leading to the following optimization problem

$$\underset{\mathbf{X}^{\sharp},\mathbf{X}}{\text{minimize}} \frac{1}{2}\|\mathbf{W} - \mathbf{RX}\|^2_{\mathcal{F}} + \mu\|\mathbf{X}^{\sharp}\|_{r=N,\theta}; \text{ subject to: } \mathbf{X}^{\sharp} = \mathbf{\Phi}(\mathbf{X}) \qquad (10)$$

We use $N = 1$ for all our experiments and assign the weights θ using Eq. (9) for the rest of the singular values in the shape matrix optimization via ADMM [7].

Shape Optimization. We optimized Eq. (10) using ADMM [7]. Introducing the Lagrange multiplier in Eq. (10) gives us

$$\begin{aligned}
\mathcal{L}_\rho(\mathbf{X}^{\sharp}, \mathbf{X}) &= \frac{1}{2}\|\mathbf{W} - \mathbf{RX}\|^2_{\mathcal{F}} + \mu\|\mathbf{X}^{\sharp}\|_{r=N,\theta} \\
&+ \frac{\rho}{2}\|\mathbf{X}^{\sharp} - \mathbf{\Phi}(\mathbf{X})\|^2_{\mathcal{F}} + <\mathbf{Y}, \mathbf{X}^{\sharp} - \mathbf{\Phi}(\mathbf{X})>
\end{aligned} \qquad (11)$$

$\mathbf{Y} \in \mathbb{R}^{F \times 3P}$ is the Lagrange multiplier and $\rho > 0$ is the penalty parameter. We obtain the solution to each variable solving the following sub-problems over iterations (indexed with the variable t):

$$\mathbf{X}_{t+1} = \underset{\mathbf{X}}{\text{argmin }} \mathcal{L}_{\rho t}(\mathbf{X}^{\sharp}, \mathbf{X}_t); \; \mathbf{X}^{\sharp}_{t+1} = \underset{\mathbf{X}^{\sharp}}{\text{argmin }} \mathcal{L}_{\rho t}(\mathbf{X}^{\sharp}_t, \mathbf{X}) \qquad (12)$$

Using Eq. (11)–Eq. (12), we derive the following expression for $\mathbf{X}$, assuming $\mathbf{X}^{\sharp}$ is constant.

$$\mathbf{X} \simeq \underset{\mathbf{X}}{\text{argmin}}\frac{1}{2}\|\mathbf{W} - \mathbf{RX}\|^2_{\mathcal{F}} + \frac{\rho}{2}\left\|\mathbf{X} - \left(\mathbf{\Phi}^{-1}(\mathbf{X}^{\sharp}) + \frac{\mathbf{\Phi}^{-1}(\mathbf{Y})}{\rho}\right)\right\|^2_{\mathcal{F}} \qquad (13)$$

The closed form solution for $\mathbf{X}$ is obtained by taking the derivative of Eq. (13) w.r.t the corresponding variable and equating it to zero. The closed form expression is used during the ADMM iteration until convergence to recover optimal $\mathbf{X}$. Similarly, rewriting the Eq. (11) by assuming $\mathbf{X}^{\sharp}$ as variable and $\mathbf{X}$ as constant, we get the following expression for $\mathbf{X}^{\sharp}$

$$\mathbf{X}^{\sharp} \simeq \underset{\mathbf{X}^{\sharp}}{\text{argmin }} \mu\|\mathbf{X}^{\sharp}\|_{r=N,\theta} + \frac{\rho}{2}\left\|\mathbf{X}^{\sharp} - \left(\mathbf{\Phi}(\mathbf{X}) - \frac{\mathbf{Y}}{\rho}\right)\right\|^2_{\mathcal{F}} \qquad (14)$$

To solve Eq. (14), we used the theory of Partial Singular Value Thresholding (PSVT) [40]. Let $\mathcal{P}_{N,\tau}[\mathbf{Q}]$ denote the PSVT operator operating on matrix $\mathbf{Q}$. The

Table 2. Statistical comparison on the MoCap dataset [3]. Our method provides favorable 3D reconstruction results. Contrary to the R-BMM [28], our approach provides a methodical way to solve NRS*f*M factorization irrespective of the camera motion assumption. The value of K used is generally same as [12,13]. The 2nd best results are underlined. To have clear spacing, we put comparison with other methods as suggested by the reviewers in the supplementary material.

Dataset↓ / Method→	MP[42]	PTA[3]	CSF1[18]	CSF2[20]	KSTA[19]	PND[36]	CNS [37]	BMM[13]	R-BMM[28]	Ours
Drink	0.0443	0.0250	0.0223	0.0223	0.0156	**0.0037**	0.0431	0.0266	0.0119	<u>0.0071</u> ($K = 12$)
Pickup	0.0667	0.2369	0.2301	0.2277	0.2322	0.0372	0.1281	0.1731	0.0198	**0.0152** ($K = 12$)
Yoga	0.2331	0.1624	0.1467	0.1464	0.1476	0.0140	0.1845	0.1150	0.0129	**0.0122** ($K = 10$)
Stretch	0.2585	0.1088	0.0710	0.0685	0.0674	0.0156	0.0939	0.1034	0.0144	**0.0124** ($K = 11$)
Dance	0.2639	0.2960	0.2705	0.1983	0.2504	0.1454	**0.0759**	0.1864	0.1491	<u>0.1209</u> ($K = 4$)
Face	0.0357	0.0436	0.0363	0.0314	0.0339	0.0165	0.0248	0.0303	0.0179	**0.0145** ($K = 7$)
Walking	0.5607	0.3951	0.1863	0.1035	0.1029	0.0465	**0.0396**	0.1298	0.0882	0.0816 ($K = 8$)
Shark	0.1571	0.1804	**0.0081**	0.0444	0.0160	0.0135	0.0832	0.2311	0.0551	0.0551 ($K = 3$)

operator preserves the leading N singular values and penalizes the others with soft-thresholding parameter τ^6. For completeness, let's go over the following:

Theorem 1. *Oh et al. [40] proposed the following optimization problem to solve*

$$\underset{\mathbf{P}}{\operatorname{argmin}} \ \tau \|\mathbf{P}\|_{r=N} + \frac{1}{2}\|\mathbf{P} - \mathbf{Q}\|_{\mathcal{F}}^2 \tag{15}$$

where, $\tau > 0$ and $\mathbf{P}, \mathbf{Q} \in \mathbb{R}^{m \times n}$ be real valued matrices which can be decomposed by Singular Value Decomposition (SVD). Then, the optimal solution can be expressed by the PSVT operator defined as:

$$\mathcal{P}_{N,\tau}[\mathbf{Q}] = \mathbf{U}_Q(\mathbf{\Sigma}_{Q1} + \mathcal{S}_\tau[\mathbf{\Sigma}_{Q2}])\mathbf{V}_Q^T \tag{16}$$

where, $\mathbf{\Sigma}_{Q1} = \mathbf{diag}(\sigma_1, \sigma_2, .., \sigma_N, .., 0)$ and $\mathbf{\Sigma}_{Q2} = \mathbf{diag}(0, ..\sigma_{N+1}, .., \max(m, n))$. Symbol $\mathcal{S}_\tau$ is the soft-thresholding operator defined as $\mathcal{S}_\tau(\sigma) = \operatorname{sign}(\sigma)\max(|\sigma| - \tau, 0)$. $\mathbf{Q} = \mathbf{U}_Q(\mathbf{\Sigma}_{Q1} + \mathbf{\Sigma}_{Q2})\mathbf{V}_Q^T$

For a detailed derivation and proof, we refer to Oh *et al.* [40]. Using the theorem, we substitute $N = 1$, $\tau = (\mu\theta)/\rho$ and write the solution of $\mathbf{X}^\sharp$ in Eq. (14) as:

$$\mathbf{X}^\sharp = \mathcal{P}_{1, \frac{\mu\theta}{\rho}}\left[\left(\mathbf{\Phi}(\mathbf{X}) - \rho^{-1}\mathbf{Y}\right)\right] \tag{17}$$

We use the above expression of $\mathbf{X}^\sharp$ during the ADMM optimization [7] to recover the optimal shape matrix. The θ values are assigned according to Eq. (9) for $N > 1$. The Lagrange multiplier ($\mathbf{Y}$) and penalty parameter (ρ) are updated over ADMM iteration (say for $t + 1$ iteration) as $\mathbf{Y}_{t+1} = \mathbf{Y}_t + \rho(\mathbf{X}_{t+1}^\sharp - \mathbf{\Phi}(\mathbf{X}_{t+1}))$; $\rho_{t+1} = \operatorname{minimum}(\rho_{\max}, \lambda\rho_t)$. Where, $\rho_{\max}$ refers to the maximum value of 'ρ' and λ is an empirical constant. $\mathbf{Y}$ and ρ are updated during the ADMM [7] iteration until convergence criteria is satisfied. The criteria for the ADMM iteration to stop are $\|\mathbf{X}^\sharp - \mathbf{\Phi}(\mathbf{X})\|_\infty < \epsilon$, or, $\rho_{t+1} \geq \rho_{\max}$.

---

[6] For more discussion on partial sum minimization of singular values, cf. the supplementary material. For a comprehensive theory refer to [40].

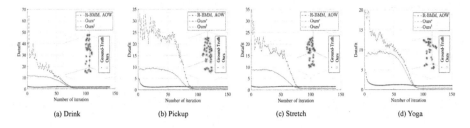

(a) Drink   (b) Pickup   (c) Stretch   (d) Yoga

Fig. 2. Datafit curve shows the value of Eq. (10) cost function over iteration compared to R-BMM [28] and AOW [24] WNN formulation on Mocap dataset [3]. Ours* show the Eq. (10) datafit value using [13] rotation whereas, Ours† show the datafit curve using our rotation initialization. Our shape optimization gives better minima, and using our rotation as initialization, we have faster and stable convergence response (Ours†).

4   Experiments

(a) Implementation Details and Initialization. We implemented our method on a desktop machine with 32 GB RAM using C++/MATLAB software. Initial rotation filtering parameter δ is set to 0.05. All the K rotations $\mathbf{R}^k \in \mathbb{R}^{2F \times 3}$ can be solved in parallel, so the minor increase in processing time compared to [13], is due to registration, filtering and rotation averaging. For e.g., a 357 frame pickup sequence takes 7.46 s. for registration, 0.012 s. for filtering and 0.93 s. for computing $\mathbf{R}_{avg}$. We ran 50 iterations of SRA (Algorithm 1) for each frame. The weights (θ) in Eq. (10) is initialized using Eq. (9) with $\xi = 5e^{-3} * \mathrm{sqrt}(\sigma_1(\mathbf{X}_{init}^{\sharp}))$ generally and $\gamma = 1e^{-6}$. For Eq. (10) optimization via ADMM, we use $\rho = 1e^{-4}$, $\lambda = 1.1$, $\rho_{max} = 1e^{10}$, $\mathbf{Y} = \mathrm{zeros}(F, 3P)$, $\epsilon_t = 1e^{-10}$, and $\epsilon = 1e^{-10}$ (see supp.).

(b) Evaluation Metric. We used the popular mean normalized 3D reconstruction error metric to report our statistical results on motion capture (MoCap) benchmark [3,50] and Garg et al. [15] dense NRSfM benchmark dataset. It is defined as $e_{3d} = \frac{1}{F} \sum_{i=1}^{F} \|\mathbf{X}_i^{est} - \mathbf{X}_i^{gt}\|_{\mathcal{F}} / \|\mathbf{X}_i^{gt}\|_{\mathcal{F}}$ with $\mathbf{X}_i^{est}$, $\mathbf{X}_i^{gt}$ symbolizing per frame estimated shape and its ground-truth (GT) value, respectively. For evaluation on recent NRSfM benchmark dataset [25], we used their supplied error evaluation metric script, which is inspired from Taylor et al. work [48]. The 3D reconstruction accuracy is computed after registering the recovered shape to the ground-truth shape due to global ambiguity [3,25]. To evaluate rotation estimate accuracy, we use the mean rotation error metric $e_{\mathbf{R}} = \frac{1}{F} \sum_{i=1}^{F} \|\mathbf{R}_i^{GT} - \mathbf{R}_i^{est}\|_{\mathcal{F}}$. Here, $\mathbf{R}_i^{GT}$, $\mathbf{R}_i^{est}$ denotes the ground-truth and estimated per frame rotation.

4.1   Dataset and Evaluation

(a) MoCap Benchmark Dataset. Introduced by Akther et al. [3] and Torresani et al. [50], this dataset has become a standard benchmark for any NRSfM algorithm evaluation. It is composed of 8 real sequences, namely Drink (1102, 41), Pickup (357, 41), Yoga (307, 41), Stretch (370, 41), Dance (264, 75),

Table 3. 3D reconstruction accuracy on dense NRSfM dataset [15]. We observed superior results compared to the well-known sparse NRSfM methods. It is interesting to observe that our results compares favorably to carefully crafted dense NRSfM methods such as DV, GM and others. The 2nd best performance of our method is underlined.

Method Type →			Sparse NRSfM Methods						Dense NRSfM Methods			
Dataset	MP [42]	PTA [3]	CSF1 [18]	CSF2 [20]	BMM [13]	Ours	DV [15]	SMSR [5]	CMDR [17]	GM [29]	ND [47]	Ours
Face Seq.1	0.0926	0.1559	0.5325	0.4677	0.4263	**0.0624**	0.0531	0.1893	-	**0.0443**	-	0.0624
Face Seq.2	0.0819	0.1503	0.9266	0.7909	0.6062	**0.0451**	0.0457	0.2133	-	**0.0381**	-	<u>0.0451</u>
Face Seq.3	0.1057	0.1252	0.5274	0.5474	0.0784	**0.0279**	0.0346	0.1345	0.0373	**0.0294**	0.0450	**0.0279**
Face Seq.4	0.0717	0.1348	0.5392	0.5292	0.0918	**0.0419**	0.0379	0.0984	0.0369	**0.0309**	0.0490	0.0419

Walking (260, 55), Face (316, 40) and Shark (240, 91). The last 3 sequences were introduced by Torresani *et al.* [50]. The numbers presented in bracket correspond to number of frames and points (F, P). Table 2 shows the comparison of our method with other competing methods. For evaluation, we keep the value of K generally same as BMM [13]. From Table 2, it is easy to observe that more often than not, our approach performs best or second-best than other methods, thus showing a consistent superior performance over a diverse set of object deformation type.

Compared to BMM [13], which also makes no assumption other than low-rank, our «organic prior» based method dramatically improves 3D reconstruction accuracy, thereby validating our claims made in the paper. Figure 2 shows few qualitative results along with the convergence curve comparison with the current methods such as R-BMM [28], AOW [24]. The results show recovery of better minima and stable convergence curve using our rotation estimate initialization.

(b) Dense NRSfM Benchmark Dataset. Introduced by Garg *et al.* [15,16], it is a standard dataset to evaluate dense NRSfM methods. It comprises of 4 synthetic face sequences and 3 real video sequences of heart, back, and face deformation. The synthetic face dataset is composed of 28,880 tracked feature points. Face sequence 1 and Face sequence 2 are 10 frames long video, whereas Face sequence 3 and Face sequence 4 are 99 frames video. The video sequence for heart, back, and face dataset is 80, 150, and 120 frames long with 68295, 20561, and 28332 feature track points. Table 3 provides the statistical results of our approach compared to well-known dense NRSfM algorithms. For better comprehension, we classified the comparison into two sets *i.e.*, sparse NRSfM methods and dense NRSfM methods. From Table 3, it is easy to observe the advantage of our approach compared to well-known sparse NRSfM methods. For evaluation of our method, we use $K = 1$ for all the four sequence. For other methods [3,13], we iterate over different K and put its best possible results.

The interesting point to note is that without using any extra assumptions about the dense deforming surface such as union of linear subspaces [26,29], variation in the deformation over frame should be smooth [16], dynamic shape prior [17], smooth trajectory constraint [5], and recent deep neural network based latent space constraint [47], our method provide impressive results and it is close to the best method [29]. Note that, contrary to our simple approach, GM [29] is a complex geometric method to implement. To conclude, our results reveal the strength of classical NRSfM factorization if organic priors are exploited sensibly.

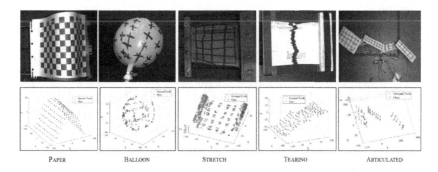

PAPER   BALLOON   STRETCH   TEARING   ARTICULATED

Fig. 3. Qualitative Results on NRSfM challenge dataset [25]. **Top row.** Subject image. **Bottom row.** 3D reconstruction of the respective object shape.

(c) **NRSfM Challenge Dataset.** Jensen *et al.* [25] recently proposed this dataset. It comprises 5 different subjects, namely Articulated, Paper, Balloon, Stretch, and Tear-

Table 4. Comparison of our method with state-of-the-art on recent benchmark [25]. Results are reported in millimeters.

Data	BMM [13]	R-BMM [28]	AOW [24]	BP [41]	Ours
Articul.	18.49	16.00	15.03	16.10	**12.18** ($K = 8$)
Balloon	10.39	7.84	8.05	8.29	**6.29** ($K = 5$)
Paper	8.94	10.69	10.45	**6.70**	8.86 ($K = 2$)
Stretch	10.02	7.53	9.01	7.66	**6.36** ($K = 6$)
Tearing	14.23	16.34	16.20	11.26	**10.91** ($K = 6$)

ing. Each subject's deformations is captured under 6 varying camera trajectories *i.e.*, circle, flyby, line, semi-circle, tricky and zigzag, making the dataset interesting yet challenging. For evaluation, the dataset provide a single frame ground-truth 3D shape for each subject. Table 4 show the average 3D reconstruction accuracy comparison in millimeters with the recent and earlier state-of-the-art on this dataset *i.e.*, BMM [13], R-BMM [28], AOW [24], BP [41]. For comparison, we used the orthogonal sequence of the dataset. The value of K used by our method for comparison is provided in the bracket. Statistical results indicate that our approach provides better non-rigid shape reconstruction for most of the subject categories on this dataset. Figure 3 show visual results obtained on this dataset.

(d) **Rotation Estimation.** To validate that the single rotation averaging gives meaningful rotation, we validate our results using the ground-truth rotation available in the Akther *et al.* [3] dataset.

Table 5 provide the average camera rotation error $e_{\mathbf{R}}$ results on yoga, pickup, stretch, and drink sequence. The statistics show that

Table 5. $e_{\mathbf{R}}$ comparison with other factorization methods.

Data	MP [42]	PTA [3]	CSF [18]	BMM [13]	R-BMM [28]	Ours
Yoga	0.8343	0.1059	0.1019	0.0883	0.0883	0.0888
Pickup	0.2525	0.1549	0.1546	0.1210	0.1217	**0.1144**
Stretch	0.8185	0.0549	0.0489	0.0676	0.0676	0.0671
Drink	0.2699	0.0058	0.0055	0.0071	0.0243	0.0072

using our approach, we can have fine rotation estimate[7]. Further, advantage of

---

[7] With $\mathbf{W} = \mathbf{RS}$ theory, even GT rotation cannot provide GT shape, cf. [13] Table 3.

Table 6. 2nd **row:** Our e_{3d} results using Dai *et al.* rotation [13]. 3rd **row:** e_{3d} using our rotation. Indeed using organic rotation priors help improve overall performance.

Dataset	Drink	Pickup	Yoga	Stretch	Dance	Face	Walking	Shark
BMM [13]	0.0266	0.1731	0.1150	0.1034	0.1864	0.0303	0.1298	0.2357
e_{3d} ([13] rotation)	0.0101	0.0164	0.0126	0.0126	0.1382	0.0152	0.0880	0.0563
e_{3d} (our rotation)	**0.0071**	**0.0152**	**0.0122**	**0.0124**	**0.1209**	**0.0145**	**0.0816**	**0.0550**

our rotation estimation on clean sequence, noisy trajectories and pseudo inverse solution can be inferred from Table 6 Fig. 4(a), and Table 1, respectively.

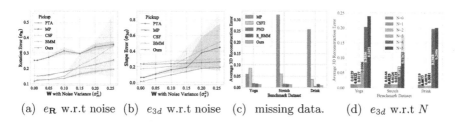

(a) $e_{\mathbf{R}}$ w.r.t noise   (b) e_{3d} w.r.t noise   (c) missing data.   (d) e_{3d} w.r.t N

Fig. 4. (a)–(b) Rotation and shape error on the noisy Pickup trajectories. Our method show stable behaviour consistently. Mean and standard deviation is shown with bold and light shaded regions, respectively. (c) Avg. 3D reconstruction for missing data experiment. (d) $N = 0$ show results when all the singular values are penalized using WNN. Our approach *i.e.*, $N = 1$ gives better results overall under same rotation.

(e) Other Experiments and Ablations

(i) *Performance with noisy trajectory.* Figure 4(a), Fig. 4(b) shows the rotation ($e_{\mathbf{R}}$) and shape error (e_{3d}) comparison on the noisy trajectory, respectively. We introduce noise to the 2D point trajectory with the standard deviation varying from 0.01–0.25 using `normrand()` function from MATLAB. We ran the different methods 10 times for each standard deviation value and plotted the method's mean and variance. Statistical results show that our method is quite robust to noisy sequence and show much stable behaviour (both in rotation and shape estimation) than the other prior or prior-free approaches (see Fig. 4(a)–4(b)).

(ii) *Performance on missing trajectory cases.* For this experiment, we used Lee *et al.* [36] and Kumar [28] setup, where we randomly set 30% of the trajectory missing from the **W**. We perform matrix completion using [11] optimization and then ran our algorithm on the recovered matrix. The results are shown in Fig. 4(c). Our method outperforms the state-of-the-art in most of the cases.

(iii) *Performance with change in value of N.* To show that $N = 1$ generally works best for Eq. (10), we conducted this experiment. First, we penalize all the singular values using WNN optimization ($N = 0$) and then we vary the value of N from 1 to 5 and recorded the results. Figure 4(d) shows the reconstruction results using different values of N. We observed that by penalizing all the singular values using WNN, we are unnecessarily hurting the performance. On the contrary, if we increase N value greater than 1, more often than not, it starts to reduce the performance. Refer supplementary material for more results and discussions.

5   Conclusion

This work reveals organic priors for NRSfM factorization irrespective of camera motion and shape deformation type. It exhibited that mindful use of such fundamental priors gives better accuracy than the prior-free methods. That said, our method uses an orthographic camera model with a low-rank shape assumption in NRSfM. Hence, by construction, it has some limitations *for e.g.*, our method may perform inadequately on high perspective distortion images having large object deformation. A recent idea by Graßhof et al. [21] can be used to overcome such a limitation. Finally, we conclude that the clever use of organic priors with matrix factorization theory is sufficient to provide excellent 3D reconstruction accuracy for both sparse and dense NRSfM.

Acknowledgement. The authors thank Google for their generous gift (ETH Zürich Foundation, 2020-HS-411).

References

1. Aanæs, H., Kahl, F.: Estimation of deformable structure and motion. In: Proceedings of the Vision and Modelling of Dynamic Scenes Workshop, vol. 2, pp. 3. Citeseer (2002)
2. Akhter, I., Sheikh, Y., Khan, S.: In defense of orthonormality constraints for non-rigid structure from motion. In: IEEE Conference on Computer Vision and Pattern Recognition, 2009. CVPR 2009, pp. 1534–1541. IEEE (2009)
3. Akhter, I., Sheikh, Y., Khan, S., Kanade, T.: Nonrigid structure from motion in trajectory space. In: Advances in Neural Information Processing Systems, pp. 41–48 (2008)
4. Akhter, I., Sheikh, Y., Khan, S., Kanade, T.: Trajectory space: a dual representation for nonrigid structure from motion. IEEE Trans. Pattern Anal. Mach. Intell. **33**(7), 1442–1456 (2011)
5. Ansari, M.D., Golyanik, V., Stricker, D.: Scalable dense monocular surface reconstruction. In: 2017 International Conference on 3D Vision (3DV), pp. 78–87. IEEE (2017)
6. Bartoli, A., Gay-Bellile, V., Castellani, U., Peyras, J., Olsen, S., Sayd, P.: Coarse-to-fine low-rank structure-from-motion. In: 2008 IEEE Conference on Computer Vision and Pattern Recognition, pp. 1–8. IEEE (2008)
7. Boyd, S., Parikh, N., Chu, E., Peleato, B., Eckstein, J.: Distributed optimization and statistical learning via the alternating direction method of multipliers. Found. Trends® Mach. Learn. **3**(1), 1–122 (2011)

8. Brand, M.: A direct method for 3D factorization of nonrigid motion observed in 2D. In: 2005 IEEE Computer Society Conference on Computer Vision and Pattern Recognition (CVPR 2005), vol. 2, pp. 122–128. IEEE (2005)
9. Bregler, C., Hertzmann, A., Biermann, H.: Recovering non-rigid 3D shape from image streams. In: IEEE Conference on Computer Vision and Pattern Recognition, vol. 2, pp. 690–696. IEEE (2000)
10. Bronstein, A.M., Bronstein, M.M., Kimmel, R.: Numerical Geometry Of Non-rigid Shapes. Springer Science & Business Media, Heidelberg (2008)
11. Cabral, R., De la Torre, F., Costeira, J.P., Bernardino, A.: Unifying nuclear norm and bilinear factorization approaches for low-rank matrix decomposition. In: Proceedings of the IEEE International Conference on Computer Vision, pp. 2488–2495 (2013)
12. Dai, Y., Li, H., He, M.: A simple prior-free method for non-rigid structure-from-motion factorization. In: Computer Vision and Pattern Recognition (CVPR), pp. 2018–2025. IEEE (2012)
13. Dai, Y., Li, H., He, M.: A simple prior-free method for non-rigid structure-from-motion factorization. Int. J. Comput. Vision **107**(2), 101–122 (2014). https://doi.org/10.1007/s11263-013-0684-2
14. Fayad, J., Agapito, L., Del Bue, A.: Piecewise quadratic reconstruction of nonrigid surfaces from monocular sequences. In: Daniilidis, K., Maragos, P., Paragios, N. (eds.) ECCV 2010. LNCS, vol. 6314, pp. 297–310. Springer, Heidelberg (2010). https://doi.org/10.1007/978-3-642-15561-1_22
15. Garg, R., Roussos, A., Agapito, L.: Dense variational reconstruction of non-rigid surfaces from monocular video. In: IEEE Conference on Computer Vision and Pattern Recognition, pp. 1272–1279 (2013)
16. Garg, R., Roussos, A., Agapito, L.: A variational approach to video registration with subspace constraints. Int. J. Comput. Vision **104**(3), 286–314 (2013). https://doi.org/10.1007/s11263-012-0607-7
17. Golyanik, V., Jonas, A., Stricker, D., Theobalt, C.: Intrinsic dynamic shape prior for dense non-rigid structure from motion. In: 2020 International Conference on 3D Vision (3DV), pp. 692–701. IEEE (2020)
18. Gotardo, P.F., Martinez, A.M.: Computing smooth time trajectories for camera and deformable shape in structure from motion with occlusion. IEEE Trans. Pattern Anal. Mach. Intell. **33**(10), 2051–2065 (2011)
19. Gotardo, P.F., Martinez, A.M.: Kernel non-rigid structure from motion. In: IEEE International Conference on Computer Vision, pp. 802–809. IEEE (2011)
20. Gotardo, P.F., Martinez, A.M.: Non-rigid structure from motion with complementary rank-3 spaces. In: 2011 IEEE Conference on Computer Vision and Pattern Recognition (CVPR), pp. 3065–3072. IEEE (2011)
21. Graßhof, S., Brandt, S.S.: Tensor-based non-rigid structure from motion. In: Proceedings of the IEEE/CVF Winter Conference on Applications of Computer Vision, pp. 3011–3020 (2022)
22. Hartley, R., Aftab, K., Trumpf, J.: L1 rotation averaging using the weiszfeld algorithm. In: CVPR 2011, pp. 3041–3048. IEEE (2011)
23. Hartley, R., Trumpf, J., Dai, Y., Li, H.: Rotation averaging. Int. J. Comput. Vision **103**(3), 267–305 (2013). https://doi.org/10.1007/s11263-012-0601-0
24. Iglesias, J.P., Olsson, C., Valtonen Örnhag, M.: Accurate optimization of weighted nuclear norm for non-rigid structure from motion. In: Vedaldi, A., Bischof, H., Brox, T., Frahm, J.-M. (eds.) ECCV 2020. LNCS, vol. 12372, pp. 21–37. Springer, Cham (2020). https://doi.org/10.1007/978-3-030-58583-9_2

25. Jensen, S.H.N., Doest, M.E.B., Aanæs, H., Del Bue, A.: A benchmark and evaluation of non-rigid structure from motion. Int. J. Comput. Vision (IJCV) **129**(4), 882–899 (2021). https://doi.org/10.1007/s11263-020-01406-y

26. Kumar, S.: Jumping manifolds: geometry aware dense non-rigid structure from motion. In: Proceedings of the IEEE/CVF Conference on Computer Vision and Pattern Recognition, pp. 5346–5355 (2019)

27. Kumar, S.: Non-rigid structure from motion. Ph.D. thesis, College of Engineering & Computer Science, The Australian National University (2019)

28. Kumar, S.: Non-rigid structure from motion: prior-free factorization method revisited. In: Winter Conference on Applications of Computer Vision (WACV 2020), pp. 51–60 (2020)

29. Kumar, S., Cherian, A., Dai, Y., Li, H.: Scalable dense non-rigid structure-from-motion: a Grassmannian perspective. In: Proceedings of the IEEE Conference on Computer Vision and Pattern Recognition, pp. 254–263 (2018)

30. Kumar, S., Dai, Y., Li, H.: Spatio-temporal union of subspaces for multi-body non-rigid structure-from-motion. Pattern Recogn. **71**, 428–443 (2017)

31. Kumar, S., Dai, Y., Li, H.: Multi-body non-rigid structure-from-motion. In: 2016 Fourth International Conference on 3D Vision (3DV), pp. 148–156. IEEE (2016)

32. Kumar, S., Dai, Y., Li, H.: Monocular dense 3D reconstruction of a complex dynamic scene from two perspective frames. In: IEEE International Conference on Computer Vision, pp. 4649–4657 (2017)

33. Kumar, S., Dai, Y., Li, H.: Superpixel soup: monocular dense 3D reconstruction of a complex dynamic scene. IEEE Trans. Pattern Anal. Mach. Intell. **43**(5), 1705–1717 (2019)

34. Kumar, S., Ghorakavi, R.S., Dai, Y., Li, H.: Dense depth estimation of a complex dynamic scene without explicit 3D motion estimation. arXiv preprint arXiv:1902.03791 (2019)

35. Kumar, S., Van Gool, L., de Oliveira, C.E., Cherian, A., Dai, Y., Li, H.: Dense non-rigid structure from motion: a manifold viewpoint. arXiv preprint arXiv:2006.09197 (2020)

36. Lee, M., Cho, J., Choi, C.H., Oh, S.: Procrustean normal distribution for non-rigid structure from motion. In: IEEE Conference on Computer Vision and Pattern Recognition, pp. 1280–1287 (2013)

37. Lee, M., Cho, J., Oh, S.: Consensus of non-rigid reconstructions. In: IEEE Conference on Computer Vision and Pattern Recognition, pp. 4670–4678 (2016)

38. Lee, S.H., Civera, J.: Robust single rotation averaging. arXiv preprint arXiv:2004.00732 (2020)

39. Matthews, I., Xiao, J., Baker, S.: 2D vs. 3D deformable face models: representational power, construction, and real-time fitting. Int. J. Comput. Vision **75**(1), 93–113 (2007). https://doi.org/10.1007/s11263-007-0043-2

40. Oh, T.H., Tai, Y.W., Bazin, J.C., Kim, H., Kweon, I.S.: Partial sum minimization of singular values in robust PCA: algorithm and applications. IEEE Trans. Pattern Anal. Mach. Intell. **38**(4), 744–758 (2016)

41. Ornhag, M.V., Iglesias, J.P., Olsson, C.: Bilinear parameterization for non-separable singular value penalties. In: Proceedings of the IEEE/CVF Conference on Computer Vision and Pattern Recognition, pp. 3897–3906 (2021)

42. Paladini, M., Del Bue, A., Stosic, M., Dodig, M., Xavier, J., Agapito, L.: Factorization for non-rigid and articulated structure using metric projections. In: 2009 IEEE Conference on Computer Vision and Pattern Recognition, pp. 2898–2905. IEEE (2009)

43. Rabaud, V., Belongie, S.: Re-thinking non-rigid structure from motion. In: IEEE Conference on Computer Vision and Pattern Recognition, pp. 1–8. IEEE (2008)
44. Recht, B., Fazel, M., Parrilo, P.A.: Guaranteed minimum-rank solutions of linear matrix equations via nuclear norm minimization. SIAM Rev. **52**(3), 471–501 (2010)
45. Russell, C., Fayad, J., Agapito, L.: Energy based multiple model fitting for non-rigid structure from motion. In: CVPR 2011, pp. 3009–3016. IEEE (2011)
46. Salzmann, M., Fua, P.: Deformable surface 3D reconstruction from monocular images. Synth. Lect. Comput. Vision **2**(1), 1–113 (2010)
47. Sidhu, V., Tretschk, E., Golyanik, V., Agudo, A., Theobalt, C.: Neural dense non-rigid structure from motion with latent space constraints. In: Vedaldi, A., Bischof, H., Brox, T., Frahm, J.-M. (eds.) ECCV 2020. LNCS, vol. 12361, pp. 204–222. Springer, Cham (2020). https://doi.org/10.1007/978-3-030-58517-4_13
48. Taylor, J., Jepson, A.D., Kutulakos, K.N.: Non-rigid structure from locally-rigid motion. In: IEEE Conference on Computer Vision and Pattern Recognition, pp. 2761–2768. IEEE (2010)
49. Tomasi, C., Kanade, T.: Shape and motion from image streams under orthography: a factorization method. Int. J. Comput. Vision **9**(2), 137–154 (1992). https://doi.org/10.1007/BF00129684
50. Torresani, L., Hertzmann, A., Bregler, C.: Nonrigid structure-from-motion: estimating shape and motion with hierarchical priors. IEEE Trans. Pattern Anal. Mach. Intell. **30**(5), 878–892 (2008)
51. Torresani, L., Hertzmann, A., Bregler, C.: Learning non-rigid 3D shape from 2D motion. In: Advances in Neural Information Processing Systems, pp. 1555–1562 (2004)
52. Valmadre, J., Sridharan, S., Denman, S., Fookes, C., Lucey, S.: Closed-form solutions for low-rank non-rigid reconstruction. In: 2015 International Conference on Digital Image Computing: Techniques and Applications (DICTA), pp. 1–6. IEEE (2015)
53. Xiao, J., Chai, J., Kanade, T.: A closed-form solution to non-rigid shape and motion recovery. In: Pajdla, T., Matas, J. (eds.) ECCV 2004. LNCS, vol. 3024, pp. 573–587. Springer, Heidelberg (2004). https://doi.org/10.1007/978-3-540-24673-2_46
54. Zhu, Y., Huang, D., De La Torre, F., Lucey, S.: Complex non-rigid motion 3D reconstruction by union of subspaces. In: IEEE Conference on Computer Vision and Pattern Recognition, pp. 1542–1549 (2014)

Perspective Flow Aggregation for Data-Limited 6D Object Pose Estimation

Yinlin Hu[1,2(✉)], Pascal Fua[1], and Mathieu Salzmann[1,2]

[1] EPFL CVLab, Lausanne, Switzerland
huyinlin@gmail.com, {pascal.fua,mathieu.salzmann}@epfl.ch
[2] ClearSpace SA, Renens, Switzerland

Abstract. Most recent 6D object pose estimation methods, including unsupervised ones, require many real training images. Unfortunately, for some applications, such as those in space or deep under water, acquiring real images, even unannotated, is virtually impossible. In this paper, we propose a method that can be trained solely on synthetic images, or optionally using a few additional real ones. Given a rough pose estimate obtained from a first network, it uses a second network to predict a dense 2D correspondence field between the image rendered using the rough pose and the real image and infers the required pose correction. This approach is much less sensitive to the domain shift between synthetic and real images than state-of-the-art methods. It performs on par with methods that require annotated real images for training when not using any, and outperforms them considerably when using as few as twenty real images.

Keywords: 6D object pose estimation · 6D object pose refinement · Image synthesis · Dense 2D correspondence · Domain adaptation

1 Introduction

Estimating the 6D pose of a target object is at the heart of many robotics, quality control, augmented reality applications, among others. When ample amounts of annotated real images are available, deep learning-based methods now deliver excellent results [7,31,32,38,46]. Otherwise, the most common approach is to use synthetic data instead [14,25,49]. However, even when sophisticated domain adaptations techniques are used to bridge the domain gap between the synthetic and real data [14,26,34], the results are still noticeably worse than when training with annotated real images, as illustrated by Fig. 1.

Pose refinement offers an effective solution to this problem: An auxiliary network learns to correct the mistakes made by the network trained on synthetic data when fed with real data [23,25,33,51]. The most common refinement strategy is to render the object using the current pose estimate, predict the 6D difference with an auxiliary network taking as input the rendered image and the

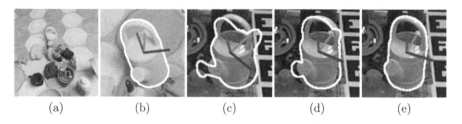

(a)   (b)   (c)   (d)   (e)

Fig. 1. Data-limited 6D object pose estimation. (a) In the absence of real data, one can train a model using synthesized images [9]. **(b)** Although the resulting accuracy on synthetic data is great, **(c)** that on real images is significantly worse. **(d)** While the common iterative pose refinement approach can help, it still suffers from the synthetic-to-real domain gap [25]. **(e)** Our non-iterative strategy generalizes much better to real images despite being trained only on synthetic data.

input one, and correct the estimate accordingly. As illustrated by Fig. 2(a), this process is performed iteratively. Not only does this involve a potentially expensive rendering at each iteration, but it also is sensitive to object occlusions and background clutter, which cannot be modeled in the rendering step. Even more problematically, most of these methods still require numerous real images for training purposes, and there are applications for which such images are simply not available. For example, for 6D pose estimation in space [14,20] or deep under water [17,36], no real images of the target object may be available, only a CAD model and conjectures about what it now looks like after decades in a harsh environment. These are the scenarios we will refer to as *data-limited*.

To overcome these problems, we introduce the non-iterative pose refinement strategy depicted by Fig. 2(b). We again start from a rough initial pose but, instead of predicting a delta pose, we estimate a dense 2D correspondence field between the image rendered with the initial pose and the input one. We then use these correspondences to compute the 6D correction algebraically. Our approach is simple but motivated by the observation that predicting dense 2D-to-2D matches is much more robust to the synthetic-to-real domain gap than predicting a pose difference directly from the image pair, as shown in Fig. 1(d–e). Furthermore, this strategy naturally handles the object occlusions and is less sensitive to the background clutter.

Furthermore, instead of synthesizing images given the rough initial pose, which requires on-the-fly rendering, we find nearest neighbors among pre-rendered exemplars and estimate the dense 2D correspondences between these neighbors and the real input. This serves several purposes. First, it makes the computation much faster. Second, it makes the final accuracy less dependent on the quality of the initial pose, which only serves as a query for exemplars. Third, as multiple exemplars are independent of each other, we can process them simultaneously. Finally, multiple exemplars deliver complementary perspectives about the real input, which we combine for increased robustness.

(a) The iterative strategy   (b) Our non-iterative strategy

Fig. 2. Different pose refinement paradigms. (a) Given an initial pose P_0, existing refinement strategies estimate a pose difference ΔP_0 from the input image and the image rendered according to P_0, generating a new intermediate pose P_1. They then iterate this process until it converges to the final pose $\hat{P}$ [23,25]. This strategy relies on estimating a delta *pose* from the input images by extracting global object features. These features contain high-level information, and we observed them not to generalize well across domains. **(b)** By contrast, our strategy queries a set of discrete poses $\{P_1, P_2, P_3, \dots\}$ that are near the initial pose P_0 from pre-rendered exemplars, and computes the final pose $\hat{P}$ in one shot by combining all the correspondences $\{C_i\}$ established between the exemplars and the input. Estimating *dense 2D-to-2D local correspondences* forces the supervision of our training to occur at the pixel-level, not at the image-level as in **(a)**. This makes our DNN learn to extract features that contain lower-level information and thus generalize across domains. In principle, our method can easily be extended into an iterative strategy, using the refined pose as a new initial one. However, we found a single iteration to already be sufficiently accurate.

We evaluate our pose refinement framework on the challenging Occluded-LINEMOD [22] and YCB-V [49] datasets, and demonstrate that it is significantly more efficient and accurate than iterative frameworks. It performs on par with state-of-the-art methods that require annotated real images for training when not using any, and outperforms them considerably when using as few as twenty real images.

2   Related Work

6D pose estimation is currently dominated by neural network-based methods [2,11,14,32,37,38]. However, most of their designs are still consistent with traditional techniques. That is, they first establish 3D-to-2D correspondences [27, 44,45] and then use a Perspective-n-Points (PnP) algorithm [3,21,24,52]. In practice, these correspondences are obtained by predicting either the 2D locations of predefined 3D keypoints [16,19,29,33,43], or the 3D positions of the pixels within the object mask [8,26,51]. These methods have been shown to outperform those that directly regress the 6D pose [49], which are potentially sensitive to object occlusions. Nevertheless, most of these methods require large amounts of annotated real training data to yield accurate predictions. Here, we propose a pose refinement strategy that allows us to produce accurate pose estimates using only synthetic training data.

6D pose refinement [19,33,40,51] aims to improve an initial rough pose estimate, obtained, for example, by a network trained only on synthetic data. In this context, DeepIM [25] and CosyPose [23] iteratively render the object in the current pose estimate and predict the 6D pose difference between the rendered and input images. However, learning to predict a pose difference directly does not easily generalize to different domains, and these methods thus also require annotated data. Furthermore, the on-the-fly rendering performed at each iteration makes these algorithms computationally demanding. Finally, these methods are sensitive to object occlusions and background clutter, which cannot be modeled in the rendering process. Here, instead, we propose a non-iterative method based on dense 2D correspondences. Thanks to our use of offline-generated exemplars and its non-iterative nature, it is much more efficient than existing refinement methods. Furthermore, it inherently handles occlusions and clutter, and, as we will demonstrate empirically, generalizes easily to new domains. The method in [28] also uses 2D information for pose refinement. Specifically, it iteratively updates the pose so as to align the model's contours with the image ones. As such, it may be sensitive to the target shape, object occlusion and background clutter. Instead, we use dense pixel-wise correspondences, which are more robust to these disturbances and only need to be predicted once.

Optical flow estimation, which provides dense 2D-to-2D correspondences between consecutive images [12,13,15,35,39,42], is a building block of our framework. Rather than estimating the flow between two consecutive video frames, as commonly done by optical flow methods, we establish dense 2D correspondences between offline-generated synthetic exemplars and the real input image. This is motivated by our observation that establishing dense correspondences between an image pair depends more strongly on the local differences between these images, rather than the images themselves, making this strategy more robust to a domain change. This is evidenced by the fact that our network trained only on synthetic data remains effective when applied to real images.

Domain adaptation constitutes the standard approach to bridging the gap between different domains. However, most domain adaptation methods assume the availability of considerable amounts of data from the target domain, albeit unsupervised, to facilitate the adaptation [1,4,30,41]. Here, by contrast, we focus on the scenario where capturing such data is difficult. As such, domain generalization, which aims to learn models that generalize to unseen domains [5], seems more appropriate for solving our task. However, existing methods typically assume that multiple source domains are available for training, which is not fulfilled in our case. Although one can generate many different domains by augmentation techniques [48,50,53], we observed this strategy to only yield rough 6D pose estimates in the test domain. Therefore, we use this approach to obtain our initial pose, which we refine with our method.

3   Approach

We aim to estimate the 6D pose of a known rigid object from a single RGB image in a data-limited scenario, that is, with little or even no access to real images during training. To this end, we use a two-step strategy that first estimates a rough initial pose and then refines it. Where we differ from other methods is

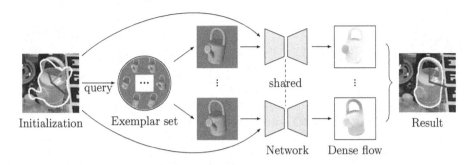

Fig. 3. Overview of our framework. We first obtain an initial pose of the target using a pose network trained only on synthetic data. We then retrieve the N closest exemplars from the offline-rendered exemplar set and estimate their dense 2D displacement fields with respect to the target. Finally, we combine all these flow results into a set of 3D-to-2D correspondences to obtain a robust final pose estimate.

in our approach to refinement. Instead of using the usual iterative strategy, we introduce a non-iterative one that relies on an optical flow technique to estimate 2D-to-2D correspondences between an image rendered using the object's 3D model in the estimated pose and the target image. The required pose correction between the rough estimate and the correct one can then be computed algebraically using a PnP algorithm. Figure 3 depicts our complete framework.

3.1   Data-Limited Pose Initialization

Most pose refinement methods [23,25,51] assume that rough pose estimates are provided by another approach trained on a combination of real and synthetic data [49], often augmented in some manner [10,14,32]. In our data-limited scenarios, real images may not be available, and we have to rely on synthetic images alone to train the initial pose estimation network.

We will show in the results section that it requires very substantial augmentations for methods trained on synthetic data alone to generalize to real data, and that they only do so with a low precision. In practice, this is what we use to obtain our initial poses.

3.2   From Optical Flow to Pose Refinement

Given an imprecise estimate of the initial pose, we seek to refine it. To this end, instead of directly regressing a 6D pose correction from an image rendered using the pose estimate, we train a network to output a dense 2D-to-2D correspondence field between the rendered image and the target one, that is, to estimate optical flow [42]. From these dense 2D correspondences, we can then algebraically compute the 6D pose correction using a PnP algorithm. In the results section, we will show that this approach generalizes reliably to real images even when trained only on synthetic ones.

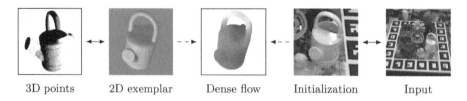

| 3D points | 2D exemplar | Dense flow | Initialization | Input |

Fig. 4. Establishing 3D-to-2D correspondences from exemplars. After retrieving an exemplar based on the initial pose, we estimate the 2D-to-2D correspondences between the exemplar and the input image within their respective region of interest. This implicitly generates a set of 3D-to-2D correspondences.

More formally, let $\mathbf{I}^t$ be the image of the target object and let $\mathbf{I}^r$ be the one rendered using the rough pose estimate. We train a network to predict the 2D flow image $\mathbf{F}^{r \to t}$ such that

$$\forall i \in \mathcal{M}, \quad \mathbf{u}_i^t = \mathbf{u}_i^r + \mathbf{f}_i^{r \to t}, \tag{1}$$

where $\mathcal{M}$ contains the indices of the pixels in $\mathbf{I}^r$ for which a corresponding pixel in $\mathbf{I}^t$ exists, $\mathbf{u}_i^t$ and $\mathbf{u}_i^r$ denote the pixel locations of matching points in both images, and $\mathbf{f}_i^{r \to t}$ is the corresponding 2D flow vector.

Because $\mathbf{I}^r$ has been rendered using a known 6D pose, the 2D image locations $\mathbf{u}^r$ are in known correspondence with 3D object points $\mathbf{p}$. Specifically, the 3D point $\mathbf{p}_i$ corresponding to the 2D location $\mathbf{u}_i^r$ can be obtained by intersecting the camera ray passing through $\mathbf{u}_i^r$ and the 3D mesh model transformed by the initial 6D pose [18], as shown in the left of Fig. 4. For each such correspondence, which we denote as $\{\mathbf{p}_i \leftrightarrow \mathbf{u}_i^r\}$, we have

$$\lambda_i \begin{bmatrix} \mathbf{u}_i^r \\ 1 \end{bmatrix} = \mathbf{K}(\mathbf{R}\mathbf{p}_i + \mathbf{t}), \tag{2}$$

where λ_i is a scale factor encoding depth, $\mathbf{K}$ is the matrix of camera intrinsic parameters, and $\mathbf{R}$ and $\mathbf{t}$ are the rotation matrix and translation vector representing the 6D pose.

To simplify the discussion, let us for now assume that the intrinsic matrix $\mathbf{K}$ used to render $\mathbf{I}^r$ is the same as that of the real camera, which is assumed to be known by most 6D pose estimation methods. We will discuss the more general case in Sect. 3.4. Under this assumption, the flow vectors predicted for an input image provide us with 2D-to-3D correspondences between the input image and the 3D model. That is, for two image locations $(\mathbf{u}_i^t, \mathbf{u}_i^r)$ deemed to be in correspondence according to the optical flow, we have

$$\{\mathbf{p}_i \leftrightarrow \mathbf{u}_i^r\} \Leftrightarrow \{\mathbf{p}_i \leftrightarrow \mathbf{u}_i^t\}. \tag{3}$$

Given enough such 3D-to-2D correspondences, the 6D pose in the input image can be obtained algebraically using a PnP algorithm [24]. In other words, we transform the pose refinement problem as a 2D optical flow one, and the 3D-to-2D correspondence errors will depend only on the 2D flow field $\mathbf{f}^{r \to t}$. Figure 5 shows an example of dense correspondences between the synthetic and real domains.

3.3 Exemplar-Based Flow Aggregation

The above-mentioned flow-based strategy suffers from the fact that it relies on an expensive rendering procedure, which slows down both training and testing. To address this, we use exemplars rendered offline. Instead of synthesizing the image from the initial pose directly, which requires on-the-fly rendering, we then retrieve the exemplar with 6D pose nearest to the initial pose estimate and compute the 2D displacements between this exemplar and the input image.

Exemplar   PBR input   Real input   Prediction   Ground truth

Fig. 5. Estimating dense 2D-to-2D correspondences across domains. We train a flow network to model the differences of images rendered using OpenGL (Exemplar) and using a PBR (Physically-based rendering) technique, respectively. Although our network accesses no real data during training, it generalizes well to estimating the flow between the exemplar and a real input image, as shown in the last two subfigures.

The resulting speed increase comes at the cost of a slight accuracy loss. However, it is compensated by the fact that this approach enables to exploit *multiple* rendered views, while only needing a single input image. That is, we do not use a single exemplar but multiple ones rendered from different viewpoints to make our pose refinement more robust. During inference, we use the initial pose to find the N closest exemplars and combine their optical flow. In short, instead of having one set of 3D-to-2D correspondences, we now have N such sets, which we write as

$$\{\mathbf{p}_{k,i} \leftrightarrow \mathbf{u}_{k,i}^t\} \quad 1 \leq i \leq n_k , \quad k \in \{1, \ldots, N\} , \tag{4}$$

where n_k is the number of correspondences found for exemplar k. Because the exemplars may depict significantly different viewpoints, this allows us to aggregate more information and adds both robustness and accuracy, as depicted by Fig. 6. Finally, we use a RANSAC-based PnP algorithm [24] to derive the final pose based on these complementary correspondences.

3.4 Dealing with Small Objects

In practice, even when using multiple exemplars, the approach described above may suffer from the fact that estimating the optical flow of small objects is

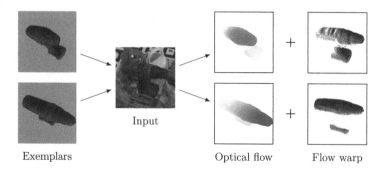

Exemplars   Optical flow   Flow warp

Fig. 6. Multi-view flow aggregation. The multiple exemplars provide 3D-to-2D correspondences that are complementary since they are rendered from different viewpoints. These correspondences are then combined to make the final pose estimates more robust.

challenging. To tackle this, inspired by other refinement methods [23,25,51], we work on image crops around the objects. Specifically, because we know the ground-truth pose for the exemplars and have a rough pose estimate for the input image, we can define 2D transformation matrices $\mathbf{M}_r$ and $\mathbf{M}_t$ that will map the object region in the exemplar and in the input image to a common size. We can then compute the flow between the resulting transformed images.

Formally, let $\tilde{\mathbf{u}}_i^r = \mathbf{M}_r \mathbf{u}_i^r$ be an exemplar 2D image location after transformation. Furthermore, accounting for the fact that the intrinsic camera matrices used to render the exemplars and acquire the input image may differ, let $\tilde{\mathbf{u}}_i^t = \mathbf{M}_t \mathbf{K}_r \mathbf{K}_t^{-1} \mathbf{u}_i^t$ be an input image location after transformation, where $\mathbf{K}_r$ is the intrinsic matrix used for the exemplars and $\mathbf{K}_t$ the one corresponding to the input image. We then estimate a flow field $\{\tilde{\mathbf{f}}_i^{r \to t} = \tilde{\mathbf{u}}_i^t - \tilde{\mathbf{u}}_i^r\}$ using the flow network. For two transformed image locations $(\tilde{\mathbf{u}}_i^t, \tilde{\mathbf{u}}_i^r)$ found to be in correspondence, following the discussion in Sect. 3.2, we can establish 3D-to-2D correspondences in the transformed image as

$$\{\mathbf{p}_i \leftrightarrow \tilde{\mathbf{u}}_i^r\} \Leftrightarrow \{\mathbf{p}_i \leftrightarrow \tilde{\mathbf{u}}_i^t\} . \tag{5}$$

We depict this procedure in Fig. 4. We can then recover the corresponding $\mathbf{u}_i^r$ in the original input image by applying the inverse transformation, which then lets us combine the correspondences from multiple exemplars.

3.5 Implementation Details

We use the WDR-Pose network [14] as our initialization network, and RAFT [42] as our 2D correspondence network. We first train WDR-Pose on the BOP synthetic data [7,9], which contains multiple rendered objects and severe occlusions in each frame to simulate real images. Before training the flow network, we generate a set of exemplars for each object type by offline rendering. To avoid computing a huge set of exemplars by densely sampling the 6D pose space, we fix the 3D translation and randomly sample a small set of 3D rotations. Specifically, we set the 3D translation to $(0, 0, \bar{z})$, where $\bar{z}$ is approximately the average depth of the working range. In our experiments, we found that 10K exemplars for each object type yields a good accuracy. We generate our exemplar images using the method of [18] with a fixed light direction pointing from the camera center to the object center.

To build image pairs to train the flow network, we pick one image from the exemplar set and the other from the BOP synthetic dataset. Specifically, we query the closest exemplar in terms of 6D pose. To simulate the actual query process, we first add some pose jitter to the target instance. Specifically we add a random rotation angle within 20° and a random translation leading to a reprojection offset smaller than 10 pixels. Note that this randomness only affects the query procedure; it does not affect the supervision of the flow network, which relies on the selected exemplar and the synthetic image.

In practice, to account for small objects, we first extract the object instances from the exemplar and target images using the transformation matrices $\mathbf{M}_r$ and $\mathbf{M}_t$ discussed above. We then resize the resulting object crops to 256×256 and build the ground-truth flow according to Eq. 5. We only supervise the flow of pixels located within the exemplar's object mask. Furthermore, during training, we also discard all pixels without explicit correspondence because of occlusions or because they fall outside the crops.

Finally, during training, we apply two main categories of data augmentation techniques. The first is noise (NS) augmentation. We add a random value between -25 to 25 to the pixels in each image channel. We then blur the resulting image with a random kernel size between 1 and 5. The second is color (HSV) augmentation. We convert the input image from RGB to HSV and add random jitter to each channel. Specifically, we add 20%, 50%, 50% of the maximum value of each channel as the random noise to the H, S, and V channel, respectively. We then convert the image back to RGB.

4   Experiments

In this section, we first compare our approach to the state of the art on standard datasets including LINEMOD ("LM") [6], Occluded-LINEMOD ("OLM") [22] and YCB-V ("YCB") [49]. We then evaluate the influence of different components of our refinement network. We defer the evaluation of the initialization network trained only on synthetic data to Sect. 4.3. The source code is publicly available at https://github.com/cvlab-epfl/perspective-flow-aggregation.

Datasets and Experimental Settings. LINEMOD comprises 13 sequences. Each one contains a single object annotated with the ground-truth pose. There are about 1.2K images for each sequence. We train our model only on the exemplars and the BOP synthetic dataset, and test it on 85% of the real LINEMOD data as in [25,33]. We keep the remaining 15% as supplementary real data for our ablation studies. Occluded-LINEMOD has 8 objects, which are a subset of the

LINEMOD ones. It contains only 1214 images for testing, with multiple objects in the same image and severe occlusions, making it much more challenging.

Most methods train their models for LINEMOD and Occluded-LINEMOD separately [11,26], sometimes even one model per object [32,47], which yields better accuracy but is less flexible and does not scale well. As these two datasets share the same 3D meshes, we train a single model for all 13 objects and test it on LINEMOD and Occluded-LINEMOD without retraining. When testing on Occluded-LINEMOD, we only report the accuracy of the corresponding 8 objects. We show that our model still outperforms most methods despite this generalization that makes it more flexible.

YCB-V is a more recent dataset that contains 92 video sequences and about 130K real images depicting 21 objects in cluttered scenes with many occlusions and complex lighting conditions. As for LINEMOD, unless stated otherwise, we train our model only on the exemplars and the BOP synthetic dataset and test on the real data.

Table 1. Comparing against the state of the art. Our method trained without accessing any real images (+0) performs on par with most methods that use *all* real data (hundreds of images per object for LM and OLM, and thousands for YCB). After accessing only 20 real images per object (+20), our method yields the best results.

Data	Metrics	PoseCNN	SegDriven	PVNet	GDR-Net	DeepIM	CosyPose	Ours (+0)	Ours (+20)
LM	ADD-0.1d	62.7	–	86.3	93.7	88.6	–	84.5	**94.4**
OLM	ADD-0.1d	24.9	27.0	40.8	62.2	55.5	–	48.2	**64.1**
YCB	ADD-0.1d	21.3	39.0	–	60.1	–	–	56.4	**62.8**
	AUC	61.3	–	73.4	84.4	81.9	84.5	76.8	**84.9**

Evaluation Metrics. We compute the 3D error as the average distance between 3D points on the object surface transformed by the predicted pose and by the ground-truth one. We then report the standard ADD-0.1d metric [49], that is, the percentage of samples whose 3D error is below 10% of the object diameter. For more detailed comparisons, we use ADD-0.5d, which uses a larger threshold of 50%. Furthermore, to compare with other methods on YCB-V, we also report the AUC metric as in [23,32,47], which varies the threshold with a maximum of 10cm and accumulates the area under the accuracy curve. For symmetric objects, the 3D error is taken to be the distance of each 3D point to its nearest model point after pose transformation.

4.1 Comparison with the State of the Art

We now compare our method to the state-of-the-art ones, PoseCNN [49], Seg-Driven [11], PVNet [32], GDR-Net [47], DeepIM [25], and CosyPose [23], where DeepIM and CosyPose are two refinement methods based on an iterative strategy. We train our initialization network WDR-Pose only on synthetic data and use its predictions as initial poses. To train the optical flow network, we generate 10K exemplars for each object and use the $N = 4$ closest exemplars during

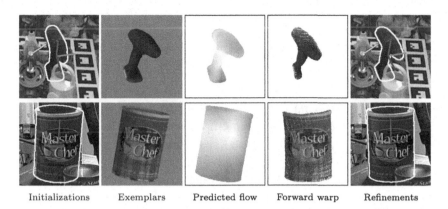

| Initializations | Exemplars | Predicted flow | Forward warp | Refinements |

Fig. 7. Visualization of the results. Although the predicted flows contain some errors (e.g., the flow at the bottom of the drill, which is occluded), aggregating multiple flows and using a RANSAC-based PnP make the final pose estimation robust. Here we show results obtained with one exemplar and by training purely on synthetic data.

| Annotation | Reprojection | Difference | Our result |

Fig. 8. An example of inaccurate annotation in YCB-V. The last two images show the difference between the input and the reprojection image rendered from the corresponding pose. Our predicted pose aligns the object more accurately here.

inference. As shown in Table 1, even without accessing any real images during training, our method already outperforms most of the baselines, which all use real training data, and performs on par with the most recent ones. Figure 7 depicts some qualitative results. Note that YCB-V contains some inaccurate pose annotations, and, as shown in Fig. 8, we sometimes predict more accurate poses than the annotations, even when training without accessing any real data.

In Table 1, we also report the results we obtain by adding 20 real images to the synthetic ones during the training of our refinement network. In this case, we train each model by mixing the BOP synthetic data with the real images, balancing their ratio to be 0.5:0.5 by dynamic sampling during training. Note that we still use the same pose initializations trained only on synthetic images. With only 20 real images, our method outperforms all the baselines by a significant margin, even though they all use *all* the real images during training.

Most existing refinement methods, including DeepIM and CosyPose, employ pose initializations trained using all real images, which is impractical in our data-limited scenario. To have a fair comparison of our refinement method with

Table 2. Comparing different refinement frameworks on OLM. We train the models with different numbers of additional real images. With as few as 20 real images, our model achieves even higher accuracy than the baselines with more than 100 real images.

	0	10	20	90	180
DeepIM	41.1	45.6	48.2	58.1	61.4
CosyPose	42.4	46.8	48.9	58.8	61.9
Ours	**48.2**	**59.5**	**64.1**	**64.9**	**65.3**

Table 3. Pose refinement with different initializations on LM. With only one exemplar ($N = 1$), our refinement framework already yields a significant improvement over the initialization. More exemplars make it more accurate.

Initialization		$N = 1$	$N = 2$	$N = 4$	$N = 8$
NS	54.1	82.0	82.7	**84.3**	84.1
HSV	52.7	81.1	81.2	83.3	**83.9**
NS+HSV	60.2	82.0	83.4	84.5	**84.9**
FPS		~32	~25	~20	~14

them, we use the same synthetic-only pose initializations for them as for our approach. We then train the refinement networks according to their open-source official code, based on synthetic data only. Furthermore, we also evaluate them when trained with different numbers of additional real images. Note that, while CosyPose can use multiple views as input, we only evaluate it in the monocular case to make it comparable with the other methods. In Table 2, we report the ADD-0.1d on the challenging Occluded-LINEMOD dataset. As expected, using more real images yields more accurate pose estimates for all methods. However, with as few as 20 real images, our model achieves even higher accuracy than the baselines with more than 100 real images. Since all methods use the same initial poses, giving an accuracy of 37.9%, as shown in Table 5, this means that DeepIM and CosyPose can only increase the initialization accuracy by 3–4% when not accessing any real image data. By contrast, our method increases accuracy by over 10% in this case, demonstrating the robustness of our method to the domain gap in cluttered scenarios.

4.2   Ablation Studies

Let us now analyze more thoroughly the exemplar-based flow aggregation in our pose refinement framework. To this end, we conduct more ablation studies on the standard LINEMOD dataset. We train our refinement model only on synthetic data [9], and report ADD-0.1d accuracies on real test data.

Flow Aggregation. We first evaluate our flow aggregation strategy given different pose initializations. We use three initialization sets with varying levels of accuracy, corresponding to the results from the initialization network under NS, HSV, and NS+HSV augmentations, respectively. Furthermore, we evaluate the accuracy using different numbers of retrieved exemplars, also reporting the corresponding running speed on a typical workstation with a 3.5G CPU and an NVIDIA V100 GPU.

As shown in Table 3, the refinement network improves the accuracy of the initial pose significantly even with only one exemplar. More exemplars boost it further, thanks to the complementarity of their different viewpoints. Interestingly, although the different pose initializations have very different pose accuracies, they all reach a similar accuracy after our pose refinement, demonstrating the robustness of our refinement network to different initial poses. As the exemplars can be processed in parallel, the running time with 4 exemplars is only about 1.6 slower than that with a single exemplar. This slight speed decrease is related to the throughput of the GPU and could be optimized further in principle. Nevertheless, our approach is still more than 3 times faster than the iterative DeepIM [25] method, which runs at only about 6 FPS using 4 iterations. Since the version with 8 exemplars yields only a small improvement over the one with 4 exemplars, we use $N = 4$ in the previous experiments. Furthermore, we use the results of NS+HSV for pose initialization.

Exemplar Set. While using an exemplar set eliminates the need for online rendering, the accuracy of our approach depends on its granularity, leading to a tradeoff between accuracy and IO storage/speed. We therefore evaluate the performance of our approach with varying numbers of exemplars during inference. To better understand the query process, we also report the numbers just after the query but before the refinement, denoted as "Before Ref.".

Table 4. Effect of exemplar sets of different sizes on LM. An exemplar set with less than 5K exemplars suffers from the large distance between the nearest exemplars. By contrast, using more than 10K exemplars does not bring much improvement.

	2.5K	5K	10K	20K	40K	Online
Before Ref	55.2	57.0	58.0	58.9	59.9	**60.2**
After Ref	81.9	83.2	84.5	**85.0**	84.8	84.9
Image preparation	16 ms	19 ms	29 ms	52 ms	81 ms	184 ms

Table 4 shows that larger exemplar sets yield more accurate queries before the refinement, leading to more accurate pose refinement results. Note that because we have a discrete set of exemplars, the ADD-0.1d scores before refinement are lower than those obtained by on-the-fly rendering from the initial pose, which reaches 60.2%. While fewer exemplars in the set translates to lower accuracy before refinement, the accuracy after refinement saturates beyond 10K exemplars, reaching a similar performance to online rendering. We therefore use 10K exemplars for each object in the previous experiments. This only requires about

200MB of disk space for storing the exemplar set for each object. We also report the timings of image preparation for each setting. Although there is a powerful GPU for the online rendering, our offline exemplar retrieval is much faster.

4.3   Pose Initialization Network

We now evaluate our pose initialization network based on WDR-Pose [14]. Unlike in [14], we train it only on the BOP synthetic data [7,9] and study the performance on real images. To fill the domain gap between the synthetic and real domains, we use simple data augmentation strategies during training.

Specifically, we evaluate 3 groups of data augmentations. The first one consists of random shifts, scales, and rotations within a range of $(-50\,\mathrm{px}, 50\,\mathrm{px})$, $(0.9, 1.1)$, and $(-45°, 45°)$, respectively. We refer to this as SSR augmentations. The second group incudes random noise and smoothness, and corresponds to the NS augmentations discussed in Sect. 4.2. The final group performs color augmentations, and corresponds to the HSV augmentations presented in Sect. 4.2.

Table 5. Data augmentation in pose initialization. We study both geometric (SSR) and non-geometric (NS, HSV) augmentation strategies for pose initialization trained only on synthetic data but tested on real images.

Data	Metrics	No	SSR	NS	HSV	NS+HSV
LM	ADD-0.1d	48.9	39.0	56.6	58.1	**60.2**
	ADD-0.5d	93.2	80.7	98.8	97.0	**98.9**
OLM	ADD-0.1d	28.6	20.9	36.0	34.4	**37.9**
	ADD-0.5d	74.8	69.2	83.0	81.3	**86.1**
YCB	ADD-0.1d	0.1	0	17.0	7.4	**27.5**
	ADD-0.5d	2.9	0	59.0	36.6	**72.3**

Table 5 summarizes the results of the model trained with these different data augmentations on LINEMOD, Occluded-LINEMOD, and YCB-V. We report the accuracy in terms of both ADD-0.1d and ADD-0.5d. In short, training on synthetic data without data augmentation ("No") yields poor performance on the real test data, with an accuracy of almost zero in both metrics on the YCB-V dataset. Interestingly, although the NS and HSV augmentations can considerably increase the performance, the SSR augmentations degrade it consistently on all three datasets. We believe this to be due to the geometric nature of the SSR augmentations. More precisely, after shifting, scaling, or rotating the input image, the resulting inputs do not truly correspond to the original 6D poses, which inevitably introduces errors in the learning process. However, the NS and HSV augmentations do not suffer from this problem, as the ground-truth annotations before and after augmentation are the same.

Note that, although the NS and HSV augmentations significantly outperform no augmentation, the accuracy remains rather low in terms of ADD-0.1d.

However, the ADD-0.5d numbers evidence that most of the predictions have an error of less than 50% of the diameter of the object. This indicates that the resulting rough initialization can indeed serve as a good starting point for our pose refinements, as demonstrated before.

5   Conclusion

We have introduced a simple non-iterative pose refinement strategy that can be trained only on synthetic data and yet still produce good results on real images. It relies on the intuition that, using data augmentation, one can obtain a rough initial pose from a network trained on synthetic images, and that this initialization can be refined by predicting dense 2D-to-2D correspondences between an image rendered in approximately the initial pose and the input image. Our experiments have demonstrated that our approach yields results on par with the state-of-the-art methods that were trained on real data, even when we don't use any real images, and outperforms these methods when we access as few as 20 images. In other words, our approach provides an effective and efficient strategy for data-limited 6D pose estimation. Nevertheless, our method remains a two-stage framework, which may limit its performance. In the future, we will therefore investigate the use of a differentiable component to replace RANSAC PnP and make our method end-to-end trainable.

Acknowledgment. This work was supported by the Swiss Innovation Agency (Innosuisse). We would like to thank Sébastien Speierer and Wenzel Jakob in EPFL Realistic Graphics Lab (RGLab) for the helpful discussions on rendering.

References

1. Cui, S., Wang, S., Zhuo, J., Su, C., Huang, Q., Tian, Q.: Gradually vanishing bridge for adversarial domain adaptation. In: Conference on Computer Vision and Pattern Recognition (2020)
2. Di, Y., Manhardt, F., Wang, G., Ji, X., Navab, N., Tombari, F.: SO-pose: exploiting self-occlusion for direct 6D pose estimation. In: International Conference on Computer Vision (2021)
3. Ferraz, L., Binefa, X., Moreno-Noguer, F.: Very fast solution to the pnp problem with algebraic outlier rejection. In: Conference on Computer Vision and Pattern Recognition, pp. 501–508 (2014)
4. Gu, X., Sun, J., Xu, Z.: Spherical space domain adaptation with robust pseudo-label loss. In: Conference on Computer Vision and Pattern Recognition (2020)
5. Gulrajani, I., Lopez-Paz, D.: In search of lost domain generalization. In: International Conference on Learning Representations (2021)
6. Hinterstoisser, S., et al.: Model based training, detection and pose estimation of texture-less 3D objects in heavily cluttered scenes. In: Lee, K.M., Matsushita, Y., Rehg, J.M., Hu, Z. (eds.) ACCV 2012. LNCS, vol. 7724, pp. 548–562. Springer, Heidelberg (2013). https://doi.org/10.1007/978-3-642-37331-2_42

7. Hodaň, T., et al.: BOP: benchmark for 6D object pose estimation. In: Ferrari, V., Hebert, M., Sminchisescu, C., Weiss, Y. (eds.) ECCV 2018. LNCS, vol. 11214, pp. 19–35. Springer, Cham (2018). https://doi.org/10.1007/978-3-030-01249-6_2

8. Hodan, T., Barath, D., Matas, J.: EPOS: estimating 6D pose of objects with symmetries. In: Conference on Computer Vision and Pattern Recognition (2020)

9. Hodan, T., et al.: Photorealistic image synthesis for object instance detection. In: International Conference on Image Processing (2019)

10. Hu, Y., Fua, P., Wang, W., Salzmann, M.: Single-stage 6D object pose estimation. In: Conference on Computer Vision and Pattern Recognition (2020)

11. Hu, Y., Hugonot, J., Fua, P., Salzmann, M.: Segmentation-driven 6D object pose estimation. In: Conference on Computer Vision and Pattern Recognition (2019)

12. Hu, Y., Li, Y., Song, R.: Robust interpolation of correspondences for large displacement optical flow. In: Conference on Computer Vision and Pattern Recognition (2017)

13. Hu, Y., Song, R., Li, Y.: Efficient coarse-to-fine PatchMatch for large displacement optical flow. In: Conference on Computer Vision and Pattern Recognition (2016)

14. Hu, Y., Speierer, S., Jakob, W., Fua, P., Salzmann, M.: Wide-depth-range 6D object pose estimation in space. In: Conference on Computer Vision and Pattern Recognition (2021)

15. Ilg, E., Mayer, N., Saikia, T., Keuper, M., Dosovitskiy, A., Brox, T.: FlowNet 2.0: evolution of optical flow estimation with deep networks. In: Conference on Computer Vision and Pattern Recognition (2017)

16. Hosseini Jafari, O., Mustikovela, S.K., Pertsch, K., Brachmann, E., Rother, C.: iPose: instance-aware 6D pose estimation of partly occluded objects. In: Jawahar, C.V., Li, H., Mori, G., Schindler, K. (eds.) ACCV 2018. LNCS, vol. 11363, pp. 477–492. Springer, Cham (2019). https://doi.org/10.1007/978-3-030-20893-6_30

17. Joshi, B., et al.: DeepURL: deep pose estimation framework for underwater relative localization. In: International Conference on Intelligent Robots and Systems (2020)

18. Kato, H., Ushiku, Y., Harada, T.: Neural 3D mesh renderer. In: Conference on Computer Vision and Pattern Recognition (2018)

19. Kehl, W., Manhardt, F., Tombari, F., Ilic, S., Navab, N.: SSD-6D: Making RGB-based 3D detection and 6D pose estimation great again. In: International Conference on Computer Vision (2017)

20. Kisantal, M., Sharma, S., Park, T.H., Izzo, D., Märtens, M., D'Amico, S.: Satellite pose estimation challenge: dataset, competition design and results. IEEE Trans. Aerosp. Electron. Syst. **56**, 4083–4098 (2020)

21. Kneip, L., Li, H., Seo, Y.: UPnP: an optimal $O(n)$ solution to the absolute pose problem with universal applicability. In: Fleet, D., Pajdla, T., Schiele, B., Tuytelaars, T. (eds.) ECCV 2014. LNCS, vol. 8689, pp. 127–142. Springer, Cham (2014). https://doi.org/10.1007/978-3-319-10590-1_9

22. Krull, A., Brachmann, E., Michel, F., Yang, M.Y., Gumhold, S., Rother, C.: Learning analysis-by-synthesis for 6D pose estimation in RGB-D images. In: International Conference on Computer Vision (2015)

23. Labbé, Y., Carpentier, J., Aubry, M., Sivic, J.: CosyPose: consistent multi-view multi-object 6D pose estimation. In: Vedaldi, A., Bischof, H., Brox, T., Frahm, J.-M. (eds.) ECCV 2020. LNCS, vol. 12362, pp. 574–591. Springer, Cham (2020). https://doi.org/10.1007/978-3-030-58520-4_34

24. Lepetit, V., Moreno-Noguer, F., Fua, P.: EPnP: an accurate O(n) solution to the PnP problem. Int. J. Comput. Vision **81**, 155–166 (2009)

25. Li, Y., Wang, G., Ji, X., Xiang, Yu., Fox, D.: DeepIM: deep iterative matching for 6D pose estimation. In: Ferrari, V., Hebert, M., Sminchisescu, C., Weiss, Y. (eds.) ECCV 2018. LNCS, vol. 11210, pp. 695–711. Springer, Cham (2018). https://doi.org/10.1007/978-3-030-01231-1_42

26. Li, Z., Wang, G., Ji, X.: CDPN: coordinates-based disentangled pose network for real-time RGB-based 6-DoF object pose estimation. In: International Conference on Computer Vision (2019)

27. Lowe, D.G.: Distinctive image features from scale-invariant keypoints. Int. J. Comput. Vision **20**(2), 91–110 (2004)

28. Manhardt, F., Kehl, W., Navab, N., Tombari, F.: Deep model-based 6D pose refinement in RGB. In: Ferrari, V., Hebert, M., Sminchisescu, C., Weiss, Y. (eds.) Computer Vision – ECCV 2018. LNCS, vol. 11218, pp. 833–849. Springer, Cham (2018). https://doi.org/10.1007/978-3-030-01264-9_49

29. Oberweger, M., Rad, M., Lepetit, V.: Making deep heatmaps robust to partial occlusions for 3D object pose estimation. In: Ferrari, V., Hebert, M., Sminchisescu, C., Weiss, Y. (eds.) ECCV 2018. LNCS, vol. 11219, pp. 125–141. Springer, Cham (2018). https://doi.org/10.1007/978-3-030-01267-0_8

30. Pan, F., Shin, I., Rameau, F., Lee, S., Kweon, I.: Unsupervised intra-domain adaptation for semantic segmentation through self-supervision. In: Conference on Computer Vision and Pattern Recognition (2020)

31. Park, K., Patten, T., Vincze, M.: Pix2Pose: pixel-wise coordinate regression of objects for 6d pose estimation. In: International Conference on Computer Vision (2019)

32. Peng, S., Liu, Y., Huang, Q., Zhou, X., Bao, H.: PVNet: pixel-wise voting network for 6dof pose estimation. In: Conference on Computer Vision and Pattern Recognition (2019)

33. Rad, M., Lepetit, V.: BB8: a scalable, accurate, robust to partial occlusion method for predicting the 3D poses of challenging objects without using depth. In: International Conference on Computer Vision (2017)

34. Rad, M., Oberweger, M., Lepetit, V.: Feature mapping for learning fast and accurate 3D pose inference from synthetic images. In: Conference on Computer Vision and Pattern Recognition (2018)

35. Revaud, J., Weinzaepfel, P., Harchaoui, Z., Schmid, C.: EpicFlow: edge-preserving interpolation of correspondences for optical flow. In: Conference on Computer Vision and Pattern Recognition (2015)

36. Risholm, P., Ivarsen, P.O., Haugholt, K.H., Mohammed, A.: Underwater marker-based pose-estimation with associated uncertainty. In: International Conference on Computer Vision (2021)

37. Sock, J., Garcia-Hernando, G., Armagan, A., Kim, T.K.: Introducing pose consistency and warp-alignment for self-supervised 6d object pose estimation in color images. In: International Conference on 3D Vision (2020)

38. Song, C., Song, J., Huang, Q.: HybridPose: 6D object pose estimation under hybrid representations. In: Conference on Computer Vision and Pattern Recognition (2020)

39. Sun, D., Yang, X., Liu, M., Kautz, J.: PWC-Net: CNNs for optical flow using pyramid, warping, and cost volume. In: Conference on Computer Vision and Pattern Recognition (2018)

40. Sundermeyer, M., et al.: Multi-path learning for object pose estimation across domains. In: Conference on Computer Vision and Pattern Recognition (2020)

41. Tang, H., Chen, K., Jia, K.: Unsupervised domain adaptation via structurally regularized deep clustering. In: Conference on Computer Vision and Pattern Recognition (2020)

42. Teed, Z., Deng, J.: RAFT: recurrent all-pairs field transforms for optical flow. In: Vedaldi, A., Bischof, H., Brox, T., Frahm, J.-M. (eds.) ECCV 2020. LNCS, vol. 12347, pp. 402–419. Springer, Cham (2020). https://doi.org/10.1007/978-3-030-58536-5_24

43. Tekin, B., Sinha, S.N., Fua, P.: Real-time seamless single shot 6D object pose prediction. In: Conference on Computer Vision and Pattern Recognition (2018)

44. Tola, E., Lepetit, V., Fua, P.: DAISY: an efficient dense descriptor applied to wide baseline stereo. IEEE Trans. Pattern Anal. Mach. Intell. **32**(5), 815–830 (2010)

45. Trzcinski, T., Christoudias, C.M., Lepetit, V., Fua, P.: Learning image descriptors with the boosting-trick. In: Advances in Neural Information Processing Systems (2012)

46. Wang, C., et al.: DenseFusion: 6D object pose estimation by iterative dense fusion. In: Conference on Computer Vision and Pattern Recognition (2019)

47. Wang, G., Manhardt, F., Tombari, F., Ji, X.: GDR-Net: geometry-guided direct regression network for monocular 6D object pose estimation. In: Conference on Computer Vision and Pattern Recognition (2021)

48. Wang, Z., Luo, Y., Qiu, R., Huang, Z., Baktashmotlagh, M.: Learning to diversify for single domain generalization. In: International Conference on Computer Vision (2021)

49. Xiang, Y., Schmidt, T., Narayanan, V., Fox, D.: PoseCNN: a convolutional neural network for 6D object pose estimation in cluttered scenes. In: Robotics: Science and Systems Conference (2018)

50. Xu, Q., Zhang, R., Zhang, Y., Wang, Y., Tian, Q.: A Fourier-based framework for domain generalization. In: Conference on Computer Vision and Pattern Recognition (2021)

51. Zakharov, S., Shugurov, I., Ilic, S.: DPOD: 6D pose object detector and refiner. In: International Conference on Computer Vision (2019)

52. Zheng, Y., Kuang, Y., Sugimoto, S., Åström, K., Okutomi, M.: Revisiting the PnP problem: a fast, general and optimal solution. In: International Conference on Computer Vision (2013)

53. Zhou, K., Yang, Y., Qiao, Y., Xiang, T.: Domain generalization with mixstyle. In: International Conference on Learning Representations (2021)

DANBO: Disentangled Articulated Neural Body Representations via Graph Neural Networks

Shih-Yang Su[1]([⊠]), Timur Bagautdinov[2], and Helge Rhodin[1]

[1] University of British Columbia, Vancouver, Canada
shihyang@cs.ubc.ca
[2] Reality Labs Research, Pittsburgh, USA

Fig. 1. DANBO enables learning volumetric body models from scratch, only requiring a single video as input, yet enable driving by unseen poses (inset) that are out of the training distribution, showing better robustness than existing surface-free approaches. **Real faces are blurred for anonymity.**

Abstract. Deep learning greatly improved the realism of animatable human models by learning geometry and appearance from collections of 3D scans, template meshes, and multi-view imagery. High-resolution models enable photo-realistic avatars but at the cost of requiring studio settings not available to end users. Our goal is to create avatars directly from raw images without relying on expensive studio setups and surface tracking. While a few such approaches exist, those have limited generalization capabilities and are prone to learning spurious (chance) correlations between irrelevant body parts, resulting in implausible deformations and missing body parts on unseen poses. We introduce a three-stage method that induces two inductive biases to better disentangled pose-dependent deformation. First, we model correlations of body parts explicitly with a graph neural network. Second, to further reduce the effect of chance correlations, we introduce localized per-bone features that use a factorized volumetric representation and a new aggregation function. We demonstrate that our model produces realistic body shapes under challenging unseen poses and shows high-quality

Supplementary Information The online version contains supplementary material available at https://doi.org/10.1007/978-3-031-20086-1_7.

image synthesis. Our proposed representation strikes a better trade-off between model capacity, expressiveness, and robustness than competing methods. Project website: https://lemonatsu.github.io/danbo.

Keywords: 3D computer vision · Body models · Monocular · Neural fields · Deformation

1   Introduction

Animating real-life objects in the digital world is a long-pursued goal in computer vision and graphics, and recent advances already enable 3D free-viewpoint video, animation, and human performance retargeting [17,41,53]. Nevertheless, animating high-definition virtual avatars with user-specific appearance and dynamic motion still remains a challenge: human body and clothing deformation are inherently complex, unique, and modeling their intricate effects require dedicated approaches. Recent solutions achieve astonishing results [10,29,44,47,48] when grounding on 3D data capture in designated studio settings, e.g., with multi-camera capture systems and controlled illumination—inaccessible to the general public for building personalized models (Fig. 1).

Less restrictive are methods relying on parametric body models [31] that learn plausible body shape, pose, and deformation from a collection of 3D scans. These methods can thereby adapt to a wide range of body shapes [4,11,36], in particular when using neural approaches to model details as a dynamic corrective [6,8,14]. Even though subject-specific details such as clothing can be learned, it remains difficult to generalize to shapes vastly different from the original scans. Moreover, the most widely used body models have restrictive commercial licenses [31] and 3D scan datasets to train these afresh are expensive.

Our goal is to learn a high-quality model with subject-specific details directly from images. Recent approaches in this class [35,46] use a neural radiance field (NeRF) that is attached to a human skeleton initialized with an off-the-shelf 3D human pose estimator. Similar to the original NeRF, the shape and appearance are modeled implicitly with a neural network that takes as input a query location and outputs density and radiance, and is only supervised with images through differentiable volume rendering. However, unlike the original that models static scenes, articulated NeRFs model time-varying body shape deformations by conditioning on per-frame body pose and representing each frame with the same underlying body model albeit in a different state. This results in an animatable full-body model that is trained directly from videos and can then can be driven with novel skeleton poses.

Not using an explicit surface poses a major difficulty as surface-based solutions exploit surface points to anchor neural features locally as vertex attributes [41], and leverage skinning weights to associate points on or close to the surface to nearby body parts [29,40]. In absence of such constraints, A-NeRF [46] uses an overparametrization by encoding 3D position relative to all body parts. Thereby dependencies between a point and body parts are learned implicitly. By contrast, NARF [35] explicitly predicts probabilities for the association of 3D points to body parts, similar to NASA [15]. However, this probability predictor is conditioned on the entire skeleton pose and is itself prone to poor generalization. Therefore, both approaches rely on large training datasets and generalization to unseen poses is limited—in particular because unrelated body parts remain weakly entangled.

In this paper, we introduce *Disentangled Articulated Neural BOdy* (DANBO), a surface-free approach that explicitly disentangles independent body parts for learning a generalizable personalized human model from unlabelled videos. It extends the established articulated NeRF-based body modeling with two additional stages, a body part-specific volumetric encoding that exploits human skeleton structure as a prior using Graph Neural Networks (GNN) [23], and a new aggregation module. Both designs are tailored for learning from few examples and optimized to be parameter efficient. Our main contributions are the following:

- A surface-free human body model with better texture detail and improved generalization when animated.
- GNN-based encoding that disentangles features from different body parts and relies on factorized per-bone volumes for efficiency.
- A part-based feature aggregation strategy that improves on and is informed by a detailed evaluation of existing aggregation functions.

We demonstrate that our proposed DANBO results in a generalizable neural body model, with quality comparable to surface-based approaches.

2 Related Work

We start our review with general-purpose neural fields and then turn to human body modeling with a focus on animatable neural representations.

Neural Fields. Neural fields [34,37,45] have attracted recent attention due to their ability to capture astonishing levels of detail. Instead of relying on explicit geometry representations such as triangle meshes or voxel grids, these methods represent the scene implicitly - as a continuous function - that maps every point in the 3D space to quantities of interest such as radiance, density, or signed distance. This approach was popularized with Neural Radiance Fields (NeRF) [34] demonstrating impressive results on reconstructing static 3D scene presentation directly from calibrated multi-view images. Various subsequent works focused on improving performance on static scenes in terms of generalization [59], level of detail [5,38], camera self-calibration [27,57], and resource efficiency [28,58]. Most relevant are deformable models that capture non-static scenes with deformation fields [16,17,43,49,53]. However, general deformation fields are unsuitable for animation and no one demonstrated that they can generalize to strongly articulated motion in monocular video.

Template-Based Body Models. The highest level of detail can be attained with specialized performance capture systems, e.g., with dozens of cameras or a laser scanner [19]. The resulting template mesh can then be textured and deformed for capturing high-quality human performances, even from a single video [61]. Neural approaches further enable learning pose-dependent appearance and geometries [3], predict vertex displacements [20] or local primitive volumes [30] for creating fine-grained local geometry and appearance including cloth wrinkles and freckles. The most recent ones use neural fields to learn implicit body models with the mesh providing strong supervision signals [2,10,44,51,54]. However, template creation is limited to expensive controlled studio environments, often entails manual cleaning, and high-quality ground truth annotations.

Parametric Human Body Models. learn common shape and pose properties from a large corpus of 3D scans [4,11,31,36]. For classical approaches the result are factorized parameters for controlling pose, shape [11,31,36,55] and even clothing [47] that can fit to a new subject. Most prevalent is the SMPL [11,31] mesh model with a linear shape space and pose-dependent deformation. However, most existing models have restrictive commercial licenses and modeling person-specific details from images requires additional reconstruction steps.

Personalized Body Models. Learning personalized body models given only videos of a single actor is particularly challenging. Most existing approaches start from estimating a parametric surface model such as SMPL and extend it to learn specifics. For instance, one can anchor neural features spatially by associating each SMPL vertex with a learnable latent feature, and then either diffuse vertex features to the 3D space [26,41] or project the 3D query point to the SMPL surface for feature retrieval. Incorrect shape estimates and missing details can then be corrected by a subsequent neural rendering step. As texturing improves classical approaches, neural texture mapping provides additional rendering quality [29]. Another line of work makes use of SMPL blend skinning weights as initialization for learning deformation fields [40]. The deformation field maps 3D points from 3D world space to canonical space, which enables learning a canonical neural body field that predicts the radiance and density for rendering as for the classical NeRF on static scenes. While the skinning weights in SMPL provide an initialization, [40] showed that fine-tuning the deformation fields via self-supervision helps rendering unseen poses. However, relying on body models imposes the previously discussed limitations.

There are few methods that target learning neural body fields from images without relying on an explicit surface model. Closest to our method are NARF [35] and A-NeRF [46], that learn articulated body models directly from image sequences, leveraging 3D body pose estimates produced by off-the-shelf approaches [24,25]. These methods encode 3D query points with respect to each bone on the posed skeleton, and either explicitly predict blending weights [35] to select the parts of influence or rely on a neural network to learn the assignment implicitly by feeding it a large stack of all relative positions [46]. However, lacking a prior for part assignments leads to spurious dependencies between irrelevant

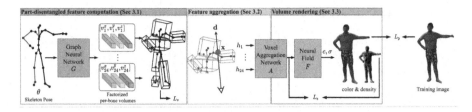

Fig. 2. Overview. The final image is generated via volume rendering by sampling points **x** along the ray **d** as in the original NeRF. Different is the conditioning on pose. First, pose features are encoded locally to every bone of a skeleton with a graph neural network using factorized volumes to increase efficiency (green boxes). Second, these disentangled features are queried and aggregated with learned weights (red module). Finally, the body shape and appearance are predicted via density and radiance fields σ and c (blue module). (Color figure online)

body parts when the training poses are scarce and have low diversity [3,44]. Our approach follows the same surface-free setting but improves upon these by introducing body part disentangled representations and a new aggregation function that achieves better rendering quality and improved generalization on novel body poses. A concurrent work COAP [33] shares a similar part-disentangle concept, but differs significantly. COAP models part geometries separately from 3D scans, whereas DANBO leverages the skeleton structure as a prior to fuse information from neighboring body parts, and learns both appearance and body geometry from images without 3D supervisions.

3 Method

Our goal is to learn an animatable avatar from a collections of N images $[\mathbf{I}_k]_{k=1}^{N}$ and the corresponding body pose in terms of skeleton joint angles $[\theta_k]_{k=1}^{N}$ that can stem from an off-the-shelf estimator [24,25], without using laser scans or surface tracking. We represent the human body as a neural field that moves with the input body pose. The neural field maps each 3D location to color and density to generate a free-viewpoint synthetic image via volume rendering. See Fig. 2 for an overview. Our approach consists of three stages that are trained end-to-end. The first stage predicts a localized volumetric representation for each body part with a Graph Neural Network (GNN). GNN has a limited receptive field and encodes only locally relevant pose information—which naturally leads to better disentangling between body parts in the absence of surface priors. This stage is independent of the query locations and is thus executed only once per frame. Additional performance is gained by using a factorized volume and encouraging the volume bounds to be compact. The second stage retrieves a feature code for each query point by sampling volume features for all body parts that enclose the point and then aggregating the relevant ones using a separate network that predicts blend weights. Finally, the third stage maps the resulting per-query feature code to the density and radiance at that location, followed by the volume rendering as in the original NeRF.

3.1   Stage I: Part-disentangled Feature Computation

Given a pose $\theta = [\omega_1, \omega_2, \cdots, \omega_{24}]$, where $\omega_i \in \mathbb{R}^6$ [62] defines the rotation of the bone $i = 1, 2, \cdots, 24$, we represent the body part attached to each bone i with a coarse volume V (green boxes in Fig. 2), predicted by a neural network G,

$$[V_1, V_2, \cdots, V_{24}] = G(\theta). \tag{1}$$

We design G as a GNN operating on the skeleton graph with nodes initialized to the corresponding joint angles in θ. In practice, we use two graph convolutional layers followed by per-node 2-layer MLPs. Because the human skeleton is irregular, we learn individual MLP weights for every node. See the supplemental for additional details on the graph network.

Factorized Volume. A straight-forward way to represent a volume is via a dense voxel grid, which has cubic complexity with respect to its resolution. Instead, we propose to factorize each volume $V_i = (v_i^x, v_i^y, v_i^z)$ as one vector $v_i \in \mathbf{R}^{H \times M}$ for each 3D axis, where H is the voxel feature channel, and is M the volume resolution. This is similar to [42] doing a factorization into 2D planes.

Figure 3 shows how to retrieve a feature for a given 3D point $\hat{\mathbf{x}}_i$ from the volume by projecting to each axis and interpolating,

$$h_i^x = v_i^x \left[s_i^x \hat{\mathbf{x}}_i(x) \right] \in \mathbf{R}^H, \tag{2}$$

where s_i^x is a learnable scaling factor to control the volume size along the x-axis, and $v_i^x [\cdot]$ returns the interpolated feature when the projected and scaled coordinate falls in $[-1, 1]$, and $\mathbf{0}$ otherwise. The extraction for y and z axes follows the same procedure.

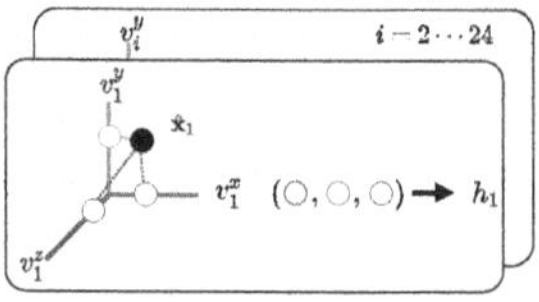

The GNN attaches one factorized volume to every bone i and is computed only once for every pose.

Fig. 3. We retrieve the voxel feature by projecting $\hat{\mathbf{x}}$ to the three axes and linearly interpolating the feature neighboring the projected location.

In Sect. 4.4, we show that the factorized volumes compare favorably against full 3D volumes on short video sequences with sparse or single views, while having 2x lower parameter counts.

3.2   Stage II: Global Feature Aggregation

Given a query location $\mathbf{x} \in \mathbf{R}^3$ in global coordinates, the corresponding voxel feature can be retrieved by first mapping the 3D points to the bone-relative space of i via the world-to-bone coordinates transformation $T(\omega_i)$,

$$\begin{bmatrix} \hat{\mathbf{x}}_i \\ 1 \end{bmatrix} = T(\omega_i) \begin{bmatrix} \mathbf{x} \\ 1 \end{bmatrix}, \tag{3}$$

and then retrieving the factorized features with equation Eq. 2. However, multiple volumes can overlap.

Windowed Bounds. To facilitate learning volume dimensions s_x that adapt to the body shape and to mitigate seam artifacts, we apply a window function

$$w_i = \exp(-\alpha(\hat{\mathbf{x}}_i(x)^\beta + \hat{\mathbf{x}}_i(y)^\beta + \hat{\mathbf{x}}_i(z)^\beta)) \tag{4}$$

that attenuates the feature value $h_i = w_i [h_i^x, h_i^y, h_i^z]$ for $\hat{\mathbf{x}}_i$ towards the boundary of the volume, with $\alpha = 2$ and $\beta = 6$ similar to [30]. Still, multiple volumes will overlap near joints and when body parts are in contact. Moreover, the overlap changes with varying skeleton pose, demanding for an explicit aggregation step.

Voxel Aggregation Network. Since an $\mathbf{x}$ that is close to the body falls into multiple volumes, we employ a voxel aggregation network A to decide which per-bone voxel features to pass on to the downstream neural field for rendering. We explore several strategies, and conduct ablation studies on each of the options. Our aggregation network A consists of a graph layer followed by per-node 2-layer MLPs with a small network width (32 per layer). We predict the weight p_i for the feature retrieved from bone i and compute the aggregated features via

$$p_i = A_i(h_i), \text{ and aggregated feature } \hat{h} = \sum_{i=1}^{24} p_i h_i. \tag{5}$$

Below, we discuss the three strategies for computing the aggregation weights.

Concatenate. Simply concatenating all features lets the network disentangle individual factors, which is prone to overfitting as no domain knowledge is used.

Softmax-OOB. Instead of simply using Softmax to obtain sparse and normalized weights as in [15,35], we can make use of our volume representation to remove the influence of irrelevant bones

$$p_i = \frac{(1 - o_i)\exp(a_i)}{\sum_{j=1}^{24}(1 - o_i)\exp(a_j)}, \tag{6}$$

where o_i is the out-of-bound (OOB) indicator which equals to 1 when $\hat{\mathbf{x}}_i$ is not inside of V_i. The potential caveat is that $\hat{h}$ is still susceptible to features from irrelevant volumes. For instance, Fig. 4 shows that Softmax-OOB produces artifacts when the hand gets close to the chest.

Soft-Softmax. Due to the design of A, the output logit a_i of bone i is only dependent on itself. We can leverage this design to obtain the weight for each V_i independently and normalize their range to $[0, 1]$ with a sigmoid function,

SoftmaxOOB Soft-softmax

$$p_i = (1 - o_i) \cdot S(a_i), \text{ where } S = \frac{1}{1 + \exp(-a_i)}. \tag{7}$$

Fig. 4. The influence of aggregation strategies.

To nevertheless ensure that aggregated features are in the same range irrespectively of the number of contributors, we introduce a *soft-softmax* constraint

$$L_s = \sum_{\mathbf{x}} \left(\sum_{i=1}^{24} (1 - o_i) p_i - l_{\mathbf{x}} \right)^2 , \tag{8}$$

that acts as a soft normalization factor opposed to the hard normalization in softmax. By setting $l_{\mathbf{x}} = 1$ if $T_{\mathbf{x}} \cdot \sigma_{\mathbf{x}} > 0$ and 0 otherwise, the loss enforces the sum of weights of the activated bones to be close to 1 when the downstream neural field has positive density prediction σ (e.g., when $\mathbf{x}$ belong to the human body), and 0 otherwise. The results is a compromise between an unweighted sum and softmax that attained the best generalization in our experiments. A representative improvement on softmax is shown in Fig. 4-right.

3.3   Stage III: Neural Field and Volume Rendering

The aggregated features $\hat{h}$ contain the coarse, pose-dependent body features at location $\mathbf{x}$. To obtain high-quality human body, we learn a neural field F to predict the refined radiance c and density σ for $\mathbf{x}$

$$(c, \sigma) = F(\hat{h}, \mathbf{d}), \tag{9}$$

where $\mathbf{d} \in \mathbf{R}^2$ is the view direction. We can then render the image of the human subject by volume rendering as in the original NeRF [34],

$$\hat{\mathbf{I}}(u, v; \theta) = \sum_{q=1}^{Q} T_q (1 - \exp(-\sigma_q \delta_q)) c_q, \quad T_q = \exp \left(- \sum_{j=1}^{q-1} \sigma_j \delta_j \right). \tag{10}$$

Given the pose θ, the predicted image color at the 2D pixel location $\hat{\mathbf{I}}(u, v; \theta)$ is computed by integrating the predicted color c_q of the Q 3D samples along $\mathbf{d}$. δ_q is the distance between neighboring samples, and T_q represents the accumulated transmittance at sample q.

3.4   Training

Our model is directly supervised with ground truth images via photometric loss

$$L_p = \sum_{(u,v) \in \mathbf{I}} |\hat{\mathbf{I}}(u, v; \theta) - \mathbf{I}(u, v; \theta)|. \tag{11}$$

We use L1 loss to avoid overfitting to appearance changes that cannot be explained by pose deformation alone. To prevent the per-bone volumes from growing too large and taking over other volumes, we employ a volume loss on the scaling factors as in [30]

$$L_v = \sum_{i=1}^{24} (s^x \cdot s^y \cdot s^z). \tag{12}$$

For Soft-softmax in Sect. 3.2, we further regularize the output weights via the self-supervised loss L_s.

To summarize, the training objective of our approach is

$$L = L_p + \lambda_v L_v + \lambda_s L_s. \tag{13}$$

We set both λ_v and λ_s to 0.001 for all experiments. See the supplemental for more implementation details.

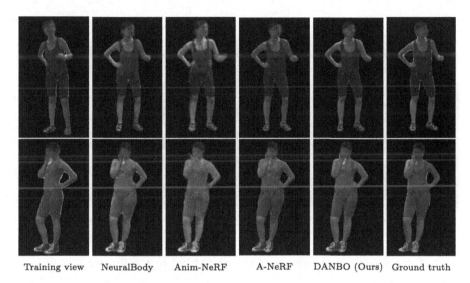

| Training view | NeuralBody | Anim-NeRF | A-NeRF | DANBO (Ours) | Ground truth |

Fig. 5. Novel-view synthesis results on Human3.6M [21]. DANBO renders more complete limbs and clearer facial features than the baselines.

4 Experiments

In the following, we evaluate the improvements upon the most recent surface-free neural body model A-NeRF [46], and compare against recent model-based solutions NeuralBody [41] and Anim-NeRF [40]. An ablation study further quantifies the improvement of using the proposed aggregation function, local GNN features, and factorized volumes over simpler and more complex [30] alternatives, including the effects on model capacity. The supplemental materials provide additional quantitative and qualitative results, including videos of retargeting applications.

Metrics and Protocols. Our goal is to analyze the quality of synthesizing novel views and separately the rendering of previously unseen poses. We quantify improvements by PSNR, SSIM [52], and perceptual metrics KID [7,39] and LPIPS [60] that are resilient to slight misalignments. All scores are computed over frames withheld from training: (1) Novel view synthesis is evaluated on multi-view datasets by learning the body model from a subset of cameras with

Table 1. Novel-view synthesis comparisons on Human3.6M [21]. The disentangled feature enables DANBO to achieve better novel view synthesis.

	NeuralBody [41]				Anim-NeRF [40]				A-NeRF [46]				DANBO (Ours)			
	PSNR ↑	SSIM ↑	KID ↓	LPIPS ↓	PSNR ↑	SSIM ↑	KID ↓	LPIPS ↓	PSNR ↑	SSIM ↑	KID ↓	LPIPS ↓	PSNR ↑	SSIM ↑	KID ↓	LPIPS ↓
S1	22.88	0.897	0.048	0.153	22.74	0.896	0.106	0.156	23.93	0.912	0.042	0.153	**23.95**	**0.916**	**0.033**	**0.148**
S5	24.61	0.917	0.033	0.146	23.40	0.895	0.087	0.151	24.67	0.919	0.036	0.147	**24.86**	**0.924**	**0.029**	**0.142**
S6	22.83	0.888	0.050	0.146	22.85	0.871	0.113	0.151	23.78	0.887	0.051	0.164	**24.54**	**0.903**	**0.035**	**0.143**
S7	23.17	0.915	0.043	0.134	21.97	0.891	0.054	0.140	24.40	0.917	**0.025**	0.139	**24.45**	**0.920**	0.028	**0.131**
S8	21.72	0.894	0.071	0.177	22.82	0.900	0.095	0.178	22.70	0.907	0.086	0.196	**23.36**	**0.917**	**0.068**	**0.173**
S9	24.29	0.911	**0.035**	0.141	24.86	0.911	0.057	0.145	25.58	0.916	0.039	0.150	**26.15**	**0.925**	0.040	**0.137**
S11	23.70	0.896	0.080	0.155	24.76	0.907	0.077	0.158	24.38	0.905	**0.057**	0.164	**25.58**	**0.917**	0.060	**0.153**
Ãvg	23.31	0.903	0.051	0.150	23.34	0.896	0.084	0.154	24.21	0.909	0.048	0.159	**24.70**	**0.917**	**0.042**	**0.146**

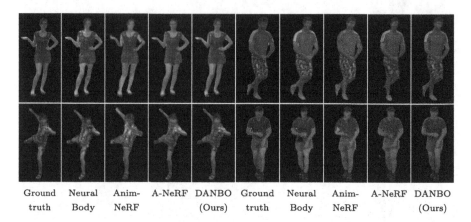

| Ground truth | Neural Body | Anim-NeRF | A-NeRF | DANBO (Ours) | Ground truth | Neural Body | Anim-NeRF | A-NeRF | DANBO (Ours) |

Fig. 6. Unseen pose synthesis on Human3.6M [21] **test split**. Our disentangled representation enables DANBO to generate plausible geometry and deformation for held-out testing poses, and achieve better visual quality than both surface-free and surface-based baselines. Note that, unlike Anim-NeRF [40], we do not require test-time finetuning for unseen poses.

the remaining ones used as the test set, i.e. rendering the same pose from the unseen view, and (2) novel pose synthesis quality is measured by training on the first part of a video and testing on the latter frames, given their corresponding 3D pose as input. This assumes that only the pose changes as the person moves. Hence, view-dependent illumination changes in (1) but stays similar in (2).

As the background image is not our focus, we report scores on tight bounding boxes either provided by the dataset or computed from the 3D poses.

Datasets. We compare our DANBO using the established benchmarks for neural bodies, covering indoor and outdoor, and single and multi-view settings:

- **Human3.6M**[1] [21,22]: We follow the same evaluation protocol as in Anim-NeRF [40], with a total of 7 subjects for evaluation. The foreground maps are computed using [18].

---

[1] Meta did not have access to the Human3.6M dataset.

Source   A-NeRF   DANBO (Ours)   Source   A-NeRF   DANBO (Ours)

Fig. 7. Motion retargeting on Mixamo [1] **and Surreal** [12,50] **dataset** with body models trained on various subjects. DANBO shows better robustness and generalization than the surface-free approach A-NeRF.

- **MonoPerfCap** [56] features multiple outdoor sequences, recorded using a single high-resolution camera. We use the same two sequences and setting as in A-NeRF [46]: Weipeng_outdoor and Nadia_outdoor with 1151 and 1635 images, respectively, of resolution 1080 × 1920. Human and camera pose is estimated by SPIN [25] and refined with [46]. Foreground masks are obtained by DeepLabv3 [9].

We further include the challenging motion such as dancing and gymnastic poses from Mixamo [1] and Surreal+CMU-Mocap dataset [12,50] for motion retargeting (detailed in the supplemental). In total, we evaluate on 9 different subjects and 11 different sequences.

4.1   Novel View Synthesis

View synthesis of poses seen during training is simpler as the interplay between body parts is observable. Hence, our explicit disentanglement of body parts is less crucial but still beneficial. Compared to the baselines, higher detail is present and body shape is better preserved, such as visible at facial features and arm contours in Fig. 5. Anim-NeRF shows slightly distorted arms and cloud-like artifacts, potentially caused by incorrectly estimated deformation fields. Table 1 verifies these improvements on the test set of Anim-NeRF [40].

Reference   A-NeRF   Ours   Reference   A-NeRF   Ours

Fig. 8. DANBO better preserves body geometry, showing a less noisy surface than A-NeRF. We extract the isosurface using Marching cubes [32] with voxel resolution 256. See the supplemental for more results.

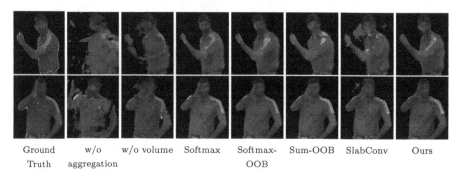

Ground   w/o   w/o volume   Softmax   Softmax-   Sum-OOB   SlabConv   Ours
Truth   aggregation   OOB

Fig. 9. Ablation study on Human3.6M [21] test split novel pose (top row) and novel view (bottom row). Our proposed designs together achieve better results with less distortion on the body parts, particularly in the limbs and face.

Table 2. Novel-pose synthesis comparisons on Human3.6M [21] (row 1-8) and MonoPerfCap [56] (row 9-11) . Our part-disentangled design enables DANBO to generalize better to unseen poses with superior perceptual qualities.

	NeuralBody [41]				Anim-NeRF [40]				A-NeRF [46]				DANBO (Ours)			
	PSNR ↑	SSIM ↑	KID ↓	LPIPS ↓	PSNR ↑	SSIM ↑	KID ↓	LPIPS ↓	PSNR ↑	SSIM ↑	KID ↓	LPIPS ↓	PSNR ↑	SSIM ↑	KID ↓	LPIPS ↓
S1	22.10	0.878	0.110	0.140	21.37	0.868	0.163	0.141	22.67	0.883	0.178	0.143	**23.03**	**0.895**	**0.081**	**0.135**
S5	23.52	0.897	**0.039**	0.151	22.29	0.875	0.123	0.155	22.96	0.888	0.081	0.157	**23.66**	**0.903**	0.049	**0.147**
S6	23.42	0.892	0.095	0.165	22.59	0.884	0.131	0.172	22.77	0.869	0.169	0.198	**24.57**	**0.906**	**0.052**	0.158
S7	22.59	0.893	0.046	0.140	22.22	0.878	0.066	0.143	22.80	0.880	0.059	0.152	**23.08**	**0.897**	**0.036**	**0.136**
S8	20.94	0.876	0.137	0.173	21.78	0.882	0.107	0.172	21.95	0.886	0.142	0.203	**22.60**	**0.904**	**0.092**	**0.167**
S9	23.05	0.885	0.043	0.141	23.73	0.886	0.068	0.141	24.16	0.889	0.074	0.152	**24.79**	**0.904**	**0.042**	**0.136**
S11	23.72	0.884	0.060	0.148	23.92	0.889	0.087	0.149	23.40	0.880	0.079	0.164	**24.57**	**0.901**	**0.040**	**0.144**
Avg	22.76	0.886	0.076	0.151	22.56	0.880	0.106	0.153	22.96	0.882	0.112	0.167	**23.76**	**0.902**	**0.056**	**0.146**
Nadia	-	-	-	-	-	-	-	-	24.88	0.931	0.048	0.115	24.44	0.921	**0.026**	**0.111**
Weipeng	-	-	-	-	-	-	-	-	22.45	0.893	0.039	0.125	22.07	0.885	**0.024**	**0.117**
Avg	-	-	-	-	-	-	-	-	23.67	0.912	0.044	0.120	23.25	0.903	**0.025**	**0.114**

4.2 Unseen Pose Synthesis and Animation

Rendering of unseen poses tests how well the learned pose-dependent deformations generalize. Figure 6 shows how differences are most prominent on limbs and faces. DANBO achieves better rendering quality and retains more consistent geometric details, generalizing well to both held out poses and out-of-distribution poses (see Fig. 7). Table 2 reports the quantitative results. DANBO consistently outperforms other baselines on Human3.6M. On MonoPerCap, the high-frequency details generated by DANBO yield lower PSNR and SSIM scores, as they penalize slightly misaligned details more than the overly smoothed results by A-NeRF. The perceptual metrics properly capture DANNO's significant quality improvement by 43% on KID and 5% on LPIPS. We attribute the boost in generalization and visual quality to the improved localization via graph neural networks as well as the Soft-softmax that outperforms the default softmax baseline as used in [15,35]. The ablation study below provides further insights.

Table 3. Ablation on each of the proposed modules.

Method variant	PSNR ↑	SSIM ↑
Ours w/o aggregation	17.08	0.627
Ours w/o volume	24.24	0.892
Ours w/o GNN	23.87	0.896
Ours full	**24.38**	**0.899**

Table 4. Ablation on different aggregation methods.

Aggregation methods	PSNR ↑	SSIM ↑
Softmax	23.80	0.896
Softmax-OOB	24.00	0.897
Sum-OOB	23.22	0.890
Sigmoid-OOB	23.75	0.896
Soft-softmax (Ours)	**24.38**	**0.899**

Table 5. Ablation study of different coarse volumes.

Volume type	PSNR ↑	SSIM ↑
3D Volume (SlabConv) [30]	24.17	0.892
Factorized Volume (Ours)	**24.38**	**0.899**

Manual animation and driving of virtual models, e.g., in VR, requires such pose synthesis, for which Fig. 7 provides animation examples. Note that no quantitative evaluation is possible here as no ground truth reference image is available in this mode. Note also that the more difficult outdoor sequences are trained from a monocular video, a setting supported only by few existing approaches. The qualitative examples validate that DANBO achieves better rendering quality on most subjects, and the poses generated by DANBO are sharper, with more consistent body parts, and suffer from less floating artifacts.

4.3 Geometry Comparisons

To further validate that DANBO improves the body shape reconstruction, we visualize the learned body geometry of DANBO and A-NeRF on unseen poses of the Human3.6M [21] dataset in Fig. 8. DANBO captures better body shapes and per-part geometry despite also being surface-free. A-NeRF suffers from missing and shrinking body parts, and predicts noisy density near the body surface. Besides the improved completeness, DANBO shows a smoother surface, which we attribute to our coarse per-bone volumetric representation.

4.4   Ablation Study

We conduct the ablation study on S9 of Human3.6M using the same splits as before. To speed up iteration cycles, we reduce the training iterations to 100k, and use every other pose in the training set from the default configuration. We furthermore decreased the factorized volume resolution to $M = 10$. Figure 9 shows results on both novel pose and novel view for all variants.

Proposed Modules. In Table 3, we report how each of our proposed modules contributes to the final performance. For Ours w/o learned aggregation, we simply concatenate all the retrieved voxel features as inputs to the NeRF network, which is similar to A-NeRF but using GNN features. This leads to poor generalization, and the w/o aggregation model predicts many floating artifacts in empty space. For Ours w/o volume, the GNN predicts per-bone feature vector instead of factorized volumes. In this variant, the aggregation network takes as input $\hat{\mathbf{x}}_i$ to predict per-bone weights. The feature to neural field F is the aggregated GNN feature and local coordinates. While the w/o volume variant achieves comparable results, the model suffers from overfitting, and produces distorted results on joints. In sum, both our aggregation network and per-bone volume designs provide useful inductive biases for learning robust and expressive models.

Aggregation Strategy. In Table 4, we show the evaluation results with different aggregation methods in Sect. 3.2. Note that the Softmax variant is equivalent to NARF [35] with our GNN backbone. Strategy with out-of-bound handling shows better robustness to unseen poses, with our Soft-softmax aggregation works better than Softmax-OOB, and the unweighted variant SUM-OOB being the worst.

Choice of Volume Representation. In Table 5, we show the results of using both our factorized volumes, and full 3D volume predicted using SlabConv [30]. We observe that SlabConv, while capturing finer texture details as the model is more expressive, is prone to noises in the empty space. We conclude that more views and pose data are required for using SlabConv as the volume representation.

5   Limitations and Discussion

Similar to other neural field-based approaches, the computation time for DANBO remains the limiting factor for real-time applications. While DANBO offers better generalization to unseen poses, we show in Fig. 10 that in extreme cases it sometimes mixes the parts around joints together leading to deformation

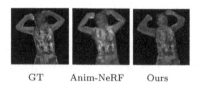

GT   Anim-NeRF   Ours

Fig. 10. Unseen local poses create artifacts around the joints.

and blur. Handling such cases remains an open problem as also the surface-based method Anim-NeRF produces candy wrap artifacts around the elbow. It is also worth noting that DANBO is a person-specific model that needs to be trained individually for each person, which is desirable so long as sufficient training time and data is available.

6   Conclusion

We presented a surface-free approach for learning an animatable human body model from video. This is practical as it applies to monocular recordings, alleviates the restrictions of template or parametric models, and works in indoor and outdoor conditions. Our contributions on encoding pose locally with a GNN, factorized volumes, and a soft aggregation function improve upon existing models in the same class and even rival recent surface-based solutions.

Acknowledgment. Shih-Yang Su and Helge Rhodin were supported by Compute Canada, Advanced Research Computing at UBC [13], and NSERC DC.

References

1. Adobe: Mixamo (2020). https://www.mixamo.com/
2. Alldieck, T., Xu, H., Sminchisescu, C.: imghum: implicit generative models of 3D human shape and articulated pose. In: ICCV (2021)
3. Bagautdinov, T., et al.: Driving-signal aware full-body avatars. ACM TOG (Proc. SIGGRAPH) **40**, 1–17 (2021)
4. Balan, A.O., Sigal, L., Black, M.J., Davis, J.E., Haussecker, H.W.: Detailed human shape and pose from images. In: CVPR, pp. 1–8 (2007)
5. Barron, J.T., Mildenhall, B., Tancik, M., Hedman, P., Martin-Brualla, R., Srinivasan, P.P.: Mip-nerf: a multiscale representation for anti-aliasing neural radiance fields. In: ICCV (2021)
6. Bhatnagar, B.L., Sminchisescu, C., Theobalt, C., Pons-Moll, G.: Combining implicit function learning and parametric models for 3D human reconstruction. In: Vedaldi, A., Bischof, H., Brox, T., Frahm, J.-M. (eds.) ECCV 2020. LNCS, vol. 12347, pp. 311–329. Springer, Cham (2020). https://doi.org/10.1007/978-3-030-58536-5_19
7. Bińkowski, M., Sutherland, D.J., Arbel, M., Gretton, A.: Demystifying mmd gans. In: ICLR (2018)
8. Burov, A., Nießner, M., Thies, J.: Dynamic surface function networks for clothed human bodies. In: ICCV (2021)
9. Chen, L.C., Papandreou, G., Schroff, F., Adam, H.: Rethinking atrous convolution for semantic image segmentation. arXiv preprint arXiv:1706.05587 (2017)
10. Chen, X., Zheng, Y., Black, M.J., Hilliges, O., Geiger, A.: Snarf: differentiable forward skinning for animating non-rigid neural implicit shapes. In: ICCV (2021)
11. Choutas, V., Pavlakos, G., Bolkart, T., Tzionas, D., Black, M.J.: Monocular expressive body regression through body-driven attention. In: Vedaldi, A., Bischof, H., Brox, T., Frahm, J.-M. (eds.) ECCV 2020. LNCS, vol. 12355, pp. 20–40. Springer, Cham (2020). https://doi.org/10.1007/978-3-030-58607-2_2. https://expose.is.tue.mpg.de
12. CMU Graphics Lab Motion Capture Database. http://mocap.cs.cmu.edu
13. Computing, U.A.R.: Ubc arc sockeye (2019). https://doi.org/10.14288/SOCKEYE
14. Corona, E., Pumarola, A., Alenyà, G., Pons-Moll, G., Moreno-Noguer, F.: Smplicit: topology-aware generative model for clothed people. In: CVPR (2021)
15. Deng, B., et al.: Nasa: neural articulated shape approximation. arXiv preprint arXiv:1912.03207 (2019)

16. Gafni, G., Thies, J., Zollhöfer, M., Nießner, M.: Dynamic neural radiance fields for monocular 4D facial avatar reconstruction. In: CVPR (2021)
17. Gao, C., Saraf, A., Kopf, J., Huang, J.B.: Dynamic view synthesis from dynamic monocular video. In: ICCV (2021)
18. Gong, K., Liang, X., Li, Y., Chen, Y., Yang, M., Lin, L.: Instance-level human parsing via part grouping network. In: Ferrari, V., Hebert, M., Sminchisescu, C., Weiss, Y. (eds.) ECCV 2018. LNCS, vol. 11208, pp. 805–822. Springer, Cham (2018). https://doi.org/10.1007/978-3-030-01225-0_47
19. Guo, K., et al.: The relightables: volumetric performance capture of humans with realistic relighting. ACM TOG (Proc. SIGGRAPH) **38**, 1–19 (2019)
20. Habermann, M., Liu, L., Xu, W., Zollhoefer, M., Pons-Moll, G., Theobalt, C.: Real-time deep dynamic characters. ACM TOG (Proc. SIGGRAPH) **40**, 1–16 (2021)
21. Ionescu, C., Carreira, J., Sminchisescu, C.: Iterated second-order label sensitive pooling for 3D human pose estimation. In: CVPR (2014)
22. Ionescu, C., Li, F., Sminchisescu, C.: Latent structured models for human pose estimation. In: ICCV (2011)
23. Kipf, T.N., Welling, M.: Semi-supervised classification with graph convolutional networks. In: ICLR (2017)
24. Kocabas, M., Athanasiou, N., Black, M.J.: Vibe: video inference for human body pose and shape estimation. In: CVPR (2020)
25. Kolotouros, N., Pavlakos, G., Black, M.J., Daniilidis, K.: Learning to reconstruct 3D human pose and shape via model-fitting in the loop. In: ICCV (2019)
26. Kwon, Y., Kim, D., Ceylan, D., Fuchs, H.: Neural human performer: learning generalizable radiance fields for human performance rendering. In: NeurIPS (2021)
27. Lin, C.H., Ma, W.C., Torralba, A., Lucey, S.: Barf: bundle-adjusting neural radiance fields. arXiv preprint arXiv:2104.06405 (2021)
28. Lindell, D.B., Martel, J.N., Wetzstein, G.: Autoint: automatic integration for fast neural volume rendering. In: CVPR (2021)
29. Liu, L., Habermann, M., Rudnev, V., Sarkar, K., Gu, J., Theobalt, C.: Neural actor: neural free-view synthesis of human actors with pose control. ACM TOG (Proc. SIGGRAPH Asia) **40**, 1–16 (2021)
30. Lombardi, S., Simon, T., Schwartz, G., Zollhoefer, M., Sheikh, Y., Saragih, J.: Mixture of volumetric primitives for efficient neural rendering. ACM TOG (Proc. SIGGRAPH) **40**, 1–13 (2021)
31. Loper, M., Mahmood, N., Romero, J., Pons-Moll, G., Black, M.J.: Smpl: a skinned multi-person linear model. ACM TOG (Proc. SIGGRAPH) **34**(6), 1–16 (2015)
32. Lorensen, W.E., Cline, H.E.: Marching cubes: a high resolution 3D surface construction algorithm. ACM TOG (Proc. SIGGRAPH) **21**, 163–169 (1987)
33. Mihajlovic, M., Saito, S., Bansal, A., Zollhoefer, M., Tang, S.: COAP: compositional articulated occupancy of people. In: CVPR (2022)
34. Mildenhall, B., Srinivasan, P.P., Tancik, M., Barron, J.T., Ramamoorthi, R., Ng, R.: NeRF: representing scenes as neural radiance fields for view synthesis. In: Vedaldi, A., Bischof, H., Brox, T., Frahm, J.-M. (eds.) ECCV 2020. LNCS, vol. 12346, pp. 405–421. Springer, Cham (2020). https://doi.org/10.1007/978-3-030-58452-8_24
35. Noguchi, A., Sun, X., Lin, S., Harada, T.: Neural articulated radiance field. In: ICCV (2021)
36. Osman, A.A.A., Bolkart, T., Black, M.J.: STAR: sparse trained articulated human body regressor. In: Vedaldi, A., Bischof, H., Brox, T., Frahm, J.-M. (eds.) ECCV 2020. LNCS, vol. 12351, pp. 598–613. Springer, Cham (2020). https://doi.org/10.1007/978-3-030-58539-6_36

37. Park, J.J., Florence, P., Straub, J., Newcombe, R., Lovegrove, S.: Deepsdf: learning continuous signed distance functions for shape representation. In: CVPR (2019)
38. Park, K., et al.: Hypernerf: a higher-dimensional representation for topologically varying neural radiance fields. ACM TOG (Proc. SIGGRAPH) (2021)
39. Parmar, G., Zhang, R., Zhu, J.Y.: On aliased resizing and surprising subtleties in gan evaluation. In: CVPR (2022)
40. Peng, S., et al.: Animatable neural radiance fields for modeling dynamic human bodies. In: ICCV (2021)
41. Peng, S., et al.: Neural body: implicit neural representations with structured latent codes for novel view synthesis of dynamic humans. In: CVPR (2021)
42. Peng, S., Niemeyer, M., Mescheder, L., Pollefeys, M., Geiger, A.: Convolutional occupancy networks. In: Vedaldi, A., Bischof, H., Brox, T., Frahm, J.-M. (eds.) ECCV 2020. LNCS, vol. 12348, pp. 523–540. Springer, Cham (2020). https://doi.org/10.1007/978-3-030-58580-8_31
43. Pumarola, A., Corona, E., Pons-Moll, G., Moreno-Noguer, F.: D-NeRF: neural radiance fields for dynamic scenes. In: CVPR (2020)
44. Saito, S., Yang, J., Ma, Q., Black, M.J.: SCANimate: weakly supervised learning of skinned clothed avatar networks. In: CVPR (2021)
45. Sitzmann, V., Martel, J., Bergman, A., Lindell, D., Wetzstein, G.: Implicit neural representations with periodic activation functions. In: NeurIPS, vol. 33 (2020)
46. Su, S.Y., Yu, F., Zollhöfer, M., Rhodin, H.: A-nerf: articulated neural radiance fields for learning human shape, appearance, and pose. In: NeurIPS (2021)
47. Tiwari, G., Bhatnagar, B.L., Tung, T., Pons-Moll, G.: SIZER: a dataset and model for parsing 3D clothing and learning size sensitive 3D clothing. In: Vedaldi, A., Bischof, H., Brox, T., Frahm, J.-M. (eds.) ECCV 2020. LNCS, vol. 12348, pp. 1–18. Springer, Cham (2020). https://doi.org/10.1007/978-3-030-58580-8_1
48. Tiwari, G., Sarafianos, N., Tung, T., Pons-Moll, G.: Neural-gif: neural generalized implicit functions for animating people in clothing. In: ICCV (2021)
49. Tretschk, E., Tewari, A., Golyanik, V., Zollhöfer, M., Lassner, C., Theobalt, C.: Non-rigid neural radiance fields: reconstruction and novel view synthesis of a dynamic scene from monocular video. In: ICCV (2021)
50. Varol, G., et al.: Learning from synthetic humans. In: CVPR (2017)
51. Wang, S., Mihajlovic, M., Ma, Q., Geiger, A., Tang, S.: Metaavatar: learning animatable clothed human models from few depth images. In: NeurIPS (2021)
52. Wang, Z., Bovik, A.C., Sheikh, H.R., Simoncelli, E.P.: Image quality assessment: from error visibility to structural similarity. TIP **13**, 600–612 (2004)
53. Xian, W., Huang, J.B., Kopf, J., Kim, C.: Space-time neural irradiance fields for free-viewpoint video. In: CVPR (2021)
54. Xu, H., Alldieck, T., Sminchisescu, C.: H-nerf: neural radiance fields for rendering and temporal reconstruction of humans in motion. In: NeurIPS (2021)
55. Xu, H., Bazavan, E.G., Zanfir, A., Freeman, W.T., Sukthankar, R., Sminchisescu, C.: Ghum & ghuml: generative 3D human shape and articulated pose models. In: CVPR (2020)
56. Xu, W., et al.: Monoperfcap: human performance capture from monocular video. TOG **37**(2), 27 (2018)
57. Yen-Chen, L., Florence, P., Barron, J.T., Rodriguez, A., Isola, P., Lin, T.Y.: inerf: inverting neural radiance fields for pose estimation. In: IROS (2020)
58. Yu, A., Li, R., Tancik, M., Li, H., Ng, R., Kanazawa, A.: PlenOctrees for real-time rendering of neural radiance fields. In: ICCV (2021)
59. Yu, A., Ye, V., Tancik, M., Kanazawa, A.: pixelNeRF: neural radiance fields from one or few images. In: CVPR (2021)

60. Zhang, R., Isola, P., Efros, A.A., Shechtman, E., Wang, O.: The unreasonable effectiveness of deep features as a perceptual metric. In: CVPR (2018)
61. Zhou, X., Zhu, M., Pavlakos, G., Leonardos, S., Derpanis, K.G., Daniilidis, K.: Monocap: monocular human motion capture using a cnn coupled with a geometric prior. PAMI **41**, 901–914 (2018)
62. Zhou, Y., Barnes, C., Lu, J., Yang, J., Li, H.: On the continuity of rotation representations in neural networks. In: CVPR, pp. 5745–5753 (2019)

CHORE: Contact, Human and Object Reconstruction from a Single RGB Image

Xianghui Xie[2]([✉]), Bharat Lal Bhatnagar[1,2], and Gerard Pons-Moll[1,2]

[1] University of Tübingen,Tübingen, Germany
bbhatnag@mpi-inf.mpg.de, gerard.pons-moll@uni-tuebingen.de
[2] Max Planck Institute for Informatics, Saarland Informatics Campus, Saarbrücken, Germany
xxie@mpi-inf.mpg.de

Abstract. Most prior works in perceiving 3D humans from images reason human in isolation without their surroundings. However, humans are constantly interacting with the surrounding objects, thus calling for models that can reason about not only the human but also the object and their interaction. The problem is extremely challenging due to heavy occlusions between humans and objects, diverse interaction types and depth ambiguity. In this paper, we introduce CHORE, a novel method that learns to jointly reconstruct the human and the object from a single RGB image. CHORE takes inspiration from recent advances in implicit surface learning and classical model-based fitting. We compute a neural reconstruction of human and object represented implicitly with two unsigned distance fields, a correspondence field to a parametric body and an object pose field. This allows us to robustly fit a parametric body model and a 3D object template, while reasoning about interactions. Furthermore, prior pixel-aligned implicit learning methods use synthetic data and make assumptions that are not met in the real data. We propose a elegant depth-aware scaling that allows more efficient shape learning on real data. Experiments show that our joint reconstruction learned with the proposed strategy significantly outperforms the SOTA. Our code and models are available at https://virtualhumans.mpi-inf.mpg.de/chore

1 Introduction

In order to deploy robots and intelligent systems in the real world, they must be able to perceive and understand humans interacting with the real world from visual input. While there exists a vast literature in perceiving humans in 3D from single images, the large majority of works perceive humans in isolation [6, 37,40,54,63,75]. The joint 3D perception of humans and objects has received much less attention and is the main focus of this work. Joint reconstruction of humans and objects is extremely challenging. The object and human occlude each other making inference hard; it is difficult to predict their relative size and spatial arrangement in the 3D world, and the visual evidence for contacts and interactions consists of only a very small region in the image Fig. 1.

Supplementary Information The online version contains supplementary material available at https://doi.org/10.1007/978-3-031-20086-1_8.

Input Image	Human, object and contact	Side views

Fig. 1. From a single image, our method jointly reconstructs the 3D human coherently with the object by reasoning about their interactions. Instead of predicting human and object independently and imposing coherency post-hoc [79], we reconstruct both jointly including contacts, leading to significant improvements over the state-of-the-art.

Recent work [79] addresses these challenges by reconstructing 3D objects and humans separately, and imposing hand-crafted rules like manually defined object contact regions. However, heuristics cannot scale as it is difficult to specify all possible human-object contacts beforehand. Consider the chair in Fig. 3: one can sit, lean, move it from the handle, back or legs, which constitutes different pairs of human-object contacts that are not easy to manually enumerate. Furthermore, human and object provide strong cues about their relative spatial arrangement for each other during interaction. Reasoning human and object separately does not exploit these cues and can produce errors that cannot be corrected afterwards, see Fig. 4. This motivates a method that can jointly reconstruct humans and objects and learn the interactions from data, without hand-crafted rules.

In this work, we introduce CHORE, a novel method to jointly recover a 3D parametric body model and the 3D object, from a single image. CHORE is built on two high-level ideas. First, instead of reconstructing human and object separately, we argue for jointly reasoning about them in the first place. Secondly, we learn spatial configuration priors of interacting human and object from data without using heuristics. Instead of regressing human parameters directly from image, we first obtain pixel-aligned neural fields predictions (CHORE fields), which consist of two unsigned distance fields to human and object surfaces, a correspondence field to the SMPL [49] body model and an object pose field. This allows us to formulate a more robust optimization energy to fit the SMPL model and the object template to the image. To train our network on real data, we propose a training strategy that enables us to effectively learn pixel-aligned implicit functions with perspective cameras, which leads to more accurate prediction and joint fitting. In summary, our key contributions are:

- We propose CHORE, the first end-to-end learning approach that can reconstruct human, object and contacts from a single RGB image. Our CHORE neural fields predictions allow us to accurately register a controllable body model and 3D object to the image.
- Different from prior works that use weak perspective cameras and learn from synthetic data, we use full perspective camera model, which is crucial to train on real data. To this end, we propose a new training strategy that allows effective pixel-aligned implicit learning with perspective cameras.

– Through our effective training and joint reconstruction, our model achieves a remarkable performance improvement of over 50% compared to prior art [79]. Our code and models are publicly available to foster future research.

2   Related Work

We propose the first learning-based approach to jointly reconstruct 3D human, object and contacts from a single image. In this regard, we first review recent advances in separate human or object reconstructions. We then discuss approaches that can jointly reason about human-object interaction.

Human Reconstruction from Images. One common approach to reconstruct 3D humans from images is to fit a parametric model such as SMPL [49] to the image [4,5,11,19,44,55,57]. Learning-based approaches have also been used to directly regress model parameters such as pose and shape [3,26,38,40,43,54, 56] as well as clothing [3,9,27–29,36,69]. More recently, implicit function based reconstruction are applied to capture fine-grained details including clothing and hair geometry [34,62,63,75,80]. These methods however cannot reconstruct 3D objects, let alone human-object interaction.

Object Reconstruction from Images. Given a single image, 3D objects can be reconstructed as voxels [18,35,72], point clouds [22,45] and meshes [41,58,70]. Similar to human reconstruction, implicit functions have shown huge success for object reconstruction as well [50,53,76]. The research in this direction has been significantly aided by large scale datasets [15,66,74]. We urge the readers to see the recent review [25] of image-based 3D reconstruction of objects. These approaches have shown great promise in rigid object reconstruction but articulated humans are significantly more challenging and human-object interaction even more so. Unlike these methods, our approach can jointly reconstruct humans, objects and their interactions.

Human Object Interactions. Modelling 3D human-object interactions is extremely challenging. Recent works have shown impressive performance in modelling hand-object interactions from 3D [13,67,86], 2.5D [12,14] and images [20, 21,32,42,77]. Despite being quite impressive, these works have a shortcoming in that they are restricted to only hand-object interactions and cannot predict the full body. Modelling full-body interactions is even more challenging, with works like PROX [30] being able to reconstruct [30,71] or synthesize [31,64,81,82] 3D humans to satisfy the 3D scene constraints. There are also works capturing interaction from multi-view [10,39,65] or reconstructing 3D scene based on human-scene interactions [78]. Recently, this direction has also been extended to model human-human interaction [24], self-contacts [23,52]. Broadly speaking, these works can model human-object interactions to satisfy scene constraints but cannot jointly reconstruct human-object contacts from single images. Few works

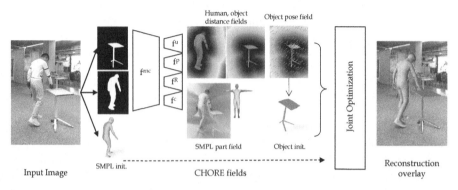

Fig. 2. We present an approach to jointly reconstruct human, object and contacts from a single RGB image. Given an image, human and object masks, we predict CHORE fields: unsigned distance fields to human and object surfaces (f^u), SMPL part (f^p) and object pose (f^R, f^c) fields. We then leverage the neural fields to robustly fit the SMPL model and the object mesh to the image while reasoning about human-object contacts.

directly reason about 3D contacts from images [16,33,85] and video [46,51,59] but do not reconstruct 3D human and object from a single RGB image.

Closest to our work are [71] and PHOSA [79] . Weng *et al.* [71] predict 3D human and scene layout separately and use scene constraints to optimize human reconstruction. They use predefined contact weights on SMPL-X [55] vertices, which is prone to errors. PHOSA first fits SMPL and object meshes separately and then uses hand crafted heuristics like predefined contact pairs to reason about human-object interaction. These heuristics are neither scale-able nor very accurate. Our method does not rely on heuristics and can learn joint reconstruction and contact priors directly from data. Experiments show that our learning based method easily outperforms heuristic-based PHOSA and [71].

3 Method

We describe here the components of CHORE, a method for 3D reconstruction of the human, object and their contacts from a single RGB image. This work focuses on a single person in close interaction with one dynamic movable object. Our approach is inspired by the classical image based model fitting methods [5,11], which fit a body model parameterized by shape and pose θ, β by minimizing an energy:

$$E(\theta, \beta) = E_{data} + E_{J2D} + E_{reg}, \qquad (1)$$

where E_{data} is a 2D image based loss like a silhouette loss, E_{J2D} is re-projection loss for body joints, and E_{reg} is a loss on body pose and shape priors learned from data [49,55,68]. Estimating the human and the object jointly however is significantly more challenging. The relative configuration of human and object needs to be accurately estimated despite occlusions, lack of depth, and hard to detect contacts. Hence, a plain extension of a hand-crafted 2D objective to incorporate the object is far too prone to local minima. Our idea is to jointly predict, based on a single image, 3D neural fields (CHORE fields) for the human, object and their relative pose and contacts, to formulate a learned robust 3D data term. We then fit a parametric body model and a template object mesh to the predicted CHORE neural fields, see overview Fig. 2.

In this section, we first explain our CHORE neural fields in Sect. 3.1, and then describe our novel human-object fitting formulation using learned CHORE neural fields in Sect. 3.2. Unlike prior works on pixel-aligned neural implicit reconstruction [62] which learns from synthetic data and assume a weak perspective camera, we learn from real data captured with full perspective cameras. This poses new challenges which we address with a simple and effective deformation of the captured real 3D surfaces to account for perspective effects (Sect. 3.3).

3.1   CHORE Neural Fields from Single Images

As representation, we use the SMPL body model $H(\boldsymbol{\theta}, \boldsymbol{\beta})$ [60] which parameterizes the 3D human as a function of pose $\boldsymbol{\theta}$ (including global translation) and shape $\boldsymbol{\beta}$, and a template mesh for the object. Our idea is to leverage a stronger 3D data term coming from learned CHORE neural fields to fit SMPL and the object templates (one template per class) to the images. In contrast to a plain joint surface reconstruction of human and object, the resulting SMPL and object mesh can be further controlled and edited. To obtain a good fit to the image, we would ideally i) minimize the distance between the optimized meshes and the corresponding ground truth human and object surfaces, and ii) enforce that human-object contacts of the meshes are consistent with input. Obviously, ground truth human and object surfaces are unknown at test time. Hence, we approximate them with CHORE fields. Specifically, a learned neural model predicts 1) the unsigned distance fields of the object and human surfaces, and 2) a part correspondence field to the SMPL model, for more robust SMPL fitting and contact modeling, and 3) an object pose field, to initialize the object pose.

This constitutes a complex multi-task learning problem which we address with a single neural network. We first use a CNN to extract an image-aligned feature grid. For a query point $\mathbf{p} \in \mathbb{R}^3$ we project it to image plane and extract pixel-aligned features, from which we predict the distance, part-correspondence and object pose fields. We explain the details of our network below.

Input Encoding. f^{enc}. We stack RGB image with human and object masks in separate channels as input and use a leaned feature extractor f^{enc} [62]to extract image feature grid $\mathbf{F}$. Given a query point $\mathbf{p} \in \mathbb{R}^3$, and the image feature $\mathbf{F}$, we extract a pixel-aligned point feature $\mathbf{F}[\pi_{3D \mapsto 2D}(\mathbf{p})]$ by projecting the 3D point to the image. We concatenate the 3D point coordinate $\mathbf{p}$ to the pixel-aligned feature, allowing the network to distinguish points at different depth along the same ray, hence $\mathbf{F_p} = (\mathbf{F}[\pi_{3D \mapsto 2D}(\mathbf{p})], \mathbf{p})$. The feature extractor f^{enc} is trained with losses defined on neural fields predictions which we explain later.

Human and Object Distance Fields. f^u. Based on the point feature $\mathbf{F_p}$, we use a point decoder f^u to predict the unsigned distances $u_h(\mathbf{p}) \in \mathbb{R}^+$ and

$u_o(\mathbf{p}) \in \mathbb{R}^+$ from the point to the human and object surface respectively. This allows to model non-watertight meshes as well. From an unsigned distance field the 3D surface $\mathcal{S}$ can be reconstructed by projecting points to it [17]:

$$\mathcal{S}_i = \{\mathbf{p} - f_i^u(\mathbf{F_p})\nabla_\mathbf{p}f_i^u(\mathbf{F_p}) \,|\, \mathbf{p} \in \mathbb{R}^3\} \tag{2}$$

where f_i^u can be human (f_h^u) or object (f_o^u) UDF predictor. In practice, points $\mathbf{p}$ are initialized from a fixed 3D volume and projection is done iteratively [17].

To train neural distance function f_i^u, we sample a set of points $\mathcal{P}_i$ near the ground truth surfaces and compute the ground truth distance $\mathrm{UDF_{gt}}(\mathbf{p})$. The decoder f_i^u is then trained to minimize the L_1 distance between clamped prediction and ground truth distance:

$$L_{u_i} = \sum_{\mathbf{p} \in \mathcal{P}_i} |\min(f_i^u(\mathbf{F_p}), \delta) - \min(\mathrm{UDF_{gt}}(\mathbf{p}), \delta)| \tag{3}$$

where δ is a small clamping value to focus on the volume nearby the surface.

Part Field f^p and Contacts. While the unsigned distance predictions can reconstruct the human and object surface, they do not tell which human or object points are in contact, and fitting template SMPL meshes using only distance fields often fails [7]. Hence we use another decoder to predict a part correspondence field to the SMPL model with two purposes: i) to formulate a robust SMPL fitting objective [7,8] and ii) to derive which body parts are in contact with the object points. Mathematically, given the point feature $\mathbf{F_p}$ for a point $\mathbf{p} \in \mathbb{R}^3$, we predict its corresponding SMPL part $\mathbf{l_p} = f^p(\mathbf{F_p}) \in \{1, 2, ... K\}$. $K = 14$ is the total number of SMPL parts. The part prediction decoder is trained with standard categorical cross entropy, L_p.

Object Pose Fields f^R and f^c. Accurate object fitting to the CHORE UDF requires good initialization for the object pose. We learn a predictor $f^R : \mathbf{F_p} \mapsto \mathbb{R}^{3\times3}$ that takes the point feature $\mathbf{F_p}$ as input and predicts the rotation matrix $\mathbf{R}$. Predicting the object translation in camera coordinates directly is more tricky due to the well known depth-scale ambiguity. Hence our predictions are relative to the human. We train a decoder $f^c : \mathbf{F_p} \mapsto \mathbb{R}^5$ which predicts the x, y coordinate of SMPL center (at fixed depth) in camera coordinates, and the object center relative to the SMPL center based on the point feature $\mathbf{F_p}$. Both f^R and f^c are trained with mean squared loss L_R and L_c.

Our feature encoder f^{enc} and neural predictors f^u, f^p, f^R, f^c are trained jointly with the objective: $L = \lambda_u(L_{u_h} + L_{u_o}) + \lambda_p L_p + \lambda_R L_R + \lambda_c L_c$. See supplementary for more details on our network architecture and training.

3.2   3D Human and Object Fitting with CHORE Fields

With CHORE fields, we reformulate Eq. (1) to include a stronger data term E_{data} in 3D, itself composed of 3 different terms for human, object, and contacts which we describe next.

3D Human Term. This term consists of the sum of distances from SMPL vertices to the CHORE neural UDF for the human f_h^u, and a part based term leveraging the part fields f^p discussed in Sect. 3.1:

$$E_{\text{data}}^h(\boldsymbol{\theta}, \boldsymbol{\beta}) = \sum_{\mathbf{p} \in H(\boldsymbol{\theta}, \boldsymbol{\beta})} (\lambda_h \min(f_h^u(\mathbf{F_p}), \delta) + \lambda_{p'} L_p(l_\mathbf{p}, f^p(\mathbf{F_p}))), \qquad (4)$$

Here, $L_p(\cdot, \cdot)$ is the standard categorical cross entropy loss function and $l_\mathbf{p}$ denotes our predefined part label on SMPL vertex $\mathbf{p}$. $\lambda_h, \lambda_{p'}$ are the loss weights. The part-based term $L_p(\cdot, \cdot)$ is effective to avoid, for example, matching a person's arm to the torso or a hand to the head. To favour convergence, we initialize the human pose estimated from the image using [61].

3D Object Term. We assume a known object mesh template with vertices $\mathbf{O} \in \mathbb{R}^{3 \times N}$ and optimize the object rotation $\mathbf{R}_o \in SO(3)$, translation $\mathbf{t}_o \in \mathbb{R}^3$ and scale $s_o \in \mathbb{R}$ leveraging the neural fields predictions. Given template vertices and object pose, we compute the posed object as $\mathbf{O}' = s_o(\mathbf{R}_o \mathbf{O} + \mathbf{t}_o)$. Intuitively, the distance between object vertices $\mathbf{O}'$ and underlying object surface should be minimized. Furthermore, the projected 2D silhouette should match the observed object mask $\mathbf{M}_o$, yielding the following objective:

$$E_{\text{data}}^o(\mathbf{R}_o, \mathbf{t}_o, s_o) = \sum_{\mathbf{p} \in \mathbf{O}'} (\lambda_o \min(f_o^u(\mathbf{F_p}), \delta) + \lambda_{\text{occ}} L_{\text{occ-sil}}(\mathbf{O}', \mathbf{M}_o) + \lambda_{\text{reg}} L_{\text{reg}}(\mathbf{O}')),$$

$$(5)$$

The first term computes the distance between fitted object and corresponding surface represented implicitly with the network f_o^u. The second term $L_{\text{occ-sil}}$ is an occlusion-aware silhouette loss [79]. We additionally use L_{reg} computed as the distance between predicted object center and center of $\mathbf{O}'$. This regularization prevents the object from being pushed too far away from predicted object center.

The object rotation is initialized by first averaging the rotation matrices of the object pose field near the object surface (points with $f_o^u(\mathbf{F_p}) < 4mm$): $\mathbf{R}_o = \frac{1}{M} \sum_{k=1}^M \mathbf{R}_k$. We further run SVD on $\mathbf{R}_o$ to project the matrix to $SO(3)$. Object translation $\mathbf{t}_o$ is similarly initialized by averaging the translation part of the pose field nearby the surface. Our experiments show that pose initialization is important for accurate object fitting, see Sect. 4.6.

Joint Fitting with Contacts. While Eq. (4) and Eq. (5) allow fitting human and object meshes coherently, fits will not necessarily satisfy fine-grained contact constraints. Our key idea here is to jointly reconstruct and fit humans and objects while reasoning about contacts. We minimize a joint objective as follows:

$$E_{\text{data}}(\boldsymbol{\theta}, \boldsymbol{\beta}, \mathbf{R_o}, \mathbf{t_o}, s_o) = E_{\text{data}}^h + E_{\text{data}}^o + \lambda_c E_{\text{data}}^c, \qquad (6)$$

where E_{data}^h and E_{data}^o are defined in Eq. (4) and Eq. (5) respectively. The contact term E_{data}^c consists of the chamfer distance $d(\cdot, \cdot)$ between the sets of human H_j^c

and object points O_j^c predicted to be in contact:

$$E_{\text{data}}^c(\mathbf{R}_o, \mathbf{t}_o, s_o) = \sum_{j=1}^{K} d(H_j^c(\boldsymbol{\theta}, \boldsymbol{\beta}), O_j^c). \tag{7}$$

Points on the $j-th$ body part of SMPL $(H_j(\boldsymbol{\theta}, \boldsymbol{\beta}))$ are considered to be in contact when their UDF $f_o^u(\mathbf{F_p})$ to the object is smaller than a threshold: $H_j^c(\boldsymbol{\theta}, \boldsymbol{\beta}) = \{\mathbf{p} \,|\, \mathbf{p} \in H_j(\boldsymbol{\theta}, \boldsymbol{\beta}) \text{ and } f_o^u(\mathbf{F_p}) \leq \epsilon\}$. Analogously, object points are considered to be in contact with body part j when their UDF to the body is small and they are labelled as part j: $O_j^c = \{\mathbf{p} \,|\, \mathbf{p} \in \mathbf{O}' \text{ and } f_h^u(\mathbf{F_p}) \leq \epsilon \text{ and } f^p(\mathbf{F_p}) = j\}$. The contact term E_{data}^c encourages the object to be close with the corresponding SMPL parts in contact. The loss is zero when no contacts detected. This is important to have a physically plausible and consistent reconstruction, see Sect. 4.5.

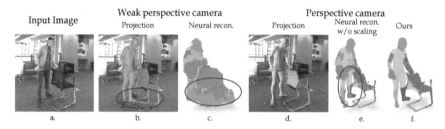

Fig. 3. Learning neural fields on real data. We show projections of GT meshes overlapped with input image using different camera models in b and d. The neural reconstructions (colored based on predicted part labels f^p) are shown in c, e and f. Weak perspective projection is not accurately aligned (b) with image hence network trained with this predicts noisy output (c). Perspective camera projection is accurately aligned (d) but directly applying it, without accounting for depth-scale ambiguity, makes learning hard. Training with this is still not optimal (e). Our proposed method reduces depth ambiguity while maintaining accurate alignment, leading to better predictions (f). (Color figure online)

Substituting our data term into Eq. (1), we can now write our complete optimization energy as: $E(\boldsymbol{\theta}, \boldsymbol{\beta}, \mathbf{R_o}, \mathbf{t_o}, s_o) = E_{data}^o + E_{data}^h + \lambda_c E_{data}^c + \lambda_J E_{J2D} + \lambda_r E_{\text{reg}}$. See Supp. for details about different loss weights λ's.

3.3   Learning Pixel-Aligned Neural Fields on Real Data

Our training data consists of real images paired with reference SMPL and object meshes. Here, we want to follow the pixel-aligned training paradigm, which has been shown effective for 3D shape reconstruction. Since both depth and scale determine the size of objects in images this makes learning from single images ambiguous. Hence, existing works place the objects at a fixed distance to the camera, and render them using a weak perspective [62,63,84] or perspective camera model [72,73,76,83]. This effectively allows the network to reason about only scale, instead of both scale and depth at the same time.

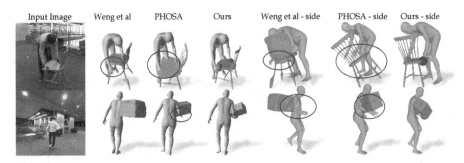

Fig. 4. Comparison with Weng *et al.* [71] and PHOSA [79] on BEHAVE. The contact spheres are placed automatically at the contact centers. [71] uses predefined contact weights and fails to reconstruct spatial arrangement properly. PHOSA's post-hoc also fails to correct errors from separate human-object reconstructions. Our network is trained jointly to reconstruct the human and the object and learns a strong prior on the relative arrangement, allowing for more accurate reconstruction.

This strategy to generate training pairs is only possible when learning from *synthetic data*, which allows to move objects and re-render the images. Instead, we learn from *real* images paired with meshes. Re-centering meshes to a fixed depth breaks the pixel alignment with the real images. An alternative is to adopt a weak perspective camera model (assume all meshes are centered at a constant depth), but the alignment is still not accurate as images are recorded with a full perspective camera, leading to inaccurate learning, see Fig. 3 b) and c). Alternatively, attempting to learn a model directly from the original pixel-aligned data with the intrinsic depth-scale ambiguity leads to poor results, as we show in Fig. 3 e). Hence, our idea is to adopt a full perspective camera model, and transform the data such that it is centered at a fixed depth, while preserving pixel alignment with the real images. We demonstrate that this can be effectively achieved by applying depth-dependent scale factor.

Our first observation is that scaling the mesh vertices $\mathbf{V}$ by s does not change its projection to the image. *Proof:* Let $\mathbf{v} = (\mathbf{v}_x, \mathbf{v}_y, \mathbf{v}_z) \in \mathbf{V}$ be a vertex of the original mesh, and $\mathbf{v}' = (s\mathbf{v}_x, s\mathbf{v}_y, s\mathbf{v}_z) \in s\mathbf{V}$ a vertex of the scaled mesh. For a camera with perspective focal length f_x, f_y and camera center c_x, c_y, the vertex $\mathbf{v}$ is projected to the image as $\pi(\mathbf{v}) = (f_x \frac{\mathbf{v}_x}{\mathbf{v}_z} + c_x, f_y \frac{\mathbf{v}_y}{\mathbf{v}_z} + c_y)$. The scaled vertices will be projected to the exact same pixels, $\pi(\mathbf{v}') = (f_x \frac{s\mathbf{v}_x}{s\mathbf{v}_z} + c_x, f_y \frac{s\mathbf{v}_y}{s\mathbf{v}_z} + c_y) = \pi(\mathbf{v})$ because the scale cancels out. This result might appear un-intuitive at first. What happens is that the object size gets scaled, but its center is also scaled, hence making the object bigger/smaller and pushing it further/closer to the camera at the same time. This effects cancel out to produce the same projection.

Given this result, all that remains to be done, is to find a scale factor which centers objects at a *fixed* depth z_0 to the camera. The desired scale factor that satisfies this condition is $s = \frac{z_0}{\mu_z}$, where $\mu_z = \frac{1}{n} \sum_{i=1}^{n} \mathbf{v}_z^i$ is the mean of the un-scaled mesh vertices depth. *Proof:* The proof follows immediately from the linearity property of the empirical mean. The depth of the transformed mesh center is:

$$\mu'_z = \frac{1}{n} \sum_{i=1}^{n} \mathbf{v}_z^{i\prime} = \frac{1}{n} \sum_i^n \mathbf{v}_z^i \frac{z_0}{\mu_z} = \mu_z \frac{z_0}{\mu_z} = z_0 \qquad (8)$$

This shows that the depth μ'_z of the scaled mesh center is fixed at z_0 and its image projection remains unchanged, as desired.

We scale all meshes in our training set as described above to center them at $z_0 = 2.2$ m and recompute GT labels. To maintain pixel alignment we use the camera intrinsic from the dataset. At test time, the images have various resolution and *unknown* intrinsic with person at large range of depth (see Fig. 6). We hence crop and resize the human-object patch such that the person in the resized patch appears as if they are at z_0 under the camera intrinsic we use during training. We leverage the human mesh reconstructed from [61] as a reference to determine the patch resizing factor. Please see supplementary for details.

4   Experiments

Datasets. We conducted experiments on the BEHAVE [10], COCO [47] and NTU-RGBD [48] dataset. BEHAVE captures 8 subjects interacting with 20 different objects in natural environments using RGBD cameras. Each image is paired with (pseudo) ground truth SMPL and object fits. CHORE is trained on 10.7k frames at 4 locations from BEHAVE and tested on 4.5k frames from one unseen location. All 20 categories are seen in both training and test set but at test time the object instances maybe different. As PHOSA [79] relies on 2D object mask for pose estimation, we exclude images where the object is occluded more than 70% for fair comparison, which leads to 4.1k test frames. To compare with Weng *et al.* [71], we select 10 common object categories between BEHAVE and their method (in total 2.6k images) and compare our method with them on this smaller set, denoted as BEHAVE^{--}.

To verify the generalization ability, we also test our method on COCO [47] where each image contains at least one instance of the object categories in BEHAVE and the object should not be occluded more than 50%. Images where there is no visible contact between human and object are also excluded. There are four overlapping categories between BEHAVE and COCO (backpack, suitcase, chair and sports ball) and in total 913 images are tested.

We additionally test on the NTU-RGBD dataset, which is quite interesting since it features human-object interactions. We select images from the NTU-RGBD dataset following the same criteria for COCO and in total 1.5k images of chair or backpack interactions are tested.

Evaluation and Baselines. To the best of our knowledge, PHOSA [79] and Weng *et al.* [71] are our closest baselines. To compare with PHOSA, we annotated object templates with contact part labels and intrinsic scales according to PHOSA's convention. [71] focuses on reconstructing the human in static scenes, hence their objects are mainly from indoor environments. Therefore, we only compare with it on the BEHAVE^{--} set and the indoor NTU-RGBD dataset.

For BEHAVE, we compute the Chamfer distance separately on SMPL and object meshes after Procrustes alignment using the combined mesh. Since [71] uses a different object template, we perform Procrustes alignment using only SMPL vertices for BEHAVE^{--}. As there are no 3D ground truth available in COCO and NTU-RGBD for thorough quantitative comparison, we compare our method with baselines through anonymous user study surveys.

4.1   Comparison on BEHAVE dataset

We compare our method against PHOSA [79] and [71] in Table 1. Note that the Procrustes alignment is performed on combined mesh for BEHAVE and on SMPL mesh only for BEHAVE^{--} for a fair comparison with [71]. Table 1 clearly shows that our learning based approach outperforms the heuristic optimization based PHOSA and [71].

We also compare our method qualitatively with PHOSA and [71] in Fig. 4. It can be seen that PHOSA fails to reconstruct the object at the correct position relative to the human. [71] also fails quite often as it uses predefined contact weights on SMPL vertices instead of predicting contacts from inputs. On the other hand, CHORE works well because it learns a 3D prior over human-object configurations based on the input image. See supplementary for more examples.

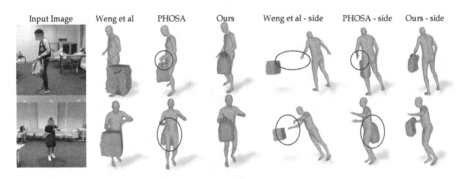

Fig. 5. Comparing our methods with [79] and [71] on NTU-RGBD dataset [48]. Our method trained on BEHAVE generalizes to NTU-RGBD and outperforms baselines.

Table 1. The mean and standard deviation of the Chamfer distance (cm) for SMPL and object reconstruction on [10]. Our approach that jointly reasons about the human, object and the contacts outperforms [71] and heuristics based PHOSA [79].

Dataset	Methods	SMPL ↓	Object ↓
BEHAVE	PHOSA [79]	12.17 ± 11.13	26.62 ± 21.87
	Ours	**5.58 ± 2.11**	**10.66 ± 7.71**
BEHAVE^{--}	PHOSA [79]	6.09 ± 1.98	182.67 ± 319.64
	Weng et al. [71]	7.86 ± 3.48	51.86 ± 96.38
	Ours	**5.22 ± 2.03**	**13.15 ± 10.60**

4.2   Generalisation Beyond BEHAVE

To verify our model trained on the BEHAVE dataset can generalize to other datasets, we further test it on the NTU-RGBD [48] as well as COCO dataset [47] and compare with [71,79].

Comparison with PHOSA [79]. We test our method and PHOSA on the selected COCO images discussed above. We then *randomly* select 50 images and render ours and PHOSA reconstruction results side by side. The results are collected in an anonymous user study survey and we ask 50 people on Amazon Mechanical Turk (AMT [1]) to select which reconstruction is better. Notably, people think our reconstruction is better than PHOSA on 72% of the images. A similar user study for images from the NTU-RGBD dataset is released to AMT and on average 84% of people prefer our reconstruction. Sample images are shown in Fig. 6 and Fig. 5. See supplementary for details on the user study and more qualitative examples.

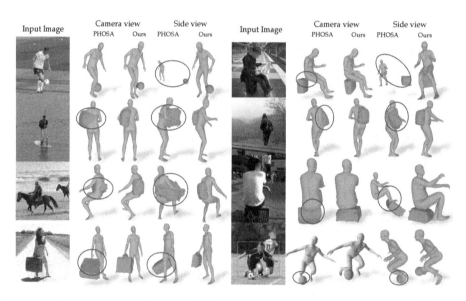

Fig. 6. Comparison with PHOSA [79] on COCO dataset [47]. For images with more than one person, the reconstructed human and object are highlighted by green and red boxes. Our model trained on BEHAVE outperforms PHOSA on 'in the wild' images. (Color figure online)

Comparison with Weng *et al.* [71]. One limitation of [71] is that they use indoor scene layout assumptions, which makes it unsuitable to compare on 'in the wild' COCO images. Instead, we only test it on the NTU-RGBD dataset. Similar to the comparison with PHOSA, we release a user study on AMT and ask 50 users to select which reconstruction is better. Results show that our method is preferred by 94% people. Our method clearly outperforms [71], see Fig. 5 and supplementary for more examples.

4.3   Comparison with a Human Reconstruction Method

Our method takes SMPL pose predicted from FrankMocap [61] as initialization and fine tunes it together with object using network predictions. We compare the human reconstruction performance with FrankMocap and PHOSA [79] in Table 2. It can be seen that our joint reasoning of human and object does not deteriorate the human reconstruction. Conversely, it slightly improves the human reconstruction as it takes cues from the interacting object into account.

4.4   Pixel-aligned Learning on Real Data

CHORE is trained with the depth-aware scaling strategy described in Sect. 3.3 for effective pixel aligned implicit surface learning on real data. To evaluate its importance, we compare with two baseline models trained with weak perspective and direct perspective (no depth-aware scaling on GT data) camera. Qualitative comparison of the neural reconstruction is shown in Fig. 3. We further fit SMPL and object meshes using these baseline models (with object pose prediction) on BEHAVE test set and compute the errors for reconstructed meshes, see Table 3 b) and c). It can be clearly seen that our proposed training strategy allows effective learning of implicit functions and significantly improves the reconstruction.

Table 2. Mean vertex to vertex (v2v) and Chamfer distance for human reconstruction results after Proscrustes alignment on SMPL mesh. Our method that jointly reasons about human and object performs on par with human only FrankMocap [61].

Metric (cm)	PHOSA	FrankMocap	Ours
v2v ↓	6.90 ± 2.68	6.91 ± 2.75	$\mathbf{5.46 \pm 3.47}$
Chamfer ↓	6.11 ± 1.98	6.12 ± 2.00	$\mathbf{5.27 \pm 1.98}$

4.5   Contacts Modeling

We have argued that contacts between human and the object are crucial for accurately modelling interaction. Quantitatively, the contact term E^c_{data} only reduces the object error slightly (Table 3 f, g) as contacts usually constitute a small region of the full body. Nevertheless, it makes significant difference qualitatively, as can be seen in Fig. 7. Without the contact information, the object cannot be fit correctly to the contact location. Our contact prediction helps snap the object to the correct contact location, leading to a more physically plausible and accurate reconstruction.

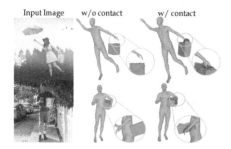

Input Image   w/o contact   w/ contact

Fig. 7. Accurate human and object reconstruction requires modeling contacts explicitly. Without contact information, the human and the objects are not accurately aligned and the resulting reconstruction is not physically plausible.

Table 3. Ablation studies. We can see that neither weak perspective (b) nor direct perspective camera (c) can work well on real data. Our proposed training strategy, together with rotation and translation prediction achieves the best results.

Methods	SMPL ↓	Object ↓
a. Neural recon	14.06	15.34
b. Weak persp	9.14	25.24
c. Direct persp	7.63	15.58
d. w/o f^R	6.58	17.54
e. w/o f^c	6.26	14.25
f. w/o contact	**5.51**	10.86
g. Full model	5.58	**10.66**

4.6   Other Ablation Studies

We further ablate our design choices in Table 3. Note that all numbers in Table 3 are Chamfer distances (cm) and computed on meshes after joint fitting except a) which is computed on the neural reconstructed point clouds. We predict object rotation and translation to initialize and regularize object fitting, which are important for accurate reconstruction. In Table 3, it can be seen that fitting results without rotation d) or without translation initialization e) are worse compared to our full model g). Without initialization the object gets stuck in local minima. See supplementary for qualitative examples.

We also compute the Chamfer distance of the neural reconstructed point clouds (Eq. (2)) using alignments computed from fitted meshes. It can be seen that this result is much worse than the results after joint fitting (Table 3g). This is because network predictions can be noisy in some regions while our joint fitting incorporates priors of human and object making the model more robust.

5   Limitations and Future Work

We introduce the first learning based method to reconstruct 3D humans and objects from single RGB images. Although the results are promising, there are some limitations. For instance, we assume known object template for the objects shown in the images. Future works can remove this assumption by selecting template from 3D CAD database or reconstructing shape directly from image. Non-rigid deformation, multiple objects, multi-person interactions are exciting avenues for future research. Please also refer to supp. for failure case discussion.

6   Conclusion

In this work we presented CHORE, the first method to *learn* a *joint* reconstruction of human, object and contacts from single images. CHORE combines powerful neural implicit predictions for human, object and its pose with robust model-based fitting. Unlike prior works on pixel-aligned implicit surface learning, we learn from real data instead of synthetic scans, which requires a different training strategy. We proposed a simple and elegant depth-aware scaling that reduces the depth-scale ambiguity while preserving pixel alignment.

Experiments on three different datasets demonstrate the superiority of CHORE compared to the SOTA. Quantitative experiments on BEHAVE dataset evidence that joint reasoning leads to a remarkable improvement of over 50% in terms of Chamfer distance compared to PHOSA. User studies on the NTU-RGBD and the challenging COCO dataset (no ground truth) show that our method is preferred over PHOSA by 84% and 72% users respectively. We also conducted extensive ablations, which reveal the effectiveness of the different components of CHORE, and the proposed depth-aware scaling for pixel-aligned learning on real data. Our code and models are released to promote further research in this emerging field of single image 3D human-object interaction capture.

Acknowledgements. We would like to thank RVH group members [2] for their helpful discussions. Special thanks to Beiyang Li for supplementary preparation. This work is funded by the Deutsche Forschungsgemeinschaft (DFG, German Research Foundation) - 409792180 (Emmy Noether Programme, project: Real Virtual Humans), and German Federal Ministry of Education and Research (BMBF): Tübingen AI Center, FKZ: 01IS18039A. Gerard Pons-Moll is a member of the Machine Learning Cluster of Excellence, EXC number 2064/1 - Project number 390727645.

References

1. https://www.mturk.com
2. http://virtualhumans.mpi-inf.mpg.de/people.html
3. Alldieck, T., Magnor, M., Bhatnagar, B.L., Theobalt, C., Pons-Moll, G.: Learning to reconstruct people in clothing from a single RGB camera. In: IEEE/CVF Conference on Computer Vision and Pattern Recognition (CVPR), pp. 1175–1186 (2019)
4. Alldieck, T., Magnor, M., Xu, W., Theobalt, C., Pons-Moll, G.: Detailed human avatars from monocular video. In: International Conference on 3D Vision, pp. 98–109, September 2018
5. Alldieck, T., Magnor, M., Xu, W., Theobalt, C., Pons-Moll, G.: Video based reconstruction of 3D people models. In: IEEE Conference on Computer Vision and Pattern Recognition, pp. 8387–8397 (2018)
6. Alldieck, T., Pons-Moll, G., Theobalt, C., Magnor, M.: Tex2shape: detailed full human body geometry from a single image. In: IEEE International Conference on Computer Vision (ICCV), pp. 2293–2303. IEEE, October 2019

7. Bhatnagar, B.L., Sminchisescu, C., Theobalt, C., Pons-Moll, G.: Combining implicit function learning and parametric models for 3D human reconstruction. In: Vedaldi, A., Bischof, H., Brox, T., Frahm, J.-M. (eds.) ECCV 2020. LNCS, vol. 12347, pp. 311–329. Springer, Cham (2020). https://doi.org/10.1007/978-3-030-58536-5_19

8. Bhatnagar, B.L., Sminchisescu, C., Theobalt, C., Pons-Moll, G.: Loopreg: self-supervised learning of implicit surface correspondences, pose and shape for 3D human mesh registration. In: Advances in Neural Information Processing Systems (NeurIPS), December 2020

9. Bhatnagar, B.L., Tiwari, G., Theobalt, C., Pons-Moll, G.: Multi-garment net: learning to dress 3D people from images. In: IEEE International Conference on Computer Vision (ICCV), pp. 5420–5430. IEEE, Ovtober 2019

10. Bhatnagar, B.L., Xie, X., Petrov, I., Sminchisescu, C., Theobalt, C., Pons-Moll, G.: Behave: dataset and method for tracking human object interactions. In: IEEE Conference on Computer Vision and Pattern Recognition (CVPR), pp. 15935–15946, June 2022

11. Bogo, F., Kanazawa, A., Lassner, C., Gehler, P., Romero, J., Black, M.J.: Keep It SMPL: automatic estimation of 3D human pose and shape from a single image. In: Leibe, B., Matas, J., Sebe, N., Welling, M. (eds.) ECCV 2016. LNCS, vol. 9909, pp. 561–578. Springer, Cham (2016). https://doi.org/10.1007/978-3-319-46454-1_34

12. Brahmbhatt, S., Ham, C., Kemp, C.C., Hays, J.: ContactDB: analyzing and predicting grasp contact via thermal imaging. In: The IEEE Conference on Computer Vision and Pattern Recognition (CVPR), pp. 8709–8719 (2019). https://contactdb.cc.gatech.edu

13. Brahmbhatt, S., Handa, A., Hays, J., Fox, D.: Contactgrasp: functional multi-finger grasp synthesis from contact. In: IROS, pp. 2386–2393 (04 2019)

14. Brahmbhatt, S., Tang, C., Twigg, C.D., Kemp, C.C., Hays, J.: ContactPose: a dataset of grasps with object contact and hand pose. In: Vedaldi, A., Bischof, H., Brox, T., Frahm, J.-M. (eds.) ECCV 2020. LNCS, vol. 12358, pp. 361–378. Springer, Cham (2020). https://doi.org/10.1007/978-3-030-58601-0_22

15. Chang, A.X., et al.: ShapeNet: an information-rich 3D model repository. Tech. Rep. arXiv:1512.03012 [cs.GR], Stanford University – Princeton University – Toyota Technological Institute at Chicago (2015)

16. Chen, Y., Huang, S., Yuan, T., Qi, S., Zhu, Y., Zhu, S.C.: Holistic++ scene understanding: single-view 3D holistic scene parsing and human pose estimation with human-object interaction and physical commonsense. In: The IEEE International Conference on Computer Vision (ICCV), pp. 8648–8657 (2019)

17. Chibane, J., Mir, A., Pons-Moll, G.: Neural unsigned distance fields for implicit function learning. In: Neural Information Processing Systems (NeurIPS), December 2020

18. Choy, C.B., Xu, D., Gwak, J.Y., Chen, K., Savarese, S.: 3D-R2N2: a unified approach for single and multi-view 3D object reconstruction. In: Leibe, B., Matas, J., Sebe, N., Welling, M. (eds.) ECCV 2016. LNCS, vol. 9912, pp. 628–644. Springer, Cham (2016). https://doi.org/10.1007/978-3-319-46484-8_38

19. Corona, E., Pons-Moll, G., Alenya, G., Moreno-Noguer, F.: Learned vertex descent: a new direction for 3D human model fitting. In: European Conference on Computer Vision (ECCV). Springer (October 2022)

20. Corona, E., Pumarola, A., Alenya, G., Moreno-Noguer, F., Rogez, G.: Ganhand: predicting human grasp affordances in multi-object scenes. In: Proceedings of the IEEE/CVF Conference on Computer Vision and Pattern Recognition (CVPR), pp. 5031–5041, June 2020

21. Ehsani, K., Tulsiani, S., Gupta, S., Farhadi, A., Gupta, A.: Use the force, luke! learning to predict physical forces by simulating effects. In: CVPR, pp. 224–233 (2020)

22. Fan, H., Su, H., Guibas, L.J.: A point set generation network for 3D object reconstruction from a single image. In: Proceedings of the IEEE Conference on Computer Vision and Pattern Recognition (CVPR), pp. 605–613, July 2017

23. Fieraru, M., Zanfir, M., Oneata, E., Popa, A., Olaru, V., Sminchisescu, C.: Learning complex 3D human self-contact. CoRR abs/2012.10366 (2020). https://arxiv.org/abs/2012.10366

24. Fieraru, M., Zanfir, M., Oneata, E., Popa, A.I., Olaru, V., Sminchisescu, C.: Three-dimensional reconstruction of human interactions. In: Proceedings of the IEEE/CVF Conference on Computer Vision and Pattern Recognition (CVPR), pp. 7214–7223, June 2020

25. Fu, K., Peng, J., He, Q., Zhang, H.: Single image 3D object reconstruction based on deep learning: a review. Multimedia Tools Appl. **80**(1), 463–498 (2020). https://doi.org/10.1007/s11042-020-09722-8

26. Guler, R.A., Kokkinos, I.: Holopose: holistic 3D human reconstruction in-the-wild. In: Proceedings of the IEEE/CVF Conference on Computer Vision and Pattern Recognition (CVPR), pp. 10884–10894, June 2019

27. Guo, C., Chen, X., Song, J., Hilliges, O.: Human performance capture from monocular video in the wild. In: 2021 International Conference on 3D Vision (3DV), pp. 889–898. IEEE (2021)

28. Habermann, M., Xu, W., Zollhoefer, M., Pons-Moll, G., Theobalt, C.: Deepcap: monocular human performance capture using weak supervision. In: IEEE Conference on Computer Vision and Pattern Recognition (CVPR), pp. 5052–5063. IEEE, June 2020

29. Habermann, M., Xu, W., Zollhöfer, M., Pons-Moll, G., Theobalt, C.: Livecap: real-time human performance capture from monocular video. ACM Trans. Graph. **38**(2), 14:1–14:17, March 2019. https://doi.org/10.1145/3311970

30. Hassan, M., Choutas, V., Tzionas, D., Black, M.J.: Resolving 3D human pose ambiguities with 3D scene constraints. In: International Conference on Computer Vision, pp. 2282–2292 (2019)

31. Hassan, M., Ghosh, P., Tesch, J., Tzionas, D., Black, M.J.: Populating 3D scenes by learning human-scene interaction. In: Proceedings IEEE/CVF Conference on Computer Vision and Pattern Recognition (CVPR), pp. 14708–14718, June 2021

32. Hasson, Y., et al.: Learning joint reconstruction of hands and manipulated objects. In: CVPR, pp. 11807–11816 (2019)

33. Huang, C.H.P., et al.: Capturing and inferring dense full-body human-scene contact. In: IEEE/CVF Conference on Computer Vision and Pattern Recognition (CVPR), pp. 13274–13285, June 2022

34. Huang, Z., Xu, Y., Lassner, C., Li, H., Tung, T.: Arch: animatable reconstruction of clothed humans. ArXiv abs/2004.04572 (2020)

35. Häne, C., Tulsiani, S., Malik, J.: Hierarchical surface prediction for 3D object reconstruction. In: 2017 International Conference on 3D Vision (3DV), pp. 412–420 (2017). https://doi.org/10.1109/3DV.2017.00054

36. Jiang, B., Zhang, J., Hong, Y., Luo, J., Liu, L., Bao, H.: Bcnet: learning body and cloth shape from a single image. In: European Conference on Computer Vision, pp. 18–35. Springer (2020). https://doi.org/10.1007/978-3-030-58565-5_2

37. Jiang, J., et al.: Avatarposer: articulated full-body pose tracking from sparse motion sensing. In: European Conference on Computer Vision (2022)

38. Jiang, W., Kolotouros, N., Pavlakos, G., Zhou, X., Daniilidis, K.: Coherent reconstruction of multiple humans from a single image. In: CVPR, pp. 5579–5588 (2020)
39. Jiang, Y., et al.: Neuralfusion: neural volumetric rendering under human-object interactions. arXiv preprint arXiv:2202.12825 (2022)
40. Kanazawa, A., Black, M.J., Jacobs, D.W., Malik, J.: End-to-end recovery of human shape and pose. In: IEEE Conference on Computer Vision and Pattern Recognition, pp. 7122–7131. IEEE Computer Society (2018)
41. Kar, A., Tulsiani, S., Malik, J.: Category-specific object reconstruction from a single image. In: IEEE Conference on Computer Vision and Pattern Recognition, pp. 1966–1974 (2015)
42. Karunratanakul, K., Yang, J., Zhang, Y., Black, M., Muandet, K., Tang, S.: Grasping field: learning implicit representations for human grasps. In: 8th International Conference on 3D Vision, pp. 333–344. IEEE, November 2020. https://doi.org/10.1109/3DV50981.2020.00043
43. Kocabas, M., Athanasiou, N., Black, M.J.: Vibe: video inference for human body pose and shape estimation. In: Proceedings IEEE Conference on Computer Vision and Pattern Recognition (CVPR), pp. 5252–5262. IEEE, June 2020. https://doi.org/10.1109/CVPR42600.2020.00530
44. Kolotouros, N., Pavlakos, G., Black, M.J., Daniilidis, K.: Learning to reconstruct 3D human pose and shape via model-fitting in the loop. In: ICCV, pp. 2252–2261 (2019)
45. Lei, J., Sridhar, S., Guerrero, P., Sung, M., Mitra, N., Guibas, L.J.: Pix2Surf: learning parametric 3D surface models of objects from images. In: Vedaldi, A., Bischof, H., Brox, T., Frahm, J.-M. (eds.) ECCV 2020. LNCS, vol. 12363, pp. 121–138. Springer, Cham (2020). https://doi.org/10.1007/978-3-030-58523-5_8
46. Li, Z., Sedlar, J., Carpentier, J., Laptev, I., Mansard, N., Sivic, J.: Estimating 3D motion and forces of person-object interactions from monocular video. In: Proceedings of the IEEE/CVF Conference on Computer Vision and Pattern Recognition (CVPR), pp. 8640–8649, June 2019
47. Lin, T.-Y.: Microsoft COCO: common objects in context. In: Fleet, D., Pajdla, T., Schiele, B., Tuytelaars, T. (eds.) ECCV 2014. LNCS, vol. 8693, pp. 740–755. Springer, Cham (2014). https://doi.org/10.1007/978-3-319-10602-1_48
48. Liu, J., Shahroudy, A., Perez, M., Wang, G., Duan, L.Y., Kot, A.C.: Ntu rgb+d 120: a large-scale benchmark for 3D human activity understanding. IEEE Trans. Pattern Anal. Mach. Intell. 42(10), 2684–2701 (2019). https://doi.org/10.1109/TPAMI.2019.2916873
49. Loper, M., Mahmood, N., Romero, J., Pons-Moll, G., Black, M.J.: SMPL: A skinned multi-person linear model. In: ACM Trans. Graph. 34(6), 1–16. ACM (2015)
50. Mescheder, L., Oechsle, M., Niemeyer, M., Nowozin, S., Geiger, A.: Occupancy networks: learning 3D reconstruction in function space. In: Proceedings IEEE Conference on Computer Vision and Pattern Recognition (CVPR), pp.4460–4470 (2019)
51. Monszpart, A., Guerrero, P., Ceylan, D., Yumer, E., J. Mitra, N.: iMapper: interaction-guided scene mapping from monocular videos. In: ACM SIGGRAPH (2019)
52. Müller, L., Osman, A.A.A., Tang, S., Huang, C.H.P., Black, M.J.: On self-contact and human pose. In: Proceedings IEEE/CVF Confernce on Computer Vision and Pattern Recognition (CVPR), 9990–9999 (2021)
53. Mller, N., Wong, Y.S., Mitra, N.J., Dai, A., Niessner, M.: Seeing behind objects for 3D multi-object tracking in RGB-D sequences. In: Proceedings of the Computer Vision and Pattern Recognition (CVPR), pp. 6071–6080. IEEE (2021)

54. Omran, M., Lassner, C., Pons-Moll, G., Gehler, P., Schiele, B.: Neural body fitting: unifying deep learning and model based human pose and shape estimation. In: International Conference on 3D Vision, pp. 484–494 (2018)

55. Pavlakos, G., et al.: Expressive body capture: 3D hands, face, and body from a single image. In: Proceedings IEEE Conference on Computer Vision and Pattern Recognition (CVPR), pp. 10975–10985 (2019)

56. Pavlakos, G., Zhu, L., Zhou, X., Daniilidis, K.: Learning to estimate 3D human pose and shape from a single color image. In: IEEE Conference on Computer Vision and Pattern Recognition, pp. 459–468 (2018)

57. Pons-Moll, G., Rosenhahn, B.: Model-based pose estimation, chap. 9, pp. 139–170. Springer (2011). https://doi.org/10.1007/978-0-85729-997-0_9

58. Pontes, J.K., Kong, C., Sridharan, S., Lucey, S., Eriksson, A., Fookes, C.: Image2mesh: a learning framework for single image 3D reconstruction. In: ACCV, pp. 365–381. Springer International Publishing (2019)

59. Rempe, D., Guibas, L.J., Hertzmann, A., Russell, B., Villegas, R., Yang, J.: Contact and human dynamics from monocular video. In: Vedaldi, A., Bischof, H., Brox, T., Frahm, J.-M. (eds.) ECCV 2020. LNCS, vol. 12350, pp. 71–87. Springer, Cham (2020). https://doi.org/10.1007/978-3-030-58558-7_5

60. Romero, J., Tzionas, D., Black, M.J.: Embodied hands: Modeling and capturing hands and bodies together. ACM Trans. Graphics, (Proc. SIGGRAPH Asia) **36**(6) (2017)

61. Rong, Y., Shiratori, T., Joo, H.: Frankmocap: a monocular 3D whole-body pose estimation system via regression and integration. In: IEEE International Conference on Computer Vision Workshops (2021)

62. Saito, S., Huang, Z., Natsume, R., Morishima, S., Kanazawa, A., Li, H.: Pifu: pixel-aligned implicit function for high-resolution clothed human digitization. In: IEEE International Conference on Computer Vision (ICCV). IEEE (2019)

63. Saito, S., Simon, T., Saragih, J., Joo, H.: Pifuhd: multi-level pixel-aligned implicit function for high-resolution 3D human digitization. In: Proceedings of the IEEE Conference on Computer Vision and Pattern Recognition (2020)

64. Savva, M., Chang, A.X., Hanrahan, P., Fisher, M., Nießner, M.: PiGraphs: Learning Interaction Snapshots from Observations. ACM Trans. Graphics (TOG) **35**(4) (2016)

65. Sun, G., et al.: Neural free-viewpoint performance rendering under complex human-object interactions. In: Proceedings of the 29th ACM International Conference on Multimedia (2021)

66. Sun, X., et al.: Pix3d: dataset and methods for single-image 3D shape modeling. In: Proceedings of the IEEE Conference on Computer Vision and Pattern Recognition (CVPR) (2018)

67. Taheri, O., Ghorbani, N., Black, M.J., Tzionas, D.: GRAB: a dataset of whole-body human grasping of objects. In: Vedaldi, A., Bischof, H., Brox, T., Frahm, J.-M. (eds.) ECCV 2020. LNCS, vol. 12349, pp. 581–600. Springer, Cham (2020). https://doi.org/10.1007/978-3-030-58548-8_34

68. Tiwari, G., Antic, D., Lenssen, J.E., Sarafianos, N., Tung, T., Pons-Moll, G.: Pose-ndf: Modeling human pose manifolds with neural distance fields. In: European Conference on Computer Vision (ECCV). Springer, October 2022

69. Tiwari, G., Bhatnagar, B.L., Tung, T., Pons-Moll, G.: Sizer: A dataset and model for parsing 3d clothing and learning size sensitive 3D clothing. In: European Conference on Computer Vision (ECCV), pp. 1–18. Springer (August 2020). https://doi.org/10.1007/978-3-030-58580-8_1

70. Wang, N., Zhang, Y., Li, Z., Fu, Y., Liu, W., Jiang, Y.-G.: Pixel2Mesh: generating 3D mesh models from single RGB images. In: Ferrari, V., Hebert, M., Sminchisescu, C., Weiss, Y. (eds.) ECCV 2018. LNCS, vol. 11215, pp. 55–71. Springer, Cham (2018). https://doi.org/10.1007/978-3-030-01252-6_4

71. Weng, Z., Yeung, S.: Holistic 3D human and scene mesh estimation from single view images. arXiv preprint arXiv:2012.01591 (2020)

72. Wu, J., Wang, Y., Xue, T., Sun, X., Freeman, W.T., Tenenbaum, J.B.: Marrnet: 3D shape reconstruction via 2.5D sketches. In: Advances In Neural Information Processing Systems (2017)

73. Wu, J., Zhang, C., Zhang, X., Zhang, Z., Freeman, W.T., Tenenbaum, J.B.: Learning 3D shape priors for shape completion and reconstruction. In: European Conference on Computer Vision (ECCV), pp. 646–662 (2018)

74. Xiang, Y., et al.: Objectnet3D: a large scale database for 3D object recognition. In: Leibe, B., Matas, J., Sebe, N., Welling, M. (eds.) Computer Vision - ECCV 2016, pp. 160–176. Springer International Publishing (2016). https://doi.org/10.1007/978-3-319-46484-8_10

75. Xiu, Y., Yang, J., Tzionas, D., Black, M.J.: ICON: implicit clothed humans obtained from normals. In: Proceedings of the IEEE/CVF Conference on Computer Vision and Pattern Recognition (CVPR), pp. 13296–13306, Jun 2022

76. Xu, Q., Wang, W., Ceylan, D., Mech, R., Neumann, U.: Disn: deep implicit surface network for high-quality single-view 3D reconstruction. In: Wallach, H., Larochelle, H., Beygelzimer, A., d'Alché-Buc, F., Fox, E., Garnett, R. (eds.) Advances in Neural Information Processing Systems. vol. 32. Curran Associates, Inc. (2019). https://proceedings.neurips.cc/paper/2019/file/39059724f73a9969845dfe4146c5660e-Paper.pdf

77. Yang, L., Zhan, X., Li, K., Xu, W., Li, J., Lu, C.: CPF: learning a contact potential field to model the hand-object interaction. In: ICCV, pp. 11097–11106 (2021)

78. Yi, H., et al.: Human-aware object placement for visual environment reconstruction. In: IEEE/CVF Conference on Computer Vision and Pattern Recognition (CVPR), pp. 3959–3970, June 2022

79. Zhang, J.Y., Pepose, S., Joo, H., Ramanan, D., Malik, J., Kanazawa, A.: Perceiving 3D human-object spatial arrangements from a single image in the wild. In: European Conference on Computer Vision (ECCV), pp. 34–51 (2020). https://doi.org/10.1007/978-3-030-58610-2_3

80. Zhang, S., Liu, J., Liu, Y., Ling, N.: Dimnet: dense implicit function network for 3D human body reconstruction. Comput. Graph. **98**, 1–10 (2021). https://doi.org/10.1016/j.cag.2021.04.035

81. Zhang, S., Zhang, Y., Ma, Q., Black, M.J., Tang, S.: Place: proximity learning of articulation and contact in 3D environments. In: International Conference on 3D Vision (3DV), pp. 642–651, November 2020

82. Zhang, X., Bhatnagar, B.L., Guzov, V., Starke, S., Pons-Moll, G.: Couch: towards controllable human-chair interactions. arXiv preprint arXiv:2205.00541 (May 2022)

83. Zhang, X., Zhang, Z., Zhang, C., Tenenbaum, J.B., Freeman, W.T., Wu, J.: Learning to reconstruct shapes from unseen classes. In: Advances in Neural Information Processing Systems (NeurIPS) (2018)

84. Zhao, F., Wang, W., Liao, S., Shao, L.: Learning anchored unsigned distance functions with gradient direction alignment for single-view garment reconstruction. In: Proceedings of the IEEE/CVF International Conference on Computer Vision, pp. 12674–12683 (2021)

85. Cao, Z., Gao, H., Mangalam, K., Cai, Q.-Z., Vo, M., Malik, J.: Long-term human motion prediction with scene context. In: Vedaldi, A., Bischof, H., Brox, T., Frahm, J.-M. (eds.) ECCV 2020. LNCS, vol. 12346, pp. 387–404. Springer, Cham (2020). https://doi.org/10.1007/978-3-030-58452-8_23
86. Zhou, K., Bhatnagar, B.L., Lenssen, J.E., Pons-Moll, G.: Toch: spatio-temporal object correspondence to hand for motion refinement. In: European Conference on Computer Vision (ECCV). Springer, October 2022

Learned Vertex Descent: A New Direction for 3D Human Model Fitting

Enric Corona[1(✉)], Gerard Pons-Moll[2,3], Guillem Alenyà[1],
and Francesc Moreno-Noguer[1]

[1] Institut de Robòtica i Informàtica Industrial, CSIC -UPC, Barcelona, Spain
enriccorona93@gmail.com
[2] University of Tübingen, Tübingen, Germany
[3] Max Planck Institute for Informatics, Saarbrücken, Germany

Abstract. We propose a novel optimization-based paradigm for 3D
human model fitting on images and scans. In contrast to existing
approaches that directly regress the parameters of a low-dimensional statistical body model (*e.g.*SMPL) from input images, we train an ensemble
of per vertex neural fields network. The network predicts, in a distributed
manner, the vertex descent direction towards the ground truth, based on
neural features extracted at the current vertex projection. At inference,
we employ this network, dubbed LVD, within a gradient-descent optimization pipeline until its convergence, which typically occurs in a fraction of a second even when initializing all vertices into a single point. An
exhaustive evaluation demonstrates that our approach is able to capture
the underlying body of clothed people with very different body shapes,
achieving a significant improvement compared to state-of-the-art. LVD
is also applicable to 3D model fitting of humans and hands, for which
we show a significant improvement to the SOTA with a much simpler
and faster method. Code is released at https://www.iri.upc.edu/people/
ecorona/lvd/

1 Introduction

Fitting 3D human models to data (single images/video/scans) is a highly
ambiguous problem. The standard approach to overcome this is by introducing
statistical shape priors [5,44,82] controlled by a reduced number of parameters.
Shape recovery then entails estimating these parameters from data. There exist
two main paradigms for doing so.

On the one side, optimization-based methods iteratively search for the model
parameters that best match available image cues, like 2D keypoints [6,11,37,57],
silhouettes [41,75] or dense correspondences [29]. On the other side, data-driven
regression methods for mesh recovery leverage deep neural networks to directly

---

Supplementary Information The online version contains supplementary material
available at https://doi.org/10.1007/978-3-031-20086-1_9.

S. Avidan et al. (Eds.): ECCV 2022, LNCS 13662, pp. 146–165, 2022.
https://doi.org/10.1007/978-3-031-20086-1_9

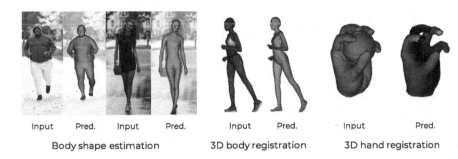

Fig. 1. Learned Vertex Descent (LVD) is a novel optimization strategy in which a network leverages local image or volumetric features to iteratively predict per-vertex directions towards an optimal body/hand surface. The proposed approach is directly applicable to different tasks with minimal changes on the network, and we show it can fit a much larger variability of body shapes than previous state-of-the-art. The figure depicts results on the three tasks where we have evaluated LVD: body shape reconstruction from a single image, and 3D fitting of body and hand scans.

predict the model parameters from the input [4,19,26,29,35,53,58]. In between these two streams, there are recent approaches that build hybrid methods combining optimization-regression schemes [34,37,77,83].

Regardless of the inference method, optimization or regression, and input modality, 2D evidence based on the entire image, keypoints, silhouettes, pointclouds, all these previous methods aim at estimating the parameters of a low-dimensional model (typically based on SMPL [44]). However, as we will show in the experimental section, these models struggle in capturing detailed body shape, specially for morphotypes departing from the mean (overweight or skinny people) or when the person is wearing loose clothing. We hypothesize that this is produced by two main reasons: 1) the models induce a bias towards the mean shape; and 2) the mapping from local image/pointcloud features to *global shape* parameters is highly non-linear. This makes optimization-based approaches prone to get stuck at local minima and have slow run times. Global shape regression methods lack the error-feedback loop of optimization methods (comparing the current estimate against image/scan input), and hence exhibit an even more pronounced bias towards mean shapes. Overcoming this problem would require immense amounts of training data, which is infeasible for 3D bodies.

To recover more detail, recent works regress or optimize a set of displacements on top of SMPL global shape [1,3,4,10,56], local surface elements [45] or points [47]. Like us, [38] by-pass the regression of global shape parameters and regress model vertices directly. However, similar to displacement-based methods [1,4], the proposed regression scheme [38] predicts the position of all points in a single pass and lacks an error-feedback loop. Hence, these methods regress a global shape based on global features and also suffer from bias towards the mean. Works based on implicit surfaces [17,70,71] address these limitations by making point-wise distributed predictions. Being more local, they require less training data. However, these methods do not produce surfaces with a coherent parameterization (e.g. SMPL vertices), and hence control is only possible with subsequent model fitting, which is hard if correspondences are not known [8,9,31,33].

In this paper, we propose a significantly different approach to all prior model fitting methods. Inspired by classical model-based fitting, where image gradients drive the direction of vertices and in turn global shape parameters, we propose to iteratively learn where 3D vertices should move based on neural features. For that purpose, we devise a novel data-driven optimization in which an ensemble of per-vertex neural fields is trained to predict the optimal 3D vertex displacement towards the ground-truth, based on local neural features extracted at the current vertex location. We dub this network LVD, from 'Learned Vertex Descent'. At inference, given an input image or scan, we initialize all mesh vertices into a single point and iteratively query LVD to estimate the vertex displacement in a gradient descent manner.

We conduct a thorough evaluation of the proposed learning-based optimization approach. Our experiments reveal that LVD combines the advantages of classical optimization and learning-based methods. LVD captures off-mean shapes significantly more accurately than all prior work, unlike optimization approaches it does not suffer from local minima, and converges in just 6 iterations. We attribute the better performance to the *distributed per-vertex predictions* and to the *error feedback loop* – the current vertex estimate is iteratively verified against the image evidence, a feature present in all optimization schemes but missing in learning-based methods for human shape estimation.

We demonstrate the usefulness of LVD for the tasks of 3D human shape estimation from images, and 3D scan registration(see Fig 1). In both problems, we surpass existing approaches by a considerable margin.

Our key contributions can be summarized as follows:

- A novel learning-based optimization where vertices *descent* towards the correct solution according to learned neural field predictions. This optimization is fast, does not require gradients and hand-crafted objective functions, and is not sensitive to initialization.
- We empirically show that our approach achieves state-of-the-art results in the task of human shape recovery from a single image.
- The LVD formulation can be readily adapted to the problem of 3D scan fitting. We also demonstrate state-of-the-art results on fitting 3D scans of full bodies and hands.
- By analysing the variance of the learned vertex gradient in local neighborhoods we can extract uncertainty information about the reconstructed shape. This might be useful for subsequent downstream applications that require confidence measures on the estimated body shape.

2   Related Work

2.1   Parametric Models for 3D Body Reconstruction

The *de-facto* approach for reconstructing human shape and pose is by estimating the parameters of a low-rank generative model [44,57,68,82], being SMPL [44] or SMPL-X [57] the most well known. We next describe the approaches to perform model fitting from images.

Optimization. Early approaches on human pose and shape estimation from images used optimization-based approaches to estimate the model parameters from 2D image evidence. Sigal *et al.* [75] did so for the SCAPE [5] human model, and assuming 2D input silhouettes. Guan *et al.* [28], combined silhouettes with manually annotated 2D skeletons. More recently, the standard optimization relies on 2D skeletons [11,57,77], estimated by off-the-shelf and robust deep methods [14]. This is typically accompanied by additional pose priors to ensure anthropomorphism of the retrieved pose [11,57]. Subsequent works have devised approaches to obtain better initialization from image cues [37], more efficient optimization pipelines [77], focused on multiple people [24] or extended the approach to multi-view scenarios [24,42].

While optimization-based approaches do not require images with 3D annotation for training and achieve relatively good registration of details to 2D observations, they tend to suffer from the non-convexity of the problem, being slow and falling into local minima unless provided with a good initialization and accurate 2D observations. In this work, we overcome both these limitations. From one side we only use as input a very coarse person segmentation and image features obtained with standard encoder-decoder architectures. And from the other side, the learned vertex displacements help the optimizer to converge to good solutions (empirically observed) in just a few iterations. On the downside, our approach requires 3D training data, but as we will show in the experimental section, by using synthetic data we manage to generalize well to real images.

Regression. Most current approaches on human body shape recovery consider the direct regression of the shape and pose parameters of the SMPL model [6,18,26,29,36,38,39,58,69,73,74]. As in optimization-based methods, different sorts of 2D image evidence have been used, *e.g.*keypoints [41], keypoints plus silhouette [59] or part segmentation maps [53]. More recently, SMPL parameters have been regressed directly from entire images encoded by pretrained deep networks (typically ResNet-like) [19,26,29,35,58]. However, regressing the parameters of a low-dimensional parametric model from a single view is always a highly ambiguous problem. This is alleviated by recent works that explore the idea of using hybrid approaches combining optimization and regression [34,37,43,51,77,83]. Very recently, [39] proposed regressing a distribution of parameters instead of having a regression into a single pose and shape representation. In any event, all these works still rely on representing the body shape through low-rank models.

We argue that other shape representations are necessary to model body shape details. This was already discussed in [38], which suggested representing the body shape using all vertices of a template mesh. We will follow the same spirit, although in a completely different learning paradigm. Specifically, [38] proposed regressing all points of the body mesh in one single regression pass of a Graph Convolutional Network. This led to noisy outputs that required post-processing to smooth the results by fitting the SMPL model. Instead, we propose a novel optimization framework, that leverages on a pre-learned prior that maps image evidence to vertex displacements towards the body shape. We will show that despite its simplicity, this approach surpasses by considerable margins all prior work, and provides smooth while accurate meshes without any post-processing.

2.2 Fitting Scans

Classical ICP-based has been used for fitting SMPL with no direct correspondences [12,13,25,32,61,63] or for registration of garments [10,40,62]. Integrating additional knowledge such as pre-computed 3D joints, facial key points [2] and body part segmentation [8] significantly improves the registration quality but these pre-processing steps are prone to error and often require human supervision. Other works initialize correspondences with a learned regressor [27,50,65,78] and later optimize model parameters. Like us, more recent methods also propose predicting correspondences [9] or body part labels [8] extracted via learnt features. Even though we do not explicitly propose a 3D registration method, LVD is a general algorithm that predicts parametric models. By optimizing these predictions without further correspondences, we surpass other methods that are explicitly designed for 3D registration.

2.3 Neural Fields for Parametric Models

Neural fields [20,21,54,66,79,86] have recently shown impressive results in modeling 3D human shape [15,22,23,52,54,85]. However, despite providing the level of detail that parametric models do not have, they are computationally expensive and difficult to integrate within pose-driven applications given the lack of correspondences. Recent works have already explored possible integrations between implicit and parametric representations for the tasks of 3D reconstruction [33,81], clothed human modeling [45,46,72], or human rendering [60].

We will build upon this direction by framing our method in the pipeline of neural fields. Concretely, we will take the vertices of an unfit mesh and use image features to learn their optimal displacement towards the optimal body shape.

3   Method

We next present our new paradigm for fitting 3D human models. For clarity, we will describe our approach in the problem of 3D human shape reconstruction from a single image. Yet, the formulation we present here is generalizable to the problem of fitting 3D scans, as we shall demonstrate in the experimental section.

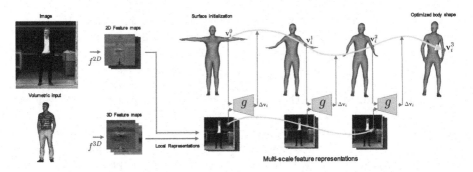

Fig. 2. LVD is a novel framework for estimation of 3D human body where local features drive the direction of vertices iteratively by predicting a per-vertex neural field. At each step t, g takes an input vertex $\mathbf{v}_i^t$ with its corresponding local features, to predict the direction towards its groundtruth position. The surface initialization here follows a T-Posed body, but the proposed approach is very robust to initialization.

3.1   Problem Formulation

Given a single-view image $\mathbf{I} \in \mathbb{R}^{H \times W}$ of a person our goal is to reconstruct his/her full body. We represent the body using a 3D mesh $\mathbf{V} \in \mathbb{R}^{N \times 3}$ with N vertices. For convenience (and compatibility with SMPL-based downstream algorithms) the mesh topology will correspond to that of the SMPL model, with $N = 6.890$ vertices and triangular connectivity (13.776 faces). It is important to note that our method operates on the vertices directly and hence it is applicable to other models (such as hands [68]). In particular, we do not use the low dimensional pose and shape parameterizations of such models.

3.2   LVD: Learning Vertex Descent

We solve the model fitting problem via an iterative optimization approach with learned vertex descent. Concretely, let $\mathbf{v}_i^t$ be the i-th vertex of the estimated mesh $\mathbf{V}$ at iteration t. Let us also denote by $\mathbf{F} \in \mathbb{R}^{H' \times W' \times F}$ the pixel aligned image features, and by $\mathbf{f}_i$ the F-dimensional vector of the specific features extracted at the projection of $\mathbf{v}_i^t$ on the image plane.

We learn a function $g(\cdot)$ that given the current 3D vertex position, and the image features at its 2D projection, predicts the magnitude and direction of steepest descent towards the ground truth location of the i-th vertex, which we shall denote as $\hat{\mathbf{v}}_i$. Formally:

$$g : (\mathbf{v}_i^t, \mathbf{f}_i) \mapsto \Delta\mathbf{v}_i . \tag{1}$$

where $\Delta\mathbf{v}_i \in \mathbb{R}^3$ is a vector with origin at $\mathbf{v}_i^t$ and endpoint at the ground truth $\hat{\mathbf{v}}_i$. In practice, during training, we will apply a component-wise clipping to the ground truth displacements with threshold λ. This stabilizes convergence during the first training iterations.

We learn the vertex descent function $g(\cdot)$ using a joint ensemble of per-vertex neural field networks, which we describe in Sect. 3.3. Once this mapping is learned, we can define the following update rule for our learned optimization:

$$\mathbf{v}_i^{t+1} = \mathbf{v}_i^t + \Delta\mathbf{v}_i \, . \tag{2}$$

The reconstruction problem then entails iterating over Eq. 2 until the convergence of $\Delta\mathbf{v}_i$. Fig. 2 depicts an overview of the approach.

Note that in essence we are replacing the standard gradient descent rule with a learned update that is locally computed at every vertex. As we will empirically demonstrate in the results section, despite its simplicity, the proposed approach allows for fast and remarkable convergence rates, typically requiring only 4 to 6 iterations no matter how the mesh vertices are initialized.

Uncertainty Estimation. An interesting outcome of our approach is that it allows estimating the uncertainty of the estimated 3D shape, which could be useful in downstream applications that require a confidence measure. For estimating the uncertainty of a vertex $\mathbf{v}_i$, we compute the variance of the points after perturbing them and letting the network converge. After this process, we obtain the displacements $\Delta\mathbf{x}_j^i$ between perturbed points $\mathbf{x}_j^i$ and the mesh vertex $\mathbf{v}_i$ predicted initially. We then define the uncertainty of $\mathbf{v}_i$ as:

$$U(\mathbf{v}_i) = \mathrm{std}(\{\mathbf{x}_j^i + \Delta\mathbf{x}_j^i\}_{j=1}^M) \, . \tag{3}$$

In Figs. 1 and 4 we represent the uncertainty of the meshes in dark blue. Note that the most uncertain regions are typically localized on the feet and hands.

3.3   Network Architecture

The LVD architecture has two main modules, one that is responsible of extracting local image features and the other of learning the optimal vertices' displacement.

Local Features. Following recent approaches [70,71], the local features $\mathbf{F}$ are learned with an encoder-decoder Hourglass network trained from scratch. Given a vertex $\mathbf{v}_i^t = (x_i^t, y_i^t, z_i^t)$ and the input image $\mathbf{I}$, these features are estimated as:

$$f : (\mathbf{I}, \pi(\mathbf{v}_i^t), z_i^t) \mapsto \mathbf{f}_i \, , \tag{4}$$

where $\pi(\mathbf{v})$ is a weak perspective projection of $\mathbf{v}$ onto the image plane. We condition $f(\cdot)$ with the depth z_i^t of the vertex to generate depth-aware local features. A key component of LVD is Predicting vertex displacements based on local features, which have been shown to produce better geometric detail, even from small training sets [16,70,71]. Indeed, this is one of our major differences compared to previous learning approaches for human shape estimation relying on parametric body models. These methods learn a mapping from a full image to global shape parameters (two disjoint spaces), which is hard to learn, and therefore they are unable to capture the local details. This results in poor image overlap between the recovered shape and the image as can be seen in Fig. 1.

Network Field. In order to implement the function $g(\cdot)$ in Eq. 1 we follow recent neural field approaches [49,55] and use a simple 3-layer MLP that takes as input the current estimate of each vertex $\mathbf{v}_i^t$ plus its local F-dimensional local feature $\mathbf{f}_i$ and predicts the displacement $\Delta\mathbf{v}_i$.

3.4   Training LVD

Training the proposed model entails learning the parameters of the functions $f(\cdot)$ and $g(\cdot)$ described above. For this purpose, we will leverage a synthetic dataset of images of people under different clothing and body poses paired with the corresponding SMPL 3D body registrations. We will describe this dataset in the experimental section.

In order to train the network, we proceed as follows: Let us assume we are given a ground truth body mesh $\hat{\mathbf{V}} = [\hat{\mathbf{v}}_1, \ldots, \hat{\mathbf{v}}_N]$ and its corresponding image $\mathbf{I}$. We then randomly sample M 3D points $\mathcal{X} = \{\mathbf{x}_1, \ldots, \mathbf{x}_M\}$, using a combination of points uniformly sampled in space and points distributed near the surface. Each of these points, jointly with the input image $\mathbf{I}$ is fed to the LVD model which predicts its displacement w.r.t. all ground truth SMPL vertices. Then, the loss associated with $\mathbf{x}_i$ is computed as:

$$\mathcal{L}(\mathbf{x}_i) = \sum_{j=1}^{N} \|\Delta\mathbf{x}_i^j - \hat{\Delta}\mathbf{x}_i^j\|_1 \,, \tag{5}$$

where $\Delta\mathbf{x}_i^j$ is the predicted displacement between $\mathbf{x}_i$ and $\hat{\mathbf{v}}_j$ and $\hat{\Delta}\mathbf{x}_i^j$ the ground truth displacement. $\|\cdot\|_1$ is the L1 distance. Note that by doing this, we are teaching our network to predict the displacement of any point in space to all vertices of the mesh. We found that this simple loss was sufficient to learn smooth but accurate body prediction. Remarkably, no additional regularization losses enforcing geometry consistency or anthropomorphism were required.

The reader is referred to the Supplemental Material for additional implementation and training details.

3.5   Application to 3D Scan Registration

The pipeline we have just described can be readily applied to the problem of fitting the SMPL mesh to 3D scans of clothed people or fitting the MANO model [68] to 3D scans of hands. The only difference will be in the feature extractor $f(\cdot)$ of Eq. 4, which will have to account for volumetric features. If $\mathbf{X}$ is a 3D voxelized scan, the feature extractor for a vertex $\mathbf{v}_i$ will be defined as:

$$f^{3D} : (\mathbf{X}, \mathbf{v}_i) \mapsto \mathbf{f}_i \,, \tag{6}$$

where again, $\mathbf{f}_i$ will be an F-dimensional feature vector. For the MANO model, the number of vertices of the mesh is $N = 778$. In the experimental section, we will show the adaptability of LVD to this scan registration problem.

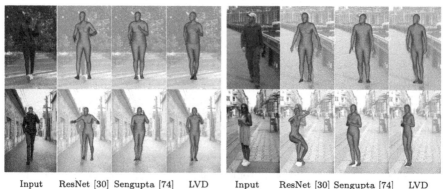

Input   ResNet [30] Sengupta [74]   LVD   Input   ResNet [30] Sengupta [74]   LVD

Fig. 3. Comparison of LVD to body shape estimation baselines. We first train a ResNet [30] on the same dataset to predict SMPL parameters. This approach fails to generalize to novel poses and shapes. We also compare LVD to Sengupta *et al.* [74], which perform well on real images, even though the predicted shapes do not fit perfectly the silhouettes of the people. See also quantitative results in Table 1.

4   Connection to Classical Model Based Fitting

Beyond its good performance, we find the connection of LVD to classical optimization based methods interesting, and understanding its relationship can be important for future improvements and extensions of LVD. Optimization methods for human shape recovery optimize model parameters to match image features such as correspondences [11,28,57], silhouettes [75,76]. See [64] for an in-depth discussion of optimization-based model based fitting.

Optimization Based. These methods minimize a scalar error $e(\mathbf{p}) \in \mathbb{R}$ with respect to human body parameters $\mathbf{p}$. Such scalar error is commonly obtained from a sum of squares error $e = \mathbf{e}(\mathbf{p})^T \mathbf{e}(\mathbf{p})$. The error vector $\mathbf{e} \in \mathbb{R}^{dN}$ contains the d dimensional residuals for the N vertices of a mesh, which typically correspond to measuring how well the projected $i - th$ vertex in the mesh fits the image evidence (*e.g.*, matching color of the rendered mesh vs image color). To minimize e one can use gradient descent, Gauss-Newton or Levenberg-Marquadt (LM) optimizer to find a descent direction for human parameters $\mathbf{p}$, but ultimately the direction is obtained from local image gradients as we will show. Without loss of generality, we can look at the individual residual incurred by one vertex $\mathbf{e}_i \in \mathbb{R}^d$, although bear in mind that an optimization routine considers all residuals simultaneously (the final gradient will be the sum of individual residual gradients or step directions in the case of LM type optimizers). The gradient of a single residual can be computed as

$$\nabla_{\mathbf{p}} e_i = \frac{\partial (\mathbf{e}_i^T \mathbf{e}_i)}{\partial \mathbf{p}} = 2 \left[\frac{\partial \mathbf{e}_i}{\partial \mathbf{v}_i} \frac{\partial \mathbf{v}_i}{\partial \mathbf{p}} \right]^T \mathbf{e}_i \qquad (7)$$

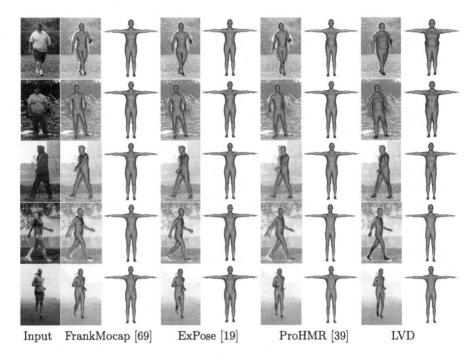

Input   FrankMocap [69]   ExPose [19]   ProHMR [39]   LVD

Fig. 4. SMPL reconstruction on images on-the-wild. For each method, we show the reconstruction in posed and canonical space. While previous works focus on pose estimation, they are prone to generate always an average body shape. In contrast, LVD generates a much richer distribution of body shapes as shown in the right-most column.

where the matrices that play a critical role in finding a good direction are the error itself $\mathbf{e}_i$, and $\frac{\partial \mathbf{e}_i}{\partial \mathbf{v}_i}$ which is the Jacobian matrix of the i-th residual with respect to the i-th vertex (the Jacobian of the vertex w.r.t. to parameters $\mathbf{p}$ is computed from the body model and typically helps to restrict (small) vertex displacements to remain within the space of human shapes). When residuals are based on pixel differences (common for rendering losses and silhouette terms) obtaining $\frac{\partial \mathbf{e}_i}{\partial \mathbf{v}_i}$ requires computing image gradients via finite differences. Such classical gradient is only meaningful once we are close to the solution.

Learned Vertex Descent. In stark contrast, our neural fields compute a learned vertex direction, with image features that have a much higher receptive field than a classical gradient. This explains why our method converges much faster and more reliably than classical approaches. To continue this analogy, our network learns to minimize the following objective error (for a single vertex)

$$e_i^{LVD} = \mathbf{e}_i^T \mathbf{e}_i = (\mathbf{v}_i - \mathbf{v}_i^{gt})^T (\mathbf{v} - \mathbf{v}_i^{gt}) \tag{8}$$

whose vertex gradient $\nabla_{\mathbf{v}_i} e_i^{LVD}$ points directly to the ground truth vertex $\mathbf{v}_i^{gt}$. In fact, our LVD is trained to learn the step size as well as the direction. What is even more remarkable, and surprising to us, is that we do not need a body model to constraint the vertices. That is, during optimization, we do not need to compute $\frac{\partial \mathbf{v}_i}{\partial \mathbf{p}}$, and project the directions to the space of valid human shapes. Since LVD has been learned from real human shapes, it automatically learns a prior, making the model very simple and fast during inference.

5   Experiments

We next evaluate the performance of LVD in the tasks of 3D human reconstruction from a single image and 3D registration. Additionally, we will provide empirical insights about the convergence of the algorithm and its shape expressiveness compared to parametric models.

Data. We use the RenderPeople, AXYZ and Twindom datasets [7,67,80], which consist of 767 3D scans. We first obtain SMPL registrations and manually annotate the correct fits. Then, we perform an aggressive data augmentation by synthetically changing body pose, shape and rendering several images per mesh from different views and illuminations. By doing, this we collect a synthetic dataset of $\sim 600k$ images which we use for training and validation. Test will be performed on real datasets. Please see Suppl. Mat. for more details.

5.1   3D Body Shape Estimation from a Single Image

We evaluate LVD in the task of body shape estimation and compare it against Sengupta et al. [74], which uses 2D edges and joints to extract features that are used to predict SMPL parameters. We also compare it against a model that

Table 1. Single-view SMPL estimation from LVD and baselines [19,37,39, 57,69,74] in the BUFF Dataset [84], in mm. The experiments take into account front, side and back views from the original scans and show that LVD outperforms all baselines in all scenarios and metrics except for back views. *We also report the results of PIFu, although note that this is a model-free approach in contrast to ours and the rest of the baselines, which recover the SMPL model.

Viewing angle:	Vertex-to-Vertex				Vertex-to-Surface				V2V	V2S
	0°	90°	180°	270°	0°	90°	180°	270°	Avg.	Avg.
*PIFu [70]	36.71	40.55	72.57	39.23	35.16	39.04	71.38	38.51	47.18	46.05
SMPL-X [57]	41.30	77.03	61.40	92.50	40.00	75.68	60.27	91.30	68.07	66.81
SPIN [37]	31.96	42.10	53.93	44.54	30.68	40.87	52.86	43.30	43.13	41.92
FrankMocap [69]	27.24	43.33	47.36	42.36	25.70	41.93	46.15	40.85	40.07	38.66
ExPose [19]	26.07	40.83	54.42	44.34	24.61	39.60	53.23	43.16	41.41	40.15
ProHMR [39]	39.55	49.26	55.42	46.03	38.42	48.18	54.41	44.88	47.56	46.47
Sengupta [74]	27.70	51.10	**40.11**	53.28	25.96	49.77	**38.80**	52.03	43.05	41.64
LVD	**25.44**	**38.24**	54.55	**38.10**	**23.94**	**37.05**	53.55	**36.94**	**39.08**	**37.87**

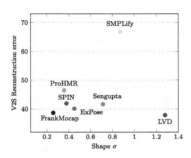 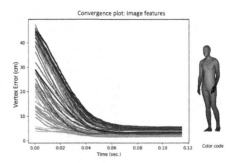

Fig. 5. *Left:* Variability of predicted body shape parameters (x-axis) with respect to vertex error (y-axis, lower is better) for works that fit SMPL to images. Previous approaches have mostly focused on the task of pose estimation. LVD, instead, aims to represent a more realistic distribution of predicted body shapes. *Right:* Convergence analysis of the proposed optimization, showing the distance from each SMPL vertex to the groundtruth scan during optimization, averaged for 200 examples of the BUFF dataset. The first iteration also includes the time to obtain the feature maps used during the rest of the optimization. Each line color encodes a different body region and the black line shows the average error of all vertices.

estimates SMPL pose and shape parameters given an input image. We use a pre-trained ResNet-18 [30] that is trained on the exact same data as LVD. This approach fails to capture the variability of body shapes and does not generalize well to new poses. We attribute this to the limited amount of data (only a few hundred 3D scans), with every image being a training data point, while in LVD every sampled 3D point counts as one training example. Figure 3 shows qualitative results on in-the-wild images. The predictions of LVD also capture the body shape better than those of Sengupta *et al.* [74] and project better to the silhouette of the input person.

Even though our primary goal is not pose estimation, we also compare LVD against several recent state-of-the-art model-based methods [19,37,39,57, 69] on the BUFF dataset, which has 9612 textured scans of clothed people. We have uniformly sampled 480 scans and rendered images at four camera views. Table 1 summarizes the results in terms of the Vertex-to-Vertex (V2V) and Vertex-to-Surface (V2S) distances. The table also reports the results of PIFu [70], although we should take this merely as a reference, as this is a model-free approach, while the rest of the methods in the Table are model-based. Figure 4 shows qualitative results on in-the-wild images. With this experiment, we want to show that previous works on pose and shape estimation tend to predict average body shapes. In contrast, our approach is able to reconstruct high-fidelity bodies for different morphotypes. It should be noted that our primary goal is to estimate accurate body shape, and our training data does not include extreme poses. Generalizing LVD to complex poses will most likely require self-supervised frameworks with in the wild 2D images like current SOTA [19,35,37,39], but this is out of the scope of this paper, and leave it for future work.

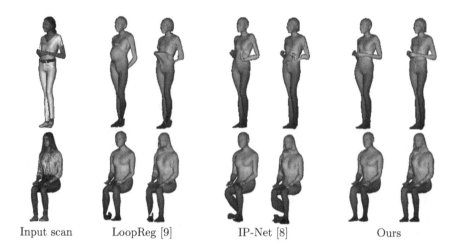

Input scan   LoopReg [9]   IP-Net [8]   Ours

Fig. 6. SMPL and SMPL+D registration of 3D scans from LVD in comparison to LoopReg and IP-Net.

Finally, it is worth to point that some of the baselines [19,37,57,69] require 2D keypoint predictions, for which we use the publicly available code of Open-Pose [14]. In contrast, our work requires coarse image segmentations to mask the background out because we trained LVD on renders of 3D scans without background. In any event, we noticed that our model is not particularly sensitive to the quality of input masks, and can still generate plausible body shapes with noisy masks (see Supp. Mat.).

5.2   Shape Expressiveness and Convergence Analysis

We further study the ability of all methods to represent different body shapes. For this, we obtain the SMPL shape for our model and pose estimation baselines in Table 1 and fit the SMPL model with 300 shape components. We then calculate the standard deviation σ_2 of the second PCA component, responsible for the shape diversity. Figure 5 (left) depicts the graph of shape σ_2 vs. V2S error. It is clearly shown that LVD stands out in its capacity to represent different shapes. In contrast, most previous approaches have a much lower capacity to recover different body shapes, with a σ_2 value 3 times smaller than ours.

We also perform an empirical convergence analysis of LVD. Figure 5 (right) plots the average V2V error (in mm) vs time, computed when performing shape inference for 200 different samples of the BUFF dataset. Note that the optimization converges at a tenth of a second using a GTX 1080 Ti GPU. The total computation time is equivalent to 6 iterations of our algorithm. The color-coded 3D mesh on the side of Fig. 5 (right) shows in which parts of the body the algorithm suffers the most. These areas are concentrated on the arms. Other regions that hardly become occluded, such as torso or head have the lowest error. The average vertex error is represented with a thicker black line.

Table 2. Evaluation on SMPL and SMPL+D registration on the RenderPeople Dataset [67]. The initial SMPL estimation from LVD is already very competitive against baselines [8,9]. By using these predictions as initialization for SMPL/SMPL+D registration, we obtain $\sim 28.4\%$ and $\sim 37.7\%$ relative improvements with respect to the second-best method [8] in joint and SMPL vertex distances respectively.

		Forward pass	SMPL Registration				SMPL+D Registration			
		LVD	No corresp.	LoopReg [9]	IP-Net [8]	LVD	No corresp.	LoopReg [9]	IP-Net [8]	LVD
SMPL error	Joint [cm]	5.89	16.6	9.33	3.60	**2.53**	16.6	9.32	3.63	**2.60**
	Vertex [cm]	6.27	21.3	12.2	5.03	**3.00**	21.3	12.3	5.20	**3.24**
Recons. to Scan	V2V [mm]	8.98	12.51	10.35	8.84	**8.16**	1.45	1.43	1.21	**1.14**
	V2S [mm]	6.61	10.53	8.19	6.61	**5.87**	0.72	0.69	0.53	**0.47**
Scan to Recons.	V2V [mm]	12.6	16.92	14.27	12.25	**11.31**	8.53	8.01	7.22	**6.88**
	V2S [mm]	9.31	13.75	10.49	8.45	**7.43**	4.22	3.47	2.78	**2.44**

Finally, we measure the sensitiveness of the convergence to different initializations of the body mesh. We randomly sampled 1K different initializations from the AMASS dataset [48] and analized the deviation of the converged reconstructions, obtaining a standard deviation of the SMPL surface vertices of only $\sigma = 1.2\,\text{mm}$ across all reconstructions. We credit this robustness to the dense supervision during training, which takes input points from a volume on the 3D space, as well as around the groundtruth body surface.

5.3 3D Body Registration

LVD is designed to be general and directly applicable for different tasks. We analyze the performance of LVD on the task of SMPL and SMPL+D registration on 3D point-clouds of humans. This task consists in initially estimating the SMPL mesh (which we do iterating our approach) and then running a second minimization of the Chamfer distance to fit SMPL and SMPL+D. The results are reported in Table 2, where we compare against LoopReg [9], IP-Net [8], and also against the simple baseline of registering SMPL with no correspondences starting from a T-Posed SMPL. Besides the V2V and V2S metrics (bi-directional), we also report the Joint error (predicted using SMPL's joint regressor), and the distance between ground truth SMPL vertices and their correspondences in the registered mesh (Vertex distance). Note that again, LVD consistently outperforms the rest of the baselines. This is also qualitatively shown in Fig. 6.

5.4 3D Hand Registration

The proposed approach is directly applicable to any statistical model, thus we also test it in the task of registration of MANO [68] from input point-clouds of hands, some of them incomplete. For this experiment, we do not change the network hyperparameters and only update the number of vertices to predict (778 for MANO). We test this task on the MANO [68] dataset, where the approach also outperforms IP-Net [8], trained on the same data. Table 3 summarizes the performance of LVD and baselines, and qualitative examples are shown in Fig. 7. Note that LVD shows robustness even in situations with partial point clouds.

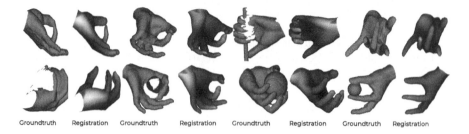

Groundtruth   Registration   Groundtruth   Registration   Groundtruth   Registration   Groundtruth   Registration

Fig. 7. Registration of MANO from input pointclouds. We include more visuals and qualitative comparisons with baselines in Supplementary Material.

Table 3. Registration of MANO [68] from input 3D pointclouds of hands.

	MANO error		Reconstruction to scan		Scan to reconstruction	
Method	Joint [cm]	Vertex [cm]	V2V [mm]	V2S [mm]	V2V [mm]	V2S [mm]
No corresp.	6.49	7.05	5.31	5.28	8.06	6.40
IP-Net [8]	1.44	1.73	3.29	3.23	6.17	4.08
LVD	**.76**	**.96**	**2.73**	**2.65**	**5.62**	**3.33**

6   Conclusion

We have introduced Learned Vertex Descent, a novel framework for human shape recovery where vertices are iteratively displaced towards the predicted body surface. The proposed method is lightweight, can work real-time and surpasses previous state-of-the-art in the tasks of body shape estimation from a single view or 3D scan registration, of both the full body and hands. Being so simple, easy to use and effective, we believe LVD can be an important building block for future model-fitting methods. Future work will focus in self-supervised training formulations of LVD to tackle difficult poses, scenes and multi-person scenarios.

Acknowledgment. This work is supported in part by the Spanish government with the project MoHuCo PID2020-120049RB-I00, by the "European Union NextGenerationEU/PRTR" through CSIC's Thematic Platforms (PTI+ Neuro-Aging), the Deutsche Forschungsgemeinschaft (DFG, German Research Foundation) - 409792180 (Emmy Noether Programme, project: Real Virtual Humans) and German Federal Ministry of Education and Research (BMBF): Tübingen AI Center, FKZ: 01IS18039A. Gerard Pons-Moll is a member of the Machine Learning Cluster of Excellence, EXC number 2064/1 - Project number 390727645. We thank NVIDIA for donating GPUs.

References

1. Alldieck, T., Magnor, M., Bhatnagar, B.L., Theobalt, C., Pons-Moll, G.: Learning to reconstruct people in clothing from a single RGB camera. In: CVPR, (2019)

2. Alldieck, T., Magnor, M., Bhatnagar, B.L., Theobalt, C., Pons-Moll, G.: Learning to reconstruct people in clothing from a single rgb camera. In: Proceedings of the IEEE/CVF Conference on Computer Vision and Pattern Recognition, pp. 1175–1186 (2019)

3. Alldieck, T., Magnor, M., Xu, W., Theobalt, C., Pons-Moll, G.: Video based reconstruction of 3d people models. In: CVPR, (2018)

4. Alldieck, T., Pons-Moll, G., Theobalt, C., Magnor, M.: Tex2shape: detailed full human body geometry from a single image. In: ICCV, IEEE (2019)

5. Anguelov, D., Srinivasan, P., Koller, D., Thrun, S., Rodgers, J., Davis, J.: SCAPE: shape completion and animation of people. SIGGRAPH **24**, 408–416 (2005)

6. Arnab, A., Doersch, C., Zisserman, A.: Exploiting temporal context for 3d human pose estimation in the wild. In: CVPR, pp. 3395–3404 (2019)

7. Axyz dataset. https://secure.axyz-design.com/

8. Bhatnagar, B.L., Sminchisescu, C., Theobalt, C., Pons-Moll, G.: Combining implicit function learning and parametric models for 3D human reconstruction. In: Vedaldi, A., Bischof, H., Brox, T., Frahm, J.-M. (eds.) ECCV 2020. LNCS, vol. 12347, pp. 311–329. Springer, Cham (2020). https://doi.org/10.1007/978-3-030-58536-5_19

9. Bhatnagar, B.L., Sminchisescu, C., Theobalt, C., Pons-Moll, G.: LoopReg: Self-supervised learning of implicit surface correspondences, pose and shape for 3d human mesh registration. NeurIPS **33**, 12909-12922(2020)

10. Bhatnagar, B.L., Tiwari, G., Theobalt, C., Pons-Moll, G.: Multi-garment net: learning to dress 3d people from images. In: ICCV, pp. 5420-5430 (2019)

11. Bogo, F., Kanazawa, A., Lassner, C., Gehler, P., Romero, J., Black, M.J.: Keep It SMPL: automatic estimation of 3D human pose and shape from a single image. In: Leibe, B., Matas, J., Sebe, N., Welling, M. (eds.) ECCV 2016. LNCS, vol. 9909, pp. 561–578. Springer, Cham (2016). https://doi.org/10.1007/978-3-319-46454-1_34

12. Bogo, F., Romero, J., Loper, M., Black, M.J.: FAUST: dataset and evaluation for 3d mesh registration. In: CVPR, pp. 3794–3801 (2014)

13. Bogo, F., Romero, J., Pons-Moll, G., Black, M.J.: Dynamic FAUST: registering human bodies in motion. In: CVPR, pp. 6233–6242 (2017)

14. Cao, Z., Hidalgo, G., Simon, T., Wei, S.E., Sheikh, Y.: Openpose: realtime multi-person 2D pose estimation using part affinity fields. PAMI **43**(1), 172–186 (2019)

15. Chen, X., Zheng, Y., Black, M.J., Hilliges, O., Geiger, A.: SNARF: differentiable forward skinning for animating non-rigid neural implicit shapes. In: ICCV, pp. 11594-11604 (2021)

16. Chibane, J., Pons-Moll, G.: Implicit feature networks for texture completion from partial 3D data. In: Bartoli, A., Fusiello, A. (eds.) ECCV 2020. LNCS, vol. 12536, pp. 717–725. Springer, Cham (2020). https://doi.org/10.1007/978-3-030-66096-3_48

17. Chibane, J., Pons-Moll, G., et al.: Neural unsigned distance fields for implicit function learning. NeurIPS **33**, 21638-21652 (2020)

18. Choutas, V., Müller, L., Huang, C.H.P., Tang, S., Tzionas, D., Black, M.J.: Accurate 3d body shape regression using metric and semantic attributes. In: CVPR, pp. 2718–2728 (2022)

19. Choutas, V., Pavlakos, G., Bolkart, T., Tzionas, D., Black, M.J.: Monocular expressive body regression through body-driven attention. In: Vedaldi, A., Bischof, H., Brox, T., Frahm, J.-M. (eds.) ECCV 2020. LNCS, vol. 12355, pp. 20–40. Springer, Cham (2020). https://doi.org/10.1007/978-3-030-58607-2_2

20. Corona, E., et al.: LISA: Learning implicit shape and appearance of hands. arXiv preprint arXiv:2204.01695 (2022)

21. Corona, E., Pumarola, A., Alenya, G., Pons-Moll, G., Moreno-Noguer, F.: SMPlicit: topology-aware generative model for clothed people. In: CVPR, pp. 11875–11885 (2021)
22. Deng, B., Lewis, J.P., Jeruzalski, T., Pons-Moll, G., Hinton, G., Norouzi, M., Tagliasacchi, A.: NASA neural articulated shape approximation. In: Vedaldi, A., Bischof, H., Brox, T., Frahm, J.-M. (eds.) ECCV 2020. LNCS, vol. 12352, pp. 612–628. Springer, Cham (2020). https://doi.org/10.1007/978-3-030-58571-6_36
23. Deprelle, T., Groueix, T., Fisher, M., Kim, V.G., Russell, B.C., Aubry, M.: Learning elementary structures for 3D shape generation and matching. arXiv preprint arXiv:1908.04725 (2019)
24. Dong, Z., Song, J., Chen, X., Guo, C., Hilliges, O.: Shape-aware multi-person pose estimation from multi-view images. In: ICCV, pp. 11158–11168 (2021)
25. Dyke, R.M., Lai, Y.K., Rosin, P.L., Tam, G.K.: Non-rigid registration under anisotropic deformations. Comput. Aided Geom. Des. **71**, 142–156 (2019)
26. Georgakis, G., Li, R., Karanam, S., Chen, T., Košecká, J., Wu, Z.: Hierarchical kinematic human mesh recovery. In: Vedaldi, A., Bischof, H., Brox, T., Frahm, J.-M. (eds.) ECCV 2020. LNCS, vol. 12362, pp. 768–784. Springer, Cham (2020). https://doi.org/10.1007/978-3-030-58520-4_45
27. Groueix, T., Fisher, M., Kim, V.G., Russell, B.C., Aubry, M.: 3D-CODED: 3D correspondences by deep deformation. In: Ferrari, V., Hebert, M., Sminchisescu, C., Weiss, Y. (eds.) ECCV 2018. LNCS, vol. 11206, pp. 235–251. Springer, Cham (2018). https://doi.org/10.1007/978-3-030-01216-8_15
28. Guan, P., Weiss, A., Balan, A.O., Black, M.J.: Estimating human shape and pose from a single image. In: ICCV, IEEE (2009)
29. Guler, R.A., Kokkinos, I.: Holopose: holistic 3d human reconstruction in-the-wild. In: CVPR, pp. 10884-10894 (2019)
30. He, K., Zhang, X., Ren, S., Sun, J.: Deep residual learning for image recognition. In: CVPR, (2016)
31. He, T., Xu, Y., Saito, S., Soatto, S., Tung, T.: Arch++: animation-ready clothed human reconstruction revisited. In: Proceedings of the IEEE/CVF International Conference on Computer Vision, pp. 11046–11056 (2021)
32. Hirshberg, D.A., Loper, M., Rachlin, E., Black, M.J.: Coregistration: simultaneous alignment and modeling of articulated 3D shape. In: Fitzgibbon, A., Lazebnik, S., Perona, P., Sato, Y., Schmid, C. (eds.) ECCV 2012. LNCS, vol. 7577, pp. 242–255. Springer, Heidelberg (2012). https://doi.org/10.1007/978-3-642-33783-3_18
33. Huang, Z., Xu, Y., Lassner, C., Li, H., Tung, T.: Arch: animatable reconstruction of clothed humans. In: CVPR, (2020)
34. Joo, H., Neverova, N., Vedaldi, A.: Exemplar fine-tuning for 3d human model fitting towards in-the-wild 3D human pose estimation. arXiv preprint arXiv:2004.03686 (2020)
35. Kanazawa, A., Black, M.J., Jacobs, D.W., Malik, J.: End-to-end recovery of human shape and pose. In: CVPR, (2018)
36. Kocabas, M., Athanasiou, N., Black, M.J.: Vibe: video inference for human body pose and shape estimation. In: CVPR, pp. 5253–5263 (2020)
37. Kolotouros, N., Pavlakos, G., Black, M.J., Daniilidis, K.: Learning to reconstruct 3d human pose and shape via model-fitting in the loop. In: ICCV, (2019)
38. Kolotouros, N., Pavlakos, G., Daniilidis, K.: Convolutional mesh regression for single-image human shape reconstruction. In: CVPR, (2019)
39. Kolotouros, N., Pavlakos, G., Jayaraman, D., Daniilidis, K.: Probabilistic modeling for human mesh recovery. In: ICCV, pp. 11605–11614 (2021)

40. Lähner, Z., Cremers, D., Tung, T.: DeepWrinkles: accurate and realistic clothing modeling. In: Ferrari, V., Hebert, M., Sminchisescu, C., Weiss, Y. (eds.) ECCV 2018. LNCS, vol. 11208, pp. 698–715. Springer, Cham (2018). https://doi.org/10.1007/978-3-030-01225-0_41

41. Lassner, C., Romero, J., Kiefel, M., Bogo, F., Black, M.J., Gehler, P.V.: Unite the people: Closing the loop between 3d and 2d human representations. In: CVPR, (2017)

42. Li, Z., Oskarsson, M., Heyden, A.: 3d human pose and shape estimation through collaborative learning and multi-view model-fitting. In: WCACV, pp. 1888–1897 (2021)

43. Lin, K., Wang, L., Liu, Z.: End-to-end human pose and mesh reconstruction with transformers. In: CVPR, pp. 1954–1963 (2021)

44. Loper, M., Mahmood, N., Romero, J., Pons-Moll, G., Black, M.J.: SMPL: a skinned multi-person linear model. ToG **34**, 1–16 (2015)

45. Ma, Q., Saito, S., Yang, J., Tang, S., Black, M.J.: Scale: modeling clothed humans with a surface codec of articulated local elements. In: CVPR, pp. 16082–16093 (2021)

46. Ma, Q., et al.: Learning to dress 3d people in generative clothing. In: CVPR, pp. 6469–6478 (2020)

47. Ma, Q., Yang, J., Tang, S., Black, M.J.: The power of points for modeling humans in clothing. In: ICCV, pp. 10974–10984 (2021)

48. Mahmood, N., Ghorbani, N., Troje, N.F., Pons-Moll, G., Black, M.J.: Amass: archive of motion capture as surface shapes. In: ICCV, (2019)

49. Mescheder, L., Oechsle, M., Niemeyer, M., Nowozin, S., Geiger, A.: Occupancy networks: Learning 3d reconstruction in function space. In: CVPR, (2019)

50. Mir, A., Alldieck, T., Pons-Moll, G.: Learning to transfer texture from clothing images to 3d humans. In: IEEE Conference on Computer Vision and Pattern Recognition (CVPR), IEEE (2020)

51. Moon, G., Lee, K.M.: I2L-MeshNet: image-to-lixel prediction network for accurate 3d human pose and mesh estimation from a single rgb image. In: Vedaldi, A., Bischof, H., Brox, T., Frahm, J.-M. (eds.) ECCV 2020. LNCS, vol. 12352, pp. 752–768. Springer, Cham (2020). https://doi.org/10.1007/978-3-030-58571-6_44

52. Niemeyer, M., Mescheder, L., Oechsle, M., Geiger, A.: Occupancy flow: 4d reconstruction by learning particle dynamics. In: CVPR, pp. 5379–5389 (2019)

53. Omran, M., Lassner, C., Pons-Moll, G., Gehler, P., Schiele, B.: Neural body fitting: unifying deep learning and model based human pose and shape estimation. In: 3DV. IEEE (2018)

54. Pan, J., Han, X., Chen, W., Tang, J., Jia, K.: Deep mesh reconstruction from single rgb images via topology modification networks. In: ICCV, pp. 9964–9973 (2019)

55. Park, J.J., Florence, P., Straub, J., Newcombe, R., Lovegrove, S.: DeepSDF: learning continuous signed distance functions for shape representation. In: CVPR, (2019)

56. Patel, C., Liao, Z., Pons-Moll, G.: TailorNet: predicting clothing in 3d as a function of human pose, shape and garment style. In: CVPR, IEEE (2020)

57. Pavlakos, G., et al.: Expressive body capture: 3d hands, face, and body from a single image. In: CVPR, (2019)

58. Pavlakos, G., Kolotouros, N., Daniilidis, K.: Texturepose: supervising human mesh estimation with texture consistency. In: ICCV, pp. 803–812 (2019)

59. Pavlakos, G., Zhu, L., Zhou, X., Daniilidis, K.: Learning to estimate 3d human pose and shape from a single color image. In: CVPR, pp. 459–468 (2018)

60. Peng, S., et al.: Neural body: Implicit neural representations with structured latent codes for novel view synthesis of dynamic humans. In: CVPR, pp. 9054–9063 (2021)
61. Pishchulin, L., Wuhrer, S., Helten, T., Theobalt, C., Schiele, B.: Building statistical shape spaces for 3d human modeling. Pattern Recogn. **67**, 276–286 (2017)
62. Pons-Moll, G., Pujades, S., Hu, S., Black, M.: ClothCap: seamless 4D clothing capture and retargeting. SIGGRAPH **36**(4), 1–15 (2017)
63. Pons-Moll, G., Romero, J., Mahmood, N., Black, M.J.: Dyna: A model of dynamic human shape in motion. ToG **34**(4), 1–14 (2015)
64. Decker, P., Paulus, D.: Model based pose estimation using SURF. In: Koch, R., Huang, F. (eds.) ACCV 2010. LNCS, vol. 6469, pp. 11–20. Springer, Heidelberg (2011). https://doi.org/10.1007/978-3-642-22819-3_2
65. Pons-Moll, G., Taylor, J., Shotton, J., Hertzmann, A., Fitzgibbon, A.: Metric regression forests for correspondence estimation. IJCV **113**(3), 163–175 (2015)
66. Prokudin, S., Black, M.J., Romero, J.: SMPLpix: neural avatars from 3d human models. In: WCACV, pp. 1810–1819 (2021)
67. Renderpeople dataset. https://renderpeople.com/
68. Romero, J., Tzionas, D., Black, M.J.: Embodied hands: Modeling and capturing hands and bodies together. ToG **36**, 1–17 (2017)
69. Rong, Y., Shiratori, T., Joo, H.: FrankMocap: fast monocular 3d hand and body motion capture by regression and integration. arXiv preprint arXiv:2008.08324 (2020)
70. Saito, S., Huang, Z., Natsume, R., Morishima, S., Kanazawa, A., Li, H.: PIFu: pixel-aligned implicit function for high-resolution clothed human digitization. In: ICCV, (2019)
71. Saito, S., Simon, T., Saragih, J., Joo, H.: PIFuHD: multi-level pixel-aligned implicit function for high-resolution 3d human digitization. In: CVPR, (2020)
72. Saito, S., Yang, J., Ma, Q., Black, M.J.: SCANimate: weakly supervised learning of skinned clothed avatar networks. In: CVPR, pp. 2886–2897 (2021)
73. Sengupta, A., Budvytis, I., Cipolla, R.: Synthetic training for accurate 3d human pose and shape estimation in the wild. BMVC (2020)
74. Sengupta, A., Budvytis, I., Cipolla, R.: Hierarchical kinematic probability distributions for 3d human shape and pose estimation from images in the wild. In: ICCV, pp. 11219–11229 (2021)
75. Sigal, L., Balan, A., Black, M.: Combined discriminative and generative articulated pose and non-rigid shape estimation. NeurIPS **20**, 1337–1344 (2007)
76. Sminchisescu, C., Triggs, B.: Covariance scaled sampling for monocular 3d body tracking. In: CVPR. vol. 1, pp. I-I. IEEE (2001)
77. Song, J., Chen, X., Hilliges, O.: Human body model fitting by learned gradient descent. In: Vedaldi, A., Bischof, H., Brox, T., Frahm, J.-M. (eds.) ECCV 2020. LNCS, vol. 12365, pp. 744–760. Springer, Cham (2020). https://doi.org/10.1007/978-3-030-58565-5_44
78. Taylor, J., Shotton, J., Sharp, T., Fitzgibbon, A.: The vitruvian manifold: inferring dense correspondences for one-shot human pose estimation. In: CVPR, pp. 103–110. IEEE (2012)
79. Tiwari, G., Antic, D., Lenssen, J.E., Sarafianos, N., Tung, T., Pons-Moll, G.: Posendf: Modeling human pose manifolds with neural distance fields. In: European Conference on Computer Vision (ECCV). Springer (2022)
80. Twindom dataset. https://web.twindom.com/
81. Xie, X., Bhatnagar, B.L., Pons-Moll, G.: Chore: Contact, human and object reconstruction from a single rgb image. In: European Conference on Computer Vision (ECCV). Springer (2022)

82. Xu, H., Bazavan, E.G., Zanfir, A., Freeman, W.T., Sukthankar, R., Sminchisescu, C.: GHUM& GHUML: Generative 3d human shape and articulated pose models. In: CVPR, pp. 6184–6193 (2020)
83. Zanfir, A., Bazavan, E.G., Zanfir, M., Freeman, W.T., Sukthankar, R., Sminchisescu, C.: Neural descent for visual 3d human pose and shape. In: CVPR, pp. 14484–14493 (2021)
84. Zhang, C., Pujades, S., Black, M.J., Pons-Moll, G.: Detailed, accurate, human shape estimation from clothed 3d scan sequences. In: CVPR, (2017)
85. Zheng, Z., Yu, T., Liu, Y., Dai, Q.: PaMIR: Parametric model-conditioned implicit representation for image-based human reconstruction. PAMI (2021)
86. Zhou, K., Bhatnagar, B., Lenssen, J.E., Pons-Moll, G.: TOCH: Spatio-temporal object correspondence to hand for motion refinement. arXiv preprint arXiv:2205.07982 (2022)

Self-calibrating Photometric Stereo
by Neural Inverse Rendering

Junxuan Li$^{(\boxtimes)}$ and Hongdong Li

Australian National University, Canberra, Australia
{junxuan.li,hongdong.li}@anu.edu.au

Abstract. This paper tackles the task of uncalibrated photometric
stereo for 3D object reconstruction, where both the object shape, object
reflectance, and lighting directions are unknown. This is an extremely
difficult task, and the challenge is further compounded with the existence of the well-known generalized bas-relief (GBR) ambiguity in photometric stereo. Previous methods to resolve this ambiguity either rely
on an overly simplified reflectance model, or assume special light distribution. We propose a new method that jointly optimizes object shape,
light directions, and light intensities, all under general surfaces and lights
assumptions. The specularities are used explicitly to solve uncalibrated
photometric stereo via a neural inverse rendering process. We gradually fit specularities from shiny to rough using novel progressive specular bases. Our method leverages a physically based rendering equation by minimizing the reconstruction error on a per-object-basis. Our
method demonstrates state-of-the-art accuracy in light estimation and
shape recovery on real-world datasets.

Keywords: Uncalibrated photometric stereo · Generalized bas-relief
ambiguity · Neural network · Inverse rendering

1 Introduction

Photometric Stereo (PS) aims to reconstruct the 3D shape of an object given a
set of images taken under different lights. Calibrated photometric stereo methods assume the light directions are known in all images [7,15,17,31,36,45–47].
However, it is quite a tedious and laborious effort to calibrate the light sources in
all input images in practice, often requiring instrumented imaging environment
and expert knowledge. How to solve uncalibrated photometric stereo is therefore
a crucial milestone to bring PS to practical use.

Recovering the surface shape with unknown light sources and general
reflectance is difficult. Previous methods tackle this problem by assuming the
Lambertian surfaces. However, Lambertian surfaces in uncalibrated photometric
stereo have an inherent 3×3 parameters ambiguity in normals and light directions [3]. When the surface integrability constraint is introduced, this ambiguity

Supplementary Information The online version contains supplementary material
available at https://doi.org/10.1007/978-3-031-20086-1_10.

can be further reduced to a 3-parameter generalized bas-relief (GBR) ambiguity. Additional information is required to further resolve this ambiguity.

Existing methods to resolve the GBR ambiguity resort to introducing additional knowledge, such as priors on the albedo distribution [2], color intensity profiles [27,38], and symmetric BRDFs [26,28,48]. Drbohlav *et al.* [11] leveraged the mirror-like specularities on a surface to resolve the ambiguity. But they need to manually label the mirror-like specularities for computation. Georghiades [12] addressed the ambiguity by using the TS reflectance model [42]. However, to avoid the local minima, they further assumed the uniformly distributed albedos. These methods either rely on unrealistic assumptions or are unstable to solve. Hence, there is still a gap in applying this technique to more generalized real-world datasets. Recent deep learning-based methods push the boundary of light estimation and surface normal estimation [6,19]. These methods treated light estimation as a classification task. Hence, they lose the ability to continuously represent the lights.

In this paper, we present an inverse rendering approach for uncalibrated photometric stereo. We propose a model which explicitly uses specular effects on the object's surface to estimate both the lights and surface normals. We show that by incorporating our model, the GBR ambiguity can be resolved up to a binary convex/concave ambiguity. Our neural network is optimized via the inverse rendering error. Hence, there is no need to manually label the specular effects during the process. To avoid local minima during the optimization, we propose *progressive specular bases* to fit the specularities from shiny to rough. The key idea of the above technique is to leverage the mirror-like specularities to reduce GBR ambiguity in the early stage of optimization. We propose a neural representation to continuously represent the lighting, normal and spatially-varying albedos. By fitting both the specular and diffuse photometric components via the inverse rendering process, our neural network can jointly optimize and refine the estimation of light directions, light intensities, surface normals, and spatially-varying albedos. In summary, our contributions in this paper are:

- We propose a neural representation that jointly estimates surface normals, light sources, and albedos via inverse rendering.
- We propose progressive specular bases to guide the network during optimization, effectively escaping local minima.

Extensive evaluations on challenging real-world datasets show that our method achieves state-of-the-art performance on lighting estimation and shape recovery.

2   Related Work

Calibrated Photometric Stereo. By assuming the surface of objects to be ideal Lambertian, shapes can be revealed in closed-form with three or more known lights [45]. This restricted assumption is gradually relaxed by following studies [17,31,46,47], where error terms were introduced to account for the deviations from the Lambertian assumption. A regression-based inverse rendering framework [16] was also used for dealing with more general surfaces. Also, in recent years, deep learning-based methods have been widely used in the context of photometric stereo [7,15,22,36,44,49,50]. Santo *et al.* [36] proposed the first photometric stereo neural network, which feeds image pixels into the network in a predetermined order. Some later works rearranged the pixels into an observation map and then solved the problem per-pixelly [15,22,24,50]. Other deep learning-based approaches used both local and global images cues for normal estimation [7,14,18,44,49]. However, their works assumed both the light directions and intensities to be known. Calibrating light sources may be a tedious process that requires professional knowledge. It will be more convenient to the public if no ground truth light directions are needed for photometric stereo.

Uncalibrated Photometric Stereo. Under the Lambertian surface assumption, there is an inherent generalized bas-relief ambiguity in solving uncalibrated photometric stereo [3]. Traditional works explored many directions to resolve this ambiguity by providing additional knowledge to the system, such as specularities [11], TS model [12], priors on the albedo distribution [2], shadows [40], color intensity profiles [27,38], perspective views [32], inter-reflections [5], local diffuse reflectance maxima [33], symmetric BRDFs [26,28,48], and total variation [34]. In the presence of inaccurate lighting, Quéau *et al.* [35] refined the initial lighting estimation by explicitly modeling the outliers among Lambertian assumption. Other works aim at solving the uncalibrated photometric stereo under natural illumination [13,30]; and semi-calibrated lighting where light directions are known but light intensities are unknown [10,25]. With the advance of the neural network, deep learning-based methods produced state-of-the-art performance in this area. Chen *et al.* [8] proposed a neural network that directly takes images as input, and outputs the surface normal. Later works [6,9] further improved this pipeline by predicting both the light directions and surface normal at the same time. A recent work [37] proposes a way to search for the most efficient neural architecture for uncalibrated photometric stereo. These neural network methods learn prior information for solving the GBR ambiguity from a large amount of training data with ground truth.

Neural Inverse Rendering. Taniai *et al.* [41] proposed the first neural inverse rendering framework for photometric stereo. They proposed a convolutional neural network that takes images at the input and directly outputs the surface normal. Li *et al.* [21] proposed an MLP framework for solving the geometry and reflectance via the reconstruction errors. But their works require the light direction at inputs. Kaya *et al.* [19] use a pre-trained light estimation network to deal with unknown lights. However, their work cannot propagate the reconstruction error back to the light directions and intensities.

In this paper, we propose a neural representation that explicitly models the specularities and uses it for resolving the GBR ambiguity via an inverse rendering process. Our model allows the re-rendered errors to be back-propagated to the light sources and refines them jointly with the normals. Hence, our method is also robust when accounting for inaccurate lighting.

3   Specularities Reduce GBR Ambiguity

In this section, we introduce the notations and formulations of image rendering in the context of uncalibrated photometric stereo under general surfaces. We discuss the GBR ambiguity under Lambertian surfaces. We further demonstrate that the GBR ambiguity can be resolved under non-Lambertian surfaces with the presence of specularities.

3.1   GBR Ambiguity

Given any point in an object's surface, we assume its surface normal to be $n \in \mathbb{R}^3$. It is illuminated by a distant light with direction to be $l \in \mathbb{R}^3$ and light intensity to be $e \in \mathbb{R}^+$. If we observe the surface point from view direction $v \in \mathbb{R}^3$, its pixel intensity $m \in \mathbb{R}^+$ can be modeled as: $m = e\rho(n, v, l)\max(n^T l, 0)$. Here, the $\rho(n, v, l)$ denotes a surface point's BRDF function, which is influenced by the surface normal, view direction, and lighting direction. The noise, interreflections, and cast-shadows that deviate from the rendering equation are ignored.

In the above equation, traditional methods assume the surface material to be ideal Lambertian, which makes the BRDF function to be a constant: $\rho(n, v, l) = \rho_d \in \mathbb{R}$. For simplicity, we omit the attached-shadows operator $\max(\cdot)$, and incorporate the diffuse albedo and light intensities into the surface normal and light direction. The equation can be rewrite as

$$M = B^T S, \tag{1}$$

where $B = [\rho_{d_1} n_1, \cdots, \rho_{d_p} n_p] \in \mathbb{R}^{3 \times p}$ denotes the normal matrix with p different pixels in a image; $S = [e_1 l_1, \cdots, e_n l_n] \in \mathbb{R}^{3 \times n}$ denotes the light matrix with n different light sources; $M \in \mathbb{R}^{p \times n}$ denotes the p pixels' intensities under n different light sources. Under this simplified assumption, once the surface point is illuminated by three or more known light sources, the equation has a closed-form solution on surface normals [45].

Under the uncalibrated photometric stereo setting, both the light directions and light intensities are unknown. The above equation will have a set of solutions in a 3×3 linear space. By applying the surface integration constraints, it can be further reduced to a 3 parameters space, which is also known as the generalize bas-relief (GBR) ambiguity in the form as below

$$G = \begin{bmatrix} 1 & 0 & 0 \\ 0 & 1 & 0 \\ \mu & \nu & \lambda \end{bmatrix} \tag{2}$$

where $\lambda \neq 0; \mu, \nu \in \mathbb{R}$. The transformed normal $\widehat{B} = G^{-T} B$, transformed light $\widehat{S} = GS$. So that both sides of $M = B^T G^{-1} GS$ remain equivalent after the transformation. Additional knowledge need to be introduced for solving the GBR ambiguity above.

3.2   Resolving the Ambiguity with Specularities

We now explain how specularities on object surfaces provide additional information for reducing the GBR ambiguity. For simplicity, we incorporate the diffuse
albedo into surface normal $\boldsymbol{b} = \rho_d \boldsymbol{n}$, and incorporate the light intensity into light
direction $\boldsymbol{s} = e\boldsymbol{l}$, and only consider the illuminated points. As stated above, the
GBR ambiguity exists when we assume the surface to be Lambertian. There
exists a transformed surface normal and light direction $\widehat{\boldsymbol{b}} = \boldsymbol{G}^{-T}\boldsymbol{b}$, $\widehat{\boldsymbol{s}} = \boldsymbol{G}\boldsymbol{s}$, so
that the transformed surface and lights will compose the identical pixel obser-
vation $\widehat{m} = \widehat{\boldsymbol{b}}^T\widehat{\boldsymbol{s}} = \boldsymbol{b}^T\boldsymbol{G}^{-1}\boldsymbol{G}\boldsymbol{s} = m$.

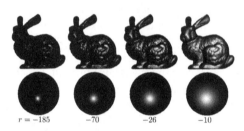

Fig. 1. Rendered "Bunny" and "Sphere" using different specular bases with different
roughness. The roughness term controls the sharpness of a specular lobe. The basis
presents narrow specular spikes when roughness is small, which is close to the mirror-
like reflection.

However, in the presence of specularities, the surface BRDF is not constant
anymore. Georghiades [12] models the reflectance as the combination of the
diffuse and specular parts as below[1]

$$\rho(\boldsymbol{n}, \boldsymbol{v}, \boldsymbol{l}) = \rho_d + \rho_s \exp(r(1 - \boldsymbol{n}^T\boldsymbol{h})), \tag{3}$$

where the ρ_d is the diffuse albedo, ρ_s denotes the specular albedo, and the $r \in \mathbb{R}^-$
denotes the roughness. $\boldsymbol{h} = \frac{\boldsymbol{v}+\boldsymbol{l}}{||\boldsymbol{v}+\boldsymbol{l}||}$ is the half-unit-vector between view direction
$\boldsymbol{v}$ and light direction $\boldsymbol{l}$. Therefore, with the specular terms, the image intensity
after the GBR transformation is

$$\widehat{m} = \widehat{\boldsymbol{b}}^T\widehat{\boldsymbol{s}} + \rho_s||\widehat{\boldsymbol{s}}||\exp(r(1 - \frac{\widehat{\boldsymbol{b}}^T}{||\widehat{\boldsymbol{b}}||}\frac{\boldsymbol{v}+\frac{\widehat{\boldsymbol{s}}}{||\widehat{\boldsymbol{s}}||}}{||\boldsymbol{v}+\frac{\widehat{\boldsymbol{s}}}{||\widehat{\boldsymbol{s}}||}||}))$$

$$= \boldsymbol{b}^T\boldsymbol{G}^{-1}\boldsymbol{G}\boldsymbol{s} + \rho_s||\boldsymbol{G}\boldsymbol{s}||\exp(r(1 - \frac{\boldsymbol{b}^T\boldsymbol{G}^{-1}}{||\boldsymbol{G}^{-T}\boldsymbol{b}||}\frac{\boldsymbol{v}+\frac{\boldsymbol{G}\boldsymbol{s}}{||\boldsymbol{G}\boldsymbol{s}||}}{||\boldsymbol{v}+\frac{\boldsymbol{G}\boldsymbol{s}}{||\boldsymbol{G}\boldsymbol{s}||}||})), \tag{4}$$

where $|| \cdot ||$ denotes the length of a vector. In general, $m = \widehat{m}$ only holds for
all pixels in the images when the GBR transformation matrix $\boldsymbol{G}$ is identity
matrix. Theoretical proof was made by Georghiades [12] that when providing
with four different $(\boldsymbol{b}, \boldsymbol{s})$ pairs, it is sufficient to solve the GBR ambiguity up

---

[1] For simplicity, we omit some terms from [12] without affecting the correctness of
their proof.

to the binary convex/concave ambiguity, $i.e.\lambda = \pm 1; \mu, \nu = 0$. However, even a global minimum exists on G, there is no guarantee that no local minima in the 3 parameters space of λ, μ and ν. Solving the above equation is still challenging given the existence of noise, shadows and inter-reflections in real world images. To avoid the local minima, Georghiades [12] assumed that the specular albedo ρ_s is uniform across the surface. This uniform specular albedo assumption prevents their method from being applied to more general objects. In this paper, we are aiming to solve this problem in more general surfaces, $i.e.$under spatially-varying diffuse and spatially-varying specular albedo.

Resolving the GBR Ambiguity by Specular Spikes. In fact, the GBR ambiguity can also be resolved by merely four or more pairs of mirror-like reflection effects ($i.e.$specular spikes) on a surface [11]. The roughness term r in (3) controls the sharpness of a specular lobe. As shown in Fig. 1, when roughness is small, the resulted material is very close to a mirror-like material (see $r_i = -185$). The specular basis reaches its highest value when $1 - n^T \frac{v+l}{||v+l||} = 0$. Since all the three vectors here are unit vectors, the above equation holds when surface normal n is a bisector between the viewing direction v and the light direction l. Hence, we have the following equation when the basis function reach its highest value, $i.e.$where the mirror-like specularities happens

$$v = 2(l^T n)n - l. \tag{5}$$

From the *consistent viewpoint constraint* [11], the GBR ambiguity can be reduced to two-parameteric group of transformations (rotation around the viewing vector and isotropic scaling). However, the mirror-like specular spikes needed to be manually labeled in previous method [11]. While in our paper, these mirror-like specular effects can be automatically fitted via our neural network.

4 Proposed Method

We propose a neural network based method that aims at inverse rendering the object by factoring the lighting, surface normal, diffuse albedo, and specular components. This section describes our model for solving uncalibrated photometric stereo in the presence of specularities.

4.1 Proposed Image Rendering Equation

Following previous works on uncalibrated photometric stereo, we make the following assumptions on the problem. We assume that the images are taken in orthographic views. Hence the view direction are consistent across the object surface, $v = [0,0,1]^T$. The object is only illuminated once by distance lights with unknown direction l and intensities e. Given the above assumptions, we now rewrite the rendering equation as

$$m = e\rho(n,l) \max(n^T l, 0). \tag{6}$$

Here, the only information we have is the observation of the surface point's pixel intensity m. Our target is to inverse this rendering equation to get all the other unknown terms, such as surface normal n, light direction l, light intensity e, and surface BRDF function $\rho(\cdot)$. In the following sections, we present our model to parameterize and optimize these terms.

4.2   BRDF Modeling

As discussed by (2) above, the Lambertian surface assumption alone will lead to GBR ambiguity in solving uncalibrated photometric stereo problem. Hence, we model the reflectance as the combination of the diffuse and specular parts as $\rho(n, l) = \rho_d + \rho_s(n, l)$, where the ρ_d is the diffuse albedo, and $\rho_s(n, l)$ is the specular terms. We further model the specular term as the summation of a set of specular bases as below

$$\rho_s(n, l) = \sum_{i=1}^{k} \rho_{s_i} \exp(r_i(1 - n^T h)), \qquad (7)$$

where $h = \frac{v+l}{||v+l||}$ is the half-unit-vector between view direction v and light direction l; k is the number of bases. Here, we adopted the Spherical Gaussian [43] as our basis function. The ρ_{s_i} denotes the specular albedo, and the $r_i \in \mathbb{R}^-$ denotes the roughness. The lower the roughness, the more shiny the material will be. We rendered two objects with the proposed specular basis, as shown in Fig. 1.

In summary, our BRDF modeling takes both the diffuse and specular component into consideration and estimate them jointly. We also model the specularities as a summation of a set of bases, which enable the material to range from shiny to rough. We can now rewrite the rendering equation as below

$$m = e(\rho_d + \sum_{i=1}^{k} \rho_{s_i} \exp(r_i(1 - n^T h))) \max(n^T l, 0). \qquad (8)$$

4.3   Progressive Specular Bases

Inspired by the two ways of resolving GBR in Sect. 3.2, we proposed the novel *progressive specular bases* to solve the uncalibrated photometric stereo robustly. The key idea of progressive specular bases is to first fit the surface with only mirror-like specular bases (bases with small roughness term r_i); then, we gradually enable the other specular bases for more diffuse effects (bases with large roughness).

At the early stage of optimization, we only enable mirror-like specular bases, the network will attempt to solve uncalibrated photometric stereo using only the mirror-like specular spikes. Then, as the optimization progresses, other specular bases for the network are gradually enabled to fit those diffuse effects. Our progressive specular bases will guide the network away from local minima at the early stage of optimization, resulting better optimized results in the end.

The progressive specular bases is achieved by applying a smooth mask on the different specular basis (from small roughness with mirror-like effects to large roughness with less sharp effects) over the course of optimization. The weights applied to the different specular bases are defined as below

$$\rho_s(\boldsymbol{n}, \boldsymbol{l}) = \sum_{i=1}^{k} \omega_i(\alpha) \rho_{s_i} \exp(r_i(1 - \boldsymbol{n}^T \boldsymbol{h})), \tag{9}$$

where the weight $\omega_i(\alpha)$ is defined as

$$\omega_i(\alpha) = \begin{cases} 0 & \text{if } \alpha < i \\ \frac{1 - \cos((\alpha - i)\pi)}{2} & \text{if } 0 \le \alpha - i < 1 \\ 1 & \text{if } \alpha - i \ge 1 \end{cases} \tag{10}$$

$\alpha \in [0, k]$ will gradually increase during the optimization progress. The defined weights above are inspired by a recent coarse-to-fine positional encoding strategy on camera pose estimation [23]. In the early stage of optimization, the α is small, hence the weight $\omega(\alpha) = 0$ will be zero for those specular bases with roughness r_i, where $i > \alpha$. As the optimization progress, we gradually activate the specular bases one by one. When $\alpha = k$, all the specular bases is used, hence, (9) is identical to (7) in the final stage. In practice, we set the specular roughness terms $\boldsymbol{r} = \{r_i | i \in \{1, \cdots, k\}\}$ in ascending order. So that the above weight will gradually activate the specular bases from small roughness to large roughness.

To sum up, when applying progressive specular bases, the network will focus on fitting the bright specular spikes at an early stage; then, as the optimization progress, more specular bases are available for the network to fit on the diffuse effects.

4.4   Neural Representation for Surfaces

Here, we describe our neural representation for object surface modeling. Inspired by the recently proposed coordinately-based multilayer-perceptron (MLP) works [29], we proposed two coordinately-based networks which take only the pixel coordinates (x, y) at input, and output the corresponding surface normal and diffuse albedos and specular albedos.

$$\boldsymbol{n} = N_\Theta(x, y), \tag{11}$$

$$\rho_d, \boldsymbol{a} = M_\Phi(x, y). \tag{12}$$

where $N_\Theta(\cdot), M_\Phi(\cdot)$ are MLPs with Θ, Φ to be their parameters respectively. Given a image pixel coordinates (x, y), the two MLPs directly output the surface normal $\boldsymbol{n}$, diffuse albedo ρ_d, and specular albedos $\boldsymbol{a} = \{\rho_{s_i} | i \in \{1, \cdots, k\}\}$ of that position.

4.5   Neural Representation for Lighting

Next, we describe the parameterization of the light direction and intensity. Let $\boldsymbol{I} \in \mathbb{R}^{h \times w}$ denotes the image taken under a light source, where h, w denote the height and width of the input image. The direction and intensity of that light source are directly predicted by feeding this image into a convolutional neural network:

$$e, \boldsymbol{l} = L_{\Psi}(\boldsymbol{I}). \qquad (13)$$

where $L_{\Psi}(\cdot)$ is a convolutional neural network with its parameters Ψ. The network $L_{\Psi}(\cdot)$ takes only the image $\boldsymbol{I}$ as input, directly output the corresponding light direction $\boldsymbol{l}$ and light intensity e. Unlike previous deep learning based lighting estimation network [6,9,19], we do not fix the lighting estimation at testing. Instead, the lighting estimation is further refined (i.e.fine-tuned) on the testing images by jointly optimizing the lighting, surface normals, and albedos via the reconstruction loss.

5   Implementation

This section describes the detail of network architectures, hyperparameters selection, and loss functions.

Network Architectures. The surface normal net $N_{\Theta}(\cdot)$ uses 8 fully-connected layers with 256 channels, followed by a ReLU activation function except for the last layer. The material net $M_{\Phi}(\cdot)$ uses the same structure but with 12 fully-connected ReLU layers. We apply a positional encoding strategy with 10 levels of Fourier functions to the input pixel coordinates (x, y) before feeding them to the normal and material MLPs. The lighting network $L_{\Psi}(\cdot)$ consists of 7 convolutional ReLU layers and 3 fully connected layers. Please see the supplementary material for detailed network architectures.

For the choices of specular bases, we initialize the roughness value for each basis range from $-r_t$ to $-r_b$ with logarithm intervals

$$r_i = -\exp(\ln r_t - (\ln r_t - \ln r_b)\frac{i-1}{k-1}), \qquad (14)$$

where $i \in [1, \cdots, k]$ denotes the index of basis. In testing, we empirically set the number of bases $k = 12$, $r_t = 300$, and $r_b = 10$.

Pre-training Light Model. The light model $L_{\Psi}(\cdot)$ is pre-trained on a public available synthetic dataset, Blobby and Sculpture datasets [8]. We trained the $L_{\Psi}(\cdot)$ for 100 epoches, with batch size to be 64. We adopt the Adam optimizer [20] for updating the network parameter Ψ with learning rate 5.0×10^{-4}. The light network is pre-trained for once, based on the pre-train loss $\mathcal{L}_{\mathrm{pre}} = (1 - \boldsymbol{l}^T \bar{\boldsymbol{l}}) + (e - \bar{e})^2$, where the first term is cosine loss for light directions, the second term is mean-square-error for intensities. The same network is then used for all other testing datasets at test time.

Testing. At testing stage, we continue refining the lighting from pre-trained light net $L_\Psi(\cdot)$, while the proposed normal-MLP $N_\Theta(\cdot)$ and material-MLP $M_\Phi(\cdot)$ are optimized from scratch via the reconstruction loss. As the reconstruction loss, we use the mean absolute difference, which is the absolute difference between observed intensity $M \in \mathbb{R}^{p \times n}$ and re-rendered intensity $\overline{M}$.

$$\mathcal{L} = \frac{1}{pn} \sum_{i=1}^{p} \sum_{j=1}^{n} |M_{i,j} - \overline{M}_{i,j}|, \tag{15}$$

Table 1. Ablation study on effectiveness of progressive specular bases (PSB). We compare the models with and without progressive specular bases. Applying progressive specular bases will consistently improve estimation accuracy.

Model	Direction	Intensity	Normal
r	5.30	0.0400	9.39
r + PSB	4.42	0.0382	7.71
Trainable r	4.75	0.0372	8.57
Trainable r + PSB	**4.02**	**0.0365**	**7.05**

Table 2. Quantitative results on DiLi-GenT where our model takes different lighting as initialization. Our model performs consistently well when varying levels of noise are applied to the lighting estimation. It shows that our model is robust against the errors in lighting estimation.

	L_Ψ	$+20°$	$+30°$	$+50°$	$+70°$
Direction	4.02	4.07	4.14	4.34	4.40
Intensity	0.0365	0.0337	0.0356	0.0358	0.0355
Normal	7.05	7.40	7.40	7.40	7.44

where the above summation is over all p pixels under n different light sources. At each iteration, we sampled pixels from 8 images and feed them to the networks. The iterations per-epoch depends on the number of images of the scene. We run 2000 epoches in total. The Adam optimizer is used with the learning rate being 10^{-3} for all parameters.

Training and Testing Time. Our framework is implemented in PyTorch and runs on a single NVIDIA RTX3090 GPU. The pre-training time of our light model L_Ψ only takes around 2 h. In comparison, previous deep methods [9,19] take more than 22 h in training light models. The reason is that we shift part of the burden of solving lightings from the neural light model to the inverse rendering procedural. Hence, our light model can be relatively lightweight and easy to train compared to previous deep learning based light estimation networks [9,19].

In testing, our method takes an average of 16 min to process each of the ten objects in DiLiGenT [39] benchmark, ranging from 13 min to 21 min. In comparison, previous CNN-based inverse rendering methods [19,41] take on average 53 min per object in testing. The reason is that both of our object modeling net N_Θ, M_Φ are simple MLPs. Hence, we can achieve a much faster forward-backward time when optimizing the MLP-based network than previous CNN-based methods.

6 Experiments

6.1 Testing Dataset

We conduct experiments in following public real-world datasets: DiLiGenT [39], Gourd&Apple dataset [1], and Light Stage Data Gallery [4]. They all provide calibrated light directions and light intensities as ground truth for evaluation. DiLiGenT contains 10 objects; each object has 96 images captured under different lighting conditions; a high-end laser scanner captured ground truth surface normal is available for evaluation. Gourd&Apple contains three objects; each object has around 100 images captured under different lighting conditions; Light Stage Data Gallery contains 252 images per object; following previous works [6], we select in total 133 images illuminated by forward-facing lights for photometric stereo. Unfortunately, Gourd&Apple and Light Stage Data Gallery did not provide ground truth surface normal for quantitative evaluation.

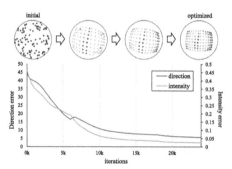

Fig. 2. Visualization of the lighting optimization under noised input. The predicted light distribution over a sphere is represented as the spheres above. The left-most lighting sphere shows the noised lighting estimation at the start of optimization. Our model gradually refines the incorrect lighting during optimization (from left to right) and provides the optimized result.

6.2 Evaluation Metrics

In this paper, we use mean angular errors (MAE) as an evaluation metric for surface normal estimate and light direction estimation. Lower MAE is preferred.

As light intensities among different images can only be estimated up to a scale factor, we follow previous work [6] to use scale-invariant relative error

$$E_{si} = \frac{1}{n} \sum_i^n \frac{|se_i - \overline{e_i}|}{\overline{e_i}}, \tag{16}$$

where $e_i, \overline{e_i}$ denote the estimated and ground truth light intensity of i-th light respectively; s is the scale factor computed by solving $\mathrm{argmin}_s \sum_i^n (se_i - \overline{e_i})^2$ with least squares. Lower scale-invariant relative error is preferred.

6.3   Ablation Study

Effectiveness of the Progressive Specular Bases. To show the effectiveness of the proposed progressive specular bases, we conduct the ablation study as shown in Table 1. The models are evaluated in the DiLiGenT dataset. In the first and second row of the table, we evaluate the model with and without the progressive specular bases. It shows that the model with progressive specular bases achieves lower error in both lighting and normal estimation. In the third and fourth row of the table, instead of using fixed (as defined by (14)) roughness terms, we set these roughness terms as trainable parameters. Results also demonstrate that when the roughness terms are trainable, progressive specular bases consistently improve the estimation accuracy. We also observe that the trainable roughness with progressive specular bases achieves the best performance. Our analysis is that, by relaxing the training of specular roughness, the network can adjust these terms for more accurate material estimation. Hence, it also leads to more accurate lighting and normals (Table 3).

Table 3. Evaluation results on DiLiGenT benchmark. Here, **bold** indicates the best results and <u>underline</u> denotes the second best results.

(a) Normal estimation results on DiLiGenT benchmark.

Method	Ball	Bear	Buddha	Cat	Cow	Goblet	Harvest	Pot1	Pot2	Reading	Average
SM10[38]	8.90	11.98	15.54	19.84	22.73	48.79	73.86	16.68	50.68	26.93	29.59
WT13[48]	4.39	6.42	13.19	36.55	19.75	20.57	55.51	9.39	14.52	58.96	23.93
PF14[33]	4.77	9.07	14.92	9.54	19.53	29.93	29.21	9.51	15.90	24.18	16.66
LC18[26]	9.30	10.90	19.00	12.60	15.00	18.30	28.00	12.40	15.70	22.30	16.30
UPS-FCN[8]	6.62	11.23	15.87	14.68	11.91	20.72	27.79	13.98	14.19	23.26	16.02
BK21[19]	3.78	5.96	13.14	7.91	10.85	11.94	25.49	8.75	10.17	18.22	11.62
SDPS-Net[6]	2.77	6.89	<u>8.97</u>	8.06	8.48	11.91	17.43	8.14	7.50	14.90	9.51
SK21[37]	3.46	<u>5.48</u>	10.00	8.94	<u>6.04</u>	9.78	17.97	7.76	<u>7.10</u>	15.02	9.15
GCNet[9]+PS-FCN[8]	<u>2.50</u>	5.60	**8.60**	<u>7.90</u>	7.80	<u>9.60</u>	<u>16.20</u>	<u>7.20</u>	<u>7.10</u>	<u>14.90</u>	<u>8.70</u>
Ours	**1.24**	**3.82**	9.28	**4.72**	**5.53**	**7.12**	**14.96**	**6.73**	**6.50**	**10.54**	**7.05**

(b) Light intensity estimation results on DiLiGenT benchmark.

Method	Ball	Bear	Buddha	Cat	Cow	Goblet	Harvest	Pot1	Pot2	Reading	Average
PF14[33]	0.0360	0.0980	0.0530	<u>0.0590</u>	0.0740	0.2230	0.1560	**0.0170**	**0.0440**	0.1220	0.0882
LCNet[6]	0.0390	<u>0.0610</u>	0.0480	0.0950	0.0730	0.0670	0.0820	0.0580	<u>0.0480</u>	0.1050	0.0676
GCNet[9]	<u>0.0270</u>	0.1010	<u>0.0320</u>	0.0750	**0.0310**	<u>0.0420</u>	<u>0.0650</u>	0.0390	0.0590	<u>0.0480</u>	<u>0.0519</u>
Ours	**0.0194**	**0.0186**	**0.0206**	**0.0321**	<u>0.0621</u>	**0.0418**	**0.0230**	<u>0.0303</u>	0.0816	**0.0352**	**0.0365**

(l) Light direction estimation results on DiLiGenT benchmark.

Method	Ball	Bear	Buddha	Cat	Cow	Goblet	Harvest	Pot1	Pot2	Reading	Average
PF14[33]	4.90	5.24	9.76	5.31	16.34	33.22	24.99	2.43	13.52	21.77	13.75
LCNet[6]	3.27	3.47	4.34	**4.08**	<u>4.52</u>	10.36	<u>6.32</u>	5.44	2.87	**4.50**	4.92
GCNet[9]	<u>1.75</u>	<u>2.44</u>	**2.86**	4.58	**3.15**	<u>2.98</u>	**5.74**	**1.41**	2.81	5.47	**3.32**
Ours	**1.43**	**1.56**	<u>4.22</u>	<u>4.41</u>	4.94	**2.26**	6.41	<u>3.46</u>	4.19	7.34	<u>4.02</u>

Robustness on Light Modeling. As stated above, our model shifts part of the burden of solving lightings from the neural light modeling to the later inverse rendering procedural. Hence, even if our pre-trained light model L_Ψ does not provide perfect lighting estimations, our later procedural can continue refining its estimation via the reconstruction error. To demonstrate the robustness of our model against the errors of the light model, we conduct the experiments where different levels of noise are added to the lightings, as shown in Table 2 and Fig. 2. In Table 2, the first column shows the results of our model on DiLiGenT with the pre-trained L_Ψ. From the second column, different levels of noise (noise that is up to certain degrees) are applied to the lightings. The light directions are randomly shifted, and the light intensities are all re-set to ones. Then, we further refined this noised lighting estimation via the inverse rendering procedural at the testing stage. As illustrated in Table 2, even when the light directions are randomly shifted up to 70°, our model still achieves comparable performance after the optimization. In Fig. 2, we visualize how our model gradually refines the lighting estimation during the course of optimization.

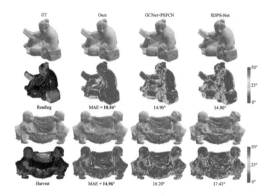

Fig. 3. Visualized comparisons of normal estimation for "Reading" and "Harvest" in DiLiGenT. Our method produces better normal estimation than others, particularly in regions with specularities (*e.g.* see the head of "reading", the golden sack of "Harvest").

6.4   Evaluation on DiLiGenT Benchmark

Results on Normal Estimation. We evaluate our method on the challenging DiLiGenT benchmark and compare our method with previous works. The quantitative result on normal estimation is shown in Table 3. We achieve the best average performance, and we outperform the second-best method by 1.65° on average. Thanks to the proposed progressive specular bases, our method performs particularly well on those objects with specularities. There are a large number of specularities in "Reading" and "Goblet", where our method outperforms the others by 4.36 and 2.48°, respectively. Figure 3 shows qualitative comparison on "Reading" and "Harvest'. Our method produces much better results on those specular regions.

Results on Light Estimation. The quantitative results on light intensity estimation are shown in Table 3. Our model achieves the best performance on average, which is 0.0365 in relative error. The results on light direction estimation are presented in Table 3, where we also demonstrate a comparable result to previous methods. Figure 4 showcases the visualization of the lighting results. As LCNet [6] discretely represents the light direction into bins, their estimation looks very noisy (see lighting in "Reading"). In contrast, our model can continuously refine the lights. Hence, our lighting estimation preserves smoother pattern overall.

6.5   Evaluation on Other Real World Dataset

We then evaluate our method on other challenging real-world datasets. Table 4 shows that our method achieves the best performance in lighting estimation in the Gourd&Apple dataset. In Fig. 4, We visualized the estimated lighting in "Apple" from Gourd&Apple dataset, and "Helmet Front" from Light Stage dataset. These results manifest that our method can also reliably recover the lighting in different light distributions. Our specular modeling is also applicable to different datasets under different materials. Please refer to supplementary material for more results.

Table 4. Evaluation results on Gourd&Apple dataset.

(a) Results on light intensity.

Method	Apple	Gourd1	Gourd2	Avg.
PF14[33]	0.1090	0.0960	0.3290	0.1780
LCNet[6]	0.1060	0.0480	**0.1860**	0.1130
GCNet[9]	0.0940	0.0420	0.1990	0.1120
Ours	**0.0162**	**0.0272**	0.2330	**0.0921**

(b) Results on light direction.

Method	Apple	Gourd1	Gourd2	Avg.
PF14[33]	6.68	21.23	25.87	17.92
LCNet[6]	9.31	4.07	7.11	6.83
GCNet[9]	10.91	4.29	7.13	7.44
Ours	**1.87**	**2.34**	**2.01**	**2.07**

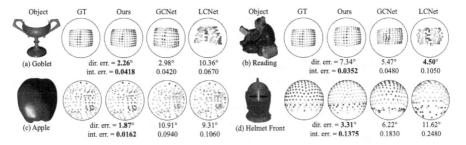

	Object	GT	Ours	GCNet	LCNet
(a) Goblet		dir. err. = **2.26°** int. err. = **0.0418**	2.98° 0.0420	10.36° 0.0670	
(b) Reading		dir. err. = 7.34° int. err. = **0.0352**	5.47° 0.0480	**4.50°** 0.1050	
(c) Apple		dir. err. = **1.87°** int. err. = **0.0162**	10.91° 0.0940	9.31° 0.1060	
(d) Helmet Front		dir. err. = **3.31°** int. err. = **0.1375**	6.22° 0.1830	11.62° 0.2480	

Fig. 4. Visualized comparisons of the ground-truth and estimated lighting distribution for the DiLiGenT dataset, Gourd&Apple dataset, and light stage dataset. It demonstrates that our lighting estimation is also robust in different datasets under different lighting distributions.

7 Discussions and Conclusions

In this paper, we propose a neural representation for lighting and surface normal estimation via inverse rendering. The surface is explicitly modeled with diffuse and specular components, and the GBR ambiguity is resolved by fitting on these photometric cues. To avoid local minima during optimization, we propose *progressive specular bases* for fitting the specularities. Our method provides state-of-the-art performance on lighting estimation and shape recovery on challenging real-world datasets.

Limitations and Future Work: The inter-reflections, subsurface scattering, and image noises are not considered in our image rendering (6). Our model may fail if these terms are prominent on an object's surface. Explicitly modeling these terms and jointly refining them within the same framework will be an intriguing direction to pursue.

Acknowledgements. This research is funded in part by ARC-Discovery grants (DP190102261 and DP220100800), a gift from Baidu RAL, as well as a Ford Alliance grant to Hongdong Li.

References

1. Alldrin, N., Zickler, T., Kriegman, D.: Photometric stereo with non-parametric and spatially-varying reflectance. In: 2008 IEEE Conference on Computer Vision and Pattern Recognition, pp. 1–8. IEEE (2008)
2. Alldrin, N.G., Mallick, S.P., Kriegman, D.J.: Resolving the generalized bas-relief ambiguity by entropy minimization. In: 2007 IEEE Conference on Computer Vision and Pattern Recognition, pp. 1–7. IEEE (2007)
3. Belhumeur, P.N., Kriegman, D.J., Yuille, A.L.: The bas-relief ambiguity. Int. J. Comput. Vision **35**(1), 33–44 (1999)
4. Chabert, C.F., et al.: Relighting human locomotion with flowed reflectance fields. In: ACM SIGGRAPH 2006 Sketches, p. 76-es (2006)
5. Chandraker, M.K., Kahl, F., Kriegman, D.J.: Reflections on the generalized bas-relief ambiguity. In: 2005 IEEE Computer Society Conference on Computer Vision and Pattern Recognition (CVPR 2005), vol. 1, pp. 788–795. IEEE (2005)
6. Chen, G., Han, K., Shi, B., Matsushita, Y., Wong, K.Y.K.: Self-calibrating deep photometric stereo networks. In: Proceedings of the IEEE/CVF Conference on Computer Vision and Pattern Recognition, pp. 8739–8747 (2019)
7. Chen, G., Han, K., Shi, B., Matsushita, Y., Wong, K.Y.K.: Deep photometric stereo for non-lambertian surfaces. IEEE Trans. Pattern Anal. Mach. Intell. **44**, 129–142 (2020)
8. Chen, G., Han, K., Wong, K.-Y.K.: PS-FCN: a flexible learning framework for photometric stereo. In: Ferrari, V., Hebert, M., Sminchisescu, C., Weiss, Y. (eds.) ECCV 2018. LNCS, vol. 11213, pp. 3–19. Springer, Cham (2018). https://doi.org/10.1007/978-3-030-01240-3_1

9. Chen, G., Waechter, M., Shi, B., Wong, K.-Y.K., Matsushita, Y.: What is learned in deep uncalibrated photometric stereo? In: Vedaldi, A., Bischof, H., Brox, T., Frahm, J.-M. (eds.) ECCV 2020. LNCS, vol. 12359, pp. 745–762. Springer, Cham (2020). https://doi.org/10.1007/978-3-030-58568-6_44

10. Cho, D., Matsushita, Y., Tai, Y.W., Kweon, I.S.: Semi-calibrated photometric stereo. IEEE Trans. Pattern Anal. Mach. Intell. **42**(1), 232–245 (2018)

11. Drbohlav, O., Šára, R.: Specularities reduce ambiguity of uncalibrated photometric stereo. In: Heyden, A., Sparr, G., Nielsen, M., Johansen, P. (eds.) ECCV 2002. LNCS, vol. 2351, pp. 46–60. Springer, Heidelberg (2002). https://doi.org/10.1007/3-540-47967-8_4

12. Georghiades, A.S.: Incorporating the torrance and sparrow model of reflectance in uncalibrated photometric stereo. In: IEEE International Conference on Computer Vision, vol. 3, pp. 816. IEEE Computer Society (2003)

13. Haefner, B., Ye, Z., Gao, M., Wu, T., Quéau, Y., Cremers, D.: Variational uncalibrated photometric stereo under general lighting. In: Proceedings of the IEEE/CVF International Conference on Computer Vision, pp. 8539–8548 (2019)

14. Honzátko, D., Türetken, E., Fua, P., Dunbar, L.A.: Leveraging spatial and photometric context for calibrated non-lambertian photometric stereo. arXiv preprint arXiv:2103.12106 (2021)

15. Ikehata, S.: CNN-PS: CNN-based photometric stereo for general non-convex surfaces. In: Ferrari, V., Hebert, M., Sminchisescu, C., Weiss, Y. (eds.) ECCV 2018. LNCS, vol. 11219, pp. 3–19. Springer, Cham (2018). https://doi.org/10.1007/978-3-030-01267-0_1

16. Ikehata, S., Aizawa, K.: Photometric stereo using constrained bivariate regression for general isotropic surfaces. In: Proceedings of the IEEE Conference on Computer Vision and Pattern Recognition, pp. 2179–2186 (2014)

17. Ikehata, S., Wipf, D., Matsushita, Y., Aizawa, K.: Robust photometric stereo using sparse regression. In: 2012 IEEE Conference on Computer Vision and Pattern Recognition (CVPR), pp. 318–325. IEEE (2012)

18. Ju, Y., Dong, J., Chen, S.: Recovering surface normal and arbitrary images: a dual regression network for photometric stereo. IEEE Trans. Image Process. **30**, 3676–3690 (2021)

19. Kaya, B., Kumar, S., Oliveira, C., Ferrari, V., Van Gool, L.: Uncalibrated neural inverse rendering for photometric stereo of general surfaces. In: Proceedings of the IEEE/CVF Conference on Computer Vision and Pattern Recognition, pp. 3804–3814 (2021)

20. Kingma, D.P., Ba, J.: Adam: a method for stochastic optimization. arXiv preprint arXiv:1412.6980 (2014)

21. Li, J., Li, H.: Neural reflectance for shape recovery with shadow handling. In: Proceedings of the IEEE/CVF Conference on Computer Vision and Pattern Recognition, pp. 16221–16230 (2022)

22. Li, J., Robles-Kelly, A., You, S., Matsushita, Y.: Learning to minify photometric stereo. In: Proceedings of the IEEE/CVF Conference on Computer Vision and Pattern Recognition, pp. 7568–7576 (2019)

23. Lin, C.H., Ma, W.C., Torralba, A., Lucey, S.: Barf: bundle-adjusting neural radiance fields. In: IEEE International Conference on Computer Vision (ICCV) (2021)

24. Logothetis, F., Budvytis, I., Mecca, R., Cipolla, R.: Px-net: simple and efficient pixel-wise training of photometric stereo networks. In: Proceedings of the IEEE/CVF International Conference on Computer Vision, pp. 12757–12766 (2021)

25. Logothetis, F., Mecca, R., Cipolla, R.: Semi-calibrated near field photometric stereo. In: Proceedings of the IEEE Conference on Computer Vision and Pattern Recognition, pp. 941–950 (2017)
26. Lu, F., Chen, X., Sato, I., Sato, Y.: Symps: brdf symmetry guided photometric stereo for shape and light source estimation. IEEE Trans. Pattern Anal. Mach. Intell. **40**(1), 221–234 (2017)
27. Lu, F., Matsushita, Y., Sato, I., Okabe, T., Sato, Y.: Uncalibrated photometric stereo for unknown isotropic reflectances. In: Proceedings of the IEEE Conference on Computer Vision and Pattern Recognition, pp. 1490–1497 (2013)
28. Lu, F., Sato, I., Sato, Y.: Uncalibrated photometric stereo based on elevation angle recovery from brdf symmetry of isotropic materials. In: Proceedings of the IEEE Conference on Computer Vision and Pattern Recognition, pp. 168–176 (2015)
29. Mildenhall, B., Srinivasan, P.P., Tancik, M., Barron, J.T., Ramamoorthi, R., Ng, R.: NeRF: representing scenes as neural radiance fields for view synthesis. In: Vedaldi, A., Bischof, H., Brox, T., Frahm, J.-M. (eds.) ECCV 2020. LNCS, vol. 12346, pp. 405–421. Springer, Cham (2020). https://doi.org/10.1007/978-3-030-58452-8_24
30. Mo, Z., Shi, B., Lu, F., Yeung, S.K., Matsushita, Y.: Uncalibrated photometric stereo under natural illumination. In: 2018 IEEE/CVF Conference on Computer Vision and Pattern Recognition (CVPR), pp. 2936–2945. IEEE Computer Society (2018)
31. Mukaigawa, Y., Ishii, Y., Shakunaga, T.: Analysis of photometric factors based on photometric linearization. JOSA A **24**(10), 3326–3334 (2007)
32. Papadhimitri, T., Favaro, P.: A new perspective on uncalibrated photometric stereo. In: Proceedings of the IEEE Conference on Computer Vision and Pattern Recognition, pp. 1474–1481 (2013)
33. Papadhimitri, T., Favaro, P.: A closed-form, consistent and robust solution to uncalibrated photometric stereo via local diffuse reflectance maxima. Int. J. Comput. Vision **107**(2), 139–154 (2014)
34. Quéau, Y., Lauze, F., Durou, J.D.: Solving uncalibrated photometric stereo using total variation. J. Math. Imaging Vision **52**(1), 87–107 (2015)
35. Quéau, Y., Wu, T., Lauze, F., Durou, J.D., Cremers, D.: A non-convex variational approach to photometric stereo under inaccurate lighting. In: Proceedings of the IEEE Conference on Computer Vision and Pattern Recognition, pp. 99–108 (2017)
36. Santo, H., Samejima, M., Sugano, Y., Shi, B., Matsushita, Y.: Deep photometric stereo network. In: 2017 IEEE International Conference on Computer Vision Workshop (ICCVW), pp. 501–509. IEEE (2017)
37. Sarno, F., Kumar, S., Kaya, B., Huang, Z., Ferrari, V., Van Gool, L.: Neural architecture search for efficient uncalibrated deep photometric stereo. arXiv preprint arXiv:2110.05621 (2021)
38. Shi, B., Matsushita, Y., Wei, Y., Xu, C., Tan, P.: Self-calibrating photometric stereo. In: 2010 IEEE Computer Society Conference on Computer Vision and Pattern Recognition, pp. 1118–1125. IEEE (2010)
39. Shi, B., Mo, Z., Wu, Z., Duan, D., Yeung, S.K., Tan, P.: A benchmark dataset and evaluation for non-lambertian and uncalibrated photometric stereo. IEEE Trans. Pattern Anal. Mach. Intell. (2018)
40. Sunkavalli, K., Zickler, T., Pfister, H.: Visibility subspaces: uncalibrated photometric stereo with shadows. In: Daniilidis, K., Maragos, P., Paragios, N. (eds.) ECCV 2010. LNCS, vol. 6312, pp. 251–264. Springer, Heidelberg (2010). https://doi.org/10.1007/978-3-642-15552-9_19

41. Taniai, T., Maehara, T.: Neural inverse rendering for general reflectance photometric stereo. In: International Conference on Machine Learning, pp. 4864–4873 (2018)
42. Torrance, K.E., Sparrow, E.M.: Theory for off-specular reflection from roughened surfaces. JOSA **57**(9), 1105–1114 (1967)
43. Wang, J., Ren, P., Gong, M., Snyder, J., Guo, B.: All-frequency rendering of dynamic, spatially-varying reflectance. ACM Trans. Graph. (TOG) **28**(5), 1–10 (2009)
44. Wang, X., Jian, Z., Ren, M.: Non-lambertian photometric stereo network based on inverse reflectance model with collocated light. IEEE Trans. Image Process. **29**, 6032–6042 (2020)
45. Woodham, R.J.: Photometric method for determining surface orientation from multiple images. Opt. Eng. **19**(1), 191139 (1980)
46. Wu, L., Ganesh, A., Shi, B., Matsushita, Y., Wang, Y., Ma, Y.: Robust photometric stereo via low-rank matrix completion and recovery. In: Kimmel, R., Klette, R., Sugimoto, A. (eds.) ACCV 2010. LNCS, vol. 6494, pp. 703–717. Springer, Heidelberg (2011). https://doi.org/10.1007/978-3-642-19318-7_55
47. Wu, T.P., Tang, C.K.: Photometric stereo via expectation maximization. IEEE Trans. Pattern Anal. Mach. Intell. **32**(3), 546–560 (2010)
48. Wu, Z., Tan, P.: Calibrating photometric stereo by holistic reflectance symmetry analysis. In: Proceedings of the IEEE Conference on Computer Vision and Pattern Recognition, pp. 1498–1505 (2013)
49. Yao, Z., Li, K., Fu, Y., Hu, H., Shi, B.: Gps-net: graph-based photometric stereo network. Adv. Neural Inf. Process. Syst. **33** (2020)
50. Zheng, Q., Jia, Y., Shi, B., Jiang, X., Duan, L.Y., Kot, A.C.: Spline-net: sparse photometric stereo through lighting interpolation and normal estimation networks. In: Proceedings of the IEEE/CVF International Conference on Computer Vision, pp. 8549–8558 (2019)

3D Clothed Human Reconstruction in the Wild

Gyeongsik Moon[1], Hyeongjin Nam[2], Takaaki Shiratori[1],
and Kyoung Mu Lee[2,3(✉)]

[1] Meta Reality Labs Research, Pittsburgh, PA, USA
{mks0601,tshiratori}@fb.com
[2] Department of ECE and ASRI, Seoul National University, Seoul, South Korea
{namhjsnu28,kyoungmu}@snu.ac.kr
[3] IPAI, Seoul National University, Seoul, South Korea

Abstract. Although much progress has been made in 3D clothed human reconstruction, most of the existing methods fail to produce robust results from in-the-wild images, which contain diverse human poses and appearances. This is mainly due to the large domain gap between training datasets and in-the-wild datasets. The training datasets are usually synthetic ones, which contain rendered images from GT 3D scans. However, such datasets contain simple human poses and less natural image appearances compared to those of real in-the-wild datasets, which makes generalization of it to in-the-wild images extremely challenging. To resolve this issue, in this work, we propose ClothWild, a 3D clothed human reconstruction framework that firstly addresses the robustness on in-the-wild images. First, for the robustness to the domain gap, we propose a weakly supervised pipeline that is trainable with 2D supervision targets of in-the-wild datasets. Second, we design a DensePose-based loss function to reduce ambiguities of the weak supervision. Extensive empirical tests on several public in-the-wild datasets demonstrate that our proposed ClothWild produces much more accurate and robust results than the state-of-the-art methods. The codes are available in https://github.com/hygenie1228/ClothWild_RELEASE.

1 Introduction

3D clothed human reconstruction aims to reconstruct humans with various poses, body shapes, and clothes in 3D space from a single image. It is an essential task for various applications, such as 3D avatars and virtual try-on. Most of the recent 3D clothed human reconstruction methods [2,3,6,7,13–15,17,33,34,37]

G. Moon and H. Nam—Equal contribution.
This work was primarily done while Gyeongsik Moon was in SNU.

Supplementary Information The online version contains supplementary material available at https://doi.org/10.1007/978-3-031-20086-1_11.

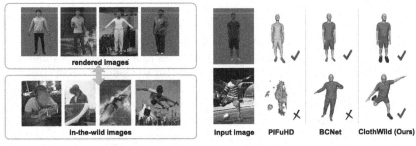

(a) Domain gap (pose, appearance, occlusion, etc)   (b) Qualitative comparison

Fig. 1. (a) Domain gap between rendered images and in-the-wild images. (b) Due to the large domain gap, existing methods (*e.g.* PIFuHD [34] and BCNet [17]) fail on in-the-wild images, while our ClothWild successfully reconstructs. Colors of reconstructed 3D clothes are manually assigned to represent cloth types.

require 3D scans for the training; hence, they are trained on synthetic datasets, which consist of 3D scans [4,31] and rendered images from the scans. Although significant progress has been made by utilizing such synthetic datasets, all of them fail to produce robust results on in-the-wild images.

The in-the-wild images are taken in our daily environments, such as cluttered offices and concert halls, and have diverse human poses, appearances, and severe human occlusions. On the other hand, the 3D scans are captured from restricted environments, such as motion capture studios. To ease 3D scan capturing, subjects are often instructed to take simple poses. Therefore, rendered images from the 3D scans have artificial appearances and simple human poses compared to those of in-the-wild images, as shown in Fig. 1(a). This large domain gap between in-the-wild and rendered images makes the methods trained on synthetic datasets fail to generalize to in-the-wild images, as shown in Fig. 1(b).

For the robustness to the domain gap, we present ClothWild, a 3D clothed human reconstruction framework that leverages a weak-supervision strategy to learn 3D clothed humans from in-the-wild datasets. Here, the weak supervision means that the supervision target is not full 3D data, but 2D data defined only in the single-camera viewpoint (*i.e.*, 2D cloth segmentations [9]). For the weak-supervision strategy, our reconstruction pipeline is divided into two networks: a cloth generative model and a regressor, ClothNet. The cloth generative model generates 3D cloth geometry around the T-posed 3D body of SMPL [23] from the cloth latent codes, where the 3D cloth geometry is animatable using a skinning function of SMPL. It is fully supervised on the synthetic datasets beforehand, and we freeze it during the weakly supervised training. Although the cloth generative model covers various cloth types and styles, it does not cover complicated human poses and diverse image appearances of in-the-wild datasets. For the robustness to such in-the-wild datasets, we design a regressor, called ClothNet, and weakly supervise it on in-the-wild datasets to predict latent codes of the cloth generative model. The final output can be obtained by passing the output of the ClothNet to the cloth generative model. As the cloth generative model is fixed during the weakly supervised training, we can protect the generative model from being hurt by imperfect 2D supervision targets of in-the-wild datasets, while making our ClothNet robust to diverse human poses and image appearances of in-the-wild images. Our weak-supervision strategy can recover full 3D geometry only from the evidence of the single-camera viewpoint by regularizing the predicted cloth latent codes to be in the cloth latent space. Note that such regularization is not possible for previous approaches [3,33,34,36] as they do not model cloth latent space.

For the weak supervision, we can enforce the projection of 3D reconstruction results to be close to 2D supervision targets (*i.e.*, cloth segmentations [9]) of in-the-wild datasets. However, naively adopting such a strategy has three difficulties in learning 3D clothed humans. First, the 2D supervision targets provide information for only a single camera viewpoint. Therefore, there is no guarantee that the weak supervision can recover 3D geometry of other viewpoints. Second, severe depth ambiguity of the cloth segmentations hampers learning accurate 3D clothes. Since each pixel in cloth segmentations corresponds to innumerable points in 3D space, it is difficult to specify 3D points corresponding to clothes. Third, pixel-level misalignment can occur between projected 3D reconstruction results and 2D cloth segmentation. As camera parameters are not available for in-the-wild images, we should additionally predict the camera parameters to project the 3D clothed humans. This is a highly ill-posed problem as various combinations of camera parameters and 3D clothed humans correspond to the same 2D cloth segmentation. Due to the ill-posedness, camera prediction can often fail, which results in the wrong projection to the 2D image space.

In this regard, we design a DensePose-based loss function to resolve the issues which can occur when weakly supervising 3D clothed human reconstructions based on their projections. DensePose [10] informs where each human pixel corresponds to the 3D human body surface of SMPL. Using DensePose, our DensePose-based loss function obtains 3D points that correspond to the cloth segmentations around the SMPL surface. Then, it enforces such 3D points to be a part of the 3D cloth surface. As the DensePose effectively limits possible positions of 3D points around the SMPL surface, it significantly reduces the depth ambiguity. In addition, DensePose is already aligned with cloth segmentations in the image space; therefore, we do not have to predict camera parameters and project 3D reconstructions to the 2D image space. Hence, our DensePose-based loss function does not suffer from pixel-level misalignment.

We show that the proposed ClothWild produces far more robust and better results than the previous 3D clothed human reconstruction methods from in-the-wild images. As robustness on in-the-wild images has not been extensively studied in the 3D human reconstruction community, we believe ours can give useful insights to the following research.

Our contributions can be summarized as follows.

- We present ClothWild, which reconstructs robust 3D clothed humans from a single in-the-wild image. To the best of our knowledge, it is the first to explicitly address robustness on in-the-wild images.
- For the robustness to the domain gap between synthesized and in-the-wild datasets, we propose a weakly supervised pipeline that is trainable with 2D supervision targets of in-the-wild datasets.
- Our DensePose-based loss function resolves the ambiguities of weak supervision by effectively limiting possible positions of 3D points using DensePose.
- ClothWild largely outperforms previous methods on in-the-wild images.

2   Related Works

3D Clothed Human Reconstruction. Varol et al. [35] and Jackson et al. [16] proposed volumetric regression networks that directly predict a voxel representation of a 3D clothed human from a single image. Saito et al. [33,34] and He et al. [13] presented a pixel-aligned implicit function that predicts 3D occupancy fields of clothed humans. Alldieck et al. [1] utilized displacement vectors between a human body surface and clothes for reconstruction. Alldieck et al. [2] presented a method estimating normal and displacement maps on top of a human body model, such as SMPL [23]. Bhatnagar et al. [6] and Jiang et al. [17] presented 3D clothed human reconstruction systems that predict PCA coefficients of cloth generative model space. Huang et al. [15] and He et al. [14] handle implicit function representation of 3D clothed humans in arbitrary poses and produce animatable reconstruction results. Xiu et al. [36] presented ICON, which utilizes local features for robust 3D clothed human reconstruction. Alldieck et al. [3] proposed PHORHUM to photorealistically reconstruct the 3D geometry and appearance of a dressed person. As all of the above methods require 3D scans for training, they are trained on synthetic datasets, which consist of 3D scans and the rendered images from the scans. As the synthetic datasets mainly contain simple human poses with artificial appearances, the methods trained on such datasets fail to generalize to in-the-wild datasets. In contrast, our ClothWild is the first work that can be weakly supervised with 2D supervision targets of in-the-wild datasets, which results in robust outputs on in-the-wild images.

Recently, Corona et al. [7] presented a fitting framework that fits their cloth generative model to 2D cloth segmentations. Although their fitting framework handles reconstruction on in-the-wild images, there are two major differences from ours. First, their fitting framework is not a learning-based system; hence, it cannot utilize image features. As it only relies on 2D cloth segmentations for fitting, it produces wrong results when cloth segmentations are not available due to truncations or occlusions. On the other hand, ClothWild is a learning-based system that utilizes image features; hence, it is much more robust to occlusions and truncations by considering contextual information of image features, as shown in Fig. 5. Second, their fitting framework suffers from the depth ambiguity and pixel-misalignment as described in Sect. 1, since it projects 3D reconstruction results to the 2D image space and compares the projected one with

2D cloth segmentations. On the other hand, ClothWild leverages our newly proposed DensePose-based loss function. Hence, ClothWild suffers much less from the depth ambiguity and is free from the pixel-misalignment issue. The detailed description of it is provided in Sect. 6.4.

3D Cloth Generative Model. 3D cloth generative models parameterize 3D clothes by embedding acquired 3D cloth scans in a latent space. Bhatnagar et al. [6] and Jiang et al. [17] used the PCA algorithm to represent clothes in a latent space. Ma et al. [25] used a graph convolutional neural network-based generative model to embed the clothes in a latent space. Bertiche et al. [5] embedded displacements from the human body surface to registered cloth meshes and cloth types as latent codes. Patel et al. [29] decomposed 3D clothes into low- and high-frequency components and represented them as a function of human poses, shapes and cloth styles. Corona et al. [7] presented a cloth generative model, SMPLicit, which embeds 3D clothes as latent codes that represent cloth styles and cloth cuts. SMPLicit covers a wide variety of clothes, which differ in their geometric properties, such as sleeve length and looseness. In our framework, we employ SMPLicit as a cloth generative model.

3D Human Body Reconstruction. 3D human body reconstruction methods predict parameters of the SMPL [23] body model from a single image. They perform well on in-the-wild images via weakly supervision with 2D GTs of in-the-wild images. Kanazawa et al. [18] proposed an end-to-end framework that utilizes adversarial loss to reconstruct plausible human bodies. Kolotouros et al. [20] combined a regressor and iterative fitting framework. Moon et al. [27] presented Pose2Pose utilizing local and global image features. We use Pose2Pose as an off-the-shelf 3D human body reconstruction method of our ClothWild due to its superior accuracy compared to other works.

3   ClothWild

Figure 2 shows the overall pipeline of our ClothWild, which consists of ClothNet and BodyNet. We provide a detailed description of each module below.

3.1   ClothNet

Given an input image $\mathbf{I}$, ClothNet predicts cloth existence scores $\mathbf{c} = (c_1, \ldots, c_{N_c})$, a set of cloth latent codes $\{\mathbf{z}_i\}_{i=1}^{N_c}$, and a gender $\mathbf{g}$. $N_c = 5$ denotes the number of clothes we consider, which include upper cloth, coat, pants, skirt, and shoes. The ith cloth existence score c_i represents the probability that a human is wearing ith cloth. The ith cloth latent code $\mathbf{z}_i \in \mathbb{R}^{d_i}$ represents a low-dimensional code of ith 3D cloth, embedded in latent space of the 3D cloth model, SMPLicit [7]. We set $d_i = 4$ for shoes and $d_i = 18$ for other clothes following SMPLicit [7]. The gender $\mathbf{g} \in \mathbb{R}^2$ is a one-hot encoded vector that represents

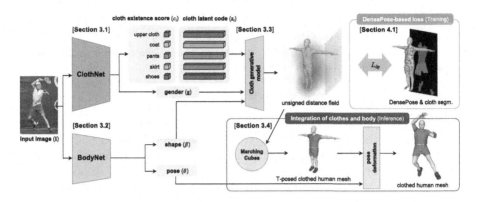

Fig. 2. The overall pipeline of ClothWild. ClothNet predicts cloth latent codes of the cloth generative model, SMPLicit, and produces an unsigned distance field by passing the codes to the SMPLicit. BodyNet predicts SMPL pose and shape parameters. At the training stage, the unsigned distance field is supervised with a combination of Dense-Pose and cloth segmentations with our DensePose-based loss function. At the inference stage, the final 3D clothed human reconstruction is obtained through Marching Cubes and pose deformation steps.

a label for the appropriate human body model (*i.e.*, male and female). We use ResNet-50 [12] to extract an image feature vector $\mathbf{f} \in \mathbb{R}^{2048}$ from the input image after removing the fully-connected layer of the last part of the original ResNet. The image feature vector $\mathbf{f}$ is passed into a fully-connected layer, followed by a sigmoid activation function, to predict the cloth existence scores $\mathbf{c}$. In addition, we use N_c fully-connected layers to predict a set of cloth latent codes $\{\mathbf{z}_i\}_{i=1}^{N_c}$ from $\mathbf{f}$, where ith fully-connected layer predicts the latent codes of ith cloth, $\mathbf{z}_i$. Finally, another fully-connected layer, followed by a softmax activation function, predicts the gender from $\mathbf{f}$. The predicted set of cloth latent codes $\{\mathbf{z}_i\}_{i=1}^{N_c}$ and gender $\mathbf{g}$ are passed to SMPLicit.

3.2   BodyNet

The BodyNet takes the input image $\mathbf{I}$ and predicts a shape parameter $\beta \in \mathbb{R}^{10}$ and a pose parameter $\theta \in \mathbb{R}^{72}$ of the SMPL human body model [23]. The shape parameter β represents PCA coefficients of T-posed human body shape space, and the pose parameter θ represents 3D rotations of human body joints. The shape parameter β is forwarded to SMPLicit that is described in Sect. 3.3. The pose parameter θ is used in the inference stage, of which detailed descriptions are in Sect. 3.4. We use Pose2Pose [27] as the BodyNet, which achieves state-of-the-art performance on in-the-wild benchmarks.

3.3   Cloth Generative Model

The cloth generative model embeds 3D clothes in the latent space. We use SMPLicit [7] as our cloth generative model, which produces a continuous unsigned distance field of a 3D cloth from a cloth latent code, gender, and human shape. We use the pre-trained SMPLicit and fix it while training ClothWild. Given the cloth latent codes $\{z_i\}_{i=1}^{N_c}$, gender g, and human shape β, SMPLicit outputs the unsigned distance field for the ith cloth, as follows:

$$C(\mathbf{x}, \mathbf{z}_i, \mathbf{g}, \beta) \longrightarrow \mathbb{R}^+, \quad i = 1, 2, \ldots, N_c, \tag{1}$$

where $\mathbf{x} \in \mathbb{R}^3$ is a 3D query point in a canonical 3D space where the human is in a T-pose. In the canonical 3D space, a T-posed naked human body mesh is founded by deriving from the gender $\mathbf{g}$ and human shape β. Around the T-posed naked human body, a set of 3D query points indicate the closest distance to the 3D cloth surface as the unsigned distance field. The above step only proceeds for the ith cloth when its cloth existence score c_i is larger than a threshold, which we empirically set to 0.25.

3.4   Integration of Clothes and Body

Marching Cubes. In the inference stage, we obtain cloth meshes using Marching Cubes [24], which extracts a mesh of an isosurface from a 3D discrete scalar field, such as the unsigned distance field. We calculate the unsigned distance field by densely sampling 3D query points in the 3D space and forwarding them to the SMPLicit model. Then, we extract cloth meshes on the T-pose from the unsigned distance field by Marching Cubes. At the end of this step, we obtain a T-posed clothed human mesh that comprises a T-posed naked human body mesh and cloth meshes.

Pose Deformation. Finally, we apply the pose deformation to the naked human body mesh and cloth meshes of the T-posed clothed human mesh, respectively, following Corona et al. [7]. To deform the naked human body, we use the skinning deformation of SMPL with the pose parameter θ predicted by the BodyNet. To deform cloth meshes, we allocate each cloth vertex of the cloth meshes to its closest naked human body vertex and apply the same pose deformation of the human body vertex. Such the SMPL-driven pose deformation has the strength that the reconstruction results can be deformed with an arbitrary pose instead of the predicted pose, which enables an animation.

4   Learning from In-the-wild Datasets

In this section, we describe loss functions to train our framework on in-the-wild datasets without any 3D scan GTs. ClothNet is the only trainable module in our framework, and all other modules, including BodyNet and SMPLicit, are fixed during the training. The overall loss function is

$$L_{\text{total}} = \lambda_{\text{dp}} L_{\text{dp}} + \lambda_{\text{reg}} L_{\text{reg}} + \lambda_{\text{exist}} L_{\text{exist}} + \lambda_{\text{gender}} L_{\text{gender}}, \tag{2}$$

where $\lambda_{\text{dp}} = 1$, $\lambda_{\text{reg}} = 0.1$, $\lambda_{\text{exist}} = 0.01$, and $\lambda_{\text{gender}} = 0.01$.

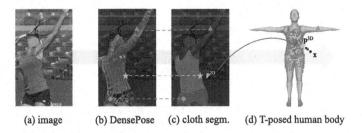

(a) image   (b) DensePose   (c) cloth segm.   (d) T-posed human body

Fig. 3. The procedure of the cloth-to-body mapping step. From (a) an in-the-wild image, we exploit 2D supervision targets: (b) DensePose and (c) cloth segmentations. (d) We sample a 2D cloth point $\mathbf{p}^{2D}$ of the cloth segmentations, and map the 2D cloth point $\mathbf{p}^{2D}$ to the 3D cloth point $\mathbf{p}^{3D}$ on the T-posed human body surface. We select the 3D query point $\mathbf{x}$ within constant distance from the 3D cloth points, and the DensePose-based loss function supervises the selected 3D query point.

4.1 DensePose-based Loss Function

The DensePose-based loss function L_{dp}, which uses a combination of cloth segmentations and DensePose, makes reconstructed clothes close to cloth segmentations. The loss is computed in three steps: cloth-to-body mapping, query point selection, and loss calculation.

Cloth-to-Body Mapping. In the first step, we place pixels of 2D cloth segmentations in 3D space. Figure 3 shows the procedure of the cloth-to-body mapping step. In the area where DensePose is defined, we sample 2D cloth points $\{\mathbf{p}_k^{2D}\}_{k=1}^{N_p}$ on cloth segmentations, where $N_p = 196$ is the number of the sampled 2D points. We utilize DensePose that informs where each human pixel corresponds to the 3D human body surface of SMPL to map the 2D cloth points $\{\mathbf{p}_k^{2D}\}_{k=1}^{N_p}$ to 3D cloth points $\{\mathbf{p}_k^{3D}\}_{k=1}^{N_p}$ on the T-posed human body surface. Each of the mapped 3D cloth points represents a cloth label (*e.g.*, upper cloth, pants, or non-cloth) elicited from the cloth segmentations.

Query Point Selection. In this step, we select 3D query points around the T-posed human body for loss calculation. For each cloth type, we uniformly sample 3D query points at a resolution of $21 \times 21 \times 21$ from a 3D bounding box, where the sampling strategy is described in the supplementary material. We select 3D query points $\{\mathbf{x}_j\}_{j=1}^{N_q}$ within a distance threshold τ from the 3D cloth points $\{\mathbf{p}_k^{3D}\}_{k=1}^{N_p}$ on the 3D human body surface, where N_q is the number of the sampled 3D query points. The distance threshold τ is set 10 cm for the coat and 3 cm for others.

Loss Calculation. To the formal description of the loss function, we define a cloth binary function $S_i(\cdot)$. If the closest 3D cloth point from a 3D query point

$\mathbf{x}_j$ belongs to the ith cloth, $S_i(\mathbf{x}_j)$ becomes 1 and 0 else. With the cloth binary function $S_i(\cdot)$, the DensePose-based loss function follows:

$$L_{dp} = \frac{1}{N_c N_q} \sum_{i=1}^{N_c} \sum_{j=1}^{N_q} (S_i(\mathbf{x}_j)|C(\mathbf{x}_j, \mathbf{z}_i, \mathbf{g}, \beta)|$$

$$+ (1 - S_i(\mathbf{x}_j))|C(\mathbf{x}_j, \mathbf{z}_i, \mathbf{g}, \beta) - d_{max}|), \tag{3}$$

where d_{max} is a maximum cut-off distance of the unsigned distance fields, set to 0.01 for shoes and 0.1 for others. The first loss term forces the 3D query point $\mathbf{x}$ to belong to ith cloth by making its unsigned distance close to zero when the 3D point matches cloth label i. The second loss term forces the 3D query point $\mathbf{x}$ to not belong to ith cloth when the 3D point does not match cloth label i. As a result, the DensePose-based loss function supervises the 3D query points established by the above steps without the depth ambiguity of the cloth segmentations.

4.2 Other Loss Functions

Regularization Loss. The regularization loss function L_{reg} makes predicted latent codes close to the mean of the cloth latent space, which results in plausible 3D clothes. The regularization loss function is defined as follows: $L_{reg} = \sum_{i=1}^{N_c} \alpha_i \|\mathbf{z}_i\|_2$, where α_i is set 0.1 for shoes and 1.0 for others. As the DensePose-based loss supervises 3D points that belong to partial areas of clothes, there is a possibility to learn implausible clothes (*e.g.*, overly thick cloth or torn cloth) that only rely on the areas. The regularization loss prevents it by constraining output clothes to be close to the mean.

Cloth Existence Loss. For the cloth existence prediction, we calculate a binary cross-entropy as follows: $L_{exist} = -\frac{1}{N_c} \sum_{i=1}^{N_c} (c_i^* \log c_i + (1 - c_i^*)(1 - \log c_i))$, where the asterisk denotes the groundtruth.

Gender Classification Loss. For the gender classification, we calculate a cross-entropy as follows: $L_{gender} = -(g_m^* \log g_m + g_f^* \log g_f)$, where g_m and $g_f = 1 - g_m$ is the probability of being male and female of the input human, respectively. The asterisk denotes the groundtruth.

5 Implementation Details

PyTorch [28] is used for implementation. The backbone part is initialized with the publicly released ResNet50 [12] pre-trained on ImageNet [32]. The weights are updated by Adam optimizer [19] with a mini-batch size of 8. The human body region is cropped using a GT box in both training and testing stages following previous works [33,34]. The cropped image is resized to 256×192. Data augmentations, including scaling, rotation, random horizontal flip, and color jittering, are performed in training. The initial learning rate is set to 10^{-4} and reduced by a factor of 10 after the 5th epoch. We train the model for 8 epochs with an NVIDIA GTX 2080 Ti GPU.

6   Experiment

6.1   Datasets

MSCOCO. MSCOCO [22] is a large-scale in-the-wild dataset, which provides in-the-wild images with diverse human poses and appearances. We train ours on the training split and evaluate on the validation split. We use outputs of the DensePose regression model [10] for the DensePose-based loss function as GT DensePose provides only sparse annotations. For the cloth segmentations, we use LIP [9], which contains cloth segmentation annotations of MSCOCO images. We acquire gender annotations by running Homogenus [30] on MSCOCO and use its predictions as supervision targets.

DeepFashion2. DeepFashion2 [8] is a comprehensive dataset that focuses on capturing clothed humans with a wide variety of cloth styles, and we use it as the additional train set along with the MSCOCO. We obtain DensePose and gender annotations by the same procedure as MSCOCO, described above. For cloth segmentation annotations, we use SCHP [21] to obtain cloth segmentations of the dataset.

3DPW. 3DPW [26] is an in-the-wild dataset, and we use it only for the evaluation purpose after sampling every 25th frame of test set videos. We use two

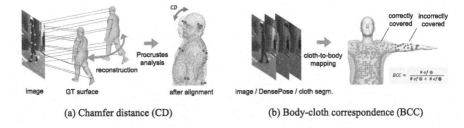

(a) Chamfer distance (CD)   (b) Body-cloth correspondence (BCC)

Fig. 4. Descriptions of our evaluation metrics. (a) Chamfer distance (CD) is a 3D distance between reconstruction and GT surface. It is measured after aligning them based on each 2D projection. (b) BCC is a proportion of 3D points that have correctly matched cloth types. The purple and red points on the right body surface are 3D points that are mapped from cloth segmentations using DensePose. The purple points represent 3D points that are covered with a correct type of reconstructed 3D clothes, while the red points represent others. It is measured after normalizing 3D poses. (Color figure online)

items of 3DPW: T-posed clothed human meshes registered to each subject's 3D scan and SMPL pose parameters of humans in images. As the registered 3D clothed human meshes have the same mesh topology as that of SMPL body mesh, we deform the registered ones with SMPL pose parameters following the same skinning algorithm of SMPL. We use the posed registered meshes as GT 3D clothed humans of 3DPW.

6.2   Evaluation Metrics

Figure 4 shows our two evaluation metrics. Since there has been no work dealing with 3D clothed human reconstruction on the in-the-wild dataset, we propose two evaluation metrics in the following.

Chamfer Distance (CD). Chamfer Distance (CD) is a 3D distance between the 3D clothed human reconstruction and the GT surface, widely used in previous works [17,33,34]. Before measurement, we rigidly align global rotation, scale, and translation of the reconstruction to the GT surface. The alignment is not trivial as there are no semantically matching pairs between the reconstruction and GT surface. For the alignment, we assume that the same human parts (*e.g.*, shoulders and knees) of both the reconstruction and the GT surface are projected to the same pixel in the image. We rasterize both the reconstruction and GT surface and pair two vertices (*i.e.*, one from the reconstruction and the other from the GT surface) that correspond to the same pixel. Based on the matching pairs, we align the reconstruction and measure the Chamfer distance (CD) in millimeter. More details of CD metric is described in the supplementary material.

Body-Cloth Correspondence (BCC). Body-cloth correspondence (BCC) is a proportion of 3D points that have correct cloth types on the T-posed naked human body surface. It only considers 3D cloth predictions, excluding 3D human pose predictions. With cloth-to-body mapping described in Sect. 4.1, we map 2D points in a GT cloth segmentation for one cloth label to 3D points on the T-posed human body surface with the cloth-to-body mapping. We consider 3D points are correctly covered ones if the distance between them and reconstructed cloth is shorter than 3 cm. We calculate the proportion of the correctly covered points and average the proportions for all cloth labels (*e.g.*, upper cloth, pants, or non-cloth). This metric is used for methods that support cloth-to-body mapping based on the T-posed naked body of SMPL. For example, as PIFu [33], PIFuHD [34], and ICON [36] do not tell us cloth type which points belong, we could not evaluate them using the BCC metric.

6.3   Comparison with State-of-the-art Methods

We compare our ClothWild with recent 3D clothed human reconstruction methods: PIFu [33], PIFuHD [34], ICON [36], BCNet [17], and the fitting framework of

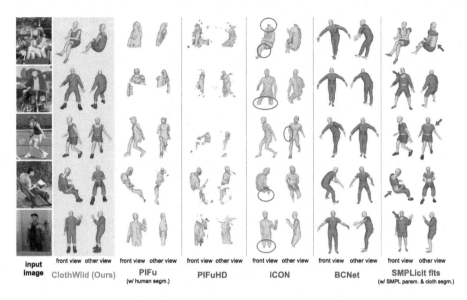

Fig. 5. Qualitative result comparisons on MSCOCO validation set. PIFu additionally uses human segmentation obtained from Mask R-CNN [11] for reconstruction. SMPLicit fits use SMPL parameter and cloth segmentations obtained from our BodyNet and SCHP [21], respectively. Colors of reconstructed 3D clothes are manually assigned to represent cloth types.

SMPLicit [7]. For the inference, PIFu requires human segmentation, and the fitting framework of SMPLicit requires SMPL parameter and cloth segmentations. We provide human segmentation, obtained by Mask R-CNN [11], to PIFu. The same SMPL parameters of our BodyNet and cloth segmentations from SCHP [21] are provided to the SMPLicit fitting framework. All of their results are obtained by using their officially released codes and pre-trained weights. Please note that the fitting framework of SMPLicit fits their cloth latent codes to the cloth segmentations. We call the fitting results of their framework as SMPLicit fits.

Qualitative Results. Figure 5 shows that our ClothWild produces much better reconstruction results than previous state-of-the-art 3D clothed human reconstruction methods on MSCOCO [22]. PIFu [33], PIFuHD [34], and ICON [36] suffer from undesirable results on in-the-wild images with diverse human poses and appearances, especially in the occluded human scene. ICON produces better results than PIFu and PIFuHD; however, it still suffers from missing human parts. On the other hand, our ClothWild successfully reconstructs invisible parts of clothed humans even when the input human is occluded or truncated. Like PIFu, PIFuHD, and ICON, BCNet [17] also requires 3D scans for the training. Accordingly, it is trained on synthetic datasets without in-the-wild images, the reason for weak results on in-the-wild images. SMPLicit fits [7] does not utilize image features, which provide contextual information of occluded and truncated

Table 1. CD comparison with state-of-the-art methods on 3DPW. Methods with *
and † additionally use human segmentation and cloth segmentations as an input for
the inference, respectively.

Methods	CD ↓
PIFuHD [34]	137.50
BCNet [17]	118.75
ICON [36]	75.00
PIFu [33]*	67.25
SMPLicit fits [7]†	45.66
ClothWild (Ours)	**40.34**

Table 2. BCC comparison with state-of-the-art methods on MSCOCO. Methods with
† additionally use cloth segmentations as an input for the inference.

Methods	Upper body	Lower body	Non-cloth	Average
BCNet [17]	0.415	0.729	0.800	0.648
SMPLicit fits [7]†	0.645	0.493	**0.961**	0.700
ClothWild (Ours)	**0.830**	**0.820**	0.887	**0.846**

Table 3. Running time (seconds per image) comparisons.

PIFuHD [34] (CVPR 20)	SMPLicit fits [7] (CVPR 21)	ICON [36] (CVPR 22)	**ClothWild (Ours)**
20.43	105.43	87.88	**10.21**

human parts. Hence, it cannot reconstruct clothes at occluded or truncated human parts. In addition, the depth ambiguity and pixel-level misalignment of their silhouette-based loss function make the fitting attain the incorrect cloth styles. Our ClothWild resolves such issues by utilizing image features and the DensePose-based loss function.

Quantitative Results. Table 1 shows that ClothWild achieves the best CD on 3DPW [22]. Also, Table 2 shows that ClothWild produces much better BCC than previous methods on MSCOCO [22]. Unlike ours, BCNet [17] handles only three cloth types (*i.e.*, upper cloth, pants, and skirt). Hence, we categorize upper cloth and coat into the upper body and pants and skirts into the lower body for a fair comparison. Then, we calculate BCC only for such clothes and exclude shoes. As the BCC evaluates only predicted 3D clothes without considering 3D human poses, the comparisons show that our ClothWild predicts the cloth styles of the image accurately, such as sleeveless and length of upper cloth and pants.

Running Time. Table 3 shows that ours takes the shortest computational time to process a single image than recently presented works. The running times are measured in the same environment with Intel Xeon Gold 6248R CPU and NVIDIA RTX 2080 Ti GPU. We exclude pre-processing stages, such as 3D body pose estimation, human segmentation, and cloth segmentations. The fitting framework of SMPLicit takes a much longer time, although it is based on the same cloth generative model [7] as ours. This is because the fitting framework of SMPLicit forwards the cloth generative model about 200 iterations to fit its cloth latent codes to cloth segmentations. ICON suffers from a similar problem as it iteratively fits initial results based on normal maps and silhouettes. In contrast, our ClothWild performs the feed-forward only a single time. The above methods, including ours, require Marching Cubes to obtain final 3D geometry, one of the main bottlenecks of the running time. The running time of ClothWild's each component will be reported in the supplementary material.

6.4 Ablation Study

Effectiveness of DensePose-Based Loss. The top block of Table 4 shows that the proposed DensePose-based loss has a vital role in properly learning 3D clothed humans. Figure 6 (a) and (b) additionally shows the effectiveness of our DensePose-based loss compared to previous silhouette loss [7]. The silhouette loss enforces 3D cloth reconstruction results to be projected onto the 2D cloth segmentations. The top block of the table shows that using the DensePose-based loss achieves better BCC than using the silhouette loss. The silhouette loss suffers

Table 4. BCC comparison among different loss configurations.

DensePose	Silhouette	Regularization	BCC ↑
* Effectiveness of DensePose-based loss			
✗	✓	✓	0.644
✓	✓	✓	0.684
✓	✗	✓	**0.689 (Ours)**
* Effectiveness of regularization loss			
✓	✗	✗	0.381
✓	✗	✓	**0.689 (Ours)**

(a) DP. + Reg. **(Ours)** (b) Sil. + Reg. (c) Ours – Reg.   (a) DP. + Reg. **(Ours)** (b) Sil. + Reg. (c) Ours – Reg.

Fig. 6. Comparison of three different loss configurations: (a) our proposed loss configuration, (b) replacing our DensePose-based loss with the silhouette loss, and (c) removing the regularization loss.

from depth ambiguity and pixel-misalignment, as described in Sect. 1. On the other hand, the proposed DensePose-based suffers much less from the depth ambiguity and is free from the misalignment issue as it designates accurate 3D points around the human body surface. Hence, it has significant benefits to learning precise 3D clothes.

Effectiveness of Regularization Loss. The bottom block of Table 4 shows the effectiveness of the regularization loss. Figure 6(b) and (c) additionally demonstrates the effectiveness. The regularization loss makes predicted clothes be in the latent space of the 3D cloth model. It is necessary because 2D supervision targets, such as cloth segmentations, only provide information of partial areas of clothes. Such limited information can lead our ClothWild to produce implausible clothes, such as overly thick cloth and torn cloth. The regularization loss prevents such improper learning and encourages reconstructing reasonable 3D clothes, despite only information of partial areas of clothes.

7   Conclusion

We propose ClothWild, a 3D clothed human reconstruction framework that produces significantly robust results from in-the-wild images. For the robustness to the domain gap between synthesized and in-the-wild datasets, we propose a weakly supervised pipeline and a DensePose-based loss function. As a result, our ClothWild outperforms previous 3D clothed human reconstruction methods on in-the-wild images.

Acknowledgement. This work was supported in part by IITP grant funded by the Korea government (MSIT) [No. 2021-0-01343, Artificial Intelligence Graduate School Program (Seoul National University), No.2022-0-00156], and in part by the Bio & Medical Technology Development Program of NRF funded by the Korean government (MSIT) [No. 2021M3A9E4080782].

References

1. Alldieck, T., Magnor, M., Bhatnagar, B.L., Theobalt, C., Pons-Moll, G.: Learning to reconstruct people in clothing from a single RGB camera. In: CVPR (2019)
2. Alldieck, T., Pons-Moll, G., Theobalt, C., Magnor, M.: Tex2shape: detailed full human body geometry from a single image. In: ICCV (2019)
3. Alldieck, T., Zanfir, M., Sminchisescu, C.: Photorealistic monocular 3D reconstruction of humans wearing clothing. In: CVPR (2022)
4. aXYZ: (2018). https://secure.axyz-design.com
5. Bertiche, H., Madadi, M., Escalera, S.: CLOTH3D: clothed 3D humans. In: Vedaldi, A., Bischof, H., Brox, T., Frahm, J.-M. (eds.) ECCV 2020. LNCS, vol. 12365, pp. 344–359. Springer, Cham (2020). https://doi.org/10.1007/978-3-030-58565-5_21
6. Bhatnagar, B.L., Tiwari, G., Theobalt, C., Pons-Moll, G.: Multi-garment net: learning to dress 3D people from images. In: ICCV (2019)

7. Corona, E., Pumarola, A., Alenya, G., Pons-Moll, G., Moreno-Noguer, F.: SMPLicit: topology-aware generative model for clothed people. In: CVPR (2021)
8. Ge, Y., Zhang, R., Wang, X., Tang, X., Luo, P.: Deepfashion2: a versatile benchmark for detection, pose estimation, segmentation and re-identification of clothing images. In: CVPR (2019)
9. Gong, K., Liang, X., Zhang, D., Shen, X., Lin, L.: Look into person: self-supervised structure-sensitive learning and a new benchmark for human parsing. In: CVPR (2017)
10. Güler, R.A., Neverova, N., Kokkinos, I.: DensePose: dense human pose estimation in the wild. In: CVPR (2018)
11. He, K., Gkioxari, G., Dollár, P., Girshick, R.: Mask R-CNN. In: ICCV (2017)
12. He, K., Zhang, X., Ren, S., Sun, J.: Deep residual learning for image recognition. In: CVPR (2016)
13. He, T., Collomosse, J., Jin, H., Soatto, S.: Geo-PIFu geometry and pixel aligned implicit functions for single-view human reconstruction. In: NeurIPS (2020)
14. He, T., Xu, Y., Saito, S., Soatto, S., Tung, T.: ARCH++: animation-ready clothed human reconstruction revisited. In: ICCV (2021)
15. Huang, Z., Xu, Y., Lassner, C., Li, H., Tung, T.: ARCH: animatable reconstruction of clothed humans. In: CVPR (2020)
16. Jackson, A.S., Manafas, C., Tzimiropoulos, G.: 3D human body reconstruction from a single image via volumetric regression. In: Leal-Taixé, L., Roth, S. (eds.) ECCV 2018. LNCS, vol. 11132, pp. 64–77. Springer, Cham (2019). https://doi.org/10.1007/978-3-030-11018-5_6
17. Jiang, B., Zhang, J., Hong, Y., Luo, J., Liu, L., Bao, H.: BCNet: learning body and cloth shape from a single image. In: Vedaldi, A., Bischof, H., Brox, T., Frahm, J.-M. (eds.) ECCV 2020. LNCS, vol. 12365, pp. 18–35. Springer, Cham (2020). https://doi.org/10.1007/978-3-030-58565-5_2
18. Kanazawa, A., Black, M.J., Jacobs, D.W., Malik, J.: End-to-end recovery of human shape and pose. In: CVPR (2018)
19. Kingma, D.P., Ba, J.: Adam: a method for stochastic optimization. In: ICLR (2014)
20. Kolotouros, N., Pavlakos, G., Black, M.J., Daniilidis, K.: Learning to reconstruct 3D human pose and shape via model-fitting in the loop. In: ICCV (2019)
21. Li, P., Xu, Y., Wei, Y., Yang, Y.: Self-correction for human parsing. IEEE TPAMI (2020)
22. Lin, T.-Y., et al.: Microsoft COCO: common objects in context. In: Fleet, D., Pajdla, T., Schiele, B., Tuytelaars, T. (eds.) ECCV 2014. LNCS, vol. 8693, pp. 740–755. Springer, Cham (2014). https://doi.org/10.1007/978-3-319-10602-1_48
23. Loper, M., Mahmood, N., Romero, J., Pons-Moll, G., Black, M.J.: SMPL: a skinned multi-person linear model. ACM TOG 34, 1–16 (2015)
24. Lorensen, W.E., Cline, H.E.: Marching cubes: a high resolution 3D surface construction algorithm. ACM Siggraph Comput. Graph. 21, 163–169 (1987)
25. Ma, Q., et al.: Learning to dress 3D people in generative clothing. In: CVPR (2020)
26. von Marcard, T., Henschel, R., Black, M.J., Rosenhahn, B., Pons-Moll, G.: Recovering accurate 3D human pose in the wild using IMUs and a moving camera. In: Ferrari, V., Hebert, M., Sminchisescu, C., Weiss, Y. (eds.) ECCV 2018. LNCS, vol. 11214, pp. 614–631. Springer, Cham (2018). https://doi.org/10.1007/978-3-030-01249-6_37
27. Moon, G., Choi, H., Lee, K.M.: Accurate 3D hand pose estimation for whole-body 3D human mesh estimation. In: CVPRW (2022)
28. Paszke, A., et al.: Automatic differentiation in pytorch (2017)

29. Patel, C., Liao, Z., Pons-Moll, G.: TailorNet: predicting clothing in 3D as a function of human pose, shape and garment style. In: CVPR (2020)
30. Pavlakos, G., et al.: Expressive body capture: 3D hands, face, and body from a single image. In: CVPR (2019)
31. Renderpeople: (2018). https://renderpeople.com/3d-people
32. Russakovsky, O., et al.: ImageNet large scale visual recognition challenge (2015)
33. Saito, S., Huang, Z., Natsume, R., Morishima, S., Kanazawa, A., Li, H.: PIFu: pixel-aligned implicit function for high-resolution clothed human digitization. In: ICCV (2019)
34. Saito, S., Simon, T., Saragih, J., Joo, H.: PIFuHD: multi-level pixel-aligned implicit function for high-resolution 3D human digitization. In: CVPR (2020)
35. Varol, G.: BodyNet: volumetric inference of 3D human body shapes. In: Ferrari, V., Hebert, M., Sminchisescu, C., Weiss, Y. (eds.) ECCV 2018. LNCS, vol. 11211, pp. 20–38. Springer, Cham (2018). https://doi.org/10.1007/978-3-030-01234-2_2
36. Xiu, Y., Yang, J., Tzionas, D., Black, M.J.: ICON: implicit clothed humans obtained from normals. In: CVPR (2022)
37. Zheng, Z., Yu, T., Wei, Y., Dai, Q., Liu, Y.: DeepHuman: 3D human reconstruction from a single image. In: ICCV (2019)

Directed Ray Distance Functions for 3D Scene Reconstruction

Nilesh Kulkarni$^{(\boxtimes)}$, Justin Johnson , and David F. Fouhey

University of Michigan, Ann Arbor, MI 48105, USA
{nileshk,justincj,fouhey}@umich.edu

Abstract. We present an approach for full 3D scene reconstruction from a single unseen image. We trained on dataset of realistic non-watertight scans of scenes. Our approach uses a predicted distance function, since these have shown promise in handling complex topologies and large spaces. We identify and analyze two key challenges for predicting such image conditioned distance functions that have prevented their success on real 3D scene data. First, we show that predicting a conventional scene distance from an image requires reasoning over a large receptive field. Second, we analytically show that the optimal output of the network trained to predict these distance functions does not obey all the distance function properties. We propose an alternate distance function, the *Directed Ray Distance Function* (DRDF), that tackles both challenges. We show that a deep network trained to predict DRDFs outperforms all other methods quantitatively and qualitatively on 3D reconstruction from single image on Matterport3D, 3DFront, and ScanNet. (Project Page: https://nileshkulkarni.github.io/scene_drdf)

Keywords: Single image 3D · Distance functions

1 Introduction

Consider the image in Fig. 1. What happens if you look behind the kitchen counter? To a layman, this single image shows a rich 3D world in which the floor continues behind the counter, and there are cabinets below the kitchen top. Our work aims to learn a mapping from a single image to the complete 3D, including visible *and* occluded surfaces. We learn such mapping from real, unstructured scans like Matterport3D [5] or ScanNet [11]. Unstructured scans are currently one of the richest sources of real-world 3D ground truth, and as more sensors like LIDAR scanners become ubiquitous, their importance will only grow.

Learning from these real-world scans poses significant challenges to the existing methods in computer vision. Voxel-based methods [10,18] scale poorly with size due to their memory requirements, and mesh-based ones [61] struggle with varying topology. Implicit functions [37,47] show promise for overcoming these

Supplementary Information The online version contains supplementary material available at https://doi.org/10.1007/978-3-031-20086-1_12.

(a) Image   (b) 3D outputs rendered from our model   (c) Ray through the scene

Fig. 1. Given a single input image (a) our model generates its full 3D shown in (b) as two rendered novel views of our method's 3D output revealing the predicted occluded cabinet and floor. Visible surfaces are colored with image pixels; occluded ones show surface normals (pink: upwards; lavender: towards camera). In (c) we show a third person view of the scene with a red-ray from camera. The ray projects at the yellow-dot in the image (a). Nearest points to the ray shown as green spheres. (Color figure online)

size and topology challenges, but mostly focus on watertight data [8,37,42,47,52] with a well-defined inside and outside regions for objects. This watertightness property enables *signed distance functions* (SDF) or occupancy functions, but limits them to data like ShapeNet [6], humans [47], or memorizing single watertight scenes [52]. Real 3D scans like Matterport3D [5] are off-limits for these methods. Exceptions include [9], which fits a single model with *unsigned distance function* (UDF) to a scene, and SAL [1,2] which learns SDFs on objects with well-defined insides and outsides that have scan holes. We believe that the lack of success in predicting implicit functions conditioned on previously unseen single image on datasets like Matterport3D [5] stems from two key challenges.

First, conventional distance functions depend on the distance to the nearest point in the full 3D scene. We show that this requires complex reasoning across an image. To see this, consider Fig. 1. The yellow point in (a) is the projection of the red ray in (c). We show the nearest point in the scene to each point on the ray in green. Near the camera, these are all over the kitchen counter to the right. Closer to the refrigerator, they finally are on the refrigerator. This illustrates that the projection of the nearest points to a point is often far from the projection of that point. Models estimating scene distances must integrate information across vast receptive fields to find the nearest points, which makes learning hard. We examine this in more detail in Sect. 4.1.

We propose to overcome these issues with a new distance-like function named the *Directed Ray Distance Function* (DRDF). Unlike the *Unsigned Distance Function* (defined by the nearest points in the scene), the DRDF is defined by points along the ray through a pixel; these project to the same pixel, facilitating learning. Unlike standard distance functions, DRDF's expected value under uncertainty behaves like a true distance function close to the surface. We learn to predict the DRDF with a PixelNerf [65]-style architecture and compare it with other distance functions. We also compare it to other conventional methods such as Layered Depth Images (LDI) [51]. Our experiments (Sect. 5) on Matterport3D [5], 3DFront [17], and ScanNet [11] show that the DRDF is substantially better at 3D scene recovery (visible and occluded) across all (three) metrics.

2   Related Work

Our approach aims to infer the full 3D structure of a scene from a single image using implicit functions, which relates with many tasks in 3D computer vision.

Scenes from a Single Image. Reconstructing the 3D scene from image cues is a long-term goal of computer vision. Most early work in 3D learning focuses on 2.5D properties [4] that are visible in the image, like qualitative geometry [15, 24], depth [49] and normals [16]. Our work instead aims to infer the full 3D of the scene, including invisible parts. Most work on invisible surfaces focuses on single objects with voxels [10,18,21], point-clouds [14,35], CAD models [27] and meshes [19,20]. These approaches are often trained with synthetic data, e.g., ShapeNet [6] or images that have been aligned with synthetic ground-truth 3D [54]. Existing scene-level work, e.g., [33,34,41,58] trains on synthetic datasets with pre-segmented, watertight objects like SunCG [53]. Our work instead can be learned on real 3D like Matterport3D [5]. In summary, our work aims to understand the interplay between 3D, uncertainty, and learning [3,30,44] that has largely been explored in the depth-map space.

Implicit Functions for 3D Reconstruction. We approach the problem with learning implicit functions [8,37,42,43], which have shown promise in addressing scale and varying topology. These implicit functions have also been used in novel view synthesis [36,38,65,66], collision prediction [45], which differs from our work in goals. In reconstruction, implicit functions have shown impressive results on two styles of task: fitting to a single model to a fixed 3D scene (e.g., SIREN [9,52]) and predicting new single objects (e.g., PIFu [47,64]). Our work falls in the latter category as it predicts new scenes. While implicit functions have shown results on humans [47,48] and ShapeNet objects [64], most work relies on watertight meshes. Our non-watertight setting is more challenging. Few solutions have been proposed: assuming the SDF's existence and supervising it indirectly (SAL: [1, 2],), voxelization of surfaces([69]), or predicting an unsigned distance function (UDF) [9] – we stress that [9] does not predict from RGB images. Our work can be trained with non-watertight 3D meshes and outperforms these approaches.

Recovering Occluded Surfaces. Our system produces the full 3D of a scene, including occluded parts, from a single image. This topic has been of interest to the community beyond previously mentioned volumetric 3D work (e.g., [10,18]). Early work often used vanishing-point-aligned box [12,23] trained on annotated data. While our approach predicts floors, this is learned, not baked in, unlike modern inheritors that have explicit object and layout components [28,57] or the ability to query for two layers [26,28]. An alternate approach is layered depth images (LDI) [13,51] or multi-plane depthmaps. LDIs can be learned without supervision [59], but when trained directly, they fare worse than our method.

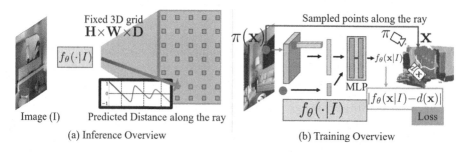

(a) Inference Overview   (b) Training Overview

Fig. 2. Approach Overview. (a) At inference our model, $f_\theta(\cdot|I)$, conditioned on an input image (I) predicts a pixel conditioned distance for each point in a 3D grid. This frustum volume is then converted to surface locations using a decoding strategy. (b) At training time, our model takes an image and set of 3D points. It is supervised with the ground truth distance function for scene at these points. More details in Sect. 3.

3   Learning Pixel Aligned Distance Functions

We aim to reconstruct the full 3D of an unseen scene, including occluded parts, from a single RGB image while training on real scene captures [5]. Towards this goal we train an image-conditioned neural network to predict distance functions for 3D points in the camera frustum. Our training set consists of images and corresponding 3D meshes for supervision. We supervise our network with any ground-truth distance function *e.g.*, the *Unsigned Distance Function* (UDF).

At test time, we consider only a single input image and a fixed set of 3D points in the camera view frustum. Our network predicts the distance function for each point using pixel aligned image features. The inference produces a grid of distances instead of a surface; we extract a surface with a *decoding strategy* (e.g., a thresholding strategy that defines values close to zero as surface locations).

Our setup is generic and can be paired with any distance function and a decoding strategy. We will discuss particular distance functions and decoding strategies later while discussing experiments. Experimentally, we will show that commonly used distance functions [1,9] do not work well when they are predicted in pixel conditioned way from a single image when trained on raw 3D data.

Inference. Given a input image like in Fig. 2 (left), we evaluate our model $f_\theta(\mathbf{x}; I)$ on pre-defined grid of points, $H \times W \times D$, in the 3D camera frustum to predict the distance function. It is then *decoded* to recover surface locations.

Training. At train time we are given n samples $\{(\mathbf{x}_i, I_i, d(\mathbf{x}_i)\}_{i=1}^n$ representing the 3D points ($\mathbf{x}_i$), input image (I_i) and the ground truth distance, $d(\mathbf{x}_i)$, computed using the 3D mesh. We find parameters θ that minimize the empirical risk $\frac{1}{n}\sum_{i=1}^n \mathcal{L}(f_\theta(\mathbf{x}_i, I_i), d(\mathbf{x}_i))$ with a loss function $\mathcal{L}$ *e.g.* the L1-Loss.

Model Architecture. We use a PixelNerf [65]-like architecture containing an encoder and multi layer perceptron (MLP). The encoder maps the image I to a

(a) Image with ray center   (b) Third person 3D views with the red ray and nearest points   (c) Plot of Dist. Func.

Fig. 3. Scene vs ray distances . (a) The red ray intersects the scene at the black and yellow point in the image. Scene vs Ray distances along the points on red-shaded ray through the camera. (b) Two different 3D views showing intersections between the ray and the scene (which define the ray distance) in blue and the nearest points in the scene to the ray in green. These nearest scene points define scene distance. A network predicting scene distance must look all over the image (e.g., looking at the bed and chair to determine it for the ray). (c) Ground truth scene vs.ray distance functions for points on the ray. There are occluded intersections not visible in the image. (Color figure online)

feature map $\mathbf{B}$. Given a point $\mathbf{x}$ and the camera (π) we compute its projection on the image $\pi(\mathbf{x})$. We extract a feature at $\pi(\mathbf{x})$ from $\mathbf{B}$ with bilinear interpolation; the MLP uses the extracted image feature and a positional encoding [38] of $\mathbf{x}$ to make a final prediction $f_\theta(\mathbf{x}; I)$. Our code is hosted at https://github. com/nileshkulkarni/scene_drdf for reproducibility. Other details appear in the supplement.

4   Behavior of Pixel Conditioned Distance Functions

Recent works have demonstrated overfitting of neural networks to single scenes [1,2,9,52] but none attempt to predict *scene-level 3D* conditioned on an image. We believe this problem has not been tackled due to two challenges. First, predicting a standard scene distance from a single image requires reasoning about large portions of the image. As we will show in Sect. 4.1, this happens because predicting scene distance for a point $\mathbf{x}$ requires finding the nearest point to $\mathbf{x}$ in the scene. This nearest point often projects to a part of the image that is far from $\mathbf{x}$'s projection in the image. Secondly, we will show in Sect. 4.3 that the uncertainty present in predicting pixel conditioned distance function incentivizes networks to produce outputs that lack basic distance function properties. These distorted distance functions do not properly decode into surfaces. To overcome the above challenges, we introduce a new distance function, the *Directed Ray Distance Function (DRDF)*. We will show analytically that DRDF retains distance-function like properties near the 3D surface under uncertainty. Yes

All distance functions are denoted with $d(\mathbf{x})$ where $\mathbf{x}$ is the query point in 3D space. We use M to denote the mesh of the 3D scene and $\overrightarrow{\mathbf{r}}$ to denote the ray originating from the camera passing through $\mathbf{x}$.

4.1   Scene *vs.* Ray Distances

A standard scene distance for a point $\mathbf{x}$ in a 3D scene M is the minimum distance from $\mathbf{x}$ to the points in M. If there are no modifications, this distance is called the *Unsigned Distance Function* (UDF) and can be operationalized by finding the nearest point $\mathbf{x}'$ in M to $\mathbf{x}$ and returning $||\mathbf{x} - \mathbf{x}'||$. We now define a *ray distance* for a point $\mathbf{x}$ as the minimum distance of $\mathbf{x}$ to any of the intersections between $\overrightarrow{\mathbf{r}}$ and M, which is operationalized similarly. The main distinction between scene *vs.* ray distances boils down to which points define the distance. When calculating scene distances, all points in M are candidates for the nearest point. When calculating ray distances, only the intersections of $\overrightarrow{\mathbf{r}}$ and M are candidates for the nearest point. These intersections are a much smaller set.

We will now illustrate the above observation qualitatively with Fig. 3. We show in Fig 3(a) the projection of $\overrightarrow{\mathbf{r}}$ (and all points on it) onto the image as the yellow-center. We show in (b) a third person view of the scene with $\overrightarrow{\mathbf{r}}$ as the red-shaded-ray. We show the intersection point of $\overrightarrow{\mathbf{r}}$ with the scene M as blue points. For each point on the red ray, we show the nearest point on the mesh in green with an arrow going to that green point. The scene distance for points on the ray is defined by these nearest points in green. These nearest points are distributed all over M including the floor, bed, and chair, *etc.*. A pixel conditioned neural network predicting scene distances needs to integrate information of all the green regions to estimate scene distance for points projecting to the yellow ray projection. To show that this is not an isolated case, we quantify the typical projection of nearest points for scene distance to get an estimate of the minimum receptive field need to predict a distance using a neural network. We measure the distance between projections of the nearest points from the ray center. The average maximum distance to the ray center is $0.375 \times image\ width$ – averaged over 50K rays on Matterport3D [5]. Thus, a neural network predicting the scene distance needs to look at least this far to predict it.

This problem of integrating evidence over large regions vanishes for a ray distance function. By definition, the only points involved in defining a ray distance function for a point $\mathbf{x}$ lie on the ray $\overrightarrow{\mathbf{r}}$ since they are at the intersection of the mesh and the ray; these points project to the same location as $\mathbf{x}$. This simplifies a network's job considerably. We define the *Unsigned Ray Distance Function* (URDF) as the Euclidean distance to the nearest of these ray intersections.

We finally plot the UDF (scene) and URDF (ray) for the points along the red $\overrightarrow{\mathbf{r}}$, both truncated at 1m, in Fig 3(c). The UDF is fairly complex because different parts of the scene are nearest to the points along the ray at different distances. In contrast, the URDF is piecewise linear due to the few points defining it. We hypothesize this simplified form of a ray distance aids learning. More details in the supp.

4.2   Ray Distance Functions

It is convenient when dealing with a ray $\overrightarrow{\mathbf{r}}$ to parameterize each point $\mathbf{x}$ on the ray by a scalar multiplier z such that $\mathbf{x} = z\overrightarrow{\mathbf{r}}$. Now the distance functions are purely defined via the scalar multiplier along the ray. Suppose we define the set of scalars along the ray $\overrightarrow{\mathbf{r}}$ that correspond to intersections as $D_{\overrightarrow{\mathbf{r}}} = \{s_i\}_0^k$ (i.e., each point $s\overrightarrow{\mathbf{r}}$ for $s \in D_{\overrightarrow{\mathbf{r}}}$ is an intersection location). We can then define a variety of ray distances using these intersections. For instance, given any point along the ray, $z\overrightarrow{\mathbf{r}}$, we can define $d_{\mathrm{UR}}(z) = \min_{s \in D_{\overrightarrow{\mathbf{r}}}} \|s - z\|$ as the minimum distance to the intersections. As described earlier, we call this *Unsigned Ray Distance Function* (URDF) – R here indicates it is a ray distance function. For watertight meshes, one can have a predicate inside(**x**) that is 1 when **x** is *inside* an object and -1 otherwise. We can then define the *Signed Ray Distance Function* (SRDF) as $d_{\mathrm{SR}}(z) = -\mathrm{inside}(z\overrightarrow{\mathbf{r}})d_{\mathrm{UR}}(z)$. Signed functions are standard in the literature but since our setting is non-watertight, the SRDF is impossible. Now we show how we can modify the SRDF for non-watertight settings.

Directed Ray Distance Function. We introduce a new ray based distance function called the *Directed Ray Distance Function* (DRDF). This can be seen as a modification to both URDF and SRDF; We define $d_{\mathrm{DRDF}}(z) = \mathrm{direction}(z)d_{\mathrm{UR}}(z)$ where our predicate *direction*(z) is $\mathrm{sgn}(s - z)$ where s is the nearest intersection to z. In practice DRDF is positive before the nearest intersection and negative after the nearest intersection. We call it *Directed* because the sign depends on the positioning along the ray. Unlike SRDF, there is no notion of inside, so the DRDF can be used with unstructured

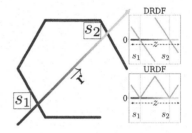

Fig. 4. DRDF *vs.* URDF in case of two intersections along the ray. Unlike URDF, DRDF is positive and negative

scans. Near an intersection, DRDF behaves like SRDF and crosses zero. DRDF has a sharp discontinuity midway between two intersections due to a sign change. We will analyze the importance of adding directional behavior to DRDF in the subsequent sections. Figure 4 shows the difference between DRDF *vs.* URDF for multiple intersections on a ray.

4.3 Modeling Uncertainty in Ray Distance Functions

When we predict distances in a single RGB image, the distance to an object in the scene is intrinsically uncertain. We may have a sense of the general layout of the scene and a rough distance, but the precise location of each object to the millimeter is not known. We investigate the consequences of this uncertainty for neural networks that predict distance functions conditioned on single view images. We analyze a simplified setup that lets us derive their optimal behavior.

In particular, if the network minimizes the MSE (mean-squared-error), its optimal behavior is to produce the expected value. In many cases, the expected value is precisely what is desired like in object detection [56,68] or in ARIMA models [40], weather prediction [63] but in others it leads to poor outcomes. For instance, in colorization [25,67], where one is uncertain of the precise hue, the expected value averages the options, leading to brown results; similar effects happen in rotation [7,32,39] and 3D estimation [29,31,62].

We now gain insights into the optimal output by analyzing the expected distance functions under uncertainty about the location of a surface. For simplicity, we derive results along a ray, although the supplement shows similar results hold true for scene distances. Since there is uncertainty about the surface location, the surface location is no longer a fixed scalar s but instead a random variable S. The distance function now depends on the value s that the random variable S takes on. We denote the ray distance at z if the intersection is at s as $d(z; s)$.

The network's output at a location z is optimal in this setting if it equals the expected distance under S or $E_S[d(z; s)] = \int_{\mathbb{R}} d(z; s)p(s)ds$, where $p(s)$ is the density of S. Thus, by analyzing $E_S[d(z; s)]$ we can understand the optimal behavior. We note that this expectation is also optimal for other losses: under many conditions (see supp) $E_S[d(z; s)]$ also is optimal for the L1 loss, and if $d(z; s)$ is $\{0, 1\}$ such as in an occupancy function, then $E_S[d(z; s)]$ is optimal for a cross-entropy loss. For ease of derivation, we derive results for when S is Gaussian distributed with its mean μ at the true intersection, standard deviation σ and CDF $\Phi(s)$. Since distance

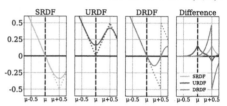

Fig. 5. True *vs.* Expected distance functions under uncertainty. Suppose the surface's location is normally distributed with mean μ at its true location and $\sigma=0.2$, and the next surface 1 is unit away. We plot the expected (solid) and true (dashed) distance functions for the SRDF, URDF, and DRDF and their difference (expected - true). The SRDF and DRDF closely match the true distance near the surface; the URDF does not.

functions also depend on the next intersection, we assume it is at $S+n$ for some constant $n \in R^+$.

We summarize salient results here, and a detailed analysis appears in the supplement. Figure 5 shows $E_S[d(z; s)]$ for three ray distance functions (for $n = 1, \sigma = 0.2$). No expected distance function perfectly matches its true function, but each varies in where the distortion occurs. At the intersection, the expected SRDF and DRDF closely match the true function while the expected URDF is grossly distorted. Full derivations appear in the supplemental. The expected URDF has a minimum value of $\approx\sigma\sqrt{2/\pi}$ rather than 0. Similarly, its previously sharp derivative is now $\approx 2\Phi(z) - 1$, which is close to ± 1 *only* when z is far from the intersection. In contrast, the expected DRDF's distortion occurs at $\mu + \frac{n}{2}$, and its derivative $(np(z - \frac{n}{2}) - 1)$ is close to -1, except when z is close to $\mu + \frac{n}{2}$.

These distortions in expected distance function disrupt the decoding of distance functions to surfaces. For instance, a true URDF can turned into to a surface by thresholding, but the expected URDF has an uncertainty-dependent minimum value $\approx\sigma\sqrt{2/\pi}$, not 0. Since a nearby intersection often has less uncertainty than a far intersection, a threshold that works for near intersections may miss far intersections. Conversely, a threshold for far intersections may dilate nearby intersections. One may try alternate schemes, e.g., using the zero-crossing of the derivative. However, the expected URDF's shape is blunted; our empirical results suggest that finding its zero-crossing is ineffective in practice.

DRDF is more stable under uncertainty and requires just finding a zero-crossing. The zero-crossing at the intersection is preserved except when σ is large (e.g., $\sigma = \frac{n}{3}$) in such cases other distance functions also break down. This is because the distortion for DRDF occur halfway to the other intersection. The only nuance is to filter out second zero-crossing after the intersection based on the crossing direction. Further analysis appears in the supplemental.

5   Experiments

We evaluate DRDF on real images of scenes and compare it to alternate choices of distance functions as well as conventional approaches such as Layered Depth Images [51]. We extensively optimize decoding schemes for our baseline methods. Their detailed description appear in the supplemental.

Our experiments evaluate each method's ability to predict the visible and occluded parts of the scene using standard metrics and a new metric that evaluates along rays.

Metrics. We use three metrics. A single metric cannot properly quantify reconstruction performance as each metric captures a different aspect of the task [55]. The first is scene Chamfer errors. The others are accuracy/completeness [50] and their harmonic mean, F1-score [55], for scenes and rays (on occluded points).

Chamfer L1. We compute Symmetric Chamfer L1 error for each scene with 30K points sampled from the ground truth and the prediction. We plot the fraction of scenes with Symmetric Chamfer L1 errors that are less than t for $t \in [0, 1]$m. It is more informative than just the mean across the dataset and compares performance over multiple thresholds.

Scene (Acc/Cmp/F1). Like [50,55], we report accuracy/Acc (% of predicted points within t of the ground-truth), completeness/Cmp (% of ground-truth points within t of the prediction), and their harmonic mean, F1-score. This gives a overall summary of scene-level reconstruction.

Rays (Acc/Cmp/F1), Occluded Points. We also evaluate reconstruction performance along each ray independently, measuring Acc/Cmp/F1 on each ray and reporting the mean. The paper shows results for occluded points, defined as all surfaces past the first intersection; the supplement contains full results. Evaluating each ray independently is a more stringent test for occluded surfaces than a scene metric: with scene-level evaluation on a image, a prediction can miss a surface (e.g., the 2nd intersection) on every other pixel. These missing predictions will be covered for by hidden surfaces on adjacent rays. Ray-based evaluation, however, requires each pixel to have all surfaces present to receive full credit.

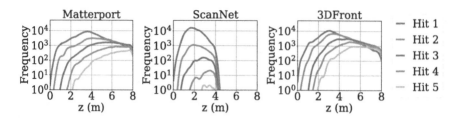

Fig. 6. Ray hit count distribution. We compare the distribution over surface hit (intersection) locations for first 4 hits over 1M rays. ScanNet has $\leq 1\%$ rays as compared to Matterport and 3DFront which have $\geq 25\%$ rays with more than 2 hits

Datasets. We see three key properties for datasets: the images should be real to avoid networks using rendering artifacts; the mesh should be a real capture since imitating capture holes is a research problem; and there should be lots of occluded regions. Our main dataset is Matterport3D [5], which satisfies all properties.

We also evaluate on 3DFront [17] and ScanNet [11]. While 3DFront has no capture holes, cutting it with a view frustum creates holes. ScanNet [11] is a popular in 3D reconstruction, but has far less occluded geometry compared to the other datasets. A full description of the datasets appears in the supplement.

Matterport3D [5]. We use the *raw images* captured with the Matterport camera. We split the 90 scenes into train/val/test (60/15/15) and remove images that are too close to the mesh ($\geq 60\%$ of image within 1m) or are $>20°$ away from level. We then sample 13K/1K/1K images for train/val/test set.

3DFront [17]. This is a synthetic dataset of houses created by artists with a hole-free 3D geometry. We collect 4K scenes from 3DFront [17] after removing scenes with missing annotations. We select 20 camera poses and filter for bad camera poses similar to Matterport3D [5]. Our train set has 3K scenes with approximately 47K images. Val/Test sets have 500 scenes with 1K images each.

ScanNet [11]. We use splits from [11] (1045/156/312 train/val/test scenes) and randomly select 5 images per scene for train, and 10 images per scene for val/test. We then sample to a set of 33K/1K/1K images per train/val/test.

Dataset Scene Statistics. To give a sense of scene statistics, we plot the frequency of the locations of the first 5 ray hits (intersections) for each dataset (computed on 1M rays each) in Fig. 6. We show 99% of ScanNet rays have 1 or 2 hits, while $\geq 24\%$ of Matterport3D [5] and 3DFront [17] rays have more than 2 hits.

5.1 Baselines

We compare against baselines to test our contributions. For fair comparison, all approaches use the same ResNet-34 [22] backbone and the same MLP. We extract features from multiple layers via bilinear interpolation [65]. Thus, different distance functions are trained identically by replacing the target distance. Each

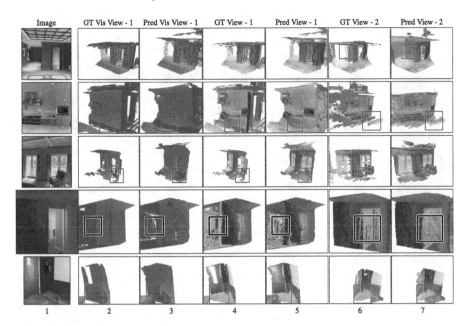

Fig. 7. Outputs from DRDF and ground-truth from new viewpoints. Columns 2,3 show visible points in red and occluded points in blue. Other columns, show the visible regions with the image and occluded regions with computed surface normals (■, scheme from camera inside a cube). DRDF recovers occluded regions, such as a room behind the door (row 1 & 4), a floor behind the kitchen counter (row 2), and a wall and floor behind the chair/couch (row 3 & 5). Rows 1–3: Matterport3D; 4: 3DFront; 5: ScanNet. (Color figure online)

method's description consists of two parts: a prediction space parameterization and a decoding strategy to convert the inferred distances to surfaces.

Picking Decoding Strategies. Most baselines predict a distance function rather than a set of intersections and need a decoding strategy to convert distances to a set of surface locations. Some baselines have trivial strategies (e.g., direct prediction or zero-crossings); others are more sensitive and have parameters.

We tried multiple strategies for each baseline based on past work and theoretical analysis of their behavior. We report the best one by Scene F1 on Matterport3D [5]. When there are parameters, we tune them to ensure similar completeness to our method. Accuracy and completeness have a trade-off; fixing one ensures that methods are compared at similar operating points, making F1 score meaningful.

Layered Depth Images (LDI). To test the value of framing the problem as implicit function prediction, we train a method to predict a k-channel depthmap where the ith output predicts the ith intersection along the pixels. We use a L1 loss per pixel and intersection. We set $k = 4$, the same number of intersections the proposed approach uses. *Decoding.* LDI directly predicts surface locations.

Image	GT	DRDF (ours)	URDF	LDI	UDF

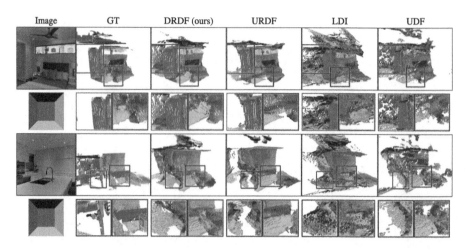

Fig. 8. We render the generated 3D outputs in a new view (rotated ←) with 2 crops for better visual comparison. Visible regions show the image; occluded regions show surface normals (legend shows a camera in a cube). DRDF produces higher quality results compared to LDI and UDF (row 1, 2, more consistency, smoother surface, no blobs). URDF misses parts of the floor (row 1/crop 2) and the green colored side of the kitchen counter (row2/crop 2). See supp. for more results. (Color figure online)

Layered Depth Images with Confidence (LDI + C). We augment the LDI baseline with k additional channels that represent the likelihood the ith intersection exists. These added channels are trained with binary cross-entropy. *Decoding.* For each pixel we accept layers with predicted probability ≥ 0.5.

Unsigned Distance Function (UDF) [9]. Chibane *et al.* [9] fit UDF to a single 3D scene. We predict it from images. *Decoding.* We use `scipy.argrelextrema` [60] to find local extrema. We find local minima of the distance function within a 1m window along the ray. We found this works better than absolute thresholding (by 14.7 on F1). Sphere tracing and gradient-based optimization proposed by [9] performs substantially worse (25.7 on F1), likely since it assumes the predicted UDF behaves similar to a GT UDF.

Unsigned Ray Distance Function (URDF). Inspired from Chibane *et al.* [9] we compare UDF against its ray based version(URDF). Now, for direct comparison between ray distance functions we compare URDF against DRDF.

Decoding . We do NMS on thresholded data with connected components on the ray with predicted distance below a tuned constant τ, and keep the first prediction. This outperforms: thresholding (by 5.3 on F1); finding 0-crossings of the numerical gradient (by 11 on F1); and sphere tracing and optimization [9] (by 6.6 on F1).

Ray Sign-Agnostic Learning Loss (SAL) [1]. Traditional SDF learning is impossible due to the non-watertightness of the data and so we use the sign

Table 1. Acc/Comp/F1Score. Thresholds: 0.5m (MP3D [5], 3DFront [17]), 0.2m (ScanNet [11]). **Bold is best,** underline is 2nd best per column. DRDF is best in F1 and accuracy in case of both metrics. For scene based it is comparable to the best in completeness and for ray based is occasionally 2nd best on Cmp. Gains on F1 score for occluded points are even larger than the full scene.

| | Scene based | | | | | | | | | Ray based (Occluded) | | | | | | | | |
| | MP3D [5] | | | 3DFront [17] | | | ScanNet [11] | | | MP3D [5] | | | 3DFront [17] | | | ScanNet [11] | | |
Method	Acc.	Cmp.	F1	Acc.	Cmp.	F1	Acc.	Cmp.	F1	Acc.	Cmp.	F1	Acc.	Cmp.	F1	Acc.	Cmp.	F1
LDI [51]	66.2	72.4	67.4	68.6	46.5	52.7	19.3	28.6	21.5	13.9	**42.8**	19.3	17.8	35.8	22.2	0.5	9.0	2.4
LDI +C	64.8	55.1	57.7	70.8	45.1	52.4	19.9	32.0	23.3	18.7	21.7	19.3	17.7	22.6	19.9	1.1	2.4	3.5
SAL [1]	66.1	25.5	34.3	80.7	28.5	39.5	51.2	**70.0**	57.7	5.5	0.5	3.5	24.1	4.3	11.4	2.4	**38.7**	5.6
UDF [9]	58.7	**76.0**	64.7	70.1	51.9	57.4	44.4	62.6	50.8	15.5	23.0	16.6	29.3	21.3	23.4	1.8	7.8	5.5
ORF	73.4	69.4	69.6	86.4	48.1	59.6	51.5	58.5	53.7	26.2	20.5	21.6	53.2	22.0	31.0	6.6	12.3	11.4
URDF	74.5	67.1	68.7	85.0	47.7	58.7	61.0	57.8	58.2	24.9	20.6	20.7	47.7	23.3	30.2	8.4	11.6	13.8
DRDF	**75.4**	72.0	**71.9**	**87.3**	**52.6**	**63.4**	**62.0**	62.7	**60.9**	**28.4**	30.0	**27.3**	54.6	**56.0**	**52.6**	9.0	20.4	**16.0**

agnostic approach proposed by [1]. We initialize our architecture with the SAL initialization and train with the SAL loss. The SAL approach assumes that while the data may not be watertight due to noisy capture, the underlying model is watertight. In this case, rays start and end *outside* objects (and thus the number of hits along each ray is even). This is not necessarily the case on Matterport3D [5] and 3DFront [17].

Decoding. Following [1], we find surfaces as zero-crossings of the predicted distance function along the ray.

Ray Occupancy (ORF). Traditional interior/exterior occupancy is not feasible on non-watertight data, but one can predict whether a point is within r of a surface as a classification problem. This baseline tests the value of predicting ray distances, and not just occupancy. We tried several values of r ([0.1, 0.25, 0.5, 1]m) and report the best-performing version.

Decoding. Each surface, in theory, produces two locations with probability 0.5: an onset and offset crossing. Finding all 0.5-crossings leads to doubled predictions. Instead, we consider all adjacent and nearby pairs of offsets and onsets, and average them; unpaired crossings are kept. This outperforms keeping just a single 0.5-crossing (by 4.7 on F1).

5.2 Results

Qualitative Results. Qualitative results of our method appear throughout the paper (by itself in Fig. 7 and compared to baselines in Fig. 8). Our approach is is often able to generate parts of the occluded scene, such as a room behind a door, cabinets and floor behind kitchen counters, and occluded regions behind furniture. Sometimes the method completes holes in the ground-truth that are due to scanning error. On the other hand we see our method sometimes fails to characterize the missing parts as detailed occluded 3D *e.g.* plants. Compared to baselines, our approach does qualitatively better. LDI and UDF often have floating blobs or extruded regions, due to either predicting too many layers (LDI) or having a distance function that is challenging to predict (UDF). URDF produces qualitatively better results, but often misses points in occluded regions.

Quantitative Results. These results are borne out in the quantitative results. Figure 9 shows the Chamfer plot and Table. 1 reports the scene distance and occluded surfaces metrics along rays. DRDF consistently does at least as well, or substantially better than the baselines on Chamfer. In general, DRDF does substantially better than all baselines. In a few situations, a baseline beats DRDF in completeness at the cost of substantially worse accuracy. However, a single baseline is not competitive with DRDF *across* datasets: SAL works well on ScanNet [11] and LDI works well on Matterport3D [5].

LDI performs worse than DRDF because it cannot vary its number of intersections; simply adding a second stack of outputs (LDI + C.) is insufficient. This is because DRDF can learn *where* things tend to be, while LDI-based methods have to learn the order in which things occur (e.g., is the floor 2nd or the 3rd intersection at a pixel?). SAL performs competitively on ScanNet, likely because of the relatively limited variability in numbers of intersections per ray; when tested on Matterport3D and 3DFront, its performance drops substantially.

We compare against a Monocular Depth Estimation (MDE) baseline with a pre-trained MiDaS [46] model. It has been trained on more datasets and has an optimal scale and translation fit per-image (which our models do not get). As it predicts one intersection its F1 is lower, 57.2 *vs.* 71.9 for DRDF on Matterport3D [5]. Nonetheless, we see advances in MDE complementary to advances in DRDF.

The most straightforward way to learn on non-watertight data is to predict unsigned scene distances [9] which has been shown to work with memorizing 3D scenes. However, predicting it from a single image is a different problem entirely, and scene distances require integration of information over large areas. This leads to poor performance. Predicting distances on rays alleviates this challenge, but recovering intersections remains hard even with multiple

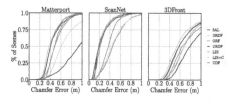

Fig. 9. Chamfer L1: % of scenes on Y-axis as a function of symmetric Chamfer L1 error $\leq t$ on X-axis. DRDF is better on Matterport and 3DFront, and comparable to the best other method on ScanNet.

decoding strategies. Thus, DRDF outperforms URDF. ORF similarly requires decoding strategies and is sensitive to training parameters. In contrast, by accounting for the uncertainty in surface location, DRDF requires a simple decoding strategy and outperforms other methods.

Conclusions. This paper introduced a new distance function, DRDF, for 3D reconstruction from an unseen image. We use real 3D, non-watertight data at training. We showed that DRDF does not suffer from pitfalls of other distance functions and outperforms other conventional methods. DRDF achieves substantially better qualitative results and has a simple *decoding strategy* to recover intersections – thanks to its stable behavior near intersections. DRDF's progress in learning 3D from real data is extendable to learning from multi-view data. Our approach, however, has societal limitations as our data does not reflect most peoples' reality: Matterport3D for instance, has many lavish houses and this may widen the technological gap. However, we are optimistic that our system will enable learning from scans collected by ordinary people rather than experts.

Acknowledgement. We would like the thank Alexandar Raistrick and Chris Rockwell for their help with the 3DFront dataset. We like to thank Shubham Tulsiani, Ekdeep Singh Lubana, Richard Higgins, Sarah Jabour, Shengyi Qian, Linyi Jin, Karan Desai, Mohammed El Banani, Chris Rockwell, Alexandar Raistrick, Dandan Shan, Andrew Owens for comments on the draft versions of this paper. NK was supported by TRI. Toyota Research Institute ("TRI") provided funds to assist the authors with their research but this article solely reflects the opinions and conclusions of its authors and not TRI or any other Toyota entity

References

1. Atzmon, M., Lipman, Y.: Sal: sign agnostic learning of shapes from raw data. In: Proceedings of the IEEE/CVF Conference on Computer Vision and Pattern Recognition, pp. 2565–2574 (2020)
2. Atzmon, M., Lipman, Y.: Sal++: sign agnostic learning with derivatives. arXiv preprint arXiv:2006.05400 (2020)
3. Bae, G., Budvytis, I., Cipolla, R.: Estimating and exploiting the aleatoric uncertainty in surface normal estimation. In: Proceedings of the IEEE/CVF International Conference on Computer Vision, pp. 13137–13146 (2021)
4. Barrow, H., Tenenbaum, J., Hanson, A., Riseman, E.: Recovering intrinsic scene characteristics. Comput. Vis. Syst **2**(3–26), 2 (1978)
5. Chang, A., et al.: Matterport3D: learning from rgb-d data in indoor environments. arXiv preprint arXiv:1709.06158 (2017)
6. Chang, A.X., et al.: Shapenet: an information-rich 3D model repository. arXiv preprint arXiv:1512.03012 (2015)
7. Chen, K., Snavely, N., Makadia, A.: Wide-baseline relative camera pose estimation with directional learning. In: Proceedings of the IEEE/CVF Conference on Computer Vision and Pattern Recognition (CVPR), pp. 3258–3268 (2021)
8. Chen, Z., Zhang, H.: Learning implicit fields for generative shape modeling. In: Proceedings of the IEEE/CVF Conference on Computer Vision and Pattern Recognition, pp. 5939–5948 (2019)
9. Chibane, J., Mir, A., Pons-Moll, G.: Neural unsigned distance fields for implicit function learning. In: Advances in Neural Information Processing Systems (NeurIPS) (2020)

10. Choy, C.B., Xu, D., Gwak, J.Y., Chen, K., Savarese, S.: 3D-R2N2: a unified approach for single and multi-view 3D object reconstruction. In: Leibe, B., Matas, J., Sebe, N., Welling, M. (eds.) ECCV 2016. LNCS, vol. 9912, pp. 628–644. Springer, Cham (2016). https://doi.org/10.1007/978-3-319-46484-8_38

11. Dai, A., Chang, A.X., Savva, M., Halber, M., Funkhouser, T., Nießner, M.: Scannet: richly-annotated 3D reconstructions of indoor scenes. In: Proceedings of the IEEE Conference on Computer Vision and Pattern Recognition, pp. 5828–5839 (2017)

12. Del Pero, L., Bowdish, J., Kermgard, B., Hartley, E., Barnard, K.: Understanding bayesian rooms using composite 3D object models. In: Proceedings of the IEEE Conference on Computer Vision and Pattern Recognition (CVPR) (2013)

13. Dhamo, H., Navab, N., Tombari, F.: Object-driven multi-layer scene decomposition from a single image. In: Proceedings of the IEEE/CVF International Conference on Computer Vision, pp. 5369–5378 (2019)

14. Fan, H., Su, H., Guibas, L.J.: A point set generation network for 3D object reconstruction from a single image. In: Proceedings of the IEEE Conference on Computer Vision and Pattern Recognition, pp. 605–613 (2017)

15. Fidler, S., Dickinson, S., Urtasun, R.: 3D object detection and viewpoint estimation with a deformable 3D cuboid model. In: Advances in Neural Information Processing Systems, pp. 611–619 (2012)

16. Fouhey, D.F., Gupta, A., Hebert, M.: Data-driven 3D primitives for single image understanding. In: Proceedings of the IEEE International Conference on Computer Vision, pp. 3392–3399 (2013)

17. Fu, H., et al.: 3D-front: 3D furnished rooms with layouts and semantics. arXiv preprint arXiv:2011.09127 (2020)

18. Girdhar, R., Fouhey, D.F., Rodriguez, M., Gupta, A.: Learning a predictable and generative vector representation for objects. In: Leibe, B., Matas, J., Sebe, N., Welling, M. (eds.) ECCV 2016. LNCS, vol. 9910, pp. 484–499. Springer, Cham (2016). https://doi.org/10.1007/978-3-319-46466-4_29

19. Gkioxari, G., Malik, J., Johnson, J.: Mesh r-cnn. In: Proceedings of the IEEE International Conference on Computer Vision, pp. 9785–9795 (2019)

20. Groueix, T., Fisher, M., Kim, V.G., Russell, B.C., Aubry, M.: A papier-mâché approach to learning 3D surface generation. In: Proceedings of the IEEE Conference on Computer Vision and Pattern Recognition, pp. 216–224 (2018)

21. Häne, C., Tulsiani, S., Malik, J.: Hierarchical surface prediction for 3D object reconstruction. In: 2017 International Conference on 3D Vision (3DV), pp. 412–420. IEEE (2017)

22. He, K., Zhang, X., Ren, S., Sun, J.: Deep residual learning for image recognition. In: Proceedings of the IEEE Conference on Computer Vision and Pattern Recognition, pp. 770–778 (2016)

23. Hedau, V., Hoiem, D., Forsyth, D.: Recovering the spatial layout of cluttered rooms. In: 2009 IEEE 12th International Conference on Computer Vision, pp. 1849–1856. IEEE (2009)

24. Hoiem, D., Efros, A.A., Hebert, M.: Geometric context from a single image. In: Tenth IEEE International Conference on Computer Vision (ICCV 2005), vol. 1, pp. 654–661. IEEE (2005)

25. Isola, P., Zhu, J.Y., Zhou, T., Efros, A.A.: Image-to-image translation with conditional adversarial networks. In: CVPR (2017)

26. Issaranon, T., Zou, C., Forsyth, D.: Counterfactual depth from a single rgb image. In: Proceedings of the IEEE/CVF International Conference on Computer Vision Workshops (2019)

27. Izadinia, H., Shan, Q., Seitz, S.M.: Im2cad. In: Proceedings of the IEEE Conference on Computer Vision and Pattern Recognition, pp. 5134–5143 (2017)
28. Jiang, Z., Liu, B., Schulter, S., Wang, Z., Chandraker, M.: Peek-a-boo: occlusion reasoning in indoor scenes with plane representations. In: Proceedings of the IEEE/CVF Conference on Computer Vision and Pattern Recognition, pp. 113–121 (2020)
29. Jin, L., Qian, S., Owens, A., Fouhey, D.F.: Planar surface reconstruction from sparse views. In: International Conference on Computer Vision (ICCV) (2021)
30. Kendall, A., Gal, Y.: What uncertainties do we need in bayesian deep learning for computer vision? In: Proceedings of the 31st International Conference on Neural Information Processing Systems, pp. 5580–5590 (2017)
31. Ku, J., Pon, A.D., Waslander, S.L.: Monocular 3D object detection leveraging accurate proposals and shape reconstruction. In: Proceedings of the IEEE/CVF Conference on Computer Vision and Pattern Recognition, pp. 11867–11876 (2019)
32. Kulkarni, N., Gupta, A., Tulsiani, S.: Canonical surface mapping via geometric cycle consistency. In: Proceedings of the IEEE/CVF International Conference on Computer Vision, pp. 2202–2211 (2019)
33. Kulkarni, N., Misra, I., Tulsiani, S., Gupta, A.: 3D-relnet: joint object and relational network for 3d prediction. In: Proceedings of the IEEE International Conference on Computer Vision, pp. 2212–2221 (2019)
34. Li, L., Khan, S., Barnes, N.: Silhouette-assisted 3D object instance reconstruction from a cluttered scene. In: ICCV Workshops (2019)
35. Lin, C.H., Kong, C., Lucey, S.: Learning efficient point cloud generation for dense 3d object reconstruction. arXiv preprint arXiv:1706.07036 (2017)
36. Martin-Brualla, R., Radwan, N., Sajjadi, M.S., Barron, J.T., Dosovitskiy, A., Duckworth, D.: Nerf in the wild: neural radiance fields for unconstrained photo collections. arXiv preprint arXiv:2008.02268 (2020)
37. Mescheder, L., Oechsle, M., Niemeyer, M., Nowozin, S., Geiger, A.: Occupancy networks: learning 3D reconstruction in function space. In: Proceedings of the IEEE Conference on Computer Vision and Pattern Recognition, pp. 4460–4470 (2019)
38. Mildenhall, B., Srinivasan, P.P., Tancik, M., Barron, J.T., Ramamoorthi, R., Ng, R.: Nerf: representing scenes as neural radiance fields for view synthesis. arXiv preprint arXiv:2003.08934 (2020)
39. Mousavian, A., Anguelov, D., Flynn, J., Kosecka, J.: 3D bounding box estimation using deep learning and geometry. In: Proceedings of the IEEE conference on Computer Vision and Pattern Recognition, pp. 7074–7082 (2017)
40. Newbold, P.: Arima model building and the time series analysis approach to forecasting. J. Forecast. **2**(1), 23–35 (1983)
41. Nie, Y., Han, X., Guo, S., Zheng, Y., Chang, J., Zhang, J.J.: Total3dunderstanding: joint layout, object pose and mesh reconstruction for indoor scenes from a single image. In: Proceedings of the IEEE/CVF Conference on Computer Vision and Pattern Recognition, pp. 55–64 (2020)
42. Park, J.J., Florence, P., Straub, J., Newcombe, R., Lovegrove, S.: Deepsdf: learning continuous signed distance functions for shape representation. In: Proceedings of the IEEE Conference on Computer Vision and Pattern Recognition, pp. 165–174 (2019)
43. Peng, S., Niemeyer, M., Mescheder, L., Pollefeys, M., Geiger, A.: Convolutional occupancy networks. In: Vedaldi, A., Bischof, H., Brox, T., Frahm, J.-M. (eds.) ECCV 2020. LNCS, vol. 12348, pp. 523–540. Springer, Cham (2020). https://doi.org/10.1007/978-3-030-58580-8_31

44. Poggi, M., Aleotti, F., Tosi, F., Mattoccia, S.: On the uncertainty of self-supervised monocular depth estimation. In: Proceedings of the IEEE/CVF Conference on Computer Vision and Pattern Recognition, pp. 3227–3237 (2020)

45. Raistrick, A., Kulkarni, N., Fouhey, D.F.: Collision replay: what does bumping into things tell you about scene geometry? arXiv preprint arXiv:2105.01061 (2021)

46. Ranftl, R., Lasinger, K., Hafner, D., Schindler, K., Koltun, V.: Towards robust monocular depth estimation: mixing datasets for zero-shot cross-dataset transfer. IEEE Trans. Pattern Anal. Mach. Intell. (TPAMI) (2020)

47. Saito, S., Huang, Z., Natsume, R., Morishima, S., Kanazawa, A., Li, H.: Pifu: pixel-aligned implicit function for high-resolution clothed human digitization. In: Proceedings of the IEEE International Conference on Computer Vision, pp. 2304–2314 (2019)

48. Saito, S., Simon, T., Saragih, J., Joo, H.: Pifuhd: multi-level pixel-aligned implicit function for high-resolution 3D human digitization. In: Proceedings of the IEEE/CVF Conference on Computer Vision and Pattern Recognition, pp. 84–93 (2020)

49. Saxena, A., Sun, M., Ng, A.Y.: Make3d: learning 3D scene structure from a single still image. IEEE Trans. Pattern Anal. Mach. Intell. $31(5)$, 824–840 (2008)

50. Seitz, S.M., Curless, B., Diebel, J., Scharstein, D., Szeliski, R.: A comparison and evaluation of multi-view stereo reconstruction algorithms. In: 2006 IEEE Computer Society Conference on Computer Vision and Pattern Recognition (CVPR 2006), vol. 1, pp. 519–528. IEEE (2006)

51. Shade, J., Gortler, S., He, L.W., Szeliski, R.: Layered depth images. In: Proceedings of the 25th Annual Conference on Computer Graphics and Interactive Techniques, pp. 231–242 (1998)

52. Sitzmann, V., Martel, J., Bergman, A., Lindell, D., Wetzstein, G.: Implicit neural representations with periodic activation functions. Adv. Neural Inf. Process. Syst. 33 (2020)

53. Song, S., Yu, F., Zeng, A., Chang, A.X., Savva, M., Funkhouser, T.: Semantic scene completion from a single depth image. In: Proceedings of the IEEE Conference on Computer Vision and Pattern Recognition, pp. 1746–1754 (2017)

54. Sun, X., et al.: Pix3d: dataset and methods for single-image 3D shape modeling. In: Proceedings of the IEEE Conference on Computer Vision and Pattern Recognition, pp. 2974–2983 (2018)

55. Tatarchenko, M., Richter, S.R., Ranftl, R., Li, Z., Koltun, V., Brox, T.: What do single-view 3D reconstruction networks learn? In: Proceedings of the IEEE Conference on Computer Vision and Pattern Recognition, pp. 3405–3414 (2019)

56. Tian, Z., Shen, C., Chen, H., He, T.: FCOS: a simple and strong anchor-free object detector. TPAMI 44, 1922–1933 (2020)

57. Tulsiani, S., Gupta, S., Fouhey, D.F., Efros, A.A., Malik, J.: Factoring shape, pose, and layout from the 2D image of a 3D scene. In: Proceedings of the IEEE Conference on Computer Vision and Pattern Recognition, pp. 302–310 (2018)

58. Tulsiani, S., Su, H., Guibas, L.J., Efros, A.A., Malik, J.: Learning shape abstractions by assembling volumetric primitives. In: Proceedings of the IEEE Conference on Computer Vision and Pattern Recognition, pp. 2635–2643 (2017)

59. Tulsiani, S., Tucker, R., Snavely, N.: Layer-structured 3D scene inference via view synthesis. In: Ferrari, V., Hebert, M., Sminchisescu, C., Weiss, Y. (eds.) ECCV 2018. LNCS, vol. 11211, pp. 311–327. Springer, Cham (2018). https://doi.org/10.1007/978-3-030-01234-2_19

60. Virtanen, P., et al.: SciPy 1.0 contributors: SciPy 1.0: fundamental algorithms for scientific computing in python. Nat. Methods **17**, 261–272 (2020). https://doi.org/10.1038/s41592-019-0686-2

61. Wang, N., Zhang, Y., Li, Z., Fu, Y., Liu, W., Jiang, Y.-G.: Pixel2Mesh: generating 3D mesh models from single RGB images. In: Ferrari, V., Hebert, M., Sminchisescu, C., Weiss, Y. (eds.) ECCV 2018. LNCS, vol. 11215, pp. 55–71. Springer, Cham (2018). https://doi.org/10.1007/978-3-030-01252-6_4

62. Wang, X., Fouhey, D.F., Gupta, A.: Designing deep networks for surface normal estimation. In: CVPR (2015)

63. Weyn, J.A., Durran, D.R., Caruana, R.: Improving data-driven global weather prediction using deep convolutional neural networks on a cubed sphere. J. Adv. Model. Earth Syst. **12**(9), e2020MS002109 (2020)

64. Xu, Q., Wang, W., Ceylan, D., Mech, R., Neumann, U.: DISN: deep implicit surface network for high-quality single-view 3D reconstruction. Adv. Neural Inf. Process. Syst., 492–502 (2019)

65. Yu, A., Ye, V., Tancik, M., Kanazawa, A.: pixelNeRF: neural radiance fields from one or few images. In: CVPR (2021)

66. Zhang, K., Riegler, G., Snavely, N., Koltun, V.: Nerf++: analyzing and improving neural radiance fields. arXiv preprint arXiv:2010.07492 (2020)

67. Zhang, R., Isola, P., Efros, A.A.: Colorful image colorization. In: Leibe, B., Matas, J., Sebe, N., Welling, M. (eds.) ECCV 2016. LNCS, vol. 9907, pp. 649–666. Springer, Cham (2016). https://doi.org/10.1007/978-3-319-46487-9_40

68. Zhou, X., Wang, D., Krähenbühl, P.: Objects as points. arXiv preprint arXiv:1904.07850 (2019)

69. Zhu, S., Ebrahimi, S., Kanazawa, A., Darrell, T.: Differentiable gradient sampling for learning implicit 3D scene reconstructions from a single image. In: International Conference on Learning Representations (2021)

Object Level Depth Reconstruction for Category Level 6D Object Pose Estimation from Monocular RGB Image

Zhaoxin Fan[1], Zhenbo Song[2], Jian Xu[4], Zhicheng Wang[4], Kejian Wu[4], Hongyan Liu[3], and Jun He[1(✉)]

[1] Key Laboratory of Data Engineering and Knowledge Engineering of MOE, School of Information, Renmin University of China, Beijing 100872, China
{fanzhaoxin,hejun}@ruc.edu.cn
[2] School of Computer Science and Engineering, Nanjing University of Science and Technology, Nanjing 210094, China
songzb@njust.edu.cn
[3] Department of Management Science and Engineering, Tsinghua University, Beijing 100084, China
hyliu@tsinghua.edu.cn
[4] Nreal, Beijing, China
{jianxu,zcwang,kejian}@nreal.ai

Abstract. Recently, RGBD-based category-level 6D object pose estimation has achieved promising improvement in performance, however, the requirement of depth information prohibits broader applications. In order to relieve this problem, this paper proposes a novel approach named **Ob**ject **L**evel **D**epth reconstruction Network (**OLD-Net**) taking only RGB images as input for category-level 6D object pose estimation. We propose to directly predict object-level depth from a monocular RGB image by deforming the category-level shape prior into object-level depth and the canonical NOCS representation. Two novel modules named Normalized Global Position Hints (NGPH) and Shape-aware Decoupled Depth Reconstruction (SDDR) module are introduced to learn high fidelity object-level depth and delicate shape representations. At last, the 6D object pose is solved by aligning the predicted canonical representation with the back-projected object-level depth. Extensive experiments on the challenging CAMERA25 and REAL275 datasets indicate that our model, though simple, achieves state-of-the-art performance.

Keywords: Category-level 6D pose estimation · Object-level depth · Position hints · Decoupled depth reconstruction

1 Introduction

Category-level 6D object pose estimation that predicts the full degrees of rotation and translation of an object w.r.t the camera is an significant yet challenging

Supplementary Information The online version contains supplementary material available at https://doi.org/10.1007/978-3-031-20086-1_13.

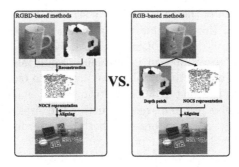

Fig. 1. Difference between RGBD-based methods and our RGB-based method. RGBD-based methods take RGB image and depth channel as inputs, and the output is a canonical NOCS representation. While our RGB-based method only takes RGB images as input, and predict the NOCS representation as well as the object-level depth simultaneously.

task. It has a wide range of applications including robotic grasping [5,26,29], augmented reality [18,21,23,36], and autonomous driving [1,9,22,33,34]. As shown in Fig. 1 left, the mainstream framework of this task includes two steps : 1) Predicting a canonical representation to represent the canonical category-level object shape. 2) Aligning the canonical representation with the back-projected object depth to predict the object pose. Wang et al. [31] first introduces a model named NOCS to do this task. Then, many following works [2,3,16,25,31] are proposed to improve the performance from various perspectives, such as, canonical representations [2], learning shape priors [25], and new augmentation strategies [3]. All these methods have achieved promising object pose estimation accuracy. Nevertheless, they are all RGBD-based, whose performance are dominated by features learned from the depth channel. Since the depth information is always not available in many scenarios, it seriously limits broader applications for these methods. Lee et al. [13] proposes to take only monocular RGB image as input for category-level 6D object pose estimation. It predicts a depth map from the RGB image for information reinforcement. One limitation of Lee et al. [13] is that it needs to reconstruct a metric-scale mesh for each object first, making the pipeline redundant. In this paper, we explore to directly predict the object-level depth from an input RGB image patch without relying on any intermediate representation, for instance, a mesh, in a simple yet effective way.

This paper proposes a novel approach named **O**bject **L**evel **D**epth reconstruction **N**etwork (**OLD-Net**) for RGB-based category-level 6D object pose estimation. Figure 1 right illustrates the main pipeline of the OLD-Net. In detail, object-level depth and the NOCS representation are simultaneously predicted from the input RGB image, and aligned together to predict the 6D object pose. Different from the previous method [13] that predicts the depth of the object region by reconstructing a mesh, the object's observed depth is directly predicted from the RGB image in an end-to-end manner in this paper.

To obtain the depth of the object region, a straight-forward way is to predict the scene-level depth. However, due to variety and diversity of field of view, the predicted scene-level depth is usually coarse, resulting in the loss of object shape details. The pose estimation performance would also suffer from it (as shown in Table 3). To release the problem, we propose to reconstruct the object-level depth directly by learning to deform category-level shape priors. In contrast to predict a scene-level depth map, reconstructing the object-level depth is more computational friendly and can preserve better shape details, benefiting the subsequent depth-NOCS alignment process.

To delicately reconstruct the object-level depth, a novel module named Normalized Global Position Hints (NGPH) is proposed in OLD-Net to balance scene-level global information and local feature-level shape details. NGPH is the normalized 2D detection results with camera intrinsics, providing global position cues about the object's absolute depth in the scene, as well as the generalization ability towards images captured by different cameras. Furthermore, a Shape-aware Decoupled Depth Reconstruction (SDDR) scheme is utilized to predict the shape details and absolute depth. In particular, SDDR decouples and predicts the absolute depth into shape points and depth translation with two independent deep networks. Intuitively, the shape points are to preserve shape details while the depth translation is designed for predicting absolute object center.

Apart from depth, we further predict the NOCS representation [31] of the target object following the RGBD-based methods [25,31]. A discriminator is utilized during training to improve reconstruction quality. We back-project the object-level depth into a point cloud after both the NOCS representation and the observed object-level depth are predicted. They are aligned by a Umeyama algorithm [27] to solve for the 6D object pose as shown in Fig. 1. We conduct extensive experiments on the famous CAMERA25 [31] dataset and REAL275 [31] dataset. Experimental results demonstrate that our method achieves state-of-the-art performance.

Our main contributions are:

– We propose OLD-Net, a novel deep learning approach for category-level 6D object pose estimation, which aims at directly predicting object-level depth from a monocular RGB image in a simple yet effective way.
– We propose the Normalized Global Position Hints and the Shape-aware Decoupled Depth Reconstruction scheme. Both modules are tailored for RGB-based category-level 6D object pose estimation.
– We conduct extensive experiments on two challenging datasets to verify the effectiveness of our method. Our model achieves state-of-the-art performance in both synthetic and real world scenarios.

2   Related Work

2.1   Instance-Level 6D Object Pose Estimation

We broadly classify instance-level 6D object pose estimation methods into RGB-based methods and RGBD-based methods according to input data format. For

RGB-based methods, PoseNet [11] is a pioneering network that introduces a CNN architecture to directly regress a 6D camera pose from a single RGB image. Then, PoseCNN [32] proposes to first locate the object in the image then predicts the depth of the object for more accurate pose estimation. However, directly estimating the object pose from an RGB image is challenging due to the non-linearity of the rotation space. Therefore, to overcome this, methods like [24] propose to first predict 2D keypoints as intermediate representations and then solve a PnP problem [14] to recover the accurate object pose. To improve keypoint detection performance, PVNet [17] formulates a voting scheme, which is more robust towards occlusion and truncation. Hybridpose [19] improves PVNet by adding more constraints such as edges. In contrast to predicting sparse keypoints, methods like DPOD [35] predict dense-correspondence for 6D object pose estimation. There are also some methods like [15] propose to refine the predicted object pose through iteratively comparing observed and rendered images. For RGBD-based methods, PVN3D [10] proposes a Hough voting network to predict 3D keypoints. The object pose is recovered by aligning these keypoints with the object models using ICP. Wang et al. [30] introduce DenseFusion, which densely fuses RGB features and point cloud features for 6D object pose detection. MoreFusion [28] uses a more compact fusion strategy for further performance improvement.

Though having achieved promising performance, instance-level methods suffer from limited generalization ability because one model only works for a particular object in their settings. In this paper, we study the more general category-level 6D object pose estimation.

2.2   Category-Level 6D Object Pose Estimation

NOCS [31] may be the first work that uses deep learning models for category-level 6D object pose estimation. The prevalent CAMERA25 and REAL275 datasets are released in NOCS. The canonical NOCS representation are used to recover the 6D object pose. Chen et al. [2] propose another canonical representation named CASS and this work also designs a deep learning approach to cope with this task. SPD [25] claims that the NOCS representation's potential is not fully explored yet. Therefore, it presents the Shape Prior Deformation idea to better predict the NOCS representation. We also use the Shape Prior Deformation, however, to predict the object-level depth, apart from predicting the NOCS representation. Chen et al. [3] propose a novel augmentation method in FS-Net to improve training quality. Lin et al. [16] introduce a dual network architecture in their work DualPoseNet to improve the 6D object pose estimation performance. One observation is that most of category-level methods solving the pose estimation problem by a estimation-by-aligning scheme, which may partly due to that alternative solutions like PnP+RANSAC or direct pose parameters prediction are hard to deal with ambiguities caused by shape variations. In this paper, we also follow the mainstream of estimation-by-aligning scheme.

Though with good performance, the above-mentioned methods all need to take an RGBD observation as input, which severely limits their application

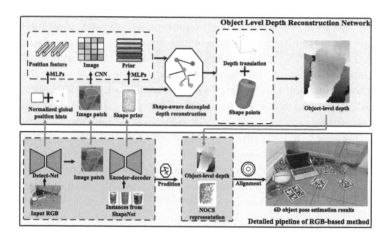

Fig. 2. The bottom figure is the pipeline of this paper, we first train a Detect-Net and an encoder-decoder network to crop image patches and generate the shape prior respectively. Then, we predict the object-level depth and the NOCS representation. 6D object pose is recovered by aligning the depth and the NOCS representation. To predict high-quality object-level depth, we design the novel OLD-Net as shown in the top figure.

scenarios. To the best of our knowledge, [13] is the only work tailored for RGB-based category-level 6D object pose estimation. It first uses Mesh-RCNN [8] to predict a metric-scale object mesh. Then the mesh is rendered into a depth map for pose estimation. Our method is significantly different from [8]. First, we propose a more simple way to directly predict the object-level depth from the monocular RGB image. Second, we design the novel SDDR and NGPH. Third, we verify the importance of using shape prior to better cope with intra-class variation. The object-level depth predicted by our approach is of higher quality, significantly improves the 6D pose estimation performance.

3   Pipeline

We illustrate the pipeline of our work in Fig. 2 (bottom). The network architecture of our main contribution OLD-Net is shown in Fig. 2 (top).

Our pipeline takes an image patch $I_{patch} \in R^{W \times H \times 3}$ and a shape prior $P_{pri} \in R^{N_m \times 3}$ as input. The image patch is cropped by a trained detector called Detect-Net, which represents object specific information. The shape prior of the target category is predicted by an encoder-decoder network using the mean embedding, which is used to alleviate category-variation [25].

Subsequently, the image patch and shape prior are input into the proposed OLD-Net to reconstruct the object-level depth as shown in Fig. 2 top. Besides, OLD-Net also takes the 2D detection results from the Detect-Net as well as the camera intrinsics as inputs, which are normalized as NGPH. A Shape-aware

Decouple Depth Reconstruction scheme is occupied in OLD-Net to preserve shape details and absolute object center.

Finally, The NOCS representation [31] is predicted using a deep network following [25]. Then, we back-project the object-level depth into a point cloud and adopt the Umeyama algorithm [27] to recover the object pose as in [31].

Next, we first introduce the OLD-Net at length. Then, we describe how we predict the NOCS representation. Finally, we introduce the loss function used in this paper.

4   OLD-Net

The most serious difficulty for category-level object pose estimation is how to deal with shape variations. RGBD-based methods like [25] have demonstrated that directly predicting the canonical NOCS representation is not promising. Therefore, for each category, they learn a category-level shape prior as an intermediate representation to ease the task. Compared to directly estimating the NOCS representation, problems caused by shape variation can be largely mitigated by utilizing the learned shape prior. In our work, we follow this framework to build OLD-Net owing to shape-prior's superiority. Further more, we extend it to predict the object-level depth. In addition, two novel modules technically designed for RGB-based methods named NGPH and SDDR are proposed to better capture useful information.

In particular, as shown in Fig. 2 top, taking the image patch, the shape prior, and the NGPH as input, OLD-Net first uses two MLPs and a CNN to learn high-level image feature $I_p \in R^{W \times H \times C}$, prior feature $f_{pri} \in R^{N_m \times C}$, and position feature $f_{pos} \in R^{2C}$ first. Then, utilizing these features, the shape points as well as the depth translation are concurrently predicted by the Shape-aware Decoupled Depth Reconstruction (SDDR) scheme. Lastly, the shape points and depth translation are reassembled together to obtain the object-level depth. Next, we introduce NGPH and SDDR in detail.

4.1   Normalized Global Position Hints

We are motivated that the object-level depth can be directly predicted from an image with high quality. The most straightforward way to achieve this goal is to predict a scene-level depth map. However, predicting the scene-level depth map from the raw image is computational costly. Furthermore, it may cause the loss of object's shape detail. Note the shape detail is very important for our pipeline since we need to align two 3D representations to recover the object pose. Therefore, we choose to take the image patch of a particular object as input to predict the object-level depth. Nevertheless, the image patch has lost the absolute global position information of the object due to the crop and resize operation, resulting in the predict depth being suffered from scale ambiguities. To this end, we propose the NGPH, which properly solves this problem by providing absolute global position information and solving scale ambiguities.

Inspired by [20], we choose the parameters of the 2D bounding box (l, t, r, b) output by the Detect-Net to form NGPH, which represents the left, top, right, and bottom image coordinates of the 2D bounding box. This information is effective enough to be supplied to the network to infer scale clues, i.e. recovering the absolute object depth if all images are captured by the same camera. However, it is common that images would be collected by different cameras. And it is a common sense that the absolute object depth would be influenced by the camera intrinsic if it is inferred from a single monocular RGB image. Therefore, we propose to inject the camera intrinsics into NGPH. Hence, the trained network can also be generalized into other images captured by different cameras. We make use of the 2D bounding box and the camera intrinsics by normalizing them into canonical coordinates:

$$g = [\frac{f_x}{r-l}, \frac{f_y}{b-t}, \frac{l-c_x}{f_x}, \frac{t-c_y}{f_y}, \frac{r-c_x}{f_x}, \frac{b-c_y}{f_y}] \tag{1}$$

where g represents the final NGPH we use, c_x and c_y represent coordinates of the camera optical center, and f_x and f_y represent focal lengths. The first two terms normalize the size of the object's bounding box with the focal length, eliminating scale ambiguity caused by object size. The later four terms normalize the center of the object using the focal length and size of the bounding box, removing ambiguity but preserving the position information.

The proposed NGPH, validated by experimental results that, though simple, is indispensable in object-level depth reconstruction.

4.2   Shape-Aware Decoupled Depth Reconstruction

We apply an estimation-by-aligning scheme to recover the 6D object pose in our pipeline. Therefore, we have to estimate the observed 3D representation of the object first. In our work, we choose to reconstruct the object-level depth to form the "observed" 3D representation. We hope the reconstructed object-level depth to be as similar as the one captured by a depth camera as possible. Besides, the object's shape detail should be well described because we need to align the depth with the NOCS representation for recovering accurate 6D object poses. To achieve so, we propose a SDDR scheme. Specifically, in SDDR, we propose to decouple the object-level depth into shape points and depth translation. The former preserves relative position information between "observed" points, where the shape detail of the observed object is expected to be delicately predicted along with it. While the latter describes the positional information of the object center. We use two different modules to predict them separately.

The features used in the OLD-Net are the reshaped image feature matrix $f_I \in R^{N_p \times C}$ (where N_p is the number of pixels), the position feature $f_{pos} \in R^{2C}$ and the prior feature $f_{pri} \in R^{N_m \times C}$. We also apply MLPs and adaptive average pooling to obtain the global image feature $f_I^g \in R^{C_g}$ and the global prior feature $f_{pri}^g \in R^{C_g}$.

Shape Points Prediction. We adopt the Shape Prior Deformation (SPD) idea [6,25] to reconstruct shape points, which would provide the model with more constraints on object shape. Specifically, utilizing the above features, the network would learn a deform field $D_{depth} \in R^{N_m \times 3}$ and an assign field $M_{depth} \in R^{N_n \times N_m}$ to deform and assign the shape prior into the back-projected point cloud of the object-level depth:

$$P_{depth} = M_{depth}(P_{pri} + D_{depth}) \qquad (2)$$

To learn D_{depth}, we repeat f_I^g, f_{pri}^g and f_{pos} for N_m times and concatenate them with f_{pri}. The concatenated features are input into a MLP to learn D_{depth}. Similarly, to learn M_{depth}, we repeat f_I^g, f_{pri}^g and f_{pos} for N_p times and concatenate them with f_I. Another MLP is used to learn M_{depth}. Note that in the literature of category-level tasks [7], shape prior is easily accessible and is widely employed for predicting canonical representations. In this paper, we use it to predict object-level depth to provide a guidance for future RGB-based works.

Depth Translation Prediction. To learn the absolute position of the object center, we propose to use an independent head to learn the depth translation, which is implemented as a MLP. We use the concatenation of f_{pos} and f_I^g as the input. The output is a single value that represents the absolute depth of the object center. We name it as Z_t.

The SDDR scheme mainly benefits from three aspects to preserve object shape details. First, since we only take image patches to reconstruct the object-level depth, the model can concentrate on the object's shape rather than the whole scene geometry. Second, the shape prior provides powerful constraints about the shape of the object, making it easier to recover shape details. Third, absolute object center and object shape are learned separately and would be paid with different attention.

After both P_{depth} and Z_t are predicted. The object-level depth can be represented as $Z = Z_{depth} + Z_t$, where Z_{depth} is the third component of P_{depth}. Note that we choose to supervise Z rather than the back-projected point cloud. It is because on the one hand, it is easier for the network to learn Z during training, on the other hand, back-projecting Z to a point cloud for aligning, the 2D coordinates of the object would provide additional constraints for the global position, which would also benefit the final pose recovery step.

5 NOCS Representation Prediction

We also predict the NOCS representation [31] of the target object in our pipeline, which is a canonical representation that is used to align with the object-level depth to recover the 6D object pose. To predict the NOCS representation, we back-project Z into a point cloud and input it into a MLP to learn depth features $f_{depth} \in R^{N_p \times C}$. Taking f_{depth}, f_{pri} and f_I as input, similar to reconstruct the object-level depth, we use SPD to predict the NOCS representation:

$$P_{nocs} = M_{nocs}(P_{pri} + D_{nocs}) \qquad (3)$$

However, we find that in some cases, P_{nocs} is not realistic enough, which would affect the final 6D object pose estimation accuracy. Therefore, we adopt the adversarial training strategy [12] to train the network. Specifically, we design a discriminator $\mathbb{D}$ to judge whether the predicted NOCS representation is real enough or not. The optimization goal of the discriminator can be represented as:

$$L_d = (\mathbb{D}(\hat{P_{nocs}}) - 1)^2 + (\mathbb{D}(P_{nocs}))^2 \tag{4}$$

where $\hat{P_{nocs}}$ is the ground-truth NOCS representation.

Similarly, the optimization goal of the NOCS prediction network is P_{nocs} is:

$$L_g = (\mathbb{D}(P_{nocs}) - 1)^2 \tag{5}$$

During training, we iteratively update the parameters of the discriminator and the NOCS prediction network. Both networks would become stronger and stronger through confrontation. Therefore, the predicted NOCS representation would also become more and more realistic.

6   Loss Function

For the object-level depth reconstruction, we use the $L1$ loss between Z and the ground-truth:

$$L_z = |z - \hat{z}|_1 \tag{6}$$

For the NOCS representation prediction, we use the same loss function as [25] due to its excellent performance. This loss function includes a smooth L1 loss L_{corr} between the reconstructed NOCS representation and ground-truth to encourage better one-to-one correspondence, the chamfer distance loss L_{cd} between the deformed shape prior $P_{pri} + D_{nocs}$ and the object's canonical instance model to preserve object shape, a cross-entropy loss L_{entro} to encourage peak distribution of the assignment matrix M_{nocs}, and a L2 regularization loss L_{reg} on M_{nocs} to avoid collapsing deformation.

The overall loss function we use is:

$$L = \gamma_1 L_z + \gamma_2 L_d + \gamma_3 L_g + \gamma_4 L_{corr} + \gamma_6 L_{cd} + \gamma_6 L_{entro} + \gamma_7 L_{reg} \tag{7}$$

where γ_1 to γ_7 are balance terms.

7   Experiment

To verify the effectiveness of our method. We conduct experiments on the CAMERA25 dataset [31] and REAL275 dataset [31]. More details about implementation, datasets and metrics can be found in the SuppMat.

Table 1. Reconstruction quality evaluation. The evaluation metric is chamfer distance.

Data	Reconstructions	Bottle	Bowl	Camera	Can	Laptop	Mug
CAMERA25	Depth	0.0532	0.0360	0.0596	0.0407	0.0371	0.0422
	NOCS	0.0225	0.0142	0.0192	0.0251	0.0150	0.0178
REAL275	Depth	0.0179	0.0200	0.0136	0.0162	0.0151	0.0129
	NOCS	0.0247	0.0174	0.0215	0.0205	0.0203	0.0203

Table 2. Quantitative comparison with state-of-the-art methods on the CAMERA25 and REAL275 dataset.

Data	Methods	IoU25	IoU50	IoU75	10 cm	10°	10° 10 cm
CAMERA25	lee et al. [13]	**75.5**	**32.4**	5.1	29.7	60.8	19.2
	OLD-Net(Ours)	74.3	32.1	**5.4**	**30.1**	**74.0**	**23.4**
REAL275	Synthesis [4]	–	–	–	34.0	14.2	4.8
	lee et al. [13]	62.0	23.4	**3.0**	**39.5**	29.2	9.6
	OLD-Net(Ours)	**68.7**	**25.4**	1.9	38.9	**37.0**	**9.8**

7.1 Results

Reconstruction Quality Evaluation: In our work, the main idea is to reconstruct the object-level depth and the NOCS representation. Therefore, we first evaluate the reconstruction quality of our method in Table 1. We compute the chamfer distance between back-projected depth and the ground-truth to validate the depth reconstruction quality. We also compute the chamfer distance between the predicted and ground-truth NOCS representations to evaluate the NOCS prediction quality. It can be seen from Table 1, for object-level depth reconstruction, the errors are less than 2 cm in the REAL275 dataset. For the NOCS prediction, the error is also close to 2 cm in the REAL275 dataset. 2 cm is a relatively small scale error compared to our large object size and scene depth. Therefore, we can conclude that our method indeed achieves good object-level depth reconstruction quality and NOCS representation prediction quality. On the CAMERA25 dataset, the NOCS representation prediction error is still below 2cm for most of the categories. However, the object-level depth construction error is increased to 3 cm to 5 cm. The reason may be that there exists a larger depth distribution variance in the larger synthetic dataset. This observation also indicates that reconstructing object-level depth is harder than predicting the NOCS representation.

Quantitative Results of 6D Pose Estimation: We quantitatively compare our method with state-of-the-art methods in Table 2. We first compare our method with Lee et al. [13] on the CAMERA25 dataset. Lee et al. [13] predict the depth by first reconstructing a mesh and then rendering the mesh into a depth map. In contrast, we choose to directly reconstruct the object-level depth, which is more simple yet more effective. We can see that our method outperforms Lee et al. [13] at 4 metrics among the 6. In the most strict 10 °10cm metric, our

Table 3. Quantitative comparison with state-of-the-art scene-level depth prediction baselines on the CAMERA25 dataset.

Data	Methods	IoU25	IoU50	IoU75	10 cm	10°	10° 10 cm
CAMERA25	Scene-level baseline (shared)	47.7	12.9	0.8	17.8	8.0	1.6
	Scene-level baseline (independent)	50.4	14.0	0.9	17.7	10.0	2.2
	OLD-Net(Ours)	**74.3**	**32.1**	**5.4**	**30.1**	**74.0**	**23.4**

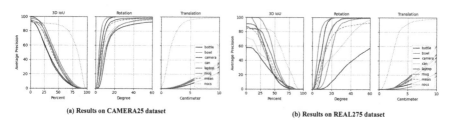

(a) Results on CAMERA25 dataset   (b) Results on REAL275 dataset

Fig. 3. The average precision (AP) vs. different thresholds on 3D IoU, rotation error, and translation error.

method exceeds Lee et al. [13] for 4.2 points, which is a significant improvement. On the IoU25 and IoU50 metrics, though our results are slightly lower than Lee et al. [13], we still achieve comparable performance. These results demonstrate that reconstructing object-level depth using our SDDR scheme and NGPH is a better choice than reconstructing the object mesh. The main reason may be it is much easier for the network to learn useful information, such as the object's shape detail or the absolute object center, if depth translation and shape points are decoupled.

Then, we compare our method with Synthesis [4] and Lee et al. [13] on REAL275. To avoid overfitting, we finetune our model trained on CAMERA25 train set on the REAL275 train set for 1500 steps rather than training on REAL275 from scratch. It can be seen from the table that our method is only slightly outperformed by Lee et al. [13] at the IoU75 metric and the 10 cm metric. While for another 4 metrics, our model performs the best. Especially at the IoU25 metric and the 10 °metric, our model outperforms the second-best model for 6.7 points and 7.8 points respectively. Our model performs much better than previous methods in terms of the IoU25 metric and the 10 °metric mainly because the SDDR and the NGPH could equip our model with the ability of concentrating on the object's shape detail and absolute object center independently.

To further verify our motivation and the benefit of reconstructing object-level depth over estimating scene-level depth, we compare our methods with two scene-level depth estimation baselines in Table 3. Both scene-level baseline (shared) and scene-level baseline (independent) share the same encoder-decoder network architecture. The difference is that during training, scene-level baseline (shared) shared the encoder with the NOCS reconstruction branch while scene-level baseline (independent) independently train the depth estimator. Both networks are carefully tuned to achieve their best performance. Table 3 shows that

Fig. 4. Qualitative results of successful cases. Top two rows are results on CAMERA25 dataset and bottom two rows are results on REAL275 dataset. Our method can accurately estimate the pose and size of the object taking a single RGB image as input.

Table 4. Results of ablation study. We remove a module from a network architecture each time to investigate its impact.

Versions	IoU25	IoU50	IoU50	10 cm	10°	10° 10 cm
Vanilla SPD	54.9	12.6	0.6	6.4	55.0	4.4
w/o Depth translation design	72.7	31.1	**5.5**	29.8	74.6	23.2
w/o Shape points design	70.0	28.4	4.5	27.7	70.8	20.7
w/o NGPH	71.2	29.4	4.6	28.3	61.6	18.7
w/o Adversarial training	71.8	29.6	5.0	28.3	**75.1**	22.1
Full model	**74.3**	**32.1**	5.4	**30.1**	74.0	**23.4**

OLD-Net significantly outperforms both scene-level baselines. The reason could be that the object-level depth predicted by OLD-Net is much better at preserving shape details than the coarse scene-level depth, while shape details are critical to the NOCS-depth aligning process.

All the above results have demonstrated the superiority of our method compared to SOTA RGB-based methods. Moreover, we also exhibit the picture of the average precision (AP) vs. different thresholds on 3D IoU, rotation error, and translation error in Fig. 3. We compare our method with NOCS [31], an RGBD-based method. It can be seen from the figure that our method performs excellently in terms of IoU and rotation on all categories. The excellent performance on rotation prediction largely due to that we decouple the shape points out of the depth to preserve shape detail. In alignment, whether the rotation is accurate or not is mostly dependent on the quality of the object's shape. Therefore, our model even achieves comparable performance with the RGBD-based

Fig. 5. Qualitative results of failure cases.

method in terms of rotation prediction. In contrast, the translation prediction results are relatively low compared to RGBD-based methods. This is because recovering the absolute global position z_t of the object from a monocular RGB image is an ill-posed problem. The relatively inaccurate translation is the main reason why the most strict 10 °10 cm metric is not high. Therefore, future works should pay more attention to obtaining more precise absolute depth prediction.

We also test the running time complexity of our method. The deep network runs 64 FPS on a 3090 GPU, and the Umeyama algorithm runs 30FPS on a normal AMD EPYC 7702 CPU. The overall pipeline runs 22FPS. Our method is potential of being real time.

Qualitative Results of 6D Pose Estimation: To qualitatively analyze the effectiveness of our method, we visualize the estimated bounding boxes in Fig. 4. Results on both synthetic data and real data are shown. It can be seen that OLD-Net can predict tight object bounding boxes, which are accurate enough for augmented reality products. In Fig 5, we also show some failure cases. OLD-Net may miss objects or detect ghosts sometimes. We leave solving it as our future work. More visualizations are in the SuppMat.

7.2   Ablation Study

In this section, we study the impact of our key designs by removing them out of our network architecture each time unless otherwise stated.

Vanilla SPD: We adopt SPD to learn shape points in SDDR. One may wonder whether the good performance of our model comes from the SPD rather than other modules we design. Therefore, we show the performance when we only use a vanilla SPD module (without OLD-Net, without SDDR, and only directly predict the back-projected point cloud of the object-level depth using SPD). Without our other designs, the performance of the vanilla SPD is poor. This demonstrates that the SPD itself can't undertake the object-level depth prediction task. In contrast, it is the proposed SDDR and NGPH being the key components that make our method work.

Impact of SDDR Scheme: In this paper, SDDR is introduced to decouple the object-level depth into depth translation and shape points. Compared to the Vanilla SPD, all versions of our models in Table 4 adopt the SDDR scheme, therefore, their performances are largely improved. Then, in Table 4 row 3, instead of using two separate modules to learn the depth translation and the shape points independently, we directly predict the absolute object-level depth using a single module. We find that the IoU25 metric and IoU50 metric are decreased a lot. That may be because without decoupling depth translation out, the network may lose object details like the length-width-height ratio of the object or some particular object components. Besides, in Table 4 row 4, we show the result of replacing the SPD with a MLP to predict shape points, i.e. directly regressing NOCS and object-level depth. It is obvious all metrics are decreased significantly. The result proves that it is very necessary to adopt SPD in SDDR. The SPD provides the model with strong constraints about object shape. Note in Table 4 row 3 and row 4, though we remove some designs, the 2D coordinates of pixels belonging to the object are still utilized for back-projection (it is also a part of SDDR), which would provide additional constraints for absolute depth. Otherwise, the performance would be even worse as shown in Table 4 row 2, which directly predicts back-projected object point clouds. In summary, the SDDR scheme plays an significant role in OLD-Net for both object shape detail preservation and absolute object center prediction.

Impact of NGPH: Since our model only takes an RGB image patch to predict depth to preserve shape details, the global position information would be lost. To make up for this defect, we inject the NGPH into our network. In Table 4 row 5, we remove the NGPH out of our network to investigate its impact. When it is removed, all metrics are decreased a lot. That is because, without NGPH, it is hard for the network to predict absolute depth. Though relative position between 3D points may be inferred from image patches, wrong absolute depth would make it hard to accurately recover the object pose through aligning.

Impact of Adversarial Training: We adopt an adversarial training strategy to increase the quality of the predicted NOCS representation. When it is removed, as shown in the second last row of Table 4, all metrics except the 10 °metric are decreased. This result evidences that adversarial training is necessary for performance improvement. It also indicates that both the quality of the NOCS representation and the object-level depth are important. Neither can be ignored.

8   Conclusion

In this paper, we propose a novel network named OLD-Net for RGB-based category-level 6D object pose estimation. Directly predicting object-level depth using shape prior is the key insight of our work. To reconstruct high-quality object-level depth, we introduce the Normalized Global Position Hints and Shape-aware Decoupled Depth Reconstruction Scheme in OLD-Net. We also predict the canonical NOCS representation of the object in our pipeline using adversarial training. Extensive experiments on both real and synthetic datasets have demonstrated that our method can achieve new state-of-the-art performance. Additional limitations and future works are presented in the SuppMat.

Acknowledgement. This work was supported in part by National Key Research and Development Program of China under Grant No. 2020YFB2104101 and National Natural Science Foundation of China (NSFC) under Grant Nos. 62172421, 71771131, and 62072459.

References

1. Caesar, H., et al.: nuscenes: a multimodal dataset for autonomous driving. In: Proceedings of the IEEE/CVF Conference on Computer Vision and Pattern Recognition, pp. 11621–11631 (2020)
2. Chen, D., Li, J., Wang, Z., Xu, K.: Learning canonical shape space for category-level 6d object pose and size estimation. In: Proceedings of the IEEE/CVF Conference on Computer Vision and Pattern Recognition, pp. 11973–11982 (2020)
3. Chen, W., Jia, X., Chang, H.J., Duan, J., Shen, L., Leonardis, A.: Fs-net: fast shape-based network for category-level 6d object pose estimation with decoupled rotation mechanism. In: Proceedings of the IEEE/CVF Conference on Computer Vision and Pattern Recognition, pp. 1581–1590 (2021)
4. Chen, X., Dong, Z., Song, J., Geiger, A., Hilliges, O.: Category level object pose estimation via neural analysis-by-synthesis. In: Vedaldi, A., Bischof, H., Brox, T., Frahm, J.-M. (eds.) ECCV 2020. LNCS, vol. 12371, pp. 139–156. Springer, Cham (2020). https://doi.org/10.1007/978-3-030-58574-7_9
5. Du, G., Wang, K., Lian, S.: Vision-based robotic grasping from object localization, pose estimation, grasp detection to motion planning: a review. arXiv preprint arXiv:1905.06658 (2019)
6. Fan, Z., et al.: ACR-pose: adversarial canonical representation reconstruction network for category level 6d object pose estimation. arXiv preprint arXiv:2111.10524 (2021)
7. Fan, Z., Zhu, Y., He, Y., Sun, Q., Liu, H., He, J.: Deep learning on monocular object pose detection and tracking: a comprehensive overview. arXiv preprint arXiv:2105.14291 (2021)
8. Gkioxari, G., Malik, J., Johnson, J.: Mesh R-CNN. In: Proceedings of the IEEE/CVF International Conference on Computer Vision, pp. 9785–9795 (2019)
9. Grigorescu, S., Trasnea, B., Cocias, T., Macesanu, G.: A survey of deep learning techniques for autonomous driving. J. Field Robot. **37**(3), 362–386 (2020)
10. He, Y., Sun, W., Huang, H., Liu, J., Fan, H., Sun, J.: Pvn3d: a deep point-wise 3D keypoints voting network for 6DoF pose estimation. In: Proceedings of the IEEE/CVF Conference on Computer Vision and Pattern Recognition, pp. 11632–11641 (2020)
11. Kendall, A., Grimes, M., Cipolla, R.: PoseNet: a convolutional network for real-time 6-DoF camera relocalization. In: Proceedings of the IEEE International Conference on Computer Vision, pp. 2938–2946 (2015)
12. Ledig, C., et al.: Photo-realistic single image super-resolution using a generative adversarial network. In: Proceedings of the IEEE Conference on Computer Vision and Pattern Recognition, pp. 4681–4690 (2017)
13. Lee, T., Lee, B.U., Kim, M., Kweon, I.S.: Category-level metric scale object shape and pose estimation. IEEE Robot. Automa. Lett. **6**(4), 8575–8582 (2021)
14. Lepetit, V., Moreno-Noguer, F., Fua, P.: EPnP: an accurate O (n) solution to the PnP problem. Int. J. Comput. Vis. **81**(2), 155 (2009). https://doi.org/10.1007/s11263-008-0152-6

15. Li, Y., Wang, G., Ji, X., Xiang, Y., Fox, D.: DeepIM: deep iterative matching for 6D pose estimation. In: Proceedings of the European Conference on Computer Vision (ECCV), pp. 683–698 (2018)

16. Lin, J., Wei, Z., Li, Z., Xu, S., Jia, K., Li, Y.: DualPoseNet: category-level 6D object pose and size estimation using dual pose network with refined learning of pose consistency. arXiv preprint arXiv:2103.06526 (2021)

17. Peng, S., Liu, Y., Huang, Q., Zhou, X., Bao, H.: Pvnet: Pixel-wise voting network for 6dof pose estimation. In: Proceedings of the IEEE/CVF Conference on Computer Vision and Pattern Recognition. pp. 4561–4570 (2019)

18. Rambach, J., Pagani, A., Schneider, M., Artemenko, O., Stricker, D.: 6DoF object tracking based on 3D scans for augmented reality remote live support. Computers **7**(1), 6 (2018)

19. Song, C., Song, J., Huang, Q.: Hybridpose: 6D object pose estimation under hybrid representations. In: Proceedings of the IEEE/CVF Conference on Computer Vision and Pattern Recognition, pp. 431–440 (2020)

20. Song, Z., Lu, J., Zhang, T., Li, H.: End-to-end learning for inter-vehicle distance and relative velocity estimation in ADAS with a monocular camera. In: 2020 IEEE International Conference on Robotics and Automation (ICRA), pp. 11081–11087. IEEE (2020)

21. Su, Y., Rambach, J., Minaskan, N., Lesur, P., Pagani, A., Stricker, D.: Deep multistate object pose estimation for augmented reality assembly. In: 2019 IEEE International Symposium on Mixed and Augmented Reality Adjunct (ISMAR-Adjunct), pp. 222–227. IEEE (2019)

22. Sun, P., et al.: Scalability in perception for autonomous driving: Waymo open dataset. In: Proceedings of the IEEE/CVF Conference on Computer Vision and Pattern Recognition, pp. 2446–2454 (2020)

23. Tan, D.J., Navab, N., Tombari, F.: 6D object pose estimation with depth images: a seamless approach for robotic interaction and augmented reality. arXiv preprint arXiv:1709.01459 (2017)

24. Tekin, B., Sinha, S.N., Fua, P.: Real-time seamless single shot 6D object pose prediction. In: Proceedings of the IEEE Conference on Computer Vision and Pattern Recognition, pp. 292–301 (2018)

25. Tian, M., Ang, M.H., Lee, G.H.: Shape prior deformation for categorical 6D object pose and size estimation. In: Vedaldi, A., Bischof, H., Brox, T., Frahm, J.-M. (eds.) ECCV 2020. LNCS, vol. 12366, pp. 530–546. Springer, Cham (2020). https://doi.org/10.1007/978-3-030-58589-1_32

26. Tremblay, J., To, T., Sundaralingam, B., Xiang, Y., Fox, D., Birchfield, S.: Deep object pose estimation for semantic robotic grasping of household objects. arXiv preprint arXiv:1809.10790 (2018)

27. Umeyama, S.: Least-squares estimation of transformation parameters between two point patterns. IEEE Trans. Pattern Anal. Mach. Intell. **13**(04), 376–380 (1991)

28. Wada, K., Sucar, E., James, S., Lenton, D., Davison, A.J.: MoreFusion: multiobject reasoning for 6D pose estimation from volumetric fusion. In: Proceedings of the IEEE/CVF Conference on Computer Vision and Pattern Recognition, pp. 14540–14549 (2020)

29. Wang, C., et al.: Feature sensing and robotic grasping of objects with uncertain information: a review. Sensors **20**(13), 3707 (2020)

30. Wang, C., Xu, D., Zhu, Y., Martín-Martín, R., Lu, C., Fei-Fei, L., Savarese, S.: Densefusion: 6d object pose estimation by iterative dense fusion. In: Proceedings of the IEEE/CVF conference on computer vision and pattern recognition. pp. 3343–3352 (2019)

31. Wang, H., Sridhar, S., Huang, J., Valentin, J., Song, S., Guibas, L.J.: Normalized object coordinate space for category-level 6D object pose and size estimation. In: Proceedings of the IEEE/CVF Conference on Computer Vision and Pattern Recognition, pp. 2642–2651 (2019)
32. Xiang, Y., Schmidt, T., Narayanan, V., Fox, D.: PoseCNN: a convolutional neural network for 6d object pose estimation in cluttered scenes. arXiv preprint arXiv:1711.00199 (2017)
33. Xu, R., Xiang, H., Tu, Z., Xia, X., Yang, M.H., Ma, J.: V2x-vit: vehicle-to-everything cooperative perception with vision transformer. arXiv preprint arXiv:2203.10638 (2022)
34. Xu, R., Xiang, H., Xia, X., Han, X., Liu, J., Ma, J.: Opv2v: an open benchmark dataset and fusion pipeline for perception with vehicle-to-vehicle communication. arXiv preprint arXiv:2109.07644 (2021)
35. Zakharov, S., Shugurov, I., Ilic, S.: DPOD: 6D pose object detector and refiner. In: Proceedings of the IEEE/CVF International Conference on Computer Vision, pp. 1941–1950 (2019)
36. Zhao, Z., Wu, Z., Zhuang, Y., Li, B., Jia, J.: Tracking objects as pixel-wise distributions (2022)

Uncertainty Quantification in Depth Estimation via Constrained Ordinal Regression

Dongting Hu[1], Liuhua Peng[1], Tingjin Chu[1], Xiaoxing Zhang[2], Yinian Mao[2], Howard Bondell[1], and Mingming Gong[1(✉)]

[1] The University of Melbourne, Parkville, Australia
dongting@student.unimelb.edu.au,
{liuhua.peng,tingjin.chu,howard.bondell,mingming.gong}@unimelb.edu.au
[2] Meituan, Beijing, China
{zhangxiaoxing,maoyinian}@meituan.com

Abstract. Monocular Depth Estimation (MDE) is a task to predict a dense depth map from a single image. Despite the recent progress brought by deep learning, existing methods are still prone to errors due to the ill-posed nature of MDE. Hence depth estimation systems must be self-aware of possible mistakes to avoid disastrous consequences. This paper provides an uncertainty quantification method for supervised MDE models. From a frequentist view, we capture the uncertainty by predictive variance that consists of two terms: error variance and estimation variance. The former represents the noise of a depth value, and the latter measures the randomness in the depth regression model due to training on finite data. To estimate error variance, we perform constrained ordinal regression (ConOR) on discretized depth to estimate the conditional distribution of depth given image, and then compute the corresponding conditional mean and variance as the predicted depth and error variance estimator, respectively. Our work also leverages bootstrapping methods to infer estimation variance from re-sampled data. We perform experiments on both simulated and real data to validate the effectiveness of the proposed method. The results show that our approach produces accurate uncertainty estimates while maintaining high depth prediction accuracy. The code is available at https://github.com/timmy11hu/ConOR

Keywords: Monocular depth estimation · Frequentist uncertainty quantification · Constrained ordinal regression · Bootstrapping

1 Introduction

Estimating depth from 2D images has received much attention due to its vital role in various vision applications, such as autonomous driving [15] and

Supplementary Information The online version contains supplementary material available at https://doi.org/10.1007/978-3-031-20086-1_14.

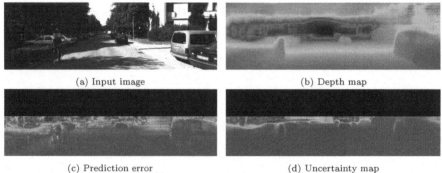

(a) Input image   (b) Depth map

(c) Prediction error   (d) Uncertainty map

Fig. 1. From a single input image (1a) we estimate depth (1b) and uncertainty (1d) maps. (1c) is the actual error as the difference between (1b) and ground truth. The black parts do not have ground truth depth value

augmented reality [41]. In the past decade, a variety of works have successfully addressed MDE by using supervised and self-supervised approaches [6,18,19,24,50,54,57,78]. Yet, the ill-posed nature of the task leads to more uncertainty in the depth distribution, resulting in error-prone models. In practice, overconfident incorrect predictions can be harmful or offensive; hence it is crucial for depth estimation algorithms to be self-aware of possible errors and provide trustworthy uncertainty information to assist decision making.

This work aims to estimate the uncertainty of a supervised single-image depth prediction model. From a frequentist perspective, we quantify the uncertainty of depth prediction by using the predictive variance, which can be decomposed into two terms: (i) error variance and (ii) estimation variance. Error variance describes the inherent uncertainty of the data, i.e. depth variations that the input image cannot explain, also known as aleatoric uncertainty [37]. Estimation variance arises from the randomness of the network parameters caused by training on finite data, which is conventionally called epistemic uncertainty [37].

One straightforward method to estimate the error variance is to predict the conditional variance as well as the expected depth value by optimizing the heteroskedastic Gaussian Likelihood (GL) with input-dependent variance parameters [65]. However, this approach often leads to unstable and slow training due to the potentially small variances for specific inputs. Moreover, directly regressing depth value on the input images has been shown sub-optimal prediction performance [6,24,25]. Alternatively, Yang et al. formulate MDE as a classification problem and measure the uncertainty by Shannon entropy [86]. However, the classification model also leads to sub-optimal prediction performance due to ignorance of the ordinal relation in depth. Moreover, there is a gap between Shannon entropy and the uncertainty of the regression model.

To estimate the error variance without sacrificing the prediction accuracy, we base our work on the deep ordinal regression (OR) model [24]. The original OR model was trained on discretized depth values with ordinal regression loss, which showed a significant boost in prediction accuracy compared to vanilla regression approaches. However, due to the discretization of depth, an optimal method to estimate the error variance for this model remains elusive. To tackle this problem, we take the advantage of the recent progress on distributional regression [54] to learn a likelihood-free conditional distribution by performing constrained ordinal regression (ConOR) on the discretized depth values. Compared to OR [24], ConOR guarantees the learning of conditional distributions of the original continuous depth given input images. Thus, we can take the expectation from the conditional distribution estimator as predicted depth, and the variance as the estimate of error variance.

Estimation variance is a long-standing problem in statistics and machine learning. If the model is simple, e.g. a linear model, one could easily construct confidence intervals of the parameters via asymptotic analysis. In our case, as the asymptotic theory for deep neural networks is still elusive, we leverage the idea of bootstrap to approximate the estimation variance by the sample variance of depth estimation calculated from re-sampled datasets. More specifically, we utilize two types of re-sampling schemes: Wild Bootstrap [84] (WBS) and Multiplier Bootstrap [10] (MBS). While the WBS performs re-weighting on the residuals to generate resamples, the MBS samples the weights that act as a multiplier of the training loss. To speed up training, we first train a single model on the entire training set and use the model parameters as initialization for training the bootstrap models. We evaluate our proposed method on both simulated and real datasets, using various metrics to demonstrate the effectiveness of our approach. Figure 1 shows the masked output of our uncertainty estimator, against the mistake made by our predicted depth.

2   Related Work

Monocular Depth Estimation. Early MDE approaches tackle the problem by applying hand-handcrafted filters to extract features [3,11,26,34,47,49,55, 69,73,74,76,88]. Since those features alone can only capture the local information, a Markov Random Field model is often trained in a supervised manner to estimate the depth value. Thanks to representation learning power of CNNs, recent approaches design various neural network architectures to estimate depth in an end-to-end manner [2,4,18,19,38,50,52,53,57,63,72,75,82,87]. Eigen et al. [19] formulate the problem as a supervised regression problem and propose a multi-scale network architecture. By applying recent progress in CNN technology, Laina et al. [50] solve the problem by using a reverse Huber loss and train a fully convolutional residual network with up-convolutional blocks to increase the output resolution. Cao et al. [6] address the problem as a classification problem and use a fully connected Conditional Random Fields to smooth the depth estimation. To utilize the ordinal nature of the discretized depth class, Fu et al. [24] formulate the problem as ordinal regression [23], and use a standard encoder-decoder architecture to get rid of previous costly up-sampling techniques. Their network consists of multiple heads, and each head solves a independent binary classification problem whether a pixel is either closer or further away from a certain depth threshold. However, the network does not output a valid distribution since the probabilities across the thresholds are not guaranteed to be monotonic.

Aside from supervised learning, many works try to eliminate the need for labeled data, as depth sensors are usually needed to obtain groundtruth depth. One direction is to use self-supervised learning, which takes a pair of images and estimate a disparity map for one of the images as an intermediate step to minimize the reconstruction loss [29,32,70,71,81,89]. Another direction is to consider depth estimation problem in a weakly-supervised manner by estimating the relative depth instead of the absolute metric value [7,9,25,56,61,85,90].

Uncertainty Quantification via Bayesian Inference. Uncertainty quantification is a fundamental problem in machine learning. There is a growing interest in quantifying the uncertainty of deep neural networks via Bayesian neural networks [8,43,58,83], as the Bayesian posterior naturally captures uncertainty. Despite the effectiveness in representing uncertainty, computation of the exact posterior is intractable in Bayesian deep neural networks. As a result, one must resort to approximate inference techniques, such as Markov Chain Monte Carlo [8,16,48,59,62,64] and Variational Inference [5,13,14,22,31,40,45,79]. To reduce computational complexity, Deep Ensemble [36,51] (DE) is proposed to sample multiple models as from the posterior distribution of network weights to estimate model uncertainty. In addition, the connection between Dropout and Bayesian inference is explored and results in the Monte Carlo Dropout [27,28] (MCD). Despite its efficiency, [21] points out that MCD changes the original Bayesian model; thus cannot be considered as approximate Bayesian inference.

Distributional Regression. Over the past few years, there has been increasing interest in distributional regression, which captures aspects of the response distribution beyond the mean [17,35,46,60,66,68]. Recently, Li et al. [54] propose a two-stage framework that estimates the conditional cumulative density function (CDF) of the response in neural networks. Their approach randomly discretizes the response space and obtains a finely discretized conditional distribution by combining an ensemble of random partition estimators. However, this method is not scalable to the deep CNNs used in MDE. Therefore, we modify their method to obtain a well-grounded conditional distribution estimator by using one single network with the Spacing-Increasing Discretization [24].

3   Method

To illustrate our method, we first show our formulation of the uncertainty as predictive variance and decompose it into error variance and estimation variance. We then introduce how to make prediction and estimate error variance via learning a conditional probability mass function (PMF) from a constrained ordinal regression (ConOR). Finally, we discuss how we infer estimation variance using re-sampling methods. Figure 2 demonstrate a brief idea of the training and testing phase of our method.

3.1 Uncertainty as Predictive Variance

Variance is commonly used in machine learning to measure uncertainty, which describes how far a set of real observations is dispersed from the expected value. To quantify how much uncertainty is in the depth prediction, for simplicity let us consider the depth prediction network as a general location-scale model [20]. We then formulate the model as:

$$y_i = g(x_i) + \sqrt{V(x_i)}\epsilon_i, \quad \text{for } i = 1, \ldots, n, \tag{1}$$

where x_i, y_i denote the feature and the response variable respectively, $g(x)$ stands for the mean function, ϵ_i represents the random errors with zero mean and unit variance, and $V(x)$ denotes the variance function. Suppose $\hat{g}$ is an estimator of g based on the training observations $\{(x_i, y_i)\}_{i=1}^n$. With x_* as a new input, the corresponding unknown response value is

$$y_* = g(x_*) + \sqrt{V(x_*)}\epsilon_*, \tag{2}$$

where ϵ_* is a random variable with zero mean and unit variance. Given the estimator $\hat{g}$, the value of y_* is predicted by $\hat{y}_* = \hat{g}(x_*)$, thus the predictive variance can be written as:

$$\text{Var}\left[y_* - \hat{y}_*\right] = \text{Var}\left[g(x_*) + \sqrt{V(x_*)}\epsilon_* - \hat{g}(x_*)\right]. \tag{3}$$

Since y_* is a new observation and $\hat{g}$ only depends on the training observations $\{(x_i, y_i)\}_{i=1}^n$, the random noise ϵ_* and $\hat{g}$ can be seen as independent. This gives

$$\text{Var}\left[y_* - \hat{y}_*\right] = \underbrace{V(x_*)}_{\text{error variance}} + \underbrace{\text{Var}\left[\hat{g}(x_*)\right]}_{\text{estimation variance}}. \tag{4}$$

The first component is known as error variance [12], and we refer to the second component as the estimation variance. Therefore, one can estimate two terms separately and quantify the total uncertainty by the summation of two terms. In the following sections, we present how to obtain their empirical estimators $\hat{V}(x_*)$ and $\widehat{\text{Var}}\left[\hat{g}(x_*)\right]$.

3.2 Constrained Ordinal Regression

Discretization. To learn a likelihood-free distribution, we first discretize continuous depth into discrete categories with ordinal nature. Considering that computer vision systems as well as humans are less capable of making precise prediction for large depths, we apply the Spacing-Increasing Discretization (SID) [24,25], which partitions the range of depth $[\alpha, \beta]$ uniformly on the log space by $K + 1$ thresholds $t_0 < t_1 < t_2 < \cdots < t_K$ into K bins, where

$$t_k = \exp\left[\log(\alpha) + k \log(\beta/\alpha)/K\right], \text{ for } k \in \{0, 1, \ldots, K\}. \tag{5}$$

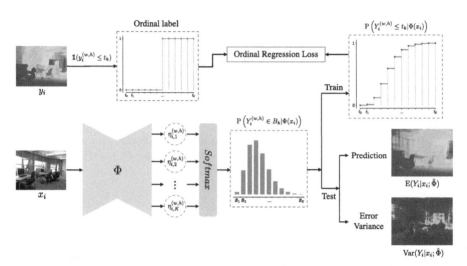

Fig. 2. Our approach first uses an encoder-decoder network Φ to extract pixel-wise features $\eta_i^{(w,h)}$ from input image x_i, and output the conditional PMF. During training, we obtain conditional CDF and construct an ordinal regression loss with the ground truth depth. In the test phase, we compute the expectation and variance from the conditional PMF estimator as depth prediction and error variance

Let $B_k = (t_{k-1}, t_k]$ denote the kth bin, for $k \in \{1, 2, \ldots, K\}$, we recast the problem to a discrete classification task that predicts the probability of pixel's depth falling into each bin. Let x_i denote an image of size $W \times H \times C$ and Φ indicate a feature extractor. The $W \times H \times K$ feature map obtained from the network can be written as $\eta_i = \Phi(x_i)$, and $\eta_i^{(w,h)}$ points to the features of (w, h) pixel. The conditional PMF, probabilities that $Y_i^{(w,h)}$ belongs to the kth bin, can be predicted by feeding K-dimensional feature $\eta_i^{(w,h)}$ into a softmax layer:

$$\mathrm{P}\left(Y_i^{(w,h)} \in B_k | \Phi(x_i)\right) = \frac{e^{\eta_{i,k}^{(w,h)}}}{\Sigma_{j=1}^K e^{\eta_{i,j}^{(w,h)}}}, \text{ for } k \in \{1, 2, \ldots, K\}, \qquad (6)$$

where $\eta_{i,k}^{(w,h)}$ represents the kth element of $\eta_i^{(w,h)}$ (also known as logits). The softmax normalization ensures the validity of output conditional distributions.

Learning. During the training, to incorporate the essential ordinal relationships among the discretized classes into the supervision, we obtain the conditional CDF in a staircase form by cumulatively summing the value of conditional PMF:

$$\mathrm{P}\left(Y_i^{(w,h)} \leq t_k | \Phi(x_i)\right) = \sum_{j=1}^k \mathrm{P}\left(Y_i^{(w,h)} \in B_j | \Phi(x_i)\right), \text{ for } k \in \{1, 2, \ldots, K\}.$$

$$(7)$$

This can be regarded as the probabilities of $Y_i^{(w,h)}$ less than or equal to the kth threshold. Given the ground truth depth value $y_i^{(w,h)}$, we construct an ordinal regression loss by solving a pixel-wise binary classification across K thresholds:

$$\ell\left(x_i, y_i^{(w,h)}, \varPhi\right) = -\sum_{k=1}^{K}\left\{\mathbb{1}\left(y_i^{(w,h)} \leq t_k\right)\log\left(\mathrm{P}(Y_i^{(w,h)} \leq t_k|\varPhi(x_i))\right)\right.$$
$$\left. + \left[1 - \mathbb{1}\left(y_i^{(w,h)} \leq t_k\right)\right]\left[1 - \log\left(\mathrm{P}(Y_i^{(w,h)} \leq t_k|\varPhi(x_i))\right)\right]\right\}, \quad (8)$$

where $\mathbb{1}$ is the indicator function. We optimize the network to minimize the ordinal regression loss over all the training examples with respective to $\varPhi$:

$$\mathcal{L}\left(\varPhi\right) = \sum_{i=1}^{n}\sum_{w=1}^{W}\sum_{h=1}^{H}\ell\left(x_i, y_i^{(w,h)}, \varPhi\right). \quad (9)$$

Prediction. After training, we obtain an estimator $\hat{\varPhi} = \arg\min_{\varPhi}\mathcal{L}\left(\varPhi\right)$. In the test phase, considering the multi-modal nature of the predicted distribution, given a new image x_*, for each pixel, we take the expectation of the conditional PMF as our prediction:

$$\hat{g}^{(w,h)}(x_*) = \mathrm{E}\left[Y_*^{(w,h)}|x_*;\hat{\varPhi}\right] = \sum_{k=1}^{K}\mu_k\mathrm{P}\left(Y_*^{(w,h)} \in B_k|\hat{\varPhi}(x_*)\right), \quad (10)$$

where $\mu_k = (t_{k-1}+t_k)/2$ is the expected value of kth bin. This gives a smoother depth prediction, compared to the hard bin assignment used by [24]. More importantly, the expected value suits well the following uncertainty inference using variance.

3.3   Error Variance Inference

The inherent variability of response value $Y_*^{(w,h)}$ comes from the noisy nature of the data, which is irreducible due to the randomness in the real world. While the expected value describes the central tendency of the depth distribution, the variance can provide information about the spread of predicted probability mass. Thus we use the variance from estimated conditional PMF to infer the variance of the response error:

$$\widehat{V}^{(w,h)}(x_*) = \mathrm{Var}\left[Y_*^{(w,h)}|x_*;\hat{\varPhi}\right] \quad (11)$$

$$= \sum_{k=1}^{K}\left(\mu_k - \mathrm{E}\left[Y_*^{(w,h)}|x_*;\hat{\varPhi}\right]\right)^2\mathrm{P}\left(Y_*^{(w,h)} \in B_k|\hat{\varPhi}(x_*)\right). \quad (12)$$

Hence our ConOR can predict the depth value together with error variance in the test phase.

3.4 Estimation Variance Inference

The second component, estimation variance, represents the discrepancy of our model prediction $\mathrm{E}\big[Y_*^{(w,h)} \mid x_*; \hat{\Phi}\big]$, which is usually caused by finite knowledge of training observations $\mathcal{D}$. Ideally, if we have the access to the entire population, given a model class Φ and M i.i.d. datasets $\{\mathcal{D}_m\}_{m=1}^M$, we can have M independent empirical estimators:

$$\hat{\Phi}_m = \underset{\Phi}{\operatorname{argmin}} \sum_{i=1}^n \sum_{w=1}^W \sum_{h=1}^H \ell\left(x_{m,i}, y_{m,i}^{(w,h)}, \Phi\right), \text{ for } m = 1, 2, \ldots, M, \quad (13)$$

where $(x_{m,i}, y_{m,i})$ represents ith training pair in $\mathcal{D}_m$. Then the estimation variance $\mathrm{Var}\big[\mathrm{E}[Y_*^{(w,h)}|x_*; \hat{\Phi}]\big]$ could be approximated by the sample variance of prediction from different estimators:

$$\frac{1}{M-1} \sum_{m=1}^M \left(\mathrm{E}\left[Y_*^{(w,h)}|x_*; \hat{\Phi}_m\right] - \frac{1}{M} \sum_{j=1}^M \mathrm{E}\left[Y_*^{(w,h)}|x_*; \hat{\Phi}_j\right]\right)^2. \quad (14)$$

However in practice, we cannot compute the estimation variance as we do not have a large number of datasets from the population. To address this problem, we adapt re-sampling methods. As a frequentist inference technique, bootstrapping a regression model gives insight into the empirical distribution of a function of the model parameters [84]. In our case, the predicted depth can be seen as a function of the network parameters. Thus we use the idea of bootstrap to achieve M empirical estimators $\{\hat{\Phi}_m\}_{m=1}^M$ and then use them to approximate $\mathrm{Var}\big[\mathrm{E}[Y_*^{(w,h)}|x_*; \hat{\Phi}]\big]$. To speed up training, we initialize the M models with the parameters of the single pre-trained model for prediction and error variance estimation. We discuss the details of the re-sampling approaches below.

Wild Bootstrap (WBS). The idea of Wild Bootstrap proposed by Wu et al. [84] is to keep the inputs x_i at their original value but re-sample the response variable $y_i^{(w,h)}$ based on the residuals values. Given $\hat{y}_i^{(w,h)} = \mathrm{E}[Y_i^{(w,h)}|x_i; \hat{\Phi}]$ as the fitted value, and $\hat{\epsilon}_i^{(w,h)} = y_i^{(w,h)} - \hat{y}_i^{(w,h)}$ as the residual, we re-sample a new response value for mth replicate based on

$$v_{m,i}^{(w,h)} = \hat{y}_i^{(w,h)} + \hat{\epsilon}_i^{(w,h)} \cdot \tau_{m,i}^{(w,h)}, \quad (15)$$

where $\tau_{m,i}^{(w,h)}$ is sampled from standard Gaussian distribution. For each replicate, we train the model on the new sampled training set:

$$\hat{\Phi}_m = \underset{\Phi}{\operatorname{argmin}} \sum_{i=1}^n \sum_{w=1}^W \sum_{h=1}^H \ell\left(x_i, v_{m,i}^{(w,h)}, \Phi\right), \text{ for } m = 1, 2, \ldots, M, \quad (16)$$

The overall procedure is outlined in Supplementary Material (SM) Sect. 1.

Multiplier Bootstrap (MBS). The idea the Multiplier Bootstrap [80] is to sample different weights used to multiply the individual loss of each observation. Here, we maintain the value of training data but re-construct the loss function for the mth replicate by putting different sampled weights across observations:

$$\hat{\Phi}_m = \underset{\Phi}{\mathrm{argmin}} \sum_{i=1}^{n} \sum_{w=1}^{W} \sum_{h=1}^{H} \omega_i^{(w,h)} \ell(x_i, y_i^{(w,h)}, \Phi), \text{ for } m = 1, 2, \ldots, M, \qquad (17)$$

where $\omega_i^{(w,h)}$ is the weight sampled from Gaussian distribution with unit mean and unit variance. Details are given in SM Sect. 1.

4 Experiment

To verify the validity of our method, we first conduct intuitive simulation experiments on toy datasets, by which we straightly compare our estimated uncertainty with the ground truth value. The qualitative and quantitative results can be found in SM Sect. 2. In this section, we evaluate on two real datasets, i.e., KITTI [30] and NYUv2 [77]. Some ablation studies are performed to give more detailed insights into our method.

4.1 Datasets

KITTI. The KITTI dataset [30] contains outdoor scenes (1–80 m) captured by the cameras and depth sensors in a driving vehicle. We follow Eigen's split [19] for training and testing, where the train set contains 23,488 images from 32 scenes and the test set has 697 images. The ground-truth depth maps improved from raw LIDAR are used for learning and evaluating. We train our model on a random crop of size 370×1224 and evaluate the result on a center crop of the same size with the depth range of 1 m to 80 m.

NYUv2. The NYU Depth v2 [77] dataset consists of video sequences from a variety of indoor scenes (0.5–10 m) and depth maps taken from the Microsoft Kinect. Following previous works [1,4], we train the models using a 50K subset, and test on the official 694 test images. The models are trained on a random crop size of 440×590 and tested based on the pre-defined center crop by [19] with the depth range of 0 m to 10 m.

4.2 Evaluation Metrics

The evaluation metrics of the depth prediction follow the previous works [19,57]. For the comparison of uncertainty estimation, as there is no ground truth label, we follow the idea of sparsification error [39]. That is, when pixels with the highest uncertainty are removed progressively, the error should decrease monotonically. Therefore, given an error metric ξ, we iteratively remove a subset (1%)

of pixels according to the descending order of estimated uncertainty and compute ξ on the remaining pixels to plot a curve. An ideal sparsification (oracle) is obtained by sorting pixels in descending order of true errors; hence we measure the difference between estimated and oracle sparsification by the Area Under the Sparsification Error (AUSE) [39]. We also calculate the Area Under the Random Gain (AURG) [67], which measures the difference between the estimated sparsification and a random sparsification without uncertainty modelling. We adopt root mean square error (rmse), absolute relative error (rel), and $1 - \delta_1$ as ξ. Both AUSE and AURG are normalized over the considered metrics to eliminate the factor of prediction accuracy, for the sake of fair comparison [39].

4.3   Implementation Details

We use ResNet-101 [33] and the encoder-decoder architecture proposed in [24] as our network backbone. We add a shift γ to both α and β so that $\alpha + \gamma = 1.0$, then apply SID on $[\alpha + \gamma, \beta + \gamma]$. We set α, β, γ to $1, 80, 0$ for KITTI [30] and $0, 10, 1$ for NYUv2 [77]. The batch size is set to 4 for KITTI [30] and 8 for NYUv2 [77]. The networks are optimized using Adam [44] with a learning rate of 0.0001 and trained for 10 epochs. We set our bootstrapping number to 20. To save computational time, we finetune the bootstrapping model for two epochs from the pre-trained model. This speedup yields only a subtle effect on the result.

For comparison, we implement Gaussian Likelihood (GL) and Log Gaussian Likelihood (LGL) for estimating the error variance and apply Monte Carlo Dropout (MCD) [28] and Deep Ensemble (DE) [51] for approximating estimation variance. Following previous works [42,51], we adapt MCD [28] and DE [51] on GL and LGL, which is designed under Bayesian framework. We also implement Gaussian and Log Gaussian in our framework with WBS and MBS. We incorporate a further comparison to the other methods that model the uncertainty on supervised monocular depth prediction, including Multiclass Classification [6,25] (MCC) and Binary Classification [86] (BC), applying the same depth discretization strategy as ours. Using softmax confidence (MCC) and entropy (BC) is generally seen as a total uncertainty [37], thus they are not adapted in any framework. We make sure the re-implemented models for comparison have an identical architecture to ours but only with a different prediction head.

4.4   Results

Table 1 and Table 2 give the results on KITTI [30] and NYUv2 [77], respectively. Here we only show three standard metrics of depth evaluation, more details can be found in SM Sect. 3.1. We put the plots of the parsification curve in SM Sect. 3.2. Firstly, our methods achieve the best result on the depth prediction in terms of all the metrics. Secondly, our methods outperform others in both AUSE and AURG. This strongly suggests that our predicted uncertainty has a better understanding of the error our model would make. The results show our method applies to both indoor and outdoor scenarios. Qualitative results are illustrated in Fig. 3 and Fig. 4, more results can be found in SM Sect. 3.3.

Table 1. Performance on KITTI

Method	Prediction			Uncertainty: AUSE(ξ) $\downarrow$			Uncertainty: AURG(ξ) $\uparrow$		
	rmse$\downarrow$	rel$\downarrow$	δ_1 $\uparrow$	rmse	rel	$1-\delta_1$	rmse	rel	$1-\delta_1$
MCC [6,25]	3.011	0.081	0.915	0.180	0.421	0.566	0.673	0.248	0.460
BC [86]	2.878	0.078	0.919	0.179	0.292	0.304	0.674	0.398	0.658
GL+MCD [28]	3.337	0.102	0.875	0.111	0.216	0.137	0.726	0.456	0.787
GL+DE [51]	2.900	0.089	0.908	0.100	0.233	0.131	0.751	0.447	0.829
GL+WBS	3.064	0.083	0.906	0.095	0.243	0.132	0.739	0.433	0.818
GL+MBS	3.064	0.083	0.906	0.096	0.242	0.131	0.739	0.435	0.817
LGL+MCD [28]	3.219	0.158	0.836	0.160	0.531	0.452	0.558	0.146	0.558
LGL+DE [51]	2.852	0.132	0.873	0.159	0.548	0.397	0.538	0.132	0.601
LGL+WBS	2.965	0.132	0.870	0.212	0.528	0.396	0.559	0.130	0.602
LGL+MBS	2.965	0.132	0.870	0.158	0.524	0.384	0.557	0.131	0.597
ConOR+WBS	**2.709**	**0.075**	**0.928**	0.095	0.181	0.107	**0.754**	0.500	0.849
ConOR+MBS	**2.709**	**0.075**	**0.928**	**0.094**	**0.180**	**0.106**	**0.754**	**0.501**	**0.851**

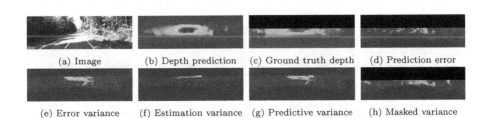

(a) Image   (b) Depth prediction   (c) Ground truth depth   (d) Prediction error

(e) Error variance   (f) Estimation variance   (g) Predictive variance   (h) Masked variance

Fig. 3. Depth prediction and uncertainty estimation on KITTI using ConOR and MBS. The masked variance is obtained from predictive variance. The black parts do not have ground truth depth in KITTI. Navy blue and crimson indicate lower and higher values respectively (Color figure online)

4.5 Ablation Studies

In this section, we study the effectiveness of modelling the error variance and the estimation variance. We first inspect the dominant uncertainty in our predictive variance, then illustrate the advantage of ConOR and analyze the performance between bootstrapping and previous Bayesian approaches. Lastly, we perform a sensitivity study of ConOR on KITTI [30].

Dominant Uncertainty. The uncertainty evaluation of our proposed method is based on the estimated predictive variance, which is composed of error variance and estimation variance. Table 3 reports the performance of uncertainty evaluation by applying different variances. We can notice that using predictive variance can achieve the best performance on AUSE and AURG for both datasets. In the predictive variance, the error variance is more influential than the estimation variance since its individual score is significantly close to the final scores of pre-

Table 2. Performance on NYUv2

Method	Prediction			Uncertainty: AUSE(ξ) ↓			Uncertainty: AURG(ξ) ↑		
	rmse↓	rel↓	δ_1 ↑	rmse	rel	$1 - \delta_1$	rmse	rel	$1 - \delta_1$
MCC [6,25]	3.658	1.518	0.017	0.341	0.817	0.437	−0.001	−0.422	−0.004
BC [86]	0.519	0.141	0.815	0.369	0.368	0.362	0.273	0.221	0.524
GL+MCD [28]	0.533	0.168	0.770	0.353	0.405	0.513	0.247	0.175	0.343
GL+DE [51]	0.503	0.158	0.790	0.333	0.367	0.418	0.258	0.205	0.450
GL+WBS	0.534	0.171	0.770	0.335	0.399	0.502	0.267	0.180	0.357
GL+MBS	0.534	0.171	0.770	0.333	0.393	0.487	0.269	0.186	0.372
LGL+MCD [28]	0.773	0.222	0.618	0.349	0.668	0.855	0.240	−0.140	−0.112
LGL+DE [51]	0.746	0.216	0.621	0.365	0.691	0.889	0.204	−0.164	−0.136
LGL+WBS	0.756	0.221	0.618	0.370	0.675	0.858	0.199	−0.149	−0.115
LGL+MBS	0.756	0.221	0.618	0.370	0.674	0.857	0.199	−0.149	−0.114
ConOR+WBS	**0.490**	**0.132**	**0.832**	**0.297**	**0.340**	**0.333**	**0.343**	**0.245**	**0.559**
ConOR+MBS	**0.490**	**0.132**	**0.832**	**0.297**	0.343	0.336	0.340	0.243	0.557

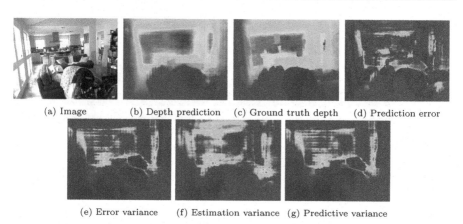

   (a) Image   (b) Depth prediction   (c) Ground truth depth   (d) Prediction error

     (e) Error variance   (f) Estimation variance (g) Predictive variance

Fig. 4. Depth prediction and uncertainty estimation on NYUv2 using ConOR and WBS. Navy blue and crimson indicate lower and higher values respectively (Color figure online)

dictive variance. This indicates that the error variance estimated by ConOR (aleatoric uncertainty) can already explain most of the predictive uncertainty, and our approach can further enhance the uncertainty understanding using re-sampling methods. This result is reasonable because the large sample size of KITTI [30] and NYUv2 [77] training set leads to low estimation variance.

ConOR. We then conduct a comparison between ConOR and other methods that capture the error variance. We also re-implement OR [25] for contrast by taking the variance from the estimated distribution. Although we observe the invalid CDFs from the OR model, our purpose is to investigate how the per-

Table 3. Comparison of uncertainty evaluation on ConOR applying different variance

Dataset	Variance	AUSE(ξ) ↓			AURG(ξ) ↑		
		rmse	rel	$1 - \delta_1$	rmse	rel	$1 - \delta_1$
KITTI	Error	0.097	0.184	0.109	0.751	0.496	0.846
	Estimation (WBS)	0.103	0.188	0.132	0.745	0.493	0.823
	Estimation (MBS)	0.101	0.183	0.120	0.745	0.498	0.835
	Predictive (w/ WBS)	0.095	0.181	0.107	**0.754**	0.500	0.849
	Predictive (w/ MBS)	**0.094**	**0.180**	**0.106**	**0.754**	**0.501**	**0.851**
NYUv2	Error	0.305	0.350	0.349	0.333	0.235	0.544
	Estimation (WBS)	0.340	0.370	0.415	0.297	0.215	0.478
	Estimation (MBS)	0.326	0.365	0.396	0.311	0.220	0.497
	Predictive (w/ WBS)	**0.297**	**0.340**	**0.333**	**0.343**	**0.245**	**0.559**
	Predictive (w/ MBS)	**0.297**	0.343	0.336	0.340	0.243	0.557

Table 4. Performance of different models for depth and error variance estimation

Dataset	Method	Prediction			AUSE(ξ) ↓			AURG(ξ) ↑		
		rmse ↓	rel ↓	δ_1 ↑	rmse	rel	$1 - \delta_1$	rmse	rel	$1 - \delta_1$
KITTI	GL	3.064	0.083	0.906	0.103	0.259	0.143	0.734	0.423	0.802
	LGL	2.965	0.132	0.870	0.157	0.540	0.427	0.557	0.135	0.602
	OR [24]	2.766	0.095	0.919	0.108	0.261	0.117	0.694	0.335	0.834
	ConOR	**2.709**	**0.075**	**0.928**	**0.097**	**0.184**	**0.109**	**0.751**	**0.496**	**0.846**
NYUv2	GL	0.534	0.171	0.770	0.344	0.413	0.528	0.258	0.167	0.330
	LGL	0.756	0.221	0.618	0.370	0.675	0.859	0.198	-0.150	-0.116
	OR [24]	0.509	0.146	0.814	0.314	0.392	0.411	0.289	0.172	0.468
	ConOR	**0.490**	**0.132**	**0.832**	**0.305**	**0.350**	**0.349**	**0.333**	**0.235**	**0.544**

formance is affected by the ill-grounded distribution estimator. Table 4 shows that ConOR yields the best performance in terms of both depth prediction and uncertainty estimation. Moreover, ConOR surpasses OR by a large margin on the uncertainty evaluation, which indicates the significance to make statistical inference based on a valid conditional distribution.

Bootstrapping. To analyze the strength of bootstrapping methods, we also apply ConOR under other frameworks i.e. MCD [28] and DE [51]. From Table 5 we can conclude that, compared to the baseline ConOR, MCD [28] does not provide correct estimation variance as the performance of uncertainty evaluation slightly decreases. DE [51] can improve some of the metrics for the uncertainty estimation. By using bootstrapping methods our predictive variance learns a

Table 5. Comparison of different methods to capture the estimation variance of ConOR

Dataset	Method	AUSE(ξ) $\downarrow$			AURG(ξ) $\uparrow$		
		rmse	rel	$1-\delta_1$	rmse	rel	$1-\delta_1$
KITTI	ConOR	0.097	0.184	0.109	0.751	0.496	0.846
	ConOR+MCD	0.104	0.185	0.128	0.740	0.499	0.814
	ConOR+DE	0.096	0.181	0.112	0.749	0.500	0.848
	ConOR+WBS	0.095	0.181	0.107	**0.754**	0.500	0.849
	ConOR+MBS	**0.094**	**0.180**	**0.106**	**0.754**	**0.501**	**0.851**
NYUv2	ConOR	0.305	0.350	0.349	0.333	0.235	0.544
	ConOR+MCD	0.305	0.351	0.350	0.331	0.233	0.542
	ConOR+DE	0.303	0.351	0.343	0.327	0.229	0.557
	ConOR+WBS	**0.297**	**0.340**	**0.333**	**0.343**	**0.245**	**0.559**
	ConOR+MBS	**0.297**	0.343	0.336	0.340	0.243	0.557

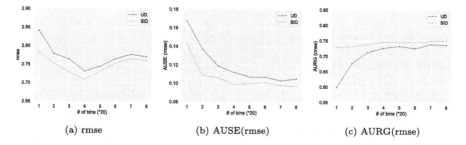

(a) rmse   (b) AUSE(rmse)   (c) AURG(rmse)

Fig. 5. Performance of UD and SID with a range of different bin numbers on KITTI (Color figure online)

better estimation variance approximation since all the metrics of uncertainty estimation have been boosted.

Discretization. To examine the sensitivity of ConOR to the discretization strategy, we compare SID with another common scheme, uniform discretization (UD), and apply the partition with a various number of bins. In Fig. 5, we can see that SID can improve the performance of both prediction and uncertainty estimation on ConOR. In addition, ConOR is robust to a large span of bin numbers regarding the prediction accuracy since the rmse ranges between 2.7 and 2.8 (orange line in Fig. 5a). We also find that increasing the number of bins tends to boost the performance of uncertainty estimation (Fig. 5b and 5c) due to a more finely-discretized distribution estimator. However, excessively increasing the bin number leads to diminishing returns but adds more computational burden. Hence, it is better to fit more bins within the computational budget.

5   Conclusions

In this paper, we have explored uncertainty modelling in supervised monocular depth estimation from a frequentist perspective. We have proposed a framework to quantify the uncertainty of depth prediction models by predictive variance which can be estimated by the aggregation of error variance and estimation variance. Moreover, we have developed a method to predict the depth value and error variance using a conditional distribution estimator learned from the constrained ordinal regression (ConOR) and approximated the estimation variance by performing bootstrapping on our model. Our approach has shown promising performance regarding both uncertainty and prediction accuracy.

Acknowledgments. This research was mainly undertaken using the LIEF HPC-GPGPU Facility hosted at the University of Melbourne. This Facility was established with the assistance of LIEF Grant LE170100200. This work was partially supported by the NCI Adapter Scheme, with computational resources provided by NCI Australia, an NCRIS-enabled capability supported by the Australian Government. This research was also partially supported by the Research Computing Services NCI Access scheme at The University of Melbourne. MG was supported by ARC DE210101624.

References

1. Alhashim, I., Wonka, P.: High quality monocular depth estimation via transfer learning. arXiv preprint arXiv:1812.11941 (2018)
2. Alp Guler, R., Trigeorgis, G., Antonakos, E., Snape, P., Zafeiriou, S., Kokkinos, I.: DenseReg: fully convolutional dense shape regression in-the-wild. In: Proceedings of the IEEE Conference on Computer Vision and Pattern Recognition, pp. 6799–6808 (2017)
3. Baig, M.H., Torresani, L.: Coupled depth learning. In: 2016 IEEE Winter Conference on Applications of Computer Vision (WACV), pp. 1–10. IEEE (2016)
4. Bhat, S.F., Alhashim, I., Wonka, P.: AdaBins: depth estimation using adaptive bins. In: Proceedings of the IEEE/CVF Conference on Computer Vision and Pattern Recognition, pp. 4009–4018 (2021)
5. Blundell, C., Cornebise, J., Kavukcuoglu, K., Wierstra, D.: Weight uncertainty in neural network. In: International Conference on Machine Learning, pp. 1613–1622. PMLR (2015)
6. Cao, Y., Wu, Z., Shen, C.: Estimating depth from monocular images as classification using deep fully convolutional residual networks. IEEE Trans. Circuits Syst. Video Technol. **28**(11), 3174–3182 (2017)
7. Cao, Z., Qin, T., Liu, T.Y., Tsai, M.F., Li, H.: Learning to rank: from pairwise approach to listwise approach. In: Proceedings of the 24th International Conference on Machine Learning, pp. 129–136 (2007)
8. Chen, T., Fox, E., Guestrin, C.: Stochastic gradient Hamiltonian monte Carlo. In: International Conference on Machine Learning, pp. 1683–1691. PMLR (2014)
9. Chen, W., Fu, Z., Yang, D., Deng, J.: Single-image depth perception in the wild. Adv. Neural. Inf. Process. Syst. **29**, 730–738 (2016)
10. Chen, X., Zhou, W.X.: Robust inference via multiplier bootstrap. Ann. Stat. **48**(3), 1665–1691 (2020)

11. Choi, S., Min, D., Ham, B., Kim, Y., Oh, C., Sohn, K.: Depth analogy: data-driven approach for single image depth estimation using gradient samples. IEEE Trans. Image Process. **24**(12), 5953–5966 (2015)
12. Colman, A.M.: A Dictionary of Psychology. Oxford University Press, USA (2015)
13. Dadaneh, S.Z., Boluki, S., Yin, M., Zhou, M., Qian, X.: Pairwise supervised hashing with Bernoulli variational auto-encoder and self-control gradient estimator. In: Conference on Uncertainty in Artificial Intelligence, pp. 540–549. PMLR (2020)
14. Daxberger, E., Hernández-Lobato, J.M.: Bayesian variational autoencoders for unsupervised out-of-distribution detection. arXiv preprint arXiv:1912.05651 (2019)
15. Dijk, T.V., Croon, G.D.: How do neural networks see depth in single images? In: Proceedings of the IEEE/CVF International Conference on Computer Vision, pp. 2183–2191 (2019)
16. Ding, N., Fang, Y., Babbush, R., Chen, C., Skeel, R.D., Neven, H.: Bayesian sampling using stochastic gradient thermostats. In: Advances in Neural Information Processing Systems, vol. 27 (2014)
17. Duan, T., Anand, A., Ding, D.Y., Thai, K.K., Basu, S., Ng, A., Schuler, A.: Ngboost: Natural gradient boosting for probabilistic prediction. In: International Conference on Machine Learning. pp. 2690–2700. PMLR (2020)
18. Eigen, D., Fergus, R.: Predicting depth, surface normals and semantic labels with a common multi-scale convolutional architecture. In: Proceedings of the IEEE International Conference on Computer Vision, pp. 2650–2658 (2015)
19. Eigen, D., Puhrsch, C., Fergus, R.: Depth map prediction from a single image using a multi-scale deep network. arXiv preprint arXiv:1406.2283 (2014)
20. Fan, J., Gijbels, I.: Local Polynomial Modelling and Its Applications. Routledge, London (2018)
21. Folgoc, L.L., et al.: Is mc dropout Bayesian? arXiv preprint arXiv:2110.04286 (2021)
22. Fortunato, M., Blundell, C., Vinyals, O.: Bayesian recurrent neural networks. arXiv preprint arXiv:1704.02798 (2017)
23. Frank, E., Hall, M.: A simple approach to ordinal classification. In: De Raedt, L., Flach, P. (eds.) ECML 2001. LNCS (LNAI), vol. 2167, pp. 145–156. Springer, Heidelberg (2001). https://doi.org/10.1007/3-540-44795-4_13
24. Fu, H., Gong, M., Wang, C., Batmanghelich, K., Tao, D.: Deep ordinal regression network for monocular depth estimation. In: Proceedings of the IEEE Conference on Computer Vision and Pattern Recognition, pp. 2002–2011 (2018)
25. Fu, H., Gong, M., Wang, C., Tao, D.: A compromise principle in deep monocular depth estimation. arXiv preprint arXiv:1708.08267 (2017)
26. Furukawa, R., Sagawa, R., Kawasaki, H.: Depth estimation using structured light flow-analysis of projected pattern flow on an object's surface. In: Proceedings of the IEEE International Conference on Computer Vision, pp. 4640–4648 (2017)
27. Gal, Y., Ghahramani, Z.: Bayesian convolutional neural networks with Bernoulli approximate variational inference. arXiv preprint arXiv:1506.02158 (2015)
28. Gal, Y., Ghahramani, Z.: Dropout as a Bayesian approximation: representing model uncertainty in deep learning. In: International Conference on Machine Learning, pp. 1050–1059. PMLR (2016)
29. Garg, R., B.G., V.K., Carneiro, G., Reid, I.: Unsupervised CNN for single view depth estimation: geometry to the rescue. In: Leibe, B., Matas, J., Sebe, N., Welling, M. (eds.) ECCV 2016. LNCS, vol. 9912, pp. 740–756. Springer, Cham (2016). https://doi.org/10.1007/978-3-319-46484-8_45
30. Geiger, A., Lenz, P., Stiller, C., Urtasun, R.: Vision meets robotics: the KITTI dataset. Int. J. Robot. Res. **32**(11), 1231–1237 (2013)

31. Ghosh, P., Sajjadi, M.S., Vergari, A., Black, M., Schölkopf, B.: From variational to deterministic autoencoders. arXiv preprint arXiv:1903.12436 (2019)
32. Godard, C., Mac Aodha, O., Brostow, G.J.: Unsupervised monocular depth estimation with left-right consistency. In: Proceedings of the IEEE Conference on Computer Vision and Pattern Recognition, pp. 270–279 (2017)
33. He, K., Zhang, X., Ren, S., Sun, J.: Deep residual learning for image recognition. In: Proceedings of the IEEE Conference on Computer Vision and Pattern Recognition, pp. 770–778 (2016)
34. Hoiem, D., Efros, A.A., Hebert, M.: Recovering surface layout from an image. Int. J. Comput. Vision **75**(1), 151–172 (2007). https://doi.org/10.1007/s11263-006-0031-y
35. Hothorn, T., Zeileis, A.: Transformation forests. arXiv preprint arXiv:1701.02110 (2017)
36. Huang, G., Li, Y., Pleiss, G., Liu, Z., Hopcroft, J.E., Weinberger, K.Q.: Snapshot ensembles: train 1, get m for free. arXiv preprint arXiv:1704.00109 (2017)
37. Hüllermeier, E., Waegeman, W.: Aleatoric and epistemic uncertainty in machine learning: an introduction to concepts and methods. Mach. Learn. **110**(3), 457–506 (2021). https://doi.org/10.1007/s10994-021-05946-3
38. Huynh, L., Nguyen-Ha, P., Matas, J., Rahtu, E., Heikkilä, J.: Guiding monocular depth estimation using depth-attention volume. In: Vedaldi, A., Bischof, H., Brox, T., Frahm, J.-M. (eds.) ECCV 2020. LNCS, vol. 12371, pp. 581–597. Springer, Cham (2020). https://doi.org/10.1007/978-3-030-58574-7_35
39. Ilg, E., et al.: Uncertainty estimates and multi-hypotheses networks for optical flow. In: Proceedings of the European Conference on Computer Vision (ECCV), pp. 652–667 (2018)
40. Jin, L., Lu, H., Wen, G.: Fast uncertainty quantification of reservoir simulation with variational U-Net. arXiv preprint arXiv:1907.00718 (2019)
41. Kalia, M., Navab, N., Salcudean, T.: A real-time interactive augmented reality depth estimation technique for surgical robotics. In: 2019 International Conference on Robotics and Automation (ICRA), pp. 8291–8297. IEEE (2019)
42. Kendall, A., Badrinarayanan, V., Cipolla, R.: Bayesian segNet: model uncertainty in deep convolutional encoder-decoder architectures for scene understanding. arXiv preprint arXiv:1511.02680 (2015)
43. Kendall, A., Gal, Y.: What uncertainties do we need in Bayesian deep learning for computer vision? arXiv preprint arXiv:1703.04977 (2017)
44. Kingma, D.P., Ba, J.: Adam: a method for stochastic optimization. arXiv preprint arXiv:1412.6980 (2014)
45. Kingma, D.P., Welling, M.: Auto-encoding variational Bayes. arXiv preprint arXiv:1312.6114 (2013)
46. Klein, N., Nott, D.J., Smith, M.S.: Marginally calibrated deep distributional regression. J. Comput. Graph. Stat. **30**(2), 467–483 (2021)
47. Konrad, J., Wang, M., Ishwar, P., Wu, C., Mukherjee, D.: Learning-based, automatic 2D-to-3D image and video conversion. IEEE Trans. Image Process. **22**(9), 3485–3496 (2013)
48. Kupinski, M.A., Hoppin, J.W., Clarkson, E., Barrett, H.H.: Ideal-observer computation in medical imaging with use of Markov-chain monte Carlo techniques. JOSA A **20**(3), 430–438 (2003)
49. Ladicky, L., Shi, J., Pollefeys, M.: Pulling things out of perspective. In: Proceedings of the IEEE Conference on Computer Vision and Pattern Recognition, pp. 89–96 (2014)

50. Laina, I., Rupprecht, C., Belagiannis, V., Tombari, F., Navab, N.: Deeper depth prediction with fully convolutional residual networks. In: 2016 Fourth International Conference on 3D Vision (3DV), pp. 239–248. IEEE (2016)

51. Lakshminarayanan, B., Pritzel, A., Blundell, C.: Simple and scalable predictive uncertainty estimation using deep ensembles. arXiv preprint arXiv:1612.01474 (2016)

52. Lee, J.H., Han, M.K., Ko, D.W., Suh, I.H.: From big to small: multi-scale local planar guidance for monocular depth estimation. arXiv preprint arXiv:1907.10326 (2019)

53. Li, J., Klein, R., Yao, A.: A two-streamed network for estimating fine-scaled depth maps from single RGB images. In: Proceedings of the IEEE International Conference on Computer Vision, pp. 3372–3380 (2017)

54. Li, R., Reich, B.J., Bondell, H.D.: Deep distribution regression. Comput. Stat. Data Anal. **159**, 107203 (2021)

55. Li, X., Qin, H., Wang, Y., Zhang, Y., Dai, Q.: DEPT: depth estimation by parameter transfer for single still images. In: Cremers, D., Reid, I., Saito, H., Yang, M.-H. (eds.) ACCV 2014. LNCS, vol. 9004, pp. 45–58. Springer, Cham (2015). https://doi.org/10.1007/978-3-319-16808-1_4

56. Lienen, J., Hullermeier, E., Ewerth, R., Nommensen, N.: Monocular depth estimation via listwise ranking using the plackett-luce model. In: Proceedings of the IEEE/CVF Conference on Computer Vision and Pattern Recognition, pp. 14595–14604 (2021)

57. Liu, F., Shen, C., Lin, G., Reid, I.: Learning depth from single monocular images using deep convolutional neural fields. IEEE Trans. Pattern Anal. Mach. Intell. **38**(10), 2024–2039 (2015)

58. MacKay, D.J.: A practical Bayesian framework for backpropagation networks. Neural Comput. **4**(3), 448–472 (1992)

59. McClure, P., Kriegeskorte, N.: Representing inferential uncertainty in deep neural networks through sampling (2016)

60. Meinshausen, N., Ridgeway, G.: Quantile regression forests. J. Mach. Learn. Res. **7**(6) (2006)

61. Mertan, A., Sahin, Y.H., Duff, D.J., Unal, G.: A new distributional ranking loss with uncertainty: illustrated in relative depth estimation. In: 2020 International Conference on 3D Vision (3DV), pp. 1079–1088. IEEE (2020)

62. Nair, T., Precup, D., Arnold, D.L., Arbel, T.: Exploring uncertainty measures in deep networks for multiple sclerosis lesion detection and segmentation. Med. Image Anal. **59**, 101557 (2020)

63. Narihira, T., Maire, M., Yu, S.X.: Learning lightness from human judgement on relative reflectance. In: Proceedings of the IEEE Conference on Computer Vision and Pattern Recognition, pp. 2965–2973 (2015)

64. Neal, R.M.: Bayesian Learning for Neural Networks, vol. 118. Springer, Cham (2012)

65. Nix, D.A., Weigend, A.S.: Estimating the mean and variance of the target probability distribution. In: Proceedings of 1994 IEEE International Conference on Neural Networks (ICNN 1994), vol. 1, pp. 55–60. IEEE (1994)

66. O'Malley, M., Sykulski, A.M., Lumpkin, R., Schuler, A.: Multivariate probabilistic regression with natural gradient boosting. arXiv preprint arXiv:2106.03823 (2021)

67. Poggi, M., Aleotti, F., Tosi, F., Mattoccia, S.: On the uncertainty of self-supervised monocular depth estimation. In: Proceedings of the IEEE/CVF Conference on Computer Vision and Pattern Recognition, pp. 3227–3237 (2020)

68. Pospisil, T., Lee, A.B.: Rfcde: random forests for conditional density estimation. arXiv preprint arXiv:1804.05753 (2018)
69. Ranftl, R., Vineet, V., Chen, Q., Koltun, V.: Dense monocular depth estimation in complex dynamic scenes. In: Proceedings of the IEEE Conference on Computer Vision and Pattern Recognition, pp. 4058–4066 (2016)
70. Ranjan, A., et al.: Competitive collaboration: joint unsupervised learning of depth, camera motion, optical flow and motion segmentation. In: Proceedings of the IEEE/CVF Conference on Computer Vision and Pattern Recognition, pp. 12240–12249 (2019)
71. Ren, Z., Lee, Y.J.: Cross-domain self-supervised multi-task feature learning using synthetic imagery. In: Proceedings of the IEEE Conference on Computer Vision and Pattern Recognition, pp. 762–771 (2018)
72. Roy, A., Todorovic, S.: Monocular depth estimation using neural regression forest. In: Proceedings of the IEEE Conference on Computer Vision and Pattern Recognition, pp. 5506–5514 (2016)
73. Saxena, A., Sun, M., Ng, A.Y.: Make3D: Learning 3D scene structure from a single still image. IEEE Trans. Pattern Anal. Mach. Intell. **31**(5), 824–840 (2008)
74. Scharstein, D., Szeliski, R.: A taxonomy and evaluation of dense two-frame stereo correspondence algorithms. Int. J. Comput. Vision **47**(1), 7–42 (2002)
75. Shashua, A., Levin, A.: Ranking with large margin principle: two approaches. In: Advances in Neural Information Processing Systems, vol. 15 (2002)
76. Shi, J., Tao, X., Xu, L., Jia, J.: Break ames room illusion: depth from general single images. ACM Trans. Graph. (TOG) **34**(6), 1–11 (2015)
77. Silberman, N., Hoiem, D., Kohli, P., Fergus, R.: Indoor segmentation and support inference from RGBD images. In: Fitzgibbon, A., Lazebnik, S., Perona, P., Sato, Y., Schmid, C. (eds.) ECCV 2012. LNCS, vol. 7576, pp. 746–760. Springer, Heidelberg (2012). https://doi.org/10.1007/978-3-642-33715-4_54
78. Song, M., Lim, S., Kim, W.: Monocular depth estimation using Laplacian pyramid-based depth residuals. IEEE Trans. Circ. Syst. Video Technol. (2021)
79. Swiatkowski, J., et al.: The k-tied normal distribution: a compact parameterization of gaussian mean field posteriors in Bayesian neural networks. In: International Conference on Machine Learning, pp. 9289–9299. PMLR (2020)
80. Wellner, J.: Weak Convergence and Empirical Processes: With Applications to Statistics. Springer, Heidelbrg (1996)
81. Wang, C., Buenaposada, J.M., Zhu, R., Lucey, S.: Learning depth from monocular videos using direct methods. In: Proceedings of the IEEE Conference on Computer Vision and Pattern Recognition, pp. 2022–2030 (2018)
82. Wang, X., Fouhey, D., Gupta, A.: Designing deep networks for surface normal estimation. In: Proceedings of the IEEE Conference on Computer Vision and Pattern Recognition, pp. 539–547 (2015)
83. Welling, M., Teh, Y.W.: Bayesian learning via stochastic gradient Langevin dynamics. In: Proceedings of the 28th International Conference on Machine Learning (ICML-11), pp. 681–688. Citeseer (2011)
84. Wu, C.F.J.: Jackknife, bootstrap and other resampling methods in regression analysis. Ann. Stat. **14**(4), 1261–1295 (1986)
85. Xian, K., Zhang, J., Wang, O., Mai, L., Lin, Z., Cao, Z.: Structure-guided ranking loss for single image depth prediction. In: Proceedings of the IEEE/CVF Conference on Computer Vision and Pattern Recognition, pp. 611–620 (2020)
86. Yang, G., Hu, P., Ramanan, D.: Inferring distributions over depth from a single image. In: 2019 IEEE/RSJ International Conference on Intelligent Robots and Systems (IROS), pp. 6090–6096. IEEE (2019)

87. Zhang, Z., Schwing, A.G., Fidler, S., Urtasun, R.: Monocular object instance segmentation and depth ordering with CNNs. In: Proceedings of the IEEE International Conference on Computer Vision, pp. 2614–2622 (2015)
88. Zhou, H., Ummenhofer, B., Brox, T.: Deeptam: Deep tracking and mapping. In: Proceedings of the European conference on computer vision (ECCV), pp. 822–838 (2018)
89. Zhou, T., Brown, M., Snavely, N., Lowe, D.G.: Unsupervised learning of depth and ego-motion from video. In: Proceedings of the IEEE Conference on Computer Vision and Pattern Recognition, pp. 1851–1858 (2017)
90. Zoran, D., Isola, P., Krishnan, D., Freeman, W.T.: Learning ordinal relationships for mid-level vision. In: Proceedings of the IEEE International Conference on Computer Vision, pp. 388–396 (2015)

CostDCNet: Cost Volume Based Depth Completion for a Single RGB-D Image

Jaewon Kam⬭, Jungeon Kim⬭, Soongjin Kim⬭, Jaesik Park⬭, and Seungyong Lee(✉)⬭

POSTECH, Pohang-si, South Korea
{jwkam95,jungeonkim,kimsj0302,jaesik.park,leesy}@postech.ac.kr

Abstract. Successful depth completion from a single RGB-D image requires both extracting plentiful 2D and 3D features and merging these heterogeneous features appropriately. We propose a novel depth completion framework, *CostDCNet*, based on the cost volume-based depth estimation approach that has been successfully employed for multi-view stereo (MVS). The key to high-quality depth map estimation in the approach is constructing an accurate cost volume. To produce a quality cost volume tailored to single-view depth completion, we present a simple but effective architecture that can fully exploit the 3D information, three options to make an RGB-D feature volume, and per-plane pixel shuffle for efficient volume upsampling. Our *CostDCNet* framework consists of lightweight deep neural networks (∼1.8M parameters), running in real time (∼30 ms). Nevertheless, thanks to our simple but effective design, *CostDCNet* demonstrates depth completion results comparable to or better than the state-of-the-art methods.

Keywords: Depth completion · Cost volume · 3D convolution · Single RGB-D image

1 Introduction

Recently, RGB-D cameras have been widely used in many applications that need 3D geometry information, such as augmented reality (AR), virtual reality (VR), autonomous driving, and robotics. However, various depth sensors, including LiDAR, Kinect, and RealSense, suffer from missing measurements. Depth completion is the task of filling missing areas in depth images obtained from sensors (Fig. 1).

Learning-based depth completion methods mainly employ 2D convolutions to extract RGB and depth feature maps from an input RGB-D image, regarding the depth image as a 2D image. Then, they fuse two heterogeneous 2D feature maps

Supplementary Information The online version contains supplementary material available at https://doi.org/10.1007/978-3-031-20086-1_15.

S. Avidan et al. (Eds.): ECCV 2022, LNCS 13662, pp. 257–274, 2022.
https://doi.org/10.1007/978-3-031-20086-1_15

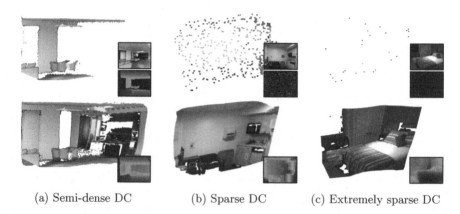

(a) Semi-dense DC   (b) Sparse DC   (c) Extremely sparse DC

Fig. 1. Our results of depth completion for three different types of input depth. The top row visualizes the input RGB-D images and their colored point clouds, and the bottom row shows our completed depth images and their colored point clouds.

in the 2D feature space to infer a completed depth image [2,18,25,26,31,33]. However, these 2D convolutions do not directly consider depth-axis information of 3D positions. To fully exploit the 3D geometry information, 3D convolutions could be an alternative, but naïvely applying standard 3D convolutions to input 3D points would be inappropriate due to their sparsity and irregularity.

Multi-view stereo (MVS) and stereo matching methods that use deep neural networks have taken a cost volume concept to infer depth by considering 3D spatial information [13,14,37,45]. These methods have shown compelling depth estimation accuracy. In the methods, a cost volume is constructed in the multiple-depth-plane representation (Fig. 3b), and is commonly regarded as containing matching costs between RGB images captured at different viewpoints. Inspired by MVS, some single-view depth completion methods using a cost volume have been proposed [22,25]. They use 2D convolutional neural networks (CNNs) to directly predict the cost volume from a single RGB-D input. However, the predicted cost volume is produced only using cascaded 2D convolutions that cannot properly utilize 3D information from the input depth.

In this paper, we propose a cost volume based depth completion network (CostDCNet) that can fully exploit 3D information by performing 3D convolutions of heterogeneous 2D and 3D features in the multiple-depth-plane representation. Our method is basically based on the cost volume-based depth estimation framework in the MVS domain. However, unlike aforementioned depth completion methods [22,25] that use multiple depth planes to represent an inferred depth, our framework uses multiple depth planes as a representation for a volume to be convolved. This approach enables our framework to use 3D convolutions like existing MVS studies. To infer a cost volume, MVS methods need an input feature volume that is commonly constructed by aggregating 2D feature maps of RGB images at multiple viewpoints. Similarly, our framework also requires a feature volume to generate a cost volume. We present three viable options to construct the feature volume, called an RGB-D feature volume, from a single RGB-D image. We experimentally showed that a proper design choice of an RGB-D feature volume is vital to produce a quality cost volume, consequently resulting in the high-quality completed depth. Various methods, including MVS, that rely on 3D convolutions typically suffer from memory and computational complexity due to the volume data usage. To handle the problem, we adopt an approach to process low-resolution volumes and then to upsample them. For such volume upsampling, we use an adapted version of pixel shuffle [38], which we call per-plane pixel shuffle, that increases volume resolution by rearranging its feature values along spatial dimensions. The upsampling scheme performs only rearrangement operations, so it works in highly memory- and computation-efficient manner.

Our *CostDCNet* framework consists of three parts: (1) construction of RGB-D feature volume from RGB-D image, (2) prediction of cost volume by a modified 3D UNet, (3) final completed depth regression. Due to our effective network design that can exploit 3D geometry and RGB information both fully and collectively, our *CostDCNet*, albeit using the small number of network parameters ($\sim$1.8M), outperforms or is comparable to state-of-the-art (SOTA) methods on both semi-dense and sparse depth datasets. Our codes are publicly available[1].

To summarize, our key contributions are as follows:

- We propose a single-view depth completion method that is based on but adapted from the cost volume-based depth estimation pipeline in the multi-view stereo (MVS) field.
- The proposed method can fully exploit heterogeneous 2D and 3D features of an input RGB-D image due to our scheme for producing RGB-D feature volume from a single RGB-D image, the multiple-depth-plane representation, and 3D convolution operation in the representation.
- We propose the depth completion framework, *CostDCNet*, that is merely composed of lightweight CNNs ($\sim$1.8M parameters) and our efficient volume upsampling module without any complex architecture.
- Due to our highly effective and efficient network design, *CostDCNet* runs in real time ($\sim$30 ms) and achieves qualitative and quantitative results that are better than or comparable to SOTA methods in both semi-dense and sparse depth datasets.

2   Related Work

We review representative approaches that are closely related to the technical components in our framework.

Depth Completion. We classify depth completion studies that use a single RGB-D image as input into two classes according to the sparsity of the input

---

[1] https://github.com/kamse/CostDCNet.

depth that they target: semi-dense depth completion and sparse depth completion. We firstly review studies on semi-dense depth completion.

Zhang et al. [48] predicted surface normals and occlusion boundaries by using two 2D CNNs, then conducted global linear optimization to obtain completed depth. Using the surface normals and occlusion boundaries predicted by Zhang et al., Huang et al. [18] adopted a self-attention mechanism to conserve and sharpen structures in the inferred depth image. These methods train their models in a supervised manner by using rendered depth from 3D reconstructed scenes as ground truth (GT). However, the poor 3D reconstruction quality leads to inaccurate GT depth images. To avoid this problem, Cao et al. [2] introduced an adaptive sampling strategy for self-supervised training to simulate missing depths in the capturing process. They trained their model with self-supervision but showed comparable results to the supervised methods.

Early sparse depth completion studies that use deep learning regarded a depth image as a 2D image and used 2D CNNs that took a typical encoder-decoder architecture with minor variations [27,31]. A few advanced methods focused on effectively extracting and fusing multi-modal features from RGB-D image [11,41,49]. Several methods that use spatial propagation networks (SPN) [5,6,33] iteratively refine initial depth regression by using affinity kernels. These methods that use 2D CNNs show highly encouraging results, but they require a large number of network parameters and might rely on pretrained models from other tasks. Rather than regarding depth images as 2D images, some methods [4,19] attempted to consider 3D geometry information explicitly, by consolidating 2D and 3D features. To extract 3D features from an input depth, they used point cloud convolutions [1,42]. However, in their methods, 3D spatial information is not fully utilized because they applied 3D convolutions only to valid pixels in depth. In addition, the methods are not suitable for semi-dense or dense depth, because they search neighbors by using the k-NN algorithm, which slows down as the number of input points increases.

In this paper, our proposed method can process both semi-dense and sparse depth completion classes, and provides comparable or better results than SOTA methods in both classes. It can fully exploit 3D geometry and context information by aggregating 2D and 3D features in a volumetric manner.

Cost Volume Based Depth Regression. Multi-view depth estimation approaches, such as stereo matching and MVS, have been studied for inferring depth from two or multiple views. They usually build a cost volume, which contains the matching costs of all pixels computed for all possible disparities, to predict the depth. Various matching costs, such as sum of absolute difference (SAD), sum of squared difference (SSD), and normalized cross-correlation (NCC), have been used for building a cost volume. Matching costs have also been computed using deep neural networks [30,46] due to the robustness. Recent methods [13,14,37,47] aggregate the cost volume with a 3D CNN. However, since 3D convolution requires high amount of computation, it is not easy to operate in real time.

Inspired by MVS works, some single-view depth completion methods attempted to borrow the cost volume concept to regress depth [22,25]. However, they could not directly calculate cost volume, because no other view is available for matching. Therefore, they inferred the cost volume by using 2D CNNs without matching between multi-views. However, since their neural network still is based on only 2D convolutions, they cannot deal with 3D information appropriately and only generate cost maps rather than a cost volume in 3D space. In contrast, we devise *CostDCNet* to effectively handle the 3D geometry information contained in the input depth using 3D convolution.

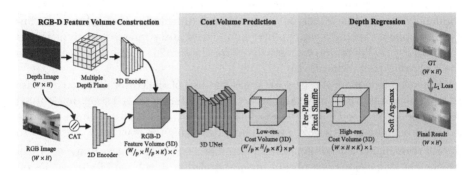

Fig. 2. Overview of *CostDCNet*. Our framework consists of three components. (1) RGB-D feature volume construction, (2) Cost volume prediction, (3) Depth regression.

3 Cost Volume Based Depth Completion Network

3.1 Overall Process and Network Design

CostDCNet infers a completed depth from a single RGB-D frame by sequentially performing three steps (Fig. 2): (1) RGB-D feature volume construction (Sect. 3.2), (2) Cost volume prediction and (3) Depth regression (Sect. 3.3). We outline these steps below.

RGB-D Feature Volume Construction. To produce an RGB-D feature volume, first of all, we extract 2D and 3D feature maps from an input RGB-D image by using 2D and 3D encoders. Unlike the 2D encoder that directly uses an RGB-D image as input, the 3D encoder requires a depth image to be converted into a multiple-depth-plane representation (Fig. 3c). We use 3D sparse convolution [8] to compute the 3D feature only for valid 3D points having non-zero depth. Both 2D and 3D encoders produce feature maps of the p times-reduced width and height to avoid the high memory footprint and heavy computation amount of a 3D CNN. Finally, we consolidate the reduced 2D and 3D feature maps into a single 3D feature volume, which we call an RGB-D feature volume (Sect. 3.2).

Cost Volume Prediction and Depth Regression. We feed the produced RGB-D feature volume into our 3D CNN to obtain a cost volume. At this time, the 3D CNN has the architecture of a 3D UNet [9] and additionally adopts pseudo 3D convolutions [35] to relieve the computational overhead of standard 3D convolutions. Because the RGB-D feature volume has the width and height lower than the original image, the predicted cost volume also has a reduced resolution. To recover the reduced resolution to the original one, a naïve option is to use 3D deconvolutions. However, feature volume upsampling by such 3D deconvolutions is computationally costly, so some multi-view depth estimation studies [20,37,45] commonly employ linear interpolation. We experimentally observed that the linear interpolation tends to cause blurry boundaries in the inferred depth image, as shown in Fig. 7. Therefore, we instead opt for the shuffle scheme [38] to upsample the cost volume of reduced size.

Our per-plane pixel shuffle rearranges features of the cost volume to increase its spatial resolution. For example, let the resolution of a target upsampled volume be $W \times H \times D$, and the resolution of the reduced cost volume that the 3D UNet outputs be $\frac{W}{p} \times \frac{H}{p} \times D \times C$. Then, by setting the feature dimension C to p^2 and rearranging a p^2-dimensional feature of a cell of the cost volume to width and height dimensions, we obtain an upsampled cost volume of the resolution $W \times H \times D \times 1$. The method requires only feature vector rearrangement without heavy computation, and shows good visual quality while running fast (Sect. 4.3, Fig. 7). Finally, we estimate the completed depth image by performing the soft-argmax based depth regression like [23] (Sect. 3.3).

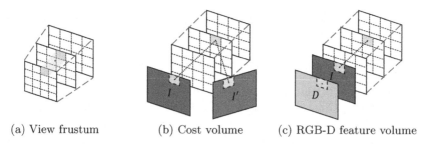

(a) View frustum   (b) Cost volume   (c) RGB-D feature volume

Fig. 3. Multiple-depth-plane representation. (a) View frustum in 3D space. (b) and (C) show a cost volume of multi-view stereo and our RGB-D feature volume in the multiple-depth-plane representation, respectively.

3.2   RGB-D Feature Volume

An RGB-D feature volume is constructed by consolidating 2D and 3D features extracted from a single RGB-D frame, where the consolidation is performed in the multiple-depth-plane representation. In this section, we introduce the multiple-depth-plane representation, how to convert an input depth to the representation, and three different types of methods to merge 2D and 3D features in this representation.

Depth to Multiple Depth Planes. A pixel position $\mathbf{u} = (x, y)$ in a depth image $D(\cdot)$ is related to a 3D position $\mathbf{x} \in \mathbb{R}^3$ within a view frustum of the image as $\mathbf{x} = D(\mathbf{u})\mathbb{K}^{-1}\tilde{\mathbf{u}}$, where $\mathbb{K}$ is a 3×3 matrix that includes depth camera intrinsic parameters, $\tilde{\mathbf{u}}$ is homogeneous coordinates $[\mathbf{u}, 1]^T$ of $\mathbf{u}$, and $D(\mathbf{u})$ is the depth value at the pixel position $\mathbf{u}$ (Fig. 3a). We can represent 3D position $\mathbf{x}$ as a 3D position in the multiple-depth-plane representation. Then, we quantize the 3D positions in the representation into a voxel grid so that 3D convolutions can be performed (Fig. 3c).

To construct the voxel grid, we need to predefine only the number K of uniformly-spaced depth planes $\{d_k\}_{k=1:K}$ because x- and y-axes resolution can be naturally determined to be the same as in the depth image. Maximum and minimum positions of the planes are determined by considering maximum and minimum depth values that a depth sensor can measure. The resolution of the voxel grid then becomes $W \times H \times K$. The 3D position $\mathbf{x} = (x, y, D(x, y))$ of a depth image pixel in the representation is easily quantized to a cell $\mathbf{x}_c$ of the voxel grid as

$$\mathbf{x}_c = (x, y, k') \tag{1}$$
$$k' = \arg\min_k |D(x, y) - d_k|.$$

By applying Eq. (1) to all valid pixels having non-zero depths, we obtain a set of valid cells $\{\mathbf{x}_c^n\}_{n=1:N}$ in the voxel grid, where N is the number of valid cells. Then, we construct an input geometry feature volume $f_g^{in} \in \mathbb{R}^{W \times H \times K \times M}$ on the voxel grid as

$$f_g^{in}(\mathbf{x}') = \begin{cases} \mathbf{s}_n, & \mathbf{x}' \in \{\mathbf{x}_c^n\}_{n=1:N} \\ \vec{0}, & \text{otherwise} \end{cases}, \tag{2}$$

where $\mathbf{x}'$ is a cell within f_g^{in}. If $\mathbf{x}'$ corresponds to a valid depth pixel $\mathbf{x}_c^n$, we store $\mathbf{s}_n$ in $\mathbf{x}'$, where $\mathbf{s}_n$ is a M-dimensional feature vector. Otherwise, a M-dimensional zero vector is stored in $\mathbf{x}'$. We set M to one and $\mathbf{s}_n$ to $D(x, y) - d_{k'}$, which is the residual of a depth pixel from the nearest predefined depth plane. Consequently, we can cover a view frustum using a regular voxel grid in the multiple-depth-plane representation, thereby enabling standard 3D convolution operations to be directly applied (Fig. 3). Performing standard 3D convolutions on the voxel grid has the effect of adjusting spatial coverage of a 3D convolution kernel accordingly to the distance from a depth camera.

Three Types of RGB-D Feature Volume. An RGB-D feature volume is a feature volume in the multiple-depth-plane representation, which is defined as element-wise concatenation of a geometric feature volume f_g and an image

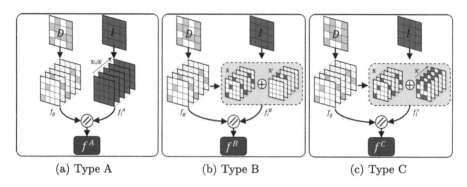

(a) Type A   (b) Type B   (c) Type C

Fig. 4. Three designs of RGB-D feature volume. The RGB-D feature volumes are represented by multiple depth planes and are classified into three types according to the structure of the image feature volume.

feature volume f_I. To obtain f_g, we first convert a depth image to the input geometry feature volume, and then feed it to our 3D encoder (Fig. 2). To obtain f_I, we first extract a 2D feature map from the input RGB-D image using our 2D encoder. Then, the 2D feature map is placed into the multiple-depth-plane representation to form f_I in three different ways (Types A, B, C), where the type of f_I determines the type of the final RGB-D feature volume. Below is the description of the three different types (Fig. 4).

(i) **Type A.** Several studies for 3D reconstruction, multi-view stereo, and 3D semantic segmentation generate a feature volume by unprojecting multi-view image features into a 3D volume, then integrating them [10,32,40]. In these methods, all the volume cells that are intersected by a ray starting from the camera's center of projection through an image pixel accumulate the same feature of the pixel. Similarly, we generate an image feature volume f_I^A to be filled with the same image features along the depth-axis as follows:

$$f_I^A(x, y, k') = I(x, y), \forall k' \in \{k\}_{k=1:K}, \tag{3}$$

where I denotes a 2D image feature map calculated by feeding an input RGB-D image into a 2D encoder (Fig. 2).

(ii) **Type B.** Since a Type A feature volume allocates image features to its all cells regardless of whether the corresponding depth pixels are valid or not, it does not consider 3D positional information of image features explicitly. In contrast, Type B considers the valid depth values of pixels for image feature allocation. To be specific, for a pixel with a valid depth, we allocate its 2D image feature to only the corresponding 3D cell in the image feature volume f_I^B. For pixels with invalid depths, we allocate their 2D image features to the corresponding cells in the middle depth plane of f_I^B. Formally,

$$f_I^B(x, y, k) = \begin{cases} I(x, y), & (x, y, k) \in \mathbb{X} \cup \mathbb{X}' \\ \vec{0}, & \text{otherwise} \end{cases}, \qquad (4)$$

where $\mathbb{X}$ is the set of cells determined by Eq. (1) from the valid depth pixels. $\mathbb{X}'$ is the set of cells corresponding to pixels (x, y) with invalid depths, where k is set to $K/2$, the center depth plane.

(iii) **Type C.** A Type C feature volume is generated in the same manner as Type B except that the image feature of each pixel with invalid depth is repeatedly allocated to the cells of f_I^C, traversing along the depth-axis.

The three types of RGB-D feature volumes have the same geometric feature volume, but their image feature volumes are defined differently. We experimentally demonstrated that using the Type C feature volume achieves the best performance (Sect. 4).

3.3 Final Depth Regression and Training Loss

Like the MVS works [20,23], we can regress a completed depth map $D'(\cdot)$ by applying the softmax operator $\sigma(\cdot)$ to the upsampled cost volume $V_c \in \mathbb{R}^{W \times H \times K}$ along the depth-axis and using the following equation

$$D'(x, y) = \sum_{k=1}^{K} d_k \times \mathbf{p}_{x,y}^k, \quad \mathbf{p}_{x,y} = \sigma(V_c(x, y, :)), \qquad (5)$$

where d_k is the predefined depth value of the k-th plane, (x, y) is an image pixel position, K is the number of depth planes, $V_c(x, y, :)$ is a K-dimensional vector along the depth-axis within the cost volume, and $\mathbf{p}_{x,y}$ is a probability vector obtained by the softmax operator $\sigma(\cdot)$ for K depth planes at (x, y).

We train our *CostDCNet* in an end-to-end manner by using only the L1 loss function as

$$L = \sum_{(x,y) \in \mathbb{G}} |D'(x, y) - D_{gt}(x, y)|, \qquad (6)$$

where D_{gt} is the GT depth, D' is an inferred depth by Eq. (5), and $\mathbb{G}$ is a set of valid pixels of D_{gt}.

4 Experiments

4.1 Experimental Setup

Datasets. We evaluated semi-dense depth completion on Matterport3D [3] dataset and sparse depth completion on NYUv2 [39], VOID [43], and KITTI DC [12] datasets.

- Matterport3D is a large-scale indoor dataset, including 194,400 RGB-D images captured by a Matterport camera. With GT depth images provided by Zhang et al. [48], we used training (∼100K images) and test (474 images) sets as in [18]. We use images downsized into size of 320 × 256 for both training and testing.
- NYUv2 includes RGB-D videos of 464 indoor scenes collected using a Kinect sensor. We randomly sample points to obtain input sparse depth images. We downscaled images into size of 320 × 240 and then center-cropped them to be size of 304 × 228. We constructed the training set (∼48K images) and the test set (654 images) as in previous studies [31].
- VOID provides 640 × 480 RGB-D images containing sequences of 56 indoor and outdoor scenes acquired from RealSense D435i camera. We used sparse depth images with about 1500 depth points as input. We train our model on the training set (∼47K images) and test on the test set (800 images) by following the previous protocol of [43].
- KITTI DC is an outdoor scene dataset that provides paired RGB and sparse depth images obtained by projecting Velodyne LiDAR sensor measurements onto 2D space. It utilizes 11 consecutive frames to generate denser depth images as GT. For training, we center-cropped the images with size of 1216 × 240 to ignore the regions with no LiDAR measurements. We used ∼93K image pairs for training and 1K pairs for testing as in the previous works.

Table 1. Quantitative comparisons with SOTA semi-dense depth completion methods on the Matterport3D dataset. The numbers are excerpted from each paper except for [26], of which the number was reported by [2].

Method	RMSE(m)↓	MAE(m)↓	SSIM↑	$\delta_{1.05}$ ↑	$\delta_{1.10}$ ↑	$\delta_{1.25}$ ↑	$\delta_{1.25^2}$ ↑	$\delta_{1.25^3}$ ↑
MRF [15]	1.675	0.618	0.692	50.6	55.6	65.1	78.0	85.6
AD [28]	1.653	0.610	0.696	50.3	56.0	66.3	79.2	86.1
Zhang et al. [48]	1.316	0.461	0.762	65.7	70.8	78.1	85.1	88.8
Cao et al. [2]	1.187	0.385	0.736	66.5	72.5	79.9	87.1	91.1
Huang et al. [18]	1.092	0.342	0.799	66.1	75.0	85.0	91.1	93.6
MSG-CHN [26]	1.068	0.347	0.778	65.0	73.2	83.3	90.3	93.4
Ours	**1.019**	**0.290**	**0.838**	71.3	78.6	87.1	92.8	94.8

Evaluation Metrics. We followed the standard metrics to evaluate the performance: root mean squared error (RMSE), mean absolute error (MAE), structural similarity index map (SSIM), relative mean absolute error (REL), and percentages δ_x of inlier pixels with the less than x meters error.

Implementation Detail. Our 3D encoder and 2D encoder are composed of 3 and 6 residual blocks [16], respectively. We used the simplified 3D UNet [9] to extract cost volumes. For the detailed network architecture, refer to the supplementary material. We used $K = 16$ depth planes and $p^2 = 16$ feature dimension of a cost volume. The maximum depth d_{max} is set to 5 m, 10 m, 15 m, and 90 m

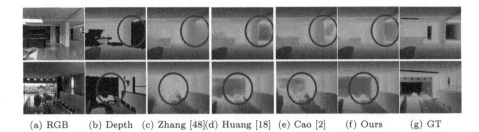

(a) RGB   (b) Depth   (c) Zhang [48](d) Huang [18] (e) Cao [2]   (f) Ours   (g) GT

Fig. 5. Qualitative comparisons with SOTA semi-dense depth completion methods on the Matterport3D dataset. The results of [18,48] were borrowed from the paper [18] and results of [2] were taken from their project page.

for VOID, NYUv2, Matterport3D and KITTI DC datasets, respectively. We used the ADAM optimizer [24] with an initial learning rate of 0.5×10^{-3}, then divided it in half every 20 epochs for network training. We set the batch size to 16 and the training epoch to 50, and trained neural networks using a single NVIDIA RTX 3090 GPU.

4.2   Comparisons with SOTA

Semi-dense Depth Completion. We compared our method with previous semi-dense depth completion methods on the Matterport3D dataset. Table 1 shows quantitative comparisons with SOTA methods. Our network outperformed all other methods significantly in all metrics by a large margin. Especially, Hwang et al. [18], which is the previous SOTA method, additionally require the normal and boundary maps predicted by Zhang et al. [48] and their network size (19.8M) is 11 times larger than ours. MSG-CHN [26] is the backbone network used by Cao et al. [2], trained by supervised learning. It has slightly better RMSE compared to [18], but our method outperforms it across all metrics. In qualitative comparisons with other methods (Fig. 5), our method better expresses details and has clearer boundaries.

Sparse Depth Completion. We conducted experiments on the NYUv2 dataset to compare our framework with SOTA methods for the sparse depth completion task (Fig. 6). Table 2 shows the quantitative results on a few standard metrics. When using 500 depth points as the input, our approach achieved the second and third best performance on REL and RMSE metrics, respectively. However, our *CostDCNet* uses merely 20% of network parameters of Point-Fusion [19] and 7% of NLSPN [33], respectively. We also notice that our method obtained higher accuracy, compared to PRNet [25] and DCoeff [22] that utilize multiple depth planes as representation for an inferred depth map and perform only 2D convolutions. These results show that our framework exploits 3D information much better than PRNet and DCeoff. In addition, even for extremely sparse input depths (32 points), our method achieves SOTA performance in both Rel and RMSE metrics.

Table 2. Quantitative comparisons with SOTA sparse depth completion methods on the NYUv2 dataset. The numbers are excerpted from respective papers.

Method	#points	#params↓	RMSE(m)↓	REL(m)↓	$\delta_{1.25}$ ↑	$\delta_{1.25^2}$ ↑	$\delta_{1.25^3}$ ↑
DCoeff [22]		45.7M	0.118	0.013	99.4	99.9	-
CSPN [7]		18.5M	0.117	0.016	99.2	99.9	100
CSPN++ [5]		28.8M	0.116	-	-	-	-
DeepLiDAR [34]		53.4M	0.115	0.022	99.3	99.9	100
PRNet [25]		14.3M	0.104	0.014	99.4	99.9	100
GuideNet [41]	500	63.3M	0.101	0.015	99.5	99.9	100
TWISE [21]		5.8M	0.097	0.013	99.6	99.9	100
NLSPN [33]		25.8M	0.092	**0.012**	99.6	99.9	100
Point-Fusion [19]		8.7M	**0.090**	0.014	99.6	99.9	100
Ours		**1.8M**	0.096	0.013	99.5	99.9	100
Point-Fusion [19]	32	8.7M	0.319	0.057	96.3	99.2	99.8
Ours		**1.8M**	**0.258**	**0.048**	96.4	99.1	99.7

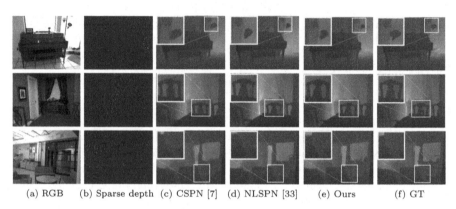

(a) RGB   (b) Sparse depth   (c) CSPN [7]   (d) NLSPN [33]   (e) Ours   (f) GT

Fig. 6. Qualitative results on NYUv2 dataset. The results of other methods [7,33] are obtained from the authors' project page.

We also compared our method with SOTA unsupervised (KBNet) and supervised (NLSPN [33], PENet [17]) methods on VOID (test set) and KITTI DC (validation set) datasets. Most of unsupervised depth completion methods, including KBNet, do not use GT depths and train networks with additional photometric loss using adjacent views. For fast experiments, we did not use the photometric loss and simply trained our networks with the original input as GT and random samples from the original input as input data. We used L1 + L2 losses for KITTI DC datasets. Table 3 shows experimental results. The numbers of other methods are borrowed from the previous paper [29]. Our method outperforms SOTA unsupervised and supervised methods across all metrics, even running in real time (~30FPS). While KBNet uses 3D position vectors to leverage 3D information, it is still based on 2D CNN. Therefore, its computational costs are lower than ours, but its inductive bias in 3D space could be weaker than 3D CNNs.

Collectively considering the overall performance, the total number of network parameters, robustness in extreme cases, we believe that our framework could be the best option.

Table 3. Quantitative comparisons with SOTA sparse depth completion methods on VOID test set and KITTI DC validation set.

Dataset	Method	Train	#Param↓	Runtime↓	MAE↓	RMSE↓	iMAE↓	iRMSE↓
VOID	KBNet [44]	U	6.9M	**13 ms**	39.80	95.86	21.16	49.72
	Ours	U	**1.8M**	30 ms	**27.19**	**79.19**	**13.02**	**35.17**
	PENet [17]	S	132M	226 ms	34.6	82.01	18.89	40.36
	NLSPN [33]	S	25.8M	122 ms	26.7	79.12	12.70	33.88
	Ours	S	**1.8M**	**30 ms**	**25.84**	**76.28**	**12.19**	**32.13**
KITTI DC	KBNet [44]	U	6.9M	**16 ms**	260.44	1126.85	1.03	3.20
	Ours	U	**1.8M**	34 ms	**242.64**	**868.62**	**0.99**	**2.39**

4.3 Ablation Study

In this section, we analyze the role of each component of our framework. For the analysis, we conducted sparse depth completion on the NYUv2 dataset. To speed up the experiments, we set the resolution of input RGB-D image to $\frac{1}{4}$ size of the original before adding the encoders and trained each model up to 20 epochs.

Network. To verify the effect of inferring depth in 3D space, we compare our 3D UNet [9] with 2D UNet [36]. The 2D UNet takes a concatenated RGB-D image as input, and 3D UNet takes as input the RGB-D feature volume. When 2D UNet was replaced with our tiny 3D Unet, even though it has only 2.5% of network parameters of 2D UNet, the accuracy was significantly improved by ~62% (Table 4a&b). The result implies that considering 3D information with the RGB-D feature volume as an appropriate representation is helpful for inferring high-quality cost volume. We also replaced the 3D convolution of 3D UNet with a pseudo-3D convolution (P3D) [35] to reduce the computational cost. P3D showed similar accuracy to 3D convolution while reducing the number of network parameters by half (Table 4b&c). Therefore, P3D was used in our 3D UNet.

Effectiveness of Explicit Positional Conditioning. To construct a RGB-D feature volume, a geometric feature volume f_g is element-wisely concatenated with an image feature volume f_I. We verify that exploiting such explicit positional cues from input depths in RGB-D feature volume construction results in performance improvement. To this end, we compared the results of using only the image feature volume f_I^A (without f_g) (Table 4d) and Type A (with f_g) (Table 4c). f_I^A leads to a poorer accuracy than Type A because it does not use 3D geometry information at all. It suggests that it is necessary to assign geometry features to the proper positions in 3D space for accurate depth completion.

Table 4. Ablation study for each component of our network. The results were evaluated on the NYUv2 dataset.

Method	Network			RGB-D Vol.				Encoder		Upsample			RMSE(m)↓	#param↓
	2D	3D	P3D	f_f^A	A	B	C	2D	3D	BL	BG	PS		
(a)	✓									✓			0.195	17.3M
(b)		✓		✓						✓			0.121	1.0M
(c)			✓	✓						✓			0.123	0.5M
(d)		✓		✓						✓			0.186	0.5M
(e)		✓			✓					✓			0.131	0.5M
(f)		✓					✓			✓			0.122	0.5M
(g)		✓					✓	✓		✓			0.108	1.5M
(h)		✓					✓	✓	✓	✓			0.106	1.8M
(i)		✓					✓	✓	✓		✓		0.102	3.1M
(j)		✓					✓	✓	✓			✓	0.099	1.8M

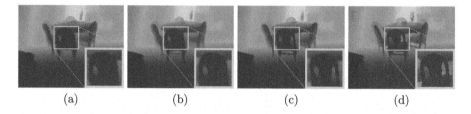

(a)　　　　　　(b)　　　　　　(c)　　　　　　(d)

Fig. 7. Different upsampling methods. (a) Bilinear upsampling, (b) Bilateral grid learning [45], (c) Per-plane pixel shuffle, and (d) Ground truth.

Three Designs of RGB-D Feature Volume. We also quantified the effect of the design of RGB-D feature volume. Type A (Table 4c) and Type C (Table 4f) had higher accuracy than Type B (Table 4e). We argue 3D information can be inferred better by assigning 2D features of unknown depth values to all possible depth planes rather than to a specific depth plane. In addition, Type C had slightly higher accuracy than Type A. This result means that ambiguity can be reduced by assigning 2D features of valid depths to the correct depth positions.

2D and 3D Encoders. We evaluated the effectiveness of the 2D and 3D encoders (Table 4g&h). Compared to a model without encoders (Table 4f), the accuracy was significantly improved when our 2D and 3D encoders are added. These results indicate that the 2D and 3D encoders can enrich the information of our RGB-D feature volumes.

Upsampling. We quantified the effect of upsampling layers, using bilinear (BL, Table 4h), bilateral grid learning (BG, Table 4i) [45], and per-plane pixel shuffle (PS, Table 4j) upsampling. BG and PS achieved better accuracy than BL. However, BG requires an additional network, which increases the number of parameters, whereas PS rearranges the volume, which is simple and fast. In qualitative results (Fig. 7), BL generally blurred the boundary, BG gave clean boundaries, but caused artifacts that break the structure, whereas PS gives clear boundaries and restores the overall structure well. These results indicate PS can reliably up-scale cost volume to the original resolution at low computational cost.

5   Conclusion

In this paper, we proposed a single-view depth completion framework, *CostD-CNet*, that can fully exploit 3D information by performing 3D convolutions of heterogeneous 2D and 3D features in the multiple-depth-plane representation. We introduced three designs of RGB-D feature volume to represent a single RGB-D image into 3D space. Furthermore, we employed the per-plane pixel shuffle to upsample the low-resolution cost volume on which 3D convolutions are performed efficiently. We demonstrated that our system is lightweight ($\sim$1.8M parameters), runs in real time ($\sim$30 ms), and achieves qualitatively and quantitatively SOTA or comparable performance in depth completion for semi-dense depths, sparse depths (500 points), and even extremely sparse depths (32 points).

Limitation and Future Work. Although our framework showed impressive results in indoor sparse and semi-dense depth completion, we have a few limitations. Our framework has a fixed number of depth planes, so in outdoor scenes such as the KITTI DC dataset, the distance between the planes becomes wider, and expressive power decreases. To tackle this problem, we plan to closely consolidate the sparse convolution and coarse-to-fine approach with our *CostDCNet*.

Acknowledgment. This work was supported by the Ministry of Science and ICT, Korea, through IITP grants (SW Star Lab, 2015-0-00174; AI Innovation Hub, 2021-0-02068; Artificial Intelligence Graduate School Program (POSTECH), 2019-0-01906).

References

1. Boulch, A., Puy, G., Marlet, R.: FKAConv: feature-kernel alignment for point cloud convolution. In: Proceedings of Asian Conference on Computer Vision (ACCV) (2020)
2. Cao, Z., Li, A., Yuan, Z.: Self-supervised depth completion via adaptive sampling and relative consistency. In: Proceedings of IEEE International Conference on Image Processing (ICIP), pp. 3263–3267 (2021)
3. Chang, A., et al.: Matterport3D: learning from RGB-D data in indoor environments. arXiv preprint arXiv:1709.06158 (2017)
4. Chen, Y., Yang, B., Liang, M., Urtasun, R.: Learning joint 2D–3D representations for depth completion. In: Proceedings of IEEE International Conference on Computer Vision (ICCV), pp. 10023–10032 (2019)
5. Cheng, X., Wang, P., Guan, C., Yang, R.: CSPN++: learning context and resource aware convolutional spatial propagation networks for depth completion. In: Proceedings of AAAI Conference on Artificial Intelligence, vol. 34, pp. 10615–10622 (2020)
6. Cheng, X., Wang, P., Yang, R.: Depth estimation via affinity learned with convolutional spatial propagation network. In: Proceedings of European Conference on Computer Vision (ECCV), pp. 103–119 (2018)

7. Cheng, X., Wang, P., Yang, R.: Learning depth with convolutional spatial propagation network. IEEE Trans. Pattern Anal. Mach. Intell. (TPAMI) **42**(10), 2361–2379 (2019)

8. Choy, C., Gwak, J., Savarese, S.: 4d spatio-temporal convnets: minkowski convolutional neural networks. In: Proceedings of IEEE Computer Vision and Pattern Recognition (CVPR), pp. 3075–3084 (2019)

9. Çiçek, Ö., Abdulkadir, A., Lienkamp, S.S., Brox, T., Ronneberger, O.: 3D U-Net: learning dense volumetric segmentation from sparse annotation. In: Ourselin, S., Joskowicz, L., Sabuncu, M.R., Unal, G., Wells, W. (eds.) MICCAI 2016. LNCS, vol. 9901, pp. 424–432. Springer, Cham (2016). https://doi.org/10.1007/978-3-319-46723-8_49

10. Dai, A., Nießner, M.: 3DMV: joint 3D-multi-view prediction for 3D semantic scene segmentation. In: Proceedings of European Conference on Computer Vision (ECCV), pp. 452–468 (2018)

11. Fu, C., Dong, C., Mertz, C., Dolan, J.M.: Depth completion via inductive fusion of planar lidar and monocular camera. In: Proceedings of IEEE/RSJ International Conference on Intelligent Robots and Systems (IROS), pp. 10843–10848 (2020)

12. Geiger, A., Lenz, P., Urtasun, R.: Are we ready for autonomous driving? the KITTI vision benchmark suite. In: Proceedings of IEEE Computer Vision and Pattern Recognition (CVPR), pp. 3354–3361 (2012)

13. Gu, X., Fan, Z., Zhu, S., Dai, Z., Tan, F., Tan, P.: Cascade cost volume for high-resolution multi-view stereo and stereo matching. In: Proceedings of IEEE Computer Vision and Pattern Recognition (CVPR), pp. 2495–2504 (2020)

14. Guo, X., Yang, K., Yang, W., Wang, X., Li, H.: Group-wise correlation stereo network. In: Proceedings of IEEE Computer Vision and Pattern Recognition (CVPR), pp. 3273–3282 (2019)

15. Harrison, A., Newman, P.: Image and sparse laser fusion for dense scene reconstruction. In: Howard, A., Iagnemma, K., Kelly, A. (eds) Proceedings of Field and Service Robotics (FSR), vol 62, pp. 219–228. Springer, Heidelberg (2010). DOIurlhttps://doi.org/10.1007/978-3-642-13408-1_20

16. He, K., Zhang, X., Ren, S., Sun, J.: Deep residual learning for image recognition. In: Proceedings of IEEE Computer Vision and Pattern Recognition (CVPR), pp. 770–778 (2016)

17. Hu, M., Wang, S., Li, B., Ning, S., Fan, L., Gong, X.: PeNet: towards precise and efficient image guided depth completion. In: Proceedings of IEEE International Conference on Robotics and Automation (ICRA), pp. 13656–13662 (2021)

18. Huang, Y.K., Wu, T.H., Liu, Y.C., Hsu, W.H.: Indoor depth completion with boundary consistency and self-attention. In: Proceedings of IEEE International Conference on Computer Vision Workshops (ICCVW) (2019)

19. Huynh, L., Nguyen, P., Matas, J., Rahtu, E., Heikkilä, J.: Boosting monocular depth estimation with lightweight 3D point fusion. In: Proceedings of IEEE International Conference on Computer Vision (ICCV), pp. 12767–12776 (2021)

20. Im, S., Jeon, H.G., Lin, S., Kweon, I.S.: DPSNet: End-to-end deep plane sweep stereo. arXiv preprint arXiv:1905.00538 (2019)

21. Imran, S., Liu, X., Morris, D.: Depth completion with twin surface extrapolation at occlusion boundaries. In: Proceedings of IEEE Computer Vision and Pattern Recognition (CVPR), pp. 2583–2592 (2021)

22. Imran, S., Long, Y., Liu, X., Morris, D.: Depth coefficients for depth completion. In: Proceedings of IEEE Computer Vision and Pattern Recognition (CVPR), pp. 12438–12447 (2019)

23. Kendall, A., et al.: End-to-end learning of geometry and context for deep stereo regression. In: Proceedings of IEEE International Conference on Computer Vision (ICCV), pp. 66–75 (2017)

24. Kingma, D.P., Ba, J.: Adam: a method for stochastic optimization. arXiv preprint arXiv:1412.6980 (2014)

25. Lee, B.U., Lee, K., Kweon, I.S.: Depth completion using plane-residual representation. In: Proceedings of IEEE Computer Vision and Pattern Recognition (CVPR), pp. 13916–13925 (2021)

26. Li, A., Yuan, Z., Ling, Y., Chi, W., Zhang, C., et al.: A multi-scale guided cascade hourglass network for depth completion. In: Proceedings of IEEE Winter Conference on Applications of Computer Vision (WACV), pp. 32–40 (2020)

27. Liao, Y., Huang, L., Wang, Y., Kodagoda, S., Yu, Y., Liu, Y.: Parse geometry from a line: monocular depth estimation with partial laser observation. In: Proceedings of IEEE International Conference on Robotics and Automation (ICRA), pp. 5059–5066 (2017)

28. Liu, J., Gong, X.: Guided depth enhancement via anisotropic diffusion. In: Huet, B., Ngo, C.-W., Tang, J., Zhou, Z.-H., Hauptmann, A.G., Yan, S. (eds.) PCM 2013. LNCS, vol. 8294, pp. 408–417. Springer, Cham (2013). https://doi.org/10.1007/978-3-319-03731-8_38

29. Liu, T.Y., Agrawal, P., Chen, A., Hong, B.W., Wong, A.: Monitored distillation for positive congruent depth completion. arXiv preprint arXiv:2203.16034 (2022)

30. Luo, W., Schwing, A.G., Urtasun, R.: Efficient deep learning for stereo matching. In: Proceedings of IEEE Computer Vision and Pattern Recognition (CVPR), pp. 5695–5703 (2016)

31. Ma, F., Karaman, S.: Sparse-to-dense: Depth prediction from sparse depth samples and a single image. In: Proceedings of IEEE International Conference on Robotics and Automation (ICRA), pp. 4796–4803 (2018)

32. Murez, Z., van As, T., Bartolozzi, J., Sinha, A., Badrinarayanan, V., Rabinovich, A.: Atlas: end-to-end 3D scene reconstruction from posed images. In: Vedaldi, A., Bischof, H., Brox, T., Frahm, J.-M. (eds.) ECCV 2020. LNCS, vol. 12352, pp. 414–431. Springer, Cham (2020). https://doi.org/10.1007/978-3-030-58571-6_25

33. Park, J., Joo, K., Hu, Z., Liu, C.-K., So Kweon, I.: Non-local spatial propagation network for depth completion. In: Vedaldi, A., Bischof, H., Brox, T., Frahm, J.-M. (eds.) ECCV 2020. LNCS, vol. 12358, pp. 120–136. Springer, Cham (2020). https://doi.org/10.1007/978-3-030-58601-0_8

34. Qiu, J., et al.: Deeplidar: deep surface normal guided depth prediction for outdoor scene from sparse lidar data and single color image. In: Proceedings of IEEE Computer Vision and Pattern Recognition (CVPR), pp. 3313–3322 (2019)

35. Qiu, Z., Yao, T., Mei, T.: Learning spatio-temporal representation with pseudo-3D residual networks. In: Proceedings of IEEE International Conference on Computer Vision (ICCV), pp. 5533–5541 (2017)

36. Ronneberger, O., Fischer, P., Brox, T.: U-Net: convolutional networks for biomedical image segmentation. In: Navab, N., Hornegger, J., Wells, W.M., Frangi, A.F. (eds.) MICCAI 2015. LNCS, vol. 9351, pp. 234–241. Springer, Cham (2015). https://doi.org/10.1007/978-3-319-24574-4_28

37. Shen, Z., Dai, Y., Rao, Z.: CFNet: cascade and fused cost volume for robust stereo matching. In: Proceedings of IEEE Computer Vision and Pattern Recognition (CVPR), pp. 13906–13915 (2021)

38. Shi, W., Caballero, J., Huszár, F., Totz, J., Aitken, A.P., Bishop, R., Rueckert, D., Wang, Z.: Real-time single image and video super-resolution using an efficient

sub-pixel convolutional neural network. In: Proceedings of IEEE Computer Vision and Pattern Recognition (CVPR). pp. 1874–1883 (2016)

39. Silberman, N., Hoiem, D., Kohli, P., Fergus, R.: Indoor segmentation and support inference from RGBD images. In: Proceedings of European Conference on Computer Vision (ECCV). pp. 746–760. Springer (2012)

40. Sun, J., Xie, Y., Chen, L., Zhou, X., Bao, H.: NeuralRecon: real-time coherent 3D reconstruction from monocular video. In: Proceedings of IEEE Computer Vision and Pattern Recognition (CVPR), pp. 15598–15607 (2021)

41. Tang, J., Tian, F.P., Feng, W., Li, J., Tan, P.: Learning guided convolutional network for depth completion. IEEE Trans. Image Process. (TIP) **30**, 1116–1129 (2020)

42. Wang, S., Suo, S., Ma, W.C., Pokrovsky, A., Urtasun, R.: Deep parametric continuous convolutional neural networks. In: Proceedings of IEEE Computer Vision and Pattern Recognition (CVPR), pp. 2589–2597 (2018)

43. Wong, A., Fei, X., Tsuei, S., Soatto, S.: Unsupervised depth completion from visual inertial odometry. IEEE Robot. Autom. Lett. (RA-L) **5**(2), 1899–1906 (2020)

44. Wong, A., Soatto, S.: Unsupervised depth completion with calibrated backprojection layers. In: Proceedings of IEEE International Conference on Computer Vision (ICCV), pp. 12747–12756 (2021)

45. Xu, B., Xu, Y., Yang, X., Jia, W., Guo, Y.: Bilateral grid learning for stereo matching networks. In: Proceedings of IEEE Computer Vision and Pattern Recognition (CVPR), pp. 12497–12506 (2021)

46. Zbontar, J., LeCun, Y.: Computing the stereo matching cost with a convolutional neural network. In: Proceedings of IEEE Computer Vision and Pattern Recognition (CVPR), pp. 1592–1599 (2015)

47. Zhang, F., Prisacariu, V., Yang, R., Torr, P.H.: GA-Net: guided aggregation net for end-to-end stereo matching. In: Proceedings of IEEE Computer Vision and Pattern Recognition (CVPR), pp. 185–194 (2019)

48. Zhang, Y., Funkhouser, T.: Deep depth completion of a single RGB-D image. In: Proceedings of IEEE Computer Vision and Pattern Recognition (CVPR), pp. 175–185 (2018)

49. Zhong, Y., Wu, C.Y., You, S., Neumann, U.: Deep RGB-D canonical correlation analysis for sparse depth completion. In: Advances in Neural Information Processing Systems (NeurIPS), vol. 32 (2019)

ShAPO: Implicit Representations for Multi-object Shape, Appearance, and Pose Optimization

Muhammad Zubair Irshad[1]([⊠]) [iD], Sergey Zakharov[2] [iD], Rares Ambrus[2] [iD], Thomas Kollar[2] [iD], Zsolt Kira[1] [iD], and Adrien Gaidon[2] [iD]

[1] Georgia Institute of Technology, Atlanta, USA
{mirshad7,zkira}@gatech.edu
[2] Toyota Research Institute, Palo Alto, USA
{sergey.zakharov,rares.ambrus,thomas.kollar,adrien.gaidon}@tri.global

Input Image	Detection Heatmaps	3D Bounding Boxes

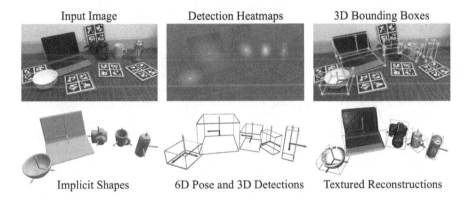

Implicit Shapes	6D Pose and 3D Detections	Textured Reconstructions

Fig. 1. Given a single RGB-D observation, our method, **ShAPO**, infers 6D pose and size, 3D shapes and appearance of all objects in the scene. Results shown on novel real-world scene in NOCS [54].

Abstract. Our method studies the complex task of object-centric 3D understanding from a single RGB-D observation. As it is an ill-posed problem, existing methods suffer from low performance for both 3D shape and 6D pose and size estimation in complex multi-object scenarios with occlusions. We present ShAPO, a method for joint multi-object detection, 3D textured reconstruction, 6D object pose and size estimation. Key to ShAPO is a single-shot pipeline to regress shape, appearance and pose latent codes along with the masks of each object instance, which is then further refined in a sparse-to-dense fashion. A novel disentangled shape and appearance database of priors is first learned to embed objects in their respective shape and appearance space. We also

M. Z. Irshad and S. Zakharov—Equal contribution.

Supplementary Information The online version contains supplementary material available at https://doi.org/10.1007/978-3-031-20086-1_16.

propose a novel, octree-based differentiable optimization step, allowing us to further improve object shape, pose and appearance simultaneously under the learned latent space, in an analysis-by-synthesis fashion. Our novel joint implicit textured object representation allows us to accurately identify and reconstruct novel unseen objects without having access to their 3D meshes. Through extensive experiments, we show that our method, trained on simulated indoor scenes, accurately regresses the shape, appearance and pose of novel objects in the real-world with minimal fine-tuning. Our method significantly out-performs all baselines on the NOCS dataset with an 8% absolute improvement in mAP for 6D pose estimation.

Keywords: Implicit representations · 3D shape and texture reconstruction · 6D pose estimation · Octree-based differentiable optimization

1   Introduction

Holistic 3D object understanding [31,60] from a single RGB-D observation has remained a popular yet challenging problem in computer vision [11,14,61] and robotics [9,16,19,25]. The capability to infer complete object-centric 3D scene information has benefits in robotic manipulation [6,16,19,25], navigation [17,18] and augmented reality. This task demands that the autonomous robot reasons about the 3D geometry of objects from partially observed single-view visual data, infer a 3D shape and 6D pose and size (i.e. 3D orientation and position) and estimate the appearance of novel object instances. Despite recent progress, this problem remains challenging since inferring 3D shape from images is an ill-posed problem and predicting the 6D pose and 3D scale can be extremely ambiguous without having any prior information about the objects of interest.

Prior works on object-centric scene understanding have attempted to address this challenge in various ways: *object pose understanding* methods obtain 3D bounding box information without shape details. Most prior works in object-pose estimation cast it as an instance-level [21,41,57] 3D object understanding task as opposed to category-level. Such methods [39,50,53], while achieving impressive results, rely on provided 3D reconstructions or prior CAD models for successful detection and pose estimation. Category-level approaches [47,51,54], on the other hand, rely on learned shape and scale priors during training, making them much more challenging. Despite great progress in category-level pose estimation, the performance of these approaches is limited due to their incapacity to express shape variations explicitly. *Object-centric scene-level reconstruction* methods [20,33,55] recover object shapes using 2D or partial 3D information for scene reconstruction. However, most methods are limited in their ability to reconstruct high quality shapes in a fast manner (i.e. the studied representation is either voxel-based which is computationally inefficient [13] or point-based which results in poor reconstruction quality [5,8]).

For holistic scene-level reconstruction, only predicting shapes in an isolated manner [13,24,58] may not yield good results due to the challenges of aligning objects in the 3D space, reasoning about occlusions and diverse backgrounds. To the best our knowledge, fewer works have tackled the problem of joint shape reconstruction with appearance and object-centric scene context (i.e. 3D bounding boxes and object pose and sizes) for a holistic object-centric scene understanding.

Motivated by the above, we present ShAPO: Implicit Representations for Multi-Object Shape, Appearance, and Pose Optimization, an end-to-end method unifying accurate shape prediction and alignment with object-centric scene context. As shown in Fig. 1, we infer the complete 3D information of novel object instances (i.e. 3D shape along with appearance and 6D pose and sizes) from a single-view RGB-D observation; the results shown in Fig. 1 are on a novel scene from the NOCS [54] dataset. In essence, our method represents object instances as center key-points [7,16,25] in a spatial 2D grid. We regress the complete 3D information i.e. object shape and appearance codes along with the object masks and 6D pose and sizes at each objects' spatial center point. A novel joint implicit shape and appearance database of signed distance and texture field priors is utilized, to embed object instances in a unique space and learn from a large collection of CAD models. We further utilize differentiable optimization of implicit shape and appearance representation to iteratively improve shape, pose, size and appearance jointly in an analysis-by-synthesis fashion. To alleviate the sampling inefficiency inherent in signed distance field shape representations, we propose a novel octree-based point sampling which leads to significant time and memory improvements as well as increased reconstruction quality.

Our contributions are summarized as follows:

- **A generalizable, disentangled shape and appearance space** coupled with **an efficient octree-based differentiable optimization procedure** which allows us to identify and reconstruct novel object instances without access to their ground truth meshes.
- **An object-centric scene understanding pipeline** relying on learned joint appearance and implicit differentiable shape priors which achieves state-of-the-art reconstruction and pose estimation results on benchmark datasets.
- Our proposed approach significantly outperforms all baselines for 6D pose and size estimation on NOCS benchmark, showing over 8% absolute improvement in mAP for 6D pose at $10°$ 10 cm.

2   Related Work

In essence, our proposed method infers 3D shape along with predicting the 3D appearance and 6D pose and sizes of multiple object instances to perform object-centric scene reconstruction from a single-view RGB-D, so it relates to multiple areas in 3D scene reconstruction, object understanding and pose estimation.
Neural Implicit Representations: 3D shape and appearance reconstructions has recently seen a new prominent direction to use neural nets as scalar fields approximators instead of ConvNets. The first works of this class are notably DeepSDF [36], Occ-Net [29], and IM-Net [4]. These works use *coordinate based representation* to output either an occupancy estimate or a continuous SDF

value, encoding the object's surface given a 3D coordinate. Improving this direction further, MeshSDF [42], NGLOD [48] and Texture fields [34] employed end-to-end differentiable mesh representation, efficient octree representation and implicitly representing high frequency textures respectively. In our pipeline, we build a differentiable database of shape and appearance priors based on the latest advances in neural implicit representations. Our pipeline is end-to-end differentiable and abstains from the expensive Marching Cubes computation at every optimization step. Our database stores not only the geometries of the objects in the form of signed distance fields, but also their appearance in the form of texture fields, allowing us to model multiple categories through a single network while also considering test-time optimization of shape, pose and appearance.

Object-centric Reconstruction: 3D object reconstruction from a single-view observation has seen great progress to output pointclouds, voxels or meshes [4, 29,36]. Similarly, scene representation has been extended to include appearance. SRN [45], DVR [33] learn from multi-view images by employing ray-marching routine and differentiable rendering respectively. Recently, NeRF [30] propose to regress density and color along a ray and perform volumetric rendering to obtain true color value. Most NeRF-based methods [27,32,35] overfit to a single scene, do not promise generalizability and requires dense viewpoint annotations. Our pipeline, on the other hand, is capable of reconstructing shapes, appearances and inferring the 6D pose and sizes of objects never seen during training from a single-view RGB-D and is also not limited to viewpoints seen during training.

6DoF Object Pose and size estimation works use direct pose regression [16, 21,53,57], template matching [22,46,49] and establishing correspondences [12, 15,37,43,54]. However, most works focus only on pose estimation and do not deal with shape and appearance retrieval and their connection to 6D pose. We instead propose a differentiable pipeline to improve the initially regressed pose, along with the shape and appearance, using our novel octree-base differentiable test-time optimization.

3   Method

ShAPO is an end-to-end learning-based holistic object-centric scene understanding method that infers 3D shape along with the 6D pose, size and appearance of multiple unknown objects in an RGB-D observation. ShAPO tackles the detection, localization and reconstruction of all unknown object instances in 3D space. Such a goal is made possible by three components: 1) A single-shot detection and 3D prediction module that detects multiple objects based on their center points in the 2D spatial grid and recovers their complete 3D shapes, 6D pose and sizes along with appearance from partial observations. 2) An implicit joint differentiable database of shape and appearances priors which is used to embed objects in a unique space and represent shapes as signed distance fields (SDF) and appearance as continuous texture fields (TF). 3) A 2D/3D refinement method utilizing an octree-based coarse-to-fine differentiable optimization to improve shape, pose, size and appearance predictions iteratively.

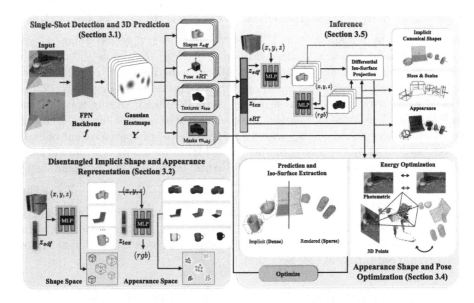

Fig. 2. ShAPO Method: Given a single-view RGB-D observation, our method jointly predicts shape, pose, size and appearance codes along with the masks of each object instances in a single-shot manner. Leveraging a novel octree-based differentiable optimization procedure, we further optimize for shape, pose, size and appearance jointly in an analysis by synthesis manner.

Formally, given a single-view RGB-D observation ($I \in \mathbb{R}^{h_o \times w_o \times 3}$, $D \in \mathbb{R}^{h_o \times w_o}$) as input, ShAPO infers the complete 3D information of multiple objects including the shape (represented as a zero-level set of an implicit signed distance field, $\boldsymbol{SDF}$), 6D pose and scales ($\tilde{\mathcal{P}} \in SE(3)$, $\hat{s} \in \mathbb{R}^3$) and appearance (represented as a continuous texture field, $\boldsymbol{TF}$). To achieve the above goal, we employ an end-to-end trainable method. As shown in Fig. 2, we first formulate object detection as a spatial per-pixel point detection [16,25,61]. A backbone comprising of feature pyramid networks [10] is employed with a specialized head to predict object instances as heatmaps in a per-pixel manner. Second, joint shape, pose, size and appearance codes along with instance masks are predicted for detected object centers using specialized heads (Sect. 3.1). Our combined shape and appearance implicit differentiable database of priors is described in Sect. 3.2 and the corresponding zero iso-surface based differentiable rendering is detailed in Sect. 3.4. Lastly, 3D shapes along with their appearance, coupled with 6D pose and sizes of novel objects are jointly optimized during inference to predict accurate shapes, poses and sizes of novel object instances (Sect. 3.5).

3.1 Single-Shot Detection and 3D Prediction

ShAPO represents object instances along with their complete 3D information including shape, pose, appearance and size codes along with corresponding 2D masks through their 2D location in the spatial RGB image, following [7,16,25,

61]. Given an RGB-D observation ($I \in \mathbb{R}^{h_o \times w_o \times 3}$, $D \in \mathbb{R}^{h_o \times w_o}$), ShAPO predicts object-centric heat maps $\hat{Y} \in [0,1]^{\frac{h_o}{R} \times \frac{w_o}{R} \times 1}$ where each detected point $(\hat{x}_i, \hat{y}_i)$ denotes the local maxima in the heatmap ($\hat{Y}$). Here R denotes the heatmap down-sampling factor, and is set to 8 in all our experiments. To predict these heatmaps, a feature backbone based on feature pyramid networks (FPN) [23] is utilized along with a specialized heatmap prediction head. During training, we find the target heatmaps by splatting the ground truth center points (x_i, y_i) using the gaussian kernel $\mathcal{N}(x_i, y_i, \sigma_i)$ where σ_i is relative to the spatial extent of each object (as defined by the corresponding ground truth bounding box annotation). The network is trained to predict ground-truth heatmaps (Y) by minimizing MSE loss over all pixels (x, y) in the heatmap, $\mathcal{L}_{inst} = \sum_{xyg} \left(\hat{Y} - Y \right)^2$. The network also predicts object instance masks ($\hat{M}$) using a specialized head (f_{θ_m}) to output $\hat{M} \in \mathbb{R}^{h_o \times w_o}$, similar to the semantic segmentation head described in [23]. Note that it is crucial for the network to predict masks for accurate downstream optimization (see Sect. 3.4).

3.2   Joint Implicit Shape, Pose and Appearance Prediction

Once the network detects objects, it then predicts their complete 3D information (i.e. 3D shape, 6D pose and size along with the 3D appearance) all in a single-forward pass using specialized heads ($f_{\theta_{sdf}}$, f_{θ_P} and $f_{\theta_{tex}}$) with outputs ($Y_{sdf} \in \mathbb{R}^{\frac{h_o}{R} \times \frac{w_o}{R} \times 64}$, $Y_P \in \mathbb{R}^{\frac{h_o}{R} \times \frac{w_o}{R} \times 13}$ and $Y_{tex} \in \mathbb{R}^{\frac{h_o}{R} \times \frac{w_o}{R} \times 64}$ respectively). During training, the task-specific heads output shape code z_{sdf}, 6D pose $\hat{\mathcal{P}}$, scale $\hat{s}$ and appearance z_{tex} information at each pixel in the down-sampled map ($\frac{h_o}{R} \times \frac{w_o}{R}$). For each object's Pose ($\tilde{\mathcal{P}}$) with respect to the camera coordinate frame, we regress a 3D rotation $\hat{\mathcal{R}} \in SO(3)$, a 3D translation $\hat{t} \in \mathbb{R}^3$ and 1D scales $\hat{s}$ (totaling thirteen numbers). These parameters are used to transform the object shape from canonical frame to the 3D world. We select a 9D rotation $\hat{\mathcal{R}} \in SO(3)$ representation since the neural network can better fit a continuous representation and to avoid discontinuities with lower rotation dimensions, as noted in [62]. Furthermore, we employ a rotation mapping function following [40] to handle ambiguities caused by rotational symmetries. The rotation mapping function is used only for symmetric objects *(bottle, bowl, and can)* in our database during training and it maps ambiguous ground-truth rotations to a single canonical rotation by normalizing the pose rotation. Note that during training, ground-truth shape codes z_{sdf} and appearance codes z_{tex} for each object are obtained from our novel implicit textured differentiable representation (further described in Sect. 3.3).

During training, we jointly optimize for shape, pose, appearance and mask prediction. Specifically, we minimize the masked L_1 loss for shape, pose and appearance prediction, denoted as $\mathcal{L}_{sdf}, \mathcal{L}_{tex}, \mathcal{L}_P$ and a pixel-wise cross-entropy loss for mask prediction $\mathcal{L}_M = \sum_{i=1}^{h_o \cdot w_o} -\log \hat{M}_i \left(M_i^{gt} \right)$ where M_i^{gt} denotes the ground truth category label for each pixel.

During training, we minimize a combination of these losses as follows:

$$\mathcal{L} = \lambda_{inst}\mathcal{L}_{inst} + \lambda_{sdf}\mathcal{L}_{sdf} + \lambda_{tex}\mathcal{L}_{tex} + \lambda_M\mathcal{L}_M + \lambda_P\mathcal{L}_P \qquad (1)$$

where λ is a weighting co-efficient with values determined empirically as $lambda_{inst} = 100$ and $\lambda_{sdf} = \lambda_{tex} = \lambda_P = 1.0$. Note that for shape, appearance and pose predictions, we enforce the L_1 loss based on the probability estimates of the Gaussian heatmaps (Y) i.e. the loss is only applied where Y has a score greater than 0.3 to prevent ambiguity in the space where no object exists. We now describe the shape and appearance representation utilized by our method.

3.3   Implicit Textured Differentiable Database of Priors

We propose a novel joint implicit textured representation to learn from a large variety of CAD models and embed objects in a concise space. This novel representation (as shown in Fig. 2 and Fig. 3) is also used as a strong inductive prior to efficiently optimize the shape and appearance along with the pose and size of objects in a differentiable manner (Sect. 3.4). In our implicit textured database of shape and appearance priors, each object shape is represented as a Signed Distance Field (SDF) where a neural network learns a signed distance function $G(x, z_{sdf}) = s : z_{sdf} \in \mathbb{R}^{64}, s \in \mathbb{R}$ for every 3D point $x \in \mathbb{R}^3$ and the appearance is represented as Texture Fields ($t_\theta : \mathbb{R}^3 \to \mathbb{R}^3$) which maps a 3D point $x \in \mathbb{R}^3$ to an RGB value $c \in \mathbb{R}^3$. Since the mapping between coordinates and colors is ambiguous without shape information, we propose to learn a texture field only at the predicted shape i.e. $t_\theta(x, z_{sdf}, z_{tex}) = c, z_{tex} \in \mathbb{R}^{64}$. The SDF function ($G$) implicitly defines the surface of each object shape by the zero-level set $G(.) = 0$. To learn a shape-code (z_{sdf}) and texture code (z_{tex}) for each object instance, we design a single MLP (multi-layer perceptron) each for shape (to reason about the different geometries in the database) and texture (to predict color information given shape and texture codes). Through conditioning the MLP output on the latent vector, we allow modeling multiple geometries and appearances using a single network each for shape and appearance. Each MLP is trained separately using the supervised ground-truth reconstruction loss L_{SDF} and L_{RGB} as follows:

$$L_{SDF} = |\text{clamp}\,(G(x, z_{sdf}), \delta) - \text{clamp}\,(s_{gt}, \delta)| + L_{contrastive}(z_{sdf}) \quad (2)$$

$$L_{RGB} = \sum_{n=1}^{N} \|c_{gt} - t_\theta(x, z_{sdf}, z_{tex})\|_2^2 \quad (3)$$

where L_{SDF} is a combination of a clipped L_1 loss between ground-truth signed-distance values s_{gt} and predicted SDF $G(x, z_{sdf})$ and a contrastive loss $L_{contrastive} = [m_{pos} - s_p]_+ + [s_n - m_{neg}]_+$. As shown by the t-SNE embeddings [28] (Fig. 3) for the latent shape-code (z_{sdf}), the contrastive loss helps with disentangling the shape space nicely and leads to better downstream regression in the single-shot model (Sect. 3.2). Once we train the implicit shape auto-decoder, we use the learned shape space z_{sdf} to minimize the color loss L_{RGB} which is defined as an MSE loss between predicted color at the surface $t_\theta(x, z_{sdf}, z_{tex})$ and ground-truth color c_{gt}.

We use 3D textured models from the CAD model repository Shapenet [1] to learn our databse of shape and texture priors. Once trained, the MLP networks for both shape and appearance find a disentangled space for color and geometry while keeping semantically-similar objects together (Fig. 3) and provides us with strong priors to be used for 2D and 3D optimization (described in Sect. 3.4).

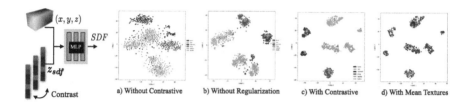

Fig. 3. Deep Implicit shape space for NOCS object Categories

3.4 Differentiable Optimization

A key component of ShAPO is the optimization scheme allowing to refine initial object predictions with respect to the pose, scale, shape, and appearance. Inspired by sdflabel [59], we develop a new differentiable and fast optimization method. Instead of using mesh-based representations, we rely entirely on implicit surfaces, which not only helps us avoid common connectivity and intersection problems, but also provides us full control over sampling density.

Surface Projection. Given input grid points x_i and estimated SDF values s_i, we aim to find a differentiable transformation to extract the object surface encoded in $\mathbf{z}_{sdf}$. A trivial solution would be to simply threshold points with SDF values more than a certain threshold. However, this procedure is not differentiable with respect to the input latent vector $\mathbf{z}_{sdf}$. Instead, we utilize the fact that deriving an SDF value s_i with respect to its input coordinate x_i yields a normal at this point, which can be computed in a single backward pass:

$$n_i = \frac{\partial G(x_i; \mathbf{z}_{sdf})}{\partial x_i}. \quad \text{and} \quad p_i = x_i - \frac{\partial G(x_i; \mathbf{z}_{sdf})}{\partial x_i} G(x_i; \mathbf{z}_{sdf}). \qquad (4)$$

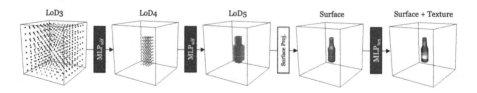

Fig. 4. Octree-based object extraction.

Algorithm 1: Octree-based implicit surface extraction

Input: $\mathbf{x} \in \mathbb{R}^3$ grid points, $l \in \mathbb{L}$ grid levels, $\mathbf{z}_{sdf}$ and $\mathbf{z}_{tex} \in \mathbb{R}^{64}$ latent vectors
Output: $\mathbf{pcd} \in \mathbb{R}^3$ surface points, $\mathbf{nrm} \in \mathbb{N}^3$ normals, $\mathbf{col} \in \mathbb{C}^3$ colors
```
/* Extract object grid (no grad)                                      */
```
1 **for** $l \in \{1, \ldots, N_{LoD}\}$ **do**
2     $\mathbf{sdf} \leftarrow G(\mathbf{x}_l, \mathbf{z}_{sdf})$;   `// regress sdf values`
3     $\mathbf{occ} \leftarrow \mathbf{sdf} < getCellSize(l)$;   `// estimate cell occupancy`
4     $\mathbf{x}_{l_{occ}} \leftarrow \mathbf{x}_l[occ]$;   `// remove unoccupied cells`
5     $\mathbf{x}_{l+1} \leftarrow subdivide(\mathbf{x}_{l_{occ}})$;   `// subdivide cells to go to next LoD`
6 **end**
```
/* Extract object shape and appearance                                */
```
7 $\mathbf{nrm} \leftarrow \text{backprop}(\mathbf{sdf})$;   `// analytically estimate surface normals`
8 $\mathbf{pcd} \leftarrow \mathbf{x} - \mathbf{nrm} * \mathbf{sdf}$;   `// project points onto the surface`
9 $\mathbf{col} \leftarrow t_\theta(\mathbf{pcd}, \mathbf{z}_{sdf}, \mathbf{z}_{tex})$;   `// regress surface texture`
10 **return** *pcd, nrm, col*

Octree-Based Point Sampling. The brute force solution to recover shapes from a learned SDF representation can be obtained by estimating SDF values for a large collection of grid points similar to the procedure used in [59]. To obtain clean surface projections one would then disregard all points x_i outside a narrow band ($|s_i| > 0.03$) of the surface. However, this procedure is extremely inefficient both memory- and compute-wise—For a grid size of $60^3 = 216000$ points, only around 1600 surface points are extracted (accounting to 0.7% of the total number of points). We propose an Octree-based procedure to efficiently extract points. We define a coarse voxel grid and estimate SDF values for each of the points using our trained SDF network. We then disregard voxels whose SDF values are larger than the voxel grid size for this resolution level. The remaining voxels are subdivided each generating eight new voxels. We repeat this procedure until the desired resolution level is reached. In our implementation, we start from level of detail (LoD) 3 and traverse up to LoD 6 depending on the desired resolution level. Finally, when points are extracted we estimate their SDF values and normals and project them onto the object surface. The pseudo-code implementation of the Octree-based surface extraction is provided in Algorithm 1 with the visualization shown in Fig. 4.

3.5 Inference

During inference, we first perform predictions using our single-shot model. Object detection is performed using peak detection [61] on the outputs of predicted heatmaps ($\hat{Y}$). Each detected center point ($\boldsymbol{x}_i, \boldsymbol{y}_i$) corresponds to maxima in the heatmap output ($\hat{Y}$). Second, we sample shape, pose and appearance codes of each object from the output of task-specific heads at the detected center location (x_i, y_i) via $\boldsymbol{z}_{sdf} = Y_{sdf}(\boldsymbol{x}_i, \boldsymbol{y}_i)$, $\boldsymbol{z}_{tex} = Y_{tex}(\boldsymbol{x}_i, \boldsymbol{y}_i)$ and $\tilde{\mathcal{P}} = Y_P(\boldsymbol{x}_i, \boldsymbol{y}_i)$.

    We utilize the predicted shape, pose, size and appearance codes as an initial estimate to further refine through our differentiable optimization pipeline.

Table 1. Quantitative comparison of 6D pose estimation and 3D object detection on NOCS [54]: Comparison with strong baselines. Best results are highlighted in **bold**. * denotes the method does not report IOU metrics since size and scale is not evaluated. We report metrics using nocs-level class predictions for a fair comparison with all baselines.

	Method	CAMERA25						REAL275					
		IOU25	IOU50	5° 5 cm	5° 10 cm	10° 5 cm	10° 10 cm	IOU25	IOU50	5° 5 cm	5° 10 cm	10° 5 cm	10° 10 cm
1	NOCS [54]	91.1	83.9	40.9	38.6	64.6	65.1	84.8	78.0	10.0	9.8	25.2	25.8
2	Synthesis* [3]	–	.	–	–	–	–	–	–	0.9	1.4	2.4	5.5
3	Metric Scale [26]	93.8	90.7	20.2	28.2	55.4	58.9	81.6	68.1	5.3	5.5	24.7	26.5
4	ShapePrior [51]	81.6	72.4	59.0	59.6	81.0	81.3	81.2	77.3	21.4	21.4	54.1	54.1
5	CASS [2]	–	–	–	–	–	–	84.2	77.7	23.5	23.8	58.0	58.3
6	CenterSnap [16]	93.2	92.3	63.0	69.5	79.5	87.9	83.5	80.2	27.2	29.2	58.8	64.4
7	CenterSnap-R [16]	93.2	92.5	66.2	71.7	81.3	87.9	83.5	**80.2**	29.1	31.6	64.3	70.9
8	ShAPO (Ours)	**94.5**	**93.5**	**66.6**	**75.9**	**81.9**	**89.2**	**85.3**	79.0	**48.8**	**57.0**	**66.8**	**78.0**

Our optimizer takes as input the predicted implicit shapes in the canonical frame of reference along with the masks predictions ($\hat{M}$), color codes (z_{tex}) and extracted 3×3 rotation $\hat{\mathcal{R}}_i^p$, 3D translation vector $\hat{t}_i^p$ and 1D scales $\hat{s}_i^p$ from recovered Pose $\tilde{\mathcal{P}}$. Although a variety of related works consider mean class predictions as initial priors, we mainly utilize the regressed outputs of shape, appearance and pose for the optimization pipeline since the initial estimates are very robust (see Table 1). We utilize the predicted SDF to recover the complete surface of each object, in a coarse-to-fine manner, using the proposed differentiable zero-isosurface projection (Sect. 3.4). After fixing the decoder (G) parameters, we optimize the feature vector z_{sdf} by estimating the nearest neighbour between the predicted projected pointclouds and masked pointclouds obtained from depth map and predicted masks ($\hat{M}$) of each object. In essence, a shape code z_{sdf} is refined using the Maximum-a-Posterior (MAP) estimation as follows:

$$z_{sdf} = \arg\min_{z}(\mathcal{L}\left(D(G(z,x)), P_d\right) \tag{5}$$

where D() denotes the differentiable iso-surface projection described in Sect. 3.4 and P_d denotes the pointclouds obtained from masked depth maps. We further optimize the RGB component similarly by optimizing the difference in colors between the masked image color values (C_d) and colors obtained using the regressed color codes decoded by the texture field (t_θ) $z_{tex} = \arg\min_{z}(\mathcal{L}\left(D(t_\theta(z,x)), C_d\right)$. We further allow t_θ weights to change to allow for a finer level of reconstruction. For qualitative results please consult supplementary material.

4   Experiments

In this section, we empirically validate the performance of our method. In essence, our goal is to answer these questions: 1) How well does ShAPO recover pose and sizes of novel objects. 2) How well does ShAPO perform in terms of reconstructing geometry and appearance of multiple objects from a single-view

RGB-D observation? 3) How well does our differentiable iterative improvement and multi-level optimization impact shape, appearance, pose and size?

Datasets. We utilize the **NOCS** [54] dataset for both shape reconstruction and category-level 6D pose and size estimation evaluation. For training, we utilize the CAMERA dataset which comprises 300K synthetic images, of which 25K are hold-out for evaluation. The training dataset includes 1085 object models from 6 different categories - *bottle, bowl, camera, can, laptop and mug* whereas the evaluation dataset includes 184 different models. The REAL dataset train-set comprises of 7 scenes with 4300 images, and test-set comprises of 6 scenes with 2750 real-world images.

Table 2. Quantitative comparison of 3D shape reconstruction on NOCS [54]: Evaluated with **CD** metric (10^{-2}). Lower is better.

	Method	CAMERA25							REAL275						
		Bottle	Bowl	Camera	Can	Laptop	Mug	Mean	Bottle	Bowl	Camera	Can	Laptop	Mug	Mean
1	Reconstruction [51]	0.18	0.16	0.40	0.097	0.20	0.14	0.20	0.34	0.12	0.89	0.15	0.29	0.10	0.32
2	ShapePrior [51]	0.34	0.22	0.90	0.22	0.33	0.21	0.37	0.50	0.12	0.99	0.24	0.71	0.097	0.44
3	CenterSnap	0.11	0.10	0.29	0.13	0.07	0.12	0.14	0.13	0.10	0.43	0.09	0.07	0.06	0.15
3	**ShAPO (Ours)**	0.14	0.08	0.2	0.14	0.07	0.11	0.16	0.1	0.08	0.4	0.07	0.08	0.06	0.13

Metrics. We evaluate the performance of 3D object detection and 6D pose estimation independently following [54]. We use the following key metrics: 1) Average-precision for different IOU-overlap thresholds (**IOU25 and IOU50**). 2) Average precision for which the error is less than $n°$ for rotation and m cm for translation (**5°5 cm, 5°10 cm and 10°10 cm**). We use Chamfer distance (CD) for shape reconstruction following [58].

4.1 Implementation Details

ShAPO is sequentially trained first on the CAMERA set with minimal fine-tuning on Real training set. For SDF, we use an MLP with 8 layers and hidden

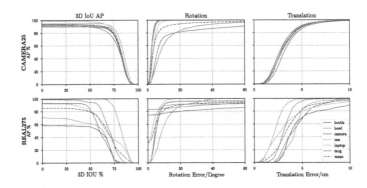

Fig. 5. Average precision of ShAPO for various IOU, rotation and translation thresholds on NOCS CAMERA25 and REAL275 dataset.

size of 512. For color, we utilize a Siren MLP [44] as it can fit higher frequencies better. We train the SDF and Color MLPs on all categories for 2000 epochs. We use Pytorch [38] for our models and training pipeline implementation. For optimization, we use an adaptive learning rate which varies with the obtained masks of each object since we believe masks capture the confidence of heatmap prediction during detection. We optimize each object for 200 iterations.

4.2 NOCS 6D Pose and Size Estimation Benchmark

NOCS Baselines: We compare eight model variants to show effectiveness of our method: (1) **NOCS** [54]: Regresses NOCS map and predicts poses using similarity transform with depth maps. We report the best pose estimation configuration in NOCS (i.e. 32-bin classification) (2) **Shape Prior** [51]: Estimates shape deformation for inter-class variation. (3) **CASS** [2]: Regress the pose and size with first detecting 2D bounding boxes. (4) **Metric-Scale** [26]: Estimates the object center and metric scale (5) **CenterSnap** [16]: Single-shot approach to predict pose and size (6) **CenterSnap-R** [16]: ICP optimization done with the predicted point-cloud based shape. Following [16], we do not compare against 6D pose tracking baselines such as [52,56] which need pose initializations and are not end-to-end detection based (i.e. they do not report mAP metrics)

Comparison with Strong Baselines on NOCS: Table 1 and Fig. 5 shows the result of our proposed ShAPO method. ShAPO consistently outperforms all the baseline methods on 6D pose and size estimation and 3D object detection. Specifically, ShAPO method shows superior generalization on the REAL test-set by achieving a mAP of 85.3% for 3D IOU at 0.25, 57.0% for 6D pose at 5° 10 cm and 78.0% for 6D pose at 10° 10 cm, hence demonstrating an absolute improvement of 1.8%, 25.4% and 7.1% over the best-performing baseline on the Real dataset. Our method also achieves better generalization on the never-seen CAMERA evaluation set. We achieve a mAP of 94.5% for 3D IOU at 0.25, 75.9% for 6D pose at 5° 10 cm and 89.2% for 6D pose at 10° 10 cm, demonstrating an absolute improvement of 1.3%, 4.2% and 1.3% over the best-performing baseline.

4.3 Generalizable Implicit Object Representation

In this experiment, we evaluate the effectiveness of our generalizable implicit object representation as well as the efficiency of our octree-based differentiable optimization. To do that, we isolate our implicit representation from the detection pipeline and consider the 3D reconstruction/identification task - given a novel object from NOCS test split, we optimize our representation for 200 iterations, while keeping f_{sdf} and f_{rgb} weights frozen, to find the best fitting model in terms of both shape and texture. We initialize the optimization using the average latent feature per class. The standard Adam solver with the learning rate of 0.001 for both for both shape and appearance losses (L2 norms) is used

Table 3. Generalizable Implicit Representation Ablation: We evaluate the efficiency (point sampling/time(s)/memory(MB)) and generalization (shape(CD) and texture(PSNR) reconstruction) capabilities of our implicit object representation as well as its sampling efficiency for different levels of detail (LoDs) and compare it to the ordinary grid sampling. All ablations were executed on NVIDIA RTX A6000 GPU.

Grid type	Resolution	Point Sampling		Efficiency (per object)		Reconstruction	
		Input	Output	Time (s)	Memory (MB)	Shape (CD)	Texture (PSNR)
Ordinary	40	64000	412	10.96	3994	0.30	10.08
	50	125000	835	18.78	5570	0.19	12.83
	60	216000	1400	30.51	7850	0.33	**19.52**
OctGrid	LoD5	1521	704	**5.53**	**2376**	0.19	9.27
	LoD6	5192	3228	6.88	2880	**0.18**	13.63
	LoD7	20246	13023	12.29	5848	0.24	16.14

with weight factors 1 and 0.3 respectively. We use three different octree resolution levels - from LoD5 to LoD7. Additionally, we show three different resolution levels for the standard ordinary grid sampling [59] (40, 50, 60).

Table 3 summarizes the results of the ablation by comparing different modalities with respect to the average point sampling (input vs output) and time efficiency, average GPU memory consumption, as well as reconstruction for shape (Chamfer distance) and texture (PSNR). One can see that our representation is significantly more efficient than the ordinary grid representation with respect to all metrics. While LoD7 provides best overall results, we use LoD6 for our experiments since it results in the optimal speed/memory/reconstruction trade-off. We show an example optimization procedure in Fig. 6.

4.4 NOCS Object Reconstruction Benchmark

To quantitatively analyze the reconstruction accuracy, we measure the Chamfer distance (CD) between our reconstructed pointclouds and the ground-truth CAD model in NOCS. Our results are reported in Table 2. Our results show consistently lower CD metrics for all class categories which shows superior reconstruction performance on novel object instances. We report a lower mean Chamfer distance of 0.14 on CAMERA25 and 0.15 on REAL275 compared to 0.20 and 0.32 reported by the competitive baseline [51].

5   Qualitative Results

We qualitatively analyze the performance of our method **ShAPO** on the NOCS Real275 dataset [54]. As shown in Fig. 7, our method reconstructs accurate 3D shapes and appearances of multiple novel objects along with estimating the 6D pose and sizes without requiring 3D CAD models of these novel instances (Results shown on 4 different real-world scenes containing novel object instances using different camera-view points i.e. orange and green backgrounds). For further qualitative results, please consult supplementary materials.

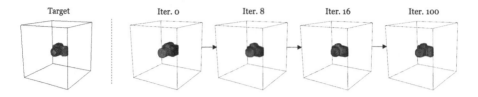

Fig. 6. Shape/Appearance optimization

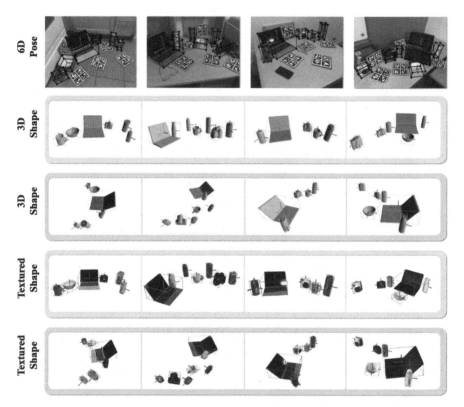

Fig. 7. ShAPO Qualitative 6D pose estimation and 3D Shape Reconstructions including Appearance: Given a single-view RGB-D observation, our method reconstructs accurate 3D shapes along with appearances and estimates the 6D pose and sizes of multiple objects in the scene. Here, reconstructions are shown with different camera view-points i.e. orange and green backgrounds.

6   Conclusion

In this paper we proposed ShAPO , an end-to-end method for joint multi-object detection, 3D textured reconstruction, 6D object pose and size estimation. Our method detects and reconstructs novel objects without having access to their ground truth 3D meshes. To facilitate this, we proposed a novel, generalizable shape and appearance space that yields accurate textured 3D reconstructions of objects in the wild. To alleviate sampling inefficiencies leading to increased time and memory requirements, we proposed a novel octree-based differentiable optimization procedure that is significantly more efficient than alternative grid based representations. For future work we will explore how the proposed method can be used to build object databases in new environments, to alleviate the cost and time required to construct high-quality 3D textured assets. A second avenue of future work consists of extensions to multi-view settings and integrating our work with SLAM pipelines for joint camera motion and object pose, shape and texture estimation in static and dynamic scenes.

References

1. Chang, A.X., et al.: ShapeNet: an information-rich 3d model repository. arXiv preprint arXiv:1512.03012 (2015)
2. Chen, D., Li, J., Wang, Z., Xu, K.: Learning canonical shape space for category-level 6d object pose and size estimation. In: Proceedings of the IEEE/CVF Conference on Computer Vision and Pattern Recognition, pp. 11973–11982 (2020)
3. Chen, X., Dong, Z., Song, J., Geiger, A., Hilliges, O.: Category level object pose estimation via neural analysis-by-synthesis. In: Vedaldi, A., Bischof, H., Brox, T., Frahm, J.-M. (eds.) ECCV 2020. LNCS, vol. 12371, pp. 139–156. Springer, Cham (2020). https://doi.org/10.1007/978-3-030-58574-7_9
4. Chen, Z., Zhang, H.: Learning implicit fields for generative shape modeling. In: Proceedings of the IEEE/CVF Conference on Computer Vision and Pattern Recognition, pp. 5939–5948 (2019)
5. Choy, C.B., Xu, D., Gwak, J.Y., Chen, K., Savarese, S.: 3D-R2N2: a unified approach for single and multi-view 3D object reconstruction. In: Leibe, B., Matas, J., Sebe, N., Welling, M. (eds.) ECCV 2016. LNCS, vol. 9912, pp. 628–644. Springer, Cham (2016). https://doi.org/10.1007/978-3-319-46484-8_38
6. Cifuentes, C.G., Issac, J., Wüthrich, M., Schaal, S., Bohg, J.: Probabilistic articulated real-time tracking for robot manipulation. IEEE Robot. Autom. Lett. 2(2), 577–584 (2016)
7. Duan, K., Bai, S., Xie, L., Qi, H., Huang, Q., Tian, Q.: CenterNet: keypoint triplets for object detection. In: Proceedings of the IEEE/CVF International Conference on Computer Vision, pp. 6569–6578 (2019)
8. Fan, H., Su, H., Guibas, L.J.: A point set generation network for 3d object reconstruction from a single image. In: Proceedings of the IEEE Conference on Computer Vision and Pattern Recognition, pp. 605–613 (2017)
9. Ferrari, C., Canny, J.F.: Planning Optimal Grasps. In: ICRA, vol. 3, p. 6 (1992)
10. Girshick, R., Donahue, J., Darrell, T., Malik, J.: Rich feature hierarchies for accurate object detection and semantic segmentation. In: Computer Vision and Pattern Recognition (2014)
11. Gkioxari, G., Malik, J., Johnson, J.: Mesh R-CNN. In: Proceedings of the IEEE/CVF International Conference on Computer Vision, pp. 9785–9795 (2019)
12. Goodwin, W., Vaze, S., Havoutis, I., Posner, I.: Zero-shot category-level object pose estimation. arXiv preprint (2022)
13. Groueix, T., Fisher, M., Kim, V.G., Russell, B., Aubry, M.: AtlasNet: A Papier-Mâché Approach to Learning 3D Surface Generation. In: Proceedings IEEE Conference on Computer Vision and Pattern Recognition (CVPR) (2018)

14. He, K., Gkioxari, G., Dollár, P., Girshick, R.B.: Mask R-CNN. In: ICCV (2017)
15. Hodan, T., Barath, D., Matas, J.: Epos: estimating 6d pose of objects with symmetries. In: CVPR (2020)
16. Irshad, M.Z., Kollar, T., Laskey, M., Stone, K., Kira, Z.: Centersnap: single-shot multi-object 3d shape reconstruction and categorical 6d pose and size estimation. In: IEEE International Conference on Robotics and Automation (ICRA) (2022). https://arxiv.org/abs/2203.01929
17. Irshad, M.Z., Ma, C.Y., Kira, Z.: Hierarchical cross-modal agent for robotics vision-and-language navigation. In: 2021 IEEE International Conference on Robotics and Automation (ICRA), pp. 13238–13246 (2021). https://doi.org/10.1109/ICRA48506.2021.9561806
18. Irshad, M.Z., Mithun, N.C., Seymour, Z., Chiu, H.P., Samarasekera, S., Kumar, R.: Sasra: semantically-aware spatio-temporal reasoning agent for vision-and-language navigation in continuous environments (2022). https://arxiv.org/abs/2108.11945
19. Jiang, Z., Zhu, Y., Svetlik, M., Fang, K., Zhu, Y.: Synergies between affordance and geometry: 6-Dof grasp detection via implicit representations. Robotics: science and systems (2021)
20. Kato, H., Ushiku, Y., Harada, T.: Neural 3d mesh renderer. In: Proceedings of the IEEE Conference on Computer Vision and Pattern Recognition, pp. 3907–3916 (2018)
21. Kehl, W., Manhardt, F., Tombari, F., Ilic, S., Navab, N.: Ssd-6d: making rgb-based 3d detection and 6d pose estimation great again. In: ICCV (2017)
22. Kehl, W., Milletari, F., Tombari, F., Ilic, S., Navab, N.: Deep learning of local RGB-D patches for 3D object detection and 6D pose estimation. In: Leibe, B., Matas, J., Sebe, N., Welling, M. (eds.) ECCV 2016. LNCS, vol. 9907, pp. 205–220. Springer, Cham (2016). https://doi.org/10.1007/978-3-319-46487-9_13
23. Kirillov, A., Girshick, R., He, K., Dollár, P.: Panoptic feature pyramid networks. In: Proceedings of the IEEE/CVF Conference on Computer Vision and Pattern Recognition, pp. 6399–6408 (2019)
24. Kuo, W., Angelova, A., Lin, T.-Y., Dai, A.: Mask2CAD: 3D shape prediction by learning to segment and retrieve. In: Vedaldi, A., Bischof, H., Brox, T., Frahm, J.-M. (eds.) ECCV 2020. LNCS, vol. 12348, pp. 260–277. Springer, Cham (2020). https://doi.org/10.1007/978-3-030-58580-8_16
25. Laskey, M., Thananjeyan, B., Stone, K., Kollar, T., Tjersland, M.: SimNet: enabling robust unknown object manipulation from pure synthetic data via stereo. In: 5th Annual Conference on Robot Learning (2021)
26. Lee, T., Lee, B.U., Kim, M., Kweon, I.S.: Category-level metric scale object shape and pose estimation. IEEE Robot. Autom. Lett. 6(4), 8575–8582 (2021)
27. Li, Z., Niklaus, S., Snavely, N., Wang, O.: Neural scene flow fields for space-time view synthesis of dynamic scenes. In: CVPR (2021)
28. Van der Maaten, L., Hinton, G.: Visualizing data using t-SNE. J. Mach. Learn. Res. 9(11) (2008)
29. Mescheder, L., Oechsle, M., Niemeyer, M., Nowozin, S., Geiger, A.: Occupancy networks: learning 3d reconstruction in function space. In: CVPR (2019)
30. Mildenhall, B., Srinivasan, P.P., Tancik, M., Barron, J.T., Ramamoorthi, R., Ng, R.: NeRF: representing scenes as neural radiance fields for view synthesis. In: Vedaldi, A., Bischof, H., Brox, T., Frahm, J.-M. (eds.) ECCV 2020. LNCS, vol. 12346, pp. 405–421. Springer, Cham (2020). https://doi.org/10.1007/978-3-030-58452-8_24

31. Nie, Y., Han, X., Guo, S., Zheng, Y., Chang, J., Zhang, J.J.: Total3dunderstanding: joint layout, object pose and mesh reconstruction for indoor scenes from a single image. In: IEEE/CVF Conference on Computer Vision and Pattern Recognition (CVPR), June 2020

32. Niemeyer, M., Geiger, A.: Giraffe: Representing scenes as compositional generative neural feature fields. In: Proceedings of IEEE Conference on Computer Vision and Pattern Recognition (CVPR) (2021)

33. Niemeyer, M., Mescheder, L., Oechsle, M., Geiger, A.: Differentiable volumetric rendering: learning implicit 3d representations without 3d supervision. In: CVPR (2020)

34. Oechsle, M., Mescheder, L., Niemeyer, M., Strauss, T., Geiger, A.: Texture fields: learning texture representations in function space. In: Proceedings IEEE International Conference on Computer Vision (ICCV) (2019)

35. Ost, J., Mannan, F., Thuerey, N., Knodt, J., Heide, F.: Neural scene graphs for dynamic scenes. In: Proceedings of the IEEE/CVF Conference on Computer Vision and Pattern Recognition (CVPR), pp. 2856–2865, June 2021

36. Park, J.J., Florence, P., Straub, J., Newcombe, R., Lovegrove, S.: Deepsdf: learning continuous signed distance functions for shape representation. In: CVPR (2019)

37. Park, K., Patten, T., Vincze, M.: Pix2pose: Pixel-wise coordinate regression of objects for 6d pose estimation. In: ICCV (2019)

38. Paszke, A., et al.: Pytorch: an imperative style, high-performance deep learning library. In: Wallach, H., Larochelle, H., Beygelzimer, A., d' Alché-Buc, F., Fox, E., Garnett, R. (eds.) Advances in Neural Information Processing Systems 32, pp. 8024–8035. Curran Associates, Inc. (2019)

39. Peng, S., Liu, Y., Huang, Q., Zhou, X., Bao, H.: Pvnet: pixel-wise voting network for 6dof pose estimation. In: CVPR (2019)

40. Pitteri, G., Ramamonjisoa, M., Ilic, S., Lepetit, V.: On object symmetries and 6d pose estimation from images. In: 2019 International Conference on 3D Vision (3DV), pp. 614–622. IEEE (2019)

41. Rad, M., Lepetit, V.: Bb8: a scalable, accurate, robust to partial occlusion method for predicting the 3d poses of challenging objects without using depth. In: ICCV (2017)

42. Remelli, E., Lukoianov, A., Richter, S., Guillard, B., Bagautdinov, T., Baque, P., Fua, P.: Meshsdf: differentiable iso-surface extraction. In: Larochelle, H., Ranzato, M., Hadsell, R., Balcan, M.F., Lin, H. (eds.) Advances in Neural Information Processing Systems, vol. 33, pp. 22468–22478. Curran Associates, Inc. (2020), https://proceedings.neurips.cc/paper/2020/file/fe40fb944ee700392ed51bfe84dd4e3d-Paper.pdf

43. Shugurov, I., Zakharov, S., Ilic, S.: Dpodv2: Dense correspondence-based 6 dof pose estimation. TPAMI (2021)

44. Sitzmann, V., Martel, J., Bergman, A., Lindell, D., Wetzstein, G.: Implicit neural representations with periodic activation functions. NeurIPS (2020)

45. Sitzmann, V., Zollhoefer, M., Wetzstein, G.: Scene representation networks: Continuous 3d-structure-aware neural scene representations. NeurIPS (2019)

46. Sundermeyer, M., Marton, Z.-C., Durner, M., Brucker, M., Triebel, R.: Implicit 3D orientation learning for 6D object detection from RGB images. In: Ferrari, V., Hebert, M., Sminchisescu, C., Weiss, Y. (eds.) ECCV 2018. LNCS, vol. 11210, pp. 712–729. Springer, Cham (2018). https://doi.org/10.1007/978-3-030-01231-1_43

47. Sundermeyer, M., Marton, Z.C., Durner, M., Triebel, R.: Augmented autoencoders: implicit 3D orientation learning for 6d object detection. Int. J. Comput. Vision **128**(3), 714–729 (2020)

48. Takikawa, T., et al.: Neural geometric level of detail: Real-time rendering with implicit 3d shapes. In: CVPR (2021)

49. Tejani, A., Tang, D., Kouskouridas, R., Kim, T.-K.: Latent-class hough forests for 3D object detection and pose estimation. In: Fleet, D., Pajdla, T., Schiele, B., Tuytelaars, T. (eds.) ECCV 2014. LNCS, vol. 8694, pp. 462–477. Springer, Cham (2014). https://doi.org/10.1007/978-3-319-10599-4_30

50. Tekin, B., Sinha, S.N., Fua, P.: Real-time seamless single shot 6d object pose prediction. In: CVPR (2018)

51. Tian, M., Ang, M.H., Lee, G.H.: Shape prior deformation for categorical 6D object pose and size estimation. In: Vedaldi, A., Bischof, H., Brox, T., Frahm, J.-M. (eds.) ECCV 2020. LNCS, vol. 12366, pp. 530–546. Springer, Cham (2020). https://doi.org/10.1007/978-3-030-58589-1_32

52. Wang, C., et al.: 6-pack: category-level 6d pose tracker with anchor-based keypoints. In: 2020 IEEE International Conference on Robotics and Automation (ICRA), pp. 10059–10066. IEEE (2020)

53. Wang, C., et al.: Densefusion: 6d object pose estimation by iterative dense fusion. In: CVPR (2019)

54. Wang, H., Sridhar, S., Huang, J., Valentin, J., Song, S., Guibas, L.J.: Normalized object coordinate space for category-level 6d object pose and size estimation. In: CVPR (2019)

55. Wang, N., Zhang, Y., Li, Z., Fu, Y., Liu, W., Jiang, Y.-G.: Pixel2Mesh: generating 3D mesh models from single RGB images. In: Ferrari, V., Hebert, M., Sminchisescu, C., Weiss, Y. (eds.) ECCV 2018. LNCS, vol. 11215, pp. 55–71. Springer, Cham (2018). https://doi.org/10.1007/978-3-030-01252-6_4

56. Wen, B., Bekris, K.E.: Bundletrack: 6d pose tracking for novel objects without instance or category-level 3d models. In: IEEE/RSJ International Conference on Intelligent Robots and Systems (2021)

57. Xiang, Y., Schmidt, T., Narayanan, V., Fox, D.: Posecnn: a convolutional neural network for 6d object pose estimation in cluttered scenes. In: RSS (2018)

58. Yuan, W., Khot, T., Held, D., Mertz, C., Hebert, M.: PCN: Point completion network. In: 3D Vision (3DV), 2018 International Conference on (2018)

59. Zakharov, S., Kehl, W., Bhargava, A., Gaidon, A.: Autolabeling 3d objects with differentiable rendering of sdf shape priors. In: CVPR (2020)

60. Zhang, C., Cui, Z., Zhang, Y., Zeng, B., Pollefeys, M., Liu, S.: Holistic 3d scene understanding from a single image with implicit representation. In: CVPR (2021)

61. Zhou, X., Wang, D., Krähenbühl, P.: Objects as points. arXiv preprint arXiv:1904.07850 (2019)

62. Zhou, Y., Barnes, C., Lu, J., Yang, J., Li, H.: On the continuity of rotation representations in neural networks. In: CVPR (2019)

3D Siamese Transformer Network for Single Object Tracking on Point Clouds

Le Hui, Lingpeng Wang, Linghua Tang, Kaihao Lan, Jin Xie[✉],
and Jian Yang[✉]

Key Lab of Intelligent Perception and Systems for High-Dimensional Information
of Ministry of Education Jiangsu Key Lab of Image and Video Understanding
for Social Security PCA Lab, School of Computer Science and Engineering,
Nanjing University of Science and Technology, Nanjing, China
{le.hui,cslpwang,tanglinghua,lkh,csjxie,csjyang}@njust.edu.cn

Abstract. Siamese network based trackers formulate 3D single object
tracking as cross-correlation learning between point features of a template and a search area. Due to the large appearance variation between
the template and search area during tracking, how to learn the robust
cross correlation between them for identifying the potential target in the
search area is still a challenging problem. In this paper, we explicitly
use Transformer to form a 3D Siamese Transformer network for learning robust cross correlation between the template and the search area of
point clouds. Specifically, we develop a Siamese point Transformer network to learn shape context information of the target. Its encoder uses
self-attention to capture non-local information of point clouds to characterize the shape information of the object, and the decoder utilizes
cross-attention to upsample discriminative point features. After that, we
develop an iterative coarse-to-fine correlation network to learn the robust
cross correlation between the template and the search area. It formulates
the cross-feature augmentation to associate the template with the potential target in the search area via cross attention. To further enhance the
potential target, it employs the ego-feature augmentation that applies
self-attention to the local k-NN graph of the feature space to aggregate target features. Experiments on the KITTI, nuScenes, and Waymo
datasets show that our method achieves state-of-the-art performance on
the 3D single object tracking task. Source code is available at https://
github.com/fpthink/STNet.

Keywords: 3D single object tracking · Siamese network ·
Transformer · Point clouds

1 Introduction

Object tracking is a classic task in computer vision, and contributes to various
applications, such as autonomous driving [34,39,41], visual surveillance [59,72],

Supplementary Information The online version contains supplementary material
available at https://doi.org/10.1007/978-3-031-20086-1_17.

robotics vision [8,38]. Early efforts [1,11,32,33,61] focus on visual object tracking that uses RGB images obtained by cameras. Recently, with the development of 3D sensors, such as LiDAR, 3D data is easy to acquire and set up 3D object tracking. Single object tracking is an important task in 3D computer vision. For example, it can improve the safety of autonomous vehicles by predicting the trajectory of key targets. However, due to the sparsity and irregular distribution of 3D points, existing popular schemes on 2D visual tracking cannot be directly applied to 3D single object tracking. Therefore, how to effectively track 3D objects in the complex scene is still a challenging problem.

Recently, Siamese network based trackers have raised much attention in the 3D single object tracking task. In [19], Giancola *et al.* first proposed a shape completion based 3D Siamese tracker, which encodes shape information into a template to improve the matching accuracy between the template and candidate proposals in the search area. However, it is time-consuming and not an end-to-end method. To this end, Qi *et al.* [50] proposed the point-to-box (P2B) network, which can be trained end-to-end and has a shorter inference time. Based on PointNet++ [49], P2B employs a target-specific feature augmentation module for the cross-correlation operation and adopts VoteNet [47] to regress the target center from the search area. Based on P2B, zheng *et al.* [78] proposed a box-aware tracker by inferring the size and the part priors of the target object from the template to capture the structure information of the target. Shan *et al.* [52] added a self-attention module in the VoteNet. Due to sparse point clouds, VoteNet is not suitable for regressing the target center in outdoor scenes. Lately, based on the bird's eye view feature map, Cui *et al.* [9] used cross-attention to learn the 2D relationship between the template and search to localize the target. In addition, Hui *et al.* [26] proposed a voxel-to-BEV tracker, which regresses the target center from the dense BEV feature map after performing shape completion in the search area. Nonetheless, due to the large appearance variation between template and search area, these simple cross-correlation feature learning cannot effectively characterize the correlation between them well.

In this paper, we propose a novel 3D Siamese Transformer tracking framework, which explicitly uses Transformer to learn the robust cross correlation between the template and search area in 3D single object tracking. Specifically, we first develop a Siamese point Transformer network by learning long-range contextual information of point clouds to extract discriminative point features for the template and search area, respectively. Our Siamese point Transformer network is an encoder-decoder structure. On each layer of the encoder, after aggregating the local features of the point cloud, we develop a non-local feature embedding module, which uses self-attention to capture the non-local information of point clouds. It is desired that the points can utilize the non-local features from the same instance to capture the whole structure of the object, *i.e.*, shape information. In the decoder, we propose an adaptive feature interpolation module to propagate features from subsampled points to the original points to generate discriminative point features. Compared with the commonly used distance-based interpolation [49], the adaptive feature interpolation can effectively obtain discriminative point features through the learnable weights of the attention. Once we obtain discriminative point features of the template and the search area, we further develop an iterative coarse-to-fine correlation network to learn the cross-correlation between them for localizing the target in the search area. It consists of a cross-feature augmentation module and an ego-feature augmentation module. In the cross-feature augmentation module, we fuse the two feature maps from the template and search area by building cross-correlation between them via cross-attention. In this way, the template information is embedded into the search area for localizing the potential target. Once we localize the potential target, we use ego-feature augmentation to further enhance the potential target by applying self-attention to the local k-NN graph in the feature space instead of using the common self-attention over the whole point clouds. By applying self-attention to the k-NN graph in the feature space, the point features with similar semantic information can be aggregated, thereby enhancing the potential target. By iteratively performing the cross-feature and ego-feature modules, we can obtain a more discriminative feature fusion map for identifying the target from the search area. Finally, we integrate the Siamese point Transformer network, the iterative cross-correlation network, and the detection network [26] to form the Siamese Transformer tracking framework. Experiments on the KITTI [18], nuScenes [4], and Waymo [57] datasets demonstrate the effectiveness of the proposed method on the 3D single object tracking task.

The contributions of this paper are as follows:

- We present a Siamese point Transformer network that explicitly uses the attention mechanism to form an encoder-decoder structure to learn the shape context information of the target.
- We develop an iterative coarse-to-fine correlation network that iteratively applies the attention mechanism to the template and the search area for learning robust cross-correlation between them.
- The proposed 3D Siamese Transformer network achieves state-of-the-art performance on the KITTI, nuScenes, and Waymo datasets in 3D single object tracking.

2 Related Work

3D Single Object Tracking. Early single object tracking approaches [3,24] focus on 2D images. Recently, Siamese network based trackers [22,23,60,63,80] have significantly improved tracking performance compared to the traditional correlation filtering based trackers [12,13,25,75]. However, due to the lack of accurate depth information in RGB images, visual object tracking may not be able to accurately estimate the depth to the target.

Previous methods [2,40,46,56] adopt RGB-D data for 3D single object tracking. RGB-D based trackers [28,29,36] heavily rely on RGB information and adopt the same schemes used in visual object tracking with additional depth information. Although these approaches can produce very promising results, they may fail when critical RGB information is degraded. Recently, researchers [19,45] have focused on using 3D point clouds for single object tracking. Giancola *et al.* [19] first proposed a shape completion based 3D Siamese tracker (SC3D) for single object tracking. It performs template matching between the template and plenty of candidate proposals generated by Kalman filter [20] in the search area, where a shape completion network is applied to the template for capturing the shape information of the object. Based on SC3D, Feng *et al.* [17] proposed a two-stage framework called Re-Track to re-track the lost objects of the coarse stage in the fine stage. However, SC3D cannot be end-to-end trained. To achieve end-to-end training, point-to-box (P2B) [50] first localizes the potential target center in the search area and then generates candidate proposals for verification. Due to incomplete targets in point clouds, box-aware tracker [78] based on P2B proposes a box-aware feature fusion module to embed the bounding box information given in the first frame to enhance the object features, where the size and part information of the template are encoded. Shan *et al.* [52] improved P2B by adding a self-attention module in the detector VoteNet [47] to generate refined attention features for increasing tracking accuracy. In addition, Cui *et al.* [9] proposed a Transformer-based method that first uses 3D sparse convolution to extract features to form a 2D BEV feature map and then uses Transformer to learn the 2D relationship between the template and search to localize the target. Lately, to handle sparse point clouds, Hui *et al.* [26] proposed a Siamese voxel-to-BEV tracker, which contains a Siamese shape-ware feature learning network and a voxel-to-BEV target localization network. It performs shape generation in the search area by generating a dense point cloud to capture the shape information of the target.

3D Multi-object Tracking. Different from 3D single object tracking, 3D multi-object tracking (MOT) usually adopts the tracking-by-detection paradigm [31,51,53,71]. 3D MOT trackers usually first use 3D detectors [47, 54,55] to detect object instances for each frame and then associate the detected objects across all frames. Early 3D multi-object tracking approaches [7,68] adopt 3D Kalman filters to predict the state of associated trajectories and objects instances. In [68], Weng *et al.* first used PointRCNN [54] to obtain 3D detections from a LiDAR point cloud, and then combined 3D Kalman filter and Hungarian algorithm for state estimation and data association. With the wide adoption of deep neural networks, recent methods [65,70,76] use neural networks to learn the 3D appearance and motion features for increasing accuracy. Lately, Weng *et al.* [69] proposed a graph neural network that uses a graph neural network for feature interaction by simultaneously considering the 2D and 3D spaces. Yin *et al.* [74] first proposed CenterPoint to detect 3D objects on the point clouds and then used a greedy closest-point matching algorithm to associate objects frame by frame.

Transformer and Attention. Transformer is first introduced in [62], which uses a self-attention mechanism [35] to capture long-range dependences of language sequences. Based on the Transformer, some further improvements have been proposed in various sequential tasks, including natural language processing [10,14,73], speech processing [42,58]. Recently, Dosovitskiy *et al.* [15] first

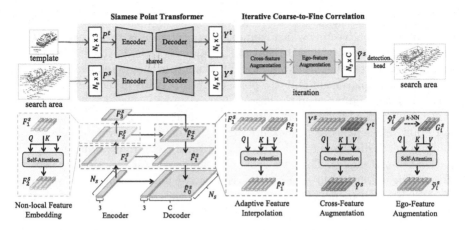

Fig. 1. The framework of our Siamese Transformer network. Given the template P^t and search area P^s, we first use the Siamese point Transformer network to extract features Y^t and Y^s for the template and search area, respectively. Then, we perform the iterative coarse-to-fine correlation network to obtain a feature fusion map $\widetilde{Y}^s$. Finally, we apply the detection head on the feature fusion map to localize the target. Note that Q, K, and V denote query, key, and value in Transformer, respectively.

proposed a vision Transformer for image recognition, which introduces a Transformer to handle non-sequential problems. The key idea is to split an image into patches, and feed the sequence of linear embeddings of these patches into a Transformer. After that, the Transformer is extended to various visual tasks, such as semantic segmentation [37,64], object detection [5,79], object tracking [6]. Recently, Liu *et al.* [37] proposed a hierarchical Transformer based on shifted windows to greatly reduce the computational cost while maintaining the capability to capture long-range dependencies in the data. For point cloud processing, Zhao *et al.* [77] first proposed a point Transformer that applies the self-attention mechanism on the local neighborhood of point clouds to extract local features for 3D semantic segmentation. Lately, inspired by point Transformer, different 3D vision tasks apply Transformer to yield good performance, such as point cloud classification [21], point cloud based place recognition [27], 3D object detection [43,44], 3D object tracking [9,52], and 3D action recognition [16].

3 Method

3.1 Siamese Point Transformer Network

In 3D single object tracking, given the target (*i.e.*, template) $P^t = \{p_i^t\}_{i=1}^{N_t}$ in the first frame, it aims to localize the 3D bounding box (3D BBox) of the same target in the search area $P^s = \{p_i^s\}_{i=1}^{N_s}$ frame by frame. N_t and N_s denote the number of points in the template and search area, and p_i^t and p_i^s are 3D coordinates. With a slight abuse of notations we use the same symbols for the sets of points and for their corresponding matrices $\boldsymbol{P}^t \in \mathbb{R}^{N_t \times 3}$ and $\boldsymbol{P}^s \in \mathbb{R}^{N_s \times 3}$. The 3D BBox is formed as a 7-dimensional vector, which contains box center (x, y, z), box size (w, l, h), and yaw angle θ. Since the 3D BBox of the target is given in the first frame, we only need to regress the target center and yaw angle in the subsequent frames. By applying the displacement and yaw angle on the 3D BBox in the previous frame, the 3D BBox of the target in the current frame can be localized.

Most of existing Siamese trackers use local descriptors (such as PointNet [48] and PointNet++ [49]) as the feature extraction network. However, it lacks the ability to learn discriminative features by capturing long-range contextual information of point clouds. Thus, we propose a Siamese point Transformer network by utilizing attention to generate discriminative point features. As shown in Fig. 1, it is a hierarchical feature learning network, consisting of two key modules: non-local feature embedding and adaptive feature interpolation.

Non-local Feature Embedding. The encoder consists of three non-local feature embedding modules. The non-local feature embedding module executes self-attention on feature maps at different scales, capturing the contextual information at different scales of the point cloud, respectively. Given the search area $\boldsymbol{P}^s$ of N_s points, we follow P2B [50] to downsample the point cloud to generate point clouds at different scales by using random sampling. The number of the subsampled points in the l-th layer is $\frac{N_s}{2^l}$.

Specifically, in the l-th layer, we first execute the local feature embedding to capture local geometric structures of point clouds. Inspired by [66], we apply edge convolution on the k-nearest neighbors (k-NN) in the coordinate space to aggregate local features, denoted by $\boldsymbol{E}_l^s \in \mathbb{R}^{\frac{N_s}{2^l} \times C_l}$. Then, we perform the self-attention on the feature map $\boldsymbol{E}_l^s$ to learn long-range context information of the point cloud. Formally, the attention mechanism is defined as:

$$\boldsymbol{F}_l^s = \text{SelfAttention}(\boldsymbol{E}_l^s + \boldsymbol{X}_l^s, \boldsymbol{E}_l^s + \boldsymbol{X}_l^s, \boldsymbol{E}_l^s + \boldsymbol{X}_l^s) \tag{1}$$

where $\boldsymbol{X}_l^s \in \mathbb{R}^{\frac{N_s}{2^l} \times C_l}$ denotes the position embedding of the sampled points in the l-th layer. Note that position information of the point cloud is very important, and thus we add the positional embedding to all matrices. In Eq. (1), the three inputs from left to right are used as query, key, and value, respectively. The obtained feature map $\boldsymbol{F}_l^s$ in the l-th layer will be used as the input of the $(l+1)$-th layer. In this way, we can obtain feature maps $\boldsymbol{F}_1^s$, $\boldsymbol{F}_2^s$, and $\boldsymbol{F}_3^s$ at three scales.

Adaptive Feature Interpolation. After the encoder, the original point set is subsampled. As the number of points on the target is reduced, it is difficult to identify the target accurately. Although the distance based interpolation [49] can be used to interpolate new points, it cannot effectively interpolate high-quality point features for the target, especially in sparse point clouds. Thus, we design a learnable interpolation module to interpolate point features from the subsampled points to the original points through the learnable weights of the attention.

We define $\boldsymbol{F}_0 \in \mathbb{R}^{N_s \times 3}$ (*i.e.*, 3D coordinates) as the point feature of the original point with a size of N_s. Given the obtained feature maps $\boldsymbol{F}_1^s \in \mathbb{R}^{\frac{N_s}{2} \times C_1}$, $\boldsymbol{F}_2^s \in$

$\mathbb{R}^{\frac{N_s}{4} \times C_2}$, $\boldsymbol{F}_3^s \in \mathbb{R}^{\frac{N_s}{8} \times C_3}$, and $\widehat{\boldsymbol{F}}_3^s = \boldsymbol{F}_3^s$, we gradually execute the adaptive feature interpolation to generate new point features from the low-resolution point cloud to the high-resolution point cloud, which is written as:

$$\widehat{\boldsymbol{F}}_l^s = \text{CrossAttention}(\boldsymbol{F}_l^s, \widehat{\boldsymbol{F}}_{l+1}^s, \widehat{\boldsymbol{F}}_{l+1}^s + \boldsymbol{X}_{l+1}^s) \tag{2}$$

where $l \in \{2, 1, 0\}$ and $\widehat{\boldsymbol{F}}_l^s \in \mathbb{R}^{\frac{N_s}{2^l} \times C_l}$ is the interpolated feature map. $\boldsymbol{X}_{l+1}^s \in \mathbb{R}^{\frac{N_s}{2^l} \times C_l}$ is the positional embedding. Note that the query $\boldsymbol{F}_l^s$ is the high-resolution feature map features, while the key ($\widehat{\boldsymbol{F}}_{l+1}^s$) and value ($\widehat{\boldsymbol{F}}_{l+1}^s + \boldsymbol{X}_{l+1}^s$) are the low-resolution feature maps. In Eq. (2), the feature map $\widehat{\boldsymbol{F}}_l^s$ is interpolated by weighting point features of the low-resolution (value) point cloud, considering the similarity between the high-resolution (query) and the low-resolution (key) point clouds. Finally, by applying the Siamese point Transformer on the template and search area, we obtain the feature maps $\widehat{\boldsymbol{F}}_0^t \in \mathbb{R}^{N_t \times C_0}$ and $\widehat{\boldsymbol{F}}_0^s \in \mathbb{R}^{N_s \times C_0}$ for the original point sets of the template and search area. For simplicity, we denote the obtained feature maps of the template and search area by $\boldsymbol{Y}^t \in \mathbb{R}^{N_t \times C}$ and $\boldsymbol{Y}^s \in \mathbb{R}^{N_s \times C}$. Note that $\boldsymbol{Y}^t = \widehat{\boldsymbol{F}}_0^t$ and $\boldsymbol{Y}^s = \widehat{\boldsymbol{F}}_0^s$.

3.2   Iterative Coarse-to-Fine Correlation Network

In 3D Siamese trackers, a cross-correlation operation is used to compute the similarity between the template and search area to generate a feature fusion map for identifying the target. Most of existing trackers use the cosine distance to generate the similarity map. Due to the large appearance variation between template and search area, this simple operation cannot effectively associate the template with the search area. Thus, we develop an iterative coarse-to-fine correlation network to learn the similarity in a coarse-to-fine manner to mitigate large appearance variation between them through the attention mechanism. Figure 1 shows the detailed structure.

Cross-feature Augmentation. We employ the cross-feature augmentation module to fuse the template and the search area by learning similarity between them. Given the template feature $\boldsymbol{Y}^t \in \mathbb{R}^{N_t \times C}$ and search area feature $\boldsymbol{Y}^s \in \mathbb{R}^{N_s \times C}$, we use the cross-attention mechanism between the template and search area to generate a coarse feature fusion map. Specifically, the cross-feature augmentation operation is formulated as:

$$\widehat{\boldsymbol{Y}}^s = \text{CrossAttention}(\boldsymbol{Y}^s, \boldsymbol{Y}^t, \boldsymbol{Y}^t + \boldsymbol{X}^t) \tag{3}$$

where $\widehat{\boldsymbol{Y}}^s \in \mathbb{R}^{N_s \times C}$ is the obtained coarse feature fusion map. Since the 3D coordinates of the template provide the positional relationship of the target, we add the positional embedding of the template $\boldsymbol{X}^t \in \mathbb{R}^{N_s \times C}$ to the value $\boldsymbol{Y}^t \in \mathbb{R}^{N_s \times C}$. By learning the similarity between the template (key) and search area (query), we embed the template (value) into the search area to generate the feature fusion map $\widehat{\boldsymbol{Y}}^s$. In this way, the potential target in the feature fusion map can be associated with the template.

Ego-Feature Augmentation. Furthermore, we design an ego-feature augmentation module to enhance target information by considering the internal association in the coarse feature fusion map. Specifically, we first construct the k-nearest neighbor (k-NN) for each point in the feature space. Given the coarse feature fusion map $\widehat{\boldsymbol{Y}}^s \in \mathbb{R}^{N_s \times C}$ with N_s feature vectors $\widehat{\boldsymbol{y}}_i^s \in \mathbb{R}^C$, the similarity between points i and j is denoted as:

$$a_{i,j} = \exp(-\|\widehat{\boldsymbol{y}}_i^s - \widehat{\boldsymbol{y}}_j^s\|_2^2) \tag{4}$$

where $a_{i,j}$ is the similarity metric. For the point i, we select K nearest points in the feature space as its neighborhood by using the defined similarity. Thus, we obtain the local k-NN feature map for the point i, denoted by $\boldsymbol{G}_i^s \in \mathbb{R}^{K \times C}$. Since the points in the same instance have similar appearances, they are close to each other in the feature space. By aggregating local k-NN graphs in the feature space, the differences between different instances can be further magnified. Therefore, we then use the self-attention on the local k-NN graph to capture local association to aggregate discriminative point features. Specifically, given the point feature $\widehat{\boldsymbol{y}}_i^s \in \mathbb{R}^C$ and its k-NN feature map $\boldsymbol{G}_i^s \in \mathbb{R}^{K \times C}$, the local association is defined as:

$$\widetilde{\boldsymbol{y}}_i^s = \mathrm{SelfAttention}(\widehat{\boldsymbol{y}}_i^s + \boldsymbol{x}_i^s, \boldsymbol{G}_i^s + \boldsymbol{Z}_i^s, \boldsymbol{G}_i^s + \boldsymbol{Z}_i^s) \tag{5}$$

where $\boldsymbol{x}_i^s \in \mathbb{R}^C$ and $\boldsymbol{Z}_i^s \in \mathbb{R}^{K \times C}$ are the positional embeddings of the i-th point and its k-NN neighborhood, and $\widetilde{\boldsymbol{y}}_i^s \in \mathbb{R}^C$ is the extracted point feature. In this way, we obtain the refined feature fusion map $\widetilde{\boldsymbol{Y}}^s \in \mathbb{R}^{N_s \times C}$.

We iteratively perform the coarse cross-feature augmentation module and the fine ego-feature augmentation module to generate a discriminative feature fusion map for identifying the target. Note that the output in the previous iteration will replace the search area input in the next iteration. By capturing the external (template) and internal (search area itself) relationships, our iterative coarse-to-fine correlation network can gradually generate a discriminative feature fusion map for identifying the target. Based on the feature fusion map, we use the 3D detector [26] to regress the target center and yaw angle.

4   Experiments

4.1   Experimental Settings

Datasets. We use the KITTI [18], nuScenes [4], and Waymo [57] datasets for single object tracking. For the KITTI dataset, it contains 21 video sequences. Following [19], we split the sequences into three parts: sequences 0–16 for training, 17–18 for validation, and 19–20 for testing. For the nuScenes dataset, it contains 700 sequences for training and 150 sequences for validation. Since the ground truth for the test set in nuScenes is inaccessible offline, we use its validation set to evaluate our method. For the Waymo dataset, we follow LiDAR-SOT [45] to use 1,121 tracklets, which are split into easy, medium, and hard subsets according to the number of points in the first frame of each tracklet. Following [26], we

Table 1. The performance of different methods on the KITTI and nuScenes datasets. Note that the results on the nuScenes dataset are obtained by using the pre-trained model on the KITTI dataset. "Mean" denotes the average results of four categories.

	Method			Success					Precision			
	Category	Car	Pedestrian	Van	Cyclist	Mean	Car	Pedestrian	Van	Cyclist	Mean
	Frame Num	6424	6088	1248	308	14068	6424	6088	1248	308	14068
KITTI	SC3D [19]	41.3	18.2	40.4	41.5	31.2	57.9	37.8	47.0	70.4	48.5
	P2B [50]	56.2	28.7	40.8	32.1	42.4	72.8	49.6	48.4	44.7	60.0
	MLVSNet [67]	56.0	34.1	52.0	34.3	45.7	74.0	61.1	61.4	44.5	66.6
	LTTR [9]	65.0	33.2	35.8	66.2	48.7	77.1	56.8	45.6	89.9	65.8
	BAT [78]	60.5	42.1	52.4	33.7	51.2	77.7	70.1	67.0	45.4	72.8
	PTT [52]	67.8	44.9	43.6	37.2	55.1	81.8	72.0	52.5	47.3	74.2
	V2B [26]	70.5	48.3	50.1	40.8	58.4	81.3	73.5	58.0	49.7	75.2
	STNet (ours)	**72.1**	**49.9**	**58.0**	**73.5**	**61.3**	**84.0**	**77.2**	**70.6**	**93.7**	**80.1**
	Category	Car	Pedestrian	Truck	Bicycle	Mean	Car	Pedestrian	Truck	Bicycle	Mean
	Frame Num	15578	8019	3710	501	27808	15578	8019	3710	501	27808
nuScenes	SC3D [19]	25.0	14.2	**25.7**	17.0	21.8	27.1	16.2	**21.9**	18.2	23.1
	P2B [50]	27.0	15.9	21.5	20.0	22.9	29.2	22.0	16.2	26.4	25.3
	BAT [78]	22.5	17.3	19.3	17.0	20.5	24.1	24.5	15.8	18.8	23.0
	V2B [26]	31.3	17.3	21.7	**22.2**	25.8	35.1	23.4	16.7	19.1	29.0
	STNet (ours)	**32.2**	**19.1**	22.3	21.2	**26.9**	**36.1**	**27.2**	16.8	**29.2**	**30.8**

use the trained model on the KITTI dataset to test on the nuScenes and Waymo datasets for evaluating the generalization ability of our 3D tracker.

Evaluation Metrics. We use *Success* and *Precision* defined in one pass evaluation [33] as the evaluation metrics for 3D single object tracking. Specifically, *Success* measures the intersection over union (IOU) between the predicted 3D bounding box (BBox) and ground truth (GT) box, while *Precision* measures the AUC for the distance between both two boxes' centers from 0 to 2 m.

Network Architecture. Following [50], we randomly sample $N_t = 512$ for each template P^t and $N_s = 1024$ for each search area P^s. For the Siamese point Transformer network, it consists of a three-layer encoder (three non-local feature embedding modules) and a three-layer decoder (three adaptive feature interpolation modules). In each encoder layer, the number of points is reduced by half. For example, if we feed the search area of 1024 points to the encoder, the number of points in each layer is 512, 256, and 128, respectively. Besides, the neighborhood sizes used to extract local feature are 32, 48, and 48, respectively. In the decoder, it gradually aggregates feature maps layer by layer to obtain a discriminative feature map. The obtained feature map sizes of the template Y^t and search area Y^s are 512×32 and 1024×32, respectively. For the iterative coarse-to-fine correlation network, we use two iterations considering the computational complexity and inference time. The hyperparameter K of the neighborhood size is set to 48. The size of the output feature fusion map $\widetilde{Y}^s$ is 1024×32. Note that in this paper, we adopt the linear Transformer [30] and employ $n = 2$ attention heads for all experiments.

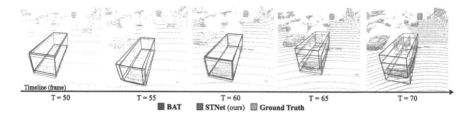

Fig. 2. The visualization results of our STNet and BAT on the car category of the KITTI dataset. The points on the target car are colored in red.

4.2 Results

Quantitative Results. As shown in the top half of Table 1, we make comprehensive comparisons on the KITTI dataset with the previous state-of-the-art methods, including SC3D [19], P2B [50], MLVSNet [67], BAT [78], LTTR [9], PTT [52], and V2B [26]. Following [50], we report the results over four categories, including car, pedestrian, van, and cyclist. From the table, it can be found that our method outperforms other methods on the mean results of four categories. For the car category, our method can significantly improve the precision from 81.8% to 84.0% with a gain of about 2% on the car category. In addition to the large targets, our method can still achieve higher performance for those small targets, such as cyclists. For the cyclist category, compared with LTTR, our method obtains a gain of about 3% on the precision. In Fig. 2, we also show the visualization results of our method and BAT. It can be observed that our method (red boxes) can accurately localize the target. Most existing methods use local descriptors to extract point features. Due to the large appearance variation between template and search area, the extracted features cannot characterize the differences between them well. Thus, we propose a Siamese point Transformer network to learn the dense and discriminative point features with a learnable point interpolation module, where the shape context information of the target can be captured. Furthermore, we use an iterative coarse-to-fine correlation network to learn the similarity between the template and search area in a coarse-to-fine manner to mitigate large appearance variations in sparse point clouds for accurate object localization.

Visualization of Attention Maps. In Fig. 3, we show the attention maps generated by our method on the KITTI dataset, including car, pedestrian, van, and cyclist. The points marked with the red color can obtain high attentional weights. It can be observed that our method can accurately focus on the target in the search area. The visualization results show that when there are multiple objects, the target can be distinguished from the non-target objects. It means that the learned shape context information of the object can help to learn the discriminative relationship between the template and search area by Transformer.

Generalization Ability. To verify the generalization ability of our method, we transfer the trained model of the KITTI dataset to obtain the testing results on

Table 2. The performance of different methods on the Waymo dataset. Each category is split into three levels of difficulty: "Easy", "Medium", and "Hard". "Mean" denotes the average results of three levels. Note that except for our STNet, the results of other methods are obtained by running the official codes.

	Method	Vehicle				Pedestrian			
	Split	Easy	Medium	Hard	Mean	Easy	Medium	Hard	Mean
	Frame Num	67832	61252	56647	185731	85280	82253	74219	241752
Success	P2B [50]	57.1	52.0	47.9	52.6	18.1	17.8	17.7	17.9
	BAT [78]	61.0	53.3	48.9	54.7	19.3	17.8	17.2	18.2
	V2B [26]	64.5	55.1	52.0	57.6	27.9	22.5	20.1	23.7
	STNet (ours)	**65.9**	**57.5**	**54.6**	**59.7**	**29.2**	**24.7**	**22.2**	**25.5**
Precision	P2B [50]	65.4	60.7	58.5	61.7	30.8	30.0	29.3	30.1
	BAT [78]	68.3	60.9	57.8	62.7	32.6	29.8	28.3	30.3
	V2B [26]	71.5	63.2	62.0	65.9	43.9	36.2	33.1	37.9
	STNet (ours)	**72.7**	**66.0**	**64.7**	**68.0**	**45.3**	**38.2**	**35.8**	**39.9**

the nuScenes and Waymo datasets. Following [26], we use the pre-trained models on four categories (car, pedestrian, van, cyclist) of the KITTI dataset to evaluate the corresponding categories (car, pedestrian, truck, bicycle) on the nuScenes dataset. The results are listed in the bottom half of Table 1. Note that except for our results, the results of other methods are taken from paper [26]. It can be observed that our method outperforms other methods on the mean results of four categories. In addition, Table 2 shows the results of vehicle and pedestrian categories on the Waymo dataset. It can be observed that our method outperforms other methods in terms of different subsets, including easy, medium, and hard. KITTI and Waymo datasets are built by 64-beam LiDAR, while nuScenes dataset is built by 32-beam LiDAR. Due to the large discrepancy between data distributions of datasets caused by different LiDAR sensors and sparsity of point clouds, it is very challenging to directly use the pre-trained model of the KITTI dataset to generalize it on nuScenes. The previous method V2B only achieves the performance of 25.8%/29.0% on the average of four categories. Our method achieves the gains of +1.1%/+1.8% over V2B. However, due to similar data distributions of the KITTI and Waymo datasets, the generalization results of the Waymo dataset are higher than those in the nuScenes dataset. The generalization results further demonstrate the effectiveness of our method for unseen scenes.

Ability to Handle Sparse Scenes. We report the results of different methods in the sparse scenarios. Following [26], we divide the number of points into four intervals, including $[0, 150)$, $[150, 1000)$, $[1000, 2500)$, and $[2500, +\infty)$. In Table 3, we report average *Success* and *Precision* for each interval on the car category of the KITTI dataset. Note that except for our results, other results are taken from [26]. It can be observed that our method achieves the best performance on all four intervals. Especially in the sparse point clouds below 150 points, our method can improve the performance by about 2% on both *Success* and *Precision* compared with V2B. Moreover, as the number of points increases, the

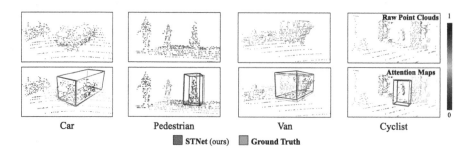

Fig. 3. The attention maps generated by our method on the KITTI dataset.

Table 3. The average *Success* and *Precision* for each interval on the car category in the KITTI dataset.

Method	Success				Precision			
Intervals	[0, 150)	[150, 1k)	[1k, 2.5k)	[2.5k, +∞)	[0, 150)	[150, 1k)	[1k, 2.5k)	[2.5k, +∞)
Frame Num	3293	2156	693	282	3293	2156	693	282
SC3D [19]	37.9	36.1	33.8	23.7	53.0	53.1	48.7	35.3
P2B [50]	56.0	62.3	51.9	43.8	70.6	78.6	68.1	61.8
BAT [78]	60.7	71.8	69.1	61.6	75.5	83.9	81.0	72.9
V2B [26]	64.7	77.5	72.3	82.2	77.4	87.1	81.5	90.1
STNet (ours)	**66.3**	**77.9**	**79.3**	**83.1**	**79.9**	**87.8**	**89.6**	**91.0**

performance of our method gradually increases. Due to the good results of our method in sparse point clouds, it will lead to more accurate template updates on the subsequent dense frames, resulting in better performance.

Running Speed. We also report the average running time of all test frames in the car category on the KITTI dataset. Specifically, we evaluate our model on a single TITAN RTX GPU. Our method achieves 35 FPS, including 4.6 ms for processing point clouds, 22.7 ms for network forward propagation, and 1.3 ms for post-processing. In addition, on the same platform, V2B, P2B and SC3D in default settings run with 37 FPS, 46 FPS, and 2 FPS, respectively. Due to Transformer, the forward time of our method is longer than that in P2B. However, the performance of our method is significantly better than that of P2B.

4.3   Ablation Study

In this section, we conduct the ablation study to validate the effectiveness of the designed modules. Due to a large number of test samples in the car category of the KITTI dataset, the ablated experiments on it can truly reflect the impact of different settings on the tracking accuracy.

Non-local Embedding and Adaptive Interpolation. To verify the effectiveness of our Siamese point Transformer network, which adopts the non-local feature embedding and the adaptive feature interpolation, we conduct experiments to study their effects on performance. Specifically, we use PointNet++ [49]

as the baseline and add the non-local embedding (dubbed "NL emb.") and the adaptive feature interpolation (dubbed "AF inte.") to conduct experiments. The results are listed in Table 4. It can be observed that the performance of only PointNet++ is worse than using both non-local feature embedding and adaptive feature interpolation ("NL emb. + AF inte."). According to the results in the ablation study, capturing shape context information of the object can effectively improve tracking performance.

Coarse-to-Fine Correlation. Here we conduct experiments to study the effects of coarse-to-fine correlation on performance. Specifically, we perform the simple feature augmentation used in P2B [50], only cross-feature augmentation (dubbed "CF aug."), and cross- and ego-feature augmentations (dubbed "CF aug. + EF aug."), respectively. The results are listed in Table 4. It can be found that when the cross- and ego-feature augmentations are used at the same time, we can obtain the best results. Since P2B's feature augmentation only uses the cosine distance to measure the similarity between the template and search area, it cannot obtain a high-quality feature fusion map. However, our method iteratively learns the similarity in a coarse-to-fine manner between them, so the target information in the feature fusion map can be further enhanced.

Comparison of Attention Maps of Different Components. In Fig. 4, we show the attention maps of the extracted features using our proposed different components. It can be observed that only using the Siamese point Transformer or only using the iterative coarse-to-fine correlation cannot effectively focus on the target object, while STNet using all components is able to effectively distinguish the car from the background. Furthermore, it can be observed that the target car can be clearly recognized from three cars since learned shape information of the target is helpful to learn the discriminative relationship between the template and search area by Transformer.

Table 4. The ablation study results of different components.

Method	Success	Precision
PointNet++ [49]	66.1	76.9
Only NL emb.	69.9	81.8
Only AF inte.	68.1	80.9
NL emb. + AF inte.	**72.1**	**84.0**
Feature aug. in P2B [50]	69.4	80.8
CF aug.	71.0	82.4
CF aug. + EF aug.	**72.1**	**84.0**

Table 5. The ablation study results of different hyperparameters.

STNet	Parameters	Success	Precision
Neighbors	$K = 16$	68.1	79.6
	$K = 32$	71.0	82.4
	$K = 48$	**72.1**	**84.0**
	$K = 64$	69.6	81.7
	$K = 80$	68.7	80.5
	$K = 96$	67.2	78.6
Iterations	iter. = 1	69.1	81.7
	iter. = 2	**72.1**	84.0
	iter. = 3	71.8	**84.2**
	iter. = 4	72.0	84.0

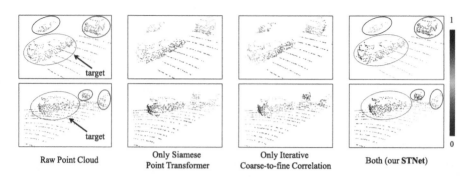

Raw Point Cloud   Only Siamese   Only Iterative   Both (our **STNet**)
                    Point Transformer   Coarse-to-fine Correlation

Fig. 4. The attention maps generated by different components of our STNet on the KITTI dataset. The leftmost column shows the input raw point cloud, and we circle the target object to distinguish the background.

Different K in Ego-Feature Augmentation. The neighbor size K is a key parameter in the ego-feature augmentation. Here we study the effects of different values of K on tracking accuracy. In Table 5, we report the performance in the cases of different neighbor sizes, including 16, 32, 48, 64, 80, and 96, respectively. It can be observed that when the neighbor size is set to 48, we can obtain the best results. If K is too small, our transformer cannot characterize the local geometry structures of point clouds, while if K is too large, background points in the scene are incorporated to localize the target.

Different Numbers of Iterations. We also study the effects of the number of iterations of coarse-to-fine correlation on performance. In Table 5, we list the quantitative results in the cases of different numbers of iterations. It can be observed that the performance of our method with two iterations is comparable to that of our method with three or four iterations. As the number of iterations increases, the GPU memory will gradually increase. Thus, considering the memory consumption, we choose to iterate twice.

5   Conclusions

In this paper, we proposed a 3D Siamese Transformer framework for single object tracking on point clouds. We developed a Siamese point Transformer network that uses the attention mechanism to formulate a encoder-decoder structure to learn shape context information of the target. Also, we constructed an iterative coarse-to-fine correlation network to produce a feature fusion map by using the attention mechanism on the template and the search area. In this way, we can effectively associate the template and the search area in a coarse-to-fine manner so as to mitigate large appearance variations between them in sparse point clouds. The experiments show that the proposed method achieves state-of-the-art performance on the KITTI, nuScenes, and Waymo datasets on 3D single object tracking.

Acknowledgment. The authors would like to thank reviewers for their detailed comments and instructive suggestions. This work was supported by the National Science Fund of China (Grant Nos. U1713208, 61876084).

References

1. Bertinetto, L., Valmadre, J., Henriques, J.F., Vedaldi, A., Torr, P.H.S.: Fully-convolutional siamese networks for object tracking. In: Hua, G., Jégou, H. (eds.) ECCV 2016. LNCS, vol. 9914, pp. 850–865. Springer, Cham (2016). https://doi.org/10.1007/978-3-319-48881-3_56

2. Bibi, A., Zhang, T., Ghanem, B.: 3D part-based sparse tracker with automatic synchronization and registration. In: CVPR (2016)

3. Bolme, D.S., Beveridge, J.R., Draper, B.A., Lui, Y.M.: Visual object tracking using adaptive correlation filters. In: CVPR (2010)

4. Caesar, H., et al.: nuScenes: a multimodal dataset for autonomous driving. arXiv preprint arXiv:1903.11027 (2019)

5. Carion, N., Massa, F., Synnaeve, G., Usunier, N., Kirillov, A., Zagoruyko, S.: End-to-end object detection with transformers. In: Vedaldi, A., Bischof, H., Brox, T., Frahm, J.-M. (eds.) ECCV 2020. LNCS, vol. 12346, pp. 213–229. Springer, Cham (2020). https://doi.org/10.1007/978-3-030-58452-8_13

6. Chen, X., Yan, B., Zhu, J., Wang, D., Yang, X., Lu, H.: Transformer tracking. In: CVPR (2021)

7. Chiu, H.k., Prioletti, A., Li, J., Bohg, J.: Probabilistic 3D multi-object tracking for autonomous driving. arXiv preprint arXiv:2001.05673 (2020)

8. Comport, A.I., Marchand, É., Chaumette, F.: Robust model-based tracking for robot vision. In: IROS (2004)

9. Cui, Y., Fang, Z., Shan, J., Gu, Z., Sifan, Z.: 3D object tracking with Transformer. In: BMVC (2021)

10. Dai, Z., Yang, Z., Yang, Y., Carbonell, J., Le, Q.V., Salakhutdinov, R.: Transformer-XL: attentive language models beyond a fixed-length context. arXiv preprint arXiv:1901.02860 (2019)

11. Danelljan, M., Bhat, G., Shahbaz Khan, F., Felsberg, M.: ECO: efficient convolution operators for tracking. In: CVPR (2017)

12. Danelljan, M., Hager, G., Shahbaz Khan, F., Felsberg, M.: Learning spatially regularized correlation filters for visual tracking. In: ICCV (2015)

13. Danelljan, M., Shahbaz Khan, F., Felsberg, M., Van de Weijer, J.: Adaptive color attributes for real-time visual tracking. In: CVPR (2014)

14. Devlin, J., Chang, M.W., Lee, K., Toutanova, K.: BERT: pre-training of deep bidirectional transformers for language understanding. arXiv preprint arXiv:1810.04805 (2018)

15. Dosovitskiy, A., et al.: An image is worth 16×16 words: transformers for image recognition at scale. arXiv preprint arXiv:2010.11929 (2020)

16. Fan, H., Yang, Y., Kankanhalli, M.: Point 4D Transformer networks for spatio-temporal modeling in point cloud videos. In: CVPR

17. Feng, T., Jiao, L., Zhu, H., Sun, L.: A novel object re-track framework for 3D point clouds. In: ACM MM (2020)

18. Geiger, A., Lenz, P., Urtasun, R.: Are we ready for autonomous driving? the KITTI vision benchmark suite. In: CVPR (2012)

19. Giancola, S., Zarzar, J., Ghanem, B.: Leveraging shape completion for 3D Siamese tracking. In: CVPR (2019)

20. Gordon, N., Ristic, B., Arulampalam, S.: Beyond the Kalman filter: particle filters for tracking applications. Artech House, London **830**(5), 1–4 (2004)

21. Guo, M.H., Cai, J.X., Liu, Z.N., Mu, T.J., Martin, R.R., Hu, S.M.: PCT: point cloud transformer. arXiv preprint arXiv:2012.09688 (2020)

22. Guo, Q., Feng, W., Zhou, C., Huang, R., Wan, L., Wang, S.: Learning dynamic Siamese network for visual object tracking. In: ICCV (2017)

23. Held, D., Thrun, S., Savarese, S.: Learning to track at 100 FPS with deep regression networks. In: Leibe, B., Matas, J., Sebe, N., Welling, M. (eds.) ECCV 2016. LNCS, vol. 9905, pp. 749–765. Springer, Cham (2016). https://doi.org/10.1007/978-3-319-46448-0_45

24. Henriques, J.F., Caseiro, R., Martins, P., Batista, J.: Exploiting the circulant structure of tracking-by-detection with kernels. In: Fitzgibbon, A., Lazebnik, S., Perona, P., Sato, Y., Schmid, C. (eds.) ECCV 2012. LNCS, vol. 7575, pp. 702–715. Springer, Heidelberg (2012). https://doi.org/10.1007/978-3-642-33765-9_50

25. Henriques, J.F., Caseiro, R., Martins, P., Batista, J.: High-speed tracking with kernelized correlation filters. IEEE Trans. Pattern Anal. Mach. Intell. **37**(3), 583–596 (2014)

26. Hui, L., Wang, L., Cheng, M., Xie, J., Yang, J.: 3D Siamese voxel-to-BEV tracker for sparse point clouds. In: NeurIPS (2021)

27. Hui, L., Yang, H., Cheng, M., Xie, J., Yang, J.: Pyramid point cloud Transformer for large-scale place recognition. In: ICCV (2021)

28. Kart, U., Kämäräinen, J.-K., Matas, J.: How to make an RGBD tracker? In: Leal-Taixé, L., Roth, S. (eds.) ECCV 2018. LNCS, vol. 11129, pp. 148–161. Springer, Cham (2019). https://doi.org/10.1007/978-3-030-11009-3_8

29. Kart, U., Lukezic, A., Kristan, M., Kämäräinen, J., Matas, J.: Object tracking by reconstruction with view-specific discriminative correlation filters. In: CVPR (2019)

30. Katharopoulos, A., Vyas, A., Pappas, N., Fleuret, F.: Transformers are RNNs: fast autoregressive Transformers with linear attention. In: ICML (2020)

31. Kim, A., Ošep, A., Leal-Taixé, L.: EagerMOT: 3D multi-object tracking via sensor fusion. arXiv preprint arXiv:2104.14682 (2021)

32. Kristan, M., et al.: The visual object tracking VOT2016 challenge results. In: Hua, G., Jégou, H. (eds.) ECCV 2016. LNCS, vol. 9914, pp. 777–823. Springer, Cham (2016). https://doi.org/10.1007/978-3-319-48881-3_54

33. Kristan, M., Matas, J., Leonardis, A., Vojíř, T., Pflugfelder, R., Fernandez, G., Nebehay, G., Porikli, F., Čehovin, L.: A novel performance evaluation methodology for single-target trackers. IEEE Trans. Pattern Anal. Mach. Intell. **38**(11), 2137–2155 (2016)

34. Lee, K.H., Hwang, J.N.: On-road pedestrian tracking across multiple driving recorders. IEEE Trans. Multimedia **17**(9), 1429–1438 (2015)

35. Lin, Z., et al.: A structured self-attentive sentence embedding. arXiv preprint arXiv:1703.03130 (2017)

36. Liu, Y., Jing, X.Y., Nie, J., Gao, H., Liu, J., Jiang, G.P.: Context-aware three-dimensional mean-shift with occlusion handling for robust object tracking in RGB-D videos. IEEE Trans. Multimedia **21**(3), 664–677 (2018)

37. Liu, Z., et al.: Swin Transformer: hierarchical vision transformer using shifted windows. In: ICCV (2021)

38. Liu, Z., Chen, W., Lu, J., Wang, H., Wang, J.: Formation control of mobile robots using distributed controller with sampled-data and communication delays. IEEE Trans. Control Syst. Technol. **24**(6), 2125–2132 (2016)

39. Liu, Z., Suo, C., Liu, Y., Shen, Y., Qiao, Z., Wei, H., Zhou, S., Li, H., Liang, X., Wang, H., et al.: Deep learning-based localization and perception systems: approaches for autonomous cargo transportation vehicles in large-scale, semiclosed environments. IEEE Robot. Autom. Mag. **27**(2), 139–150 (2020)

40. Luber, M., Spinello, L., Arras, K.O.: People tracking in RGB-D data with on-line boosted target models. In: IROS (2011)

41. Luo, W., Yang, B., Urtasun, R.: Fast and furious: Real time end-to-end 3D detection, tracking and motion forecasting with a single convolutional net. In: CVPR (2018)

42. Lüscher, C., et al.: RWTH ASR Systems for LibriSpeech: Hybrid vs attention-w/o data augmentation. arXiv preprint arXiv:1905.03072 (2019)

43. Mao, J., et al.: Voxel Transformer for 3D object detection. In: ICCV (2021)

44. Pan, X., Xia, Z., Song, S., Li, L.E., Huang, G.: 3D object detection with point-former. In: CVPR (2021)

45. Pang, Z., Li, Z., Wang, N.: Model-free vehicle tracking and state estimation in point cloud sequences. In: IROS (2021)

46. Pieropan, A., Bergström, N., Ishikawa, M., Kjellström, H.: Robust 3D tracking of unknown objects. In: 2015 IEEE International Conference on Robotics and Automation (ICRA), pp. 2410–2417. IEEE (2015)

47. Qi, C.R., Litany, O., He, K., Guibas, L.J.: Deep hough voting for 3D object detection in point clouds. In: ICCV (2019)

48. Qi, C.R., Su, H., Mo, K., Guibas, L.J.: PointNet: deep learning on point sets for 3D classification and segmentation. In: CVPR (2017)

49. Qi, C.R., Yi, L., Su, H., Guibas, L.J.: PointNet++: deep hierarchical feature learning on point sets in a metric space. In: NeurIPS (2017)

50. Qi, H., Feng, C., Cao, Z., Zhao, F., Xiao, Y.: P2B: point-to-box network for 3D object tracking in point clouds. In: CVPR (2020)

51. Scheidegger, S., Benjaminsson, J., Rosenberg, E., Krishnan, A., Granström, K.: Mono-camera 3D multi-object tracking using deep learning detections and PMBM filtering. In: IV (2018)

52. Shan, J., Zhou, S., Fang, Z., Cui, Y.: PTT: point-track-Transformer module for 3D single object tracking in point clouds. In: IROS (2021)

53. Shenoi, A., et al.: JRMOT: a real-time 3D multi-object tracker and a new large-scale dataset. In: IROS (2020)

54. Shi, S., Wang, X., Li, H.: PointRCNN: 3D object proposal generation and detection from point cloud. In: CVPR (2019)

55. Shi, S., Wang, Z., Shi, J., Wang, X., Li, H.: From points to parts: 3D object detection from point cloud with part-aware and part-aggregation network. IEEE Trans. Pattern Anal. Mach. Intell. (2020)

56. Spinello, L., Arras, K., Triebel, R., Siegwart, R.: A layered approach to people detection in 3D range data. In: AAAI (2010)

57. Sun, P., et al.: Scalability in perception for autonomous driving: Waymo open dataset. In: CVPR (2020)

58. Synnaeve, G., et al.: End-to-end ASR: from supervised to semi-supervised learning with modern architectures. arXiv preprint arXiv:1911.08460 (2019)

59. Tang, S., Andriluka, M., Andres, B., Schiele, B.: Multiple people tracking by lifted multicut and person re-identification. In: CVPR (2017)

60. Tao, R., Gavves, E., Smeulders, A.W.: Siamese instance search for tracking. In: CVPR (2016)

61. Valmadre, J., Bertinetto, L., Henriques, J., Vedaldi, A., Torr, P.H.: End-to-end representation learning for correlation filter based tracking. In: CVPR (2017)

62. Vaswani, A., et al.: Attention is all you need. arXiv preprint arXiv:1706.03762 (2017)
63. Wang, Q., Gao, J., Xing, J., Zhang, M., Hu, W.: DCFNet: discriminant correlation filters network for visual tracking. arXiv preprint arXiv:1704.04057 (2017)
64. Wang, W., et al.: Pyramid vision Transformer: a versatile backbone for dense prediction without convolutions. In: ICCV (2021)
65. Wang, Y., Weng, X., Kitani, K.: Joint detection and multi-object tracking with graph neural networks. arXiv preprint arXiv:2006.13164 (2020)
66. Wang, Y., Sun, Y., Liu, Z., Sarma, S.E., Bronstein, M.M., Solomon, J.M.: Dynamic graph cnn for learning on point clouds. arXiv preprint arXiv:1801.07829 (2018)
67. Wang, Z., Xie, Q., Lai, Y.K., Wu, J., Long, K., Wang, J.: MLVSNet: multi-level voting Siamese network for 3D visual tracking. In: ICCV (2021)
68. Weng, X., Wang, J., Held, D., Kitani, K.: 3D multi-object tracking: a baseline and new evaluation metrics. In: IROS (2020)
69. Weng, X., Wang, Y., Man, Y., Kitani, K.M.: GNN3DMOT: graph neural network for 3D multi-object tracking with 2D–3D multi-feature learning. In: CVPR (2020)
70. Weng, X., Yuan, Y., Kitani, K.: Joint 3D tracking and forecasting with graph neural network and diversity sampling. arXiv preprint arXiv:2003.07847 (2020)
71. Wu, H., Han, W., Wen, C., Li, X., Wang, C.: 3D multi-object tracking in point clouds based on prediction confidence-guided data association. IEEE Trans. Intell. Transp. Syst. (2021)
72. Xing, J., Ai, H., Lao, S.: Multiple human tracking based on multi-view upper-body detection and discriminative learning. In: ICPR (2010)
73. Yang, Z., Dai, Z., Yang, Y., Carbonell, J., Salakhutdinov, R., Le, Q.V.: XLNet: Generalized autoregressive pretraining for language understanding. arXiv preprint arXiv:1906.08237 (2019)
74. Yin, T., Zhou, X., Krahenbuhl, P.: Center-based 3D object detection and tracking. In: CVPR (2021)
75. Zhang, M., Xing, J., Gao, J., Shi, X., Wang, Q., Hu, W.: Joint scale-spatial correlation tracking with adaptive rotation estimation. In: ICCV Workshops (2015)
76. Zhang, W., Zhou, H., Sun, S., Wang, Z., Shi, J., Loy, C.C.: Robust multi-modality multi-object tracking. In: CVPR (2019)
77. Zhao, H., Jiang, L., Jia, J., Torr, P., Koltun, V.: Point transformer. In: ICCV (2021)
78. Zheng, C., et al.: Box-aware feature enhancement for single object tracking on point clouds. In: ICCV (2021)
79. Zhu, X., Su, W., Lu, L., Li, B., Wang, X., Dai, J.: Deformable DETR: deformable transformers for end-to-end object detection. arXiv preprint arXiv:2010.04159 (2020)
80. Zhu, Z., Wang, Q., Li, B., Wu, W., Yan, J., Hu, W.: Distractor-aware siamese networks for visual object tracking. In: Ferrari, V., Hebert, M., Sminchisescu, C., Weiss, Y. (eds.) ECCV 2018. LNCS, vol. 11213, pp. 103–119. Springer, Cham (2018). https://doi.org/10.1007/978-3-030-01240-3_7

Object Wake-Up: 3D Object Rigging from a Single Image

Ji Yang[1]([envelope]), Xinxin Zuo[1], Sen Wang[1,2], Zhenbo Yu[3], Xingyu Li[1],
Bingbing Ni[2,3], Minglun Gong[4], and Li Cheng[1]

[1] University of Alberta, Edmonton, Canada
{jyang7,xzuo,sen9,xingyu,lcheng5}@ualberta.ca
[2] Huawei HiSilicon, Shenzhen, China
[3] Shanghai Jiao Tong University, Shanghai, China
[4] University of Guelph, Guelph, Canada

Abstract. Given a single chair image, could we wake it up by reconstructing its 3D shape and skeleton, as well as animating its plausible articulations and motions, similar to that of human modeling? It is a new problem that not only goes beyond image-based object reconstruction but also involves articulated animation of generic objects in 3D, which could give rise to numerous downstream augmented and virtual reality applications. In this paper, we propose an automated approach to tackle the entire process of reconstruct such generic 3D objects, rigging and animation, all from single images. two-stage pipeline has thus been proposed, which specifically contains a multi-head structure to utilize the deep implicit functions for skeleton prediction. Two in-house 3D datasets of generic objects with high-fidelity rendering and annotated skeletons have also been constructed. Empirically our approach demonstrated promising results; when evaluted on the related sub-tasks of 3D reconstruction and skeleton prediction, our results surpass those of the state-of-the-arts by a noticeable margin. Our code and datasets are made publicly available at the dedicated project website.

Keywords: Object reconstruction · Object rigging

1 Introduction

Presented with a single image of a generic object, say an airplane or a chair, our goal is to wake it up in the 3D virtual world: this entails reconstructing its 3D shape and the skeleton, as well as animating its plausible articulations and motions, such as an airplane flapping its wings or a chair walking as a quadruped,

---

J. Yang and X. Zuo—Equal contribution.
Project website: https://kulbear.github.io/object-wakeup/.

Supplementary Information The online version contains supplementary material available at https://doi.org/10.1007/978-3-031-20086-1_18.

as illustrated in Fig. 1. This is a relatively new problem that may have many downstream applications in virtual and augmented reality scenarios. It is worth noting that there has been research efforts [15] performing 3D manipulations from single input images, where the main focus is toward rigid body transformations. To generate non-rigid shape deformations, it is usually necessary to involve intensive user interactions and dedicated software tools. Instead, our aim in this paper is to automate the entire process of object 3D reconstruction, rigging, and animation. The generic objects considered here are articulated, such that their shapes are capable of being deformed by a set of skeletal joints. In a way, our problem may be considered as a generalization of image-based 3D human shape and pose reconstruction to generic objects encountered in our daily life, as long as they could be endowed with a skeleton.

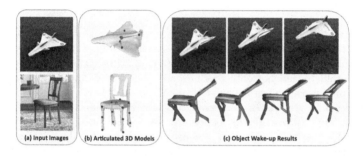

Fig. 1. Two exemplar visual results of our approach: presented with an input image of an airplane or a chair, our approach is capable of reconstructing its 3D shape and skeleton, then animating its plausible articulated motions.

Compared with the more established tasks of human shape and pose estimation [40], there are nevertheless new challenges to tackle with. To name one, there is no pre-existing parametric 3D shape model for generic objects. Besides, the human template naturally comes with its skeletal configuration for 3D motion control, and the precise skinning weights designed by professionals. However, such skeletal joints are yet to be specified not to mention the skinning weights in the case of generic objects, which usually possess rather diverse geometric structures even within the same object category.

These observations have motivated us to propose an automated pipeline consisting of two stages. Stage one involves 3D shape reconstruction from a single image. It includes a transformer-based [34] encoder as the feature extractor, followed by a location occupancy prediction decoder and an auxiliary 3D voxel decoder module with improved loss function [21]. Stage two focuses on predicting the corresponding skeleton. By formulating it as estimating the multi-head probability field, a novel multi-head skeleton prediction module is proposed, inspired by the deep implicit functions of [21]. Specifically, compared with previous skeleton prediction methods with voxel-based [44] or mesh-based representations [43], our approach predict occupancy probability of joints and bones in a continuous

3D space. Moreover, a joint-aware instance segmentation module is also used as an auxiliary task to incorporate regional features of neighboring points.

Our major contributions are two folds. 1) A new object wake-up problem is considered, for which an automated pipeline is proposed to reconstruct 3D objects and their skeletons from single images. 2) A novel and effective skeleton prediction approach with a multi-head structure is developed by utilizing the deep implicit functions. Moreover, two in-house 3D datasets (SSkel & ShapeRR) of typical objects are constructed, containing annotated 3D skeletal joints and photo-realistic re-rendered images, respectively. Empirically our approach is shown to achieve promising results. Quantitative evaluations on benchmark datasets also demonstrate the superior performance of our approach on the related sub-tasks of image-based shape reconstruction and skeleton prediction.

2   Related Work

Image-Based Object Reconstruction. There exist numerous studies on image-based 3D object reconstruction with various 3D shape representations, including voxel, octree [29,33,38], deep implicit function, mesh and point cloud [9,18,22,28]. Methods based on different representations have their own benefits and shortcomings. For example, as a natural extension of 2D pixels, voxel representation [10,36] has been widely used in early efforts due to its simplicity of implementation and compatibility with the convolutional neural network. However, these approaches often yield relatively coarse results, at the price of significant memory demand and high computational cost. Mesh-based representations [13,16,20,37], on the other hand, become more desirable in real applications, as they are able to model fine shape details, and are compatible with various geometry regularizers. It is however still challenging to work with topology changes [25,37]. Deep implicit 3D representations [6,19,26,35] have recently attracted wide attention as a powerful technique in modeling complex shape topologies at arbitrary resolutions.

Skeleton Prediction and Rigging. The task of skeleton prediction has been investigated in various fields and utilized in a variety of applications for shape modeling and analysis. The best-known example is the medial axis [1,2], which is an effective means for shape abstraction and manipulation. Curve skeleton or meso-skeleton [12,45] have been popular in computer graphics, mostly due to their compactness and ease of manipulation. It is worth noting the related research around detecting 3D keypoints from input point clouds, such as skeleton merger [31]. Pinocchio [3] is perhaps the earliest work on automatic rigging, which fits a pre-defined skeletal template to a 3D shape, with skinning obtained through heat diffusion. These fittings, unfortunately, tend to fail as the input shapes become less compatible with the skeletal template. On the other hand, hand-crafting templates for every possible structural variation of an input character is cumbersome. More recently, Xu et al. [44] propose to learn a volumetric network for inferring skeletons from input 3D characters, which however often suffers from the limited voxel resolution. Exploiting the mesh representation,

RigNet [43] utilizes a graph neural network to produce the displacement map for joint estimation, which is followed by the additional graph neural networks to predict joint connectivity and skinning weights. Its drawback is they assume strong requirements for the input mesh such as a watertight surface with evenly distributed vertices can be satisfied. Besides, they predict the joints and kinematic chains successively causing error propagation from stages. In contrast, a deep implicit function representation [21] which is capable of predicting the joints and bones over a continuous 3D space is considered in this paper for inferring skeleton.

Image Based Object Animation. An established related topic is photo editing, which has already been popular with professional tools such as PhotoShop. Existing tools are however often confined to 2D object manipulations in performing basic functions such as cut-and-paste and hole-filling. A least-square method is considered in [30] to affine transform objects in 2D. The work of [11] goes beyond linear transformation, by presenting an as-rigid-as-possible 2D animation of a human character from an image, it is however manual intensive. In [42], 2D instances of the same visual objects are ordered and grouped to form an instance-based animation of non-rigid motions. Relatively few research activities concern 3D animations, where the focus is mostly on animals, humans, and human-like objects. For example, photo wake-up [40] considers reconstruction, rig, and animate 3D human-like shapes from input images. This line of research benefits significantly from the prior work establishing the pre-defined skeletal templates and parametric 3D shape models for humans and animals. On the other hand, few efforts including [5,15] consider 3D manipulations of generic objects from images, meanwhile, they mainly focus on rigid transformations. Our work could be regarded as an extension of automated image-based human shape reconstruction & animation to reconstruct & articulate generic lifeless objects from single images.

3   Our Approach

Given an input image, usually in the form of a segmented object, first the 3D object shape is to be reconstructed; its skeletons are then extracted to form a rigged model. In this section, we will present the stage-wise framework in detail.

3.1   Image-Based 3D Shape Reconstruction

A Transformer-based occupancy prediction network is developed here, which performs particularly well on real images when compared with existing methods [17,21,41]. As illustrated in Fig. 2, it consists of a 2D transformer encoder, an auxiliary 3D CNN decoder, and an occupancy decoder. The DeiT-Tiny [34] is used as our transformer encoder network. Similar to the Vision Transformer [8], the encoder first encodes fixed-size patches splitted from the original image and processes extract localized information from each of the patches, then outputs a universal latent representation for the entire image by jointly learning the

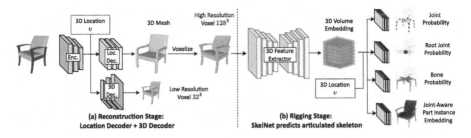

Fig. 2. An illustration of our overall pipeline. (a) a DeiT image encoder, an auxiliary 3D CNN voxel prediction branch and the location occupancy decoder; (b) SkelNet accepts a high resolution 3D shape voxel based on the reconstructed 3D mesh, and predicts articulated skeleton with a multi-head architecture.

patch representation with multi-head attention. An auxiliary 3D CNN decoder is used for reconstructing a low-resolution voxel-based 3D model as well as helping to encode 3D information for the latent representation extracted from the Transformer encoder. The occupancy decoder then uses the latent representation as the conditional prior to predict the occupancy probability for each point by introducing fully connected residual blocks and conditional batch normalization [24,27].

It is worth noting that although the voxel prediction branch is only used for auxiliary training, the highly unbalanced labels where most of the voxel occupancy are zeros will always make the training more difficult. To this end, while most of the methods for voxel-based 3D reconstruction simply use the (binary) cross-entropy loss which is directly related to IoU metric [32], in this work, the Dice loss is extended to gauge on both the 3D voxel prediction and the point-based occupancy prediction,

$$\mathcal{L}_{dice} = 1 - \frac{\sum_{n=1}^{N^3} \hat{y}_n y_n}{\sum_{n=1}^{N^3} \hat{y}_n + y_n} - \frac{\sum_{n=1}^{N^3}(1 - \hat{y}_n)(1 - y_n)}{\sum_{n=1}^{N^3} 2 - \hat{y}_n - y_n}, \tag{1}$$

where y_n is the ground-truth occupancy score, $\hat{y}_n$ is the predicted occupancy score of the n-th element.

3.2 Skeleton Prediction and Automatic Rigging

Our key insight here is instead of predicting the joints inside fixed voxel locations [44] or indirectly regressing the joints location by estimating the displacement from the mesh [43], we train a neural network utilizing the deep implicit function to assign every location with a probability score in $[0, 1]$, indicating the existence of a skeletal joint and bone. Taking the 3D model and any sampled 3D point location as input, the network produces the joint and bone existence probabilities. In addition, we incorporate joint-aware instance segmentation as an auxiliary task considering the regional features over neighboring points. In inference, the feature embedding output from the instance segmentation branch is further used in the subsequent step to infer joint locations from the incurred joints' probability maps.

As in Fig. 2, four output heads are utilized, which are for predicting the probability of skeletal joints, the root joint, the bones, and the joint-aware instance segmentation, respectively. The output from the instance segmentation is a feature embedding.

Feature Extraction. The predicted 3D shape, represented as an occupancy grid with the dimension of 128^3, is converted to a 3D feature embedding grid by a 3D UNet structure. Inspired by the design of Squeeze and Excitation (SE) block in 2D image classification, a 3D adaptive channel activation module is developed as a plug-in module, to be attached after each of the encoder and decoder blocks of the 3D UNet, detailed design is described in the supplementary. The ablative study demonstrated the usefulness of this 3D adaptive channel activation module.

Multi-head Implicit Functions. Given aggregated features from the feature extraction, we acquire the feature vector for any 3D point v via the trilinear interpolation from 3D feature embedding. For each of the output heads, a fully-connected network (empirically it is implemented as 5 fully-connected ResNet blocks and ReLU activation [24,27]) is engaged to take as input the point v and its feature vector. The concurrent multi-head strategy eliminates the possible issue with error propagation of successive prediction [43].

Sampling. In general, the animation joints and bones should lie inside the convex hull of the object. Therefore, different from previous efforts that uniformly sample points in a 3D volume [21,27], points in our 3D space are adaptively sampled. Specifically, for each sample in the training batch, we sampled K points with 10% of the points lying outside but near the surface, and the rest 90% points entirely inside the object.

Joints and Bones Loss. First, for every query point, its joint probability is computed under a 3D Gaussian distribution measured by its distance to nearest annotated joint locations. To generate the bone probability field, for every query point we compute a point-to-line distance to its nearest line segment of the bones, and the bone probability is computed under the Gaussian distribution of the measured distance. In training, with the query points $v \in \mathbb{R}^3$ acquired through sampling, the network predicts their probabilities of being a joint or lying on bones. Different from the occupancy prediction [21] task where the binary cross-entropy loss is used, we use the L1 loss to measure the difference of the predicted joint probability and their ground-truth values as we are dealing with the continuous probability prediction: for the i-th sample in training, the loss function is defined as,

$$\mathcal{L}_{joint}^i(\hat{P}_J, P_J) = \sum_{v \in \mathcal{V}^i} |\hat{P}_J(v) - P_J(v)|$$

$$\mathcal{L}_{jointR}^i(\hat{P_{JR}}, P_{JR}) = \sum_{v \in \mathcal{V}^i} |\hat{P_{JR}}(v) - P_{JR}(v)| \tag{2}$$

In the above equation, $\hat{P}_J$ is the predicted joints probability field, and P_J is the ground-truth probability field. $\hat{P}_{JR}$ and P_{JR} denote for the probability field of the root joint. $\mathcal{V}^i$ denotes the sampled points for the i-th model.

Similarly, for the sampled points, L1 loss is also applied between predicted bones probability $\hat{P}_B$ and the ground-truth P_B. The loss function of the bones is denoted as $\mathcal{L}^i_{bone}(\hat{P}_B, P_B)$.

Symmetry Loss. Since the objects of interest often possess symmetric 3D shapes, a symmetry loss is used here to regularize the solution space, as follows,

$$\mathcal{L}^i_{sym}(\hat{P}_J, \hat{P}_B) = \mathbf{1}_{\Omega'}(i) \sum_{v \in \mathcal{V}^i} |\hat{P}_J(v) - \hat{P}_J(\phi(v))| + \mathbf{1}_{\Omega'}(i) \sum_{v \in \mathcal{V}^i} |\hat{P}_B(v) - \hat{P}_B(\phi(v))|,$$

(3)

Here $\phi(v)$ denotes the mapping from point v to its symmetric point. To detect the symmetry planes, as the input 3D mesh models are in the canonical coordinates, we flip the mesh model according to the xy-, xz- and yz-planes. The symmetry plane is set as the one with the smallest Chamfer distance computed between the flipped model and the original model. $\mathbf{1}_{\Omega'}$ is an indicator function where Ω' is the subset of training models with symmetry planes detected.

Joint-Aware Instance Segmentation Loss. The joint-aware instance segmentation maps the sampled point from Euclidean space to a feature space, where 3D points of the same instance are closer to each other than those belonging to different instances. To maintain consistency between the clustered feature space and the joints probability maps, the part instance is segmented according to the annotated ground-truth joints. Basically, for each sampled point we assign an instance label as the label or index of its closest joint. Following the instance segmentation method of [39], our joint-aware instance segmentation loss is defined as a weighted sum of three terms: (1) $\mathcal{L}_{var}$ is an intra-cluster variance term that pulls features belonging to the same instance towards the mean feature; (2) $\mathcal{L}_{dist}$ is an inter-cluster distance term that pushes apart instances with different part labels; and (3) $\mathcal{L}_{reg}$ is a regularization term that pulls all features towards the origin in order to bound the activation.

$$\mathcal{L}^i_{var}(\mu, x) = \frac{1}{|J^i|} \sum_{c=1}^{|J^i|} \frac{1}{N_c} \sum_{j=1}^{N_c} [\, \|\mu^i_c - x^i_j\| - \delta_{var} \,]^2_+,$$

$$\mathcal{L}^i_{dist}(\mu) = \frac{1}{|J^i|(|J^i| - 1)} \sum_{c_a=1}^{|J^i|} \sum_{\substack{c_b=1 \\ c_b \neq c_a}}^{|J^i|} [\, 2\delta_{dist} - \|\mu^i_{c_a} - \mu^i_{c_b}\| \,]^2_+,$$

$$\mathcal{L}^i_{reg}(\mu) = \frac{1}{|J^i|} \sum_{c=1}^{|J^i|} \|\mu^i_c\|.$$

(4)

Here $|J^i|$ denotes the number of joints or clusters for the i-th sample model. N_c is the number of elements in cluster c. x^i_j is the output feature vector for the query point. $[x]_+$ is the hinge function. The parameter δ_{var} describes the maximum allowed distance between a feature vector and the cluster center. Likewise, $2\delta_{dist}$ is the minimum distance between different cluster centers to avoid overlap.

Joints and Kinematic Tree Construction. In inference, the joints and bones are obtained from the corresponding probability maps by mean-shift clustering. Instead of clustering over the euclidean space as in classical mean-shift clustering, we implement the clustering on the feature space with the kernel defined over the feature embedding output from the joint-aware instance segmentation. In this way, the points belonging to the same joint-aware instance will all shift towards the corresponding joints. The kernel is also modulated by the predicted joint probability to better localize the joint location. Mathematically, at each mean-shift iteration, for any point v it is displaced according to the following vector:

$$m(v) = \frac{\sum_{u \in \mathcal{N}(v)} P_J(v)\kappa(\|x(u) - x(v)\|)u}{\sum_{u \in N(v)} P_J(v)\kappa(\|x(u) - x(v)\|)} - v \tag{5}$$

where $\mathcal{N}(v)$ denotes the neighboring points of v, $x(v)$ is the feature embedding output from our joint-aware instance segmentation. Besides, $\kappa()$ is a kernel function and in our case we choose to use the RBF kernel. Following [44], the object kinematic tree (or chains) are constructed using a minimum spanning tree by minimizing a cost function defined over the edges connecting the joints pairwisely. It is realized as a graph structure, with the detected joints as the graph nodes, and the edges connecting the pairwise joints computed from the probability maps. Specifically, for every edge, its weight is set by the negative-log function of the integral of the bones probability for the sampled points over the edge. The MST problem is solved using Prim's algorithm [7].

Skinning Weight Computation. For automatic rigging of the reconstructed 3D model, the last issue is to compute the skinning weights that bind each vertex to the skeletal joints. To get meaningful animation, instead of computing the skinning weights according to the Euclidean distance [3], we choose to assign the skinning weights by utilizing the semantic part segmentation [39]. Specifically, for every segmented part, we assign its dominant control joint to the one closest to the center of the part. In some cases where the center of the part could have about the same distance to more than one skeletal joint, we choose the parent joint as the control joint. The skinning weights around the segmentation boundaries are smoothed out afterwards. It is worth noting that some semantic parts are further segmented if skeleton joints are detected inside the part.

3.3   Our In-House Datasets

As there is no existing dataset of general 3D objects with ground-truth skeletons, we collect such a dataset (named SSkel for *ShapeNet skeleton*) by designing an annotation tool to place joints and build kinematic trees for the 3D shapes. To ensure consistency, a predefined protocol is used for all object categories. For example, for chairs, we follow the part segmentation in PartNet dataset [23] to segment a chair into the chair seat, back, and legs. The root joint is annotated at the center of the chair seat, followed by child joints which are the intersection between chair seat and back, chair seat and legs. More details about the annotation tool and some sampled annotations are presented in the supplementary. Without loss of generality, we only consider four categories of objects from ShapeNet [4], namely *chair, table, lamp* and *airplane*. Our SSkel dataset contains a total of 2,150 rigged 3D shapes including 700 for chair, 700 for table, 400 for lamp and 350 for airplane.

Moreover, in improving the input image resolution and quality of the original ShapeNet, we use the UNREAL 4 Engine to re-render photo-realistic images of the 3D ShapeNet models with diverse camera configuration, lighting conditions, object materials, and scenes, named ShapeRR dataset for *ShapeNet of realistic rendering*. More details are relegated to the supplementary file.

4   Experiments

Datasets. A number of datasets are considered in our paper. In terms of image-based reconstruction, it contains our ShapeRR dataset for synthetic images and the Pix3D dataset of real images. In terms of rigging performance, we use the RigNetv1 dataset for 3D shape-based rigging, and our SSkel dataset for image-based rigging.

Table 1. Image-based 3D mesh reconstruction on ShapeRR (i.e. re-rendered ShapeNet dataset) and Pix3D dataset. Metrics are Chamfer Distance (×0.001, the smaller the better) and Volumetric IoU (the larger the better). Best results are in **bold face**.

ShapeNet	Chamfer Distance (↓)					Volumetric IoU (↑)				
	Chair	Table	Lamp	Airplane	Avg.	Chair	Table	Lamp	Airplane	Avg.
OccNet [21]	1.9347	1.9903	4.5224	1.3922	2.3498	0.5067	0.4909	0.3261	0.5900	0.4918
DVR [24]	1.9188	2.0351	4.7426	1.3814	2.5312	0.4794	0.5439	0.3504	0.5741	0.5029
D^{2}IM-Net [17]	**1.8847**	1.9491	4.1492	1.4457	2.0346	**0.5487**	0.5332	0.3755	0.6123	0.5231
Ours	1.8904	**1.7392**	**3.9712**	**1.2309**	**1.9301**	0.5436	**0.5541**	**0.3864**	**0.6320**	**0.5339**
Pix3D	Table	Chair	Desk	Sofa	Avg.	Table	Chair	Desk	Sofa	Avg.
OccNet [21]	7.425	9.399	15.726	14.126	11.625	0.215	0.201	0.143	0.152	0.190
DVR [24]	8.782	6.452	12.826	11.543	9.901	0.187	0.237	0.165	0.187	0.185
D^{2}IM-Net [17]	8.038	7.592	11.310	9.291	9.057	0.205	0.244	0.183	0.207	0.215
Ours	**6.449**	**6.028**	**8.452**	**8.201**	**7.282**	**0.239**	**0.277**	**0.219**	**0.241**	**0.242**

The Pix3D dataset contains 3D object shapes aligned with their real-world 2D images. Similar to ShapeRR, we focus on a subset of 4 categories in the dataset, i.e. chair, sofa, desk, and table. The RigNetv1 dataset (i.e. ModelsResource-RigNetv1 [44]), on the other hand, contains 2,703 rigged 3D characters of humanoids, quadrupeds, birds, fish, robots, and other fictional characters.

4.1   Evaluation on Image-Based Reconstruction

For evaluation metrics, we follow the previous works [21] and use volumetric
IoU and Chamfer-L1 distance. We first compare with several state-of-the-art
methods with released source code on single image object reconstruction where
each of the methods is trained and tested, namely OccNet [21], DVR [24] and
D^{2}IM-Net [17]. We follow the common test protocol on ShapeNet as it has been
a standard benchmark in the literature. All methods are re-implemented (when
the code is not available) and re-trained then evaluated directly on the test split.
We can observe that our method performs reasonably well compared with other
recent methods, and outperforms existing methods in 3 of the 4 categories. And
we are able to achieve a significant advantage over other methods in terms of
the average performance across all 4 categories of our interests.

Considering that our 3D reconstruction is primarily for supporting rigging
and animation purposes on real images, to better compare the generalization
ability with such a situation, we use the complete Pix3D dataset as the test set.

We report both quantitative and visual comparison on Pix3D in Table 1 and
in Fig. 3 respectively. As shown in Table 1, our proposed method has outperformed all previous approaches on Pix3D with a large margin in terms of the
two metrics. To validate the effectiveness of our feature encoder and the incorporated auxiliary voxel prediction task, we also conduct a group of ablative studies,
and the experiment results are included in the supplementary material.

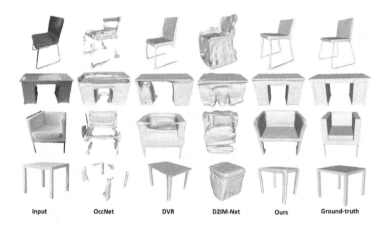

Input   OccNet   DVR   D2IM-Net   Ours   Ground-truth

Fig. 3. Visualization of image-based 3D reconstruction on the Pix3D dataset. Our
method shows excellent generalization performance on the real images.

4.2   Evaluation on Skeleton Prediction

The evaluation is conducted on both the RigNetv1 dataset and our SSkel dataset,
where our approach is compared with two state-of-the-art methods, RigNet [43]
and VolumetricNets [44].

Metrics. First, we measure the accuracy of the predicted joints by computing the Chamfer distance between the predicted joints and the ground-truth which is denoted as CD-J2J. Similarly, the predicted bones are evaluated by computing the Chamfer distance between the densely sampled points over the estimated bones and the ground-truth, which is denoted as CD-B2B. CD-J2B is also considered here by computing the Chamfer distance between predicted joints to bones. For all metrics, the lower the better.

Table 2. Comparison of skeleton prediction on the RigNetv1 dataset.

	CD-J2J ($\downarrow$)	CD-J2B ($\downarrow$)	CD-B2B ($\downarrow$)
Pinocchino [3]	0.072	0.055	0.047
Volumetric [44]	0.045	0.029	0.026
RigNet [43]	0.039	0.024	0.022
Ours	**0.029**	**0.019**	**0.017**

Quantitative Evaluation. In Table 2 we show the comparison results of the predicted skeleton on the RigNetv1 dataset [44]. For the RigNetv1 dataset, we follow the same train and test split as previous works [43, 44]. In Table 3 we show the quantitative evaluation and comparison results of the predicted skeleton on our SSkel dataset. We have re-trained the RigNet [43], which is the most current work on auto-rigging, on our SSkel dataset. As shown in the tables, our proposed skeleton prediction method has outperformed the current state-of-the-art approaches with the smallest error on all reported metrics on both the RigNetv1 dataset and our SSkel dataset.

Table 3. Quantitative comparison of skeleton prediction on our SSkel dataset. The J2J, J2B, B2B are the abbreviation for CD-J2J, CD-J2B and CD-B2B respectively. For these values, the smaller the better. Best results are in **bold face**.

Metrics	Chair			Table			Lamp			Airplane			Average		
	J2J	J2B	B2B	J2J	J2B	B2B	J2J	J2B	B2B	J2J	J2B	B2B	J2J	J2B	B2B
RigNet-GT	0.052	0.042	0.035	0.061	0.049	0.040	0.132	0.110	0.098	0.096	0.081	0.073	0.061	0.046	0.041
Ours-GT	**0.030**	**0.023**	**0.021**	**0.044**	**0.032**	**0.028**	**0.097**	**0.071**	**0.063**	**0.075**	**0.062**	**0.056**	**0.047**	**0.038**	**0.033**
RigNet-rec	0.048	0.035	0.033	0.060	0.046	0.038	0.143	0.116	0.102	0.103	0.084	0.076	0.063	0.047	0.042
Ours-rec	**0.036**	**0.024**	**0.022**	**0.047**	**0.033**	**0.029**	**0.101**	**0.073**	**0.065**	**0.081**	**0.065**	**0.059**	**0.051**	**0.041**	**0.036**

It is worth noting that the evaluation on the SSkel dataset is conducted with two different inputs. First, we report the skeleton error(RigNet-GT, Ours-GT) when taking the ground-truth 3D models as input. To evaluate the performance of the overall pipeline, we also calculate the skeleton error(RigNet-rec, Ours-rec) when 3D models reconstructed from the color images are taken as input. Our skeleton prediction performance on the reconstructed 3D models degraded slightly due to imperfect reconstruction.

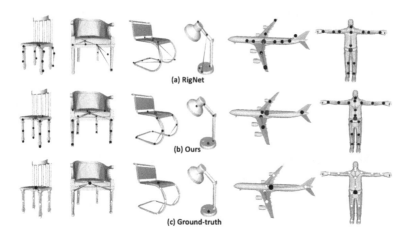

Fig. 4. Visual comparison on skeleton prediction. The rightmost model comes from the RigNetv1 dataset and the others are from our SSkel dataset.

Visual Results on Skeleton Prediction. In Fig. 4 and Fig. 5 we demonstrate the qualitative comparison of the predicted skeleton. First, in Fig. 4, the skeletons are predicted with ground-truth 3D models as input. We also evaluated the overall pipeline when taking a single image as input, and the results are shown in Fig. 5. As shown in the figures, compared with the most current work, our proposed approach can produce more reasonable results that correctly predicted the joints' location and constructed the kinematic chains. On the other hand, the RigNet method fails to localize the joints. The reason is that their mesh-based approach requires the vertices to be evenly distributed over the mesh and they rely on the mesh curvature to pre-train an attention model. But for the models from the SSkel dataset, there is no close connection between the mesh curvature and the joint locations.

Table 4. Ablation study on joints prediction. CD-J2J metric is used.

	RigNetv1	SSkel
Baseline	0.037	0.065
Baseline + joint-aware seg	0.033	0.055
Baseline + symmetry loss	0.034	0.058
Baseline + 3D adaptive activation	0.033	0.056
Ours	**0.029**	**0.047**

Ablation Study. To validate the effectiveness of several key components of the proposed method, we conduct several ablation studies with the quantitative evaluation results shown in Table 4. We denote our method without the 3D channel

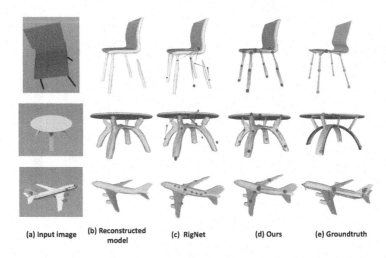

(a) Input image   (b) Reconstructed model   (c) RigNet   (d) Ours   (e) Groundtruth

Fig. 5. Visual results on articulated 3D models from input images. Taking the color image (a) as input, we reconstruct the 3D model (b) and predict its skeleton (d), and also compare with the RigNet [43] on skeleton prediction (c).

adaptive activation, symmetry loss, and joint-aware instance segmentation as the Baseline method.

4.3   Applications on Animation

After obtaining the rigged 3D models from the input images, in this section, we present interesting applications of animating the rigged 3D objects. To get the texture for the 3D models, similar to [41] we have trained a deep neural network to predict the projection matrix represented as a 6D rotation vector aligning the 3D models from canonical space to image space. Our reconstructed 3D model is further refined and deformed according to the object silhouettes [40]. The mirrored texture is applied to the invisible part of the 3D model.

In Fig. 6, we demonstrate the animation of objects as driven by the source motion of reference articulated models. Specifically, in the upper rows of Fig. 6 we map the motion of a Jumping human to two Chairs as well as a Lamp. The details of the skeleton mapping from the human template to the animated objects are shown in each corresponding row of Fig. 6(d). Likewise, in the lower part of Fig. 6, we demonstrate the manipulation of a Chair and Table driven by a quadruped. It is conducted by mapping the joints of four legs on the Dog skeleton to the legs of the chair and table. In addition, the joint of the neck is mapped to the joint on the chair back. The motion sequence of the dog is from RGBD-Dog dataset [14]. More results can be seen in the supplementary video.

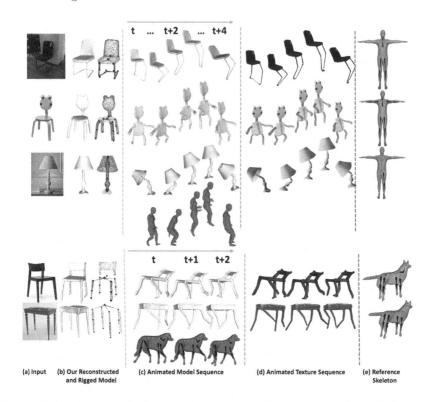

Fig. 6. Object animation. Given an input image (i.e. the object segment), its 3D shape is reconstructed and rigged, followed by the animated sequence (re-targeted from human or quadruped motions, which is not the main focus of this work). We map the joints from the human or quadruped skeleton to the objects, and the mapped joints are marked in red (c). The source human/dog motion is shown in the bottom row. (Color figure online)

5   Conclusion and Limitations

We consider an interesting task of waking up a 3D object from a single input image. An automated pipeline is proposed to reconstruct the 3D object, predict the articulated skeleton to animate the object with plausible articulations. Quantitative and qualitative experiments demonstrate the applicability of our work when unseen real-world images are presented at test time.

Limitations. First, the domain gap between synthetic to real images still exists. Second, in our current stage-wise framework, the skeleton prediction and final animation rely on the success of 3D shape reconstruction. For future work, we would like to combine shape reconstruction and skeleton prediction in a unified network structure to facilitate each task. Moreover, the collected SSkel dataset is limited in the number of objects and the range of object categories. For future work, we plan to work with a large-scale dataset containing a much broader range of generic object categories.

Acknowledgements. This research was partly supported by the NSERC Discovery, CFI-JELF and UAHJIC grants. We also thank Priyal Belgamwar for her contribution to the dataset annotation.

References

1. Amenta, N., Bern, M.: Surface reconstruction by voronoi filtering. Discrete Comput. Geom. **22**(4), 481–504 (1999)
2. Attali, D., Montanvert, A.: Computing and simplifying 2D and 3D continuous skeletons. Comput. Vis. Image Underst. **67**(3), 261–273 (1997)
3. Baran, I., Popović, J.: Automatic rigging and animation of 3d characters. ACM Trans. Graph. (TOG) **26**(3), 72 (2007)
4. Chang, A.X., et al.: Shapenet: an information-rich 3D model repository. arXiv preprint arXiv:1512.03012 (2015)
5. Chen, T., Zhu, Z., Shamir, A., Hu, S.M., Cohen-Or, D.: 3-sweep: extracting editable objects from a single photo. ACM Trans. Graph. (TOG) **32**(6), 1–10 (2013)
6. Chen, Z., Zhang, H.: Learning implicit fields for generative shape modeling. In: IEEE/CVF Conference on Computer Vision and Pattern Recognition (2019)
7. Cheriton, D., Tarjan, R.E.: Finding minimum spanning trees. SIAM J. Comput. **5**(4), 724–742 (1976)
8. Dosovitskiy, A., et al.: An image is worth 16×16 words: transformers for image recognition at scale. In: International Conference on Learning Representations (ICLR) (2021)
9. Fan, H., Su, H., Guibas, L.J.: A point set generation network for 3d object reconstruction from a single image. In: IEEE Conference on Computer Vision and Pattern Recognition (2017)
10. Gkioxari, G., Malik, J., Johnson, J.: Mesh R-CNN. In: IEEE/CVF International Conference on Computer Vision (2019)
11. Hornung, A., Dekkers, E., Kobbelt, L.: Character animation from 2d pictures and 3d motion data. ACM Trans. Graph. (TOG) **26**(1), 1 (2007)
12. Huang, H., Wu, S., Cohen-Or, D., Gong, M., Zhang, H., Li, G., Chen, B.: L1-medial skeleton of point cloud. ACM Trans. Graph. (TOG) **32**(4), 65:1–65:8 (2013)
13. Kato, H., Ushiku, Y., Harada, T.: Neural 3d mesh renderer. In: IEEE Conference on Computer Vision and Pattern Recognition (2018)
14. Kearney, S., Li, W., Parsons, M., Kim, K.I., Cosker, D.: Rgbd-dog: predicting canine pose from rgbd sensors. In: IEEE/CVF Conference on Computer Vision and Pattern Recognition, pp. 8336–8345 (2020)
15. Kholgade, N., Simon, T., Efros, A., Sheikh, Y.: 3d object manipulation in a single photograph using stock 3D models. ACM Trans. Graph. (TOG) **33**(4), 1–12 (2014)
16. Kulon, D., Guler, R.A., Kokkinos, I., Bronstein, M.M., Zafeiriou, S.: Weakly-supervised mesh-convolutional hand reconstruction in the wild. In: IEEE/CVF Conference on Computer Vision and Pattern Recognition (2020)
17. Li, M., Zhang, H.: D2im-net: Learning detail disentangled implicit fields from single images. In: IEEE/CVF Conference on Computer Vision and Pattern Recognition, pp. 10246–10255 (2021)

18. Lin, C.H., Kong, C., Lucey, S.: Learning efficient point cloud generation for dense 3D object reconstruction. In: AAAI Conference on Artificial Intelligence (2018)
19. Lin, C.H., Wang, C., Lucey, S.: Sdf-srn: Learning signed distance 3D object reconstruction from static images. In: Advances in Neural Information Processing Systems (2020)
20. Liu, S., Li, T., Chen, W., Li, H.: Soft rasterizer: a differentiable renderer for image-based 3d reasoning. In: IEEE/CVF International Conference on Computer Vision (2019)
21. Mescheder, L., Oechsle, M., Niemeyer, M., Nowozin, S., Geiger, A.: Occupancy networks: learning 3d reconstruction in function space. In: IEEE/CVF Conference on Computer Vision and Pattern Recognition (2019)
22. Mi, Z., Luo, Y., Tao, W.: Ssrnet: scalable 3D surface reconstruction network. In: IEEE/CVF Conference on Computer Vision and Pattern Recognition (2020)
23. Mo, K., et al.: Partnet: a large-scale benchmark for fine-grained and hierarchical part-level 3d object understanding. In: IEEE/CVF Conference on Computer Vision and Pattern Recognition (2019)
24. Niemeyer, M., Mescheder, L., Oechsle, M., Geiger, A.: Differentiable volumetric rendering: learning implicit 3D representations without 3D supervision. In: IEEE/CVF Conference on Computer Vision and Pattern Recognition (2020)
25. Pan, J., Han, X., Chen, W., Tang, J., Jia, K.: Deep mesh reconstruction from single rgb images via topology modification networks. In: IEEE International Conference on Computer Vision (2019)
26. Park, J.J., Florence, P., Straub, J., Newcombe, R., Lovegrove, S.: Deepsdf: learning continuous signed distance functions for shape representation. In: IEEE/CVF Conference on Computer Vision and Pattern Recognition (2019)
27. Peng, S., Niemeyer, M., Mescheder, L., Pollefeys, M., Geiger, A.: Convolutional occupancy networks. In: Vedaldi, A., Bischof, H., Brox, T., Frahm, J.-M. (eds.) ECCV 2020. LNCS, vol. 12348, pp. 523–540. Springer, Cham (2020). https://doi.org/10.1007/978-3-030-58580-8_31
28. Qi, C.R., Yi, L., Su, H., Guibas, L.J.: Pointnet++: deep hierarchical feature learning on point sets in a metric space. In: Advances in Neural Information Processing Systems (2017)
29. Riegler, G., Osman Ulusoy, A., Geiger, A.: Octnet: learning deep 3D representations at high resolutions. In: IEEE Conference on Computer Vision and Pattern Recognition (2017)
30. Schaefer, S., McPhail, T., Warren, J.: Image deformation using moving least squares. ACM Trans. Graph. (TOG) 25(3), 533–540 (2006)
31. Shi, R., Xue, Z., You, Y., Lu, C.: Skeleton merger: an unsupervised aligned keypoint detector. In: IEEE Conference on Computer Vision and Pattern Recognition (2021)
32. Shi, Z., Meng, Z., Xing, Y., Ma, Y., Wattenhofer, R.: 3d-retr: end-to-end single and multi-view 3D reconstruction with transformers. In: The British Machine Vision Conference (2021)
33. Tatarchenko, M., Dosovitskiy, A., Brox, T.: Octree generating networks: efficient convolutional architectures for high-resolution 3d outputs. In: IEEE International Conference on Computer Vision (2017)
34. Touvron, H., Cord, M., Douze, M., Massa, F., Sablayrolles, A., Jegou, H.: Training data-efficient image transformers and distillation through attention. In: International Conference on Machine Learning, vol. 139, pp. 10347–10357 (2021)

35. Tretschk, E., Tewari, A., Golyanik, V., Zollhöfer, M., Stoll, C., Theobalt, C.: PatchNets: patch-based generalizable deep implicit 3D shape representations. In: Vedaldi, A., Bischof, H., Brox, T., Frahm, J.-M. (eds.) ECCV 2020. LNCS, vol. 12361, pp. 293–309. Springer, Cham (2020). https://doi.org/10.1007/978-3-030-58517-4_18

36. Tulsiani, S., Efros, A.A., Malik, J.: Multi-view consistency as supervisory signal for learning shape and pose prediction. In: IEEE Conference on Computer Vision and Pattern Recognition (2018)

37. Wang, N., Zhang, Y., Li, Z., Fu, Y., Liu, W., Jiang, Y.-G.: Pixel2Mesh: generating 3D mesh models from single RGB images. In: Ferrari, V., Hebert, M., Sminchisescu, C., Weiss, Y. (eds.) ECCV 2018. LNCS, vol. 11215, pp. 55–71. Springer, Cham (2018). https://doi.org/10.1007/978-3-030-01252-6_4

38. Wang, P.S., Liu, Y., Tong, X.: Deep octree-based cnns with output-guided skip connections for 3D shape and scene completion. In: IEEE/CVF Conference on Computer Vision and Pattern Recognition Workshops (2020)

39. Wang, W., Yu, R., Huang, Q., Neumann, U.: Sgpn: similarity group proposal network for 3D point cloud instance segmentation. In: Proceedings of the IEEE Conference on Computer Vision and Pattern Recognition, pp. 2569–2578 (2018)

40. Weng, C.Y., Curless, B., Kemelmacher-Shlizerman, I.: Photo wake-up: 3d character animation from a single photo. In: IEEE/CVF Conference on Computer Vision and Pattern Recognition, pp. 5908–5917 (2019)

41. Xu, Q., Wang, W., Ceylan, D., Mech, R., Neumann, U.: DISN: deep implicit surface network for high-quality single-view 3d reconstruction. In: Advances in Neural Information Processing Systems (2019)

42. Xu, X., Wan, L., Liu, X., Wong, T.T., Wang, L., Leung, C.S.: Animating animal motion from still **27**(5), 1–8 (2008)

43. Xu, Z., Zhou, Y., Kalogerakis, E., Landreth, C., Singh, K.: Rignet: neural rigging for articulated characters. ACM Trans. Graph. (TOG) **39**(58) (2020)

44. Xu, Z., Zhou, Y., Kalogerakis, E., Singh, K.: Predicting animation skeletons for 3d articulated models via volumetric nets. In: International Conference on 3D Vision, pp. 298–307 (2019)

45. Yin, K., Huang, H., Cohen-Or, D., Zhang, H.: P2p-net: bidirectional point displacement net for shape transform. ACM Trans. Graph. (TOG) **37**(4), 1–13 (2018)

IntegratedPIFu: Integrated Pixel Aligned Implicit Function for Single-View Human Reconstruction

Kennard Yanting Chan[1,2,3]([✉]), Guosheng Lin[3], Haiyu Zhao[2], and Weisi Lin[1,3]

[1] S-Lab, Nanyang Technological University, Singapore, Singapore
`kenn0042@e.ntu.edu.sg`
[2] SenseTime Research, Singapore, Singapore
`zhaohaiyu@sensetime.com`
[3] Nanyang Technological University, Singapore, Singapore
`{gslin,wslin}@ntu.edu.sg`

Abstract. We propose IntegratedPIFu, a new pixel-aligned implicit model that builds on the foundation set by PIFuHD. IntegratedPIFu shows how depth and human parsing information can be predicted and capitalized upon in a pixel-aligned implicit model. In addition, IntegratedPIFu introduces depth-oriented sampling, a novel training scheme that improve any pixel-aligned implicit models ability to reconstruct important human features without noisy artefacts. Lastly, IntegratedPIFu presents a new architecture that, despite using less model parameters than PIFuHD, is able to improves the structural correctness of reconstructed meshes. Our results show that IntegratedPIFu significantly outperforms existing state-of-the-arts methods on single-view human reconstruction. We provide the code in our supplementary materials. Our code is available at https://github.com/kcyt/IntegratedPIFu.

Keywords: Single-view human reconstruction · Implicit function · Depth prediction · Human parsing prediction

1 Introduction

Human digitization is an important topic with applications in areas like virtual reality, game production, and medical imaging. While high precision reconstruction of human body is already possible using high-end, multi-view capturing systems [5,6,17], it is largely inaccessible to general consumers. Increasingly, the research community has shown interest in developing deep learning models for human digitization from simple inputs such as a single image [1,20,27,28].

Many methods have been proposed for single-image clothed human reconstruction, but one class of approaches that have captured significant interest is pixel-aligned implicit models [8,26,27]. These methods model a human body

Supplementary Information The online version contains supplementary material available at https://doi.org/10.1007/978-3-031-20086-1_19.

as an implicit function, from which a mesh can be obtained using Marching Cubes algorithm [19]. One recent and notable pixel-aligned implicit model is PIFuHD [27] proposed by Saito *et al.*. Unlike previous pixel-aligned implicit models, PIFuHD is able to capture fine-level geometric details such as clothes wrinkles.

However, pixel-aligned implicit models, including PIFuHD, are observed to be prone to problems such as depth ambiguity and generation of meshes with broken limbs [10, 23]. In particular, depth ambiguity can lead to unnaturally elongated human features in the reconstructed meshes.

In order to overcome these issues, we propose IntegratedPIFu, which is a new and improved pixel-aligned implicit model that builds on the foundations set by PIFuHD. In order to mitigate the problem of depth ambiguity and broken limbs in reconstructed human meshes, IntegratedPIFu dedicates specialized networks for depth and human parsing predictions from a single RGB image. Predicted depth information mitigates depth ambiguity by serving as a proxy for actual depth. Human parsing predictions provide structural information critical for reconstructing human limbs without breakages or gaps.

In addition, IntegratedPIFu introduces depth-oriented sampling, a novel training scheme suitable for training any pixel-aligned implicit model. We show that this scheme is able to significantly improve the model's ability to capture important human features. Furthermore, IntegratedPIFu introduces High-resolution integrator, a new architecture that ensures coarse and fine-level components in a pixel-aligned implicit model can work together in closer tandem. We later show that our new architecture can improve the structural correctness of the reconstructed meshes.

The main contributions of our work consist of the following:

1. To the best of our knowledge, we are the first to introduce a method to predict and incorporate relative depth and human parse maps into pixel-aligned implicit models for single-view clothed human reconstruction.
2. Depth-oriented sampling, a novel training scheme that replaces the original spatial sampling scheme used to train pixel-aligned implicit models. Our scheme is able to capture small but important human features, such as fingers and ears, that are often ignored by the original scheme. In addition, unlike the original scheme, depth-oriented sampling does not cause highly noticeable wavy artefacts on reconstructed meshes.
3. High-resolution integrator, a newly coined neural architecture that enables much stronger interactions between the coarse and fine-level components in a pixel-aligned implicit model. It is also an efficient architecture that improves the structure of the reconstructed meshes despite using 39% less model parameters than its direct predecessor.

All three of our contributions can be applied to any existing pixel-aligned implicit model.

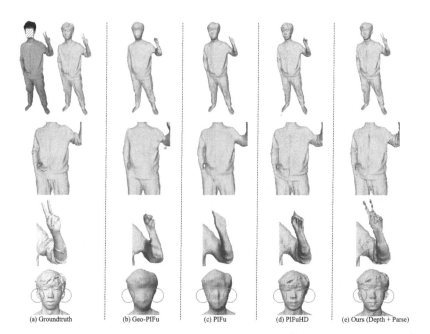

(a) Groundtruth   (b) Geo-PIFu   (c) PIFu   (d) PIFuHD   (e) Ours (Depth + Parse)

Fig. 1. Compared with state-of-the-art methods, including (b) Geo-PIFu [8], (c) PIFu [26], and (d) PIFuHD [27], our proposed model can precisely reconstruct various parts of a clothed human body without noisy artefacts. Subject's face censored as required by dataset's owner

2   Related Work

2.1   Single-View Human Reconstruction

Several methods have been proposed to reconstruct human body shape from a single image. The methods can be classified into parametric and non-parametric approaches. Parametric approaches, such as [13–15], recover human body shapes by estimating the parameters of a human parametric model (e.g. SMPL [18]) from an input image. However, these parametric methods are only able to reconstruct "naked" (without geometry of clothes) human meshes. Bhatnagar *et al.* [3] and Jiang *et al.* [12] additionally estimate the clothes on top of a human parametric model. However, these methods are unable to reconstruct high-fidelity geometry shapes.

Non-parametric approaches, on the other hand, do not require a human parametric model. For example, [28] use a 3D CNN to directly estimate a volumetric body shape from a single image. Notably, a subclass of non-parametric approaches that have garner significant interest is pixel-aligned implicit models [8,10,26,27]. One of the first pixel-aligned implicit models is the Pixel-Aligned Implicit Function (PIFu) proposed by Saito *et al.* [26]. PIFu is memory efficient and capable of producing high-fidelity 3D reconstructions of clothed human meshes.

Building from PIFu, there have been other pixel-aligned implicit models being proposed. Examples include GeoPIFu [8] and StereoPIFu [10] that make use of latent voxel features and an additional view respectively to improve the quality of their reconstructed meshes. However, GeoPIFu is unable to reconstruct fine geometry details of a human body, and StereoPIFu requires an additional view and careful calibration of a binocular camera. On the other hand, PIFuHD [27], which is a multi-scale variant of PIFu and a follow-up work by Saito *et al.*, is able to reconstruct very fine geometry details such as clothes wrinkles.

2.2 PIFu and PIFuHD

PIFu [26] can be interpreted as having two separate parts - 1. Encoder and 2. Decoder. An illustration of the PIFU architecture is given in Fig. 2 (under "Low-Resolution PIFu"). The encoder is a 2D convolutional network that extract feature maps from a RGB image. Points are sampled from the 3D camera space (of the RGB image), and their (x,y) coordinates are used to index the feature maps to retrieve a set of feature vectors. The z value of a point, together with the feature vector retrieved by the point, would then be used by the decoder (usually a multi-layer perceptron or MLP) to predict the binary occupancy value of that point. By evenly sampling the 3D camera space and employing the Marching Cube algorithm [19], a PIFu can reconstruct a 3D mesh.

PIFuHD [27] improves upon PIFu by using two PIFu modules that works at different resolutions. Additionally, PIFuHD also predicts frontal and rear normal maps from a single RGB image. In PIFuHD, the first PIFu (i.e. low-res PIFu) is given a downsampled RGB image and a rear and frontal normal maps as input. The second PIFu (i.e. high-res PIFu) is given the same inputs but at the original resolution. For each point sampled from the 3D camera space, the high-res PIFu's decoder would obtain the point's corresponding feature vector from the encoder before combining that feature vector with additional features obtained from the low-res PIFu's decoder. The high-res PIFu's decoder would then predict the binary occupancy value of that point. A 3D mesh can then be generated using the same approach as PIFu.

2.3 Signed Distance Field

Our depth-oriented sampling technique drew inspiration from DeepSDF [22], which also employs a continuous signed distance function. But in our supplementary materials, we explain why DeepSDF, unlike DOS, is not a suitable solution for a pixel-aligned implicit model.

3 Method

Our method builds on PIFuHD, which we consider to be the current state-of-the-art in this field. An overview of IntegratedPIFu is shown in Fig. 2. We train specialised networks to predict frontal normal, relative depth, and human parsing

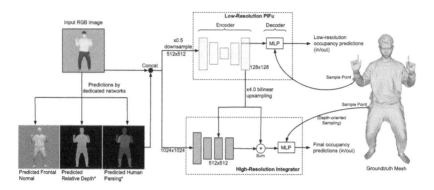

Fig. 2. Overview of our IntegratedPIFu framework. The Low-Resolution PIFu produces coarse feature maps that are further refined by High-Resolution Integrator. The High-Resolution Integrator will then use a MLP to generate a reconstructed mesh. *We recommend the use of predicted depth and human parsing maps in the Low-Resolution PIFu, but the use of them in the High-Resolution Integrator is optional and depends heavily on the quality of the two maps.

maps from a single 1024×1024 RGB image. Along with the image, these maps are downsampled (to 512×512 resolution), concatenated, and given to a PIFu. The feature maps produced by the PIFu's encoder is then upsampled bilinearly before being fed into our High-Resolution Integrator. Our High-Resolution Integrator combines the upsampled feature maps with **only** the 1024×1024 RGB image and predicted frontal normal map before producing occupancy predictions using a MLP. We train IntegratedPIFu using our newly proposed depth-oriented sampling scheme.

We like to highlight that, unlike PIFuHD, IntegratedPIFu does not use a rear normal map as input as it tends to cause hallucinations of creases or wrinkles on the rear-side of a reconstructed mesh (More details in supplementary materials).

In short, IntegratedPIFu offers three new contributions: 1. Incorporating depth and parsing information 2. Depth-oriented sampling 3. High-resolution integrator. We will explain the motivations for and inner workings of each of them in the following sections.

3.1 Prediction and Incorporation of Relative Depth and Human Parse Information

Similar to PIFuHD [27], we use a pix2pixHD [29] network to predict a frontal normal map from a single RGB image. Additionally, we find that using this normal map as an additional input for relative depth and human parse prediction (carried out by specialised networks) helps to predict more accurate depth and human parse maps (shown in our supplementary materials).

Depth Prediction. In our dataset, each input RGB image is rendered from a realistic human mesh. In order to reconstruct the 3D mesh shown in a single

RGB image, a pixel-aligned implicit model is implicitly required to predict the depth of each mesh vertex in the 3D camera space. This is not an easy task due to depth ambiguity in a 2D RGB image. Also, 3D mesh vertices, when being projected onto an image, can have very similar RGB values, and yet have very different depth values in the 3D space.

Thus, we decided to partially shift the burden of depth prediction from a pixel-aligned implicit model to a separate, specialised network. This network (called depth predictor) would predict the relative depth values of mesh vertices that are visible in a RGB image (i.e. camera-facing vertices). The usefulness of incorporating relative depth information into a pixel-aligned implicit model has been soundly demonstrated in StereoPIFu [10], though in their case they used two different, carefully positioned views of the mesh to generate a highly accurate relative depth map via triangulation.

The inputs to the depth predictor is a 2D RGB image, a predicted frontal normal map, and a center indicator map. The output is a 2D relative depth map (same size as RGB image), where each pixel contains a depth value that indicates how near it is to the camera compared to a reference mesh vertex on the mesh. Our reference vertex is the front-most vertex that is located at the centre of the image, and it should always have a relative depth value of zero. We will elaborate on the center indicator map.

The depth predictor is fundamentally a fully convolutional network with spatial invariance property. However, we require the center pixel in the relative depth map produced by depth predictor to have a value of zero (Since it is where the reference vertex is). To solve this, we introduce what we call a center indicator map, which is simply a map of zero values except its center pixel (has value of one). It has the same size as the RGB image. This helps the depth predictor to locate and predict a zero for the center pixel of all relative depth maps it generates.

The depth predictor consists of a two-staged U-Net [25]. Using the aforementioned inputs, the first stage U-Net would produce a coarse relative depth map. The second stage U-Net then refines the coarse relative depth map. The second U-Net is given the same inputs except that a coarse relative depth map replaces the center indicator map. In our supplementary material, we show the importance of having this two-staged process.

Human Parse Prediction. As observed by [10,23], pixel-aligned implicit models, such as PIFu and PIFuHD, has a tendency to produce broken limbs in some of its reconstructed 3D meshes. We argue that by feeding human parsing information into a pixel-aligned implicit model, the model can better understand the general shape and location of human's limbs and parts. For example, the model should learn from a human parsing map that a normal human arm is a continuous (no gap or breakage in between) and elongated structure.

Rather than manually labelling each pixel in every RGB image with human parsing information, we use a Self-Correction for Human Parsing model [16] that has been pre-trained on the Pascal-Person-Part dataset [4] to automatically generate human parsing maps from images. We find that the human parsing results, while not perfect, is reasonably correct in majority of the cases. The pre-trained model is used only to generate human parsing maps of training instances.

We treat these generated human parsing maps as the groundtruths, and use these groundtruths to train a separate network (called human parsing predictor or HPP) that would be used in IntegratedPIFu. We do this to ensure that only the necessary information from the Pascal-Person-Part dataset is transmitted to HPP. HPP is a U-Net that takes in a RGB image and predicted frontal normal map and outputs a corresponding human parsing map.

Depth-Oriented Sampling. Pixel-aligned implicit models need to be trained with 3D sample points. Each sample point is given a scalar label. Sample points outside the mesh are given a label of zero, and sample points inside the mesh are given a label of one. During training, a pixel-aligned implicit model will learn to assign a prediction of one to points it believes is inside the mesh and a prediction of zero to points outside of the mesh. As discussed by Saito *et al.* in [26], the scheme that is used to generate the sample points is very important as it can adversely affect the quality of the reconstructed mesh.

To the best of our knowledge, all existing pixel-aligned implicit models, including PIFu [26], PIFuHD [27], GeoPIFu [8], and StereoPIFu [10], use what is called the spatial sampling scheme during training. Spatial sampling scheme is the original sampling scheme developed by Saito *et al.* in [26] to generate sample points to train a PIFu. Two types of sample points exist in spatial sampling. The first type of sample points are points that are sampled directly on the mesh's surface. These points are then perturbed with normal-distributed noise (See Fig. 3). The second type of sample points are points that are uniformly sampled from a 3D camera space. Typically, the ratio of the first type of sample points to the second type is set to 16:1. Regardless of whether a sample point is of the first or second type, if it is inside a mesh, it would be given a label of one. Otherwise, it will have a label of zero.

The first problem with spatial sampling is that if a sample point is only just slightly inside a mesh, it is given a label of one. If a similarly located sample point is just slightly outside of the mesh, then it is given a very different label of zero. On the other hand, both a sample point that is slightly outside of the mesh and a sample point that is very far away from the mesh is given the same label of zero. This problem is illustrated in Fig. 3

We argue that this scheme confuses a pixel-aligned implicit model and make it harder to train it, leading to noises in reconstructed meshes. We believe that this is the cause of noisy, wavy-like artefacts on the reconstructed mesh surfaces as seen in Fig. 6b.

The second problem with spatial sampling is that it tends to ignore small but important human body features such as human ears or fingers and reconstruct meshes that have neither ears nor fingers. Small human body features like an ear have very small volume and, consequently, very few sample points would be located inside that small body feature. Instead, most sample points would be

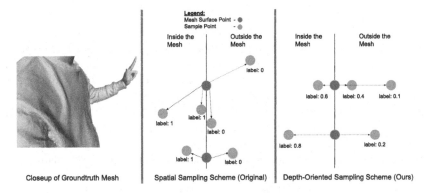

Fig. 3. Illustration of Depth-Oriented Sampling. The red dots represent points that are exactly on the mesh surface. These red dots are then randomly displaced. The blue dots represent the possible locations of the red dots after displacement (Color figure online)

located outside of it and have a label of zero. This means that a pixel-aligned implicit model trained with spatial sampling tends to predict labels of zero for the region containing an ear (i.e. the model predicts the region to be a pure empty space rather than containing a surface of a mesh).

These two problems inspired us to develop a new sampling scheme called depth-oriented sampling (DOS). In DOS, we sample points on the mesh surface and displace them only in the z-direction (i.e. camera direction. See Fig. 3). We use a normal distribution to determine the **magnitude** of displacement. In addition, rather than limiting labels to either value of zero or one, DOS allows labels to range from 0.0 to 1.0 (i.e. soft labels). The value of the label is indicative of the distance between a particular sample point and the mesh's surface in the z-direction. A label of 0.5 indicates that the sample point is exactly on the mesh surface. A label of 0.0 indicates that the sample point is very far away from the mesh surface and is outside of the mesh body. A label of 1.0 indicates that the sample point is very far away from the mesh surface but is inside the mesh body.

This new scheme naturally solves the first problem (similarly located points being given very different labels), and it also resolves the second problem since points that are outside but in front of a small human feature (e.g. a ear) will have labels that indicates how near the surface of the human feature is, rather than completely dismissing the existence of the human feature.

High-Resolution Integrator. PIFuHD [27] consists of two PIFu modules working at different resolution levels. The low-resolution PIFu (low-PIFu) would reconstruct a coarse, general shape of the human mesh, and the high-resolution PIFu (high-PIFu) would add details onto the coarse human mesh. As aforementioned, each PIFu module consists of an image encoder (uses stacked hourglass network [21]) and a MLP (See "Low-Resolution PIFu" in Fig. 2).

The first problem with this is that stacked hourglass network is heavy in parameters and would take up a significant amount of GPU memory during training. Consequently, given a 1024×1024 RGB image, the high-PIFu can only be trained using image crops (as discussed in [27]). Due to this, the high-PIFu does not have access to global information from the entire 1024×1024 image. Even if the high-PIFu is given enough number of image crops such that the original 1024×1024 image could be pieced together, the high-PIFu does not have information of where, in the original image, the crops are taken from.

The first problem would not be a problem if the high-PIFu has direct and early access to information generated by the low-PIFu, and this leads us to the second problem. The low-PIFu is trained on 512×512 low-resolution images in its entirety. Thus, the low-PIFu is aware of the global information in an image. However, the high-PIFu has no opportunity to use any information from the low-PIFu until late in its pipeline. Specifically, the high-PIFu's encoder does not get to interact with information from the low-PIFu. That information is given only to the high-PIFu's MLP component. This means that the high-PIFu's image encoder does not actually know what information it should be looking for in the 1024×1024 image. Ideally, the high-PIFu's image encoder should collect complementary information that is not already captured by the low-PIFu.

In order to solve the two problems mentioned above, we introduce a new architecture, High-resolution Integrator (HRI), to replace the high-PIFu. Similar to high-PIFu, the HRI has a encoder and a MLP. But rather than using a parameter-heavy stacked hourglass network for its encoder, the HRI's encoder adopts a shallow architecture consisting of only four convolutional layers. Thus, it consumes less GPU memory and can be trained using entire images (rather than image crops).

A distinguishing feature of HRI is how these four layers are being used (refer to "High-Resolution Integrator" in Fig. 2). The first and second convolutional layers are used to process the 1024×1024 high-resolution input image into a 512×512 feature map F. Then, using bilinear upsampling, we upscale the 128×128 feature map from the low-PIFu's encoder by a factor of 4. This upscaled feature map (denoted as U) is then concatenated with F. The concatenated feature map is then processed by the third and fourth convolutional layers. The output of the fourth convolutional layer is then added with U. In other words, we are using the principle of residual networks [7] to train the HRI's encoder to collect only complementary information not captured by low-PIFu. Crucially, HRI's encoder directly interacts with the output from low-PIFu before producing its own output, allowing it to infer what information is missing from low-PIFu.

4   Experiments

4.1   Datasets

We train our models and other competing models on the THuman2.0 dataset [31], which consists of high-quality scans of Chinese human models. We remove scans or meshes that contain obvious scanning errors. Scanning errors tend to occur on the female meshes due to their free-flowing hairs. We also remove meshes that suffer from extreme self-occlusion because we do not hope to reduce the task into a guessing game. This data cleaning process is done before any of the models is trained to ensure fair comparison between the models. In all, we use 362 human meshes from the THuman2.0 dataset. We adopted a 80–20 train-test split of these meshes. For each training mesh, we render 10 RGB images at different yaw angles using a weak-perspective camera.

In addition, we also use the BUFF dataset [32] to evaluate the different models. No model is trained on the BUFF dataset. Systematic sampling based on sequence number is done on the BUFF dataset to obtain 93 human meshes for testing the different models. Systematic sampling ensures that, for the same human subject, meshes of different poses are obtained and repeated poses are avoided. More implementation details is in our supplementary materials.

4.2   Comparison with State-of-the-Art

We compare our method against the existing methods on single-view clothed human reconstruction qualitatively and then quantitatively. As in [8, 26, 27], the metrics in our quantitative evaluation include Chamfer distance (CD), Point-to-Surface (P2S), and Normal reprojection error (Normal). We observe that CD and P2S tends to contain a degree of noise due to the lack of depth information in a 2D RGB image. Specifically, although depth ambiguity in RGB image allows multiple plausible 3D reconstruction outputs, CD and P2S assume that only one 3D mesh output with very specific depth values for each mesh vertex can be correct.

Existing methods that we compared against include PIFu [26], Geo-PIFu [8], and PIFuHD [27]. We did not include parametric approaches, such as Deep-Human [33] and Tex2shape [2], because [8], [27], and [10] have all shown that pixel-aligned implicit approaches outperformed parametric ones.

In addition, we did not compare our method with hybrid approaches (e.g. ARCH [11] and ARCH++ [9]) that combine parametric approaches with pixel-aligned implicit function approaches because of two reasons. The first reason is that ARCH and ARCH++ are solving the problem of generating animatable meshes, which is a different problem from ours. The second reason is that these approaches make use of information from an additional dataset. ARCH and ARCH++ both make use of parametric human body models estimated by DenseRaC [30] using 4,400 human scans from the CAESAR dataset [24]. Furthermore, our approach can be easily slotted into ARCH and ARCH++ as both methods make use of a pixel-aligned implicit model, and our approach is centred around techniques to improve a pixel-aligned implicit model.

Qualitative Evaluation. We present a qualitative comparison of our IntegratedPIFu (i.e. HRI + DOS + predicted depth and parsing maps) with the other existing methods in Fig. 1 and Fig. 4. In Fig. 1, we observe that only PIFuHD and our approach are able to reconstruct human facial features with great details.

However, PIFuHD tends to suffer from wavy artefacts. Moreover, only our app-roach can reconstruct small but important human body parts like fingers and ears.

In Fig. 4, we observe that Geo-PIFu, PIFu, and PIFuHD tend to generate floating artefacts that are very clearly visible from the side-view or top view. In contrast, IntegratedPIFu is able to generate a clean, natural structure of human body. As we have seen earlier, only PIFuHD and our method can reconstruct facial features of the human mesh in great details. However, PIFuHD remains prone to generating noisy, wavy artefacts on the body of reconstructed meshes, and only our method can reconstruct the ears of the human body mesh properly. Moreover, in the fourth row, we observe that only IntegratedPIFu managed to produce a non-broken, naturally-looking wrist.

We also provide a qualitative evaluation of our method against PIFuHD using real Internet photos in our supplementary materials.

Quantitative Evaluation. In addition, we show a quantitative evaluation of our method against the state-of-the-arts methods in Table 1.

In the first five rows of In Table 1, we compare the state-of-the-art methods with ours without the use of predicted depth or human parsing maps. We exclude these maps to allow for a fairer assessment. As seen from the table, with HRI and DOS, we are able to outperform the existing methods in all metrics.

In addition, in the last three rows of Table 1, we also show the results of incor-porating depth (D) or human parsing (P) maps. The results seems to suggest that our approach works best when only human parsing map is given or when neither of the maps are given. However, our ablation studies later will show that IntegratedPIFu with both predicted depth maps and human parsing maps would be a more robust strategy. We show there that using only human parsing maps or neither of the maps would lead to broken limbs or floating artefacts around reconstructed meshes. These phenomena are not obvious if we consider only the quantitative metrics.

Table 1. Quantitative evaluation of our methods against the state-of-the-arts in the THuman2.0 test set and BUFF dataset. (HRI = High-resolution Integrator, DOS = Depth-Oriented Sampling, D = depth, P = human parsing)

Methods	THuman2.0			BUFF		
	CD (10^{-4})	P2S (10^{-4})	Normal	CD (10^3)	P2S (10^3)	Normal
Geo-PIFu	5.816	9.657	2.452	6.250	10.757	2.912
PIFu	3.135	3.072	1.731	2.639	3.367	1.947
PIFuHD	2.800	2.540	1.698	2.031	2.029	2.010
Ours- HRI	2.841	2.177	**1.622**	2.083	1.931	**1.762**
Ours- HRI+DOS	**2.711**	**2.139**	1.643	**2.029**	**1.925**	1.800
Ours- HRI+DOS (D+P)	3.040	2.259	1.641	2.287	2.224	1.842
Ours- HRI+DOS (D)	3.003	2.387	**1.633**	2.182	2.094	1.858
Ours- HRI+DOS (P)	**2.734**	**2.153**	1.780	**2.030**	**1.897**	**1.789**

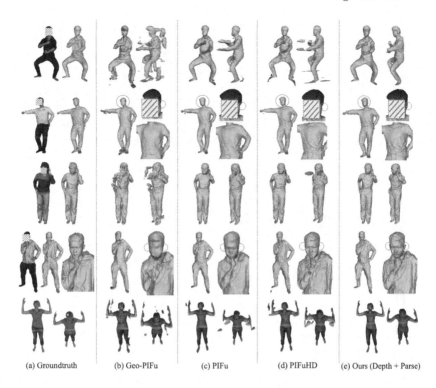

| (a) Groundtruth | (b) Geo-PIFu | (c) PIFu | (d) PIFuHD | (e) Ours (Depth + Parse) |

Fig. 4. Qualitative evaluation with SOTA methods, including (b) Geo-PIFu [8], (c) PIFu [26], and (d) PIFuHD [27]. The input RGB image is shown as the first object in each row. For each method, we show the frontal view and an alternative view. For the last row, the reconstructed meshes are colored by projecting the RGB values from the input image onto the generated meshes. The coloring serves as visual aids only. (Color figure online)

4.3 Ablation Studies

Comparison of Different Backbones in PIFuHD. Both PIFuHD and IntegratedPIFu use a low-resolution PIFu (also called the "backbone") to provide a coarse structure of a human mesh. IntegratedPIFu incorporates predicted depth and human parse map into its backbone. In order to evaluate the impact of these maps, we try out different possible backbones and show the results in Fig. 5.

In the first row of the figure, we observe that (b) a PIFu with neither predicted depth nor human parsing maps (i.e. vanilla PIFu) produced a left arm with a very noticeable breakage. But when either (c) predicted depth, (d) human parsing, or (e) both maps are added to the PIFu module, the left arm is reconstructed properly without any breakage. Reconstructed meshes of the vanilla PIFu have similar breakage in the second and fourth rows in the figure. In the third row, vanilla PIFu produces floating artefacts near the foot of the reconstructed mesh. Furthermore, the reconstructed arms are unnaturally elongated. All of these problems are not replicated by both (c) and (e).

We find that while (d) a PIFu with human parse map only may mitigate the problems, it does not always solve all of them. Qualitatively, we find that (e) produce the most natural-looking human meshes (explained in supplementary materials). Also, we observe that errors in the backbone would usually be propagated to the PIFuHD (or IntegratedPIFu). To show this, we deliberately pick the same human model for the third row of Fig. 5 and the first row of Fig. 4. When the backbone of PIFuHD erroneously produced elongated human arms, the PIFuHD would also replicate this error. More results in supp. materials.

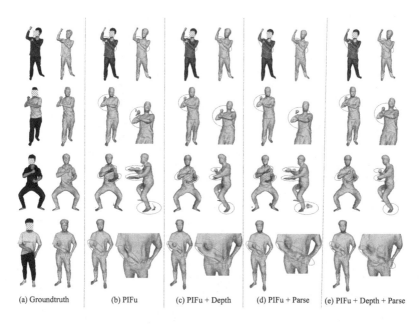

(a) Groundtruth   (b) PIFu   (c) PIFu + Depth   (d) PIFu + Parse   (e) PIFu + Depth + Parse

Fig. 5. Comparison with different backbones. (b) is a vanilla PIFu, (c) is given predicted depth map as additional input, (d) is given predicted human parsing, (e) is given both maps. To aid visualization, some reconstructed meshes are colored by projecting the RGB values from the input image onto the generated meshes (Color figure online)

Evaluation of Depth-Oriented Sampling. In order to evaluate the impact of using depth-oriented sampling (DOS), we train a PIFuHD using the original spatial sampling scheme and compare that with a PIFuHD trained with DOS. Neither models are given depth or human parsing maps. We evaluate the two PIFuHDs in Fig. 6. From the figure, we see the two advantages DOS has over spatial sampling scheme. The first is capturing small but important human features such as fingers and ears. The second advantage is that, unlike spatial sampling, DOS does not produce wavy artefacts on the reconstructed meshes' body.

Evaluation of High-Resolution Integrator. In order to evaluate our High-Resolution Integrator (HRI), we train a vanilla PIFuHD and a PIFuHD that

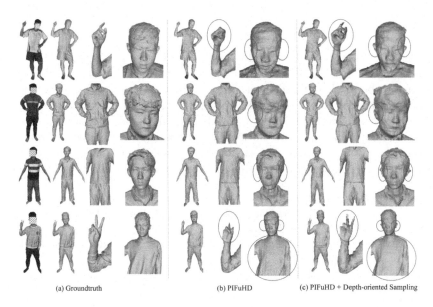

(a) Groundtruth   (b) PIFuHD   (c) PIFuHD + Depth-oriented Sampling

Fig. 6. Evaluation of the effect of depth-oriented sampling. Depth-oriented sampling captures small important features (e.g. fingers, ears) without producing wavy artefacts

(a) Groundtruth   (b) PIFuHD   (c) High-Res Integrator

Fig. 7. Comparison of PIFuHD with our HRI. Coloring serves as visual aids only

has its high-PIFu replaced with our HRI. Both models use the original spatial sampling scheme and are not given depth or human parsing maps. We present the results on Fig. 7. We find that a PIFuHD modified with our HRI is better at capturing the structure of human meshes compared to the vanilla PIFuHD, which often produces floating artefacts.

5   Conclusion

We have presented three novel techniques to improve any existing pixel-aligned implicit models. Firstly, we showed how relative depth and human parsing information can be predicted and incorporated into a pixel-aligned implicit model. Next, we described depth-oriented sampling, a new training scheme that gives more precise supervision signals than the original spatial sampling scheme. Finally, we introduce High-resolution Integrator, a new architecture that can work in closer tandem with the backbone to reconstruct structurally accurate human meshes. Together, these techniques form our IntegratedPIFu framework.

Acknowledgements. This study is supported under the RIE2020 Industry Alignment Fund - Industry Collaboration Projects (IAF-ICP) Funding Initiative, as well as cash and in-kind contribution from the industry partner(s). G. Lin's participation is supported by the Ministry of Education, Singapore, under its Academic Research Fund Tier 2 (MOE-T2EP20220-0007).

References

1. Alldieck, T., Magnor, M., Bhatnagar, B.L., Theobalt, C., Pons-Moll, G.: Learning to reconstruct people in clothing from a single rgb camera. In: Proceedings of the IEEE/CVF Conference on Computer Vision and Pattern Recognition, pp. 1175–1186 (2019)
2. Alldieck, T., Pons-Moll, G., Theobalt, C., Magnor, M.: Tex2shape: detailed full human body geometry from a single image. In: Proceedings of the IEEE/CVF International Conference on Computer Vision. pp. 2293–2303 (2019)
3. Bhatnagar, B.L., Tiwari, G., Theobalt, C., Pons-Moll, G.: Multi-garment net: learning to dress 3d people from images. In: Proceedings of the IEEE/CVF International Conference on Computer Vision, pp. 5420–5430 (2019)
4. Chen, X., Mottaghi, R., Liu, X., Fidler, S., Urtasun, R., Yuille, A.: Detect what you can: detecting and representing objects using holistic models and body parts. In: Proceedings of the IEEE Conference on Computer Vision and Pattern Recognition, pp. 1971–1978 (2014)
5. Collet, A., Chuang, M., Sweeney, P., Gillett, D., Evseev, D., Calabrese, D., Hoppe, H., Kirk, A., Sullivan, S.: High-quality streamable free-viewpoint video. ACM Trans. Graph. (ToG) **34**(4), 1–13 (2015)
6. Guo, K., et al.: The relightables: volumetric performance capture of humans with realistic relighting. ACM Trans. Graph. (ToG) **38**(6), 1–19 (2019)
7. He, K., Zhang, X., Ren, S., Sun, J.: Deep residual learning for image recognition. In: Proceedings of the IEEE Conference on Computer Vision and Pattern Recognition, pp. 770–778 (2016)
8. He, T., Collomosse, J., Jin, H., Soatto, S.: Geo-pifu: geometry and pixel aligned implicit functions for single-view human reconstruction. Adv. Neural. Inf. Process. Syst. **33**, 9276–9287 (2020)
9. He, T., Xu, Y., Saito, S., Soatto, S., Tung, T.: Arch++: animation-ready clothed human reconstruction revisited. In: Proceedings of the IEEE/CVF International Conference on Computer Vision, pp. 11046–11056 (2021)

10. Hong, Y., Zhang, J., Jiang, B., Guo, Y., Liu, L., Bao, H.: Stereopifu: depth aware clothed human digitization via stereo vision. In: Proceedings of the IEEE/CVF Conference on Computer Vision and Pattern Recognition, pp. 535–545 (2021)

11. Huang, Z., Xu, Y., Lassner, C., Li, H., Tung, T.: Arch: animatable reconstruction of clothed humans. In: Proceedings of the IEEE/CVF Conference on Computer Vision and Pattern Recognition, pp. 3093–3102 (2020)

12. Jiang, B., Zhang, J., Hong, Y., Luo, J., Liu, L., Bao, H.: BCNet: learning body and cloth shape from a single image. In: Vedaldi, A., Bischof, H., Brox, T., Frahm, J.-M. (eds.) ECCV 2020. LNCS, vol. 12365, pp. 18–35. Springer, Cham (2020). https://doi.org/10.1007/978-3-030-58565-5_2

13. Kanazawa, A., Black, M.J., Jacobs, D.W., Malik, J.: End-to-end recovery of human shape and pose. In: Proceedings of the IEEE Conference on Computer Vision and Pattern Recognition, pp. 7122–7131 (2018)

14. Kolotouros, N., Pavlakos, G., Black, M.J., Daniilidis, K.: Learning to reconstruct 3d human pose and shape via model-fitting in the loop. In: Proceedings of the IEEE/CVF International Conference on Computer Vision, pp. 2252–2261 (2019)

15. Kolotouros, N., Pavlakos, G., Daniilidis, K.: Convolutional mesh regression for single-image human shape reconstruction. In: Proceedings of the IEEE/CVF Conference on Computer Vision and Pattern Recognition, pp. 4501–4510 (2019)

16. Li, P., Xu, Y., Wei, Y., Yang, Y.: Self-correction for human parsing. IEEE Trans. Pattern Anal. Mach. Intell. (2020). https://doi.org/10.1109/TPAMI.2020.3048039

17. Lombardi, S., Saragih, J., Simon, T., Sheikh, Y.: Deep appearance models for face rendering. ACM Trans. Graph. (ToG) 37(4), 1–13 (2018)

18. Loper, M., Mahmood, N., Romero, J., Pons-Moll, G., Black, M.J.: Smpl: a skinned multi-person linear model. ACM Trans. Graph. (TOG) 34(6), 1–16 (2015)

19. Lorensen, W.E., Cline, H.E.: Marching cubes: a high resolution 3d surface construction algorithm. ACM siggraph Comput. Graph. 21(4), 163–169 (1987)

20. Natsume, R., Saito, S., Huang, Z., Chen, W., Ma, C., Li, H., Morishima, S.: Siclope: silhouette-based clothed people. In: Proceedings of the IEEE/CVF Conference on Computer Vision and Pattern Recognition, pp. 4480–4490 (2019)

21. Newell, A., Yang, K., Deng, J.: Stacked hourglass networks for human pose estimation. In: Leibe, B., Matas, J., Sebe, N., Welling, M. (eds.) ECCV 2016. LNCS, vol. 9912, pp. 483–499. Springer, Cham (2016). https://doi.org/10.1007/978-3-319-46484-8_29

22. Park, J.J., Florence, P., Straub, J., Newcombe, R., Lovegrove, S.: Deepsdf: learning continuous signed distance functions for shape representation. In: Proceedings of the IEEE/CVF Conference on Computer Vision and Pattern Recognition, pp. 165–174 (2019)

23. Peng, S., et al.: Neural body: implicit neural representations with structured latent codes for novel view synthesis of dynamic humans. In: Proceedings of the IEEE/CVF Conference on Computer Vision and Pattern Recognition, pp. 9054–9063 (2021)

24. Robinette, K.M., Blackwell, S., Daanen, H., Boehmer, M., Fleming, S.: Civilian American and European surface anthropometry resource (caesar), final report. volume 1. summary. Technical report, Sytronics Inc Dayton Oh (2002)

25. Ronneberger, O., Fischer, P., Brox, T.: U-Net: convolutional networks for biomedical image segmentation. In: Navab, N., Hornegger, J., Wells, W.M., Frangi, A.F. (eds.) MICCAI 2015. LNCS, vol. 9351, pp. 234–241. Springer, Cham (2015). https://doi.org/10.1007/978-3-319-24574-4_28

26. Saito, S., Huang, Z., Natsume, R., Morishima, S., Kanazawa, A., Li, H.: Pifu: Pixel-aligned implicit function for high-resolution clothed human digitization. In: Proceedings of the IEEE/CVF International Conference on Computer Vision, pp. 2304–2314 (2019)

27. Saito, S., Simon, T., Saragih, J., Joo, H.: Pifuhd: Multi-level pixel-aligned implicit function for high-resolution 3d human digitization. In: Proceedings of the IEEE/CVF Conference on Computer Vision and Pattern Recognition, pp. 84–93 (2020)

28. Varol, G., Ceylan, D., Russell, B., Yang, J., Yumer, E., Laptev, I., Schmid, C.: BodyNet: volumetric inference of 3D human body shapes. In: Ferrari, V., Hebert, M., Sminchisescu, C., Weiss, Y. (eds.) ECCV 2018. LNCS, vol. 11211, pp. 20–38. Springer, Cham (2018). https://doi.org/10.1007/978-3-030-01234-2_2

29. Wang, T.C., Liu, M.Y., Zhu, J.Y., Tao, A., Kautz, J., Catanzaro, B.: High-resolution image synthesis and semantic manipulation with conditional gans. In: Proceedings of the IEEE Conference on Computer Vision and Pattern Recognition, pp. 8798–8807 (2018)

30. Xu, Y., Zhu, S.C., Tung, T.: Denserac: joint 3d pose and shape estimation by dense render-and-compare. In: Proceedings of the IEEE/CVF International Conference on Computer Vision, pp. 7760–7770 (2019)

31. Yu, T., Zheng, Z., Guo, K., Liu, P., Dai, Q., Liu, Y.: Function4d: real-time human volumetric capture from very sparse consumer rgbd sensors. In: IEEE Conference on Computer Vision and Pattern Recognition (CVPR2021), June 2021

32. Zhang, C., Pujades, S., Black, M.J., Pons-Moll, G.: Detailed, accurate, human shape estimation from clothed 3d scan sequences. In: The IEEE Conference on Computer Vision and Pattern Recognition (CVPR), July 2017

33. Zheng, Z., Yu, T., Wei, Y., Dai, Q., Liu, Y.: Deephuman: 3d human reconstruction from a single image. In: Proceedings of the IEEE/CVF International Conference on Computer Vision, pp. 7739–7749 (2019)

Realistic One-Shot Mesh-Based Head Avatars

Taras Khakhulin[1,2](✉) (iD), Vanessa Sklyarova[1,2] (iD), Victor Lempitsky[3] (iD),
and Egor Zakharov[1,2] (iD)

[1] Samsung AI Center – Moscow, Moscow, Russia
t.khakhulin@gmail.com
[2] Skolkovo Institute of Science and Technology, Moscow, Russia
[3] Yandex Armenia, Yerevan, Armenia
https://samsunglabs.github.io/rome/

Abstract. We present a system for the creation of realistic one-shot mesh-based (ROME) human head avatars. From a single photograph, our system estimates the head mesh (with person-specific details in both the facial and non-facial head parts) as well as the neural texture encoding, local photometric and geometric details. The resulting avatars are rigged and can be rendered using a deep rendering network, which is trained alongside the mesh and texture estimators on a dataset of in-the-wild videos. In the experiments, we observe that our system performs competitively both in terms of head geometry recovery and the quality of renders, especially for cross-person reenactment.

1 Introduction

Personalized human avatars are becoming a key technology across several application domains, such as telepresence, virtual worlds, and online commerce. In many practical cases, it is sufficient to personalize only a part of the avatar's body, while the remaining areas can then be picked from a pre-defined library of assets or omitted from the interface. Towards this end, many applications require personalization at the head level, i.e., the creation of person-specific head models, thus making it an important and viable intermediate step between personalizing only the face and the entire body. Alone, face personalization is often insufficient, while the full-body reconstruction remains a complicated task and leads to the reduced quality of the models or requires cumbersome data collection.

Acquiring human avatars from a single photograph (in a "one-shot" setting) offers the highest convenience for the end-user. However, their creation process is particularly challenging and requires strong priors on human geometry and appearance. To this end, parametric models are long known to offer good personalization solutions [3] and were recently adapted to one-shot performance [9,13,41]. Such models can be learned from a relatively small dataset

---

Supplementary Information The online version contains supplementary material available at https://doi.org/10.1007/978-3-031-20086-1_20.

Fig. 1. Our system creates realistic mesh-based avatars from a single **source** photo. These avatars are rigged, i.e., they can be driven by the animation parameters from a different **driving** frame. At the same time, our obtained **meshes** and **renderes** achieve a high degree of personalization in both appearance and geometry and are trained in an end-to-end fashion on a dataset of in-the-wild videos without any additional 3D supervision.

of 3D scans and represent geometry and appearance via textured meshes, making them compatible with many computer graphics applications and pipelines. However, they cannot be trivially expanded to the whole head region due to the large geometric variability of the non-facial parts such as hair and neck.

Our proposed system addresses this issue and allows parametric face models to represent the non-facial parts. In order to handle the increased geometric and photometric variability, we train our method on a large dataset of in-the-wild videos [6] and use neural networks to parameterize both the geometry and the appearance. For the appearance modeling, we follow the deferred neural rendering [46] paradigm and employ a combination of neural textures and rendering networks. In addition, a neural rendering framework [36] is used to enable end-to-end training and achieve high visual realism of the resulting head models. After training, the geometric and appearance networks can be conditioned on the information extracted from a single photograph, enabling one-shot realistic avatar generation.

To the best of our knowledge, our system is the first that is capable of creating realistic personalized human head models in a rigged mesh format from a single photograph. This distinguishes our model from a growing class of approaches that a) recover neural head avatars without explicit geometry [42,49,52,53], b) can personalize the face region but not the whole head [3,9,20,45], and c) from commercial systems that create non-photorealistic mesh avatars from a single image [1,33]. Alongside our main model, we also discuss its simplified version based on a linear blendshapes basis and show how to train it using the same video dataset. Below, we refer to the avatars generated by our system as ROME avatars (Realistic One-shot Mesh-based avatars).

2   Related Work

Parametric Models of Human Faces. Over the recent decades, 3D face reconstruction methods have been actively employed to tackle the problems of face tracking and alignment [13,15], face recognition [2,47], and generative modelling [20,25,26,29,35,45]. In all these scenarios, statistical mesh-based models, aka parametric models [3], remain one of the widely used tools [8,34]. State-of-the-art parametric models for human heads consist of rigged meshes [23] which support a diverse range of animations via disentangled shape and expression blendshapes and rigid motions for the jaw, neck, and eyeballs. However, they only provide reconstructions for the face, ears, neck, and forehead regions, limiting the range of applications. Including full head reconstruction (i.e., hair and shoulders) into these parametric models is possible, but existing approaches require significantly more training data to be gathered in the form of 3D scans. Instead, in our work, we propose to leverage existing large-scale datasets [6] of in-the-wild videos via the learning-by-synthesis paradigm without any additional 3D annotations.

Neural 3D Human Head Models. While parametric models provide sufficient reconstruction quality for many downstream applications, they are not able to depict the fine appearance details that are needed for photorealistic modelling. In recent years, the problem of representing complex geometry and appearance of humans started being addressed using high-capacity deep neural networks. Some of these works use strong human-specific priors [9,27,35,39], while others fit high-capacity networks to data without the use of such priors [19,25,26,28,29,31,32]. The latter methods additionally differ by the type of data structure used to represent the geometry, namely, mesh-based [9,12,25,26], point-based [28,51], and implicit models [27,29,31,32,35,39,50]. Additionally, recently there have emerged the hybrid models [10,55] where authors integrate face priors from parametric models with implicit representations to learn geometry and rendering for the specific person from the video.

However, mesh-based models arguably represent the most convenient class of methods for downstream applications. They provide better rendering quality and better temporal stability than point-based neural rendering. Also, unlike methods based on implicit geometry, mesh-based methods preserve topology and rigging capabilities and are much faster during fitting and rendering. However, current mesh-based methods either severely limit the range of deformations [9], making it infeasible to learn more complex geometry like hair and clothed shoulders, operate in the multi-shot setting [12] or require 3D scans as training data [25,26]. Our proposed method is also mesh-based, but we allow the prediction of complex deformations without 3D supervision and using a single image, lifting the limitations of the previous and concurrent works.

One-Shot Neural Head Models. Advances in neural networks also led to the development of methods that directly predict images using large ConvNets operating in the 2D image domain, with effectively no underlying 3D geometry [42,52,53] or very coarse 3D geometry [49]. These methods achieve state-of-the-art realism [49], use in-the-wild images or videos with no 3D annotations for training, and can create avatars from a single image. However, the lack of an explicit geometric model makes these models incompatible with many real-world applications and limits the span of camera poses that these methods can handle.

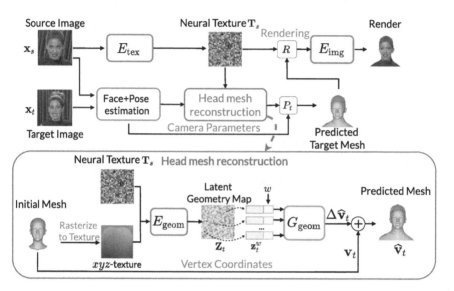

Fig. 2. Overview of our approach and the detailed scheme of the head mesh reconstruction. Given the source photo, we first estimate a *neural texture* that encodes local geometric and photometric details of visible and occluded parts. We then use a pre-trained system [9] for face reconstruction to estimate an initial mesh with a reconstructed facial part. We call this step face and 3D pose estimation. During head mesh reconstruction (bottom), using the estimated neural texture and the initial mesh, we predict the offsets for the mesh vertices, which do not correspond to a face. The offsets are predicted with a combination of a convolutional network E_{geom} and a perceptron network G_{geom}. We then render the personalized head mesh using the camera parameters, estimated by a pre-trained regressor [9] while superimposing the predicted neural texture. Finally, the rendering network E_{img} estimates the RGB image and the mask from the render. (Color figure online)

Neural Mesh Rendering. Recently, approaches that combine explicit data structures (point clouds or meshes) with neural image generation have emerged. These methods gained popularity thanks to the effectiveness of the pioneering Deferred Neural Rendering system [46], as well as recent advances in differentiable mesh rendering [22,24,36]. Neural mesh rendering uses 2D convolutional networks to model complex photometric properties of surfaces. It achieves high realism of renders with fine details present even when they are missing in the underlying geometric model. In this work, we adapt these advances to human head modelling while training using a large dataset of in-the-wild videos.

3   Method

Our goal is to build a system that jointly learns to produce photorealistic renders of human heads and estimate their 3D meshes using only a *single image* without any 3D supervision.

To achieve that, we use a large-scale dataset [6] of in-the-wild videos with talking speakers. All frames in each video are assumed to depict the same person in the same environment (defined by lighting, hairstyle, and person's clothing). At each training step, we sample two random frames $\mathbf{x}_s$ and $\mathbf{x}_t$ from a random training video. Our goal is to reconstruct and render the target image $\hat{\mathbf{x}}_t$ given a) the personal details and the face shape extracted from the source image $\mathbf{x}_s$, as well as b) the head pose, the facial expression, and the camera pose estimated from the target image $\mathbf{x}_t$. The final reconstruction loss is backpropagated and used to update the parameters of the model's components.

After training, we can create a personalized head model by estimating all parameters from a single image. This model can then be *animated* using face tracking parameters extracted from any talking head sequence and rendered from a range of viewpoints similar to those present in the training dataset (Fig. 1).

3.1 Model Overview

In our model, we jointly train multiple neural networks that perform rendering and mesh reconstruction. The training pipeline proceeds as follows (Fig. 2):

Neural Texture Estimation. The source image $\mathbf{x}_s$ is encoded into a neural texture $\mathbf{T}_s$, which describes both person-specific appearance and geometry. The encoding is done by a convolutional neural network E_{tex}.

Face and 3D Pose Estimation. In parallel, we apply a pre-trained DECA system [9] for face reconstruction to both the source and the target image, which estimates facial shape, expression, and head pose. Internally, it uses the FLAME parametric head model [23], which includes mesh topology, texture mapping, and blendshapes. We use the face shape from the source image $\mathbf{x}_s$ as well as the facial expression and the camera pose from the target image $\mathbf{x}_t$ for further processing.

Head Mesh Reconstruction. The vertices of the DECA mesh with personalized face region and generic non-facial parts are rendered into an xyz-coordinate texture using the predefined texture mapping. The xyz-texture and the neural texture $\mathbf{T}_s$ are concatenated and processed with the U-Net network [37] E_{geom} into a new texture map $\mathbf{Z}_t$, called *latent geometry* map. The 3D displacements for each mesh vertex are then decoded independently by the multi-layer perceptron G_{geom} that predicts a 3D offset $\Delta\hat{\mathbf{v}}$ for each vertex. This step reconstructs the personalized model for non-face parts of the head mesh. The obtained reconstructions are compatible with the topology/connectivity of the FLAME mesh [23].

Deferred Neural Rendering. The personalized head mesh is rendered using the pose estimated by DECA for the target image and with the superimposed neural texture. The rendered neural texture and the rasterized surface normals are concatenated and processed by the decoding (rendering) U-Net network E_{img} to predict the rendered image $\hat{\mathbf{x}}_t$ and the segmentation mask $\hat{\mathbf{s}}_t$. During training, the difference between the predictions and the ground truths is used to update all components of our system.

Below we discuss our system and its training process in more detail. We also describe a training procedure for a simplified version of our model, which represents head geometry using a linear basis of blendshapes.

3.2   Parametric Face Modeling

Our method uses a predefined head mesh with the corresponding topology, texture coordinates w, and rigging parameters, which remain fixed for all avatars. More specifically, we use FLAME [23] head model that has N base vertices $\mathbf{v}_{\text{base}} \in \mathbb{R}^{3N}$, and two sets of K and L basis vectors (blendshapes) that encode shape $\mathcal{B} \in \mathbb{R}^{3N \times K}$ and expression $\mathcal{D} \in \mathbb{R}^{3N \times L}$. The reconstruction process is carried out in two stages. First, the basis vectors are blended using the person- and expression-specific vectors of linear coefficients ϕ and ψ. Then, the linear blend skinning [23] function $\mathcal{W}$ is applied, parameterized by the angles θ, which rotates the predefined groups of vertices around linearly estimated joints. The final reconstruction in world coordinates can be expressed as follows:

$$\mathbf{v}(\phi, \psi, \theta) = \mathcal{W}\left(\mathbf{v}_{\text{base}} + \mathcal{B}\phi + \mathcal{D}\psi, \ \theta\right).$$

In previous works [45], a similar set of parameters for the 3DMM [3] parametric model was obtained via photometric optimization. More recently, learning-based methods [9,13] capable of feed-forward estimation started to emerge. In our work, given an input image, we use a pre-trained feed-forward DECA system [9] to estimate ϕ, ψ, θ, and the camera parameters.

During training, we apply DECA to both source image $\mathbf{x}_s$ and the target image $\mathbf{x}_t$. The face shape parameters ϕ_s from the source image $\mathbf{x}_s$ alongside the expression ψ_t, head pose θ_t and camera parameters from the target image $\mathbf{x}_t$ are then used to reconstruct the initial FLAME vertices $\mathbf{v}_t = \mathbf{v}(\phi_s, \psi_t, \theta_t)$, as well as camera transform $\mathcal{P}_t$.

3.3   Head Mesh Reconstruction

The FLAME vertices $\mathbf{v}_t$ estimated by DECA provide good reconstructions for the face region but lack any person-specific details in the remaining parts of the head (hair and shoulders). To alleviate that, we predict person-specific mesh offsets for non-facial regions while preserving the face shape predicted by DECA. We additionally exclude ear regions since their geometry in the initial mesh is too complex to be learned from in-the-wild video datasets.

These mesh offsets are estimated in two steps. First, we encode both the xyz-coordinate texture and the neural texture $\mathbf{T}_s$ into the latent geometry texture map $\mathbf{Z}_t$ via a U-Net network E_{geom}. It allows the produced latent map to contain both positions of the initial vertices $\mathbf{v}_t$ and their semantics, provided by the neural texture.

From $\mathbf{Z}_t$ we obtain the vectors $\mathbf{z}_t^w$ by bilinear interpolation at the fixed texture coordinates w. The vectors $\mathbf{z}_t^w$ and their coordinates w are then concatenated and passed through a multi-layer perceptron G_{geom} to predict the coefficients $\hat{\mathbf{m}}_t \in \mathbb{R}^{3N \times 3}$ independently for each vertex in the mesh. These coefficients are multiplied elementwise by the normals $\mathbf{n}_t$, calculated for each vertex in $\mathbf{v}_t$, to obtain the displacements: $\Delta\hat{\mathbf{v}}_t = \hat{\mathbf{m}} \odot \mathbf{n}_t$. These displacements are then zeroed out for face and ear regions, and the final reconstruction in world coordinates is obtained as follows: $\hat{\mathbf{v}}_t = \mathbf{v}_t + \Delta\hat{\mathbf{v}}_t$.

3.4 Deferred Neural Rendering

We render the reconstructed head vertices $\hat{\mathbf{v}}_t$ using the topology and texture coordinates w from the FLAME model with the superimposed neural texture $\mathbf{T}_s$. For that, we use a differentiable mesh renderer $\mathcal{R}$ [36] with the camera transform $\mathcal{P}_t$ estimated by DECA for the target image $\mathbf{x}_t$.

The resulting rasterization, which includes both the neural texture and the surface normals, is processed by the rendering network E_{img} to obtain the predicted image $\hat{\mathbf{x}}_t$ and the segmentation mask $\hat{\mathbf{s}}_t$. E_{img} consists of two U-Nets that separately decode an image and a mask. The result of the deferred neural rendering is the reconstruction of the target image $\hat{\mathbf{x}}\hat{\mathbf{x}}_t$ and its mask $\hat{\mathbf{s}}_t$, which are compared to the ground-truth image $\mathbf{x}_t$ and mask $\mathbf{s}_t$ respectively.

3.5 Training Objectives

In our approach, we learn the geometry of hair and shoulders, which are not reconstructed by the pre-trained DECA estimator, without any ground-truth 3D supervision during training. For that we utilize two types of objectives: segmentation-based geometric losses $\mathcal{L}_{\text{geom}}$ and photometric losses $\mathcal{L}_{\text{photo}}$.

We found that explicitly assigning subsets of mesh vertices to the neck and the hair regions helps a lot with the quality of final deformations. It allows us to introduce a topological prior for the predicted offsets, which is enforced by.

To evaluate the geometric losses, we calculate two separate occupancy masks using a soft rasterization operation [24]. First, $\hat{\mathbf{o}}_t^{\text{hair}}$ is calculated with detached neck vertices, so that the gradient flows through that mask only to the offsets corresponding to the hair vertices, and then $\hat{\mathbf{o}}_t$ is calculated with detached hair vertices. We match the hair occupancy mask to the ground-truth mask $\mathbf{s}_t^{\text{hair}}$ (which covers the hair, face, and ears), and the estimated occupancy mask to the whole segmentation mask $\mathbf{s}_t$: $\mathcal{L}_{\text{occ}} = \lambda_{\text{hair}}\left\|\hat{\mathbf{o}}_t^{\text{hair}} - \mathbf{s}_t^{\text{hair}}\right\|_2^2 + \lambda_{\text{o}}\left\|\hat{\mathbf{o}}_t - \mathbf{s}_t\right\|_2^2$.

We also use an auxiliary Chamfer loss to ensure that the predicted mesh vertices cover the head more uniformly. Specifically, we match the 2D coordinates of the mesh vertices projected into the target image to the head segmentation mask. We denote the subset of predicted mesh vertices, visible in the target image, as $\hat{\mathbf{p}}_t = \mathcal{P}'_t(\hat{\mathbf{v}}_t)$, and the number of these vertices as N_t, so that $\hat{\mathbf{p}}_t \in \mathbf{R}^{N_t \times 2}$. Notice that operator $\mathcal{P}'_t$ here not only does the camera transformation but also discards the z coordinate of the projected mesh vertices. To compute the loss, we then sample N_t 2D points from the segmentation mask $\mathbf{s}_t$ and estimate the Chamfer distance between the sampled set of points $\mathbf{p}_t$ and the vertex projections:

$$\mathcal{L}_{\text{chm}} = \frac{1}{2N_t} \sum_{\hat{p}_t \in \hat{\mathbf{p}}_t} \left\| \hat{p}_t - \arg\min_{p \in \mathbf{p}_t} \|p - \hat{p}_t\| \right\| +$$

$$\frac{1}{2N_t} \sum_{p_t \in \mathbf{p}_t} \left\| p_t - \arg\min_{\hat{p} \in \hat{\mathbf{p}}_t} \|\hat{p} - p_t\| \right\|.$$

Lastly, we regularize the learned geometry using the Laplacian penalty [43]. Initially, we found that regularizing offsets $\Delta\hat{\mathbf{v}}$ worked better than regularizing full coordinates $\hat{\mathbf{v}}$ and stuck to that approach for all experiments. Our version of the Laplacian loss can be written as:

$$\mathcal{L}_{\text{lap}} = \frac{1}{V} \sum_{i=1}^{V} \left\| \Delta\hat{\mathbf{v}}_i - \frac{1}{\mathcal{N}(i)} \sum_{j \in \mathcal{N}(i)} \Delta\hat{\mathbf{v}}_j \right\|_1,$$

where $\mathcal{N}(i)$ denotes a set indices for vertices adjacent to the i-th vertex in the mesh.

We also use photometric optimization that matches the predicted and the ground truth images. This allows us to obtain photorealistic renders and aid in learning proper geometric reconstructions. We utilize perceptual loss $\mathcal{L}_{\text{per}}$ [18], the face recognition loss $\mathcal{L}_{\text{idt}}$ [5] and adversarial loss $\mathcal{L}_{\text{adv}}$ [11,48]. We also use the Dice loss $\mathcal{L}_{\text{seg}}$ [30] to match the predicted segmentation masks.

The final objective is weighted sum of the geometric and the photometric losses described above.

3.6   Linear Deformation Model

In addition to the full non-linear model introduced above, we consider a simplified parametric model with a linear basis of offsets $\Delta\hat{\mathbf{v}}$. While this model is similar to parametric models [23,56], we still do not use 3D scans for training and instead obtain our linear model by "distilling" the non-linear model. Additionally, we train a feed-forward estimator that predicts the linear coefficients from the input image.

The motivation for training this additional model is to show that the deformations learned by our method can be approximated using a system with a significantly lower capacity. Such a simple regression model can be easier to apply for inference on low-performance devices.

To train the linear model, we first obtain the basis of offsets $\mathcal{F} \in \mathbb{R}^{3N \times K}$, which is similar to the blendshapes used in the FLAME parametric model. This basis is obtained by applying a low-rank PCA [14] to the matrix of offsets $\Delta\hat{\mathbf{v}} \in \mathbb{R}^{3N \times M}$, calculated using M images from the dataset. Following [23], we discard most of the basis vectors and only keep K components corresponding to maximal singular values. The approximated vertex offsets $\tilde{\mathbf{v}}$ for each image can then be estimated as following $\tilde{\mathbf{v}} = \mathcal{F}\eta$, where η is obtained by applying the pseudo-inverse of a basis matrix $\mathcal{F}$ to the corresponding offsets $\Delta\hat{\mathbf{v}}$: $\eta = \left(\mathcal{F}^T \mathcal{F}\right)^{-1} \mathcal{F}^T \Delta\hat{\mathbf{v}}$

We then train the regression network by estimating a vector of basis coefficients η_t, given an image $\mathbf{x}_t$. For that, we minimize the mean squared error (MSE) loss $\|\hat{\eta}_t - \eta_t\|_2^2$ between the estimated coefficients and the ground truth, as well as the segmentation loss $\mathcal{L}_{\mathrm{occ}}$ and a Chamfer distance between predicted and ground truth meshes.

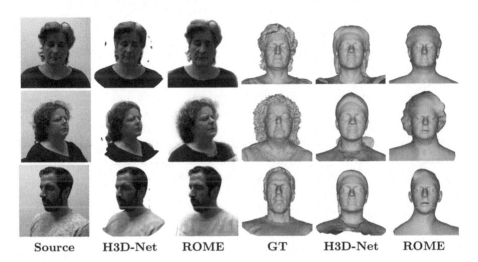

| Source | H3D-Net | ROME | GT | H3D-Net | ROME |

Fig. 3. Qualitative comparison of the representative cases from the H3DS dataset. While neither of the two methods achieves perfect results, arguably, ROME achieves more realistic renders and better matches the head geometry than H3D-Net in the single-shot mode. Furthermore, an important advantage of ROME is that the resulting avatars are ready for animation and are obtained in a feed-forward manner without the lengthy fine-tuning process employed by H3D-Net.

4   Experiments

We train our models on the VoxCeleb2 [6] dataset of videos. This large-scale dataset contains an order of 10^5 videos of 10^3 different speakers. It is widely used [7,49,52] to train talking head models. However, the main drawback of this dataset is the mixed quality of videos and the heavy bias towards frontal poses.

To address these well-known limitations, we process this dataset using an off-the-shelf image quality analysis model [44] and a 3D face-alignment network [4]. We then filter out the data which has poor quality and non-diverse head rotations. Our final training dataset has ≈ 15000 sequences. We note that filtering/pruning does not fully solve the problem of head rotation bias, and our method still works best in frontal views. For more details, please refer to the supplementary materials.

We also use the H3DS [35] dataset of photos with associated 3D scans to evaluate the quality of head reconstructions.

Table 1. Evaluation results on the H3DS dataset in the one-shot scenario for our models, H3D-Net, and DECA. We compute Chamfer distance (lower is better) across all available scans, reconstructed from three different viewpoints. Both of the ROME variants significantly exceed H3D-Net in the one-shot reconstruction quality.

Method	DECA	H3D-Net	ROME	LinearROME
Chamfer Distance	15.0	15.1	12.6	12.5

4.1   Implementation Details

In the experiments, unless noted otherwise, we train all architectures jointly and end-to-end. We use the following weights: $\lambda_{hair} = 10$, $\lambda_{per} = 1$, $\lambda_{idt} = 0.1$, $\lambda_{adv} = 0.1$, $\lambda_{seg} = 10$, and enable the neck and the 2D Chamfer loss $\lambda_{chm} = 0.01$) and $\lambda_{lap} = 10$. We ablate all geometry losses and method parts below.

We train our models at 256×256 resolution using ADAM [21] with the fixed learning rate of 10^{-4}, $\beta_1 = 0$, $\beta_2 = 0.999$, and a batch size of 32. For more details, please refer to the supplementary materials.

4.2   Evaluation

3D Reconstruction. We evaluate our head reconstruction quality using a novel H3DS dataset [35]. We compare against the state-of-the-art head reconstruction method H3D-Net [35], which uses signed distance functions to represent the geometry. While providing great reconstruction quality in the sparse-view scenario, their approach has several limitations. For example, H3D-Net requires a dataset of full head scans to learn the prior on head shapes. Additionally, its results do not have fixed topology or rigging and their method requires fine-tuning per scene, while our method works in a feed-forward way.

We carry out the comparison with H3D-Net in a single-view scenario, which is native for our method but is beyond the capabilities stated by the authors in the original publication [35]. However, to the best of our knowledge, H3D-Net is the closest system to ours in single-view reconstruction capabilities (out of all systems with either their code or results available). Additionally, we tried to compare our system with PIFuHD [38], which unfortunately failed to work with heads images without body (see supplementary).

We show qualitative comparison in Fig. 3. We evaluate our method and H3D-Net both for frontal- and side-view reconstruction. We note the significant over-fitting of H3D-Net to the visible hair geometry, while our model provides reconstructions more robust to the change of viewpoint.

In total, we compared our models on all scans available in the test set of the H3DS dataset, and each scan was reconstructed from three different viewpoints. We provide the measured mean Chamfer distance both for our method and baselines across all scans in Table 1.

| Source | Driver | FOMM | Bi-Layer | FLAMETex | ROME |

Fig. 4. Comparison of renders on a VoxCeleb2 dataset. The task is to reenact the **source** image with the expression and pose of the **driver** image. Here, we picked diverse examples in terms of pose variation to highlight the differences in performance of compared methods. We observe that for the large head pose rotations, purely neural-based methods (**FOMM**, **Bi-Layer**) struggle to maintain consistent quality. In contrast, our rendering method produces images that are more robust to pose changes. Admittedly, for small pose changes, neural-based methods exhibit a smaller identity gap than ROME (bottom row) and overall outperform our method in terms of rendering quality. As a reference, we also include a non-neural **FLAMETex** rendering method, which is employed in state-of-the-art one-shot face reconstruction systems [9] but is not able to personalize the avatar at the head level.

Rendering. We evaluate the quality of our renders on the hold-out subset Vox-Celeb2 dataset. We use a cross-driving comparison scenario for qualitative comparison to highlight the animation capabilities of our method, and self-driving scenario for quantitative comparison.

First, we compare with a FLAMETex [23] rendering system, which works explicitly with mesh rendering. From the source image, FLAMETex estimates the albedo via a basis of RGB textures, and then combines it with predicted scene-specific shading. On the contrary, our method predicts a rendered image directly and avoids the complexity of explicit albedo-shading decomposition.

We then compare with publicly available geometry-free rendering methods, which were trained on the same dataset. For that, we use the First-Order Motion Model (FOMM) [42], the Bi-Layer Avatar Model [52] and recently proposed Thin-Plate-Spline-Motion-Mode (TPSMM) [54]. Both these systems bypass explicit 3D geometry estimation and rely only on learning the scene structure via the parameters of generative ConvNets. Other methods [7,49], which internally utilize some 3D structures, like camera rotations, were out of the scope of our comparison due to the unavailability of pre-trained models.

Table 2. Here we present the quantitative results on the VoxCeleb2-HQ dataset in the self-reenactment and cross-reenactment modes. Our ROME system performs on par with FOMM and TPSMM in self-reenactment, notably outperforming them in the most perceptually-plausible LPIPS metrics. On the contrary, in the cross-driving scenario, when the task is complex for pure neural-based systems, our method obtains better results.

Method	Self-reenactment			Cross-reenactment		
	LPIPS ↓	SSIM ↑	PSNR ↑	FID ↓	CSIM ↑	IQA ↑
FOMM	0.09	0.87	25.8	52.95	0.53	55.9
Bi-Layer	0.08	0.83	23.7	51.4	0.56	50.48
TPSMM	0.09	0.85	26.1	49.27	0.57	59.5
ROME	0.08	0.86	26.2	45.32	0.62	66.3

We present the qualitative comparison in Fig. 4, and a quantitative comparison across a randomly sampled hold-out VoxCeleb2 subset in Table 2. We restrict the comparison to the face and hair region as the shoulder pose is not controlled by our method (driven by DECA parameters), which is admittedly a limitation of our system. We thus mask the results according to the face and hair mask estimated from the ground truth image.

Generally, we observe that over the entire test set, the quality of ROME avatars in the self-reenactment mode is similar to FOMM and better than the Bi-layer model. For the cross-reenactment scenario, our model is clearly better than both alternatives according to three metrics, that help to asses unsupervised quality of the images in three aspects: realism, identity preservation and blind quality of the image. The huge gap for IQA [44] and FID [17] is also noticeable in the qualitative comparison, especially for strong pose change (see CSIM [53] column in Table 2). The PSNR and SSIM metrics penalize slight misalignments between the sharp ground truth and our renderings much stronger than the blurriness in FOMM reconstructions. The advantage of ROME avatar is noticable even for self-driving case according to LPIPS. We provide a more extensive qualitative evaluation in the supplementary materials.

4.3   Linear Basis Experiments

As discussed above, we distill our ROME head reconstruction model into a linear parametric model. To do that, we set the number of basis vectors to 50 for the hair and 10 for the neck offsets and run low-rank Principle Component Analysis (PCA) to estimate them. The number of components is chosen to obtain a low enough approximation error. Interestingly, the offsets learned by our model can be compressed by almost two orders of magnitude in terms of degrees of freedom without any practical loss in quality (Figure 6a), which suggests that the capacity of the offset generator is underused in our model. We combine estimated basis vectors with the original basis of the FLAME.

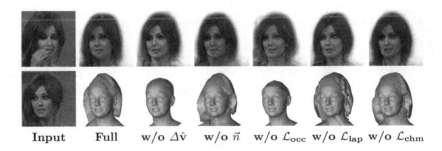

Input   Full   w/o $\Delta\hat{v}$ w/o $\vec{n}$ w/o $\mathcal{L}_{occ}$ w/o $\mathcal{L}_{lap}$ w/o $\mathcal{L}_{chm}$

Fig. 5. Ablation study. We qualitatively evaluate the individual components of our *full* model. w/o $\Delta\hat{v}$: without the per-vertex displacements, we obtain a significantly worse render quality. w/o $\vec{n}$: when we apply per-vertex deformations instead of per-vertex displacements (i.e., deformations alongside the normals), we obtain noisy reconstructions in neck area and worse renders. w/o $\mathcal{L}_{occ}$: without silhouette-based losses, our model fails to learn proper reconstructions. w/o $\mathcal{L}_{lap}$: Laplacian regularization smooths the reconstructions. w/o $\mathcal{L}_{chm}$: chamfer loss allows us to constrain the displaced vertices to lie inside the scene boundaries, which positively affects the smoothness of the visible part of the reconstruction.

After that, we train feed-forward encoders that directly predict the coefficients of the two basis from the source image. The prediction is performed in two stages. First, face expression, pose and camera parameters are predicted with a MobileNetV2 [40] encoder. Then a slower ResNet-50 encoder [16] is used to predict hair, neck and shape coefficients. The choice of architectures are motivated by the fact that in many practical scenarios only the first encoder needs to be invoked frequently (per-frame), while the second can run at much lower rate or even only at the model creation time.

4.4   Ablation Study

We demonstrate results of ablation study at Fig. 5. As expected, predicting more accurate geometry affect the renders (first row). Also, we verify the necessity of all terms of geometry loss. We observe significant improvement in quality of renders with additional geometry (see supplementary), which leads us to an optimistic conclusion that our learned coarse mesh may be integrated into other neural rendering systems [49] to improve their quality. Additionally, we observe that geometry losses allows to correctly model coarse details on the hair without noise and reconstruct the hair without sticking with neck. Similar artifacts are removed by adding shifts along the normals.

Our current model is trained at roughly fixed scale, though explicit geometry modeling allows it to generalize to adjacent scale reasonably well. Still, strong changes of scale lead to poor performance (Fig. 6b). More examples are provided in the supplementary materials. Addressing this issue via mip-mapping and multi-scale GAN training techniques remains future work.

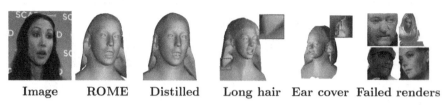

| Image | ROME | Distilled | Long hair | Ear cover | Failed renders |

(a) Linear model   (b) Limitations

Fig. 6. Linear model results and the examples of limitations. On the left, we show how reconstructions learned by our method, **ROME**, could be **distilled** using a linear parametric model. We are able to compress the learned offsets into a small basis, reducing the degrees of freedom by two orders of magnitude. We can then **distill** these offsets using a much faster regression network with a small gap in terms of the reconstruction quality. On the right, we highlight the main limitations of our method, which include the failure related to **long hair** modelling, caused by an incorrect topological prior, no **coverage of ears** and **unrealistic renders** under a significant change of scales.

Lastly, our model can have artifacts with long hair (Fig. 6b, left) or ears (Fig. 6b, middle). Handling such cases gracefully are likely to require a departure from the predefined FLAME mesh connectivity to new person-specific mesh topology. Handling such issues using a limited set of pre-designed hair meshes is an interesting direction for future research.

5   Summary

We have presented ROME avatars: a system for creating realistic one-shot mesh-based human head models that can be animated and compatible with FLAME head models. We compare our model with representative state-of-the-art models from different classes, and show that it is highly competitive both in terms of geometry estimation and the quality of rendering.

Crucially, our system can learn to model head geometry without direct supervision in the form of 3D scans. Despite that, we have observed it to achieve state-of-the-art results in head geometry recovery from a single photograph. At the same time, it also performs better than previous one-shot neural rendering approaches in the cross- and self-driving scenario. We have thus verified that the resulting geometry could be used to improve the rendering quality.

As neural rendering becomes more widespread within graphics systems, ROME avatars and similar systems can become directly applicable, while their one-shot capability and the simplicity of rigging derived from DECA and FLAME could become especially important in practical applications.

Acknowledgements. We sincerely thank Eduard Ramon for providing us the one-shot H3D-Net reconstructions. We also thank Arsenii Ashukha for comments and suggestions regarding the text contents and clarity, as well as Julia Churkina for helping us with proof-reading. The computational resources for this work were mainly provided by Samsung ML Platform.

References

1. AvatarSDK. https://avatarsdk.com/
2. Blanz, V., Romdhani, S., Vetter, T.: Face identification across different poses and illuminations with a 3d morphable model. In: Proceedings of Fifth IEEE International Conference on Automatic Face Gesture Recognition, pp. 202–207 (2002)
3. Blanz, V., Vetter, T.: A morphable model for the synthesis of 3d faces. In: SIGGRAPH 1999 (1999)
4. Bulat, A., Tzimiropoulos, G.: How far are we from solving the 2D & 3D face alignment problem? (and a dataset of 230,000 3D facial landmarks). In: International Conference on Computer Vision (2017)
5. Cao, Q., Shen, L., Xie, W., Parkhi, O.M., Zisserman, A.: VGGFace2: a dataset for recognising faces across pose and age. In: 2018 13th IEEE International Conference on Automatic Face and Gesture Recognition (FG 2018), pp. 67–74 (2018)
6. Chung, J.S., Nagrani, A., Zisserman, A.: VoxCeleb2: deep speaker recognition. In: INTERSPEECH (2018)
7. Doukas, M.C., Zafeiriou, S., Sharmanska, V.: HeadGAN: video-and-audio-driven talking head synthesis (2021)
8. Egger, B., et al.: 3d morphable face models-past, present, and future. ACM Trans. Graph. (TOG) **39**, 1–38 (2020)
9. Feng, Y., Feng, H., Black, M.J., Bolkart, T.: Learning an animatable detailed 3D face model from in-the-wild images. ACM Trans. Graph. (TOG) **40**, 1–13 (2020)
10. Gafni, G., Thies, J., Zollhöfer, M., Nießner, M.: Dynamic neural radiance fields for monocular 4D facial avatar reconstruction. In: Proceedings of the IEEE/CVF Conference on Computer Vision and Pattern Recognition (CVPR) (2021)
11. Goodfellow, I.J., et al.: Generative adversarial nets. In: NIPS (2014)
12. Grassal, P.W., Prinzler, M., Leistner, T., Rother, C., Nießner, M., Thies, J.: Neural head avatars from monocular RGB videos. In: Proceedings of the IEEE/CVF Conference on Computer Vision and Pattern Recognition (CVPR) (2022)
13. Guo, J., Zhu, X., Yang, Y., Yang, F., Lei, Z., Li, S.Z.: Towards fast, accurate and stable 3D dense face alignment. In: Vedaldi, A., Bischof, H., Brox, T., Frahm, J.-M. (eds.) ECCV 2020. LNCS, vol. 12364, pp. 152–168. Springer, Cham (2020). https://doi.org/10.1007/978-3-030-58529-7_10
14. Halko, N., Martinsson, P.G., Tropp, J.A.: Finding structure with randomness: probabilistic algorithms for constructing approximate matrix decompositions. SIAM Rev. **53**, 217–288 (2011)
15. Hassner, T., Harel, S., Paz, E., Enbar, R.: Effective face frontalization in unconstrained images. In: 2015 IEEE Conference on Computer Vision and Pattern Recognition (CVPR), pp. 4295–4304 (2015)
16. He, K., Zhang, X., Ren, S., Sun, J.: Deep residual learning for image recognition. In: 2016 IEEE Conference on Computer Vision and Pattern Recognition (CVPR), pp. 770–778 (2016)
17. Heusel, M., Ramsauer, H., Unterthiner, T., Nessler, B., Hochreiter, S.: GANs trained by a two time-scale update rule converge to a local Nash equilibrium. In: Advances in Neural Information Processing Systems (2017)
18. Johnson, J., Alahi, A., Fei-Fei, L.: Perceptual losses for real-time style transfer and super-resolution. In: Leibe, B., Matas, J., Sebe, N., Welling, M. (eds.) ECCV 2016. LNCS, vol. 9906, pp. 694–711. Springer, Cham (2016). https://doi.org/10.1007/978-3-319-46475-6_43

19. Kellnhofer, P., Jebe, L., Jones, A., Spicer, R.P., Pulli, K., Wetzstein, G.: Neural lumigraph rendering. In: 2021 IEEE/CVF Conference on Computer Vision and Pattern Recognition (CVPR) (2021)

20. Kim, H., et al.: Deep video portraits. ACM Trans. Graph. (TOG) 37(4), 163 (2018)

21. Kingma, D.P., Ba, J.: Adam: a method for stochastic optimization. In: International Conference for Learning Representations (2015)

22. Laine, S., Hellsten, J., Karras, T., Seol, Y., Lehtinen, J., Aila, T.: Modular primitives for high-performance differentiable rendering. ACM Trans. Graph. 39(6) (2020)

23. Li, T., Bolkart, T., Black, M.J., Li, H., Romero, J.: Learning a model of facial shape and expression from 4D scans. ACM Trans. Graph. (TOG) 36, 1–17 (2017)

24. Liu, S., Li, T., Chen, W., Li, H.: Soft rasterizer: a differentiable renderer for image-based 3D reasoning. In: 2019 IEEE/CVF International Conference on Computer Vision (ICCV), pp. 7707–7716 (2019)

25. Lombardi, S., Saragih, J.M., Simon, T., Sheikh, Y.: Deep appearance models for face rendering. ACM Trans. Graph. (TOG) 37, 1–13 (2018)

26. Lombardi, S., Simon, T., Saragih, J.M., Schwartz, G., Lehrmann, A.M., Sheikh, Y.: Neural volumes. ACM Trans. Graph. (TOG) 38, 1–14 (2019)

27. Lombardi, S., Simon, T., Schwartz, G., Zollhoefer, M., Sheikh, Y., Saragih, J.M.: Mixture of volumetric primitives for efficient neural rendering. ACM Trans. Graph. (TOG) 40, 1–13 (2021)

28. Ma, Q., Saito, S., Yang, J., Tang, S., Black, M.J.: Scale: modeling clothed humans with a surface codec of articulated local elements. In: CVPR (2021)

29. Mildenhall, B., Srinivasan, P.P., Tancik, M., Barron, J.T., Ramamoorthi, R., Ng, R.: NeRF: representing scenes as neural radiance fields for view synthesis. In: Vedaldi, A., Bischof, H., Brox, T., Frahm, J.-M. (eds.) ECCV 2020. LNCS, vol. 12346, pp. 405–421. Springer, Cham (2020). https://doi.org/10.1007/978-3-030-58452-8_24

30. Milletari, F., Navab, N., Ahmadi, S.A.: V-net: fully convolutional neural networks for volumetric medical image segmentation. In: 2016 Fourth International Conference on 3D Vision (3DV), pp. 565–571 (2016)

31. Oechsle, M., Peng, S., Geiger, A.: UniSurf: unifying neural implicit surfaces and radiance fields for multi-view reconstruction. In: International Conference on Computer Vision (ICCV) (2021)

32. Park, J.J., Florence, P.R., Straub, J., Newcombe, R.A., Lovegrove, S.: DeepSDF: learning continuous signed distance functions for shape representation. In: 2019 IEEE/CVF Conference on Computer Vision and Pattern Recognition (CVPR), pp. 165–174 (2019)

33. Pinscreen. https://www.pinscreen.com/

34. Ploumpis, S., et al.: Towards a complete 3D morphable model of the human head. IEEE Trans. Pattern Anal. Mach. Intell. (2021)

35. Ramon, E., et al.: H3D-Net: few-shot high-fidelity 3D head reconstruction. Proceedings of the IEEE/CVF International Conference on Computer Vision (2021)

36. Ravi, N., et al.: Accelerating 3D deep learning with PyTorch3D. arXiv:2007.08501 (2020)

37. Ronneberger, O., Fischer, P., Brox, T.: U-net: convolutional networks for biomedical image segmentation. In: Navab, N., Hornegger, J., Wells, W.M., Frangi, A.F. (eds.) MICCAI 2015. LNCS, vol. 9351, pp. 234–241. Springer, Cham (2015). https://doi.org/10.1007/978-3-319-24574-4_28

38. Saito, S., Simon, T., Saragih, J., Joo, H.: PifuHD: multi-level pixel-aligned implicit function for high-resolution 3D human digitization. In: Proceedings of the IEEE Conference on Computer Vision and Pattern Recognition, June 2020
39. Saito, S., Simon, T., Saragih, J.M., Joo, H.: PifuHD: multi-level pixel-aligned implicit function for high-resolution 3D human digitization. In: 2020 IEEE/CVF Conference on Computer Vision and Pattern Recognition (CVPR), pp. 81–90 (2020)
40. Sandler, M., Howard, A.G., Zhu, M., Zhmoginov, A., Chen, L.C.: MobileNetv 2: inverted residuals and linear bottlenecks. In: 2018 IEEE/CVF Conference on Computer Vision and Pattern Recognition (2018)
41. Sanyal, S., Bolkart, T., Feng, H., Black, M.J.: Learning to regress 3D face shape and expression from an image without 3D supervision. In: 2019 IEEE/CVF Conference on Computer Vision and Pattern Recognition (CVPR), pp. 7755–7764 (2019)
42. Siarohin, A., Lathuilière, S., Tulyakov, S., Ricci, E., Sebe, N.: First order motion model for image animation. In: Advances in Neural Information Processing Systems (NeurIPS) (2019)
43. Sorkine-Hornung, O.: Laplacian mesh processing. In: Eurographics (2005)
44. Su, S., et al.: Blindly assess image quality in the wild guided by a self-adaptive hyper network. In: 2020 IEEE/CVF Conference on Computer Vision and Pattern Recognition (CVPR) (2020)
45. Thies, J., Zollhöfer, M., Stamminger, M., Theobalt, C., Nießner, M.: Face2Face: real-time face capture and reenactment of RGB videos. In: Proceedings of Computer Vision and Pattern Recognition (CVPR). IEEE (2016)
46. Thies, J., Zollhöfer, M., Nießner, M.: Deferred neural rendering: image synthesis using neural textures. arXiv: Computer Vision and Pattern Recognition (2019)
47. Tran, A., Hassner, T., Masi, I., Medioni, G.G.: Regressing robust and discriminative 3D morphable models with a very deep neural network. In: 2017 IEEE Conference on Computer Vision and Pattern Recognition (CVPR), pp. 1493–1502 (2017)
48. Wang, T.C., Liu, M.Y., Zhu, J.Y., Tao, A., Kautz, J., Catanzaro, B.: High-resolution image synthesis and semantic manipulation with conditional GANs. In: 2018 IEEE/CVF Conference on Computer Vision and Pattern Recognition, pp. 8798–8807 (2018)
49. Wang, T.C., Mallya, A., Liu, M.Y.: One-shot free-view neural talking-head synthesis for video conferencing. In: 2021 IEEE/CVF Conference on Computer Vision and Pattern Recognition (CVPR), pp. 10034–10044 (2021)
50. Yenamandra, T., et al.: I3DMM: deep implicit 3D morphable model of human heads. In: 2021 IEEE/CVF Conference on Computer Vision and Pattern Recognition (CVPR), pp. 12798–12808 (2021)
51. Zakharkin, I., Mazur, K., Grigoriev, A., Lempitsky, V.S.: Point-based modeling of human clothing. In: 2021 IEEE/CVF International Conference on Computer Vision (ICCV) (2021)
52. Zakharov, E., Ivakhnenko, A., Shysheya, A., Lempitsky, V.: Fast bi-layer neural synthesis of one-shot realistic head avatars. In: Vedaldi, A., Bischof, H., Brox, T., Frahm, J.-M. (eds.) ECCV 2020. LNCS, vol. 12357, pp. 524–540. Springer, Cham (2020). https://doi.org/10.1007/978-3-030-58610-2_31
53. Zakharov, E., Shysheya, A., Burkov, E., Lempitsky, V.S.: Few-shot adversarial learning of realistic neural talking head models. In: 2019 IEEE/CVF International Conference on Computer Vision (ICCV) (2019)

54. Zhao, J., Zhang, H.: Thin-plate spline motion model for image animation. In: 2022 IEEE/CVF Conference on Computer Vision and Pattern Recognition (CVPR) (2022)
55. Zheng, Y., Abrevaya, V.F., Bühler, M.C., Chen, X., Black, M.J., Hilliges, O.: I m avatar: implicit morphable head avatars from videos. In: 2022 IEEE Conference on Computer Vision and Pattern Recognition (CVPR) (2022)
56. Zuffi, S., Kanazawa, A., Berger-Wolf, T., Black, M.J.: Three-D safari: learning to estimate zebra pose, shape, and texture from images "in the wild" (2019)

A Kendall Shape Space Approach to 3D Shape Estimation from 2D Landmarks

Martha Paskin[1]([✉]) [iD], Daniel Baum[1] [iD], Mason N. Dean[2] [iD],
and Christoph von Tycowicz[1,3] [iD]

[1] Zuse Institute Berlin, Berlin, Germany
{paskin,baum,vontycowicz}@zib.de
[2] City University of Hong Kong, Hong Kong, China
mndean@cityu.edu.hk
[3] Freie Universität Berlin, Berlin, Germany

Abstract. 3D shapes provide substantially more information than 2D images. However, the acquisition of 3D shapes is sometimes very difficult or even impossible in comparison with acquiring 2D images, making it necessary to derive the 3D shape from 2D images. Although this is, in general, a mathematically ill-posed problem, it might be solved by constraining the problem formulation using prior information. Here, we present a new approach based on Kendall's shape space to reconstruct 3D shapes from single monocular 2D images. The work is motivated by an application to study the feeding behavior of the basking shark, an endangered species whose massive size and mobility render 3D shape data nearly impossible to obtain, hampering understanding of their feeding behaviors and ecology. 2D images of these animals in feeding position, however, are readily available. We compare our approach with state-of-the-art shape-based approaches, both on human stick models and on shark head skeletons. Using a small set of training shapes, we show that the Kendall shape space approach is substantially more robust than previous methods and results in plausible shapes. This is essential for the motivating application in which specimens are rare and therefore only few training shapes are available.

Keywords: 3D shape estimation · 2D-to-3D · Shape space approach · Kendall's shape space · Sparse data

1   Introduction

The reconstruction of a 3D shape from 2D images is an important problem of computer vision that has been the subject of research for decades [6,34]. It is a widespread challenge with sample applications including motion recognition and tracking, autonomous driving, as well as robot-assisted surgery and navigation. Generally, estimating the 3D shape of an object from single monocular 2D images is an ill-posed problem in the sense of Hadamard. To tackle this problem, several approaches have been proposed, the choice of which greatly depends on the type and amount of data, and the application.

© The Author(s), under exclusive license to Springer Nature Switzerland AG 2022
S. Avidan et al. (Eds.): ECCV 2022, LNCS 13662, pp. 363–379, 2022.
https://doi.org/10.1007/978-3-031-20086-1_21

One common approach is to use a series of 2D images [7,15] or multiple cameras [16,19,24]. This is used, for example, in photogrammetry. In order to calculate the depth, corresponding points in 2D images need to be identified [1, 7,29].

Another approach is based on physical modeling of the object to be estimated [2,32]. Here, the object is described as a kinematic tree consisting of segments connected by joints. Each joint contains some degrees of freedom (DOF), indicating the directions it is allowed to move. The object is modeled by the DOF of all joints. Length constraints can also be added, such as limb lengths constraints in a human pose. This helps reduce the depth ambiguity by constraining the relative position of the joints.

In lieu of additional viewpoints or physical models, another line of work regularizes the estimation problem by employing prior knowledge learned from examples of the respective object class. Some works in this category are based on the concept of shape spaces. Here, the 3D shape of an object is estimated by interpolating through a set of pre-defined 3D shapes, called training shapes, that represent possible deformations of the object. Given a 2D projection of the object, the aim is to find the ideal camera parameters and the shape coefficients describing the interpolation. Most commonly, *active shape model* (ASM) techniques are used [14,23,30,35,37,38]. ASM has been used intensively for the purpose of recognizing and locating non-rigid objects in the presence of noise and occlusion [4,13]. It aims at providing a robust approach, which accommodates shape variability by arguing that when the objects deform in ways characteristic to the class of objects they represent, the method should be able to recognize them. Here, the *shape* of a class of objects is described by a set of labeled *landmark* points, each representing a particular part of the object or its boundary. Given a set of pre-defined *basis shapes* of an object, the assumption is that any shape of the object can be described by linearly interpolating between basis shapes. The legitimacy of the model is determined by the set of training shapes, which needs to include the variability in the shape of the object.

Apart from these more classical approaches, recent years have mostly been devoted to the development of deep learning-based methods that exploit domain-specific data repositories with abundant samples (e.g., *ShapeNet, Human3.6M*). In 2017, a kinematic skeleton fitting method using a *convolutional neural network* (CNN) was proposed that regresses 2D and 3D joint positions jointly in real-time [21]. More recently, *Procrustean regression networks* (PRN) were proposed [26]. Using a novel loss function, they solve the problem of automatically determining the rotation. Another recent deep learning-based method, *KShapeNet* [11], makes use of Kendall's shape space by modeling shape sequences first as trajectories on Kendall's non-linear shape space, which are then mapped to the linear tangent space. The authors report [11] that the non-linear motion can be captured better using their approach than using previous geometric deep-learning methods.

In general, the training of deep neural network models requires a considerable amount of data. While the generalization of learned models to new classes with few available examples has become a highly popular research topic (see e.g. [22]),

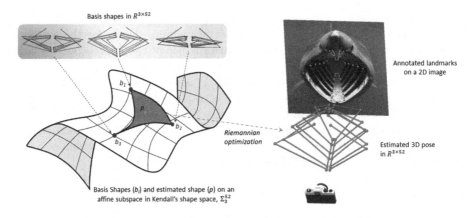

Fig. 1. Methodology diagram for the proposed method.

such base models are rarely available in many applications. There is therefore a strong impetus to develop so-called shallow learning approaches that can be applied even if few-shot learning is not an option.

Our work contributes to this area by deriving a novel shape space-based approach. We demonstrate the effectiveness of the proposed scheme in an application to the study of marine animal behavior. In this application, we are faced with the retrieval of the 3D shape of a non-rigid (biological) object - the head skeleton of a basking shark - from single monocular 2D images. Basking sharks (*Cetorhinus maximus*) are massive animals and thought to be one of the most efficient filter-feeding fish in terms of the throughput of water filtered through their gill rakers [31]. Details about the underlying morphology of the basking shark filter apparatus and particularly how it is configured when the animal feeds have not been studied due to various challenges in acquiring real-world data. In this study, we address this issue, using several computed-tomography (CT) scans to create skeletal representations of basking shark head structure. From these, and known aspects of the biology (e.g. shark cranial anatomy, feeding behaviors), we semi-automatically created plausible configurations of the skeleton which we use as training shapes to describe the shape space. The ultimate goal is, given a photograph of a basking shark in feeding position, to estimate a plausible 3D shape of the skeletal representation from the training data and annotations of the skeletal joints in the form of 2D landmarks.

Since the number of training shapes is very limited in our application, deep learning-based methods cannot be applied. When using only a single 2D image, photogrammetry-based methods also cannot be applied. And for a physical modeling-based approach, information about the movement of the skeletal elements that is supported by the joints would be necessary. This information is not available. We therefore resort to shape space-based methods. In particular, we develop a new *Kendall shape space* (KSS) approach for the reconstruction of 3D shape from 2D landmarks. Our overall workflow is sketched in Fig. 1. In order to evaluate our approach, we compare it qualitatively and quantitatively with state-of-the-art ASM approaches [37] on both human poses and basking shark skeletons. Due to the limited number of training shapes for the basking sharks, we are mainly interested in the performance of the approaches w.r.t. a small number of training shapes.

The results of our experiments suggest that our method is substantially more robust than previous shape space-based methods. This is particularly true for real world data both of human beings and shark data. It is also computationally very efficient and provides plausible interpolations without auxiliary regularization since the estimated shape will always lie on a subspace in Kendall's shape space spanned by the training data.

The source code of the proposed method together with the derived basking shark shapes have been made publicly available [27].

2   Methods

In this work, we approach the problem of estimating the shape of 3D objects from single images. To this end, we employ a landmark-based representation, viz. a set of ordered 3D points $(x_i)_{i=1,\ldots,k}$ that correspond to homologous points (e.g. joint centers in a skeleton) common to all subjects belonging to the object class under study. By assuming the weak perspective camera model, the projection or forward map is given by the linear system

$$W = \Pi RX + t\mathbf{1}_k^T, \tag{1}$$

where $X \in \mathbb{R}^{3 \times k}$ and $W \in \mathbb{R}^{2 \times k}$ denote the matrices of stacked landmarks and their 2D projections, respectively. The rotation $R \in SO(3)$ and translation $t \in \mathbb{R}^2$ encode the camera coordinate system while the projection is carried out by the matrix

$$\Pi = \begin{pmatrix} \alpha\ 0\ 0 \\ 0\ \alpha\ 0 \end{pmatrix},$$

where the scalar α depends only on the focal length and distance to the object. The inverse problem of finding the 3D configuration corresponding to given projections is commonly formulated in terms of a least-squares problem. However, the underdeterminedness renders such a problem ill-posed requiring inclusion of prior knowledge in order to obtain feasible solutions. An established strategy based on the active shape model [9] is to restrict the search space to linear combinations of basis shapes $B_1, \ldots, B_n \in \mathbb{R}^{3 \times k}$, i.e.

$$X = \sum_{j=1}^{n} c_j B_j, \tag{2}$$

with weights c_j satisfying the constraint $\sum_j c_j = 1$. The quality of this approach, however, depends on the validity of the assumption that instances of the object class are well approximated by a hyper-planar manifold. In general, the shape of an object is considered to be invariant under rotation, translation and scaling and, hence, takes values in a nonlinear space with quotient structure. In particular, for landmark-based representations, this concept gives rise to the well-known Kendall shape space [17]. The non-Euclidean nature of shape space not only violates the linearity assumption but furthermore prevents direct application of algebraic expressions such as Eq. (2) due to the lack of a global vector space structure. Nevertheless, the framework of (computational) differential geometry provides us with a rich toolset to generalize the ASM approach for use within the reconstruction problem.

2.1   Geometric Model

Before we formulate a manifold version of the least-squares estimation, we first recall essential notions and properties from Kendall's shape space. We refer the reader to the comprehensive work [18] for an in-depth introduction.

Let $X \in \mathbb{R}^{m \times k}$ be the matrix holding k landmarks $x_i \in \mathbb{R}^m$ as columns. We remove the effect of translations and scaling by subtracting the row-wise mean from each landmark and then dividing X by its *Frobenius norm* (denoted $\| \cdot \|$). The set of all such configurations constitutes the *pre-shape space*

$$\mathcal{S}_m^k = \{X \in \mathbb{R}^{m \times k} : \sum_{i=1}^k x_i = 0\,,\, \|x\| = 1\}.$$

Now, the left action of $SO(m)$ on $\mathcal{S}_m^k$ given by $(R, X) \mapsto RX$ defines an equivalence relation given by $X \sim Y$ if and only if $Y = RX$ for some $R \in SO(m)$. Kendall's shape space is defined as the quotient $\Sigma_m^k = \mathcal{S}_m^k / \sim$. Now, denoting the canonical projection of $\sim$ by π and the spherical distance by $d_{\mathcal{S}}(X, Y) = \arccos \langle X, Y \rangle$, the induced distance between any two shapes $\pi(X)$ and $\pi(Y)$ is given by

$$d_{\Sigma}(X, Y) := \min_{R \in SO(m)} d_{\mathcal{S}}(X, RY) = \arccos \sum_{i=1}^n \lambda_i, \qquad (3)$$

where $\lambda_1 \geq \lambda_2 \geq \cdots \geq \lambda_{m-1} \geq |\lambda_m|$ are the pseudo-singular values of YX^T [25]. The points X and Y are said to be *well-positioned* (denoted by $X \overset{w}{\sim} Y$), if and only if, YX^T is symmetric and $d_{\mathcal{S}}(X, Y) = d_{\Sigma}(X, Y)$. Note that for $m \geq 3$, the shape space Σ_m^k contains singularities making it a strata of manifolds with varying dimensions.

In order to generalize the ASM approach, we first note that Eq. (2) effectively parametrizes the affine subspace spanned by the basis shapes. A common approach to obtain equivalent notions in Riemannian manifolds is to define *geodesic subspaces* that are spanned by generalized straight lines (geodesics) emanating from a reference point and with directions restricted to a linear subspace of the tangent space [10]. However, as geodesic subspaces rely on tangent vectors, they can only be defined within regular strata of the shape space. Therefore, we opt for an alternative construction by Pennec [28] called *barycentric subspaces*, which are defined as the locus of points that are weighted means of the basis shapes. Specifically, let $b_1 = \pi(B_1), \ldots, b_n = \pi(B_n) \in \Sigma_m^k$ be a set of n distinct basis shapes, then the *Fréchet barycentric subspace* is given by

$$FBS_{(b_j)_j} = \left\{ \operatorname*{arg\,min}_{p \in \Sigma_m^k} \sum_{j=1}^n c_j\, d_{\Sigma}^2(p, b_j) : \sum_{j=1}^n c_j \neq 0 \right\}.$$

With a notion of affine submanifold at hand, we next derive a reprojection error that is defined on Kendall's shape space. Consistently to the 3D case, we will treat the 2D projections as points in shape space Σ_2^k and employ the geodesic distance as objective for the reconstruction problem. To this end, we re-formulate the projection (1) as a map from 3D KSS to 2D KSS by

$$p \in \Sigma_3^k \mapsto \pi \circ \nu(R_{[1,2]}\pi^\dagger(p)) \in \Sigma_2^k, \tag{4}$$

where ν performs normalization (i.e. projects onto the sphere) and the subscript $[1,2]$ refers to the first two rows of $R \in SO(3)$. To assure class invariance under $\sim$, we introduce the map $\pi^\dagger$, which yields a unique representative for a shape by well-positioning to a fixed reference pre-shape $X \in \mathcal{S}_3^k$, viz.

$$\pi^\dagger : p \in \Sigma_m^k \mapsto P \in \mathcal{S}_m^k \quad s.t. \quad \pi(P) = p, P \overset{w}{\sim} X. \tag{5}$$

Note that due to the quotient structure, the re-formulation no longer depends on the scaling and translation camera parameters α and t found in the original formulation (1).

We are now in the position to obtain a geometry-aware counterpart of the estimation problem in terms of the projection (4) and the Fréchet barycentric subspace resulting in the following optimization problem

$$\min_{p,R} d_\Sigma^2 \left(W, \nu(R_{[1,2]}\pi^\dagger(p)) \right) \quad s.t. \quad p \in FBS_{(b_j)_j}, R \in SO(3). \tag{6}$$

2.2   Algorithmic Treatment

In order to solve the reconstruction problem (6), we employ an alternating optimization strategy taking advantage of the product structure of the search space, viz. $FBS_{(B_j)_j} \times SO(3)$. Each outer iteration thus consists of two steps: First, rotation R is minimized while considering the current shape estimate p fixed. To this end, we perform Riemannian optimization on the *Stiefel* manifold

$$V_2(\mathbb{R}^3) := \{X \in \mathbb{R}^{3\times 2} : X^T X = I_2\} \cong SO(3)$$

utilizing the Pymanopt [5] library. Second, we fix the rotation R and solve the resulting sub-problem w.r.t. shape p parametrized by barycentric weights. For Riemannian computations on Kendall's space space, we employ Morphomatics [3]. As both steps are guaranteed to weakly decrease the reconstruction objective, we obtain a simple, yet convergent optimization scheme. In particular, both sub-problems are solved employing steepest descent strategies, where gradients are computed via automatic differentiation with JAX [12].

Due to the non-Euclidean structure of the shape space, there are no closed-form expressions for determining the (weighted) Fréchet mean of a given collection of sample points. Here, we adopt an efficient, inductive estimator to derive a parameterization of the Fréchet barycentric subspace that exhibits only a linear computational cost in the number of basis shapes. In particular, let

$b_1, \ldots, b_n \in \Sigma_3^k$ and $w_1, \ldots, w_n \in \mathbb{R}$ such that $\sum_{j=1}^{n} w_j \neq 0$, then the parameterization $(w_j)_j \mapsto \mu_n \in \Sigma_3^k$ is given by the recursion

$$\mu_1 = b_1 \qquad \mu_j = \gamma_{\mu_{j-1}}^{b_j} \left(\frac{w_j}{\sum_{l=1}^{j} w_l} \right), \qquad (7)$$

where $\gamma_{\mu_{j-1}}^{b_j}$ denotes the shortest geodesic from μ_{j-1} to b_j. Note that under certain conditions (cf. [8]) the recursion can be shown to converge to the actual weighted Fréchet mean. In any case, we expect the Fréchet barycentric subspace to be contained in the image of the above parameterization.

3   Experiments

We perform qualitative and quantitative evaluation of the proposed Kendall shape space (*KSS*) approach in experiments concerning the estimation of human poses as well as head skeletons of basking sharks. Throughout the experiments, we additionally provide results for the vanilla ASM approach as well as a recent convex relaxation thereof presented by Zhou et al. [37]. We will refer to the former and latter as *ASM non-convex* and *ASM convex*, respectively.

3.1   Human Pose Estimation

The design of this experiment closely follows the setup proposed in [37] in order to provide comparability. In particular, we employ the MoCap dataset[1] for defining training and test shapes. Sequences from subject 86 are used as training data and sequences from subjects 13, 14 and 15 are used as testing data. All sequences are composed of a variety of poses, including running, climbing, jumping, and dancing, and can hence be used to define a comprehensive set of basis shapes. While 41 landmarks are used to encode human poses in the MoCap database, we use a reduced representation comprising a subset of 15 landmarks mimicking the construction in [37]. To reduce the effects of rotation and translation as much as possible for the Euclidean approaches, we perform generalized Procrustes analysis of the data during pre-processing.

   As this dataset features abundant training data, we apply a strategy to learn an appropriate set of a restricted number of basis shapes. An immediate choice to determine such a set would be to perform barycentric subspace analysis [28], thus finding an optimal subspace w.r.t. unexplained variance. However, as this could introduce a positive bias for our approach when comparing to the Euclidean ones, we opt for the established k-means clustering [20]. Specifically, we set the basis shapes as the arithmetic means of each determined cluster thereby providing a homogeneous sampling according to the Euclidean metric.

---

[1] Carnegie Mellon University - Graphics Lab - motion capture library http://mocap. cs.cmu.edu/.

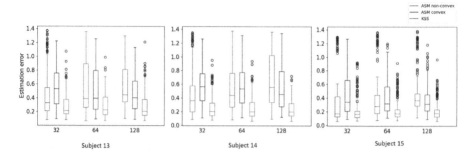

Fig. 2. Boxplots of shape estimation errors of human pose test shapes using the three approaches.

Quantitative Testing. Similar to the creation of basis shapes, 200 shapes were chosen for each of the test subjects by performing k-means clustering on the pose sequences. The shapes were then projected along the z-direction to create the 2D landmarks. We then estimated the 3D shapes from the 2D landmarks for all approaches with different numbers of basis shapes (32, 64, and 128) and computed for each reconstruction the estimation error as the Procrustes distance (3) between the true and estimated shapes. Figure 2 shows boxplots of estimation errors obtained for the derived test shapes for the ASM non-convex, ASM convex, and our approach (listed as KSS), respectively. Table 1 gives an overview of the error distribution. Statistical Friedman tests were conducted for the different combinations of test subjects and number of basis shapes to examine the effect that the reconstruction methods had on estimation errors. Results showed that the methods lead to statistically significant differences in estimation errors ($p < 0.001$). The Kendall shape space approach out-performs the other approaches by estimating the unknown 3D shapes with consistently lower errors for all sets of basis shapes and test subjects. The accuracy of the approach is directly proportional to the number of basis shapes used.

Table 1. Mean(variance) estimation errors for human pose test shapes.

	#Basis shapes	32	64	128
Subject 13	ASM NC	0.462(0.121)	0.548(0.142)	0.571(0.104)
	ASM Conv	0.550(0.071)	0.513(0.100)	0.461(0.059)
	KSS	**0.295(0.031)**	**0.295(0.031)**	**0.288(0.038)**
Subject 14	ASM NC	0.475(0.129)	0.544(0.127)	0.644(0.128)
	ASM Conv	0.583(0.066)	0.566(0.077)	0.533(0.087)
	KSS	**0.267(0.029)**	**0.258(0.028)**	**0.242(0.019)**
Subject 15	ASM NC	0.358(0.136)	0.406(0.122)	0.457(0.089)
	ASM Conv	0.450(0.092)	0.416(0.069)	0.366(0.043)
	KSS	**0.221(0.034)**	**0.231(0.027)**	**0.221(0.021)**

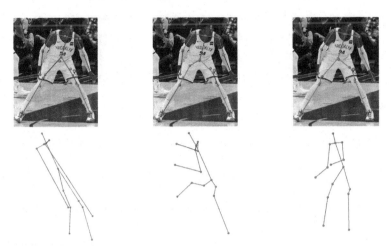

Fig. 3. Comparison of the three approaches for 3D shape estimation applied to an image of a basket ball player. Top row: Fitting of the estimated shapes (green) to the landmarks (yellow). Bottom row: side views of the estimated shapes. Left: ASM non-convex approach. Middle: ASM convex approach. Right: KSS approach (ours). (Color figure online)

Qualitative Testing. Next, we investigate the performance of the approaches in estimating the 3D pose of people in real-world images with manually labelled landmarks. Figure 3 shows the estimated 3D poses of a basket ball player from different viewpoints using all three approaches. The ASM approaches perform very well in estimating a 3D shape that fits to the 2D landmarks, but the estimated shapes are implausible, which can be seen by viewing them from the side. Moreover, they are vastly different from the basis shapes. The proposed approach, although compromising an exact fit to the 2D landmarks, is able to estimate the 3D pose with greater plausibility. This may be attributed to more consistent interpolation between the basis shapes adhering to the Kendall shape space constraints, which lead to reduced distortion of the basis shapes.

A similar scenario is shown in Fig. 4. Here, however, even though the KSS results in a plausible shape, it does not fit to the shape we would expect to obtain. This is most likely attributed to the fact that the ballet pose cannot be estimated from the given basis shapes.

3.2   Estimating Head Skeletons of Basking Sharks

In this section, we give the results for the application that motivated the new approach for shape estimation, that is, the estimation of the shape of the head skeletons of basking sharks in feeding position. As specimens are hard to come by and the species is heavily protected under conservation laws in many countries, the ability to extract the 3D structure of the head region non-invasively, using real-world underwater images is a great contribution to the field of biol-

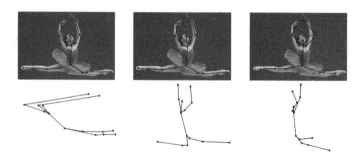

Fig. 4. Comparison of the three approaches for 3D shape estimation applied to an image of a ballet dancer. Top row: Fitting of the estimated shapes (green) to the landmarks (yellow). Bottom row: side views of the estimated shapes. Left: ASM non-convex approach. Middle: ASM convex approach. Right: KSS approach (ours). (Color figure online)

ogy. We use computed tomography (CT) scans of the heads of three basking sharks (*Cetorhinus maximus*) from two museum collections (BMNH: British Museum of Natural History; ZMUC: Zoological Museum, University of Copenhagen); sample and scan information are as follows: BS1: BMNH 1978.6.22.1, size: $512 \times 512 \times 1389$; BS2: BMNH 2004.4.15.30, size: $512 \times 512 \times 1654$; BS3: ZMUC (no accession number), size: $512 \times 512 \times 1862$. BS1 and BS2 were scanned at the Royal Brompton Hospital, BS3 at the Aarhus University Hospital. CT data were used to derive basis shapes and test the methods on real-world images of the species with manually labelled landmarks. BS3 is shown in Fig. 5a.

Basking sharks feed by holding their mouths agape and ballooning the pharynx (throat region), allowing water to flow out the gill slits on the sides of the head [31,33,36]. The pharynx is supported by jointed branchial arches, comprising rod-like skeletal elements linked together to form a mobile skeletal basket around the throat, which can expand and collapse. The kinematics of the pharyngeal skeleton are key to the filtering mechanism, but cannot be visualized from outside the body. From the CT scans of basking sharks, the relevant elements of the head skeleton (the jaw, hyoid and branchial arches, skull, and spine) are isolated using manual and automatic segmentation techniques. These isolated elements are then used to create a piece-wise linear skeleton of the sharks' pharyngeal region by labelling the start and end points of each skeletal element (e.g. the rod-like ceratobranchial cartilages; Fig. 5b) and connecting each point pair via a linear segment. Due to preservation conditions (e.g. specimens fixed in non-physiological positions), sharks in the CT scans showed non-physiological deformations (e.g. the branchial basket collapsed asymmetrically under the shark's weight), structures needed correction before creating the set of basis shapes. Due to the bilateral symmetry of basking sharks, their right and left halves

(a) CT scan of a basking shark (BS3) in left lateral view.

(b) (left) Segmented CT scan of the head skeleton of a basking shark (BS3, ventral view). (middle) Piece-wise linear skeleton created by selecting end points of each region.(right) Skeleton split into right and left halves.

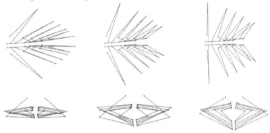

(c) Basking shark skeleton shapes created by mirroring optimized half skeletons. (top) Top/dorsal-view showing the expansion of gill arches. (bottom) Front/anterior-view showing varying degrees of openness of the mouth.

Fig. 5. From CT scan to skeletal representation of shark head. (a) Volume rendering of CT scan. (b) Segmentation, skeletonization, and separation of left and right parts of the skeleton. (c) Opening of skeleton to create open-mouth configurations of the head.

are essentially identical: skeletons were split into right and left halves which could later be mirrored to create full skeletons. A set of optimization problems which aim to conserve the lengths of segments were used to move the spine and the ventral plate (a portion of the branchial basket) of the half skeletons into an anatomically plausible position [36]. The mouth of the skeleton was opened using the same method. The corrected skeletons were then mirrored w.r.t. the sagittal plane. Figure 5c visualizes this process. The anatomical arrangements of the final skeletons were approved by experts in the field (M. Dean & F. Mollen, personal communication).

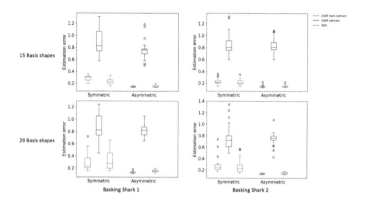

Fig. 6. Boxplots of shape estimation errors of basking shark test shapes for the three approaches using the basis shapes from BS3.

Analysis of Reconstruction Accuracy. Similar to human pose estimation, quantitative and qualitative analyses were performed for all approaches. In the quantitative experiments, we used the head skeleton shapes (29 in total) of one of the basking sharks to estimate the shapes (28/29) of the other two. Two types of projections, bilaterally symmetric and asymmetric, are used to estimate the 3D shape. The former is the case when viewing the shark anteriorly (from the front) and the latter when viewing from the side (e.g. where one side of the throat is more visible than the other). Both scenarios are equally important when extracting the 3D shape from images. Figure 6 shows the errors in estimation using all the approaches and Table 2 provides some error statistics. Again, statistically significant differences have been confirmed via Friedmann tests ($p < 0.001$) for each combination of subject and viewpoints. Contrary to the human pose estimation, the ASM non-convex and our approach provide similar estimation errors for the basking shark experiment with the former being slightly superior for 5 out of the 8 cases. These results indicate that the basking shark data might

Table 2. Mean(variance) estimation errors for basking shark test shapes for symmetric and asymmetric projections using (15/29) basis shapes from Basking Shark 3.

	#Basis shapes	15 (sym)	15 (asym)	29 (sym)	29 (asym)
BS1	ASM NC	0.231(0.002)	**0.146(3e−04)**	**0.306(0.020)**	**0.136(2e−04)**
	ASM Conv	0.854(0.030)	0.836(0.013)	0.857(0.036)	0.820(0.011)
	KSS	**0.215(0.001)**	0.151(3e−04)	0.336(0.025)	0.156(0.0003)
BS2	ASM NC	0.286(0.001)	**0.145(1e−04)**	0.281(0.014)	**0.137(9.7e−05)**
	ASM Conv	0.906(0.041)	0.757 (0.021)	0.755(0.041)	0.747(0.013)
	KSS	**0.236(0.001)**	0.153(3e−04)	**0.256(0.012)**	0.150(3.5e−04)

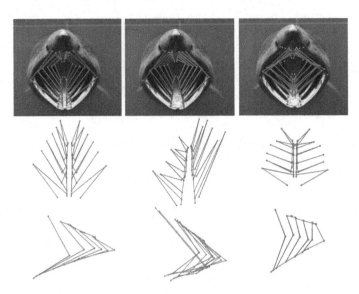

Fig. 7. Comparison of the three approaches for 3D shape estimation applied to an under-water image[5] of a basking shark. Top row: Fitting of the estimated shapes (green) to the landmarks (yellow). Middle row: top views of the estimated shapes. Bottom row: side views. Left: ASM non-convex approach. Middle: ASM convex approach. Right: KSS approach (ours). (Color figure online)

be located in a region of relatively low curvature in shape space that is well approximated by a hyper-plane.

Qualitative Validation on Underwater Imagery. We investigated the performances of the approaches in estimating the 3D structure of basking shark heads in underwater images with manually placed landmarks. Shapes from all three sharks (86 in total) were used as basis shapes. Figures 7 and 8 show the results obtained using the two ASM approaches and the novel KSS approach. Similarly to the results for the estimation of real-world human poses, the shape estimations obtained from the two ASM approaches fit the 2D landmarks very well but fail to produce convincing results when looking from a different view. This is particularly striking for the ASM convex approach but is also noticeable for the ASM non-convex method—the estimated shape of which is unnaturally elongated. In contrast, applying the KSS approach results in 3D shapes that are very plausible and show a widely opened mouth.

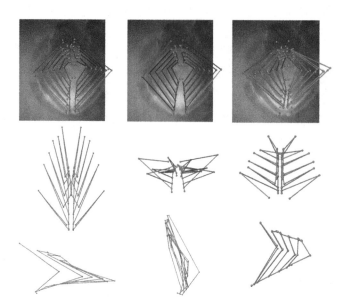

Fig. 8. Comparison of the three approaches for 3D shape estimation applied to an under-water image[9] of a basking shark. Top row: Fitting of the estimated shapes (green) to the landmarks (yellow). Middle row: top views of the estimated shapes. Bottom row: side views. Left: ASM non-convex approach. Middle: ASM convex approach. Right: KSS approach (ours). (Color figure online)

4   Conclusion

In this work, we have proposed a novel, non-Euclidean approach for the estimation of 3D shapes from single monocular 2D images. In particular, we generalized the established active shape model approach to Kendall's shape space combining concepts from geometric statistics and computational differential geometry. The resulting geometric model provides efficient, yet highly consistent estimation of 3D shapes due to a natural encoding of constraints.

We have demonstrated the performance of our approach in experiments on the reconstruction of human poses as well as head skeletons of basking sharks. The advantages of the proposed scheme are particularly apparent in qualitative comparison to previous approaches that rely on assumptions of linearity. While former approaches attained lower reprojection errors, the corresponding 3D shapes show defects like non-physiological distortions indicating a need for further domain-specific regularization. For example, the convex relaxation of the ASM proposed in [37] developed strong asymmetries although basis shapes are symmetric. In contrast, our geometric method yielded highly physiological results even in challenging situations where the target shape differed greatly from the training distribution.

In future work, we plan to extend our approach to more advanced camera models to be able to account for strong perspective effects. Furthermore, while we use the 2D Kendall shape space distance as reprojection error, weighted or ℓ^1-like extensions could be employed to incorporate uncertainty in 2D landmark detection or to increase robustness against outliers, respectively.

Acknowledgments. We are grateful for the funding by Deutsche Forschungsgemeinschaft (DFG) through Germany's Excellence Strategy – The Berlin Mathematics Research Center MATH+ (EXC-2046/1, project ID: 390685689) and by Bundesministerium für Bildung und Forschung (BMBF) through BIFOLD – The Berlin Institute for the Foundations of Learning and Data (ref. 01IS18025A and ref. 01IS18037A). The basking shark work was funded in part by an HFSP Program Grant (RGP0010-2020 to M.N.D.). We also want to thank the British Museum of Natural History and Zoological Museum, University of Copenhagen for providing basking shark specimens, Pepijn Kamminga, James Maclaine, Allison Luger and Henrik Lauridsen for help acquiring CT data, and Alex Mustard (Underwater Photography) and Maura Mitchell (Manx Basking Shark Watch) for granting us permission to use their underwater images of basking sharks.

References

1. Agudo, A., Agapito, L., Calvo, B., Montiel, J.M.: Good vibrations: a modal analysis approach for sequential non-rigid structure from motion. In: Proceedings of IEEE Computer Vision and Pattern Recognition, pp. 1558–1565 (2014)
2. Akhter, I., Black, M.J.: Pose-conditioned joint angle limits for 3D human pose reconstruction. In: Proceedings of IEEE Computer Vision and Pattern Recognition, pp. 1446–1455 (2015)
3. Ambellan, F., Hanik, M., von Tycowicz, C.: Morphomatics: geometric morphometrics in non-Euclidean shape spaces (2021). https://doi.org/10.12752/8544
4. Ambellan, F., Lamecker, H., von Tycowicz, C., Zachow, S.: Statistical shape models: understanding and mastering variation in anatomy. In: Rea, P.M. (ed.) Biomedical Visualisation. AEMB, vol. 1156, pp. 67–84. Springer, Cham (2019). https://doi.org/10.1007/978-3-030-19385-0_5
5. Boumal, N., Mishra, B., Absil, P.A., Sepulchre, R.: ManOPT, a MATLAB toolbox for optimization on manifolds. J. Mach. Learn. Res. **15**(1), 1455–1459 (2014)
6. Bregler, C., Hertzmann, A., Biermann, H.: Recovering non-rigid 3D shape from image streams. In: Proceedings of IEEE Computer Vision and Pattern Recognition, vol. 2, pp. 690–696. IEEE (2000)
7. Cao, C., Weng, Y., Lin, S., Zhou, K.: 3D shape regression for real-time facial animation. ACM Trans. Graph. (TOG) **32**(4), 1–10 (2013)
8. Chakraborty, R., Bouza, J., Manton, J., Vemuri, B.C.: Manifoldnet: a deep neural network for manifold-valued data with applications. IEEE Trans. Pattern Anal. Mach. Intell. (2020)
9. Cootes, T.F., Taylor, C.J., Cooper, D.H., Graham, J.: Active shape models-their training and application. Comput. Vis. Image Underst. **61**(1), 38–59 (1995)
10. Fletcher, P.T., Lu, C., Pizer, S.M., Joshi, S.: Principal geodesic analysis for the study of nonlinear statistics of shape. IEEE Trans. Med. Imaging **23**(8), 995–1005 (2004)
11. Friji, R., Drira, H., Chaieb, F., Kurtek, S., Kchok, H.: KshapeNet: Riemannian network on Kendall shape space for skeleton based action recognition. arXiv preprint arXiv:2011.12004 (2020)

12. Frostig, R., Johnson, M.J., Leary, C.: Compiling machine learning programs via high-level tracing. Syst. Mach. Learn. **4**(9) (2018)
13. Heimann, T., Meinzer, H.P.: Statistical shape models for 3D medical image segmentation: a review. Med. Image Anal. **13**(4), 543–563 (2009)
14. Hejrati, M., Ramanan, D.: Analyzing 3D objects in cluttered images. In: Advances in Neural Information Processing Systems, vol. 25 (2012)
15. Howe, N.R.: Silhouette lookup for automatic pose tracking. In: 2004 Conference on Computer Vision and Pattern Recognition Workshop, pp. 15–22. IEEE (2004)
16. Jiang, H., Liu, H., Tan, P., Zhang, G., Bao, H.: 3D reconstruction of dynamic scenes with multiple handheld cameras. In: Fitzgibbon, A., Lazebnik, S., Perona, P., Sato, Y., Schmid, C. (eds.) ECCV 2012. LNCS, vol. 7573, pp. 601–615. Springer, Heidelberg (2012). https://doi.org/10.1007/978-3-642-33709-3_43
17. Kendall, D.G.: Shape manifolds, procrustean metrics, and complex projective spaces. Bull. Lond. Math. Soc. **16**(2), 81–121 (1984)
18. Kendall, D.G., Barden, D., Carne, T.K., Le, H.: Shape and Shape Theory. Wiley, Hoboken (2009)
19. Larsen, E.S., Mordohai, P., Pollefeys, M., Fuchs, H.: Temporally consistent reconstruction from multiple video streams using enhanced belief propagation. In: 2007 IEEE 11th International Conference on Computer Vision, pp. 1–8. IEEE (2007)
20. Lloyd, S.: Least squares quantization in PCM. IEEE Trans. Inf. Theory **28**(2), 129–137 (1982)
21. Mehta, D., et al.: VNect: real-time 3D human pose estimation with a single RGB camera. ACM Trans. Graph. (TOG) **36**(4), 1–14 (2017)
22. Michalkiewicz, M., Parisot, S., Tsogkas, S., Baktashmotlagh, M., Eriksson, A., Belilovsky, E.: Few-shot single-view 3-D object reconstruction with compositional priors. In: Vedaldi, A., Bischof, H., Brox, T., Frahm, J.-M. (eds.) ECCV 2020. LNCS, vol. 12370, pp. 614–630. Springer, Cham (2020). https://doi.org/10.1007/978-3-030-58595-2_37
23. Mori, G., Malik, J.: Recovering 3D human body configurations using shape contexts. IEEE Trans. Pattern Anal. Mach. Intell. **28**(7), 1052–1062 (2006)
24. Mustafa, A., Kim, H., Guillemaut, J.Y., Hilton, A.: General dynamic scene reconstruction from multiple view video. In: Proceedings of the IEEE International Conference on Computer Vision, pp. 900–908 (2015)
25. Nava-Yazdani, E., Hege, H.C., Sullivan, T.J., von Tycowicz, C.: Geodesic analysis in Kendall's shape space with epidemiological applications. J. Math. Imaging Vision **62**(4), 549–559 (2020)
26. Park, S., Lee, M., Kwak, N.: Procrustean regression networks: learning 3D structure of non-rigid objects from 2D annotations. In: Vedaldi, A., Bischof, H., Brox, T., Frahm, J.-M. (eds.) ECCV 2020. LNCS, vol. 12374, pp. 1–18. Springer, Cham (2020). https://doi.org/10.1007/978-3-030-58526-6_1
27. Paskin, M., Dean, M., Baum, D., von Tycowicz, C.: A Kendall shape space approach to 3D shape estimation from 2D landmarks - source code and data (2022). https://doi.org/10.12752/8730
28. Pennec, X.: Barycentric subspace analysis on manifolds. Ann. Stat. **46**(6A), 2711–2746 (2018)
29. Plänkers, R., Fua, P.: Tracking and modeling people in video sequences. Comput. Vis. Image Underst. **81**(3), 285–302 (2001)
30. Ramakrishna, V., Kanade, T., Sheikh, Y.: Reconstructing 3D human pose from 2D image landmarks. In: Fitzgibbon, A., Lazebnik, S., Perona, P., Sato, Y., Schmid, C. (eds.) ECCV 2012. LNCS, vol. 7575, pp. 573–586. Springer, Heidelberg (2012). https://doi.org/10.1007/978-3-642-33765-9_41

31. Sanderson, S.L., Roberts, E., Lineburg, J., Brooks, H.: Fish mouths as engineering structures for vortical cross-step filtration. Nat. Commun. **7**(1), 1–9 (2016)
32. Sanzari, M., Ntouskos, V., Pirri, F.: Bayesian image based 3D pose estimation. In: Leibe, B., Matas, J., Sebe, N., Welling, M. (eds.) ECCV 2016. LNCS, vol. 9912, pp. 566–582. Springer, Cham (2016). https://doi.org/10.1007/978-3-319-46484-8_34
33. Sims, D.W.: Sieving a living: a review of the biology, ecology and conservation status of the plankton-feeding basking shark Cetorhinus maximus. Adv. Mar. Biol. **54**, 171–220 (2008)
34. Tomasi, C., Kanade, T.: Shape and motion from image streams under orthography: a factorization method. Int. J. Comput. Vis. **9**(2), 137–154 (1992)
35. Wang, C., Wang, Y., Lin, Z., Yuille, A.L., Gao, W.: Robust estimation of 3d human poses from a single image. In: Proceedings of IEEE Computer Vision and Pattern Recognition, pp. 2361–2368 (2014)
36. Wegner, N.C.: Elasmobranch gill structure. In: Fish Physiology, vol. 34, pp. 101–151. Elsevier, Amsterdam (2015)
37. Zhou, X., Leonardos, S., Hu, X., Daniilidis, K.: 3d shape estimation from 2d landmarks: A convex relaxation approach. In: Proc. IEEE Comput. Vis. Pattern Recognit. pp. 4447–4455 (2015)
38. Zia, M.Z., Stark, M., Schiele, B., Schindler, K.: Detailed 3D representations for object recognition and modeling. IEEE Trans. Pattern Anal. Mach. Intell. **35**(11), 2608–2623 (2013)

Neural Light Field Estimation for Street Scenes with Differentiable Virtual Object Insertion

Zian Wang[1,2,3]($\boxtimes$), Wenzheng Chen[1,2,3], David Acuna[1,2,3], Jan Kautz[1], and Sanja Fidler[1,2,3]

[1] NVIDIA, Santa Clara, USA
{zianw,wenzchen,dacunamarrer,jkautz,sfidler}@nvidia.com
[2] University of Toronto, Toronto, Canada
[3] Vector Institute, Toronto, Canada

Abstract. We consider the challenging problem of outdoor lighting estimation for the goal of photorealistic virtual object insertion into photographs. Existing works on outdoor lighting estimation typically simplify the scene lighting into an environment map which cannot capture the spatially-varying lighting effects in outdoor scenes. In this work, we propose a neural approach that estimates the 5D HDR light field from a single image, and a differentiable object insertion formulation that enables end-to-end training with image-based losses that encourage realism. Specifically, we design a hybrid lighting representation tailored to outdoor scenes, which contains an HDR sky dome that handles the extreme intensity of the sun, and a volumetric lighting representation that models the spatially-varying appearance of the surrounding scene. With the estimated lighting, our shadow-aware object insertion is fully differentiable, which enables adversarial training over the composited image to provide additional supervisory signal to the lighting prediction. We experimentally demonstrate that our hybrid lighting representation is more performant than existing outdoor lighting estimation methods. We further show the benefits of our AR object insertion in an autonomous driving application, where we obtain performance gains for a 3D object detector when trained on our augmented data.

Keywords: Lighting estimation · Image editing · Augmented reality

1 Introduction

In this work, we address the task of outdoor lighting estimation from monocular imagery, specifically focusing on street scenes, as shown in Fig. 1. This is an important task, as it enables virtual object insertion that can cater to many

Supplementary Information The online version contains supplementary material available at https://doi.org/10.1007/978-3-031-20086-1_22.

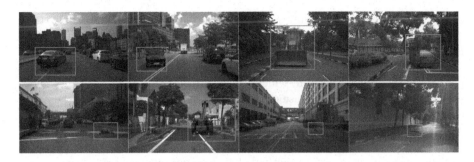

Fig. 1. We estimate lighting and perform virtual objects insertion in real street scenery. We insert cars and heavy vehicles (top), and composite rare but safety-critical scenarios with garbage, construction site, a dog, and debris (bottom).

downstream domains [8,10,18,28,35], such as virtually inserting newly planned buildings for architectural visualization, realistically rendering game characters into surroundings, or as a way to augment real datasets with objects that are otherwise hard to record in the real world, such as road debris and exotic animals, for the purpose of training more robust and performant computer vision models.

Lighting estimation for AR applications needs to account for complex 5D light transport [1], *i.e.* a function of spatial location and viewing direction. With usually a limited field-of-view observed from input, the task of estimating the light field is challenging and ill-posed. An additional challenge encountered for outdoor scenes, in contrast to indoor scenes, is the extreme high dynamic range (HDR) of the sun, which is critical to estimate correctly in order to render cast shadows. Existing literature on lighting estimation usually tackles a simplified problem setting. [34,37] focus on spatially-varying effects but do not handle HDR intensities. In contrast, methods that focus on HDR and predict parametric sky [17,39] or utilize learned sky models [16] typically ignore the spatially-varying effects and lack high-frequency details. These limitations not only result in inaccurate lighting estimation but also hamper virtual object insertion effects.

In this paper, we propose a unified approach that overcomes the previously mentioned limitations, estimating the HDR scene light field from a single image. Tailored to outdoor scenes, we estimate a hybrid lighting representation that comprises of two components: an HDR sky dome and a volumetric lighting representation for the surrounding scene. We employ a learned latent vector to represent the sky dome inspired by [16], which can be decoded into an HDR environment map that is designed to model the strong intensity of the sun. We adopt the volumetric spherical Gaussian representation [37] to represent the non-infinity surroundings such as road and buildings. The two components naturally combine with volume rendering and demonstrate superiority over prior works [16,37]. We further design a physics-based object insertion formulation that renders the inserted objects and their shadows cast on the scene. We utilize ray-tracing to capture the second-order lighting effects, which is fully differentiable with respect to the lighting parameters. We train our method with supervised and self-supervised losses, and show that adversarial training over the composited AR images provides complementary supervisory signal to improve lighting estimation.

Our method outperforms prior work in the tasks of lighting estimation and photorealistic object insertion, which we show through numerical results and a user study. We further showcase our virtual object insertion through the application of 3D object detection in autonomous driving. Our approach, which can render synthetic 3D objects into real imagery in a realistic way, provides useful data augmentation that leads to notable performance gains over the vanilla dataset, and a naive insertion method that does not account for lighting.

2   Related Work

Lighting Estimation aims to predict an HDR light field from image observations. Due to the ill-posed nature of the problem, prior works often tackle a simplified task and ignore spatially-varying effects, using lighting representations such as spherical lobes [3,24], light probes [21], sky parameters [16,17,39], and environment maps [12,31,32,38]. Recent works explored various representations for capturing spatially-varying lighting, including per-pixel spherical lobes [13,23,41], light source parameters [11], per-location environment map [33,43] and 3D volumetric lighting [34,37]. These works usually train with synthetic data due to the scarcity of available groundtruth HDR light field on real-world captures.

Outdoor scenes require special attention for the extreme High Dynamic Range (HDR) lighting intensity, *e.g.* the sun's intensity, which is several orders higher in magnitude than typical light sources found in indoor scenes. Prior works employed sky parameters [17,39], or learned sky models [16] with an encoder-decoder architecture for modeling HDR sky. However, these works typically only focus on modeling the sky, and ignore the high-frequency and spatially-varying effects, which are equally important to get right for AR applications. In this work, we propose a unified representation that can handle both HDR sky intensity as well as spatially varying effects in outdoor scenes to achieve better performance.

Self-supervised lighting estimation methods apply differentiable rendering to provide gradient for lighting estimation [6,7,22,27,40]. Differentiable rasterization-based renderers [6,7,40] are typically limited to images of single objects and ignores the spatially-varying effects. Physically-based rendering (PBR) methods [22,27] require intensive memory and running time, and are thus limited to optimization tasks. Note that existing differentiable renderers [6,7,27] typically do not provide direct functionality for object insertion, which is an image editing task. We propose a novel differentiable object insertion formulation, providing valuable supervision signal for lighting estimation.

Image Manipulation. Related to ours is also work that aims to insert synthetic objects into images using alternative techniques, such as adversarial methods [20,

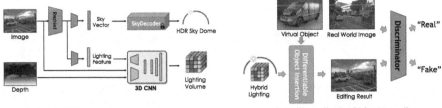

(a) Hybrid Lighting Joint Estimation   **(b) Differentiable Object Insertion**

Fig. 2. Model overview. Our monocular lighting estimation model (a) predicts a hybrid lighting representation containing an HDR sky dome (top) representing sky and sun at infinity, and a lighting volume (bottom) representing the surrounding scene. The depth (a, left) for lighting volume prediction comes from off-the-shelf monocular depth estimator [14]. With the predicted lighting, our object insertion module (b) renders a 3D asset into a given image and is fully differentiable w.r.t. lighting parameters, thus enabling end-to-end training with adversarial objective for photorealism.

25], or by perturbing real scenes using recent advances in neural rendering [28]. Alhaija *et al.* [2] assumes known lighting and propose to use AR as a data generation technique by inserting synthetic assets into real world scenes. Naive copy-paste object insertion has also been shown to boost downstream object recognition accuracy [10,35]. Neural Scene Graph [28] optimize neural implicit functions for each object in the scene. Despite realistic editing results, lighting effects are baked into the representation and thus swapping assets from one scene to another is not easily possible. GeoSim [8] reconstructs assets such as cars from real-world driving sequences, and inserts them into a given image using a classical renderer followed by a shallow neural renderer that fixes errors such as unrealistic compositing effects. While achieving impressive results on car insertion, it remains difficult to apply on less frequent objects. In contrast, our method supports inserting 3D assets of various classes (Fig. 1).

3 Method

We aim to estimate scene lighting so as to render synthetic 3D assets into images realistically. In what follows, we introduce the hybrid representation, which comprises an HDR sky dome and a volumetric scene lighting (Sect. 3.1), the hybrid lighting prediction model (Sect. 3.2, Fig. 2a), the differentiable object insertion module that renders a virtual object into an image (Sect. 3.3, Fig. 2b), and the training schema (Sect. 3.4).

3.1 Hybrid Lighting Representation

Our goal is to model the 5D light field, which maps a spatial location $\mathbf{x} \in \mathbb{R}^3$ and light direction $\mathbf{l} \in \mathcal{S}^2$ into an HDR radiance value $\mathbf{r} \in \mathbb{R}^3_+$. In contrast to indoor, outdoor scenes require simultaneously modeling the extreme HDR sky as well

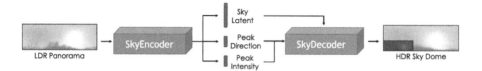

Fig. 3. Sky modeling network takes as input an LDR panorama and produces an HDR sky with an encoder-decoder structure, where the network also learns to compress sky information into the intermediate vector representation $\mathbf{f} \in \mathbb{R}^d$. The sky vector consists of explicit feature of peak intensity and direction, and a latent feature vector.

as the surrounding environment. The peak magnitude of the former (sun) can be several orders higher than the latter. To address this, we propose to use a hybrid lighting representation that separately models the sky at infinity and the surrounding scene. This decomposition allows us to capture both, the extreme intensity of the sky while preserving the spatially-varying effects of the scene.

HDR Sky Representation. The sky dome typically contains a relatively simple structure, *i.e.* sun, sky, and possibly clouds, which affords a much lower dimensional representation than that of a typical environment map. Thus, instead of directly predicting a high resolution 2D environment map, we learn a feature space of the sky, and represent the sky dome with a sky feature vector $\mathbf{f} \in \mathbb{R}^d$, which can further be passed to a pretrained CNN decoder to decode into an HDR environment map, as shown in Fig. 2a (top). The sky feature space learning is described in Sect. 3.2, *sky modeling* part.

Spatially-varying Surrounding Scene Representation. The outdoor scenes generally consist of complex geometric structures resulting in location-dependent lighting effects like shadows and reflections, which cannot be simply modeled as an environment map. To address this, we use a volumetric spherical Gaussian (VSG) [37] to represent the nearby surrounding scene. VSG is a 8-channel volumetric tensor $L_{\text{VSG}} \in \mathbb{R}^{8 \times X \times Y \times Z}$, augmenting the RGB$\alpha$ volume with view-dependent spherical Gaussian lobes. Each voxel of VSG contains a spherical Gaussian lobe $G(\mathbf{l}) = ce^{-(1-\mathbf{l}\cdot\boldsymbol{\mu})/\sigma^2}$, where $\mathbf{l}$ is viewing direction and $\boldsymbol{\xi} = \{c, \boldsymbol{\mu}, \sigma\}$ are 7-dimensional parameters to model the exiting radiance of the corresponding 3D location. Each voxel also has an alpha channel $\alpha \in [0, 1]$ to represent occupancy. The 5D light field can be queried with volume rendering which we detail below.

Radiance Query Function. With our hybrid lighting representation utilizing both sky dome and volumetric lighting, the lighting intensity at any 3D point along any ray direction can be queried. To compute the radiance of a ray that starts inside the volume, we first shoot the ray through the lighting volume L_{VSG} and finally hit the HDR sky dome L_{env}. We adopt alpha compositing to combine the two lighting effects. Specifically, to compute the lighting intensity for the ray emitted from the location $\mathbf{x} \in \mathbb{R}^3$ in the direction $\mathbf{l} \in \mathcal{S}^2$, we select K equi-spaced locations along the ray and use nearest neighbor interpolation to get the voxel values $\{\alpha_k, \boldsymbol{\xi}_k\}_{k=1}^K$ from L_{VSG}. We then query the intensity of L_{env} in the direction $\mathbf{l}$, referred to as $L_{\text{env}}(\mathbf{l})$, via bilinear interpolation. The final HDR light intensity $L(\mathbf{x}, \mathbf{l}) \in \mathbb{R}_+^3$ can be computed using volume rendering:

$$L(\mathbf{x}, \mathbf{l}) = \left(\sum_{k=1}^K \tau_{k-1} \alpha_k G(-\mathbf{l}; \boldsymbol{\xi}_k) \right) + \tau_K L_{\text{env}}(\mathbf{l}) \tag{1}$$

where $\tau_k = \prod_{i=1}^k (1 - \alpha_i)$ is the transmittance. This function will be used for rendering object insertion in Eq. 2 and shadows in Eq. 4.

3.2 Network Architecture

In this section, we introduce the network architecture for the pre-trained sky model and lighting prediction.

Sky Modeling. To learn the sky feature space, we design a sky modeling network as shown in Fig. 3. Specifically, the encoder compresses the input LDR panorama into a feature vector, then the decoder decode it to the original HDR sky dome. Our sky feature vector $\mathbf{f}$ contains explicit HDR peak intensity $\mathbf{f}_{\text{intensity}} \in \mathbb{R}^3$, peak direction $\mathbf{f}_{\text{dir}} \in \mathbb{R}^3$, and a latent vector $\mathbf{f}_{\text{latent}} \in \mathbb{R}^{d-6}$ encoding the content of the sky dome. This design allows us to control the lighting of the sun by controlling $\mathbf{f}_{\text{dir}}$ and $\mathbf{f}_{\text{intensity}}$, which is convenient for applications that allow manual editing.

We pre-train the sky encoder-decoder network on a set of outdoor HDR panoramas and keep it freezed. Once trained, we integrate the fixed decoder into the sky prediction branch (Fig. 2a top). The pre-trained sky modeling network, which maps an LDR panorama into HDR, will also be used to generate HDR pseudo labels for supervision (Sect. 3.4) due to the lack of HDR data.

Hybrid Lighting Prediction. As shown in Fig. 2, we use a two-branch network to predict the sky dome and the lighting volume. We detail each branch below.
HDR Sky Prediction Branch. Given an input image, the sky branch directly predicts the sky feature vector $\mathbf{f}$ from the ResNet [15] backbone. The pre-trained fixed sky decoder then maps $\mathbf{f}$ to an HDR sky environment map.
Lighting Volume Prediction Branch. We adapt from a subnetwork of [37] for VSG prediction. Specifically, we first use an MLP [26] to map the lighting feature extracted by ResNet backbone into a feature volume, and then unproject the input image into a RGBα volume. We adopt a 3D UNet to fuse the two volumes and predict the VSG lighting representation. Since unprojection requires depth information, we adopt an off-the-shelf monocular depth estimator PackNet [14] to predict a dense depth map. Architecture details are included in the Appendix.

3.3 Differentiable Object Insertion

We now study the task of realistic object insertion, which is key in AR and our main final objective. Given an estimated lighting representation L, our goal is to composite a virtual object with known geometry $\mathcal{M}$ and material Θ into a real image I with known depth D and camera intrinsics. To achieve realistic lighting effects in this process, not only the inserted object should be influenced by the scene lighting, but it should also affect the scene to create cast shadows.

In our work, we aim to make this insertion module differentiable, including shadow rendering, such that it can afford gradient backpropagation from the losses defined on the composited image, back to our lighting parameters. Since groundtruth light field is not easily available for outdoor scenes, we argue that a plausible complementary supervision signal is to use the quality of object insertion as an objective. Thus, carefully designed adversarial training on the composite images can be a powerful approach to supervise lighting estimation. We also argue that even if groundtruth lighting information would be available, optimizing for the quality of object insertion end-to-end will likely lead to improved results.

Foreground Object Appearance Rendering. We render the virtual object with our predicted hybrid lighting representation L using a physically-based renderer. We adopt the Disney BRDF [4,7,19] for enhanced realism.

Specifically, we first shoot rays from the camera origin to the scene, where we apply ray-mesh intersection detection for the rays and the inserted object $\mathcal{M}$. For each intersected ray, we create a G-buffer for the location of the intersection $\mathbf{x}$, the surface normal $\mathbf{n}$ and the material properties θ. We bounce multiple rays at $\mathbf{x}$ and render with Monte-Carlo numerical integration:

$$I_{\mathbf{x}} = \frac{1}{N} \sum_{k=1}^{N} \frac{f(\mathbf{l}_k, \mathbf{v}; \theta) L(\mathbf{x}, \mathbf{l}_k)(\mathbf{n} \cdot \mathbf{l}_k)^+}{p(\mathbf{l}_k)} \tag{2}$$

where $L(\cdot, \cdot)$ is the radiance query function as defined in Eq. 1, N and $\mathbf{l}_k$ is the number and direction of sampled lighting, $\mathbf{v}$ is the viewing direction of the camera ray, and f is the Disney BRDF.

Background Shadow Map Rendering. The inserted object changes the light transport in the scene and affects the appearance of the background scene pixels, which typically causes shadows. We adopt ray tracing to generate faithful ratio shadow maps for the inserted object, inspired by classic ratio imaging techniques [29]. Specifically, for each scene pixel p, we compute its 3D location $\mathbf{x}$ from the depth map D. We first compute the lighting distribution before object insertion $\{L(\mathbf{x}_s, \mathbf{l}_k)\}_{k=1}^{N_s}$, where $\{\mathbf{l}_k\}_{k=1}^{N_s}$ are uniformly selected light directions on the upper hemisphere. After object insertion, the rays may potentially get occluded by the inserted objects, resulting in a post-insertion lighting distribution $\{L^{'}(\mathbf{x}_s, \mathbf{l}_k)\}_{k=1}^{N_s}$. To compute $\{L^{'}(\mathbf{x}_s, \mathbf{l}_k)\}_{k=1}^{N_s}$, we perform ray-mesh query for all rays. If ray $(\mathbf{x}_s, \mathbf{l}_k)$ is occluded by the inserted object, we set the lighting intensity value to an ambient value I_a which we empirically set to 0.1, while the lighting intensities of unoccluded rays remain the same as the original radiance. We then define the shadow effects as the ratio of the pixel intensity values before (I) and after (I') object insertion,

$$S_p = \frac{I'_p}{I_p} = \frac{\sum_{k=1}^{N_s} f_{\text{scene}}(\mathbf{x}_s, \mathbf{l}_k, \mathbf{v}; \theta) L'(\mathbf{x}_s, \mathbf{l}_k)(\mathbf{n} \cdot \mathbf{l}_k)^+}{\sum_{k=1}^{N_s} f_{\text{scene}}(\mathbf{x}_s, \mathbf{l}_k, \mathbf{v}; \theta) L(\mathbf{x}_s, \mathbf{l}_k)(\mathbf{n} \cdot \mathbf{l}_k)^+} \tag{3}$$

where the BRDF of the scene pixel f_{scene} and normal direction $\mathbf{n}$ are unknown. As our object insertion and shadows occur on flat surfaces in typical street scenes we consider, we simplify it by assuming the normal direction is pointing upward, and assume the scene surface is Lambertian with constant diffuse albedo $f_{\text{scene}}(\mathbf{x}_s, \mathbf{l}_k, \mathbf{v}) = f_d$. As a result, we can move the BRDF term outside the sum in Eq. 3 and cancel it out to obtain a simpler term:

$$S_p = \frac{f_d \sum_{k=1}^{N_s} L'(\mathbf{x}_s, \mathbf{l}_k)(\mathbf{n} \cdot \mathbf{l}_k)^+}{f_d \sum_{k=1}^{N_s} L(\mathbf{x}_s, \mathbf{l}_k)(\mathbf{n} \cdot \mathbf{l}_k)^+} = \frac{\sum_{k=1}^{N_s} L'(\mathbf{x}_s, \mathbf{l}_k)(\mathbf{n} \cdot \mathbf{l}_k)^+}{\sum_{k=1}^{N_s} L(\mathbf{x}_s, \mathbf{l}_k)(\mathbf{n} \cdot \mathbf{l}_k)^+} \tag{4}$$

which can be computed with the estimated lighting L. Scene pixels after insertion can then be computed by multiplying the ratio shadow map $I' = S \odot I$.

Gradient Propagation. We design the forward rendering process to be differentiable for both foreground object and background shadows, which allows us to back propagate gradients from image pixels to the lighting parameters.

For each foreground pixel, the rendered appearance of the inserted object is differentiable via Eq. 2. Gradients from background pixels I' with respect to the lighting L, i.e. $\frac{\partial I'}{\partial L}$, can be computed via $\frac{\partial I'}{\partial L} = \frac{\partial S}{\partial L} I$, where the shadow ratio S in Eq. 4 is also differentiable wrt. lighting L. Intuitively, if we want the shadows around the object to be perceptually darker, this will encourage the occluded light directions to have stronger intensity.

3.4   Training

We first pre-train the sky modeling network on a collection of outdoor HDR panoramas, and then keep it fixed in the following training process for our hybrid lighting prediction. The supervision for our hybrid lighting joint estimation module comes from two parts: (1) the direction supervision that learns lighting information from the training data, and (2) the adversarial supervision that applies on the final editing results and optimizes for realism.

Sky Modeling Supervision. We train the sky modeling encoder-decoder network (Fig. 3) on a collection of outdoor HDR panoramas. For each HDR panorama I_{HDR}, we compute its ground-truth peak intensity $\mathbf{f}_{intensity}$ and direction $\mathbf{f}_{dir}$. We train the encoder-decoder with the LDR-HDR pair (I_{LDR}, I_{HDR}), where the input LDR panorama I_{LDR} is converted from the HDR panorama via gamma correction and intensity clipping. We supervise the network with a combination of three losses, including peak direction loss $\mathcal{L}_{dir}$ with L1 angular error, and peak intensity loss $\mathcal{L}_{intensity}$ and HDR reconstruction loss $\mathcal{L}_{hdr}$ using log-encoded L2 error defined as $\text{LogEncodedL2}(\hat{x}, x) = ||\log(1+\hat{x}) - \log(1+x)||_2^2$.

Supervision for Hybrid Lighting Prediction. To supervise lighting prediction, we use two complementary datasets: the self-driving dataset nuScenes [5], and the panoramic street view dataset HoliCity [42]. As both datasets are LDR, we predict HDR pseudo labels from the pre-trained modeling network (Fig. 3) by lifting HoliCity LDR panoramas into HDR. In what follows, we descibe the supervision for the sky prediction branch, the lighting volume prediction branch, and the loss signal to combine the two representation.

HDR Sky Branch Losses. We train our sky branch on HoliCity [42], which contains LDR panoramas I_{pano} with sky masks M_{sky} and sun location $\mathbf{f}_{dir}$. To compute HDR pseudo labels, we feed the LDR panorama I_{pano} into the pre-trained sky network, and get the estimated sky peak intensity $\tilde{\mathbf{f}}_{intensity}$ and latent code $\tilde{\mathbf{f}}_{latent}$ as pseudo groundtruth to supervise our sky prediction branch. In a training step, we crop a perspective image I_{crop} from the panorama as input to our lighting estimation network, and predict the sky vector output $(\hat{\mathbf{f}}_{intensity}, \hat{\mathbf{f}}_{dir}, \hat{\mathbf{f}}_{latent})$ and the reconstructed HDR sky image $\hat{I}_{pano}$. We use a combination of the log-encoded L2 loss for peak intensity $(\hat{\mathbf{f}}_{intensity}, \tilde{\mathbf{f}}_{intensity})$, L1 loss for latent code $(\hat{\mathbf{f}}_{latent}, \tilde{\mathbf{f}}_{latent})$, L1 angular loss for peak direction $(\hat{\mathbf{f}}_{dir}, \mathbf{f}_{dir})$, and L1 reconstruction loss between $(\hat{I}_{pano} \odot M_{sky}, I_{pano} \odot M_{sky})$ within the LDR sky region indicated by M_{sky}.

Lighting Volume Branch Loss. Recall that images in the datasets are inherently groundtruth of a subset of the light field captured by camera sensor rays, e.g. the videos captured by self-driving cars in nuScenes [5] and the panoramas in HoliCity [42]. Meanwhile, the predicted hybrid lighting representation supports radiance query along arbitrary rays as shown in Eq. 1. Thus, we can enforce the consistency of radiance between our predicted light field and captured image groundtruth, given known camera pose and intrinsics.

Specifically, we sample images from nuScenes, and crop perspective images from HoliCity panoramas as input images. We then predict the corresponding lighting volume together with the sky dome, query the radiance of the camera rays, and enforce consistency with ground truth captured images using L2 loss. Following [37], we also render the alpha channel into a depth map and enforce consistency with groundtruth depth.

Sky Separation Loss. Intuitively, the real world camera rays that directly reach the sky should also transmit through the lighting volume and hit the sky environment map. With the losses mentioned above, the model may still fall into the degenerate case where the lighting volume completely occludes the sky. To address this, we use the sky mask M_{sky} information to supervise the sky transmittance τ_K in Eq. 1 with binary cross entropy loss.

Training Lighting via Object Insertion. Our final goal is to realistically insert virtual objects into images. We formulate the object insertion process in an end-to-end fashion and use a discriminator to supervise the perceptual lighting effects on the image editing results.

Specifically, we collect a set of high quality 3D car models from Turbosquid[1]. Given an input image, we estimate scene lighting, randomly select a 3D asset, and insert it into the scene using our object insertion module to get $\hat{I}_{edit}$. We use the map information available in nuScenes to place the car on a driveable surface. We also perform collision and occlusion checking with the depth map to avoid unrealistic object insertion due to erroneous placement. As shown in Fig. 2b, we use a discriminator to judge the quality of $\hat{I}_{edit}$ compared to real cars, and employ adversarial supervision to optimize for realism of insertion: $\mathcal{L}_{adv} = -\mathcal{D}(\hat{I}_{edit})$. Intuitively, a discriminator could easily detect erroneous shadow direction and intensity, and error in specular highlights. Through the adversarial supervision, the estimated lighting is encouraged to produce object insertion results similar to real world image samples. We refer to further analysis in the Appendix.

4 Experiments

We extensively evaluate our method both qualitatively and quantitatively. We first provide experiment details (Sect. 4.1). We then compare lighting estimation, evaluate the quality of object insertion (Sect. 4.2) and perform ablation study (Sect. 4.3). Finally, we show that our AR data helps downstream self-driving perception tasks (Sect. 4.4).

Table 1. Quantitative results of peak direction on HoliCity [42]. We outperform past work, and each component (sky modeling, adversarial supervision) helps.

Method	Median angular error ↓
Hold-Geoffroy *et al.* [16]	24.88°
Wang *et al.* [37]	53.86°
Ours	**22.43°**
Ours (w/o sky modeling)	31.45°
Ours (w/o adv. supervision)	24.16°

---

[1] www.turbosquid.com.

Table 2. Quantitative results of LDR appearance on the nuScenes dataset [5]. * indicates constraining the evaluation on the upper hemisphere.

Method	PSNR ↑	si-PSNR ↑
Hold-Geoffroy *et al.* [16]	9.33	10.73
Hold-Geoffroy *et al.* [16]*	10.81	14.20
Wang *et al.* [37]	14.06	15.28
Ours (w/o adv. supervision)	14.23	15.31
Ours	**14.49**	**15.35**

4.1 Experimental Details

Lighting Estimation. Our lighting representation combines a sky feature vector and a VSG lighting volume. We set the dimension of the sky vector to be 64 and decode it to a 64×256 HDR sky dome. Different from [37], we tailor the size of VSG lighting volume to be $256 \times 256 \times 64$ (xyz) to accommodate $300 \times 300 \times 80$ (meters^3) outdoor scenes. As outdoor scenes are larger in scale while visible scene surfaces are relatively dense in close-to-camera regions, we employ log projection to map the volume representation to a 3D scene location. Inference time of the lighting estimation network is 180 ms per image, clocked on a TITAN V GPU.

Object Insertion. Our object insertion module relies on a differentiable rendering process of both foreground object and background shadows. During training, we sample 5000 rays for foreground objects. For background shadows, we render a 160×90 resolution shadow map and sample 450 rays per pixel to save memory and computation. After training, we do importance sampling for each pixel in foreground and can afford a high resolution shadow map for background to generate more realistic effects. During inference time, we also have the option to use commercial renderer such as Blender [9], which we detail in the Appendix.

Datasets. We collected 724 outdoor HDR panoramas from online HDRI databases to train the sky encoder-decoder. We train the full model with nuScenes [5] and HoliCity [42]. For nuScenes, we use the official split containing 700 scenes for training and 150 scenes for evaluation. For HoliCity dataset, we apply 90% v.s. 10% data split for training and evaluation.

Multi-view Extension. While we focus on monocular estimation, our model is extendable to multi-view input. It can consume multi-view images to predict more accurate lighting, as shown in Fig. 6. For the HDR sky prediction branch, we apply max pooling for $f_{intensity}$, f_{latent}, and average pooling to f_{dir} after rotating f_{dir} in different views to the canonical view. As for the volumetric lighting, since it is defined in the "world" coordinate space, we unproject and fuse multi-view images into a common lighting volume representation, akin to [30].

Table 3. Quantitative results of user study. Users compare baseline methods to an ablated version of our method (Ours w/o adv. supervision) in a pair-wise comparison. Each row reports the percentage of images that Ours w/o adv. supervision is preferred. Our method outperforms baselines, and adv. supervision improves performance.

Approach	% Ours (w/o adv. sup.) is preferred ↓
Hold-Geoffroy *et al.* [16]	68.1 ± 5.4 %
Wang *et al.* [37]	94.2 ± 2.0 %
Ours	**40.6 ± 10.2 %**

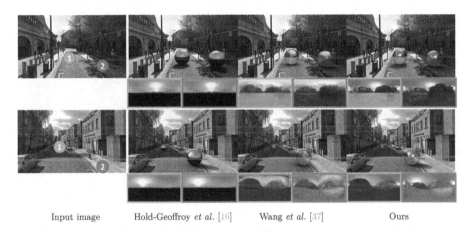

Input image   Hold-Geoffroy *et al.* [16]   Wang *et al.* [37]   Ours

Fig. 4. Qualitative comparison of lighting estimation. We insert a purely specular sphere into the image to visualize the lighting prediction, and display the environment maps on the bottom. Note the sun and environment map changes between locations.

4.2 Evaluation of Lighting Estimation

Baselines. We compare with current state-of-the-art lighting estimation methods [16,37]. Hold-Geoffroy *et al.* [16] estimates the HDR sky environment map from a single image. Wang *et al.* [37] predicts Volumetric Spherical Gaussian. We re-train or finetune these methods on the same data sources we used for our method to ensure a fair comparison.

HDR Evaluation of Peak Direction. We evaluate peak direction prediction on HoliCity dataset [42]. We report the median angular error between the predicted direction and GT in Table 1. Wang *et al.* [37] predicts HDR component in a self-supervised manner and cannot learn strong peaks. We also outperform Hold-Geoffroy *et al.* [16], which separately predicts a sky dome and its azimuth.

LDR Evaluation of Novel View Reconstruction. Recall that any lighting representation, such as environment map and our hybrid lighting, aims to

| Input image | Hold-Geoffroy *et al.* [16] | Wang *et al.* [37] | Ours |

Fig. 5. Qualitative comparison of virtual object insertion. Our method produces realistic cast shadows and high-frequency "clear coat" effects.

| Input image | Inside shadow | Shadow boundary | Outside shadow |

Fig. 6. Qualitative results of spatially-varying shadow effects. Our method can handle the spatial changes of shadow intensity around shadow boundary, not possible previously. (Results take six surrounding perspective views as input.)

represent the complete or a subset of the light field, which can be rendered into images by querying the radiance function with specified camera rays. Prior work [34,37] proposed to use novel view radiance reconstruction PSNR as quantitative evaluation of the quality of lighting estimation, which we report on nuScenes dataset [5].

As the nuScenes-captured images may have different exposure values, we report both PSNR and scale invariant PSNR (si-PSNR) in Table 2. For the latter, we multiply the predicted novel view with a scaling factor that minimizes L2 error. Since Hold-Geoffroy *et al.* [16] only predicts lighting on the upper hemisphere, we also constrain the evaluation on the upper hemisphere to make a fair comparison. Our method outperforms both baselines with a large margin, as [16] ignores spatially-varying effects and usually predicts a sky dome with little high-frequency details. Our method also outperforms Wang *et al.* [37] which cannot handle high HDR intensity of an outdoor scene.

Human Study. To quantitatively evaluate the quality of object insertion, we perform a human study with Amazon Mechanical Turk, where we show two augmented images, randomly permuted, produced by our method and by the baseline. We then ask users to compare the realism of the inserted object, e.g. the cast shadows and the reflections, and select the more realistic image. For each comparison, we invite 15 users to judge 23 examples. We adopt majority vote for the preference of each example, and run three times to report mean and stan-

Initial editing   After optimization   Initial editing   After optimization

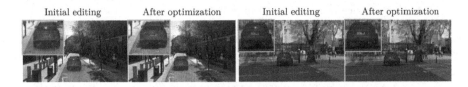

Fig. 7. Discriminator test-time optimization. Note the discriminator corrects the shadow direction (left), and removes erroneous specular highlight (right). The pixelated effect is due to low-resolution rendering during end-to-end training.

dard deviation in Table 3. The ablated version of Ours (w/o adv. supervision) outperforms baselines, indicating the hybrid lighting representation improves upon prior works. Comparing Ours and Ours (w/o adv. supervision), the results indicate including adversarial supervision leads to more visually realistic editing.

Qualitative Comparison. We first visualize the environment maps at different scene locations and insertion of a purely specular sphere in Fig. 4. Hold-Geoffroy *et al.* [16] only predicts one environment lighting and ignored spatially-varying effects. For inserted spheres around shadowed region, it still produces strong cast shadows. Also, the high-frequency details are not well preserved in the sky prediction. Wang *et al.* [37] can generate high-frequency details but fails to handle the extreme HDR intensity of the outdoor scene, and thus cannot generate realistic cast shadows. Our method is the only one that handles extreme HDR, angular details and spatially-varying lighting. We show virtual object insertion results in Fig. 5. Our lighting prediction preserves high-frequency details with HDR intensity, producing realistic highlights and clear coating effects, while prior method cannot generate such effects.

Spatially-Varying Shadows. Benefiting from the accurate HDR sky and surrounding scene estimation, our method can produce spatially-varying shadow effects. As shown in Fig. 6, the car casts an intense shadow when outside the shadow of the building, while the shadow caused by the car is much weaker when the car is inside the shadow region. Especially, it also shows reasonably different shadow intensity around the shadow boundary. This challenging effect requires accurate prediction of direction, intensity and geometry of HDR lighting, and will not occur with an incapable lighting representation.

4.3   Ablation Study

We verify the effectiveness of the sky decoder module and the adversarial supervision. In Table 1, compared to the ablated version that directly predict sky dome as an environment map (denoted as "Ours w/o sky modeling"), the full model reduces the error by around 50%, which demonstrates the sky modeling network is important for achieving accurate sun position prediction in outdoor scenes.

Table 4. Performance of a SOTA 3D object detector [36] on nuScenes benchmark. mAP represents the mean for the 10 object categories. We report individual categories that saw a significant boost (full table in the Appendix).

Method	mAP	Car	Bus	Trailer	Const.vehicle	Bicycle
Real data	0.190	0.356	0.124	0.011	0.016	0.116
+ Aug no light	0.201	0.363	0.163	0.029	<u>0.021</u>	0.120
+ Aug light	**0.211**	<u>0.369</u>	<u>0.182</u>	<u>0.036</u>	0.020	<u>0.146</u>

Adversarial supervision improves the performance on quantitative evaluation in Tables 1, 2, especially for peak direction estimation, which indicates that discriminating on the final image editing result is complementary to existing supervision and benefits lighting prediction. In the user study (Table 3), adversarial supervision improves perceptual realism and receives a higher user preference. We also qualitatively visualize the behaviour of the discriminator in Fig. 7. To understand the "photorealism" implicitly perceived by the discriminator during the training process, we perform test-time optimization on the object insertion results to minimize the adversarial loss, and show the optimized results in Fig. 7. In the first example, the initial editing results fail to predict the correct sun location and produce wrong shadows. After test-time optimization, the shadow direction points to the bottom-left of the image and the shadow intensity also matches the visual cues from the rest of the scene. In the second example, the initial editing results contain an obviously erroneous highlight, and the discriminator detects the artifact and removes it. This agrees with the intuition that a neural discriminator have the capacity to catch lighting effects such as cast shadows and incorrect specular highlights. Further details are included in the Appendix.

4.4   Downstream Perception Task

We investigate the benefits of our object insertion as data augmentation for a downstream 3D object detection task on nuScenes. The goal of this task is to place a 3D bounding box for 10 different object categories. We first train a state-of-the-art monocular 3D detector [36] on a 10% subset of real data from the nuScenes training set. This subset was chosen randomly across all scenes but in a way that the number of objects per category resembles the original nuScenes training set. We then augment the front-camera images of this subset with our method. Specifically, we collect a set of 3D models with categories of *car* and *construction vehicles*, and randomly insert one object per image. Our augmented dataset has approximately 15K augmented (new) images. We use the same training strategy and model hyperparameters as [36] but do not supervise attributes or velocity as these are not present for the augmented data. Quantitatively, in Table 4 we can observe that the performance of the detector improves by 2% when comparing to real data. Moreover, we can also see that while naively adding objects leads to a 1% improvement, another 1% is a result of having better light estimation. Interestingly, we can also notice that the performance of the object detector also improves in different categories even though we do not directly augment those.

5 Discussion

In this paper, we proposed a hybrid representation of lighting and a novel differentiable object insertion module that allows end-to-end optimization of AR objectives. In a variety of comparisons, we demonstrate the effectiveness of our approach in lighting estimation. Furthermore, we showcase performance gains on a 3D object detection task when training the detector on our augmented dataset.

While our method presents an effective way of rendering 3D assets into images, some limitations remain for future work. Currently, the inserted virtual object pixels do not pass the same capturing process as the background scene, and the shadow rendering assumes Lambertian surface. Modeling of camera ISP, weather, and non-Lambertian scene materials can be interesting directions for future work.

References

1. Adelson, E.H., Bergen, J.R.: The plenoptic function and the elements of early vision. In: Computational Models of Visual Processing, pp. 3–20. MIT Press (1991)
2. Alhaija, H.A., Mustikovela, S.K., Mescheder, L., Geiger, A., Rother, C.: Augmented reality meets computer vision: efficient data generation for urban driving scenes. Int. J. Comput. Vis. **126**(9), 961–972 (2018)
3. Boss, M., Jampani, V., Kim, K., Lensch, H., Kautz, J.: Two-shot spatially-varying BRDF and shape estimation. In: Proceedings of the IEEE/CVF Conference on Computer Vision and Pattern Recognition, pp. 3982–3991 (2020)
4. Burley, B., Studios, W.D.A.: Physically-based shading at disney. In: ACM SIGGRAPH, vol. 2012, pp. 1–7 (2012)
5. Caesar, H., et al.: nuscenes: a multimodal dataset for autonomous driving. arXiv preprint arXiv:1903.11027 (2019)
6. Chen, W., et al.: Learning to predict 3D objects with an interpolation-based differentiable renderer. In: NeurIPS (2019)
7. Chen, W., et al.: DIB-R++: learning to predict lighting and material with a hybrid differentiable renderer. In: Advances in Neural Information Processing Systems (NeurIPS) (2021)
8. Chen, Y., et al.: GeoSim: realistic video simulation via geometry-aware composition for self-driving. In: CVPR (2021)
9. Community, B.O.: Blender - a 3D modelling and rendering package. Blender Foundation, Stichting Blender Foundation, Amsterdam (2018). http://www.blender.org
10. Dwibedi, D., Misra, I., Hebert, M.: Cut, paste and learn: Surprisingly easy synthesis for instance detection. In: The IEEE International Conference on Computer Vision (ICCV), October 2017

11. Gardner, M.A., Hold-Geoffroy, Y., Sunkavalli, K., Gagné, C., Lalonde, J.F.: Deep parametric indoor lighting estimation. In: Proceedings of the IEEE International Conference on Computer Vision, pp. 7175–7183 (2019)
12. Gardner, M.A., et al.: Learning to predict indoor illumination from a single image. arXiv preprint arXiv:1704.00090 (2017)
13. Garon, M., Sunkavalli, K., Hadap, S., Carr, N., Lalonde, J.F.: Fast spatially-varying indoor lighting estimation. In: Proceedings of the IEEE Conference on Computer Vision and Pattern Recognition, pp. 6908–6917 (2019)
14. Guizilini, V., Ambrus, R., Pillai, S., Raventos, A., Gaidon, A.: 3D packing for self-supervised monocular depth estimation. In: IEEE Conference on Computer Vision and Pattern Recognition (CVPR) (2020)
15. He, K., Zhang, X., Ren, S., Sun, J.: Deep residual learning for image recognition. CoRR abs/1512.03385 (2015). arxiv.org:1512.03385
16. Hold-Geoffroy, Y., Athawale, A., Lalonde, J.F.: Deep sky modeling for single image outdoor lighting estimation. In: Proceedings of the IEEE/CVF Conference on Computer Vision and Pattern Recognition, pp. 6927–6935 (2019)
17. Hold-Geoffroy, Y., Sunkavalli, K., Hadap, S., Gambaretto, E., Lalonde, J.F.: Deep outdoor illumination estimation. In: Proceedings of the IEEE Conference on Computer Vision and Pattern Recognition, pp. 7312–7321 (2017)
18. Hong, S., Yan, X., Huang, T.E., Lee, H.: Learning hierarchical semantic image manipulation through structured representations. In: Advances in Neural Information Processing Systems, pp. 2713–2723 (2018)
19. Karis, B., Games, E.: Real shading in unreal engine 4. Proc. Phys. Based Shading Theory Pract. 4(3), 1 (2013)
20. Kim, S.W., Philion, J., Torralba, A., Fidler, S.: DriveGAN: towards a controllable high-quality neural simulation. In: IEEE Conference on Computer Vision and Pattern Recognition (CVPR) (2021)
21. LeGendre, C., et al.: DeepLight: learning illumination for unconstrained mobile mixed reality. In: Proceedings of the IEEE Conference on Computer Vision and Pattern Recognition, pp. 5918–5928 (2019)
22. Li, T.M., Aittala, M., Durand, F., Lehtinen, J.: Differentiable monte Carlo ray tracing through edge sampling. ACM Trans. Graph. (Proc. SIGGRAPH Asia) 37(6), 222:1–222:11 (2018)
23. Li, Z., Shafiei, M., Ramamoorthi, R., Sunkavalli, K., Chandraker, M.: Inverse rendering for complex indoor scenes: shape, spatially-varying lighting and SVBRDF from a single image. In: Proceedings of the IEEE/CVF Conference on Computer Vision and Pattern Recognition, pp. 2475–2484 (2020)
24. Li, Z., Xu, Z., Ramamoorthi, R., Sunkavalli, K., Chandraker, M.: Learning to reconstruct shape and spatially-varying reflectance from a single image. ACM Trans. Graph. (TOG) 37(6), 1–11 (2018)
25. Ling, H., Acuna, D., Kreis, K., Kim, S.W., Fidler, S.: Variational a modal object completion. Adv. Neural Inf. Process. Syst. 33, 16246–16257 (2020)
26. Mescheder, L., Oechsle, M., Niemeyer, M., Nowozin, S., Geiger, A.: Occupancy networks: learning 3D reconstruction in function space. In: Proceedings of the IEEE Conference on Computer Vision and Pattern Recognition, pp. 4460–4470 (2019)
27. Nimier-David, M., Vicini, D., Zeltner, T., Jakob, W.: Mitsuba 2: a retargetable forward and inverse renderer. Trans. Graph. (Proceedings of SIGGRAPH Asia) 38(6) (2019). https://doi.org/10.1145/3355089.3356498

28. Ost, J., Mannan, F., Thuerey, N., Knodt, J., Heide, F.: Neural scene graphs for dynamic scenes. In: Proceedings of the IEEE/CVF Conference on Computer Vision and Pattern Recognition (CVPR), pp. 2856–2865, June 2021
29. Peers, P., Tamura, N., Matusik, W., Debevec, P.: Post-production facial performance relighting using reflectance transfer. ACM Trans. Graph. (TOG) **26**(3), 52-es (2007)
30. Philion, J., Fidler, S.: Lift, splat, shoot: Encoding images from arbitrary camera rigs by implicitly unprojecting to 3D. arXiv preprint arXiv:2008.05711 (2020). https://doi.org/10.1007/978-3-030-58568-6_12
31. Sengupta, S., Gu, J., Kim, K., Liu, G., Jacobs, D.W., Kautz, J.: Neural inverse rendering of an indoor scene from a single image. In: International Conference on Computer Vision (ICCV) (2019)
32. Somanath, G., Kurz, D.: HDR environment map estimation for real-time augmented reality. In: Proceedings of the IEEE/CVF Conference on Computer Vision and Pattern Recognition (2021)
33. Song, S., Funkhouser, T.: Neural illumination: lighting prediction for indoor environments. In: Proceedings of the IEEE Conference on Computer Vision and Pattern Recognition, pp. 6918–6926 (2019)
34. Srinivasan, P.P., Mildenhall, B., Tancik, M., Barron, J.T., Tucker, R., Snavely, N.: Lighthouse: predicting lighting volumes for spatially-coherent illumination. In: Proceedings of the IEEE/CVF Conference on Computer Vision and Pattern Recognition, pp. 8080–8089 (2020)
35. Su, H., Qi, C.R., Li, Y., Guibas, L.J.: Render for CNN: viewpoint estimation in images using CNNs trained with rendered 3d model views. In: The IEEE International Conference on Computer Vision (ICCV), December 2015
36. Wang, T., Zhu, X., Pang, J., Lin, D.: FCOS3D: fully convolutional one-stage monocular 3D object detection. arXiv preprint arXiv:2104.10956 (2021)
37. Wang, Z., Philion, J., Fidler, S., Kautz, J.: Learning indoor inverse rendering with 3D spatially-varying lighting. In: Proceedings of International Conference on Computer Vision (ICCV) (2021)
38. Wei, X., Chen, G., Dong, Y., Lin, S., Tong, X.: Object-based illumination estimation with rendering-aware neural networks. arXiv preprint arXiv:2008.02514 (2020). https://doi.org/10.1007/978-3-030-58555-6_23
39. Zhang, J., Sunkavalli, K., Hold-Geoffroy, Y., Hadap, S., Eisenman, J., Lalonde, J.F.: All-weather deep outdoor lighting estimation. In: Proceedings of the IEEE Conference on Computer Vision and Pattern Recognition, pp. 10158–10166 (2019)
40. Zhang, Y., et al.: Image GANs meet differentiable rendering for inverse graphics and interpretable 3D neural rendering. In: International Conference on Learning Representations (2021)
41. Zhao, Y., Guo, T.: Pointar: Efficient lighting estimation for mobile augmented reality. arXiv preprint arXiv:2004.00006 (2020). https://doi.org/10.1007/978-3-030-58592-1_40
42. Zhou, Y., Huang, J., Dai, X., Luo, L., Chen, Z., Ma, Y.: HoliCity: A city-scale data platform for learning holistic 3D structures (2020). arXiv:2008.03286 [cs.CV]
43. Zhu, Y., Zhang, Y., Li, S., Shi, B.: Spatially-varying outdoor lighting estimation from intrinsics. In: CVPR (2021)

Perspective Phase Angle Model for Polarimetric 3D Reconstruction

Guangcheng Chen[1,2] (ID), Li He[2,3] (ID), Yisheng Guan[1] (ID), and Hong Zhang[2,3(✉)] (ID)

[1] Guangdong University of Technology, Guangzhou, China
2112001004@mail2.gdut.edu.cn
[2] Southern University of Science and Technology, Shenzhen, China
{hel,hzhang}@sustech.edu.cn
[3] Shenzhen Key Laboratory of Robotics and Computer Vision, Shenzhen, China
ysguan@gdut.edu.cn
https://github.com/GCChen97/ppa4p3d

Abstract. Current polarimetric 3D reconstruction methods, including those in the well-established shape from polarization literature, are all developed under the orthographic projection assumption. In the case of a large field of view, however, this assumption does not hold and may result in significant reconstruction errors in methods that make this assumption. To address this problem, we present the *perspective phase angle (PPA) model* that is applicable to perspective cameras. Compared with the orthographic model, the proposed PPA model accurately describes the relationship between polarization phase angle and surface normal under perspective projection. In addition, the PPA model makes it possible to estimate surface normals from only one single-view phase angle map and does not suffer from the so-called π-ambiguity problem. Experiments on real data show that the PPA model is more accurate for surface normal estimation with a perspective camera than the orthographic model.

Keywords: Polarization image · Phase angle · Perspective projection · 3D Reconstruction

1 Introduction

The property that the polarization state of light encodes geometric information of object surfaces has been researched in computer vision for decades. With the development of the division-of-focal-plane (DoFP) polarization image sensor [23] in recent years, there has been a resurgent interest in 3D reconstruction with polarization information. In the last decade, it has been shown that polarization information can be used to enhance the performance of traditional reconstruction methods of textureless and non-Lambertian surfaces [2,17,21,26]. For accurate reconstruction of objects, shape from polarization and photo-polarimetric

Supplementary Information The online version contains supplementary material available at https://doi.org/10.1007/978-3-031-20086-1_23.

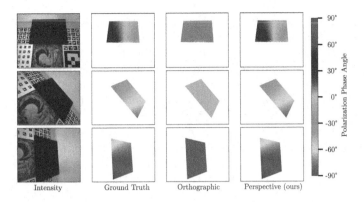

Fig. 1. Comparison of polarization phase angle maps of a black glossy board in three views. The first column shows intensity images. The second column shows the ground-truth phase angle maps calculated from polarization images. The third and the fourth columns show the phase angle maps calculated from the OPA model and our proposed PPA model, respectively.

stereo can recover fine-grain details [10,26] of the surfaces. For dense mapping in textureless or specular scenes, multi-view stereo can also be improved with polarimetric cues [5,7,21,30].

In computer vision and robotics, the use of perspective cameras is common. However, in all the previous literature on polarimetric 3D reconstruction, to the best of our knowledge, the use of polarization and its derivation are without exception under the orthographic projection assumption. Therefore, the dense maps or shapes generated by these methods from polarization images captured by perspective cameras will be flawed without considering the perspective effect. In this paper, we present an accurate model of perspective cameras for polarimetric 3D reconstruction.

One of the key steps in polarimetric 3D reconstruction is the optimization of depth maps with a linear constraint on surface normals by the polarization phase angles. In this paper, we refer to this constraint as the *phase angle constraint*. This constraint was first proposed in [27] under the orthographic projection assumption and has become a standard practice of utilizing the phase angles. In the literature, this constraint has been derived from a model, which we refer to as the *orthographic phase angle (OPA) model* in this paper, where the azimuth of the normal is equivalent to the phase angle [7,20]. If observed objects are in the middle of the field of view in a 3D reconstruction application, orthographic projection could be a reasonable assumption. However, for dense mapping and large objects, this assumption is easily violated.

In this work, an alternative *perspective phase angle (PPA) model* is developed to solve this problem. The PPA model is inspired by the geometric properties of a polarizer in [13]. Different from the OPA model, the proposed PPA model defines the phase angle as the direction of the intersecting line of the image plane and the plane of incident (PoI) spanned by the light ray and the surface normal (see Fig. 2 for details). As shown in Fig. 1, given the ground-truth normal of the black board in the images, the phase angle maps calculated using the proposed PPA model are much more accurate than those using the OPA model. Under perspective projection, we also derive a new linear constraint on the surface normal by the phase angle, which we refer to as the *PPA constraint*. As a useful by-product of our PPA model, the PPA constraint makes it possible to estimate surface normal using only one single-view phase angle map without suffering from the well-known π-ambiguity problem, which requires at least two views to resolve as shown in previous works [19,27]. In addition, the PPA constraint leads to improved the accuracy of normal estimation from phase angle maps of multiple views [15,27]. The main contributions of this paper are summarized as follows:

- A perspective phase angle model and a corresponding constraint on surface normals by polariztion phase angles are proposed. The model and the constraint serve as the basis for accurately estimating surface normals from phase angles.
- A novel method is developed to estimate surface normals from a *single-view* phase angle map. The method does not suffer from the π-ambiguity problem as does a method using the orthographic phase angle model.
- We make use of the proposed model and the corresponding constraint to improve surface normal estimation from phase angle maps of *multiple views*.

The rest of this paper is organized as follows. Section 2 overviews related works. Section 3 reviews the utilization of polarization phase angles under orthographic projection. Section 4 describes our proposed PPA model, PPA constraint and normal estimation methods. Experimental evaluation is presented in Sect. 5. The conclusion of this paper and the discussions of our future work are presented in Sect. 6.

2   Related Works

The proposed PPA model is fundamental to polarimetric 3D reconstruction and thus it is related to the following three topics: 1) shape and depth estimation from single-view polarization images, 2) multi-view reconstruction with additional polarization information and 3) camera pose estimation with polarization information.

2.1   Polarimetric Single-View Shape and Depth Estimation

This topic is closely related to two lines of research: shape from polarization (SfP) and photo-polarimetric stereo. SfP first estimates surface normals that are parameterized in the OPA model by azimuth and zenith angles from polarization phase angles and degree of linear polarization and then obtains Cartesian height maps by integrating the normal maps [2,17]. With additional spectral cues, refractive distortion [12] of SfP can be solved [11]. Alternatively, it has been shown that the surface normals, refractive indexes, and light directions can be estimated from photometric and polarimetric constraints [18]. The recent work of DeepSfP [4] is the first attempt to use a convolutional neural network (CNN) to estimate normal maps from polarization images. It is reasonable to expect more accurate surface normal estimation when these methods parameterize the surface normal with the help of the proposed PPA model in perspective cameras. In fact, a recent work shows that learning-based SfP can benefit from considering the perspective effect [14]. Regardless, as a two-stage method, SfP is sensitive to noise.

As a one-stage method, photo-polarimetric stereo directly estimates a height map from polarization images and is able to avoid cumulative errors and suppress noise. By constructing linear constraints on surface heights from illumination and polarization, height map estimation is solved through the optimization of a non-convex cost function [22]. Yu et al. [31] derives a fully differentiable method that is able to optimize a height map through non-linear least squares optimization. In [26], variations of the photo-polarimetric stereo method are unified as a framework incorporating different optional photometric and polarimetric constraints. In these works, the OPA constraint is a key to exploiting polarization during height map estimation. In perspective cameras, the proposed PPA constraint can provide a more accurate description than the OPA constraint.

2.2   Polarimetric Multi-View 3D Reconstruction

Surface reconstruction can be solved by optimizing a set of functionals given phase angle maps of three different views [20]. To address transparent objects, a two-view method [17] exploits phase angles and degree of linear polarization to solve correspondences and polarization ambiguity. Another two-view method [3] uses both polarimetric and photometric cues to estimate reflectance functions and reconstruct shapes of practical and complex objects. By combining space carving and normal estimation, [16] is able to solve polarization ambiguity problems and obtain more accurate reconstructions of black objects than pure space carving. Fukao et al. [10] models polarized reflection of mesoscopic surfaces and proposes polarimetric normal stereo for estimating normals of mesoscopic surfaces whose polarization depends on illumination (i.e., polarization by light [6]). These works are all based on the OPA model without considering the perspective effect.

Recently, traditional multi-view 3D reconstruction methods enhanced by polarization prove to be able to densely reconstruct textureless and non-Lambertian surfaces under uncalibrated illumination [7,21,30]. Cui et al. [7] proposes polarimetric multi-view stereo to handle real-world objects with mixed polarization and solve polarization ambiguity problems. Yang et al. [30] proposes a polarimetric monocular dense SLAM system that propagates sparse depths in textureless scenes in parallel. Shakeri et al. [21] uses relative depth maps generated by a CNN to solve the $\pi/2$-ambiguity problem robustly and efficiently in polarimetric dense map reconstruction. In these works, iso-depth contour tracing [33] is a common step to propagate sparse depths on textureless or specular surfaces. It is based on the proposition that, with the OPA model, the direction perpendicular to the phase angle is the tangent direction of an iso-depth contour [7]. However, in a perspective camera, this proposition is only an approximation.

Besides, the OPA constraint can be integrated in stereo matching [5], depth optimization [30] and mesh refinement [32]. However, only the first two components of the surface normal are involved in the constraint, in addition to its inaccuracy in perspective cameras. With the proposed PPA model, all three components of a surface normal are constrained and the constraint is theoretically accurate for a perspective camera.

2.3   Polarimetric Camera Pose Estimation

The polarization phase angle of light emitted from a surface point depends on the camera pose. Therefore, it is intuitive to use this cue for camera pose estimation. Chen *et al.* [6] proposes polarimetric three-view geometry that connects the phase angle and three-view geometry and theoretically requires six triplets of corresponding 2D points to determine the three rotations between the views. Different from using only phase angles in [6], Cui *et al.* [8] exploits full polarization information including degree of linear polarization to estimate relative poses so that only two 2D-point correspondences are needed. The method achieves competitive accuracy with the traditional five 2D-point method. Since both works are developed without considering the perspective effect, the proposed PPA model can be used to generalize them to a perspective camera.

3   Preliminaries

In this section, we review methods for phase angle estimation from polarization images, as well as the OPA model and the corresponding OPA constraint that are commonly adopted in the existing literature.

3.1   Phase Angle Estimation

As a function of the orientation of the polarizer ϕ, the intensity of unpolarized light is attenuated sinusoidally as $I(\phi) = I_{avg} + \rho I_{avg} \cos(2(\phi - \varphi))$. The parameters of polarization state are the average intensity I_{avg}, the degree of linear polarization (DoLP) ρ and the phase angle φ. The phase angle is also called the angle of linear polarization (AoLP) in [21, 24, 28, 32]. In this paper, we uniformly use the term "phase angle" to refer to AoLP.

Given images captured through a polarizer at a minimum of three different orientations, the polarization state can be estimated by solving a linear system [30]. For a DoFP polarization camera that captures four images $I(0), I(\frac{\pi}{4}), I(\frac{\pi}{2})$ and $I(\frac{3\pi}{4})$ in one shot, the polarization state can be extracted from the Stokes vector $\mathbf{s} = [s_0, s_1, s_2]^T$ as follows:

$$I_{avg} = \frac{s_0}{2}, \; \varphi = \frac{1}{2}\text{arctan2}(s_2, s_1), \; \rho = \frac{\sqrt{s_1^2 + s_2^2}}{s_0} \tag{1}$$

where $s_o = I(0) + I(\frac{\pi}{2})$, $s_1 = I(0) - I(\frac{\pi}{2})$ and $s_1 = I(\frac{\pi}{4}) - I(\frac{3\pi}{4})$. Although it has been shown that further optimization of the polarization state from multi-channel polarization images is possible [25], for this paper, Eq. (1) is sufficiently accurate for us to generate ground-truth phase angle maps from polarization images.

3.2 The OPA Model

The phase angles estimated from polarization images through Eq. (1) are directly related to the surface normals off which light is reflected. It is this property that is exploited in polarimetric 3D reconstruction research to estimate surface normal from polarization images. Model of projection, which defines how light enters the camera, is another critical consideration in order to establish the relationship between the phase angle and the surface normal.

The OPA model assumes that all light rays enter the camera in parallel, as shown by the blue plane in Fig. 2, so that the azimuth angle of the surface normal $\mathbf{n}$ is equivalent to the phase angle φ_o up to a $\pi/2$-ambiguity and a π-ambiguity [32]. Specifically, $\mathbf{n}$ can be parameterized by the phase angle φ_o and the zenith angle θ in the camera coordinate system:

$$\mathbf{n} = \begin{bmatrix} n_x, n_y, n_z \end{bmatrix}^T = \begin{bmatrix} \cos\varphi_o \sin\theta, \; -\sin\varphi_o \sin\theta, \; \cos\theta \end{bmatrix}^T \tag{2}$$

With this model, φ_o can be calculated from $\mathbf{n}$ as

$$\varphi_o = -\text{arctan2}(n_y, n_x) \tag{3}$$

We can use Eq. (3) to evaluate the accuracy of the OPA model. I.e., if the OPA model is accurate, then the phase angle calculated by Eq. (3) should agree with that estimated from the polarization images. Although this model is based on the orthographic projection assumption, it is widely adopted in polarimetric 3D reconstruction methods even when polarization images are captured by a camera with perspective projection. In addition, Eq. (2) defines a constraint on $\mathbf{n}$ by φ_o, i.e., the OPA constraint:

$$\begin{bmatrix} \sin\varphi_o, \cos\varphi_o, 0 \end{bmatrix} \cdot \mathbf{n} = 0 \tag{4}$$

This linear constraint is commonly integrated in depth map optimization [7,26, 30]. It is also the basis of iso-depth contour tracing [1,7] as it gives the tangent direction of an iso-depth contour. Obviously, this constraint is strictly valid only in the case of orthographic projection.

4 Phase Angle Model Under Perspective Projection

In the perspective camera model, light rays that enter the camera are subject to the perspective effect as illustrated by the red plane in Fig. 2. As a result, the

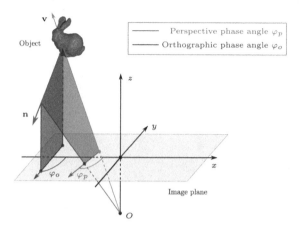

Fig. 2. Definitions of the polarization phase angle of the two models under orthographic projection (φ_o) and perspective projection (φ_p). O is the optical center of the camera. The blue plane and the red plane are the two PoIs, corresponding to the two (orthographic and perspective) projection models. (Color figure online)

estimated phase angle by Eq. (1) not only depends on the direction of the surface normal **n** but also on the direction **v** in which the light ray enters the camera. In this section, the PPA model is developed to describe the relationship between the polarization phase angle and the surface normal. The PPA constraint naturally results from the PPA model as well as two methods for normal estimation from the phase angles.

4.1   The PPA Model

The geometric properties of a polarizer in [13] inspire us to model the phase angle as the direction of the intersecting line of the image plane and the PoI spanned by the light ray and the surface normal. As shown in Fig. 2, there is an obvious difference between the two definitions of the phase angle, depending upon the assumed type of projection.

Specifically, let the optical axis be $\mathbf{z} = [0,0,1]^T$ and the light ray be $\mathbf{v} = [v_x, v_y, v_z]^T = K^{-1}\mathbf{x}/\|K^{-1}\mathbf{x}\|$, for an image point at the pixel coordinates $\mathbf{x} = [u, v, 1]^T$ and a camera with intrinsic matrix K. From Fig. 2, the PPA model can be formulated as follows:

$$\mathbf{z} \times (\mathbf{v} \times \mathbf{n}) = \left[-v_z n_x + v_x n_z, \ -v_z n_y + v_y n_z, \ 0\right]^T = c \cdot \mathbf{d} \tag{5}$$

where **z**, **v** and **n** are normalized to 1, c is a constant and $\mathbf{d} = [\cos\varphi_p, -\sin\varphi_p, 0]^T$. From Eq. (5), the phase angle φ_p can be obtained from **n** and **v** as:

$$\varphi_p = -\arctan2(-v_z n_y + v_y n_z, \ -v_z n_x + v_x n_z) \tag{6}$$

Similar to Eq. (3), Eq. (6) can also be used for evaluating the accuracy of the PPA model. Different from φ_o, φ_p not only depends on the surface normal $\mathbf{n}$ but also on the light ray $\mathbf{v}$.

In addition, $\mathbf{n}$ can be parameterized by φ_p and θ as $\mathbf{n} = -(e^{\theta \mathbf{a}_p^\wedge})\mathbf{v}$ where $\mathbf{a}_p = \mathbf{d} \times \mathbf{v}/\|\mathbf{d} \times \mathbf{v}\|$ is the normal of the PoI and $\mathbf{r}^\wedge$ represents the skew-symmetric matrix of $\mathbf{r} \in \mathbb{R}^3$. Equation (2) can also be reformulated into a similar form as $\mathbf{n} = -(e^{\theta \mathbf{a}_o^\wedge})\mathbf{v}$ where $\mathbf{a}_o = [-\sin \varphi_o, \cos \varphi_o, 0]^T$. Obviously, the difference of the two parameterizations of $\mathbf{n}$ is the axis about which $\mathbf{v}$ rotates.

With the PPA model, the PPA constraint can be derived from Eq. (5) as follows:

$$\left[\sin \varphi_p, \cos \varphi_p, -\frac{(v_y \cos \varphi_p + v_x \sin \varphi_p)}{v_z} \right] \cdot \mathbf{n} = 0 \qquad (7)$$

Note that Eq. (7) can be used just as the OPA constraint Eq. (4), without the knowledge of object geometry since $\mathbf{v}$ is a scene-independent directional vector. Compared with Eq. (4), Eq. (7) has an additional constraint on the third component of the normal. This additional constraint is critical in allowing us to estimate $\mathbf{n}$ of a planar surface from a single view as we will show in the next section. Table 1 summaries the definitions of the phase angle, the normal and the constraint of the OPA and PPA models.

Table 1. Summary of the OPA and PPA models

	OPA model	PPA model
Phase angle	$-\arctan2(n_y, n_x)$	$-\arctan2(-v_z n_y + v_y n_z, \\ -v_z n_x + v_x n_z)$
Normal	$\mathbf{n} = -e^{\theta \mathbf{a}_o^\wedge} \cdot \mathbf{v}$	$\mathbf{n} = -e^{\theta \mathbf{a}_p^\wedge} \cdot \mathbf{v}$
Constraint	$\begin{bmatrix} \sin \varphi_o \\ \cos \varphi_o \\ 0 \end{bmatrix}^T \cdot \mathbf{n} = 0$	$\begin{bmatrix} \sin \varphi_p \\ \cos \varphi_p \\ -\dfrac{(v_y \cos \varphi_p + v_x \sin \varphi_p)}{v_z} \end{bmatrix}^T \cdot \mathbf{n} = 0$

4.2   Relations with the OPA Model

Comparing the two constraints in Table 1, the coefficient $-(v_y \cos \varphi_p + v_x \sin \varphi_p)/v_z$ implies that there exist four cases in which the two models are equivalent:

1. $\mathbf{v} = [0, 0, 1]^T$, when the light ray is parallel to the optical axis, which corresponds to orthographic projection.

2. $[v_x, v_y]^T \parallel [\cos \varphi_p, -\sin \varphi_p]^T \parallel [n_x, n_y]^T$, when the PoI is perpendicular to the image plane.

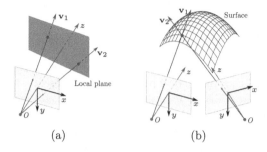

Fig. 3. Two cases of surface normal estimation from phase angle map(s). (a) Single-view normal estimation and (b) Multi-view normal estimation.

3. $n_z \rightarrow 1$, when the normal tends to be parallel to the optical axis. In this case, the PoI is also perpendicular to the image plane.

4. $n_z = 0$, when the normal is perpendicular to the optical axis.

Besides, according to Eq. (3) and Eq. (4), if $n_z = 1$, the OPA model and the OPA constraint will become degenerate whereas ours will still be useful.

4.3   Normal Estimation

Theoretically, a surface normal can be solved from at least its two observations with the PPA constraint. The observations can either be the phase angles from multiple pixels in the same phase angle map or from phase angle maps of multiple views as shown in Fig. 3. The two cases lead to the following two methods.

Single-View Normal Estimation. In the same phase angle map, if a set of phase angles of the points share the same surface normal, e.g., points in a local plane or points in different parallel planes, they can be used for estimating the normal. Let $\mathbf{m}$ denote the coefficients in Eq. (7) as $\mathbf{m} = [\sin \varphi_p, \cos \varphi_p, -(v_y \cos \varphi_p + v_x \sin \varphi_p)/v_z]^T$. Given P points that have the same normal $\mathbf{n}$, a coefficient matrix $\mathbf{M}_1$ can be constructed from their coefficients:

$$\mathbf{M}_1 = \begin{bmatrix} \mathbf{m}_1^T, \cdots, \mathbf{m}_P^T \end{bmatrix}^T \tag{8}$$

then $\mathbf{n}$ can be obtained by the eigen decomposition of $\mathbf{M}_1^T \mathbf{M}_1$. This method directly solves $\mathbf{n}$ with only one single-view phase angle map and does not suffer from the π-ambiguity problem, while previous works based on the OPA model require at least two views [19,27]. Ideally the rank of $\mathbf{M}_1$ should be exactly two so that $\mathbf{n}$ can be solved. In practice, with image noise, we can construct a well-conditioned $\mathbf{M}_1$ with more than two points that are on the same plane for solving $\mathbf{n}$ as we will show in Sect. 5.3.

Fig. 4. The capture setup of polarization images of the dataset. The glossy and black plastic board is captured by the DoFP polarization camera at random view points. The AR tags are used for estimating the ground-truth poses of the camera and the board.

Multi-view Normal Estimation. If a point is observed in K views, another coefficients matrix $\mathbf{M}_2$ can be constructed as follows:

$$\mathbf{M}_2 = \begin{bmatrix} \mathbf{m}_1^T \mathbf{R}_1, & \cdots, & \mathbf{m}_K^T \mathbf{R}_K \end{bmatrix}^T \tag{9}$$

where $\mathbf{R}_k$ $(k = 1, 2, \cdots, K)$ is a camera rotation matrix. The normal $\mathbf{n}$ can be solved as in the case of single-view normal estimation above. Similar to $\mathbf{M}_1$, $\mathbf{n}$ can be solved if the rank of $\mathbf{M}_2$ is two and well conditioned. Therefore, observations made from sufficiently different camera poses are desirable. This method is the generalization of the method proposed in [15,27] to the case of perspective projection. We will verify that a method using the PPA constraint is more accurate in a perspective camera than using the OPA constraint in Sect. 5.3.

5   Experimental Evaluation

In this section, we present the experimental results that verify the proposed PPA model and PPA constraint in a perspective camera. Details on the experimental dataset and experimental settings are provided in Sect. 5.1. In Sect. 5.2, we evaluate the accuracy of the PPA model and analyze its phase angle estimation error. To verify that the PPA model is beneficial to polarimetric 3D reconstruction, we conduct experiments on normal estimation in Sect. 5.3 and on contour tracing in Sect. 5.4.

5.1   Dataset and Experimental Settings

An image capture setup is shown in Fig. 4. Our camera has a lens with a focal length of 6 mm and a field of view of approximately 86.6°. Perspective projection is therefore appropriate to model its geometry. We perform camera calibration first to obtain its intrinsics, and use the distortion coefficients to undistort the images before they are used in our experiments. The calibration matrix K is used to generate the light ray $\mathbf{v}$ in homogeneous coordinates.

We capture a glossy and black plastic board with a size of 300 mm by 400 mm on a table by a handheld DoFP polarization camera [9]. The setting is such that: 1) the board is specular-reflection-dominant so that the $\pi/2$ ambiguity problem can be easily solved and 2) the phase angle maps of the board can be

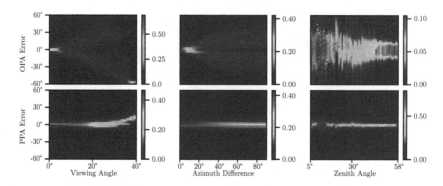

Fig. 5. The phase angle error distributions of the two models. The first row shows the distributions of the OPA model and the second row corresponds to the PPA model. Each column in one subfigure represents the one-dimension error distribution of a specific angle. The density is expressed in the form of pseudo color.

reasonably estimated. Although this setting could be perceived as being limited, it is carefully chosen to verify the proposed model accurately and conveniently.

We create a dataset that contains 282 groups of grayscale polarization images (four images per group) of the board captured at random view points. The camera poses and the ground-truth normal of the board are estimated with the help of AR tags placed on the table. Ground-truth phase angle maps are calculated from polarization images by Eq. (1). To reduce the influence of noise, we only use the pixels with DoLP higher than 0.1 in the region of the board, and apply Gaussian blur to the images before calculating phase angle maps and DoLP maps. This dataset is used in all the following experiments.

5.2   Accuracy of the PPA Model

To evaluate the accuracy of the OPA model and the PPA model, we calculate the phase angle of every pixel with Eq. (3) and Eq. (6), respectively, given the ground-truth normals, and compare the results to the estimated phase angle by Eq. (1). The mean and the root mean square error (RMSE) of the phase angle errors of the OPA model are $-0.18°$, and $20.90°$ respectively, and the ones of our proposed PPA model are $0.35°$ and $5.90°$ respectively. Although the phase angle error of both the OPA and the PPA models is unbiased with a mean that is close to zero, the RMSE of the phase angle estimated by the PPA model is only 28% of that by the OPA model in relative terms, and small in absolute terms from a practical point of view. As shown in Fig. 1, the PPA model accurately describes the spatial variation of the phase angle while the phase angle maps of the OPA model are spatially uniform and inaccurate, in comparison with the ground truth.

In addition, we plot the error distributions with respect to the viewing angle (the angle between the light ray and the normal), the azimuth difference (the angle between the azimuths of the light ray and the normal) and the zenith

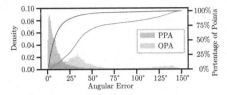

Fig. 6. Histogram and cumulative distribution function curves of angular errors of three-view normal estimation.

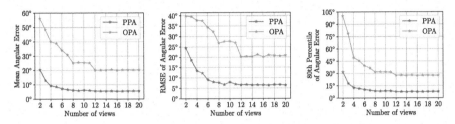

Fig. 7. Angular error with the increase of the number of views.

angle of the normal. As shown in Fig. 5, the deviations of the PPA error are much smaller than those of the OPA error. It is shown that pixels closer to the edges of the views have larger errors with the OPA model. Additionally, the errors are all close to zeros in the first three equivalent cases stated in Sect. 4.2. The high density at viewing angles near 40° in the first column of Fig. 5 is likely a result of the nonuniform distribution of the positions of the board in the images since they correspond to the pixels at the edges of the views.

5.3 Accuracy of Normal Estimation

Single-View Normal Estimation. As has been mentioned, it is possible to estimate surface normal from a single view by a polarization camera. Methods based on the OPA model however suffer from the π-ambiguity problem. In contrast, given a single-view phase angle map, surface normal estimation can be solved with the proposed PPA constraint without suffering from the π-ambiguity problem. Therefore, we only evaluate our method developed in Sect. 4.3 with the PPA constraint for the normal of a planar surface.

In this experiment, for every image in the dataset introduced in Sect. 5.1, we use the phase angles of the pixels in the region of the black board in Fig. 4 to estimate its normal. The number of the pixels contributing to the normal in one estimation varies from 100,000 to 300,000, depending on the size of area of the board in the image. We obtain 282 estimated normals among the 282 images (see the estimated normals in our supplementary video). The mean and the RMSE of the angular errors of these estimated normals are 2.68° and 1.16°, respectively. Such excellent performance is in part due to our highly accurate PPA model in

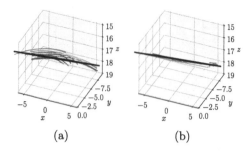

Fig. 8. Contours of a plane generated by the iso-depth contour tracing and our method respectively. (a) Contours from iso-depth tracing using the OPA model and (b) Contours using our PPA model. The viewing direction is parallel to the plane and the black line represents the plane.

describing the image formation process and in part due to the simplicity of the scene (planar surface) and a large number of measurements available.

Multi-view Normal Estimation. As well, it is possible to estimate surface normal from multiple views of a polarization camera. To establish the superiority of our proposed model, we compare the accuracy of multi-view normal estimation with the proposed method using the PPA constraint developed in Sect. 4.3 and the one using the OPA constraint proposed in [19,27], respectively.

In this experiment, we randomly sample $10,000$ 3D points on the board among the 282 images and individually estimate the normals of the points from multiple views. For every point, the number of views for its normal estimation varies from two to 20, and the views are selected using the code of ACMM [29] and the ground-truth poses of the camera and the board are used to resolve the pixel correspondences among the multiple views.

Figure 6 shows the distribution of the angular errors of the three-view case. 80% of the results of our method have errors smaller than 25° compared with only 26% of the one using the OPA constraint. Figure 7 shows the normal estimation errors with different number of views. Although the accuracy of these two methods can be improved with the increase of the number of views, the errors of our method with three views are already 50% smaller than those using the OPA model with more than ten views. The results of this experiment can be visualized in our supplementary video. Note that the error of the estimated normal in this case is significantly larger than that in the single-view case, mostly because of the small number of measurements (2–20) used in estimating each normal and the uncertainty in the relative camera poses used to solve data association. Nonetheless, the superiority of the PPA model over the OPA model is clearly established.

5.4 Comparison of Contour Tracing

This experiment is designed to illustrate the influence of the perspective effect on the iso-depth surface contour tracing with the OPA model and to show the accuracy of the proposed PPA model. We sample 20 seed 3D points on the edge of the board and propagate their depths to generate contours of the board. With the OPA model, the iso-depth contour tracing requires only the depths and a single-view phase angle map. However, according to the proposed PPA model, the iso-depth contour tracing is infeasible in perspective cameras. Therefore, we estimate the normals of the points through the method developed in Sect. 4.3 with two views for generating surface contours. To clearly compare the quality of the contours, our method is set to generate 3D contours that have the same 2D projections on the image plane as those by iso-depth contour tracing. The propagation step size is set to 0.5 pixel, which is the same as that in [7].

The iso-depth contours of the board are expected to be straight in perspective cameras. However, as shown in Fig. 8, the contours generated by iso-depth contour tracing using the OPA model are all curved and lie out of the ground-truth plane, while those generated by our PPA model are well aligned with the ground-truth plane. We also compute the RMSE of the distances between the points on the contours and the plane. The RMSE of the contours using our PPA model is 2.2 mm, 25% of that using the OPA model which is 9.6 mm.

6 Conclusions and Future Work

In this paper, we present the perspective phase angle (PPA) model as a superior alternative to the orthographic phase angle (OPA) model for accurately utilizing polarization phase angles in 3D reconstruction with perspective polarization cameras. The PPA model defines the polarization phase angle as the direction of the intersecting line of the image plane and the plane of incident, and hence allows the perspective effect to be considered in estimating surface normals from the phase angles and in defining the constraint on surface normal by the phase angle. In addition, a novel method for surface normal estimation from a single-view phase angle map naturally results from the PPA model that does not suffer from the well-known π-ambiguity problem as in the traditional orthographic model. Experimental results on real data validate that our PPA model is more accurate than the commonly adopted OPA model in perspective cameras. Overall, we demonstrate the necessity of considering the perspective effect in polarimetric 3D reconstruction and propose the PPA model for realizing it.

As a limitation of our work, we have so far only conducted experiments on surface normal estimation and contour tracing. We have not used our model in solving other problems related to polarimetric 3D reconstruction. Our immediate future plan includes improving polarimetric 3D reconstruction methods with the proposed PPA model. We are also interested in synthesizing polarization images with open-source datasets and the PPA model for data-driven approaches. We leave the above interesting problems as our future research.

Acknowledgments. We thank the reviewers for their valuable feedback. This work was done while Guangcheng Chen was a visiting student at Southern University of Science and Technology. This work was supported in part by the National Natural Science Foundation of China under Grant No. 62173096, in part by the Leading Talents Program of Guangdong Province under Grant No. 2016LJ06G498 and 2019QN01X761, in part by Guangdong Province Special Fund for Modern Agricultural Industry Common Key Technology R&D Innovation Team under Grant No. 2019KJ129, in part by Guangdong Yangfan Program for Innovative and Entrepreneurial Teams under Grant No. 2017YT05G026.

References

1. Alldrin, N.G., Kriegman, D.J.: Toward reconstructing surfaces with arbitrary isotropic reflectance: a stratified photometric stereo approach. In: 2007 IEEE 11th International Conference on Computer Vision, pp. 1–8. IEEE (2007)
2. Atkinson, G.A., Hancock, E.R.: Recovery of surface orientation from diffuse polarization. IEEE Trans. Image Process. **15**(6), 1653–1664 (2006)
3. Atkinson, G.A., Hancock, E.R.: Shape estimation using polarization and shading from two views. IEEE Trans. Pattern Anal. Mach. Intell. **29**(11), 2001–2017 (2007)
4. Ba, Y., et al.: Deep shape from polarization. In: Vedaldi, A., Bischof, H., Brox, T., Frahm, J.-M. (eds.) ECCV 2020. LNCS, vol. 12369, pp. 554–571. Springer, Cham (2020). https://doi.org/10.1007/978-3-030-58586-0_33
5. Berger, K., Voorhies, R., Matthies, L.H.: Depth from stereo polarization in specular scenes for urban robotics. In: 2017 IEEE International Conference on Robotics and Automation (ICRA), pp. 1966–1973. IEEE (2017)
6. Chen, L., Zheng, Y., Subpa-Asa, A., Sato, I.: Polarimetric three-view geometry. In: Proceedings of the European Conference on Computer Vision (ECCV), pp. 20–36 (2018)
7. Cui, Z., Gu, J., Shi, B., Tan, P., Kautz, J.: Polarimetric multi-view stereo. In: Proceedings of the IEEE Conference on Computer Vision and Pattern Recognition, pp. 1558–1567 (2017)
8. Cui, Z., Larsson, V., Pollefeys, M.: Polarimetric relative pose estimation. In: Proceedings of the IEEE/CVF International Conference on Computer Vision, pp. 2671–2680 (2019)
9. FLIR: Blackfly s usb3. https://www.flir.com.au/products/blackfly-s-usb3/?model=BFS-U3-51S5P-C. Accessed 14 Feb 2022
10. Fukao, Y., Kawahara, R., Nobuhara, S., Nishino, K.: Polarimetric normal stereo. In: Proceedings of the IEEE/CVF Conference on Computer Vision and Pattern Recognition, pp. 682–690 (2021)
11. Huynh, C.P., Robles-Kelly, A., Hancock, E.: Shape and refractive index recovery from single-view polarisation images. In: 2010 IEEE Computer Society Conference on Computer Vision and Pattern Recognition, pp. 1229–1236. IEEE (2010)
12. Kadambi, A., Taamazyan, V., Shi, B., Raskar, R.: Polarized 3D: high-quality depth sensing with polarization cues. In: Proceedings of the IEEE International Conference on Computer Vision, pp. 3370–3378 (2015)
13. Korger, J., et al.: The polarization properties of a tilted polarizer. Opt. Express **21**(22), 27032–27042 (2013)
14. Lei, C., Qi, C., Xie, J., Fan, N., Koltun, V., Chen, Q.: Shape from polarization for complex scenes in the wild. In: Proceedings of the IEEE/CVF Conference on Computer Vision and Pattern Recognition (CVPR), pp. 12632–12641, June 2022

15. Miyazaki, D., Shigetomi, T., Baba, M., Furukawa, R., Hiura, S., Asada, N.: Polarization-based surface normal estimation of black specular objects from multiple viewpoints. In: 2012 Second International Conference on 3D Imaging, Modeling, Processing, Visualization & Transmission, pp. 104–111. IEEE (2012)

16. Miyazaki, D., Shigetomi, T., Baba, M., Furukawa, R., Hiura, S., Asada, N.: Polarization-based surface normal estimation of black specular objects from multiple viewpoints. In: 2012 Second International Conference on 3D Imaging, Modeling, Processing, Visualization & Transmission, pp. 104–111. IEEE (2012)

17. Miyazaki, D., Tan, R.T., Hara, K., Ikeuchi, K.: Polarization-based inverse rendering from a single view. In: IEEE International Conference on Computer Vision, vol. 3, pp. 982–982. IEEE Computer Society (2003)

18. Thanh, T.N., Nagahara, H., Taniguchi, R.I.: Shape and light directions from shading and polarization. In: Proceedings of the IEEE Conference on Computer Vision and Pattern Recognition, pp. 2310–2318 (2015)

19. Rahmann, S.: Polarization images: a geometric interpretation for shape analysis. In: Proceedings 15th International Conference on Pattern Recognition. ICPR-2000, vol. 3, pp. 538–542. IEEE (2000)

20. Rahmann, S., Canterakis, N.: Reconstruction of specular surfaces using polarization imaging. In: Proceedings of the 2001 IEEE Computer Society Conference on Computer Vision and Pattern Recognition. CVPR 2001, vol. 1, p. I. IEEE (2001)

21. Shakeri, M., Loo, S.Y., Zhang, H., Hu, K.: Polarimetric monocular dense mapping using relative deep depth prior. IEEE Robot. Autom. Lett. **6**(3), 4512–4519 (2021)

22. Smith, W.A.P., Ramamoorthi, R., Tozza, S.: Linear depth estimation from an uncalibrated, monocular polarisation image. In: Leibe, B., Matas, J., Sebe, N., Welling, M. (eds.) ECCV 2016. LNCS, vol. 9912, pp. 109–125. Springer, Cham (2016). https://doi.org/10.1007/978-3-319-46484-8_7

23. Sony: Polarization image sensor with four-directional on-chip polarizer and global shutter function. https://www.sony-semicon.co.jp/e/products/IS/industry/product/polarization.html. Accessed 14 Feb 2022

24. Ting, J., Wu, X., Hu, K., Zhang, H.: Deep snapshot HDR reconstruction based on the polarization camera. In: 2021 IEEE International Conference on Image Processing (ICIP), pp. 1769–1773. IEEE (2021)

25. Tozza, S., Smith, W.A., Zhu, D., Ramamoorthi, R., Hancock, E.R.: Linear differential constraints for photo-polarimetric height estimation. In: Proceedings of the IEEE International Conference on Computer Vision, pp. 2279–2287 (2017)

26. Tozza, S., Zhu, D., Smith, W., Ramamoorthi, R., Hancock, E.: Uncalibrated, two source photo-polarimetric stereo. IEEE Trans. Patt. Anal. Mach. Intell. **44**, 5747–5760 (2021)

27. Wolff, L.B.: Surface orientation from two camera stereo with polarizers. In: Optics, Illumination, and Image Sensing for Machine Vision IV, vol. 1194, pp. 287–297. SPIE (1990)

28. Wu, X., Zhang, H., Hu, X., Shakeri, M., Fan, C., Ting, J.: HDR reconstruction based on the polarization camera. IEEE Robot. Autom. Lett. **5**(4), 5113–5119 (2020)

29. Xu, Q., Tao, W.: Multi-scale geometric consistency guided multi-view stereo. Comput. Vis. Patt. Recogn. (CVPR), 5483–5492 (2019)

30. Yang, L., Tan, F., Li, A., Cui, Z., Furukawa, Y., Tan, P.: Polarimetric dense monocular slam. In: Proceedings of the IEEE Conference on Computer Vision and Pattern Recognition, pp. 3857–3866 (2018)

31. Yu, Y., Zhu, D., Smith, W.A.: Shape-from-polarisation: a nonlinear least squares approach. In: Proceedings of the IEEE International Conference on Computer Vision Workshops, pp. 2969–2976 (2017)
32. Zhao, J., Monno, Y., Okutomi, M.: Polarimetric multi-view inverse rendering. In: Vedaldi, A., Bischof, H., Brox, T., Frahm, J.-M. (eds.) ECCV 2020. LNCS, vol. 12369, pp. 85–102. Springer, Cham (2020). https://doi.org/10.1007/978-3-030-58586-0_6
33. Zhou, Z., Wu, Z., Tan, P.: Multi-view photometric stereo with spatially varying isotropic materials. In: Proceedings of the IEEE Conference on Computer Vision and Pattern Recognition, pp. 1482–1489 (2013)

DeepShadow: Neural Shape from Shadow

Asaf Karnieli$^{(\boxtimes)}$, Ohad Fried , and Yacov Hel-Or

School of Computer Science, Reichman University, Herzliya, Israel
asafkarnieli@gmail.com,
{ofried,toky}@idc.ac.il

(a) (b) (c)

Fig. 1. Results on the rose object. (a) Input shadow maps, which were used for supervision (b) Depth produced by the algorithm. (c) Surface normals extracted from the depth map.

Abstract. This paper presents 'DeepShadow', a one-shot method for recovering the depth map and surface normals from photometric stereo shadow maps. Previous works that try to recover the surface normals from photometric stereo images treat cast shadows as a disturbance. We show that the self and cast shadows not only do not disturb 3D reconstruction, but can be used alone, as a strong learning signal, to recover the depth map and surface normals. We demonstrate that 3D reconstruction from shadows can even outperform shape-from-shading in certain cases. To the best of our knowledge, our method is the first to reconstruct 3D shape-from-shadows using neural networks. The method does not require any pre-training or expensive labeled data, and is optimized during inference time.

Keywords: Shape from shadow · One-shot · Inverse graphics

1 Introduction

The photometric stereo setting was first defined in [25]. The setting includes a single camera viewpoint, and multiple varying illumination sources. Most works try to extract the underlying per-pixel normal map from the input images. The original problem assumed Lambertian objects, which only have a diffuse reflectance component. More recent works solve a more general setting, with various light and material properties, including specular components.

Supplementary Information The online version contains supplementary material available at https://doi.org/10.1007/978-3-031-20086-1_24.

S. Avidan et al. (Eds.): ECCV 2022, LNCS 13662, pp. 415–430, 2022.
https://doi.org/10.1007/978-3-031-20086-1_24

To date, most works extract the required information from the local illumination effect, defined by the bidirectional reflectance distribution function (BRDF), and either ignored the global cast shadow effect, or model it in a statistical way. Almost all recent works use Conv Nets to recover the 3D structure from photometric stereo. Since Conv Nets have limited receptive fields, global information can only be aggregated in the deeper layers where accurate spatial resolution is limited.

In our work, we extract the depth information directly from the cast shadows. As far as we know, this is the first attempt to do so using neural networks. In the photometric stereo setting, cast and attached shadow detection is a relatively easy learning task. The shadow maps are binary inputs, i.e., have a 0 or 1 value. To extract depth, we initially predict per-pixel depth information in 2D and thereafter produce a point-cloud in 3D from this prediction. The 3D points are then used to calculate global cast shadows, by tracing the light source to all destination pixels. The input images are used as supervision for the produced shadow maps. The entire process is differentiable, and the predicted depth can be learned using optimization. Our process is physics based and can aggregate global information while keeping the full resolution of the image.

Most previous works assume directional lights due to its simplicity, although this is usually not the case. Many scenes consist of point light sources, thus depth information should be extracted using a point light shading model. In this work, we assume images generated by point light sources, but we can easily extend our method to handle directional lights. Although the inputs in this work are only shadow maps, our method can be integrated with existing shape-from-shading models, in order to improve their results in complex shadowed scenes. Our code and data are available at https://asafkar.github.io/deepshadow/.

2   Related Work

Shape Reconstruction from Shadows. Extracting shape information from shadows has been attempted in various works. This was mostly done before the deep learning era. An early attempt was performed in [8], which initializes a shadow map and sets lower and upper bounds on expected illuminated or shadowed pixels, which are then optimized until reaching a predicted height map. In [28], a graph-based representation is used to incorporate constraints induced by the shadow maps. This work also optimizes the height map using iteration based on low and high bounds. The ShadowCuts [2] work performs Lambertian photometric stereo with shadows present. It initially uses a graph-cut method for estimating light source visibility for every pixel. Then it uses the produced shadow maps along with shading information to perform surface normal integration, to produce the final predicted surface. In [26], the authors use 1D shadow graphs to speed up the 3D reconstruction process. 1D slices (i.e., rows or columns of the shadow images) are used, assuming the light source moves in two independent circular orbits. Each such slice can be solved independently, to retrieve the corresponding 1D slice of the underlying height map. This method only handles light sources that are on a unit sphere, and the trajectories of the light sources must be perpendicular to each other. All the above works extract the shadow maps from the images using a hand-picked threshold. A recent method [16] uses an initial approximation of the 3D geometry as input to optimize object deformations by using soft shadow information. In contrary, our method does not require an initial approximation of the geometry. The method uses spherical harmonics to approximate the surface occlusion whereas we use implicit representations along with a linear-time tracing method.

Implicit Representations. Implicit representations have recently been used to replace voxel grids or meshes with continues parameterization using neural networks. These are used in [17] to query the color and opacity of a certain point in space, to produce the pixel color of an image acquired from a specific viewing position. Lately, implicit representations have also been used in works such as [1,23,30] to recover various underlying geometric and photometric properties such as albedo, normals, etc. These have all been done in multi-view settings and take many hours and days to optimize.

Viewshed Analysis. Viewshed analysis solves the problem of which areas are visible from a specific viewpoint, and solved in [7,10] using a line-of-sight (LOS) algorithm. This algorithm tracks along a ray from the viewpoint to the target point, while verifying that the target point is not occluded by the height points along the ray. Shapira [21] proposed the R3 method for viewshed computation, by generating LOS rays from the viewpoint to all other cells (pixels) in a height map. Franklin et al. [9] introduced the R2 algorithm, which optimizes the R3 method by launching LOS rays only to the outer cells (boundary pixels), while computing and storing the intermediate results of all cells on the way. This method is considered an approximation since some rays will encounter the same cells during the process.

Photometric Stereo. In the past few years, various learning-based methods have been proposed to solve calibrated and uncalibrated photometric stereo problems [4,5,12,15,27]. Most existing methods solve the problem in a supervised manner, i.e., given inputs of N images and their associated light directions and intensities, the methods predict the surface normals as an output. The ground-truth normals are needed as supervision in order to train the network. In the uncalibrated scenarios, the light intensities and directions are not required. Works such as [5,6] first regress the light direction and light intensities, and then solve the calibrated photometric stereo problem using the predicted lights. Methods such as [12,24] solve the problem in an unsupervised manner, using a reconstruction loss. These methods only require the input images, which are used as self-supervision in the reconstruction loss.

Most of the above-mentioned methods use the pixelwise information to solve the problem. No inter-pixel relations are taken into account, besides the obvious local dependencies resulting from the local filtering. There are also methods such as [15,27] that use local neighborhood pixels as well by feature aggregation. In [27], the authors use a graph-based neural network to unify all-pixel and per-pixel information, while in [15] the authors use each pixel as a data-point to learn interactions between pixels. Although the latter method does handle cast shadows, it does so within a bound area of the observation map and in a statistical manner. Apart from this method, the previous methods ignore the cast shadows as a source of information, and treat them as a disturbance.

Some work solve the near-field photometric stereo problem, which assumes that the lights are close to the object, and thus cannot use directional lights. In [20], the authors use a hybrid approach that utilizes both distant and near-field models. The surface normals of a local area are computed by assuming they are illuminated by a distant light source, and the reconstruction error is based on the near field model. This method yields good results for close range lights, although it requires knowing the mean depth for initialization. It also requires the location of the point lights as well as the ambient lighting. The work in [14] also uses a far and near hybrid method, by first predicting the surface normals assuming far light sources, and then computing the depth by integrating the normal fields. The normal fields are then used to estimate light directions and attenuation that are used to compute the reflectance.

We also mention [11,19], which produce high resolution depth maps by using low resolution depth maps and photometric stereo images. Since few photometric stereo-based methods target depth outputs, we will compare our work with [19].

In summary, most previous shape-from-shading methods need a large amount of data for training. Also, they ignore the cast shadow instead of using it as a source of information. The main contributions of our method are:

- We propose the first deep-learning based method for recovering depth and surface normals from shadow maps.
- Our method includes a shadow calculation component, which globally aggregates information in the spatial space.
- Our method uses linear-time calculation rather than quadratic complexity in [17] and its follow-up works. We also use 2D parameterization for depth maps, avoiding the expensive 3D parameterization in NeRF like works.
- In contrast to most shape-from-shading methods, which use photometric stereo data, our method is insensitive to non-diffuse reflectance (specular highlights) or varying intensity lights, which also enables it to generate good results in both from the near-field and far-light photometric stereo settings.
- Lastly, our method estimates the depth-map in a one-shot manner, avoiding costly data collection and supervised training.

3   Shape-From-Shadow Method

DeepShadow is a technique that estimates the shape of an object or a scene from cast and attached shadows. The input data are multiple shadow maps and the location of their associated point light sources. In our work, these can later be relaxed to input images alone. Similarly to photometric stereo, the data are generated or captured with a single viewpoint and multiple illuminations. We assume each input shadow map is a byproduct of a single image taken under

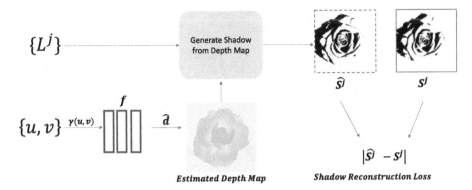

Fig. 2. Algorithm Overview. DeepShadow takes the light source location L^j and pixel coordinates (u, v) as inputs, along with the estimated depth $\hat{d}$ from the MLP, and outputs an estimate of the shadow map $\hat{S}^j$ at each pixel location. The ground-truth shadow map S^j is then used as a supervision to optimize the learned depth map.

a single light source. In contrast to other methods that use directional lights, we do not enforce the location of the point light to be on a unit sphere. Our algorithm can also work with directional light, which models a light source at infinity.

Figure 2 shows our framework. First, a multi-layer perceptron (MLP) predicts the depth at each given location $\mathbf{u} = (u, v)$ in the image. Positional encoding $\gamma(\mathbf{u})$ is used at the input of the MLP. Then, the predicted depth $\hat{d}$ along with an input light location L^j are used to estimate a shadow map $\hat{S}^j$. This is a physics based component which is differentiable but not trainable. The associated ground-truth shadow map S^j is used for supervision to optimize the MLP.

3.1 Shadow Map Estimation

To calculate the shadow of a pixel with respect to a specific light source L^j, the 'shadow line scan' algorithm is used. This algorithm traces a light ray from the light source to the destination pixel, and determines whether the pixel is illuminated or shadowed. More details are provided in Sect. 3.2.

To produce a shadow map from an estimated depth map, we use both world coordinates[1] $\mathbf{X} = \{x, y, z\}$ and image coordinates[1] $\mathbf{u} = \{u, v\}$ on the image plane. We assume the calibrated camera model is known. During the process, we use perspective projection and unprojection to go from one coordinate system to the other. Thus for a certain pixel location $\mathbf{u}_i$, $\mathbf{u}_i = P\mathbf{X}_i$, where P is the projection matrix $P = K \cdot [R|\mathbf{t}]$, K is the intrinsic matrix and $[R|\mathbf{t}]$ is the extrinsic matrix.

For a given light source $L^j = (L^j_x, L^j_y, L^j_z)$ in world coordinates, we initially map the light source to a point $\ell^j = P \cdot L^j$ on the image plane. To estimate the

---

[1] We omit the homogeneous coordinates for the sake of clarity.

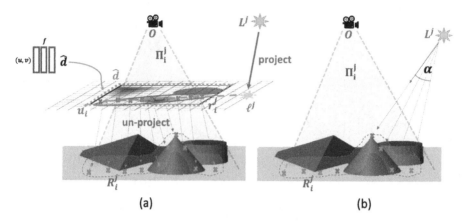

Fig. 3. Flow of shape-from-shadow. (a) The light source L^j is projected onto the image plane to receive ℓ^j. A ray $\mathbf{r}_i^j$ of (u, v) points is created between ℓ^j and $\mathbf{u}_i$. Then, each point with its estimated depth $\hat{d}$ is unprojected to world coordinates. (b) The shadow line scan algorithm is used on points in 3D space to calculate shadowed pixels. Red points are shadowed, since their angle to the light source is smaller than α. (Color figure online)

shadow for a chosen pixel $\mathbf{u}_i = (u_i, v_i)$ in the image, a line $\mathbf{r}_i^j$ of points in the image plane is generated between ℓ^j and $\mathbf{u}_i$:

$$\mathbf{r}_i^j(\alpha) = (1 - \alpha)\ell^j + \alpha\mathbf{u}_i, \quad \alpha \in [0, 1] \tag{1}$$

Points on $\mathbf{r}_i^j$ that are outside the image frame are excluded. For each pixel in $\mathbf{r}_i^j(\alpha)$, we estimate the depth $\hat{d}_i^j(\alpha)$ by querying the MLP model at the pixel's coordinates. Each such triplet $(\mathbf{r}_i^j(\alpha)[x], \mathbf{r}_i^j(\alpha)[y], \hat{d}_i^j(\alpha))$ is then unprojected to world coordinates to receive its 3D location $R_i^j(\alpha)$ as described in Eq. (2) and illustrated in Fig. 3a.

$$R_i^j(\alpha) = P^{-1}\mathbf{r}_i^j(\alpha) \cdot \hat{d}_i^j(\alpha) , \quad \alpha \in [0, 1] \tag{2}$$

Once the 3D coordinates for each pixel in R_i^j are obtained, we can solve this as a 1D line-of-sight problem, as illustrated in Fig. 3b. Note, that this process will determine, *for each* point in R_i^j, whether it is shadowed or illuminated (and not only for the point $\mathbf{u}_i$). We use the image plane coordinates for parameterization of the depth, thus avoiding a costly full 3D parameterization (as in [17] and follow up works). This process assumes the object's depth is a function of (u, v), which is a justifiable assumption since we are solving for the case of a single viewpoint.

Note that the light source L^j, viewer location O and a given point $\mathbf{u}_i$ create a plane Π_i^j in 3D, as can be seen in Fig. 3b. ℓ^j is also located on Π_i^j, as are all the points in $\mathbf{r}_i^j$ and all the points in R_j^j. This enables us to use a 1D line-of-sight algorithm between L^j and all points in R_i^j (elaborated in Sect. 3.2).

We emphasize that the shadow calculation depends only on the locations of the light source and the depth map. The camera's center of projection (COP) O is used to generate the scan order for points along a 1D ray, and to expedite calculations as will be described in the next section.

3.2   Shadow Line Scan Algorithm

Given a height map and a viewer location, one can analyze all points visible to the viewer using a 'line-of-sight' calculation. This process identifies which areas are visible from a given point. It can be naively achieved by sending 1D rays to every direction from the viewer, and calculating the line-of-sight visibility for each ray. This is analogous to producing shade maps – the viewer is replaced with a light source L^j, and every pixel is analyzed to determine whether it is shadowed (visible from L^j) or not, in the same manner. We refer to this process as 'shadow line scan'.

Calculating the visibility of each pixel point is time consuming and may take many hours to train. Instead, we propose to calculate the visibility of entire lines in the image. Each line R_i^j is calculated using a single scan. Each line includes the projections of all the points in 3D that are in the plane Π_i^j that is formed by the COP O, L^j and $\mathbf{u}_i$.

As is illustrated in Fig. 4, we define a vector from the light source L^j to each point in R_i^j, as

$$V_i^j(\alpha) = L^j - R_i^j(a). \tag{3}$$

Since we use the shadow maps as supervision and the shadow maps are composed of discrete pixels, we use discrete alpha values $\alpha \rightarrow \{\alpha_i\}_{i=0}^T$. We calculate all the angles between $V_i^j[a_0]$ and each of the points. The angle for the ith point is defined as

$$ang[i] = \arccos\left(\frac{V_i^j[\alpha_0] \cdot V_i^j[\alpha_i]}{\|V_i^j[\alpha_0]\| \cdot \|V_i^j[\alpha_i]\| + \epsilon}\right) \tag{4}$$

For numerical stability, ϵ is added to the denominator. $ang[i]$ is then compared to all previous angles $\{ang[k] \mid k \leq i\}$. If the current angle is larger than all previous angles, the current point is visible from the light source location and thus has no shadow. Otherwise, the point (pixel) is shadowed. A visualization of the process can be seen in Fig. 4.

This process can be reduced to a cumulative maximum function as defined in Eq. (5). To achieve the final shadow estimate in Eq. (6) we use a Sigmoid function to keep the final values between 0 and 1.

$$s_L[\alpha_i] = \max\left(ang[\alpha_i], s_L[\alpha_{i-1}]\right) \tag{5}$$

$$s[\alpha_i] = 2\sigma\left(ang[\alpha_i] - s_L[\alpha_i]\right) \tag{6}$$

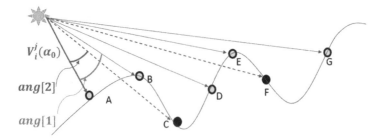

Fig. 4. 1D Shadow Line Scan Algorithm for Shadow Calculation. Points A–B are visible to the viewer, thus have no shadows. The angle $ang[2]$ between A and C (red) is smaller than the angle $ang[1]$ between A and B (green), thus C is not visible. Similarly, the angle between A and F is smaller than the last encountered largest angle, A–E, making F shadowed as well. (Color figure online)

The cumulative maximum function was chosen since it is differentiable, similar to the well-known ReLU function. The rest of the process is also differentiable, and can be used to learn the depth map similar to what is done in inverse rendering methods.

3.3 Learning Depth from Shadows

For a given light source L^j, a dense estimated shadow map is produced by generating the shadow prediction for each pixel. The shadow line scan algorithm is applied for many lines in the image, covering the entire set of pixels, in order to generate a dense shadow map $\hat{S}^j$. The ground-truth shadow map can then be used for supervision, to learn the depth. Once finished, the optimized MLP can be used to generate a dense predicted depth map.

3.4 Computational Aspects

In [17] and similar follow-up works, to predict the pixel color, an integral must be calculated along a ray of samples. This requires quadratic computation complexity relative to the image size. In our work, the calculation takes linear time, since shadow predictions for all pixels along a shadow line scan can be calculated in a cumulative manner. The intermediate shadow results for a particular pixel and the maximum angle thus far are stored and used in the next pixel calculation along the line. We used the boundary sampling method (R2) [9], which sends LOS rays from the light source to the boundary of image only, instead of sending rays to all pixels. Although this method is considered less accurate than the R3 [21] method which calculates results for all pixels, it requiring an order of magnitude fewer calculations. The R2 method can also be sub-sampled using a coarse-to-fine sampling scheme. In the early iterations, rather than taking all pixels in the boundary, one can take every k_{th} pixel. Since the light locations vary, we will most likely use all pixels in the depth map at least once.

3.5   Loss Function

We used a loss composed of the reconstruction loss and a depth-guided regularization loss. The general loss is:

$$\mathcal{L} = \frac{1}{N} \sum_j \mathcal{L}_{rec}^j + \lambda \mathcal{L}_d \tag{7}$$

where $\mathcal{L}_{rec}^j$ is the reconstruction loss:

$$\mathcal{L}_{rec}^j = \frac{1}{HW} |S^j - \hat{S}^j|. \tag{8}$$

$\mathcal{L}_d$ is a depth regularization term:

$$\mathcal{L}_d = \sum_{ij} \left| \partial_x \hat{d}_{ij} \right| e^{-\|\partial_x \bar{I}_{ij}\|} + \left| \partial_y \hat{d}_{ij} \right| e^{-\|\partial_y \bar{I}_{ij}\|}, \tag{9}$$

where $\hat{d}_{ij} = \hat{d}(u_i, v_j)$ is the estimated depth at pixel (u_i, v_j), ∂_x and ∂_y are gradients in the horizontal and vertical directions, and $\bar{I}$ is the average color over all input images. Similar to [29], we assume that the average image edges provide a signal for the object discontinuity. This regularization term helps the depth map to converge faster.

4   Experimental Results

We compare our method to several shape-from-shading methods[2]. While these methods require illuminated images as input (and we only require binary shadow maps) we find that this comparison illustrates the complementary nature of our method to shape-from-shading. As we will show, results depend on the statistics of the input objects, and for several classes of objects we achieve superior results to shape-from-shading even though we use less data.

4.1   Implementation Details

We represent the continuous 2D depth map as a function of $\mathbf{u} = (u, v)$. Similar to [17], we approximate this function with an MLP $F_w(\mathbf{u}) = \hat{d}$. We used six-layer MLP with a latent dimension of 128, along with *sine* activation functions, similar to [22]. The MLP was initialized according to [22].

We implemented this using PyTorch [18]. We optimized the neural network using the Adam optimizer [13] with an initial learning rate of 5×10^{-5}, which was decreased every 15 epochs by a factor of 0.9. We reduce the temperature of the Sigmoid function 3 times during the optimization process, using a specific

---

[2] Shape from *shadow* was previously studied (Sect. 2). However, all works precede the deep learning era and only target simple objects. We compare to shape from *shading* methods that can be applied to the complex shapes in our datasets.

schedule. We run the optimization until the loss plateaus, which typically takes an hour on an input of 16 images with spatial resolution of 256×256, using an Intel i9-10900X CPU and an NVIDIA GeForce RTX 2080 Ti. The current implementation uses a single-process and contains many occurrences of native Python indexing, thus is sub-optimal and can be further optimized.

Photometric-stereo data is not usually accompanied by labeled shadow masks. Thus, for datasets which have no ground-truth shadows or light directions, we implement a model to estimate these. We use the Blobby and Sculptures datasets from [3] along with our own shadow dataset in order to train the model. Details can be found in the supplementary material.

4.2   Datasets

We show results on nine synthetic objects: 3 from previous work [12] and 6 curated and rendered by us from Sketchfab[3]. The objects we selected span various shapes and sizes, and they also possess one key property: many 3D features that cast shadows. As we will show, when this property holds, our method outperforms shape-from-shading methods and thus complements them. Our objects were each rendered with 16 different illumination conditions. Scenes are illuminated by a single point-light source.

Since shadow maps are not available in the dataset of Kaya et al. [12], we have our previously mentioned shadow-extraction model to estimate these. For our rendered objects, we use the ground-truth shadow maps as inputs. Qualitative results on real objects (without ground-truth) are available in the supplementary material.

4.3   Comparisons

We compare to the state-of-the-art methods of Chen et al. [5], Santo et al. [20], and Peng et al. [19], that use photometric stereo inputs, with the latter requiring a down-sampled depth map as an additional input. We compare both depth maps [19,20] and normals [5,20] (according to the generated outputs of each method).

Figure 5 shows a qualitative evaluation of depth map result quality. The method of Santo et al. produces a low frequency estimation of depth, but does not contain any high frequency details. The method of Peng et al. produces results which are closer to the ground truth, but still lacking in sharpness (e.g., in *Relief* and *Cactus*). Our method is overall closest to the ground truth depth. Quantitatively, we measure normalized mean depth error (nMZE)[4] in Table 1. We achieve lower nMZE on 5 out of the 6 objects, with an overall average nMZE which is 1.7 times [19] and 4.9 times [20] lower than the alternative.

Figure 6 shows a qualitative evaluation of surface normal result quality. The method of Santo et al. produces overly smooth normals, with some examples

---

[3] https://sketchfab.com/.

[4] we normalize each depth map by its own std and bias, in order to make the comparisons scale and bias invariant.

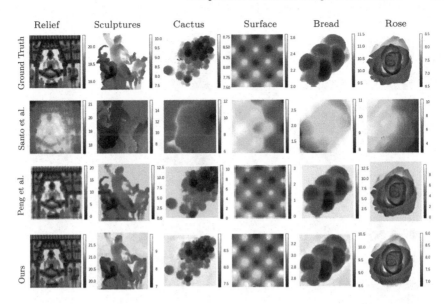

Fig. 5. Comparison of depth maps. Each row refers to a specific method.

relatively close to the ground truth (e.g., *Relief*) but others farther away (e.g., *Rose*). The method of Chen et al. is comparable to ours, with generally good results that resemble the ground truth normals, but lack sharp transitions. Quantitatively, we measure mean angle error (MAE in degrees) in Table 1. Our results are comparable to (albeit slightly better than) those of Chen et al., and 1.6 times better than those of Santo et al.

Table 1. Quantitative evaluation. The top three rows are depth map results, and the bottom rows are surface normal results. All methods but Peng et al. were given ground-truth light location, and Peng et al. was given a down-scaled depth map.

Method	Metric	Cactus	Rose	Bread	Sculptures	Surface	Relief	Avg
Santo et al. [20]	nMZE	0.96	1.16	0.77	0.81	0.75	0.75	0.87
Peng et al. [19]	nMZE	0.43	**0.05**	0.40	0.20	0.33	0.42	0.31
Chen et al. [5]	nMZE	N/A	N/A	N/A	N/A	N/A	N/A	N/A
Ours	nMZE	**0.33**	0.11	**0.16**	**0.19**	**0.10**	**0.18**	**0.18**
Santo et al. [20]	MAE	32.79	50.23	33.95	54.49	22.21	21.93	35.93
Peng et al. [19]	MAE	N/A	N/A	N/A	N/A	N/A	N/A	N/A
Chen et al. [5]	MAE	24.61	**25.12**	**18.31**	**26.43**	18.91	25.46	23.14
Ours	MAE	**22.60**	26.27	20.43	27.50	**17.16**	**21.80**	**22.63**

Note that [12] refers to a *rose* object as an object with 'complex geometry and high amount of surface discontinuity', where their method fails due to their assumption of a continuous surface and due to a high amount of cast shadows.

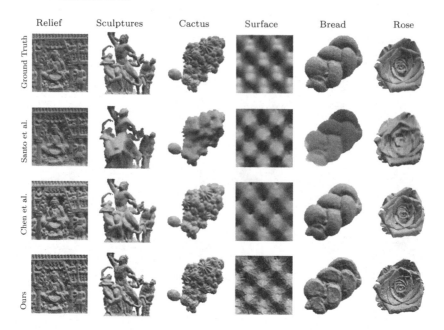

Fig. 6. Comparison of surface normals estimated by each of the compared methods. Each row represents a different method.

Table 2. Comparison of surface normal estimation on the dome dataset in [12] using calibrated methods (known light locations). Compared results were used from the original paper.

Method	Metric	Vase	Golf Ball	Face
Chen et al. [3]	MAE	27.11	15.99	16.17.81
Kaya et al. [12]	MAE	16.40	**14.23**	**14.24**
Ours	MAE	**11.24**	16.51	18.70

We render a similar object and show that our method does not require such assumptions. Visual results can be seen in Fig. 1.

Besides our own generated dataset, we compare our results to three different shape-from-shading results reported in [12][5] which can be seen in Table 2. Since the *vase* object is concave, it has a strong cast shadow affect, which is a strong learning signal. We can also see that the shape-from-shading methods fail to deal with this. The *golf* and *face* objects have sparse cast shadows, which is likely the reason why our method does not perform well there.

---

[5] The code was not available at the time of writing this paper, so the reported results in [12] were used as-is.

Table 3. Average shadow pixels in image analysis. We measure MAE of estimated surface normals for increasing amount of average shadows. These are calculated by taking the average amount of shadowed pixels in each rendered object.

Avg. Shadow	A(48%)	B(60%)	C(66%)	D(69%)	E(60%)*	Avg
Chen et al. [5]	18.63	18.71	20.43	21.44	22.99	20.44
Santo et al. [20]	**16.18**	**17.25**	**17.19**	18.25	42.70	22.31
Ours	20.43	18.53	17.95	**17.53**	**18.68**	**18.62**

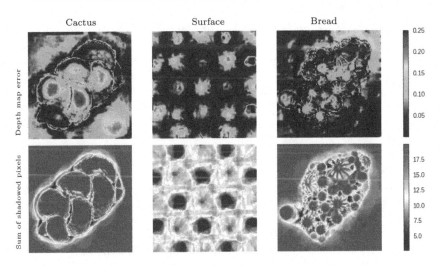

Fig. 7. Comparison of Depth Estimation Error (top) vs. Number of Shadowed Pixels (bottom). In the bottom row, we can observe pixels that are mostly shadowed (blue) or mostly illuminated (red) in all renderings. These pixels have higher depth estimation errors (top row). Pixels that are balanced, i.e., shadowed and illuminated in roughly equal proportions (white, bottom row) have a smaller depth estimation error. (Color figure online)

4.4   Analysis and Ablation

Performance on Various Shadow Amounts. To further test our method, we generated the *surface* object using 16 lights placed at different incidence angles, thus creating inputs with increasing amount of shadows. We rendered this by placing the object at a constant location, and increasing the distance of the lights from the object at each different scene. We observe in Table 3 that DeepShadow's accuracy improves as the amount of shadow present in the image increases, as opposed to the other tested methods, in which the accuracy degrades as the amount of shadowed pixels increases. Note that objects A–D were rendered with lights at a constant distance, and object E was rendered with lights at varying distances. We observe that [20] does not handle this scenario well.

Shadowed and Illuminated Pixels. We analyze the effects of the number of shadowed and illuminated pixels on the final depth estimation. In Fig. 7 we compare the error map (top) to the number of illuminated pixels across all lighting conditions (bottom). Our method works best if this sum is balanced, i.e., if pixels are illuminated in some samples and shadowed in other samples. If pixels are always shadowed or always illuminated, reconstruction is ill-posed and our method does not perform well.

4.5   Failure Cases

Our algorithm is based on the line of sight algorithm, thus it relies on shadow gradients to reconstruct the underlying depth map. In objects such as the *face* in Table 2, the algorithm fails in flat areas, e.g., as the forehead, since the latter is relatively smooth and convex - and thus has no shadow from which to learn from. This is also true for the *bread object* in Table 1, which has large areas that are flat, as can be seen in Fig. 7. In contrast, the *vase* in Table 2 is relatively smooth yet also concave, and has many cast shadows, which enables our method to succeed.

5   Conclusions

In this work we proposed DeepShadow, a deep-learning based method for recovering shape from shadows. We show that in various scenarios, the shadow maps serve as good learning signals that enable the underlying depth and surface normals to be recovered. Experiments have shown that this method achieves results equal to or better than those generated by the various shape-from-shading algorithms, for severely shadowed objects, while using fewer or no data—since we are not using any training data besides the shadow maps. An additional benefit of our method is that we do not require knowing the light intensity, since the shadow maps are of binary values. Even though previous works have shown this can be estimated, the estimation may be erroneous, which affects the final result.

Our method fails on convex objects or objects with sparse shadows. In future work, this method should be combined with shape-from-shading methods in order for both methods to benefit from each other. Another possible research direction is producing super-resolution depth maps using the shadow clues, which would combine our work and [19]. Since we are using implicit representations, this may work well.

Acknowledgements. This work was supported by the Israeli Ministry of Science and Technology under The National Foundation for Applied Science (MIA), and by the Israel Science Foundation (grant No. 1574/21).

References

1. Boss, M., Braun, R., Jampani, V., Barron, J.T., Liu, C., Lensch, H.P.A.: NeRD: neural reflectance decomposition from image collections. In: IEEE International Conference on Computer Vision (ICCV) (2021)

2. Chandraker, M., Agarwal, S., Kriegman, D.: ShadowCuts: photometric stereo with shadows. In: 2007 IEEE Conference on Computer Vision and Pattern Recognition, pp. 1–8 (2007). https://doi.org/10.1109/CVPR.2007.383288

3. Chen, G., Han, K., Wong, K.-Y.K.: PS-FCN: a flexible learning framework for photometric stereo. In: ECCV (2018)

4. Chen, G., Han, K., Shi, B., Matsushita, Y., Wong, K.-Y.K.: Deep photometric stereo for non-lambertian surfaces (2020a)

5. Chen, G., Han, K., Shi, B., Matsushita, Y., Wong, K.-Y.K.: Self-calibrating deep photometric stereo networks (2019)

6. Chen, G., Waechter, M., Shi, B., Wong, K.-Y.K., Matsushita, Y.: What is learned in deep uncalibrated photometric stereo? In: Vedaldi, A., Bischof, H., Brox, T., Frahm, J.-M. (eds.) ECCV 2020. LNCS, vol. 12359, pp. 745–762. Springer, Cham (2020). https://doi.org/10.1007/978-3-030-58568-6_44

7. Cole, R., Sharir, M.: Visibility problems for polyhedral terrains. J. Symbol. Comput. **7**(1), 11–30 (1989)

8. Daum, M., Dudek, G.: On 3-D surface reconstruction using shape from shadows. In: Proceedings of the 1998 IEEE Computer Society Conference on Computer Vision and Pattern Recognition (Cat. No.98CB36231), pp. 461–468 (1998). https://doi.org/10.1109/CVPR.1998.698646

9. Franklin, W.R., Ray, C.: Higher isn't necessarily better: visibility algorithms and experiments. In: Advances in GIS Research: Sixth International Symposium on Spatial Data Handling, vol. 2, pp. 751–770. Taylor & Francis Edinburgh (1994)

10. Goodchild, M.F., Lee, J.: Coverage problems and visibility regions on topographic surfaces. Ann. Oper. Res. **18**(1), 175–186 (1989). https://doi.org/10.1007/BF02097802

11. Haefner, B., Peng, S., Verma, A., Quéau, Y., Cremers, D.: Photometic depth super-resolution. IEEE Trans. Patt. Anal. Mach. Intell. **42**, 2453–2464 (2019)

12. Kaya, B., Kumar, S., Oliveira, C., Ferrari, V., Van Gool, L.: Uncalibrated neural inverse rendering for photometric stereo of general surfaces (2021)

13. Kingma, D.P., Ba, J.: A method for stochastic optimization, Adam (2017)

14. Logothetis, F., Budvytis, I., Mecca, R., Cipolla, R.: A CNN based approach for the near-field photometric stereo problem (2020)

15. Logothetis, F., Budvytis, I., Mecca, R., Cipolla, R.: Simple and efficient pixel-wise training of photometric stereo networks, Px-net (2021)

16. Lyu, L., Habermann, M., Liu, L., Mallikarjun B.R, Tewari, A., Theobalt, C.: Efficient and differentiable shadow computation for inverse problems. In: Proceedings of the IEEE/CVF International Conference on Computer Vision (ICCV), pp. 13107–13116, October 2021

17. Mildenhall, B., Srinivasan, P.P., Tancik, M., Barron, J.T., Ramamoorthi, R., Ng, R.: Representing scenes as neural radiance fields for view synthesis. In: ECCV, Nerf (2020)

18. Paszke, A., et al.: Pytorch: an imperative style, high-performance deep learning library. In: Wallach, H., Larochelle, H., Beygelzimer, A., d' Alché-Buc, F., Fox, E., Garnett, R. (eds.) Advances in Neural Information Processing Systems, vol. 32, pp. 8024–8035. Curran Associates Inc (2019). http://papers.neurips.cc/paper/9015-pytorch-an-imperative-style-high-performance-deep-learning-library.pdf

19. Peng, S., Haefner, B., Quéau, Y., Cremers, D.: Depth super-resolution meets uncalibrated photometric stereo. In: IEEE International Conference on Computer Vision (ICCV) Workshop (2017)

20. Santo, H., Waechter, M., Matsushita, Y.: Deep near-light photometric stereo for spatially varying reflectances. In: Vedaldi, A., Bischof, H., Brox, T., Frahm, J.-M. (eds.) Computer Vision - ECCV 2020, pp. 137–152, Cham (2020). Springer International Publishing. ISBN 978-3-030-58598-3. https://doi.org/10.1007/978-3-030-58598-3_9

21. Shapira, A.: Visibility and terrain labeling. PhD thesis, Rensselaer Polytechnic Institute, May 1990

22. Sitzmann, V., Martel, J.N.P., Bergman, A.W., Lindell, D.B., Wetzstein, G.: Implicit neural representations with periodic activation functions. In: Proceedings of NeurIPS (2020)

23. Srinivasan, P.P., Deng, B., Zhang, X., Tancik, M., Mildenhall, B., Barron, J.T.: Neural reflectance and visibility fields for relighting and view synthesis, Barron. Nerv (2020)

24. Taniai, T., Maehara, T.: Neural inverse rendering for general reflectance photometric stereo (2018)

25. Woodham, R.J.: Photometric method for determining surface orientation from multiple images. Opt. Eng. **19**(1), 139–144 (1980) https://doi.org/10.1117/12.7972479

26. Yamashita, Y., Sakaue, F., Sato, J.: Recovering 3D shape and light source positions from non-planar shadows. In: 2010 20th International Conference on Pattern Recognition, pp. 1775–1778 (2010). https://doi.org/10.1109/ICPR.2010.1153

27. Yao, Z., Li, K., Fu, Y., Hu, H., Shi, B.: GPS-Net: graph-based photometric stereo network. Adv. Neural Inf. Process. Syst. **33**, 10306–10316 (2020)

28. Yu, Y., Chang, J.: Shadow graphs and 3D texture reconstruction. Int. J. Comput. Vis. **62**, 35–60 (2005). https://doi.org/10.1023/B:VISI.0000046588.02227.3b

29. Zhan, H., Weerasekera, C.S., Garg, R., Reid, I.D.: Self-supervised learning for single view depth and surface normal estimation. CoRR, abs/1903.00112 (2019). arxiv:1903.00112

30. Zhang, X., Srinivasan, P.P., Deng, B., Debevec, P., Freeman, W.T., Barron, J.T.: Nerfactor. ACM Trans. Graph. **40**(6), 1–18 (2021). ISSN 1557–7368. https://doi.org/10.1145/3478513.3480496

Camera Auto-calibration from the Steiner Conic of the Fundamental Matrix

Yu Liu[1,2] and Hui Zhang[2(✉)]

[1] Department of Computer Science, Hong Kong Baptist University, Hong Kong SAR, China
[2] Guangdong Key Laboratory of Interdisciplinary Research and Application for Data Science, BNU-HKBU United International College, Zhuhai, China
{yuliu,amyzhang}@uic.edu.cn

Abstract. This paper addresses the problem of camera auto-calibration from the fundamental matrix under general motion. The fundamental matrix can be decomposed into a symmetric part (a Steiner conic) and a skew-symmetric part (a fixed point), which we find useful for fully calibrating camera parameters. We first obtain a fixed line from the image of the symmetric, skew-symmetric parts of the fundamental matrix and the image of the absolute conic. Then the properties of this fixed line are presented and proved, from which new constraints on general eigenvectors between the Steiner conic and the image of the absolute conic are derived. We thus propose a method to fully calibrate the camera. First, the three camera intrinsic parameters, i.e., the two focal lengths and the skew, can be solved from our new constraints on the imaged absolute conic obtained from at least three images. On this basis, we can initialize and then iteratively restore the optimal pair of projection centers of the Steiner conic, thereby obtaining the corresponding vanishing lines and images of circular points. Finally, all five camera parameters are fully calibrated using images of circular points obtained from at least three images. Experimental results on synthetic and real data demonstrate that our method achieves state-of-the-art performance in terms of accuracy.

Keywords: Auto-calibration · Steiner conic · Fundamental matrix · General motion

1 Introduction

Camera calibration is a very critical step in image measurement or machine vision applications such as 3D reconstruction [5,23,36], vision metrology [22] and robot navigation [4]. The accuracy and stability of the calibration algorithm directly affect its usability. In the past few decades, researchers have proposed many methods to solve the problem of camera calibration, which can be roughly divided into two categories: calibration with objects [10,35,37] and without objects [7,12,30,34,36]. Calibration methods with objects always require

© The Author(s), under exclusive license to Springer Nature Switzerland AG 2022
S. Avidan et al. (Eds.): ECCV 2022, LNCS 13662, pp. 431–446, 2022.
https://doi.org/10.1007/978-3-031-20086-1_25

highly accurate tailor-made calibration objects, such as lines [37], 2D planar patterns [10,15,36] or 3D objects [24,32,35], etc. These methods can accurately calibrate the camera parameters according to the geometric constraints provided by the calibration objects. However, the calibration process is manually cumbersome, which greatly limits the scope of application of these methods. In contrast, auto-calibration methods can recover the camera intrinsic parameters through corresponding points [3,7,12,21,31] or object contours in the scene images [19,26,30,33,34]. Since no specific objects are required, auto-calibration methods can avoid the tedious manual process, greatly expanding its application and can even be applied to pre-shot videos.

Researchers have successfully proposed closed-form solutions for auto-calibration under constrained motion, such as rotational motion [1,2], planar motion [6,16,29,34], etc. For pure rotation, the camera intrinsic parameters can be calibrated using the rotational conjugation of the infinite homography of the image pair [13]. For planar motion [6,16], the translation is always perpendicular to the rotation axis. The vanishing point of the translation direction and the image of the rotation axis can be derived from the fundamental matrix, which provides a pole-polar relationship with respect to the image of the absolute conic for auto-calibration. In [29,34], the authors calibrate the three intrinsic parameters using the imaged silhouettes of an object under turntable motion. However, due to insufficient geometric constraints, most of these existing methods can only calibrate a limited number of camera intrinsic parameters.

The first auto-calibration method for general motion used the Kruppa equation to obtain the camera intrinsic parameters [3,7,12,13,21,31]. It uses the fundamental matrix as input to obtain the constraints on the dual image of the absolute conic, which is used for camera calibration. The Kruppa equation contains two independent constraints on the five unknown camera intrinsic parameters from two views under general motion. Therefore, at least three images can be used to fully calibrate the camera. Although algebraic solutions [7,13,28] are available, there are still 2^5 possible solutions for the five unknowns from the five quadratic equations [13]. Later in [21], a hybrid method of GA [17] & PSO [18] was proposed to optimize the accuracy of camera auto-calibration, which heavily depends on the initial values. Other approaches attempt to simplify the Kruppa equation by eliminating the scale coefficients by some specific operations, such as applying singular value decomposition (SVD) to the fundamental matrix [7,11,13,21] or using the rank constraint on the coefficient matrix [11,20]. However, there is still several ambiguity in the obtained constraints for camera auto-calibration. Therefore, the inaccuracy and ambiguity of these methods have made them lose their popularity.

This paper presents a two-step solution to the problem of camera auto-calibration using the fundamental matrix under general motion. The method is based on a newly discovered constraint derived from the Steiner conic, the symmetric part of the fundamental matrix. Inspired by the general eigenvectors of two separate conics [14,15], we first obtain a fixed line from the image of the Steiner conic, the skew-symmetric part of the fundamental matrix and the image of the absolute conic. Then the properties of this fixed line are presented and proved, from which new constraints on general eigenvectors between the Steiner conic and the image of the absolute conic are derived. We thus propose a method to fully calibrate the camera. First, the three parameters of the camera intrinsics, namely the two focal lengths and the skew, can be recovered by our new constraints on the imaged absolute conic from at least three images. On this basis, we can initialize and iteratively restore the optimal pair of projection centers of the Steiner conic, thereby obtaining the corresponding vanishing lines and images of circular points. Finally, the five camera parameters are fully calibrated using images of circular points obtained from at least three images. We summarize our contributions as follows:

1. We find that a new fixed line can be obtained from the image, which is an invariant under general motion;
2. New constraints are derived from the general eigenvectors of the image of the absolute conic and the Steiner conic for calibrating the three intrinsic parameters of the camera;
3. We obtain the optimal pair of projection centers of the Steiner conic for fully calibrating all five intrinsic parameters of the camera, and our method achieves state-of-the-art accuracy for auto-calibration under general motion.

The paper is organized as follows. Section 2 introduces some basic concepts that will be used in the following sections. Section 3 proposes a method for determining a fixed line under general motion. Section 3 and 4 describe the two properties of the fixed line and the derived calibration method, respectively. Section 5 lists the degenerate cases. Synthetic and real experiments on the proposed method are shown in Sect. 6. Conclusions are given in Sect. 7.

2   Preliminary

This section briefly introduces the basic concepts that will be used for camera calibration. We use a pinhole camera model to represent camera intrinsics.

2.1   The Pinhole Camera Model

A 3D point $\mathbf{P} = [X, Y, Z, 1]^T$ is projected into the image at $\mathbf{p} = [u, v, 1]^T$ by

$$\mu \mathbf{p} = \mathbf{K} [\mathbf{R}|\mathbf{t}] \, \mathbf{P}, \tag{1}$$

where μ is a non-zero scalar, $[\mathbf{R}|\mathbf{t}]$ denotes the rigid body transformation, and $\mathbf{K}$ is the camera intrinsic matrix, as

$$\mathbf{K} = \begin{bmatrix} f_x & s & u_0 \\ 0 & f_y & v_0 \\ 0 & 0 & 1 \end{bmatrix}. \tag{2}$$

Here f_x and f_y are the focal lengths along x- and y-axis, respectively. s is the skew parameter, (u_0, v_0) is the principal point.

The absolute conic is a conic at infinity [13], which is projected into the image of the absolute conic (IAC) $\omega = \mathbf{K}^{-T}\mathbf{K}^{-1}$, whose dual is $\omega^* = \mathbf{K}\mathbf{K}^T$. Once at least five independent constraints on ω is obtained, the intrinsic matrix $\mathbf{K}$ can be determined by the Cholesky decomposition [9,13] of ω.

2.2   The Steiner Conic from the Fundamental Matrix

The fundamental matrix $\mathbf{F}$ can be decomposed into a symmetric part $\mathbf{F}_s$ and a skew-symmetric part $\mathbf{F}_a$ [13], i.e.,

$$\mathbf{F}_s = \frac{\mathbf{F} + \mathbf{F}^T}{2}, \quad \mathbf{F}_a = \frac{\mathbf{F} - \mathbf{F}^T}{2}, \tag{3}$$

so that $\mathbf{F} = \mathbf{F}_s + \mathbf{F}_a$. Geometrically, $\mathbf{F}_s$ is a Steiner conic, which is the image of the horopter curve $(\mathbf{x} = \mathbf{x}')$ formed by a series of intersection points $\mathbf{x}_c$ of the corresponding epipolar lines $\mathbf{l}$ and $\mathbf{l}'$ in the two views (see Fig. 1).

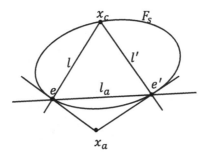

Fig. 1. Geometric representation F. The fundamental matrix $\mathbf{F}$ is decomposed into a symmetric part $\mathbf{F}_s$ and a skew-symmetric part $\mathbf{F}_a$. Under general motion, $\mathbf{F}_s$ is the Steiner conic formed by the horopter points $\mathbf{x}_c$, which are the intersections of the corresponding epipolar lines $\{\mathbf{l}, \mathbf{l}'\}$ in the two views. The line $\mathbf{l}_a$ is polar of $\mathbf{x}_a$, the null-vector of $\mathbf{F}_a$, and intersects $\mathbf{F}_s$ at the epipoles $\mathbf{e}, \mathbf{e}'$ of the two views.

$\mathbf{F}_a$ can be written as $\mathbf{F}_a = [\mathbf{x}_a]_\times$, where the point $\mathbf{x}_a$ is the null-vector of $\mathbf{F}_a$. The polar of $\mathbf{x}_a$ with respect to $\mathbf{F}_s$ is the line $\mathbf{l}_a = \mathbf{F}_s\mathbf{x}_a$, intersects with $\mathbf{F}_s$ at the two epipoles $\{\mathbf{e}, \mathbf{e}'\}$, i.e., $\mathbf{l}_a = \mathbf{e} \times \mathbf{e}'$. Here $\mathbf{e}$ and $\mathbf{e}'$ are the null vectors of $\mathbf{F}$ and $\mathbf{F}^T$, respectively. Consequently, once $\mathbf{F}$ is determined by the normalized eight-point algorithms [13] or the five-point method [3], $\mathbf{F}_s$, the epipoles $\{\mathbf{e}, \mathbf{e}'\}$, the skew-symmetric point $\mathbf{x}_a$ and its polar $\mathbf{l}_a$ can be uniquely defined.

3   The Fixed Line and Camera Calibration

This section introduces a fixed line and its property, which can be used for camera calibration. For a pair of views under general motion, let $\mathbf{v}_\perp = \omega^*\mathbf{l}_a$ is

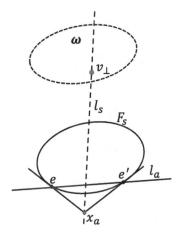

Fig. 2. The fixed line l_s of two views under general motion. The point $v_\perp$ is the pole of the line l_a w.r.t the IAC ω. The lines l_s and l_a are orthogonal with respect to ω, where the line l_s is obtained by connecting the points $v_\perp$ and x_a.

the pole of the line l_a with respect to the IAC ω, the line l_s (see Fig. 2) be the fixed line connecting the points x_a and $v_\perp$, as

$$l_s = x_a \times v_\perp$$
$$= [x_a]_\times v_\perp \qquad (4)$$
$$= F_a \omega^* l_a.$$

As F_a is skew-symmetric, left-multiplying $l_a^T \omega^*$ on both sides of Eq. 4, we obtain

$$l_a^T \omega^* l_s = l_a^T \omega^* F_a \omega^* l_a = 0. \qquad (5)$$

Hence the lines l_a and l_s are orthogonal with respect to ω, where l_s and l_a can be regarded as the vanishing lines of two perpendicular planes in 3D space [13].

3.1   General Eigenvectors of IAC ω and F_s

Here we introduce the location of general eigenvectors of IAC ω and F_s.

Proposition 1. *Under general motion, one of the general eigenvectors of the IAC ω and Steiner conic F_s lies on the line l_a, and the other two are on l_s.*

Proof. For two views captured by the same camera under general motion, the IAC ω and the Steiner conic F_s can be drawn as two separated conics (see Fig. 3). Inspired by [13–15,29], there is a unique common self-polar triangle $\triangle v_1 v_2 v_3$ with respect to these two conics, whose vertices are the general eigenvectors of $\omega^* F_s$, as

$$F_s v_i \sim \omega v_i \Rightarrow (\omega^* F_s - \gamma_i I) v_i = 0_{3\times 1}, \qquad (6)$$

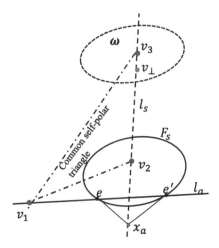

Fig. 3. Location of the general eigenvectors of the IAC ω and the Steiner conic $\mathbf{F}_s$. Under general motion, the IAC ω and Steiner conic $\mathbf{F}_s$ can be drawn as two fixed but separate conics. There is only one common self-polar triangle $\triangle \mathbf{v}_1 \mathbf{v}_2 \mathbf{v}_3$, whose vertices are the general eigenvectors of $\omega^* \mathbf{F}_s$. The general eigenvector $\mathbf{v}_1$ is on the line $\mathbf{l}_a$. The other two, $\mathbf{v}_2$ and $\mathbf{v}_3$, lie on the fixed line $\mathbf{l}_s$.

where γ_i is the non-zero eigenvalues with $i = 1$, 2, and 3. As demonstrated in [14,15], the position of $\triangle \mathbf{v}_1 \mathbf{v}_2 \mathbf{v}_3$ is fixed with respect to the two conics. The vertex $\mathbf{v}_1$ locates apart from the two conics, and the other two vertices $\mathbf{v}_2$ and $\mathbf{v}_3$ are located inside the two conics, respectively. In addition, based on the pole-polar relationship, the general eigenvectors $(\mathbf{v}_1, \mathbf{v}_2, \mathbf{v}_3)$ satisfy with

$$\begin{cases} \mathbf{v}_i \sim \mathbf{F}_s^{-1} (\mathbf{v}_j \times \mathbf{v}_k), & \text{(7a)} \\ \mathbf{v}_i \sim \omega^* (\mathbf{v}_j \times \mathbf{v}_k), & \text{(7b)} \end{cases}$$

where $\{i, j, k\} = \{1, 2, 3\}$. Let $\mathbf{l}_v$ be the line joining $\mathbf{v}_2$ and $\mathbf{v}_3$, $\mathbf{v}_\perp$ satisfies with

$$\begin{aligned} \mathbf{v}_\perp^T \mathbf{l}_v &\sim \mathbf{v}_\perp^T (\mathbf{v}_2 \times \mathbf{v}_3) \\ &\sim \mathbf{v}_\perp^T \mathbf{F}_s \mathbf{F}_s^{-1} (\mathbf{v}_2 \times \mathbf{v}_3) \\ &\sim \mathbf{l}_a^T \omega^* \mathbf{F}_s \mathbf{v}_1 \\ &\sim \mathbf{l}_a^T \mathbf{v}_1. \end{aligned} \qquad (8)$$

And from Eq. 7, the point $\mathbf{x}_a = \mathbf{F}_s^{-1} \mathbf{l}_a$ satisfies

$$\begin{aligned} \mathbf{x}_a^T \mathbf{l}_v &\sim \left(\mathbf{F}_s^{-1} \mathbf{l}_a\right)^T (\mathbf{v}_2 \times \mathbf{v}_3) \\ &\sim \left(\mathbf{F}_s^{-1} \mathbf{l}_a\right)^T \omega \omega^* (\mathbf{v}_2 \times \mathbf{v}_3) \\ &\sim \mathbf{l}_a^T \mathbf{F}_s^{-1} \omega \mathbf{v}_1 \\ &\sim \mathbf{l}_a^T \mathbf{v}_1. \end{aligned} \qquad (9)$$

From Eqs. 8 and 9, we can have $\mathbf{x}_a^T \mathbf{l}_v = \kappa \mathbf{v}_\perp^T \mathbf{l}_v \Rightarrow \left(\mathbf{x}_a^T - \kappa \mathbf{v}_\perp^T \right) \mathbf{l}_v = 0$, where κ is a non-zero scalar. Hence, the line $\mathbf{l}_s$ connecting $\mathbf{x}_a$ and $\mathbf{v}_\perp$ aligns with the line $\mathbf{l}_v$, thus both $\mathbf{v}_2$ and $\mathbf{v}_3$ lies on $\mathbf{l}_s$, i.e., $\mathbf{l}_s \sim \mathbf{v}_2 \times \mathbf{v}_3$. Furthermore, it can be easily derived that $\mathbf{l}_a^T \mathbf{v}_1 \sim \mathbf{x}_a^T \mathbf{l}_s = 0$, which indicates the eigenvector $\mathbf{v}_1$ lies on $\mathbf{l}_a$. □

3.2 Calibration of the Focal Lengths and the Skew

In order to eliminate the unknown eigenvalues γ_i in Eq. 6, we can substitute the skew-symmetric matrix of the corresponding eigenvectors on both sides of the equation. Furthermore, since the general eigenvector $\mathbf{v}_1$ lies on the line $\mathbf{l}_a$, the constraints on the IAC $\boldsymbol{\omega}$ for calibrating the camera can be obtained as

$$\begin{cases} \mathbf{l}_a^T \mathbf{v}_1 = 0, & (10a) \\ [\mathbf{v}_1]_\times \, \boldsymbol{\omega}^* \mathbf{F}_s \mathbf{v}_1 = \mathbf{0}_{3\times 1}, & (10b) \end{cases}$$

which include three independent constraints. Let $\mathbf{v}_1$ have two unknown coordinates (v_{1x}, v_{1y}) and the camera have only one unknown focal length f. The three unknowns, i.e., f, v_{1x}, and v_{1y}, can therefore be uniquely recovered by solving Eq. 10. Furthermore, for a camera with the known principal point, the focal length (f_x, f_y), skew s, and six parameters of three distinct $\mathbf{v}_1$ for each pair of views can be recovered through the nine independent constraints (Eq. 10) that are obtained from three images.

4 Full Calibration Using the Centers of the Steiner Conic

This section presents the properties of the centers of the Steiner conic $\mathbf{F}_s$ and then introduces a method to calibrate all the five camera intrinsic parameters.

4.1 The Centers of the Steiner Conic $\mathbf{F}_s$

Proposition 2. *Suppose the Steiner conic $\mathbf{F}_s$ is the projection of a circle on the image plane. Its two projected centers $\mathbf{o}_{1,2}$ are associated with two opposite viewing directions of $\mathbf{F}_s$, both lying on the fixed line $\mathbf{l}_s$. They correspond to the two planes containing the circle. Furthermore, the general eigenvector $\mathbf{v}_1$, which lies outside the two conic $\mathbf{F}_s$ and $\boldsymbol{\omega}$ coincides with the intersection of the vanishing lines of these two planes $\mathbf{l}_{h1,2}$.*

Proof. In projective geometry, any non-degenerate conic is projectively equivalent to a circle [13]. Therefore, based on different viewing directions, there are two projected centers of the Steiner conic $\mathbf{F}_s$ [13,29]. One is along the camera's viewing direction, and the other is on the opposite viewing direction. Inspired by [14,15,24,35], IAC $\boldsymbol{\omega}$ and the Steiner conic $\mathbf{F}_s$ intersect at four distinct circular points $\mathbf{i}_i, \mathbf{j}_i$, forming two vanishing lines $\mathbf{l}_{hi}$ as (see Fig. 4(a))

$$\mathbf{l}_{hi} = \mathbf{i}_i \times \mathbf{j}_i, \tag{11}$$

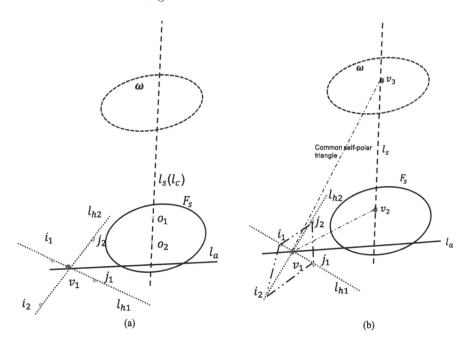

Fig. 4. The projected centers of Steiner conic F_s are on the line l_s. (a) The intersection points of IAC ω and the Steiner conic F_s are two pairs of circular points i_i, j_i, and form two vanishing lines l_{hi}, where $i = 1, 2$. Accordingly, based on the pole-polar relationship with respect to F_s, two projected centers o_i associated with l_{hi} and lie on the line l_s. (b) The general eigenvector v_1, which lies outside the two conics F_s and ω, coincides with the intersection of the two vanishing lines l_{hi}.

where $i = 1, 2$. The two pairs of circular points form a quadrangle, $i_1 i_2 j_1 j_2$ (see Fig. 4(b)). The diagonal triangle $\triangle v_1 v_2 v_3$ is self-polar triangle for the IAC ω [13,14], where the point v_1 is the intersection point of the diagonals of the quadrangle, and the points v_2 and v_3 are the intersection of two opposite sides of the quadrilateral. Therefore, we can get $v_1 = l_{h1} \times l_{h2}$.

According to the pole-polar relationship, these two projected centers of F_s can be obtained by $o_i \sim F_s^{-1} l_{hi}$, which form a line l_c as

$$
\begin{aligned}
l_c &\sim o_1 \times o_2 \\
&\sim F_s^{-1} l_{h1} \times F_s^{-1} l_{h2} \\
&\sim (F_s^{-1})^* (l_{h1} \times l_{h2}) \\
&\sim F_s v_1.
\end{aligned}
\tag{12}
$$

From Proposition 1, we can get $l_s \sim l_c \sim o_1 \times o_2$.

$\square$

Therefore, once the projected centers $\mathbf{o}_i$ of the Steiner conic $\mathbf{F}_s$ are obtained, the polar lines $\mathbf{l}_{hi}$ with respect to $\mathbf{F}_s$ can be recovered. They intersect $\mathbf{F}_s$ at two pairs of circular points $\mathbf{i}_i$, $\mathbf{j}_i$, which lie on the image of the absolute conic $\boldsymbol{\omega}$ as

$$\mathbf{i}_i^T \boldsymbol{\omega} \mathbf{i}_i = \mathbf{j}_i^T \boldsymbol{\omega} \mathbf{j}_i = 0. \tag{13}$$

4.2 Recovery of the Centers of the Steiner Conic $\mathbf{F}_s$

When the principal point is known, Sect. 3.2 introduces a method to calibrate three camera intrinsic parameters using three views. When the principal point is unknown, it is theoretically possible to fully recover the camera intrinsic parameters using the method in Sect. 3.2. However, due to the high order of ambiguity, full camera calibration is not easy to achieve [13]. Instead, as described in Sect. 4.1, the intersection of the IAC $\boldsymbol{\omega}$ and the Steiner conic $\mathbf{F}_s$ are two pairs of imaged circular points, which provide four linear orthogonal constraints on IAC $\boldsymbol{\omega}$ (Eq. 13). Therefore, from three views, six pairs of imaged circular points are sufficient to calibrate the five camera intrinsic parameters.

Taking the center of the image as the initial value of the principal point, we can first get the initial focal length $\hat{f}_x$, $\hat{f}_y$, the skew $\hat{s}$ from three images, using the method in Sect. 3.2, and thus the initial IAC $\hat{\boldsymbol{\omega}}$. For any two views, the image of circular points $\hat{\mathbf{i}}_i, \hat{\mathbf{j}}_i$ can be found by intersecting the initial $\hat{\boldsymbol{\omega}}$ with $\mathbf{F}_s$, so as the vanishing lines $\hat{\mathbf{l}}_{hi}$, by connecting the $\hat{\mathbf{i}}_i, \hat{\mathbf{j}}_i$, respectively. The two initial projected centers $\hat{\mathbf{o}}_i$ of $\mathbf{F}_s$ can then be recovered by $\hat{\mathbf{o}}_i = \mathbf{F}_s^{-1}\hat{\mathbf{l}}_{hi}$ ($i = 1, 2$).

Next, we set the search range for the optimal solution centered on the two initial centers $\hat{\mathbf{o}}_i$. We generate a series of uniformly distributed sample points within these ranges. For each pair of the sample points $\tilde{\mathbf{o}}_i$, we can get the line $\tilde{\mathbf{l}}_s = \tilde{\mathbf{o}}_1 \times \tilde{\mathbf{o}}_2$. We can also get the corresponding vanishing line $\tilde{\mathbf{l}}_{hi}$ using the pole-polar relationship $\tilde{\mathbf{l}}_{hi} = \mathbf{F}_s\tilde{\mathbf{o}}_i$ with respect to $\mathbf{F}_s$. Then, we can calculate the new imaged circular points $\tilde{\mathbf{i}}_i, \tilde{\mathbf{j}}_i$, which are the intersections of the vanishing line $\tilde{\mathbf{l}}_{hi}$ and $\mathbf{F}_s$. We then use Eq. 13 to recover the corresponding image of the absolute conic $\tilde{\boldsymbol{\omega}}$. Finally, all the obtained parameters, the conic centers $\tilde{\mathbf{o}}_i$, the image of circular points $\tilde{\mathbf{i}}_i, \tilde{\mathbf{j}}_i$, the corresponding IAC $\tilde{\boldsymbol{\omega}}$, the Steiner conics $\mathbf{F}_s$, the lines $\mathbf{l}_a$, and the points $\mathbf{x}_a$, are regarded as the input value to substitute into the *cost function* for an iterative optimization.

According to the properties of the line $\mathbf{l}_s$ and its Euclidean geometry property, our cost function for the optimal conic centers $\tilde{\mathbf{o}}_i$ by the Levenberg-Marquardt optimization [27] is

$$cost = \sum_{3}^{N} (\tilde{\mathbf{l}}_s^T \tilde{\boldsymbol{\omega}}^* \mathbf{l}_a + \tilde{\mathbf{l}}_s^T \mathbf{x}_a + \mathbf{l}_l^T \tilde{\boldsymbol{\omega}}^* \mathbf{l}_r), \tag{14}$$

where N is the number of images. $\tilde{\mathbf{l}}_s^T \tilde{\boldsymbol{\omega}}^* \mathbf{l}_a$ contains the orthogonality between $\tilde{\mathbf{l}}_s$ and $\mathbf{l}_a$, where $\tilde{\mathbf{l}}_s$ is obtained by connecting the two center $\tilde{\mathbf{o}}_i$. $\tilde{\mathbf{l}}_s^T \mathbf{x}_a$ indicates $\tilde{\mathbf{l}}_s$ defined by the projected centers of $\mathbf{F}_s$ should also pass through the fixed point $\mathbf{x}_a$. $\mathbf{l}_l^T \tilde{\boldsymbol{\omega}}^* \mathbf{l}_r$ contains the orthogonality between the lines $\mathbf{l}_l$ and $\mathbf{l}_r$ (see Fig. 5) since $\tilde{\mathbf{l}}_s$ passes through the two centers of the conic $\mathbf{F}_s$. Let $\mathbf{x}_c$ be an arbitrary point on $\mathbf{F}_s$, $\mathbf{l}_l = \mathbf{p}_1 \times \mathbf{x}_c$, $\mathbf{l}_r = \mathbf{p}_2 \times \mathbf{x}_c$, where the point $\mathbf{p}_1$ and $\mathbf{p}_2$ are the image of the terminal vertexes of the diameter and can be obtained as the intersections of the line $\tilde{\mathbf{l}}_s$ and $\mathbf{F}_s$.

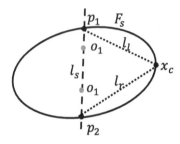

Fig. 5. The illustration for $\mathbf{l}_l^T \tilde{\omega}^* \mathbf{l}_r$. The points $\mathbf{p}_1$ and $\mathbf{p}_2$ are the intersections of $\mathbf{l}_s$ and $\mathbf{F}_s$, and are also the endpoints of the diameter. $\mathbf{x}_c$ is an arbitrary point on $\mathbf{F}_s$. The lines $\mathbf{l}_l$ and $\mathbf{l}_r$ are formed by connecting $\mathbf{x}_c$ with $\mathbf{p}_1$ and $\mathbf{p}_2$, respectively. Moreover, hence $\mathbf{l}_l^T \tilde{\omega}^* \mathbf{l}_r$ contains the orthogonality between the lines $\mathbf{l}_l$ and $\mathbf{l}_r$.

Once the iterative optimization converges, we can obtain three pairs of optimized conic centers $\mathbf{o}_i$. Based on the pole-polar relationship, the corresponding vanishing lines $\mathbf{l}_{hi}$ can be recovered with the optimized conic centers $\mathbf{o}_i$ with respect to the Steiner conic $\mathbf{F}_s$, i.e., $\mathbf{l}_{hi} = \mathbf{F}_s \mathbf{o}_i$, and then further obtain the pairs of the image of circular points $\mathbf{i}_i, \mathbf{j}_i$. The IAC ω with five unknown parameters can be recovered from three or more images by the linear orthogonality constraint in Eq. 13. Finally, the intrinsic matrix $\mathbf{K}$ can be obtained through Cholesky decomposition on the IAC ω [9].

5   Degenerate Cases

The proposed method cannot be used for camera calibration when the camera performs degenerate motions such as pure translation, rotation, and planar motion. Because in these cases, although the point $\mathbf{x}_a$ and its polar line $\mathbf{l}_a$ can be recovered from $\mathbf{F}_s$, $\mathbf{F}_s$ is degenerate, and we cannot recover the complete Steiner conic to get the image of the circular points. Another work will be carried out to introduce detailed camera calibration methods for degenerate motion using different constraints.

6   Experiments and Results

Experiments are carried out on synthetic and real data to evaluate the feasibility of the proposed methods.

6.1   Synthetic Data

In synthetic experiments, a cube mesh containing 3000 3D points (see Fig. 6) was projected into images using predefined projection matrices. Image size is 520 × 480. The camera focal lengths are $f_x = 1000$, $f_y = 800$, the skew is $s = 0.1$, and the principal point is $(u_0, v_0) = (270, 250)$. The external parameters of general motion are randomly set. We add 0 to 3 pixels of uniform random noise to each image point with a noise step size of 0.1. For each noise level, 100 independent trials were conducted to evaluate the feasibility of the proposed method.

Cube Mesh

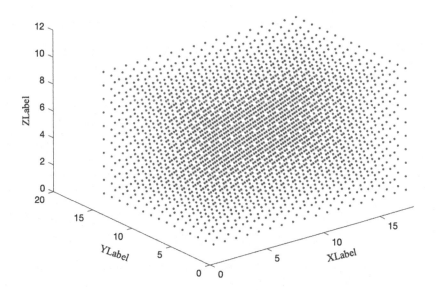

Fig. 6. The synthetic object is a cube mesh containing 3000 3D points.

Known Principal Point. The camera is calibrated from three images using the method described in Sect. 3.2, with the known principal point. Figure 7 shows the results of calibrated focal length f_x, f_y and the skew s versus different image noise levels. It can be seen that the medians of the three calibrated parameters are accurate, all close to the ground truth. The relative errors at noise level 1.0 are $f_x = 0.02\%$, $f_y = 0.17\%$. Since the scale of the skew s is much smaller than that of the focal length, its direct estimation tends to be unstable. However, the errors of skew angle θ in $s = -f_x \cot \theta$ [7] is less than 0.2° (0.017%) compared to the ground truth angle.

Full Camera Auto-calibration. In this case, the camera is first calibrated from three images using the method described in Sect. 3.2, assuming the initial

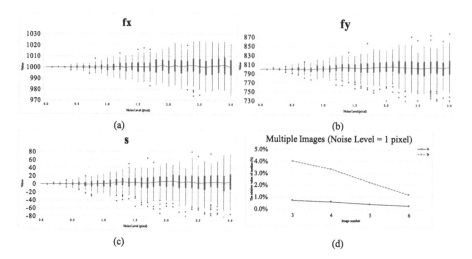

Fig. 7. (a)–(c) Boxplots of known principal points, calibrated focal length f_x, f_y and skew s under different image noise levels. (d) The relative errors of the calibrated focal length f_x and f_y with respect to the number of images under the noise level 1.0.

principal point is at the center of the image. The pair of projected centers of the Steiner conic are then initialized and used to set the searching ranges for optimal solutions using the methods described in Sect. 4.2. In each searching range, 100 uniformly distributed sample image points are generated. Finally, the five camera intrinsic parameters are fully calibrated. Figure 8 shows the results of calibrated focal length f_x, f_y, u_0, v_0 and the skew s versus different image noise levels. It can be seen that the medians of the calibrated parameters are accurate, all close to the ground truth. The relative errors at noise level 1.0 are $f_x = 0.13\%$, $f_y = 0.33\%$, $u_0 = 2.35\%$, and $v_0 = 4.01\%$. The errors of skew angle θ in $s = -f_x \cot \theta$ is less than $0.9°$ (1.0%) compared to the ground truth angle.

Furthermore, the estimate of skew s in this case is worse than when the principal points are known. In addition to the scale issue we mentioned earlier, in this case the instability of the principal point here makes f_y worse, further affecting the skewed s estimate. Fortunately, we can adopy the general zero skew s assumption to provide more stable calibration results [8,13,25,36].

Increased Number of Images. As mentioned in [36], the error decreases when more images are used. At noise level 1.0, we use more images to verify the accuracy of the camera calibration for three (see Fig. 7(d)) or five parameters (Fig. 8(f)), respectively. The median value of each obtained camera parameter is regarded as the best result. As can be seen from Fig. 7(d) and Fig. 8(f), the relative error of the camera intrinsic parameters decreases as the number of images increases. For both cases, an optimal result can be obtained when at least six images are used.

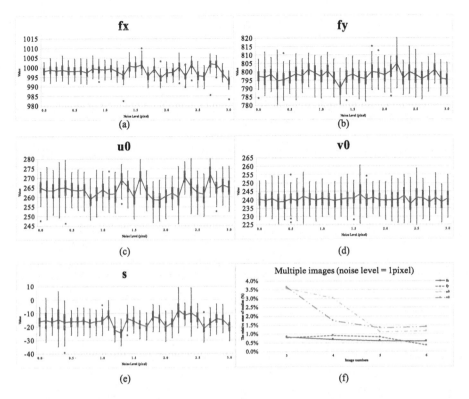

Fig. 8. (a)–(e) Boxplots of calibrated focal length f_x, f_y, principal point u_0, v_0 and skew s under different image noise levels. (f) The relative errors of the calibrated focal length f_x, f_y, and principal point u_0, v_0 with respect to the number of images under the noise level 1.0.

6.2   Real Scenes

In the real experiment, a set of images is captured by Nikon D300s with the image size 4032 × 3024. The ground truth is obtained as the calibration results of the chessboard method [36] from 12 images.

Known Principal Point. The Nikon D300s is calibrated with 3, 6, 10 images respectively, using the image center as the principal point. The calibration results of focal length f_x, f_y and skew s are shown in Table 1. It can be seen that our method can obtain accurate focal length calibration results, and the relative error of focal length is about 4%. The skew s is not accurately estimated, but can be assumed to be zero to provide more stable calibration results. Meanwhile, as more images are used in the calibration, the relative error decreases.

Full Camera Auto-calibration of Intrinsic Parameters. Using the method in Sect. 4.2, we fully calibrate five camera intrinsic parameters with 3, 6, 10 images, respectively. We also provide a comparison with the widely used auto-calibration method GA-PSO [21] and the results are shown in Table 2. It can be

Table 1. Results with the known principal point.

Methods	f_x	f_y	s
GT (12 images) [36]	4486.74	4493.00	−4.07
Ours (3 images)	4213.02 (6.10%)	4722.08 (5.10%)	57.20
Ours (6 images)	4703.82 (4.84%)	4291.95 (4.48%)	−46.40
Ours (10 images)	4692.24 (4.58%)	4301.74 (4.25%)	−12.46

Table 2. Results of full auto-calibration of intrinsic parameters.

Methods	f_x	f_y	s	u_0	v_0
GT (12)	4486.70	4493.00	-4.07	2162.40	1464.70
GA-PSO (3)	4073.27 (9.22%)	4059.92 (9.63%)	251.13	1944.27 (10.08%)	1278.97 (12.68%)
Ours (3)	4287.14 (4.45%)	4234.33 (5.76%)	172.72	2005.88 (7.24%)	1334.47 (8.89%)
GA-PSO (6)	4252.29 (5.22%)	4171.24 (7.16%)	148.49	2389.43 (10.50%)	1319.74 (9.90%)
Ours (6)	4343.96 (3.18%)	4730.33 (5.28%)	142.68	2019.71 (6.60%)	1380.54 (5.75%)
GA-PSO (10)	4699.22(4.74%)	4234.33 (5.76%)	104.05	1990.95 (7.92%)	1354.28 (7.53%)
Ours (10)	4333.79 (3.41%)	4678.82 (4.14%)	108.62	2050.43 (5.18%)	1391.40 (5.01%)

seen that the relative errors achieve better accuracy compared with GA-PSO. The skew s is not accurately estimated, but can be assumed to be zero to provide more stable calibration results [8]. Meanwhile, as more images are used in the calibration, the relative error decreases.

7   Conclusions

This paper proposes new constraints derived from the Steiner conic, the symmetric part of the fundamental matrix, to solve the problem of camera auto-calibration. A method has been presented to determine a fixed line between two views under general motion. We then introduced and proved two properties of the fixed line that can be used for calibration. Based on a known principal point and the new constraints, we presented a method that can calibrate the focal lengths and the skew from three images. Moreover, we proposed a method to fully calibrate the five camera intrinsic parameters through iterative optimization from at least three images, by recovering the pair of the projected centers of the Steiner conic. Finally, we verified the feasibility and accuracy of the proposed method through synthetic and real experiments and achieved state-of-the-art calibration results.

Acknowledgement. This work was supported by the National Key Research and Development Program of China (2022YFE0201400), the National Natural Science Foundation of China (62076029), Guangdong Science and Technology Department (2022B1212010006, 2017A030313362) and internal funds of the United International College (R202012, R201802, UICR0400025-21).

References

1. Agapito, L., Hartley, R., Hayman, E.: Linear calibration of a rotating and zooming camera. In: Proceedings. 1999 IEEE Computer Society Conference on Computer Vision and Pattern Recognition (Cat. No PR00149) (1999)
2. Agapito, L., Hayman, E., Reid, I.D.: Self-calibration of rotating and zooming cameras. Int. J. Comput. Vision **47**, 287 (2005)
3. Barath, D.: Five-point fundamental matrix estimation for uncalibrated cameras. In: 2018 IEEE/CVF Conference on Computer Vision and Pattern Recognition, pp. 235–243 (2018)
4. Chen, H.Y., Matsumoto, K., Ota, J., Arai, T.: Self-calibration of environmental camera for mobile robot navigation. Robot. Auton. Syst. **55**, 177–190 (2007)
5. Dyer, C.R.: Volumetric scene reconstruction from multiple views. In: Foundations of Image Understanding. pp. 469–489. Springer, New York (2001). https://doi.org/10.1007/978-1-4615-1529-6
6. Espuny, F.: A new linear method for camera self-calibration with planar motion. J. Math, Imag. Vis. **27**, 81–88 (2006)
7. Faugeras, O.D., Luong, Q.-T., Maybank, S.J.: Camera self-calibration: theory and experiments. In: Sandini, G. (ed.) ECCV 1992. LNCS, vol. 588, pp. 321–334. Springer, Heidelberg (1992). https://doi.org/10.1007/3-540-55426-2_37
8. Fetzer, T., Reis, G., Stricker, D.: Stable intrinsic auto-calibration from fundamental matrices of devices with uncorrelated camera parameters. In: 2020 IEEE Winter Conference on Applications of Computer Vision (WACV), pp. 221–230 (2020)
9. Gentle, J.: Numerical Linear Algebra for Applications in Statistics. Springer New York (1998). https://doi.org/10.1007/978-1-4612-0623-1
10. Gurdjos, P., Sturm, S., Wu, Y.H.: Euclidean structure from n $\geq$ 2 parallel circles: Theory Algorithms, pp. 238–252 (2006)
11. Habed, A., Boufama, B.: Camera self-calibration from triplets of images using bivariate polynomials derived from Kruppa's equations. In: IEEE International Conference on Image Processing, 2005 2, II-1174 (2005)
12. Hartley, R.: Kruppa's equations derived from the fundamental matrix. IEEE Trans. Pattern Anal. Mach. Intell. **19**, 133–135 (1997)
13. Hartley, R., Zisserman, A.: Multiple View Geometry in Computer Vision, 2nd edn,. Cambridge University Press, Cambridge (2003)
14. Huang, H.F., Zhang, H., Cheung, Y.M.: The common self-polar triangle of separate circles: properties and applications to camera calibration. In: 2016 IEEE International Conference on Image Processing (ICIP), pp. 1170–1174 (2016)
15. Huang, H.F., Zhang, H., Cheung, Y.M.: Homography estimation from the common self-polar triangle of separate ellipses. In: 2016 IEEE Conference on Computer Vision and Pattern Recognition (CVPR), pp. 1737–1744 (2016)
16. Jaynes, C.: Multi-view calibration from planar motion trajectories. Image Vis. Comput. **22**, 535–550 (2004)
17. Ji, Q., Zhang, Y.M.: Camera calibration with genetic algorithms. IEEE Trans. Syst. Man Cybern, Part A Syst. Hum. **31**, 120–130 (2001)
18. Jiang, Z.T., Wu, W.H., Wu, M.: Camera autocalibration from Krupp's equations using particle swarm optimization. In: CSSE (2008)
19. Koch, R., Gool, L.V.: 3D structure from multiple images of large-scale environments. In: Lecture Notes in Computer Science (1998)
20. Lei, C.: A novel camera self-calibration technique based on the Krupp equations. Chinese J. Comput. (2003)

21. Li, J., Yang, Y.M., Fu, G.P.: Camera self-calibration method based on ga-pso algo-rithm. 2011 IEEE International Conference on Cloud Computing and Intelligence Systems pp. 149–152 (2011). https://doi.org/10.1109/CCIS.2011.6045050

22. Liang, B.J., Chen, Z.Z., Pears, N.: Uncalibrated two-view metrology. In: Proceed-ings of the 17th International Conference on Pattern Recognition, vol. 1, pp. 96–99 (2004)

23. Liang, C., Wong, K.: Robust recovery of shapes with unknown topology from the dual space. IEEE Trans. Pattern Anal. Mach. Intell. 29(12), 2205 (2007)

24. Liu, Y., Yang, J.Y., Zhou, X.Y., Ma, Q.Q., Zhang, H.: Intrinsic calibration of a camera to a line-structured light using a single view of two spheres. In: Advanced Concepts for Intelligent Vision Systems. pp. 87–98. Springer, Cham (2018)

25. Mendonca, P.R.S.: Multiview geometry: profiles and self-calibration. Ph.D. thesis, University of Cambridge (2001)

26. Mendonca, P.R.S., Wong, K.Y., Cipolla, R.: Epipolar geometry from profiles under circular motion. IEEE Trans. Pattern Anal. Mach. Intell. 23, 604–616 (2001)

27. Moré, J.J.: The Levenberg-marquardt algorithm: implementation and theory. In: Watson, G.A. (ed.) Numerical Analysis. LNM, vol. 630, pp. 105–116. Springer, Heidelberg (1978). https://doi.org/10.1007/BFb0067700

28. Projectibe, C.Z.: Affine and euclidean calibration in computer vision and the appli-cation of three dimensional perception. Ph.D. thesis, Robot Vis Group. INRIA Sophia - Antipolis (1996)

29. Semple, J., Kneebone, G.: Algebraic Projective Geometry. Oxford University Press, Oxford (1998)

30. Sinha, S.N., Pollefeys, M., McMillan, L.: Camera network calibration from dynamic silhouettes. in: Proceedings of the 2004 IEEE Computer Society Conference on Computer Vision and Pattern Recognition, 2004. CVPR 2004, pp. 235–243 (2004)

31. Wang, G.H., Wu, Q.M., Zhang, W.: Kruppa equation based camera calibration from homography induced by remote plane. Pattern Recogn. Lett. 29, 2137–2144 (2008)

32. Wilczkowiak, M., Boyer, E., Sturm, P.F.: Camera calibration and 3D reconstruc-tion from single images using parallelepipeds. In: Proceedings Eighth IEEE Inter-national Conference on Computer Vision, ICCV 2001, vol. 1, pp. 142–148 (2001)

33. Wong, K.Y., Zhang, G.Q., Liang, C., Zhang, H.: 1D camera geometry and its application to the self-calibration of circular motion sequences. IEEE Trans. Pat-tern Anal. Mach. Intell. 30(12), 2243–2248 (2009)

34. Zhang, H., Wong, K.Y.: Self-calibration of turntable sequences from silhouettes. IEEE Trans. Pattern Anal. Mach. Intell. 31, 5–14 (2009)

35. Zhang, H., Zhang, G.Q., Wong, K.Y.: Camera calibration with spheres: linear approaches. In: IEEE International Conference on Image Processing, vol. 2 (2005)

36. Zhang, Z.Y.: A flexible new technique for camera calibration. IEEE Trans. Pattern Anal. Mach. Intell. 22, 1330–1334 (2000)

37. Zhang, Z.Z.: Camera calibration with one-dimensional objects. In: IEEE, pp. 892–899 (2004)

Super-Resolution 3D Human Shape from a Single Low-Resolution Image

Marco Pesavento[(✉)], Marco Volino, and Adrian Hilton

Centre for Vision, Speech and Signal Processing (CVSSP), University of Surrey,
Guildford, UK
{m.pesavento,m.volino,a.hilton}@surrey.ac.uk

Abstract. We propose a novel framework to reconstruct super-resolution human shape from a single low-resolution input image. The approach overcomes limitations of existing approaches that reconstruct 3D human shape from a single image, which require high-resolution images together with auxiliary data such as surface normal or a parametric model to reconstruct high-detail shape. The proposed framework represents the reconstructed shape with a high-detail implicit function. Analogous to the objective of 2D image super-resolution, the approach learns the mapping from a low-resolution shape to its high-resolution counterpart and it is applied to reconstruct 3D shape detail from low-resolution images. The approach is trained end-to-end employing a novel loss function which estimates the information lost between a low and high-resolution representation of the same 3D surface shape. Evaluation for single image reconstruction of clothed people demonstrates that our method achieves high-detail surface reconstruction from low-resolution images without auxiliary data. Extensive experiments show that the proposed approach can estimate super-resolution human geometries with a significantly higher level of detail than that obtained with previous approaches when applied to low-resolution images. https://marcopesavento.github.io/SuRS/.

1 Introduction

The demand for user-friendly frameworks to create virtual 3D content is increasing at the same pace as the rise in the application of immersive technologies. This has led research to a focus on finding practical solutions to replace existing sophisticated multi-view systems for 3D reconstruction, which are impractical and expensive to build for the general community. With the recent advance of 3D deep learning, several approaches have been proposed to estimate the 3D shape directly from a single RGB image for specific object classes such as human bodies, faces or man made objects. Although consumer cameras are nowadays able to capture high-resolution (HR) images, there are several scenarios where the image

Supplementary Information The online version contains supplementary material available at https://doi.org/10.1007/978-3-031-20086-1_26.

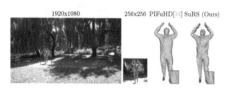

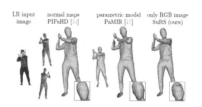

Fig. 1. Person capture in a large space in a HR image [22]. Our approach is able to represent significant higher level of fine details compared to PIFuHD [34] even if these are not clear in the LR input image.

Fig. 2. 3D human digitization of a low-resolution (256 × 256) image. Our approach result represents significant higher level of details compared to related approaches that leverage auxiliary data.

of a single person is not at the full camera image resolution but at a relatively low-resolution (LR) sub-image. Reconstruction of high quality shape from LR images of people is therefore important for example for images of multiple people, scenes requiring a large capture volume or when people are distant from the camera (Fig. 1). Since the LR image contains little detail information, state-of-the-art approaches cannot represent fine details in the reconstructed shape. The introduction of pixel-aligned implicit function (PIFu [33]) improved the quality of human shapes reconstructed from a single image. However, it is highly dependent in the level of details represented on the input image and it fails to reconstruct HR shape from a LR image that does not contain information on fine details. Recent works leverage auxiliary information such as displacement or normal maps together with HR images (1024 × 1024) to retrieve fine details [4,34]. Other methods combine the implicit function with 3D information by using voxel alignment and 3D convolution [11,20,47]. However, none of these works can reconstruct high quality shapes by only using a single LR RGB image.

To tackle this problem, we introduce a new framework that generates Super-Resolution Shape (SuRS) via a high-detail implicit function which learns the mapping from low to high-resolution shape. If a low-resolution shape S_{LR} is compared with its high-resolution counterpart S_{HR}, the primary difference is in the fine details that represent the information lost between S_{LR} and S_{HR}. This information is retrieved by learning the mapping from low to high-resolution shape such that corresponding fine details can be reproduced in the super-resolution shape S_{SR}. We apply SuRS to the task of 3D human digitization to estimate high-detail 3D human shape from a single LR RGB image (256 × 256) without assisting the training with auxiliary data such as normal maps or parametric models. Our approach learns the missing information of S_{LR} in order to estimate fine shape details from a LR image even if these details are not clearly visible in the input image. The final high-detail shape is represented with an implicit representation, which is learned by a novel end-to-end trainable framework with a new loss that estimates the information missing in the low-resolution shape S_{LR} by computing the difference between the implicit representation of high-resolution shape S_{HR} and the estimated implicit representation of the reconstructed super-resolution shape S_{SR}. This loss facilitates the learning of the map as shown in Sect. 4.2. Low and high-resolution features are extracted from the LR input image and then given as input to two multi-layer perceptrons (MLPs), which estimate the probability field over the 3D space. The pixel-alignment feature used in previous approaches [33,34] is adopted by SuRS to preserve local details and infer plausible shape detail in unseen regions. Extensive experiments show that SuRS reconstructs significantly higher resolution human shape detail compared to previous single image human reconstruction approaches when LR images are given as input (Fig. 1). The level of details on the reconstructed surfaces is also much higher to that achieved by state-of-the-art approaches that leverage auxiliary data in the reconstruction process (Fig. 2).

The main contributions of this work are:

- An end-to-end trainable approach for implicit function learning of super-resolution shape for 3D human digitization from single low-resolution image.
- Introduction of a novel loss to learn the mapping between low and high resolution shapes based on the information loss between their representations.
- Improved quantitative and perceptual performance for human shape reconstruction from a single LR image compared with state-of-the-art approaches.

2 Related Works

3D Super Resolution: The concept of super resolution (SR) is well established in the 2D domain. On the other hand, there is considerably less work related to super resolution applied to the 3D domain. Most approaches focus on super-resolving 2.5D data such as texture maps [19,28–30], depth maps [25,35,38, 40], or light field images [32,46]. All of these methods apply similar network architectures to the ones used to super-resolve 2D images. They consider the 2.5D data as a RGB image and leverage a modified convolutional neural network (CNN) architecture with additional data such as normal maps or edge images as input. Sinha et al. [37] and Chen et al. [7] first retrieve a geometry image that embeds geometric information and then super-resolve it with a standard SR CNN, reconstructing the final HR mesh. In this case, the super-resolution task consists of creating the HR mesh by subdividing the LR mesh through remeshing and super-resolving the extracted geometry images. In other methods [9,42], the super-resolution task is formulated for point cloud data as increasing the number of points in the final model, achieved by applying graph networks. Li et al. [20] first retrieve a coarse estimation of human shape from multi-view images and then refine the reconstruction by voxelizing the shape and applying 3D convolution to super-resolve the voxel. The SR voxel is obtained by subdividing each voxel grid in order to increase their total number in the final voxel. We introduce a new concept for super-resolution of shape represented via high-detail implicit function. In this paper, super resolution is defined as the reproduction of high quality details in the reconstructed shape even if they are not embedded in the input. To overcome the resolution limitation of previous methods, we propose a novel approach that learns to map a LR shape to its HR counterpart.

3D Human Digitization: Early 3D human digitization strategies such as fitting the input image by a parametric model [6,16,17,27,43], using a 3D CNN to regress volumetric representation [39,48] or adding a displacement on each vertex of the mesh [2–4], mainly aim to recover the naked body's shape with only approximate representation of shape details such as clothing and hairs. With the ground-breaking introduction of implicit functions for 3D reconstruction [8,12,14,23,26], deep learning approaches that estimate 3D human shape, started to adopt this form of representation because it can represent fine-scale details on the reconstructed surfaces. The first work to adopt the implicit representation for 3D human digitization from a single image was PIFu [33], which exploits pixel-aligned image features rather than global features. The local details present in the input image are preserved since the occupancy of any 3D point is predicted.

There are two main problems with this approach that are addressed from other works: it may generate incorrect body structures and struggle to recover fine-scale geometric details. With regards to the first problem, several frameworks combine the implicit function with either a parametric model [14,47] or geometry-aligned shape feature [11] to improve the stability of prediction since they serve as a shape prior for the reconstruction. These works focus on improving the parts of the reconstructed geometry that are not seen in the input image, deliberately neglecting the representation of fine details. To increase the quality of the reconstructed shape, PIFuHD [34] leverages HR images (>1k resolution) as well as front and back normal maps in the reconstruction process. The normal maps need to be predicted from the HR input image with an additional network. The use of HR images and normal maps increases the computation cost and memory use. Other approaches reconstruct high-detail shape using multiple images [13,20,45,49], which is a different objective from single image 3D reconstruction.

Our proposed framework aims to reconstruct super-resolution geometries from a single LR image (256 × 256) without leveraging auxiliary data.

3   Methodology

We introduce a novel framework that aims to learn a high-detail implicit shape representation to recover Super-Resolution Shape (SuRS) from a single LR RGB image. A LR image does not contain significant information about fine details and previous approaches for shape reconstruction from a single image cannot reconstruct detailed shape if the fine detail are not embedded in the input (Sect. 4.3). Inspired by the 2D image super-resolution objective of mapping LR images to their HR counterparts, SuRS learns to map a LR surface S_{LR} to its HR counterpart S_{HR}. By learning the missing information of S_{LR} with respect to S_{HR}, our approach can reproduce the fine details of the HR shape even if they are not embedded in the input. We define Super-Resolution shape S_{SR} as a shape with fine details reconstructed from a LR input image.

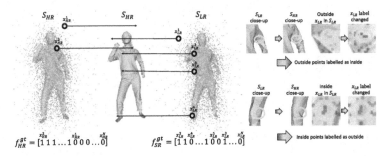

Fig. 3. On the left, comparison between ordinary implicit representation of 3D points x_{HR} sampled from the HR surface S_{HR} space and implicit function representation of super-resolution shape with 3D points x_{LR} sampled from the LR surface S_{LR} space and classified with respect to S_{HR}. The red points are 'inside' the surfaces while the green ones are 'outside'. On the right, close-up of the labelling process: some points 'outside' S_{LR} are represented as 'inside' points (first row) while some other points 'inside' S_{LR} are labelled as 'outside' (second row).

3.1   Implicit Function Representations of Super-Resolution Shape

An implicit function defines a surface as a level set of a function f, e.g. $f(X) = 0$ [36] where X is a set of 3D points in $\Re^3$. To represent a 3D surface S, this function $f(X)$ is modelled with a Multi-Layer Perceptron (MLP) that classifies the 3D points as either 'inside' or 'outside' the 3D surface S. A HR surface S_{HR} can be represented as a 0.5 level-set of a continuous 3D occupancy field:

$$f_{HR}^{gt}(x_{HR}) = \begin{cases} 1, \text{if } x_{HR} \text{ is inside } S_{HR} \\ 0, \text{otherwise} \end{cases} \tag{1}$$

where x_{HR} is a point in the 3D space around the HR surface S_{HR}. This means that f_{HR}^{gt} is a vector of length N, where N is the total number of 3D points x_{HR} that are sampled from S_{HR} space and classified as 'inside' or 'outside' points:

- $f_{HR}^{gt}[0 : \frac{N}{2}] = 1$ correspond to the $\frac{N}{2}$ 3D points inside S_{HR};
- $f_{HR}^{gt}[\frac{N}{2} + 1 : N] = 0$ correspond to the $\frac{N}{2}$ 3D points outside S_{HR};

To map the LR surface to the HR surface, we adapt the implicit function representation to the 3D super-resolution shape. We define a new ground truth for the high-detail implicit function of the estimated super-resolution shape S_{SR}:

$$f_{SR}^{gt}(x_{LR}) = \begin{cases} 1, \text{if } x_{LR} \text{ is inside } S_{HR} \\ 0, \text{otherwise} \end{cases} \tag{2}$$

where x_{LR} are the 3D points sampled from the space of the LR surface S_{LR}. In contrast to the common implicit function, f_{SR}^{gt} is created by classifying the 3D points x_{LR} with respect to the HR surface instead of the LR one: some x_{LR} points are labelled as 'outside' even if they are 'inside' S_{LR}, and viceversa (Fig. 3). The

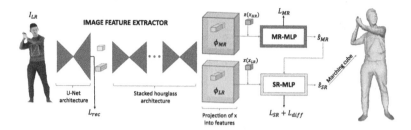

Fig. 4. Network architecture of SuRS. The image feature extractor creates an embedding from the LR input image. 3D points are projected on the embedding and classified first by MR-MLP to produce a mid-level resolution estimation and then by SR-MLP to obtain the super-resolution estimation, from which the 3D SR shape is reconstructed.

vector f_{SR}^{gt} contains $N_{inside} \neq \frac{N}{2}$ values equal to 1 and $N_{outside} \neq N_{inside} \neq \frac{N}{2}$ values equal to 0. This will lead the MLP that models f_{SR}^{gt} to classify points of the LR surface S_{LR} as points of an HR surface S_{HR}, learning a map from S_{LR} to S_{HR}. The points that change classification represent the difference between S_{HR} and S_{LR}, which is primarily in the fine details of the shapes. SuRS learns to infer this difference to estimate super-resolution shape detail from a LR image.

3.2   Super-Resolution Single-View Shape Estimation

We apply SuRS to the task of 3D human digitization from a single LR RGB image. To reconstruct a 3D human shape from a single high-resolution RGB image I_{HR}, Saito et al. [33] introduced pixel aligned implicit function (PIFu), whose objective is to predict the binary occupancy value for any given 3D position x in continuous camera space. Instead of classifying directly the 3D points X of the surface, PIFu estimates the level-set by exploiting the image feature $\phi(p)$ of the 2D projection $p = \pi(x_{HR})$ of the 3D point x_{HR} in the input image I_{HR}. The function f is represented by a MLP that is conditioned on the depth value $z(x_{HR})$ of x_{HR} in the camera coordinate space:

$$f_{HR}(\phi(p, I_{HR}), z(x_{HR})) = \hat{s}_{HR}, \hat{s}_{HR} \in \mathbb{R} \tag{3}$$

We modify the pixel-aligned implicit function representation by adapting it to the reconstruction of super-resolution shape from a low-resolution image I_{LR}:

$$f_{SR}(\phi(p_{LR}, I_{LR}), z(x_{LR}), \hat{s}_{MR}) = \hat{s}_{SR}, \hat{s}_{SR} \in \mathbb{R} \tag{4}$$

where x_{LR} are the 3D points sampled from the space of the LR surface S_{LR}, $p_{LR} = \pi(x_{LR})$, $\hat{s}_{MR}$ is a mid-resolution estimation of the shape computed with $f_{HR}^{gt}(x_{HR})$ from a LR input image and $\hat{s}_{SR}$ is a super-resolution estimation of the shape computed with $f_{SR}^{gt}(x_{LR})$. SuRS is modelled via a neural network architecture composed of 3 modules and trained end-to-end (Fig. 4).

• **Image features extractor:** an image feature embedding is extracted from the projected 2D location of the 3D points in the LR image I_{LR}. Specifically, the embedding is the concatenation of two feature vectors extracted from the input image of size $(N_I \times N_I)$: one with the resolution of $(\frac{N_I}{2} \times \frac{N_I}{2})$ to maintain holistic reasoning and the second of higher resolution $(2N_I \times 2N_I)$ to embed the fine detail of the input image. The combination of holistic reasoning and high-resolution images features is essential for high-fidelity 3D reconstruction [34].

• **Mid-resolution multi-layer perceptron (MR-MLP):** a first classification $\hat{s}_{MR}$ of the 3D points x_{HR} sampled from S_{HR} space is computed with an MLP that models the pixel aligned implicit function $f_{MR}(\phi(p, I_{LR}), z(x_{HR}))$. x_{HR} are projected through orthogonal projection to the LR input image I_{LR} and indexed to the feature embedding retrieved before. This is concatenated with the depth value $z(x_{HR})$ of x_{HR} in the camera coordinate space and given as input to MR-MLP. f_{MR} differs from f_{HR} because the input is a low-resolution image: the output representation of MR-MLP does not reconstruct high-detail shape since information is missing in the LR input image and it cannot be learned with the standard implicit function modelled by MR-MLP (Sect. 4.2).

• **Super-resolution multi-layer perceptron (SR-MLP):** the final estimation $\hat{s}_{SR}$ is obtained with a further MLP, which models the implicit function f_{SR} to represent super-resolution shape. The input of SR-MLP differs from the MR-MLP one since the 3D points x_{LR} are sampled from the space of the LR surface S_{LR}, projected to the input image and indexed to the feature embedding. Their projection is then concatenated with the depth value $z(x_{LR})$ of x_{LR}. To help the learning of a map from S_{LR} to S_{HR}, the estimation $\hat{s}_{MR}$ is concatenated with the input embedding of SR-MLP to facilitate the learning of the lost information of S_{LR}. SR-MLP trained with f_{SR}^{gt} learns to classify x_{LR} according to the difference between S_{LR} and S_{HR}. Compared to MR-MLP, SR-MLP additionally infers this difference to the estimation $\hat{s}_{SR}$, representing fine details on the SR shape even if they are not represented in the LR input image.

During inference, a LR image is given as input to the network. A set of M random 3D points x of the 3D space are projected on the extracted embedding and then classified first with MR-MLP to estimate $\hat{s}_{MR}$ and then with SR-MLP to estimate $\hat{s}_{SR}$. The final shape is obtained by extracting iso-surface $f = 0.5$ of the probability field $\hat{s}_{SR}$ at threshold 0.5 applying the Marching Cube algorithm [21].

3.3 Training Objectives

Our objective function combines 4 different losses used to train the 3 modules:

$$\mathcal{L} = \mathcal{L}_{rec} + \mathcal{L}_{MR} + \mathcal{L}_{SR} + \mathcal{L}_{diff} \tag{5}$$

2D reconstruction loss: the higher resolution feature extracted from the LR input image is double the size of the image. To ensure that the newly created features will preserve the spatial structure of the LR input image, SuRS minimises the L1 loss commonly used in the 2D image super-resolution task [41]:

$$\mathcal{L}_{rec} = ||I_{SR} - I_{GT}||_1 \tag{6}$$

I_{SR} is an image reconstructed from the HR features extracted by the feature extractor module and processed by a further convolutional layer. I_{GT} is the ground-truth of the reconstructed image I_{SR}.

MR loss: since MR-MLP represents a pixel aligned implicit function, we train the network by minimising the average of mean squared error between MR-MLP output and the canonical ground-truth of implicit functions as done in PIFu [33]:

$$\mathcal{L}_{MR} = \frac{1}{N} \sum_{i=1}^{N} |f_{MR}(\phi^i_{MR}, z(x^i_{HR})) - f^{gt}_{HR}(x^i_{HR})|^2 \tag{7}$$

where N is the number of points x_{HR} sampled from the space of S_{HR}, $\phi^i_{MR} = \phi(p, I_{LR})$ and $f_{MR}(\phi^i_{MR}, z(x^i_{HR})) = \hat{s}_{MR}$.

SR loss: to compute the final estimation, the average of mean squared error between the output of SR-MLP and SuRS ground-truth is minimised:

$$\mathcal{L}_{SR} = \frac{1}{N} \sum_{i=1}^{N} |f_{SR}(\phi^i_{LR}, z(x^i_{LR}), \hat{s}_{MR}) - f^{gt}_{SR}(x^i_{LR})|^2 \tag{8}$$

where $\phi^i_{LR} = \phi(p_{LR}, I_{LR})$, $f_{SR}(\phi^i_{LR}, z(x^i_{LR}), \hat{s}_{MR}) = \hat{s}_{SR}$ and the N points x_{LR} are sampled from the space of S_{LR}.

Difference loss: to facilitate the learning of the map from S_{LR} to S_{HR}, we design a novel loss that minimises the average of mean squared error of the difference between S_{SR} and S_{HR}, expressed as the difference between the estimated values $\hat{s}_{MR}$ and $\hat{s}_{SR}$:

$$\mathcal{L}_{diff} = \frac{1}{N} \sum_{i=1}^{N} |(f^{gt}_{HR} - f^{gt}_{SR}) - (\hat{s}_{MR} - \hat{s}_{SR})|^2 \tag{9}$$

Since f^{gt}_{SR} contains the missing information of S_{LR}, this loss leads the network to learn in which points S_{LR} differs from S_{HR}. Since these points represent the fine details, the network learns how to reproduce them in the estimated shape. This loss is important to learn the super-resolution shape detail (see Sect. 4.2).

4   Experiments

We quantitatively and qualitatively evaluate the proposed approach on the task of reconstructing 3D human shape from a single LR image. To train SuRS, LR surfaces must be retrieved from a set of HR example models. The performance will improve if the displacement between S_{HR} and S_{LR} is higher as shown in Sect. 4.2. Therefore, we use the THuman2.0 [44] dataset, which consists of 524 high-resolution surfaces which have a high level of fine details. We split the dataset into training (402 models) and testing (122 models). To evaluate the generalisation of the method, we test SuRS on 136 models taken from 3D People [1]. We evaluate the reconstruction accuracy with 3 quantitative metrics: the normal reprojection error introduced in [33], the average point-to-surface Euclidean distance (P2S) and the Chamfer distance (CD), expressed in cm.

4.1   Implementation Details

SuRS is trained with LR images I_{LR} of size $(N_I \times N_I, N_I = 256)$ obtained by downscaling by a factor of 2 ground truth images I_{GT} with bicubic degradation. We first apply [5] to make the HR surfaces watertight. For training, a LR shape S_{LR} is obtained by remeshing S_{HR} from $\sim 400k$ to $1k$ faces via quadric edge collapse decimation [10]. $N_T = 24000$ 3D points X are sampled with a mixture of uniform sampling and importance sampling around surface S_{HR} following PIFu [33]. A subset of X of $N = 6000$ x_{HR} points are sampled for S_{HR} by selecting $\frac{N}{2}$ points inside and $\frac{N}{2}$ outside S_{HR}. A different subset of X of $N = 6000$ x_{LR} points are sampled for S_{LR} by selecting $\frac{N}{2}$ points inside and $\frac{N}{2}$ outside S_{LR}. The novel architecture of the image feature extractor is a combination of U-Net [31] and stacked hourglass architectures [24]. The former retrieves the features whose resolution is double that of the input image while the second has been proved to be effective for surface reconstruction [24]. We design a novel U-Net architecture to retrieve both high and low-resolution features from the input image (see supplementary material). The HR features are then processed by a convolution layer while the LR features by 3 stacks. The outputs of the image feature extractor are a HR feature vector of size $(2N_I \times 2N_I \times 64)$ and a LR one of size $(\frac{N_I}{2} \times \frac{N_I}{2} \times 256)$. The final embedding is obtained with the concatenation of these two vectors. MR-MLP has the number of neurons of (321, 1024, 512, 256, 128, 1) while SR-MLP of (322, 1024, 512, 256, 128, 1) with skip connections at 3rd, 4th and 5th layers.

4.2   Ablation Studies

Training Configurations. In the first ablation study we demonstrate that training the losses of the network in an end-to-end manner improves the performance of SuRS. We evaluate the network by training separately the three modules; by training first the feature extractor ($\mathcal{L}_{rec}$) and then the two MLPs together ($\mathcal{L}_{diff} + \mathcal{L}_{MR} + \mathcal{L}_{SR}$); by first training the feature extractor and the MR-MLP together ($\mathcal{L}_{rec} + \mathcal{L}_{MR}$) and then the SR-MLP ($\mathcal{L}_{diff} + \mathcal{L}_{SR}$). $\mathcal{L}_{diff}$ is always trained with $\mathcal{L}_{SR}$ since it depends on the output of SR-MLP. The values of the considered metrics are the highest when the end-to-end training is adopted (Table 1). This is confirmed by the qualitative evaluation (Fig. 5). The worst results are obtained when the feature extractor ($\mathcal{L}_{rec}$) is trained separately from the MLPs (case 1, 2). In these cases, the feature extractor learns how to create the embedding without being influenced by the classification part of the network: the extracted features embed information that is meaningless for the task of 3D human reconstruction. When the feature extractor is trained along with the MLPs (case 3, 4), the extracted features are influenced by the other losses and they are more informative for the objective of 3D human digitization. This proves that just applying a 2D image super-resolution network to upscale the input image as a pre-processing step is less efficient than the proposed approach. Training SR-MLP separately introduces noise in the reconstructed shapes while the end-to-end configuration produces the best results.

Table 1. Quantitative results obtained by training SuRS with different configurations.

Training Configuration	THuman2.0			3D people		
	CD	Normal	P2S	CD	Normal	P2S
1: $\mathcal{L}_{rec};\mathcal{L}_{MR};\mathcal{L}_{SR} + \mathcal{L}_{disp}$	1.375	0.1360	1.454	1.509	0.1261	1.636
2: $\mathcal{L}_{rec};\mathcal{L}_{MR} + \mathcal{L}_{SR} + \mathcal{L}_{disp}$	1.261	0.1347	1.496	1.243	0.1240	1.470
3: $\mathcal{L}_{rec} + \mathcal{L}_{MR};\mathcal{L}_{SR} + \mathcal{L}_{disp}$	1.035	0.1106	1.083	1.121	0.1160	1.281
4: End to end (ours)	**0.931**	**0.1065**	1.151	**1.057**	0.1127	**1.247**

Table 2. Quantitative evaluation of using different decimation factors to create the low-resolution ground-truth shape.

Nr. faces	THuman2.0			3D people		
	CD	Normal	P2S	CD	Normal	P2S
100000	0.942	0.1084	1.117	1.147	0.1123	1.331
50000	0.950	0.1079	1.117	1.118	**0.1120**	1.291
10000	0.941	0.1113	**1.116**	1.084	0.1133	1.276
1000 (ours)	**0.931**	**0.1065**	1.151	**1.057**	0.1127	**1.247**

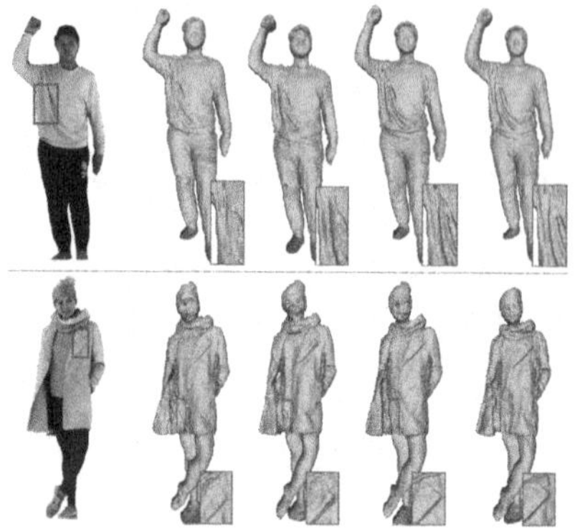

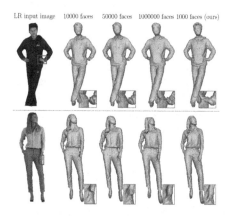

Fig. 5. Visual results obtained by changing the configuration of training. 1, 2, 3 and 4 are different configurations (refer to Table 1). The upper model is from THuman2.0, the below one from 3DPeople.

Fig. 6. Qualitative results obtained by using different decimation factors to create the low-resolution ground-truth shape. The upper model is from THuman2.0, the below one from 3DPeople.

Decimation Factors. To create the LR geometry from the HR shape, we apply quadric edge collapse decimation that reduces the number of faces. We evaluate our approach by changing the decimation factor of the number of faces of S_{LR}. Low-resolution geometries with 100000, 50000, 10000 and 1000 faces are created (examples are illustrated in the supplementary material). Both the quantitative (Table 2) and qualitative (Fig. 6) results show that the performance increases when the number of faces of S_{LR} is the lowest, with significantly sharper details on the output shapes. Our approach is more efficient if the difference between the HR ground-truth shape and the LR ground-truth one is higher. SuRS learns to estimate missing information to obtain the SR shape by mapping S_{LR} to S_{HR}. As S_{LR} is coarser, the information loss increases while if S_{LR} is similar to S_{HR}, there is no missing information, hence nothing to learn. The LR shapes with 1000 faces are the ones with the highest displacement from their HR counterparts, hence the improvement in the performance.

Table 3. Quantitative results obtained by changing the architecture of the approach.

Architecture	THuman2.0			3D people		
	CD	Normal	P2S	CD	Normal	P2S
W/o U-Net	1.090	0.1228	1.204	1.260	0.1296	1.364
Only MR-MLP	1.044	0.1066	1.077	1.240	0.1129	1.276
Only SR-MLP	1.039	0.1146	**1.051**	1.223	0.1215	1.255
W/o $\mathcal{L}_{diff}$	1.020	0.1138	1.196	1.127	0.1200	1.255
SuRS (ours)	**0.931**	**0.1065**	1.151	**1.057**	**0.1127**	**1.247**

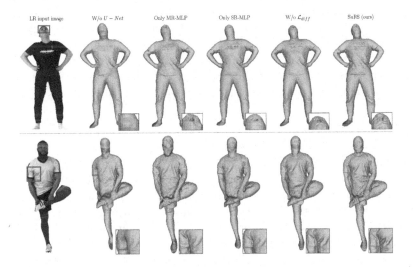

Fig. 7. Visual results obtained by changing the architecture of our approach. The upper model is from THuman2.0 while the below is from 3DPeople.

Efficiency of the Proposed Architecture and Displacement Loss. We demonstrate the significant improvement achieved by the combination of the 3 modules and by the introduction of $\mathcal{L}_{diff}$. We train and test 4 frameworks obtained by modifying the architecture of SuRS:

- **Without U-Net:** the U-Net architecture of the feature extractor is not implemented. The feature embedding, extracted only by the stacked hourglass part of the future extractor, is composed by two feature vectors of size $(N_I \times N_I \times 64)$ and $(\frac{N_I}{2} \times \frac{N_I}{2} \times 256)$. $\mathcal{L}_{rec}$ is not minimised during training.
- **Only MR-MLP:** this framework consists only of the image feature extractor and MR-MLP. SR-MLP is not implemented and the shape is reconstructed from $\hat{s}_{MR}$. $\mathcal{L}_{SR}$ and $\mathcal{L}_{diff}$ are not considered during training.
- **Only SR-MLP:** the feature embedding is directly processed by SR-MLP that outputs the estimation $\hat{s}_{SR}$ without being conditioned on $\hat{s}_{MR}$. $\mathcal{L}_{MR}$ and $\mathcal{L}_{diff}$ are not minimised during training.

– **Without** $\mathcal{L}_{diff}$: this framework is the same as the proposed one but it is trained without considering $\mathcal{L}_{diff}$ to check the importance of this loss.

Both the quantitative (Table 3) and the qualitative (Fig. 7) evaluations show the importance of implementing all the different modules of SuRS. If the HR features are not extracted (W/o U-Net), the fine details are lost in the reconstructed shape, which is just a coarse representation of the input image. Less sharp details are obtained when only MR-MLP is applied, with a lower resolution of the final reconstruction. This configuration does not use either the f_{SR}^{gt} ground-truth or the L_{diff} and this deteriorates the performance. In this case, the network does not learn the map from S_{LR} to S_{HR} and the lost information is not retrieved. Similarly, this map is not learned when only SR-MLP is applied and significant lower resolution shapes are obtained compared to when the map is learned (combination of SR-MLP and MR-MLP with HR features), confirming the efficiency of SuRS. The difference between training SuRS with or without L_{diff} is significant proving its efficiency: the wrinkles of the dress are sharper and human body parts are more realistic when L_{diff} is minimised.

4.3 Comparisons

We compare SuRS with related works on 3D human digitization from a single image. We evaluate DeepHuman [48], which do not use implicit representation but leverage parametric models to facilitate the reconstruction. We then compare SuRS with approaches that represent the 3D surfaces with implicit representation. Among these, PIFu [33] is the only one which uses only single RGB images. PIFuHD [34] exploits front and back normal maps while PaMIR [47] and Geo-PIFu [11] leverage parametric models. We train and test PIFuHD without using normal maps (PIFuHD$_{no}$). These approaches are trained and tested with the same datasets as SuRS except for Geo-PIFu, which cannot pre-processed THuman2.0 shapes. See supplementary material for further comparisons.

Qualitative Evaluation: Figure 8 illustrates two shapes reconstructed from a LR input image of sizes $N_I = 256$. Compared to other methods, SuRS reconstructs significantly higher resolution shapes, which contain the highest level of fine details in clothes and faces. Related works produce coarse shapes with smooth details even if other data such as normal maps or parametric models is leveraged.

Quantitative Evaluation: Our approach outperforms related works when only LR input images are used in both training and testing. SuRS achieves the highest values of the considered metrics, proving its superiority over all the considered approaches (Table 4). SuRS outperforms also all the other approaches that use auxiliary data for the CD and Normal metrics. PiFUHD achieves lower values of P2S due to its use of back normal maps, which improve its performance on parts of the model that are not seen in just a single image.

Real Data: We qualitatively evaluate our approach on images of people captured in real scenarios. More specifically, we reconstruct the 3D shape of a person from an HR image (>1024) where the person resolution is at a relatively

Table 4. Quantitative comparisons between state-of-the-art approaches with LR input image for training and testing. The highest scores are highlighted in red while the second highest scores are blue.

N_I	Methods	THuman2.0			3D people		
		CD	Normal	P2S	CD	Normal	P2S
256	DeepHuman [48]	1.956	0.1465	2.063	1.703	0.1253	1.733
	PIFu [33]	1.518	0.1218	1.647	1.519	0.1198	1.581
	PIFuHD$_{no}$	1.308	0.1237	1.346	1.440	0.1595	1.464
	PIFuHD [34]	1.032	0.1116	1.046	1.062	0.1257	1.037
	PaMIR [47]	1.713	0.1341	1.818	1.644	0.1410	1.740
	Geo-PIFu [11]	1.786	0.1473	1.724	1.853	0.1658	1.652
	SuRS (ours)	0.931	0.1065	1.151	1.057	0.1127	1.247

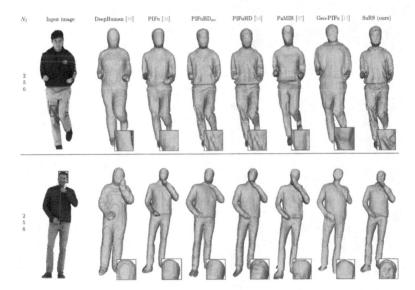

Fig. 8. Visual comparisons using LR input image for training and testing. The upper model is from THuman2.0, the below one is from 3DPeople.

low-resolution sub-image of the original HR image ($< 350 \times 350$). We select random images from various datasets [15,18] and we compare SuRS with only the approaches that do not use auxiliary data in the reconstruction, namely PiFU and PIFuHD$_{no}$. For the reconstruction, a LR human body patch is cropped from the HR image. SuRS significantly outperforms the other approaches, reproducing higher level of fine details on the reconstructed shapes, which are coarser with smoother details if reconstructed by the other approaches (Fig. 9).

Limitations: our method cannot super-resolve parts of the human body that are not visible on the input image: since no auxiliary data are provided, SuRS

HR image   LR patch   PiFu[33]   PIFuHD$_{no}$[34]   SuRS (ours)

Fig. 9. Human shapes reconstructed from LR patches of HR images of people.

reconstructs a coarse geometry of the hidden parts of the body. Like existing works, it may generate incorrect body structures when the input model presents features that significantly differ from the ones seen during training. It may also suffer problems related to depth ambiguity. Examples in supplementary material.

5   Conclusion

We propose Super-Resolution shape represented by an high-detail implicit representation and we tackle the problem of 3D human digitization from a single low-resolution image. To achieve this, we propose a novel architecture with a customised novel loss that can reconstruct super-resolution shape from a low-resolution image. As demonstrated by the evaluation, the reconstructed surfaces contain significantly higher level of details compared to the outputs of related methods when low-resolution images are used. The resolution of the shape obtained from a low-resolution image is significantly higher than the one obtained by state-of-the-art works that leverage also auxiliary data such as normal maps and parametric models. As future works, a super-resolution texture representation will be investigated and the approach will be extended to dynamic shape.

Acknowledgement. This research was supported by UKRI EPSRC Platform Grant EP/P022529/1.

References

1. 3D people. https://3dpeople.com/en/. Accessed 6 Oct 2021
2. Alldieck, T., Magnor, M., Bhatnagar, B.L., Theobalt, C., Pons-Moll, G.: Learning to reconstruct people in clothing from a single RGB camera. In: Proceedings of the IEEE/CVF Conference on Computer Vision and Pattern Recognition, pp. 1175–1186 (2019)
3. Alldieck, T., Magnor, M., Xu, W., Theobalt, C., Pons-Moll, G.: Video based reconstruction of 3d people models. In: Proceedings of the IEEE Conference on Computer Vision and Pattern Recognition, pp. 8387–8397 (2018)
4. Alldieck, T., Pons-Moll, G., Theobalt, C., Magnor, M.: Tex2shape: detailed full human body geometry from a single image. In: Proceedings of the IEEE/CVF International Conference on Computer Vision, pp. 2293–2303 (2019)
5. Barill, G., Dickson, N., Schmidt, R., Levin, D.I., Jacobson, A.: Fast winding numbers for soups and clouds. ACM Trans. Graph. **37**, 1–12 (2018)
6. Bogo, F., Kanazawa, A., Lassner, C., Gehler, P., Romero, J., Black, M.J.: Keep It SMPL: automatic estimation of 3D human pose and shape from a single image. In: Leibe, B., Matas, J., Sebe, N., Welling, M. (eds.) ECCV 2016. LNCS, vol. 9909, pp. 561–578. Springer, Cham (2016). https://doi.org/10.1007/978-3-319-46454-1_34
7. Chen, L., Ye, J., Jiang, L., Ma, C., Cheng, Z., Zhang, X.: Synthesizing cloth wrinkles by CNN-based geometry image superresolution. Comput. Anim. Vir. Worlds **29**(3–4), e1810 (2018)

8. Chen, Z., Zhang, H.: Learning implicit fields for generative shape modeling. In: Proceedings of the IEEE/CVF Conference on Computer Vision and Pattern Recognition, pp. 5939–5948 (2019)

9. Dinesh, C., Cheung, G., Bajić, I.V.: Super-resolution of 3D color point clouds via fast graph total variation. In: ICASSP 2020–2020 IEEE International Conference on Acoustics, Speech and Signal Processing (ICASSP), pp. 1983–1987. IEEE (2020)

10. Garland, M., Heckbert, P.S.: Simplifying surfaces with color and texture using quadric error metrics. In: Proceedings Visualization'98 (Cat. No. 98CB36276), pp. 263–269. IEEE (1998)

11. He, T., Collomosse, J., Jin, H., Soatto, S.: Geo-PIFU: geometry and pixel aligned implicit functions for single-view human reconstruction. arXiv preprint arXiv:2006.08072 (2020)

12. He, T., Xu, Y., Saito, S., Soatto, S., Tung, T.: Arch++: animation-ready clothed human reconstruction revisited. In: Proceedings of the IEEE/CVF International Conference on Computer Vision, pp. 11046–11056 (2021)

13. Hong, Y., Zhang, J., Jiang, B., Guo, Y., Liu, L., Bao, H.: StereoPiFu: depth aware clothed human digitization via stereo vision. In: Proceedings of the IEEE/CVF Conference on Computer Vision and Pattern Recognition, pp. 535–545 (2021)

14. Huang, Z., Xu, Y., Lassner, C., Li, H., Tung, T.: ARCH: animatable reconstruction of clothed humans. In: Proceedings of the IEEE/CVF Conference on Computer Vision and Pattern Recognition, pp. 3093–3102 (2020)

15. Johnson, S., Everingham, M.: Clustered pose and nonlinear appearance models for human pose estimation. In: Proceedings of the British Machine Vision Conference (2010). https://doi.org/10.5244/C.24.12

16. Kanazawa, A., Black, M.J., Jacobs, D.W., Malik, J.: End-to-end recovery of human shape and pose. In: Proceedings of the IEEE Conference on Computer Vision and Pattern Recognition, pp. 7122–7131 (2018)

17. Kocabas, M., Athanasiou, N., Black, M.J.: VIBE: video inference for human body pose and shape estimation. In: Proceedings of the IEEE/CVF Conference on Computer Vision and Pattern Recognition, pp. 5253–5263 (2020)

18. Li, L.J., Fei-Fei, L.: What, where and who? classifying events by scene and object recognition. In: 2007 IEEE 11th International Conference on Computer Vision, pp. 1–8. IEEE (2007)

19. Li, Y., Tsiminaki, V., Timofte, R., Pollefeys, M., Gool, L.V.: 3D appearance super-resolution with deep learning. In: Proceedings of the IEEE/CVF Conference on Computer Vision and Pattern Recognition, pp. 9671–9680 (2019)

20. Li, Z., Oskarsson, M., Heyden, A.: Detailed 3d human body reconstruction from multi-view images combining voxel super-resolution and learned implicit representation. arXiv preprint arXiv:2012.06178 (2020)

21. Lorensen, W.E., Cline, H.E.: Marching cubes: a high resolution 3d surface construction algorithm. ACM SIGGRAPH Comput. Graph. **21**(4), 163–169 (1987)

22. Malleson, C., Collomosse, J., Hilton, A.: Real-time multi-person motion capture from multi-view video and imus. Int. J. Comput. Vision **128**(6), 1594–1611 (2020)

23. Mescheder, L., Oechsle, M., Niemeyer, M., Nowozin, S., Geiger, A.: Occupancy networks: learning 3D reconstruction in function space. In: Proceedings of the IEEE/CVF Conference on Computer Vision and Pattern Recognition, pp. 4460–4470 (2019)

24. Newell, A., Yang, K., Deng, J.: Stacked hourglass networks for human pose estimation. In: Leibe, B., Matas, J., Sebe, N., Welling, M. (eds.) ECCV 2016. LNCS, vol. 9912, pp. 483–499. Springer, Cham (2016). https://doi.org/10.1007/978-3-319-46484-8_29

25. Ni, M., Lei, J., Cong, R., Zheng, K., Peng, B., Fan, X.: Color-guided depth map super resolution using convolutional neural network. IEEE Access **5**, 26666–26672 (2017)

26. Park, J.J., Florence, P., Straub, J., Newcombe, R., Lovegrove, S.: DeepSDF: learning continuous signed distance functions for shape representation. In: Proceedings of the IEEE/CVF Conference on Computer Vision and Pattern Recognition, pp. 165–174 (2019)

27. Pavlakos, G., et al.: Expressive body capture: 3D hands, face, and body from a single image. In: Proceedings of the IEEE/CVF Conference on Computer Vision and Pattern Recognition, pp. 10975–10985 (2019)

28. Pesavento, M., Volino, M., Hilton, A.: Attention-based multi-reference learning for image super-resolution. In: Proceedings of the IEEE/CVF International Conference on Computer Vision, pp. 14697–14706 (2021)

29. Pesavento, M., Volino, M., Hilton, A.: Super-resolution appearance transfer for 4D human performances. In: Proceedings of the IEEE/CVF Conference on Computer Vision and Pattern Recognition, pp. 1791–1801 (2021)

30. Richard, A., Cherabier, I., Oswald, M.R., Tsiminaki, V., Pollefeys, M., Schindler, K.: Learned multi-view texture super-resolution. In: 2019 International Conference on 3D Vision (3DV), pp. 533–543. IEEE (2019)

31. Ronneberger, O., Fischer, P., Brox, T.: U-Net: convolutional networks for biomedical image segmentation. In: Navab, N., Hornegger, J., Wells, W.M., Frangi, A.F. (eds.) MICCAI 2015. LNCS, vol. 9351, pp. 234–241. Springer, Cham (2015). https://doi.org/10.1007/978-3-319-24574-4_28

32. Rossi, M., Frossard, P.: Geometry-consistent light field super-resolution via graph-based regularization. IEEE Trans. Image Process. **27**(9), 4207–4218 (2018)

33. Saito, S., Huang, Z., Natsume, R., Morishima, S., Kanazawa, A., Li, H.: PIFU: Pixel-aligned implicit function for high-resolution clothed human digitization. In: Proceedings of the IEEE/CVF International Conference on Computer Vision, pp. 2304–2314 (2019)

34. Saito, S., Simon, T., Saragih, J., Joo, H.: PIFuHD: multi-level pixel-aligned implicit function for high-resolution 3D human digitization. In: Proceedings of the IEEE/CVF Conference on Computer Vision and Pattern Recognition, pp. 84–93 (2020)

35. Sang, L., Haefner, B., Cremers, D.: Inferring super-resolution depth from a moving light-source enhanced RGB-D sensor: a variational approach. In: Proceedings of the IEEE/CVF Winter Conference on Applications of Computer Vision, pp. 1–10 (2020)

36. Sclaroff, S., Pentland, A.: Generalized implicit functions for computer graphics. ACM SIGGRAPH Comput. Graph. **25**(4), 247–250 (1991)

37. Sinha, A., Unmesh, A., Huang, Q., Ramani, K.: SurfNet: generating 3D shape surfaces using deep residual networks. In: Proceedings of the IEEE Conference on Computer Vision and Pattern Recognition, pp. 6040–6049 (2017)

38. Song, X., et al.: Channel attention based iterative residual learning for depth map super-resolution. In: Proceedings of the IEEE/CVF Conference on Computer Vision and Pattern Recognition, pp. 5631–5640 (2020)

39. Varol, G., et al.: BodyNet: volumetric inference of 3D human body shapes. In: Ferrari, V., Hebert, M., Sminchisescu, C., Weiss, Y. (eds.) ECCV 2018. LNCS, vol. 11211, pp. 20–38. Springer, Cham (2018). https://doi.org/10.1007/978-3-030-01234-2_2

40. Voynov, O., et al.: Perceptual deep depth super-resolution. In: Proceedings of the IEEE/CVF International Conference on Computer Vision, pp. 5653–5663 (2019)

41. Wang, Z., Chen, J., Hoi, S.C.: Deep learning for image super-resolution: a survey. IEEE Trans. Pattern Anal. Mach. Intell. **43**(10), 3365–3387 (2020)
42. Wu, H., Zhang, J., Huang, K.: Point cloud super resolution with adversarial residual graph networks. arXiv preprint arXiv:1908.02111 (2019)
43. Xu, X., Chen, H., Moreno-Noguer, F., Jeni, L.A., De la Torre, F.: 3D human pose, shape and texture from low-resolution images and videos. IEEE Trans. Pattern Anal. Mach. Intell. (99), 1–1 (2021)
44. Yu, T., Zheng, Z., Guo, K., Liu, P., Dai, Q., Liu, Y.: Function4d: real-time human volumetric capture from very sparse consumer RGBD sensors. In: IEEE Conference on Computer Vision and Pattern Recognition (CVPR2021), June 2021
45. Zhang, S., Liu, J., Liu, Y., Ling, N.: DimNet: dense implicit function network for 3d human body reconstruction. Comput. Graph. **98**, 1–10 (2021)
46. Zhang, S., Chang, S., Lin, Y.: End-to-end light field spatial super-resolution network using multiple epipolar geometry. IEEE Trans. Image Process. **30**, 5956–5968 (2021)
47. Zheng, Z., Yu, T., Liu, Y., Dai, Q.: PaMIR: parametric model-conditioned implicit representation for image-based human reconstruction. IEEE Trans. Pattern Anal. Mach. Intell. (2021)
48. Zheng, Z., Yu, T., Wei, Y., Dai, Q., Liu, Y.: DeepHuman: 3D human reconstruction from a single image. In: Proceedings of the IEEE/CVF International Conference on Computer Vision, pp. 7739–7749 (2019)
49. Zins, P., Xu, Y., Boyer, E., Wuhrer, S., Tung, T.: Data-driven 3D reconstruction of dressed humans from sparse views. In: 2021 International Conference on 3D Vision (3DV), pp. 494–504. IEEE (2021)

Minimal Neural Atlas: Parameterizing Complex Surfaces with Minimal Charts and Distortion

Weng Fei Low[1,2,3]($\boxtimes$) (iD) and Gim Hee Lee[1,2,3] (iD)

[1] Institute of Data Science (IDS), National University of Singapore,
Singapore, Singapore
{wengfei.low,gimhee.lee}@comp.nus.edu.sg
[2] NUS Graduate School's Integrative Sciences and Engineering Programme (ISEP),
Singapore, Singapore
[3] Department of Computer Science, National University of Singapore,
Singapore, Singapore
https://github.com/low5545/minimal-neural-atlas

Abstract. Explicit neural surface representations allow for exact and efficient extraction of the encoded surface at arbitrary precision, as well as analytic derivation of differential geometric properties such as surface normal and curvature. Such desirable properties, which are absent in its implicit counterpart, makes it ideal for various applications in computer vision, graphics and robotics. However, SOTA works are limited in terms of the topology it can effectively describe, distortion it introduces to reconstruct complex surfaces and model efficiency. In this work, we present *Minimal Neural Atlas*, a novel atlas-based explicit neural surface representation. At its core is a fully learnable parametric domain, given by an implicit probabilistic occupancy field defined on an open square of the parametric space. In contrast, prior works generally predefine the parametric domain. The added flexibility enables charts to admit arbitrary topology and boundary. Thus, our representation can learn a minimal atlas of 3 charts with distortion-minimal parameterization for surfaces of arbitrary topology, including closed and open surfaces with arbitrary connected components. Our experiments support the hypotheses and show that our reconstructions are more accurate in terms of the overall geometry, due to the separation of concerns on topology and geometry.

Keywords: Surface representation · 3D shape modeling

1 Introduction

An explicit neural surface representation that can faithfully describe surfaces of arbitrary topology at arbitrary precision is highly coveted for various down-

Supplementary Information The online version contains supplementary material available at https://doi.org/10.1007/978-3-031-20086-1_27.

stream applications. This is attributed to some of its intrinsic properties that are absent in implicit neural surface representations.

Specifically, the explicit nature of such representations entail that the encoded surface can be sampled exactly and efficiently, irrespective of its scale and complexity. This is particularly useful for inference-time point cloud generation, mesh generation and rendering directly from the representation. In contrast, implicit representations rely on expensive and approximate isosurface extraction and ray casting. Furthermore, differential geometric properties of the surface can also be derived analytically in an efficient manner [5]. Some notable examples of such properties include surface normal, surface area, mean curvature and Gaussian curvature. Implicit neural representations can at most infer such quantities at approximated surface points. Moreover, explicit representations are potentially more scalable since a surface is merely an embedded 2D submanifold of the 3D Euclidean space.

Despite the advantages of explicit representations, implicit neural surface representations have attracted most of the research attention in recent years. Nevertheless, this is not unwarranted, given its proven ability to describe general surfaces at high quality and aptitude for deep learning. This suggests that explicit representations still have a lot of potential yet to be discovered. In this work, we aim to tackle various shortcomings of existing explicit neural representations, in an effort to advance it towards the goal of a truly faithful surface representation.

State-of-the-art explicit neural surface representations [5,13,18,27] mainly consists of neural *atlas*-based representations, where each *chart* is given by a *parameterization* modeled with neural networks, as well as a predefined open square *parametric domain*. In other words, such representations describe a surface with a collection of neural network-deformed planar square patches.

In theory, these representations cannot describe surfaces of arbitrary topology, especially for surfaces with arbitrary connected components. This is clear from the fact that an atlas with 25 deformed square patches cannot represent a surface with 26 connected components. In practice, these works also cannot faithfully represent single-object or single-connected component surfaces of arbitrary topology, although it is theoretically capable given sufficient number of charts. Furthermore, these atlas-based representations generally admits a distortion-minimal surface parameterization at the expense of representation accuracy. For instance, distortion is inevitable to deform a square patch into a circular patch. Some of these works also require a large number of charts to accurately represent general surfaces, which leads to a representation with low model efficiency.

The root cause of all limitations mentioned above lies in predefining the parametric domain, which unnecessarily constrains its boundary and topology, and hence also that of the chart. While [27] has explored "tearing" an initial open square parametric domain at regions of high distortion, the limitation on distortion remains unaddressed. Our experiments also show that its reconstructions still incur a relatively high topological error on general single-object surfaces.

Contributions. We propose a novel representation, *Minimal Neural Atlas*, where the core idea is to model the parametric domain of each chart via an implicit *probabilistic occupancy field* [24] defined on the $(-1,1)^2$ open square of the *parametric space*. As a result, each chart is free to admit any topology and boundary, as we only restrict the bounds of the parametric domain. This enables the learning of a distortion-minimal parameterization, which is important for high quality texture mapping and efficient uniform point cloud sampling. A separation of concerns can also be established between the occupancy field and parameterization, where the former focuses on topology and the latter on geometry and distortion. This enables the proposed representation to describe surfaces of arbitrary topology, including closed and open surfaces with arbitrary connected components, using a *minimal atlas* of 3 charts. Our experiments on ShapeNet and CLOTH3D++ support this theoretical finding and show that our reconstructions are more accurate in terms of the overall geometry.

2 Related Work

Point clouds, meshes and voxels have long been the *de facto* standard for surface representation. Nonetheless, these *discrete surface representations* describe the surface only at sampled locations with limited precision. First explored in [18,35], *neural surface representations* exploits the universal approximation capabilities of neural networks to describe surfaces continuously at a low memory cost.

Explicit Neural Surface Representations. Such representations provide a closed form expression describing exact points on the surface. [18,35] first proposed to learn an atlas for a surface by modeling the chart parameterizations with a neural network and predefining the parametric domain of each chart to the open unit square. Building on [5,18] introduced novel training losses to regularize for chart degeneracy, distortion and the amount of overlap between charts. [13] additionally optimizes for the quality of overlaps between charts. Such atlas-based representations have also been specialized for surface reconstruction [3,26,34]. However, these representations suffer from various limitations outlined in Sect. 1, as a consequence of predefining the parametric domain. Hence, [27] proposed to adapt to the target surface topology by "tearing" an initial unit square parametric domain. In addition to the drawbacks mentioned in Sect. 1, this single-chart atlas representation also theoretically cannot describe general single-object surfaces. Moreover, the optimal tearing hyperparameters are instance-dependent, as they are determined by the scale, sampling density and area of the surface, which cannot be easily normalized.

Implicit Neural Surface Representations. These representations generally encode the surface as a level set of a scalar field defined on the 3D space, which is parameterized by a neural network. Some of the first implicit representations proposed include the *Probabilistic Occupancy Field* (POF) [9,24] and *Signed Distance Field* (SDF) [28]. These representations can theoretically describe closed surfaces of arbitrary topology and they yield accurate watertight reconstructions in practice. However, these works require ample access to watertight meshes for training, which might not always be possible. [1,2,4,7,17]

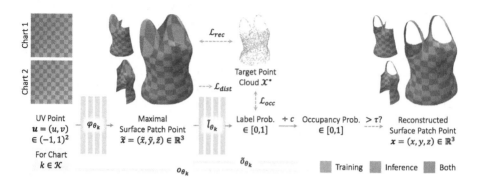

Fig. 1. Overview of our proposed method.

proposed various approaches to learn such representations from unoriented point clouds. Nevertheless, POF and SDF are only restricted to representing closed surfaces. [10] proposed to model an *Unsigned Distance Field* (UDF) so that both open and closed surfaces can be represented as the zero level set. While this is true in theory, surface extraction is generally performed with respect to a small epsilon level set, which leads to a double or crusted surface, since there is no guarantee that the zero level set exists in practice. Consequently, UDF cannot truly represent general surfaces.

3   Our Method

We first present our proposed surface representation and its theoretical motivation (Sect. 3.1, 3.2). Next, we detail how to learn this representation (Sect. 3.3) and describe an approach for extracting point clouds and meshes of a specific size during inference (Sect. 3.4). An illustration of our method is given in Fig. 1.

3.1   Background

A *manifold* $\mathcal{M}$ is a topological space that locally resembles an Euclidean space. A *surface* $\mathcal{S}$ is merely a 2-dimensional manifold, or 2-manifold in short. In general, a manifold can be explicitly described using an *atlas*, which consists of *charts* that each describe different regions of the manifold. Formally, a chart on an n-manifold $\mathcal{M}$ can be denoted by an ordered pair (U, φ), whereby $U \subset \mathbb{R}^n$ is an open subset of the n-dimensional Euclidean space and $\varphi_k : U \mapsto \mathcal{M}$ is a *homeomorphism* or *parameterization* from U to an open subset of $\mathcal{M}$. An atlas for $\mathcal{M}$ is given by an indexed family of charts $\{(U_k, \varphi_k) \mid k \in \mathcal{K}\}$ which forms an *open cover* of $\mathcal{M}$ (*i.e.* $\bigcup_{k \in \mathcal{K}} \varphi_k(U_k) = \mathcal{M}$).

It is well-known that the *Lusternik-Schnirelmann category* [11,16,21] of a general n-manifold is at most $n + 1$. This implies that irrespective of its complexity, a general n-manifold always admits an atlas of $n+1$ charts. Consequently, this defines the notion of a *minimal atlas* for a general n-manifold.

3.2   Surface Representation

Motivated by such a theoretical guarantee, we propose to represent general surfaces S with a minimal atlas of 3 charts modeled using neural networks. Specifically, we model the surface parameterization of each chart k with a *Multi-Layer Perceptron* (MLP) parameterized by θ_k, which we denote as φ_{θ_k}. Furthermore, we employ a *probabilistic occupancy field* [24] defined on the $\mathbb{R}^2$ *parametric space* to implicitly model the *parametric domain* U_{θ_k} of each chart k.

More precisely, we model a probabilistic occupancy field o_{θ_k} with an MLP parameterized by θ_k on the $(-1, 1)^2$ open square of the parametric space. This allows us to implicitly represent the parametric domain U_{θ_k} as regions in the parametric space with occupancy probability larger than a specific threshold τ, or *occupied* regions in short. Our proposed *Minimal Neural Atlas* surface representation is formally given as:

$$\{(U_{\theta_k}, \varphi_{\theta_k}) \mid k \in \mathcal{K}\} , \tag{1}$$

where:

$$U_{\theta_k} = \{\boldsymbol{u} \in (-1, 1)^2 \mid o_{\theta_k}(\boldsymbol{u}) > \tau\} , \tag{2}$$

$$\varphi_{\theta_k} : U_{\theta_k} \mapsto S , \tag{3}$$

$$o_{\theta_k} : (-1, 1)^2 \mapsto [0, 1] . \tag{4}$$

While we have formulated the proposed representation in the context of representing a single surface, conditioning the representation on a *latent code* $z \in \mathcal{Z}$ encoding any surface of interest facilitates the modeling of a family of surfaces. The latent code z can be inferred from various forms of inputs describing the associated surface, such as a point cloud or an image, via an appropriate encoder.

The key component that contrasts this atlas-based representation from the others is the flexibility of the parametric domain. In contrast to predefining the parametric domain, we only restrict its bounds. This eliminates redundant constraints on the boundaries and topology of the parametric domain and hence the chart. As a result, the proposed representation can learn a minimal atlas for general surfaces with arbitrary topology, including closed and open surfaces with arbitrary connected components. This also enables the learning of a distortion-minimal surface parameterization. A *separation of concerns* can thus be achieved, where o_{θ_k} mainly addresses the concern of discovering and representing the appropriate topology, and φ_{θ_k} addresses the concern of accurately representing the geometry with minimum distortion.

Decoupling Homeomorphic Ambiguity. Learning a minimal neural atlas in the present form possesses some difficulties. For a given *surface patch* described by a chart (U, φ), there exists infinitely many other charts (U', φ') such that $U' = \phi(U)$ and $\varphi' = \varphi \circ \phi^{-1}$, where ϕ is a homeomorphism in the open square of the parametric space, that can describe the same surface patch. This statement is true because $\varphi'(U') = (\varphi \circ \phi^{-1})(\phi(U)) = \varphi(U)$. This coupled ambiguity of ϕ

presents a great challenge during the learning of the two relatively independent components o_{θ_k} and φ_{θ_k}.

To decouple this homeomorphic ambiguity, we reformulate o_{θ_k} as:

$$o_{\theta_k} = \tilde{o}_{\theta_k} \circ \varphi_{\theta_k} , \tag{5}$$

where:

$$\tilde{o}_{\theta_k} : \varphi_{\theta_k}((-1,1)^2) \mapsto [0,1] \tag{6}$$

is an auxiliary probabilistic occupancy field defined on the *maximal surface patch* $\varphi_{\theta_k}((-1,1)^2) \subset \mathbb{R}^3$. This also requires us to extend the domain and codomain of φ_{θ_k} to the open square and $\mathbb{R}^3$, respectively. Nonetheless, this is just a matter of notation since φ_{θ_k} is modeled using an MLP with a *natural domain* of $\mathbb{R}^2$ and codomain of $\mathbb{R}^3$. Under this reformulation that conditions o_{θ_k} on φ_{θ_k}, $\tilde{o}_{\theta_k}$ can be learned such that it is invariant to ambiguities in ϕ. Particularly, since the same surface patch is described irrespective of the specific ϕ, it is sufficient for $\tilde{o}_{\theta_k}$ to be occupied only within that surface patch and *vacant* elsewhere (*i.e.* "trim away" arbitrary *surface patch excess*). This enables the learning of φ_{θ_k} with arbitrary ϕ that is independent of $\tilde{o}_{\theta_k}$.

3.3   Training

To learn the minimal neural atlas of a target surface $\mathcal{S}^*$, we only assume that we are given its raw unoriented point cloud during training, which we denote as the set $\mathcal{X}^*$. For training, we uniformly sample a common fixed number of points or *UV samples* in the open square of each chart k to yield the set $\mathcal{V}_k$.

Due to the lack of minimal atlas annotations (*e.g.* target point cloud for each chart of a minimal atlas), a straightforward supervision of the surface parameterization and (auxiliary) probabilistic occupancy field for each chart is not possible. To mitigate this problem, we introduce the reconstruction loss $\mathcal{L}_{rec}$, occupancy loss $\mathcal{L}_{occ}$ and metric distortion loss $\mathcal{L}_{dist}$. Without a loss of generality, the losses are presented similar to Sect. 3.2 in the context of fitting a single target surface. The total training loss is then given by their weighted sum:

$$\mathcal{L} = \lambda_{rec}\mathcal{L}_{rec} + \lambda_{occ}\mathcal{L}_{occ} + \lambda_{dist}\mathcal{L}_{dist} , \tag{7}$$

where $\lambda_{rec}, \lambda_{occ}$ and λ_{dist} are the hyperparameters to balance the loss terms.

Reconstruction Loss. The concern of topology is decoupled from the parameterization in our proposed surface representation. As a result, we can ensure that the geometry of the target surface is accurately represented as long as the *maximal surface* $\tilde{\mathcal{S}}$, given by the collection of all maximal surface patches $\bigcup_{k \in \mathcal{K}} \varphi_{\theta_k}((-1,1)^2)$, forms a *cover* of the target surface $\mathcal{S}^*$. To this end, we regularize the surface parameterization of each chart with the unidirectional *Chamfer Distance* [15] that gives the mean squared distance of the target point cloud and its *maximal surface point cloud* $\bigcup_{k \in \mathcal{K}} \varphi_{\theta_k}(\mathcal{V}_k)$ nearest neighbor:

$$\mathcal{L}_{rec} = \frac{1}{|\mathcal{X}^*|} \sum_{x^* \in \mathcal{X}^*} \min_{k \in \mathcal{K}} \min_{u \in \mathcal{V}_k} \|x^* - \varphi_{\theta_k}(u)\|_2^2 . \tag{8}$$

Occupancy Loss. To truly represent the target surface with the correct topology, it is necessary for the auxiliary probabilistic occupancy field of each chart $\tilde{o}_{\theta_k}$ to "trim away" only the *surface excess* given by $\tilde{S} \setminus S^*$.

Naïve Binary Classification Formulation. This is achieved by enforcing an occupancy of '1' at the nearest neighbors of the target point cloud, and '0' at other non-nearest neighbor maximal surface points, which effectively casts the learning of $\tilde{o}_{\theta_k}$ as a binary classification problem. However, this form of annotation incorrectly assigns an occupancy of '0' at some maximal points which also form the target surface. Such mislabeling can be attributed to the difference in sampling density as well as distribution between the target and maximal surface, and effects of random sampling on the nearest neighbor operator.

Positive-Unlabeled Learning Formulation. Instead of the interpretation of mislabeling, we can take an alternative view of partial labeling. Specifically, a maximal point annotated with a label of '1' is considered as a labeled positive (occupied) sample and a maximal point annotated with a label of '0' is considered as an unlabeled sample instead of a labeled negative (vacant) sample. This interpretation allows us to cast the learning of $\tilde{o}_{\theta_k}$ as a *Positive and Unlabeled Learning* (PU Learning) problem [6,14] (also called *learning from positive and unlabeled examples*).

Our labeling mechanism satisfies the *single-training-set scenario* [6,14] since the maximal points are *independent and identically distributed* (i.i.d.) on the maximal surface and are either labeled positive (occupied) or unlabeled to form the "training set". Following [14], we assume that our labeling mechanism satisfies the *Selected Completely at Random* (SCAR) assumption, which entails that the labeled maximal points are i.i.d. to, or selected completely at random from, the maximal points on the target surface. Under such an assumption, the auxiliary probabilistic occupancy field defined on can be factorized as:

$$\tilde{o}_{\theta_k}(\tilde{x}) = \frac{\tilde{l}_{\theta_k}(\tilde{x})}{c} , \tag{9}$$

where:

$$\tilde{l}_{\theta_k} : \varphi_{\theta_k}((-1,1)^2) \mapsto [0,1] \tag{10}$$

returns the probability that the given maximal point $\tilde{x}$ is labeled, and c is the constant probability that a maximal point on the target surface is labeled. In the PU learning literature, $\tilde{l}_{\theta_k}$ and c are referred to as a *non-traditional classifier* and *label frequency* respectively. Note that c is proportional to the relative sampling density between the target and maximal point cloud.

$\tilde{l}_{\theta_k}$ can now be learned in the standard supervised binary classification setting with the *Binary Cross Entropy* (BCE) loss as follows:

$$\mathcal{L}_{occ} = -\frac{1}{\sum_{k \in \mathcal{K}} |\mathcal{V}_k|} \sum_{k \in \mathcal{K}} \sum_{u \in \mathcal{V}_k} \text{BCE}(\mathbb{1}_{\mathcal{V}_k^*}(u), \tilde{l}_{\theta_k} \circ \varphi_{\theta_k}(u)) , \tag{11}$$

where $\mathcal{V}_k^* \subseteq \mathcal{V}_k$ is the set of UV samples corresponding to the target point cloud nearest neighbors. As a result of the reformulation of the probabilistic occupancy field, it can be observed that the surface parameterization of each chart directly contributes to the occupancy loss. In practice, we prevent the backpropagation of the occupancy loss gradients to the surface parameterizations. This enables the parameterizations to converge to a lower reconstruction loss since they are now decoupled from the minimization of the occupancy loss. Furthermore, this also facilitates the separation of concerns between o_{θ_k} and φ_{θ_k}.

Metric Distortion Loss. To learn a minimal neural atlas with distortion-minimal surface parameterization, we explicitly regularize the parameterization of each chart to preserve the *metric* of the parametric domain, up to a common scale. We briefly introduce some underlying concepts before going into the details of the loss function.

Let $J_k(\boldsymbol{u}) = \left[\partial\varphi_{\theta_k}/\partial u \;\; \partial\varphi_{\theta_k}/\partial v\right]$, where $\boldsymbol{u} = \left[u\;v\right]^{\top}$, be the Jacobian of the surface parameterization of chart k. It describes the tangent space of the surface at the point $\varphi_{\theta_k}(\boldsymbol{u})$. The *metric tensor* or *first fundamental form* $g_k(\boldsymbol{u}) = J_k(\boldsymbol{u})^{\top} J_k(\boldsymbol{u})$ enables the computation of various differential geometric properties, such as length, area, normal, curvature and distortion.

To quantify metric distortion up to a specific common scale of L, we adopt a scaled variant of the *Symmetric Dirichlet Energy* (SDE) [29–31], which is an isometric distortion energy, given by:

$$\frac{1}{\sum_{k\in\mathcal{K}}|\mathcal{W}_k|}\sum_{k\in\mathcal{K}}\sum_{\boldsymbol{u}\in\mathcal{W}_k}\frac{1}{L^2}\mathrm{trace}(g_k(\boldsymbol{u})) + L^2\mathrm{trace}(g_k(\boldsymbol{u})^{-1}) \,, \qquad (12)$$

where the distortion is quantified with respect to the set of UV samples denoted as $\mathcal{W}_k$. We refer this metric distortion energy as the *Scaled Symmetric Dirichlet Energy* (SSDE). As the SSDE reduces to the SDE when $L = 1$, the SSDE can be alternatively interpreted as the SDE of the derivative surface parameterization, given by post-scaling the parameterization of interest by a factor of $1/L$.

Since we are interested in enforcing metric preservation up to an arbitrary common scale, it is necessary to deduce the optimal scale L^* of the SSDE, for any given atlas (hence given g_k). To this end, we determine the L^* by finding the L that minimizes the SSDE. As the SSDE is a convex function of L, its unique global minimum can be analytically derived. Finally, the metric distortion loss used to learn a minimal neural atlas with distortion-minimal parameterization is simply given by:

$$\mathcal{L}_{dist} = 2\sqrt{\mathrm{mean}_{\mathcal{V}^*}(\mathrm{trace}\circ g_k)\,\mathrm{mean}_{\mathcal{V}^*}(\mathrm{trace}\circ g_k^{-1})} \,, \qquad (13)$$

where:

$$\mathrm{mean}_{\mathcal{W}}(f) = \frac{1}{\sum_{k\in\mathcal{K}}|\mathcal{W}_k|}\sum_{k\in\mathcal{K}}\sum_{\boldsymbol{u}\in\mathcal{W}_k}f(\boldsymbol{u}) \,. \qquad (14)$$

Note that we only regularize UV samples corresponding to nearest neighbors of the target point cloud, which are labeled as occupied. This provides more flexibility to the parameterization outside of the parametric domain. While [5] has proposed a novel loss to minimize metric distortion, our metric distortion loss is derived from the well-established SDE, which quantifies distortion based on relevant fundamental properties of the metric tensor, rather than its raw structure. We also observe better numerical stability as $\mathcal{L}_{dist}$ is given by the geometric mean of two values roughly inversely proportional to each other.

3.4 Inference

Label Frequency Estimation. The label frequency c can be estimated during inference with the *positive subdomain* assumption [6]. This requires the existence of a subset of the target surface that is uniquely covered by a chart, which we assume to be true. We refer such regions as *chart interiors* since they are generally far from the chart boundary, where overlapping between charts occur.

Similar to training, we uniformly sample the open square to infer a set of maximal surface points. Given that $\tilde{l}_{\theta_k}$ is well-calibrated [14], maximal points on a chart interior have a $\tilde{l}_{\theta_k}$ value of c under the positive subdomain assumption. In practice, we identify such points by assuming at least η percent of maximal points lie on a chart interior, and these points correspond to the maximal points with the highest confidence in $\tilde{l}_{\theta_k}$. We refer η as the *minimum interior rate*. c can then be estimated by the mean $\tilde{l}_{\theta_k}$ of the interior maximal points [6,14]. As $\tilde{l}_{\theta_k}$ is not explicitly calibrated and the SCAR assumption does not strictly hold in practice, we adopt the median estimator instead for improved robustness.

Point Cloud and Mesh Extraction. After the label frequency has been estimated, the *reconstructed minimal neural atlas* $\{(U_{\theta_k}, \varphi_{\theta_k}) \mid k \in \mathcal{K}\}$, and hence the *reconstructed surface* $\mathcal{S} = \bigcup_{k \in \mathcal{K}} \varphi_k(U_{\theta_k})$, are then well-defined. As a result, we can extract the *reconstructed surface point cloud* $\mathcal{X} = \bigcup_{k \in \mathcal{K}} \varphi_{\theta_k}(\mathcal{V}_k \cap U_{\theta_k})$. Furthermore, we can also extract a mesh from the reconstructed minimal neural atlas, similar to [18]. We refer this as the *reconstructed mesh*. This can be done by first defining a regular mesh in the open square of each chart and then discarding triangles with vertices outside of the reconstructed parametric domain. The mesh is then transferred to the reconstructed surface via the parameterization of each chart.

Nevertheless, it is often useful to extract a point cloud or mesh with a specific number of vertices. We achieve this in an approximate but efficient manner by adopting a two-step batch *rejection sampling* strategy. Firstly, we employ a small batch of UV samples to estimate the *occupancy rate*, which quantifies the extent to which the open square of all charts are occupied. Given such an estimate, we then deduce the number of additional UV samples required to eventually yield a point cloud or mesh with approximately the target size.

4 Experiments

We conduct two standard experiments: surface reconstruction (Sect. 4.1) and single-view reconstruction (Sect. 4.2) to verify that our representation can effectively learn a minimal atlas with distortion-minimal parameterization for surfaces of arbitrary topology. The first experiment considers the basic task of reconstructing the target surface given its point cloud, while the second is concerned with the complex task of surface reconstruction from a single image of the target. In addition to the benchmark experiments, we also perform ablation studies to investigate the significance of various components in our representation (Sect. 4.3).

Datasets. We perform all experiments on the widely used *ShapeNet* dataset [8], which is a large-scale dataset of 3D models of common objects. Specifically, we adopt the dataset preprocessed by ONet [24]. Instead of the default unit cube normalization on the point clouds, we follow existing atlas-based representations on a unit ball normalization. The ShapeNet dataset serves as a strong benchmark on representing general single-object closed surfaces.

Additionally, we also perform the surface reconstruction experiment on the CLOTH3D++ [23] dataset, which contains approximately 13,000 3D models of garments across 6 categories. Following ONet, we preprocess the dataset by uniformly sampling 100,000 points on the mesh of each garment. The point clouds are then similarly normalized to a unit ball. With this dataset, we are able to evaluate the representation power on general single-object open surfaces.

Metrics. We adopt a consistent set of metrics to assess the performance of a surface representation on all experiments. To quantify the accuracy of surface reconstruction, we employ the standard bidirectional Chamfer Distance (CD) [15] as well as the *F-score* at the default distance threshold of 1% (F@1%) [22,32], which has been shown to be a more representative metric than CD [32]. Following prior works on atlas-based representations, we report these two metrics on the reconstructed surface point cloud, given by regularly sampling the parametric domain of each chart. Furthermore, we also report the metrics on the *reconstructed mesh point cloud*, given by uniformly sampling the reconstructed mesh. This is similarly done in [19], as well as in implicit representation works. We refer to the first set of metrics as Point Cloud CD and F@1%, while the second as Mesh CD and F@1%. The reported reconstruction metrics are computed with a point cloud size of 25,000 for both the reconstruction and the target.

As pointed out by [28], topological errors in the reconstructed surface are better accounted for when evaluating on the reconstructed mesh point cloud. This is due to the non-uniform distribution of the reconstructed surface point cloud, especially at regions of high distortion where sampled points are sparse. Nevertheless, we still report the point cloud metrics to assess the reconstruction accuracy in the related task or setting of point cloud reconstruction.

We employ a set of metrics to quantify the distortion of the chart parameterizations. In particular, we use the SSDE at the optimal scale L^* (Eq. 13) to measure the metric distortion up to a common scale. We also quantify the area distortion up to a common scale using a distortion energy, which is derived in a similar manner from the equi-area distortion energy introduced in [12]. Lastly, we measure the *conformal* distortion, or distortion of local angles, using the MIPS energy [20]. The reported distortion metrics are computed with respect to the UV samples associated with the reconstructed surface point cloud. We offset the distortion metrics such that a value of zero implies no distortion.

Table 1. Surface reconstruction on CLOTH3D++.

No. of charts	Surface representation	Point cloud		Mesh		Distortion		
		CD, 10^{-4} ↓	F@1% ↑	CD, 10^{-4} ↓	F@1% ↑	Metric ↓	Conformal ↓	Area ↓
	AtlasNet	**4.074**	**88.56**	18.99	82.40	15.54	3.933	0.8428
	AtlasNet++	4.296	87.88	4.937	86.20	13.22	3.368	0.6767
	DSP	7.222	82.41	21.86	78.93	**1.427**	<u>0.5746</u>	**0.1032**
	TearingNet	6.872	84.99	8.321	83.40	17.40	3.407	1.149
	Ours w/o $\mathcal{L}_{dist}$	<u>4.206</u>	<u>88.38</u>	**4.373**	**87.85**	3.263	1.328	0.1516
1	Ours	4.296	88.00	<u>4.476</u>	<u>87.36</u>	<u>1.600</u>	**0.5688**	<u>0.1652</u>
	AtlasNet	3.856	89.78	7.075	86.71	6.411	1.931	0.4031
	AtlasNet++	4.106	88.62	4.734	86.93	20.65	5.095	1.116
	DSP	4.710	87.12	5.536	85.91	**0.2160**	**0.0771**	**0.0283**
	Ours w/o $\mathcal{L}_{dist}$	**3.603**	**90.78**	**3.846**	**89.91**	3.654	1.328	0.2227
2	Ours	<u>3.775</u>	<u>90.08</u>	<u>3.982</u>	<u>89.50</u>	<u>0.9227</u>	<u>0.3582</u>	<u>0.0847</u>
	AtlasNet	3.396	91.47	6.269	88.74	8.028	2.485	0.4144
	AtlasNet++	3.368	91.62	3.652	90.67	12.89	3.615	1.073
	DSP	**3.227**	**92.06**	**3.501**	**91.26**	0.4284	0.1252	0.0439
	Ours w/o $\mathcal{L}_{dist}$	3.300	91.87	3.684	90.72	4.603	1.654	0.3047
25	Ours	<u>3.299</u>	<u>91.90</u>	<u>3.554</u>	<u>91.07</u>	<u>0.5637</u>	<u>0.1770</u>	<u>0.0940</u>

Table 2. Surface reconstruction on ShapeNet.

No. of charts	Surface representation	Point cloud		Mesh		Distortion		
		CD, 10^{-4} ↓	F@1% ↑	CD, 10^{-4} ↓	F@1% ↑	Metric ↓	Conformal ↓	Area ↓
	AtlasNet	8.131	79.74	13.37	74.60	21.23	4.151	1.574
	AtlasNet++	8.467	78.46	10.82	75.69	30.40	5.687	2.017
	DSP	14.22	70.03	16.29	68.58	**0.4684**	**0.1618**	**0.0580**
	TearingNet	11.64	75.96	20.01	70.86	21.96	5.092	1.882
	Ours w/o $\mathcal{L}_{dist}$	**6.684**	**83.05**	**7.133**	**81.76**	8.264	2.654	0.4130
1	Ours	<u>7.559</u>	<u>80.45</u>	<u>7.959</u>	<u>79.39</u>	<u>2.546</u>	<u>0.8929</u>	<u>0.2246</u>
	AtlasNet	7.071	81.98	10.96	77.68	16.27	4.037	1.041
	AtlasNet++	7.516	80.59	9.280	78.17	32.39	6.252	2.626
	DSP	10.79	76.39	11.98	74.85	**0.4130**	**0.1571**	**0.0380**
	Ours w/o $\mathcal{L}_{dist}$	**6.266**	**84.04**	<u>6.875</u>	<u>82.22</u>	10.23	3.303	0.5155
3	Ours	<u>6.311</u>	<u>83.63</u>	**6.761**	**82.23**	<u>2.189</u>	<u>0.7094</u>	<u>0.2521</u>
	AtlasNet	6.285	83.98	7.855	81.25	14.48	4.522	0.9469
	AtlasNet++	6.451	83.50	7.333	81.87	20.34	5.643	1.981
	DSP	7.995	81.54	8.609	80.08	**0.9477**	**0.2900**	**0.1040**
	Ours w/o $\mathcal{L}_{dist}$	<u>5.844</u>	<u>85.11</u>	**6.646**	<u>83.52</u>	7.639	2.595	0.4464
25	Ours	**5.780**	**85.28**	<u>6.726</u>	**83.86**	<u>1.178</u>	<u>0.3760</u>	<u>0.1576</u>

Baselines. We benchmark minimal neural atlas against state-of-the-art explicit neural representations that can be learned given raw unoriented target point clouds for training. Specifically, we compare with AtlasNet [18], DSP [5] and TearingNet [27]. Furthermore, a variant of AtlasNet that is trained with the Mesh CD and SSDE at the optimal scale, in addition to the original Point Cloud CD loss, is also adopted as an additional baseline, which we refer to as AtlasNet++. It serves as a strong baseline since topological errors in the reconstructions are explicitly regularized with the Mesh CD, unlike other baselines. The remaining losses help to minimize the excessive distortion caused by optimizing the Mesh CD, as similarly mentioned in [19].

4.1 Surface Reconstruction

In this experiment, we consider the specific setting of reconstructing the target surface given an input point cloud of size 2,500. The input point cloud also serves as the target point cloud for training. This is consistent with previous works such as [5,13,18,19]. Nevertheless, we adopt a larger UV sample size of 5,000 for training in all works.

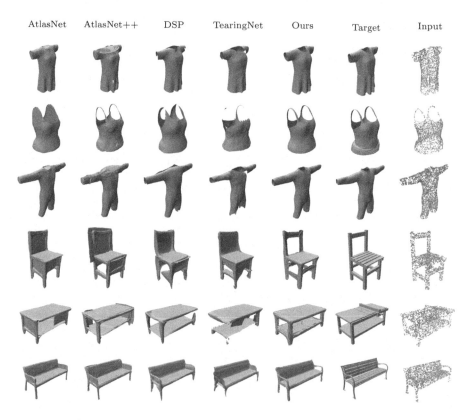

Fig. 2. Surface reconstruction on CLOTH3D++ and ShapeNet.

To evaluate whether a method can faithfully learn a minimal representation, we benchmark all surface representations at 3 different number of charts, except for TearingNet. In particular, we evaluate at 1, 2 and 25 charts on CLOTH3D++ and 1, 3 and 25 charts on ShapeNet. The inconsistency of 2 and 3 charts between both datasets is attributed to the fact that these baselines theoretically admit a

Table 3. Single-view reconstruction on ShapeNet.

No. of charts	Surface representation	Point cloud		Mesh		Distortion		
		CD, 10^{-3} ↓	F@1% ↑	CD, 10^{-3} ↓	F@1% ↑	Metric ↓	Conformal ↓	Area ↓
	AtlasNet	**3.100**	57.78	4.512	52.85	34.60	4.771	3.189
	AtlasNet++	<u>3.254</u>	55.74	4.049	54.13	33.48	6.579	3.657
	DSP	5.210	46.28	6.048	44.55	**1.113**	**0.3718**	**0.1294**
	TearingNet	3.633	55.27	5.250	51.65	30.52	5.610	2.778
	Ours w/o $\mathcal{L}_{dist}$	3.754	**61.63**	**3.891**	**60.38**	8.148	2.510	0.4778
1	Ours	3.840	<u>59.90</u>	<u>4.002</u>	<u>58.71</u>	<u>2.674</u>	<u>0.9069</u>	<u>0.2420</u>
	AtlasNet	**2.992**	59.08	4.125	54.92	25.00	4.759	2.059
	AtlasNet++	<u>3.077</u>	57.84	<u>3.706</u>	56.26	38.07	6.263	3.419
	DSP	4.447	50.12	5.096	48.11	**0.5316**	**0.1505**	**0.0901**
	Ours w/o $\mathcal{L}_{dist}$	3.582	**62.11**	**3.704**	**60.68**	9.972	3.177	0.5906
3	Ours	3.621	<u>61.90</u>	3.744	<u>60.56</u>	<u>1.776</u>	<u>0.5537</u>	<u>0.2304</u>
	AtlasNet	**2.883**	60.68	3.655	57.21	18.77	4.853	1.516
	AtlasNet++	<u>2.961</u>	59.40	<u>3.469</u>	57.88	25.76	6.201	2.522
	DSP	3.582	55.60	4.336	52.94	<u>1.492</u>	<u>0.3712</u>	<u>0.2254</u>
	Ours w/o $\mathcal{L}_{dist}$	3.413	<u>62.71</u>	**3.464**	<u>61.42</u>	6.620	2.206	0.4532
25	Ours	3.437	**63.05**	3.514	**61.93**	**1.037**	**0.3321**	**0.1497**

minimal atlas of 2 and 3 charts for general single-object open and closed surfaces respectively. Benchmarking at 1 and 25 charts, which is the default for the baselines, also allows us to assess the limiting performance of a surface representation as the number of charts decreases or increases, respectively. Furthermore, we also evaluate at 1 chart because our proposed representation admits a minimal atlas of 1 chart for general single-object open surfaces.

The quantitative results for surface reconstruction on CLOTH3D++ and ShapeNet are reported in Table 1 and 2, respectively. In general, our surface representation achieves higher point cloud reconstruction performance at any given number of charts, especially on the more complex ShapeNet dataset. This indicates that the overall surface geometry is more accurately reconstructed by our representation, which can be attributed to the separation of concerns between o_{θ_k} and φ_{θ_k}. Furthermore, minimal neural atlas significantly outperforms the baselines in terms of the mesh reconstruction accuracy at any given number of charts, which is particularly true for lower number of charts and on ShapeNet. Together with the observation that our point cloud and mesh reconstruction metrics are relatively on par with each other, this suggests that minimal neural atlas can also reconstruct the topology of the target surface more accurately. These conclusions are also supported qualitatively in Fig. 2, where we show the reconstructed meshes of all surface representations at 2 and 3 charts, except for TearingNet, on CLOTH3D++ and ShapeNet.

The reconstruction metrics of our representation are also substantially more consistent across a wide range of charts. It is also worth noting that despite using fewer charts, minimal neural atlas often outperforms the baselines in terms of reconstruction accuracy. This affirms the ability of our representation to learn a minimal atlas for general surfaces. Moreover, the chart parameterizations of minimal neural atlas exhibit inherently lower distortion as it achieves lower metric values compared to AtlasNet, TearingNet and even AtlasNet++ without explicit regularization of distortion. Unlike DSP, the reported results also indicate that our representation is able to significantly reduce distortion without sacrificing reconstruction accuracy by additionally minimizing the metric distortion loss.

4.2   Single-View Reconstruction

This experiment adopts the exact same setting as the surface reconstruction experiment, except the input is an image of the target surface. The quantitative results on ShapeNet reported in Table 3 remains largely similar to the previous experiment. While our representation incurs a relatively higher point cloud CD, it consistently achieves a higher reconstruction performance on the more representative F@1% metric [32]. We can thus reach to the same conclusions, as per the previous experiment.

Table 4. Ablation study of minimal neural Atlas with $\mathcal{L}_{dist}$.

Variant	Point cloud		Mesh		Metric distortion ↓	Occupancy rate ↑
	CD, 10^{-4} ↓	F@1% ↑	CD, 10^{-4} ↓	F@1% ↑		
No o_{θ_k} reformulation	15.60	69.12	16.59	67.31	2.348	80.49
No $\tilde{o}_{\theta_k}$ factorization	327.8	29.51	386.3	27.59	4.951	6.762
No $\tilde{l}_{\theta_k}$ pos. encoding	7.419	82.04	8.050	80.23	**1.848**	**83.45**
Full model	**6.311**	**83.63**	**6.761**	**82.23**	2.189	77.48

4.3   Ablation Studies

The ablation studies are conducted in the same setting as surface reconstruction on ShapeNet using 3 charts. The results reported in Table 4 verifies the immense importance of decoupling the homeomorphic ambiguity by reformulating o_{θ_k} with Eq. 5, as well as casting the learning of $\tilde{o}_{\theta_k}$ as a PU Learning problem, which can be easily solved given the factorization of $\tilde{o}_{\theta_k}$ in Eq. 9, instead of a naïve binary classification problem. It also shows that it is crucial to apply positional embedding [25,33] on the input maximal point coordinates of $\tilde{l}_{\theta_k}$ to learn a more detailed occupancy field for better reconstructions, albeit at a minor cost of distortion.

5   Conclusion

In this paper, we propose *Minimal Neural Atlas*, a novel explicit neural surface representation that can effectively learn a minimal atlas with distortion-minimal parameterization for general surfaces of arbitrary topology, which is enabled by a fully learnable parametric domain. Despite its achievements, our representation remains prone to artifacts common in atlas-based representations, such as inter-sections and seams between charts. Severe violation of the SCAR assumption, due to imperfect modeling of the target surface, non-matching sampling distri-bution *etc.*, also leads to unintended holes on the reconstructed surface, which we leave for future work. Although we motivated this work in the context of rep-resenting surfaces, our representation naturally extends to general n-manifolds. It would thus be interesting to explore its applications in other domains.

Acknowledgements. This research/project is supported by the National Research Foundation, Singapore under its AI Singapore Programme (AISG Award No: AISG2-RP-2021-024), and the Tier 2 grant MOE-T2EP20120-0011 from the Singapore Min-istry of Education.

References

1. Atzmon, M., Lipman, Y.: SAL: sign agnostic learning of shapes from raw data. In: Proceedings of the IEEE Computer Society Conference on Computer Vision and Pattern Recognition (2020)
2. Atzmon, M., Lipman, Y.: SALD: sign agnostic learning with derivatives. In: Inter-national Conference on Learning Representations (2021)
3. Badki, A., Gallo, O., Kautz, J., Sen, P.: Meshlet priors for 3d mesh reconstruction. In: 2020 IEEE/CVF Conference on Computer Vision and Pattern Recognition (CVPR) (2020)
4. Baorui, M., Zhizhong, H., Yu-shen, L., Matthias, Z.: Neural-pull: learning signed distance functions from point clouds by learning to pull space onto surfaces. In: International Conference on Machine Learning (ICML) (2021)
5. Bednarik, J., Parashar, S., Gundogdu, E., Salzmann, M., Fua, P.: Shape recon-struction by learning differentiable surface representations. In: Proceedings of the IEEE Computer Society Conference on Computer Vision and Pattern Recognition (2020)
6. Bekker, J., Davis, J.: Learning from positive and unlabeled data: a survey. Mach. Learn. **109**, 719–760 (2020)
7. Boulch, A., Langlois, P., Puy, G., Marlet, R.: NeeDrop: self-supervised shape rep-resentation from sparse point clouds using needle dropping. In: 2021 International Conference on 3D Vision (3DV) (2021)
8. Chang, A.X., et al.: ShapeNet: an information-rich 3D model repository. Technical report. arXiv:1512.03012 [cs.GR], Stanford University – Princeton University – Toyota Technological Institute at Chicago (2015)
9. Chen, Z., Zhang, H.: Learning implicit fields for generative shape modeling. In: 2019 IEEE/CVF Conference on Computer Vision and Pattern Recognition (CVPR) (2019)
10. Chibane, J., Mir, A., Pons-Moll, G.: Neural unsigned distance fields for implicit function learning. In: Advances in Neural Information Processing Systems (2020)
11. Cornea, O., Lupton, G., Oprea, J., Tanré, D.: Lusternik-Schnirelmann Category. American Mathematical Soc. (2003)
12. Degener, P., Meseth, J., Klein, R.: An adaptable surface parameterization method. In: IMR (2003)

13. Deng, Z., Bednarik, J., Salzmann, M., Fua, P.: Better patch stitching for parametric surface reconstruction. In: Proceedings - 2020 International Conference on 3D Vision, 3DV 2020 (2020)

14. Elkan, C., Noto, K.: Learning classifiers from only positive and unlabeled data. In: Proceedings of the 14th ACM SIGKDD International Conference on Knowledge Discovery and Data Mining (2008)

15. Fan, H., Su, H., Guibas, L.: A point set generation network for 3d object reconstruction from a single image. In: 2017 IEEE Conference on Computer Vision and Pattern Recognition (CVPR) (2017)

16. Fox, R.H.: On the Lusternik-Schnirelmann category. Ann. Math., 333–370 (1941)

17. Gropp, A., Yariv, L., Haim, N., Atzmon, M., Lipman, Y.: Implicit geometric regularization for learning shapes. In: International Conference on Machine Learning (2020)

18. Groueix, T., Fisher, M., Kim, V.G., Russell, B.C., Aubry, M.: A Papier-Mâché approach to learning 3D surface generation. In: Proceedings of the IEEE Computer Society Conference on Computer Vision and Pattern Recognition (2018)

19. Gupta, K., Chandraker, M.: Neural mesh flow: 3D manifold mesh generation via diffeomorphic flows. In: Advances in Neural Information Processing Systems (2020)

20. Hormann, K., Greiner, G.: MIPS: an efficient global parametrization method, Technical report. Erlangen-Nuernberg Univ (Germany) Computer Graphics Group (2000)

21. James, I.: On category, in the sense of Lusternik-Schnirelmann. Topology **17**, 331–348 (1978)

22. Knapitsch, A., Park, J., Zhou, Q.Y., Koltun, V.: Tanks and temples: benchmarking large-scale scene reconstruction. ACM Trans. Graph. **36**, 1–13 (2017)

23. Madadi, M., Bertiche, H., Bouzouita, W., Guyon, I., Escalera, S.: Learning cloth dynamics: 3d + texture garment reconstruction benchmark. In: Proceedings of the NeurIPS 2020 Competition and Demonstration Track, PMLR (2021)

24. Mescheder, L., Oechsle, M., Niemeyer, M., Nowozin, S., Geiger, A.: Occupancy networks: learning 3d reconstruction in function space. In: 2019 IEEE/CVF Conference on Computer Vision and Pattern Recognition (CVPR) (2019)

25. Mildenhall, B., Srinivasan, P.P., Tancik, M., Barron, J.T., Ramamoorthi, R., Ng, R.: NeRF: representing scenes as neural radiance fields for view synthesis. In: Vedaldi, A., Bischof, H., Brox, T., Frahm, J.-M. (eds.) ECCV 2020. LNCS, vol. 12346, pp. 405–421. Springer, Cham (2020). https://doi.org/10.1007/978-3-030-58452-8_24

26. Morreale, L., Aigerman, N., Kim, V., Mitra, N.J.: Neural surface maps. In: 2021 IEEE/CVF Conference on Computer Vision and Pattern Recognition (CVPR) (2021)

27. Pang, J., Li, D., Tian, D.: TearingNet: point cloud autoencoder to learn topology-friendly representations. In: 2021 IEEE/CVF Conference on Computer Vision and Pattern Recognition (CVPR) (2021)

28. Park, J.J., Florence, P., Straub, J., Newcombe, R., Lovegrove, S.: DeepSDF: learning continuous signed distance functions for shape representation. In: 2019 IEEE/CVF Conference on Computer Vision and Pattern Recognition (CVPR) (2019)

29. Rabinovich, M., Poranne, R., Panozzo, D., Sorkine-Hornung, O.: Scalable locally injective mappings. ACM Trans. Graph. **36**, 1 (2017)

30. Schreiner, J., Asirvatham, A., Praun, E., Hoppe, H.: Inter-surface mapping. ACM Trans. Graph. **23**, 870–877 (2004)

31. Smith, J., Schaefer, S.: Bijective parameterization with free boundaries. ACM Trans. Graph **34**, 1–9 (2015)
32. Tatarchenko, M., Richter, S.R., Ranftl, R., Li, Z., Koltun, V., Brox, T.: What do single-view 3D reconstruction networks learn? In: 2019 IEEE/CVF Conference on Computer Vision and Pattern Recognition (CVPR) (2019)
33. Vaswani, A., et al.: Attention is all you need. In: Advances in Neural Information Processing Systems (2017)
34. Williams, F., Schneider, T., Silva, C., Zorin, D., Bruna, J., Panozzo, D.: Deep geometric prior for surface reconstruction. In: Proceedings of the IEEE Computer Society Conference on Computer Vision and Pattern Recognition (2019)
35. Yang, Y., Feng, C., Shen, Y., Tian, D.: FoldingNet: point cloud auto-encoder via deep grid deformation. In: 2018 IEEE/CVF Conference on Computer Vision and Pattern Recognition (CVPR) (2018)

ExtrudeNet: Unsupervised Inverse Sketch-and-Extrude for Shape Parsing

Daxuan Ren[1,2], Jianmin Zheng[1(✉)], Jianfei Cai[1,3], Jiatong Li[1,2],
and Junzhe Zhang[1,2]

[1] Nanyang Technological University, Singapore, Singapore
{daxuan001,asjmzheng,E180176,junzhe001}@ntu.edu.sg
[2] Sensetime Research, Singapore, Singapore
[3] Monash University, Melbourne, Australia
jianfei.cai@monash.edu

Abstract. Sketch-and-extrude is a common and intuitive modeling process in computer aided design. This paper studies the problem of learning the shape given in the form of point clouds by "inverse" sketch-and-extrude. We present *ExtrudeNet*, an unsupervised end-to-end network for discovering sketch and extrude from point clouds. Behind ExtrudeNet are two new technical components: **1)** an effective representation for sketch and extrude, which can model extrusion with freeform sketches and conventional cylinder and box primitives as well; and **2)** a numerical method for computing the signed distance field which is used in the network learning. This is the first attempt that uses machine learning to reverse engineer the sketch-and-extrude modeling process of a shape in an unsupervised fashion. ExtrudeNet not only outputs a compact, editable and interpretable representation of the shape that can be seamlessly integrated into modern CAD software, but also aligns with the standard CAD modeling process facilitating various editing applications, which distinguishes our work from existing shape parsing research. Code is released at https://github.com/kimren227/ExtrudeNet.

1 Introduction

Pen draws a line, paint roller sweeps a surface, and pasta maker extrudes Fusilli from a stencil. From a point to a line, then to a surface and to a solid shape, the process of using lower dimensional shapes to construct a higher dimensional object seems to be a human instinct. In this paper, we explore the inverse of this process by training a neural network to infer 2D drawings of a point cloud and then extrude them into 3D to reconstruct the shape.

With recent development in 3D reconstruction technologies and cheaper sensors, point clouds can be easily obtained and become a widely adopted 3D data representation [23,24,34]. However, the unordered and unstructured nature of

---

Supplementary Information The online version contains supplementary material available at https://doi.org/10.1007/978-3-031-20086-1_28.

S. Avidan et al. (Eds.): ECCV 2022, LNCS 13662, pp. 482–498, 2022.
https://doi.org/10.1007/978-3-031-20086-1_28

point clouds makes it difficult to perform high level manipulation and easy editing of their underlying geometries. Thus in recent years, the research of extracting shape features and generating high level shape representation from point clouds is very active, especially in computer vision and graphics.

We take inspiration from the process of sketch and extrude, a popular and intuitive approach widely used in the field of computer aided design (CAD) where engineers usually model shapes by first "sketching" a closed free form sketch (profile) in a 2D sketch plane and then "extruding" the sketch into 3D. We propose *ExtrudeNet*, the first of its kind end-to-end unsupervised network for learning high level (editable and interpretable) shape representation through inverse sketch and extrude process from point clouds.

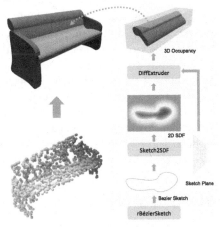

Fig. 1. ExtrudeNet studies the problem of learning the shape, given in the form of point clouds, by "inverse" sketch-and-extrude.

To realize ExtrudeNet, as shown in Fig. 1, we create three modular components: *1) rBézierSketch*, which generates a simple closed curve (i.e. no self-intersection); *2) Sketch2SDF*, a versatile numerical method for computing Signed-Distance-Field from parametric curves; and *3) DiffExtruder*, a differentiable method for extruding 2D Signed-Distance-Field (SDF) into a 3D solid shape. Built upon these components, ExtrudeNet takes a point cloud as input and outputs sketch and extrude parameters which form a compact, interpretable and editable shape representation. ExtrudeNet's outputs are highly compatible with modern CAD software [3], allowing control points based editing, which is much easier compared to directly editing triangle, polygonal meshes or even primitive based constructive solid geometry (CSG) models [26].

There are prior works on converting point clouds to high level shape representations. These representatives are discovering CSG in either a supervised or unsupervised manner. Supervised approaches [11,19,32,35] suffer issues such as invalid syntax, infeasible models, and requiring large amount of expert annotated data. Unsupervised methods [8,9,21,25,33,36] find the Boolean combinations of pre-defined geometric primitives such as box and cylinder. Our ExtrudeNet goes beyond these works. First, 2D sketch can be complex freeform curves, which allows us to model much more complex shapes using a single extrusion. Second, "Sketch-and-Extrude" is more user-friendly when it comes to editing and secondary-development, as editing a 2D sketch is more intuitive than editing 3D parameters. This Sketch-and-Extrude process happens to be a widely adopted method in CAD software for modeling 3D shapes [1–3,15], making our method highly compatible with industry standards. Moreover, extensive experiments show that our ExtrudeNet can reconstruct highly interpretable and editable representations from point clouds. We also show through qualitative visualizations and quantitative evaluation metrics that ExtrudeNet outputs better overall results. The main contributions of the paper are:

- We present an end-to-end network, ExtrudeNet, for unsupervised inverse sketch and extrude for shape parsing. To the best of our knowledge, ExtrudeNet is the first unsupervised learning method for discovering sketch and extrude from point clouds.
- We design a special rational cubic Bézier curve based representation for sketch and extrusion learning, which can model freeform extrusion shapes, and the common cylinder and box primitives as well.
- We present a simple and general numerical method for computing the signed distance field of 2D parametric curves and their 3D extrusions which is proven to be suitable for gradient-based learning.

2   Related Work

Shape Representation. There have been different representations for 3D shapes. Recently implicit representation [12,18,20], usually in the form of Occupancy or Signed Distance Field, has drawn a lot of attention. It frees from intricate data representation and can be used directly via neural networks. To extract the underlying geometry, however, further processing is required [17], which is computationally intensive. Parametric representation describes shapes by parametric equations and is widely used in industry for modeling shapes thanks to its strong edibility and infinite resolution. However, generating parametric shapes from raw data like point clouds is a non-trivial task.

High Level Shape Learning. High level shape representations are often required, which benefit various practical applications. With the advance in machine learning, learning high level shape representations from raw data structure gains popularity. There have been many works for reconstructing CAD and especially CSG from point clouds. CSG is a tree-like structure representing shapes by starting from primitive objects and iteratively combining geometric shapes through Boolean operations [16]. It is well adapted in professional CAD software.

CSGNet [32] pioneers supervised CSG learning by modeling CSG as a sequence of tokens. It processes the sequence into a valid CSG-Tree using NLP techniques. With recent NLP technologies, DeepCAD [35] and CAD-As-Language [11] employ more powerful language models, e.g. Transformer, and add additional constraints to better predict CAD models. However, modeling CAD as language gives rise to addition problems (such as producing grammatically correct but invalid representations), which are not easy to solve.

VP [33] pioneers the unsupervised approaches by using the union of a set of boxes to approximate shapes. SQ [21] takes a step further by using super quadrics instead of boxes to better approximate complex shapes. BSPNet [8] and CVXNet [9] propose to use the union of a set of convexes to represent a complex shape, where the convexes are constructed by intersecting half-spaces. These methods extend the modeling capability of using standard primitives, but abundant planes are required to approximate freeform surfaces, which also limits their edibility. UCSGNet [13] proposes CSG-Layers that iteratively selects primitives and Boolean operations for reconstruction. CSG-StumpNet [25] reformulates CSG-Tree with arbitrary depth into a fixed three layer structure similar to Disjunctive Normal Form, and uses a simple network to generate binary matrices for select fundamental products to union into the final reconstruction. However, these methods focuses on CSG operations and use only basic primitives (boxes, spheres, etc.), which is not efficient to approximate complicated shapes. CAPRI-Net [36] uses quadric implicit shapes to construct two intermediate shapes using an approach similar to BSP-Net. The two intermediate shapes are then subtracted to form the final shape. The construction process is interpretable, but the use of quadric implicit shapes reduces its edibility.

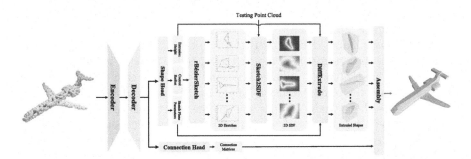

Fig. 2. Framework overview. The input point cloud first goes through the encoder-decoder phase to predict shape parameters and connection matrices via shape head and connection head. rBézierSketch is then used to generate the profile curve from the decoded sketch parameters. Sketch2SDF computes the SDF of the sketches. Sketch SDF, sketch plane parameters, and extrusion height are passed into DiffExtruder to generate the occupancy of the extrusion shapes, which together with the connection matrices are passed into CSG-Stump to generate the final shape occupancy.

3   ExtrudeNet

This section presents ExtrudeNet, an end-to-end network for unsupervised inverse sketch and extrude for compact and editable shape parsing. The input to the network is a point cloud representing a shape to be learned. ExtrudeNet outputs a set of 3D extrusions as the building blocks and their Boolean operations, which together create the shape. Each of the 3D extrusions is defined by a 2D sketch profile curve and a 3D extrusion process.

The pipeline of the entire network is illustrated in Fig. 2. The main components are briefly described below. Note that different encoder and assembly methods can be used to adapt for different use cases.

(1) **Encoder-Decoder:** ExtrudeNet first encodes the input point cloud into a latent feature using the off-the-shelf DGCNN as a backbone encoder [34]. The latent code is then enhanced by three fully connected layers with size 512, 1024, and 2048. After that, the latent feature is passed to the shape head and the connection head to decode into extruded shape parameters and connection matrices. Extruded shape parameters consist of 2D sketch parameters, sketch plane parameters, and extrusion height. Connection matrices represent Boolean operations among the extruded shapes. Since binary value is not differentiable, we use the Sigmoid function to predict a soft connection weight in $[0, 1]$ for each matrix.

(2) **rBézierSketch:** rBézierSketch is used to convert sketch parameters into a closed profile curve defined by a set of rational cubic Bézier curves for extrusion. The generated 2D sketch curve is guaranteed to be free of self-intersection and can represent free-form curves, circular arc and even polygon in a single formulation.

(3) **SDF-Generation:** This consists of Sketch2SDF and DiffExtruder. Sketch2SDF is first used to compute the Signed-Distance-Field (SDF) of the generated 2D sketch on a plane. The computed 2D sketch SDF, the sketch plane parameters, and extrusion height are then passed into DiffExtruder to compute the extruded shapes' occupancy field in 3D space.

(4) **Assembly:** Given the predicted extrusion shapes' occupancy and connection matrices, we are in a position to assemble the extrusion shapes to complete the final reconstruction. For this purpose, we choose to directly use CSG-Stump from [25] for its simplicity and learning friendly nature. CSG-Stump reformulates CSG-Trees into a three layer structure similar to Disjunctive Normal Form and use three fixed size binary matrices to generate and select fundamental products. The first layer of CSG-Stump is a complement layer indicating whether the complement of the input occupancy should be used for the down steam operations. The second layer is an intersection layer which selects and intersects complement layer's outputs into intersected shapes. The last layer selects intersected shapes to union into the final shape.

Below we describe rBézierSketch and SDF-Generation in more detail.

3.1 rBézierSketch and Extrusion

To create an extrusion shape, a profile curve should be sketched and then extruded in 3D space. We use a network to predict the sketch parameters that define the profile curve in the $XY-$plane (serving as its local coordinate system) and then extrude it along the $Z-$direction to create the extrusion shape. The shape is then transformed to the required location and orientation predicted by the network which mimics the sketch plane transform in CAD software.

rBézierSketch. Considering the common modeling practice and shapes in CAD applications, there are a few assumptions for the profile curve: (i) it is closed and has no self-intersection, which has advantages in defining a valid solid shape; (ii) it is piecewise smooth for creating quality shapes; and (iii) it can model freeform curves, and circles or polygons as well. Meanwhile, we also have to balance the capability and complexity of the representation such that it can be easily deployed into a learning pipeline. Based on these considerations, we propose the following model for our profile curve.

The basic mathematical model is a closed curve formed by N curve segments defined by special rational cubic Bézier curves $C_k(t), t \in [0,1], k = 0, 1, \cdots, N - 1$, which may explain the name *rBézierSketch*. The equation of $C_k(t)$ is:

$$C_k(t) = \frac{P_0^k B_0^3(t) + w_1^k P_1^k B_1^3(t) + w_2^k P_2^k B_2^3(t) + P_3^k B_3^3(t)}{B_0^3(t) + w_1^k B_1^3(t) + w_2^k B_2^3(t) + B_3^3(t)} \tag{1}$$

where $P_i^k = (x_i^k, y_i^k)$ are the control points on the XY-plane, weights $w_1^k \geq 0, w_2^k \geq 0$ are for the two inner control points, and $B_i^3(t) = \binom{3}{i}(1-t)^{3-i}t^i$ are Bernstein polynomials. To make sure that consecutive segments are connected to form a closed curve, the constraints $P_3^k = P_0^{(k+1)\bmod N}$ are added.

The closed curve is defined around the origin. Thus it is convenient to express each control points $P_i^k = (x_i^k, y_i^k) = (\rho_i^k \cos(\alpha_i^k), \rho_i^k \sin(\alpha_i^k))$ by the radial coordinate ρ_i^k and the polar angle α_i^k. For simplicity, we further distribute the central angles of the segments evenly. That is, each Bézier curve has the central angle $\frac{2\pi}{N}$. Within each segment $C_k(t)$, the polar angles of control points are chosen to be:

$$\alpha_1^k = \alpha_0^k + \theta, \quad \alpha_3^k = \alpha_0^k + \frac{2\pi}{N}, \quad \alpha_2^k = \alpha_3^k - \theta \tag{2}$$

where $\theta = \frac{2\pi}{4N} + \tan^{-1}\left(\frac{1}{3}\tan\left(\frac{2\pi}{4N}\right)\right)$. It is worth pointing out that these polar angles are specially designed to achieve the capability of circle recovery (see Proposition 2 below). In this way, to specify the Bézier control points, we just need to provide the radial coordinates. Connecting all the control points in order forms a polygon that is homeomorphic to the origin-centered unit circle, which assures good behavior of the generated profile curve. In summary, the network only has to estimate the radial coordinates ρ_i^k and the weights w_1^k, w_2^k in order to sketch the profile curve.

Remark 1. The proposed curve model is specially designed to deliver a few nice properties, which are outlined in the following paragraphs.

Rational cubic Bézier representation in (1) is proposed because it is a simple form of NURBS that is the industry standard in CAD and meanwhile sufficient to model freeform curves [10]. Besides freeform smooth shapes, this representation is able to represent a straight line or a polygon, for example, as long as we let all the control points P_i^k lie on a line. The reason that the rational form is chosen is that it includes polynomial curves as a special case and has the capability of exactly representing a circle. These properties enable the extrusion shapes to include box and cylinder primitive shapes as special cases.

Due to the special angular set-up of rBézierSketch, the generated profile curve is a simple closed curve, i.e., it does not self-intersect. In fact, we have an even stronger result.

Proposition 1. *The area bounded by the curve generated by rBézierSketch is a star-shaped set.*

Moreover, the special choice of angle θ in (2) makes it possible to exactly represent a circular arc using Eq. 1.

Proposition 2. *Let the polar angles be given by Eq. 2. If $\rho_0^k = \rho_3^k$, $\rho_1^k = \rho_2^k = \frac{\rho_0^k}{\cos(\theta)}$, and $w_1^k = w_2^k = \frac{1}{3}\left(1 + 2\cos\left(\frac{\pi}{N}\right)\right)$, then the rational Bézier curve of (1) defines a circular arc, as shown in Fig. 3 (left).*

The proposed curve model assures C^0 continuity among the segments since the Bézier control polygons are connected in a loop by enforcing each curve's last control point to be the same as the next curve's first control point (see Fig. 3 (middle)). Thus totally $3N$ radial coordinates and $2N$ weights need to be predicted. In case the predicted control points and weights happen to satisfy certain condition given by Proposition 3, C^1 continuity can be achieved.

Proposition 3. *If the control points and weights satisfy*

$$P_0^{k+1} = P_3^k = \frac{\rho_2^k P_1^{k+1} + \rho_1^{k+1} P_2^k}{\rho_2^k + \rho_1^{k+1}}, \quad \frac{w_2^k}{w_1^{k+1}} = \frac{\rho_1^{k+1}}{\rho_2^k}, \tag{3}$$

curve segments $C_{k+1}(t)$ and $C_k(t)$ meet at P_0^{k+1} with C^1 continuity.

The proof of above propositions is provided in the supplementary material.

If for some CAD applications we already have prior knowledge that the models should be at least C^1 continuous, then we can enforce C^1 continuity by letting P_0^k and w_2^k be computed from Eq. 3. In this case we just predict $2N$ control points P_1^k, P_2^k and N weights w_2^k, which have fewer variables (see Fig. 3 (right)).

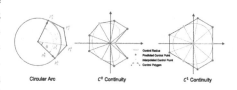

Fig. 3. Left: a circular arc. Middle: a C^0 profile curve. Right: a C^1 profile curve.

Remark 2. In CAD there have been some works to define single-valued curves in the polar coordinate system. For example, Sanchez-Reyes proposed a subset of rational Bézier curves that can be used to define single-valued curves [28] and later extended them to splines [29]. It should be pointed out that our proposed curves are different from those proposed by Sanchez-Reyes. Particularly, for a Sanchez-Reyes's curve, the control points are on radial directions regularly spaced by a constant angle and each weight must equal the inverse of the radial coordinate of the corresponding control point, which leaves very few degrees of freedom (DoF) for shape modeling. Our curves have more DoFs.

Extrusion. Once the profile curve $C(t) = (x(t), y(t))$ on the XY−plane is obtained, the extrusion shape is generated by directly extruding the curve along the Z−direction. The extrusion shape is bounded by the top and bottom planes and a side surface. The side surface has the parametric equations $(x, y, z) = ((x(t), y(t)), s)$ where $s \in [0, h]$ is the second parameter and h is the extrusion height estimated by the network.

The network also estimates a quaternion that defines a rotation matrix R and a translation vector $\mathbf{t} = (t_x, t_y, t_z)$ that defines a translation matrix T. The matrix R makes the XY−plane be in the orientation of the target sketch plane and the matrix T moves the origin to the target sketch center on the sketch plane. Thus applying matrices R and T to the upright extrusion shape gives the target extrusion shape in 3D space, as shown in Fig. 4.

3.2   SDF-Generation

Sketch2SDF. Note that the generated sketches are in parametric forms. Unlike explicit or implicit functions, computing a signed-distance-field of parametric curves is not trivial. There were a few implicitization algorithms for converting a parametric curve into an implicit representation [30, 37]. However, they require exact arithmetic computation. More-

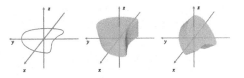

Fig. 4. Left: 2D sketch in the XY−plane; Middle: direct extrusion; Right: the target extrusion shape.

over, as observed in [31], the existence of singularity in parametric representation often makes the resulting implicit expression useless.

In this section, we present a numerical method for computing the SDF of parametric sketches. The method is general. While it applies to the rational cubic Bézier curves here, it also works for other parametric curves. This method also yields good gradients which is friendly for deep learning applications (see Sect. 4.2). The SDF of a sketch is defined by the

Fig. 5. The SDF of a curve is computed by a numerical method.

Distance-Field $DF(p)$, the smallest distance from a given testing point p to the curve, multiplied by a sign $SIGN(p)$ which indicates whether the testing point p is inside or outside of the sketch.

Distance-Field. To compute the Distance-Field of a sketch, we first sample a set of points S from the curve and take the smallest distance between the test point p and sample points S as the value of $DF(p)$. Specifically, given a parametric curve $C(t) = (x(t), y(t)), t \in [0, 1]$, the sampling points are obtained by evenly sampling the parameter values in the parameter domain:

$$S = \left\{ \left(x(\frac{i}{n}), y(\frac{i}{n}) \right) \mid i = 0, 1, \cdots, n \right\} \tag{4}$$

Then the distance between the testing point p and the set S is found by

$$DF(p) = \min_{s \in S} \|s - p\|_2 \tag{5}$$

and its corresponding closest point's parameter value is denoted by $CT(p)$.

Signed Distance-Field. To test if a point p is inside or outside of a sketch, we check whether if the displacement vector from the testing point towards the closest point in S has the same direction as the normal vector of the curve at the closest point. We assume that the curves are parameterized such that they are traced in the counter-clockwise direction. Otherwise, a simple reparameterization can correct it. Then the normal vector of the curve $C(t)$ can be computed by rotating its tangent vector by 90° clockwise:

$$N(t) = \left(\frac{dy(t)}{dt}, -\frac{dx(t)}{dt} \right) \tag{6}$$

If two consecutive curve segments of the sketch meet with C^0 continuity, the normal vectors of the two segments at the joint point are different. To ensure a consistent normal at the junction of two curves, the average of the two is used. In this way, the sign function for a testing point p can be computed:

$$SIGN(p) = \frac{N(CT(p))) \cdot (C(CT(p)) - p)}{\|N(CT(p))) \cdot (C(CT(p)) - p)\|_2 + \epsilon} \tag{7}$$

where a small positive number ϵ is added to prevent from zero division. Finally, the Signed-Distance of p is:

$$SDF_s(p) = SIGN(p) \times DF(p). \tag{8}$$

Figure 5 gives an example of a computed SDF.

DiffExtruder. Now we show how to compute the SDF of the extrusion shape. We first transform the testing point p back to a point p' by reversing the transformations that transform the XY-plane to the target sketch plane: $p' = R^{-1}(T^{-1}(p))$. Then we compute the signed distance of p' with respect to the upright extrusion shape whose base lies on the XY-plane. For this purpose, we project point p' onto the XY-plane by setting its z-value to 0 and denote the footprint by p'', and further find its nearest point $(c_x, c_y, 0)$ on the profile curve. Then the projected testing point p'', the nearest point $(c_x, c_y, 0)$ and its corresponding point (c_x, c_y, h) on the end plane of the extrusion define a vertical plane. Now, the problem of finding the SDF of the extrusion shape is reduced into computing the 2D SDF on the vertical plane.

If a point is inside of the extrusion shape, its signed distance to the shape simply becomes the minimum of the 2D sketch SDF and the distances from the point to the two planes that bound the extrusion.

$$SDF_i(p') = \max(\min(SDF_s((p'_x, p'_y)), h - p'_z, p'_z), 0) \tag{9}$$

If the point lies outside the extruded primitive, its signed distance becomes:

$$\begin{aligned} SDF_o(p') = -[(\min(h - p'_z, 0))^2 + (\min(p'_z, 0))^2 \\ + (\min(SDF_s((p'_x, p'_y)), 0))^2]^{\frac{1}{2}}. \end{aligned} \tag{10}$$

It can be seen that for a testing point outside the extruded shape, SDF_i becomes zero, and for a testing point inside the extrusion shape, SDF_o becomes zero. Therefore we can simply get the overall SDF by adding the two terms:

$$SDF(p') = SDF_i(p') + SDF_o(p'). \tag{11}$$

Occupancy of Extrusion Shape. After getting the SDF of an extrusion shape, the occupancy can be computed by a sigmoid function Φ where η indicates how sharp the conversion is taken place:

$$O(p') = \Phi(-\eta \times SDF(p')). \tag{12}$$

3.3   Training and Inference

We train ExtrudeNet in an end-to-end and unsupervised fashion as no ground truth sketch and extrusion parameters are present. The supervision signals are mainly generated by the reconstruction loss L_{re} that computes the discrepancy between the reconstructed shape's occupancy $\hat{O}$ and the ground truth shape's occupancy O^* using a set of testing points $P \subset R^3$ sampled within the shape's bounding box:

$$L_{re} = \mathbb{E}_{p \sim P} ||\hat{O}_i - O_i^*||_2^2. \tag{13}$$

As suggested in [25], when a shape is too far from any testing points, the gradient becomes extremely small due to the use of a sigmoid function. Thus a primitive loss is introduced to "poll" the primitive shapes towards testing points:

$$L_{prim} = \frac{1}{K} \sum_k^K \min_n SDF_k^2(p_n), \tag{14}$$

We enforce the weights to be close to one, which encourage the rational Bézier curves to be close to Bézier curves.

Thus, the overall objective is then defined:

$$L_{total} = L_{re} + \lambda_p \cdot L_{prim} + \lambda_w \cdot \sum_{k=0}^{N-1} \sum_{i=1}^{2} (w_i^k - 1)^2 \tag{15}$$

where λ_p and λ_w are the trade-off factors.

During inference, we discretize the connection matrices into Boolean values for interpretable construction. In addition, we implement a CAD converter that directly takes binary connection matrices and the network generated parameters as input and converts the reconstructed shape into CAD compatible format. We use OpenSCAD [15] to render the final shape into STL [27] format.

4   Experiments

In this section, we first evaluate our complete pipeline ExtrudeNet, particularly its ability to extract editable and interpretable shape representations with ablation on different settings. Then, we evaluate the key component of rBézierSketch and Sketch2SDF on 2D toy examples.

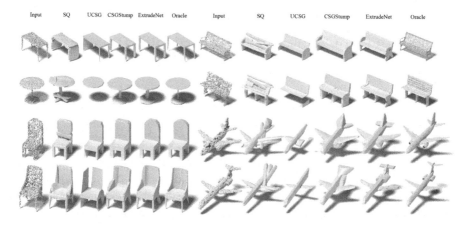

Fig. 6. Qualitative comparison between ExtrudeNet and other baselines. ExtrudeNet generates visually more pleasing outputs with curved surfaces compared to all the baselines.

4.1   Evaluations of ExtrudeNet

Dataset. We evaluate the ExtrudeNet on ShapeNet Dataset [7] with train, test, and val split aligned with prior methods. The input point clouds are sampled from the original mesh surface via Poisson Disk Sampling [6]. The testing points are sampled using [5] in a grid from the mesh bounding box with 15% of padding on each side. This padding is important to remove unwanted artifacts, see Supplementary Material.

Implementation Details. We implement ExtrudeNet using PyTorch [22], and train the network with Adam Optimizer [14] with a learning rate of 1e-4. We train each class on a single NVIDIA V100 GPU with a batch size of 16. It took about 5 days to converge.

In our experiments, each sketch is constructed with 4 Bézier curves with a sample rate of 100. We estimate 64 extruded shapes in total, and use 64 as the number of intersection nodes in Assembly (see Fig. 2) adopted from CSG-Stump [25].

Main Results - Comparisons with Baselines. We compare our method with related approaches focusing on editable shape abstraction, namely, VP [33], SQ [21], UCSG-Net [13], and CSG-Stump Net [25]. Note that BSPNet and CVXNet are excluded as they mainly focus on the reconstruction of thousands of planes that contain too many primitives and thus lack editability. For fair comparison, we align the number of available primitives to 64 for VP, SQ and UCSG. We show qualitative comparisons with the baseline methods in Fig. 6. It can be seen that our ExtrudeNet models curved surfaces more effectively compared to all the baseline methods, thus resulting in a more detailed reconstruction.

Moreover, we also conduct quantitative evaluations using symmetric L_2 Chamfer Distance (CD), volumetric IoU and surface F1 scores. The comparisons of the results are given in Table 1. We can see that ExtrudeNet achieves the best overall reconstruction quality.

Table 1. Different Metric computed between 3D reconstruction results and the ground truth shapes. ExtrudeNet outputs better overall results

	VP [33]			SQ [21]			UCSG [13]			Stump [25]			ExtrudeNet		
	CD	V-IoU	F1	CD	V-IoU	F1	CD	V-IoU	F1	CD	V-IoU	F1	CD	V-IoU	F1
Chair	**1.10**	0.28	**67.07**	2.85	0.21	41.49	3.54	0.25	61.01	1.34	**0.41**	63.33	1.47	**0.41**	60.17
Car	1.02	**0.67**	62.71	1.25	0.17	78.58	**0.64**	0.11	**82.54**	0.76	0.32	76.45	0.67	0.41	82.20
Sofa	2.18	0.29	48.75	1.27	0.37	69.14	1.30	0.29	79.59	0.85	0.61	**83.88**	**0.79**	**0.62**	83.42
Plane	5.11	0.29	37.55	**0.58**	0.23	82.94	0.71	0.10	**87.66**	0.70	**0.36**	74.57	0.66	0.33	77.95
Lamp	8.41	**0.24**	35.57	**1.79**	0.16	**63.00**	7.02	0.22	55.66	3.48	**0.24**	57.93	3.77	0.20	42.86
Telephone	2.75	0.55	48.22	0.46	0.38	88.29	**0.34**	**0.69**	**93.32**	1.60	0.58	91.24	0.56	0.62	89.00
Vessel	2.84	0.37	54.21	**0.76**	0.27	**78.52**	4.54	0.09	61.65	1.15	0.44	72.30	1.63	**0.48**	61.06
Loudspeaker	1.67	0.45	50.06	2.07	0.34	65.00	1.81	0.19	56.35	1.70	0.52	63.32	**1.21**	**0.60**	**75.04**
Cabinate	3.16	0.48	42.90	1.97	0.31	40.52	1.09	0.38	73.56	0.77	0.56	79.11	**0.73**	**0.68**	**84.94**
Table	1.62	0.26	60.05	2.89	0.17	60.01	3.64	0.30	65.09	1.35	0.35	**74.48**	**1.06**	0.45	73.49
Display	1.25	0.36	60.52	**0.72**	0.33	80.09	1.13	0.54	78.18	1.64	0.50	75.75	0.96	**0.55**	**83.66**
Bench	1.57	0.26	63.31	1.09	0.17	73.46	1.73	0.21	74.12	1.04	0.29	73.40	**0.78**	**0.39**	**81.17**
Rifle	1.35	0.35	66.06	**0.38**	0.26	**90.55**	1.05	0.29	84.38	0.78	0.37	85.61	0.76	**0.44**	84.18
Mean	2.61	0.37	53.61	1.39	0.25	70.12	2.19	0.28	73.31	1.32	0.42	74.64	**1.15**	**0.47**	**75.32**

Effect of Different Numbers of Primitives. To show that our proposed extrude shapes with freeform profile curves are highly adaptable, we train ExtrudeNet with limited numbers of extruded shapes. Table 2 reports the results on the three classes. It can be seen that even with only 8 available extruded shapes, our method can still achieve reasonable reconstruction results.

Table 2. CD results $(\times 10^{-3})$ with shapes extruded from different numbers of sketches.

#Primitives	8	16	32	64
Plane	0.89	0.96	0.81	**0.66**
Chair	2.01	1.81	1.47	**1.47**
Bench	1.41	1.18	1.30	**0.78**

Effect of Different Sketches. Our method can also use other profile curves such as polygonal and circular. Table 3 gives a comparison on the CD results under different types of profile curves. We can see that extruded shapes with the proposed freeform profile curves outperform the results using the other

Table 3. CD results ($\times 10^{-3}$) with shapes extruded from different sketches on the Airplane class.

Sketch type	Freeform	Circle	Poly
CD	**0.66**	0.877	0.838

two common profile curves by a significant margin, which indicates the strong representability of the extruded shapes with freeform profile curves.

Edibility of Sketch and Extrude. After getting the results from ExtrudeNet, a designer can do a secondary development with ease. Using the bench example in Fig. 7, we show that by editing the Bezier Control Points and reducing the extrusion height, we can easily generate an armchair from the reconstruction result.

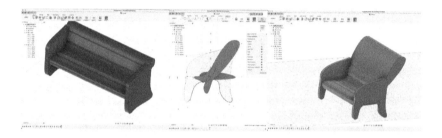

Fig. 7. As ExtrudeNet's output is directly compatible with Industrial CAD software, we can directly import the shape into Fusion360 and edit using its GUI interface. We show that a bench can be edited into an armchair by simply edit the 2D cross-section sketch by dragging the control points and adjust the extrusion height. **Left:** ExtrudeNet's output. **Middle:** Edit sketch using Fusion 360. **Right:** Result after editing.

More ablations such as sampling rate, number of curves, sketch plane placement etc., can be found in the supplementary material.

4.2   Evaluation of rBézierSketch

To demonstrate the approximation ability and the ease of learning of the proposed rBézierSketch, we conduct a fitting experiment that directly optimize for the radial coordinate that best reconstructs a given raster emoji image from [4]. As the emojis contains different color blocks, which is not suitable to be represented using occupancy or SDFs, we choose to approximate the individual boundaries instead of solid colors blocks. Given a raster emoji image, we first compute its edges using Canny edge detection, and then we compute the Distance Field for the edge image. We fit the sketch by minimizing the MSE loss between the predicted and ground truth distance fields using standard gradient decent. As shown in Fig. 8, the emoji can be reconstructed by rBézierSketch with good quality. We also show the training plot, where a smooth decrease in the loss term indicating that rBézierSketch and Sketch2Field yields good gradients and it is friendly to used in a learning setup.

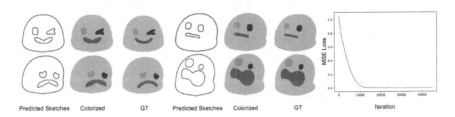

Fig. 8. Left: We show that using rBézierSketch alone we can reconstruct the emojis with good qualities. Right: Our rBézierSketch and Sketch2SDF provide low variance gradients which yields a smooth convergence.

4.3 Evaluation of Sketch2SDF

Here we demonstrate the versatility and accuracy of Sketch2SDF on computing parametric sketches' SDF by giving concrete examples.

Versatility. To show the versatility, we implemented four different kinds of parametric curves, namely polygon, ellipse, Cubic Bezier Sketchs with C^1 and C^0 continuity, see Fig. 9(Top). Note that our method is not limited to these curves, and can be easily adapted to new parametric curve types. During the implementation of these curves, only the curve sampling and normal computation need to be adapted accordingly while the rest of the code remains untouched. This indicates that our pipeline is highly reusable and can support new parametric curves with minimum effort.

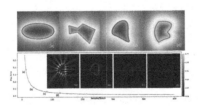

Fig. 9. Top: Sketch2SDF can be easily adapted to different parametric curve types. Bottom: Visualization of the approximation errors by comparing numerical and analytical SDFs of Bezier sketch. (a)–(d) indicate the errors at sampling rate of 20, 40, 80 and 120. We can see that error is barely noticeable with a relatively small sampling rate.

Approximation Accuracy. As Sketch2SDF is a numerical method, approximation is introduced, where the sample rate is the most influential factor. Thus, we study the degree of approximation under different sampling rates by comparing our numerical results against the analytical results using Bézier Sketches. In Fig. 9, we plot the maximum error of all testing points versus sample rate and visualize the error heat map. We can see that too few sample points will dramatically decrease the accuracy, and higher sampling rates yield more accurate approximation, which is however at the cost of higher computation and memory usage. Empirically, we find that around 400 sample points per curve is a reasonable trade-off.

5   Conclusion

In this paper, we have presented ExtrudeNet, which is an effective framework for unsupervised inverse sketch-and-extrude for shape parsing from point clouds. It not only output a compact, editable and interpretable shape representation but also a meaningful sketch-and-extrude process, which can benefit various applications. As demonstrated by extensive experiments, ExtudeNet can express complex shapes with high compactness and interpretability while achieving state-of-the-art reconstruction results both visually and quantitatively.

Discussion. Currently, ExtrudeNet requires a relatively long training time as sketches are more freeformed and have higher degrees of freedom. We also notice that some artifacts have been reconstructed due to high degrees of freedom. The current extrusion is a simple extrusion along the direction orthogonal to the sketch plane. Generalizing the extrusion to include more advanced processes such as sweeping and lofting warrants further investigation, which would have more impacts in the industry.

Acknowledgements. The work is partially supported by a joint WASP/NTU project (04INS000440C130), Monash FIT Startup Grant, and SenseTime Gift Fund.

References

1. Shapr3D: The world's most intuitive 3d design app. https://www.shapr3d.com/
2. SOLIDWORKS: 3D CAD design software. https://www.solidworks.com/
3. Fusion 360: Cloud powered 3d CAD/CAM software for product design, June 2021. https://www.autodesk.com.sg/products/fusion-360/overview
4. Color and black-and-white noto emoji fonts, and tools for working with them, March 2022. https://github.com/googlefonts/noto-emoji
5. Batty, C.: SDFGen (2015). https://github.com/christopherbatty/SDFGen
6. Bridson, R.: Fast poisson disk sampling in arbitrary dimensions. SIGGRAPH Sketches **10**, 1 (2007)
7. Chang, A.X., et al.: ShapeNet: an information-rich 3d model repository. arXiv preprint arXiv:1512.03012 (2015)

8. Chen, Z., Tagliasacchi, A., Zhang, H.: BSP-Net: generating compact meshes via binary space partitioning. In: Proceedings of the IEEE/CVF Conference on Computer Vision and Pattern Recognition, pp. 45–54 (2020)

9. Deng, B., Genova, K., Yazdani, S., Bouaziz, S., Hinton, G., Tagliasacchi, A.: CVXNet: learnable convex decomposition. In: Proceedings of the IEEE/CVF Conference on Computer Vision and Pattern Recognition, pp. 31–44 (2020)

10. Farin, G.: Curves and Surfaces for CAGD: A Practical Guide, 5th edn. Morgan Kaufmann Publishers Inc., San Francisco (2001)

11. Ganin, Y., Bartunov, S., Li, Y., Keller, E., Saliceti, S.: Computer-aided design as language. arXiv preprint arXiv:2105.02769 (2021)

12. Hao, Z., Averbuch-Elor, H., Snavely, N., Belongie, S.: DualSDF: semantic shape manipulation using a two-level representation. In: Proceedings of the IEEE/CVF Conference on Computer Vision and Pattern Recognition, pp. 7631–7641 (2020)

13. Kania, K., Zieba, M., Kajdanowicz, T.: UCSG-Net-unsupervised discovering of constructive solid geometry tree. arXiv preprint arXiv:2006.09102 (2020)

14. Kingma, D.P., Ba, J.: Adam: a method for stochastic optimization. arXiv preprint arXiv:1412.6980 (2014)

15. Kintel, M., Wolf, C.: OpenSCAD. GNU General Public License, p GNU General Public License (2014)

16. Laidlaw, D.H., Trumbore, W.B., Hughes, J.F.: Constructive solid geometry for polyhedral objects. In: Proceedings of the 13th Annual Conference on Computer Graphics and Interactive Techniques, pp. 161–170 (1986)

17. Lorensen, W.E., Cline, H.E.: Marching cubes: a high resolution 3d surface construction algorithm. ACM SIGGRAPH Comput. Graph. 21(4), 163–169 (1987)

18. Mescheder, L., Oechsle, M., Niemeyer, M., Nowozin, S., Geiger, A.: Occupancy networks: learning 3d reconstruction in function space. In: Proceedings of the IEEE/CVF Conference on Computer Vision and Pattern Recognition, pp. 4460–4470 (2019)

19. Para, W.R., et al.: SketchGen: generating constrained cad sketches. arXiv preprint arXiv:2106.02711 (2021)

20. Park, J.J., Florence, P., Straub, J., Newcombe, R., Lovegrove, S.: DeepSDF: learning continuous signed distance functions for shape representation. In: Proceedings of the IEEE/CVF Conference on Computer Vision and Pattern Recognition, pp. 165–174 (2019)

21. Paschalidou, D., Ulusoy, A.O., Geiger, A.: Superquadrics revisited: learning 3d shape parsing beyond cuboids. In: Proceedings of the IEEE/CVF Conference on Computer Vision and Pattern Recognition, pp. 10344–10353 (2019)

22. Paszke, A., et al.: PyTorch: an imperative style, high-performance deep learning library. In: Wallach, H., Larochelle, H., Beygelzimer, A., d' Alché-Buc, F., Fox, E., Garnett, R. (eds.) Advances in Neural Information Processing Systems, vol. 32, pp. 8024–8035. Curran Associates, Inc. (2019). http://papers.neurips.cc/paper/9015-pytorch-an-imperative-style-high-performance-deep-learning-library.pdf

23. Qi, C.R., Su, H., Mo, K., Guibas, L.J.: PointNet: deep learning on point sets for 3d classification and segmentation. In: Proceedings of the IEEE Conference on Computer Vision and Pattern Recognition, pp. 652–660 (2017)

24. Qi, C.R., Yi, L., Su, H., Guibas, L.J.: PointNet++: deep hierarchical feature learning on point sets in a metric space. In: Advances in Neural Information Processing Systems, vol. 30 (2017)

25. Ren, D., et al.: CSG-stump: a learning friendly CSG-like representation for interpretable shape parsing. arXiv preprint arXiv:2108.11305 (2021)

26. Requicha, A.A., Voelcker, H.B.: Constructive solid geometry (1977)
27. Roscoe, L., et al.: Stereolithography interface specification. America-3D Systems Inc **27**(2020), 10 (1988)
28. Sanchez-Reyes, J.: Single-valued curves in polar coordinates. Comput. Aided Des. **22**(1), 19–26 (1990)
29. Sánchez-Reyes, J.: Single-valued spline curves in polar coordinates. Comput. Aided Des. **24**(6), 307–315 (1992)
30. Sederberg, T.W., Anderson, D.C., Goldman, R.N.: Implicit representation of parametric curves and surfaces. Comput. Vis. Graph. Image Process. **28**(1), 72–84 (1984)
31. Sederberg, T.W., Zheng, J., Klimaszewski, K., Dokken, T.: Approximate implicitization using monoid curves and surfaces. Graph. Model. Image Process. **61**(4), 177–198 (1999). https://doi.org/10.1006/gmip.1999.0497
32. Sharma, G., Goyal, R., Liu, D., Kalogerakis, E., Maji, S.: CSGNet: neural shape parser for constructive solid geometry. In: Proceedings of the IEEE Conference on Computer Vision and Pattern Recognition, pp. 5515–5523 (2018)
33. Tulsiani, S., Su, H., Guibas, L.J., Efros, A.A., Malik, J.: Learning shape abstractions by assembling volumetric primitives. In: Proceedings of the IEEE Conference on Computer Vision and Pattern Recognition, pp. 2635–2643 (2017)
34. Wang, Y., Sun, Y., Liu, Z., Sarma, S.E., Bronstein, M.M., Solomon, J.M.: Dynamic graph CNN for learning on point clouds. ACM Trans. Graph. (ToG) **38**(5), 1–12 (2019)
35. Wu, R., Xiao, C., Zheng, C.: DeepCAD: a deep generative network for computer-aided design models. arXiv preprint arXiv:2105.09492 (2021)
36. Yu, F., et al.: CAPRI-Net: learning compact CAD shapes with adaptive primitive assembly. arXiv preprint arXiv:2104.05652 (2021)
37. Zheng, J., Sederberg, T.W.: A direct approach to computing the μ-basis of planar rational curves. J. Symb. Comput. **31**(5), 619–629 (2001). https://doi.org/10.1006/jsco.2001.0437

CATRE: Iterative Point Clouds Alignment for Category-Level Object Pose Refinement

Xingyu Liu[1], Gu Wang[2], Yi Li[3], and Xiangyang Ji[1(✉)]

[1] Tsinghua University, BNRist, Beijing, China
liuxy21@mails.tsinghua.edu.cn , xyji@tsinghua.edu.cn
[2] JD.com, Beijing, China
[3] University of Washington, Seattle, USA

Abstract. While category-level 9DoF object pose estimation has emerged recently, previous correspondence-based or direct regression methods are both limited in accuracy due to the huge intra-category variances in object shape and color, *etc.* Orthogonal to them, this work presents a category-level object pose and size refiner CATRE, which is able to iteratively enhance pose estimate from point clouds to produce accurate results. Given an initial pose estimate, CATRE predicts a relative transformation between the initial pose and ground truth by means of aligning the partially observed point cloud and an abstract shape prior. In specific, we propose a novel disentangled architecture being aware of the inherent distinctions between rotation and translation/size estimation. Extensive experiments show that our approach remarkably outperforms state-of-the-art methods on REAL275, CAMERA25, and LM benchmarks up to a speed of $\approx$85.32 Hz, and achieves competitive results on category-level tracking. We further demonstrate that CATRE can perform pose refinement on unseen category. Code and trained models are available (https://github.com/THU-DA-6D-Pose-Group/CATRE.git).

1 Introduction

Estimating the 6DoF pose, *i.e.*, 3DoF orientation and 3DoF localization, of an object in Euclidean space plays a vital role in robotic manipulation [13,49], 3D scene understanding [22,36] and augmented/virtual reality [35,46]. The vast majority of previous works [30,31,38,45,52–54,62,64] study with instance-level object pose estimation, which can be decomposed by two procedures: initial pose estimation and pose refinement. Despite considerable progress has been made in instance-level settings, the generalizability and scalability w.r.t.unseen objects

---

X. Liu and G. Wang—Equal contribution.

Supplementary Information The online version contains supplementary material available at https://doi.org/10.1007/978-3-031-20086-1_29.

S. Avidan et al. (Eds.): ECCV 2022, LNCS 13662, pp. 499–516, 2022.
https://doi.org/10.1007/978-3-031-20086-1_29

are limited due to the high dependency of known exact CAD models during both training and inference.

To alleviate this problem, recently, increasing attention has been received on category-level 9DoF pose (*i.e.*, 6DoF pose and 3DoF size) estimation which aims to handle novel instances among known categories without requiring CAD models for test. As an early proposed work, Wang *et al.* [55] predict the normalized object coordinates (NOCS) in image space and then solve the pose and size by matching NOCS against observed depth with Umeyama algorithm [50]. Afterwards, several works [7,14,47,56] attempt to deform the shape prior (*i.e.*, the mean shape) of a category towards observed instances to improve the accuracy of correspondences matching. However, those methods highly rely on the RANSAC procedure to remove outliers thus making them non-differentiable and time-consuming. Contrary to correspondence-based methods, some more recent works [9,32] propose to directly regress pose and size to achieve a higher speed during inference. Nevertheless, these end-to-end approaches are oftentimes error-prone in that they are not sufficiently aware of the inherent distinctions between rotation and translation/size estimation. To summarize, compared with the milestones achieved by state of the art in instance-level works, category-level pose estimation methods are still limited in accuracy.

Previously, when the CAD model is available, one common way of enhancing pose accuracy is to apply a post-refinement step through matching the rendered results against observed images given initial estimates, which has been widely explored in both traditional [2,44] and learning-based [25,27,30,59] methods. Being motivated by this, we seek to tackle the above problem by investigating object pose refinement at the category level. However, traditional object pose refinement methods rely on the CAD model to perform render-and-compare, which is not accessible when we conduct category-level object pose estimation.

To solve this dilemma, we propose a novel method for *CAT*egory-level object pose *RE*finement (*CATRE*), leveraging the abstract shape prior information instead of exact CAD models. As shown in Fig. 1, we aim to directly regress the relative pose and size transformations by aligning the partially observed point cloud against the transformed shape prior given initial pose and size predictions. In specific, we first use the initial pose prediction to focalize the shape prior and observed point cloud into a limited range. Then, a Siamese PointNet-based [40] encoder is employed to map the two input point clouds into a common feature space while maintaining relevant features for rigid transformation. Finally, we design two distinct heads to predict relative rotation and translation/size transformations in a disentangled manner. This is based on the observation that rotation is heavily reliant on point-level local geometry whereas translation and size reside with the object-level global feature. Besides, the procedure of refinement is conducted iteratively to achieve more accurate results.

Extensive experiments demonstrate that our proposed method can accurately yet efficiently refine and track category-level object poses. Exemplarily, we achieve a significant improvement over the baseline SPD [47] with an improve-

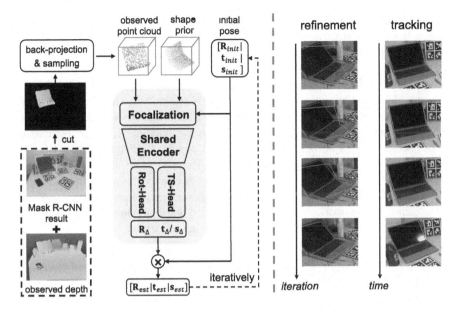

Fig. 1. The framework of CATRE. Given an initial pose and size estimate $[\mathbf{R}_{init}|\mathbf{t}_{init}|\mathbf{s}_{init}]$, CATRE predicts a relative transformation $[\mathbf{R}_\Delta|\mathbf{t}_\Delta|\mathbf{s}_\Delta]$ by iteratively aligning two focalized point clouds, *i.e.*, shape prior and observed point cloud. The framework can perform pose refinement and tracking, where blue and green contours reflect ground-truth and predicted poses, respectively. (Color figure online)

ment of 26.8% on the strict $5°\,2\,cm$ metric and 14.5% on the IoU_{75} metric on REAL275 dataset.

To sum up, our contributions are threefold: i) To the best of our knowledge, we propose the first versatile pipeline for category-level pose refinement based on point clouds leveraging abstract shape prior, without requiring exact CAD models during training or inference. ii) For the learning of relative transformation, a pose-guided focalization strategy is proposed to calibrate input point clouds. We further introduce a novel disentangled architecture being aware of the inherent attributions in pose estimation. Thanks to these key ingredients, we overcome the drawback of being error-prone while maintaining the high speed of direct regression. iii) Our versatile framework can also perform category-level pose tracking and achieve competitive performance against state of the art, whilst at $7\times$ faster speed. Meanwhile, CATRE can be naturally extended to instance-level and unseen category pose refinement leveraging appropriate shape priors.

2   Related Work

Category-level Object Pose Estimation. Category-level pose estimation aims to predict the 9DoF pose of a novel instance without the aid of its CAD model. Existing works can be generally categorized to correspondence-based [7,

47,55,56] and direct regression [6,9,32] approaches. Correspondence-based approaches first predict dense object coordinates in a normalized canonical space (NOCS) [55] and then solve the pose by Umeyama algorithm [50]. Notably, SPD [47] proposes to extract a categorical shape prior and adapt it to various instances via deformation prediction, in an effort to improve the matching of correspondences. On the other hand, direct regression methods predict object pose in an end-to-end manner, achieving a higher inference speed. For instance, FSNet [9] decouples rotation prediction into two orthogonal axes estimation. DualPoseNet [32] exploits spherical convolutions to explicitly regress the pose with an auxiliary task of canonicalizing the observed point cloud meanwhile.

While this field has emerged recently, the accuracy of estimating category-level pose is still far from satisfactory compared with instance-level settings. Orthogonally, this work builds an end-to-end category-level pose refinement pipeline which can largely enhance the performance whilst being fast.

Object Pose Refinement. In instance-level cases [27,30,45,53,59,62,64], object pose refinement has demonstrated to be very effective. Notably, DeepIM [30] predicts pose transformation by comparing the rendered image against the observed image. se(3)-TrackNet [59] further leverages this render-and-compare strategy to object tracking using RGB-D images. Extended from DeepIM, CosyPose [27] conquers the leaderboard of BOP Challenge 2020 [21], showing the powerful capability of the render-and-compare technique.

Different from the instance-level settings, category-level pose refinement is still rarely explored. DualPoseNet [32] refines their prediction by a self-adaptive pose consistency loss, which is only applicable to specific networks. However, our work is generalizable to various kinds of baselines [32,47,55] without re-training.

Category-level Object Pose Tracking. 6-PACK [51] performs category-level tracking by anchor-based keypoints generation and matching between adjacent frames. CAPTRA [60] tracks rigid and articulated objects by employing two separate networks to predict the interframe rotation and normalized coordinates respectively. Recently, iCaps [12] leverages a particle filtering framework to estimate and track category-level pose and size. Note that CAPTRA could be adapted for refinement in theory, although there are no relevant experiments. Still, there might be some limitations. First, it relies on CAD models to provide supervision signals (*i.e.*, NOCS map) for training, while CATRE does not need exact CAD models during training or inference. Moreover, it was proposed for tracking where the errors between adjacent frames are minor, so it is unclear if CAPTRA could handle noises from other estimation methods. However, as CATRE directly regresses the relative pose, it can perform iterative inference with a faster speed and more robust performance w.r.t.noises.

Point Cloud Registration. A closely related field to depth-based refinement is point cloud registration. Traditional methods like ICP [2] and its variants [3,42, 44] require reliable pose initialization. To overcome this problem, learning-based methods are proposed recently [1,10,57,58]. Works like [16,48] use the non-overlapped prior as CATRE does, but they usually learn the deformation rather

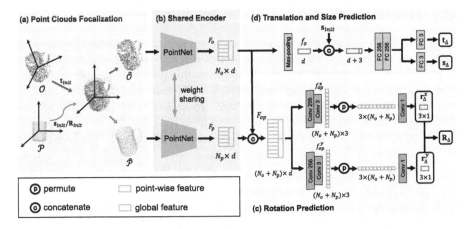

Fig. 2. The network architecture of CATRE. Taking an observed point cloud $\mathcal{O}$ and shape prior $\mathcal{P}$ as input, CATRE first focalizes them into a limited range using initial pose prediction $[\mathbf{R}_{init}|\mathbf{t}_{init}|\mathbf{s}_{init}]$. Then, we employ a Siamese geometric encoder followed by two disentangled heads to predict relative pose transformation $[\mathbf{R}_\Delta|\mathbf{t}_\Delta|\mathbf{s}_\Delta]$.

than the relative pose. Besides, shape prior in CATRE can be very different from the objects, varying from instance-specific keypoints to categorical mean shape to generic bounding box corners.

3 Category-Level Object Pose Refinement

This section first addresses the problem formulation and framework overview (Fig. 1), and then describes the key ingredients of our approach (Fig. 2) for category-level object pose refinement. Afterwards, we present the training and testing protocol and show that CATRE can be naturally applied to pose tracking.

3.1 Problem Formulation

Given an initial pose and size estimate $[\mathbf{R}_{init}|\mathbf{t}_{init}|\mathbf{s}_{init}]$ and the observed point cloud $\mathcal{O}$ of an object, our goal is to predict a relative transformation $[\mathbf{R}_\Delta|\mathbf{t}_\Delta|\mathbf{s}_\Delta]$ between the initial prediction and ground truth $[\mathbf{R}_{gt}|\mathbf{t}_{gt}|\mathbf{s}_{gt}]$ leveraging a shape prior $\mathcal{P}$, as shown in Eq. (1).

$$[\mathbf{R}_\Delta|\mathbf{t}_\Delta|\mathbf{s}_\Delta] = CATRE([\mathbf{R}_{init}|\mathbf{t}_{init}|\mathbf{s}_{init}], \mathcal{O}, \mathcal{P}). \tag{1}$$

Thereby, $\mathbf{R} \in SO(3)$, $\mathbf{t} \in \mathbb{R}^3$ and $\mathbf{s} \in \mathbb{R}^3$ respectively represents rotation, translation and size. The shape prior $\mathcal{P}$ can be the mean shape of a given category or a generic skeleton like bounding box corners. We use the categorical mean shape (*c.f.* Sect. 3.2) as the prior information in our main experiments and illustrations.

3.2   Overview of CATRE

Recapping Fig. 1, we first employ an off-the-shelf instance segmentation network (*e.g.*, Mask R-CNN [17]) to cut the object of interest from the observed depth map. Then we back-project the depth into camera space and sample N_o points within a ball near to the object following [8,60]. The center and radius of this ball are determined by the initial pose estimate. To this end, we effectively remove outliers and obtain the observed point cloud $\mathcal{O} = \{o_i \in \mathbb{R}^3\}_{i=1}^{N_o}$.

To estimate the pose and size transformations based on the observed point cloud, we leverage the publicly available shape prior $\mathcal{P} = \{p_j \in \mathbb{R}^3\}_{j=1}^{N_p}$ from [47]. Thereby, a mean shape is reconstructed from the mean latent embedding for each category trained with a large amount of synthetic point cloud models from ShapeNet [5] using an encoder-decoder framework. We normalize the size of the shape prior such that the length of each side of its bounding box is 1.

Taking the observed point cloud $\mathcal{O}$, and the prior point cloud $\mathcal{P}$ as input, our CATRE network (Fig. 2) essentially predicts the relative transformation to iteratively refine the initial estimate towards the target pose and size.

3.3   Disentangled Transformation Learning

Point Clouds Focalization. As the localization of input point clouds can vary dramatically in camera space, it would be very hard for the network to exploit useful information for learning relative transformation. Inspired by the image-space zooming in operation in DeepIM [30], we propose a novel point cloud focalization strategy to limit the range of input point clouds. Specifically, after transforming the prior point cloud $\mathcal{P}$ into camera space with the initial pose and size, we simultaneously shift the observed and estimated point clouds using the initial translation. Therefore, the input observed point cloud $\hat{\mathcal{O}}$ and prior point cloud $\hat{\mathcal{P}}$ can be obtained as follows

$$
\begin{aligned}
\hat{\mathcal{O}} &= \{\hat{o}_i \mid \hat{o}_i = o_i - \mathbf{t}_{init}\}_{i=1}^{N_o}, \\
\hat{\mathcal{P}} &= \{\hat{p}_j \mid \hat{p}_j = \mathbf{s}_{init} \odot \mathbf{R}_{init} p_j\}_{j=1}^{N_p},
\end{aligned}
\tag{2}
$$

where $\odot$ denotes element-wise product. Geometrically, $\hat{\mathcal{P}}$ and $\hat{\mathcal{O}}$ contain all the information needed for learning the relative transformation between the initial estimate and the target pose, no matter how we shift them. By fixing the center of $\hat{\mathcal{P}}$ to the origin, we can let the network focalize on the limited range around the origin, thus reducing the difficulty of learning for the network. Notice that, compared with similar strategies in image space proposed for instance-level 6D pose refinement and tracking [30,59], which rely on rendering with known CAD models and the costly operation of cropping and resizing, our point cloud focalization is much simpler yet more efficient.

Shared Encoder. Inspired by works on learning-based point cloud registration [28,43,58], we employ a shared encoder to respectively extract embeddings $F_p \in \mathbb{R}^{N_p \times d}$ and $F_o \in \mathbb{R}^{N_o \times d}$ from $\hat{\mathcal{P}}$ and $\hat{\mathcal{O}}$ for efficiently encoding the geometric information locally and globally. Here $d = 1088$ denotes the output dimension. In point cloud registration, both point-based encoder [40] and graph-based encoder [33] have been widely used. However, we experimentally find 3D-GCN [33] performing poorly in our work, as it is locally sensitive whilst the local graph structures of the partially observed point cloud and the full shape prior share little similarity. Hence we choose the simpler PointNet [40] as the backbone for better generalizability. Concretely, PointNet maps each point from $\mathbb{R}^3$ into a high-dimensional space, and generates an additional global feature by aggregating features from all points. The global feature is repeated N times and appended to each point-wise feature, where N denotes the number of input points. For details of the employed encoder, please kindly refer to the supplementary material.

By the prominent weight sharing strategy, we map $\hat{\mathcal{P}}$ and $\hat{\mathcal{O}}$ into a common feature space while remaining sensitive to relevant features for rigid transformation. Considering that rotation is different from translation and size in essence, we introduce a disentangled transformation learning strategy for them by means of two different heads namely *Rot-Head* and *TS-Head* in the following.

Rotation Prediction. As aforementioned, $\hat{\mathcal{O}}$ encodes the information of $\mathbf{R}_{gt}$, and $\hat{\mathcal{P}}$ contains $\mathbf{R}_{init}$, so the network can predict $\mathbf{R}_\Delta$ by comparing $\hat{\mathcal{O}}$ and $\hat{\mathcal{P}}$. First, we concatenate F_o and F_p along the point dimension to get a unified per-point feature $F_{op} \in \mathbb{R}^{(N_o+N_p)\times d}$. Then, the feature is fed to Rot-Head to predict a continuous 6-dimensional rotation representation $[\mathbf{r}_\Delta^x | \mathbf{r}_\Delta^y]$ following [9,66], *i.e.*, the first two columns of the rotation matrix $\mathbf{R}_\Delta$. Finally, the relative rotation matrix $\mathbf{R}_\Delta$ is recovered as in [66], and the refined rotation prediction can be computed by $\mathbf{R}_{est} = \mathbf{R}_\Delta \mathbf{R}_{init}$, where $\mathbf{R}_{est}$ is used for loss calculation and reassigned as $\mathbf{R}_{init}$ for the next iteration.

Noteworthy, since the prediction of relative rotation is sensitive to local geometry, it is crucial how the network fuses the information of F_{op} at point level. Instead of using non-parametric operations like max-pooling which loses the local information severely, we opt for a trainable way to aggregate the point-wise features in Rot-Head. In particular, we employ two parallel branches for Rot-Head to obtain axis-wise rotation predictions $\mathbf{r}_\Delta^x$ and $\mathbf{r}_\Delta^y$, respectively. Each branch is comprised of two 1D convolutional layers each followed by Group Normalization [61] and GELU [18] activation to generate an implicit per-point rotation prediction $f_{op} \in \mathbb{R}^{(N_o+N_p)\times 3}$ first. Then the explicit global axis-wise prediction is aggregated from the permuted point-wise implicit prediction $f_{op}' \in \mathbb{R}^{3\times(N_o+N_p)}$ using an extra 1D convolutional layer, reducing the dimension from $3 \times (N_o+N_p)$ to 3×1. In this way, the network can preserve the local information regarding the relative rotation between $\hat{\mathcal{P}}$ and $\hat{\mathcal{O}}$ in a trainable way.

Translation and Size Prediction. Since $\mathcal{O}$ is shifted to $\hat{\mathcal{O}}$ by $\mathbf{t}_{init}$, the translation transformation $\mathbf{t}_\Delta$ can be derived from F_o directly. Different from predicting rotation by aggregating point-level information, we argue that translation and size should be treated differently in that they are both global attributions at the object level. Therefore, TS-Head first extracts a global feature f_o from F_o by performing max-pooling along the point dimension. Then, the initial scale is explicitly appended to f_o for predicting the size transformation $\mathbf{s}_\Delta$. Afterwards, two fully connected (FC) layers are applied to the global feature, reducing the dimension from 1091 to 256. Finally, two parallel FC layers output $\mathbf{t}_\Delta$ and $\mathbf{s}_\Delta$ separately. The predicted translation and size are obtained by $\mathbf{t}_{est} = \mathbf{t}_{init} + \mathbf{t}_\Delta$ and $\mathbf{s}_{est} = \mathbf{s}_{init} + \mathbf{s}_\Delta$ accordingly. Similar to the rotation prediction, they are also re-assigned as the initial estimates for the next iteration.

3.4   Training and Testing Protocol

Pose Loss. In works for direct pose regression, the design of loss function is crucial for optimization [54]. Apart from using an angular distance based loss on rotation [23], and L_1 losses for translation and scale, we additionally leverage a novel loss modified based on point matching [30] to couple the estimation of $[\mathbf{R}|\mathbf{t}|\mathbf{s}]$. To summarize, the overall loss function can be written as

$$\mathcal{L} = \mathcal{L}_{pm} + \mathcal{L}_{\mathbf{R}} + \mathcal{L}_{\mathbf{t}} + \mathcal{L}_{\mathbf{s}}, \tag{3}$$

where

$$\begin{cases} \mathcal{L}_{pm} &= \underset{\mathbf{x}\in\mathcal{P}}{\mathrm{avg}}\|(\mathbf{s}_{gt}\odot\mathbf{R}_{gt}\mathbf{x}+\mathbf{t}_{gt})-(\mathbf{s}_{est}\odot\mathbf{R}_{est}\mathbf{x}+\mathbf{t}_{est})\|_1, \\ \mathcal{L}_{\mathbf{R}} &= \frac{3-\mathrm{Tr}(\mathbf{R}_{gt}\mathbf{R}_{est}^T)}{4}, \\ \mathcal{L}_{\mathbf{t}} &= \|\mathbf{t}_{gt}-\mathbf{t}_{est}\|_1, \\ \mathcal{L}_{\mathbf{s}} &= \|\mathbf{s}_{gt}-\mathbf{s}_{est}\|_1. \end{cases} \tag{4}$$

Here $\odot$ denotes element-wise product. For symmetric objects, we rotate $\mathbf{R}_{gt}$ along the known symmetry axis to find the best match for $\mathbf{R}_{est}$.

Iterative Training and Testing. We employ an iterative training and testing strategy for pose refinement inspired by [29], namely the current prediction is re-assigned as the initial pose for the next iteration. By repeating this procedure multiple times, i.e., 4 in this work, not only the diversity of training pose error distribution is enriched, but also more accurate and robust inference results can be obtained. To decouple CATRE from different initial pose estimation methods, during training we add random Gaussian noise to $[\mathbf{R}_{gt}|\mathbf{t}_{gt}|\mathbf{s}_{gt}]$ as initial pose in the first iteration. The network can therefore refine the pose prediction from various methods [32,47,55] consistently without re-training (see also Table 2).

3.5   Pose Tracking

It is natural to apply CATRE to tracking due to the similarity of pose refinement and tracking. Given a live point cloud stream and the 9DoF pose estimate $[\mathbf{R}_t|\mathbf{t}_t|\mathbf{s}_t]$ of an object at frame t, the target of category-level pose tracking is to estimate the object pose $[\mathbf{R}_{t+1}|\mathbf{t}_{t+1}|\mathbf{s}_{t+1}]$ of the next frame $t+1$. Similar to pose refinement, we use $[\mathbf{R}_t|\mathbf{t}_t|\mathbf{s}_t]$ as the initial pose to focalize $\mathcal{P}$ and $\mathcal{O}$, and predict the relative pose transformation between frame t and $t+1$.

During inference, we jitter the ground-truth pose of the first frame with the same Gaussian noise distribution in [60]. The pose is re-initialized if the adjacent frames are not consecutive.

4 Experiments

4.1 Experimental Setup

Implementation Details. All the experiments are implemented using PyTorch [37]. We train our model using Ranger optimizer [34,63,65] with a base learning rate of 1×10^{-4}, annealed at 72% of the training epoch using a cosine schedule [24]. The total training epoch is set to 120 with a batch size of 16. We employ some basic strategies for depth augmentation, *e.g.*, randomly dropping depth values, adding Gaussian noise, and randomly filling 0 points, as well as some pose augmentations like random scaling, random rotation and translation perturbation as in [9]. Unless otherwise specified, the size of input images are 480×640, N_o and N_p are empirically set to 1024, and a single model is trained for all categories.

Datasets. We conduct experiments on 4 datasets: REAL275 [55], CAM-ERA25 [55], LM [19], and YCB-V [62]. *REAL275* is a widely-used real-world category-level pose benchmark containing 4.3k images of 7 scenes for training, and 2.75k images of 6 scenes for testing. *CAMERA25* is a synthetic dataset generated by a context-aware mixed reality approach. There are 300k composite images of 1085 object instances in total, where 25k images and 184 instances are used for evaluation. REAL275 and CAMERA25 share the same object categories, *i.e.*, bottle, bowl, camera, can, laptop, and mug. *LM* dataset consists of 13 object instances, each of which is labeled around the center of a sequence of $\approx$1.2k cluttered images. We follow [4] to split $\approx$15% images for training and $\approx$85% images for testing. Additionally, 1k rendered images for each instance are used to assist training as in [31]. *YCB-V* dataset is very challenging due to severe occlusions and various lighting conditions. We select two objects, *i.e.*, master chef can and cracker box, out of 21 instances for unseen category refinement.

Metrics. On REAL275 and CAMERA25, we follow [55] to report the mean Average Precision (mAP) of intersection over union (IoU) metric at different thresholds[1], as well as mAP at $n°\,m\,\mathrm{cm}$ for evaluating pose accuracy. Additionally, for the task of tracking, we report mIoU, $\mathbf{R}_{err}$, and $\mathbf{t}_{err}$ as in [60], respectively standing for the mean IoU of ground-truth and predicted bounding boxes, average rotation error, and average translation error. On LM, the ADD metric [19] is used to measure whether the average offset of transformed model points is less than 10% of the object diameter. For symmetric objects, the ADD-S metric [20] is employed. On YCB-V, we use the area under the accuracy curves (AUC) of ADD(-S) metric varying the threshold from 0 to 10 cm as in [62].

4.2 Category-Level Pose Refinement

Results. The quantitative results for category-level pose refinement on REAL275 and CAMERA25 are presented in Table 1. We use the results of SPD [47] as initial poses during inference in our main experiments and ablation studies. It clearly

---

[1] Note that there is a small mistake in the original IoU evaluation code of [55], we recalculated the IoU metrics as in [39].

Table 1. Results of category-level pose refinement on REAL275 and CAMERA25. SPD* denotes our re-implementation of SPD [47].

Dataset	Method	Refine	IoU$_{75}$	5° 2 cm	5° 5 cm	10° 2 cm	10° 5 cm
REAL275	NOCS [55]		9.4	7.2	10.0	13.8	25.2
	DualPoseNet [32]	✓	30.8	29.3	35.9	50	66.8
	CR-Net [56]		33.2	27.8	34.3	47.2	60.8
	SGPA [7]		37.1	35.9	39.6	61.3	70.7
	SPD [47]		27.0	19.3	21.4	43.2	54.1
	SPD*		27.0	19.1	21.2	43.5	54.0
	SPD*+Ours	✓	**43.6**	**45.8**	**54.4**	**61.4**	**73.1**
CAMERA25	NOCS [55]		37.0	32.3	40.9	48.2	64.6
	DualPoseNet [32]	✓	71.7	64.7	70.7	77.2	84.7
	CR-Net [56]		75.0	72.0	76.4	81.0	87.7
	SGPA [7]		69.1	70.7	74.5	82.7	88.4
	SPD [47]		46.9	54.3	59.0	73.3	81.5
	SPD*		46.9	54.1	58.8	73.9	82.1
	SPD*+Ours	✓	**76.1**	**75.4**	**80.3**	**83.3**	**89.3**

Table 2. Ablation on different initial poses on REAL275. *(a)* The average precision (AP) of rotation (°) and translation (cm) at different thresholds before and after refinement. *(b)* Quantitative results. * denotes our re-implementation.

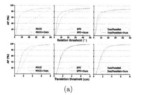

Method	Ref.	IoU$_{75}$	5° 2 cm	5° 5 cm
NOCS* [55]		9.0	7.3	9.9
w/ Ours	✓	42.6	40.7₊33.4	47.8₊37.9
SPD* [47]		27.0	19.1	21.2
w/ Ours	✓	43.6	45.8₊26.7	54.4₊33.2
DualPoseNet* [32]	✓	31.4	29.3	35.9
w/ Ours	✓	44.4	43.9₊14.6	54.8₊18.9

(a)   (b)

shows that our method surpasses the baseline by a large margin, especially on the strict 5° 2 cm metric, achieving an absolute improvement of 26.7% on the challenging REAL275 dataset and 21.3% on the CAMERA25 dataset.

The results also demonstrate the significant superiority of CATRE over state-of-the-art methods [7,32,47,55,56]. Notice that although we do not exploit any color information in the refinement procedure, we are still very competitive overall. More importantly, on the strict metrics IoU$_{75}$ and 5° 2 cm, we surpass all the previous methods. We kindly refer readers to the *supplementary material* for more qualitative analyses and detailed results for each category.

Ablation Study. Table 2 and Table 3 present the ablations on various factors.

Ablation on Different Initial Poses. To demonstrate the generalizability and robustness of our method w.r.t.different kinds of initial poses, we initialize the network with predictions of various qualities from [32,47,55] and present the

Table 3. Ablation studies on REAL275. *(a)* Accuracy and speed w.r.t.iterations. *(b)* Quantitative results, where SPD* denotes our re-implementation of SPD [47].

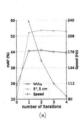

(a)

Row	Method	IoU_{75}	$5°$ 2cm	$5°$ 5cm	$5°$	2cm
A0	SPD*	27.0	19.1	21.2	23.8	68.6
B0	SPD*+Ours	43.6	**45.8**	**54.4**	58.0	75.1
C0	B0: Mean shape → 3D bounding box	42.9	39.5	47.2	52.7	73.1
C1	B0: Mean shape → 3D axes	42.2	36.7	43.1	49.6	73.2
D0	B0: TS-Head also w/ MaxPool(F_p)	**47.8**	45.7	52.8	**58.4**	75.7
D1	B0: w/o focalizing to origin	41.4	40.2	47.5	52.3	70.7
D2	B0: w/o adaptive points sampling	29.0	26.7	42.3	46.3	63.3
E0	B0: PointNet [40] → 3D-GCN [33]	28.4	36.0	43.4	47.7	68.0
E1	B0: w/o weight sharing	23.6	1.7	2.0	2.5	76.0
F0	B0: Single pose head (TS-Head style)	46.4	40.7	46.2	52.6	75.9
F1	B0: Single pose head (Rot-Head style)	45.0	41.1	50.0	55.1	69.1
F2	B0: Rot-Head conv fusion → MaxPool	45.1	41.8	49.5	55.0	76.4
F3	B0: Rot-Head conv fusion → AvgPool	44.9	41.8	48.0	53.4	**77.1**
F4	B0: TS-Head global feature→point-wise	29.8	32.3	46.3	53.0	57.5
G0	B0: w/o $\mathcal{L}_{pm}$	44.4	42.5	50.7	55.5	74.1
G1	B0: w/o $\mathcal{L}_R/\mathcal{L}_t/\mathcal{L}_s$	38.4	22.6	30.1	34.0	72.8

(b)

results in Table 2. The network achieves consistent enhancement using the same weight, no matter initialized with the early proposed methods [47,55], or recent state of the art [32]. Table 2a further shows distinct improvement on rotation estimate after refinement.

Ablation on Shape Prior. Aside from the mean shape, CATRE can use the eight corners of the 3D bounding box ($N_p = 8$) or four points constructing 3D axes ($N_p = 4$) as shape prior, the sizes of which are determined by s_{est}. As shown in Table 3b, the results using mean shape (B0) are superior to those using bounding box corners (C0) or axes (C1). However, the poses can still be refined taking bounding box corners or axes as input, which implies that the geometric encoder is able to encode the initial pose information from sparse input without categorical prior knowledge. Inspired by this, we further extend our method to pose refinement on the unseen category in Sect. 4.5.

Effectiveness of Point Cloud Focalization. To verify the efficiency and accuracy of predicting relative pose from the focalized point clouds, we conduct several experiments. Firstly, the input of TS-Head is replaced with a concatenated feature from both MaxPool(F_o) and MaxPool(F_p). Since the relative translation can be derived from $\hat{O}$ due to the focalization operation, adding feature from $\hat{P}$ introduces unnecessary noise thus leading to a slight performance drop (Table 3b B0 *vs.* D0). Moreover, we translate the center of shape prior $\mathcal{P}$ to t_{init}, and keep the pose of the observed point cloud $\mathcal{O}$ as it is in camera space. The initial translation is then appended to the input of TS-Head for better predicting t_Δ. However, we observe a larger decrease in accuracy (Table 3b B0 *vs.* D1) discarding focalization, thus limiting the absolute range of input point clouds is vital for reducing the complexity of learning relative transformation. To avoid introducing too many background points, we employed an adaptive strategy to sample points within a ball determined by the initial pose estimate. Without this step, the accuracy decreased dramatically (Table 3b B0 *vs.* D2).

Effectiveness of Shared Encoder. As mentioned in Sect. 3.3, 3D-GCN [33] performs worse than PointNet [40] in our work (Table 3b B0 *vs.* E0). Moreover, weight sharing in the encoder is prominent for capturing relevant features regarding relative transformation by embedding $\hat{\mathcal{P}}$ and $\hat{\mathcal{O}}$ into a unified space, which is especially crucial to the prediction of $\mathbf{R}_\Delta$. Otherwise, it is almost unable to perform any refinement on rotation, as shown in Table 3b (B0 *vs.* E1).

Effectiveness of Disentangled Heads. We consider two types of single pose heads, *i.e.*, extending TS-Head to estimate $[\mathbf{r}_\Delta^x | \mathbf{r}_\Delta^y]$ (F0), and adding two FC layers in Rot-Head to predict $\mathbf{t}_\Delta$ and $\mathbf{s}_\Delta$ (F1). Table 3b reveals that the disentangled design (B0) outperforms a single pose head leveraging a global feature (F0) or point-wise features (F1) consistently.

The Design Choices of Heads. When replacing the trainable point-wise features aggregation with non-parametric operation MaxPool or AvgPool in Rot-Head, the accuracy on $5°$ drops significantly (Table 3b B0 *vs.* F2, F3). Furthermore, treating $\mathbf{t}$ and $\mathbf{s}$ as global attributes rather than collecting point-wise features like Rot-Head also enhances performance (Table 3b B0 *vs.* F4).

Effectiveness of Loss Function. Table 3b (B0 *vs.* G0) evinces that $\mathcal{L}_{pm}$ coupling pose prediction brings performance enhancement, and the individual loss components designated for $[\mathbf{R}_{est} | \mathbf{t}_{est} | \mathbf{s}_{est}]$ are crucial as well (Table 3b B0 *vs.* G1).

Accuracy and Speed vs. Iteration. In Table 3a, we show the accuracy and inference speed w.r.t.iterations. Here we empirically set 4 as the maximum number of iteration to balance the performance and speed. On a machine with a TITAN XP GPU and two Intel 2.0 GHz CPUs, CATRE runs at ≈ 85.32 Hz for 4 iterations.

4.3   Category-Level Pose Tracking

Table 4 summarizes the quantitative results for category-level pose tracking, with a comparison between our methods and other tracking-based methods [12,51,60].

Leveraging a single model for tracking all objects, our method achieves competitive results with previous state-of-the-art methods. Noticeably, the pipeline can run at 89.21 Hz, which is 7× faster than the state-of-the-art method CAPTRA [60] and qualified for real-time application. Moreover, our method exceeds CAPTRA in the metric of mIoU and $\mathbf{t}_{err}$ by a large margin, in that CAPTRA solves $\mathbf{t}$ and $\mathbf{s}$ using the indirect Umeyama algorithm without RANSAC, making their method sensitive to outliers. In contrast, our network predicts $\mathbf{t}$ and $\mathbf{s}$ in an end-to-end manner. Additionally, our method deals with all the objects by a single network, while [60] needs to train separately for $\mathbf{R}$ and $\mathbf{t}/\mathbf{s}$ of each category. To sum up, although CAPTRA performs slightly better than ours w.r.t.$5°$ 5 cm and $\mathbf{R}_{err}$, we still have an edge over them in tracking speed and translation accuracy, which are vital in many robotic tasks such as grasping.

Table 4. Results of category-level pose tracking on REAL275. Following [60], we perturb the ground-truth pose of the first frame as the initial pose.

Method	Oracle ICP [60]	6-PACK [51]	iCaps [12]	CAPTRA [60]	Ours
Init.	GT	GT. Pert.	Det. and Seg.	GT. Pert	GT. Pert.
Speed (Hz) ↑	–	10	1.84	12.66	**89.21**
mIoU ↑	14.7	–	–	64.1	**80.2**
5° 5 cm↑	0.7	33.3	31.6	**62.2**	57.2
$R_{err}(°)$ ↓	40.3	16.0	9.5	**5.9**	6.8
t_{err}(cm) ↓	7.7	3.5	2.3	7.9	**1.2**

Table 5. Results on LM referring to the Average Recall (%) of ADD(-S) metric. * denotes symmetric objects. Ours(B) and Ours(F) use 8 bounding box corners and 128 FPS model points as shape priors respectively.

Method	Ref	Ape	Bvise	Cam	Can	Cat	Drill	Duck	Ebox*	Glue*	Holep	Iron	Lamp	Phone	Mean
SSD-6D [26]+ICP	✓	65	80	78	86	70	73	66	**100**	**100**	49	78	73	79	79
DenseFusion [52]	✓	92.3	93.2	94.4	93.1	96.5	87.0	92.3	99.8	**100**	92.1	97	95.3	92.8	94.3
CloudAAE [15]+ICP	✓	–	–	–	–	–	–	–	–	–	–	–	–	–	95.5
PoseCNN [62]		27.9	69.4	47.7	71.1	56.4	65.4	43.2	98.2	95.0	50.7	65.9	70.4	54.4	62.7
w/ Ours(B)	✓	63.7	98.6	89.7	96.1	84.3	98.6	63.9	99.8	99.4	93.2	98.4	98.7	97.5	90.9
w/ Ours(F)	✓	**94.1**	**99.5**	**97.9**	**99.4**	**98.0**	**99.8**	**92.9**	99.8	99.7	**98.3**	**99.0**	**99.8**	**99.5**	**98.3**

4.4 Instance-Level Pose Refinement

Different from category-level refinement, instance-level pose refinement assumes the CAD model is available. Considering this, we propose two types of shape priors, *i.e.*, the tight bounding box of CAD model or N_p model points selected by farthest point sampling (FPS) algorithm, where we choose $N_p = 128$ empirically.

Table 5 shows the experimental results on LM dataset. Our methods achieve significant improvement against the initial prediction provided by PoseCNN [62]. Noteworthy, Ours(B) utilizing the sparse bounding box corners information can still be comparable with methods refined by ICP procedure leveraging exact CAD models. Furthermore, by explicitly exploiting the shape information with 128 FPS model points, Ours(F) achieves state of the art distinctly surpassing previous RGB-D based methods [15,26,52] with refinement.

4.5 Pose Refinement on Unseen Category

As discussed before, utilizing bounding box corners as shape prior offers a possibility for pose refinement on unseen category, as long as the objects have a unified definition of the canonical view. We verify this assumption in two instances on the challenging YCB-V dataset, *i.e.*, master chef can and cracker box, and present qualitative and quantitative results in Table 6. Training with master chef can, the network is able to refine the pose of the unseen category cracker box and vice versa. It demonstrates that the network learns some general features for pose refinement exceeding the limitation of the trained category. We hope this experiment will inspire future work for unseen object refinement or tracking leveraging self-supervision or domain adaptation techniques.

Table 6. Results of unseen category pose refinement on YCB-Video. *(a)* Qualitative results, where white, red and green contours illustrate the ground-truth, initial (modified from PoseCNN [62]) and refined (Ours) poses, respectively. *(b)* Quantitative results (Metric: AUC of ADD(-S)).

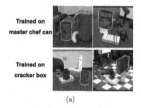

(a)

Test Train	Master Chef Can		Cracker Box	
	Init.	Ref.	Init.	Ref.
Master Chef Can	52.7	71.3	57.8	65.3↑7.5
Cracker Box	52.7	57.4↑4.7	57.8	89.6

(b)

5   Conclusion

We have presented CATRE, a versatile approach for pose refinement and tracking, which enables tackling instance-level, category-level and unseen category problems with a unified framework. The key idea is to iteratively align the focalized shape prior and observed point cloud by predicting a relative pose transformation using disentangled pose heads. Our algorithm is generalizable to various kinds of baselines and achieves significant boosts in performance over other state-of-the-art category-level pose estimation works as well as competitive results with tracking-based methods. Future work will focus on more challenging scenarios, such as tracking unseen objects, leveraging RGB information, and training with only synthetic data utilizing large-scale 3D model sets [5,11,41].

Acknowledgments. We thank Yansong Tang at Tsinghua-Berkeley Shenzhen Institute, Ruida Zhang and Haotian Xu at Tsinghua University for their helpful suggestions. This work was supported by the National Key R&D Program of China under Grant 2018AAA0102801 and National Natural Science Foundation of China under Grant 61620106005.

References

1. Aoki, Y., Goforth, H., Srivatsan, R.A., Lucey, S.: PointNetLK: robust & efficient point cloud registration using PointNet. In: IEEE/CVF Conference on Computer Vision and Pattern Recognition (CVPR), pp. 7163–7172 (2019)
2. Besl, P.J., McKay, N.D.: A method for registration of 3-D shapes. IEEE Trans. Pattern Anal. Mach. Intell. (TPAMI) **14**(2), 239–256 (1992)
3. Bouaziz, S., Tagliasacchi, A., Pauly, M.: Sparse iterative closest point. In: Computer Graphics Forum, vol. 32, pp. 113–123. Wiley Online Library (2013)

4. Brachmann, E., Michel, F., Krull, A., Ying Yang, M., Gumhold, S., Rother, C.: Uncertainty-driven 6D pose estimation of objects and scenes from a single RGB image. In: IEEE/CVF Conference on Computer Vision and Pattern Recognition (CVPR), pp. 3364–3372 (2016)
5. Chang, A.X., et al.: ShapeNet: an information-rich 3D model repository. arXiv preprint arXiv:1512.03012 (2015)
6. Chen, D., Li, J., Wang, Z., Xu, K.: Learning canonical shape space for category-level 6D object pose and size estimation. In: IEEE/CVF Conference on Computer Vision and Pattern Recognition (CVPR), pp. 11970–11979 (2020). https://doi.org/10.1109/CVPR42600.2020.01199
7. Chen, K., Dou, Q.: SGPA: structure-guided prior adaptation for category-level 6D object pose estimation. In: IEEE/CVF International Conference on Computer Vision (ICCV), pp. 2773–2782 (2021)
8. Chen, W., Jia, X., Chang, H.J., Duan, J., Leonardis, A.: G2L-Net: global to local network for real-time 6D pose estimation with embedding vector features. In: IEEE/CVF Conference on Computer Vision and Pattern Recognition (CVPR), pp. 4233–4242 (2020)
9. Chen, W., Jia, X., Chang, H.J., Duan, J., Linlin, S., Leonardis, A.: FS-Net: fast shape-based network for category-level 6D object pose estimation with decoupled rotation mechanism. In: IEEE/CVF Conference on Computer Vision and Pattern Recognition (CVPR), pp. 1581–1590, June 2021
10. Choy, C., Dong, W., Koltun, V.: Deep global registration. In: IEEE/CVF Conference on Computer Vision and Pattern Recognition (CVPR), pp. 2514–2523 (2020)
11. Collins, J., et al.: ABO: Dataset and benchmarks for real-world 3d object understanding. arXiv preprint arXiv:2110.06199 (2021)
12. Deng, X., Geng, J., Bretl, T., Xiang, Y., Fox, D.: iCaps: iterative category-level object pose and shape estimation. IEEE Robot. Autom. Lett. (RAL) **7**, 1784–1791 (2022)
13. Du, G., Wang, K., Lian, S., Zhao, K.: Vision-based robotic grasping from object localization, object pose estimation to grasp estimation for parallel grippers: a review. Artif. Intell. Rev. **54**(3), 1677–1734 (2021)
14. Fan, Z., et al.: ACR-Pose: Adversarial canonical representation reconstruction network for category level 6d object pose estimation. arXiv preprint arXiv:2111.10524 (2021)
15. Gao, G., Lauri, M., Hu, X., Zhang, J., Frintrop, S.: CloudAAE: learning 6D object pose regression with on-line data synthesis on point clouds. In: IEEE International Conference on Robotics and Automation (ICRA), pp. 11081–11087 (2021)
16. Groueix, T., Fisher, M., Kim, V.G., Russell, B.C., Aubry, M.: 3D-CODED: 3D correspondences by deep deformation. In: Ferrari, V., Hebert, M., Sminchisescu, C., Weiss, Y. (eds.) ECCV 2018. LNCS, vol. 11206, pp. 235–251. Springer, Cham (2018). https://doi.org/10.1007/978-3-030-01216-8_15
17. He, K., Gkioxari, G., Dollár, P., Girshick, R.: Mask R-CNN. In: IEEE/CVF International Conference on Computer Vision (ICCV), pp. 2961–2969 (2017)
18. Hendrycks, D., Gimpel, K.: Gaussian error linear units (GELUs). arXiv preprint arXiv:1606.08415 (2016)
19. Hinterstoisser, S., et al.: Model based training, detection and pose estimation of texture-less 3D objects in heavily cluttered scenes. In: Asian Conference on Computer Vision (ACCV) (2012)
20. Hodaň, T., Matas, J., Obdržálek, Š: On evaluation of 6D object pose estimation. In: Hua, G., Jégou, H. (eds.) ECCV 2016. LNCS, vol. 9915, pp. 606–619. Springer, Cham (2016). https://doi.org/10.1007/978-3-319-49409-8_52

21. Hodaň, T., et al.: bop challenge 2020 on 6D object localization. In: Bartoli, A., Fusiello, A. (eds.) ECCV 2020. LNCS, vol. 12536, pp. 577–594. Springer, Cham (2020). https://doi.org/10.1007/978-3-030-66096-3_39

22. Huang, S., Qi, S., Xiao, Y., Zhu, Y., Wu, Y.N., Zhu, S.C.: Cooperative holistic scene understanding: unifying 3D object, layout, and camera pose estimation. In: Advances in Neural Information Processing Systems (NeurIPS), vol. 31 (2018)

23. Huynh, D.Q.: Metrics for 3D rotations: comparison and analysis. J. Math. Imag. Vis. 35(2), 155–164 (2009)

24. Ilya Loshchilov, F.H.: SGDR: stochastic gradient descent with warm restarts. In: International Conference on Learning Representations (ICLR) (2017)

25. Iwase, S., Liu, X., Khirodkar, R., Yokota, R., Kitani, K.M.: RePOSE: fast 6D object pose refinement via deep texture rendering. In: IEEE/CVF International Conference on Computer Vision (ICCV), pp. 3303–3312 (2021)

26. Kehl, W., Manhardt, F., Tombari, F., Ilic, S., Navab, N.: SSD-6D: making RGB-based 3D detection and 6D pose estimation great again. In: IEEE/CVF International Conference on Computer Vision (ICCV), pp. 1521–1529 (2017)

27. Labbé, Y., Carpentier, J., Aubry, M., Sivic, J.: CosyPose: consistent multi-view multi-object 6D pose estimation. In: Vedaldi, A., Bischof, H., Brox, T., Frahm, J.-M. (eds.) ECCV 2020. LNCS, vol. 12362, pp. 574–591. Springer, Cham (2020). https://doi.org/10.1007/978-3-030-58520-4_34

28. Lee, D., Hamsici, O.C., Feng, S., Sharma, P., Gernoth, T.: DeepPRO: deep partial point cloud registration of objects. In: IEEE/CVF International Conference on Computer Vision (ICCV), pp. 5683–5692 (2021)

29. Li, Y., Wang, G., Ji, X., Xiang, Yu., Fox, D.: DeepIM: deep iterative matching for 6D pose estimation. In: Ferrari, V., Hebert, M., Sminchisescu, C., Weiss, Y. (eds.) ECCV 2018. LNCS, vol. 11210, pp. 695–711. Springer, Cham (2018). https://doi.org/10.1007/978-3-030-01231-1_42

30. Li, Y., Wang, G., Ji, X., Xiang, Y., Fox, D.: DeepIM: deep iterative matching for 6D pose estimation. Int. J. Comput. Vis. (IJCV) 128(3), 657–678 (2020)

31. Li, Z., Wang, G., Ji, X.: CDPN: coordinates-based disentangled pose network for real-time RGB-based 6-DoF object pose estimation. In: IEEE/CVF International Conference on Computer Vision (ICCV), pp. 7678–7687 (2019)

32. Lin, J., Wei, Z., Li, Z., Xu, S., Jia, K., Li, Y.: DualPoseNet: category-level 6D object pose and size estimation using dual pose network with refined learning of pose consistency. In: IEEE/CVF International Conference on Computer Vision (ICCV), pp. 3560–3569, October 2021

33. Lin, Z.H., Huang, S.Y., Wang, Y.C.F.: Convolution in the cloud: learning deformable kernels in 3D graph convolution networks for point cloud analysis. In: IEEE/CVF Conference on Computer Vision and Pattern Recognition (CVPR), pp. 1800–1809 (2020)

34. Liu, L., et al.: On the variance of the adaptive learning rate and beyond. In: International Conference on Learning Representations (ICLR) (2019)

35. Marchand, E., Uchiyama, H., Spindler, F.: Pose estimation for augmented reality: a hands-on survey. IEEE Trans. Vis. Comput. Graph. (TVCG) 22(12), 2633–2651 (2015)

36. Nie, Y., Han, X., Guo, S., Zheng, Y., Chang, J., Zhang, J.J.: Total3DUnderstanding: joint layout, object pose and mesh reconstruction for indoor scenes from a single image. In: IEEE/CVF Conference on Computer Vision and Pattern Recognition (CVPR), pp. 55–64 (2020)

37. Paszke, A., et al.: PyTorch: an imperative style, high-performance deep learning library. In: Advances in Neural Information Processing Systems (NeurIPS), pp. 8026–8037 (2019)

38. Peng, S., Liu, Y., Huang, Q., Zhou, X., Bao, H.: PVNet: pixel-wise voting network for 6dof pose estimation. In: IEEE/CVF Conference on Computer Vision and Pattern Recognition (CVPR), pp. 4561–4570 (2019)

39. Peng, W., Yan, J., Wen, H., Sun, Y.: Self-supervised category-level 6D object pose estimation with deep implicit shape representation. In: Proceedings of the AAAI Conference on Artificial Intelligence (AAAI), vol. 36, no. 2, pp. 2082–2090 (2022). https://doi.org/10.1609/aaai.v36i2.20104

40. Qi, C.R., Su, H., Mo, K., Guibas, L.J.: PointNet: deep learning on point sets for 3D classification and segmentation. In: IEEE/CVF Conference on Computer Vision and Pattern Recognition (CVPR), vol. 1, no. 2, p. 4 (2017)

41. Reizenstein, J., Shapovalov, R., Henzler, P., Sbordone, L., Labatut, P., Novotny, D.: Common objects in 3D: large-scale learning and evaluation of real-life 3D category reconstruction. In: IEEE/CVF International Conference on Computer Vision (ICCV) (2021)

42. Rusinkiewicz, S., Levoy, M.: Efficient variants of the ICP algorithm. In: Proceedings third International Conference on 3-D Digital Imaging and Modeling, pp. 145–152. IEEE (2001)

43. Sarode, V., et al.: PCRNet: point cloud registration network using pointnet encoding. arXiv preprint arXiv:1908.07906 (2019)

44. Segal, A., Haehnel, D., Thrun, S.: Generalized-ICP. In: Robotics: Science and Systems, Seattle, WA, vol. 2, p. 435 (2009)

45. Song, C., Song, J., Huang, Q.: HybridPose: 6D object pose estimation under hybrid representations. In: IEEE/CVF Conference on Computer Vision and Pattern Recognition (CVPR), pp. 431–440 (2020)

46. Su, Y., Rambach, J., Minaskan, N., Lesur, P., Pagani, A., Stricker, D.: Deep multi-state object pose estimation for augmented reality assembly. In: 2019 IEEE International Symposium on Mixed and Augmented Reality Adjunct (ISMAR-Adjunct), pp. 222–227 (2019)

47. Tian, M., Ang, M.H., Lee, G.H.: Shape prior deformation for categorical 6D object pose and size estimation. In: Vedaldi, A., Bischof, H., Brox, T., Frahm, J.-M. (eds.) ECCV 2020. LNCS, vol. 12366, pp. 530–546. Springer, Cham (2020). https://doi.org/10.1007/978-3-030-58589-1_32

48. Trappolini, G., Cosmo, L., Moschella, L., Marin, R., Melzi, S., Rodolà, E.: Shape registration in the time of transformers. In: Advances in Neural Information Processing Systems (NeurIPS), vol. 34, pp. 5731–5744 (2021)

49. Tremblay, J., To, T., Sundaralingam, B., Xiang, Y., Fox, D., Birchfield, S.: Deep object pose estimation for semantic robotic grasping of household objects. In: Conference on Robot Learning (CoRL), pp. 306–316 (2018)

50. Umeyama, S.: Least-squares estimation of transformation parameters between two point patterns. IEEE Trans. Pattern Anal. Mach. Intell. (TPAMI) 13(04), 376–380 (1991). https://doi.org/10.1109/34.88573

51. Wang, C., et al.: 6-PACK: category-level 6D pose tracker with anchor-based keypoints. In: IEEE International Conference on Robotics and Automation (ICRA), pp. 10059–10066 (2020)

52. Wang, C., et al.: DenseFusion: 6D object pose estimation by iterative dense fusion. In: IEEE/CVF Conference on Computer Vision and Pattern Recognition (CVPR), pp. 3343–3352 (2019)

53. Wang, G., Manhardt, F., Liu, X., Ji, X., Tombari, F.: Occlusion-aware self-supervised monocular 6D object pose estimation. IEEE Trans. Pattern Anal. Mach. Intell. (TPAMI) (2021). https://doi.org/10.1109/TPAMI.2021.3136301
54. Wang, G., Manhardt, F., Tombari, F., Ji, X.: GDR-Net: Geometry-guided direct regression network for monocular 6D object pose estimation. In: IEEE/CVF Conference on Computer Vision and Pattern Recognition (CVPR), pp. 16611–16621 (2021)
55. Wang, H., Sridhar, S., Huang, J., Valentin, J., Song, S., Guibas, L.J.: Normalized object coordinate space for category-level 6D object pose and size estimation. In: IEEE/CVF Conference on Computer Vision and Pattern Recognition (CVPR), pp. 2642–2651 (2019)
56. Wang, J., Chen, K., Dou, Q.: Category-level 6D object pose estimation via cascaded relation and recurrent reconstruction networks. In: IEEE/RJS International Conference on Intelligent Robots and Systems (IROS) (2021)
57. Wang, Y., Solomon, J.: PRNet: self-supervised learning for partial-to-partial registration. In: Advances in Neural Information Processing Systems (NeurIPS), pp. 8814–8826 (2019)
58. Wang, Y., Solomon, J.M.: Deep closest point: learning representations for point cloud registration. In: IEEE/CVF International Conference on Computer Vision (ICCV), pp. 3523–3532 (2019)
59. Wen, B., Mitash, C., Ren, B., Bekris, K.E.: se(3)-TrackNet: data-driven 6D pose tracking by calibrating image residuals in synthetic domains. In: IEEE/RJS International Conference on Intelligent Robots and Systems (IROS), pp. 10367–10373 (2020)
60. Weng, Y., et al: CAPTRA: category-level pose tracking for rigid and articulated objects from point clouds. In: IEEE/CVF International Conference on Computer Vision (ICCV), pp. 13209–13218 (2021)
61. Wu, Y., He, K.: Group normalization. In: Ferrari, V., Hebert, M., Sminchisescu, C., Weiss, Y. (eds.) ECCV 2018. LNCS, vol. 11217, pp. 3–19. Springer, Cham (2018). https://doi.org/10.1007/978-3-030-01261-8_1
62. Xiang, Y., Schmidt, T., Narayanan, V., Fox, D.: PoseCNN: a convolutional neural network for 6D object pose estimation in cluttered scenes. In: Robotics: Science and Systems Conference (RSS) (2018)
63. Yong, H., Huang, J., Hua, X., Zhang, L.: Gradient centralization: a new optimization technique for deep neural networks. In: Vedaldi, A., Bischof, H., Brox, T., Frahm, J.-M. (eds.) ECCV 2020. LNCS, vol. 12346, pp. 635–652. Springer, Cham (2020). https://doi.org/10.1007/978-3-030-58452-8_37
64. Zakharov, S., Shugurov, I., Ilic, S.: DPOD: dense 6D pose object detector in RGB images. In: IEEE/CVF International Conference on Computer Vision (ICCV) (2019)
65. Zhang, M., Lucas, J., Ba, J., Hinton, G.E.: Lookahead optimizer: k steps forward, 1 step back. In: Wallach, H., Larochelle, H., Beygelzimer, A., d' Alché-Buc, F., Fox, E., Garnett, R. (eds.) Advances in Neural Information Processing Systems (NeurIPS), vol. 32. Curran Associates, Inc. (2019)
66. Zhou, Y., Barnes, C., Lu, J., Yang, J., Li, H.: On the continuity of rotation representations in neural networks. In: IEEE/CVF Conference on Computer Vision and Pattern Recognition (CVPR), pp. 5745–5753 (2019)

Optimization over Disentangled Encoding: Unsupervised Cross-Domain Point Cloud Completion via Occlusion Factor Manipulation

Jingyu Gong[1], Fengqi Liu[1], Jiachen Xu[1], Min Wang[2], Xin Tan[3],
Zhizhong Zhang[3], Ran Yi[1], Haichuan Song[3], Yuan Xie[3(✉)],
and Lizhuang Ma[1,3,4(✉)]

[1] Shanghai Jiao Tong University, Shanghai, China
{gongjingyu,liufengqi,xujiachen,ranyi}@sjtu.edu.cn
[2] SenseTime Research, Shanghai, China
wangmin@sensetime.com
[3] East China Normal University, Shanghai, China
tanxin2017@sjtu.edu.cn, {zzzhang,hcsong,yxie}@cs.ecnu.edu.cn
[4] Qing Yuan Research Institute, SJTU, Shanghai, China
ma-lz@cs.sjtu.edu.cn

Abstract. Recently, studies considering domain gaps in shape completion attracted more attention, due to the undesirable performance of supervised methods on real scans. They only noticed the gap in input scans, but ignored the gap in output prediction, which is specific for completion. In this paper, we disentangle partial scans into three (domain, shape, and occlusion) factors to handle the output gap in cross-domain completion. For factor learning, we design view-point prediction and domain classification tasks in a self-supervised manner and bring a factor permutation consistency regularization to ensure factor independence. Thus, scans can be completed by simply manipulating occlusion factors while preserving domain and shape information. To further adapt to instances in the target domain, we introduce an optimization stage to maximize the consistency between completed shapes and input scans. Extensive experiments on real scans and synthetic datasets show that ours outperforms previous methods by a large margin and is encouraging for the following works. Code is available at https://github.com/azuki-miho/OptDE.

Keywords: Point cloud completion · Cross-domain · Disentanglement

---

J. Gong and F. Liu—Equal Contribution.

Supplementary Information The online version contains supplementary material available at https://doi.org/10.1007/978-3-031-20086-1_30.

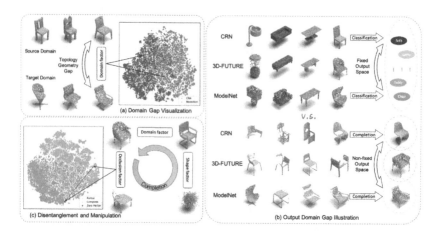

Fig. 1. (a) presents the domain gap between objects from the same category but different datasets where topology and geometry patterns vary a lot, as well as the feature distribution. (b) illustrates the output domain gap which is specific for completion task in contrast to cross-domain classification. In (c), we disentangle any partial scan into three independent factors, and completion can be simply implemented by setting occlusion factors to zero vector (red arrow) while well preserve shape and domain features. (Color figure online)

1   Introduction

Shape completion in which we infer complete shapes given partial ones, attracted lots of attention recently, for its wide application in robotics, path planning and VR/AR [6,14,42]. However, real scan completion is quite challenging due to the irregularity of point cloud and absence of complete real shapes for training.

Previous methods [15,30,35] had widely exploited completion on virtual 3D models like ShapeNet [5] and achieved desirable performance. That is attributed to the availability of complete shapes, and corresponding partial point clouds can be obtained through virtual scanning [41]. However, it is hard to use supervised methods for real point cloud completion, because complete shapes of real objects are usually unavailable for supervision. Meanwhile, completion networks trained on virtual 3D model are commonly not able to generalize well to infer complete real objects, especially when there are large domain gaps between the synthesized shapes and real objects [6]. So, the key for recovering real scans is to handle the cross-domain completion, where geometry and topology of objects from the same category are different between various datasets as shown in Fig. 1(a).

To alleviating the influence of domain gaps, pcl2pcl [6] trained two auto-encoders and an adaptation network to transform the latent code of a real scan to that of complete virtual one for each category. Then, the decoder for complete virtual shapes can map the transformed codes into complete shapes. However, they ignored a serious problem which is specific for completion task. In contrast to cross-domain shape classification whose output space (*i.e.*, categories) is invariant to different input domains, the predicted complete point cloud should correspond to the domain of input partial shapes (see Fig. 1(b)). *That means an output domain gap in completion task, as illustrated by the domain factor distribution of complete shapes from CRN [32] and ModelNet [38] after t-SNE in Fig. 1 (a).* Therefore, decoder trained to infer complete virtual shape cannot complete real scans. Recently, based on TreeGAN [27] and GAN Inversion [22], ShapeInversion [42] fine-tuned the decoder trained on virtual shapes during optimization stage for better performance. The underlying principle is that, fine-tuning according to real scans could adapt the decoder to real instances, alleviating output domain gap to some extent. However, adaptation in optimization alone is not enough, especially when the output domain gaps are quite large.

To handle the output domain gap, we assume the category of input partial shapes is known in advance as previous works [6,33,42], and introduce an intensively disentangled representation for partial shapes of each category via comprehensive consideration of both shape completion and output domain gap. Specifically, in our assumption, there are three generative factors, *i.e.*, occlusion, domain and domain-invariant shape factor, underlying a given partial cloud as shown in Fig. 1(c). For complete point clouds from the same category but different domains, they usually share the same semantic parts but quite different topology and geometry patterns. Thus, we attempt to disentangle any complete shape into a domain factor and a domain-invariant shape factor. While for a given complete shape, the partial point clouds generated from scanning vary a lot due to the occlusion caused by different scanning view-point [41]. So, we also introduce an occlusion factor which indicates the view-point for partial scans.

Based on this assumption, any partial scan can be disentangled into these factors no matter it is virtual or real, and we also assume the occlusion factor will be all-zero if the input shape is complete. Thus, point cloud completion can be simply implemented by manipulating the occlusion factor (setting to zero vector, see the occlusion factor manipulation in Fig. 1(c)), while shape and domain information can be well-preserved in the output prediction.

To thoroughly explore these three factors, we design several components to facilitate the disentanglement. (a) It is noteworthy that occlusion in partial shapes is usually caused by scanning at fixed view-point. Therefore, we introduce a self-supervised view-point prediction task for better occlusion factor/feature learning. (b) We take a domain discriminator judging whether a shape is virtual or real to extract domain factor, and employ another domain discriminator to decouple the domain information from the shape feature in an adversarial way. Additionally, we utilize the completion task to ensure the domain and domain-invariant shape factors are enough to infer complete shapes. (c) Inspired by PMP [10], for more intensive disentanglement, we derive a new factor permutation consistency regularization by randomly swapping the factors between samples, and introduce an inverse structure of auto-encoder, decoder-encoder for swapped factor reconstruction to ensure these factors independent to each other.

To further adapt our prediction to each partial instance in the target domain, we embrace a collaboration of regression and optimization. We use the trained encoder to obtain the disentangled factors of input cloud and set the occlusion factor to zero. Then, the combined factors can give a good initial prediction given the decoder. Later, Chamfer Distance between partial input and masked prediction [42] is used to fine-tune these factors and decoder within several iterations. Thanks to the collaboration, our method can give prediction 100× faster than pure optimization method like [42] and achieve much better performance.

To evaluate the performance on cross-domain completion, we test on real datasets ScanNet [8], MatterPort3D [4] and KITTI [12] like previous works [6,42]. We also utilize two additional point cloud completion datasets 3D-FUTURE [9] and ModelNet [38] with complete shapes for more comprehensive evaluation. The experimental results demonstrate our method can well cover the gap in output prediction and significantly improve cross-domain completion performance.

2   Related Works

Point Cloud Completion. Inspired by PointNet [25], PCN [41] designed an auto-encoder with folding operation [40] for shape completion. Later, a great performance boost has been brought in virtual shape completion, where paired shapes are available for training [20,23,30,34,35,39,43]. To generalize to real scans, pcl2pcl [6] trained two auto-encoders for virtual complete shapes and real partial scans, and an adaptation network to map the latent codes of real scans to that of virtual complete shapes. Cycle4Completion [33] added a reverse mapping function to maintain shape consistency. Meanwhile, ShapeInversion [42] searched for the latent code that best reconstruct the shapes during the optimization stage, given a generator for complete virtual shapes. Even though they fine-tuned the generator for better adaptation of partial scans, it is far from enough when the domain gaps are large.

Compared with these methods, we attempt to handle the domain gaps in the output prediction, which is specific for generation or completion task. In our method, we disentangle occlusion factor and domain factor for better completion of real scans while preserving domain-specific patterns.

Disentangled Representation Learning. Disentangled factor learning was explored under the concept of "discovering factorial codes" [2] by minimizing the predictability of one factor given remaining units [26]. Based on VAE [17], FactorVAE proposed to disentangle the latent code to be factorial and independent [16]. Factors can be more easily used for image manipulation and translation after disentanglement [19,21]. To reduce the domain discrepancy, domain-specific and domain-invariant features were disentangled for better recognition performance [24,37]. To ensure the disentanglement, additional constraints on factor through recombination were used in motion and 3D shape modeling [1,7].

Inspired by their works, we design a disentangled space consisting of occlusion, domain and domain-invariant shape factors for cross-domain shape completion where complete shapes in target domain are unavailable for training.

Collaboration of Regression and Optimization. Methods based on optimization and regression correspond to generative and discriminative models respectively, and recently their cooperation became prevailing for its speed and performance. In pose estimation, optimization was used on a good initial pose estimated by a regression approach [28]. Later, results obtained by optimization further supervised the regression network [18]. To speed up the process of finding latent code z of the generator that best reconstruct an image in image manipulation, an encoder is used for good initialization before further optimization [3].

Inspired by these methods, we further optimize the prediction given by disentangled encoding within several iterations to adapt to each input partial instance in the target domain, making it $100\times$ faster than optimization-based completion method and achieve much better performance.

3   Method

Overview. The framework of our two-stage method is shown in Fig. 2. In the first stage, we attempt to disentangle the input partial point cloud (unpaired source domain partial shapes generated from complete ones through real-time rendering and target domain partial scans) into three factors, naming view-based occlusion factor, domain factor, and domain-invariant shape factor as shown in Fig. 2(a). Here, we design a view-point prediction task in a self-supervised manner to disentangle the occlusion information caused by scanning. Concurrently, domain discriminators are taken to disentangle the domain-specific information from domain-invariant shape features. Later, three factors will be combined to output reconstructed partial point clouds. Meanwhile, we can simply predict the complete shapes by setting the occlusion factor to zero vector. Additionally, the independence of these three factors are ensured by randomly permuting the factors within a batch and keeping combined factors consistent after a decoder-encoder structure as presented by Fig. 2(b). In the second stage, for completion of specific partial point clouds, we optimize the disentangled factors and decoder obtained from stage 1 within several iterations to better adapt to each input partial point cloud instance (Fig. 2(c)).

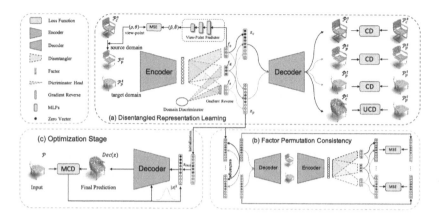

Fig. 2. Overall framework of Optimization over Disentangled Encoding. (a) shows the supervision given by view-point prediction, domain discrimination, reconstruction and completion. (b) shows the procedure of factor permutation consistency where factors are more intensively disentangled. Here, the Encoder, Decoder and Disentanglers are shared with (a). (c) shows the optimization procedure over disentangled factors of completed partial shapes and the Decoder is initialized by pre-trained model from (a).

3.1   Disentangled Representation for Completion

According to the disentanglement assumption [10,13], there are intrinsic factors $\{f_i\}_{i=1}^l$ in much lower dimension that generate the observed samples in high dimension point cloud space $\mathcal{P}(f_1, \cdots, f_l)$. In our method, we attempt to disentangle the common partial point cloud into three independent factors, including the occlusion factor f_o, domain factor f_d, and domain-invariant shape factor f_s.

View-Based Occlusion Factor. Partial shapes are mainly caused by occlusion, since a complete shape will generate various partial clouds when scanned from different view-points. So, scanning view-point plays a key role in point cloud completion and we aim to disentangle the view-based occlusion factor specially [31].

1) View-point Prediction: To disentangle the view-based occlusion factor, we design a view-point prediction task in a self-supervised manner. Here, we assume the view-point is located in a unit sphere. As shown in Fig. 2(a), we first randomly generate azimuth and elevation angles (ρ, θ) as the view-point direction, and rotate the complete point cloud accordingly. Then, based on z-buffer [29], we design a real-time implementation to render the complete shapes in a fast non-differentiable way and obtain the partial clouds in source domain.

Then, the generated partial shapes will be fed into the shared encoder to extract common features, and a specific disentangler is utilized to obtain occlusion factor f_o. For better factor learning, we introduce a view-point predictor module VP, consisting of several MLPs, to predict the view-point of point cloud $(\hat{\rho}, \hat{\theta}) = VP(f_o)$. The loss for view-point prediction can be formulated as follows:

$$\mathcal{L}_{vp} = (\rho - \hat{\rho})^2 + (\theta - \hat{\theta})^2. \tag{1}$$

Here, we choose to predict the azimuth and elevation angle directly rather than the rotation matrix due to their independence and simplicity.

2) Occlusion Factor Manipulation: Additionally, we assume it is the occlusion factor that makes the point cloud incomplete, and the decoder will predict the complete shape when the occlusion factor is zeroed out. So, for the same input partial point cloud, it can generate reconstructed partial shapes and complete objects by simply manipulating the occlusion factor. The corresponding latent factors for reconstructed partial shapes (z_p) and complete ones (z_c) are:

$$z_p = f_o \otimes f_d \otimes f_s, \quad z_c = \mathbf{0} \otimes f_d \otimes f_s, \tag{2}$$

where $\otimes$ indicates vector concatenation. Therefore, the reconstructed partial shape and completed shape are $\hat{P}_p = Dec(z_p)$ and $\hat{P}_c = Dec(z_c)$, respectively, where $Dec(\cdot)$ is the decoder. Chamfer Distance (CD) or Unidirectional Chamfer Distance (UCD) between the output prediction and target shapes are used to supervise the whole network. We take the form of CD as previous works [23,42]:

$$CD(P_1, P_2) = \frac{1}{|P_1|} \sum_{p_1 \in P_1} \min_{p_2 \in P_2} \|p_1 - p_2\|_2^2 + \frac{1}{|P_2|} \sum_{p_2 \in P_2} \min_{p_1 \in P_1} \|p_1 - p_2\|_2^2, \tag{3}$$

and UCD is formulated as follows:

$$UCD(P_1, P_2) = \frac{1}{|P_1|} \sum_{p_1 \in P_1} \min_{p_2 \in P_2} \|p_1 - p_2\|_2^2. \tag{4}$$

Here, we use $CD(\cdot)$ to supervise the reconstructed partial shape from source $\hat{P}_p^s$ and target domains $\hat{P}_p^t$, and predicted complete shape from source domains $\hat{P}_c^s$. For inferred complete shape in target domain $\hat{P}_c^t$ where GT are not available, we take UCD for guidance. Therefore, the loss function for reconstruction and completion can be expressed by

$$\mathcal{L}_{rec}^s = CD(P_p^s, \hat{P}_p^s), \quad \mathcal{L}_{rec}^t = CD(P_p^t, \hat{P}_p^t), \tag{5}$$

and

$$\mathcal{L}_{com}^s = CD(P_c^s, \hat{P}_c^s), \quad \mathcal{L}_{com}^t = UCD(P_p^t, \hat{P}_c^t), \tag{6}$$

where P_p^s and P_c^s are input partial cloud and corresponding complete shape Ground Truth (GT) from source domain respectively, and P_p^t indicates the input partial shape from the target domain.

Domain Factor. To keep the domain-specific features of input partial shapes well preserved in the output prediction, we extract the domain factor to provide domain clues for the decoder. As shown in Fig. 2(a), we utilize a specific disentangler to extract domain factors from common hidden features and introduce a domain discriminator to guide the learning of domain information. Here, our network will predict whether an input partial shape comes from the source domain or target domain according to the domain factor. Then, the domain labels, which are generated automatically, will supervise the domain prediction through cross-entropy loss, guiding the learning of domain factor.

Domain-Invariant Shape Factor. To make the shape factor domain-invariant, we also utilize the domain discriminator to distinguish the shape factor. However, a gradient reverse layer [11] is utilized between the domain discriminator and shape factor, where gradient will be reversed during back-propagation. Thus, the shape factor can learn to be domain-invariant in an adversarial way. To learn the shape information, this factor will be combined with domain factor to predict the complete point cloud, and the output prediction will be supervised in Eq. (6).

3.2   Factor Permutation Consistency

The independence of each disentangled factor is pursued for an intensive disentanglement [10,26]. To satisfy this property, we introduce a factor permutation consistency loss for the disentanglement of partial point cloud. Specifically, we first feed a batch of B samples into encoder to extract common features, then three separate disentanglers are used to extract occlusion factors $\{f_o^i\}_{i=1}^B$, domain factors $\{f_d^i\}_{i=1}^B$ and domain-invariant shape features $\{f_s^i\}_{i=1}^B$ respectively. In order to make the shape factors invariant to different domain and occlusion situations, we choose to generate random permutations of occlusion features f_o^i or domain features f_d^i to form new combinations of factors:

$$\tilde{z}^i = f_o^j \otimes f_d^i \otimes f_s^i \ \ or \ \ \tilde{z}^i = f_o^i \otimes f_d^j \otimes f_s^i, \tag{7}$$

where j is a permutation of i. In our implementation, we attempt to permute occlusion factors or domain factors alternately. As we need to make sure the extracted factors are independent to the remaining factors, an inverse structure of auto-encoder, saying decoder-encoder as shown in Fig. 2(b), is designed to keep factor permutation consistency with the following loss:

$$\mathcal{L}_{cons} = \sum_i^B \|Enc(Dec(\tilde{z}^i)) - \tilde{z}^i\|_2^2, \tag{8}$$

where Enc consists of the shared encoder and disentanglers, and Dec indicates the decoder. It is noteworthy that we only add factor permutation consistency loss halfway, when the three factors have been learned preliminarily in encoder.

3.3   Optimization over Disentangled Encoding

Based on the well-trained disentangled representation, we can obtain a complete version of partial point cloud by simply manipulating the occlusion features. To make the overlapping parts between prediction and input partial shape instance look more similar, we introduce a collaboration of regression and optimization method to fine-tune latent factors and decoders within only a few iterations.

Given the pre-trained auto-encoder from Fig. 2(a)–(b) ($Enc^\dagger$, $Dec^\dagger$) and partial point cloud $\mathcal{P}$, we first obtain the disentangled factors:

$$f_o \otimes f_d \otimes f_s = Enc^\dagger(\mathcal{P}), \tag{9}$$

and obtain the initial latent factors of complete shape through:

$$z_{init} = \mathbf{0} \otimes f_d \otimes f_s, \tag{10}$$

as shown in Fig. 2(c). Meanwhile, the pre-trained decoder is utilized to initialize the output predictor $Dec_{init} = Dec^{\dagger}$. Then, we attempt to optimize the disentangled factors and decoder together to better adapt to input partial point clouds by optimizing the following function $\mathcal{L}_{op}$:

$$z^*, Dec^* = \arg\min_{z,Dec} \mathcal{L}_{op}(Dec(z), \mathcal{P}, z), \tag{11}$$

and the final prediction can be expressed by $Dec^*(z^*)$.

To construct the loss function, for all points of $\mathcal{P}$, we first find their k nearest neighbors in $Dec(z)$ and the union of all neighboring points form the masked point cloud $M(Dec(z))$ like ShapeInversion [42]. Then, Chamfer Distance between the partial point cloud and masked complete shape $\mathcal{MCD}(\mathcal{P}_1, \mathcal{P}_2) = \mathcal{CD}(M(\mathcal{P}_1), \mathcal{P}_2)$ is used to maximize the similarity. Meanwhile, we also take a regularization of latent factors. All in all, the optimization target is:

$$\mathcal{L}_{op}(Dec(z), \mathcal{P}, z) = \mathcal{CD}(M(Dec(z)), \mathcal{P}) + \|z\|_2^2. \tag{12}$$

Compared with pure optimization method [42], our optimization stage can converge much faster and give much better predictions, since the disentangled factors and well pre-trained decoder have already covered the domain gaps in prediction and give much better initialization for further instance-level adaptation which can be evidenced obviously in Sect. 4.4.

4   Experiments

To show the effectiveness of our method and demonstrate our statement, we treat CRN [32] as our source domain and evaluate the proposed method on the target domain including real-world scans from ScanNet [8], MatterPort3D [4] and KITTI [12] as well as synthesized shape completion dataset 3D-FUTURE [9] and ModelNet [38]. Following previous works [6,42], we assume the category of partial clouds are known in advance and train a separate model for each category.

4.1   Datasets

CRN. We take CRN derived from ShapeNet [5] as our source domain. It provides 30,174 partial-complete pairs from eight categories where both partial and complete shapes contain 2,048 points. Here, we take 26,863 samples from six shared categories between CRN and other datasets for training and evaluation.

Real-World Scans. Similar to previous works [6,42], we evaluate the performance of our method on partial point cloud from real scans. There are three sources for real scans, saying ScanNet, MatterPort3D, and KITTI. The tables and chairs in ScanNet and MatterPort3D, and cars in KITTI are used for performance evaluation. We re-sample the input scans to $2,048$ points for unpaired training and inference to match the virtual dataset.

3D-FUTURE. To evaluate the performance on more realistic shapes, we generate another point cloud completion dataset from 3D-FUTURE [9]. The models in 3D-FUTURE are much more close to real objects. Similarly, we obtain partial shapes and complete ones with $2,048$ points from 5 different view-points. Because 3D-FUTURE only contains indoor furniture models, we only take five shared categories of furniture for point cloud completion.

ModelNet. We generate a shape completion dataset ModelNet using models from ModelNet40 [38]. We synthesize the partial shape through virtually scanning and generate complete ones by randomly sampling points in the surface like previous works [31,41]. $2,048$ points are taken for both partial and complete shapes to match the CRN dataset. In order to test the adaptation ability, we take the shared categories of ModelNet40 and CRN for evaluation.

4.2   Implementation

All experiments can be conducted on a machine with GTX 1080Ti and 64 GB RAM. Here, we take PointNet [25] as our encoder to extract common features with dimension $1,024$. Then, we take three separate disentanglers consisting of two MLPs to extract $f_o \in \mathbb{R}^{96}$, $f_d \in \mathbb{R}^{96}$, and $f_s \in \mathbb{R}^{96}$, and a TreeGCN [27] as our decoder. More details is available at https://github.com/azuki-miho/OptDE.

4.3   Metrics and Results

Metrics. For real scans without ground truth, we use Unidirectional Chamfer Distance (UCD) and Unidirectional Hausdorff Distance (UHD) from the partial input to the predicted complete shapes as our metric following previous works [6, 36,42]. For more comprehensive evaluation of our completion performance on cross-domain datasets, we take mean Chamfer Distance as our metric for the brand new datasets 3D-FUTURE and ModelNet like previous works [30,41] where complete shapes are available for testing.

Here, we first compare our method with the prevailing unsupervised cross-domain completion methods on real-world datasets of ScanNet, MatterPort3D and KITTI. The results are reported in Table 1 where UCD and UHD are used as metrics for evaluation. In this table, DE indicates regression method only using disentangled encoding shown in Fig. 2(a)–(b), and OptDE shows the results of optimization over disentangled encoding (Fig. 2(c)). As shown, disentangled encoding significantly improves the completion performance on real-world scans, and optimization over the disentangled encoding can further refine the results according to the input partial shapes. That is because our method can cover the domain gaps in output prediction between different datasets and adapt to various instances even within the target domain. We also show the qualitative results in Fig. 3 where our predictions correspond well to input partial scans.

Table 1. Cross-domain completion results on real scans. We take [UCD ↓/UHD ↓] as our metrics to evaluate the performance, and the scale factors are 10^4 for UCD and 10^2 for UHD. +UHD indicates UHD loss is used during training.

Methods	ScanNet		MatterPort3D		KITTI
	Chair	Table	Chair	Table	Car
pcl2pcl [6]	17.3/10.1	9.1/11.8	15.9/10.5	6.0/11.8	9.2/14.1
ShapeInversion [42]	3.2/10.1	3.3/11.9	3.6/10.0	3.1/11.8	2.9/13.8
+UHD [42]	4.0/9.3	6.6/11.0	4.5/9.5	5.7/10.7	5.3/12.5
Cycle4Compl. [33]	5.1/6.4	3.6/5.9	8.0/8.4	4.2/6.8	3.3/5.8
DE (Ours)	2.8/**5.4**	2.5/5.2	3.8/6.1	2.5/5.4	1.8/**3.5**
OptDE (Ours)	**2.6**/5.5	**1.9/4.6**	**3.0/5.5**	**1.9/5.3**	**1.6/3.5**

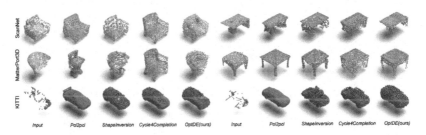

Fig. 3. Visualization results on the data of ScanNet, MatterPort3D and KITTI. Partial point clouds, predictions of pcl2pcl, ShapeInversion, Cycle4Completion and our methods are presented separately from the left to the right.

Additionally, we report the completion results of our method and previous works on target domain 3D-FUTURE in Table 2, and only complete shapes of CRN and partial point clouds of 3D-FUTURE are used for training for fair comparison. In this dataset, our method significantly outperforms other competitors. Again, collaboration of regression and optimization can improve the performance by adapting to each instance. Figure 4(a) gives the visualization results of our method and shows the qualitative improvement over previous works.

Table 2. Results of cross-domain completion on 3D-FUTURE. We evaluate the performance of each method using [CD↓] and scale-up factor is 10^4.

Methods	Cabinet	Chair	Lamp	Sofa	Table	Avg.
Pcl2pcl [6]	57.23	43.91	157.86	63.23	141.92	92.83
ShapeInversion [42]	38.54	26.30	48.57	44.02	108.60	53.21
Cycle4Compl. [33]	32.62	34.08	77.19	43.05	40.00	45.39
DE (Ours)	28.62	22.18	30.85	38.01	27.43	29.42
OptDE (Ours)	**28.37**	**21.87**	**29.92**	**37.98**	**26.81**	**28.99**

Table 3. Results of cross-domain completion on ModelNet. We take [CD↓] as our metric to evaluate the performance of each method which has been scaled by 10^4.

Methods	Plane	Car	Chair	Lamp	Sofa	Table	Avg.
Pcl2pcl [6]	18.53	17.54	43.58	126.80	38.78	163.62	68.14
ShapeInversion [42]	3.78	15.66	22.25	60.42	22.25	125.31	41.61
Cycle4Compl. [33]	5.77	11.85	26.67	83.34	22.82	21.47	28.65
DE (Ours)	2.19	**9.80**	15.11	42.94	21.45	10.26	16.96
OptDE (Ours)	**2.18**	**9.80**	**14.71**	**39.74**	**19.43**	**9.75**	**15.94**

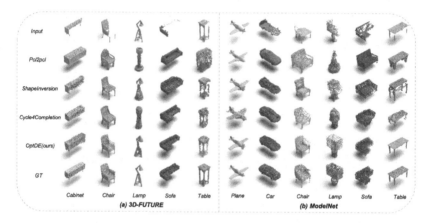

Fig. 4. Visualization results on the test set of 3D-FUTURE and ModelNet. The images from the top to bottom are input partial clouds, results given by pcl2pcl, ShapeInversion, Cycle4Completion and ours, and Ground Truth respectively.

We further compare the cross-domain completion performance on target domain dataset ModelNet. The results of cross-domain completion on this dataset are reported in Table 3 where disentangled encoding alone can outperform previous methods by a large margin. In addition, optimization over the disentangled encoding can further boost the performance especially for hard categories.

Moreover, we provide the qualitative results of different methods in Fig. 4(b). As can be seen, our method can well adapt to input partial shapes from different domains.

4.4 Ablation Study

In this section, we will conduct more experiments to evaluate the effectiveness of our proposed method from different aspects and prove our claims. Without loss of generality, we mainly utilize CRN as the source domain and evaluate on the target domain ModelNet.

Optimization over Disentangled Encoding. In order to evaluate the effectiveness of different parts in our method and test how far away from a perfect cross-domain completion method, we conduct ablation studies as follows. We first train the network with the same structure using only paired point clouds from CRN and evaluate the performance on ModelNet which is taken as our baseline. Then, we add Disentangled Representation Learning (Fig. 2(a)), Factor Permutation Consistency, and Optimization stage gradually. Additionally, we evaluate the best performance that can be brought by our backbones through training using paired data from both source domain CRN and target domain ModelNet, which is usually named as the oracle. We report all the results in Table 4.

Table 4. Ablation study of occlusion factor supervision on ModelNet. $[CD\downarrow](\times 10^4)$ is taken as our metric to evaluate the performance improvement and distance to oracle.

Methods	Plane	Car	Chair	Lamp	Sofa	Table	Avg.
Baseline	5.41	10.05	22.82	67.25	22.44	53.14	30.19
DE w/o Consistency	2.27	10.05	15.36	46.18	22.08	11.09	17.84
+ Consistency	2.19	9.80	15.11	42.94	21.45	10.26	16.96
+ Optimization	2.18	9.80	14.71	**39.74**	19.43	9.75	15.94
Oracle	**1.51**	**6.58**	**10.52**	41.98	**9.94**	**7.87**	**13.07**

It shows that our method can greatly handle the domain gaps in the output space and well preserve domain-specific patterns in predictions thanks to the disentanglement of occlusion factor and domain factor. Permutation consistency loss and optimization over the disentangled representation can both boost the performance. Even though, the improvement on car and sofa category is minor and that is because the samples in source domain have covered most samples in the target domains but the distribution is quite different. Compared with the oracle, there are still gaps to be bridged. Thus, this paper may inspire more work to focus on how to transfer the knowledge of virtual shapes to real objects given only virtual complete shapes and real partial scans.

Occlusion Factor Manipulation. In order to show the learning of disentangled occlusion factor and prove our claims, we take four original partial point clouds $\{\mathcal{P}_i\}_{i=1}^4$ that are scanned from different view-points, and then utilize the shared encoder and disentanglers to obtain the occlusion factors, domain factors and domain-invariant shape factors. After that, we replace the occlusion factors of $\mathcal{P}_1$ and $\mathcal{P}_3$ by those of $\mathcal{P}_2$ and $\mathcal{P}_4$, and obtain new generated point clouds through the decoder as shown in Fig. 5.

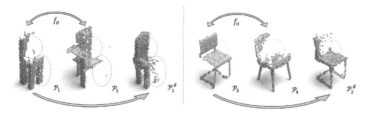

Fig. 5. Visualization of occlusion factor manipulation. The disentangled occlusion factors of $\mathcal{P}_1$ and $\mathcal{P}_3$ are replaced by the occlusion factors of $\mathcal{P}_2$ and $\mathcal{P}_4$. The new latent factors can generate brand-new partial point clouds through the pre-trained decoder. (Color figure online)

We can see the back and seat of $\mathcal{P}_1$ is occluded (blue circle), and the right front leg (red circle) of $\mathcal{P}_2$ is occluded. After replacing the occlusion factor, the right front leg of $\mathcal{P}_1^g$ is occluded due to the occlusion factor while shape and domain information is well preserved. We can also see the occlusion factor manipulation effect in $\mathcal{P}_2^g$. This indicates a disentangled representation can provide a much easier way to control the occlusion through simple factor manipulation.

Initialization in Optimization. Our method pursue a collaboration of regression and optimization where disentangled encoding provides a good initialization for optimization. Here, we provide two representative examples of optimization progression in Fig. 6 where our method can provide a desirable prediction, and the optimization can converge within about 4 iterations thanks to this good initialization of latent code and decoder. Compared with ours, ShapeInversion converges much slower and may even converge to a sub-optimal solution.

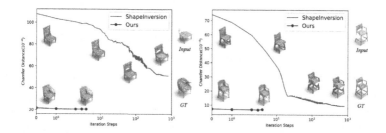

Fig. 6. Optimization progression on ModelNet test set. Compared with ShapeInversion, our method can converge 100× faster (0.12 s for 4 iterations v.s. 23.56 s for 800 iterations on a single GTX 1080Ti) and easily circumvent sub-optimal solution.

5   Conclusion

In this paper, we propose the very first method OptDE to deal with the output domain gap in shape completion. We introduce a disentangled representation consisting of three essential factors for any partial shape, and shape completion can be implemented by simply manipulating the occlusion factor while preserving shape and domain features. To further adapt to each partial instance in the target domain, we introduce a collaboration of regression and optimization to ensure the consistency between completed shapes and input scans. For comprehensive evaluation on cross-domain completion, we treat CRN as the source domain and evaluate on real-world scans in ScanNet, MatterPort3D and KITTI as well as synthesized datasets 3D-FUTURE and ModelNet. Results show that our method outperforms previous methods by a large margin which may inspire more works to focus on cross-domain point cloud completion.

Limitation and Discussion. Since all previous methods assume the category of partial shapes to be known and trained in category-specific way, we believe it will be better to train a unified model for cross-domain completion of all categories.

Acknowledgments. This work is sponsored by the National Key Research and Development Program of China (No. 2019YFC1521104), the National Natural Science Foundation of China (No. 61972157,72192821), Shanghai Municipal Science and Technology Major Project (2021SHZDZX0102), Shanghai Sailing Program (22YF1420300), Shanghai Science and Technology Commission (21511101200) and SenseTime Collaborative Research Grant.

References

1. Aberman, K., Li, P., Lischinski, D., Sorkine-Hornung, O., Cohen-Or, D., Chen, B.: Skeleton-aware networks for deep motion retargeting. ACM Trans. Graph. (TOG) **39**(4), 62-1 (2020)
2. Barlow, H.B., Kaushal, T.P., Mitchison, G.J.: Finding minimum entropy codes. Neural Comput. **1**(3), 412–423 (1989)
3. Bau, D., et al.: Semantic photo manipulation with a generative image prior. In: SIGGRAPH (2020)
4. Chang, A., et al.: Matterport3D: learning from RGB-D data in indoor environments. In: 2017 International Conference on 3D Vision (3DV), pp. 667–676. IEEE Computer Society (2017)
5. Chang, A.X., et al.: ShapeNet: an information-rich 3d model repository. arXiv preprint arXiv:1512.03012 (2015)
6. Chen, X., Chen, B., Mitra, N.J.: Unpaired point cloud completion on real scans using adversarial training. In: International Conference on Learning Representations (2020)
7. Cosmo, L., Norelli, A., Halimi, O., Kimmel, R., Rodolà, E.: LIMP: learning latent shape representations with metric preservation priors. In: Vedaldi, A., Bischof, H., Brox, T., Frahm, J.-M. (eds.) ECCV 2020. LNCS, vol. 12348, pp. 19–35. Springer, Cham (2020). https://doi.org/10.1007/978-3-030-58580-8_2
8. Dai, A., Chang, A.X., Savva, M., Halber, M., Funkhouser, T., Nießner, M.: ScanNet: richly-annotated 3d reconstructions of indoor scenes. In: Proceedings of the IEEE Conference on Computer Vision and Pattern Recognition, pp. 5828–5839 (2017)

9. Fu, H., et al.: 3d-future: 3d furniture shape with texture. arXiv preprint arXiv:2009.09633 (2020)
10. Fumero, M., Cosmo, L., Melzi, S., Rodolà, E.: Learning disentangled representations via product manifold projection. In: ICML (2021)
11. Ganin, Y., Lempitsky, V.: Unsupervised domain adaptation by backpropagation. In: International Conference on Machine Learning, pp. 1180–1189. PMLR (2015)
12. Geiger, A., Lenz, P., Urtasun, R.: Are we ready for autonomous driving? The Kitti vision benchmark suite. In: 2012 IEEE Conference on Computer Vision and Pattern Recognition, pp. 3354–3361. IEEE (2012)
13. Gonzalez-Garcia, A., van de Weijer, J., Bengio, Y.: Image-to-image translation for cross-domain disentanglement. In: NeurIPS (2018)
14. Hou, J., Dai, A., Nießner, M.: RevealNet: seeing behind objects in RGB-D scans. In: Proceedings of the IEEE/CVF Conference on Computer Vision and Pattern Recognition, pp. 2098–2107 (2020)
15. Huang, Z., Yu, Y., Xu, J., Ni, F., Le, X.: PF-Net: point fractal network for 3d point cloud completion. In: Proceedings of the IEEE/CVF Conference on Computer Vision and Pattern Recognition, pp. 7662–7670 (2020)
16. Kim, H., Mnih, A.: Disentangling by factorising. In: International Conference on Machine Learning (ICML), pp. 2649–2658. PMLR (2018)
17. Kingma, D.P., Welling, M.: Auto-encoding variational bayes. In: ICLR (2014)
18. Kolotouros, N., Pavlakos, G., Black, M.J., Daniilidis, K.: Learning to reconstruct 3d human pose and shape via model-fitting in the loop. In: Proceedings of the IEEE/CVF International Conference on Computer Vision, pp. 2252–2261 (2019)
19. Liu, A.H., Liu, Y.C., Yeh, Y.Y., Wang, Y.C.F.: A unified feature disentangler for multi-domain image translation and manipulation. In: Proceedings of the 32nd International Conference on Neural Information Processing Systems, pp. 2595–2604 (2018)
20. Liu, M., Sheng, L., Yang, S., Shao, J., Hu, S.M.: Morphing and sampling network for dense point cloud completion. In: Proceedings of the AAAI Conference on Artificial Intelligence, vol. 34, pp. 11596–11603 (2020)
21. Liu, Y.C., Yeh, Y.Y., Fu, T.C., Wang, S.D., Chiu, W.C., Wang, Y.C.F.: Detach and adapt: learning cross-domain disentangled deep representation. In: Proceedings of the IEEE Conference on Computer Vision and Pattern Recognition, pp. 8867–8876 (2018)
22. Ma, F., Ayaz, U., Karaman, S.: Invertibility of convolutional generative networks from partial measurements. In: Advances in Neural Information Processing Systems, vol. 31 (2018)
23. Pan, L., et al.: Variational relational point completion network. In: Proceedings of the IEEE/CVF Conference on Computer Vision and Pattern Recognition, pp. 8524–8533 (2021)
24. Peng, X., Huang, Z., Sun, X., Saenko, K.: Domain agnostic learning with disentangled representations. In: International Conference on Machine Learning, pp. 5102–5112. PMLR (2019)
25. Qi, C.R., Su, H., Mo, K., Guibas, L.J.: PointNet: deep learning on point sets for 3d classification and segmentation. In: The IEEE/CVF Conference on Computer Vision and Pattern Recognition (CVPR), pp. 652–660 (2017)
26. Schmidhuber, J.: Learning factorial codes by predictability minimization. Neural Comput. 4(6), 863–879 (1992)
27. Shu, D.W., Park, S.W., Kwon, J.: 3d point cloud generative adversarial network based on tree structured graph convolutions. In: Proceedings of the IEEE/CVF International Conference on Computer Vision, pp. 3859–3868 (2019)

28. Sigal, L., Balan, A., Black, M.: Combined discriminative and generative articulated pose and non-rigid shape estimation. Adv. Neural. Inf. Process. Syst. **20**, 1337–1344 (2007)

29. Straßer, W.: Schnelle kurven-und flächendarstellung auf grafischen sichtgeräten. Ph.D. thesis (1974)

30. Tchapmi, L.P., Kosaraju, V., Rezatofighi, H., Reid, I., Savarese, S.: TopNet: structural point cloud decoder. In: Proceedings of the IEEE/CVF Conference on Computer Vision and Pattern Recognition, pp. 383–392 (2019)

31. Wang, H., Liu, Q., Yue, X., Lasenby, J., Kusner, M.J.: Unsupervised point cloud pre-training via occlusion completion. In: Proceedings of the IEEE/CVF International Conference on Computer Vision, pp. 9782–9792 (2021)

32. Wang, X., Ang Jr, M.H., Lee, G.H.: Cascaded refinement network for point cloud completion. In: Proceedings of the IEEE/CVF Conference on Computer Vision and Pattern Recognition, pp. 790–799 (2020)

33. Wen, X., Han, Z., Cao, Y.P., Wan, P., Zheng, W., Liu, Y.S.: Cycle4completion: unpaired point cloud completion using cycle transformation with missing region coding. In: Proceedings of the IEEE/CVF Conference on Computer Vision and Pattern Recognition, pp. 13080–13089 (2021)

34. Wen, X., Li, T., Han, Z., Liu, Y.S.: Point cloud completion by skip-attention network with hierarchical folding. In: Proceedings of the IEEE/CVF Conference on Computer Vision and Pattern Recognition, pp. 1939–1948 (2020)

35. Wen, X., et al.: PMP-Net: point cloud completion by learning multi-step point moving paths. In: Proceedings of the IEEE/CVF Conference on Computer Vision and Pattern Recognition, pp. 7443–7452 (2021)

36. Wu, R., Chen, X., Zhuang, Y., Chen, B.: Multimodal shape completion via conditional generative adversarial networks. In: Vedaldi, A., Bischof, H., Brox, T., Frahm, J.-M. (eds.) ECCV 2020. LNCS, vol. 12349, pp. 281–296. Springer, Cham (2020). https://doi.org/10.1007/978-3-030-58548-8_17

37. Wu, X., Huang, H., Patel, V.M., He, R., Sun, Z.: Disentangled variational representation for heterogeneous face recognition. In: Proceedings of the AAAI Conference on Artificial Intelligence, vol. 33, pp. 9005–9012 (2019)

38. Wu, Z., et al.: 3d shapenets: a deep representation for volumetric shapes. In: Proceedings of the IEEE Conference on Computer Vision and Pattern Recognition, pp. 1912–1920 (2015)

39. Xie, H., Yao, H., Zhou, S., Mao, J., Zhang, S., Sun, W.: GRNet: gridding residual network for dense point cloud completion. In: Vedaldi, A., Bischof, H., Brox, T., Frahm, J.-M. (eds.) ECCV 2020. LNCS, vol. 12354, pp. 365–381. Springer, Cham (2020). https://doi.org/10.1007/978-3-030-58545-7_21

40. Yang, Y., Feng, C., Shen, Y., Tian, D.: FoldingNet: point cloud auto-encoder via deep grid deformation. In: Proceedings of the IEEE Conference on Computer Vision and Pattern Recognition, pp. 206–215 (2018)

41. Yuan, W., Khot, T., Held, D., Mertz, C., Hebert, M.: PCN: point completion network. In: 2018 International Conference on 3D Vision (3DV), pp. 728–737. IEEE (2018)

42. Zhang, J., et al.: Unsupervised 3d shape completion through GAN inversion. In: Proceedings of the IEEE/CVF Conference on Computer Vision and Pattern Recognition, pp. 1768–1777 (2021)

43. Zhang, W., Yan, Q., Xiao, C.: Detail preserved point cloud completion via separated feature aggregation. In: Vedaldi, A., Bischof, H., Brox, T., Frahm, J.-M. (eds.) ECCV 2020. LNCS, vol. 12370, pp. 512–528. Springer, Cham (2020). https://doi.org/10.1007/978-3-030-58595-2_31

Unsupervised Learning of 3D Semantic Keypoints with Mutual Reconstruction

Haocheng Yuan[1], Chen Zhao[2], Shichao Fan[1], Jiaxi Jiang[1], and Jiaqi Yang[1(✉)]

[1] Northwestern Polytechnical University, Xi'an, China
{hcyuan,fsc_smile,jshmjjx}@mail.nwpu.edu.cn, jqyang@nwpu.edu.cn
[2] CVLab EPFL, Lausanne, Switzerland
chen.zhao@epfl.ch

Abstract. Semantic 3D keypoints are category-level semantic consistent points on 3D objects. Detecting 3D semantic keypoints is a foundation for a number of 3D vision tasks but remains challenging, due to the ambiguity of semantic information, especially when the objects are represented by unordered 3D point clouds. Existing unsupervised methods tend to generate category-level keypoints in implicit manners, making it difficult to extract high-level information, such as semantic labels and topology. From a novel mutual reconstruction perspective, we present an unsupervised method to generate consistent semantic keypoints from point clouds explicitly. To achieve this, the proposed model predicts keypoints that not only reconstruct the object itself but also reconstruct other instances in the same category. To the best of our knowledge, the proposed method is the first to mine 3D semantic consistent keypoints from a mutual reconstruction view. Experiments under various evaluation metrics as well as comparisons with the state-of-the-arts demonstrate the efficacy of our new solution to mining semantic consistent keypoints with mutual reconstruction. Our code and pre-trained models are available at https://github.com/YYYYYHC/Learning-Semantic-Keypoints-with-Mutual-Reconstruction.git.

Keywords: Keypoint detection · 3D point cloud · Unsupervised learning · Reconstruction

1 Introduction

3D semantic keypoints generally refer to representative points on 3D objects, which possess category-level semantic consistency through categories. Detecting 3D semantic keypoints has a broad application scenarios, such as 3D registration [26], 3D reconstruction [15], shape abstraction [25] and deformation [10].

Supplementary Information The online version contains supplementary material available at https://doi.org/10.1007/978-3-031-20086-1_31.

S. Avidan et al. (Eds.): ECCV 2022, LNCS 13662, pp. 534–549, 2022.
https://doi.org/10.1007/978-3-031-20086-1_31

However, this task is quite challenging because of unknown shape variation among different instances in a category, unordered point cloud representations, and limited data annotations (Fig. 1).

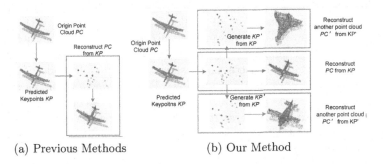

(a) Previous Methods   (b) Our Method

Fig. 1. Comparison of our method and previous methods. Previous methods focus on self-reconstruction, which may fail to mine category-level semantic consistency information. We address this issue with mutual reconstruction (the keypoints of an object also reconstruct other objects in the same category).

From the technical view, 3D keypoint detection can be divided into geometry-only [21,36] and learning-based [5,9,10,12,18]. For geometry-only ones, they generally leverage shape attributes such as normals to detect distinctive and repeatable points, however, they generally fail to mine semantic information. Learning-based methods can learn semantics from massive training data and can be further classified into supervised and unsupervised. As illustrated in previous works [10,18], supervised methods may suffer from limited human annotated data [32], which greatly limits their applicability. Unsupervised learning of 3D semantic keypoints [10,12,18], however, is particularly challenging due to the ambiguity of semantic information when labels are not given. A few trails have been made toward this line, and we divide these unsupervised methods into two classes by examining if the method employs category-level information explicitly or implicitly. 1) Implicit methods focus on self-related tasks of a single object, such as self-reconstruction [5,18], where keypoints of each object are optimized to reconstruct the original object; category-level information is ensured in an indirect way, as all objects in a specific category are fed into the model during the training process. 2) There are only a few explicit methods [9,10], which consider category information directly. The networks are usually driven by losses of specific tasks involving more than one object from a category. Both explicit and implicit methods have made great success in terms of geometric consistency and robustness, but still fail to ensure semantic consistency. For the implicit methods [5,18], this is caused by a lack of semantic information, as they only consider a single object in a whole category, e.g., reconstructing the object itself based on its own keypoints. As for explicit methods [9,10], although category-level information are taken into consideration explicitly, they still tend to pursue consistency and fail to mine the hidden semantic information within keypoints.

To this end, from a novel mutual reconstruction perspective, we propose an unsupervised method to learn category-level semantic keypoints from point clouds. *We believe that semantic consistent keypoints of an object should be able to reconstruct itself as well as other objects from the same category.* The motivation behind is to fully leverage category-level semantic information and ensure the consistency based on an explicit manner. Compared with deformation tasks [10] based on cage deformation methods, shape reconstruction from keypoints have been well investigated [5,18] and is more straightforward and simpler. In particular, only reconstruction task is involved in our model. The overall technique pipeline of our method is as follows. First, given two point clouds of the same category, keypoints are extracted by an encoder; second, the source keypoint set is reshaped according to the offset of input point clouds; then, source and reshaped keypoint sets are used as the guidance for self-reconstruction and mutual reconstruction with a decoder [18]; finally, both self-reconstruction and mutual reconstruction losses are considered to train the network. Experimental results on KeypointNet [32] and ShapeNet Part [3] have shown that the proposed model outperforms the state-of-the-arts on human annotation datasets. It can be also generalized to real-world scanned data [6] without human annotations.

Overall, our method has two key contributions:

- To the best of our knowledge, we are the first to mine semantic consistency with mutual reconstruction, which is a simple yet effective way to detect consistent 3D semantic keypoints.
- We propose a network to ensure keypoints performing both self reconstruction and mutual reconstruction. It achieves the overall best performance under several evaluation metrics on KeypointNet [32] and ShapeNet Part [3] datasets.

2   Related Work

This section first gives a review on unsupervised semantic keypoints and geometric keypoint detection. Supervised methods are not included, since the task of 3D keypoint detection is seldomly accomplished in a supervised way due to the lack of sufficient labelled datasets. Then, a recap on deep learning on point clouds is given.

2.1   Unsupervised Semantic Keypoint Detection

We divide current methods into two classes according to if the category-level information is leveraged implicitly or explicitly.

Implicit Methods. Implicit methods employ self-related metrics to measure the quality of keypoints. A typical implicit method is skeleton merger [18], whose key idea is to reconstruct skeleton-liked objects based on its keypoints through an encoder-decoder architecture. Another implicit way [5] utilizes a convex combination of local points to generate local semantic keypoints, which are then measured by how close they are to the origin point cloud. Unsupervised stable interest point (USIP) [12] predicts keypoints with a Siamese architecture, and the two inputs are two partial views from a 3D object. Implicit methods can achieve good spatial consistency and are relatively light-weight. However, they generally fail to mine semantic consistency information.

Explicit Methods. Explicit methods cope with category-level information directly. Keypoint deformer [10] employs a Siamese architecture for shape deformation to detect shape control keypoints; the difference between two input shapes is analysed by comparing their keypoint sets. The cage [31] method is crucial to keypoint deformer [10]; to deform a point cloud, cage [31] takes the origin point cloud, shape control points on point cloud, and target cage as input, the output of cage consists of a deformed cage and a deformed point cloud under the constraint of cage. Another explicit method [9] learns both category-specific shape basis and instance-specific parameters such as rotations and coefficients during training; however, the method requires a symmetric hypothesis. Different from the two previous works, our method evaluates keypoints from the self and mutual reconstruction quality by estimated keypoints and do not require additional hypotheses on inputs.

2.2 Geometric Keypoint Detection

Besides semantic keypoints, detection of geometric keypoints has been well investigated in previous works [21,36]. Different from semantic keypoints that focus on category-level semantic consistency, geometric keypoints are defined to be repeatable and distinctive keypoints on 3D surfaces. In a survey on geometric keypoints, Tombari et al. [23] divided 3D geometric detectors into two categories, i.e., fixed-scale and adaptive-scale. Fixed-scale detectors, such as LSP [4], ISS [36], KPQ [14] and HKS [22], find distinctive keypoints at a specific scale with a non-maxima suppression (NMS) procedure, which is measured by saliency. Differently, adaptive-scale detectors such as LBSS [24] and MeshDoG [35] first build a scale-space defined on the surface, and then pick up distinctive keypoints with an NMS of the saliency at the characteristic scale of each point. Geometric keypoints focus on repeatable and distinctive keypoints rather than semantically consistent keypoints.

2.3 Deep Learning on Point Clouds

Because our method relies on reconstruction, which is typically performed with an encoder-decoder network on point clouds. We will briefly discuss deep learning methods from the perspectives of encoder and decoder.

Encoder. A number of neural networks have been proposed, e.g., PointNet [16], PointNet++ [17], and PointConv [28], which directly consume 3D point clouds. PointNet [16] is a pioneering work, which extracts features from point clouds with point-wise MLPs and permutation-invariant functions. Based on PointNet, PointNet++ [17] introduces a hierarchical structure to consider both local and global features; PointNet is applied after several sampling and grouping layers; PointNet++ is also employed as an encoder by several unsupervised 3D semantic keypoint detection methods [5,18]. More recent point cloud encoders include [20, 27,28]. These encoders have achieved success in tasks like registration [26] and reconstruction [15]. Several keypoint detection methods [5,10,18] also employ PointNet++ [17] as the encoder.

Decoder. In previous point cloud learning works [1,33], MLP is frequently leveraged to generate point clouds from the encoded features. Specifically, Fold-ingNet [30] proposes a folding-based decoder to deform 2D grid onto 3D object surface of a point cloud. Many works [7,8,29] follow FoldingNet [30] and decode the features based on structure deformation. In [19], tree structure is used to decode structured point clouds. From the functional view, most decoders lever-aged by 3D semantic keypoint detection methods [5,9,12,18] focus on recon-structing the original shape of the input. An exception is keypoint deformer [10], whose decoder tries to deform the source shape into the target shape through cage-based deformation.

3   The Proposed Method

The pipeline of our method is shown in Fig. 2. Self reconstruction and mutual reconstruction are performed simultaneously through encoder-decoder architec-tures.

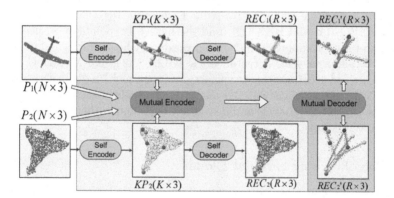

Fig. 2. Pipeline of our method. Two input point clouds (each with N points) P_1, P_2 are fed into self and mutual encoders, the outputs are two keypoint sets KP_1, KP_2 and mutual features. Self and mutual decoders then decode the source keypoint set KP_1, KP_2 into REC_1, REC_2 and REC_1', REC_2'. Reconstruction loss is calculated by Chamfer distance between P, REC (self reconstruction) and P, REC' (mutual recon-struction).

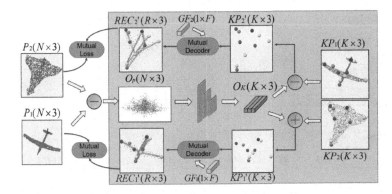

Fig. 3. Mutual reconstruction process of our method. Two predicted keypoint sets KP_1 and KP_2 are reshaped into KP_1' and KP_2' with offsets generated between input point clouds PC_1, PC_2. A **shared** decoder from Skeleton Merger [18], then decodes KP_1', KP_2' into REC_1', REC_2'. Mutual reconstruction loss is calculated by Chamfer distance between REC, REC'. (Color figure online)

3.1 Self and Mutual Reconstructions

Self and mutual reconstructions are the key components of our method. For an input point cloud P_1, self-reconstruction is supposed to reconstruct the origin point cloud P_1 from its own keypoint set KP_1; mutual reconstruction is to reconstruct another point cloud P_2 with KP_1 and the offset between P_1, P_2.

Mutual Reconstruction. Our mutual reconstruction module is depicted in Fig. 3. The mutual reconstruction process utilizes several outputs from self reconstruction, including keypoint sets KP_1, KP_2 and the global feature GF.

Mutual reconstruction is supposed to be able to extract category-level semantic consistent keypoints as illustrated in Fig. 4. The figure illustrates the semantic ambiguity of self-reconstruction, which can be resolved by the mutual reconstruction module. When the method with only self-related tasks (e.g., self reconstruction) predicts object-wise keypoints which are not semantically consistent, it may fail to notice the inconsistency as the topology information is inconsistent as well (we visualize the topology information as a sequence of connection, while some methods employ topology information implicitly); however, the mutual reconstruction model is sensitive when either the topology or semantic label prediction is not correct, as additional shapes are considered in mutual reconstruction and the constraint on keypoint consistency is much tighter.

Self Reconstruction. The self reconstruction module is presented in Fig. 5. Specifically, the point-wise feature can also be considered as point-wise score, because the keypoints are actually generated by linear combination of origin points. In other words, for the point with a higher score (feature value), it con-

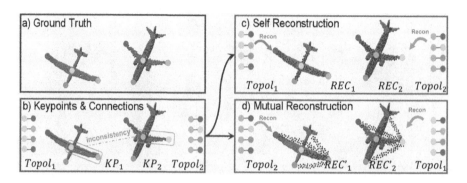

Fig. 4. Illustration of the difference between self-related tasks and mutual reconstruction. The purple points are reconstruction results REC, REC'. Loss is computed between the purple reconstruction points and the grey original input points. **a)** Consistent ground truth keypoints. **b)** Inconsistent prediction of the model. Both keypoints and the topology are inconsistent. **c)** For self-reconstruction, REC_1, REC_2 are reconstructed from KP_1, KP_2 separately with topology $Topol_1, Topol_2$. That may cause inconsistency problem as the encoder may learn to predict inconsistent $Topol$ for inconsistent KP. The Chamfer distance loss between a single REC and its original point cloud is low, **despite the inconsistency of predicted keypoints. d)** Mutual-reconstruction can alleviate this problem. The mutual reconstruction decoder first reshapes KP_1, KP_2 into KP_2', KP_1', which are predictions of KP_2, KP_1. (The visualized keypoints in mutual reconstruction are KP' instead of KP.) Then, the decoder reconstructs REC_1', REC_2' based on KP_1', KP_2' and $Topol_1, Topol_2$. The chamfer distance between reconstruction and original point cloud would be much greater due to the inconsistent topology.

tributes more to the keypoint prediction. We simply define the point-wise score to be the sum of the k-dim feature, as visualized in Fig. 3 (the airplane in red).

Self reconstruction is also a critical component for mining the semantic information from an instance [5,18]. To ensure category-level semantic consistent information, instance and cross-instance information should be mined, such that self reconstruction is utilized as complementary to mutual reconstruction.

3.2   Network Architecture

The whole pipeline of our method is illustrated in Fig. 2. All **decoders** in self and mutual reconstruction processes are shared, and the only difference between the self and mutual **encoder** is that the mutual one needs to **reshape keypoint set** after the same architecture as the self one. Thus, the core of our network architecture are encoder, reshaping keypoint set and decoder. The three technical modules are detailed in the following.

Encoder. The designed encoder is supposed to generate keypoints proposals K_1, K_2 from input point clouds P_1, P_2. First, we employ the PointNet++ [17]

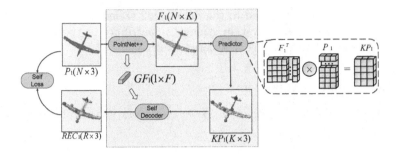

Fig. 5. Self reconstruction process of our method. The input point cloud (with N 3D points) P_1 is first fed into a shared PointNet++ encoder, whose output is a group of $K \times N$ point-wise feature F_1, where K indicates the number of keypoints. Keypoint sets KP_1 is calculated by the inner product of F_1^T and P. A shared decoder then reconstructs the source keypoint KP_1 sets into REC_1. Self reconstruction loss is calculated by Chamfer distance between P_1, REC_1. The GF_1 indicates the global feature, which consists of activation strengths and trainable offsets.

encoder and it offers a K-dimension point-wise feature for every point in the origin point cloud, thus the shape of point feature matrix F is $K \times N$. Keypoints are calculated by:

$$KP = F \cdot P. \tag{1}$$

Reshape Keypoint Set. After keypoints proposals KP are generated by the encoder, they are reshaped into new keypoint sets KP', which are utilized by the decoder for mutual reconstruction. We reshape source keypoint set KP with a point-wise offsets O_{kp} as:

$$KP_1' = KP_2 + O_K, \tag{2}$$

and

$$KP_2' = KP_1 - O_K, \tag{3}$$

where O_{kp} is calculated by feeding offsets of origin point clouds O_p into a 3-layers MLP, as in the following:

$$O_K = MLP(O_P), \tag{4}$$

and

$$O_P = P_1 - P_2. \tag{5}$$

The reshaped source keypoints are fed to the decoder for reconstruction.

Decoder. We build our decoder following skeleton merger [18]. The decoder takes keypoint sets KP, KP' and global feature (activation strengths and trainable offsets) as input. It first generates $n(n-1)/2$ line-like skeletons, each of them is composed of a series of points with fixed intervals. Second, trainable offsets are added to every point on the skeleton-like point cloud. Finally, $n(n-1)/2$

activation strengths are applied to the $n(n-1)/2$ skeletons for reconstruction; only skeletons with high activation strengths contribute to the reconstruction process. As such, shapes are reconstructed by decoders.

3.3   Losses and Regularizers

Both self and mutual reconstruction losses are employed to train our model in an unsupervised way.

Reconstruction Losses. We calculate reconstruction loss with Composite Chamfer Distance (CCD) [18]. CCD is a modified Chamfer Distance which takes the activation strengths into consideration. For fidelity loss, the CCD between $\hat{X}$ and X is given as:

$$L_f = \sum_i a_i \sum_{\hat{p} \in \hat{X}_i} \min_{p_0 \in X} \|\hat{p} - p_0\|_2, \tag{6}$$

where $\hat{X}_i$ is the i-th skeleton of point cloud $\hat{X}$, and a_i is the activation strength of $\hat{X}_i$. For the coverage loss, there is a change from the fidelity loss that more than one skeleton are considered in the order of how close they are to the given point, until the sum of their activation strengths exceeds 1 [18].

We apply the CCD loss in both self and mutual reconstruction tasks. For self reconstruction, we calculate the CCD between the input target shape P_t and output target shape P'_t:

$$L_{rec_s} = CCD(P_1, REC_1) + CCD(P_2, REC_2). \tag{7}$$

For mutual reconstruction, we calculate the CCD between the input target shape P_t and output source shape P'_s:

$$L_{rec_m} = CCD(P_1, REC'_1) + CCD(P_2, REC'_2). \tag{8}$$

The eventual reconstruction loss is a combination of the two losses:

$$L_{rec} = \lambda_s L_{rec_s} + \lambda_m L_{rec_m}, \tag{9}$$

where λ_s and λ_m are weights to control the contributions of self and mutual reconstructions.

Regularizers. The trainable offsets in our decoder are calculated by multiple MLPs. To keep the locality of every points on the skeleton, we apply an L_2 regularization on them. L_2 regularization is also imposed on the keypoint offset O_K, in order to reduce the geometric changes of keypoints when reconstructing the other shape.

4   Experiments

Experimental Setup. In our experiments, we follow [18] and report the dual alignment score (DAS), mean intersection over union (mIoU), part correspondence ratio, and robustness scores of tested methods. We choose learning-based methods including skeleton merger [18], Fernandez et al. [9], USIP [12], and D3Feat [2]; and geometric methods including ISS [36], Harris3D [21], and SIFT3D [13], for a thorough comparison. Note that there is a lack of supervised methods [34] and valid annotated datasets [32] in this field. For this reason, only several unsupervised ones are chosen. We also perform an ablation study, in which we analyze the effectiveness of our mutual-reconstruction module. For training, We employ ShapeNet [3] with the standard split of training and testing data, in which all shapes are normalized into a unit box. For evaluation, we utilize the following datasets, i.e., the human-annotated keypoint dataset KeypointNet [32], a part segmentation dataset named ShapeNet Part [3], and a real-world scanned dataset ScanNet [6].

Implementation Details. We randomly split the training dataset into two groups. Mutual reconstruction is performed by respectively taking two shapes from two different groups per time. Point clouds are down-sampled to 2048 points with farthest-point-sampling [17]. The number of keypoints for all categories is restricted to 10. The model is trained on a single NVIDIA GTX 2080Ti GPU, and the Adam [11] is used as the optimizer. We train the KeypointNet [32] for 80 epochs in 8 h. By default, the weights (λ_s and λ_m) of self reconstruction and mutual reconstruction losses are set to 0.5.

4.1   Semantic Consistency

Semantic consistency means a method can predict keypoints that are of the same semantic information. There are several popular metrics to evaluate semantic consistency, all of which are considered in the experiments for a comprehensive evaluation.

Dual Alignment Score. We first evaluate the semantic consistency on KeypointNet [32] with DAS, which is introduced by [18]. Given the estimated keypoints on a source point cloud, DAS employs a reference point cloud for keypoint quality evaluation. We predict keypoints with our model on both source and reference point clouds, and use the human annotation on the reference point cloud to align our keypoints with annotated keypoints. The closet keypoint to a human annotation point is considered to be aligned with the annotation. DAS then calculates the ratio of aligned keypoints between the source and reference point clouds.

The results are shown in Table 1. It can be found that ISS is significantly inferior to others, because it tries to find distinctive and repeatable points rather than points with semantic information. Compared with two recent unsupervised learning methods, our method also surpasses them in most categories.

Table 1. Comparative DAS performance on KeypointNet.

	Airplane	Chair	Car	Table	Bathtub	Guitar	Mug	Cap	Mean
Fernandez et al. [9]	61.4	64.3	–	–	–	–	–	–	62.85
Skeleton Merger [18]	77.7	76.8	**79.4**	70.0	69.2	**63.1**	67.2	53.0	69.55
ISS [36]	13.1	10.7	8.0	16.2	9.2	8.7	11.2	13.1	11.28
Ours	**81.0**	**83.1**	74.0	**78.5**	**71.2**	61.3	**68.2**	**57.1**	**71.8**

Table 2. Comparative mIoU performance on KeypointNet.

	Airplane	Chair	Car	Table	Bed	Skateboard	Mean
Fernandez et al. [9]	69.7	51.2	–	–	–	–	–
Skeleton Merger [18]	**79.4**	68.4	47.8	50.0	**47.2**	40.1	55.48
ISS [36]	36.3	11.6	20.3	24.1	33.7	31.0	26.16
Ours	79.1	**68.9**	**51.7**	**54.1**	45.4	**43.3**	**57.08**

Mean Intersection over Union. We report the mIoU of predicted keypoints and ground truth ones. The results are shown in Table 2.

As witnessed by the table, our method achieves the best performance on four categories. Note that Fernandez et al. [9] only reported results on the 'Airplane' and 'Chair' categories, while our method still outperforms it on these two categories.

Part Correspondence Ratio. We also test the mean part correspondence ratio on the ShapeNet Part dataset. This metric is not as strict as DAS and mIoU, because it defines two semantic keypoints as corresponding if they are in the same semantic part of objects in a category. The comparative results are shown in Table 3.

Due the that the part correspondence ratio is a loose metric, the gaps among tested methods are not as dramatic as those in Tables 1 and 2. Remarkably, our method also achieves the best performance under this metric.

Table 3. Mean correspondence ratio results on ShapeNet part dataset.

	Airplane	Chair	Table	Mean
USIP [12]	77.0	70.2	81.5	76.23
D3Feat [2]	79.9	84.0	79.1	81.00
Harris3D [21]	76.9	70.3	84.2	77.13
ISS [36]	72.2	68.1	83.3	74.53
SIFT3D [13]	73.5	70.9	84.1	76.17
Ours	**81.5**	**85.2**	**85.7**	**84.13**

Visualization. We first visualize the 3D keypoint distribution and the keypoint features based on t-SNE in Fig. 6, where different colors indicate different semantic labels. Here, we take the skeleton merger method as a comparison.

It can bee seen that our method ensures more consistent alignment of semantic keypoints, as keypoints of the same semantic label tend to be close to each other in the 3D space. Besides, the t-SNE results suggest that our encoder learns more distinctive category-level information from point clouds. Finally, we give a comparative semantic keypoint detection results in Fig. 7.

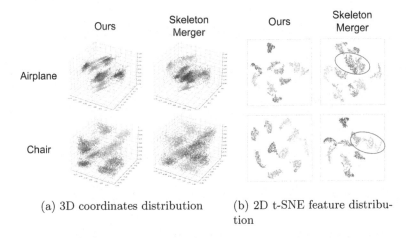

(a) 3D coordinates distribution   (b) 2D t-SNE feature distribution

Fig. 6. Distribution of semantic keypoints in the 3D space and keypoint features in the 2D space with t-SNE. Points with the same semantic label are rendered with the same color.

4.2   Robustness

We test the repeatability of predicted keypoints under Gaussian noise to show the robustness of our method. Specifically, Gaussian noise with different scales are injected to the point cloud, and if the keypoint localization error on noisy point clouds are greater than a distance threshold (0.1 in this experiment), we treat the detected keypoint is not repeatable. The results in shown in Fig. 8.

It suggests that our method holds good robustness to noise, which can be more clearly reflected by the right visualization results in Fig. 8.

We also test the generalization ability on a real-world scanned dataset [6]. We split chairs from the large scene in ScanNet [6] according to the semantic label, and perform random sampling to opt 2048 points from the raw data. Our model is trained on normalized ShapeNet, and tested on the real-world scanned chairs. The result is shown in Fig. 9. One can see that on real-world data, the model can still predict semantic consistent points without re-training.

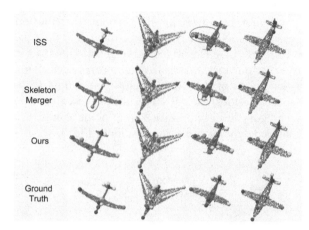

Fig. 7. Keypoints predicted by different methods. Keypoints are rendered with different colors to show semantic consistency.

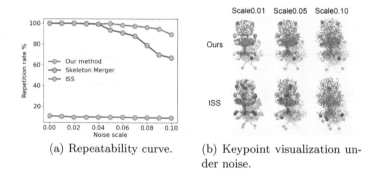

(a) Repeatability curve.   (b) Keypoint visualization under noise.

Fig. 8. Robustness test. This experiment is tested on the airplane (a) and chair (b) categories from ShapeNet [3].

4.3   Ablation Study

To verify the effectiveness of mutual reconstruction, we compare a variation of our method without mutual reconstruction ('w/o m-rec') with the original method. The results are shown in Table 4.

It can be found that mutual reconstruction can significantly improve the performance as verified by both DAS and mIoU metrics. This clearly verifies the effectiveness of mutual reconstruction for unsupervised 3D semantic keypoint detection.

Sofa Chair   Office Chair   Arm Chair

Fig. 9. Test on a real-world scanned dataset. Real-world scanned "Chairs" are taken from the ScanNet [6] dataset.

Table 4. Comparison of the full method and the one without mutual reconstruction.

	Airplane	Chair	Car	Table	Mean
Full method (DAS)	**81.0**	**83.1**	**74.0**	**78.5**	**79.15**
w/o m-rec (DAS)	67.2	61.3	60.3	71.2	65.0
Full method (mIoU)	**79.1**	**68.8**	**51.7**	54.1	**62.85**
w/o m-rec (mIoU)	77.2	52.1	48.2	**56.1**	58.4

5   Conclusions

In this paper, we proposed mutual reconstruction for 3D semantic keypoint detection. Compared with previous works, we mine *category-level semantic information* from 3D point clouds from a novel mutual reconstruction view. In particular, we proposed an unsupervised Siamese network, which first encodes input point clouds into keypoint sets, and then decoding the keypoint features to achieve both self and mutual reconstructions. In the experiments, our method delivers outstanding semantic consistency and robustness performance. Ablation study also validates the effectiveness of mutual reconstruction for unsupervised 3D semantic keypoint detection.

Though preserving global information (e.g., topology) well, the designed decoder tends to reconstruct point clouds in a skeleton-like manner, which consists limited local information. In our future work, we expect the mutual reconstruction model to be capable of detecting keypoints capturing both local and global structures.

Acknowledgment. This work is supported in part by the National Natural Science Foundation of China (NFSC) under Grant 62002295, Natural Science Basic Research Program of Shaanxi (No. 2021JCW-03).

References

1. Achlioptas, P., Diamanti, O., Mitliagkas, I., Guibas, L.: Learning representations and generative models for 3D point clouds. In: International Conference on Machine Learning, pp. 40–49. PMLR (2018)

2. Bai, X., Luo, Z., Zhou, L., Fu, H., Quan, L., Tai, C.L.: D3Feat: joint learning of dense detection and description of 3D local features. In: IEEE Conference on Computer Vision and Pattern Recognition, pp. 6359–6367 (2020)

3. Chang, A.X., et al.: Shapenet: an information-rich 3D model repository. arXiv preprint arXiv:1512.03012 (2015)

4. Chen, H., Bhanu, B.: 3D free-form object recognition in range images using local surface patches. Pattern Recogn. Lett. **28**(10), 1252–1262 (2007)

5. Chen, N., et al.: Unsupervised learning of intrinsic structural representation points. In: IEEE Conference on Computer Vision and Pattern Recognition, pp. 9121–9130 (2020)

6. Dai, A., Chang, A.X., Savva, M., Halber, M., Funkhouser, T., Nießner, M.: Scannet: richly-annotated 3D reconstructions of indoor scenes. In: IEEE Conference on Computer Vision and Pattern Recognition, pp. 5828–5839 (2017)

7. Deng, H., Birdal, T., Ilic, S.: PPF-FoldNet: unsupervised learning of rotation invariant 3D local descriptors. In: European Conference on Computer Vision, pp. 602–618 (2018)

8. Deprelle, T., Groueix, T., Fisher, M., Kim, V., Russell, B., Aubry, M.: Learning elementary structures for 3D shape generation and matching. In: Advances in Neural Information Processing Systems, vol. 32 (2019)

9. Fernandez-Labrador, C., Chhatkuli, A., Paudel, D.P., Guerrero, J.J., Demonceaux, C., Gool, L.V.: Unsupervised learning of category-specific symmetric 3D keypoints from point sets. In: Vedaldi, A., Bischof, H., Brox, T., Frahm, J.-M. (eds.) ECCV 2020. LNCS, vol. 12370, pp. 546–563. Springer, Cham (2020). https://doi.org/10.1007/978-3-030-58595-2_33

10. Jakab, T., Tucker, R., Makadia, A., Wu, J., Snavely, N., Kanazawa, A.: Keypointdeformer: unsupervised 3D keypoint discovery for shape control. In: IEEE Conference on Computer Vision and Pattern Recognition, pp. 12783–12792 (2021)

11. Kingma, D.P., Ba, J.: Adam: a method for stochastic optimization. arXiv preprint arXiv:1412.6980 (2014)

12. Li, J., Lee, G.H.: USIP: unsupervised stable interest point detection from 3D point clouds. In: Proceedings of the IEEE/CVF International Conference on Computer Vision, pp. 361–370 (2019)

13. Lowe, D.G.: Distinctive image features from scale-invariant keypoints. Int. J. Comput. Vision **60**(2), 91–110 (2004)

14. Mian, A., Bennamoun, M., Owens, R.: On the repeatability and quality of keypoints for local feature-based 3d object retrieval from cluttered scenes. Int. J. Comput. Vision **89**(2), 348–361 (2010)

15. Novotny, D., Ravi, N., Graham, B., Neverova, N., Vedaldi, A.: C3DPO: canonical 3D pose networks for non-rigid structure from motion. In: Proceedings of the IEEE/CVF International Conference on Computer Vision, pp. 7688–7697 (2019)

16. Qi, C.R., Su, H., Mo, K., Guibas, L.J.: Pointnet: deep learning on point sets for 3D classification and segmentation. In: IEEE Conference on Computer Vision and Pattern Recognition, pp. 652–660 (2017)

17. Qi, C.R., Yi, L., Su, H., Guibas, L.J.: Pointnet++: deep hierarchical feature learning on point sets in a metric space. arXiv preprint arXiv:1706.02413 (2017)

18. Shi, R., Xue, Z., You, Y., Lu, C.: Skeleton merger: an unsupervised aligned keypoint detector. In: IEEE Conference on Computer Vision and Pattern Recognition, pp. 43–52 (2021)

19. Shu, D.W., Park, S.W., Kwon, J.: 3D point cloud generative adversarial network based on tree structured graph convolutions. In: Proceedings of the IEEE/CVF International Conference on Computer Vision, pp. 3859–3868 (2019)

20. Simonovsky, M., Komodakis, N.: Dynamic edge-conditioned filters in convolutional neural networks on graphs. In: IEEE Conference on Computer Vision and Pattern Recognition, pp. 3693–3702 (2017)

21. Sipiran, I., Bustos, B.: Harris 3D: a robust extension of the harris operator for interest point detection on 3D meshes. Vis. Comput. **27**(11), 963–976 (2011)

22. Sun, J., Ovsjanikov, M., Guibas, L.: A concise and provably informative multi-scale signature based on heat diffusion. In: Computer Graphics Forum, vol. 28, pp. 1383–1392. Wiley Online Library (2009)

23. Tombari, F., Salti, S., Di Stefano, L.: Performance evaluation of 3D keypoint detectors. Int. J. Comput. Vision **102**(1), 198–220 (2013)

24. Tombari, F., Salti, S., Di Stefano, L.: Unique signatures of histograms for local surface description. In: Daniilidis, K., Maragos, P., Paragios, N. (eds.) ECCV 2010. LNCS, vol. 6313, pp. 356–369. Springer, Heidelberg (2010). https://doi.org/10.1007/978-3-642-15558-1_26

25. Tulsiani, S., Su, H., Guibas, L.J., Efros, A.A., Malik, J.: Learning shape abstractions by assembling volumetric primitives. In: IEEE Conference on Computer Vision and Pattern Recognition, pp. 2635–2643 (2017)

26. Wang, H., Guo, J., Yan, D.M., Quan, W., Zhang, X.: Learning 3D keypoint descriptors for non-rigid shape matching. In: European Conference on Computer Vision, pp. 3–19 (2018)

27. Wang, Y., Sun, Y., Liu, Z., Sarma, S.E., Bronstein, M.M., Solomon, J.M.: Dynamic graph CNN for learning on point clouds. ACM Trans. Graph. **38**(5), 1–12 (2019)

28. Wu, W., Qi, Z., Fuxin, L.: Pointconv: deep convolutional networks on 3D point clouds. In: IEEE Conference on Computer Vision and Pattern Recognition, pp. 9621–9630 (2019)

29. Yang, G., Huang, X., Hao, Z., Liu, M.Y., Belongie, S., Hariharan, B.: Pointflow: 3D point cloud generation with continuous normalizing flows. In: Proceedings of the IEEE/CVF International Conference on Computer Vision, pp. 4541–4550 (2019)

30. Yang, Y., Feng, C., Shen, Y., Tian, D.: Foldingnet: point cloud auto-encoder via deep grid deformation. In: IEEE Conference on Computer Vision and Pattern Recognition, pp. 206–215 (2018)

31. Yifan, W., Aigerman, N., Kim, V.G., Chaudhuri, S., Sorkine-Hornung, O.: Neural cages for detail-preserving 3D deformations. In: IEEE Conference on Computer Vision and Pattern Recognition, pp. 75–83 (2020)

32. You, Y., et al.: Keypointnet: a large-scale 3D keypoint dataset aggregated from numerous human annotations. In: IEEE Conference on Computer Vision and Pattern Recognition, pp. 13647–13656 (2020)

33. Yu, L., Li, X., Fu, C.W., Cohen-Or, D., Heng, P.A.: PU-Net: point cloud upsampling network. In: IEEE Conference on Computer Vision and Pattern Recognition, pp. 2790–2799 (2018)

34. Yumer, M.E., Chaudhuri, S., Hodgins, J.K., Kara, L.B.: Semantic shape editing using deformation handles. ACM Trans. Graph. **34**(4), 1–12 (2015)

35. Zaharescu, A., Boyer, E., Varanasi, K., Horaud, R.: Surface feature detection and description with applications to mesh matching. In: IEEE Conference on Computer Vision and Pattern Recognition, pp. 373–380. IEEE (2009)

36. Zhong, Y.: Intrinsic shape signatures: a shape descriptor for 3D object recognition. In: International Conference on Computer Vision Workshops, pp. 689–696. IEEE (2009)

MvDeCor: Multi-view Dense Correspondence Learning for Fine-Grained 3D Segmentation

Gopal Sharma[1], Kangxue Yin[2(✉)], Subhransu Maji[1], Evangelos Kalogerakis[1], Or Litany[2], and Sanja Fidler[2,3,4]

[1] University of Massachusetts Amherst, Amherst, USA
[2] NVIDIA, Santa Clara, USA
kangxuey@nvidia.com
[3] University of Toronto, Toronto, Canada
[4] Vector Institute, Toronto, Canada

Abstract. We propose to utilize self-supervised techniques in the 2D domain for fine-grained 3D shape segmentation tasks. This is inspired by the observation that view-based surface representations are more effective at modeling high-resolution surface details and texture than their 3D counterparts based on point clouds or voxel occupancy. Specifically, given a 3D shape, we render it from multiple views, and set up a dense correspondence learning task within the contrastive learning framework. As a result, the learned 2D representations are view-invariant and geometrically consistent, leading to better generalization when trained on a limited number of labeled shapes than alternatives based on self-supervision in 2D or 3D alone. Experiments on textured (RenderPeople) and untextured (PartNet) 3D datasets show that our method outperforms state-of-the-art alternatives in fine-grained part segmentation. The improvements over baselines are greater when only a sparse set of views is available for training or when shapes are textured, indicating that MvDeCor benefits from both 2D processing and 3D geometric reasoning. Project page: https://nv-tlabs.github.io/MvDeCor/.

1 Introduction

Part-level interpretation of 3D shapes is critical for many applications in computer graphics and vision, including 3D content editing, animation, simulation and synthesizing virtual datasets for visual perception, just to name a few. Specifically, our goal in this work is to perform fine-grained shape segmentation from

---

G. Sharma—The work was mainly done during Gopal's internship at NVIDIA.

Supplementary Information The online version contains supplementary material available at https://doi.org/10.1007/978-3-031-20086-1_32.

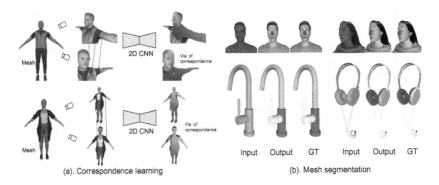

(a). Correspondence learning   (b). Mesh segmentation

Fig. 1. The MvDeCor pipeline. (a) Dense 2D representations are learned using pixel-level correspondences guided by 3D shapes. (b) The 2D representations can be fine-tuned using a few labels for 3D shape segmentation tasks in a multi-view setting.

limited available data. This poses two main challenges. First, training deep networks relies on large-scale labeled datasets that require tremendous annotation effort. For this reason, previous methods have proposed self-supervised feature extraction, however these mostly rely on point cloud or voxel-based networks. This brings us to the second challenge – these 3D networks have a limited ability to capture fine-grained surface details in their input points or voxels due to the limits on the sampling density.

We present MvDeCor, a self-supervised technique for learning dense 3D shape representations based on the task of learning correspondences across views of a 3D shape (Fig. 1). At training time we render 3D shapes from multiple views with known correspondences and setup a contrastive learning task to train 2D CNNs. In doing so, we take advantage of the excellent abilities of 2D networks to capture fine details. The learned 2D representations can be directly used for part segmentation on images, or projected onto the shape surface to produce a 3D representation for 3D tasks (Figs. 1 and 2). The approach works well in standard few-shot fine-grained 3D part segmentation benchmarks, outperforming prior work based on 2D and 3D self-supervised learning (Sect. 3, Tables 1 and 2).

Many previous representation learning methods for 3D shapes are based on self-reconstruction loss [2,6,10,15,42] or contrastive learning [20,41,44] where point clouds and voxels are the main choices of 3D data formats. In contrast, our work is motivated from the observation that view-based surface representations are more effective at modeling high-resolution surface details and texture than their 3D counterparts based on point clouds or voxel occupancy. We also benefit from recent advances in network architectures and self-supervised learning for 2D CNNs. In addition, our approach allows training the network using 2D labeled views rather than fully labeled 3D shapes. This is particularly beneficial because annotating 3D shapes for fine-grained semantic segmentation is often done using 2D projections of the shape to avoid laborious 3D manipulation operations [43].

Compared to techniques based on 3D self-supervision, MvDECOR demonstrates significant advantages. On the PartNet dataset [28] with fine-grained (Level-3) parts, our method achieves 32.6% mIOU compared to a PointContrast [41], a self-supervised learning technique that achieves 31.0% mIOU (Table 1). While some of the benefit comes from the advantages of view-based representations, e.g., off-the-self 2D CNNs trained from scratch outperform their 3D counterparts, this alone does not explain the performance gains. MvDECOR outperforms both ImageNet pretrained models (29.3% mIOU) and dense contrastive learning [39] (30.8% mIOU), suggesting that our correspondence-driven self-supervision is beneficial. These improvements over baselines are even larger when sparse view supervision is provided - MvDECOR generalizes to novel views as it has learned a view invariant local representations of shapes (Table 2).

We also present experiments on the RenderPeople [1] dataset consisting of textured 3D shapes of humans, which we label with 13 parts (Sect. 4). We observe that 2D self-supervised techniques performs better than their 3D counterparts, while MvDECOR offers larger gains over both 2D and 3D baselines (Table 4). Surprisingly on this dataset we find that when texture is available, the view-based representations do not require the use of depth and normal information, and in fact the models generalize better without those, as explained in Sect. 4.6. MvDECOR gives 17.3% mIOU improvement over training a network from scratch when only a few labeled examples are provided for supervision.

To summarize, we show that multi-view dense correspondence learning induces view-invariant local representations that generalize well on few-shot 3D part segmentation tasks. Our approach MvDECOR outperforms state-of-the art 2D contrastive learning methods, as well as 3D contrastive learning methods that operate on point cloud representations. After a discussion of prior work on 2D and 3D self-supervised learning in Sect. 2, we describe our method and experiments in Sect. 3 and Sect. 4 respectively.

2   Related Works

Our work lies at the intersection of 3D self-supervision, 2D self-supervision, and multi-view representations.

3D Self-supervision. Many self-supervised approaches in 3D shape are based on training an autoencoder with a reconstruction loss. For example, Achlioptas *et al.* [2] train a PointNet [30] with a Chamfer or EMD loss. FoldingNet [42] deforms a 2D grid using a deep network conditioned on the shape encoding to match the output shape. AtlasNet [15] uses multiple decoders to reconstruct the surface as a collection of patches. BAE-NET [6] splits reconstruction across decoding branches, but adopted an implicit field shape representation instead of point clouds. Once trained the representations from the encoder can be used for downstream tasks. Alternatives to reconstruction include prediction based on k-means [18], convex decomposition [9,26], primitive fitting [24,33,36] and 3D jigsaw puzzles [3,32]. Unsupervised learning for recovering dense correspondences between non-rigid shapes has been studied in [12,16], however it relies

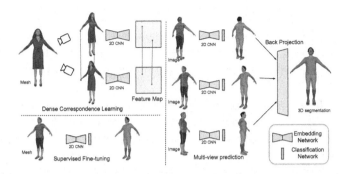

Fig. 2. Overview of MvDeCor. *Top left:* Our self-supervision approach takes two overlapping views (RGB image, with optional normal and depth maps) of a 3D shape and passes it through a network that produces per-pixel embeddings. We define a dense contrastive loss promoting similarity between matched pixels and minimizing similarity between un-matched pixels. *Bottom left:* Once the network is trained we add a segmentation head and fine-tune the entire architecture on a few labeled examples to predict per-pixel semantic labels. *Right:* Labels predicted by the 2D network for each view are back-projected to the 3D surface and aggregated using a voting scheme.

on a near-isometry assumption that does not fit clothed people and furniture parts, used in our work. We instead use partial correspondences from the 3D models to supervise 2D networks. Wang *et al.* [37] proposed a deep deformation approach that aligns a labeled template shape to unlabeled target shapes to transfer labels. However this method is not effective for fine-grained segmentation of shapes as shown in Sect. 4, since deformation often distorts surface details. A few recent works [38,41,44] have learned per-point representations for point clouds under a contrastive learning framework. Networks pre-trained in this way are further fine-tuned for 3D downstream tasks. However, point cloud based shape representations limit the ability to capture fine-grained details and texture.

2D Self-supervision. While early work focused on training networks based on proxy tasks such as image colorization, rotation prediction, and jigsaw puzzles, contrastive learning [5,14,19,40] has emerged as a popular technique. Most of these representations are based on variants of InfoNCE loss [29], where the mutual information between two views of an image obtained by applying synthetic transformations is maximized. DenseCL [39] modifies the contrastive approach to include information across locations within an image to learn dense representations. We use this method as the representative 2D self-supervised baseline. However, the above methods work on the 2D domain and lack any 3D priors incorporated either in the network or in the training losses. Correspondence learning has been used as self-supervision task to learn local descriptors for geometric matching in structure from motion applications [21,27,31,39]. However, much of this work has focused on instance matching, while our goal is to generalize across part instances within a category. The most related work to ours is Pri3D [21] that also proposes to learns geometry-aware embedding with a contrastive loss based on pixel correspondences across views. Their work focuses on improving 2D representations using 3D supervision for 2D tasks such as scene segmentation and object detection, while we deal with fine-grained 3D segmentation.

Multi-view Representation. Our method is motivated by earlier multi-view approaches for 3D shape recognition and segmentation [8,22,23,25,34]. In these approaches, multiple views of the shapes are processed by a 2D network to obtain pixel-level representations. These are back-projected to the 3D shape to produce 3D surface representations. More recently, Kundu *et al.* [25] applies multi-view fusion for 3D semantic segmentation of scenes. Genova et al. [11] leverage a pre-trained 2D segmentation network to synthesize pseudo-labels for training a 3D segmentation network. The above approaches benefit from large-scale pretraining on image dataset, and the ability of 2D CNNs to handle higher image resolutions compared to voxel grids and point clouds. They continue to outperform 3D deep networks on many 3D tasks (e.g., [13,35]). Semantic-NeRF [45] jointly reconstructs geometry and semantics of a 3D scene from multi-view images with partial or noisy labels. All the above view-based methods are trained in a supervised or weakly supervised manner, while ours is based on self-supervision.

3   Method

Our goal is to learn a multi-view representation for 3D shapes for the task of fine-grained 3D shape segmentation. For this task, we assume a large dataset of unlabeled 3D shapes and a small number of labeled examples. For the latter, we consider two settings (1) when labels are provided on the surface of the 3D shape, and (2) labels are provided on the images (projections) of the 3D shape. To that end, we use multi-view dense correspondence learning for pre-training, followed by a feature fine-tuning stage on the downstream segmentation task. In the pre-training stage described in Sect. 3.1, we have a set of unlabeled 3D shapes (either with or w/o textures) from which we render 2D views, and build ground-truth dense correspondences between them. After pre-training on the dense correspondence learning task, the network learns pixel-level features that are robust to view changes and is aware of fine-grained details.

In the fine-tuning stage (Sect. 3.2), we train a simple convolutional head on top of the pixel-level embeddings, supervised by a small number of annotated examples, to segment the multi-view renderings of the 3D shapes. The network pre-trained in this fashion produces better segmentation results under the few-shot semantic segmentation regime in comparison to baselines. We aggregate multi-view segmentation maps onto 3D surface via an entropy-based voting scheme (Sect. 3.3). Figure 2 shows the overview of our approach.

3.1   Multi-view Dense Correspondence Learning

Let us denote the set of *unlabeled* shapes as $\mathcal{X}_u$. Each shape instance $X \in \mathcal{X}_u$ can be rendered from a viewpoint i into color, normal and depth images denoted as V^i. We use a 2D CNN backbone $\boldsymbol{\Phi}$ which maps each view into pixel-wise embeddings $\{\boldsymbol{\Phi}(V^i)_p\} \in \mathbb{R}^D$, where p is an index of a pixel and D is the dimensionality of the embedding space. We pre-train the network $\boldsymbol{\Phi}$ using the following self-supervised loss:

$$\mathcal{L}_{\mathsf{ssl}} = \mathop{\mathbb{E}}_{\substack{V^i, V^j \sim \mathcal{R}(X) \\ X \sim \mathcal{X}_u}} \left[\ell_{\mathsf{ssl}}\big(\boldsymbol{\Phi}(V^i), \boldsymbol{\Phi}(V^j)\big) \right] \tag{1}$$

where $\mathcal{R}(X)$ is the set of 2D renderings of shape X, and V^i and V^j are sampled renderings in different views from $\mathcal{R}(X)$. The self-supervision loss ℓ_{ssl} is applied to the pair of sampled views V^i and V^j.

Since V^i and V^j originate from the 3D mesh, each foreground pixel in the rendered images corresponds to a 3D point on the surface of a 3D object. We find matching pixels from V^i and V^j when their corresponding points in 3D lie within a small threshold radius. We use the obtained dense correspondences in the self-supervision task. Specifically, we train the network to minimize the distance between pixel embeddings that correspond to the same points in 3D space and maximize the distance between unmatched pixel embeddings. This encourages the network to learn pixel embeddings to be invariant to views, which is a non-trivial task, as two rendered views of the same shape may look quite different, consisting of different contexts and scales. We use InfoNCE [29] as the self-supervision loss. Given two rendered images (V^i and V^j) from the same shape X and pairs of matching pixels p and q, the InfoNCE loss is defined as:

$$\ell_{\mathsf{ssl}}\big(\boldsymbol{\Phi}(V^i), \boldsymbol{\Phi}(V^j)\big) = - \sum_{(p,q) \in M} \log \frac{\exp\big(\boldsymbol{\Phi}(V^i)_p \cdot \boldsymbol{\Phi}(V^j)_q / \tau\big)}{\sum_{(.,k) \in M} \exp\big(\boldsymbol{\Phi}(V^i)_p \cdot \boldsymbol{\Phi}(V^j)_k / \tau\big)}, \tag{2}$$

where $\boldsymbol{\Phi}(V^i)_p$ is the embedding of pixel p in view i, M is the set of paired pixels between two views that correspond to the same points in 3D space, and the temperature is set to $\tau = 0.07$ in our experiments. We use two views that have at least 15% overlap. The output $\boldsymbol{\Phi}(V^i)_p$ and $\boldsymbol{\Phi}(V^j)_q$ of the embedding module are normalized to a unit hyper-sphere. Pairs of matching pixels are treated as positive pairs. The above loss also requires sampling of negative pairs. Given the matching pixels $(p, q) \in M$ from V^i and V^j respectively, for each pixel p from the first view, the rest of the pixels $k \neq q$ appearing in M and belonging to the second view, yield the negative pixel pairs (p, k).

3.2   Semantic Segmentation of 3D Shapes

In the fine-grained shape segmentation stage, the network learns to predict pixel level segmentation labels. Once the embedding module is pre-trained using the self-supervised approach, it is further fine-tuned in the segmentation stage, using a small labeled shape set $\mathcal{X}_l$ to compute a supervised loss, as follows:

$$\min_{\boldsymbol{\Phi}, \boldsymbol{\Theta}} \lambda \mathcal{L}_{\mathsf{ssl}} + \mathcal{L}_{\mathsf{sl}}, \text{ where } \mathcal{L}_{\mathsf{sl}} = \mathop{\mathbb{E}}_{(X,Y) \sim \mathcal{X}_l} \left[\mathop{\mathbb{E}}_{(V^i, L^i) \in \mathcal{R}(X,Y)} \ell_{\mathsf{sl}}\big(L^i, \boldsymbol{\Theta} \circ \boldsymbol{\Phi}(V^i)\big) \right], \tag{3}$$

and Θ is the segmentation module, λ is a hyper-parameter set to 0.001, and ℓ_{sl} is the semantic segmentation loss implemented using cross-entropy loss applied to each view of the shape separately. $\mathcal{R}(X,Y)$ is the set of renderings for shape X and its 3D label map Y. L^i represents the projected labels from the 3D shape for view V^i. Since the labeled set is much smaller than the unlabeled set, the network could overfit to the small set. To avoid this over-fitting during the fine-tuning stage, we use the self-supervision loss $\mathcal{L}_{ssl}$ as an auxiliary loss along with supervision loss $\mathcal{L}_{sl}$ as is shown in Eq. 3. In Table 5 we show that incorporating this regularization improves the performance.

During inference we render multiple overlapping views of the 3D shape and segment each view. The per-pixel labels are then projected onto the surface. We use ray-tracing to encode the triangle index of the mesh for each pixel. To aggregate labels from different views for each triangle, one option is to use majority-voting. An illustration of the process is shown in Fig. 2. However, not all views should contribute equally towards the final label for each triangle as some views may not be suitable to recognize a particular part of the shape. We instead define a weighted voting scheme based on the average entropy of the probability distribution predicted by the network for a view. Specifically, a weight $W^{(i)} = (1 - \sum_{p \in F^{(i)}} H^{(i,p)} / |F^{(i)}|)^{\gamma}$ is given to the view i, where $F^{(i)}$ is its set of foreground pixels, $H^{(i,p)}$ is the entropy of the probability distribution predicted by the network at pixel p, and γ is a hyperparameter set to 20 in our experiments. More weight is given to the view with less entropy. Consequently, for each triangle t on the mesh of the 3D shape, the label is predicted as: $l_t = \arg\max_{c \in C} \sum_{i \in I, p \in t} W^{(i)} P^{(i,p)}$, where I is the set of views where the triangle t is visible, $P^{(i,p)}$ is the probability distribution of classes at a pixel $p \in t$ in view i, and C is the set of segmentation classes. In cases where no labels are projected to a triangle due to occlusion, we assign a label to the triangle by nearest neighbor search.

3.3   Implementation Details

The embedding Φ is implemented as the DeepLabV3+ network [4] originally proposed for image segmentation with ResNet-50 backbone. We add extra channels in the first layer to incorporate depth and normal maps. Specifically, it takes a K-channel image (V^i) as input of size $H \times W \times K$ and outputs $\Phi(V^i)$ per pixel features of size $H \times W \times 64$, where the size of pixel embedding is 64. In the second stage, we add a segmentation head (a 2D convolutional layer with a softmax) on top of the pixel embedding network to produce per-pixel semantic labels. Additional architecture details are provided in the supplementary material.

To generate the dataset for the self-supervision stage, we start by placing a virtual camera at 2 unit radius around the origin-centered and unit normalized mesh. We then render a fixed number of images by placing the camera at uniform positions and adding random small perturbations in the viewing angle and scale. In practice, we use approximately 90 rendered images per shape to cover most of the surface area of the shapes. We also render depth and normal maps for each view. Normal maps are represented in a global coordinate system. Depth maps are normalized within each view. We use ray tracing to record the triangle index to which each pixel corresponds to and also the point-of-hit for each pixel. This helps in identifying correspondences between two views of the same shape. More information is provided in the supplementary material.

4   Experiments and Results

4.1   Dataset

We use the following datasets in our experiments, samples from which are visualized in the Supplement. The license information is provided in the Supplement.

PartNet [28]. This dataset provides *fine-grained* semantic segmentation annotation for various 3D shape categories, unlike the more coarse-level shape parts in the ShapeNet-Part dataset. We use 17 categories from "level-3", which denotes the finest level of segmentation. On average the categories contain 16 parts, ranging from 4 for the Display category, to 51 for Table category. For training in the few-shot framework, we use the entire training and validation set as the self-supervision dataset $\mathcal{X}_u$, and select k shapes from the train set as labeled dataset $\mathcal{X}_l$ for the fine-tuning stage.

RenderPeople [1]. This dataset contains 1000 human textured models represented as triangle meshes in two poses. We use 936 shapes of them for self-supervision. We label the remaining 64 shapes with 13 different labels, while focusing more on facial semantic parts. The 64 labeled shapes consist of 32 different identities in 2 poses. We randomly split the 32 identities into 16 and 16, so that we get 32 shapes as the labeled training set, and 32 shapes as the test set for evaluation. More details of the labeling and individual semantic parts are provided in the Supplement.

ShapeNet-Part [43]. We also show experiments on ShapeNet-Part dataset in the Supplementary material where we outperform previous works according to the class-average mIOU metric.

4.2   Experiment Settings

Segmentation Using Limited Labeled Shapes. We pre-train our 2D embedding network and fine-tune it with a segmentation head using k labeled shapes. During fine-tuning, each shape is rendered from 86 different views. We render extra 10 images for the RenderPeople dataset that focuses more on details of facial regions. Each view consists of a grayscale image for PartNet dataset and textured image for RenderPeople dataset, a normal and a depth map for both datasets. For PartNet dataset, pre-training is done using all shape categories and fine-tuning is done on individual category specific manner. All experiments in this few-shot setting are run 5 times on randomly selected k labeled training shapes and the average part mIOU is reported.

Segmentation Using Limited Labeled Views per Shape. In this setting supervision is available in 2D domain in the form of sparse set of labeled views per shape. Specifically, a small number of k shapes are provided with a small number of v labeled views per shape. For training 3D baselines, labeled views are projected to 3D mesh and corresponding points are used for supervision. Similar to the first setting, all experiments are run 5 times on randomly selected k labeled training shapes and the average part mIOU is reported.

4.3   Baselines

We compare our method against the following baselines:

- **(2D) Scratch.** In this baseline, we train our 2D networks (Φ and segmentation head Θ) directly using the small set of labeled examples, without pre-training, and apply the same multi-view aggregation.
- **(2D) ImageNet.** We create a baseline in which the backbone ResNet in our embedding network Φ is initialized with ImageNet pre-trained weights and the entire network is fine-tuned using few-labeled examples. The first layer of ResNet trained on Imagenet is adapted to take the extra channels (normal and depth maps) following the method proposed in ShapePFCN [23].
- **(2D) DenseCL.** To compare with the 2D dense contrastive learning method we also create a baseline using DenseCL [39]. We pre-train this method on our unlabeled dataset $\mathcal{X}_u$ using their original codebase. Once this network is trained, we initialize the backbone network with the pre-trained weights and fine-tune the entire architecture using the available labeled set. Further details about training these baselines are in the Supplement.
- **(3D) Scratch.** In this baseline, we train a 3D ResNet based on sparse convolutions (Minkowski Engine [7]) that takes uniformly sampled points and their normals from the surface and predicts semantic labels for each point. We train this network directly using the small set of labeled examples.
- **(3D) PointContrast.** To compare with the 3D self-supervision methods, we pre-train the above 3D ResNet (Minkowski Engine) on $\mathcal{X}_u$ using the approach proposed in PointContrast [41]. The pre-trained network is later fine-tuned by adding a segmentation head (a 3D convolution layer and softmax) on top to predict per-point semantic labels. We use the codebase provided by authors to train the network. Details are provided in the Supplement.
- **(3D) Weak supervision via learned deformation.** We use the approach by Wang *et al.* [37], which uses learning-based deformation and transfer of labels from the labeled set to unlabeled shapes. We use our labeled and unlabeled set to train this method using the code provided by the authors.

4.4   Visualization of Learned Embeddings

Our self-supervision is based on enforcing consistency in pixel embeddings across views for pixels that corresponds to the same point in 3D. In Fig. 3 we visualize correspondences using our learned embeddings between human subjects from the RenderPeople dataset in different costumes and poses. The smoothness and consistency in correspondences implies that the network can be fine-tuned with few labeled examples and still perform well on unseen examples.

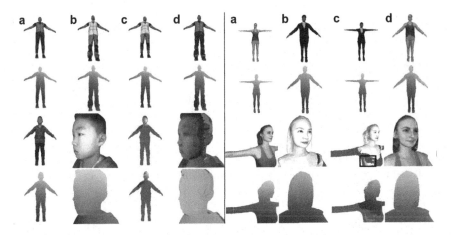

Fig. 3. Visualization of learned embeddings. Given a pair of images in (a) and (b), our network produces per-pixel embedding for each image. We map pixels from (b) to (a) according to feature similarity, resulting in (c). Similarly (d) is generated by transferring texture from (a) to (b). For pixels which have similarity below a threshold are colored red. We visualize the smoothness of our learned correspondence in the second and forth row. Our method learns to produce correct correspondences between human subject in different clothing and same human subject in different camera poses (left). Our approach also finds correct correspondences between different human subjects in different poses (right). Mistakes are highlighted using black boxes. (Color figure online)

4.5   Few-shot Segmentation on PartNet

k Fully Labeled Shapes. Table 1 shows results using the part mIOU metric on few-shot semantic segmentation on PartNet dataset using $k = 10$ fully labeled shapes. Our method performs better than the network trained from scratch by 4% (part mIOU) showing the effectiveness of our self-supervision approach. Our architecture initialized with ImageNet pre-trained weights, improves performance over training from scratch, implying pre-training on large labeled datasets is helpful even when the domain is different. The DenseCL baseline, which is trained on our dataset, improves performance over ImageNet pre-trained weights, owing to the effectiveness of contrastive learning at instance level and at dense level. Interestingly, 2D training from scratch performs better than 3D training from scratch. The learned deformation based alignment approach [37] performs worse because aligning shapes of different topology and structure does

Table 1. Few-shot segmentation on the Partnet dataset with limited labeled shapes. 10 fully labeled shapes are provided for training. Evaluation is done on the test set of PartNet using the mean part-iou metric (%). Training is done per category separately. Results are reported by averaging over 5 random runs.

Methods	Mean	Fau.	Vase	Earph.	Knife	Bed	Bot.	Dishw.	Clock	Door	Micro.	Fridge	Stor.F.	Trash	Dis
# semantic parts		12	6	10	10	15	9	7	11	5	6	7	24	11	4
(2D) Scratch	32.0	29.9	31.5	32.4	25.0	27.3	30.5	34.1	19.2	26.7	35.1	26.8	19.3	33.6	76.4
(2D) ImageNet	32.8	30.1	34.5	33.1	23.8	29.2	30.8	32.9	20.1	28.1	36.1	27.5	19.6	34.7	**78.7**
(2D) DenseCL [39]	34.2	**31.4**	35.4	33.6	22.7	30.8	33.7	36.7	19.7	28.9	41.9	30.2	21.2	34.7	78.3
(3D) Scratch	30.3	27.7	28.8	28.4	19.8	24.5	25.8	39.4	15.9	24.3	37.7	30.9	23.5	30.0	67.8
(3D) Deformation [37]	27.5	28.4	27.2	24.7	20.6	12.4	34.7	30.9	17.4	26.1	38.8	24.6	14.2	21.0	63.8
(3D) PointContrast [41]	34.1	29.0	35.8	31.0	**25.6**	27.8	32.5	39.9	**22.8**	**29.1**	41.3	**32.5**	**25.2**	31.1	73.4
(2D+3D) MvDeCor	**35.9**	31.1	**39.1**	**34.8**	25.2	**32.4**	**39.2**	**40.0**	20.7	28.7	**44.3**	29.8	22.6	**36.3**	78.2

Table 2. Few-shot segmentation on the PartNet dataset with limited labeled 2D views. 10 shapes, each containing $v = 5$ random labeled views, are used for training. Evaluation is done on the test set of PartNet using the mean part-iou metric (%). Training is done per category separately. Results are averaged over 5 random runs.

Methods	Mean	Fau.	Vase	Earph.	Knife	Bed	Bot.	Dishw.	Clock	Door	Micro.	Fridge	Stor.F.	Trash	Dis
# semantic parts		12	6	10	10	15	9	7	11	5	6	7	24	11	4
(2D) Scratch	25.9	21.7	25.2	26.1	19.3	19.8	25.0	27.3	16.6	25.0	27.9	22.3	13.2	24.2	68.7
(2D) ImageNet	27.1	23.2	27.9	28.1	20.1	21.2	25.4	28.2	16.6	25.6	29.3	23.4	12.6	27.4	70.1
(2D) DenseCL [39]	28.9	23.9	31.3	29.0	21.3	22.4	28.9	29.6	16.4	27.4	33.6	25.0	15.9	28.4	71.9
(3D) Scratch	17.1	14.8	17.6	16.4	12.1	8.2	15.7	19.0	7.7	20.7	20.9	15.8	6.8	10.6	52.9
(3D) PointContrast [41]	28.4	22.3	32.5	28.6	21.2	18.9	25.9	**31.3**	**18.9**	**28.5**	31.4	24.8	15.5	25.8	**72.1**
(2D+3D) MvDeCor	**30.3**	**25.5**	**33.7**	**31.6**	**22.4**	**24.9**	**31.7**	31.0	16.2	25.8	**35.7**	**25.6**	**17.0**	**31.4**	71.2

not align semantic parts well. Furthermore, alignment is agnostic to the difference in the set of fine-grained semantic parts between shapes. The 3D sparse convolution network pre-trained using point contrastive learning on our dataset and fine-tuned with few labeled shapes performs better than all previous baselines. Finally our approach, that uses dense contrastive learning at pixel level outperforms all baselines.

Sparse Labeled 2D Views. Table 2 shows the results on few-shot semantic segmentation on PartNet dataset using sparse 2D views for supervision. Here, the DenseCL baseline outperforms training from scratch and the ImageNet initialized network. DenseCL also outperforms the 3D PointContrast baseline, showing the effectiveness of 2D architectures and 2D self-supervision. Finally, our approach outperforms all baselines. Note that evaluation on Chairs, Lamps and Tables categories is shown separately in Table 3 with $k = 30$, because our randomly selected $k = 10$ shapes do not cover all the part labels of these classes. In this setting our approach outperforms the baselines.

4.6   Few-Shot Segmentation on RenderPeople

To evaluate our method on the textured dataset, we use the RenderPeople dataset. We use the same set of 2D and 3D baselines as described in Sect. 4.3.

Note that, we provide color and normal with point cloud input to 3D Scratch and 3D PointContrast. In addition to the settings described in Sect. 4.2, we analyze the effect of different inputs given to the network, i.e. when only RGB images are used as input for self-supervision and fine-tuning, and when both RGB images and geometry information (normal + depth maps) are available for self-supervision and fine-tuning. We train all baselines in these two settings, except 3D baselines that take geometry by construction. The results are shown in Table 4.

RGB+Geom. In the first setting when RGB is used as input along with geometry information (normal + depth), our approach outperforms all the baselines, with 3.5% and 9.7% improvement on training from scratch when only $k = 5$ labeled shapes are given and when $k = 5$ shapes with $v = 3$ views are given for supervision respectively. We use only 3 views for RenderPeople dataset because

Table 3. Few-shot segmentation on the PartNet dataset. Left: 30 fully labeled shapes are used for training. **Right:** 30 shapes are used for training, each containing $v = 5$ random labeled views. Evaluation is done on the test set of PartNet with the mean part-iou metric (%). Results are reported by averaging over 5 random runs.

Methods	$k = 30, v =$ all				$k = 30, v = 5$			
	Mean	Chair	Table	Lamp	Mean	Chair	Table	Lamp
# semantic labels		39	51	41		39	51	41
(2D) Scratch	13.7	20.8	10.1	10.3	10.6	15.2	7.3	9.2
(2D) Imagenet	13.7	20.4	9.9	10.8	11.4	16.4	7.7	10.1
(2D) DenseCL [39]	15.7	22.6	11.7	**12.6**	12.0	17.1	8.5	**10.4**
(3D) Scratch 3d	11.5	17.8	8.0	8.7	6.3	10.1	4.5	4.3
(3D) Deformation [37]	6.5	8.4	4.9	6.1	-	-	-	-
(3D) Pointcontrast [41]	14.5	23.0	10.8	9.8	11.8	**20.4**	7.8	7.1
(2D+3D) Ours	**16.6**	**25.3**	**12.9**	11.7	**12.8**	19.3	**9.8**	9.3

Table 4. Few-shot segmentation on the RenderPeople dataset. We evaluate the segmentation performance using the part mIOU metric. We experiment with two kinds of input, 1) when both RGB+Geom. (depth and normal maps) are input, and 2) when only RGB is input to the network. We evaluate all methods when $k = 5, 10$ fully labeled shapes are used for supervision and when $k = 5, 10$ shapes with 3 2D views are available for supervision. MvDeCor consistently outperform baselines on all settings.

Methods	RGB				RGB+Geom.			
	$k=5, v=$ all	$k=10, v=$ all	$k=5, v=3$	$k=10, v=3$	$k=5, v=$ all	$k=10, v=$ all	$k=5, v=3$	$k=10, v=3$
(2D) Scratch	50.2	60.5	38.7	46.3	55.3	62.6	40.6	50.4
(2D) ImageNet	58.8	67.6	48.9	58.1	55.3	63.7	44.3	51.9
(2D) DenseCL [39]	58.3	66.8	46.5	55.5	56.0	64.0	31.0	41.5
(3D) Scratch	-	48.1	-	26.1	35.0	-	14.5	-
(3D) PointContrast [41]	-	61.3	-	56.7	53.0	-	48.5	-
(2D+3D) MvDeCor	**67.5**	**73.8**	**59.6**	**67.4**	**58.8**	**65.0**	**50.3**	**55.1**

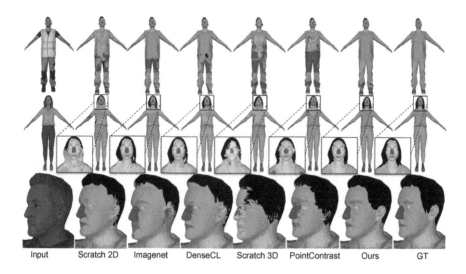

Input   Scratch 2D   Imagenet   DenseCL   Scratch 3D   PointContrast   Ours   GT

Fig. 4. Visualization of predicted semantic labels on the Renderpeople dataset in the few-shot setting when $k = 5$ fully labeled shapes are used for fine-tuning. We visualize the predictions of all baselines. Our method produces accurate semantic labels for 3D shapes even for small parts, such as ears and eyebrows.

of its simpler topology in comparison to 5 views for PartNet. The ImageNet pre-trained model, which is modified to take depth and normal maps as input performs similar to training from scratch, that implies that the domain shift is too large between ImageNet and our dataset. DenseCL applies dense correspondence learning at a coarse grid and hence does not perform well in the dense prediction task when only a few labeled examples are given.

RGB Only. In the second setting, when only RGB image is input to the network, MvDeCor gives 17.3% and 20.9% improvement over training from scratch when only $k = 5$ labeled shapes are given, and when $k = 5$ shapes with $v = 3$ views are given for supervision respectively. The ImageNet and DenseCL both perform better than training from scratch, including their counterpart which takes both RGB+geometry as input. MvDeCor with only RGB as input also performs significantly better than its RGB+geometry counterpart. We expect this behaviour is due to the following reasons: first when geometry is also used as input to the network, the pre-training task focuses more on geometry to produce consistent embeddings, as is shown in Fig. 3, where consistent embeddings are produced between the same human subject in two different costumes. However, when only RGB is input to the network, the pretraining task focuses on RGB color only to learn correspondences. Second, the semantic segmentation of human models requires high reliance on RGB features compared to geometry, and the additional geometry input tends to confuse the pre-trained network.

Figure 4 shows qualitative results of different methods. MvDeCor consistently outperforms all baselines and can segment tiny parts such as eyes, ears and nose. We also refer to the Supplement for more qualitative visualization. Figure 5 shows the effect of multi-view aggregation on 3D segmentation.

Table 5. Effect of renderings and regularization on the RenderPeople dataset. MvDeCor without closeup views for pre-training and fine-tuning performs worse compared to using closeup views. Our regularization term in the loss also shows improvement.

Method	RGB+Geom	RGB
MvDeCor w/o closeup views	51.6	57.4
MvDeCor w/o reg	58.0	67.2
MvDeCor	58.8	67.5

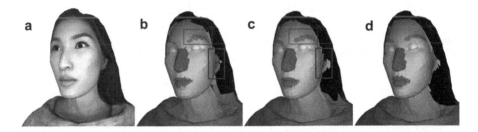

Fig. 5. View aggregation. Given the input in (a), MvDeCor produces 2D labels (b) which can further be improved by multi-view aggregation (c) as is highlighted in boxes and produces segmentation close to the ground truth (d).

Regularization. During the fine-tuning stage, we use an extra regularization term $\lambda \mathcal{L}_{ssl}$ applied on shapes from $\mathcal{X}_u$, to prevent the network from overfitting on the small training set $\mathcal{X}_l$ as described in Sect. 3.2. In Table 5, we show that this regularization improves our performance on the RenderPeople dataset.

Effect of View Selection. We also analyze the effect of view selection. In our previous experiment, we select views by placing camera farther away from the shape to obtain a full context along with placing the camera close to the shape to obtain finer details. The case of removing close-up views during pre-training and fine-tuning stage is examined in Table 5. We observe that closeup views are important for accurate segmentation of small parts. Finally, we also observe that on the RenderPeople dataset, the segmentation performance improves as more views are provided during inference. As the number of views are increased from 5 to 96, the segmentation performance improves from 54.7% to 58.8%.

5   Conclusion

In this paper, we present MvDeCor, a self-supervision method that learns a multi-view representation for 3D shapes with geometric consistency enforced across different views. We pre-train our network with a multi-view dense correspondence learning task, and show that the learned representation outperforms state-of-art methods in our experiments of few-shot fine-grained part segmentation, giving most benefits for textured 3D shapes.

Limitations. Our method relies on 2D renderings of 3D shapes, thus a few surface regions may not be covered due to self-occlusion. In this case, the label predictions in these regions are unreliable. Our self-supervision also requires rendering several views of shapes to make the representations view invariant, which increases the computational cost. Our view selection during pre-training and fine-tuning stage is heuristic-based and can be improved by a learnable approach [17]. A useful future avenue is to combine our approach of 2D correspondence learning with 3D correspondence learning [41] to obtain the best of both worlds. MvDeCor may also open up other potential supervision sources, such as reusing existing image segmentation datasets to segment 3D shapes, exploiting motion in videos to provide correspondence supervision for pre-training.

Acknowledgements.. Subhransu Maji acknowledges support from NSF grants #1749833 and #1908669.

References

1. Renderpeople. https://renderpeople.com/
2. Achlioptas, P., Diamanti, O., Mitliagkas, I., Guibas, L.J.: Learning representations and generative models for 3D point clouds. In: International Conference on Machine Learning (2018)
3. Alliegro, A., Boscaini, D., Tommasi, T.: Joint supervised and self-supervised learning for 3D real world challenges. In: 2020 25th International Conference on Pattern Recognition (ICPR), pp. 6718–6725. IEEE Computer Society (2021)
4. Chen, L.C., Zhu, Y., Papandreou, G., Schroff, F., Adam, H.: Encoder-decoder with atrous separable convolution for semantic image segmentation. In: ECCV (2018)
5. Chen, T., Kornblith, S., Norouzi, M., Hinton, G.: A simple framework for contrastive learning of visual representations. In: International Conference on Machine Learning, pp. 1597–1607 (2020)
6. Chen, Z., Yin, K., Fisher, M., Chaudhuri, S., Zhang, H.: BAE-NET: branched autoencoder for shape co-segmentation. In: International Conference on Computer Vision (ICCV), pp. 8490–8499 (2019)
7. Choy, C., Gwak, J., Savarese, S.: 4D spatio-temporal ConvNets: minkowski convolutional neural networks. In: Computer Vision and Pattern Recognition (CVPR), pp. 3075–3084 (2019)
8. Choy, C.B., Gwak, J., Savarese, S., Chandraker, M.: Universal correspondence network. In: Advances in Neural Information Processing Systems, vol. 30 (2016)

9. Gadelha, M., et al.: Label-efficient learning on point clouds using approximate convex decompositions. In: Vedaldi, A., Bischof, H., Brox, T., Frahm, J.-M. (eds.) ECCV 2020. LNCS, vol. 12355, pp. 473–491. Springer, Cham (2020). https://doi.org/10.1007/978-3-030-58607-2_28

10. Gadelha, M., Wang, R., Maji, S.: Multiresolution tree networks for 3D point cloud processing. In: ECCV (2018)

11. Genova, K., et al.: Learning 3D semantic segmentation with only 2D image supervision. In: International Conference on 3D Vision (3DV), pp. 361–372. IEEE (2021)

12. Ginzburg, D., Raviv, D.: Cyclic functional mapping: self-supervised correspondence between non-isometric deformable shapes. In: Vedaldi, A., Bischof, H., Brox, T., Frahm, J.-M. (eds.) ECCV 2020. LNCS, vol. 12350, pp. 36–52. Springer, Cham (2020). https://doi.org/10.1007/978-3-030-58558-7_3

13. Goyal, A., Law, H., Liu, B., Newell, A., Deng, J.: Revisiting point cloud shape classification with a simple and effective baseline. In: International Conference on Machine Learning (2021)

14. Grill, J.B., et al.: Bootstrap your own latent - a new approach to self-supervised learning. In: Advances in Neural Information Processing Systems, vol. 33 (2020)

15. Groueix, T., Fisher, M., Kim, V.G., Russell, B., Aubry, M.: AtlasNet: a papier-Mâché approach to learning 3D surface generation. In: Computer Vision and Pattern Recognition (CVPR) (2018)

16. Halimi, O., Litany, O., Rodola, E., Bronstein, A.M., Kimmel, R.: Unsupervised learning of dense shape correspondence. In: Proceedings of the IEEE Conference on Computer Vision and Pattern Recognition, pp. 4370–4379 (2019)

17. Hamdi, A., Giancola, S., Ghanem, B.: MVTN: multi-view transformation network for 3D shape recognition. In: Proceedings of the IEEE/CVF International Conference on Computer Vision (ICCV), pp. 1–11 (2021)

18. Hassani, K., Haley, M.: Unsupervised multi-task feature learning on point clouds. In: Proceedings of the IEEE International Conference on Computer Vision, pp. 8160–8171 (2019)

19. He, K., Fan, H., Wu, Y., Xie, S., Girshick, R.: Momentum contrast for unsupervised visual representation learning. In: 2020 IEEE/CVF Conference on Computer Vision and Pattern Recognition (CVPR), pp. 9726–9735 (2020). https://doi.org/10.1109/CVPR42600.2020.00975

20. Hou, J., Graham, B., Nießner, M., Xie, S.: Exploring data-efficient 3D scene understanding with contrastive scene contexts. In: Conference on Computer Vision and Pattern Recognition (CVPR), pp. 15587–15597 (2021)

21. Hou, J., Xie, S., Graham, B., Dai, A., Nießner, M.: Pri3d: can 3D priors help 2D representation learning? In: 2021 IEEE/CVF International Conference on Computer Vision (ICCV), pp. 5673–5682 (2021). https://doi.org/10.1109/ICCV48922.2021.00564

22. Huang, H., Kalogerakis, E., Chaudhuri, S., Ceylan, D., Kim, V.G., Yumer, E.: Learning local shape descriptors from part correspondences with multiview convolutional networks. ACM Trans. Graph. 37(1), 1–14 (2018)

23. Kalogerakis, E., Averkiou, M., Maji, S., Chaudhuri, S.: 3D shape segmentation with projective convolutional networks. In: Proceedings of CVPR (2017)

24. Kawana, Y., Mukuta, Y., Harada, T.: Neural star domain as primitive representation. In: Proceedings of the 34th International Conference on Neural Information Processing Systems, NIPS 2020. Curran Associates Inc., Red Hook (2020)

25. Kundu, A., et al.: Virtual multi-view fusion for 3D semantic segmentation. In: Vedaldi, A., Bischof, H., Brox, T., Frahm, J.-M. (eds.) ECCV 2020. LNCS, vol. 12369, pp. 518–535. Springer, Cham (2020). https://doi.org/10.1007/978-3-030-58586-0_31

26. Lien, J.M., Amato, N.M.: Approximate convex decomposition of polyhedra. In: ACM Symposium on Solid and Physical Modeling (2007)

27. Luo, W., Schwing, A.G., Urtasun, R.: Efficient deep learning for stereo matching. In: Computer Vision and Pattern Recognition (CVPR), pp. 5695–5703 (2016)

28. Mo, K., et al.: Partnet: a large-scale benchmark for fine-grained and hierarchical part-level 3D object understanding. In: Computer Vision and Pattern Recognition (CVPR) (2019)

29. Oord, A.V.D., Li, Y., Vinyals, O.: Representation learning with contrastive predictive coding. arXiv preprint arXiv:1807.03748 (2018)

30. Qi, C.R., Su, H., Mo, K., Guibas, L.J.: PointNet: deep learning on point sets for 3D classification and segmentation. In: Proceedings of CVPR (2017)

31. Sarlin, P.E., DeTone, D., Malisiewicz, T., Rabinovich, A.: SuperGlue: learning feature matching with graph neural networks. In: CVPR (2020)

32. Sauder, J., Sievers, B.: Self-supervised deep learning on point clouds by reconstructing space. In: Advances in Neural Information Processing Systems, pp. 12942–12952 (2019)

33. Sharma, G., et al.: PriFit: learning to fit primitives improves few shot point cloud segmentation. In: Computer Graphics Forum (2022). https://doi.org/10.1111/cgf.14601

34. Su, H., Maji, S., Kalogerakis, E., Learned-Miller, E.G.: Multi-view convolutional neural networks for 3D shape recognition. In: Proceedings of ICCV (2015)

35. Su, J.C., Gadelha, M., Wang, R., Maji, S.: A deeper look at 3D shape classifiers. In: European Conference on Computer Vision Workshops (ECCV) (2018)

36. Tulsiani, S., Su, H., Guibas, L.J., Efros, A.A., Malik, J.: Learning shape abstractions by assembling volumetric primitives. In: Computer Vision and Pattern Regognition (CVPR) (2017)

37. Wang, L., Li, X., Fang, Y.: Few-shot learning of part-specific probability space for 3D shape segmentation. In: Conference on Computer Vision and Pattern Recognition (CVPR), pp. 4504–4513 (2020)

38. Wang, P.S., Yang, Y.Q., Zou, Q.F., Wu, Z., Liu, Y., Tong, X.: Unsupervised 3D learning for shape analysis via multiresolution instance discrimination (2021)

39. Wang, X., Zhang, R., Shen, C., Kong, T., Li, L.: Dense contrastive learning for self-supervised visual pre-training. In: Proceedings of IEEE Conference on Computer Vision and Pattern Recognition (CVPR) (2021)

40. Wu, Z., Xiong, Y., Yu, S.X., Lin, D.: Unsupervised feature learning via non-parametric instance discrimination. In: Conference on Computer Vision and Pattern Recognition (CVPR), pp. 3733–3742 (2018)

41. Xie, S., Gu, J., Guo, D., Qi, C.R., Guibas, L., Litany, O.: PointContrast: unsupervised pre-training for 3D point cloud understanding. In: Vedaldi, A., Bischof, H., Brox, T., Frahm, J.-M. (eds.) ECCV 2020. LNCS, vol. 12348, pp. 574–591. Springer, Cham (2020). https://doi.org/10.1007/978-3-030-58580-8_34

42. Yang, Y., Feng, C., Shen, Y., Tian, D.: FoldingNet: point cloud auto-encoder via deep grid deformation. In: Computer Vision and Pattern Recognition (CVPR), pp. 206–215 (2018)

43. Yi, L., et al.: A scalable active framework for region annotation in 3D shape collections. ACM Trans. Graph. **35**(6), 1–12 (2016)

44. Zhang, Z., Girdhar, R., Joulin, A., Misra, I.: Self-supervised pretraining of 3D features on any point-cloud. In: International Conference on Computer Vision (ICCV), pp. 10252–10263 (2021)

45. Zhi, S., Laidlow, T., Leutenegger, S., Davison, A.J.: In-place scene labelling and understanding with implicit scene representation. In: International Conference on Computer Vision (ICCV), pp. 15838–15847 (2021)

SUPR: A Sparse Unified Part-Based Human Representation

Ahmed A. A. Osman[1]([✉]), Timo Bolkart[1], Dimitrios Tzionas[2],
and Michael J. Black[1]

[1] Max Planck Institute for Intelligent Systems, Tübingen, Germany
{aosman,tbolkart,black}@tuebingen.mpg.de
[2] University of Amsterdam, Amsterdam, The Netherlands
d.tzionas@uva.nl

Abstract. Statistical 3D shape models of the head, hands, and full body
are widely used in computer vision and graphics. Despite their wide use,
we show that existing models of the head and hands fail to capture
the full range of motion for these parts. Moreover, existing work largely
ignores the feet, which are crucial for modeling human movement and
have applications in biomechanics, animation, and the footwear industry. The problem is that previous body part models are trained using 3D
scans that are isolated to the individual parts. Such data does not capture
the full range of motion for such parts, e.g. the motion of head relative to
the neck. Our observation is that full-body scans provide important information about the motion of the body parts. Consequently, we propose
a new learning scheme that jointly trains a full-body model and specific
part models using a federated dataset of full-body and body-part scans.
Specifically, we train an expressive human body model called SUPR
(Sparse Unified Part-Based Representation), where each joint strictly
influences a sparse set of model vertices. The factorized representation
enables separating SUPR into an entire suite of body part models: an
expressive head (SUPR-Head), an articulated hand (SUPR-Hand), and
a novel foot (SUPR-Foot). Note that feet have received little attention
and existing 3D body models have highly under-actuated feet. Using
novel 4D scans of feet, we train a model with an extended kinematic tree
that captures the range of motion of the toes. Additionally, feet deform
due to ground contact. To model this, we include a novel non-linear
deformation function that predicts foot deformation conditioned on the
foot pose, shape, and ground contact. We train SUPR on an unprece-
dented number of scans: 1.2 million body, head, hand and foot scans. We
quantitatively compare SUPR and the separate body parts to existing
expressive human body models and body-part models and find that our
suite of models generalizes better and captures the body parts' full range
of motion. SUPR is publicly available for research purposes.

Supplementary Information The online version contains supplementary material
available at https://doi.org/10.1007/978-3-031-20086-1_33.

S. Avidan et al. (Eds.): ECCV 2022, LNCS 13662, pp. 568–585, 2022.
https://doi.org/10.1007/978-3-031-20086-1_33

1   Introduction

Generative 3D models of the human body and its parts play an important role in understanding human behaviour. Over the past two decades, numerous 3D models of the body [1–9], face [10–17] and hands [18–23] have been proposed. Such models enabled a myriad of applications ranging from reconstructing bodies [24–26], faces [27–29], and hands [30,31] from images and videos, modeling human interactions [32], generating 3D clothed humans [33–39], or generating humans in scenes [40–42]. They are also used as priors for fitting models to a wide range of sensory input measurements like motion capture markers [43,44] or IMUs [45–47].

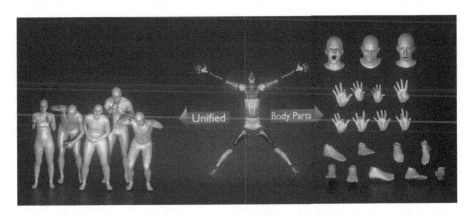

Fig. 1. Expressive part-based human body model. SUPR is a factorized representation of the human body that can be separated into a full suite of body part models.

Hand [21,22,48,49], head [12,13,49] and body [6,7] models are typically built independently. Heads and hands are captured with a 3D scanner in which a subject remains static, while the face and hands are articulated. This data is unnatural as it does not capture how the body parts move together with the body. As a consequence, the construction of head/hand models implicitly assumes a static body, and use a simple kinematic tree that fails to model the head/hand full degrees of freedom. For example, in Fig. 2a we fit the FLAME head model [13] to a pose where the subject is looking right and find that FLAME exhibits a significant error in the neck region. Similarly, we fit the MANO [21] hand model to a hand pose where the the wrist is fully bent downwards. MANO fails to capture the wrist deformation that results from the bent wrist. This is a systematic limitation of existing head/hand models, which can not be addressed by simply training on more data.

Another significant limitation of existing body-part models is the lack of an articulated foot model in the literature. This is surprising given the many applications of a 3D foot model in the design, sale, and animation of footwear.

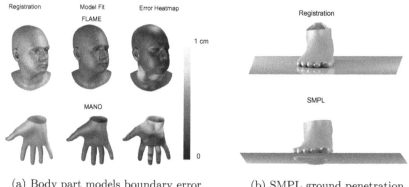

Registration   Model Fit   Error Heatmap
FLAME

Registration

1 cm

MANO

SMPL

0

(a) Body part models boundary error.   (b) SMPL ground penetration.

Fig. 2. Body part models failure cases. Left: Existing body part models such as the FLAME [13] head model and the MANO [21] hand model fail to capture the corresponding body part's shape through the full range of motion. Fitting FLAME to a subject looking left results in significant error in the neck region. Similarly, fitting MANO to hands with a bent wrist, results in significant error at the wrist region. Right: The foot of SMPL [6] fails to model deformations due to ground contact, hence penetrating the ground. Additionally, it has a limited number of joints with which to model toe articulation.

Feet are also critical for human locomotion. Any biomechanical or physics-based model must have realistic feet to be faithful. The feet on existing full body models like SMPL are overly simplistic, have limited articulation, and do not deform with contact as shown in Fig. 2b.

In contrast to the existing approaches, we propose to jointly train the full human body and body part models together. We first train a new full-body model called SUPR, with articulated hands and an expressive head using a federated dataset of body, hand, head and foot scans. This joint learning captures the full range of motion of the body parts along with the associated deformation. Then, given the learned deformations, we separate the body model into body part models. To enable separating SUPR into compact individual body parts we learn a sparse factorization of the pose-corrective blend shape function as shown in the teaser Fig. 1. The factored representation of SUPR enables separating SUPR into an entire suite of models: SUPR-Head, SUPR-Hand and SUPR-Foot. A body part model is separated by considering all the joints that influence the set of vertices defined by the body part template mesh. We show that the learned kinematic tree structure for the head/hand contains significantly more joints than commonly used by head/hand models. In contrast to the existing body part models that are learned in isolation of the body, our training algorithm unifies many disparate prior efforts and results in a suite of models that can capture the full range of motion of the head, hands, and feet.

SUPR goes beyond existing statistical body models to include a novel foot model. To do so, we extend the standard kinematic tree for the foot to allow more degrees of freedom. To train the model, we capture foot scans using a custom 4D foot scanner (see Sup. Mat.), where the foot is visible from all views, including the sole of the foot which is imaged through a glass plate. This uniquely allows us to capture how the foot is deformed by contact with the ground. We then model this deformation as a function of body pose and contact.

We train SUPR on 1.2 million hand, head, foot, and body scans, which is an order of magnitude more data than the largest training dataset reported in the literature (60K GHUM [49]). The training data contains extreme body shapes such as anorexia patients and body builders. All subjects gave informed written consent for participation and the use of their data in statistical models. Capture protocols were reviewed by the local university ethics board.

We quantitatively compare SUPR and the individual body-part models to existing models including SMPL-X, GHUM, MANO, and FLAME. We find that SUPR is more expressive, is more accurate, and generalizes better. In summary our main contributions are: (1) A unified framework for learning both expressive body models and a suite of high-fidelity body part models. (2) A novel 3D articulated foot model that captures compression due to contact. (3) SUPR, a sparse expressive and compact body model that generalizes better than existing expressive human body models. (4) An entire suite of body part models for the head, hand and feet, where the model kinematic tree and pose deformation are learned instead of being artist defined. (5) The Tensorflow and a PyTorch implementations of all the models are publicly available for research purposes.

2   Related Work

Body Models: SCAPE [2] is the first 3D model to factor body shape into separate pose and a shape spaces. SCAPE is based on triangle deformations and is not compatible with existing graphics pipelines. In contrast, SMPL [6] is the first learned statistical body model compatible with game engines SMPL is a vertex-based model with linear blend skinning (LBS) and learned pose and shape corrective blendshapes. A key drawback of SMPL is that it relates the pose corrective blendshapes to the elements of the part rotations matrices of all the model joints in the kinematic tree. Consequently, it learns spurious long-range correlations in the training data. STAR [7] addresses many of the drawback of SMPL by using a compact representation of the kinematic tree based on quaternions and learning sparse pose corrective blendshapes where each joint strictly influences a sparse set of the model vertices. The pose corrective blendshape formulation in SUPR is based on STAR. Also related to our work, the *Stitched Puppet* [50] is a part-based model of the human body. The body is segmented into 16 independent parts with learned pose and shape corrective blendshapes. A pairwise stitching function fuses the parts, but leaves visible discontinuities. While SUPR is also part-based model, we start with a unified model and learn its segmentation into parts during training from a federated training dataset.

Expressive Body Models: The most related to SUPR are expressive body models such as Frank [51], SMPL-X [52], and GHUM & GHUML [49,53]. Frank [51] merges the body of SMPL [6] with the FaceWarehouse [12] face model and an artist-defined hand rig. Due to the fusion of different models learned in isolation, Frank looks unrealistic. SMPL-X [52] learns an expressive body model and fuses the MANO hand model [21] pose blendshapes and the FLAME head model [13] expression space. However, since MANO and FLAME are learned in isolation of the body, they do not capture the full degrees of freedom of the head and hands. Thus, fusing the parameters results in artifacts at the boundaries. In contrast to the construction of Frank and SMPL-X, for SUPR, we start with a coherent full body model, trained on a federated dataset of body, hand, head and feet scans, then separate the model into individual body parts. Xu et al. [49] propose GHUM & GHUML, which are trained on a federated dataset of $60K$ head, hand and body scans and use a fully connected neural network architecture to predict the pose deformation. The GHUM model can not be separated into body parts as a result of the dense fully connected formulation that relates all the vertices to all the joints in the model kinematic tree. In contrast, the SUPR factorized representation of the pose space deformations enables seamless separation of the body into head/hand and foot models.

Head Models: There are many models of 3D head shape [54–56], shape and expression [10–12, 14–17] or shape, pose and expression [13]. We focus here on models with a full head template, including a neck. The FLAME head model [13], like SMPL, uses a dense pose corrective blendshape formulation that relates all vertices to all joints. Xu et al. [49] also propose GHUM-Head, where the template is based on the GHUM head with a retrained pose dependant corrector network (PSD). Both GHUM-Head and FLAME are trained in isolation of the body and do not have sufficient joints to model the full head degrees of freedom. In contrast to the previous methods, SUPR-Head is trained jointly with the body on a federated dataset of head and body meshes, which is critical to model the head full range of motion. It also has more joints than GHUM-Head or FLAME, which we show is crucial to model the head full range of motion.

Hand Models: MANO [21] is widely use and is based on the SMPL formulation where the pose corrective blendshapes deformations are regularised to be local. The kinematic tree of MANO is based on spherical joints allowing redundant degrees of freedom for the fingers. Xu et al. [49] introduce the GHUM-Hand model where they separate the hands from the template mesh of GHUM and train a hand-specific pose-dependant corrector network (PSD). Both MANO and GHUM-Hand are trained in isolation of the body and result in implausible deformation around the wrist area. SUPR-Hand is trained jointly with the body and has a wrist joint which is critical to model the hands full range of motion.

Foot Models: Statistical shape models of the feet are less studied than those of the body, head, and hands. Conard et al. [57] propose a statistical shape model of the human foot, which is a PCA space learned from static foot scans. However, the human feet deform with motion and models learned from static scans can not capture the complexity of 3D foot deformations. To address the limitations of static scans, Boppana et al. [58] propose the DynaMo system to capture scans of the feet in motion and learn a PCA-based model from the scans. However, the DynaMo setup fails to capture the sole of the foot in motion. In contrast, to all prior work, SUPR-Foot contains a kinematic tree, a pose deformation space, and a PCA shape space. We use a specialized 4D foot scanner, where the entire human foot is visible and accurately reconstructed, including the toes and the sole. Furthermore, we go beyond previous work to model the foot deformations resulting from ground contact, which was not possible before.

3   Model

We describe the formulation of SUPR in Sect. 3.1, followed by how we separate SUPR into body parts models in Sect. 3.2. Since existing body corrective deformation formulations fail to model foot deformations due to ground contact, we discuss a novel foot deformation network in Sect. 3.3.

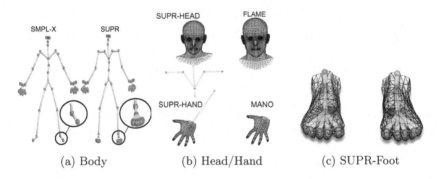

(a) Body   (b) Head/Hand   (c) SUPR-Foot

Fig. 3. The kinematic tree of SUPR and the separated body part models.

3.1   SUPR

SUPR is a vertex-based 3D model with linear blend skinning (LBS) and learned blend shapes. The blend shapes are decomposed into 3 types: *Shape Blend Shapes* to capture the subject identity, *Pose-Corrective Blend Shapes* to correct for the widely-known LBS artifacts, and *Expression Blend Shapes* to model facial expressions. The SUPR mesh topology and kinematic tree are based on the SMPL-X topology. The template mesh contains $N = 10,475$ vertices and $K = 75$ joints. The SUPR kinematic tree is shown in Fig. 3. In contrast to existing body models, the SUPR kinematic tree contains significantly more joints in the foot, ankle and toes as shown in Fig. 3a. Following the notation of SMPL, SUPR is defined by a function $M(\vec{\theta}, \vec{\beta}, \vec{\psi})$, where $\vec{\theta} \in \mathbb{R}^{75 \times 3}$ are the pose parameters corresponding to the individual bone rotations, $\vec{\beta} \in \mathbb{R}^{300}$ are the shape parameters corresponding to the subject identity, $\vec{\psi} \in \mathbb{R}^{100}$ are the expression parameters controlling facial expressions. Formally, SUPR is defined as

$$M(\vec{\theta}, \vec{\beta}, \vec{\psi}) = W(T_p(\vec{\theta}, \vec{\beta}, \vec{\psi}), J(\vec{\beta}), \vec{\theta}; \mathcal{W}), \tag{1}$$

where the 3D body, $T_p(\vec{\theta}, \vec{\beta}, \vec{\psi})$, is transformed around the joints J by the linear-blend-skinning function $W(.)$, parameterized by the skinning weights $\mathcal{W} \in \mathbb{R}^{10475 \times 75}$. The cumulative corrective blend shapes term is defined as

$$T_p(\vec{\theta}, \vec{\beta}, \vec{\psi}) = \overline{T} + B_S(\vec{\beta}; \mathcal{S}) + B_P(\vec{\theta}; \mathcal{P}) + B_E(\vec{\psi}; \mathcal{E}), \qquad (2)$$

where $\overline{T} \in \mathbb{R}^{10475 \times 3}$ is the template of the mean body shape, which is deformed by: $B_S(\vec{\beta}; \mathcal{S})$, the shape blend shape function capturing a PCA space of body shapes; $B_P(\vec{\theta}; \mathcal{P})$, the pose-corrective blend shapes that address the LBS artifacts; and $B_E(\vec{\psi}; \mathcal{E})$, a PCA space of facial expressions.

Sparse Pose Blend Shapes. In order to separate SUPR into body parts, each joint should strictly influence a subset of the template vertices $\overline{T}$. To this end, we base the pose-corrective blend shapes $B_p(.)$ in Eq. 2 on the STAR model [7]. The pose-corrective blend shape function is factored into per-joint pose corrective blend shape functions

$$B_P(\vec{q}, \mathbf{K}, \mathbf{A}) = \sum_{j=1}^{K-1} B_P^j(\vec{q}_{ne(j)}; \mathbf{K}_j; A_j), \qquad (3)$$

where the pose-corrective blend shapes are sum of $K-1$ sparse spatially-local pose-corrective blend-shape functions. Each joint-based corrective blend shape $B_P^j(.)$, predicts corrective offsets for a sparse set of the model vertices, defined by the learned joint activation weights $A_j \in \mathbb{R}^{10475}$. Each A_j is a sparse vector defining the sparse set of vertices influenced by the jth joint blend shape $B_p^j(.)$. The joint corrective blend shape function is conditioned on the normalized unit quaternions $\vec{q}_{ne(j)}$ of the jth joint's direct neighbouring joints' pose parameters. We note that the SUPR pose blend-shape formulation in Eq. 3 is not conditioned on body shape, unlike STAR, since the additional body-shape blend shape is not sparse and, hence, can not be factorized into body parts. Since the skinning weights in Eq. 1 and the pose-corrective blend-shape formulation in Eq. 3 are sparse, each vertex in the model is related to a small subset of the model joints. This sparse formulation of the pose space is key to separating the model into compact body part models.

3.2   Body Part Models

In traditional body part models like FLAME and MANO, the kinematic tree is designed by an artist and the models are learned in isolation of the body. In contrast, here the pose-corrective blend shapes of the hand (SUPR-Hand), head (SUPR-Head) and foot (SUPR-Foot) models are trained jointly with the body on a federated dataset. The kinematic tree of each part model is inferred from SUPR rather than being artist defined. To separate a body part, we first define the subset of mesh vertices of the body part $\overline{T}_{bp}$ from the SUPR template $\overline{T}_{bp} \in \overline{T}$. Since the learned SUPR skinning weights and pose-corrective blend shapes are strictly sparse, any subset of the model vertices $\overline{T}_{bp}$ is strictly influenced by a subset of the model joints. More formally, a joint $\vec{j}$ is deemed to influence a body part defined by the template $\overline{T}_{bp}$ if:

$$\mathbb{I}(T_{bp},\vec{j}) = \begin{cases} 1 & \text{if } \sum \mathcal{W}(\overline{T}_{bp},\vec{j}) \neq 0 \text{ or } \sum A_j(\overline{T}_{bp}) \neq 0 \\ 0 & \text{othewise,} \end{cases} \tag{4}$$

where $\mathbb{I}(.,.)$ is an indicator function, $\mathcal{W}(\overline{T}_{bp},\vec{j})$ is a subset of the SUPR learned skinning weights matrix, where the rows are defined by the vertices of $\overline{T}_{bp}$, the columns correspond to the jth joint, $\vec{j}$, $A_j(\overline{T}_{bp})$ corresponds to the learned activation for the jth joint and the rows defined by vertices $\overline{T}_{bp}$. The indicator function $\mathbb{I}$ returns 1 if a joint $\vec{j}$ has non-zero skinning weights or a non-zero activation for the vertices defined by $\overline{T}_{bp}$. Therefore the set of joints J_{bp} that influences the template $\overline{T}_{bp}$ is defined by:

$$J_{bp} = \left\{ \mathbb{I}(\overline{T}_{bp},j) = 1 \;\; \forall \;\; j \in \{1,\dots,K\} \right\}. \tag{5}$$

The kinematic tree defined for the body part models in Eq. 5 is implicitly defined by the learned skinning weights $\mathcal{W}$ and the per joint activation weights A_j. The resulting kinematic tree of the separated models is shown in Fig. 3b. Surprisingly, the head is influenced by substantially more joints than in the artist-designed kinematic tree used in FLAME. Similarly, SUPR-Hand has an additional wrist joint compared to MANO. We note here that the additional joints in SUPR-Head and SUPR-Hand are outside the head/hand mesh. The additional joints for the head and the hand are beyond the scanning volume of a body part head/hand scanner. This means that it is not possible to learn the influence of the shoulder and spine joints on the neck from head scans alone.

The skinning weights for a separated body are defined by $\mathcal{W}_{bp} = \mathcal{W}(\overline{T}_{bp}, J_{bp})$, where $\mathcal{W}(\overline{T}_{bp}, J_{bp})$ is the subset of the SUPR skinning weights defined by the rows corresponding to the vertices of $\overline{T}_{bp}$ and the columns defined by J_{bp}. Similarly, the pose corrective blendshapes are defined by $B_{bp} = B_p(\overline{T}_{bp}, J_{bp})$ where $B_p(\overline{T}_{bp}, J_{bp})$ corresponds to a subset of SUPR pose blend shapes defined by the vertices of $\overline{T}_{bp}$ and the quaternion features for the set of joints J_{bp}. The skinning weights $\mathcal{W}_{bp}$ and blendshapes B_{bp} are based on the SUPR learned blend shapes and skinning weights, which are trained on a federated dataset that explores each body part's full range of motion relative to the body. We additionally train a joint regressor $\mathcal{J}_{bp}$, to regress the joints $\mathcal{J}_{bp} : T_{bp} \rightarrow J_{bp}$. We learn a local body part shape space $B_S(\vec{\beta}_{bp}; \mathcal{S}_{bp})$, where $\mathcal{S}_{bp}$ is the body part PCA shape components. For the head, we use the SUPR learned expression space $B_E(\psi; \mathcal{E})$.

3.3   Foot Deformation Network

The linear pose-corrective blend shapes in Eq. 2 and Eq. 3 relate the body deformations to the body pose only. However, the human foot deforms as a function of pose, shape and ground contact. To model this, we add a foot deformation network.

The foot body part model, separated from SUPR, is defined by the pose parameters $\vec{\theta}_{bp} \in \vec{\theta}$, corresponding to the ankle and toe pose parameters in addition to $\vec{\beta}_{bp}$, the PCA coefficients of the local foot shape space. We extend the pose blend shapes in Eq. 2 to include a deep corrective deformation term for the foot vertices defined by $\overline{T}_{foot} \in \overline{T}$. With a slight abuse of notation, we will refer to the deformation function $T_p(\vec{\theta}, \vec{\beta}, \vec{\psi})$ in Eq. 2 as T_p for simplicity. The foot deformation function is defined by:

$$T'_p(\vec{\theta}, \vec{\beta}, \vec{c}) = T_p + \vec{m} \circ B_F(\vec{\theta}_{foot}, \vec{\beta}_{foot}, \vec{c}; \mathcal{F}), \tag{6}$$

where $\vec{m} \in \{0,1\}^{10475}$ is a binary vector with ones corresponding to the foot vertices and 0 elsewhere. $B_F(.)$ is a multilayer perceptron-based deformation function parameterized by $\mathcal{F}$, conditioned on the foot pose parameters $\vec{\theta}_{foot}$, foot shape parameters $\vec{\beta}_{foot}$ and foot contact state $\vec{c}$. The foot contact state variable is a binary vector $\vec{c} \in \{0,1\}^{266}$ defining the contact state of each vertex in the foot template mesh, a vertex is represented by a 1 if it is in contact with the ground, and 0 otherwise. The Hadamard product between $\vec{m}$ and $B_F(.)$ ensures the network $B_F(.)$ strictly predicts deformations for the foot vertices only.

Implementation Details. The foot contact deformation network is based on an encoder-decoder architecture. The input feature, $\vec{f} \in \mathbb{R}^{320}$, to the encoder is a concatenated feature of the foot pose, shape and contact vector. The foot pose is represented with a normalised unit quaternion representation, shape is encoded with the first two PCA coefficients of the local foot shape space. The input feature $\vec{f}$ is encoded into a latent vector $\vec{z} \in \mathbb{R}^{16}$ using fully connected layers with a leaky LReLU as an activation function with a slope of 0.1 for negative values. The latent embedding $\vec{z}$ is decoded to predict deformations for each vertex using fully connected layers with LReLU activation. The full architecture is described in detail in Supp. Mat. We train male, female and a gender-neutral versions of SUPR and the separated body part models. Training details are discussed in Supp. Mat.

4   Experiments

Our goal is to evaluate the generalization of SUPR and the separated head, hand, and foot model to unseen test subjects. We first evaluate the full SUPR body model against existing state of the art expressive human body models SMPL-X and GHUM (Sect. 4.1), then we evaluate the separated SUPR-Head model against existing head models FLAME and GHUM-Head (Sect. 4.2), and compare the hand model to GHUM-Hand and MANO (Sect. 4.3). Finally, we evaluate the SUPR-Foot (Sect. 4.4).

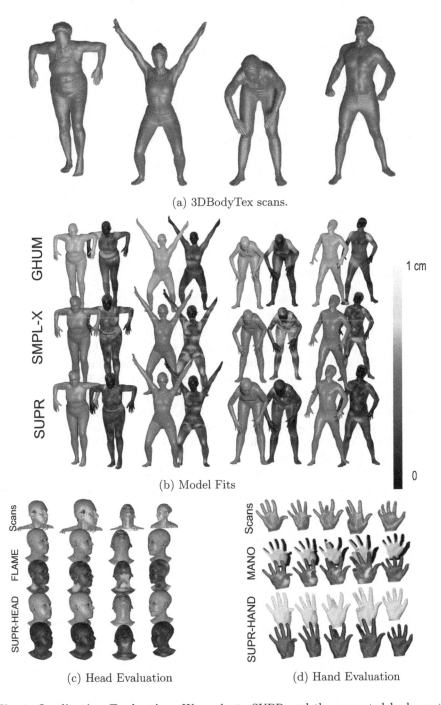

(a) 3DBodyTex scans.

(b) Model Fits

(c) Head Evaluation

(d) Hand Evaluation

Fig. 4. Qualitative Evaluation: We evaluate SUPR and the separated body part models against baselines. We use the 3DBodyTex dataset in (a) to evaluate GHUM, SMPL-X and SUPR in (b) using 16 shape components. We evaluate SUPR-Head against FLAME in (c) using 16 shape components and SUPR-Hand against MANO in (d) using 8 shape components.

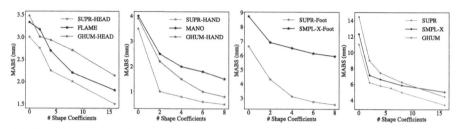

(a) Head Evaluation (b) Hand Evaluation (c) Foot Evaluation (d) Body Evaluation

Fig. 5. Quantitative Evaluation: Evaluating the generalization of the separated head, hand and foot model from SUPR against existing body part models: GHUM-HEAD and FLAME for the head (a), GHUM-HAND and MANO (b). We report the *vertex-to-vertex* error (*mm*) as a function of the number of the shape coefficients used when fitting each model to the test set.

4.1 Full-Body Evaluation

We use the publicly available 3DBodyTex dataset [59], which includes 100 male and 100 female subjects. We register the GHUM template and the SMPL-X template to all the scans; note SMPL-X and SUPR share the same mesh topology. We visually inspected all registered meshes for quality control. Given registered meshes, we fit each model by minimizing the vertex-to-vertex loss (*v2v*) between the model surface and the corresponding registration. The free optimization parameters for all models are the pose parameters $\vec{\theta}$ and the shape parameters $\vec{\beta}$. Note that, for fair comparison with GHUM, we only report errors for up to 16 shape components since this is the maximum in the GHUM release. SUPR includes 300 shape components that would reduce the errors significantly.

We follow the 3DBodyTex evaluation protocol and exclude the face and the hands when reporting the mean absolute error (*mabs*). We report the mean absolute error of each model on both male and female registrations. For the GHUM model, we use the PCA-based shape and expression space. We report the model generalization error in Fig. 5d and show a qualitative sample of the model fits in Fig. 4b. SUPR uniformly exhibits a lower error than SMPL-X and GHUM.

4.2 Head Evaluation

The head evaluation test set contains a total of 3 male and 3 female subjects, with sequences containing extreme facial expression, jaw movement and neck movement. As for the full body, we register the GHUM-Head model and the FLAME template to the test scans, and use these registered meshes for evaluation. For the GHUM-Head model, we use the linear PCA expression and shape space. We evaluate all models using a standard *v2v* objective, where the optimization free variables are the model pose, shape parameters, and expression parameters. We use 16 expression parameters when fitting all models. For GHUM-Head we exclude the internal head geometry (corresponding to a tongue-like structure) when reporting the $v2v$ error. Figure 5a shows the model generalization as a function of the number of shape components. We show a sample of the model fits in Fig. 4c. Both GHUM-Head and FLAME fail to capture head-to-neck rotations plausibly, despite each featuring a full head mesh including a neck. This is clearly highlighted by the systematic error around the neck region in Fig. 4c. In contrast, SUPR-Head captures the head deformations and the neck deformations plausibly and uniformly generalizes better.

4.3 Hand Evaluation

We use the publicly available MANO test set [21]. Since both SUPR-Hand and MANO share the same topology, we used the MANO test registrations provided by the authors to evaluate both models. To evaluate GHUM-Hand, we register the model to the MANO test set. However, the GHUM-Hand features a hand and an entire forearm, therefore to register GHUM-Hand we selected vertices on the model corresponding to the hand and only register that hand part of the model to the MANO scans. We fit all models to the corresponding registrations using a standard $v2v$ loss. For GHUM-Hand, we fit the model only to the selected hand vertices. The optimization free variables are the model pose and shape parameters. Figure 5b shows generalization as a function of the number of shape parameters, where SUPR-Hand uniformly exhibits a lower error compared to both MANO and GHUM-Hand. A sample qualitative evaluation of MANO and SUPR-Hand is shown in Fig. 4d. In addition to a lower overall fitting error, SUPR-Hand has a lower error around the wrist region than MANO.

4.4 Foot Evaluation

We evaluate SUPR-Foot generalization on a test set of held-out subjects. The test set contains 120 registrations for 5 subjects that explore the foot's full range of motion, such as ankle and toe movements. We extract the foot from the SMPL-X body model as a baseline and refer to it as SMPL-X-Foot. We register the SUPR-Foot template to the test scans and fit the SUPR-Foot and SMPL-X-Foot to the registrations using a standard $v2v$ objective. For SUPR-Foot, the optimization free variables are the model pose and shape parameters, while for SMPL-X-Foot the optimization free variables are the foot joints and the SMPL-X shape parameters. We report the models' generalization as a function of the number of shape components in Fig. 5c. A sample of the model fits are shown in Fig. 6. SUPR-Foot better captures the degrees of freedom of the foot, such as moving the ankle, curling the toes, and contact deformations.

Dynamic Evaluation. We further evaluate the foot deformation network on a dynamic sequence shown in Fig. 7. Figure 7a shows raw scanner footage of a subject performing a body rocking movement, where they lean forward then

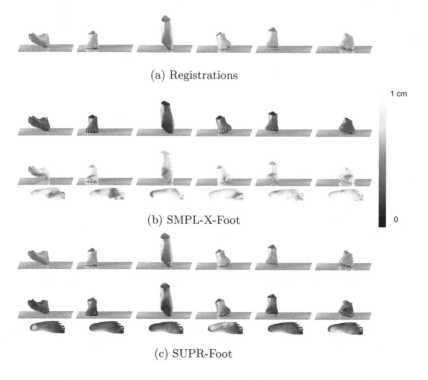

(a) Registrations

1 cm

(b) SMPL-X-Foot

0

(c) SUPR-Foot

Fig. 6. Evaluating SUPR-Foot against SMPL-X-Foot.

backward effectively changing the body center of mass. We visualise the corresponding SUPR-Foot fits and a heat map of the magnitude of predicted deformations in Fig. 7b. When the subject is leaning backward and the center of mass is directly above the ankle, the soft tissue at heel region of the foot deforms due to contact. The SUPR-Foot network predicts significant deformations localised around the heel region compared to the rest of the foot. However, when the subject leans forward the center of mass is above the toes, consequently the soft tissue at the heel is less compressed. The SUPR-Foot predicted deformations shift from the heel towards the front of the foot.

5   Conclusion

We present a novel training algorithm for jointly learning high-fidelity expressive full-body and body parts models. We highlight a critical drawback in existing body part models such as FLAME and MANO, which fail to model the full range of motion of the head/hand. We identify that the issue stems from the current practice in which body parts are modeled with a simplified kinematic tree in isolation from the body. Alternatively, we propose a holistic approach where the body and body parts are jointly trained on a federated dataset that contains the body parts' full range of motion relative to the body. Additionally, we point

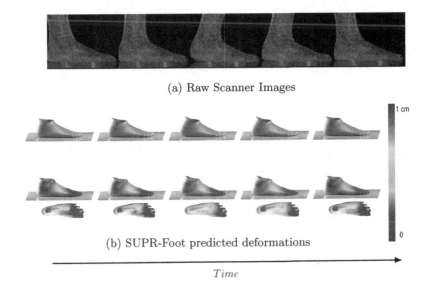

(a) Raw Scanner Images

(b) SUPR-Foot predicted deformations

Time

Fig. 7. Dynamic Evaluation: Evaluating the SUPR-Foot predicted deformations on a dynamic sequence where the subject leans backward and forward, effectively shifting their center of mass.

out the lack of any articulated foot model in the literature and show that the feet of existing full-body models do not have enough joints to model the full range of motion of the foot. Using 4D scans, we learn a foot model with a novel pose-corrective deformation formulation that is conditioned on the foot pose, its shape, and ground contact information. We train SUPR with a federated dataset of 1.2 million scans of the body, hands, and feet. The sparse formulation of SUPR enables separating the model into an entire suite of body-part models. Surprisingly, we show that the head and hand models are influenced by significantly more joints than commonly used in existing models. We thoroughly compare SUPR and the separated models against SMPL-X, GHUM, MANO and FLAME and show that the models uniformly generalize better and have a significantly lower error when fitting test data. The pose-corrective blendshapes of SUPR and the separated body part models are linearly related to the kinematic tree pose parameters, therefore our new formulation is fully compatible with the existing animation and gaming industry standards. A Tensorflow and PyTorch implementation of SUPR and the separated head (SUPR-Head), hand (SUPR-Hand) and the foot (SUPR-Foot) models is publicly available for research purposes.

Acknowledgments:. The authors thank the MPI-IS Tübingen members of the data capture team since 2012 for capturing the data used to train SUPR: S. Polikovsky, A. Keller, E. Holderness, J. Márquez, T. Alexiadis, M. Höschle, M. Landry, G. Henz, M. Safroshkin, M. Landry, T. McConnell, T. Bauch and B. Pellkofer for the IT support. The authors thank M. Safroshkin and M. Landry for configuring the foot scanner. The authors thank the International Max Planck Research School for Intelligent Systems (IMPRS-IS) for supporting Ahmed A. A. Osman. This work was done when DT was at MPI.

MJB Disclosure: https://files.is.tue.mpg.de/black/CoI_ECCV_2022.txt

References

1. Allen, B., Curless, B., Curless, B., Popović, Z.: The space of human body shapes: reconstruction and parameterization from range scans. ACM TOG **22**(3), 587–594 (2003)

2. Anguelov, D., Srinivasan, P., Koller, D., Thrun, S., Rodgers, J., Davis, J.: SCAPE: shape completion and animation of people. ACM TOG **24**(3), 408–416 (2005)

3. Chen, Y., Liu, Z., Zhang, Z.: Tensor-based human body modeling. In: Proceedings of the IEEE Conference on Computer Vision and Pattern Recognition, pp. 105–112 (2013)

4. Hasler, N., Stoll, C., Sunkel, M., Rosenhahn, B., Seidel, H.-P.: A statistical model of human pose and body shape. Comput. Graph. Forum **28**(2), 337–346 (2009)

5. Hirshberg, D.A., Loper, M., Rachlin, E., Black, M.J.: Coregistration: simultaneous alignment and modeling of articulated 3D shape. In: Fitzgibbon, A., Lazebnik, S., Perona, P., Sato, Y., Schmid, C. (eds.) ECCV 2012. LNCS, vol. 7577, pp. 242–255. Springer, Heidelberg (2012). https://doi.org/10.1007/978-3-642-33783-3_18

6. Loper, M., Mahmood, N., Romero, J., Pons-Moll, G., Black, M.J.: SMPL: a skinned multi-person linear model. ACM Trans. Graph. (Proc. SIGGRAPH Asia) **34**(6), 248:1–248:16 (2015)

7. Osman, A.A.A., Bolkart, T., Black, M.J.: STAR: sparse trained articulated human body regressor. In: Vedaldi, A., Bischof, H., Brox, T., Frahm, J.-M. (eds.) ECCV 2020. LNCS, vol. 12351, pp. 598–613. Springer, Cham (2020). https://doi.org/10.1007/978-3-030-58539-6_36

8. Pishchulin, L., Wuhrer, S., Helten, T., Theobalt, C., Schiele, B.: Building statistical shape spaces for 3D human modeling. PR **67**, 276–286 (2017)

9. Wang, H., Güler, R.A., Kokkinos, I., Papandreou, G., Zafeiriou, S.: BLSM: a bone-level skinned model of the human mesh. In: Vedaldi, A., Bischof, H., Brox, T., Frahm, J.-M. (eds.) ECCV 2020. LNCS, vol. 12350, pp. 1–17. Springer, Cham (2020). https://doi.org/10.1007/978-3-030-58558-7_1

10. Amberg, B., Knothe, R., Vetter, T.: Expression invariant 3D face recognition with a morphable model, pp. 1–6 (2008)

11. Brunton, A., Bolkart, T., Wuhrer, S.: Multilinear wavelets: a statistical shape space for human faces. In: Fleet, D., Pajdla, T., Schiele, B., Tuytelaars, T. (eds.) ECCV 2014. LNCS, vol. 8689, pp. 297–312. Springer, Cham (2014). https://doi.org/10.1007/978-3-319-10590-1_20

12. Cao, C., Weng, Y., Zhou, S., Tong, Y., Zhou, K.: Facewarehouse: a 3D facial expression database for visual computing. IEEE Trans. Visual Comput. Graphics **20**(3), 413–425 (2014)

13. Li, T., Bolkart, T., Black, M.J., Li, H., Romero, J.: Learning a model of facial shape and expression from 4D scans. ACM Trans. Graph. (Proc. SIGGRAPH Asia) **36**(6) (2017)

14. Li, R., et al.: Learning formation of physically-based face attributes. In: CVPR, pp. 3410–3419 (2020)

15. Ranjan, A., Bolkart, T., Sanyal, S., Black, M.J.: Generating 3D faces using convolutional mesh autoencoders. In: ECCV, pp. 725–741 (2018)
16. Yang, H., et al.: FaceScape: a large-scale high quality 3D face dataset and detailed riggable 3D face prediction. In: CVPR, pp. 601–610 (2020)
17. Vlasic, D., Brand, M., Pfister, H., Popovic, J.: Face transfer with multilinear models. ACM TOG **24**(3), 426–433 (2005)
18. Khamis, S., Taylor, J., Shotton, J., Keskin, C., Izadi, S., Fitzgibbon, A.: Learning an efficient model of hand shape variation from depth images. In: Proceedings of the IEEE Conference on Computer Vision and Pattern Recognition, pp. 2540–2548 (2015)
19. Kulon, D., Wang, H., Güler, R.A., Bronstein, M.M., Zafeiriou, S.: Single image 3D hand reconstruction with mesh convolutions. In: BMVC, p. 45 (2019)
20. Oikonomidis, I., Kyriazis, N., Argyros, A.A.: Efficient model-based 3D tracking of hand articulations using kinect. In: BMVC, pp. 1–11 (2011)
21. Romero, J., Tzionas, D., Black, M.J.: Embodied hands: modeling and capturing hands and bodies together. ACM Trans. Graph. (Proc. SIGGRAPH Asia) **36**(6), 245:1–245:17 (2017)
22. Smith, B., et al.: Constraining dense hand surface tracking with elasticity. ACM TOG **39**(6), 219:1–219:14 (2020)
23. Tkach, A., Pauly, M., Tagliasacchi, A.: Sphere-meshes for real-time hand modeling and tracking. ACM TOG **35**(6), 222:1–222:11 (2016)
24. Kanazawa, A., Black, M.J., Jacobs, D.W., Malik, J.: End-to-end recovery of human shape and pose. In: Proceedings of the IEEE Conference on Computer Vision and Pattern Recognition, pp. 7122–7131 (2018)
25. Kocabas, M., Athanasiou, N., Black, M.J.: Vibe: video inference for human body pose and shape estimation. arXiv preprint arXiv:1912.05656 (2019)
26. Kolotouros, N., Pavlakos, G., Black, M.J., Daniilidis, K.: Learning to reconstruct 3D human pose and shape via model-fitting in the loop. In: ICCV, pp. 2252–2261 (2019)
27. Feng, Y., Wu, F., Shao, X., Wang, Y., Zhou, X.: Joint 3D face reconstruction and dense alignment with position map regression network. In: ECCV, pp. 534–551 (2018)
28. Tewari, A., et al.: FML: face model learning from videos. In: CVPR, pp. 10812–10822 (2019)
29. Sanyal, S., Bolkart, T., Feng, H., Black, M.: Learning to regress 3D face shape and expression from an image without 3D supervision. In: CVPR, pp. 7763–7772 (2019)
30. Boukhayma, A., de Bem, R., Torr, P.H.S.: 3D hand shape and pose from images in the wild. In: CVPR, pp. 10843–10852 (2019)
31. Hasson, Y., et al.: Learning joint reconstruction of hands and manipulated objects. In: CVPR, pp. 11807–11816 (2019)
32. Fieraru, M., Zanfir, M., Oneata, E., Popa, A.I., Olaru, V., Sminchisescu, C.: Three-dimensional reconstruction of human interactions. In: CVPR, pp. 7214–7223 (2020)
33. Alldieck, T., Pons-Moll, G., Theobalt, C., Magnor, M.: Tex2Shape: detailed full human body geometry from a single image. In: ICCV, pp. 2293–2303 (2019)
34. Lassner, C., Pons-Moll, G., Gehler, P.V.: A generative model of people in clothing. In: ICCV, pp. 853–862 (2017)
35. Ma, Q., et al.: Learning to dress 3D people in generative clothing. In: CVPR, pp. 6468–6477 (2020)
36. Zhang, C., Pujades, S., Black, M., Pons-Moll, G.: Detailed, accurate, human shape estimation from clothed 3D scan sequences. In: CVPR, pp. 5484–5493 (2017)

37. Pons-Moll, G., Pujades, S., Hu, S., Black, M.: ClothCap: seamless 4D clothing capture and retargeting. ACM TOG **36**(4), 73:1–73:15 (2017)

38. Bhatnagar, B.L., Tiwari, G., Theobalt, C., Pons-Moll, G.: Multi-garment net: learning to dress 3D people from images. In: ICCV, pp. 5419–5429 (2019)

39. Patel, C., Liao, Z., Pons-Moll, G.: TailorNet: predicting clothing in 3D as a function of human pose, shape and garment style. In: CVPR, pp. 7363–7373 (2020)

40. Zanfir, M., Oneata, E., Popa, A.-I., Zanfir, A., Sminchisescu, C.: Human synthesis and scene compositing. In: AAAI, pp. 12749–12756 (2020)

41. Zhang, Y., Hassan, M., Neumann, H., Black, M., Tang, S.: Generating 3D people in scenes without people. In: CVPR, pp. 6194–6204 (2020)

42. Zhang, S., Zhang, Y., Ma, Q., Black, M.J., Tang, S.: PLACE: proximity learning of articulation and contact in 3D environments (2020)

43. Loper, M., Mahmood, N., Black, M.J.: MoSh: motion and shape capture from sparse markers. ACM Trans. Graph. (Proc. SIGGRAPH Asia) **33**(6), 220:1–220:13 (2014)

44. Mahmood, N., Ghorbani, N., Troje, N.F., Pons-Moll, G., Black, M.J.: AMASS: archive of motion capture as surface shapes. In: ICCV, pp. 5442–5451 (2019)

45. von Marcard, T., Pons-Moll, G., Rosenhahn, B.: Human pose estimation from video and IMUs. IEEE TPAMI **38**(8), 1533–1547 (2016)

46. Huang, Y., et al.: Towards accurate marker-less human shape and pose estimation over time, pp. 421–430 (2017)

47. Huang, Y., Kaufmann, M., Aksan, E., Black, M.J., Hilliges, O., Pons-Moll, G.: Deep inertial poser: learning to reconstruct human pose from sparse inertial measurements in real time. ACM Trans. Graph. (Proc. SIGGRAPH Asia) **37**, 185:1–185:15 (2018)

48. Moon, G., Shiratori, T., Lee, K.M.: DeepHandMesh: a weakly-supervised deep encoder-decoder framework for high-fidelity hand mesh modeling. In: Vedaldi, A., Bischof, H., Brox, T., Frahm, J.-M. (eds.) ECCV 2020. LNCS, vol. 12347, pp. 440–455. Springer, Cham (2020). https://doi.org/10.1007/978-3-030-58536-5_26

49. Xu, H., Bazavan, E.G., Zanfir, A., Freeman, W.T., Sukthankar, R., Sminchisescu, C.: GHUM & GHUML: generative 3D human shape and articulated pose models. In: CVPR, pp. 6184–6193 (2020)

50. Zuffi, S., Black, M.J.: The stitched puppet: a graphical model of 3D human shape and pose. In: Proceedings of the IEEE Conference on Computer Vision and Pattern Recognition, pp. 3537–3546 (2015)

51. Joo, H., Simon, T., Sheikh, Y.: Total capture: a 3D deformation model for tracking faces, hands, and bodies. In: CVPR, pp. 8320–8329 (2018)

52. Pavlakos, G., et al.: Expressive body capture: 3D hands, face, and body from a single image. In: Proceedings IEEE Conference on Computer Vision and Pattern Recognition (CVPR) (2019)

53. Zanfir, A., Bazavan, E.G., Xu, H., Freeman, W.T., Sukthankar, R., Sminchisescu, C.: Weakly supervised 3D human pose and shape reconstruction with normalizing flows. In: Vedaldi, A., Bischof, H., Brox, T., Frahm, J.-M. (eds.) ECCV 2020. LNCS, vol. 12351, pp. 465–481. Springer, Cham (2020). https://doi.org/10.1007/978-3-030-58539-6_28

54. Blanz, V., Vetter, T.: A morphable model for the synthesis of 3D faces. In: SIGGRAPH 1999, pp. 187–194 (1999)

55. Booth, J., Roussos, A., Ponniah, A., Dunaway, D., Zafeiriou, S.: Large scale 3D morphable models. IJCV **126**(2–4), 233–254 (2018)

56. Paysan, P., Knothe, R., Amberg, B., Romdhani, S., Vetter, T.: A 3D face model for pose and illumination invariant face recognition. In: 2009 Sixth IEEE International Conference on Advanced Video and Signal Based Surveillance, pp. 296–301. IEEE (2009)
57. Conrad, B.P., Amos, M., Sintini, I., Polasek, B.R., Laz, P.: Statistical shape modelling describes anatomic variation in the foot. Footwear Sci. **11**(Suppl. 1), S203–S205, 2019
58. Boppana, A., Anderson, A.P.: Dynamic foot morphology explained through 4D scanning and shape modeling. J. Biomech. **122**, 110465 (2021)
59. Saint, A., Ahmed, E., Cherenkova, K., Gusev, G., Aouada, D., Ottersten, B.: 3DBodyTex: textured 3D body dataset, pp. 495–504 (2018)

Revisiting Point Cloud Simplification:
A Learnable Feature Preserving Approach

Rolandos Alexandros Potamias$^{(\boxtimes)}$, Giorgos Bouritsas, and Stefanos Zafeiriou

Imperial College London, London, UK
{r.potamias,g.bouritsas,s.zafeiriou}@imperial.ac.uk

Abstract. The recent advances in 3D sensing technology have made possible the capture of point clouds in significantly high resolution. However, increased detail usually comes at the expense of high storage, as well as computational costs in terms of processing and visualization operations. Mesh and Point Cloud simplification methods aim to reduce the complexity of 3D models while retaining visual quality and relevant salient features. Traditional simplification techniques usually rely on solving a time-consuming optimization problem, hence they are impractical for large-scale datasets. In an attempt to alleviate this computational burden, we propose a fast point cloud simplification method by learning to sample salient points. The proposed method relies on a graph neural network architecture trained to select an arbitrary, user-defined, number of points according to their latent encodings and re-arrange their positions so as to minimize the visual perception error. The approach is extensively evaluated on various datasets using several perceptual metrics. Importantly, our method is able to generalize to out-of-distribution shapes, hence demonstrating zero-shot capabilities.

Keywords: Point clouds · Simplification · Sampling · GNN

1 Introduction

The progress in sensing technologies has significantly expedited the 3D data acquisition pipelines which in turn has increased the availability of large and diverse 3D datasets. With a single 3D sensing device [39], one can capture a target surface and represent it as a 3D object, with point clouds and meshes being the most popular representations. Several applications, ranging from virtual reality and 3D avatar generation [26,46] to 3D printing and digitization of cultural heritage [43], depend from such representations. However, in general, a 3D capturing device generates thousands of points per second, making processing, visualization and storage of captured 3D objects a computationally daunting task. Often, raw point sets contain an enormous amount of redundant and putatively noisy points of points with low visual perceptual importance, which results

---

Supplementary Information The online version contains supplementary material available at https://doi.org/10.1007/978-3-031-20086-1_34.

S. Avidan et al. (Eds.): ECCV 2022, LNCS 13662, pp. 586–603, 2022.
https://doi.org/10.1007/978-3-031-20086-1_34

into an unnecessary increase in the storage costs. Thus processing, rendering and editing applications require the development of efficient simplification methods that discard excessive details and reduce the size of the object, while preserving their significant visual characteristics. In particular, triangulation, registration and editing processes of real-world scans include an initial simplification step to achieve real-time meshing and rendering. In contrast to sampling methods that aim to preserve the overall point cloud structure, simplification methods attempt to solve the non-trival task of preserving the semantics of the input objects [8]. Visual semantics refer to the salient features of the object that mostly correlate with human perception and determine its visual appearance in terms of curvature and roughness characteristics of the shape [27,33]. As can be easily observed in an indicative case shown in Fig. 1, effortless sampling techniques, such as FPS or uniform sampling, can easily preserve the structure of a point cloud. However, the preservation of perceptually visual characteristics, especially when combined with structural preservation, remains a challenging task.

Traditional simplification methods manage to retain the structural and the salient characteristics of large point clouds [15,42,49] by constructing a point importance queue that sorts points according to their scores at every iteration. However, apart from being very time demanding, such optimizations are non-convex with increased computational requirements and can not be generalized to different topologies. On the contrary, an end-to-end dif-

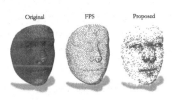

Fig. 1. Point cloud simplified using FPS (left) smooths out facial characteristics of the input whereas our method preserves salient features of the input (right).

ferentiable neural-based simplification method could leverage the parallel processing of neural networks and simplify batches of point clouds in one pass [45].

In this study, we tackle the limitations of the literature on the task of point cloud simplification and propose the first, to the best of our knowledge, learnable point cloud simplification method. Motivated by the works that showcase the importance of perceptual saliency, we propose a method that preserves both the salient features as well as the overall structure of the input and can be used for real-time point cloud simplification without any prior surface reconstruction. Given that our method is fully differentiable, it can be directly integrated to any learnable pipeline without any modification. Additionally, we introduce a fast latent space clustering using FPS that could benefit several fields (such as graph partitioning, generative models, shape interpolation, etc.), serving as a fast (non-iterative) alternative to differentiable clustering, in a way that the cluster center selection is guided by the loss function. Finally, we highlight the limitations of popular distance metrics, such as Chamfer, to capture salient details of the simplified models, and we propose several evaluation criteria, well-suited for simplification tasks. The proposed method is extensively evaluated in a series of wide range experiments.

2   Related Work

Mesh Simplification is a well studied field with long history of research. A mesh can be simplified progressively by two techniques, namely vertex decimation and edge collapse. Although the first approach is more interpretable, since it assigns importance scores to each vertex [36,51,52], it requires careful retessellation in order to fill the generated holes. Edge folding was first introduced in [18], where several transforms such as edge swap, edge split and edge collapse were introduced to minimize a simplification energy function. In the seminal works of [15,50], the authors associated each vertex with the set of planes in its 1-hop neighborhood and defined a fundamental *quadric* matrix quantifying the distance of a point from its respective set of planes. A Quadric Error Metric (QEM) was proposed to measure the error introduced when an edge collapses, ensuring that edges with the minim error are folded first. Several modification of the QEM cost function have been proposed to incorporate curvature features [22,23,38,62], mesh saliency [2,40,59] or to preserve boundary constrains [3] and spectral mesh properties [34,37]. Recently, [17] proposed a learnable edge collapse method that learns the importance of each edge, for task-driven mesh simplification. However, the edges are contracted in an inefficient iterative way and the resulting mesh can only be decimated approximately by two.

Point Cloud Simplification and Sampling: Similar to mesh simplification, iterative point selection and clustering techniques have also been proposed for point clouds [16,42,49,53,64]. In particular, *point cloud simplification* can be addressed either via mesh simplification where the points are fitted to a surface and then simplified using traditional mesh simplification objectives [1,14], or via direct optimization on the point cloud where the points are selected and decimated according to their estimated local properties [32,42,47,53,64]. However, similar to mesh simplification, computationally expensive iterative optimization is needed, making them inefficient for large scale point clouds. The point cloud simplification methodology presented in this paper attempts to address and overcome the inefficiencies of the aforementioned approaches using a learnable alternative that works with arbitrary, user-defined decimation factors.

In a different line of research, *sampling methods* rely on a point selection scheme that focuses on retaining either the overall structure of the object or specific components of the input. A huge difference between simplification and sampling is founded upon their point selection perspective. Sampling methods are usually utilized for hierarchical learning [48] in contrast to simplification methods that attempt to preserve as much of the visual appearance of the input even at very low resolutions. Farthest Point Sampling (FPS) [12], along with several modification of it, remains the most popular sampling choice and has been widely used as a building block in deep learning pipelines [47,48,61]. Nevertheless, as we experimentally showcase, FPS directly from the input xyz-space can not preserve sharp details of the input and thus is not suitable for simplification tasks. Recently, several methods [11,25] have been proposed as a learnable alternative for task-driven sampling, optimized for downstream tasks. However, they require the input point clouds to have the same size which limits their usage to datasets with different topologies. In addition, they explicitly generate the sampled output using linear layers which is not scalable to large point clouds. Although the learnable sampling methods are closely related to ours, they only sample point clouds in a task-driven manner and as a result, the preservation of the high frequency details of the point cloud is not ensured.

Assessment of Perceptual Visual Quality: Processes such as simplification, lossy compression and watermarking inevitably introduce distortion to the 3D objects. Measuring the visual cost in rendered data is a long studied problem [9,30]. Inspired by Image Quality Assessment measures, the objective of Perceptual Visual Quality (PVQ) assessment is to measure the distortion of an object in terms directly correlated with the Human Perceptual System (HPS). Several methods have been proposed, acting directly on 3D positions, to measure the PVQ using Laplacian distances [21], curvature statistics [24,28,54], dihedral angles [55] or per vertex roughness [9]. Several studies [10,13,29,63] utilized crowdsourcing platforms and user subjective assessments to identify the most relevant geometric attributes that mostly correlate with human perception. The findings demonstrated that curvature related features along with dihedral angles and roughness indicate strong similarity with the HVS. In this work, motivated by the aforementioned studies we utilized curvature related losses and quality measures to train and assess the performance of the proposed model and we refer to them as perceptual measures.

3   Method

3.1   Preliminaries: Point Curvature Estimation

Calculating the local surface properties of an unstructured point cloud is a non-trivial problem. As demonstrated in [19,42], covariance analysis can be an intuitive estimator of the surface normals and curvature. In particular, considering a neighborhood $\mathcal{N}_i$ around the point $\mathbf{p}_i \in \mathcal{R}^3$ we can define the covariance matrix:

$$\mathbf{C} = \frac{1}{k-1} \sum_{i=1}^{k} (\mathbf{p}_{i_1} - \mathbf{p}_i)^T (\mathbf{p}_{i_1} - \mathbf{p}_i), \quad \mathbf{p}_{i_j} \in \mathcal{N}_i \tag{1}$$

Solving the eigendecomposition of the covariance matrix $\mathbf{C}$ we can derive the eigenvectors corresponding to the principal eigenvalues that define an orthogonal frame at point $\mathbf{p}_i$. The eigenvalues λ_i measure the variation along the axis defined by their corresponding eigenvector. Intuitively, the eigenvectors that correspond to the largest eigenvalues span the tangent plane at point $\mathbf{p}_i$, whereas the eigenvector corresponding to the smallest eigenvalue can be used to approximate the surface normal $\mathbf{n}_i$. Thus, given that the smallest eigenvalue λ_0 measures the deviation of point $\mathbf{p}_i$ from the surface, it can be used as an estimate of point curvature. As shown in [42], we may define:

$$\kappa(\mathbf{p}_i) = \frac{\lambda_0}{\lambda_0 + \lambda_1 + \lambda_2}, \quad \lambda_0 < \lambda_1 < \lambda_2 \tag{2}$$

as the local curvature estimate at point $\mathbf{p}_i$ which is ideal for tasks such as point simplification. Using the previously estimated curvature at point $\mathbf{p}_i$ we can estimate the mean curvature as the Gaussian weighted average of the curvatures around the neighborhood $\mathcal{N}_i$:

$$\bar{\mathcal{K}}(\mathbf{p}_i) = \frac{\sum\limits_{j \in \mathcal{N}_i} \kappa(\mathbf{p}_j) \exp\left(-\|\mathbf{p}_j - \mathbf{p}_i\|^2/h\right)}{\sum\limits_{j \in \mathcal{N}_i} \exp\left(-\|\mathbf{p}_j - \mathbf{p}_i\|^2/h\right)} \tag{3}$$

where h is a constant defining the neighborhood radius. Finally, we can define an estimation of the roughness as the difference between curvature and the mean curvature at point $\mathbf{p}_i$ as: $\mathcal{R}(\mathbf{p}_i) = |\kappa(\mathbf{p}_i) - \bar{\mathcal{K}}(\mathbf{p}_i)|$

3.2 Model

The main building block of the proposed architecture is a graph neural network that receives at its input a point cloud (or a mesh) $\mathcal{P}_1$ with N points $\mathbf{p}_i$ and outputs a simplified version $\mathcal{P}_2$ with M points, $M << N$. It is important to note that the simplified point cloud $\mathcal{P}_2$ does not need to be a subset of the original point set $\mathcal{P}_1$. The proposed model is composed by three modules: the *Projection Network*, the *Point Selector* and the *Refinement Network*. Figure 2 illustrates the architecture of the proposed method.

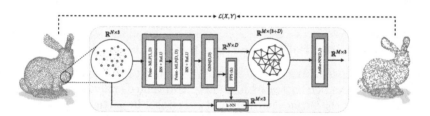

Fig. 2. Overview of the proposed method. Initially a point cloud (or a mesh) is passed through a projection network (green) and embedded to a higher dimensional latent space. FPS is used to select points from the set of latent representations (blue) that can be conceived as cluster centers of the input. Finally, a k-NN graph is constructed between the cluster centers and the input points that is used to modify their positions using the refinement layer (purple). (Color figure online)

Projection Network and Point Selector: In this study, we formulate sampling as a clustering problem. In particular, we aim to cluster points that share similar perceptual and structural features and express the simplified point cloud using the cluster centres. To do so, we designed a *Projector Network* that embeds (x, y, z) coordinates to a high dimensional space, where points with similar features are close in the latent space. In other words, instead of directly sampling from the Euclidean input space, we aim to sample points embedded to a high dimensional latent space that captures the perceptual characteristics of the input. Clustering the latent space will create clusters with latent vectors of points that share similar perceptual characteristics.

Based on the observations that Farthest Point Sampling (FPS) provides a simple and intuitive technique to select points covering the point cloud structure [48], we built a sampling module on top of this sampling strategy, where points are sampled from a high dimensional space instead of the input xyz-space. Although any clustering algorithm could be adequate, we utilized FPS module since it covers sufficiently the input space without solving any optimization problem. Intuitively, using this formulation we are allowed to interfere the selection process and transform it to a learnable module that is trained to select point embeddings that cover the perceptual latent space, enabling the preservation of both structural and perceptual salient features of the input.

Projector Network comprises of a multi-layer perceptron (MLP) applied to each point independently, followed by a Graph Neural Network (GNN) that captures the local geometric properties around each point. The update rule of the GNN layer is the following:

$$\mathbf{f}'_i = \mathbf{W}_c \mathbf{f}_i + \frac{1}{\mathcal{N}_i} \sum_{j \in \mathcal{N}_i} \mathbf{W}_n \mathbf{f}_j \tag{4}$$

where $\mathbf{f}_i$ denotes the output of the shared point-wise MLP for point $\mathbf{p}_i$ and $\mathbf{W}_c, \mathbf{W}_n$ represent learnable projection matrices. The connectivity between points can be given either by the mesh triangulation or by a k-nn query in the input space (we used a small neighborhood of $k = 7$ as in [44]). Following the Projector Network, *Point Selector* utilizes FPS to select points, i.e. cluster centers, based on their latent representations, in order to cover the latent space. Given the cluster centers selected by FPS, a k-nn graph is constructed that connects the center points with their k-nearest neighbours, based on their 3D positions.

Attention-Based Refinement Layer: Cluster centers, their neighboring point positions along with their respective embeddings from the projection networks are passed to the attention-based refinement layer (AttRef) that modifies the positions of the cluster centers. This layer can be considered as a rectification step that given a neighborhood and its corresponding latent features, displaces the cluster center points in order to minimize the visual perceptual error. Given that the latent embeddings of each point can be considered as its local descriptor, the refinement layer generates the new positions based on the vertex displacements along with the neighborhood local descriptors. The final positions of the points as predicted by *AttRef* are defined as follows:

$$\mathbf{p}'_{c_i} = \mathbf{p}_{c_i} + \gamma \left(\frac{1}{\mathcal{N}_{c_i}} \sum_{j \in \mathcal{N}_{c_i}} \alpha_{ij} \phi([\mathbf{f}_j \| \mathbf{p}_j - \mathbf{p}_{c_i}]) \right) \tag{5}$$

where γ and ϕ are MLPs, $\mathcal{N}_{c_i}$ the k-nearest neighbors of point $\mathbf{p}_{c_i}$ (we used $k = 15$), $\mathbf{f}_j$ the latent features of point $\mathbf{p}_j$ and α_{ij} the attention coefficients between center $\mathbf{p}_{c_i}$ and point $\mathbf{p}_j$. The attention coefficients α_{ij} are computed using scaled dot-product [56], i.e. $\alpha_{ij} = \mathrm{softmax}\left(\frac{\theta_q(\mathbf{f}_j)^T \theta_k(\mathbf{f}_i)}{\sqrt{d}}\right)$, where θ_q, θ_k are linear transformations mapping features $\mathbf{f}$ to a d-dimensional space.

3.3 Loss Function

The selection of the loss function to be optimized is crucial for the task of simplification since we seek for a balance between the preservation of the object's structure and its underlying salient features. A major barrier of most common distance metrics is the uniform weighting of points that can not reflect the perceptual differences between objects. As shown in many studies [20,35,58] the commonly used Chamfer distance (CD) between two point sets $\mathcal{P}_1, \mathcal{P}_2$ defined as:

$$d_{\mathcal{P}_1,\mathcal{P}_2} = \sum_{x\in\mathcal{P}_1} \min_{y\in\mathcal{P}_2} \|x - y\|^2 + \sum_{y\in\mathcal{P}_2} \min_{x\in\mathcal{P}_1} \|x - y\|^2 \tag{6}$$

can only describe the overall surface structure similarity between the two sets without taking into account the high frequency details of each point cloud. Figure 1 illustrates an example of such case. Similarly, the point to surface distance between points of a set $\mathcal{P}$ and a surface $\mathcal{M}$ as well as the Hausdorff distance can not preserve salient points of the object rather than its global appearance. To train our model task it is essential to devise a loss function that preserves both the salient features along with the structure of the point cloud.

Adaptive Chamfer Distance: As can be easily observed, the first term of Eq. (6) measures the preservation of the overall structure of $\mathcal{P}_1$ by $\mathcal{P}_2$, in a uniform way. To break the uniformity of the first term of CD we introduc a weighting factor w_x in Eq. 7 that penalizes the distances between the two sets at the points with high salient features ensuring that they will be preserved at the simplified point cloud. We define the modified adaptive Chamfer distance as:

$$d_{\mathcal{P}_1,\mathcal{P}_2}^{Adapt} = \sum_{x\in\mathcal{P}_1} w_{\bar{\mathcal{K}}(x)} \min_{y\in\mathcal{P}_2} \|x - y\|^2 + \sum_{y\in\mathcal{P}_2} \min_{x\in\mathcal{P}_1} \|x - y\|^2 \tag{7}$$

where $\mathcal{P}_1$ denotes the initial point cloud, $\mathcal{P}_2$ the simplified one, and $w_{\bar{\mathcal{K}}(x)}$ a weighting factor proportional to the mean curvature $\bar{\mathcal{K}}$ at point x^1. Since we only aim to retain salient points of $\mathcal{P}_1$, we avoid applying a similar weighting factor to the second term of Eq. (6) to prevent the optimization process from getting trapped at local minima.

Curvature Preservation: Additional to the adaptive CD, we make use of a loss term to reinforce the selection of high curvature points of the input. To quantify the preservation of salient features of the input we introduce an error to measure the average point-wise curvature distance between the two point clouds:

---

[1] We define the weights w_x using the sigmoid of the normalized curvatures divided by a temperature scalar $\tau = 10$ to amplify high curvature values.

$$\mathcal{E}_c = \left(\frac{1}{|\mathcal{P}_1|} \sum_{x \in \mathcal{P}_1} \|\bar{\mathcal{K}}_1(x) - \bar{\mathcal{K}}_2(\text{NN}(x, \mathcal{P}_2))\|^2 \right)^{1/2} \tag{8}$$

where $\text{NN}(x, \mathcal{P}_2)$ denotes the nearest neighbour of x in set $\mathcal{P}_2$, and $\bar{\mathcal{K}}(\cdot)$ the mean curvature. We refer to this error as Curvature Error (CE).

Overall Objective: We used a combination of the two aforementioned losses as the total objective to be minimized:

$$\mathcal{L}(\mathcal{P}_1, \mathcal{P}_2) = d_{\mathcal{P}_1, \mathcal{P}_2}^{Adapt} + \lambda \mathcal{E}_c, \tag{9}$$

where λ is used as a scaling factor set to 0.1. The first term ensures that the selected points cover the surface of the input, while the latter enforces the selection of high curvature points.

4   Evaluation Criteria

To assess the performance of the simplified models generated by our method in terms of visual perception we define several metrics that measure the similarity between the two point cloud models.

Roughness Preservation: Roughness describes the deviation of a point from the surface defined by its neighbours and has been identified as a salient feature in many visual perception studies [33,57]. Similar to the curvature preservation loss, we calculate the roughness preservation error by substituting the curvature values with roughness in Eq. (8). We refer to this error as RE.

Point Cloud Structural Distortion Measure: Additionally to curvature and roughness preservation metrics, we also calculate the structural similarity score between the two point clouds that has been shown to highly correlate with human perception [31]. In particular, the point cloud Structural Distortion Measure (SDM) can be defined as:

$$D(\mathcal{P}_1, \mathcal{P}_2) = \frac{\alpha \mathcal{L}(p_i, \hat{p}_i) + \beta \mathcal{C}(p_i, \hat{p}_i) + \gamma \mathcal{S}(p_i, \hat{p}_i)}{\alpha + \beta + \gamma} \tag{10}$$

$$\mathcal{L}(p_i, \hat{p}_i) = \frac{\|\bar{\mathcal{K}}_1(p_i) - \bar{\mathcal{K}}_2(\hat{p}_i)\|}{\max(\bar{\mathcal{K}}_1(p_i), \bar{\mathcal{K}}_2(\hat{p}_i))}, \quad \mathcal{C}(p_i, \hat{p}_i) = \frac{\|\sigma_{\bar{\mathcal{K}}_1}(p_i) - \sigma_{\bar{\mathcal{K}}_2}(\hat{p}_i)\|}{\max(\bar{\mathcal{K}}_1(p_i), \bar{\mathcal{K}}_2(\hat{p}_i))} \tag{11}$$

$$\mathcal{S}(p_i, \hat{p}_i) = \frac{\|\sigma_{\bar{\mathcal{K}}_1}(p_i)\sigma_{\bar{\mathcal{K}}_2}(\hat{p}_i) - \sigma_{\bar{\mathcal{K}}_{12}}(p_i, \hat{p}_i)^2\|}{\sigma_{\bar{\mathcal{K}}_1}(p_i)\sigma_{\bar{\mathcal{K}}_2}(\hat{p}_i)} \tag{12}$$

where $\mathcal{K}_1, \mathcal{K}_2, \sigma_{\bar{\mathcal{K}}_1}, \sigma_{\bar{\mathcal{K}}_2}, \sigma_{\bar{\mathcal{K}}_{12}}(p_i, \hat{p}_i)$ are the mean, the gaussian-weighted standard deviation and the covariance of the curvatures for point p_i in $\mathcal{P}_1$ and its corresponding point $\hat{p}_i$ in $\mathcal{P}_2$, respectively. We establish the correspondence between the two point clouds using the 1-nearest neighbor for each point. The global similarity score is obtained using *Minkowski pooling* as suggested in [28].

Normals Consistency: Point normals are highly related to visual appearance as indicators of sharp and smooth areas. We measure the consistency of normals' orientations between the two models using the cosine similarity loss:

$$\mathcal{E}_n = \frac{1}{|\mathcal{P}_1|} \sum_{\substack{x \in \mathcal{P}_1 \\ y \in NN(x, \mathcal{P}_2)}} 1 - \frac{\mathbf{n_x} \cdot \mathbf{n_y}}{\|\mathbf{n_x}\| \|\mathbf{n_y}\|} + \frac{1}{|\mathcal{P}_2|} \sum_{\substack{y \in \mathcal{P}_2 \\ x \in NN(y, \mathcal{P}_1)}} 1 - \frac{\mathbf{n_x} \cdot \mathbf{n_y}}{\|\mathbf{n_x}\| \|\mathbf{n_y}\|} \quad (13)$$

where $\mathbf{n_x}$ denotes the normal at point x and $NN(x, \mathcal{P}_2)$ the nearest neighbour of x in set $\mathcal{P}_2$, calculated as described in Sect. 3.1.

5   Experiments

In this section we extensively evaluate the proposed method with both quantitative and qualitative experiments.

Baselines. We compare our approach against several sampling and simplification methods including: uniform sampling (random), FPS, PointASNL adaptive sampling method [61], quadric error metric (QEM) simplification [15], spectral mesh simplification [37], feature preserving point cloud simplification [49] along with a top curvature points sampling (TCP) where the top-k curvature points are selected from the input point cloud. We failed to compare with recent simplification methods [34,41] that rely on the eigendecomposition of the Laplacian matrix, since they entail an overwhelmingly large processing run-time and memory consumption (≈ 15 min for a mesh with ≈ 15K points).

Datasets. We evaluated the proposed method using several publicly available 3D datasets, with different characteristics. The simplification benchmark TOSCA [6] dataset comprises 80 synthetic high-resolution meshes with 9 different deformable objects. It is an excellent candidate to assess feature-preserving simplification, since most of its meshes are non-smooth consisting of high curvature regions. Additionally, we used the popular ModelNet10 dataset [60] and the fixed topology high-resolution MeIn3D face dataset [5]. All datasets used were randomly split in 80%–20% train-test sets, taking care that none of the identities/shapes used for training are present in the respective test set.

Evaluation. We quantitatively evaluate the quality of the simplified point clouds in three folds. Primarily, we measure the low-level structural and perceptual measures, as described in Sect. 4, in Sect. 5.1. We additionally use an pre-trained objective classifier to measure the preservation of high-level semantics along with a user-study that aims to access the conceivable human perceptual similarity between the input and the simplified models. Furthermore, we access the importance of the major components of the proposed method using ablations studies, as well as the performance of the proposed method under noisy conditions and real-world scans. Due to space limitations several of the aforementioned experiments are reported on the supplementary material along with additional qualitative results.

5.1 Point Cloud Simplification

In this section, we showcase the simplification performance of the proposed method. For each dataset, we report both structural (i.e. CD, NC) as well as perceptual metrics (i.e. CE, RE, SDM) for the proposed and the baseline methods. Table 1 indicates the superiority of the proposed method to maintain the perceptual features of the input (i.e. low SDM) without sacrificing the overall structure (i.e. low CD) of the shape at three indicative simplification ratios. Results for larger simplification ratios can be found in the supplementary material. In contrast to TPC method where the selection of high curvature points leads to an increased Chamfer distance, the proposed method achieves a fair balance between structure (CD and NC) and saliency (SDM and RE). Additionally, the proposed method exhibits lower perceptual error (SDM) compared to FPS and PointASNL [61] methods that sample points directly from the xyz-space. This may be also observed in Fig. 3 where sampling from the perceptual latent space can effectively induce the preservation of the details of the input cloud.

Table 1. Simplification performance tested on TOSCA (top), ModelNet10 (middle) and MeIn3d (bottom) datasets. Best approaches are highlighted in **bold** and second best in red. We refer to the dataset used for training as "Proposed-*Dataset*"

TOSCA

Method	$N_s/N_{org}=0.2$				$N_s/N_{org}=0.1$				$N_s/N_{org}=0.05$			
	CD	NC	RE($\times 10^{-4}$)	SDM($\times 10^{-4}$)	CD	NC	RE($\times 10^{-4}$)	SDM($\times 10^{-4}$)	CD	NC	RE($\times 10^{-4}$)	SDM($\times 10^{-4}$)
Random	1.63	0.312	4.45	6.07	3.35	0.342	4.91	10.7	6.68	0.369	5.71	19.2
TCP	51.3	0.625	4.99	9.52	129.4	0.732	6.42	17.8	172.5	0.793	6.20	32.4
FPS	**0.81**	0.307	4.71	5.13	**1.93**	0.341	4.82	9.64	**3.94**	**0.321**	5.56	18.3
QEM	1.35	0.291	4.01	5.36	2.64	0.310	4.79	10.4	4.77	0.338	5.53	18.4
Liu et al. [37]	2.17	0.358	4.39	5.39	3.12	0.331	4.96	10.4	5.62	0.441	5.96	18.5
Qi et al. [49]	2.49	0.303	4.45	7.37	3.46	0.353	4.51	13.18	6.15	0.372	5.34	23.18
Yan et al. [61]	1.17	0.301	4.27	5.41	2.54	0.321	4.48	9.51	5.14	0.357	5.27	18.1
Proposed-MeIn3D	1.14	0.293	4.15	5.64	2.53	0.313	4.47	8.15	5.36	0.364	5.01	17.7
Proposed-ModelNet	1.15	0.310	4.01	5.53	2.51	0.312	4.81	9.72	5.19	0.341	4.99	17.4
Proposed-TOSCA	1.12	**0.290**	**3.91**	**5.01**	2.45	**0.307**	**4.41**	**7.84**	4.93	0.333	**4.93**	**16.5**

ModelNet

Method	$N_s/N_{org}=0.2$				$N_s/N_{org}=0.1$				$N_s/N_{org}=0.05$			
	CD ($\times 10^{-4}$)	NC	RE($\times 10^{-5}$)	SDM($\times 10^{-3}$)	CD($\times 10^{-5}$)	NC	RE($\times 10^{-5}$)	SDM($\times 10^{-3}$)	CD($\times 10^{-4}$)	NC	RE($\times 10^{-5}$)	SDM($\times 10^{-3}$)
Random	8.01	0.568	5.91	2.83	20.4	0.655	6.19	4.92	41.02	0.793	6.57	8.19
TCP	197.3	0.898	7.25	3.87	403.1	0.937	7.84	7.11	611.6	0.952	7.01	12.81
FPS	**3.12**	**0.505**	6.05	2.74	**7.56**	0.641	6.39	4.81	**16.01**	0.744	6.48	8.38
QEM	3.45	0.513	5.94	3.01	9.45	0.625	6.13	5.19	21.43	0.724	6.25	9.12
Liu et al. [37]	4.21	0.537	5.99	3.05	10.32	0.632	6.75	5.32	21.54	0.792	6.52	9.44
Qi et al. [49]	5.64	0.515	6.03	3.47	10.97	0.654	6.54	5.71	26.37	0.745	6.39	9.17
Yan et al. [61]	6.28	0.514	5.87	2.89	11.08	0.643	6.29	5.04	20.69	0.428	6.37	8.61
Proposed-MeIn3D	4.02	0.531	5.93	2.86	29.31	0.610	6.08	4.76	45.12	0.701	6.33	8.02
Proposed-ModelNet	3.32	0.515	5.79	**2.68**	8.24	0.606	6.06	**4.61**	17.24	0.696	6.25	**7.92**
Proposed-TOSCA	4.35	0.523	**5.77**	2.72	9.42	**0.603**	**5.91**	4.64	22.18	**0.688**	**6.04**	7.96

MeIn3D

Method	$N_s/N_{org}=0.2$				$N_s/N_{org}=0.1$				$N_s/N_{org}=0.05$			
	CD ($\times 10^{-4}$)	NC	RE($\times 10^{-5}$)	SDM($\times 10^{-3}$)	CD($\times 10^{-5}$)	NC	RE($\times 10^{-5}$)	SDM($\times 10^{-3}$)	CD($\times 10^{-4}$)	NC	RE($\times 10^{-5}$)	SDM($\times 10^{-3}$)
Random	1.42	0.198	4.15	2.81	3.46	0.313	6.73	5.92	5.52	0.481	7.05	12.4
TCP	158.3	0.801	3.46	3.73	421.1	0.910	6.02	7.38	556.0	0.934	11.87	14.2
FPS	**1.12**	**0.121**	3.64	2.96	**1.93**	0.195	6.29	5.98	3.45	0.484	7.43	11.8
QEM	2.01	0.185	4.53	3.01	2.52	0.198	6.31	5.71	3.65	0.331	8.13	11.3
Liu et al. [37]	2.92	0.215	4.92	3.12	3.14	0.199	6.67	5.92	3.88	0.392	8.46	11.9
Qi et al. [49]	3.12	0.193	4.74	3.45	3.55	0.211	6.52	5.95	4.07	0.405	8.22	12.6
Yan et al. [61]	2.75	0.193	4.70	2.95	3.05	0.205	6.34	5.41	3.76	0.374	9.17	11.4
Proposed-MeIn3D	1.24	0.128	**3.15**	**2.30**	2.01	0.192	5.69	4.91	3.25	0.305	6.47	10.6
Proposed-ModelNet	1.75	0.189	3.65	2.45	3.23	0.196	5.73	5.10	4.02	0.369	7.02	10.9
Proposed-TOSCA	1.54	0.168	3.29	2.41	2.32	0.194	5.98	5.06	3.82	0.342	6.49	10.8

Significantly, it can be observed in Table 1 and Fig. 4, the proposed method outperforms recent methods [37,49,61] under all metrics, and QEM in terms

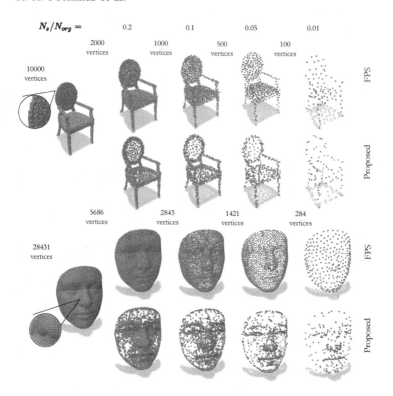

Fig. 3. Qualitative comparison between FPS (top row) and the proposed (bottom row) methods, at different simplification ratios. Differences between the two methods can be found at coarse and smooth areas, where the proposed model favours the preservation of high-frequency details of the input point cloud.

of perceptual error. Figure 5, demonstrates the superiority of our method to remarkably retain the salient points of the input using just 1% of the input is retained, in contrast to QEM that performs poorly at coarse areas of high curvature. The selection of salient points of the input is demonstrated in Fig. 3, where the proposed method favours point selection around the chair's arm, the face's eyes and nose in contrast to points at smooth areas, such as the forehead. Intuitively, smooth areas require only a few points to describe their associated planes compared to coarse areas that demand many points in order to preserve their curvature.

We also experimented with a cross-dataset generalization scenario where different datasets were used for training and testing the model (bottom rows in Table 1). Interestingly, it is observed that the proposed model can generalize well to out-of-distribution shapes and topologies indicating that it can be applied directly to any point cloud without fine-tuning, especially when trained with TOSCA or ModelNet dataset. We argue that this is due to the diversity of shapes and topologies as well as the presence of many rough regions at the training sets of these datasets that enforce the model to favour salient features.

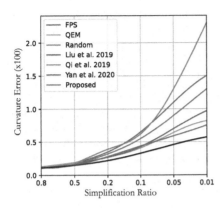

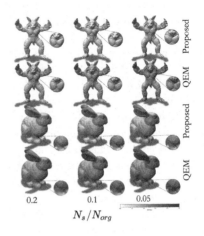

Fig. 4. Curvature preservation error comparison for the TOSCA dataset at different simplification ratios. Curvature error scales linearly for the proposed method.

Fig. 5. Colorcoded curvature error comparison between QEM and the proposed method. Blue color corresponds to larger error. (Color figure online)

5.2 Computational Time

Inevitably, in addition to salient point preservation, a proper point cloud simplification method should confront real-time executions. Although time complexity is beyond the scope of this study, we assessed the time required for simplifying 80 high-resolution meshes from the TOSCA dataset. Since FPS, Uniform and TCP baseline methods do not require any significant computations, we compare the proposed method with the popular QEM approach using a highly optimized version from the MeshLab framework [7] and the official implementations of [49] and [37]. It is important to note that the code of the proposed method could be further optimized, using parallel programming. In particular, 80% of the computational time of the proposed method is acquired by k-NN search that could be further optimized whereas FPS takes 17 % and the rest 3% of the runtime is spent on the learnable modules. Figure 7 demonstrates that the required mean runtime of the proposed method decreases drastically across all experiments, as the desired simplification increases, requiring just a few seconds to simplify the input to 1% of its original size. In contrast, the methods of [49] and [37] require approximately a minute to simplify a single mesh which makes them impractical.

5.3 Mesh Simplification

As described in Sect. 2, mesh simplification is a long studied problem that has been tackled only by greedy algorithms. In this section, we will attempt to propose an alternative method that circumvents the greedy nature of simplification using the simplification technique proposed in Sect. 3. The proposed method, without the need of any particular modification, can be easily extended for the task of mesh simplification when combined with a triangulation algorithm to transform the simplified vertices into a mesh structure. The process unfolds in two steps. Initially, mesh vertices are simplified by treating them as a point cloud but, instead of using a k-nn, the mesh adjacency matrix is utilized in order to determine point connectivity. In a second step, the remaining vertices are re-triangulated using an off-the-self triangulation algorithm such as Ball Pivoting [4]. Other triangulation algorithms, such as Delaunay, alpha shapes or Voronoi diagrams, could be also used but we observed that Ball Pivoting algorithm produces better results for small point clouds. Figure 6 shows visual results for the extension of the proposed simplification method to triangular meshes (for various simplification ratios).

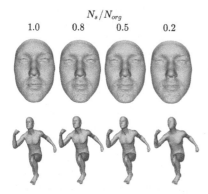

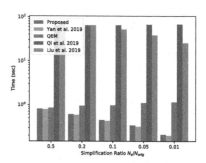

Fig. 6. Simplified meshes using the proposed method followed by Ball Pivoting Algorithm.

Fig. 7. Average time of simplification for the proposed and the baseline methods.

5.4   User-Study

To quantify the ability of the proposed method to select points that correlate with human perception we performed a user study, using the paired comparison protocol contrasting the proposed and one baseline method. In total, 50 participants were specifically asked to evaluate 18 point clouds and select one of the two simplified point clouds that mostly preserves the perceptual details of the reference one in terms of the overall shape and identity similarity. In average, as shown in Table 2, users selected 14 out of the 18 point clouds produced by the proposed method, as the ones preserving most of the visual features.

Table 2. User studies results of different methods. We average user preference scores (higher is better, results in %). Best results in bold.

Method	User choice
Ours vs QEM	**73**/27
Ours vs Liu *et al.* [37]	**78**/22
Our vs FPS	**71**/29
Average	**74**/26

5.5 Simplification Under Noise Conditions

To both quantitatively and qualitatively evaluate the performance of the proposed method in the presence of noise we fed the pretrained model with point clouds distorted with Gaussian noise ($\sigma = 1$). Quantitative experimental result are summarized in Table 3, with the proposed method to exhibit the best performance for almost all metrics (NC, RE, SDM) across all simplification ratios, and even the best second for structure preservation (CD). Such findings reveal the anti-noising capabilities of latent space sampling that, compared to xyz-space sampling, is less affected by the outlier noisy points. For qualitative comparisons along with results on LiDAR scans we refer the reader to the Supplementary material.

Table 3. Simplification performance tested on TOSCA dataset with addition of Gaussian noise. Best approaches are highlighted in **bold** and second best in red.

Method	$N_s/N_{org} = 0.2$				$N_s/N_{org} = 0.1$				$N_s/N_{org} = 0.05$			
	CD	NC	RE($\times 10^{-4}$)	SDM($\times 10^{-4}$)	CD	NC	RE($\times 10^{-4}$)	SDM($\times 10^{-4}$)	CD	NC	RE($\times 10^{-4}$)	SDM($\times 10^{-4}$)
Random	2.71	0.37	6.56	9.20	4.43	0.38	6.74	14.39	7.78	0.39	6.85	23.63
TCP	24.7	0.48	6.30	9.27	37.2	0.49	6.58	14.83	53.5	0.51	6.77	23.45
FPS	2.74	0.34	6.25	9.89	4.28	0.36	6.34	15.86	6.83	0.39	6.81	25.03
QEM	**1.92**	**0.31**	6.61	9.14	**2.57**	0.36	6.81	14.53	**3.85**	0.37	6.93	23.12
Liu *et al.* [37]	3.04	0.35	7.14	9.48	3.99	0.39	7.36	16.21	6.74	0.412	7.61	26.35
Qi *et al.* [49]	3.21	0.33	7.22	11.14	4.31	0.35	7.54	18.34	7.13	0.39	7.81	27.52
Yan *et al.* [61]	2.95	0.35	6.54	10.04	4.30	0.39	7.30	16.01	7.11	0.41	7.12	25.14
Proposed	2.50	0.33	**6.13**	**8.81**	3.96	**0.35**	**6.24**	**14.42**	6.46	**0.37**	**6.34**	**22.31**

6   Conclusion

Our work emphasises on the proposal of a learnable, neural-based simplification approach to overcome the inefficiencies of traditional greedy simplification methods. In this study we presented the first, to the best of our knowledge, learnable point cloud simplification method that aims at preserving salient features while at the same time retaining the global structural appearance of the input 3D object. Using three learnable modules we attain to simplify large-scale point clouds in real-time, addressing the literature limitations regarding computational complexity. As shown in an extensive series of both quantitative and qualitative experiments the proposed method not only outperforms its counterparts under most perceptual criteria but also exhibits zero-shot capabilities. Regarding future work, we plan to adapt the proposed method to mesh structures using a more sophisticated triangulation process. In particular, instead of using off-the-shelf triangulation algorithms on top of the point cloud simplification model, we aim to extend the proposed method to predict the triangulation of the simplified model utilizing the priors of the input mesh.

Acknowledgements.. Dr. Stefanos Zafeiriou acknowledges support from EPSRC fellowship Deform (EP/S010203/1).

References

1. Alexa, M., Behr, J., Cohen-Or, D., Fleishman, S., Levin, D., Silva, C.T.: Point set surfaces. In: Proceedings Visualization, VIS 2001, pp. 21–29. IEEE (2001)
2. An, G., Watanabe, T., Kakimoto, M.: Mesh simplification using hybrid saliency. In: 2016 International Conference on Cyberworlds (CW), pp. 231–234. IEEE (2016)
3. Bahirat, K., Lai, C., Mcmahan, R.P., Prabhakaran, B.: Designing and evaluating a mesh simplification algorithm for virtual reality. ACM Trans. Multimedia Comput. Commun. Appl. **14**(3s) (2018)
4. Bernardini, F., Mittleman, J., Rushmeier, H., Silva, C., Taubin, G.: The ball-pivoting algorithm for surface reconstruction. IEEE Trans. Visual Comput. Graphics **5**(4), 349–359 (1999)
5. Booth, J., Roussos, A., Ponniah, A., Dunaway, D., Zafeiriou, S.: Large scale 3D morphable models. Int. J. Comput. Vision **126**(2), 233–254 (2018)
6. Bronstein, A.M., Bronstein, M.M., Kimmel, R.: Numerical Geometry of Non-rigid Shapes. Springer, New York (2008). https://doi.org/10.1007/978-0-387-73301-2
7. Cignoni, P., Callieri, M., Corsini, M., Dellepiane, M., Ganovelli, F., Ranzuglia, G.: Meshlab: an open-source mesh processing tool. In: Eurographics Italian Chapter Conference, Salerno, Italy, vol. 2008, pp. 129–136 (2008)
8. Cignoni, P., Montani, C., Scopigno, R.: A comparison of mesh simplification algorithms. Comput. Graph. **22**(1), 37–54 (1998)
9. Corsini, M., Larabi, M.C., Lavoué, G., Petřík, O., Váša, L., Wang, K.: Perceptual metrics for static and dynamic triangle meshes. In: Computer Graphics Forum, vol. 32, pp. 101–125. Wiley Online Library (2013)
10. Dong, L., Fang, Y., Lin, W., Seah, H.S.: Perceptual quality assessment for 3D triangle mesh based on curvature. IEEE Trans. Multimedia **17**(12), 2174–2184 (2015)
11. Dovrat, O., Lang, I., Avidan, S.: Learning to sample. In: Proceedings of the IEEE/CVF Conference on Computer Vision and Pattern Recognition, pp. 2760–2769 (2019)
12. Eldar, Y., Lindenbaum, M., Porat, M., Zeevi, Y.Y.: The farthest point strategy for progressive image sampling. IEEE Trans. Image Process. **6**(9), 1305–1315 (1997)
13. Feng, X., Wan, W., Da Xu, R.Y., Chen, H., Li, P., Sánchez, J.A.: A perceptual quality metric for 3D triangle meshes based on spatial pooling. Front. Comp. Sci. **12**(4), 798–812 (2018)
14. Galantucci, L.M., Percoco, G.: A multilevel approach to edge detection in tessellated point clouds. CIRP Ann. **54**(1), 127–130 (2005)
15. Garland, M., Heckbert, P.S.: Surface simplification using quadric error metrics. In: Proceedings of the 24th Annual Conference on Computer Graphics and Interactive Techniques, pp. 209–216 (1997)
16. Han, H., Han, X., Sun, F., Huang, C.: Point cloud simplification with preserved edge based on normal vector. Optik Int. J. Light Electron Opt. **126**(19), 2157–2162 (2015)
17. Hanocka, R., Hertz, A., Fish, N., Giryes, R., Fleishman, S., Cohen-Or, D.: Meshcnn: a network with an edge. ACM Trans. Graph. (TOG) **38**(4), 90:1–90:12 (2019)
18. Hoppe, H.: Progressive meshes. In: Proceedings of the 23rd Annual Conference on Computer Graphics and Interactive Techniques, pp. 99–108 (1996)
19. Hoppe, H., DeRose, T., Duchamp, T., McDonald, J., Stuetzle, W.: Surface reconstruction from unorganized points. In: Proceedings of the 19th Annual Conference on Computer Graphics and Interactive Techniques, pp. 71–78 (1992)

20. Jin, J., Patil, A.G., Xiong, Z., Zhang, H.: DR-KFS: a differentiable visual similarity metric for 3D shape reconstruction. In: Vedaldi, A., Bischof, H., Brox, T., Frahm, J.-M. (eds.) ECCV 2020. LNCS, vol. 12366, pp. 295–311. Springer, Cham (2020). https://doi.org/10.1007/978-3-030-58589-1_18

21. Karni, Z., Gotsman, C.: Spectral compression of mesh geometry. In: Proceedings of the 27th Annual Conference on Computer Graphics and Interactive Techniques, pp. 279–286 (2000)

22. Kim, S., Jeong, W., Kim, C.: Lod generation with discrete curvature error metric. In: Proceedings of Korea Israel Bi-National Conference, pp. 97–104. Citeseer (1999)

23. Kim, S.J., Kim, C.H., Levin, D.: Surface simplification using a discrete curvature norm. Comput. Graph. 26(5), 657–663 (2002)

24. Kim, S.J., Kim, S.K., Kim, C.H.: Discrete differential error metric for surface simplification. In: Proceedings of 10th Pacific Conference on Computer Graphics and Applications, pp. 276–283. IEEE (2002)

25. Lang, I., Manor, A., Avidan, S.: Samplenet: differentiable point cloud sampling. In: Proceedings of the IEEE/CVF Conference on Computer Vision and Pattern Recognition, pp. 7578–7588 (2020)

26. Lattas, A., et al.: Avatarme: realistically renderable 3D facial reconstruction "in-the-wild". In: Proceedings of the IEEE/CVF Conference on Computer Vision and Pattern Recognition, pp. 760–769 (2020)

27. Lavoué, G.: A local roughness measure for 3D meshes and its application to visual masking. ACM Trans. Appl. Percept. (TAP) 5(4), 1–23 (2009)

28. Lavoué, G.: A multiscale metric for 3D mesh visual quality assessment. In: Computer Graphics Forum, vol. 30, pp. 1427–1437. Wiley Online Library (2011)

29. Lavoué, G., Cheng, I., Basu, A.: Perceptual quality metrics for 3D meshes: towards an optimal multi-attribute computational model. In: 2013 IEEE International Conference on Systems, Man, and Cybernetics, pp. 3271–3276. IEEE (2013)

30. Lavoué, G., Corsini, M.: A comparison of perceptually-based metrics for objective evaluation of geometry processing. IEEE Trans. Multimedia 12(7), 636–649 (2010)

31. Lavoué, G., Gelasca, E.D., Dupont, F., Baskurt, A., Ebrahimi, T.: Perceptually driven 3D distance metrics with application to watermarking. In: Applications of Digital Image Processing XXIX, vol. 6312, p. 63120L. International Society for Optics and Photonics (2006)

32. Leal, N., Leal, E., German, S.T.: A linear programming approach for 3D point cloud simplification. IAENG Int. J. Comput. Sci. 44(1), 60–67 (2017)

33. Lee, C.H., Varshney, A., Jacobs, D.W.: Mesh saliency. In: ACM SIGGRAPH 2005 Papers, pp. 659–666 (2005)

34. Lescoat, T., Liu, H.T.D., Thiery, J.M., Jacobson, A., Boubekeur, T., Ovsjanikov, M.: Spectral mesh simplification. Comput. Graph. Forum 39(2), 315–324 (2020)

35. Li, C.L., Simon, T., Saragih, J., Póczos, B., Sheikh, Y.: LBS autoencoder: self-supervised fitting of articulated meshes to point clouds. In: Proceedings of the IEEE/CVF Conference on Computer Vision and Pattern Recognition, pp. 11967–11976 (2019)

36. Li, W., Chen, Y., Wang, Z., Zhao, W., Chen, L.: An improved decimation of triangle meshes based on curvature. In: Miao, D., Pedrycz, W., Ślęzak, D., Peters, G., Hu, Q., Wang, R. (eds.) RSKT 2014. LNCS (LNAI), vol. 8818, pp. 260–271. Springer, Cham (2014). https://doi.org/10.1007/978-3-319-11740-9_25

37. Liu, H.T.D., Jacobson, A., Ovsjanikov, M.: Spectral coarsening of geometric operators. ACM Trans. Graph. 38(4) (2019)

38. Liu, X.L., Liu, Z.Y., Gao, P.D., Peng, X.: Edge collapse simplification based on sharp degree. Ruan Jian Xue Bao(J. Softw.) 16(5), 669–675 (2005)

39. Lu, T., Chao, T.H.: A single-camera system captures high-resolution 3D images in one shot. SPIE Newsroom (2006)

40. Luan, W., Liu, C., Pang, H.: Skeleton-bridged mesh saliency and mesh simplification. In: 2020 4th International Conference on Computer Science and Artificial Intelligence, pp. 278–283 (2020)

41. Nasikun, A., Brandt, C., Hildebrandt, K.: Fast approximation of laplace-beltrami eigenproblems. In: Computer Graphics Forum, vol. 37, pp. 121–134. Wiley Online Library (2018)

42. Pauly, M., Gross, M., Kobbelt, L.P.: Efficient simplification of point-sampled surfaces. In: IEEE Visualization, VIS 2002, pp. 163–170. IEEE (2002)

43. Pavlidis, G., Koutsoudis, A., Arnaoutoglou, F., Tsioukas, V., Chamzas, C.: Methods for 3D digitization of cultural heritage. J. Cult. Herit. 8(1), 93–98 (2007)

44. Potamias, R.A., Neofytou, A., Bintsi, K.M., Zafeiriou, S.: Graphwalks: efficient shape agnostic geodesic shortest path estimation. In: Proceedings of the IEEE/CVF Conference on Computer Vision and Pattern Recognition (CVPR) Workshops, pp. 2968–2977 (2022)

45. Potamias, R.A., Ploumpis, S., Zafeiriou, S.: Neural mesh simplification. In: Proceedings of the IEEE/CVF Conference on Computer Vision and Pattern Recognition, pp. 18583–18592 (2022)

46. Potamias, R.A., Zheng, J., Ploumpis, S., Bouritsas, G., Ververas, E., Zafeiriou, S.: Learning to generate customized dynamic 3D facial expressions. In: Vedaldi, A., Bischof, H., Brox, T., Frahm, J.-M. (eds.) ECCV 2020. LNCS, vol. 12374, pp. 278–294. Springer, Cham (2020). https://doi.org/10.1007/978-3-030-58526-6_17

47. Qi, C.R., Su, H., Mo, K., Guibas, L.J.: Pointnet: deep learning on point sets for 3D classification and segmentation. In: Proceedings of the IEEE Conference on Computer Vision and Pattern Recognition, pp. 652–660 (2017)

48. Qi, C.R., Yi, L., Su, H., Guibas, L.J.: Pointnet++: deep hierarchical feature learning on point sets in a metric space. In: Guyon, I., et al. (eds.) Advances in Neural Information Processing Systems, vol. 30. Curran Associates, Inc. (2017)

49. Qi, J., Hu, W., Guo, Z.: Feature preserving and uniformity-controllable point cloud simplification on graph. In: 2019 IEEE International Conference on Multimedia and Expo (ICME), pp. 284–289. IEEE (2019)

50. Ronfard, R., Rossignac, J.: Full-range approximation of triangulated polyhedra. In: Computer Graphics Forum, vol. 15, pp. 67–76. Wiley Online Library (1996)

51. Rossignac, J., Borrel, P.: Multi-resolution 3D approximations for rendering complex scenes. In: Falcidieno, B., Kunii, T.L. (eds.) Modeling in Computer Graphics, pp. 455–465. Springer, Heidelberg (1993). https://doi.org/10.1007/978-3-642-78114-8_29

52. Schroeder, W.J., Zarge, J.A., Lorensen, W.E.: Decimation of triangle meshes. In: Proceedings of the 19th Annual Conference on Computer Graphics and Interactive Techniques, pp. 65–70 (1992)

53. Shi, B.Q., Liang, J., Liu, Q.: Adaptive simplification of point cloud using k-means clustering. Comput. Aided Des. 43(8), 910–922 (2011)

54. Torkhani, F., Wang, K., Chassery, J.M.: A curvature tensor distance for mesh visual quality assessment. In: ICCVG (2012)

55. Váša, L., Rus, J.: Dihedral angle mesh error: a fast perception correlated distortion measure for fixed connectivity triangle meshes. In: Computer Graphics Forum, vol. 31, pp. 1715–1724. Wiley Online Library (2012)

56. Vaswani, A., et al.: Attention is all you need. In: Guyon, I., et al. (eds.) Advances in Neural Information Processing Systems, vol. 30 (2017)

57. Wang, Y., Zheng, J., Wang, H.: Fast mesh simplification method for three-dimensional geometric models with feature-preserving efficiency. Sci. Program. **2019** (2019)
58. Wen, C., Zhang, Y., Li, Z., Fu, Y.: Pixel2mesh++: multi-view 3D mesh generation via deformation. In: Proceedings of the IEEE/CVF International Conference on Computer Vision, pp. 1042–1051 (2019)
59. Wu, J., Shen, X., Zhu, W., Liu, L.: Mesh saliency with global rarity. Graph. Models **75**(5), 255–264 (2013)
60. Wu, Z., Song, S., Khosla, A., Yu, F., Zhang, L., Tang, X., Xiao, J.: 3D shapenets: a deep representation for volumetric shapes. In: Proceedings of the IEEE Conference on Computer Vision and Pattern Recognition, pp. 1912–1920 (2015)
61. Yan, X., Zheng, C., Li, Z., Wang, S., Cui, S.: Pointasnl: robust point clouds processing using nonlocal neural networks with adaptive sampling. In: Proceedings of the IEEE/CVF Conference on Computer Vision and Pattern Recognition, pp. 5589–5598 (2020)
62. Yao, L., Huang, S., Xu, H., Li, P.: Quadratic error metric mesh simplification algorithm based on discrete curvature. Math. Probl. Eng. **2015** (2015)
63. Yildiz, Z.C., Oztireli, A.C., Capin, T.: A machine learning framework for full-reference 3D shape quality assessment. Vis. Comput. **36**(1), 127–139 (2020)
64. Zhang, K., Qiao, S., Wang, X., Yang, Y., Zhang, Y.: Feature-preserved point cloud simplification based on natural quadric shape models. Appl. Sci. **9**(10), 2130 (2019)

Masked Autoencoders for Point Cloud Self-supervised Learning

Yatian Pang[2], Wenxiao Wang[3], Francis E. H. Tay[2], Wei Liu[4], Yonghong Tian[1,5], and Li Yuan[1,5(✉)]

[1] School of Electronic and Computer Engineering, Peking University, Beijing, China
`yuanli-ece@pku.edu.cn`
[2] National University of Singapore, Singapore, Singapore
`yatian_pang@u.nus.edu`
[3] Zhejiang University, Hangzhou, China
[4] Tencent Data Platform, Shenzhen, China
[5] PengCheng Laboratory, Shenzhen, China

Abstract. As a promising scheme of self-supervised learning, masked autoencoding has significantly advanced natural language processing and computer vision. Inspired by this, we propose a neat scheme of masked autoencoders for point cloud self-supervised learning, addressing the challenges posed by point cloud's properties, including leakage of location information and uneven information density. Concretely, we divide the input point cloud into irregular point patches and randomly mask them at a high ratio. Then, a standard Transformer based autoencoder, with an asymmetric design and a shifting mask tokens operation, learns high-level latent features from unmasked point patches, aiming to reconstruct the masked point patches. Extensive experiments show that our approach is efficient during pre-training and generalizes well on various downstream tasks. The pre-trained models achieve 85.18% accuracy on ScanObjectNN and 94.04% accuracy on ModelNet40, outperforming all the other self-supervised learning methods. We show with our scheme, a simple architecture entirely based on standard Transformers can surpass dedicated Transformer models from supervised learning. Our approach also advances state-of-the-art accuracies by 1.5%–2.3% in the few-shot classification. Furthermore, our work inspires the feasibility of applying unified architectures from languages and images to the point cloud. Codes are available at https://github.com/Pang-Yatian/Point-MAE.

1 Introduction

Self-supervised learning learns latent features from unlabeled data instead of building representations based on human-defined annotations. It is usually done by designing a pretext task to pre-train the model, then fine-tune on downstream tasks. Relying less on labeled data, self-supervised learning has significantly advanced natural language processing (NLP) [4,12,34,35] and computer

---

Supplementary Information The online version contains supplementary material available at https://doi.org/10.1007/978-3-031-20086-1_35.

vision [2,3,8,9,18,19,30,51]. Among them, masked autoencoding [2,18,51], illustrated in Fig. 1, is a promising scheme for both languages and images. It randomly masks a portion of input data and adopts an autoencoder to reconstruct explicit features (e.g., pixels) or implicit features (e.g., discrete tokens) corresponding to the original masked content. As masked parts do not provide data information, this reconstruction task enables the autoencoder to learn high-level latent features from unmasked parts. Besides, the powerful capability of masked autoencoding gives credit to its autoencoder's backbone, which adopts Transformers [42] architecture. For example, BERT [12] in NLP and MAE [18] in computer vision both apply masked autoencoding and adopt a standard Transformer architecture as autoencoder's backbone to achieve state-of-the-art performance.

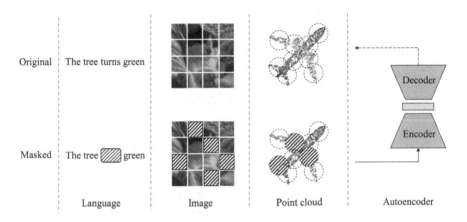

Fig. 1. Illustration of masked autoencoding. A portion of input data is masked, then an autoencoder is trained to recover the masked parts from original input data. The encoder in autoencoder is encouraged to learn high-level latent features from unmasked parts.

The idea of masked autoencoding is also applicable for point cloud self-supervised learning, as point cloud essentially shares a common property with both languages and images (see Fig. 1). Specifically, the fundamental elements (i.e., points, vocabularies, and pixels) that carry information are not independent. Instead, neighbouring elements form a meaningful subset to present local features. Together with local features, the complete set of elements makes up global features. Therefore, after embedding point subsets into tokens, the point cloud can be processed similarly with languages and images. Furthermore, considering datasets for the point cloud are relatively small, masked autoencoding as a self-supervised learning method can naturally address the large data demand of Transformers architecture, which is the autoencoder's backbone. Indeed, a recent work Point-BERT [56] attempts to design a scheme somewhat similar to masked autoencoding. It proposes a BERT-style pre-training strategy by masking input tokens of the point cloud, then adopts a Transformer architecture to predict

discrete tokens of the masked tokens. However, this method is relatively sophisticated as it is required to train a DGCNN [46] based discrete Variational AutoEncoder (dVAE) [37] before pre-training and relies heavily on contrastive learning as
well as data augmentation during pre-training. Moreover, the masked tokens from
their inputs are processed from the input of Transformers during pre-training,
leading to early leakage of location information and high consumption of computing resources. Different from their method, and more importantly, to introduce
masked autoencoding to the point cloud, we aim to design a neat and efficient
scheme of masked autoencoders. To this end, we first analyze the main challenges
of introducing masked autoencoding for point cloud from the following aspects:

(i) Lack of a unified Transformer architecture. Compared to Transformers [42]
    in NLP and Vision Transformer (ViT) [13] in computer vision, Transformer
    architectures for point cloud are less studied and relatively diverse, mainly
    because small datasets cannot meet the large data demand of Transformers.
    Different from previous methods that use dedicated Transformers or adopt
    extra non-Transformers models to assist (such as Point-BERT [56] uses an
    extra DGCNN [46]), we aim to build our autoencoder's backbone entirely
    based on standard Transformers, which can serve as a potential unified
    architecture for point cloud. This also enables further development for point
    cloud to join general multi-modality frameworks, such Data2vec [2].
(ii) Positional embeddings for mask tokens lead to leakage of location infor-
    mation. In masked autoencoders, each masked part is replaced by a share-
    weighted learnable mask token. All the mask tokens need to be provided
    with their location information in input data by positional embeddings.
    Then after processing by autoencoders, each mask token is used to recon-
    struct the corresponding masked part. Providing location information is
    not an issue for languages and images, because they do not contain location
    information. While point cloud naturally has location information in the
    data, leakage of location information to mask tokens makes the reconstruc-
    tion task less challenging, which is harmful for autoencoders learning latent
    features. We address this issue by shifting mask tokens from the input of
    the autoencoder's encoder to the input of the autoencoder's decoder. This
    delays the leakage of location information and enables the encoder to focus
    on learning features from unmasked parts.
(iii) Point cloud carries information in a different density compared to languages
    and images. Languages contain high-density information, while images con-
    tain heavy redundant information [18]. In the point cloud, information den-
    sity distribution is relatively uneven. The points that make up key local
    features (e.g., sharp corners and edges) contain a much higher density of
    information than the points that make up less important local features (e.g.,
    flat surfaces). In other words, if being masked, the points that contain high-
    density information is more difficult to be recovered in the reconstruction
    task. This can be directly observed in reconstruction examples, as shown
    in Fig. 2. Taking the last row of Fig. 2 for illustration, the masked desk sur-
    face (left) can be easily recovered, while the reconstruction of the masked

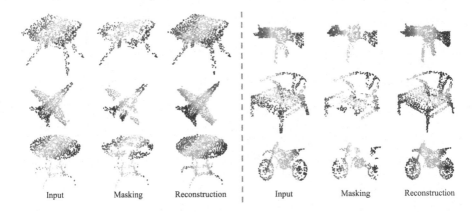

Input   Masking   Reconstruction   Input   Masking   Reconstruction

Fig. 2. Reconstruction examples on ShapeNet validation set. In each group, we show the original input (i.e., ground truth), masked point cloud, and reconstruction result from left to right. The masking ratio is 60%. It can be observed directly that reconstructions of key local features (such as sharp corners) are much worse than reconstructions of less important local features (such as flat surfaces).

motorcycle's wheel (right) is much worse. Although the point cloud contains uneven density of information, we find that random masking at a high ratio (60%–80%) works well, which is surprisingly the same as images. This indicates the point cloud is similar to images instead of languages, in terms of information density.

Driven by the analysis, we propose a novel self-supervised learning framework for **Point** cloud by designing a neat and efficient scheme of **M**asked **A**uto**E**ncoders, termed as **Point-MAE**. As shown in Fig. 3, our Point-MAE mainly consists of a point cloud masking and embedding module, and an autoencoder. The input point cloud is divided into irregular point patches, which are randomly masked at a high ratio to reduce data redundancy. Then, the autoencoder learns high-level latent features from unmasked point patches, aiming to reconstruct masked point patches in coordinate space. Specifically, our autoencoder's backbone is entirely built by standard Transformer blocks and adopts an asymmetric encoder-decoder structure [18]. The encoder only processes unmasked point patches. Then taking both encoded tokens and mask tokens as input, the lightweight decoder with a simple prediction head reconstructs masked point patches. Compared to processing mask tokens from the input of the encoder, shifting mask tokens to the lightweight decoder results in significant computational savings, and more importantly, avoiding early leakage of location information.

Our approach is effective, and pre-trained models generalize well on various downstream tasks. In object classification tasks, our Point-MAE achieves 85.18% accuracy on the hardest setting of real-world dataset ScanObjectNN and 94.04% accuracy on a clean object dataset ModelNet40, outperforming all the other self-supervised learning methods. Meanwhile, Point-MAE surpasses all the dedicated

Transformers models from supervised learning. In the few-shot object classification, Point-MAE significantly advances state-of-the-art accuracies by 1.5%–2.3% on different settings of ModelNet40. When generalized to the part segmentation task, Point-MAE largely improves the baseline by 1% mean IoU.

Our main contributions can be summarized as follows:

(1) We propose a novel scheme of masked autoencoders for point cloud self-supervised learning, addressing key issues including backbone architecture, early leakage of location information, and information density of the point cloud. Our approach is neat and efficient, with high generalization capability on various downstream tasks, outperforming all the other self-supervised learning methods.
(2) We show with our approach, a simple architecture that is entirely based on standard Transformers can surpass dedicated Transformer models from supervised learning. This result suggests that standard Transformers can serve as a potential unified architecture in the point cloud discipline.
(3) From the perspective of multimodal learning, our work inspires that unified architectures for languages and especially images, such as masked autoencoders, are also applicable for point cloud, when equipped with a modality-specific embedding module and a task-specific output head. We hope our field could be further advanced with the joint of other modality data.

2   Related Work

2.1   Self-supervised Learning

In the machine learning field, Self-supervised Learning (SSL) is defined as "the machine predicts any parts of its input for any observed part"[1]. The main ideas can be summarized as: a) supervision labels are generated from the data itself instead of human annotating, b) the model predicts parts of the data from other parts [26]. This process is usually done by designing a pretext task, which relieves the high demand for manual labeling data.

SSL for NLP and Image. In the NLP field, SSL has been well developed. Generative SSL methods such as BERT [12] gain huge success by designing pretext tasks that mask input tokens, and pre-train the model to predict original vocabularies. In computer vision for images, contrastive SSL methods [9,10,16,19,49] aim to discriminate the degree of similarities between different augmented images. These methods have dominated until recent generative SSL methods [18,47,51] result in more competitive performance. For example, MAE [18] randomly masks input patches, and pre-train the model to recover masked patches in pixel space.

SSL for Point Cloud. SSL has also been widely studied for point cloud representation learning [1,14,24,36,38,43,50,53,54,60]. Pretext tasks are relatively diverse. Among them, DepthContrast [60] sets an instance discrimination task for

---

[1] https://aaai.org/Conferences/AAAI-20/invited-speakers/.

two augmented versions of an input point cloud. OcCo [43] attempts to recover the original point cloud from the occluded point cloud in camera views. IAE [53] adopts an autoencoder to reconstruct implicit features from augmented inputs. A recent work Point-BERT [56] proposes a BERT-style pre-training strategy by masking input tokens and aims to predict discrete tokens of masked parts, with the assistance of dVAE [37]. Different from previous methods, we attempt to design a neat scheme for point cloud self-supervised learning.

2.2 Autoencoders

Generally, an autoencoder consists of an encoder followed by a decoder. The encoder is responsible for encoding inputs to high-level latent features. Then the decoder decodes latent features, aiming to reconstruct the input. The optimization goal is to make the reconstructed data as similar as possible to the original input, such as mean squared error loss in pixel space for images.

Specifically, our approach belongs to the class of denoising autoencoders. The main idea of denoising autoencoders is to enhance the robustness of the model by introducing input noise. Following the same principle, masked autoencoders introduce input noise through a masking operation. For example, in NLP, BERT [12] adopts masked language modeling. It randomly masks tokens from the input, then applies an autoencoder to predict vocabularies corresponding to masked tokens. In computer vision, both MAE [18] and SimMIM [51] propose a similar masked image modeling, which randomly masks input image patches. Then autoencoders are applied to predict the masked patches in pixel space. Inspired by the above ideas, our work aim to introduce masked autoencoders to point cloud.

2.3 Transformers

Transformers [42] model global dependencies of input through the self-attention mechanism, and have dominated in NLP [4,12,27,34,35]. Since ViT [13], Transformers architectures have been popular in computer vision [7,17,29,44,45,57, 58,61]. It also shows strength in multi-modality learning [2]. However, as backbones for masked autoencoders, Transformers architectures for point cloud representation learning are less developed. PCT [17] designs a dedicated input embedding layer and modifies the self-attention mechanism in Transformer layers. PointTransformer [61] also modifies the Transformer layer, and uses extra aggregating operations between Transformer blocks. These modifications largely limit the joint of other modality data from the perspective of multi-modality learning. Set Transformer [23] and the Perceiver line of works [5,21,22] mainly focus on supervised learning for multi-modality data. However, their experiment results for point cloud are less satisfactory. The recent work Point-BERT [56] introduces a standard Transformer architecture, but requires DGCNN [46] to assist pre-training. Different from previous works, our work presents an architecture that is entirely based on standard Transformers.

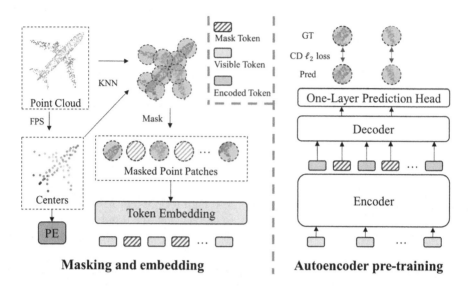

Fig. 3. Overall scheme of our Point-MAE. On the left, we show the masking and embedding process. The input cloud is divided into point patches, which are masked randomly and then embedded. Autoencoder pre-training is shown on the right. The encoder only processes visible tokens. Mask tokens are added to the input sequence of the decoder to reconstruct masked point patches.

3   Point-MAE

We aim to design a neat and efficient scheme of masked autoencoders for point cloud self-supervised learning. Figure 3 illustrates the overall scheme of our approach Point-MAE. The input point cloud is first processed by a masking and embedding module. Then a standard Transformer based autoencoder is adopted, including a simple prediction head, to reconstruct the masked parts of the input point cloud.

3.1   Point Cloud Masking and Embedding

Unlike images in computer vision that can be naturally divided into regular patches, point cloud consists of unordered points in 3D space. Based on its property, we process the input point cloud through three stages: point patches generation, masking, and embedding.

Point Patches Generation. Following Point-BERT [56], we divide input point cloud into irregular point patches (may overlap) via Farthest Point Sampling (FPS) and K-Nearest Neighborhood (KNN) algorithm. Formally, given an input point cloud with p points $X^i \in \mathbb{R}^{p \times 3}$, FPS is applied to sample n points for centers CT in point patches. Based on center points, KNN selects k nearest points from input for corresponding point patches P,

$$CT = FPS(X^i), \quad CT \in \mathbb{R}^{n \times 3}; \tag{1}$$

$$P = KNN(X^i, CT), \quad P \in \mathbb{R}^{n \times k \times 3}. \tag{2}$$

Note that in point patches, each point is represented by normalized coordinates with respect to its center point. This leads to better convergence.

Masking. Considering point patches may overlap, we mask them separately, in order to keep information complete in each point patch. With a masking ratio m, the set of masked patches is denoted as $P_{gt} \in \mathbb{R}^{mn \times k \times 3}$, which is used as ground truth in the computing of reconstruction loss. As for masking strategy, we find random masking at a high ratio (60%–80%) works well for our approach (see Sect. 4.2).

Embedding. For the embedding of each masked point patch, we replace it with a share-weighted learnable mask token. We denote the full set of mask tokens as $T_m \in \mathbb{R}^{mn \times C}$, where C is the embedding dimension. For the unmasked (visible) point patches, a naive idea is to flatten and embed them with a trainable linear projection, similar to ViT [13]. However, we argue that linear embedding fails to follow the principle of permutation invariance [31]. A more reasonable embedding method should be adopted. To keep neat, we implement a lightweight PointNet [31], which mainly consists of MLPs and max pooling layers. The visible point patches $P_v \in \mathbb{R}^{(1-m)n \times k \times 3}$ are hence embedded into visible tokens T_v,

$$T_v = PointNet(P_v), \quad T_v \in \mathbb{R}^{(1-m)n \times C}. \tag{3}$$

Considering point patches are represented in normalized coordinates, providing centers' position information to embedding tokens is essential. A simple method for Position Embedding (PE) is mapping coordinates of centers to embedding dimension with a learnable MLP, following previous works [56,61]. Note that we use two separate PE for encoder and decoder respectively in our autoencoder, introduced next.

3.2 Autoencoder's Backbone

Our autoencoder's backbone is entirely based on standard Transformers, with an asymmetric encoder-decoder design [18]. The last layer of the autoencoder adopts a simple prediction head to achieve the reconstruction target.

Encoder-Decoder. Our encoder consists of standard Transformer blocks and only encodes visible tokens T_v without mask tokens T_m. The encoded tokens are denoted as T_e. Furthermore, positional embeddings are added to every Transformer block, providing location information.

Our decoder is similar to the encoder but contains fewer Transformer blocks. It takes both encoded tokens T_e and masks tokens T_m as input. A full set of positional embeddings is added to every Transformer block, providing location information to all the tokens. After processing, the decoder only outputs the decoded mask tokens H_m, which are fed to the following prediction head. The encoder-decoder structure is formulated as,

$$T_e = Encoder(T_v), \quad T_e \in \mathbb{R}^{(1-m)n \times C}; \tag{4}$$

$$H_m = Decoder(concat(T_e, T_m)), \quad H_m \in \mathbb{R}^{mn \times C}. \tag{5}$$

In our encoder-decoder structure, we shift the mask tokens to the lightweight decoder instead of processing them from the input of the encoder. This design is beneficial from two aspects. First, as we use high masking ratios, shifting mask tokens significantly reduces the number of input tokens for the encoder. Therefore, we can save computational resources due to the quadratic complexity of Transformers. More importantly, shifting mask tokens to the decoder can avoid early leakage of location information to the encoder, making the encoder learn latent features better (see Sect. 4.2).

Prediction Head. As the last layer of backbone, the prediction head aims to reconstruct masked point patches in coordinate space. We simply use a fully connected (FC) layer as our prediction head. Taking the output H_m from the decoder, the prediction head projects it to a vector, which has the same number of dimensions as the total number of coordinates in a point patch. Then followed by a reshape operation, predicted masked point patches P_{pre} are obtained,

$$P_{pre} = Reshape(FC(H_m)), \quad P_{pre} \in \mathbb{R}^{mn \times k \times 3}. \tag{6}$$

3.3 Reconstruction Target

Our reconstruction target is to recover coordinates of the points in every masked point patch. Given the predicted point patches P_{pre} and ground truth P_{gt}, we compute the reconstruction loss by l_2 Chamfer Distance [15],

$$L = \frac{1}{|P_{pre}|} \sum_{a \in P_{pre}} \min_{b \in P_{gt}} \|a - b\|_2^2 + \frac{1}{|P_{gt}|} \sum_{b \in P_{gt}} \min_{a \in P_{pre}} \|a - b\|_2^2 \tag{7}$$

4 Experiments

We conduct the following experiments with our Point-MAE. a) Pre-training the model on ShapeNet [6] training set. b) Evaluating the pre-trained model on various downstream tasks. c) We study different masking strategies, and show the effect of shifting mask tokens. Model details and experiment details are provided in Appendix due to space limitation.

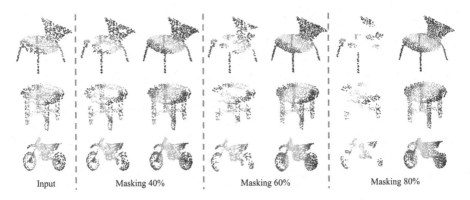

Input   Masking 40%   Masking 60%   Masking 80%

Fig. 4. Reconstruction results on ShapeNet validation set. The model is pretrained with a masking ratio of 60% but can generalize well on inputs with different masking ratios. Inputs are shown in the leftmost column. In the following columns, we show the masked input (left) and reconstruction (right) with different masking ratios.

4.1 Pre-training Setup

We pre-train the model on the ShapeNet [6] training set. To demonstrate the effectiveness of our method, we visualize reconstruction results on ShapeNet validation set in Fig. 4. The model is pre-trained with a masking ratio of 60%, but it is able to reconstruct inputs with different masking ratios. This high generalization capability can be expected, as our model learns high-level latent features well. Furthermore, our method speeds up pre-training by 1.7× compared to Point-BERT [56].

Table 1. Object classification on real-world ScanObjectNN dataset. We evaluate our approach on three variants, among which PB-T50-RS is the hardest setting.

Methods	OBJ-BG (%)	OBJ-ONLY (%)	PB-T50-RS (%)
PointNet [31]	73.3	79.2	68.0
SpiderCNN [52]	77.1	79.5	73.7
PointNet++ [32]	82.3	84.3	77.9
DGCNN [46]	82.8	86.2	78.1
PointCNN [25]	86.1	85.5	78.5
BGA-DGCNN [41]	–	–	79.7
BGA-PN++ [41]	–	–	80.2
GBNet [33]	–	–	80.5
PRANet [11]	–	–	81.0
Transformer [56]	79.86	80.55	77.24
Transformer-OcCo [56]	84.85	85.54	78.79
Point-BERT [56]	87.43	88.12	83.07
Point-MAE	**90.02**	**88.29**	**85.18**

4.2   Downstream Tasks

Object Classification on Real-World Dataset. In SSL for point cloud, one of the main concerns is that the commonly used dataset for pre-training, ShapeNet [6], only contains clean object models, without any scene context such as backgrounds. Motivated by this, we evaluate our pre-trained model on a challenging real-world dataset, ScanObjectNN [41], in which the objects are scanned from real-world indoor scene with backgrounds. We conduct experiments on three variants and show the results in Table 1. Experiment details are provided in Appendix. Our Point-MAE largely improves the baselines of standard Transformer. On the hardest variant PB-T50-RS, our model achieves 85.18% accuracy, outperforming Point-BERT [56] by 2.11%. Though being pre-trained on clean objects, Point-MAE generalizes well on real-world data, presenting a strong generalization capability.

Table 2. Object classification on ModelNet40. [T] represents the model is based on modified Transformers. [ST] represents the standard Transformers models.

Self-supervised methods	Accuracy	Supervised methods	Accuracy
		PointNet [31]	89.2%
		PointNet++ [32]	90.7%
OcCo [43]	93.0%	PointCNN [25]	92.5%
STRL [20]	93.1%	KPConv [40]	92.9%
IAE [53]	93.7%	DGCNN [25]	92.9%
[ST]Transformer-OcCo [56]	92.1%	RS-CNN [28]	92.9%
[ST]Point-BERT [56]	93.2%	[T]PCT [17]	93.2%
[ST]**Point-MAE**	**93.8%**	[T]PVT [59]	93.6%
		[T]PointTransformer [61]	93.7%
		[ST]Transformer [56]	91.4%

Object Classification on Clean Objects Dataset. We evaluate the pre-trained model on ModelNet40 [48] for object classification. For fair comparisons, we also use the standard voting method [28] during testing. Experiment results are presented in Table 2. All the reported methods are given 1024 points that only contain coordinate information without any normal information. Point-MAE achieves 93.8% accuracy, improving 2.4% accuracy compared to training from scratch (91.4%). Compared with other self-supervised learning methods, Point-MAE achieves state-of-the-art performance. Specifically, our approach with standard Transformers backbone surpasses IAE [53] that uses a more powerful DGCNN [46] as the backbone (in Table 2, DGCNN achieves a higher accuracy when training from scratch). Besides, Point-MAE outperforms sophisticated Point-BERT [56] by 0.6% accuracy. Besides, our approach surpasses all the dedicated Transformers models from supervised learning. Furthermore, given 8192 points as input, our Point-MAE achieves 94.04% accuracy.

Table 3. Few-shot classification on ModelNet40. We conduct 10 independent experiments for each setting and report mean accuracy (%) with standard deviation.

Methods	5-way, 10-shot	5-way, 20-shot	10-way, 10-shot	10-way, 20-shot
DGCNN-rand [43]	31.6 ± 2.8	40.8 ± 4.6	19.9 ± 2.1	16.9 ± 1.5
DGCNN-OcCo [43]	90.6 ± 2.8	92.5 ± 1.9	82.9 ± 1.3	86.5 ± 2.2
Transformer-rand [56]	87.8 ± 5.2	93.3 ± 4.3	84.6 ± 5.5	89.4 ± 6.3
Transformer-OcCo [56]	94.0 ± 3.6	95.9 ± 2.3	89.4 ± 5.1	92.4 ± 4.6
Point-BERT [56]	94.6 ± 3.1	96.3 ± 2.7	91.0 ± 5.4	92.7 ± 5.1
Point-MAE	$\mathbf{96.3 \pm 2.5}$	$\mathbf{97.8 \pm 1.8}$	$\mathbf{92.6 \pm 4.1}$	$\mathbf{95.0 \pm 3.0}$

Few-Shot Learning. We follow previous works [39,43,56] to conduct few-shot learning experiments on ModelNet40 [48], adopting n-way, m-shot setting. More details are provided in Appendix. The results with the setting of $n \in \{5, 10\}$ and $m \in \{10, 20\}$ are presented in Table 3. Our Point-MAE significantly advances state-of-the-art accuracies of four settings by 1.5%–2.3%, with smaller deviations.

Table 4. Part segmentation on ShapeNetPart dataset. We report mean IoU for all instances $mIoU_I$ (%), with IoU (%) for each category.

Methods	$mIoU_I$	aero	bag	cap	car	chair	e-phone	guitar	knife
		lamp	laptop	motor	mug	pistol	rocket	s-board	table
PointNet [31]	83.7	83.4	78.7	82.5	74.9	89.6	73.0	91.5	85.9
		80.8	95.3	65.2	93.0	81.2	57.9	72.8	80.6
PointNet++ [32]	85.1	82.4	79.0	87.7	77.3	90.8	71.8	91.0	85.9
		83.7	95.3	71.6	94.1	81.3	58.7	76.4	82.6
DGCNN [46]	85.2	84.0	83.4	86.7	77.8	90.6	74.7	91.2	87.5
		82.8	95.7	66.3	94.9	81.1	63.5	74.5	82.6
Transformer [56]	85.1	82.9	85.4	87.7	78.8	90.5	80.8	91.1	87.7
		85.3	95.6	73.9	94.9	83.5	61.2	74.9	80.6
Point-BERT [56]	85.6	84.3	84.8	88.0	79.8	91.0	81.7	91.6	87.9
		85.2	95.6	75.6	94.7	84.3	63.4	76.3	81.5
Point-MAE	**86.1**	84.3	85.0	88.3	80.5	91.3	78.5	92.1	87.4
		86.1	96.1	75.2	94.6	84.7	63.5	77.1	82.4

Part Segmentation. We evaluate the representation learning capability of our Point-MAE on ShapeNetPart dataset [55]. Our segmentation head is relatively simple and does not use any propagating operation or DGCNN [46]. For fair comparisons, our segmentation head has a similar weight with Point-BERT [56] and also uses learned features from $4th$, $8th$ and $12th$ layer of Transformer block. Details are provided in Appendix. Note that no voting methods or data augmentation are used during testing. As shown in Table 4, we report mean IoU (mIoU) for all instances, with IoU for each category. Our Point-MAE achieves 86.1% mIoU, improving the baseline by 1% mIoU. Point-MAE with a simple segmentation head also outperforms Point-BERT [56], which uses DGCNN [46] and propagation in their segmentation head.

Table 5. Ablation study on masking strategy. We conduct experiments using two masking strategy with different masking ratios (%), and report pre-train loss (10^{-3}) as well as fine-tune accuracy (%).

Type	Ratio	Loss	Acc.	Type	Ratio	Loss	Acc.	Type	Ratio	Loss	Acc.
Block	40	2.83	92.67	Random	40	2.49	92.46	Random	70	2.68	93.11
Block	60	2.89	92.67	Random	50	2.54	92.43	Random	80	2.77	93.03
Block	80	2.98	92.50	Random	60	2.60	**93.19**	Random	90	2.89	92.63

4.3   Ablation Study

Masking Strategy. To find a proper masking strategy for our method, we compare two masking types with different masking ratios. No voting method is used during testing. The reconstruction loss and fine-tune accuracy on Model-Net40 are presented in Table 5. We also visualize reconstructions with different masking strategies in Fig. 5.

The block masking [3,56] type masks neighbouring point patches, resulting in masked blocks. Though this strategy is harder for reconstruction, adopting a medium masking ratio can also achieve good performance.

The random masking type masks random point patches and empirically results in the best performance with a high masking ratio (i.e. 60%–80%). The performance degrades largely with low making ratios and also degrades slightly if the masking ratio is too high.

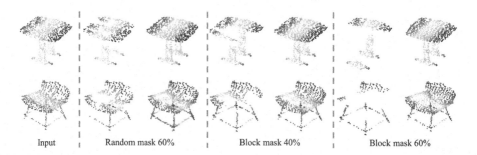

Input   Random mask 60%   Block mask 40%   Block mask 60%

Fig. 5. Reconstructions with different masking strategies. We mainly show three different masking strategies for same inputs (leftmost). In each column, masked inputs (left) and reconstructions (right) are shown. Instances are from ShapeNet validation set.

Effect of Shifting Mask Tokens. Our Point-MAE shifts mask tokens from the input of the encoder to the lightweight decoder. To demonstrate the effectiveness of this design, we conduct an experiment in which the mask tokens are processed from the input of the encoder. For fair comparisons, the autoencoder's backbone adopts the same encoder and prediction head as Point-MAE but without the decoder, resulting in the exact same model on fine-tune tasks. We use random masking at a ratio of 60% in this experiment. After pre-training, a smaller reconstruction loss is observed. However, for the fine-tune performance on ModelNet40, it achieves 92.14% accuracy, much lower than Point-MAE (93.19%). The result can be explained. At the input of the encoder, all tokens, including mask tokens, are provided with location information by positional embeddings. This causes early leakage of location information because mask tokens are processed for the reconstruction of point patches in coordinate space. The leakage of location information makes the reconstruction task less challenging, and the model cannot learn latent features well, leading to worse fine-tune performance.

4.4 Discussion

Here we attempt to analyse the reasons why our Point-MAE outperforms Point-BERT [56], which also adopts a similar mask and reconstruction framework. First, during pre-training, our reconstruction target is a part from the input data (i.e., coordinates), which is noise-free. While Point-BERT aims to reconstruct high-level latent representations, which are obtained from a frozen dVAE. If the dVAE is not well-learned to provide meaningful latent representations, the reconstruction target might be noisy. Second, Point-BERT processes masked tokens from the input. This causes leakage of location information, which is harmful for learning latent features. We address it by shifting mask tokens. Third, we argue the point cloud is similar to images instead of languages, in terms of information density. Empirically, we adopt random masking at a ratio of 60%–80%, which is largely different from Point-BERT's 25%–45% block masking.

5 Conclusions

In this paper, we present a novel scheme of masked autoencoders for point cloud self-supervised learning, termed as Point-MAE. Our Point-MAE is neat and efficient, with minimal modifications based on the properties of the point cloud. The effectiveness and high generalization capability of our approach are verified on various tasks, including object classification, few-shot learning, and part segmentation. Specifically, Point-MAE outperforms all the other self-supervised learning methods. We also show with our approach, a simple architecture that is entirely based on standard Transformers can surpass dedicated Transformer models from supervised learning. Furthermore, our work inspires the feasibility of applying unified architectures from languages and images to the point cloud.

Acknowledgments. This work was supported in part by PKU-Shenzhen Start-Up Research Fund (1270110283) and PengCheng Laboratory.

References

1. Achlioptas, P., Diamanti, O., Mitliagkas, I., Guibas, L.: Learning representations and generative models for 3D point clouds. In: International Conference on Machine Learning, pp. 40–49. PMLR (2018)
2. Baevski, A., Hsu, W.N., Xu, Q., Babu, A., Gu, J., Auli, M.: data2vec: a general framework for self-supervised learning in speech, vision and language, pp. 01–27 (2022). https://ai.facebook.com/research/data2veca-general-framework-for-self-supervised-learning-in-speech-vision-and-language/
3. Bao, H., Dong, L., Wei, F.: BEiT: BERT pre-training of image transformers. arXiv preprint arXiv:2106.08254 (2021)
4. Brown, T., et al.: Language models are few-shot learners. In: Advances in Neural Information Processing Systems, vol. 33, pp. 1877–1901 (2020)
5. Carreira, J., et al.: Hierarchical perceiver. arXiv preprint arXiv:2202.10890 (2022)
6. Chang, A.X., et al.: ShapeNet: an information-rich 3D model repository. arXiv preprint arXiv:1512.03012 (2015)
7. Chen, G., Wang, M., Yue, Y., Zhang, Q., Yuan, L.: Full transformer framework for robust point cloud registration with deep information interaction. arXiv preprint arXiv:2112.09385 (2021)
8. Chen, M., et al.: Generative pretraining from pixels. In: International Conference on Machine Learning, pp. 1691–1703. PMLR (2020)
9. Chen, T., Kornblith, S., Norouzi, M., Hinton, G.: A simple framework for contrastive learning of visual representations. In: International Conference on Machine Learning, pp. 1597–1607. PMLR (2020)
10. Chen, X., Fan, H., Girshick, R., He, K.: Improved baselines with momentum contrastive learning. arXiv preprint arXiv:2003.04297 (2020)
11. Cheng, S., Chen, X., He, X., Liu, Z., Bai, X.: PRA-Net: point relation-aware network for 3D point cloud analysis. IEEE Trans. Image Process. **30**, 4436–4448 (2021)
12. Devlin, J., Chang, M.W., Lee, K., Toutanova, K.: BERT: pre-training of deep bidirectional transformers for language understanding. arXiv preprint arXiv:1810.04805 (2018)
13. Dosovitskiy, A., et al.: An image is worth 16×16 words: transformers for image recognition at scale. arXiv preprint arXiv:2010.11929 (2020)
14. Eckart, B., Yuan, W., Liu, C., Kautz, J.: Self-supervised learning on 3D point clouds by learning discrete generative models. In: Proceedings of the IEEE/CVF Conference on Computer Vision and Pattern Recognition, pp. 8248–8257 (2021)
15. Fan, H., Su, H., Guibas, L.J.: A point set generation network for 3D object reconstruction from a single image. In: Proceedings of the IEEE Conference on Computer Vision and Pattern Recognition, pp. 605–613 (2017)
16. Grill, J.B., et al.: Bootstrap your own latent-a new approach to self-supervised learning. In: Advances in Neural Information Processing Systems, vol. 33, pp. 21271–21284 (2020)
17. Guo, M.H., Cai, J.X., Liu, Z.N., Mu, T.J., Martin, R.R., Hu, S.M.: PCT: point cloud transformer. Comput. Vis. Media **7**(2), 187–199 (2021). https://doi.org/10.1007/s41095-021-0229-5
18. He, K., Chen, X., Xie, S., Li, Y., Dollár, P., Girshick, R.: Masked autoencoders are scalable vision learners. arXiv preprint arXiv:2111.06377 (2021)
19. He, K., Fan, H., Wu, Y., Xie, S., Girshick, R.: Momentum contrast for unsupervised visual representation learning. In: Proceedings of the IEEE/CVF Conference on Computer Vision and Pattern Recognition, pp. 9729–9738 (2020)

20. Huang, S., Xie, Y., Zhu, S.C., Zhu, Y.: Spatio-temporal self-supervised representation learning for 3D point clouds. In: Proceedings of the IEEE/CVF International Conference on Computer Vision, pp. 6535–6545 (2021)
21. Jaegle, A., et al.: Perceiver IO: a general architecture for structured inputs & outputs. arXiv preprint arXiv:2107.14795 (2021)
22. Jaegle, A., Gimeno, F., Brock, A., Vinyals, O., Zisserman, A., Carreira, J.: Perceiver: general perception with iterative attention. In: International Conference on Machine Learning, pp. 4651–4664. PMLR (2021)
23. Lee, J., Lee, Y., Kim, J., Kosiorek, A., Choi, S., Teh, Y.W.: Set transformer: a framework for attention-based permutation-invariant neural networks. In: International Conference on Machine Learning, pp. 3744–3753. PMLR (2019)
24. Li, J., Chen, B.M., Lee, G.H.: SO-Net: self-organizing network for point cloud analysis. In: Proceedings of the IEEE Conference on Computer Vision and Pattern Recognition, pp. 9397–9406 (2018)
25. Li, Y., Bu, R., Sun, M., Wu, W., Di, X., Chen, B.: PointCNN: convolution on X-transformed points. In: Advances in Neural Information Processing Systems, vol. 31 (2018)
26. Liu, X., et al.: Self-supervised learning: generative or contrastive. IEEE Trans. Knowl. Data Eng. (2021)
27. Liu, Y., et al.: RoBERTa: a robustly optimized BERT pretraining approach. arXiv preprint arXiv:1907.11692 (2019)
28. Liu, Y., Fan, B., Xiang, S., Pan, C.: Relation-shape convolutional neural network for point cloud analysis. In: Proceedings of the IEEE/CVF Conference on Computer Vision and Pattern Recognition, pp. 8895–8904 (2019)
29. Liu, Z., et al.: Swin transformer: hierarchical vision transformer using shifted windows. In: Proceedings of the IEEE/CVF International Conference on Computer Vision, pp. 10012–10022 (2021)
30. Pathak, D., Krahenbuhl, P., Donahue, J., Darrell, T., Efros, A.A.: Context encoders: feature learning by inpainting. In: Proceedings of the IEEE Conference on Computer Vision and Pattern Recognition, pp. 2536–2544 (2016)
31. Qi, C.R., Su, H., Mo, K., Guibas, L.J.: PointNet: deep learning on point sets for 3D classification and segmentation. In: Proceedings of the IEEE Conference on Computer Vision and Pattern Recognition, pp. 652–660 (2017)
32. Qi, C.R., Yi, L., Su, H., Guibas, L.J.: PointNet++: deep hierarchical feature learning on point sets in a metric space. In: Advances in Neural Information Processing Systems, vol. 30 (2017)
33. Qiu, S., Anwar, S., Barnes, N.: Geometric back-projection network for point cloud classification. IEEE Trans. Multimed. **24**, 1943–1955 (2021)
34. Radford, A., Wu, J., Child, R., Luan, D., Amodei, D., Sutskever, I., et al.: Language models are unsupervised multitask learners. OpenAI Blog **1**(8), 9 (2019)
35. Raffel, C., et al.: Exploring the limits of transfer learning with a unified text-to-text transformer. arXiv preprint arXiv:1910.10683 (2019)
36. Rao, Y., Lu, J., Zhou, J.: Global-local bidirectional reasoning for unsupervised representation learning of 3D point clouds. In: Proceedings of the IEEE/CVF Conference on Computer Vision and Pattern Recognition, pp. 5376–5385 (2020)
37. Rolfe, J.T.: Discrete variational autoencoders. arXiv preprint arXiv:1609.02200 (2016)
38. Sauder, J., Sievers, B.: Self-supervised deep learning on point clouds by reconstructing space. In: Advances in Neural Information Processing Systems, vol. 32 (2019)

39. Sharma, C., Kaul, M.: Self-supervised few-shot learning on point clouds. In: Advances in Neural Information Processing Systems, vol. 33, pp. 7212–7221 (2020)

40. Thomas, H., Qi, C.R., Deschaud, J.E., Marcotegui, B., Goulette, F., Guibas, L.J.: KPConv: flexible and deformable convolution for point clouds. In: Proceedings of the IEEE/CVF International Conference on Computer Vision, pp. 6411–6420 (2019)

41. Uy, M.A., Pham, Q.H., Hua, B.S., Nguyen, T., Yeung, S.K.: Revisiting point cloud classification: a new benchmark dataset and classification model on real-world data. In: Proceedings of the IEEE/CVF International Conference on Computer Vision, pp. 1588–1597 (2019)

42. Vaswani, A., et al.: Attention is all you need. In: Advances in Neural Information Processing Systems, vol. 30 (2017)

43. Wang, H., Liu, Q., Yue, X., Lasenby, J., Kusner, M.J.: Unsupervised point cloud pre-training via occlusion completion. In: Proceedings of the IEEE/CVF International Conference on Computer Vision, pp. 9782–9792 (2021)

44. Wang, W., et al.: Pyramid vision transformer: a versatile backbone for dense prediction without convolutions. In: Proceedings of the IEEE/CVF International Conference on Computer Vision, pp. 568–578 (2021)

45. Wang, W., et al.: CrossFormer: a versatile vision transformer hinging on cross-scale attention. arXiv preprint arXiv:2108.00154 (2021)

46. Wang, Y., Sun, Y., Liu, Z., Sarma, S.E., Bronstein, M.M., Solomon, J.M.: Dynamic graph CNN for learning on point clouds. ACM Trans. Graph. (ToG) **38**(5), 1–12 (2019)

47. Wei, C., Fan, H., Xie, S., Wu, C.Y., Yuille, A., Feichtenhofer, C.: Masked feature prediction for self-supervised visual pre-training. arXiv preprint arXiv:2112.09133 (2021)

48. Wu, Z., et al.: 3D ShapeNets: a deep representation for volumetric shapes. In: Proceedings of the IEEE Conference on Computer Vision and Pattern Recognition, pp. 1912–1920 (2015)

49. Wu, Z., Xiong, Y., Yu, S.X., Lin, D.: Unsupervised feature learning via non-parametric instance discrimination. In: Proceedings of the IEEE Conference on Computer Vision and Pattern Recognition, pp. 3733–3742 (2018)

50. Xie, S., Gu, J., Guo, D., Qi, C.R., Guibas, L., Litany, O.: PointContrast: unsupervised pre-training for 3D point cloud understanding. In: Vedaldi, A., Bischof, H., Brox, T., Frahm, J.-M. (eds.) ECCV 2020. LNCS, vol. 12348, pp. 574–591. Springer, Cham (2020). https://doi.org/10.1007/978-3-030-58580-8_34

51. Xie, Z., et al.: SimMIM: a simple framework for masked image modeling. arXiv preprint arXiv:2111.09886 (2021)

52. Xu, Y., Fan, T., Xu, M., Zeng, L., Qiao, Yu.: SpiderCNN: deep learning on point sets with parameterized convolutional filters. In: Ferrari, V., Hebert, M., Sminchisescu, C., Weiss, Y. (eds.) ECCV 2018. LNCS, vol. 11212, pp. 90–105. Springer, Cham (2018). https://doi.org/10.1007/978-3-030-01237-3_6

53. Yan, S., et al.: Implicit autoencoder for point cloud self-supervised representation learning. arXiv preprint arXiv:2201.00785 (2022)

54. Yang, Y., Feng, C., Shen, Y., Tian, D.: FoldingNet: point cloud auto-encoder via deep grid deformation. In: Proceedings of the IEEE Conference on Computer Vision and Pattern Recognition, pp. 206–215 (2018)

55. Yi, L., et al.: A scalable active framework for region annotation in 3D shape collections. ACM Trans. Graph. (ToG) **35**(6), 1–12 (2016)

56. Yu, X., Tang, L., Rao, Y., Huang, T., Zhou, J., Lu, J.: Point-BERT: pre-training 3D point cloud transformers with masked point modeling. arXiv preprint arXiv:2111.14819 (2021)
57. Yuan, L., et al.: Tokens-to-Token ViT: training vision transformers from scratch on ImageNet. In: Proceedings of the IEEE/CVF International Conference on Computer Vision, pp. 558–567 (2021)
58. Yuan, L., Hou, Q., Jiang, Z., Feng, J., Yan, S.: VOLO: vision outlooker for visual recognition. arXiv preprint arXiv:2106.13112 (2021)
59. Zhang, C., Wan, H., Liu, S., Shen, X., Wu, Z.: PVT: point-voxel transformer for 3D deep learning. arXiv preprint arXiv:2108.06076 (2021)
60. Zhang, Z., Girdhar, R., Joulin, A., Misra, I.: Self-supervised pretraining of 3D features on any point-cloud. In: Proceedings of the IEEE/CVF International Conference on Computer Vision, pp. 10252–10263 (2021)
61. Zhao, H., Jiang, L., Jia, J., Torr, P.H., Koltun, V.: Point transformer. In: Proceedings of the IEEE/CVF International Conference on Computer Vision, pp. 16259–16268 (2021)

Intrinsic Neural Fields: Learning Functions on Manifolds

Lukas Koestler[1], Daniel Grittner[1] (ID), Michael Moeller[2] (ID), Daniel Cremers[1] (ID), and Zorah Lähner[2(✉)] (ID)

[1] Technische Universität München, Munich, Germany
[2] Universität Siegen, Siegen, Germany
zorah.laehner@uni-siegen.de

Abstract. Neural fields have gained significant attention in the computer vision community due to their excellent performance in novel view synthesis, geometry reconstruction, and generative modeling. Some of their advantages are a sound theoretic foundation and an easy implementation in current deep learning frameworks. While neural fields have been applied to signals on manifolds, *e.g.*, for texture reconstruction, their representation has been limited to extrinsically embedding the shape into Euclidean space. The extrinsic embedding ignores known intrinsic manifold properties and is inflexible wrt. Transfer of the learned function. To overcome these limitations, this work introduces intrinsic neural fields, a novel and versatile representation for neural fields on manifolds. Intrinsic neural fields combine the advantages of neural fields with the spectral properties of the Laplace-Beltrami operator. We show theoretically that intrinsic neural fields inherit many desirable properties of the extrinsic neural field framework but exhibit additional intrinsic qualities, like isometry invariance. In experiments, we show intrinsic neural fields can reconstruct high-fidelity textures from images with state-of-the-art quality and are robust to the discretization of the underlying manifold. We demonstrate the versatility of intrinsic neural fields by tackling various applications: texture transfer between deformed shapes & different shapes, texture reconstruction from real-world images with view dependence, and discretization-agnostic learning on meshes and point clouds.

1 Introduction

Neural fields have grown incredibly popular for novel view synthesis since the breakthrough work by Mildenhall et al. [29]. They showed that neural radiance fields together with differentiable volume rendering can be used to reconstruct scenes and often yield photorealistic renderings from novel viewpoints. This inspired work in related fields, *e.g.*, human shape modeling [34], shape and texture

---

L. Koestler and D. Grittner—Contributed equally.

Supplementary Information The online version contains supplementary material available at https://doi.org/10.1007/978-3-031-20086-1_36.

S. Avidan et al. (Eds.): ECCV 2022, LNCS 13662, pp. 622–639, 2022.
https://doi.org/10.1007/978-3-031-20086-1_36

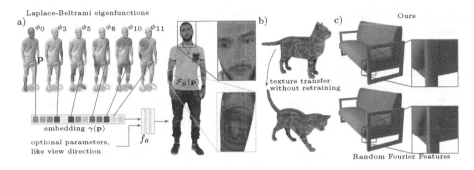

Fig. 1. (a) Overview of our method. We use the eigenfunctions ϕ_i of the Laplace-Beltrami operator (LBO) at each point as a point embedding $\gamma(\mathbf{p})$. This overcomes the spectral bias of the multilayer perceptron (MLP) f_θ, and hence the combined *intrinsic neural field* $\mathcal{F}_\theta$ can represent a high-frequency function on the surface. Notice that $\mathbf{p}$ can be inside a triangle, and the function is clearly more detailed than the discretization (*insets*). (b) An intrinsic neural texture field trained on one shape (*top*) can be transferred to a new shape (*bottom*) without retraining. (c) Due to our intrinsic approach (LBO eigenfunctions) local geometry is maintained in close but separate parts, whereas an extrinsic approach (Random Fourier Features [51]) shows bleeding artifacts when trained with sparse supervision.

generation from text [28], and texture representation on shapes [2,32], where neural fields are able to generate a wide variety of functions with high fidelity.

These methods use neural fields as functions from a point in Euclidean space to the quantity of interest. While this is valid for many applications, for others, the output actually lives on a general manifold. For example, texture mappings define a high-frequency color function on the surface of a 3D object. Texture-Fields [32] and Text2Mesh [28] solve this discrepancy by defining a mapping of each surface point to its Euclidean embedding and then learning the neural field there. Both show that they can achieve detail preservation above the discretization level, but the detour to Euclidean space has drawbacks. The Euclidean and geodesic distance between points can differ significantly. This is important on intricate shapes with fine geometric details that overlap because the local geometry prior is lost. Further, extrinsic representations cannot be used in the presence of surface deformations without retraining or applying heuristics.

Similar challenges have been solved in geometry processing by using purely intrinsic representations, most famously properties derived from the Laplace-Beltrami operator (LBO). Some of the main advantages of the LBO are its invariance under rigid and isometric deformations and reparametrization. We follow this direction by defining intrinsic neural fields on manifolds independent of the extrinsic Euclidean embedding and thus inherit the favorable properties of intrinsic representations. This is enabled by the fact that random Fourier features [51], an embedding technique that enabled the recent success of Euclidean neural fields, have an intrinsic analog based on the LBO. The result is a fully differentiable method that can learn high-frequency information on any 3D geometry representation that admits the computation of the LBO. A schematic overview of our method can be found in Fig. 1. Our main theoretical and experimental **contributions** are:

- We introduce **intrinsic neural fields**, a novel and versatile representation for neural fields on manifolds. Intrinsic neural fields combine the advantages of neural fields with the spectral properties of the Laplace-Beltrami operator.
- We extend the **neural tangent kernel analysis** of [51] to the manifold setting. This yields a proof characterizing the stationarity of the kernel induced by intrinsic neural fields and insight into their spectral properties.
- We show that intrinsic neural fields can **reconstruct high-fidelity textures** from images with state-of-the-art quality.
- We demonstrate the versatility of intrinsic neural fields by tackling **various applications**: texture transfer between isometric and non-isometric shapes, texture reconstruction from real-world images with view dependence, and discretization-agnostic learning on meshes and point clouds.

The source code can be found at github.com/tum-vision/intrinsic-neural-fields.

This work studies how a *neural field* can be defined on a manifold. Current approaches use the *extrinsic Euclidean embedding* to define the neural field on a manifold in the extrinsic embedding space – we describe this approach in Sect. 3.1. In contrast, our approach uses the well-known Laplace-Beltrami Operator (LBO), which we briefly introduce in Sect. 3.2. The final definition of *intrinsic neural fields* is given in Sect. 4. The experimental results are presented in Sect. 5.

2   Related Work

This work investigates neural fields for learning on manifolds, and we will only consider directly related work in this section. We point interested readers to the following overview articles: neural fields in visual computing [59], advances in neural rendering [52], and an introduction into spectral shape processing [25].

Neural Fields. While representing 3D objects and scenes with coordinate-based neural networks, or neural fields, has already been studied more than two decades ago [16,36,37], the topic has gained increased interest following the breakthrough work by Mildenhall et al. [29]. They show that a Neural Radiance Field (NeRF) often yields photorealistic renderings from novel viewpoints. One key technique underlying this success is positional encoding, which transforms the three-dimensional input coordinates into a higher dimensional space using sines and cosines with varying frequencies. This encoding overcomes the low-frequency bias of neural networks [3,38] and thus enables high-fidelity reconstructions. The aforementioned phenomenon is analyzed using the neural tangent kernel [20] by Tancik et al. [51], and our analysis extends theirs from Euclidean space to manifolds. Simultaneously to Tancik et al., Sitzmann et al. [48] use periodic activation functions for neural scene representation, which is similar to the above-mentioned positional encoding [4]. Additionally, many other works [19,22,26,27,40,41,55,61,64] offer insights into neural fields and their embedding functions. Most notably, [14] introduces spectral features for transformers on graphs. However, none of these works considers neural fields on manifolds.

Neural Fields on Manifolds. Prior works [2,11,18,28,30,32,34,58,60] use neural fields to represent a wide variety of quantities on manifolds. Oechsle et al. [32] use the extrinsic embedding of the manifold to learn textures as multilayer perceptrons. Their Texture Fields serve as an important baseline for this work. NeuTex by Xiang et al. [58] combines neural, volumetric scene representations with a 2D texture network to facilitate interpretable and editable texture learning. To enable this disentanglement, their method uses mapping networks from the 3D space of the object to the 2D space of the texture and back. We compare with an adapted version of their method that utilizes the known geometry of the object. Baatz et al. [2] introduce NeRF-Tex, a combination of neural radiance fields (NeRFs) and classical texture maps. Their method uses multiple small-scale NeRFs to cover the surface of a shape and represent mesoscale structures, such as fur, fabric, and grass. Because their method focuses on mesoscale and artistic editing, we believe that extending the current work to their setting is an interesting direction for future research. Further, neural fields are used to represent quantities other than texture on manifolds. Palafox et al. [34] define a neural deformation field that maps points on a canonical shape to their location on the deformed shape. This model is applied to generate neural parametric models which can be used similarly to traditional models like SMPL [24]. Yifan et al. [60] decompose a neural signed distance function (SDF) into a coarse SDF and a high-frequency implicit displacement field. Morreale et al. [30] define neural surface maps, which can be used to define surface-to-surface correspondences among other applications. Text2Mesh [28] uses a coarse mesh and a textual description to generate a detailed mesh and associated texture as neural fields.

Intrinsic Geometry Processing. Intrinsic properties are a popular tool in geometry processing, especially in the analysis of deformable objects. The most basic intrinsic features are Gauss curvature and intrinsic point descriptors based on the Laplace-Beltrami operator (LBO). They have been heavily used since the introduction of the global point signature [42] and refined since then [1,50]. Intrinsic properties are not derived from a manifold's embedding into its embedding space but instead arise from the pairwise geodesic distance on the surface. These are directly related to natural kernel functions on manifolds, *e.g.*, shown by the efficient approximation of the geodesic distance from the heat kernel [12]. Kernel functions as a measure of similarity are popular in geometry processing. They have been used in various applications, *e.g.*, in shape matching [9,23,54], parallel transport [46], and robustness wrt. discretization [44,53]. Manifold kernels naturally consider the local and global geometry [5], and our approach follows this direction by showing a natural extension of neural fields on manifolds.

3   Background

Differential geometry offers two viewpoints onto manifolds: intrinsic and extrinsic. The extrinsic viewpoint studies the manifold $\mathcal{M}$ through its *Euclidean embedding* where each point $\mathbf{p} \in \mathcal{M}$ is associated with its corresponding point in Euclidean space. In contrast, the intrinsic viewpoint considers only properties of points independent of the extrinsic embedding, such as, the geodesic distance between a point pair. Both can have advantages depending on the method and application. An intrinsic viewpoint is by design invariant against certain deformations in the Euclidean embedding, like rigid transformations but also pose variations that are hard to characterize in the extrinsic view.

3.1 Neural Fields for Euclidean Space

A Euclidean neural field $\mathcal{F}_\theta^E : \mathbb{R}^m \to \mathbb{R}^o$ is a neural network that maps points in Euclidean space to vectors and is parametrized by weights $\theta \in \mathbb{R}^p$. The network is commonly chosen to be a multilayer perceptron (MLP). Let $\mathcal{M} \subset \mathbb{R}^m$ be a manifold with a Euclidean embedding into $\mathbb{R}^m$. Naturally, the restriction of $\mathcal{F}_\theta^E$ to $\mathcal{M}$ leads to a neural field on a manifold: $\mathcal{F}_\theta : \mathcal{M} \to \mathbb{R}^o, \mathcal{F}_\theta(x) = \mathcal{F}_\theta^E(x)$.

Natural signals, such as images and scenes, are usually quite complex and contain high-frequency variations. Due to spectral bias, standard neural fields fail to learn high-frequency functions from low dimensional data [48,51] and generate blurry reconstructions. With the help of the neural tangent kernel, it was proven that the composition $\mathcal{F}_\theta^E \circ \gamma$ of a higher dimensional Euclidean neural field and a random Fourier feature (RFF) encoding γ helps to overcome the spectral bias and, consequently, enables the neural field to better represent high-frequency signals. The RFF encoding $\gamma : \mathbb{R}^m \to \mathbb{R}^d$ with $d \gg m$ is defined as

$$\gamma(\mathbf{x}) = [a_1 \cos(\mathbf{b}_1^\top \mathbf{x}), a_1 \sin(\mathbf{b}_1^\top \mathbf{x}), \dots, a_{d/2} \cos(\mathbf{b}_{d/2}^\top \mathbf{x}), a_{d/2} \sin(\mathbf{b}_{d/2}^\top \mathbf{x})], \quad (1)$$

where the coefficients $\mathbf{b}_i \in \mathbb{R}^m$ are randomly drawn from the multivariate normal distribution $\mathcal{N}(\mathbf{0}, (2\pi\sigma)^2 \mathbf{I})$. The a_i are often set to one and $\sigma > 0$ is a hyperparameter that offers a trade-off between reconstruction fidelity and overfitting.

3.2 The Laplace-Beltrami Operator

In the following, we briefly introduce the Laplace-Beltrami operator (LBO) and refer the interested reader to [42] for more details. The LBO $\triangle_\mathcal{M}$ is the generalization of the Euclidean Laplace operator on general closed compact manifolds. Its eigenfunctions $\phi_i : \mathcal{M} \to \mathbb{R}$ and eigenvalues $\lambda_i \in \mathbb{R}$ are the non-trivial solutions of the equation $\triangle_\mathcal{M} \phi_i = \lambda_i \phi_i$. The eigenvalues are non-negative and induce a natural ordering which we will use for the rest of the paper. The eigenfunctions are orthonormal to each other, build an optimal basis for the space of square-integrable functions [35], and are frequency ordered allowing a low-pass filtering by projecting onto the first k eigenfunctions. Hence, a function $f : \mathcal{M} \to \mathbb{R} \in L^2(\mathcal{M})$ can be expanded in this basis:

$$f = \sum_{i=0}^{\infty} c_i \phi_i = \sum_{i=0}^{\infty} \langle f, \phi_i \rangle \phi_i \approx \sum_{i=0}^{k} \langle f, \phi_i \rangle \phi_i, \quad (2)$$

where the quality of the last $\approx$ depends on the amount of high-frequency information in f. The projection onto the LBO basis is similar to the Fourier transform, allowing the same operations, and thus we use the LBO basis as the replacement for Fourier features. In fact, if $[0,1]^2$ is considered as a manifold, its LBO eigenfunctions with different boundary conditions are exactly combinations of sines and cosines. Furthermore, the eigenfunctions of the LBO are identical up to sign ambiguity for isometric shapes since the LBO is entirely intrinsic.

4   Intrinsic Neural Fields

We introduce *Intrinsic Neural Fields* based on the eigenfunctions of the Laplace-Beltrami operator (LBO) which can represent detailed surface information, like texture, directly on the manifold. In the presence of prior geometric information, it is more efficient than using an extrinsic embedding which is often mainly empty. Further, this representation is naturally invariant to translation, rotation, different surface discretization, as well as isometric deformations.

Definition 1 (Intrinsic Neural Field). *Let $\mathcal{M} \subset \mathbb{R}^m$ be a closed, compact manifold and $\phi_1, \ldots, \phi_d$ be the first d Laplace-Beltrami eigenfunctions of $\mathcal{M}$. We define an **intrinsic neural field** $\mathcal{F}_\theta : \mathcal{M} \to \mathbb{R}^o$ as*

$$\mathcal{F}_\theta(\mathbf{p}) = (f_\theta \circ \gamma)(\mathbf{p}) = f_\theta(a_1\phi_1(\mathbf{p}), \ldots, a_d\phi_d(\mathbf{p})). \tag{3}$$

where $\gamma : \mathcal{M} \to \mathbb{R}^d, \gamma(\mathbf{p}) = (a_1\phi_1(\mathbf{p}), \ldots, a_d\phi_d(\mathbf{p}))$, with $a_i \geq 0$ and $\lambda_i = \lambda_j \Rightarrow a_i = a_j$, is our embedding function and $f_\theta : \mathbb{R}^d \to \mathbb{R}^o$ represents a neural network with weights $\theta \in \mathbb{R}^p$.

Within this work, we will use $a_i = 1$, which has proven sufficient in praxis, and multilayer perceptrons (MLPs) for f_θ, as this architectural choice is common for Euclidean neural fields [59]. A detailed description of the architecture can be found in the supplementary material. It is possible to choose different embedding functions γ but we choose the LBO eigenfunctions as they have nice theoretical properties (see Sect. 4.1) and are directly related to Fourier features.

In Fig. 2, we apply intrinsic neural fields to the task of signal reconstruction on a 1D manifold to give an intuition about how it works and what its advantages are. The results show that the neural tangent kernel (NTK) for intrinsic neural fields exhibits favorable properties, which we prove in Sect. 4.1. We show that we can represent high-frequency signals on manifold surfaces that go far beyond the discretization level. In Sect. 5, we apply the proposed intrinsic neural fields to a variety of tasks including texture reconstruction from images, texture transfer between shapes without retraining, and view-dependent appearance modeling.

4.1   Theory

In this section, we prove that the embedding function γ proposed in Definition 1 generalizes the stationarity result of [51] to certain manifolds. Stationarity is a desirable property if the kernel is used for interpolation, for example, in novel view synthesis [51, App. C]. Fourier features induce a stationary (shift-invariant) neural tangent kernel (NTK). Namely, the composed NTK for two

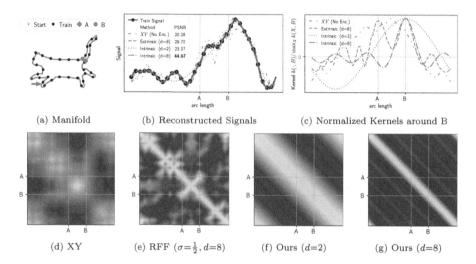

(a) Manifold   (b) Reconstructed Signals   (c) Normalized Kernels around B

(d) XY   (e) RFF ($\sigma=\frac{1}{2}$, $d=8$)   (f) Ours ($d=2$)   (g) Ours ($d=8$)

Fig. 2. Signal reconstruction. (2b) The target is sampled at 32 points and MLPs with three layers, 1024 channels, and different embeddings are trained using L^2 loss. The intrinsic neural field with $d = 8$ eigenfunctions performs best. Using only two eigenfunctions leads to oversmoothing. The reconstruction with the extrinsic embedding and random Fourier features (RFF) [51] can capture the high-frequency details, but introduces artifacts when the Euclidean distance is not a good approximation of the geodesic distance, for example, at points A & B. (2d–2g) The second row of subfigures shows the pairwise neural tangent kernel (NTK) [20,31] between all points on the manifold. (2d) The NTK using the extrinsic Euclidean embedding is not maximal along the diagonal. (2e) For the NTK with RFF embedding the maximum is at the diagonal because each point's influence is maximal onto itself. However, it has many spurious correlations between points that are close in Euclidean space but not along the manifold, for example, around B. (2f, 2g) The NTK with our intrinsic embedding is localized correctly and is stationary (c.f. Theorem 1), which makes it most suitable for interpolation.

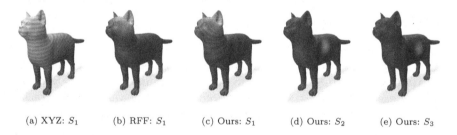

(a) XYZ: S_1 (b) RFF: S_1 (c) Ours: S_1 (d) Ours: S_2 (e) Ours: S_3

Fig. 3. Neural tangent kernels (NTKs) [20,31] with different embedding functions. The source S_1 lies directly inside the ear of the cat. (3a) The NTK using the extrinsic Euclidean embedding is not maximal at the source. (3b) The NTK using random Fourier features (RFF) [51] is localized correctly, but shows wrong behavior on the cat's body. (3c) The NTK with our intrinsic embedding is localized correctly and adapts to the local and global geometry. (3d, 3e) Additionally, the NTK with our intrinsic embedding is nearly shift-invariant, if the local geometry is approximately Euclidean: When the source is shifted from S_2 to S_3 the kernel is approximately shifted as well.

points in Euclidean space $\mathbf{x}, \mathbf{y} \in \mathbb{R}^m$ is given by $k_{\text{NTK}}(\mathbf{x}, \mathbf{y}) = (h_{\text{NTK}} \circ h_\gamma)(\mathbf{x} - \mathbf{y})$ where $h_{\text{NTK}} : \mathbb{R} \to \mathbb{R}$ is a scalar function related to the NTK of the MLP and $h_\gamma : \mathbb{R}^m \to \mathbb{R}$ is a scalar function related to the Fourier feature embedding [51, Eqn. 7, 8]. Extending this result to $\mathbf{p}, \mathbf{q} \in \mathcal{M}$ on a manifold is challenging because the point difference $\mathbf{p} - \mathbf{q}$ and, therefore, stationarity is not defined intrinsically (Fig. 3).

Stationarity on Manifolds. While one could use the Euclidean embedding of the manifold to define the difference $\mathbf{p} - \mathbf{q}$, this would ignore the local connectivity and can change under extrinsic deformations. Instead, we use an equivalent definition from Bochner's theorem which states that in Euclidean space any continuous, *stationary* kernel is the Fourier transform of a non-negative measure [39, Thm. 1]. This definition can be directly used on manifolds, and we define a kernel $k : \mathcal{M} \times \mathcal{M} \to \mathbb{R}$ to be **stationary** if it can be written as

$$k(\mathbf{p}, \mathbf{q}) = \sum_i \hat{k}(\lambda_i)\phi_i(\mathbf{p})\phi_i(\mathbf{q}), \qquad \hat{k}(\lambda_i) \geq 0 \ \forall i, \qquad (4)$$

where the function $\hat{k} : \mathbb{R} \to \mathbb{R}_0^+$ is akin to the Fourier transform. This implies that $\hat{k}(\lambda_i)$ and $\hat{k}(\lambda_j)$ for identical eigenvalues $\lambda_i = \lambda_j$ must be identical.

First, we want to point out that for inputs with $\|\mathbf{x}\| = \|\mathbf{y}\| = r$ the result of $k_{\text{NTK}}(\mathbf{x}, \mathbf{y}) = h_{\text{NTK}}(\langle \mathbf{x}, \mathbf{y} \rangle)$ shown by [20] for $r = 1$ and used in [51] still holds. We include this slight extension as Lemma 1 in the suppl. This is a prerequisite for the following theorem which requires the same setting as used in [20].

Theorem 1. *Let $\mathcal{M}$ be $\mathbb{S}^n$ or a closed 1-manifold. Let $(\lambda_i, \phi_i)_{i=1,\dots,d}$ be the positive, non-decreasing eigenvalues with associated eigenfunctions of the Laplace-Beltrami operator on $\mathcal{M}$. Let $a_i \geq 0$ be coefficients s.t. $\lambda_i = \lambda_j \Rightarrow a_i = a_j$, which define the embedding function $\gamma : \mathcal{M} \to \mathbb{R}^d$ with $\gamma(\mathbf{p}) = (a_1\phi_1(\mathbf{p}), \dots, a_d\phi_d(\mathbf{p}))$. Then, the composed neural tangent kernel $k_{NTK} : \mathcal{M} \times \mathcal{M} \to \mathbb{R}$ of an MLP with the embedding γ is stationary as defined in Eq. 4.*

Proof. Let $\mathcal{M} = \mathbb{S}^n$ and let $\mathbf{H}_l^n$ be the space of degree l spherical harmonics on $\mathbb{S}^n$. Let $Y_{lm} \in \mathbf{H}_l^n$ be the m-th real spherical harmonic of degree l with $m = 1, \dots, \dim \mathbf{H}_l^n$. Notice that the spherical harmonics are the eigenfunctions of the LBO. We will use j to linearly index the spherical harmonics and $l(j)$ for the degree. Spherical harmonics of the same degree have the same eigenvalues, thus we use $c_{l(j)} = a_j = a_i$ for $\lambda_i = \lambda_j$ to denote the equal coefficients for same degree harmonics. First, the norm of the embedding function is constant:

$$\|\gamma(\mathbf{q})\|^2 = \sum_j c_{l(j)}^2 \phi_j^2(\mathbf{q}) = \sum_l c_l^2 \sum_{m=1}^{\dim \mathbf{H}_l^n} Y_{lm}^2(\mathbf{q}) \overset{(a)}{=} \sum_l c_l^2 Z_l(\mathbf{q}, \mathbf{q}) \overset{(b)}{=} \text{const.} \quad (5)$$

Here, $Z_l(\mathbf{q}, \mathbf{q})$ is the degree l zonal harmonic and (a, b) are properties of zonal harmonics [13, Lem. 1.2.3, Lem. 1.2.7]. Due to Eq. 5 and Lemma 1 (supp.) $k_{\text{NTK}}(\gamma(\mathbf{p}), \gamma(\mathbf{q})) = h_{\text{NTK}}(\langle \gamma(\mathbf{p}), \gamma(\mathbf{q}) \rangle) \ \forall \mathbf{p}, \mathbf{q} \in \mathcal{M}$ holds. It follows:

$$\langle\gamma(\mathbf{p}),\gamma(\mathbf{q})\rangle = \sum_{j} c_{l(j)}^2 \phi_j(\mathbf{p})\phi_j(\mathbf{q}) = \sum_{l} c_l^2 \sum_{m=1}^{\dim \mathbf{H}_l^n} Y_{lm}(\mathbf{p})Y_{lm}(\mathbf{q}) \qquad (6)$$

$$\overset{(c)}{=} \sum_{l} c_l^2 Z_{\mathbf{p}}^l(\mathbf{q}) \overset{(d)}{=} \sum_{l} c_l^2 (1+l/\alpha) C_l^{\alpha}(\langle\mathbf{p},\mathbf{q}\rangle), \qquad (7)$$

where $C_l^{\alpha} : [-1,1] \to \mathbb{R}$ are the Gegenbauer polynomials which are orthogonal on $[-1,1]$ for the weighting function $w_{\alpha}(z) = (1-z^2)^{\alpha-1/2}$ with $\alpha = (n-1)/2$ [13, B.2]. Equality (c) holds again due to [13, Lem. 1.2.3]. Equality (d) holds due to a property of Gegenbauer polynomials [13, Thm. 1.2.6], here $\langle\mathbf{p},\mathbf{q}\rangle$ denotes the extrinsic Euclidean inner product. For the composed NTK we obtain

$$k_{\text{NTK}}(\gamma(\mathbf{p}),\gamma(\mathbf{q})) = h_{\text{NTK}}\left(\sum_l c_l^2 (1+l/\alpha) C_l^{\alpha}(\langle\mathbf{p},\mathbf{q}\rangle)\right). \qquad (8)$$

We see that $k_{\text{NTK}}(\gamma(\mathbf{p}),\gamma(\mathbf{q}))$ is a function depending only on $\langle\mathbf{p},\mathbf{q}\rangle$. Because the Gegenbauer polynomials are orthogonal on $[-1,1]$, this function can be expanded with coefficients $\hat{c}_l \in \mathbb{R}$, which yields

$$k_{\text{NTK}}(\gamma(\mathbf{p}),\gamma(\mathbf{q})) = \sum_l \hat{c}_l (1+l/\alpha) C_l^{\alpha}(\langle\mathbf{p},\mathbf{q}\rangle) = \sum_l \hat{c}_l Z^l(\mathbf{p},\mathbf{q}) \qquad (9)$$

$$= \sum_l \hat{c}_l \sum_{m=1}^{\dim \mathbf{H}_l^n} Y_{lm}(\mathbf{p})Y_{lm}(\mathbf{q}) = \sum_j \hat{c}_{l(j)} \phi_j(\mathbf{p})\phi_j(\mathbf{q}). \qquad (10)$$

The coefficients $\hat{c}_{l(j)}$ are non-negative as a consequence of the positive definiteness of the NTK [20, Prop. 2] and a classic result by Schoenberg [13, Thm. 14.3.3]. This shows that $k_{\text{NTK}}(\gamma(\mathbf{p}),\gamma(\mathbf{q}))$ is stationary as defined in Eq. 4.   □

The adapted proof for 1-manifolds can be found in the supplementary. A qualitative example of the stationary kernels can be seen in Fig. 2. The theorem does not hold for general manifolds, however, our experiments with different γ (Table 1) indicate the eigenfunctions are still a superior choice for complex manifolds. We leave the theoretical explanation for this behaviour to future work.

5   Experiments

We refer to the supplementary material for all experimental details and hyperparameter settings as well as further results. To facilitate fair comparisons, all methods use the same hyperparameters like learning rate, optimizer, number of training epochs, and MLP architecture except when noted otherwise. For baselines using random Fourier features (RFF), we follow [51] and tune the standard deviation σ (c.f. Eq. 1) of the random frequency matrix to obtain optimal results.

5.1   Texture Reconstruction from Images

To investigate the representation power of the proposed intrinsic neural fields, we consider the task of texture reconstruction from posed images as proposed by Oechsle et al. [32] in Table 1 and Fig. 4. The input to our algorithms is a set of five 512×512 images with their camera poses and the triangle mesh of the shape. After fitting the intrinsic neural field to the data, we render images from 200 novel viewpoints and compare them to ground-truth images for evaluation.

For each pixel, we perform ray mesh intersection between the ray through the pixel and the mesh. The eigenfunctions of the Laplace-Beltrami operator are defined only on vertices of the mesh [45]. Within triangles, we use barycentric interpolation. We employ the mean L^1 loss across a batch of rays and the RGB color channels. The eigenfunction computation and ray-mesh intersection are performed once at the start of training. Hence, our training speed is similar to the baseline method that uses random Fourier features. Training takes approx. one hour on an Nvidia Titan X with 12 GB memory.

Comparison with State of the Art Methods. We compare against Texture Fields [32] enhanced with random Fourier features (RFF) [51]. Additionally, we compare against NeuTex [58], which uses a network to map a shape to the sphere and represents the texture on this sphere. We adapt NeuTex s.t. it takes advantage of the given geometry, see supplementary. Table 1 and Fig. 4 show that intrinsic neural fields can reconstruct texture with state-of-the-art quality. This is also true if the number of training epochs is decreased from 1000 to 200.

Ablation Study. We investigate the effect of different hyperparameters on the quality of the intrinsic neural texture field. The results in Table 2 show that the number of eigenfunctions is more important than the size of the MLP, which is promising for real-time applications. A model using only 64 eigenfunctions and $17k$ parameters[1] still achieves a PSNR of 29.20 for the cat showing that intrinsic neural fields can be a promising approach for compressing manifold data. Additionally, we test the importance of the choice of Laplace-Beltrami eigenfunctions as γ for the results. Table 1 shows that popular point descriptors [43,50], that achieve great results in the difficult task of shape matching, perform worse within our framework. This indicates that, although we were not able to proof it, an extension of Theorem 1 likely holds on 2D manifolds.

5.2   Discretization-agnostic Intrinsic Neural Fields

For real-world applications, it is desirable that intrinsic neural fields can be trained for different discretizations of the same manifold. First, the training process of the intrinsic neural field should be robust to the sampling in the discretization. Second, it would be beneficial if an intrinsic neural field trained on one discretization could be transferred to another, which we show in Sect. 5.3. To quantify the discretization dependence of intrinsic neural fields, we follow the procedure proposed by Sharp et al. [44, Sec. 5.4] and rediscretize the meshes

---

[1] For reference: a 80×80 3-channel color texture image has over $17k$ pixel values.

Table 1. Texture reconstruction from images. Our intrinsic neural fields show state-of-the-art performance (*first block*), even with fewer training epochs (*Ep.↓, second block*). For a fair comparison, we improve Texture Fields by employing the same MLP architecture as our model and by using random Fourier features (*TF+RFF*). NeuTex has more parameters than our model but we increase the embedding size (*Em.↑*) to match. We adapt NeuTex to take advantage of the given geometry (see supplementary). The methods are evaluated on novel views using PSNR, DSSIM [56], and LPIPS [63]. DSSIM and LPIPS are scaled by 100. The intrinsic representation shows better results than the extrinsic representation (*TF+RFF*) as well as when mapping to a textured sphere (*NeuTex*). The last block shows the performance of our method when using point descriptors HKS [50] and SHOT [43] instead of the proposed γ input.

	Em.	Ep.	Cat			Human		
			PSNR↑	DSSIM↓	LPIPS↓	PSNR↑	DSSIM↓	LPIPS↓
NeuTex [58]	63	1000	31.60	0.242	0.504	29.49	0.329	0.715
NeuTex Em.↑	1023	1000	31.96	0.212	0.266	29.22	0.306	0.669
TF+RFF ($\sigma = 4$) [32,51]	1023	1000	33.86	0.125	0.444	32.04	0.130	0.420
TF+RFF ($\sigma = 16$)	1023	1000	34.19	0.105	0.167	31.53	0.193	0.414
TF+RFF ($\sigma = 8$)	1023	1000	34.39	0.097	0.205	32.26	0.129	0.336
Intrinsic (Ours)	1023	1000	**34.82**	**0.095**	**0.153**	**32.48**	**0.121**	**0.306**
NeuTex Ep.↓	1023	200	30.96	0.290	0.355	28.02	0.418	0.900
TF+RFF ($\sigma = 8$) Ep.↓	1023	200	34.07	0.116	0.346	31.85	0.142	0.427
Intrinsic (Ours) Ep.↓	1023	200	**34.79**	**0.100**	**0.196**	**32.37**	**0.126**	**0.346**
Ours (HKS)	352	1000	23.40	1.219	2.877	22.26	0.904	2.347
Ours (SHOT)	352	1000	26.44	0.780	1.232	28.04	0.421	0.965
Ours (Efcts.)	352	1000	**34.19**	**0.119**	**0.345**	**31.63**	**0.150**	**0.489**

used in Sect. 5.1. The qualitative results in Fig. 5 and the quantitative results in Table 3 show that intrinsic neural fields work across various discretizations. Furthermore, Fig. 6 shows that transferring pre-trained intrinsic neural fields across discretizations is possible with minimal loss in visual quality.

5.3 Intrinsic Neural Field Transfer

One advantage of the Laplace-Beltrami operator is its invariance under isometries which allows transferring a pre-trained intrinsic neural field from one manifold to another. However, this theoretic invariance does not hold completely in practice, for example, due to discretization artifacts [21]. Hence, we employ functional maps [33] computed with Smooth Shells [15] to correct the transfer of eigenfunctions from source to target shape, see Fig. 6 for results. Specifically, transfer is possible between different discretizations, deformations [49] of the same shape, and even shapes from different categories. It is, of course, possible to generate similar results with extrinsic fields by calculating a point-to-point correspondence and mapping the coordinate values. However, functional maps are naturally low-dimensional, continuous, and differentiable. This makes them a beneficial choice in many applications, especially related to learning.

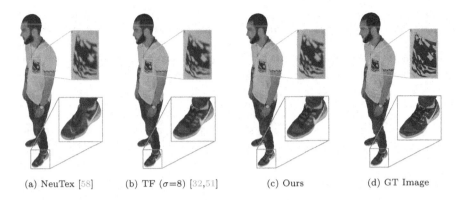

(a) NeuTex [58]   (b) TF (σ=8) [32,51]   (c) Ours   (d) GT Image

Fig. 4. Texture reconstruction from images. (4a) NeuTex uses a network to map from the shape to the sphere and represents the texture on the sphere, which yields distortions around the shoe. (4b) Texture Fields (TF) [32] with random Fourier Features (RFF) [51] learns the texture well and only around the breast pocket our method shows slightly better results. (4c) Intrinsic neural fields can reconstruct texture from images with state-of-the-art quality, which we show quantitatively in Table 1.

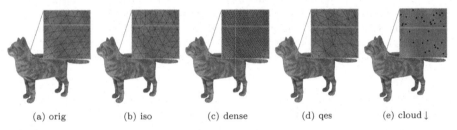

(a) orig   (b) iso   (c) dense   (d) qes   (e) cloud ↓

Fig. 5. Discretization-agnostic intrinsic neural fields. Our method produces identical results for a variety of triangular meshings and even point cloud data. For the point cloud, we use local triangulations [45, Sec. 5.7] for ray-mesh intersection. Pre-trained intrinsic neural fields can be transferred across discretizations as shown in Fig. 6.

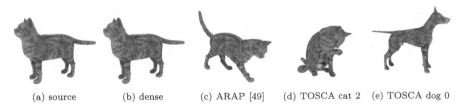

(a) source   (b) dense   (c) ARAP [49]   (d) TOSCA cat 2   (e) TOSCA dog 0

Fig. 6. Intrinsic neural field transfer. (6a) The pre-trained intrinsic neural texture field from the source mesh is transferred to the target shapes using functional maps [15,33]. (6b, 6c) The transfer across rediscretization (c.f. Fig. 5) and deformation gives nearly perfect visual quality. (6d, 6e) As a proof of concept, we show artistic transfer to a different cat shape and a dog shape from the TOSCA dataset [8]. Both transfers work well but the transfer to the dog shows small visual artifacts in the snout area due to locally different geometry. Overall, the experiment shows the advantage of the intrinsic formulation which naturally incorporates field transfer through functional maps.

Table 2. Ablation study based on the texture reconstruction experiment (c.f. Sect. 5.1). The number of eigenfunctions is more important than the size of the MLP which is promising for real-time applications. A model using only 64 eigenfunctions and only 17k parameters still achieves a PSNR of 29.20 for the cat, which shows that intrinsic neural fields can be a promising approach for compressing manifold data.

	#Params	#φ	Cat			Human		
			PSNR ↑	DSSIM ↓	LPIPS ↓	PSNR ↑	DSSIM ↓	LPIPS ↓
Full model	329k	1023	**34.82**	**0.095**	**0.153**	**32.48**	**0.121**	**0.306**
Smaller MLP	140k	1023	34.57	0.108	0.205	32.20	0.134	0.379
Fewer eigenfunctions	83k	64	31.18	0.284	0.927	28.95	0.312	1.090
Smaller MLP & fewer efs	17k	64	29.20	0.473	1.428	26.72	0.493	1.766
Just 4 eigenfunctions	68k	4	22.84	1.367	3.299	20.60	1.033	2.756

Table 3. Discretization-agnostic intrinsic neural fields. We employ the procedure proposed by Sharp et al. [44, Sec. 5.4] to generate different discretizations of the original meshes (*orig*): uniform isotropic remeshing (*iso*), densification around random vertices (*dense*), refinement and subsequent quadric error simplification [17] (*qes*), and point clouds sampled from the surfaces with more points than vertices (*cloud* ↑) and with fewer points (*cloud* ↓). The discretizations are then used for texture reconstruction as in Sect. 5.1. For the point clouds, we use local triangulations [45, Sec. 5.7] for ray-mesh intersection. This table and the qualitative results in Fig. 5 show that intrinsic neural fields can be trained for a wide variety of discretizations. Furthermore, pre-trained intrinsic neural fields can be transferred across discretizations as shown in Fig. 6.

Method	Cat						Human					
	orig	iso	dense	qes	cloud ↑	cloud ↓	orig	iso	dense	qes	cloud ↑	cloud ↓
PSNR ↑	34.82	34.85	34.74	**35.07**	34.91	33.17	32.48	**32.63**	32.57	32.49	32.45	31.99
DSSIM ↓	0.095	**0.093**	0.096	0.096	0.096	0.130	0.121	**0.117**	0.120	0.121	0.123	0.135
LPIPS ↓	0.153	0.152	0.159	**0.147**	0.152	0.220	0.306	0.300	0.301	**0.297**	0.307	0.323

5.4   Real-World Data and View Dependence

We validate the effectiveness of intrinsic neural fields in a real-world setting on the BigBIRD dataset [47]. The dataset provides posed images and reconstructed meshes, and we apply a similar pipeline as in Sect. 5.1. However, the objects here are not perfectly Lambertian, and thus, view dependence must be considered. For this, we use viewing direction as an additional input to the network, as done in [29]. At first glance, using the viewing direction in its extrinsic representation opposes our intrinsic definition of neural fields. However, view dependence arises from extrinsic effects, such as lighting, which cannot be represented purely intrinsically. Figure 7 shows that we can reconstruct high-quality textures from real-world data with imprecise calibration and meshes, quantitative results are shown in the supplementary. Decomposing the scene into intrinsic properties of the object, like the BRDF, and the influence of the environment, like light sources, is an interesting future application for our method, similar to what has been done in the context of neural radiance fields [6,7,10,57,62].

(a) Baseline [47]   (b) Ours   (c) GT Image   (d) Baseline   (e) Ours   (f) GT Image

Fig. 7. Texture reconstruction from real-world data. (7b, 7e) Intrinsic neural fields can reconstruct high quality textures from the real-world BigBIRD dataset [47] with imprecise calibration and imprecise meshes. (7a, 7d) The baseline texture mapped meshes provided in the dataset show notable seams due to the non-Lambertian material, which are not present in our reconstruction that utilizes view dependence as proposed by [29].

6   Conclusion

Discussion. The proposed intrinsic formulation of neural fields outperforms the extrinsic formulation in the presented experiments. However, if the data is very densely sampled, and the kernel is thus locally limited, the extrinsic method can overcome many of its weaknesses. In practice, dense sampling often leads to increased runtime of further processing steps, and thus we consider our intrinsic approach still superior. Further, we provided the proof for a stationary NTK on n-spheres. Our experiments and intuition imply that even for general manifolds, it is advantageous how the NTK takes local geometry into account. The details leave an interesting direction for further theoretical analysis.

Conclusion. We present intrinsic neural fields, an elegant and direct generalization of neural fields for manifolds. Intrinsic neural fields can represent high-frequency functions on manifold surfaces independent of discretization by making use of the Laplace-Beltrami eigenfunctions. We introduce a new definition for stationary kernels on manifolds, and our theoretic analysis shows that the derived neural tangent kernel is stationary under specific conditions. We conduct experiments to investigate the capabilities of our framework on the application of texture reconstruction from a limited number of views. Furthermore, the learned functions can be transferred to new examples using functional maps without any retraining, and view-dependent changes can be incorporated. Intrinsic neural fields outperform competing methods in all settings. Additionally, they add flexibility, especially in settings with deformable objects due to the intrinsic nature of our approach.

Acknowledgements. We thank Florian Hofherr, Simon Klenk, Dominik Muhle and Emanuele Rodolà for useful discussions and proofreading. ZL is funded by a KI-Starter grant from the Ministerium für Kultur und Wissenschaft NRW.

References

1. Aubry, M., Schlickewei, U., Cremers, D.: The wave kernel signature: a quantum mechanical approach to shape analysis. In: IEEE International Conference on Computer Vision (ICCV) (2011)
2. Baatz, H., Granskog, J., Papas, M., Rousselle, F., Novák, J.: NeRF-Tex: neural reflectance field textures. In: Eurographics Symposium on Rendering (EGSR) (2021)
3. Basri, R., Galun, M., Geifman, A., Jacobs, D.W., Kasten, Y., Kritchman, S.: Frequency bias in neural networks for input of non-uniform density. In: International Conference on Machine Learning (ICML) (2020)
4. Benbarka, N., Höfer, T., ul Moqeet Riaz, H., Zell, A.: Seeing implicit neural representations as fourier series. In: IEEE Winter Conference of Applications on Computer Vision (WACV) (2022)
5. Boscaini, D., Masci, J., Rodolà, E., Bronstein, M.M., Cremers, D.: Anisotropic diffusion descriptors. In: Computer Graphics Forum (CGF), vol. 35 (2016)
6. Boss, M., Braun, R., Jampani, V., Barron, J.T., Liu, C., Lensch, H.: NeRD: neural reflectance decomposition from image collections. In: IEEE International Conference on Computer Vision (ICCV) (2021)
7. Boss, M., Jampani, V., Braun, R., Liu, C., Barron, J.T., Lensch, H.P.A.: Neural-PIL: neural pre-integrated lighting for reflectance decomposition. CoRR abs/2110.14373 (2021)
8. Bronstein, A.M., Bronstein, M.M., Kimmel, R.: Numerical Geometry of Non-Rigid Shapes. Springer, Berlin (2009). https://doi.org/10.1007/978-0-387-73301-2
9. Burghard, O., Dieckmann, A., Klein, R.: Embedding shapes with green's functions for global shape matching. Comput. Graph. **68**, 1–10 (2017)
10. Chen, Z., Nobuhara, S., Nishino, K.: Invertible neural BRDF for object inverse rendering. In: Vedaldi, A., Bischof, H., Brox, T., Frahm, J.-M. (eds.) ECCV 2020. LNCS, vol. 12350, pp. 767–783. Springer, Cham (2020). https://doi.org/10.1007/978-3-030-58558-7_45
11. Chibane, J., Pons-Moll, G.: Implicit feature networks for texture completion from partial 3D data. In: Bartoli, A., Fusiello, A. (eds.) ECCV 2020. LNCS, vol. 12536, pp. 717–725. Springer, Cham (2020). https://doi.org/10.1007/978-3-030-66096-3_48
12. Crane, K., Weischedel, C., Wardetzky, M.: The heat method for distance computation. Commun. ACM **60**, 90–99 (2017)
13. Dai, F., Xu, Y.: Approximation Theory and Harmonic Analysis on Spheres and Balls. Springer, Berlin (2013)
14. Dwivedi, V.P., Bresson, X.: A generalization of transformer networks to graphs. In: AAAI Workshop on Deep Learning on Graphs: Methods and Applications (2021)
15. Eisenberger, M., Lähner, Z., Cremers, D.: Smooth shells: multi-scale shape registration with functional maps. In: IEEE Conference on Computer Vision and Pattern Recognition (CVPR) (2020)
16. Gargan, D., Neelamkavil, F.: Approximating reflectance functions using neural networks. In: Drettakis, G., Max, N. (eds.) EGSR 1998. E, pp. 23–34. Springer, Vienna (1998). https://doi.org/10.1007/978-3-7091-6453-2_3
17. Garland, M., Heckbert, P.S.: Surface simplification using quadric error metrics. In: International Conference on Computer Graphics and Interactive Techniques (SIGGRAPH) (1997)

18. Hertz, A., Perel, O., Giryes, R., Sorkine-Hornung, O., Cohen-Or, D.: Mesh draping: parametrization-free neural mesh transfer. CoRR abs/2110.05433 (2021)
19. Hertz, A., Perel, O., Giryes, R., Sorkine-Hornung, O., Cohen-Or, D.: SAPE: spatially-adaptive progressive encoding for neural optimization. In: Conference on Neural Information Processing Systems (NeurIPS) (2021)
20. Jacot, A., Hongler, C., Gabriel, F.: Neural tangent kernel: convergence and generalization in neural networks. In: Conference on Neural Information Processing Systems (NeurIPS) (2018)
21. Kovnatsky, A., Bronstein, M.M., Bronstein, A.M., Glashoff, K., Kimmel, R.: Coupled quasi-harmonic bases. In: Computer Graphics Forum, vol. 32 (2013)
22. Lee, J., Jin, K.H.: Local texture estimator for implicit representation function. CoRR abs/2111.08918 (2021)
23. Liu, X., Donate, A., Jemison, M., Mio, W.: Kernel functions for robust 3D surface registration with spectral embeddings. In: International Conference on Pattern Recognition (ICPR) (2008)
24. Loper, M., Mahmood, N., Romero, J., Pons-Moll, G., Black, M.J.: SMPL: a skinned multi-person linear model. ACM Trans. Graph. (TOG) **34**, 1–16 (2015)
25. Marin, R., Cosmo, L., Melzi, S., Rampini, A., Rodolá, E.: Spectral geometry in practice. 3DV Tutorial (2021)
26. Mehta, I., Gharbi, M., Barnes, C., Shechtman, E., Ramamoorthi, R., Chandraker, M.: Modulated periodic activations for generalizable local functional representations. CoRR abs/2104.03960 (2021)
27. Meronen, L., Trapp, M., Solin, A.: Periodic activation functions induce stationarity. CoRR abs/2110.13572 (2021)
28. Michel, O., Bar-On, R., Liu, R., Benaim, S., Hanocka, R.: Text2Mesh: text-driven neural stylization for meshes. CoRR abs/2112.03221 (2021)
29. Mildenhall, B., Srinivasan, P.P., Tancik, M., Barron, J.T., Ramamoorthi, R., Ng, R.: NeRF: representing scenes as neural radiance fields for view synthesis. In: Vedaldi, A., Bischof, H., Brox, T., Frahm, J.-M. (eds.) ECCV 2020. LNCS, vol. 12346, pp. 405–421. Springer, Cham (2020). https://doi.org/10.1007/978-3-030-58452-8_24
30. Morreale, L., Aigerman, N., Kim, V.G., Mitra, N.J.: Neural surface maps. In: IEEE Conference on Computer Vision and Pattern Recognition (CVPR) (2021)
31. Novak, R., et al.: Neural tangents: fast and easy infinite neural networks in Python. In: International Conference on Learning Representations (ICLR) (2020)
32. Oechsle, M., Mescheder, L.M., Niemeyer, M., Strauss, T., Geiger, A.: Texture fields: learning texture representations in function space. In: IEEE International Conference on Computer Vision (ICCV) (2019)
33. Ovsjanikov, M., Ben-Chen, M., Solomon, J., Butscher, A., Guibas, L.: Functional maps: a flexible representation of maps between shapes. ACM Trans. Graph. (TOG) **31**, 1–11 (2012)
34. Palafox, P., Bozic, A., Thies, J., Nießner, M., Dai, A.: Neural parametric models for 3D deformable shapes. In: IEEE International Conference on Computer Vision (ICCV) (2021)
35. Parlett, B.N.: The Symmetric Eigenvalue Problem. SIAM (1998)
36. Peng, L.W., Shamsuddin, S.M.H.: 3D object reconstruction and representation using neural networks. In: International Conference on Computer Graphics and Interactive Techniques in Australia and Southeast Asia (GRAPHITE) (2004)
37. Piperakis, E., Kumazawa, I.: Affine transformations of 3D objects represented with neural networks. In: IEEE International Conference on 3-D Digital Imaging and Modeling (2001)

38. Rahaman, N., et al.: On the spectral bias of neural networks. In: International Conference on Machine Learning (ICML) (2019)

39. Rahimi, A., Recht, B.: Random features for large-scale kernel machines. In: Conference on Neural Information Processing Systems (NeurIPS) (2007)

40. Ramasinghe, S., Lucey, S.: Beyond periodicity: towards a unifying framework for activations in coordinate-MLPs. CoRR abs/2111.15135 (2021)

41. Ramasinghe, S., Lucey, S.: Learning positional embeddings for coordinate-MLPs. CoRR abs/2112.11577 (2021)

42. Rustamov, R.M.: Laplace-Beltrami eigenfunctions for deformation invariant shape representation. In: Symposium on Geometry Processing (SGP) (2007)

43. Salti, S., Tombari, F., Di Stefano, L.: SHOT: unique signatures of histograms for surface and texture description. Comput. Vis. Image Underst. **125**, 251–264 (2014)

44. Sharp, N., Attaiki, S., Crane, K., Ovsjanikov, M.: DiffusionNet: discretization agnostic learning on surfaces. ACM Trans. Graph. (TOG) **41**(3), 1–16 (2022)

45. Sharp, N., Crane, K.: A Laplacian for nonmanifold triangle meshes. In: Computer Graphics Forum, vol. 39 (2020)

46. Sharp, N., Soliman, Y., Crane, K.: The vector heat method. ACM Trans. Graph. (TOG) **38**, 1–19 (2019)

47. Singh, A., Sha, J., Narayan, K.S., Achim, T., Abbeel, P.: BigBIRD: a large-scale 3D database of object instances. In: IEEE International Conference on Robotics and Automation (ICRA) (2014)

48. Sitzmann, V., Martel, J.N.P., Bergman, A.W., Lindell, D.B., Wetzstein, G.: Implicit neural representations with periodic activation functions. In: Conference on Neural Information Processing Systems (NeurIPS) (2020)

49. Sorkine, O., Alexa, M.: As-rigid-as-possible surface modeling. In: Symposium on Geometry Processing (SGP) (2007)

50. Sun, J., Ovsjanikov, M., Guibas, L.: A concise and provably informative multi-scale signature based on heat diffusion. In: Symposium on Geometry Processing (SGP) (2009)

51. Tancik, M., et al.: Fourier features let networks learn high frequency functions in low dimensional domains. In: Conference on Neural Information Processing Systems (NeurIPS) (2020)

52. Tewari, A., et al.: Advances in neural rendering. CoRR abs/2111.05849 (2021)

53. Vaxman, A., Ben-Chen, M., Gotsman, C.: A multi-resolution approach to heat kernels on discrete surfaces. ACM Trans. Graph. (TOG) **29**, 1–10 (2010)

54. Vestner, M., et al.: Efficient deformable shape correspondence via kernel matching. In: International Conference on 3D Vision (3DV) (2017)

55. Wang, P., Liu, Y., Yang, Y., Tong, X.: Spline positional encoding for learning 3D implicit signed distance fields. In: International Joint Conference on Artificial Intelligence (IJCAI) (2021)

56. Wang, Z., Bovik, A.C., Sheikh, H.R., Simoncelli, E.P.: Image quality assessment: from error visibility to structural similarity. IEEE Trans. Image Process. **13**, 600–612 (2004)

57. Wimbauer, F., Wu, S., Rupprecht, C.: De-rendering 3D objects in the wild. CoRR abs/2201.02279 (2022)

58. Xiang, F., Xu, Z., Hasan, M., Hold-Geoffroy, Y., Sunkavalli, K., Su, H.: NeuTex: neural texture mapping for volumetric neural rendering. In: IEEE Conference on Computer Vision and Pattern Recognition (CVPR) (2021)

59. Xie, Y., et al.: Neural fields in visual computing and beyond (2021)

60. Yifan, W., Rahmann, L., Sorkine-hornung, O.: Geometry-consistent neural shape representation with implicit displacement fields. In: International Conference on Learning Representations (ICLR) (2022)
61. Yüce, G., Ortiz-Jiménez, G., Besbinar, B., Frossard, P.: A structured dictionary perspective on implicit neural representations. CoRR abs/2112.01917 (2021)
62. Zhang, K., Luan, F., Wang, Q., Bala, K., Snavely, N.: PhySG: inverse rendering with spherical gaussians for physics-based material editing and relighting. In: IEEE Conference on Computer Vision and Pattern Recognition (CVPR) (2021)
63. Zhang, R., Isola, P., Efros, A.A., Shechtman, E., Wang, O.: The unreasonable effectiveness of deep features as a perceptual metric. In: IEEE Conference on Computer Vision and Pattern Recognition (CVPR) (2018)
64. Zheng, J., Ramasinghe, S., Lucey, S.: Rethinking positional encoding. CoRR abs/2107.02561 (2021)

Skeleton-Free Pose Transfer for Stylized 3D Characters

Zhouyingcheng Liao[1]([✉]), Jimei Yang[2], Jun Saito[2], Gerard Pons-Moll[3,4], and Yang Zhou[2]

[1] Saarland University, Saarbrücken, Germany
zycliao@gmail.com
[2] Adobe Research, Munich, Germany
[3] University of Tübingen, Tübingen, Germany
[4] Max Planck Institute for Informatics, Saarland Informatics Campus, Saarbrücken, Germany
https://zycliao.github.io/sfpt

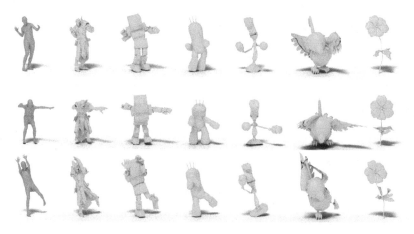

Fig. 1. Stylized 3D characters pose transfer. Given source pose characters as input (left), our model automatically transfers their poses to target subject characters with different body proportions and topologies (right). Our method does not require rigging, skinning, or correspondence labeling for both source and target characters.

Abstract. We present the first method that automatically transfers poses between stylized 3D characters without skeletal rigging. In contrast to previous attempts to learn pose transformations on fixed or topology-equivalent skeleton templates, our method focuses on a novel scenario to handle skeleton-free characters with diverse shapes, topologies, and mesh connectivities. The key idea of our method is to represent the characters in a unified articulation model so that the pose can be transferred

Z. Liao—Work done during an internship at Adobe.

Supplementary Information The online version contains supplementary material available at https://doi.org/10.1007/978-3-031-20086-1_37.

through the correspondent parts. To achieve this, we propose a novel pose transfer network that predicts the character skinning weights and deformation transformations jointly to articulate the target character to match the desired pose. Our method is trained in a semi-supervised manner absorbing all existing character data with paired/unpaired poses and stylized shapes. It generalizes well to unseen stylized characters and inanimate objects. We conduct extensive experiments and demonstrate the effectiveness of our method on this novel task.

1 Introduction

Humans and animals evolved naturally with intrinsic articulation structures to facilitate their movements in complex environments. As a result, the articulated poses become an important part of their behaviors and emotions. Based on this observation, 3D artists create highly-stylized characters in movies and games, from human-like, anthropomorphic to even inanimate objects (e.g. Pixar's Luxo Jr.). Posing and animating these characters like humans is key to conveying human-understandable expressions and emotions but actually requires many costly and sophisticated manual processes. Furthermore, once animations are created, artists often want to re-use them in novel characters and scenarios. A large number of existing studies have addressed the problem of automatically transferring poses between human-like characters [2,16,24,46,47], as they often share a similar or same skeletal rig. Very few works were devoted to animating non-human characters from human data [7,15], but they either require correspondence, or need to be trained for every pair of shapes. In this paper, we propose a learning-based method that automatically transfers poses between characters of various proportion and topology without skeletal rigs as a prerequisite (Fig. 1).

Given that most articulated 3D characters have piecewise rigid structures, the animation of characters is usually controlled by a set of sparse deformation primitives (rigs) [20] instead of manipulating the 3D mesh directly. With the deformation primitives, one has to bind them to the character mesh to build the correspondences between the primitives and the mesh vertices. This process is referred to as skinning. The skinning weight is used to describe how each deformation primitive affects the mesh deformation.

For characters deformed by sparse primitives, transferring poses between them faces two challenges. First, rigging and skinning is a laborious manual process, which requires high expertise. Second, rigs must have correspondence to each other so that the primitives are paired to enable pose transfer from source to target characters. Most existing works require the rigs to be exactly the same [46–48], e.g., a pre-defined human skeleton template. However, in practice, the rig definition is arbitrary and the rig topology could differ a lot [49]. Thus, most existing pose transfer methods [2,25,46,47] cannot be directly applied to a new character without a rig or with a rig in a different topology. While recent works [27,49] achieve automatic rigging and skinning for characters, their output, i.e., hierarchical skeletons, do not have correspondence across different characters and cannot be directly used for pose transfer.

To address the above issues, we propose a novel pose transfer method to predict correspondence-preserving deformation primitives, skinning weights, and rigid transformations to jointly deform the target character so that its pose is similar to the one of the source character.

Specifically, we define a character articulation model in terms of a set of deformation body parts but without commonly-used hierarchical structures. Each part can be deformed by its own rigid transformation based on skinning weights. Besides, since there is no hierarchical structure to connect the body parts, they can be associated with any part of the character regardless of the shape topology. Given such an articulation model, we propose a novel deep learning based method to transfer poses between characters. It first generates skinning weights for both source and target characters, leading to a consistent segmentation of both into a set of corresponding deformation body parts. It then predicts a rigid transformation for each deformation body part. Finally, linear blending skinning (LBS) [23] is applied to deform the target mesh based on predicted rigid transformations. As the deformation body parts and their rigid transformations are automatically generated by the network by analyzing the source and target meshes, they tend to be robust and adaptive to very stylized characters.

A lack of diverse data makes it hard to train our network. Most public character datasets with ground truth pose transfer data only contain natural human shapes [19,30,54] or characters of limited shape varieties [1]. The datasets with stylized characters [49] contain a single mesh in the rest pose for each character. We propose a semi-supervised training mechanism based on cycle consistency [56] to ease the requirement of ground truth pose transfer data on the stylized characters. This makes it possible to use arbitrary static characters with various shapes and topologies in training to improve the robustness of the method. Overall, our contributions can be summarized as follows:

1. We propose the first automatic method for pose transfer between rig-free 3D characters with diverse shapes, topologies, and mesh connectivities.
2. Our method parameterises the character pose as a set of learned independent body part deformations coherent across characters. We do not require any manual intervention or preprocessing, e.g., rigging, skinning, or correspondence labeling.
3. Our model is trained end-to-end and in a semi-supervised manner. We do not require neither annotations nor mesh correspondences for training and can make use of large amounts of static characters.

2   Related Work

Skeleton-Based Pose Transfer. Transferring poses based on skeletal rigs was intensively studied in the past. Gleicher [16] pioneered skeleton-based pose transfer through space-time optimization. Follow-up work [3,4,12,24,44] mostly incorporated various physics and kinematics constraints into this framework. Generalization to arbitrary objects has been proposed by [34,51], but they require example poses from users. Recent deep learning methods [26, 46, 47] trained neural networks with forward kinematics layers to directly estimate hierarchical transformations of the target skeleton. However, their models require the source and target skeletons to be the same while only allowing for different proportions. [6, 25] fit a predefined template skeleton and derive the skinning weights for character pose transfer within the same category, e.g., humanoid, quadruped, etc. [32] relaxed the singular template constraint through a multi-resolution topology graph. [2] proposed skeleton-aware pooling operators which supports skeletal pose transfer with a different number of joints. Yet, these methods still require the skeletons to be topologically equivalent. However, even these relaxed skeleton constraints cannot be guaranteed through state-of-the-art automated rigging and skinning methods [27, 49, 50]. Our method does not require skeletal rigging and can transfer poses across characters with different topologies.

Mesh Deformation Transfer. Character pose transfer can also be achieved by mesh deformation transfer without relying on rigs. Traditional methods [5, 7, 8, 43] require accurate correspondences through manual annotation. [52] proposed a keypoint detection method to characterize the deformation, but still required user effort to specify corresponding keypoints from the source to target. Recent deep learning based methods analyzed the mesh deformation primitives and embedded the mesh into latent spaces [45, 53]. However, their latent spaces are not shared across subjects and thus cannot be used for pose transfer between different characters. [15] trained a GAN-based model with unpaired data in two shape sets to perform pose transfer. But it is limited to shape deformation in the training set and does not generalize to unseen characters. [48, 55] disentangled the shape identity and pose information and made it possible to transfer poses to unseen characters. However, they can only handle characters with limited shape varieties, e.g., human bodies with minimal clothing. Our method automatically generates consistent deformation body parts across different character meshes and deforms the target mesh with part-wise rigid transformations in an LBS manner. Hence, no manual correspondence is needed. Once trained, our network can generalize to unseen characters with various shapes and topologies.

Correspondence Learning. Correspondence learning is crucial in pose transfer and motion retargeting tasks [2, 17, 21, 35, 37, 38, 41]. [21, 37, 38] detected 2D keypoints on images as correspondences for human video reposing. [18, 39, 40] found corresponding regions and segments for pose transfer. [33] performed analogies on 2D character sprites and transferred animations between them. They worked on image domain by utilizing deep image features to locate corresponding body parts. [22, 28, 36] proposed unsupervised methods to discover corresponding 3D keypoints as deformation handles. They generate plausible shapes, e.g., chairs, airplanes, via shape deformation but are not suitable for character posture articulation. [41] found per-vertex correspondence between human meshes via correlation matrices. But its generalization is limited to shapes close to training data [10, 11]. Our method discovers part-level shape correspondence by learning through the pose transfer task. It does not need correspondence annotation for supervision and can generalize to unseen stylized characters.

3   Method

3.1   Overview

Given a source 3D character mesh $\mathbf{V}^s$ with the desired pose and its mesh $\bar{\mathbf{V}}^s$ in rest pose and a different target 3D character mesh $\bar{\mathbf{V}}^t$ in rest pose, the goal of our method is to deform the target mesh to a new pose $\hat{\mathbf{V}}^t$ which matches the input source pose $\{\mathbf{V}^s, \bar{\mathbf{V}}^s, \bar{\mathbf{V}}^t\} \mapsto \hat{\mathbf{V}}^t$. Here, we use the bar symbol $\bar{\mathbf{V}}$ to indicate the character in rest pose. To solve this problem, we propose an end-to-end neural network that learns part-level mesh correspondences and transformations between characters to achieve pose transfer. The overview is shown in Fig. 2.

We first define a character articulation model to represent the mesh deformation in terms of a set of deformation parts (Sect. 3.2). Unlike existing methods [2,6,47] requiring skeletal rigging to deform character body parts hierarchically, our model deforms body parts independently without the kinematic chain. Our method parameterises the character pose as a set of learned independent body part deformations coherent across characters, which is the foundation for the following pose transfer network to overcome topology constraints.

We propose a novel skeleton-free pose transfer network to predict the skinning weights and the transformations for each deformation part defined in the above character articulation model so that the target character can be transformed by linear blending skinning (LBS) to match the input pose (Sect. 3.3).

The pose transfer network consists of three modules: *skinning weight predictor*, *mesh encoder*, and *transformation decoder*. The skinning weight predictor estimates per-vertex skinning weights that segment the mesh into K deformation parts (see examples in Fig. 3). The *mesh encoder* encodes the input mesh into a latent feature that embeds both pose and shape information. The *transformation decoder* predicts a set of part-wise rigid transformations, which are further used to articulate the target mesh into the desired pose.

We train our framework end-to-end in a semi-supervised manner (Sect. 3.4). For characters with pairwise animation sequences [1,30], i.e. different subjects with the same animation poses, we train our network directly with cross-subject reconstruction. There also exist datasets with stylized characters of diverse shapes, topologies, and mesh connectivities. However, such data usually contains only a static rest pose and thus cannot be directly used in training. We propose a cycle-consistency loss to train on such data unsupervised, which turns out to improve our model robustness significantly.

3.2   Character Articulation Model

We propose to represent the mesh deformation in a unified way so that the pose can be easily transferred between characters with various shapes and topologies. We define K deformation parts for a mesh $\bar{\mathbf{V}}$ with N vertices. Each part can be deformed based on the skinning weight $\mathbf{W} \in \mathbb{R}^{N \times K}$ associated with it. The K deformation parts are not character-specific but consistent across characters (Fig. 3). $\mathbf{W}$ satisfies the partition of unity condition where $0 \le w_{i,k} \le 1$ and

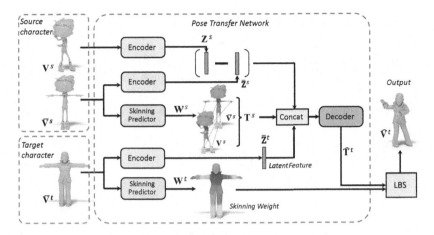

Fig. 2. Overview. Given a posed source character and a target character as input, the pose transfer network estimates character skinning weights and part-wise transformations which articulate the target character through LBS to match the pose of the source.

$\sum_{k=1}^{K} w_{i,k} = 1$. Here i is the vertex index and k is the deformation part index. Different characters may have different shapes and topologies, so ideally the number of deformation parts should vary. We define $K = 40$ as the maximum number of parts for all the characters in our experiment. Depending on the shape of the character, we allow some parts to be degenerate, i.e. having zero coverage: $w_{i,k} = 0, \forall i$. Meanwhile, the number of vertices N is not fixed and can vary from character to character during either training or testing phases.

Given rigid transformations for K body parts $\mathbf{T} = \{\mathbf{T}_1, ..., \mathbf{T}_K\}$, we use LBS [23] to deform the character mesh,

$$\mathbf{V}_i = \sum_{k=1}^{K} w_{i,k} \mathbf{T}_k (\bar{\mathbf{V}}_i - \mathbf{C}_k), \quad \forall \bar{\mathbf{V}}_i \in \bar{\mathbf{V}} \tag{1}$$

where $\mathbf{C}_k$ is the center of deformation part k in terms of the average position of vertices weighted by the skinning weight,

$$\mathbf{C}_k = \frac{\sum_{i=1}^{N} w_{i,k} \bar{\mathbf{V}}_i}{\sum_{i=1}^{N} w_{i,k}} \tag{2}$$

We do not connect the center of deformations parts $\mathbf{C}_k$ to form a skeleton since the skeleton connectivity varies in characters with different topology [50]. Our transformation $\mathbf{T}_k$ is applied independently on each deformation part without the kinematic chain. A consistent deformation part segmentation together with part-wise transformations forms a more general way of articulation than the commonly-used skeleton-based methods [2], which is crucial for achieving the skeleton-free pose transfer.

3.3   Skeleton-Free Pose Transfer Network

We propose a skeleton-free pose transfer network to transfer the pose from a source character to a different target character (see Fig. 2). It predicts skinning weights of both source and target characters through the skinning weight predictor and estimates the corresponding transformation matrices jointly from the mesh encoder and transformation decoder network.

Fig. 3. Visualization of deformation parts based on predicted skinning weights. Each color represents a deformation part. The deformation part is semantically consistent across characters with various shapes and topologies.

Skinning Weight Predictor. Given a character mesh $\bar{\mathbf{V}}$, we design a graph convolution network g_s to predict its skinning weight $\mathbf{W} \in \mathbb{R}^{N \times K}$,

$$\mathbf{W} = g_s(f(\bar{\mathbf{V}}); \phi_s) \tag{3}$$

where $f(\bar{\mathbf{V}}) \in \mathbb{R}^{N \times 6}$ is the vertex feature vector consisting of position and normal. ϕ_s are learnable parameters. Each row of $\mathbf{W}$ indicates each vertex skinning weight association to K deformation parts. The network architecture follows [49] and can process meshes with arbitrary number of vertices and connectivities. We modify the last layer as a softmax layer to satisfy the skinning weight convex condition. The detailed structure can be found in the supplementary.

Mesh Encoder. We use another graph convolution network g_e to encode the input mesh $\mathbf{V}$ into a latent feature $\mathbf{Y} \in \mathbb{R}^{N \times C}$,

$$\mathbf{Y} = g_e(f(\mathbf{V}); \phi_e) \tag{4}$$

where C is the dimension of the latent space and ϕ_e are learnable parameters.

Instead of pooling $\mathbf{Y}$ into a global latent feature, we multiply it with the predicted skinning weight as an attention map to convert the feature dimension $\mathbb{R}^{N \times C} \mapsto \mathbb{R}^{K \times C}$. This conversion can be interpreted as an aggregation function to gather deformation part features from relevant vertices. After that, a 1D convolution layer is further applied to transform the feature to be the attended latent feature $\mathbf{Z} \in \mathbb{R}^{K \times C}$,

$$\mathbf{Z} = \text{Conv1d}(\mathbf{W}^{\mathsf{T}} \cdot \mathbf{Y}, \phi_c) \tag{5}$$

where ϕ_c are learnable parameters and $C = 128$ in our experiment. Note that the mesh encoder is applied to all three input meshes $\mathbf{V}^s, \bar{\mathbf{V}}^s, \bar{\mathbf{V}}^t$ to obtain their attended latent features $\mathbf{Z}^s, \bar{\mathbf{Z}}^s, \bar{\mathbf{Z}}^t$ with corresponding skinning weights.

Transformation Decoder. The goal of the decoder is to predict transformations $\hat{\mathbf{T}}^t = \{\hat{\mathbf{T}}_1^t, ..., \hat{\mathbf{T}}_K^t\}$ on each deformation part of the target mesh $\bar{\mathbf{V}}^t$. Hence, the target mesh $\bar{\mathbf{V}}^t$ can be reposed to $\hat{\mathbf{V}}^t$ which matches the desired pose mesh $\mathbf{V}^s$. The decoder takes as input three component:

- the latent feature of the target mesh $\bar{\mathbf{Z}}^t$. It is derived from the target mesh $\bar{\mathbf{V}}^t$ with the mesh encoder. It encodes the target mesh shape information.
- the difference between the latent features of the posed source mesh and itself in rest pose $\mathbf{Z}^s - \bar{\mathbf{Z}}^s$.
- the transformation of each deformation part $\mathbf{T}^s = \{\mathbf{T}_1^s, ..., \mathbf{T}_K^s\}$ between the pair of source meshes. This explicit transformation serves as an initial guess and helps the network focus on estimating residuals. It is analytically calculated by [9].

To summarize, the decoder takes the concatenation of $\mathbf{Z}^t, \mathbf{Z}^s - \bar{\mathbf{Z}}^s, \mathbf{T}^s$ as input and predicts the transformation $\hat{\mathbf{T}}^t$:

$$\hat{\mathbf{T}}^t = g_d(\bar{\mathbf{Z}}^t, \mathbf{Z}^s - \bar{\mathbf{Z}}^s, \mathbf{T}^s; \phi_d) \qquad (6)$$

where ϕ_d are learnable parameters for the decoder. With the predicted skinning weights $\mathbf{W}^t$ and transformation $\hat{\mathbf{T}}^t$, we can use the proposed articulation model to deform the target mesh $\bar{\mathbf{V}}^t$ to the new pose $\hat{\mathbf{V}}^t$.

3.4   Training and Losses

We propose the following losses to train our network in a semi-supervised manner to make the best use of all possible data.

Mesh Reconstruction Loss. For characters with paired pose data in [1,30], we use a reconstruction loss as direct supervision. We apply a per-vertex L1 loss between the predicted mesh $\hat{\mathbf{V}}^t$ and the ground truth mesh $\mathbf{V}^t$,

$$L_{rec} = ||\hat{\mathbf{V}}^t - \mathbf{V}^t||_1 \qquad (7)$$

Transformation Loss. With the predicted skinning weight $\mathbf{W}^t$ of the target mesh, we group the vertices into K deformation parts by performing $\text{argmax}_k \, w_{i,k}$. Then we calculate the ground truth transformation $\mathbf{T}^t$ on the approximated parts between the input rest pose mesh $\bar{\mathbf{V}}^t$ and the ground truth mesh $\mathbf{V}^t$. We apply an L1 loss between the ground truth and predicted transformation $\hat{\mathbf{T}}^t$,

$$L_{trans} = ||\hat{\mathbf{T}}^t - \mathbf{T}^t||_1 \qquad (8)$$

Cycle Loss. When paired data are not available, or just a single rest pose mesh is provided, e.g., in [49], we use the cycle consistency loss for training [56]. Given a pair of source meshes $\mathbf{V}^s, \bar{\mathbf{V}}^s$ and a target mesh $\bar{\mathbf{V}}^t$ in rest pose, we first transfer the pose from source to target: $\{\mathbf{V}^s, \bar{\mathbf{V}}^s, \bar{\mathbf{V}}^t\} \mapsto \hat{\mathbf{V}}^t$, and then transfer the pose from the predicted target back to the source mesh: $\{\hat{\mathbf{V}}^t, \bar{\mathbf{V}}^t, \bar{\mathbf{V}}^s\} \mapsto \hat{\mathbf{V}}^s$. The predicted source mesh $\hat{\mathbf{V}}^s$ should be the same as $\mathbf{V}^s$. We apply L1 loss between them for the cycle reconstruction.

Through experiments, we found that training only with this loss leads to mode collapse. In existing datasets, characters with multiple poses are usually human characters, while most stylized characters are only in rest pose. These stylized characters can only be used as the target mesh $\bar{\mathbf{V}}^t$ in the cycle loss instead of interchangeably as $\mathbf{V}^s$. Thus the network tends to collapse and results in $\hat{\mathbf{V}}^t$ with limited pose variance. To solve this problem, we apply the transformations calculated from the source meshes $\mathbf{T}^s$ to the target mesh $\bar{\mathbf{V}}^t$ to obtain a pseudo-ground truth $\tilde{\mathbf{V}}^t$ for $\hat{\mathbf{V}}^t$. The complete cycle loss is

$$L_{cyc} = ||\hat{\mathbf{V}}^s - \mathbf{V}^s||_1 + w_{\text{pseudo}}||\hat{\mathbf{V}}^t - \tilde{\mathbf{V}}^t||_1 \tag{9}$$

where $w_{pseudo} = 0.3$ is used in our experiment. To note that $\hat{\mathbf{V}}^t$ is an approximated pseudo-ground truth mesh and sometimes may not be well-deformed if the transformation $\mathbf{T}^s$ is large. We introduce this term as a regularization which helps prevent the model from collapsing.

Skinning Weight Loss. In existing rigged character datasets [1,30,49], the skeletons and skinning weights are defined independently for each character. Therefore, we cannot use them directly as ground truth to supervise the training of our skinning weight predictor because of their lack of consistency. We thus propose a contrastive learning method to make use of such diverse skinning data. Our assumption is if two vertices belong to the same body part based on the ground truth skinning weight, they should also belong to the same deformation part in the predicted skinning. We select vertices with $w_{i,k} > 0.9$, $\exists k$ and use the KL divergence to enforce similarity between skinning weights of two vertices,

$$L_{skin} = \gamma_{i,j} \sum_{k=1}^{K} (w_{i,k} log(w_{i,k}) - w_{i,k} log(w_{j,k})) \tag{10}$$

where i, j indicate two randomly sampled vertices. γ is an indicator function: $\gamma_{i,j} = 1$ if vertices i and j belong to the same part in the ground truth skinning weight and $\gamma_{i,j} = -1$ if not. This loss holds only when the ground truth skinning is available.

Edge Length Loss. The desired deformation should be locally rigid and preserve the character shape, e.g., limb lengths and other surface features. Thus, we apply an edge length loss between the predicted mesh and input target mesh to prevent undesired non-rigid deformations,

$$L_{edge} = \sum_{\{i,j\} \in \mathcal{E}} | \, ||\hat{\mathbf{V}}_i^t - \hat{\mathbf{V}}_j^t||_2 - ||\mathbf{V}_i^t - \mathbf{V}_j^t||_2 \, | \tag{11}$$

where $\mathcal{E}$ denotes the set of edges on the mesh.

4   Experiments

4.1   Datasets

We train our model on three datasets: AMASS [30], Mixamo [1] and RigNet [49]. We additionally use MGN [10] for evaluation.

AMASS [30] is a large human motion dataset that fits SMPL [29] to real-world human motion capture data. SMPL disentangles and parameterizes the human pose and shape. Therefore, we can obtain paired pose data by switching different shape parameters while keeping the pose parameter the same. We follow the train-test split protocol in [55].

Mixamo [1] contains over a hundred humanoid characters and over two thousand corresponding motion sequences. Since the motion sequences are shared across all characters, the paired pose data is also available. We use 98 characters for training and 20 characters for testing. The detailed split can be found in the supplementary.

RigNet [49] contains 2703 rigged characters with a large shape variety, including humanoids, quadrupeds, birds, fish, etc. All characters have their skeletal rigging. Each character only has one mesh in the rest pose. We remove character categories that can not be animated by the human pose, e.g., fish. We follow the train-test split protocol in [49] on the remaining 1268 characters.

MGN [10] contains 96 scanned clothed human registered to SMPL topology. We evaluation on this dataset to further demonstrate the robustness on human model with larger shape variety.

4.2   Comparison Methods

Pinocchio [6] is a pioneering work in automatic 3D character rigging and skinning. It fits a predefined skeleton to the target mesh and calculates skinning weights. As the skeleton is fixed, it achieves pose transfer by retargeting the joint rotations estimated by [9]. Pinocchio has a strict requirement on the mesh connectivity: non-watertight, multi-component, or non-manifold meshes are not allowed. We manually preprocessed meshes to match its requirement in our evaluation. **Skeleton-aware Network (SAN)** [2] transfers the pose between two humanoid characters with the same skeleton topology. However, they require the motion statistics for both source and target characters to remap the predicted motion, e.g., an animation sample for the test subject mesh. This is not available in our task where only one instance of the subject character is provided. To make a fair comparison, we used the average statistics from the training set for test meshes. The ground truth skeleton and skinning is also assumed given for this method. **Neural Blend Shape (NBS)** [25] is the state-of-the-art method that achieves pose transfer between skeleton-free human shapes. They adopt SMPL skeleton template and can only work on human characters. **Shape Pose Disentanglement (SPD)** [55] can disentangle pose and shape information for 3D meshes from the same category. The pose transfer can be achieved by applying the pose information from one mesh to the other while keeping the shape information. Their model can only work on meshes with the same connectivity and thus we evaluate it only on SMPL-based dataset. **Ours (AMASS)** represents the reposing results from our proposed framework. It is trained only with AMASS data with limited character shapes. It is used for evaluating the generalization of the proposed network architecture. **Ours (full)** is our full result trained on all three datasets mentioned above.

4.3 Pose Transfer Evaluation

We evaluate our skeleton-free pose transfer results on different stylized characters both qualitatively and quantitatively.

Figure 4 shows comparison results of the reposed characters from each of the comparison methods. SAN [2] fails on our task where only a single test mesh is given. It relies a lot on the motion statistics for test characters. Pinocchio [6] does not preserve the character shape well, e.g., the limbs have undesired non-rigid deformations. NBS [25] results in collapsed shapes and cannot generalize well to stylized characters. Our results match the source pose the best and work well on various character shapes. More visual comparisons and animation videos can be found in the supplementary.

Quantitatively, we use the Point-wise Mesh Euclidean Distance (PMD) [48, 55] as the evaluation metric. We first evaluate the results on MGN dataset [10] with all competing methods (the first row of Table 1). SAN [2] is not compared because it is trained on Mixamo [1] and cannot generalize to the unseen skeleton. SPD [55] trained only on naked human data fails to generalize to clothed human. NBS [25] directly trained on MGC and thus achieves relatively good result. Our full model achieves the best result by using all possible stylized characters.

In addition, we evaluate our method and competing methods on a more challenging dataset Mixamo [1], with more stylized test characters. The results are reported in the second row of Table 1. SPD [55] is not compared since it can only handle meshes with the same mesh connectivity. All competing methods cannot generalize well to stylized characters in Mixamo and fail significantly in terms of PMD. Our full model results in the lowest PMD which demonstrates the performance of our model on more stylized characters. Our ablation model trained only on AMASS data also scores better than other methods. It shows the generalization of our method when being only trained on limited data.

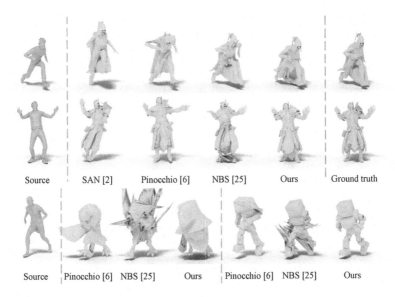

Fig. 4. Pose transfer results for human (top) and stylized characters (bottom).

Table 1. Quantitative comparison of pose transfer results on MGN and Mixamo.

	Pinocchio [6]	SAN [2]	NBS [25]	SPD [55]	Ours (AMASS)	Ours (full)
PMD ↓ on MGN [10]	3.145	–	1.498	5.649	2.878	**1.197**
PMD ↓ on Mixamo [1]	6.139	5.581	3.875	–	3.412	**2.393**

4.4   Deformation Part Semantic Consistency

Our predicted deformation parts denote the same body region across different characters. Although this can be demonstrated by our pose transfer results, we further validate it by conducting an explicit semantic consistency evaluation.

In Sect. 3.4, we define the vertex belongings to each deformation part by selecting the vertex maximum skinning weight. Therefore, each deformation part can be defined as a mesh semantic part with a group of vertices belonging to it. Then our goal is to evaluate such semantic part consistency across subjects. Because existing ground truth annotation, i.e., traditional skeletal skinning weights, cannot be directly used for evaluation, we design an evaluation protocol similar to [13,22] for semantic part consistency. More specifically, first, we get our and ground truth mesh semantic parts based on the predicted and ground truth skinning weights respectively. Second, we calculate the *correlation* from the semantic parts of prediction to the ones of ground truth: a predicted semantic part is *correlated* with the ground truth part with the most number of overlapped vertices. Then we can derive the *"consistency score"* of each predicted part as the maximum percentage of the correlated ground truth parts with the same semantics from all characters in the dataset. The final metric is the average of the consistency score over all predicted parts. We denote the above evaluation metric as Pred → GT since we find the correlation from predictions to ground truth. GT → Pred can be calculated in the opposite direction, i.e., for each ground truth part, we find the most correlated predicted part.

Fig. 5. Visualization of deformation parts based on predicted skinning weights from each method (in row). Each part is denoted by a unique color.

Table 2. Semantic consistency scores for deformation part prediction. We compare with Pinocchio [6] and NBS [25] on Mixamo [1] in both correlation directions.

	Pinocchio [6]	NBS [25]	Ours (AMASS)	Ours (full)
Pred → GT ↑ on Mixamo [1]	0.833	0.870	0.886	**0.993**
GT → Pred ↑ on Mixamo [1]	0.886	0.808	0.827	**0.947**

We compare our results with Pinocchio and NBS which rely on a fixed skeleton template and thus can predict skinning weights with the same semantic parts for different characters. The comparison result on Mixamo characters is shown in Table 2. Our full model achieves the best and close to 1 correlation accuracy compared to others. Ours trained only on AMASS achieves a similar average performance to comparison methods. We note that NBS used predefined skeleton [29] for training, while ours is not supervised by any body part labels.

We also visualize the skinning weights predicted from ours and comparison methods in Fig. 5. For each method, we used consistent color for deformation parts to reflect the same semantic. Our skinning paints characters consistently on semantic regions while the comparison methods fail on some body parts.

4.5   Ablation Study

We conduct ablation studies on Mixamo dataset to investigate the effectiveness of each component. **w/o edge loss** is trained without the edge length constraint. **w/o pseudo** is trained without cycle loss from the pseudo-ground truth. **w/o skinning** is trained with out skinning weight loss. Table 3 shows the evaluation results on Mixamo data. Our full model achieves the best performance.

Table 3. Quantitative evaluation results on ablation methods.

	w/o edge loss	w/o pseudo	w/o skinning loss	Ours (full)
PMD ↓ on Mixamo [1]	2.450	2.601	2.978	**2.393**

5   Conclusion and Future Work

We present a novel learning-based framework to automatically transfer poses between stylized 3D characters without skeletal rigging. Our model can handle characters with diverse shapes, topologies, and mesh connectivities. We achieve this by representing the characters in a unified articulation model and predicting the deformation skinning and transformations when given the desired pose. Our model can utilize all types of existing character data, e.g., with motion or static, and thus can have great generalization to various unseen stylized characters.

Limitations and Future Work. Our model focuses on pose transfer and is not optimized for motion transfer in the temporal domain. Jittering and penetration problems [46] may occur when using our proposed method for animation. We apply the edge length constraint to prevent the mesh from breaking but no other explicit controls are involved. Data-driven deformation constraints [14] and better geometric regularizations [42] could prevent the implausible deformations further. Our current framework requires the rest pose mesh as an additional input. Canonicalization methods [31] might be helpful to ease this requirement. We are looking for automating the process of the character pose transfer, yet in real content authoring scenarios, user input is still desired to increase tool usability and content diversity. We look forward to future endeavors on expressive pose transfer animations with intuitive user controls.

Acknowledgement. This work is funded by a gift from Adobe Research and the Deutsche Forschungsgemeinschaft (DFG, German Research Foundation) - 409792180 (Emmy Noether Programme, project: Real Virtual Humans). Gerard Pons-Moll is a member of the Machine Learning Cluster of Excellence, EXC number 2064/1 - Project number 390727645.

References

1. Mixamo (2022). http://www.mixamo.com/
2. Aberman, K., Li, P., Lischinski, D., Sorkine-Hornung, O., Cohen-Or, D., Chen, B.: Skeleton-aware networks for deep motion retargeting. ACM Trans. Graph. (TOG) **39**(4), 1–14 (2020)
3. Al Borno, M., Righetti, L., Black, M.J., Delp, S.L., Fiume, E., Romero, J.: Robust physics-based motion retargeting with realistic body shapes. In: Computer Graphics Forum, vol. 37, pp. 81–92. Wiley Online Library (2018)
4. Aristidou, A., Lasenby, J.: FABRIK: a fast, iterative solver for the inverse kinematics problem. Graph. Models **73**(5), 243–260 (2011)

5. Avril, Q., et al.: Animation setup transfer for 3D characters. In: Computer Graphics Forum, vol. 35, pp. 115–126. Wiley Online Library (2016)
6. Baran, I., Popović, J.: Automatic rigging and animation of 3D characters. ACM Trans. Graph. (TOG) **26**(3), 72–es (2007)
7. Baran, I., Vlasic, D., Grinspun, E., Popović, J.: Semantic deformation transfer. In: ACM SIGGRAPH 2009 Papers, pp. 1–6 (2009)
8. Ben-Chen, M., Weber, O., Gotsman, C.: Spatial deformation transfer. In: Proceedings of the 2009 ACM SIGGRAPH/Eurographics Symposium on Computer Animation, pp. 67–74 (2009)
9. Besl, P.J., McKay, N.D.: Method for registration of 3D shapes. In: Sensor Fusion IV: Control Paradigms and Data Structures (1992)
10. Bhatnagar, B.L., Tiwari, G., Theobalt, C., Pons-Moll, G.: Multi-garment net: learning to dress 3D people from images. In: Proceedings of the IEEE/CVF International Conference on Computer Vision, pp. 5420–5430 (2019)
11. Bogo, F., Romero, J., Loper, M., Black, M.J.: FAUST: dataset and evaluation for 3D mesh registration. In: Proceedings of the IEEE Conference on Computer Vision and Pattern Recognition, pp. 3794–3801 (2014)
12. Choi, K.J., Ko, H.S.: Online motion retargetting. J. Vis. Comput. Animat. **11**(5), 223–235 (2000)
13. Fernandez-Labrador, C., Chhatkuli, A., Paudel, D.P., Guerrero, J.J., Demonceaux, C., Gool, L.V.: Unsupervised learning of category-specific symmetric 3D keypoints from point sets. In: Vedaldi, A., Bischof, H., Brox, T., Frahm, J.-M. (eds.) ECCV 2020. LNCS, vol. 12370, pp. 546–563. Springer, Cham (2020). https://doi.org/10.1007/978-3-030-58595-2_33
14. Gao, L., Lai, Y.K., Yang, J., Zhang, L.X., Xia, S., Kobbelt, L.: Sparse data driven mesh deformation. IEEE TVCG **27**, 2085–2100 (2019)
15. Gao, L., et al.: Automatic unpaired shape deformation transfer. ACM Trans. Graph. (TOG) **37**(6), 1–15 (2018)
16. Gleicher, M.: Retargetting motion to new characters. In: Proceedings of the 25th Annual Conference on Computer Graphics and Interactive Techniques, pp. 33–42 (1998)
17. Groueix, T., Fisher, M., Kim, V.G., Russell, B.C., Aubry, M.: 3D-CODED: 3D correspondences by deep deformation. In: Ferrari, V., Hebert, M., Sminchisescu, C., Weiss, Y. (eds.) ECCV 2018. LNCS, vol. 11206, pp. 235–251. Springer, Cham (2018). https://doi.org/10.1007/978-3-030-01216-8_15
18. Hung, W.C., Jampani, V., Liu, S., Molchanov, P., Yang, M.H., Kautz, J.: SCOPS: self-supervised co-part segmentation. In: Proceedings of the IEEE/CVF Conference on Computer Vision and Pattern Recognition, pp. 869–878 (2019)
19. Ionescu, C., Papava, D., Olaru, V., Sminchisescu, C.: Human3.6M: large scale datasets and predictive methods for 3D human sensing in natural environments. IEEE Trans. Pattern Anal. Mach. Intell. **36**(7), 1325–1339 (2013)
20. Jacobson, A., Deng, Z., Kavan, L., Lewis, J.P.: Skinning: real-time shape deformation (full text not available). In: ACM SIGGRAPH 2014 Courses, p. 1 (2014)
21. Jakab, T., Gupta, A., Bilen, H., Vedaldi, A.: Unsupervised learning of object landmarks through conditional image generation. In: Advances in Neural Information Processing Systems, vol. 31 (2018)
22. Jakab, T., Tucker, R., Makadia, A., Wu, J., Snavely, N., Kanazawa, A.: KeypointDeformer: unsupervised 3D keypoint discovery for shape control. In: Proceedings of the IEEE/CVF Conference on Computer Vision and Pattern Recognition, pp. 12783–12792 (2021)

23. Kavan, L.: Direct skinning methods and deformation primitives. In: ACM SIG-GRAPH Courses (2014)
24. Lee, J., Shin, S.Y.: A hierarchical approach to interactive motion editing for human-like figures. In: Proceedings of the 26th Annual Conference on Computer graphics and Interactive Techniques, pp. 39–48 (1999)
25. Li, P., Aberman, K., Hanocka, R., Liu, L., Sorkine-Hornung, O., Chen, B.: Learning skeletal articulations with neural blend shapes. ACM Trans. Graph. (TOG) **40**(4), 1–15 (2021)
26. Lim, J., Chang, H.J., Choi, J.Y.: PMnet: learning of disentangled pose and movement for unsupervised motion retargeting. In: BMVC, vol. 2, p. 7 (2019)
27. Liu, L., Zheng, Y., Tang, D., Yuan, Y., Fan, C., Zhou, K.: NeuroSkinning: automatic skin binding for production characters with deep graph networks. ACM TOG **38**, 1–12 (2019)
28. Liu, M., Sung, M., Mech, R., Su, H.: DeepMetaHandles: learning deformation meta-handles of 3D meshes with biharmonic coordinates. In: Proceedings of the IEEE/CVF Conference on Computer Vision and Pattern Recognition, pp. 12–21 (2021)
29. Loper, M., Mahmood, N., Romero, J., Pons-Moll, G., Black, M.J.: SMPL: a skinned multi-person linear model. ACM Trans. Graph. (TOG) **34**(6), 1–16 (2015)
30. Mahmood, N., Ghorbani, N., Troje, N.F., Pons-Moll, G., Black, M.J.: AMASS: archive of motion capture as surface shapes. In: International Conference on Computer Vision, pp. 5442–5451 (2019)
31. Musoni, P., Marin, R., Melzi, S., Castellani, U.: Reposing and retargeting unrigged characters with intrinsic-extrinsic transfer. In: Smart Tools and Applications in Graphics (2021)
32. Poirier, M., Paquette, E.: Rig retargeting for 3D animation. In: Graphics Interface, pp. 103–110 (2009)
33. Reed, S.E., Zhang, Y., Zhang, Y., Lee, H.: Deep visual analogy-making. In: Proceedings of the NeurIPS (2015)
34. Rhodin, H., et al.: Generalizing wave gestures from sparse examples for real-time character control. ACM Trans. Graph. **34**(6), 1–12 (2015)
35. Saito, S., Yang, J., Ma, Q., Black, M.J.: SCANimate: weakly supervised learning of skinned clothed avatar networks. In: Proceedings of the IEEE/CVF Conference on Computer Vision and Pattern Recognition, pp. 2886–2897 (2021)
36. Shi, R., Xue, Z., You, Y., Lu, C.: Skeleton merger: an unsupervised aligned keypoint detector. In: Proceedings of the IEEE/CVF Conference on Computer Vision and Pattern Recognition, pp. 43–52 (2021)
37. Siarohin, A., Lathuilière, S., Tulyakov, S., Ricci, E., Sebe, N.: Animating arbitrary objects via deep motion transfer. In: Proceedings of the IEEE/CVF Conference on Computer Vision and Pattern Recognition, pp. 2377–2386 (2019)
38. Siarohin, A., Lathuilière, S., Tulyakov, S., Ricci, E., Sebe, N.: First order motion model for image animation. In: Advances in Neural Information Processing Systems, vol. 32 (2019)
39. Siarohin, A., Roy, S., Lathuilière, S., Tulyakov, S., Ricci, E., Sebe, N.: Motion-supervised co-part segmentation. arXiv preprint arXiv:2004.03234 (2020)
40. Siarohin, A., Woodford, O.J., Ren, J., Chai, M., Tulyakov, S.: Motion representations for articulated animation. In: Proceedings of the IEEE/CVF Conference on Computer Vision and Pattern Recognition, pp. 13653–13662 (2021)
41. Song, C., Wei, J., Li, R., Liu, F., Lin, G.: 3D pose transfer with correspondence learning and mesh refinement. In: Advances in Neural Information Processing Systems, vol. 34 (2021)

42. Sorkine, O., Alexa, M.: As-rigid-as-possible surface modeling. In: Symposium on Geometry Processing (2007)
43. Sumner, R.W., Popović, J.: Deformation transfer for triangle meshes. ACM Trans. Graph. (TOG) **23**(3), 399–405 (2004)
44. Tak, S., Ko, H.S.: A physically-based motion retargeting filter. ACM Trans. Graph. (TOG) **24**(1), 98–117 (2005)
45. Tan, Q., Gao, L., Lai, Y.K., Xia, S.: Variational autoencoders for deforming 3D mesh models. In: Proceedings of the IEEE Conference on Computer Vision and Pattern Recognition, pp. 5841–5850 (2018)
46. Villegas, R., Ceylan, D., Hertzmann, A., Yang, J., Saito, J.: Contact-aware retargeting of skinned motion. In: Proceedings of the IEEE/CVF International Conference on Computer Vision, pp. 9720–9729 (2021)
47. Villegas, R., Yang, J., Ceylan, D., Lee, H.: Neural kinematic networks for unsupervised motion retargetting. In: Proceedings of the IEEE Conference on Computer Vision and Pattern Recognition, pp. 8639–8648 (2018)
48. Wang, J., et al.: Neural pose transfer by spatially adaptive instance normalization. In: Proceedings of the IEEE/CVF Conference on Computer Vision and Pattern Recognition, pp. 5831–5839 (2020)
49. Xu, Z., Zhou, Y., Kalogerakis, E., Landreth, C., Singh, K.: RigNet: neural rigging for articulated characters. arXiv preprint arXiv:2005.00559 (2020)
50. Xu, Z., Zhou, Y., Kalogerakis, E., Singh, K.: Predicting animation skeletons for 3D articulated models via volumetric nets. In: 3DV (2019)
51. Yamane, K., Ariki, Y., Hodgins, J.: Animating non-humanoid characters with human motion data. In: Proceedings of the 2010 ACM SIGGRAPH/Eurographics Symposium on Computer Animation, pp. 169–178 (2010)
52. Yang, J., Gao, L., Lai, Y.K., Rosin, P.L., Xia, S.: Biharmonic deformation transfer with automatic key point selection. Graph. Models **98**, 1–13 (2018)
53. Yang, J., Gao, L., Tan, Q., Huang, Y., Xia, S., Lai, Y.K.: Multiscale mesh deformation component analysis with attention-based autoencoders. arXiv preprint arXiv:2012.02459 (2020)
54. Zhang, X., Bhatnagar, B.L., Starke, S., Guzov, V., Pons-Moll, G.: COUCH: towards controllable human-chair interactions. In: European Conference on Computer Vision (ECCV). Springer (2022)
55. Zhou, K., Bhatnagar, B.L., Pons-Moll, G.: Unsupervised shape and pose disentanglement for 3D meshes. In: Vedaldi, A., Bischof, H., Brox, T., Frahm, J.-M. (eds.) ECCV 2020. LNCS, vol. 12367, pp. 341–357. Springer, Cham (2020). https://doi.org/10.1007/978-3-030-58542-6_21
56. Zhu, J.Y., Park, T., Isola, P., Efros, A.A.: Unpaired image-to-image translation using cycle-consistent adversarial networks. In: Proceedings of the IEEE International Conference on Computer Vision, pp. 2223–2232 (2017)

Masked Discrimination for Self-supervised Learning on Point Clouds

Haotian Liu$^{(\boxtimes)}$, Mu Cai, and Yong Jae Lee

University of Wisconsin–Madison, Madison, USA
{lht,mucai,yongjaelee}@cs.wisc.edu

Abstract. Masked autoencoding has achieved great success for self-supervised learning in the image and language domains. However, mask based pretraining has yet to show benefits for point cloud understanding, likely due to standard backbones like PointNet being unable to properly handle the training versus testing distribution mismatch introduced by masking during training. In this paper, we bridge this gap by proposing a discriminative mask pretraining Transformer framework, *Mask-Point*, for point clouds. Our key idea is to represent the point cloud as discrete occupancy values (1 if part of the point cloud; 0 if not), and perform simple binary classification between masked object points and sampled noise points as the proxy task. In this way, our approach is robust to the point sampling variance in point clouds, and facilitates learning rich representations. We evaluate our pretrained models across several downstream tasks, including 3D shape classification, segmentation, and real-word object detection, and demonstrate state-of-the-art results while achieving a significant pretraining speedup (e.g., 4.1× on ScanNet) compared to the prior state-of-the-art Transformer baseline. Code is available at https://github.com/haotian-liu/MaskPoint.

1 Introduction

Learning rich feature representations without human supervision, also known as self-supervised learning, has made tremendous strides in recent years. We now have methods in NLP [12,39,40] and computer vision [2,5,8,19,20] that can produce stronger features than those learned on labeled datasets.

In particular, masked autoencoding, whose task is to reconstruct the masked data from the unmasked input (e.g., predicting the masked word in a sentence or masked patch in an image, based on surrounding unmasked context) is the dominant self-supervised learning approach for text understanding [12,24,25,61] and has recently shown great promise in image understanding [2,19] as well. Curiously, for point cloud data, masked autoencoding has not yet been able to produce a similar level of performance [51,59,63]. Self-supervised learning

---

Supplementary Information The online version contains supplementary material available at https://doi.org/10.1007/978-3-031-20086-1_38.

S. Avidan et al. (Eds.): ECCV 2022, LNCS 13662, pp. 657–675, 2022.
https://doi.org/10.1007/978-3-031-20086-1_38

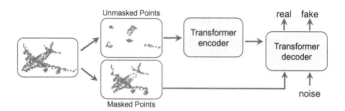

Fig. 1. Main Idea. We randomly partition the point cloud into masked and unmasked sets. We only feed the visible portion of the point cloud into the encoder. Then, a set of real query points are sampled from the masked points, and a set of fake query points are randomly sampled from 3D space. We train the decoder so that it distinguishes between the real and fake points. After pre-training, we discard the decoder and use the encoder for downstream tasks.

would be extremely beneficial for point cloud data, as obtaining high-quality annotations is both hard and expensive, especially for real-world scans. At the same time, masked autoencoding should also be a good fit for point cloud data, since each point (or group of points) can easily be masked or unmasked.

We hypothesize that the primary reason why masked autoencoding has thus far not worked well for point cloud data is because standard point cloud backbones are unable to properly handle the distribution mismatch between training and testing data introduced by masking. Specifically, PointNet type backbones [36–38] leverage local aggregation layers that operate over local neighborhoods (e.g., k-nearest neighbors) of each point. The extent of the local neighborhoods can change drastically with the introduction of masking, creating a discrepancy between the distribution of local neighborhoods seen on masked training scenes versus unmasked test scenes. Transformers [50], on the other hand, can perform self-attention (a form of aggregation) on either all or selective portions of the input data. This means that it has the ability to only process the unmasked portions of the scene in the training data, without being impacted by the masked portions. This property suggests that Transformers could be an ideal backbone choice for self-supervised masked autoencoding for point clouds.

For image understanding, the state-of-the-art masked autoencoding Transformer approach MAE [19] masks out a large random subset of image patches, applies the Transformer encoder to the unmasked patches, and trains a small Transformer decoder that takes in the positional encodings of the masked patches to reconstruct their original pixel values. However, this approach cannot be directly applied to point cloud data, because the raw representation of each 3D point is its spatial xyz location. Thus, training the decoder to predict the xyz coordinates of a masked point would be trivial, since its positional encoding would leak the correct answer. In this case, the network would simply take a shortcut and not learn meaningful features.

To address this, we propose a simple binary point classification objective as a new pretext task for point cloud masked autoencoding. We first group points into local neighborhoods, and then mask out a large random subset of those groups.

The Transformer encoder takes in the unmasked point groups, and encodes each group through self-attention with the other groups. The Transformer decoder takes in a set of real and fake query points, where the real queries are sampled from the *masked* points, while the fake queries are randomly sampled from the full 3D space. We then perform cross attention between the decoder queries and encoder outputs. Finally, we apply a binary classification head to the decoder's outputs and require it to distinguish between the real and fake queries. We find this simple design to be effective, as it creates a difficult and meaningful pretext task that requires the network to deduce the 3D shape of the object from only a small amount of visible point groups.

Among prior self-supervised point cloud approaches, Point-BERT [63] is the most related. It trains a discrete Variational AutoEncoder (dVAE) [42] to encode the input point cloud into discrete point token representations, and performs BERT-style pretraining over them. To aid training, it uses point patch mixing augmentation, together with an auxiliary MoCo [20] loss. However, the dependency on a pretrained dVAE together with other auxiliary techniques, creates a significant computational overhead in pretraining – our experiments show that its pre-training is significantly slower (e.g., 4.1× on ScanNet [9]) than ours even without taking into account the training time of the dVAE module. The large speedup is also due to our design of the Transformer encoder processing only the unmasked points.

In sum, our main contributions are: (1) A novel masked point classification Transformer, *MaskPoint*, for self-supervised learning on point clouds. (2) Our approach is simple and effective, achieving state-of-the-art performance on a variety of downstream tasks, including object classification on Model-Net40 [56]/ScanObjectNN [49], part segmentation on ShapeNetPart [62], object detection on ScanNet [9], and few-shot object classification on ModelNet40 [56]. (3) Notably, for the first time, we show that a standard Transformer architecture can outperform sophisticatedly designed point cloud backbones.

2   Related Work

Transformers. Transformers were first proposed to model long-term dependencies in NLP tasks [50], and have achieved great success [12,40,50]. More recently, they have also shown promising performance on various image and video understanding tasks [3,14,23,39,45,48,52]. There have also been attempts to adopt transformers to 3D point cloud data. PCT [18] and Point Transformer [68] propose new attention mechanisms for point cloud feature aggregation. 3DETR [32] uses Transformer blocks and the parallel decoding strategy from DETR [3] for 3D object detection. However, it is still hard to get promising performance using the standard Transformer. For example, in 3D object detection, there is a large performance gap between 3DETR [32] and state-of-the-art point based [66] and convolution based [10] methods. In this paper, we show that self-supervised learning using a novel masked point classification objective can aid a standard

Transformer to learn rich point cloud feature representations, and in turn largely improve its performance on various downstream tasks.

Self-supervised Learning. Self-supervised learning (SSL) aims to learn meaningful representations from the data itself, to better serve downstream tasks. Traditional methods typically rely on pretext tasks, such as image rotation prediction [17], image colorization [64], and solving jigsaw puzzles [33]. Recent methods based on contrastive learning (e.g., MoCo [20], SimCLR [5], SimSiam [8]) have achieved great success in the image domain, sometimes producing even better downstream performance compared to supervised pretraining on ImageNet [11].

Self-supervised learning has also begun to be explored for point cloud data. Pretext methods include deformation reconstruction [1], geometric structure prediction [46], and orientation estimation [35]. Contrastive learning approaches include PointContrast [57], which learns corresponding points from different camera views, and DepthContrast [65], which learns representations by comparing transformations of a 3D point cloud/voxel. OcCo [51] learns an autoencoder to reconstruct the scene from the occluded input. However, due to the sampling variance of the underlying 3D shapes, explicitly reconstructing the original point cloud will inevitably capture such variance. In this paper, we explore a simple but effective discriminative classification pretext task to learn representations that are robust to the sampling variance.

Mask Based Pretraining. Masking out content has been used in various ways to improve model robustness including as a regularizer [16,44], data augmentation [13,43,69], and self-supervised learning [7,12,19]. For self-supervised learning, the key idea is to train the model to predict the masked content based on its surrounding context. The most successful approaches are built upon the Transformer [50], due in part to its token-based representation and ability to model long-range dependencies.

In masked language modeling, BERT [12] and its variants [24,25] achieve state-of-the-art performance across nearly all NLP downstream tasks by predicting masked tokens during pretraining. Masked image modeling works [2,19] adopt a similar idea for image pretraining. BEiT [2] maps image patches into discrete tokens, then masks a small portion of patches, and feeds the remaining visible patches into the Transformer to reconstruct the tokens of the masked patches. Instead of reconstructing tokens, the recent Masked AutoEncoder (MAE) [19] reconstructs the masked patches at the pixel level, and with a much higher mask ratio of $\geq 70\%$. Following works try to predict higher-level visual features such as HoG [54], or improve the representation capability of the encoder by aligning the feature from both visible patches and masked patches [7]. To our knowledge, the only self-supervised mask modeling Transformer approach for point clouds is Point-BERT [63], which adopts a similar idea as BEiT [2]. However, to obtain satisfactory performance, it requires a pretrained dVAE and other auxiliary techniques (e.g., a momentum encoder [20]), which slow down training. Our masked point discrimination approach largely accelerates training (4.1× faster than Point-BERT) while achieving state-of-the-art performance for various downstream tasks.

Finally, some concurrent works [34] also explore adopting the masked autoencoding pretraining objective on point clouds. Our key novelty over these contemporary approaches is the discriminative point classification objective which helps to address the sampling variance issue in point clouds.

3   Approach

The goal is to learn semantic feature representations without human supervision that can perform well on downstream point cloud recognition tasks. We motivate our self-supervised learning design with a qualitative example. Figure 1 "Unmasked Points" shows a point cloud with a large portion (90%) of its points masked out. Still, based on our prior semantic understanding of the world, we as humans are able to say a number of things about it: (1) it might be an airplane; (2) if so, it should consist of a head, body, tail, and wings; and even (3) roughly where these parts should be present. In other words, because we already know what airplanes are, we can recover the missing information from the small visible subset of the point cloud. In a similar way, training a model to recover information about the masked portion of the point cloud given the visible portion could force the model to learn object semantics.

However, even as humans, it can be difficult or impossible to precisely reconstruct all missing points, since there are several ambiguous factors; e.g., the precise thickness of the wings or the precise length of the airplane. If we are instead given a sampled 3D point in space, and are asked to answer whether it likely belongs to the object or not, we would be more confident in our answer. This discriminative point classification task is much less ambiguous than the reconstruction task, yet still requires a deep understanding of object semantics in order to deduce the masked points from the small number of visible points.

3.1   Masked Point Discrimination

Our approach works as follows. We randomly partition each input point cloud $\mathcal{P} \in \mathbb{R}^{N \times 3}$ into two groups: masked $\mathcal{M}$ and unmasked $\mathcal{U}$. We use the Transformer encoder to model the correlation between the sparsely-distributed unmasked tokens $\mathcal{U}$ via self-attention. Ideally, the resulting encoded latent representation tokens $\mathcal{L}$ should not only model the relationship between the unmasked points $\mathcal{U}$, but also recover the latent distribution of masked points $\mathcal{M}$, so as to perform well on the pretraining task. We next sample a set of *real* query points $\mathbf{Q}_{real}$ and a set of *fake* query points $\mathbf{Q}_{fake}$. The real query points are sampled from the masked point set $\mathcal{M}$, while the fake query points are randomly sampled from the full 3D space. We then perform cross attention between each decoder query $\mathbf{q} \in \{\mathbf{Q}_{real}, \mathbf{Q}_{fake}\}$ and the encoder outputs, $\mathtt{CA}(\mathbf{q}, \mathcal{L})$, to model the relationship between the masked query point and the unmasked points. Finally, we apply a binary classification head to the decoder's outputs and require it to distinguish between the real and fake queries.

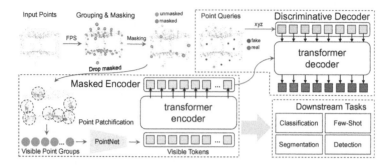

Fig. 2. MaskPoint architecture. We first uniformly sample point groups from the point cloud, and partition them to masked and unmasked. We patchify the visible point groups to token embeddings with PointNet and feed these visible tokens into the encoder. Then, a set of real query points are sampled from the masked points, and a set of fake query points are randomly sampled from 3D space. We train the decoder so that it distinguishes between the real and fake points. After pre-training, we discard the decoder and use the encoder for downstream tasks. See Sect. 3.1 for details.

We show in our experiments that our approach is both simple and effective, as it creates a pretext task that is difficult and meaningful enough for the model to learn rich semantic point cloud representations.

Discarding Ambiguous Points. Since we sample fake query points uniformly at random over the entire space, there will be some points that fall close to the object's surface. Such points can cause training difficulties since their target label is 'fake' even though they are on the object. In preliminary experiments, we find that such ambiguous points can lead to vanishing gradients in the early stages of training. Thus, to stabilize training, we simply remove all fake points $\hat{\mathbf{p}} \in \mathbf{Q}_{fake}$ whose euclidean distance is less than γ to any object (masked or unmasked) point $\mathbf{p}_i \in \mathcal{P}$: $\min_i ||\hat{\mathbf{p}} - \mathbf{p}_i||_2 < \gamma$. To address the size variance of the input point cloud, γ is dynamically selected per point cloud $\mathcal{P}$: $\hat{\mathcal{P}} = \mathrm{FPS}(\mathcal{P}), \gamma = \min_{j \neq i} ||\hat{\mathcal{P}}_i - \hat{\mathcal{P}}_j||_2$.

3D Point Patchification. Feeding every single point into the Transformer encoder can yield an unacceptable cost due to the quadratic complexity of self-attention operators. Following [14,63], we adopt a patch embedding strategy that converts input point clouds into 3D point patches.

Given the input point cloud $\mathcal{P} \in \mathbb{R}^{N \times 3}$, S points $\{\mathbf{p}_i\}_{i=1}^{S}$ are sampled as patch centers using farthest point sampling [38]. We then gather the k nearest neighbors for each patch center to generate a set of 3D point patches $\{\mathbf{g}_i\}_{i=1}^{S}$. A PointNet [37] is then applied to encode each 3D point patch $\mathbf{g}_i \in \mathbb{R}^{k \times 3}$ to a feature embedding $\mathbf{f}_i \in \mathbb{R}^d$. In this way, we obtain S tokens and their corresponding features $\{\mathbf{f}_i\}_{i=1}^{S}$ and center coordinates $\{\mathbf{p}_i\}_{i=1}^{S}$.

Transformer Architecture. Our network architecture is shown in Fig. 2. We adopt the standard Transformer encoder [50] as the encoding backbone, where each Transformer encoder block consists of a multi-head self-attention (MSA) layer and a feed forward network (FFN). As noted earlier, we construct patch-wise features $\{\mathbf{f}_i\}_{i=1}^M$ from the input point cloud $\mathcal{P} \in \mathbb{R}^{N \times 3}$. Following [63], we apply the MLP positional embedding $\{\mathbf{pos}_i\}_{i=1}^M$ to the patch features $\{\mathbf{f}_i\}_{i=1}^M$. Then, the class token $\mathbf{E}[s]$, which will be used for downstream classification tasks, is stacked to the top of the patch features $\{\mathbf{f}_i\}_{i=1}^M$; i.e., the input to the Transformer encoder is $I_0 = \{\mathbf{E}[s], \mathbf{f}_1 + \mathbf{pos}_1, \cdots, \mathbf{f}_M + \mathbf{pos}_M\}$. After n Transformer blocks, we get the feature embedding for each point patch $I_n = \{\mathbf{E}^n[s], \mathbf{f}_1^n, \cdots, \mathbf{f}_M^n\}$.

During the decoding stage, N_q *real* query points $\mathbf{Q}_{real}$ and N_q *fake* query points $\mathbf{Q}_{fake}$ are sampled. We pass the encoder output I_n and its positional embedding $\{\mathbf{pos}_i\}_{i=1}^M$, $\mathbf{Q}_{real}$, $\mathbf{Q}_{fake}$ and their positional embedding $\{\mathbf{pos}_i^{\mathbf{Q}}\}_{i=1}^{2N}$ into a one-layer Transformer decoder. Cross attention is only performed between the queries and encoder keys/values, but not between different queries. Finally, the decoder output goes through an MLP classification head, which is trained with the binary focal loss [27], since there can be a large imbalance between positive and negative samples.

For downstream tasks, the point patchification module and Transformer encoder will be used with their pretrained weights as initialization.

An Information Theoretic Perspective. Here, we provide an information theoretic perspective to our self-supervised learning objective, using mutual information. The mutual information between random variables X and Y, $I(X;Y)$, measures the amount of information that can be gained about random variable X from the knowledge about the other random variable Y.

Ideally, we would like the model to learn a rich feature representation of the point cloud: the latent representation $\mathcal{L}$ from our encoder $\mathcal{E}$ should contain enough information to recover the original point cloud $\mathcal{P}$, *i.e.*, we would like to maximize the mutual information $I(\mathcal{P};\mathcal{L})$. However, directly estimating $I(\mathcal{P};\mathcal{L})$ is hard since we need to know the exact probability distribution of $P(\mathcal{P}|\mathcal{L})$. Following [6], we instead use auxiliary distribution Q to approximate it:

$$
\begin{aligned}
I(\mathcal{P};\mathcal{L}) &= -H(\mathcal{P}|\mathcal{L}) + H(\mathcal{P}) \\
&= \mathbb{E}_{x \sim \mathcal{L}}[\mathbb{E}_{p' \sim P(\mathcal{P}|\mathcal{L})}[\log P(p'|x)]] + H(\mathcal{P}) \\
&= \mathbb{E}_{x \sim \mathcal{L}}[\underbrace{D_{\mathrm{KL}}(P(\cdot|x)\|Q(\cdot|x))}_{\geq 0} + \mathbb{E}_{p' \sim P(\mathcal{P}|\mathcal{L})}[\log Q(p'|x)]] + H(\mathcal{P}) \quad (1) \\
&\geq \mathbb{E}_{x \sim \mathcal{L}}[\mathbb{E}_{p' \sim P(\mathcal{P}|\mathcal{L})}[\log Q(p'|x)]] + H(\mathcal{P})
\end{aligned}
$$

Lemma 3.1. For random variables X, Y and function $f(x,y)$ under suitable regularity conditions: $\mathbb{E}_{x \sim X, y \sim Y|x}[f(x,y)] = \mathbb{E}_{x \sim X, y \sim Y|x, x' \sim X|y}[f(x',y)]$.

Therefore, we can define a variational lower bound, $L_I(Q,\mathcal{L})$, of the mutual information, $I(\mathcal{P};\mathcal{L})$:

$$
\begin{aligned}
L_I(Q,\mathcal{L}) &= \mathbb{E}_{p \sim P(\mathcal{P}), x \sim \mathcal{L}}[\log Q(p|x)] + H(\mathcal{P}) \\
&= \mathbb{E}_{x \sim \mathcal{L}}[\mathbb{E}_{p' \sim P(\mathcal{P}|\mathcal{L})}[\log Q(p'|x)]] + H(\mathcal{P}) \quad (2) \\
&\leq I(\mathcal{P};\mathcal{L})
\end{aligned}
$$

Therefore, we have:

$$\max I(\mathcal{P};\mathcal{L}) \iff \max L_I(Q,\mathcal{L}) \iff \max \mathbb{E}_{x\sim\mathcal{L}}[\mathbb{E}_{p'\sim P(\mathcal{P}|\mathcal{L})}[\log Q(p'|x)]] \quad (3)$$

Previous works use the Chamfer distance to approximate such auxiliary function Q, but it has the disadvantage of being sensitive to point sampling variance (discussed in detail in Sect. 3.2). Thus, we instead represent the point cloud distribution with occupancy values within the tightest 3D bounding box of the point cloud: $\mathcal{B} \in \{x,y,z,o\}^L$, where $(x,y,z) \in \mathbb{R}^3$, $o \in \{0,1\}$, and L is the number of densely sampled points. We let the output of Q denote the continuous distribution of the occupancy value $\hat{o}$, where $Q(\cdot) \in [0,1]$. In our implementation, as discussed previously, we construct a set of real query points and fake query points, assign them with the corresponding occupancy labels, and optimize the probability outputs from the model with a binary classification objective.

3.2 Why Not Reconstruction, as in MAE?

In this section, we delve into the details on why a reconstruction objective (i.e., reconstructing the original point cloud from the unmasked points) as used in the related Masked AutoEncoder (MAE) [19] approach for images would not work for our point cloud setting.

First, in MAE, the self-supervised learning task is to reconstruct the masked patches, based on the input image's unmasked (visible) patches. Specifically, given the 2D spatial position for each masked image patch query, the objective is to generate its RGB pixel values. In our case, the analogue would be to generate the spatial xyz values for a masked 3D point patch query – which would be trivial for the model since the query already contains the corresponding spatial information. Such a trivial solution will result in perfect zero-loss, and prevent the model from learning meaningful feature representations.

Another issue with the reconstruction objective for point clouds is that there will be point sampling variance. Specifically, the true 3D shape of the object will be a continuous surface, but a point cloud will a discrete sampling of it. Suppose we sample two such point clouds, and denote the first set as the "ground truth" target, and the second set as the prediction of a model. Although both sets reflect the same geometric shape of the object, the Chamfer distance (which can be used to measure the shape difference between the two point sets) between them is non-zero (i.e., there would be a loss). Thus, minimizing the Chamfer distance would force the model to generate predictions that exactly match the first set. And since the first set is just one sampling of the true underlying distribution, this can be an unnecessarily difficult optimization problem that can lead to suboptimal model performance.

4 Experiments

We evaluate the pre-trained representation learned by the proposed model on a variety of downstream point cloud understanding tasks, including object classification, part segmentation, object detection, and few-shot object classification.

We also visualize the reconstruction results from masked point clouds, to qualitatively study the effect of our pretraining. Finally, we perform ablation studies on masking strategies and decoder designs.

Pretraining Datasets. (1) ShapeNet [4] has 50,000 unique 3D models from 55 common object categories, and is used as our pre-training dataset for object classification, part segmentation, and few-shot classification. For ShapeNet pretraining, we sample 1024 points from each 3D model as the inputs. We follow [63] to sample 64 point groups, each containing 32 points.

(2) We also use single-view depth map videos from the popular ScanNet [9] dataset, which contains around 2.5 million RGBD scans. We do not use its RGB information in this paper. We adopt similar pre-processing steps as DepthContrast [65], but we generate a smaller subset of the dataset than in [65], which we call 'ScanNet-Medium', to accelerate pretraining. ScanNet-Medium is generated by sampling every 10-th frame from ScanNet, resulting in ∼25k samples. We use ScanNet-Medium (only geometry information) as the pre-training dataset for 3D object detection. For pretraining, we sample 20k points from each 3D scene scan as the input. We follow [32] to sample 2048 groups, each containing 64 points.

Transformer Encoder. We construct a 12-layer standard Transformer encoder, named PointViT, for point cloud understanding. Following Point-BERT [63], we set the hidden dimension of each encoder block to 384, number of heads to 6, FFN expansion ratio to 4, and drop rate of stochastic depth [21] to 0.1.

Transformer Decoder. We use a single-layer Transformer decoder for pretraining. The configuration of the attention block is identical to the encoder.

Training Details. Following [63], we pretrain with the AdamW [31] optimizer with a weight decay of 0.05 and a learning rate of 5×10^{-4} with the cosine decay. The model is trained for 300 epochs with a batch size of 128, with random scaling and translation data augmentation. Following [63], MoCo loss [20] is used for ShapeNet pretraining. For finetuning and other training details, please see supp.

4.1   3D Object Classification

Datasets. We compare the performance of object classification on two datasets: the synthetic ModelNet40 [56], and real-world ScanObjectNN [49]. ModelNet40 [56] consists of 12,311 CAD models from 40 classes. We follow the official data splitting scheme in [56]. We evaluate the overall accuracy (OA) over all test samples. ScanObjectNN [49] is a more challenging point cloud benchmark that consists of 2902 unique objects in 15 categories collected from noisy real-world scans. It has three splits: OBJ (object only), BG (with background), PB (with background and manually added perturbations). We evaluate the overall accuracy (OA) over all test samples on all three splits.

ModelNet40 Results. Table 1 shows ModelNet40 [56] results. With 1k points, our approach achieves a significant 2.4% OA improvement compared to training from scratch (PointViT). It also brings a 1.7% gain over OcCo [51] pretraining,

Table 1. Shape Classification on ModelNet40 [56]. With a standard Transformer backbone, our approach significantly outperforms training-from-scratch baselines and SOTA pretraining methods. It even outperforms PointTransformer [68], which uses an attention operator specifically designed for point clouds. *SSL: Self-supervised pretraining. [T]: Transformer-based networks with special designs for point clouds. [ST]: Standard Transformer network.

Method	SSL	#point	OA
PointNet [37]		1k	89.2
PointNet++ [38]		1k	90.7
PointCNN [26]		1k	92.2
SpiderCNN [58]		1k	92.4
PointWeb [67]		1k	92.3
PointConv [55]		1k	92.5
DGCNN [53]		1k	92.9
KPConv [47]		1k	92.9
DensePoint [28]		1k	93.2
PosPool [30]		5k	93.2
RSCNN [29]		5k	93.6
[T] Point Trans. [15]		1k	92.8
[T] Point Trans. [68]		–	93.7
[T] PCT [18]		1k	93.2
[ST] PointViT		1k	91.4
[ST] PointViT-OcCo [51]	✓	1k	92.1
[ST] Point-BERT [63]	✓	1k	93.2
[ST] MaskPoint (ours)	✓	1k	**93.8**

Table 2. Shape Classification on ScanObjectNN [49]. OBJ: object-only; BG: with background; PB: BG with manual perturbation.

Method	OA		
	OBJ	BG	PB
PointNet [37]	79.2	73.3	68.0
PointNet++ [38]	84.3	82.3	77.9
PointCNN [26]	85.5	86.1	78.5
SpiderCNN [58]	79.5	77.1	73.7
DGCNN [53]	86.2	82.8	78.1
BGA-DGCNN [49]	–	–	79.7
BGA-PN++ [49]	–	–	80.2
PointViT	80.6	79.9	77.2
PointViT-OcCo [51]	85.5	84.9	78.8
Point-BERT [63]	88.1	87.4	83.1
MaskPoint (ours)	**89.7**	**89.3**	**84.6**

Table 3. Part Segmentation on ShapeNetPart [62]. Our method also works well on dense prediction tasks like segmentation.

Method	mIoU	
	cat.	ins.
PointNet [37]	80.4	83.7
PointNet++ [38]	81.9	85.1
DGCNN [53]	82.3	85.2
PointViT	83.4	85.1
PointViT-OcCo [51]	83.4	85.1
Point-BERT [63]	84.1	85.6
MaskPoint (ours)	**84.4**	**86.0**

and 0.6% gain over Point-BERT [63] pretraining. The significant improvement over the baselines indicates the effectiveness of our pre-training method. Notably, for the first time, with 1k points, a standard vision transformer architecture produces competitive performance compared to sophisticatedly designed attention operators from PointTransformer [68] (93.8% vs 93.7%).

ScanObjectNN Results. We next conduct experiments using the real-world scan dataset ScanObjectNN [49]. Table 2 shows the results. Our approach achieves SOTA performance on all three splits. On the hardest PB split, our approach achieves a large 7.4% OA improvement compared to training from scratch (Point-ViT). It achieves a 5.8% gain over OcCo [51] pretraining, and a 1.5% gain over Point-BERT [63] pretraining. The large improvement over the baselines highlights the transferability of our model's self-supervised representation,

Table 4. Few-shot classification on ModelNet40 [56].

Method	5-way		10-way	
	10-shot	20-shot	10-shot	20-shot
DGCNN [51]	91.8 ± 3.7	93.4 ± 3.2	86.3 ± 6.2	90.9 ± 5.1
DGCNN-OcCo [51]	91.9 ± 3.3	93.9 ± 3.2	86.4 ± 5.4	91.3 ± 4.6
PointViT	87.8 ± 5.3	93.3 ± 4.3	84.6 ± 5.5	89.4 ± 6.3
PointViT-OcCo [51]	94.0 ± 3.6	95.9 ± 2.3	89.4 ± 5.1	92.4 ± 4.6
Point-BERT [63]	94.6 ± 3.1	96.3 ± 2.7	91.0 ± 5.4	92.7 ± 5.1
MaskPoint (ours)	$\mathbf{95.0 \pm 3.7}$	$\mathbf{97.2 \pm 1.7}$	$\mathbf{91.4 \pm 4.0}$	$\mathbf{93.4 \pm 3.5}$

as there is a significant domain gap between the clean synthetic ShapeNet [4] dataset used for pretraining and the noisy real-world ScanObjectNN [49] dataset.

We believe the performance gain over OcCo [51] and Point-BERT [63] is mainly because of our discriminative pretext task. OcCo suffers from the sampling variance issue (Sect. 3.2) as it uses a reconstruction-based objective in pretraining. Compared to Point-BERT, we do not use the point patch mixing technique, which mixes two different point clouds. This could introduce unnecessary noise and domain shifts to pretraining and harm downstream performance.

4.2   3D Part Segmentation

Dataset. ShapeNetPart [62] consists of 16,880 models from 16 shape categories and 50 different part categories, with 14,006 models for training and 2,874 for testing. We use the sampled point sets produced by [38] for a fair comparison with prior work. We report per-category mean IoU (cat. mIoU) and mean IoU averaged over all test instances (ins. mIoU).

Results. Table 3 shows the results (per-category IoU is in supp). Our approach outperforms the training from the scratch (PointViT) and OcCo-pretraining baselines by 1.0%/0.9% in cat./ins. mIoU. It also produces a 0.3%/0.4% gain compared to Point-BERT. Thanks to our dense discriminative pretraining objective, in which we densely classify points over the 3D space, we are able to obtain good performance when scaling to dense prediction tasks.

4.3   Few-Shot Classification

We conduct few-shot classification experiments on ModelNet40 [56], following the settings in [63]. The standard experiment setting is the "K-way N-shot" configuration, where K classes are first randomly selected, and then $N + 20$ objects are sampled for each class. We train the model on $K \times N$ samples (support set), and evaluate on the remaining $K \times 20$ samples (query set). We compare our approach with OcCo and Point-BERT, which are the current state-of-the-art.

Table 5. 3D object detection results on ScanNet validation set. The backbone of our pretraining model and Point-BERT [63] is 3DETR [32]. All other methods use VoteNet [37] as the finetuning backbone. Only geometry information is fed into the downstream task. "Input" column denotes input type for the pretraining stage. "Geo" denotes geometry information. Note that DepthContrast (Geo + RGB) model uses a heavier backbone (PointNet 3x) for downstream tasks.

Methods	SSL	Pretrained input	$\mathbf{AP_{25}}$	$\mathbf{AP_{50}}$
VoteNet [36]		-	58.6	33.5
STRL [22]	✓	Geo	59.5	38.4
Implicit autoencoder [59]	✓	Geo	61.5	39.8
RandomRooms [41]	✓	Geo	61.3	36.2
PointContrast [57]	✓	Geo	59.2	38.0
DepthContrast [65]	✓	Geo	61.3	–
DepthContrast [65]	✓	Geo + RGB	**64.0**	**42.9**
3DETR [32]		-	62.1	37.9
Point-BERT [63]	✓	Geo	61.0	38.3
MaskPoint (ours)	✓	Geo	63.4	40.6
MaskPoint (ours, 12 Enc)	✓	Geo	**64.2**	**42.1**

We perform experiments with 4 settings, where for each setting, we run the train/evaluation on 10 different sampled splits, and report the mean and std over the 10 runs. Table 4 shows the results. Our approach achieves the best performance for all settings. It demonstrate an absolute gain of 7.2%/3.8%/4.6%/2.5% over the PointViT training from the scratch baseline. When comparing to pretraining baselines, it outperforms OcCo by 1.0%/1.3%/1.5%/1.0%, and outperforms Point-BERT by 0.4%/0.9%/0.4%/0.7%. It also clearly outperforms the DGCNN baselines. Our state-of-the-art performance on few-shot classification further demonstrates the effectiveness of our pretraining approach.

4.4   3D Object Detection

Our most closely related work, Point-BERT [63] showed experiments only on object-level classification and segmentation tasks. In this paper, we evaluate a model's pretrained representation on a more challenging scene-level downstream task: 3D object detection on ScanNetV2 [9], which consists of real-world richly-annotated 3D reconstructions of indoor scenes. It comprises 1201 training scenes, 312 validation scenes and 100 hidden test scenes. Axis-aligned bounding box labels are provided for 18 object categories.

For this experiment, we adopt 3DETR [32] as the downstream model for both our method and Point-BERT. 3DETR is an end-to-end transformer-based 3D object detection pipeline. During finetuning, the input point cloud is first down-sampled to 2048 points via a VoteNet-style Set Aggregation (SA) layer [36,38], which then goes through 3-layer self-attention blocks. The decoder is composed

Original   Masked   Recon.   Original   Masked   Recon.

Fig. 3. Reconstruction results. By reformulating reconstruction as a discriminative occupancy classification task, we achieve a similar learning objective to generative reconstruction while being robust to point sampling variance. Even with a high 90% mask ratio, our approach recovers the overall shape of the original point cloud, without overfitting. Visualization toolkit: Pointflow [60].

of 8-layer cross-attention blocks. For a fair comparison with the 3DETR train-from-scratch baseline, we strictly follow its architecture of SA layer and encoder during pretraining, whose weights are transferred during finetuning. Our pre-training dataset is ScanNet-Medium, as described in Sect. 4.

Table 5 shows that our method surpasses the 3DETR train-from-scratch baseline by a large margin ($+1.3AP_{25}$ and $+2.7AP_{50}$). Interestingly, Point-BERT brings nearly no improvement compared to training from scratch. The low mask rate and discrete tokens learned from dVAE may impede Point-BERT from learning meaningful representations for detection. Also, the 3DETR paper [32] finds that increasing the number of encoding layers in 3DETR brings only a small benefit to its detection performance. Here we increase the number of layers from 3 to 12, which leads to a large performance improvement ($+2.1AP_{25}$ and $+4.2AP_{50}$) for our approach compared to training from scratch. This result demonstrates that by pre-training on a large unlabeled dataset, we can afford to increase the model's encoder capacity to learn richer representations. Finally, note that we also include VoteNet based methods at the top of Table 5 as a reference, but the numbers are not directly comparable as they are using a different (non Transformer-based) detector.

4.5   Reconstruction Quality

Although our model is not trained with the reconstruction objective, we can still reconstruct the point cloud with our decoder by classifying the densely sampled points from the point cloud's full 3D bounding box space: $\mathcal{P}_{rec} = \{x | \mathcal{D}(x|\mathcal{L}) = 1\}$. Figure 3 shows that even with a large 90% mask ratio, our model is able to reconstruct the overall shape of the original point cloud, without overfitting. We also quantitatively evaluate the reconstruction quality with the L2 chamfer distance (CD-ℓ_2), a standard metric to measure the similarity between two point clouds. MaskPoint achieves a satisfactory reconstruction accuracy of 6.6×10^{-3} CD-ℓ_2 (with points $p \in [-1,1]^3$). The imperfection is expected (similar to the

Table 6. Ablations on ScanObjectNN [49] (PB split). Our findings are: a larger masking ratio generally yields better performance; random masking is slightly better than block masking; 256-query provides a good balance between information and noise; a thin decoder ensures rich feature representation in the encoder and benefits downstream performance.

Ratio	OA
0.25	83.2
0.50	83.7
0.75	84.1
0.90	**84.6**

(a) Random mask

Ratio	OA
0.25	82.4
0.50	83.8
0.75	83.7
0.90	84.1

(b) Block mask

# queries	OA
64	83.7
256	**84.6**
1024	83.9

(c) # dec. queries

# dec	OA
1	**84.6**
3	83.7
6	83.9

(d) # dec. layers

blurry reconstructed image in MAE [19]), as there can be multiple plausible reconstructions given such a large 90% mask ratio.

4.6   Ablation Studies

Masking Strategy. We show the influence of different masking strategies in Table 6a, 6b. First, we observe that a higher masking ratio generally yields better performance, regardless of sampling type. This matches our intuition that a higher masking ratio creates a harder and more meaningful pretraining task. Further, with a higher masking ratio, random masking is slightly better than block masking. Therefore, we use a high mask rate of 90% with random masking.

Pretraining Decoder Design. We study the design of the pretraining decoder in Table 6c, 6d, by varying the number of decoder queries and layers. The number of decoder queries influence the balance between the classification of the real points and fake points. We find that 256-query is the sweet spot, where more queries could introduce too much noise, and fewer queries could result in insufficient training information.

The modeling power of the decoder affects the effectiveness of the pretraining: ideally, we want the encoder to only encode the features, while the decoder only projects the features to the pre-training objective. Any imbalance in either way can harm the model's performance on downstream tasks. We find that a single-layer decoder is sufficient for performing our proposed point discrimination task, and having more decoder layers harms the model's performance.

5   Conclusion

We proposed a discriminative masked point cloud pretraining framework, which facilitates a variety of downstream tasks while significantly reducing the pre-training time compared to the prior Transformer-based state-of-the-art method. We adopted occupancy values to represent the point cloud, forming a simpler yet effective binary pretraining objective function. Extensive experiments on 3D shape classification, detection, and segmentation demonstrated the strong performance of our approach. Currently, we randomly mask local point groups to partition the point cloud into masked and unmasked sets. It could be interesting to explore ways to instead learn how to mask the points. We hope our research can raise more attention to mask based self-supervised learning on point clouds.

Acknowledgement. This work was supported in part by NSF CAREER IIS-2150012 and the Wisconsin Alumni Research Foundation. We thank Xumin Yu for the helpful discussion in reproducing the Point-BERT baselines.

References

1. Achituve, I., Maron, H., Chechik, G.: Self-supervised learning for domain adaptation on point clouds. In: Proceedings of the IEEE/CVF Winter Conference on Applications of Computer Vision, pp. 123–133 (2021)
2. Bao, H., Dong, L., Wei, F.: BEIT: BERT pre-training of image transformers. arXiv preprint arXiv:2106.08254 (2021)
3. Carion, N., Massa, F., Synnaeve, G., Usunier, N., Kirillov, A., Zagoruyko, S.: End-to-end object detection with transformers. In: Vedaldi, A., Bischof, H., Brox, T., Frahm, J.-M. (eds.) ECCV 2020. LNCS, vol. 12346, pp. 213–229. Springer, Cham (2020). https://doi.org/10.1007/978-3-030-58452-8_13
4. Chang, A.X., et al.: ShapeNet: an information-rich 3D model repository. arXiv preprint arXiv:1512.03012 (2015)
5. Chen, T., Kornblith, S., Norouzi, M., Hinton, G.: A simple framework for contrastive learning of visual representations. In: III, H.D., Singh, A. (eds.) Proceedings of the 37th International Conference on Machine Learning. Proceedings of Machine Learning Research, vol. 119, pp. 1597–1607. PMLR, 13–18 July 2020. https://proceedings.mlr.press/v119/chen20j.html
6. Chen, X., Duan, Y., Houthooft, R., Schulman, J., Sutskever, I., Abbeel, P.: InfoGAN: interpretable representation learning by information maximizing generative adversarial nets. In: Advances in Neural Information Processing Systems, vol. 29 (2016)
7. Chen, X., et al.: Context autoencoder for self-supervised representation learning. arXiv preprint arXiv:2202.03026 (2022)
8. Chen, X., He, K.: Exploring simple Siamese representation learning. In: Proceedings of the IEEE/CVF Conference on Computer Vision and Pattern Recognition, pp. 15750–15758 (2021)
9. Dai, A., Chang, A.X., Savva, M., Halber, M., Funkhouser, T., Nießner, M.: ScanNet: richly-annotated 3D reconstructions of indoor scenes. In: Proceedings of the IEEE Conference on Computer Vision and Pattern Recognition, pp. 5828–5839 (2017)
10. Danila Rukhovich, Anna Vorontsova, A.K.: FCAF3D: fully convolutional anchor-free 3D object detection. arXiv preprint arXiv:2112.00322 (2021)
11. Deng, J., Dong, W., Socher, R., Li, L.J., Li, K., Fei-Fei, L.: ImageNet: a large-scale hierarchical image database. In: 2009 IEEE Conference on Computer Vision and Pattern Recognition, pp. 248–255. IEEE (2009)

12. Devlin, J., Chang, M.W., Lee, K., Toutanova, K.: BERT: pre-training of deep bidirectional transformers for language understanding. In: Proceedings of the 2019 Conference of the North American Chapter of the Association for Computational Linguistics: Human Language Technologies, Volume 1 (Long and Short Papers), pp. 4171–4186. Association for Computational Linguistics, Minneapolis, June 2019. https://doi.org/10.18653/v1/N19-1423, www.aclanthology.org/N19-1423

13. DeVries, T., Taylor, G.W.: Improved regularization of convolutional neural networks with cutout. arXiv preprint arXiv:1708.04552 (2017)

14. Dosovitskiy, A., et al.: An image is worth 16x16 words: transformers for image recognition at scale. In: ICLR (2021)

15. Engel, N., Belagiannis, V., Dietmayer, K.: Point transformer. IEEE Access **9**, 134826–134840 (2021)

16. Ghiasi, G., Lin, T.Y., Le, Q.V.: Dropblock: a regularization method for convolutional networks. In: NeurIPS (2018)

17. Gidaris, S., Singh, P., Komodakis, N.: Unsupervised representation learning by predicting image rotations. In: International Conference on Learning Representations (2018). https://openreview.net/forum?id=S1v4N2l0

18. Guo, M.H., Cai, J.X., Liu, Z.N., Mu, T.J., Martin, R.R., Hu, S.M.: PCT: point cloud transformer. Comput. Vis. Media **7**(2), 187–199 (2021)

19. He, K., Chen, X., Xie, S., Li, Y., Doll'ar, P., Girshick, R.: Masked autoencoders are scalable vision learners. arXiv preprint arXiv:2111.06377 (2021)

20. He, K., Fan, H., Wu, Y., Xie, S., Girshick, R.: Momentum contrast for unsupervised visual representation learning. In: Proceedings of the IEEE/CVF Conference on Computer Vision and Pattern Recognition, pp. 9729–9738 (2020)

21. Huang, G., Sun, Yu., Liu, Z., Sedra, D., Weinberger, K.Q.: Deep networks with stochastic depth. In: Leibe, B., Matas, J., Sebe, N., Welling, M. (eds.) ECCV 2016. LNCS, vol. 9908, pp. 646–661. Springer, Cham (2016). https://doi.org/10.1007/978-3-319-46493-0_39

22. Huang, S., Xie, Y., Zhu, S.C., Zhu, Y.: Spatio-temporal self-supervised representation learning for 3D point clouds. arXiv preprint arXiv:2109.00179 (2021)

23. Jiang, Y., Chang, S., Wang, Z.: TransGAN: two pure transformers can make one strong GAN, and that can scale up. In: Advances in Neural Information Processing Systems, vol. 34 (2021)

24. Joshi, M., Chen, D., Liu, Y., Weld, D.S., Zettlemoyer, L., Levy, O.: SpanBERT: improving pre-training by representing and predicting spans. Trans. Assoc. Comput. Linguist. **8**, 64–77 (2020)

25. Lan, Z., Chen, M., Goodman, S., Gimpel, K., Sharma, P., Soricut, R.: Albert: a lite BERT for self-supervised learning of language representations. In: International Conference on Learning Representations (2020). https://openreview.net/forum?id=H1eA7AEtvS

26. Li, Y., Bu, R., Sun, M., Wu, W., Di, X., Chen, B.: PointCNN: convolution on x-transformed points. In: Advances in Neural Information Processing Systems, vol. 31 (2018)

27. Lin, T.Y., Goyal, P., Girshick, R., He, K., Dollar, P.: Focal loss for dense object detection. In: ICCV (2017)

28. Liu, Y., Fan, B., Meng, G., Lu, J., Xiang, S., Pan, C.: DensePoint: learning densely contextual representation for efficient point cloud processing. In: Proceedings of the IEEE/CVF International Conference on Computer Vision, pp. 5239–5248 (2019)

29. Liu, Y., Fan, B., Xiang, S., Pan, C.: Relation-shape convolutional neural network for point cloud analysis. In: Proceedings of the IEEE/CVF Conference on Computer Vision and Pattern Recognition, pp. 8895–8904 (2019)

30. Liu, Z., Hu, H., Cao, Y., Zhang, Z., Tong, X.: A closer look at local aggregation operators in point cloud analysis. In: Vedaldi, A., Bischof, H., Brox, T., Frahm, J.-M. (eds.) ECCV 2020. LNCS, vol. 12368, pp. 326–342. Springer, Cham (2020). https://doi.org/10.1007/978-3-030-58592-1_20

31. Loshchilov, I., Hutter, F.: Decoupled weight decay regularization. arXiv preprint arXiv:1711.05101 (2017)

32. Misra, I., Girdhar, R., Joulin, A.: An end-to-end transformer model for 3D object detection. In: ICCV (2021)

33. Noroozi, M., Favaro, P.: Unsupervised learning of visual representations by solving Jigsaw puzzles. In: Leibe, B., Matas, J., Sebe, N., Welling, M. (eds.) ECCV 2016. LNCS, vol. 9910, pp. 69–84. Springer, Cham (2016). https://doi.org/10.1007/978-3-319-46466-4_5

34. Pang, Y., Wang, W., Tay, F.E.H., Liu, W., Tian, Y., Yuan, L.: Masked autoencoders for point cloud self-supervised learning (2022)

35. Poursaeed, O., Jiang, T., Qiao, H., Xu, N., Kim, V.G.: Self-supervised learning of point clouds via orientation estimation. In: 2020 International Conference on 3D Vision (3DV), pp. 1018–1028. IEEE (2020)

36. Qi, C.R., Litany, O., He, K., Guibas, L.J.: Deep Hough voting for 3D object detection in point clouds. In: Proceedings of the IEEE International Conference on Computer Vision (2019)

37. Qi, C.R., Su, H., Mo, K., Guibas, L.J.: PointNet: deep learning on point sets for 3D classification and segmentation. In: Proceedings of the IEEE Conference on Computer Vision and Pattern Recognition, pp. 652–660 (2017)

38. Qi, C.R., Yi, L., Su, H., Guibas, L.J.: PointNet++: deep hierarchical feature learning on point sets in a metric space. arXiv preprint arXiv:1706.02413 (2017)

39. Radford, A., et al.: Learning transferable visual models from natural language supervision. In: International Conference on Machine Learning, pp. 8748–8763. PMLR (2021)

40. Radford, A., Sutskever, I.: Improving language understanding by generative pre-training. arXiv (2018)

41. Rao, Y., Liu, B., Wei, Y., Lu, J., Hsieh, C.J., Zhou, J.: RandomRooms: unsupervised pre-training from synthetic shapes and randomized layouts for 3D object detection. In: Proceedings of the IEEE/CVF International Conference on Computer Vision, pp. 3283–3292 (2021)

42. Rolfe, J.T.: Discrete variational autoencoders. In: ICLR (2017)

43. Singh, K.K., Lee, Y.J.: Hide-and-seek: forcing a network to be meticulous for weakly-supervised object and action localization. In: 2017 IEEE International Conference on Computer Vision (ICCV), pp. 3544–3553. IEEE (2017)

44. Srivastava, N., Hinton, G., Krizhevsky, A., Sutskever, I., Salakhutdinov, R.: Dropout: a simple way to prevent neural networks from overfitting. J. Mach. Learn. Res. 15(56), 1929–1958 (2014). https://jmlr.org/papers/v15/srivastava14a.html

45. Steiner, A., Kolesnikov, A., Zhai, X., Wightman, R., Uszkoreit, J., Beyer, L.: How to train your ViT? Data, augmentation, and regularization in vision transformers. arXiv preprint arXiv:2106.10270 (2021)

46. Thabet, A., Alwassel, H., Ghanem, B.: Self-supervised learning of local features in 3D point clouds. In: Proceedings of the IEEE/CVF Conference on Computer Vision and Pattern Recognition Workshops, pp. 938–939 (2020)

47. Thomas, H., Qi, C.R., Deschaud, J.E., Marcotegui, B., Goulette, F., Guibas, L.J.: KPConv: flexible and deformable convolution for point clouds. In: Proceedings of the IEEE/CVF International Conference on Computer Vision, pp. 6411–6420 (2019)

48. Tolstikhin, I., et al.: MLP-mixer: an all-MLP architecture for vision. arXiv preprint arXiv:2105.01601 (2021)

49. Uy, M.A., Pham, Q.H., Hua, B.S., Nguyen, T., Yeung, S.K.: Revisiting point cloud classification: a new benchmark dataset and classification model on real-world data. In: Proceedings of the IEEE/CVF International Conference on Computer Vision, pp. 1588–1597 (2019)

50. Vaswani, A., et al.: Attention is all you need. In: Guyon, I., et al. (eds.) Advances in Neural Information Processing Systems, vol. 30. Curran Associates, Inc. (2017). https://proceedings.neurips.cc/paper/2017/file/3f5ee243547dee91fbd053c1c4a845aa-Paper.pdf

51. Wang, H., Liu, Q., Yue, X., Lasenby, J., Kusner, M.J.: Unsupervised point cloud pre-training via occlusion completion. In: ICCV (2021)

52. Wang, H., Zhu, Y., Adam, H., Yuille, A., Chen, L.C.: MaX-DeepLab: end-to-end panoptic segmentation with mask transformers. In: CVPR (2021)

53. Wang, Y., Sun, Y., Liu, Z., Sarma, S.E., Bronstein, M.M., Solomon, J.M.: Dynamic graph CNN for learning on point clouds. Acm Trans. Graph. (ToG) **38**(5), 1–12 (2019)

54. Wei, C., Fan, H., Xie, S., Wu, C.Y., Yuille, A., Feichtenhofer, C.: Masked feature prediction for self-supervised visual pre-training. arXiv preprint arXiv:2112.09133 (2021)

55. Wu, W., Qi, Z., Fuxin, L.: PointConv: deep convolutional networks on 3D point clouds. In: Proceedings of the IEEE/CVF Conference on Computer Vision and Pattern Recognition, pp. 9621–9630 (2019)

56. Wu, Z., et al.: 3D shapenets: a deep representation for volumetric shapes. In: Proceedings of the IEEE Conference on Computer Vision and Pattern Recognition, pp. 1912–1920 (2015)

57. Xie, S., Gu, J., Guo, D., Qi, C.R., Guibas, L., Litany, O.: PointContrast: unsupervised pre-training for 3D point cloud understanding. In: Vedaldi, A., Bischof, H., Brox, T., Frahm, J.-M. (eds.) ECCV 2020. LNCS, vol. 12348, pp. 574–591. Springer, Cham (2020). https://doi.org/10.1007/978-3-030-58580-8_34

58. Xu, Y., Fan, T., Xu, M., Zeng, L., Qiao, Yu.: SpiderCNN: deep learning on point sets with parameterized convolutional filters. In: Ferrari, V., Hebert, M., Sminchisescu, C., Weiss, Y. (eds.) ECCV 2018. LNCS, vol. 11212, pp. 90–105. Springer, Cham (2018). https://doi.org/10.1007/978-3-030-01237-3_6

59. Yan, S., et al.: Implicit autoencoder for point cloud self-supervised representation learning. arXiv preprint arXiv:2201.00785 (2022)

60. Yang, G., Huang, X., Hao, Z., Liu, M.Y., Belongie, S., Hariharan, B.: PointFlow: 3D point cloud generation with continuous normalizing flows. arXiv (2019)

61. Yang, Z., Dai, Z., Yang, Y., Carbonell, J., Salakhutdinov, R.R., Le, Q.V.: XLNet: generalized autoregressive pretraining for language understanding. In: Advances in Neural Information Processing Systems, vol. 32 (2019)

62. Yi, L., et al.: A scalable active framework for region annotation in 3D shape collections. ACM Trans. Graph. (ToG) **35**(6), 1–12 (2016)

63. Yu, X., Tang, L., Rao, Y., Huang, T., Zhou, J., Lu, J.: Point-BERT: pre-training 3D point cloud transformers with masked point modeling. arXiv preprint arXiv:2111.14819 (2021)

64. Zhang, R., Isola, P., Efros, A.A.: Colorful image colorization. In: Leibe, B., Matas, J., Sebe, N., Welling, M. (eds.) ECCV 2016. LNCS, vol. 9907, pp. 649–666. Springer, Cham (2016). https://doi.org/10.1007/978-3-319-46487-9_40

65. Zhang, Z., Girdhar, R., Joulin, A., Misra, I.: Self-supervised pretraining of 3D features on any point-cloud. In: Proceedings of the IEEE/CVF International Conference on Computer Vision (ICCV), pp. 10252–10263, October 2021

66. Zhang, Z., Sun, B., Yang, H., Huang, Q.: H3DNet: 3D object detection using hybrid geometric primitives. In: Vedaldi, A., Bischof, H., Brox, T., Frahm, J.-M. (eds.) ECCV 2020. LNCS, vol. 12357, pp. 311–329. Springer, Cham (2020). https://doi. org/10.1007/978-3-030-58610-2_19

67. Zhao, H., Jiang, L., Fu, C.W., Jia, J.: PointWeb: enhancing local neighborhood features for point cloud processing. In: Proceedings of the IEEE/CVF Conference on Computer Vision and Pattern Recognition, pp. 5565–5573 (2019)

68. Zhao, H., Jiang, L., Jia, J., Torr, P.H., Koltun, V.: Point transformer. In: Proceedings of the IEEE/CVF International Conference on Computer Vision, pp. 16259–16268 (2021)

69. Zhong, Z., Zheng, L., Kang, G., Li, S., Yang, Y.: Random erasing data augmentation. arXiv preprint arXiv:1708.04896 (2017)

FBNet: Feedback Network for Point Cloud Completion

Xuejun Yan[1,3], Hongyu Yan[1,2], Jingjing Wang[1], Hang Du[1], Zhihong Wu[2], Di Xie[1($\boxtimes$)], and Li Lu[2($\boxtimes$)]

[1] Hikvision Research Institute, Hangzhou, China
{yanxuejun,wangjingjing9,duhang,xiedi,pushiliang.hri}@hikvision.com
[2] Sichuan University, Chengdu, China
hongyuyan@stu.scu.edu.cn,luli@scu.edu.cn
[3] Zhejiang University, Hangzhou, China

Abstract. The rapid development of point cloud learning has driven point cloud completion into a new era. However, the information flows of most existing completion methods are solely feedforward, and high-level information is rarely reused to improve low-level feature learning. To this end, we propose a novel Feedback Network (**FBNet**) for point cloud completion, in which present features are efficiently refined by rerouting subsequent fine-grained ones. Firstly, partial inputs are fed to a Hierarchical Graph-based Network (HGNet) to generate coarse shapes. Then, we cascade several Feedback-Aware Completion (FBAC) Blocks and unfold them across time recurrently. Feedback connections between two adjacent time steps exploit fine-grained features to improve present shape generations. The main challenge of building feedback connections is the dimension mismatching between present and subsequent features. To address this, the elaborately designed point Cross Transformer exploits efficient information from feedback features via cross attention strategy and then refines present features with the enhanced feedback features. Quantitative and qualitative experiments on several datasets demonstrate the superiority of proposed FBNet compared to state-of-the-art methods on point completion task. The source code and model are available at https://github.com/hikvision-research/3DVision/.

Keywords: Point cloud completion · Feedback network · Cross transformer

1 Introduction

With the rapid development of 3D sensors, point cloud has been widely used in 3D computer vision applications such as autonomous driving, augmented reality,

---

X. Yan and H. Yan—Equal contribution.

Supplementary Information The online version contains supplementary material available at https://doi.org/10.1007/978-3-031-20086-1_39.

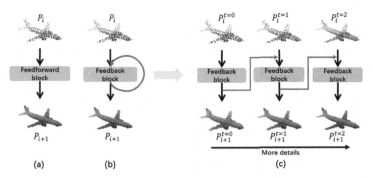

Fig. 1. The illustrations of the feedforward and feedback blocks for point completion. (a) Feedforward block in which information only flows from low-level block to high-level block. (b) Feedback mechanism in our proposed FBNet which refines present information with high-level information via feedback connections (represented by the blue arrow). (c) Unfolding feedback block across time steps. (Color figure online)

and robotics. However, due to the limitations of the resolution, occlusion, and view angles, point clouds acquired from 3D sensors are usually sparse, partial, and noisy. Therefore, recovering the complete shape from its partial observation is desirable and vital for various downstream tasks (e.g. shape classification [20], object detection [11,19], and semantic/instance segmentation [34]).

The pioneering work PCN [45] applied an encoder-decoder net to predict coarse shapes from partial inputs firstly, and then refined coarse results to fine-grained completions through a folding-based decoder. Enlightened by the success of PCN's two-stage generation fashion (coarse-to-fine), most recent point completion works [16,18,26,30,31,45] focus on enhancing the the performance of the network of coarse or fine stages to get more fruitful final results. More recent works [8,30,37] extended two-stage (coarse-to-fine) strategy to multistage point generation and achieved impressive completion performance. However, these completion networks are wholly feedforward: the information solely flows from lower stages to higher ones. It is reasonable to infer that the output of a regular completion network has more details and higher quality compared to its input, as shown in Fig. 1 (a). Similarly, for a two-stage or multistage network, higher stages also generate better results compared to lower ones. *Is it possible to utilize higher quality information to make the lower stage features more representative and informative?*

Motivated by the successful applications of the feedback mechanism on 2D vision [2,4,13,15,25,46], we propose the feedback network (FBNet) for point cloud completion. To the best of our knowledge, FBNet is the first feedback-based network for point completion task. The feedback mechanism aims to transmit high-level features to previous layers and refine low-level information. As shown in Fig. 1 (b), the feedback block reuses the output information to enhance its own feature learning via feedback connections. When unfolding it across time, the feedback block takes the state of the previous time step to enrich present feature representations, shown in Fig. 1 (c). As a result, the feedback block has the ability to refine its output recurrently across time steps.

The proposed FBNet consists of a Hierarchical Graph-based Network (HGNet) and the feedback refinement module which stacks three Feedback-Aware Completion (FBAC) blocks, as shown in Fig. 2. The HGNet is an encoder-decoder structure that encodes partial inputs to global features and then decodes them to coarse complete point clouds. The existing point cloud pooling methods [21,50] downsample point clouds via FPS algorithm and focus on pooled point feature learning. Due to unlearnability, the FPS algorithm may fail to correctly capture local structures when the input is partial and sparse. Hence, the Adaptive Graph Pooling (AdaptGP), the learnable downsampling method, is applied in the HGNet to get more fruitful and accurate global features. After getting coarse complete shapes from HGNet, the feedback refinement module with stacked FBAC blocks refine the coarse complete point clouds to fine-grained and dense ones. For each FBAC block, the high-level information is rerouted to the low layer through the feedback connection and helps to make low-layer features more representative and informative. The main challenge of fusing high-layer information with low-layer ones is the dimension mismatching between two layers. To address this problem, the proposed Cross Transformer builds the relationships between two mismatched point features, and adaptively selects useful information from rerouted features to enhance low-layer features via cross attention strategy. The stacked FBAC blocks gradually refine their outputs across time steps and finally get impressive complete shapes. The proposed FBNet achieves state-of-the-art performance on several benchmarks with various resolutions. Our key contributions are as follows:

- We propose a novel feedback network (FBNet) for point completion, which recurrently refines completion shapes across time steps. To the best of our knowledge, the proposed FBNet is the first feedback-based network for point completion task.
- We introduce the feedback-aware completion (FBAC) block to refine coarse complete point clouds to fine-grained ones. Compared with previous feedforward completion works, feedback connections in FBAC blocks reroute high-level point information back to the low layer and make low-level features more representative.
- We design the Cross Transformer to overcome the feature mismatching problem and adaptively select valuable information from feedback features for enhancing low-level features.
- Experiments on several datasets show that the proposed FBNet achieves superior performance compared to state-of-the-art methods.

2   Related Work

2.1   Point Cloud Processing

The pioneering work PointNet [20] used the shared Multi-layer Perceptions (MLPs) and symmetrical max-pooling operation to extract global features on the unorderedness point cloud, which did not take the relationships of local points into count. To solve this problem, PointNet++ [21] introduced a hierarchical architecture with local PointNet layers to capture regional information. Following point-based works [5,7,12,23,24,38,43,49] focused on how to learn local features more effectively. Recently, PCT [7] and Point Transformer [49] introduced the self-attention strategy of Transformer [28] for point feature learning and achieved impressive results. For achieving convolution-like operation in the point cloud, many convolution-based works [3,14,17,27,36,40,42] built the relationship between local centers and their neighborhoods to learn dynamic weights for convolution. Besides, graph-based methods [10,32,41,50] achieved notable performance for the local aggregation of geometric features, where DGCNN [32] proposed the EdgeConv module to dynamically update point features by learning edge features between two nodes. In this paper, we aim to design a hierarchical graph-based encoder to learn multi-scale geometric features of the partial point cloud.

2.2 Point Cloud Completion

The target of point cloud completion is to recover a complete 3D shape based on its partial observation. Recent advances based on 3D point cloud processing techniques have boosted the research of point cloud completion. PCN [45] first proposed an explicit coarse-to-fine completion framework, which generates a coarse point cloud based on learned global features from the partial inputs and then refines coarse results to fine-grained completions through a folding-based decoder. Enlightened by the success of PCN, the following methods [8,9,16,26,30,31,33–35,39,44,47] especially focused on the local feature exploitation, and the decoding operation were applied to refine their 3D completion results. Most recently, VRC-Net [18] introduced a novel variational relation point completion dual-path network, which used the probabilistic modeling network and relation enhancement network to capture local point features and structural relations between points. SnowflakeNet [37] stacked several SPD modules to generate a complete shape like the snowflake growth of points in 3D space. Although these methods achieved impressive completion performance, all of them are feedforward networks that the information flows only from low layer to high layer, and ignore that the information from fine-grained shapes can reroute back to correct previous states.

2.3 Feedback Mechanism

The feedback mechanism has been widely employed in various 2D image vision tasks [2,4,13,15,25,46]. With feedback connections, high-level features are rerouted to the low layer to refine low-level feature representations. Building feedback connections in 2D vision tasks are convenient because image-based feature maps are regular and ordered. The resolutions of high-layer feature maps can strictly align with lower ones easily. Several works [13,15,46] directly concatenate feedback features with lower ones and then employ convolution layers to fuse features. Similarly, in our work, the high-resolution point features are transmitted back to enrich low-resolution point features. Due to the unorderedness of the point cloud, it is difficult to align two point cloud features with different resolutions.

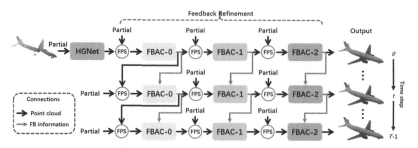

Fig. 2. The overall architecture of our FBNet consists of the Hierarchical Graph-based Network (HGNet) and the feedback refinement module that stacks three Feedback-Aware Completion (FBAC) Blocks. The HGNet aims to generate coarse completions from partial inputs. The cascaded FBAC blocks in the feedback refinement module aim to reconstruct complete and dense point clouds from partial inputs and coarse outputs. Note that, the FBAC block's weight parameters are shared across time steps.

3   Methodology

The overall architecture of FBNet is shown in Fig. 2, which consists of two modules: one Hierarchical Graph-based Network (HGNet) and the feedback refinement module with three Feedback-Aware Completion (FBAC) blocks. The HGNet generates sparse but complete shapes from partial inputs. The stacked FBAC blocks reconstruct complete and fine-grained point point clouds based on both partial inputs and HGNet's outputs. The feedback connections on these FBAC blocks reroute high resolution point information (points and features) to enrich low resolution point features. With the help of feedback mechanism, FBAC blocks can gradually refine their outputs across time steps and finally get impressive complete shapes.

3.1   Hierarchical Graph-Based Network

Hierarchical Graph-based Network (HGNet) is an encoder-decoder structure, which encodes partial inputs to global features and then decodes them to coarse complete point clouds, as shown in Fig. 3. To get more representative global features, we introduce the hierarchical encoder which stacks EdgeConv [32] and proposed Adaptive Graph Pooling alternately.

Adaptive Graph Pooling. The existing point cloud pooling methods [21,50] usually downsampled point clouds via FPS algorithm and aggregated sampled point feature by pooling their neighborhood features. However, the FPS algorithm is unstable, which may fail to pool geometric information efficiently when the input is incomplete and sparse.

Fig. 3. The architecture of Hierarchical Graph-based Network.

To overcome above drawback, we propose a novel Adaptive Graph Pooling (AdaptGP) to pool points and features for partial inputs adaptively. Specifically, AdaptGP generates the pooled points and features by weighting the neighbors of sampled points in geometric and feature space respectively. The weight matrix w is learned from the relation of key point and its neighbors, which can be defined as:

$$w = Softmax(\mathcal{M}((f_i - f_j) + \mathcal{K}(p_i - p_j)) \tag{1}$$

where $\mathcal{M}$, $\mathcal{K}$ are linear mapping functions (i.e., MLPs), which can learn both the point and feature relations between point p_i and point p_j.

The final pooled point and feature of in our AdaptGP can be represented as:

$$p'_i = \sum_{j:(i,j)\in\mathcal{E}} w_j p_j \tag{2}$$

$$f'_i = \sum_{j:(i,j)\in\mathcal{E}} w_{f,j} f_j \tag{3}$$

where $\mathcal{E} \subseteq \mathcal{V} \times \mathcal{V}$ is the edge set of the directed point graph $G(\mathcal{V},\mathcal{E})$ built by k-nearest neighbors(kNN) grouping operation. In our encoder, we use the two AdaptGP with the pooling rate (4, 2) and three EdgeConv with dimensions (64, 128, 512) to extract multi-scale point features. Finally, we employ max and avg pooling operations to generate the global feature.

Coarse Point Generator. We decode the global feature to predict a coarse output P_c via three fully-connected (FC) layers, as shown in Fig. 3.

With the help of the representative global feature generated by our hierarchical graph-based encoder, the FC layers can recover the coarse shape with more geometric details. Besides, we use FPS to gain new coarse output P'_c from aggregation of P_c and partial input, which provides a better initial input for the following feedback refinement stage.

3.2   Feedback Refinement Mechanism

The feedback refinement module aims to refine the HGNet's coarse result to the complete and fine-grained point cloud. The feedback refinement module consists of three stacked Feedback-Aware Completion (FBAC) blocks and builds multiple feedback connections at various scales to learn more effective features. As shown in Fig. 2 (left-to-right), the information firstly flows from coarse HGNet

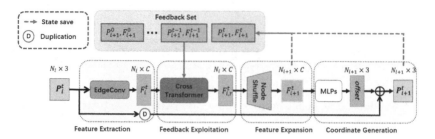

Fig. 4. The detailed architecture of proposed Feedback-Aware Completion Block which consists of four parts: feature extraction, feedback exploitation, feature expansion and coordinate generation.

to stacked FBAC blocks in a feedforward fashion. Each FBAC block takes the output of previous block as input, then refines and upsamples the shape to the denser one with more details.

In particular, for getting better input to i-th FBAC block, we aggregate partial input with feedforward output of $i-1$-th block to a new point cloud, and then downsample it to the same size of previous output via FPS algorithm. Through this initialization operation, the $i-1$-th block's outputs are refined with the original geometric information from partial shapes to get the new inputs, which make present block easier to generate fruitful results. For 0-th block, we aggregate partial input with HGNet's output to initialize its input at $t=0$ step, and aggregate partial input with its own output at $t-1$ step when $t>0$.

In our refinement module, the information also flows from high layer to low layer of same FBAC block in the feedback fashion. We unfold FBAC blocks across time steps, shown in Fig. 2 (top-to-down). The weight parameters of FBAC blocks are shared across time steps. For the i-th FBAC block at t step, its high layer features at $t-1$ step are rerouted and used for present step feature learning via the feedback connection. It is reasonable to infer that high layer features at $t-1$ step contain fine-grained information that can refine the low layer features to be more representative at present time t step. As a result, stacked FBAC blocks gradually refine their outputs across time steps and finally fruitful shapes are generated via the feedback refinement mechanism.

3.3 Feedback-Aware Completion Block

The Feedback-Aware Completion (FBAC) block aims to refine and upsample the low resolution point cloud to high resolution and fine-grained ones via aggregating the points and features from the feedback connection. As shown in Fig. 4, the detailed architecture of proposed FBAC block consists of four parts: feature extraction, feedback exploitation, feature expansion and coordinate generation. We first use EdgeConv [32] to extract local geometric features F_i^t from P_i. Then, the Cross Transformer fuses present features F_i^t with feedback information $(P_{i+1}^{t-1}, F_{i+1}^{t-1})$ generated at $t-1$ step. Subsequently, the refined features $F_{i,r}^t$

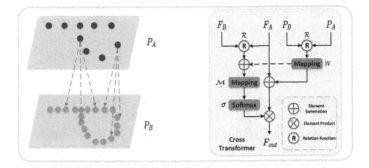

Fig. 5. The detailed structure of our Point Cross Transformer. The left figure visualize the perception process (noted as dashed arrows) of Cross Transformer between two point clouds P_A,P_B. The detail structure of Cross Transformer is shown on the right. P_A, F_A and P_B, F_B denote two different point clouds and their features. The $\mathcal{M}$ and $\mathcal{W}$ are linear mapping functions. $\mathcal{R}$ is a relation function (i.e., subtraction)

is expanded r times via the NodeShuffle [22] block, where $r = N_{i+1}/N_i$. Finally, we gain the point displacements via a series of MLPs.

The final result is calculated as:

$$P_{i+1}^t = \left\{ \mathcal{D}(P_i^t, r) + \mathcal{M}(\eta(\mathcal{T}(P_i^t, \mathcal{G}(P_i^t), P_{i+1}^{t-1}, F_{i+1}^{t-1}), r)) \right\} \tag{4}$$

where $\mathcal{D}$ is the duplication operation. $\mathcal{M}$ is a series of linear functions. η is node-shuffle operation and r is up-sampling ratio. $\mathcal{T}$ is Cross Transformer function. $\mathcal{G}$ is the feature extractor based on EdgeConv.

Cross Transformer. The cross layer feature fusion strategy is widely used for point completion methods [18,34,37]. But in most of them, low-level information flows from a low layer to a high layer with same resolution in a feed-forward fashion and the alignment between two features is required. Take the skip-transformer in SnowflakeNet [37] for example, the two skip-connected features are the displacement feature of the previous SPD and the points feature extracted from the input of the present SPD (also the output of the previous SPD). These two features have the same resolution and a strict one-to-one mapping is built between them. As a result, it is convenient to fuse them via the concatenation operation in the Skip Transformer [37].

In our FBAC block, the feedback feature F_{i+1}^{t-1} has higher resolution compared with the extracted feature F_i^t. Regular fusion strategies (e.g., Skip Transformer, Concatenation) can not be applied directly since they only process the fusion of two point clouds that have the same resolution and their features are aligned.

To address this, we propose a novel point Cross Transformer to fuse features from two point clouds with different resolutions. As shown in Fig. 5, the P_A and P_B are two point clouds with different resolutions. By constructing cross-points relations between P_A and P_B, our Cross Transformer can utilize P_B information to guide the network to learn better feature representation of P_A. The calculation of Cross Transformer can be formulated as:

$$f'_a = \sum_{b:(a,b)\in\mathcal{E}(\mathcal{A},\mathcal{B})} \sigma(\mathcal{M}(f_a - f_b + \delta)) \odot (f_b + \delta) \tag{5}$$

where $\mathcal{E}(\mathcal{A}, \mathcal{B})$ is the directed edge set from point cloud P_A to P_B. the $\mathcal{M}$ is a mapping function i.e., $\{MLP \rightarrow ReLU \rightarrow MLP\}$. The $\delta = \mathcal{W}(p_a - p_b)$ which encoding the position embedding. The σ denotes $Softmax$ function. Through building the cross point cloud graph, the proposed Cross Transformer has the ability to query useful information from reference point cloud P_B and then enrich its own features, shown in Fig. 5. When P_A, P_B are the same point cloud, our Cross Transformer degrades to a point transformer [49] with self-attention mechanism.

The Cross Transformer refines present point features with the reference point cloud information via the cross attention strategy. We apply the Cross Transformer to exploit feedback information and enrich present feature representations. In our FBAC block, we build P_A, P_B and their features as follows:

$$P_A = P_i^t, \quad F_A = F_i^t$$
$$P_B = [P_i^t, P_{i+1}^{t-1}], \quad F_B = [F_i^t, F_{i+1}^{t-1}] \tag{6}$$

where $[,]$ is the merge operation.

As a result, present features F_i^t adaptively query valuable information from the merged feature set. It should be noted that there is no feedback features at 0 step , the F_i^t queries its own features and Cross Transformer degenerate to a Point Transformer.

3.4   Training Loss

In our implementation, we use Chamfer Distance (CD) as the loss function, which can be defined as follows:

$$\mathcal{L}_{CD}(P_1, P_2) = \frac{1}{|P_1|} \sum_{x\in P_1} \min_{y\in P_2} \|x - y\|^2 + \frac{1}{|P_2|} \sum_{y\in P_2} \min_{x\in P_1} \|y - x\|^2. \tag{7}$$

where x and y denote points that belong to two point clouds P_1 and P_2, respectively.

The total training loss is formulated as:

$$\mathcal{L} = \mathcal{L}_{CD}(P_c, Y_{gt}) + \sum_{t=0}^{T} \sum_{i=1}^{n} \mathcal{L}_{CD}(P_i^t, Y_{gt}), \tag{8}$$

where P_c denotes the coarse output of HGNet. The P_i^t and Y_{gt} denote the output of $i-1$-th FBAC block at t step and ground truth, respectively. T is the number of the time steps.

Table 1. Point cloud completion results on MVP dataset (16384 points) in terms of per-point L2 Chamfer distance ($\times 10^4$). The proposed FBNet achieves the lowest reconstruction errors in 14 categories. The best results are highlighted in bold.

Methods	Airplane	Cabinet	Car	Chair	Lamp	Sofa	Table	Watercraft	Bed	Bench	Bookshelf	Bus	Guitar	Motorbike	Pistol	Skateboard	Avg.
PCN [45]	2.95	4.13	3.04	7.07	14.93	5.56	7.06	6.08	12.72	5.73	6.91	2.46	1.02	3.53	3.28	2.99	6.02
TopNet [26]	2.72	4.25	3.40	7.95	17.01	6.04	7.42	6.04	11.60	5.62	8.22	2.37	1.33	3.90	3.97	2.09	6.36
MSN [16]	2.07	3.82	2.76	6.21	12.72	4.74	5.32	4.80	9.93	3.89	5.85	2.12	0.69	2.48	2.91	1.58	4.90
CRN [30]	1.59	3.64	2.60	5.24	9.02	4.42	5.45	4.26	9.56	3.67	5.34	2.23	0.79	2.23	2.86	2.13	4.30
GRNet [39]	1.61	4.66	3.10	4.72	5.66	4.61	4.85	3.53	7.82	2.96	4.58	2.97	1.28	2.24	2.11	1.61	3.87
NSFA [47]	1.51	4.24	2.75	4.68	6.04	4.29	4.84	3.02	7.93	3.87	5.99	2.21	0.78	1.73	2.04	2.14	3.77
VRCNet [18]	1.15	3.20	**2.14**	3.58	5.57	3.58	4.17	2.47	6.90	2.76	3.45	1.78	0.59	**1.52**	1.83	1.57	3.06
SnowflakeNet [37]	0.96	3.19	2.27	3.30	4.10	3.11	3.43	2.29	5.93	2.29	3.34	1.81	0.50	1.72	1.54	2.13	2.73
FBNet (ours)	**0.81**	**2.97**	2.18	**2.83**	**2.77**	**2.86**	**2.84**	**1.94**	**4.81**	**1.94**	**2.91**	**1.67**	**0.40**	1.53	**1.29**	**1.09**	**2.29**

Table 2. Quantitative results with various resolutions on the MVP dataset. For CD ($\times 10^4$), lower is better. For F1-score, higher is better.

Method	2048		4096		8192		16384	
	CD	F1	CD	F1	CD	F1	CD	F1
PCN [45]	9.77	0.320	7.96	0.458	6.99	0.563	6.02	0.638
TopNet [26]	10.11	0.308	8.20	0.440	7.00	0.533	6.36	0.601
MSN [16]	7.90	0.432	6.17	0.585	5.42	0.659	4.90	0.710
CRN [30]	7.25	0.434	5.83	0.569	4.90	0.680	4.30	0.740
VRCNet [18]	5.96	0.499	4.70	0.636	3.64	0.727	3.12	0.791
SnowflakeNet [37]	5.71	0.503	4.40	0.661	3.48	0.743	2.73	0.796
FBNet (ours)	**5.06**	**0.532**	**3.88**	**0.671**	**2.99**	**0.766**	**2.29**	**0.822**

4 Experiments

Implementation and Evaluation Metrics. The number of time steps in our FBNet is set to 3 for low resolution (2K) task and for other higher resolution tasks (e.g., 4K, 8K, 16K) is set to 2. Full settings are detailed in the supplementary material. The model's performance is evaluated by Chamfer Distance (CD) and F1-score.

4.1 Evaluation on MVP Dataset

The MVP dataset is a multi-view partial point cloud dataset. There are 26 incomplete shapes that are captured from 26 uniformly distributed views for each CAD model. Furthermore, MVP consists of 16 shape categories of partial and complete shapes for training and testing. MVP dataset provides various resolutions (including 2048, 4096, 8192, and 16384) of ground truth which can be used to precisely evaluate the completion methods at different resolutions.

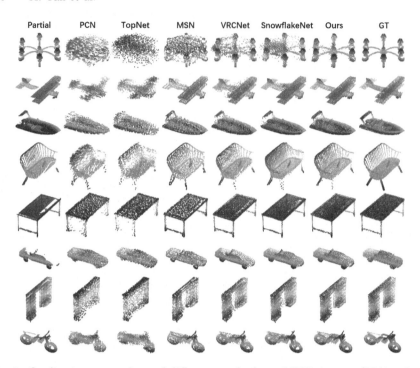

Fig. 6. Qualitative comparison of different methods on MVP dataset (2048 points). Our FBNet generates better complete shapes with fine-grained details compared to other methods.

To verify the effectiveness of our FBNet, we conduct a series of experiments on the MVP dataset. We train our FBNet and SnowflakeNet [37] on the MVP dataset and cite the results of other SOTA methods from [18]. The quantitative results on the high resolution (16384) completion task are shown in Table 1, our FBNet achieves the lowest CD distances in 14 categories. Compared with SnowflakeNet [37], FBNet reduces averaged CD error with a margin of 16%, which demonstrates the superior performance of our method.

The various resolutions completion results are shown in Table 2, our FBNet outperforms all the other methods with the lowest reconstruction error and highest F1-Score. The visualization results of 2048 points completion are shown in Fig. 6, our FBNet can not only get the lowest reconstruction errors but also recover fine-grained details of the targets. Take the second row, for example, the proposed FBNet can precisely recover the missing fuselage of the plane. PCN [45], TopNet [26] and MSN [16] can only generate coarse plane shape and fail to maintain the original geometric information of partial input. VRCNet [18] and SnowflakeNet [37] get better results compared to the previous method, however they also generates outliers during the completion processing.

Table 3. Quantitative results on PCN dataset (16384) in terms of per-point L1 Chamfer distance $\times 10^3$). Our FBNet gets the lowest reconstruction error in all 8 categories.

Methods	Airplane	Cabinet	Car	Chair	Lamp	Sofa	Table	Watercraft	Avg.
PCN [45]	5.50	22.70	10.63	8.70	11.00	11.34	11.68	8.59	9.64
TopNet [26]	7.61	13.31	10.90	13.82	14.44	14.78	11.22	11.12	12.15
CRN [30]	4.79	9.97	8.31	9.49	8.94	10.69	7.81	8.05	8.51
GRNet [41]	6.45	10.37	9.45	9.41	7.96	10.51	8.44	8.04	8.83
PMPNet [35]	5.65	11.24	9.64	9.51	6.95	10.83	8.72	7.25	8.73
NSFA [48]	4.76	10.18	8.63	8.53	7.03	10.53	7.35	7.48	8.06
VRCNet [18]	4.78	9.96	8.52	9.14	7.42	10.82	7.24	7.49	8.17
PoinTr [44]	4.75	10.47	8.68	9.39	7.75	10.93	7.78	7.29	8.38
VE-PCN [29]	4.80	9.85	9.26	8.90	8.68	9.83	7.30	7.93	8.32
SnowflakeNet [37]	4.29	9.16	8.08	7.89	6.07	9.23	6.55	6.40	7.21
FBNet (ours)	**3.99**	**9.05**	**7.90**	**7.38**	**5.82**	**8.85**	**6.35**	**6.18**	**6.94**

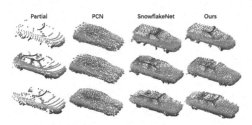

Fig. 7. Qualitative results on KITTI dataset

Table 4. Quantitative results on KITTI dataset in terms of FD ($\times 10^4$) and MMD ($\times 10^2$). Lower is better.

Methods	FD ↓	MMD ↓
PCN [45]	11.12	**2.50**
SnowflakeNet [37]	2.08	2.81
FBNet (ours)	**0.52**	2.97

4.2 Evaluation on PCN Dataset

We also evaluate our FBNet with other completion methods on the PCN dataset [45]. The PCN dataset is derived from ShapeNet dataset [1], which covers 30974 CAD models from 8 categories. The resolutions of partial input and ground truth are 2048 and 16384, respectively. The quantitative results are represented in Table 3. The proposed FBNet achieves the lowest CD errors in all 8 categories, which shows the robust generalization capability of our method across categories.

4.3 Evaluation on KITTI Dataset

We further evaluate our method on KITTI [6] dataset, which includes 2401 real-scanned partial cars captured by a LiDAR. We directly test the models trained on the MVP dataset (2048 points) without any finetuning or retraining operations. As the KITTI dataset does not have ground truth shapes, we can not directly calculate reconstruction error of different methods. The PCN [45] proposed the Fidelity Distance (FD) and the Mini Match Distance (MMD) to evaluate the

Table 5. Ablation study of feedback mechanism on MVP dataset (2048 points).

Time steps T	Feedback	CD	F1
1		5.41	0.527
2		5.36	0.526
3		5.33	0.513
2	✓	5.19	0.529
3	✓	**5.06**	**0.532**

model's performance. We also use these two metrics in our experiment. The quantitative results in terms of FD and MMD metrics are reported in Table 4. Our FBNet achieves lower FD compared with SnowflakeNet [37] and PCN [45]. In addition, we visualize the reconstructed results, as shown in Fig. 7. We can see that FBNet can not only generate the general shape of the car but also preserve the observed fine-grained details.

5   Ablation Study

5.1   Feedback Refinement Mechanism

Our ablation experiments are conducted on the MVP dataset (2048 points). We set different time steps and enable/disable the feedback connections to evaluate the effectiveness of the feedback refinement mechanism. The experiment results are shown in Table 5. When number of time steps T is set to 1, our FBNet becomes a feedforward network without unfolding operation across time steps. The FBNet with 2 and 3 time steps are reported at the bottom of Table 5. Our FBNet with feedback mechanism achieves superior performance compared with the feedforward version of FBNet ($T = 1$). The FBNet without feedback connections is also evaluated shown in the second and third rows of Table 5. Without the feedback connections, the performance only gets slightly improved as the feature refinement is invalid across time steps. The gain comes from the updated input of the first FBAC block across time steps.

5.2   Input Initialization of FBAC

As shown in Fig. 2, to synthesize the input of the present FBAC block, we aggregate partial and output of the previous block to a new point cloud and then downsample it via the FPS algorithm. Through this initialization operation, we refine the previous outputs with the original geometric information from partial shapes. We conduct ablation studies to evaluate the influence of different input initialization strategies. For the first FBAC block, we design two initialization ways: aggregation of HGNet and partial input $P_c + P_{part}$ across all steps, aggregation of feedback points and partial input $P_{fb} + P_{part}$ at $t > 0$ step. For other

Table 6. The comparison of different input initialization strategies.

Strategy	First block		Others block			CD	F1
	P_c+P_{part}	$P_{fb}+P_{part}$	P_{ff}	$P_{ff}+P_{part}$	$P_{ff}+P_{fb}$		
A	✓		✓			5.44	0.520
B	✓			✓		5.28	0.528
C		✓	✓			5.31	0.508
D		✓			✓	19.93	0.233
E (ours)		✓		✓		**5.06**	**0.532**

blocks, we design three strategies: (1) Feedforward points P_{ff} only. (2) Aggregation of feedforward points and partial input $P_{ff}+P_{part}$. (3) Aggregation of feedforward points and feedback points $P_{ff}+P_{fb}$. The experimental results are reported in Table 6, which proves the effectiveness of our initialization strategy.

5.3 Adaptive Graph Pooling

Table 7. The comparison of different pooling methods used in HGNet on the MVP dataset (2048 points).

Pooling methods	CD	F1
Graph pooling [50]	5.48	0.510
Point pooling [21]	5.23	0.521
AdaptGP (ours)	**5.06**	**0.532**

We study the effectiveness of the proposed AdaptGP method used in HGNet. The HGNet equipped with AdaptGP gets lowest CD error and best F1-score with a large margin compared with point pooling [21], regular graph pooling [50], as reported in Table 7. The AdaptGP pooling used in HGNet can improve the average performance of our FBNet.

6 Conclusion

In this paper, we propose a novel feedback network for point cloud completion, named FBNet. By introducing the feedback connection in FBAC blocks, FBNet can learn more representative and informative low-level features with the help of rerouted high-level information. As the result, the FBNet gradually refines the completion results across time steps and finally gets impressive complete shapes. Exhaustive experiments on several datasets indicate that our FBNet achieves superior performance compared to state-of-the-art methods.

References

1. Chang, A.X., et al.: ShapeNet: an information-rich 3d model repository. arXiv preprint arXiv:1512.03012 (2015)
2. Chen, C., Li, H.: Robust representation learning with feedback for single image deraining. In: 2021 IEEE/CVF Conference on Computer Vision and Pattern Recognition (CVPR), pp. 7738–7747 (2021)
3. Dai, J., et al.: Deformable convolutional networks. In: Proceedings of the IEEE International Conference on Computer Vision, pp. 764–773 (2017)
4. Feng, M., Lu, H., Ding, E.: Attentive feedback network for boundary-aware salient object detection. In: 2019 IEEE/CVF Conference on Computer Vision and Pattern Recognition (CVPR), pp. 1623–1632 (2019)
5. Gadelha, M., Wang, R., Maji, S.: Multiresolution tree networks for 3D point cloud processing. In: Ferrari, V., Hebert, M., Sminchisescu, C., Weiss, Y. (eds.) ECCV 2018. LNCS, vol. 11211, pp. 105–122. Springer, Cham (2018). https://doi.org/10.1007/978-3-030-01234-2_7
6. Geiger, A., Lenz, P., Stiller, C., Urtasun, R.: Vision meets robotics: the KITTI dataset. Int. J. Robot. Res. **32**(11), 1231–1237 (2013)
7. Guo, M.H., Cai, J.X., Liu, Z.N., Mu, T.J., Martin, R.R., Hu, S.M.: PCT: point cloud transformer. Comput. Vis. Media **7**(2), 187–199 (2021)
8. Huang, T., et al.: RFNet: recurrent forward network for dense point cloud completion. In: Proceedings of the IEEE/CVF International Conference on Computer Vision, pp. 12508–12517 (2021)
9. Huang, Z., Yu, Y., Xu, J., Ni, F., Le, X.: PF-net: point fractal network for 3D point cloud completion. In: Proceedings of the IEEE/CVF Conference on Computer Vision and Pattern Recognition, pp. 7662–7670 (2020)
10. Kipf, T.N., Welling, M.: Semi-supervised classification with graph convolutional networks. arXiv preprint arXiv:1609.02907 (2016)
11. Li, B., Ouyang, W., Sheng, L., Zeng, X., Wang, X.: GS3D: an efficient 3D object detection framework for autonomous driving. In: 2019 IEEE/CVF Conference on Computer Vision and Pattern Recognition (CVPR), pp. 1019–1028 (2019)
12. Li, J., Chen, B.M., Lee, G.H.: SO-net: self-organizing network for point cloud analysis. In: Proceedings of the IEEE Conference on Computer Vision and Pattern Recognition, pp. 9397–9406 (2018)
13. Li, Q., Li, Z., Lu, L., Jeon, G., Liu, K., Yang, X.: Gated multiple feedback network for image super-resolution. In: BMVC (2019)
14. Li, Y., Bu, R., Sun, M., Wu, W., Di, X., Chen, B.: PointCNN: convolution on x-transformed points. Adv. Neural. Inf. Process. Syst. **31**, 820–830 (2018)
15. Li, Z., Yang, J., Liu, Z., Yang, X., Jeon, G., Wu, W.: Feedback network for image super-resolution. In: 2019 IEEE/CVF Conference on Computer Vision and Pattern Recognition (CVPR), pp. 3862–3871 (2019)
16. Liu, M., Sheng, L., Yang, S., Shao, J., Hu, S.M.: Morphing and sampling network for dense point cloud completion. In: Proceedings of the AAAI Conference on Artificial Intelligence, vol. 34, pp. 11596–11603 (2020)
17. Liu, Y., Fan, B., Xiang, S., Pan, C.: Relation-shape convolutional neural network for point cloud analysis. In: Proceedings of the IEEE/CVF Conference on Computer Vision and Pattern Recognition, pp. 8895–8904 (2019)

18. Pan, L., et al..: Variational relational point completion network. In: Proceedings of the IEEE/CVF Conference on Computer Vision and Pattern Recognition, pp. 8524–8533 (2021)
19. Qi, C., Litany, O., He, K., Guibas, L.J.: Deep Hough voting for 3D object detection in point clouds. In: 2019 IEEE/CVF International Conference on Computer Vision (ICCV), pp. 9276–9285 (2019)
20. Qi, C.R., Su, H., Mo, K., Guibas, L.J.: PointNet: deep learning on point sets for 3D classification and segmentation. In: Proceedings of the IEEE Conference on Computer Vision and Pattern Recognition. pp. 652–660 (2017)
21. Qi, C.R., Yi, L., Su, H., Guibas, L.J.: PointNet++: deep hierarchical feature learning on point sets in a metric space. arXiv preprint arXiv:1706.02413 (2017)
22. Qian, G., Abualshour, A., Li, G., Thabet, A.K., Ghanem, B.: PU-GCN: point cloud upsampling using graph convolutional networks. In: 2021 IEEE/CVF Conference on Computer Vision and Pattern Recognition (CVPR), pp. 11678–11687 (2021)
23. Ran, H., Liu, J., Wang, C.: Surface representation for point clouds. In: Proceedings of the IEEE/CVF Conference on Computer Vision and Pattern Recognition, pp. 18942–18952 (2022)
24. Ran, H., Zhuo, W., Liu, J., Lu, L.: Learning inner-group relations on point clouds (2021)
25. Sam, D.B., Babu, R.V.: Top-down feedback for crowd counting convolutional neural network. In: AAAI (2018)
26. Tchapmi, L.P., Kosaraju, V., Rezatofighi, H., Reid, I., Savarese, S.: Topnet: structural point cloud decoder. In: Proceedings of the IEEE/CVF Conference on Computer Vision and Pattern Recognition, pp. 383–392 (2019)
27. Thomas, H., Qi, C.R., Deschaud, J.E., Marcotegui, B., Goulette, F., Guibas, L.J.: KPConv: flexible and deformable convolution for point clouds. In: Proceedings of the IEEE/CVF International Conference on Computer Vision, pp. 6411–6420 (2019)
28. Vaswani, A., et al.: Attention is all you need. In: Advances in Neural Information Processing Systems, vol. 30 (2017)
29. Wang, X., M.H.A.J., Lee, G.H.: Voxel-based network for shape completion by leveraging edge generation. In: ICCV (2021)
30. Wang, X., Ang Jr., M.H., Lee, G.H.: Cascaded refinement network for point cloud completion. In: Proceedings of the IEEE/CVF Conference on Computer Vision and Pattern Recognition, pp. 790–799 (2020)
31. Wang, Y., Tan, D.J., Navab, N., Tombari, F.: SoftPoolNet: shape descriptor for point cloud completion and classification. In: Vedaldi, A., Bischof, H., Brox, T., Frahm, J.-M. (eds.) ECCV 2020. LNCS, vol. 12348, pp. 70–85. Springer, Cham (2020). https://doi.org/10.1007/978-3-030-58580-8_5
32. Wang, Y., Sun, Y., Liu, Z., Sarma, S.E., Bronstein, M.M., Solomon, J.M.: Dynamic graph CNN for learning on point clouds. Acm Trans. Graph. (ToG) 38(5), 1–12 (2019)
33. Wen, X., Han, Z., Cao, Y.P., Wan, P., Zheng, W., Liu, Y.S.: Cycle4Completion: unpaired point cloud completion using cycle transformation with missing region coding. In: Proceedings of the IEEE/CVF Conference on Computer Vision and Pattern Recognition, pp. 13080–13089 (2021)
34. Wen, X., Li, T., Han, Z., Liu, Y.S.: Point cloud completion by skip-attention network with hierarchical folding. In: Proceedings of the IEEE/CVF Conference on Computer Vision and Pattern Recognition, pp. 1939–1948 (2020)

35. Wen, X., et al.: PMP-net: point cloud completion by learning multi-step point moving paths. In: Proceedings of the IEEE/CVF Conference on Computer Vision and Pattern Recognition, pp. 7443–7452 (2021)

36. Wu, W., Qi, Z., Fuxin, L.: PointConv: deep convolutional networks on 3D point clouds. In: Proceedings of the IEEE/CVF Conference on Computer Vision and Pattern Recognition, pp. 9621–9630 (2019)

37. Xiang, P., et al.: SnowFlakeNet: point cloud completion by snowflake point deconvolution with skip-transformer. In: Proceedings of the IEEE/CVF International Conference on Computer Vision, pp. 5499–5509 (2021)

38. Xiang, T., Zhang, C., Song, Y., Yu, J., Cai, W.: Walk in the cloud: learning curves for point clouds shape analysis. In: Proceedings of the IEEE/CVF International Conference on Computer Vision, pp. 915–924 (2021)

39. Xie, H., Yao, H., Zhou, S., Mao, J., Zhang, S., Sun, W.: GRNet: gridding residual network for dense point cloud completion. In: Vedaldi, A., Bischof, H., Brox, T., Frahm, J.-M. (eds.) GRnet: gridding residual network for dense point cloud completion. LNCS, vol. 12354, pp. 365–381. Springer, Cham (2020). https://doi.org/10.1007/978-3-030-58545-7_21

40. Xu, M., Ding, R., Zhao, H., Qi, X.: PAConv: position adaptive convolution with dynamic kernel assembling on point clouds. In: Proceedings of the IEEE/CVF Conference on Computer Vision and Pattern Recognition, pp. 3173–3182 (2021)

41. Xu, Q., Sun, X., Wu, C.Y., Wang, P., Neumann, U.: Grid-GCN for fast and scalable point cloud learning. In: Proceedings of the IEEE/CVF Conference on Computer Vision and Pattern Recognition, pp. 5661–5670 (2020)

42. Xu, Y., Fan, T., Xu, M., Zeng, L., Qiao, Yu.: SpiderCNN: deep learning on point sets with parameterized convolutional filters. In: Ferrari, V., Hebert, M., Sminchisescu, C., Weiss, Y. (eds.) ECCV 2018. LNCS, vol. 11212, pp. 90–105. Springer, Cham (2018). https://doi.org/10.1007/978-3-030-01237-3_6

43. Yan, X., Zheng, C., Li, Z., Wang, S., Cui, S.: PointASNL: robust point clouds processing using nonlocal neural networks with adaptive sampling. In: Proceedings of the IEEE/CVF Conference on Computer Vision and Pattern Recognition, pp. 5589–5598 (2020)

44. Yu, X., Rao, Y., Wang, Z., Liu, Z., Lu, J., Zhou, J.: PoinTR: diverse point cloud completion with geometry-aware transformers. In: Proceedings of the IEEE/CVF International Conference on Computer Vision, pp. 12498–12507 (2021)

45. Yuan, W., Khot, T., Held, D., Mertz, C., Hebert, M.: PCN: point completion network. In: 2018 International Conference on 3D Vision (3DV), pp. 728–737. IEEE (2018)

46. Zeng, Yu., Lin, Z., Yang, J., Zhang, J., Shechtman, E., Lu, H.: High-resolution image inpainting with iterative confidence feedback and guided upsampling. In: Vedaldi, A., Bischof, H., Brox, T., Frahm, J.-M. (eds.) ECCV 2020. LNCS, vol. 12364, pp. 1–17. Springer, Cham (2020). https://doi.org/10.1007/978-3-030-58529-7_1

47. Zhang, W., Yan, Q., Xiao, C.: Detail preserved point cloud completion via separated feature aggregation. In: Vedaldi, A., Bischof, H., Brox, T., Frahm, J.-M. (eds.) ECCV 2020. LNCS, vol. 12370, pp. 512–528. Springer, Cham (2020). https://doi.org/10.1007/978-3-030-58595-2_31

48. Zhao, H., Jia, J., Koltun, V.: Exploring self-attention for image recognition. In: Proceedings of the IEEE/CVF Conference on Computer Vision and Pattern Recognition, pp. 10076–10085 (2020)

49. Zhao, H., Jiang, L., Jia, J., Torr, P.H., Koltun, V.: Point transformer. In: Proceedings of the IEEE/CVF International Conference on Computer Vision, pp. 16259–16268 (2021)
50. Zhou, H., Feng, Y., Fang, M., Wei, M., Qin, J., Lu, T.: Adaptive graph convolution for point cloud analysis. In: Proceedings of the IEEE/CVF International Conference on Computer Vision, pp. 4965–4974 (2021)

Meta-sampler: Almost-Universal yet Task-Oriented Sampling for Point Clouds

Ta-Ying Cheng, Qingyong Hu$^{(\boxtimes)}$, Qian Xie, Niki Trigoni, and Andrew Markham

Department of Computer Science, University of Oxford, Oxford, UK
qingyong.hu@cs.ox.ac.uk

Abstract. Sampling is a key operation in point-cloud task and acts to increase computational efficiency and tractability by discarding redundant points. Universal sampling algorithms (*e.g.,* Farthest Point Sampling) work without modification across different tasks, models, and datasets, but by their very nature are agnostic about the downstream task/model. As such, they have no implicit knowledge about which points would be best to keep and which to reject. Recent work has shown how task-specific point cloud sampling (*e.g.,* SampleNet) can be used to outperform traditional sampling approaches by learning which points are more informative. However, these learnable samplers face two inherent issues: *i)* overfitting to a model rather than a task, and *ii)* requiring training of the sampling network from scratch, in addition to the task network, somewhat countering the original objective of down-sampling to increase efficiency. In this work, we propose an *almost-universal* sampler, in our quest for a sampler that can learn to preserve the most useful points for a particular task, yet be inexpensive to adapt to different tasks, models or datasets. We first demonstrate how training over multiple models for the same task (*e.g.,* shape reconstruction) significantly outperforms the vanilla SampleNet in terms of accuracy by not overfitting the sample network to a particular task network. Second, we show how we can train an almost-universal meta-sampler across multiple tasks. This meta-sampler can then be rapidly fine-tuned when applied to different datasets, networks, or even different tasks, thus amortizing the initial cost of training. Code is available at https://github.com/ttchengab/MetaSampler.

Keywords: Point cloud sampling · Point cloud processing · Meta-learning

1 Introduction

Modern depth sensors such as LiDAR scanners can capture visual scenes with highly dense and accurate points, expanding the real-world applications of point

Supplementary Information The online version contains supplementary material available at https://doi.org/10.1007/978-3-031-20086-1_40.

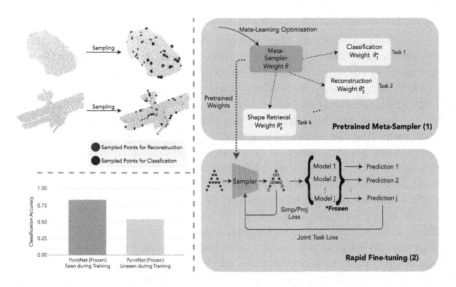

Fig. 1. Overview. Top Left: We highlight the points sampled for classification (red) and reconstruction (blue). It is apparent that classification concentrates on more generalised features across the entire point cloud whereas reconstruction focuses on denser aspects for optimisation. **Bottom Left:** We evaluate the classification performance of two frozen PointNets on 16 sampled points from SampleNet. A large performance gap is observed despite the two models (one adopted during SampleNet training and one unseen) having an identical architecture, implying overfitting onto the model instead of the task itself. **Right:** An overview of our meta-sampler as a pretrained model that can rapidly adapt with a joint-training mechanism. (Color figure online)

clouds to traditionally challenging 3D vision tasks. However, while existing deep network architectures such as PointNet [34] are capable of consuming these dense point clouds for downstream tasks (*e.g.,* classification, reconstruction), it is standard to downsample initial point cloud to reduce the computational and memory cost, especially for resource-constrained or real-time applications. As such, the objective of extracting a representative subset of points from raw point clouds while maintaining satisfactory performance over various tasks is a key problem.

Early techniques usually adopt Farthest Point Sampling (FPS) [27,35,41], Inverse Density Importance Sampling (IDIS) [13], or Random Sampling (RS) [19,20] to progressively reduce the resolution of the raw point clouds. Albeit simple and universal, these sampling schemes are inherently heuristic and task-agnostic. Recently, Dovrat et al. [8] and Lang et al. [26] explored a new domain of learning-based, task-specific, and data-driven point cloud sampling strategies. They empirically proved that leveraging the task loss can effectively optimise the sampler to preserve representative and informative features. Although remarkable progress has been achieved in several downstream tasks such as classification and reconstruction, there remain two critical issues to be further explored: 1) The learnt samplers are shown to **overfit to a specific task model** instead of being generalisable to the task itself—this causes a significant performance drop when adopting another network for the same task even when the two architectures are identical (as exemplified in Fig. 1 Bottom Left); 2) Training a sampler to fit a particular task is both time-consuming and computationally expensive, which counters the original objective of sampling to improve efficiency.

To this end, we propose an *almost-universal* sampler (Fig. 1 Right) comprising two training alterations to address the aforementioned issues accordingly. First, we suggest jointly training by forwarding the sampled points to multiple models targetting the same task instead of a single model and updating the sampler through a summation of task losses. This kind of ensemble allows us to better simulate the distribution of different task models, encouraging the sampler to truly learn the task rather than a particular instance. Second, we introduce our meta-sampler to learn how to adapt to a specific task, rather than explicitly learning a particular task model. We incorporate a set of tasks, each with multiple task models, for the meta-optimisation. Our meta-sampler can serve as a pretrained module to adhere to any tasks through fine-tuning while being *almost-universal* in the sense that it could be optimised with fewer iterations.

Extensive experimental results justify the performance and versatility of the proposed meta-sampler. In particular, there is a significant improvement in performance for several mainstream tasks with our joint-training technique compared to the best results from the conventional single-task training on SampleNet. Moreover, we thoroughly evaluate the versatility of our meta-sampler by adapting to particular tasks (both included and excluded from the meta-training), model architectures, and datasets. Our meta-sampler adapts rapidly to all challenging scenarios, making it a suitable pretrained candidate for task-specific learning-based samplers.

In summary, the key contributions of this paper are threefold:

- A joint-training scheme for the sampler to truly learn a task rather than simply overfitting to a particular instance (*i.e.*, a specific task model).
- A meta-sampler that can rapidly adapt to downstream point cloud tasks within and beyond the meta-training stage, models of varying architectures, and datasets of different domains.
- Extensive experiments validate the performance and versatility of our meta-sampler across various tasks, models, and datasets.

2   Related Work

2.1   Learning with 3D Point Clouds

Earlier pursuit of 3D computer vision tasks is mainly focused on grid-like representations of voxel volumes, as the mature convolutional neural networks (CNNs) can be directly extended to such data representation and easily introduce inductive biases such as translational equivariance [7,38]. However, voxel volume representation has the ingrained drawback of being uniform and low-resolution with densely compacted empty cells consuming vast amount of computational resources. Recently, point-based networks have attracted wide attention with the emergence of PointNet/PointNet++ [34,35]. These architectures pioneered the learning of per-point local features, circumvented the constraint of low resolution and uniform voxel representations, and hence introduced significant flexibilities and inspired a plethora of point-based architectures [13,27,29,40,45]. A number of point cloud based tasks [14] including classification [12,16,28,30,43,48], segmentation [3,17–19,25], registration [2,11,22], reconstruction [9,31], and completion [6,46] are extensively investigated. Nevertheless, few arts targeted the fundamental component of point cloud sampling in this deep learning era.

2.2 Point Cloud Sampling

Point cloud sampling, a basic component in most point-based neural architectures, is usually used to refine the raw inputs and improve computational efficiency for several downstream tasks. Widely-adopted point cloud sampling methods include RS, FPS [19,33,35], and IDIS [13]. A handful of recent works began to explore advanced and sophisticated sampling schemes [5,32,44]. Nonetheless, despite the remarkable progress in point cloud sampling, these methods are task-agnostic and rather universal, lacking awareness of the important features which a particular task may require.

Recently, Dovrat et al. [8] proposed a learnable, data-driven sampling strategy by imposing a specific task loss to enforce the sampler in learning specific-related features for a particular task. Later, Lang et al. [26] extended the learning approach by introducing a differentiable relaxation to minimise the training and inference accuracy gap for the sampling operation. Nevertheless, by introducing an additional task loss, sampling ultimately becomes constrained and prone to overfitting on a specific task model instead of the task itself. Additionally, this also requires significant extra training to fit a particular goal.

Our meta-sampler hopes to bring the best of both worlds: being task-oriented yet as universal as possible. Instead of directly overfitting onto a task model, we focus on how to learn a task through incorporating a meta-learning algorithm. By introducing a better approach of learning a particular task through joint-training, our pretrained meta-sampler be rapidly fine-tuned to any task, making it *almost-universal* while easing the computational efficiency to which sampling is targeting in the first place.

2.3 Meta-learning

Meta-learning, the process of learning the learning algorithm itself, has shown to be applicable to several challenging computer vision scenarios such as few-shot and semi-supervised classification [10,36], shape reconstruction [39], and reinforcement learning [15,23] due to its capacity for fast adaptation.

Finn et al. [10] proposed one of the most representative meta-learning methods, termed model-agnostic meta-learning (MAML), that allows the model to quickly adapt to new tasks in different domains such as classification, regression, and reinforcement learning. Later, Antoniou et al. [1] further improved the MAML learning scheme, making the learning more generalisable and stable.

Recently, Huang et al. [21] proposed MetaSets, which aims to meta-learn the different geometry of point clouds so that the model can generalize to classification tasks performed on different datasets. In contrast and being analogous to the standard meta-learning problem, our proposed meta-sampler focuses on universal point cloud sampling for different tasks, aiming to achieve fast adaptation to reduce computation efficiency through a training strategy extended from [1,10]. Our fast adaption is not just across tasks within the meta-training, but also across models, datasets and unforeseen tasks.

3   Meta-sampler and Rapid Task Adaptation

Ideally, it is desirable to learn a unified and universal point cloud sampling scheme for different tasks in a data-driven manner—this is most likely unfeasible since different tasks inherently have distinctive preferences of sampling strategies, as shown in Fig. 1 top left (for more qualitative comparisons please refer to the Appendices). For example, 3D semantic segmentation pays more attention to the overall geometrical structure, while 3D object detection naturally puts more emphasis on the foreground instance with sparse points [47]. Motivated by this, we take the next-best objective, which is to learn a highly adaptive sampling network that can adapt to a number of tasks with minimal iterations and achieve optimal performances. In particular, this fast adaptation capability allows samplers to be pretrained then quickly fine-tuned, satisfying the ultimate goal of improving computational efficiency.

3.1   Problem Setting

The goal of this paper is to develop a learning-based sampling module f_θ with trainable parameters θ, which takes in a point cloud with m points and outputs a smaller subset of n points ($m > n$). Apart from the objective of SampleNet to learn task-specific sampling (*i.e.,* particularly suitable for a single task such as shape classification or reconstruction), we take a step further and aim to propose an universal pretrained model, which can be rapidly adapted to a set of different tasks $S_T = \{T_i\}_{i=1}^{K_T}$. Formally, we define the ideal adaptation of sampling to a specific task T_i as capable of achieving satisfactory performance by integrating the sampling module into a set of K_{A_i} known networks $S_{A_i} = \{A_{i,j}\}_{j=1}^{K_{A_i}}$ (Each $A_{i,j}$ is one network trained with unsampled point clouds to solve task T_i). We split S_{A_i} into $S_{A_i}^{train}$ and $S_{A_i}^{test}$ (*i.e.,* task networks used during training are disjoint to the ones for testing) to make sure that our evaluation on f_θ is fair and not overfitting to task models instead of the task itself. Note that while $S_{A_i}^{train}$ is available during training, the weights are frozen when learning our sampler as suggested by [26].

To achieve the dual objectives of high accuracy and rapid convergence, we must first carefully evaluate the best training strategy to better learn each individual task, and then design a training strategy which is adaptive to multiple tasks. We build our sampler f_θ based on the previous state-of-the-art learnable sampling network—PointNet-based SampleNet architecture [26,34]—and then introduce our training technique in a bottom-up manner.

3.2 Single-Task Multi-model Training

For an individual task T_i, we hope that the f_θ learns to sample the best set of points $\forall A \in S_{A_i}$.

The conventional way of training the SampleNet uses a single frozen network A' as S_A^{train} for training by defining a sampling task loss $\mathcal{L}_{ST_i}$ targeting T_i as:

$$\mathcal{L}_{ST_i}(f_\theta) = \mathcal{L}_{T_i}(A'(f_\theta)), \tag{1}$$

where $\mathcal{L}_{T_i}$ is the loss when pretraining A'. We refer to this configuration as single-model, single-task training. As mentioned previously, this training method, having accomplished promising results in several tasks, still exhibits a large accuracy discrepancy between the results on A' and S_A^{test}. In other words, even though A' is frozen during the training of SampleNet, the sampling stage is overfitted onto the task network instead of the task itself.

To alleviate the issue of model-wise overfitting, we extend (1) and create a joint-training approach for a single task. Specifically, we take a set of weight-frozen models $\{A_{i,j}\}_{j=1}^k, 1 < k << K_{A_i}$ as $S_{A_i}^{train}$ and compute $\mathcal{L}_{ST_i}$ as:

$$\mathcal{L}_{ST_i}(f_\theta) = \sum_{j=1}^k \mathcal{L}_{T_i}(A_{i,j}(f_\theta)). \tag{2}$$

It is critical to understand that all the frozen task models are under inference mode (*i.e.*, not significantly sabotaging computation power) and that only a very small number of task models (easily obtainable online or by self-training with different random initial weights) would bring significant improvements to the sampler's performance. We further show in Sect. 4.2 that a very small $k > 1$ allows the sampling network generalise better across S_{A_i}, as $S_{A_i}^{train}$ becomes a vicinity distribution rather than a single specific instance to S_{A_i}.

In addition to the joint $\mathcal{L}_{ST_i}$, we also update the weights with a simplification loss comprising the average and maximum nearest neighbour distance and a projection loss to enforce the probability of projection over the points to be the Kronecker delta function located at the nearest neighbour point (identical to the SampleNet loss [26]).

3.3 Multi-task Multi-model Meta-sampler Training

Instead of restricting ourselves to a single task (*e.g.*, classification), we consider whether training the sampler over multiple tasks could lead to our vision of an almost-universal sampler. Broadly, we aim to extend the sampler beyond multi-model to multi-task, such that given any task $T_i \in S_T$, where S_T is a set of tasks, a good initial starting point could be achieved for the sampler. In this

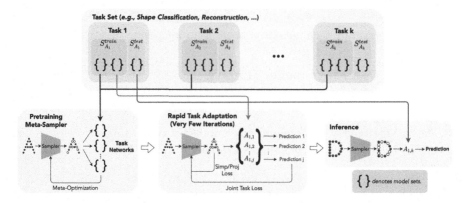

Fig. 2. The pipeline of the proposed meta-sampling. The illustration exemplifies the pretraining with multiple tasks through our meta-training strategy, then fitting onto a single task with our joint-training mechanism.

way, adapting or fine-tuning to a particular task (which may even be beyond the known set) will be rapid and cheap.

To tackle this, we draw inspiration from the MAML framework and propose a meta-learning approach for rapidly adaptive sampling [10]. In essence, we aim to utilise the set of $S_{A_i}^{train}$ to mimic the best gradients in learning a particular task T_i for meta-optimisation, such that given any task $T_i \in S_T$ or even beyond the known set of tasks, the MAML network can quickly converge within a few iterations and without additional training of the task networks.

The joint-training procedure discussed in the previous section motivates that a particular task is better solved with a set of task networks instead of just one—we transfer this idea to the meta-optimisation such that the sampler is adaptive to a number of tasks instead of just one. Formally, we first optimise the adaptation of f_θ to $T_i \in S_T$ by updating the parameters θ to $\theta'_{i,j}$ for every $A_{i,j}$ through the gradient update:

$$\theta'_{i,j} = \theta - \alpha \nabla \mathcal{L}_{T_i}(A_{i,j}(f_\theta)), \tag{3}$$

where α is the step size hyperparameter. Similar to MAML, we can directly extend the single gradient update into multi-gradient updates to optimise the effectiveness of $\theta'_{i,j}$ on T_i.

With the inner update (3), we then follow the meta-optimisation procedure through a stochastic gradient descent:

$$\theta = \theta - \beta \nabla \sum_{i=1}^{K_T} \sum_{j=1}^{k} \mathcal{L}_{T_i}(A_{i,j}(f_{\theta'_{i,j}})), \tag{4}$$

where β is the meta step size hyperparameter that could either be fixed or accompanied with annealings. Note that we apply the single task loss in the inner update (3) but sum all losses from all weights to resemble a task in the meta-update (4). Section 4.3 shows that our meta-optimisation design is sufficient in learning tasks for rapid adaptation. Simplification and projection losses are also directly optimised at this stage. They are however directly updated rather than included in the meta-update fashion as they are task-agnostic.

3.4   Overall Pipeline: Pretrained Meta-sampler to Task Adaptation

We describe the overall training pipeline of the proposed meta-sampler (Fig. 2) as the following:

Pretrained Meta-Sampler: Our pipeline begins with training a meta-sampler. First, we take a set of tasks S_T (*e.g.*, shape classification, reconstruction, retrieval) and their corresponding task networks S_{A_i} for every $T_i \in S_T$ (pretrained on the unsampled point clouds). Next, we freeze all their original weights and perform our meta-sampler training as illustrated in Sect. 3.3 to obtain a pretrained meta-sampler.

Rapid Task Adaptation: The meta-training attempts to optimise θ to a position optimal to learn any task T_i. Therefore, to adapt to a particular task, we can simply take the pretrained weights of the meta-sampler and fine-tune it with the joint-training strategy as illustrated in Sect. 3.2 along with the previously proposed simplification and projection loss.

Disjoint Task Networks for Pretraining and Training: Realistically, one should be able to directly obtain a pretrained meta-sampler without the task networks and fit to their own networks. To mimic such real-world constraints, we ensure that the meta pretraining and joint-training use disjoint sets of networks—both of which are unseen during testing.

4   Experiments

Our empirical studies comprise two major components. First, we evaluate the performance of the proposed joint-training scheme against prior training methodologies on representative individual tasks. Afterward, we justify the versatility and robustness of the meta-sampler by measuring its adaptiveness across different tasks, models, and datasets.

4.1   Experimental Setup

To comprehensively evaluate the performance of our meta-sampler, we extract a set of representative tasks on 3D point clouds, including shape classification, reconstruction, and shape retrieval. Note that all experiments are conducted on the ModelNet40 [42] (except for ShapeNet [4] used in transferring dataset analysis) to ensure fair evaluation (*i.e.*, without introducing additional information during meta-sampler training). The detailed experimental settings (*i.e.*, task network architecture, task loss) are described as follows:

Shape Classification. This is a fundamental task in 3D vision to determine the shape categories of a given point cloud. The task network set $\{A_{i,j}\}$ are pretrained PointNets [34] with random and distinct weight initialisations, and the validation accuracy converges to 89% to 90%. $\mathcal{L}_{T_i}$ is the vanilla binary cross-entropy (BCE) loss for classification.

Reconstruction. This task aims to reconstruct the complete 3D shape from partial point sets. Following [26], the goal of sampling for this task is to preserve n key points that could be reconstructed to the original unsampled point clouds. For this task, S_{A_i} is a set of Point Completion Networks (PCN) [46] trained in an autoencoder fashion to minimise the Chamfer Distance (CD) between the input and output points. We select the PCN architecture owing to its encoder and decoder mechanism that doesn't take in any structural assumptions (*e.g.,* symmetry), making it suitable for reconstruction even when missing points are randomly distributed upon the entire shape instead of a particular part. $\mathcal{L}_{T_i}$ is the two-way CD between the inputs and predicted outputs; all networks are pretrained with the loss to the chamfer distance of around 3×10^{-4}. Unlike other tasks where projection restricts the feature information, reconstruction is benefitted from projections. And thus, our results adopt the pre-projected points for both single and joint training. Using projected points boosts results for both.

Shape Retrieval. Given a sampled point cloud, the goal is to match it with the shifted/rotated original point cloud given N options (similar to the N-way evaluation in few-shot settings). Due to the existence of hard negative pairs (point clouds of the same class), this task requires more advanced learning of fine-grained features compared with the pure shape classification. In this case, S_{A_i} is a set of Siamese PointNets inspired by [24] pretrained on unsampled point clouds matching. $\mathcal{L}_{T_i}$ is a BCE loss where the ground truth is set to 1 if the point cloud is a shifted/rotated version of the other and vice versa. All networks are pretrained to achieve 100% accuracy on the simple 4-way evaluation.

4.2   Performance Evaluation on Individual Tasks

To justify the effectiveness of the proposed multiple-model training scheme, we present the quantitative comparison of incorporating multiple models training and the traditional SampleNet single-model training strategy in all three individual tasks on the ModelNet40 dataset [42]. We adopt the official train and test splits in this dataset, and follow [8,26] to pretrain all task networks with the original point clouds (1024 points by default). All the task models are under inference mode during the training of the sampling network. We evaluate our sampling on different sampling ratios calculated as $1024/n$, where n is the number of outputted points from the sampler. Note that for reconstruction and shape retrieval tasks, we were adopting a different dataset and task to prior networks. Much work is required for the adaption and thus we only compare with the previously proposed state-of-the-art SampleNet.

Shape Classification. As shown in Table 1, the classification performance achieved with our joint-training scheme consistently outperforms the single SampleNet and previous sampling strategies such as FPS across all sampling ratios.

Table 1. Joint v.s. Single Task Network Training. Single and Joint denotes the SampleNet trained through the originally proposed single task network approach [26] and through our proposed multi-model single-task training ($k = 3$), respectively. Bold texts denote best results.

Sampling ratio	Classification (accuracy ↑)				Sampling ratio	Reconstruction (CD ↓)	
	FPS	SNet[8]	Single [26]	Joint		Single [26]	Joint
8	70.4%	77.5%	83.7%	**88.0%**	8	3.29	**3.05**
16	46.3%	70.4%	82.2%	**85.5%**	16	3.32	**3.15**
32	26.3%	60.6%	80.1%	**81.5%**	32	3.61	**3.37**
64	13.5%	36.1%	54.1%	**61.6%**	64	4.43	**4.31**

Sampling ratio	Shape retrieval (accuracy ↑)					
	4-way		10-way		20-way	
	Single[26]	Joint	Single[26]	Joint	Single [26]	Joint
8	99.6%	**99.7%**	96.3%	**98.3%**	95.9%	**96.7%**
16	98.7%	**99.1%**	94.0%	**96.7%**	89.5%	**91.9%**
32	97.2%	**97.5%**	91.4%	**91.5%**	82.9%	**84.6%**
64	92.5%	**94.6%**	79.5%	**84.6%**	67.0%	**71.0%**

In particular, the classification accuracy achieved with our joint-training mechanism under a sampling ratio of 8 is very close to the upper bound accuracy (88.0% vs. 89.5%) achieved without any sampling, verifying the effectiveness of our joint-training strategy. We also notice that the performance gap between the proposed method and others is widening with a growingly aggressive sampling rate (*e.g.,* at sampling ratio 64 with 16 points left for the point clouds). This further demonstrates the superiority of the proposed training mechanism under aggressive sampling ratios.

Reconstruction. The effect of joint-training on reconstruction follows a similar trend to shape classification, outperforming other strategies in terms of the CD across all sampling ratios. The improvement seems to be consistent across all sampling ratios, further exhibiting the effectiveness of joint-training.

Shape Retrieval. Our shape retrieval results are presented under the N-way few-shot settings ($N = 4, 10, 20$). It is clear that the joint-training scheme achieves better results compared with the single SampleNet training strategy. Specifically, the advantages of our proposed joint-training scheme is more prominent with the increase of the sampling ratios, suggesting that our sampling schemes can preserve points that have high similarity to the original point cloud.

Faster Convergence with Multiple Models. Considering the sampler is exposed to more task networks during training, it is expected for the sampler to converge to stabilised accuracies with a shorter time span of training. Our empirical study generally aligns with this idea. Our joint-training taking usually around 40 epochs to converge as opposed to around 60 for single-task training.

Table 2. Classification accuracy when Increasing k. Sampling Ratio is 32.

	Number of task models (k)				
	$k = 1$	$k = 2$	$k = 3$	$k = 4$	$k = 5$
Accuracy	80.0%	81.3%	81.7%	82.8%	83.4%

The Impact of the Number of Task Models k**.** We further dive into the correlation between the number of networks k for joint-training and classification accuracy. Table 2 shows the classification results under the randomly selected sampling ratio of 32 when we slowly increase the number of task networks for ensemble. A clear trend of increments continues as k increases, implying that the wider the set of training networks the better the approximation is to the entire task distribution. Nonetheless, such increments suffer from the trade-off in computational resources time and memory-wise. We stick with 3 networks as the standard for joint-training and in later experiments unless specified.

4.3   Versatility of Meta-sampler

Versatility is a broad term with multiple dimensions requiring evaluation. To fully realize this, we begin with the critical evaluation of our meta-sampler's adaptiveness on tasks included in the meta-optimisation step. We then extend to the more challenging scenarios of changing model architecture, dataset distribution, and ultimately tasks distinct from the ones used for meta-training. All experiments are conducted with hyperparameters α and β set to 1e−3. All plots begin after one epoch as single SampleNets are not pretrained.

Converging to Meta-tasks. To investigate the impact of the meta-sampler for the performance of meta tasks, we conduct several groups of experiments in this section for the three tasks used in our meta-optimisation, including shape classification, reconstruction, and shape retrieval. We compare the task performance achieved with/without the pretrained meta-sampler under different sampling ratios in Fig. 3. Specifically, for our meta-sampling, we first deliberately select a bunch of task models unseen during meta-optimisation to fine-tuned the meta-sampler with the joint-training scheme, then evaluate the task performance with the sampled point clouds.

As shown in Fig. 3, we separately compare the task performance as the training progresses with/without our pretrained meta-sampler for different meta-tasks. It is clear that as the sampling ratio increases (*i.e.*, the task is more challenging), joint-training without meta-sampler starts at lower performance and requires more iterations to converge to a stable result. By contrast, our pretrained meta-sampler, while acting as a sampler trained without any task loss

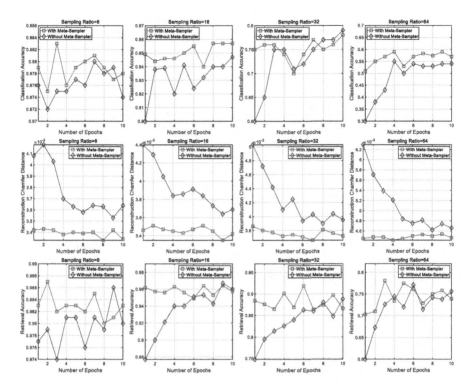

Fig. 3. The performance comparison in classification (row 1 ↑), reconstruction (row 2 ↓), and shape retrieval (row 3 ↑) with/without the meta-sampler at the initiation of training. All graphs begin after one epoch. Red is ours. (Color figure online)

at 0th epoch (similar to FPS), adapts to the task within one epoch across all sampling ratios and achieves higher accuracies after 10 epochs in most cases.

There are also two intriguing points we would like to address within this empirical study. First, we observe a relatively large fluctuation of the performance for shape classification and shape retrieval—a phenomenon we conjecture to be owing to the distribution shift between training and testing sets. Second, we notice that our meta-sampler not only converges faster, but also pushes the upper bound in some cases. For example, our shape retrieval results at sampling ratio 16 achieved the accuracy of 96.9% (the upper bound of training from scratch is 96.7%) on the 20th epoch (not plotted in the figure). This infers that by learning how to adapt, the sampling model could potentially also be trained to learn better. However, such occurrences do not take place at all times.

Transferring Model Architectures. Prior experiments focus on training from the meta-sampler with task networks of identical architecture but different weights. To further explore the versatility of our meta-sampler, we transfer the joint-training networks from PointNets to PointNet++ [34,35]. All the networks

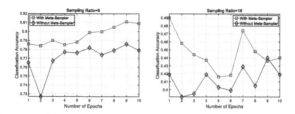

Fig. 4. Accuracy of PointNet++ for classification with joint-training. The results with and without the pretrained meta-sampler on PointNet is presented for sampling ratios at 8 and 16. All graphs begin after one epoch.

are pretrained until convergence (*i.e.*, around 92% accuracy on unsampled point clouds). Constrained by the original implementation of PointNet++ (*i.e.*, point set abstraction layer) extracting features from the 32 points neighborhoods, we only evaluate our meta-sampler upon the sampling ratio of 8 and 16, where the remaining point cloud size is greater than 32.

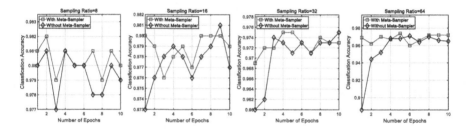

Fig. 5. Transfer to ShapeNet. We adopt the ModelNet pretrained meta-sampler to fit onto the ShapeNet dataset for classification. All graphs begin after one epoch.

The achieved results are plotted in Fig. 4. It is apparent that better performance is achieved using our meta-sampler, with a higher starting point and fast convergence speed under both sampling ratios. This further demonstrates the capacity of our meta-sampler in adapting different model architectures. Interestingly, we also notice that the classification accuracy of PointNet++ achieved on sampled points drops significantly compared with that of unsampled point clouds, especially under the sampling ratio of 16. This is likely because FPS is progressively used in each encoding layer. In this case, by adding a SampleNet in front of PointNet++, we are implicitly "double sampling" and leaving very few features for the abstraction layer.

Transferring Datasets. To verify that our ModelNet40 [42] pretrained sampler isn't applicable to just the data distribution it was expose to, we measure the effectiveness when using the same pretrained model for the same task but on a different dataset. Specifically, we evaluate the classification performance of our meta-sampler on the ShapeNetCoreV1 Dataset [4], which comprises point

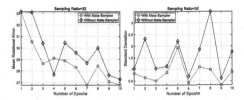

Fig. 6. **The** **performance** **comparison** **in** **point** **cloud** **registration** **with/without the meta-sampler. Left:** Rotational error comparison. **Right:** Standard deviation of rational error per epoch. All graphs begin after one epoch.

cloud objects from 16 different shape categories. Specifically, we still adopt the PointNet [34] architecture and trained three networks following the best practise, while these models can achieve around 98% accuracy on unsampled point clouds. We then show the training progress achieved by using our joint training scheme with/without the meta-sampler. As shown in Fig. 5, although the performance is similar when the sampling ratio is small (easier), we can clearly notice that the model without our meta-sampler starts at a much lower performance. By contrast, the model with our pretrained meta-sampler converges much faster (even within one epoch) and is more stable. As such, this empirical study can well prove that our meta-sampler can adapt to a completely disparate dataset distribution and serve as a better and more stabilised starting point.

Transferring Beyond Meta-Tasks. Finally, we extend to the most challenging question of whether the proposed meta sampler can generalize to unseen tasks, i.e. tasks that are not included in the meta-optimisation step. This is highly challenging since different tasks inevitably have distinct preferences in sampled points. However, this is also a critical step to validate whether the proposed meta sampler could be the universal pretrained module for all point cloud tasks.

We evaluate our meta-sampler on the point cloud registration—the task of finding the spatial transformation between two point clouds. Here, we follow the standard train-test split of PCRNet [37] to obtain pairs of source and template point clouds with templates rotated by three random Euler angles of $[-45°, 45°]$ and translated with a value in the range $[-1, 1]$. $\mathcal{L}_{T_i}$ is the CD between the source point cloud and the template point cloud with our predicted transformation. We first train three PCRNets to achieve the rotation error of around 7–9° on unsampled point clouds, then freeze the PCRNet weights and perform the proposed joint-training scheme under the conditions with/without the pretrained meta-sampler under the sampling ratio of 32. We ran each setting three times and show the mean and standard deviation of rotational error during training in Fig. 6. Even though the task objective (registration), task network (PCRNet), and even the dataset itself (pairs of point clouds from ModelNet40) are unforeseen during our meta-optimisation, we can still notice two subtle yet solid performance differences adopting our meta-sampler: 1) The pretrained model generally converges faster during the initiation of training and 2) The pretrained model is much more stabilised and improves consistently compared to the model trained from scratch that exhibits a large variance throughout every epoch (other sampling ratios also perform similarly in stabilisation).

5   Conclusion

We propose a learnable meta-sampler and a joint-training strategy for task-oriented, almost-universal point cloud sampling. The proposed multi-model joint training scheme on SampleNet achieved promising performance for various point cloud tasks, and the meta-sampler has empirically shown to be effective and stabilising when transferred to any tasks incorporated during meta-optimisation, even extending to unseen model architectures, datasets, and tasks. We hope our pretrained meta-sampler can be used as a plug-and-play module and widely deployed to point cloud downstream tasks to save computational resources.

Acknowledgements. This work was partially supported by Amazon AWS, Oxford Singapore Human-Machine Collaboration Programme, and EPSRC ACE-OPS grant.

References

1. Antoniou, A., Edwards, H., Storkey, A.J.: How to train your MAML. In: ICLR (2019)
2. Ao, S., Hu, Q., Yang, B., Markham, A., Guo, Y.: SpinNet: learning a general surface descriptor for 3D point cloud registration. In: CVPR (2021)
3. Behley, J., et al.: Towards 3D lidar-based semantic scene understanding of 3D point cloud sequences: the semanticKITTI dataset. Int. J. Robot. Res. (2021)
4. Chang, A.X., et al.: ShapeNet: an information-rich 3D model repository. arXiv preprint arXiv:1512.03012 (2015)
5. Chen, S., Tian, D., Feng, C., Vetro, A., Kovacevic, J.: Fast resampling of 3D point clouds via graphs. arXiv preprint arXiv:1702.06397 (2017)
6. Chen, X., Chen, B., Mitra, N.J.: Unpaired point cloud completion on real scans using adversarial training. In: ICLR (2020)
7. Choy, C.B., Xu, D., Gwak, J.Y., Chen, K., Savarese, S.: 3D-R2N2: a unified approach for single and multi-view 3D object reconstruction. In: Leibe, B., Matas, J., Sebe, N., Welling, M. (eds.) ECCV 2016. LNCS, vol. 9912, pp. 628–644. Springer, Cham (2016). https://doi.org/10.1007/978-3-319-46484-8_38
8. Dovrat, O., Lang, I., Avidan, S.: Learning to sample. In: CVPR (2019)
9. Fan, H., Su, H., Guibas, L.J.: A point set generation network for 3D object reconstruction from a single image. In: CVPR (2017)
10. Finn, C., Abbeel, P., Levine, S.: Model-agnostic meta-learning for fast adaptation of deep networks. In: Precup, D., Teh, Y.W. (eds.) ICML (2017)
11. Gojcic, Z., Zhou, C., Wegner, J.D., Wieser, A.: The perfect match: 3D point cloud matching with smoothed densities. In: CVPR (2019)
12. Goyal, A., Law, H., Liu, B., Newell, A., Deng, J.: Revisiting point cloud shape classification with a simple and effective baseline. In: Meila, M., Zhang, T. (eds.) ICML (2021)
13. Groh, F., Wieschollek, P., Lensch, H.P.A.: Flex-convolution - million-scale point-cloud learning beyond grid-worlds. In: Jawahar, C.V., Li, H., Mori, G., Schindler, K. (eds.) ACCV 2018. LNCS, vol. 11361, pp. 105–122. Springer, Cham (2019). https://doi.org/10.1007/978-3-030-20887-5_7

14. Guo, Y., Wang, H., Hu, Q., Liu, H., Liu, L., Bennamoun, M.: Deep learning for 3D point clouds: a survey. IEEE Trans. Pattern Anal. Mach. Intell. **43**(12), 4338–4364 (2020)
15. Gupta, A., Eysenbach, B., Finn, C., Levine, S.: Unsupervised meta-learning for reinforcement learning. arXiv preprint arXiv:1806.04640 (2020)
16. Hamdi, A., Giancola, S., Li, B., Thabet, A.K., Ghanem, B.: MVTN: multi-view transformation network for 3D shape recognition. In: ICCV (2021)
17. Hu, Q., et al.: SQN: weakly-supervised semantic segmentation of large-scale 3D point clouds with 1000x fewer labels. arXiv preprint arXiv:2104.04891 (2021)
18. Hu, Q., Yang, B., Khalid, S., Xiao, W., Trigoni, N., Markham, A.: SensaturBAN: learning semantics from urban-scale photogrammetric point clouds. Int. J. Comput. Vision, pp. 1–28 (2022)
19. Hu, Q., et al.: RandLA-net: efficient semantic segmentation of large-scale point clouds. In: CVPR (2020)
20. Hu, Q., et al.: Learning semantic segmentation of large-scale point clouds with random sampling. IEEE Trans. Pattern Anal. Mach. Intell. (2021)
21. Huang, C., Cao, Z., Wang, Y., Wang, J., Long, M.: Metasets: meta-learning on point sets for generalizable representations. In: CVPR (2021)
22. Huang, S., Gojcic, Z., Usvyatsov, M., Wieser, A., Schindler, K.: Predator: registration of 3D point clouds with low overlap. In: CVPR (2021)
23. Jabri, A., Hsu, K., Gupta, A., Eysenbach, B., Levine, S., Finn, C.: Unsupervised curricula for visual meta-reinforcement learning. In: Wallach, H.M., Larochelle, H., Beygelzimer, A., d'Alché-Buc, F., Fox, E.B., Garnett, R. (eds.) NeurIPS (2019)
24. Koch, G., Zemel, R., Salakhutdinov, R., et al.: Siamese neural networks for one-shot image recognition. In: ICML Workshop (2015)
25. Landrieu, L., Simonovsky, M.: Large-scale point cloud semantic segmentation with superpoint graphs. In: CVPR (2018)
26. Lang, I., Manor, A., Avidan, S.: SampleNet: differentiable point cloud sampling. In: CVPR (2020)
27. Li, Y., Bu, R., Sun, M., Wu, W., Di, X., Chen, B.: PointCNN: convolution on X-transformed points. In: NeurIPS (2018)
28. Liu, X., Han, Z., Liu, Y., Zwicker, M.: Point2Sequence: learning the shape representation of 3D point clouds with an attention-based sequence to sequence network. In: AAAI (2019)
29. Liu, Z., Tang, H., Lin, Y., Han, S.: Point-voxel CNN for efficient 3D deep learning. In: Wallach, H.M., Larochelle, H., Beygelzimer, A., d'Alché-Buc, F., Fox, E.B., Garnett, R. (eds.) NeurIPS (2019)
30. Ma, X., Qin, C., You, H., Ran, H., Fu, Y.: Rethinking network design and local geometry in point cloud: a simple residual MLP framework. In: ICLR (2022)
31. Mandikal, P., Navaneet, K.L., Babu, R.V.: 3D-PSRNet: part segmented 3D point cloud reconstruction from a single image. In: Leal-Taixé, L., Roth, S. (eds.) ECCV 2018. LNCS, vol. 11131, pp. 662–674. Springer, Cham (2019). https://doi.org/10.1007/978-3-030-11015-4_50
32. Nezhadarya, E., Taghavi, E., Razani, R., Liu, B., Luo, J.: Adaptive hierarchical down-sampling for point cloud classification. In: CVPR (2020)
33. Qi, C.R., Litany, O., He, K., Guibas, L.J.: Deep Hough voting for 3D object detection in point clouds. In: ICCV (2019)
34. Qi, C.R., Su, H., Mo, K., Guibas, L.J.: PointNet: deep learning on point sets for 3D classification and segmentation. In: CVPR (2017)
35. Qi, C.R., Yi, L., Su, H., Guibas, L.J.: PointNet++: deep hierarchical feature learning on point sets in a metric space. In: NeurIPS (2017)

36. Ren, M., et al.: Meta-learning for semi-supervised few-shot classification. In: ICLR (2018)
37. Sarode, V., et al.: PCRNet: point cloud registration network using pointnet encoding (2019)
38. Tatarchenko, M., Dosovitskiy, A., Brox, T.: Octree generating networks: efficient convolutional architectures for high-resolution 3D outputs. In: ICCV (2017)
39. Wallace, B., Hariharan, B.: Few-shot generalization for single-image 3D reconstruction via priors. In: ICCV (2019)
40. Wang, Y., Sun, Y., Liu, Z., Sarma, S.E., Bronstein, M.M., Solomon, J.M.: Dynamic graph CNN for learning on point clouds. ACM TOG (2019)
41. Wu, W., Qi, Z., Fuxin, L.: PointConv: deep convolutional networks on 3D point clouds. In: CVPR (2018)
42. Wu, Z., et al.: 3D shapenets: a deep representation for volumetric shapes. In: CVPR (2015)
43. Xiang, T., Zhang, C., Song, Y., Yu, J., Cai, W.: Walk in the cloud: learning curves for point clouds shape analysis. In: ICCV (2021)
44. Xu, Q., Sun, X., Wu, C., Wang, P., Neumann, U.: Grid-GCN for fast and scalable point cloud learning. In: CVPR (2020)
45. Yu, X., Tang, L., Rao, Y., Huang, T., Zhou, J., Lu, J.: Point-BERT: pre-training 3D point cloud transformers with masked point modeling. arXiv preprint arXiv:2111.14819 (2021)
46. Yuan, W., Khot, T., Held, D., Mertz, C., Hebert, M.: PCN: point completion network. In: 3DV (2018)
47. Zhang, Y., Hu, Q., Xu, G., Ma, Y., Wan, J., Guo, Y.: Not all points are equal: learning highly efficient point-based detectors for 3D lidar point clouds. In: Proceedings of the IEEE Conference on Computer Vision and Pattern Recognition (2022)
48. Zhong, J.X., Zhou, K., Hu, Q., Wang, B., Trigoni, N., Markham, A.: No pain, big gain: classify dynamic point cloud sequences with static models by fitting feature-level space-time surfaces. In: Proceedings of the IEEE Conference on Computer Vision and Pattern Recognition (2022)

A Level Set Theory for Neural Implicit Evolution Under Explicit Flows

Ishit Mehta$^{(\boxtimes)}$, Manmohan Chandraker, and Ravi Ramamoorthi

University of California San Diego, La Jolla, USA
mehtaib@gmail.com

Abstract. Coordinate-based neural networks parameterizing implicit surfaces have emerged as efficient representations of geometry. They effectively act as parametric level sets with the zero-level set defining the surface of interest. We present a framework that allows applying deformation operations defined for triangle meshes onto such implicit surfaces. Several of these operations can be viewed as energy-minimization problems that induce an instantaneous flow field on the explicit surface. Our method uses the flow field to deform parametric implicit surfaces by extending the classical theory of level sets. We also derive a consolidated view for existing methods on differentiable surface extraction and rendering, by formalizing connections to the level-set theory. We show that these methods drift from the theory and that our approach exhibits improvements for applications like surface smoothing, mean-curvature flow, inverse rendering and user-defined editing on implicit geometry.

Keywords: Implicit surfaces · Level sets · Euler-lagrangian deformation

1 Introduction

Recent successes in generative modeling of shapes [13,46,52] and inverse rendering [41,69] are largely driven by implicit representations of geometry parameterized as multi-layer perceptrons (MLPs) (or neural implicits [16]). These networks can compactly represent highly-detailed surfaces at (theoretically) infinite resolution [34,53,59,60]; they are defined continuously in $\mathbb{R}^3$ and are differentiable – enabling their usage in gradient-based optimization [25,69] and learning [2,12,37] methods. Despite these advances, there is still a large body of work in geometry processing, computer vision and graphics which relies on explicit surface representations. Often these mesh-based algorithms are a better choice than their implicit counterparts. For instance, in case of inverse rendering, differentiable renderers for triangle meshes [18,26,27,42,71] are a) faster, b) more accurate, and c) can handle more complex light-transport effects, in comparison to the

---

Supplementary Information The online version contains supplementary material available at https://doi.org/10.1007/978-3-031-20086-1_41.

S. Avidan et al. (Eds.): ECCV 2022, LNCS 13662, pp. 711–729, 2022.
https://doi.org/10.1007/978-3-031-20086-1_41

renderers designed for implicit surfaces [23,41,69]. Similarly, geometry processing algorithms for applications like surface smoothing and deformation [10,54,61] are vastly superior in terms of compute and memory requirements than the ones developed for neural implicit surfaces [67]. Most of these methods, however, are highly specific to mesh geometry and are not easily adaptable to MLP-defined surfaces. Our work is a theoretical attempt to bridge this gap.

We first introduce the following insight: several mesh-based algorithms define an energy-minimization problem that is solved using gradient descent; the gradients used by the optimizer to update the geometry can be viewed as analogous to an instantaneous explicit flow-field ($\mathbf{V}$) applied on the surface. Informed by the literature on fluid simulation [7] and level-sets [44], deformation of a surface with such a flow field depends on the geometry representation.

The *Lagrangian* representation involves tracking the surface explicitly as a set of a points ($\mathbf{x}$) and connections (like triangles). The point-set is discrete and the connectivity is *static*, which keeps the optimization relatively simple; we can separately integrate the field at each point (update vertices $\mathbf{x} \rightarrow \mathbf{x}'$). But optimization of the resolution of the surface is non-trivial and can also get unwieldy for problems which involve surfaces with unknown topology.

Alternatively, *Eulerian* descriptions can be used. Each point in space has an object-property ϕ associated with it, like the distance from the surface or its occupancy inside the enclosed volume. The surface here is implicitly defined with *dynamic* connectivity; one can smoothly vary the topology during optimization. Canonically, ϕ is defined only on a discrete voxel-grid and needs to be interpolated for points off the grid. Here, making instantaneous updates to the surface is more involved as it requires changing ϕ values for a large set of points. A neural implicit is a continuous variant of an Eulerian representation. Applying a flow field to such functions is non-trivial as updates are required in the parameter (θ) space as opposed to directly updating ϕ to ϕ'.

We propose a parametric level-set evolution method (Sect. 4) which propagates neural implicit surfaces according to an explicitly generated flow field. Our method comprises of three repeating steps, 1) A non-differentiable surface extraction method like Marching Cubes [31] or Sphere Tracing [21] is used to obtain a Lagrangian representation corresponding to a neural implicit, 2) A mesh-based algorithm is used to derive a flow field on the explicit surface (Sect. 4.1), and 3) A corresponding Eulerian flow field is used to evolve the implicit geometry (Sect. 4.2).

Previous methods [41,49,51] approach the problem of using mesh-based
energy functions on Eulerian surfaces
with the idea of differentiable extraction
of Lagrangian representations. We show
these methods are not in accordance with
the level-set theory [45] (Sect. 5). The discussion also yields a more general proof
(Sect. 5.1) for differentiable surface extrac-

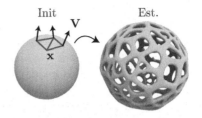

Fig. 1. Inverse-rendering recovery.

tion from level set functions with arbitrary gradient norms ($|\nabla \phi| \neq 1$). Our
method is more formally connected to the theory and we validate it with experimental observations made on three diverse problem settings, 1) Curvature-based
deformation (Sect. 6.1), where we demonstrate more accurate surface smoothing
and mean-curvature flow than previous methods [49,67], 2) Inverse rendering of
geometry (Sect. 6.2), where we show accurate recovery from multi-view images
for high-genus shapes without object masks as in [41,69] (example in Fig. 1), and
3) User-defined shape editing (Sect. 6.3), where the implicit surface is deformed
60× faster than previous work [67].

2   Related Work

Coordinate-based MLPs have become a popular choice as function approximators for signals like images, videos and shapes [13,46,53,56,60]. Our work focuses
on using MLPs for approximating implicit geometry. Such representations are
compact, continuous and differentiable. These advantages are well suited with
gradient-descent based optimization and learning problems. Recent developments in generative modeling of shapes [11,35,46,52], 3D consistent image synthesis [12,66], 3D reconstruction [5,57,72] and inverse rendering [25,43,68,69],
all rely on representing geometry using MLPs. For a more detailed discussion on
recent work regarding coordinate-based representations refer to the survey by
Xie *et al.* [65], and for inverse rendering the survey by Tewari *et al.* [63].

There is also a rich literature on geometry processing [8–10,54,55] and inverse
rendering [4,18,32,40] for explicit surface representations. Yang *et al.* [67] introduce some of the geometry processing ideas to neural implicit surfaces, but the
method could be inaccurate (Sect. 6.1) and slow (Sect. 6.3).

For inverse rendering applications, differentiable renderers for triangle meshes
are used for gradient-based optimization. Physics-based renderers differentiate through a light-simulation process [6,27,42,71] and provide accurate gradients. Alternatively, differentiable rasterization [26,30,48] can be used for high-
performance gradient computation, but only for single-bounce rendering models. However, optimizing triangle meshes with gradient-descent is non-trivial.
Careful design of the optimization method [18,40] and error functions [32] is
required for robust optimization. To circumvent some of these issues, IDR [69]
and DVR [41] use implicit surface representations like SDFs and occupancy functions [36] parameterized with MLPs. These methods mitigate some of the topological restrictions, but are not physics-based and are not in accordance with the

level-set theory (Sect. 5.2). We propose an inverse rendering method which uses explicit differentiable renderers for parametrically defined implicit surfaces. The proposed method is not as sensitive to initialization as explicit methods [18,40] are, does not require an object mask like implicit methods [41,69] do, and maintains the ability to vary topology during optimization.

Our method uses the level-set theory [45] as the foundation for optimizing and deforming parametric implicit surfaces. Previous methods [3,39,64] for the applications discussed in this work apply to non-parametric level sets. Perhaps the most related works to our method are MeshSDF [49] and RtS [15]. Compared to MeshSDF, our approach is more formally connected to the theory of level-sets (Sect. 4), applies to all parametric functions (Sect. 5.1), and works for a more diverse set of optimization problems like shape editing (Sect. 6.1, 6.3) and inverse rendering (Sect. 6.2) – deviating from experimental observations made by Remelli *et al.* [49] on learning-based settings. Compared to RtS [15], we show geometry processing applications along with theoretical parallels (Sect. 5) between parametric level-set methods like MeshSDF [49], DVR [41], IDR [69] and the classical theory [44]. Our inverse rendering method is shown to work (Sect. 6.2) for a set of high-genus shapes with a genus-0 initialization, in contrast to object-pose optimization or small genus changes shown in [15]. Recent work by Munkberg *et al.* [38] and Hasselgren *et al.* [22] also show promise in using explicit differentiable renderers with implicit geometry for inverse problems.

3   Background

Consider a closed surface of arbitrary topology $\partial\Omega$ evolving with respect to time t. We define a Lagrangian representation of this surface with a finite set of k points in $\mathbb{R}^3$ as $\partial\Omega_L = \{\mathbf{x}_i \mid \mathbf{x}_i \sim \partial\Omega; \ \forall i \in \{1, 2, 3, \ldots, k\}\}$. This point-set can be viewed as a triangle mesh if an additional set of connections between the points is provided, and as a point cloud otherwise. Implicitly this surface can also be represented with a family of level-sets $\phi : \mathbb{R}^3 \to \mathbb{R}$, the zero iso-contour of which represents the surface $\partial\Omega_E = \{\mathbf{x} \mid \phi(\mathbf{x}) = 0\}$. ϕ can be arbitrarily chosen, but a canonical choice is a signed-distance function (SDF) which satisfies:

$$\phi(\mathbf{x}) = (\pm) \min_{\mathbf{x}_C \in \partial\Omega} \{||\mathbf{x} - \mathbf{x}_C||_2\}, \tag{1}$$

where $\mathbf{x}_C$ is the closest point on the surface to $\mathbf{x}$ and the sign of $\phi(\mathbf{x})$ denotes whether $\mathbf{x}$ is enclosed $(-)$ within the shape or not $(+)$.

Parameterizing ϕ. Analytically defining ϕ for simple and regular shapes is relatively straightforward [47], but is infeasible for most objects. Recent work on 3D reconstruction [41,69] and generative shape modeling [13,46] suggests parameterizing ϕ using a multi-layer perceptron (MLP) with θ as its parameters. The networks are optimized by minimizing an energy function comprised of a distance term [46] and a gradient term [19] enforcing $|\nabla\phi|$ to be 1. We use SIREN [53] as the parametric function of choice, although our method is agnostic to the network parameterization. The network acts approximately as an SDF at the rest state $(t = 0)$, but may not retain the SDF property (Eq. 1) as the surface evolves. We denote this surface as $\partial\Omega_E(\theta) = \{\mathbf{x} \mid \Phi(\mathbf{x}; \theta) = 0\}$, where Φ is parameterized with θ as the weights and biases of the network. For clarity, we use Φ for parametric level-sets and ϕ for non-parametric.

4   Method

We begin the discussion by first characterizing the deformation of surfaces into Lagrangian (Sect. 4.1) and Eulerian (Sect. 4.2) settings. We show that gradient descent on energy functions defined for triangle meshes can be viewed as surface deformation under the dynamics of a flow field $\mathbf{V}$, which is *discretely* defined only on the surface points $\partial\Omega_L$. We can use this flow field to deform a *continuous* surface representation using the level-set equation. We extend the level-set equation to the case of parametric level-sets Φ which enables us to use loss functions defined on triangle meshes to deform MLP-defined level-sets.

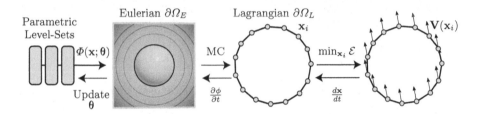

Fig. 2. Method Overview. We present a level-set method to evolve neural representations of implicit surfaces. Using Marching Cubes (MC) [31], a Lagrangian surface $\partial\Omega_L$ is extracted from an Eulerian representation $\partial\Omega_E$ encoded in the network parameters θ. An energy function $\mathcal{E}$ is defined on $\partial\Omega_L$ which is minimized using gradient-descent. The gradients of the optimizer together act as a flow-field $\mathbf{V}$ on the surface points $\mathbf{x}$, which is used to evolve the non-parametric ϕ using the level-set equation. The values of ϕ on the surface act as references to update the parameters θ of the network.

4.1   Lagrangian Deformation

As mentioned earlier, in the Lagrangian setting, the surface is defined with a finite set of points $\partial\Omega_L$. A variety of methods in geometry processing and computer vision define an energy function $\mathcal{E}$ that is minimized to make instantaneous updates to $\partial\Omega_L$. Some recent examples include optimizing point-clouds for view-synthesis [1,50] and triangle-meshes for inverse-rendering of geometry [18,40]. The surface is updated using spatial gradients $\frac{\partial\mathcal{E}}{\partial\mathbf{x}}$, which is well studied in numerical analysis [58] and optimization methods [14]. Through the lens of physics, these gradients induce an instantaneous flow field $\mathbf{V}(\mathbf{x})$, which can be used to evolve the surface by integrating the following ordinary differential equation (ODE):

$$\frac{d\mathbf{x}}{dt} = -\frac{\partial \mathcal{E}}{\partial \mathbf{x}} \rightarrow \mathbf{V}(\mathbf{x}). \qquad \lhd \text{ Lagrangian Deformation} \qquad (2)$$

Numerically, this can be done using forward-Euler steps $\mathbf{x}^{t+1} = \mathbf{x}^t + \Delta t \mathbf{V}^t(\mathbf{x})$. This is easy to accomplish if the connectivity of the points remains static. More sophisticated integration schemes can also be used [58]. Here, in case of optimization problems solved using gradient descent, Δt is equivalent to the learning rate. Several works in shape deformation [20] and inverse rendering [40] can be subsumed by this ODE with different definitions for flow $\mathbf{V}$ and time-step Δt. We next show that these readily available energy functions and optimization algorithms defined for explicit surfaces can also be used to optimize MLP-defined level-sets.

4.2   Eulerian Deformation

To avoid the topological complications associated with Lagrangian deformations, we can instead define a corresponding Eulerian deformation field. By definition, we know for points $\mathbf{x} \in \partial\Omega$, $\phi(\mathbf{x}) = 0$. Using implicit differentiation:

$$\frac{d\phi(\mathbf{x})}{dt} = \frac{\partial \phi}{\partial t} + \frac{\partial \phi}{\partial \mathbf{x}}\frac{\partial \mathbf{x}}{\partial t} = \frac{\partial \phi}{\partial t} + \nabla\phi \cdot \mathbf{V} = 0 \qquad \lhd \text{ From 2}$$

$$\Longleftrightarrow \frac{\partial \phi}{\partial t} = -\nabla\phi \cdot \mathbf{V}. \qquad \lhd \text{ Eulerian Deformation} \qquad (3)$$

This partial differential equation (PDE) is sometimes referred to as the level-set equation [45], the material derivative [7] or the G-equation [33]. We extend this PDE to obtain an evolution method for parametric level-sets Φ. First, for each time step t, we extract a Lagrangian surface representation $\partial\Omega_L^t$ from Φ using MC [31]. Depending on the task at hand, an energy function $\mathcal{E}$ (e.g., photometric error for inverse rendering) is defined on $\partial\Omega_L^t$. Assuming $\mathcal{E}$ is differentiable, we compute $\frac{\partial \mathcal{E}}{\partial \mathbf{x}} = -\mathbf{V}^t(\mathbf{x})$ for each vertex $\mathbf{x}_i \in \partial\Omega_L$. With the flow field $\mathbf{V}^t$, we update the level-set function as we would in the non-parametric case using forward-Euler steps:

$$\phi^{t+1} = \Phi^t - \Delta t \nabla\Phi^t \cdot \mathbf{V}^t. \qquad \lhd \text{ From (3)} \qquad (4)$$

The time step Δt here is a parameter which is dependent on the dynamics of the flow-field. If $\mathbf{V}$ is highly non-linear, taking smaller steps (i.e., Δt is small) is required, while for a simple field, larger values of Δt should suffice. For each time step, we take the values of non-parametric ϕ^{t+1} as the reference and update the parameters of Φ accordingly. This is achieved by minimizing the following objective:

$$\min_\theta J(\theta) = \frac{1}{|\partial\Omega_L|} \sum_{\mathbf{x} \in \partial\Omega_L} ||\phi^{t+1}(\mathbf{x}) - \Phi(\mathbf{x}; \theta)||^2 \,, \qquad (5)$$

using gradient descent. Since the surface updates are small for each time step, the number of descent steps required is in the order of 10^2. This makes the method convenient for obtaining neural representations of deformed variants of the initial geometry. After each optimization routine, we again extract the Lagrangian surface using MC [31], which is subsequently fed into a mesh-based energy-minimization problem. An overview of our method is shown in Fig. 2. For each of the applications we show in Sect. 6, we define $\mathbf{V}^t$ using a corresponding energy function, and minimize J for each time step.

5   Theoretical Comparisons

The level-set method discussed in Sect. 4.2 subsumes two related works, 1) Differentiable iso-surface extraction (MeshSDF) [49], and 2) Differentiable rendering of implicit surfaces (DVR/IDR) [41,69]. We first show that MeshSDF minimizes the level-set objective J defined in (5) with a single gradient-descent step. But the surface does not propagate in agreement with the level-set equation, as outlined in Sect. 5.1. We then show that these two seemingly disparate works (MeshSDF and DVR) are closely related in Sect. 5.2. We end the discussion with an explanation for how DVR deviates from the level-set equation.

5.1   Differentiable Iso-Surface Extraction

Result 1. *Differentiable Iso-Surface Extraction [49] takes a single gradient-descent step to minimize the level-set objective function J (Eq. 5).*

Proof. MeshSDF [49] defines a loss-function $\mathcal{L}$ on a triangle mesh extracted using Marching Cubes [31] from an SDF parameterized with an MLP. They use an MLP $\Phi(\mathbf{x}; \theta, \mathbf{z})$ conditioned on a latent-code $\mathbf{z}$ characterizing the shape. Using $\mathcal{L}$ they update the latent-code $\mathbf{z}$, which is different from our goal of updating θ for an unconditional Φ. To clarify this distinction, we use MeshSDF$^\theta$ to denote our variant which updates θ. To update the parameters of the MLP, we compute the following gradient using the chain-rule:

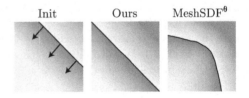

Init   Ours   MeshSDF$^\theta$

Fig. 3. MeshSDF$^\theta$ does not follow the level-set equation. (*Left*) A planar surface defined implicitly with an MLP is influenced by a flow field in the direction of its normal. The motion attained using differentiable iso-surface extraction (*Right*) is inconsistent with the field. Our method (*Center*) propagates the front as expected.

$$\frac{\partial \mathcal{L}}{\partial \theta} = \sum_{\mathbf{x} \in \partial \Omega_L} \frac{\partial \mathcal{L}}{\partial \mathbf{x}} \frac{\partial \mathbf{x}}{\partial \Phi} \frac{\partial \Phi}{\partial \theta}, \tag{6}$$

where $\mathbf{x}$ are the vertices on the mesh and Φ is an SDF. The first and the third gradient terms on the right are computed using automatic differentiation. The second term $\frac{\partial \mathbf{x}}{\partial \Phi}$ can be approximated as the inverted surface normal $-\mathbf{n}(\mathbf{x}) = -\nabla_{\mathbf{x}}\Phi$ [49], when Φ is an SDF. In the spirit of Lagrangian deformation (Eq. 2), $-\frac{\partial \mathcal{L}}{\partial \mathbf{x}}$ acts as an instantaneous flow field $\mathbf{V}$ on the vertices $\mathbf{x}$. The parameters of the MLP are then updated as:

$$\theta \leftarrow \theta - \lambda \frac{\partial \mathcal{L}}{\partial \theta} = \theta - \lambda \sum_{\mathbf{x} \in \partial \Omega_L} \mathbf{V} \cdot \nabla \Phi \frac{\partial \Phi}{\partial \theta}, \tag{7}$$

where λ is the learning rate. Alternatively, we can also update θ using the objective function defined in Eq. 5 using gradient descent:

$$\theta \leftarrow \theta - \lambda \frac{\partial J}{\partial \theta} = \theta - \lambda \sum_{\mathbf{x} \in \partial \Omega_L} 2(\phi^{t+1}(\mathbf{x}) - \Phi(\mathbf{x}; \theta)) \left(-\frac{\partial \Phi}{\partial \theta} \right)$$

$$= \theta - \epsilon \sum_{\mathbf{x} \in \partial \Omega_L} \mathbf{V} \cdot \nabla \Phi \frac{\partial \Phi}{\partial \theta}, \quad \triangleleft \text{ From (4)} \tag{8}$$

where ϵ is a constant. The last equivalency is valid when $\phi^{t+1}(\mathbf{x}) - \Phi(\mathbf{x}; \theta) = -\Delta t \mathbf{V} \cdot \nabla \Phi$ (Eq. 4), which is true only for the first gradient descent step. Subsequently, the value of $\Phi(\mathbf{x}; \theta)$ changes as the parameters get updated. Comparing (7) and (8), we conclude that the optimization in MeshSDF$^\theta$ has the effect of taking a single gradient-descent step to minimize J. Note that while the proof by Remelli *et al.* [49] assumes Φ is an SDF, the second update equation (8) does not. It is valid for all level-set functions, with no restrictions on the values of the gradient-norm ($|\nabla \Phi|$) and is also valid for occupancy functions [36].   □

However, by taking a single step to update θ, the surface does not propagate in agreement with the level-set Eq. (3). This is problematic for applications which require the surface to move as intended by the flow-field. An example application is shown in Sect. 6.1. We also illustrate this with a toy example in Fig. 3 where a planar surface propagates in the direction of its normal. A more formal discussion is in Result 2.

Result 2. *Differentiable iso-surface extraction [49] does not propagate the surface-front as dictated by the flow field.*

Proof. We show this with an example flow field. Consider the surface-front propagating with a constant speed β in the direction of the normal. The corresponding Eulerian deformation is constant across the surface:

$$\frac{\partial \phi}{\partial t} = -|\nabla \phi| \beta = -\beta. \quad \triangleleft \text{ Assuming } \phi \text{ is an SDF} \tag{9}$$

With the same flow field, we can estimate the instantaneous change in Φ (parametric) for MeshSDF$^\theta$ as:

$$\frac{\partial \Phi}{\partial t} = \frac{\partial \Phi}{\partial \theta} \frac{\partial \theta}{\partial t} = \frac{\partial \Phi}{\partial \theta} \sum_{\mathbf{x} \in \partial \Omega_L} -\beta \frac{\partial \Phi}{\partial \theta} = \frac{\partial \Phi}{\partial \theta} B. \quad \triangleleft \text{ From (7) and (9)} \tag{10}$$

The term B on the right is constant for every point $\mathbf{x}$ on the surface. The gradient $\frac{\partial \Phi}{\partial \theta}$ is dependent on the position where it is evaluated and hence front-propagation $\frac{\partial \Phi}{\partial t}$ is not constant. On the contrary, we minimize the objective function defined in (5) which ensures that the surface propagation is constant as in (9). □

For the implications of Result 1 and 2, and experimental comparisons, we defer the discussion to Sect. 6.1.

5.2 Differentiable Surface Rendering

An alternate way of extracting a Lagrangian surface $\partial \Omega_L$ from Φ is by computing ray-surface intersections using ray-marching or sphere-tracing [21]. If ray-marching is differentiable [24,29], one can backpropagate gradients from error functions defined on $\partial \Omega_L$ to the parameters θ defining the implicit surface. Recent developments in inverse rendering [36,69] rely on this idea. The explicit surface extracted using ray-marching differs from the one obtained using marching-cubes in two ways, 1) Ray-marching does not extract the connectivity (e.g., triangle faces) among the intersection points. This restricts the usage of loss functions which rely on attributes like the edge-length or differential operators like the Laplacian. 2) The intersection points depend on the camera attributes. The resolution of the image plane affects the density of points and the viewing direction determines the visibility. As a result, $\partial \Omega_L$ obtained using ray-marching could be sparser than the one obtained marching cubes. Furthermore, as we show in Result 3, by using differentiable ray-marching the parameters get updated exactly as when differentiable iso-surface extraction is used—although with a less favorable Lagrangian representation (sparser and no connectivity). This is in addition to the computational disadvantage associated with ray-marching. We also formally show in Result 4 that surface evolution with differentiable ray-marching is in disagreement with level-set theory for tangential flows.

Result 3. *Surface evolution using differentiable ray-marching of parametric implicit surfaces [36,69] is the same as using differentiable iso-surface extraction [49] when the viewing direction $\mathbf{v}_u$ is parallel to the normal $\mathbf{n}$ at the intersection point $\mathbf{x}_u$. The parameters θ for the level-set function Φ are updated as:*

$$\theta \leftarrow \theta - \lambda \sum_{\mathbf{x}_u} \mathbf{V} \cdot \nabla \Phi \frac{\partial \Phi}{\partial \theta}, \tag{11}$$

where $\mathbf{x}_u$ are the visible points and $\mathbf{V}$ is the flow field. Comparing (11) and (7), the gradient-descent step is the same. As in the case of MeshSDF$^\theta$, here the surface is evolved with a single step in the parameter space. We provide a more detailed proof for (11) in the Appendix.

Result 4. *Differentiable ray-marching of parametric implicit surfaces [36,69] disagrees with the level-set equation for tangential components* $\mathbf{V}^\perp$ *of the flow field* $\mathbf{V}$. *The change in parameters* $\Delta\theta$ *is:*

$$\Delta\theta = \lambda \sum_{\mathbf{x}_u} \pm |\mathbf{V}^\perp| \tan(\arccos(\nabla\Phi \cdot \mathbf{v}_u))\frac{\partial\Phi}{\partial\theta} \neq 0, \qquad (12)$$

which could be non-zero. A detailed proof is in the Appendix. Referring to Eq. 3, for tangential flows the surface should not undergo any deformation, i.e. $\frac{\partial\phi}{\partial t} = 0$. However, since θ gets updated as in (12), the surface *does* deform. We instead minimize the objective function J (Eq. 5) which is 0 for a tangential field. We show an example of tangential deformation in

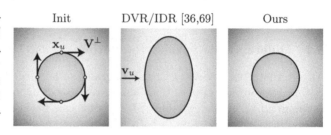

Init   DVR/IDR [36,69]   Ours

Fig. 4. Tangential flow fields may deform surfaces when DVR/IDR is used for surface extraction. (*Left*) A parametric Eulerian circle undergoes tangential deformation $\mathbf{V}^\perp$ at surface points $\mathbf{x}_u$. (*Middle*) Using differentiable surface rendering, the surface deforms incorrectly. (*Right*) Our method agrees with the level-set equation and the resultant deformation is the identity.

Fig. 4. Experimental comparisons in Sect. 6.2 validate that deforming Φ accurately is critical for applications like inverse rendering.

6 Applications

We focus on validating the proposed theory with computer graphics models in three different settings, 1) Curvature-based deformations (Sect. 6.1), which can be used to smooth/sharpen features and apply curvature defined flows on implicit surfaces, 2) Inverse rendering of geometry (Sect. 6.2), where a differentiable renderer for explicit geometry can be used to evolve implicit surfaces, and 3) User-defined deformations (Sect. 6.3), where a user can specify alterations for a given object.

6.1   Curvature-based Deformation

To apply surface smoothing on parametric implicit surfaces, we first define a corresponding explicit force field. For the extracted Lagrangian surface $\partial\Omega_L$ at each time step, we minimize the Dirichlet-energy functional on the surface. In the continuous setting, this is defined as:

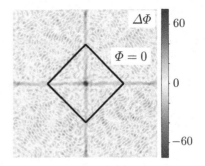

Fig. 5. The laplacian $\Delta\Phi$ of an MLP-defined level-set function is noisy. We show the mean-curvature values for a parametric level-set function of a square. Large values are observed for a zero-curvature surface.

$$\mathcal{E}(\partial\Omega) = \int_{\partial\Omega} ||\nabla\mathbf{x}||^2 \, d\mathbf{x}. \qquad (13)$$

Minimizing $\mathcal{E}$ can be shown [8] to induce the following explicit flow-field on the surface:

$$\frac{\partial\mathbf{x}}{\partial t} = \mathbf{V}(\mathbf{x}) = \lambda\Delta\mathbf{x} = -2\lambda\kappa(\mathbf{x})\mathbf{n}(\mathbf{x}), \qquad (14)$$

where λ is a scalar diffusion coefficient, Δ is the Laplace-Beltrami operator and $\mathbf{n}$ is the normal. κ is the mean-curvature, which for an implicit surface is defined as the divergence of the normalized gradient of ϕ (*i.e.*, $\nabla \cdot \frac{\nabla\phi}{|\nabla\phi|}$) [44]. It is equivalent to computing the laplacian $\Delta\Phi$ of the MLP using automatic differentiation. In Fig. 5 we show that such an estimation of the laplacian is noisy—significant magnitudes are observed even for surfaces with zero curvature.[1] Instead of using (14) as it is, which requires estimating $\Delta\Phi$, we approximate $\mathbf{V} = \lambda\Delta\mathbf{x} \approx \lambda\mathbf{L}\mathbf{x}$; where $\mathbf{L}$ is the discrete Laplacian we can compute using the Lagrangian surface. Note that this is feasible only because of the hybrid (Eulerian+Lagrangian) nature of our method. We use the flow-field to update Φ using the method outlined in Sect. 4.2. Figure 6 shows qualitative comparisons for smoothing applied on two surfaces. We show a comparison with a method which applies deformation using the continuous Laplacian ($\Delta\Phi$) (NFGP) [67]. When $\mathcal{E}$ is minimized using MeshSDF$^\theta$ [49], the deformation is not curvature based and high-frequency features are retained during the evolution.

Equation (14) is referred to as mean-curvature flow [17]. Since our method deforms the surface in accordance with the flow-field, we can use (14) to apply mean-curvature flow on a parametrically defined ϕ. Yang *et al.* [67] minimize an objective function which is handcrafted for a specific level-of-smoothness. Applying curvature-based flow is infeasible with their method since it would require a new optimization objective for each level-of-smoothness. As MeshSDF$^\theta$ [49] does not evolve the surface according to the level-set equation, the flow obtained with it is incorrect. We show an example flow on a genus-0 surface in Fig. 7.

---

[1] This might be due to the unconstrained Lipschitz constants of MLPs [28].

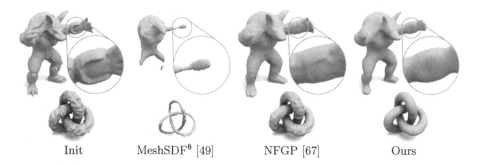

Init	MeshSDF$^\theta$ [49]	NFGP [67]	Ours

Fig. 6. Surface smoothing on parametric level-sets. We apply surface smoothing on an MLP-defined implicit surface by minimizing Dirichlet energy on the corresponding explicit surface. We use a discrete Laplacian to define a flow-field on the surface; NFGP [67] uses its continuous counterpart and preserves too many high-frequency details. MeshSDF$^\theta$ [49] fails to smoothen the surface.

6.2   Inverse Rendering of Geometry

We propose an inverse-rendering method which uses a differentiable renderer designed for triangle meshes to optimize geometry defined using parametric level-sets. As in the case of recent methods [4,41,69], we use an analysis-by-synthesis approach. A photometric error comparing the captured and the rendered images is minimized using gradient descent. The gradients of the error function are used to define an explicit flow-field. A corresponding Eulerian deformation field is obtained to evolve the level-set function Φ. As a result we can take large steps in inverse rendering of geometry with unconstrained topology and guarantees on mesh quality. The resulting optimization is robust and does not require an object-mask as in the (unlike [41,69]).

Our single-bounce forward rendering model uses a collocated camera and point-light, with a known diffuse-Phong BRDF Although we choose Nvd-iffrast [26] as the differentiable rasterizer in our method, in theory it can be

Mean-Curvature Flow

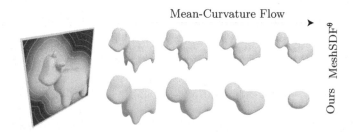

MeshSDF$^\theta$

Ours

Fig. 7. We use an explicit mean-curvature flow-field to deform a parametrically defined implicit surface. When the same flow-field is used with MeshSDF, the deformation is not curvature-based. A genus-0 surface morphs into a sphere using our method while MeshSDF retains high-curvature regions.

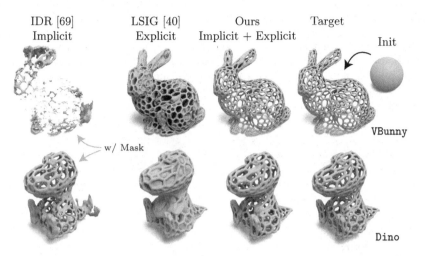

Fig. 8. Inverse rendering of high-genus shapes. A spherical surface is used for initialization. IDR [69], which uses differentiable rendering of implicit surfaces does not recover finer details. LSIG [40] uses a triangle-mesh and restricts the topology post initialization. Using an explicit differentiable renderer to optimize implicit geometry, our method can change topology during optimization and recover fine-details. Note that IDR requires an object mask and a neural renderer.

swapped with any other differentiable renderer. Starting from an initial estimate Φ, for each time-step t we first extract the triangle mesh $\partial\Omega_L^t$ and minimize a photometric error $\mathcal{E}$. We use the gradients of $\mathcal{E}$ to define the flow-field as $\mathbf{V}^t(\mathbf{x}_i) = -\frac{\partial\mathcal{E}}{\partial\mathbf{x}_i} - \lambda\mathbf{L}\mathbf{x}_i$, where $\mathbf{L}\mathbf{x}_i$ is used for smooth evolution. Taking a single descent step for θ is sufficient since the evolution does not need to follow a specific trajectory.

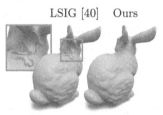

We evaluate the recovery on a diverse set of shapes, each of which is rendered from 100 random viewpoints. We use IDR [69] and LSIG [40] as baselines. We test IDR in three settings, 1) w/o Mask, 2) With known Phong shading, and 3) Using the Neural renderer in [69]. Quantitative comparisons are in Table 1 and qualitative comparisons are in Fig. 8. For a genus-0 shape (Bunny) LSIG [40] is able to recover accurate geometry, but the optimized meshes can have self intersections as shown on the left. It struggles with high-genus shapes as the mesh connectivity remains static throughout the optimization routine. Even with correct topology at initialization, the recovery is erroneous. Comparisons with IDR [69] are in Fig. 9.

Table 1. Quantitative evaluation on inverse rendering of geometry. An initial sphere is optimized to a diverse set of shapes from multi-view images. Chamfer distance is reported for geometric consistency and PSNR is reported to evaluate the visual appearance of optimized geometry. IDR [69] w/o Mask does not converge for any of the shapes. Methods marked with † require object masks. LSIG [40] works well for a genus-0 shape (**Bunny**) but struggles with high-genus shapes. Shapes recovered using our method are shown on the top.

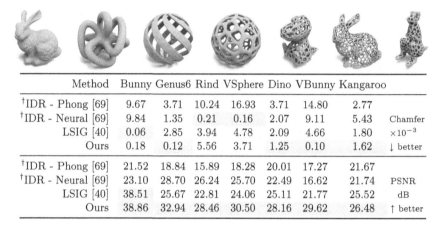

Method	Bunny	Genus6	Rind	VSphere	Dino	VBunny	Kangaroo	
†IDR - Phong [69]	9.67	3.71	10.24	16.93	3.71	14.80	2.77	
†IDR - Neural [69]	9.84	1.35	0.21	0.16	2.07	9.11	5.43	Chamfer
LSIG [40]	0.06	2.85	3.94	4.78	2.09	4.66	1.80	×10⁻³
Ours	0.18	0.12	5.56	3.71	1.25	0.10	1.62	↓ better
†IDR - Phong [69]	21.52	18.84	15.89	18.28	20.01	17.27	21.67	
†IDR - Neural [69]	23.10	28.70	26.24	25.70	22.49	16.62	21.74	PSNR
LSIG [40]	38.51	25.67	22.81	24.06	25.11	21.77	25.52	dB
Ours	38.86	32.94	28.46	30.50	28.16	29.62	26.48	↑ better

6.3   User-Defined Shape Editing

GT (Explicit) Ours (Implicit)

Fig. 10. User-defined editing on parametric level-sets.

We demonstrate deformation operations on parametric level-sets using constraints defined by a user. The problem setup is in line with the extensive literature [10, 54,55,70] on shape editing for triangle meshes. At $t = 0$, we first extract a mesh from a neural implicit surface using MC [31]. A user can specify handle regions on this surface to either rotate, translate or freeze parts of the shape along with their target locations. This generates a sparse deformation flow-field on the surface which we *densify* by minimizing a thin-shell energy function that penalizes local stretching and bending on the surface [62]. More details are in the Appendix. Estimating the flow-field requires solving a linear system $-k_S \Delta \mathbf{V} + k_B \Delta^2 \mathbf{V} = 0$, where Δ and Δ^2 are the laplacian and bi-laplacian operators. k_S and k_B are weighting terms for stretching and bending respectively. Additional constraints which adhere to user specifications are also added to the linear system [9]. With the obtained flow-field, we update the parameters of the level-set function such that the surface propagation is as intended. We also use gradient regularization as in [19]. An example deformation is shown in Fig. 10.

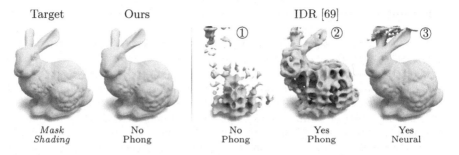

Fig. 9. **Qualitative comparison for inverse rendering using implicit representations.** We evaluate IDR in three different settings. ① Without object-mask supervision it fails to converge to a reasonable geometry. ② With a known-reflectance model (Phong) the silhouette of the object is recovered but without any details. ③ It requires a rendering network (unknown reflectance) and an object-mask for good convergence—both of which not required by our method.

7   Discussion

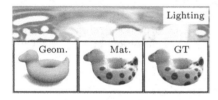

Fig. 11. Joint recovery of geometry, complex material and lighting.

Our work formulates a level-set evolution method for parametrically defined implicit surfaces. It does not require surface extraction to be differentiable and can be used to apply mesh algorithms to neural implicit surfaces. We expect the proposed method to be particularly useful for inverse problems. We showcase one example of joint recovery of geometry, material and lighting from multi-view images in Fig. 11, where we use our surface evolution method along with components from [38]. Although the surface deformation is as dictated by the flow field, the corresponding implicit function may not retain gradient characteristics during evolution. This could become a pertinent problem for algorithms like sphere tracing [21] which require reliable distance queries, and is an interesting avenue for future research. We hope this work encourages further inquiry into recent work on geometry optimization by drawing connections to methods in computer vision and graphics developed in the pre-deep-learning era.

Acknowledgements. This work was supported in part by NSF CAREER 1751365, NSF IIS 2110409, ONR grant N000142012529, NSF Chase-CI grant 1730158, Adobe, Google, an Amazon Research Award, the Ronald L. Graham Chair and UC San Diego Center for Visual Computing. We thank Ceh Jan and 3dmixers users roman_hegglin and PhormaSolutions for the 3D models. We thank the anonymous reviewers for helpful comments and discussions.

References

1. Aliev, K.A., Sevastopolsky, A., Kolos, M., Ulyanov, D., Lempitsky, V.: Neural point-based graphics (2020)
2. Alldieck, T., Xu, H., Sminchisescu, C.: imghum: implicit generative models of 3D human shape and articulated pose. In: Proceedings of the IEEE/CVF International Conference on Computer Vision, pp. 5461–5470 (2021)
3. Ambrosio, L., Soner, H.M.: Level set approach to mean curvature flow in arbitrary codimension. J. Differ. Geom. **43**(4), 693–737 (1996)
4. Azinović, D., Li, T.M., Kaplanyan, A., Nießner, M.: Inverse path tracing for joint material and lighting estimation. In: Proceedings of the Computer Vision and Pattern Recognition (CVPR). IEEE (2019)
5. Azinović, D., Martin-Brualla, R., Goldman, D.B., Nießner, M., Thies, J.: Neural RGB-D surface reconstruction. arXiv preprint arXiv:2104.04532 (2021)
6. Bangaru, S., Li, T.M., Durand, F.: Unbiased warped-area sampling for differentiable rendering. ACM Trans. Graph. **39**(6), 245:1-245:18 (2020)
7. Batchelor, C.K., Batchelor, G.: An Introduction to Fluid Dynamics. Cambridge University Press, Cambridge (2000)
8. Botsch, M., Kobbelt, L., Pauly, M., Alliez, P., Lévy, B.: Polygon Mesh Processing. CRC Press, New York (2010)
9. Botsch, M., Sorkine, O.: On linear variational surface deformation methods. IEEE Trans. Visual. Comput. Graphics **14**(1), 213–230 (2007)
10. Botsch, M., Sumner, R., Pauly, M., Gross, M.: Deformation transfer for detail-preserving surface editing. In: Vision, Modeling & Visualization, pp. 357–364. Citeseer (2006)
11. Chabra, R., et al.: Deep local shapes: learning local SDF priors for detailed 3D reconstruction. arXiv preprint arXiv:2003.10983 (2020)
12. Chan, E.R., Monteiro, M., Kellnhofer, P., Wu, J., Wetzstein, G.: pi-GAN: periodic implicit generative adversarial networks for 3d-aware image synthesis. In: Proceedings of the IEEE/CVF Conference on Computer Vision and Pattern Recognition, pp. 5799–5809 (2021)
13. Chen, Z., Zhang, H.: Learning implicit fields for generative shape modeling. In: Proceedings of the IEEE/CVF Conference on Computer Vision and Pattern Recognition (CVPR), June 2019
14. Chong, E.K., Zak, S.H.: An Introduction to Optimization. Wiley, Hoboken (2004)
15. Cole, F., Genova, K., Sud, A., Vlasic, D., Zhang, Z.: Differentiable surface rendering via non-differentiable sampling. In: Proceedings of the IEEE/CVF International Conference on Computer Vision, pp. 6088–6097 (2021)
16. Davies, T., Nowrouzezahrai, D., Jacobson, A.: On the effectiveness of weight-encoded neural implicit 3D shapes. arXiv preprint arXiv:2009.09808 (2020)
17. Desbrun, M., Meyer, M., Schröder, P., Barr, A.H.: Implicit fairing of irregular meshes using diffusion and curvature flow. In: Proceedings of the 26th Annual Conference on Computer Graphics and Interactive Techniques, pp. 317–324 (1999)
18. Goel, P., Cohen, L., Guesman, J., Thamizharasan, V., Tompkin, J., Ritchie, D.: Shape from tracing: towards reconstructing 3D object geometry and svbrdf material from images via differentiable path tracing. In: 2020 International Conference on 3D Vision (3DV), pp. 1186–1195. IEEE (2020)
19. Gropp, A., Yariv, L., Haim, N., Atzmon, M., Lipman, Y.: Implicit geometric regularization for learning shapes. In: Proceedings of Machine Learning and Systems 2020 (2020)

20. Gupta, K., Chandraker, M.: Neural mesh flow: 3D manifold mesh generation via diffeomorphic flows. In: Larochelle, H., Ranzato, M., Hadsell, R., Balcan, M.F., Lin, H. (eds.) Advances in Neural Information Processing Systems, vol. 33, pp. 1747–1758. Curran Associates, Inc. (2020). https://proceedings.neurips.cc/paper/2020/file/1349b36b01e0e804a6c2909a6d0ec72a-Paper.pdf
21. Hart, J.C.: Sphere tracing: a geometric method for the antialiased ray tracing of implicit surfaces. Visual Comput. **12**(10), 527–545 (1996)
22. Hasselgren, J., Hofmann, N., Munkberg, J.: Shape, light & material decomposition from images using monte carlo rendering and denoising. arXiv preprint arXiv:2206.03380 (2022)
23. Jiang, Y., Ji, D., Han, Z., Zwicker, M.: SDFDIFF: differentiable rendering of signed distance fields for 3d shape optimization. In: Proceedings of the IEEE/CVF Conference on Computer Vision and Pattern Recognition, pp. 1251–1261 (2020)
24. Jiang, Y., Ji, D., Han, Z., Zwicker, M.: SDFDIFF: differentiable rendering of signed distance fields for 3D shape optimization. In: The IEEE/CVF Conference on Computer Vision and Pattern Recognition (CVPR) June 2020
25. Kellnhofer, P., Jebe, L.C., Jones, A., Spicer, R., Pulli, K., Wetzstein, G.: Neural lumigraph rendering. In: Proceedings of the IEEE/CVF Conference on Computer Vision and Pattern Recognition, pp. 4287–4297 (2021)
26. Laine, S., Hellsten, J., Karras, T., Seol, Y., Lehtinen, J., Aila, T.: Modular primitives for high-performance differentiable rendering. ACM Trans. Graphics **39**(6), 1–14 (2020)
27. Li, T.M., Aittala, M., Durand, F., Lehtinen, J.: Differentiable monte carlo ray tracing through edge sampling. ACM Trans. Graph. (Proc. SIGGRAPH Asia) 37(6), 222:1–222:11 (2018)
28. Liu, H.T.D., Williams, F., Jacobson, A., Fidler, S., Litany, O.: Learning smooth neural functions via lipschitz regularization. arXiv preprint arXiv:2202.08345 (2022)
29. Liu, S., Zhang, Y., Peng, S., Shi, B., Pollefeys, M., Cui, Z.: Dist: Rendering deep implicit signed distance function with differentiable sphere tracing. In: IEEE/CVF Conference on Computer Vision and Pattern Recognition (CVPR) (June 2020)
30. Liu, S., Li, T., Chen, W., Li, H.: Soft rasterizer: a differentiable renderer for image-based 3D reasoning. In: The IEEE International Conference on Computer Vision (ICCV), October 2019
31. Lorensen, W.E., Cline, H.E.: Marching cubes: a high resolution 3D surface construction algorithm. ACM SIGGRAPH Comput. Graphics **21**(4), 163–169 (1987)
32. Luan, F., Zhao, S., Bala, K., Dong, Z.: Unified shape and SVBRDF recovery using differentiable monte Carlo rendering. ArXiv (2021)
33. Markstein, G.H.: Nonsteady flame propagation: AGARDograph. Elsevier (2014)
34. Martel, J.N.P., Lindell, D.B., Lin, C.Z., Chan, E.R., Monteiro, M., Wetzstein, G.: Acorn: adaptive coordinate networks for neural scene representation. ACM Trans. Graph. (SIGGRAPH) **40**(4) (2021)
35. Mehta, I., Gharbi, M., Barnes, C., Shechtman, E., Ramamoorthi, R., Chandraker, M.: Modulated periodic activations for generalizable local functional representations. In: Proceedings of the IEEE/CVF International Conference on Computer Vision (ICCV), pp. 14214–14223, October 2021
36. Mescheder, L., Oechsle, M., Niemeyer, M., Nowozin, S., Geiger, A.: Occupancy networks: learning 3D reconstruction in function space. In: Proceedings IEEE Conference on Computer Vision and Pattern Recognition (CVPR) (2019)

37. Mu, J., Qiu, W., Kortylewski, A., Yuille, A., Vasconcelos, N., Wang, X.: A-SDF: learning disentangled signed distance functions for articulated shape representation. In: Proceedings of the IEEE/CVF International Conference on Computer Vision, pp. 13001–13011 (2021)
38. Munkberg, J., et al.: Extracting Triangular 3D Models, Materials, and Lighting From Images. arXiv:2111.12503 (2021)
39. Museth, K., Breen, D.E., Whitaker, R.T., Barr, A.H.: Level set surface editing operators. In: Proceedings of the 29th Annual Conference on Computer Graphics and Interactive Techniques, pp. 330–338 (2002)
40. Nicolet, B., Jacobson, A., Jakob, W.: Large steps in inverse rendering of geometry. ACM Trans. Graphics (Proc. SIGGRAPH Asia) 40(6), December 2021. https://doi.org/10.1145/3478513.3480501, https://rgl.epfl.ch/publications/Nicolet2021Large
41. Niemeyer, M., Mescheder, L., Oechsle, M., Geiger, A.: Differentiable volumetric rendering: learning implicit 3D representations without 3d supervision. In: IEEE/CVF Conference on Computer Vision and Pattern Recognition (CVPR), June 2020
42. Nimier-David, M., Vicini, D., Zeltner, T., Jakob, W.: Mitsuba 2: a retargetable forward and inverse renderer. Trans. Graphics (Proc. SIGGRAPH Asia) 38(6), December 2019. https://doi.org/10.1145/3355089.3356498
43. Oechsle, M., Peng, S., Geiger, A.: UNISURF: unifying neural implicit surfaces and radiance fields for multi-view reconstruction. In: Proceedings of the IEEE/CVF International Conference on Computer Vision, pp. 5589–5599 (2021)
44. Osher, S., Fedkiw, R.P.: Level set methods: an overview and some recent results. J. Comput. Phys. 169(2), 463–502 (2001)
45. Osher, S., Sethian, J.A.: Fronts propagating with curvature-dependent speed: algorithms based on hamilton-jacobi formulations. Journal of Computational Physics 79, 12–49 (1988)
46. Park, J.J., Florence, P., Straub, J., Newcombe, R., Lovegrove, S.: DeepSDF: learning continuous signed distance functions for shape representation. In: Proceedings of the IEEE/CVF Conference on Computer Vision and Pattern Recognition (CVPR), June 2019
47. Quilez, I.: https://iquilezles.org/www/articles/distfunctions/distfunctions.htm
48. Ravi, N., et al.: Accelerating 3d deep learning with pytorch3d. http://arxiv.org/abs/2007.08501 (2020)
49. Remelli, E., et al.: MeshSDF: differentiable ISO-surface extraction. In: Larochelle, H., Ranzato, M., Hadsell, R., Balcan, M.F., Lin, H. (eds.) Advances in Neural Information Processing Systems, vol. 33, pp. 22468–22478. Curran Associates, Inc. (2020). https://proceedings.neurips.cc/paper/2020/file/fe40fb944ee700392ed51bfe84dd4e3d-Paper.pdf
50. Rückert, D., Franke, L., Stamminger, M.: ADOP: approximate differentiable one-pixel point rendering. arXiv preprint arXiv:2110.06635 (2021)
51. Shen, T., Gao, J., Yin, K., Liu, M.Y., Fidler, S.: Deep marching tetrahedra: a hybrid representation for high-resolution 3d shape synthesis. In: Advances in Neural Information Processing Systems (NeurIPS) (2021)
52. Sitzmann, V., Chan, E.R., Tucker, R., Snavely, N., Wetzstein, G.: MetaSDF: meta-learning signed distance functions. In: Proceedings of the NeurIPS (2020)
53. Sitzmann, V., Martel, J.N., Bergman, A.W., Lindell, D.B., Wetzstein, G.: Implicit neural representations with periodic activation functions. In: arXiv (2020)
54. Sorkine, O., Alexa, M.: As-rigid-as-possible surface modeling. In: Symposium on Geometry Processing, vol. 4, pp. 109–116 (2007)

55. Sorkine, O., Cohen-Or, D., Lipman, Y., Alexa, M., Rössl, C., Seidel, H.P.: Laplacian surface editing. In: Proceedings of the 2004 Eurographics/ACM SIGGRAPH symposium on Geometry Processing, pp. 175–184 (2004)
56. Stanley, K.O.: Compositional pattern producing networks: a novel abstraction of development. Genetic Program. Evol. Mach. 8(2), 131–162 (2007)
57. Sucar, E., Liu, S., Ortiz, J., Davison, A.J.: imap: implicit mapping and positioning in real-time. In: Proceedings of the IEEE/CVF International Conference on Computer Vision, pp. 6229–6238 (2021)
58. Süli, E., Mayers, D.: An Introduction to Numerical Analysis. An Introduction to Numerical Analysis, Cambridge University Press (2003). https://books.google.com/books?id=hj9weaqJTbQC
59. Takikawa, T., et al.: Neural geometric level of detail: real-time rendering with implicit 3D shapes (2021)
60. Tancik, M., et al.: Fourier features let networks learn high frequency functions in low dimensional domains. arXiv preprint arXiv:2006.10739 (2020)
61. Taubin, G.: A signal processing approach to fair surface design. In: Proceedings of the 22nd Annual Conference on Computer Graphics and Interactive Techniques, pp. 351–358 (1995)
62. Terzopoulos, D., Platt, J., Barr, A., Fleischer, K.: Elastically deformable models. In: Proceedings of the 14th Annual Conference on Computer Graphics and Interactive Techniques, pp. 205–214 (1987)
63. Tewari, A., et al.: Advances in neural rendering. arXiv preprint arXiv:2111.05849 (2021)
64. Whitaker, R.T.: A level-set approach to 3D reconstruction from range data. Int. J. Comput. Vision 29(3), 203–231 (1998)
65. Xie, Y., et al.: Neural fields in visual computing and beyond. arXiv preprint arXiv:2111.11426 (2021)
66. Xu, Y., Peng, S., Yang, C., Shen, Y., Zhou, B.: 3D-aware image synthesis via learning structural and textural representations (2021)
67. Yang, G., Belongie, S., Hariharan, B., Koltun, V.: Geometry processing with neural fields. In: Thirty-Fifth Conference on Neural Information Processing Systems (2021)
68. Yariv, L., Gu, J., Kasten, Y., Lipman, Y.: Volume rendering of neural implicit surfaces. In: Advances in Neural Information Processing Systems 34 (2021)
69. Yariv, L., et al.: Multiview neural surface reconstruction by disentangling geometry and appearance. In: Advances in Neural Information Processing Systems, vol. 33 (2020)
70. Zayer, R., Rössl, C., Karni, Z., Seidel, H.P.: Harmonic guidance for surface deformation. In: Computer Graphics Forum, vol. 24, pp. 601–609. Citeseer (2005)
71. Zhang, C., Miller, B., Yan, K., Gkioulekas, I., Zhao, S.: Path-space differentiable rendering. ACM Trans. Graph. 39(4), 143:1–143:19 (2020)
72. Zhu, Z., et al.: Nice-slam: Neural implicit scalable encoding for slam. arXiv preprint arXiv:2112.12130 (2021)

Efficient Point Cloud Analysis Using Hilbert Curve

Wanli Chen, Xinge Zhu, Guojin Chen, and Bei Yu[✉]

The Chinese University of Hong Kong, Ma Liu Shui, Hong Kong
{wlchen,gjchen21,byu}@cse.cuhk.edu.hk

Abstract. Some previous state-of-the-art research on analyzing point cloud rely on the voxelization quantization because it keeps the better spatial locality and geometry. However, these 3D voxelization methods and subsequent 3D convolution networks often bring the large computational overhead and GPU occupation. A straightforward alternative is to flatten 3D voxelization into 2D structure or utilize the pillar representation to perform the dimension reduction, while all of them would inevitably alter the spatial locality and 3D geometric information. In this way, we propose the HilbertNet to maintain the locality advantage of voxel-based methods while significantly reducing the computational cost. Here the key component is a new flattening mechanism based on Hilbert curve, which is a famous locality and geometry preserving function. Namely, if flattening 3D voxels using Hilbert curve encoding, the resulting structure will have similar spatial topology compared with original voxels. Through the Hilbert flattening, we can not only use 2D convolution (more lightweight than 3D convolution) to process voxels, but also incorporate technologies suitable in 2D space, such as transformer, to boost the performance. Our proposed HilbertNet achieves state-of-the-art performance on ShapeNet, ModelNet40 and S3DIS datasets with smaller cost and GPU occupation.

1 Introduction

Point clouds are the principal data form for 3D world; they also constitute the output of the 3D sensing device including LiDAR. Pioneering works often process point clouds directly, including PointNet [31], PointNet++ [34], SO-Net [19], etc. Point-wise methods bypass the mesh or voxelization reconstruction and possess the permutation invariance. However, in these methods the spatial locality of point clouds is not sufficiently attended. Recently, the success of deep convolutional networks for image processing has motivated the learning-based approach for point clouds and convolution is a natural function focusing on the spatial locality. One common methodology to manipulate the point cloud using convolutional neural networks is to first convert the raw point cloud into a volumetric representation, and then utilize 3D convolutional neural networks to extract the

---

Supplementary Information The online version contains supplementary material available at https://doi.org/10.1007/978-3-031-20086-1_42.

S. Avidan et al. (Eds.): ECCV 2022, LNCS 13662, pp. 730–747, 2022.
https://doi.org/10.1007/978-3-031-20086-1_42

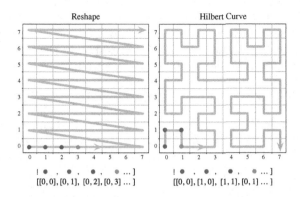

Fig. 1. Left: The mapping scheme of Reshape function. Right: The mapping scheme of Hilbert curve. Hilbert curve has better locality because it has no "**jump connections**" like reshape function.

intermediate features. This approach can keep the spatial topology and generate well-generalized features; however, it usually introduces the huge computational cost and excessive memory usage (mainly from 3D convolutional neural networks).

A natural idea to tackle this issue is to map the 3D space to the 2D representation, including flattening, range image, pillar-based bird-eye view and multi-view image, etc., and then process the resulting 2D representation with 2D convolutional neural networks. Unfortunately, this approach would inevitably alter the spatial topology and locality. Hence, a locality preserving mapping function from three to two dimension is desired.

Here, space filling curves [27], widely existing in the database [2], GIS [36] and image compression [22], provide a possible solution, where they act as a **fractal** function going through each point in a multi-dimensional space without repetition (Note that fractal function is also applicable to efficient parallel implementation). This mechanism for linking all elements in the high-dimensional space reveals a way to reduce the dimension, namely, mapping elements in the high-dimensional space into low-dimensional space (i.e. 2D and 1D) according to the mapping rule of space filling curve. There are various space filling curves, including Z-order curve [28], Gray-Code [9] and Hilbert curve [14]. In this paper, because of the good locality preserving capability as shown in Fig. fig:banner, Hilbert curve is incorporated to perform the dimension reduction and keep local topology.

Specifically, we first voxelize the point cloud to keep its 3D spatial locality. Then these voxels are flattened into 2D space via Hilbert curve in slice-level. We show an example in Eq. (5), where for 2D compression, Hilbert curve stretches voxels slice by slice to get the 2D representation.

Then, in this work, we propose a local feature collection module Hilbert pooling, and a light-weighted global feature harvesting module called Hilbert attention. Besides it, we combine 2D features (obtained using 3D Hilbert compression) with 1D point features using Hilbert interpolation, which is designed for better 2D feature gathering. The cooperation of Hilbert curve based flattening and

Hilbert curve based operations leads to the final framework, termed as Hilbert-Net. We conduct extensive experiments on various tasks, including point cloud classification and segmentation, where it reaches state-of-the-art performance on ShapeNet [4], S3DIS [1] ModelNet40 [49] dataset while the GPU occupation and computational overhead are relatively small.

The contributions of this paper can be summarized as follows:

- We propose a new perspective of efficient usage of 3D volumetric data, namely, using the Hilbert curve to collapse 3D structure into 2D with spatial locality preserving and employing the 2D convolutions for lower overhead.
- We propose Hilbert interpolation and Hilbert pooling for better feature extraction. They are designed according to the characteristics of the Hilbert curve.
- We propose Hilbert attention, a light-weighted transformer based module for exploring the cross-slice attention, providing a solution for 2D global feature extraction.
- We design a powerful framework HilbertNet, which reaches SOTA performance on segmentation and classification benchmarks.

2   Related Work

Image-Based Point Cloud Analysis. Recently, more and more 2D image-based methods are proposed for point cloud analysis. The advantages of using 2D images are 1) less computation than 3D convolution. 2) In 2D convolution, there are many excellent previous works [8,10,38,48] that have been proved to have high generalization ability, which can be applied directly to point cloud tasks. However, it is not an easy task to use 2D convolution in the point cloud. An important step is to map the point cloud to 2D images. MVCNN [38] uses the snapshot of a point cloud in a different point of view to implement point-image mapping. This method cannot get accurate spatial information of a point cloud. Therefore, its performance on the segmentation task is not as good as the classification task. Another mapping method is using range image such as RangeNet++ [25] and SqueezeSeg [47]. Such methods make up for the shortcomings of image-based methods in segmentation, but in the process of 2D projection, the spatial locality of the original 3D structure is not well preserved. Different from previous works, PolarNet [56] adopts bird view and polar coordination to convert the point cloud into the 2D image and they achieve good results in the LiDAR point cloud segmentation task. In our proposed work, we use a new point-image mapping technique. The input image we use are voxels compressed by the 2D Hilbert curve. Such input images can ensure good spatial locality in each slice, so as to avoid information loss caused by point-image mapping.

Point Cloud with Space Filling Curve. Space filling curve [27] is a series of fractal curves that can fill the entire 2D/3D space. Classical space filling curve

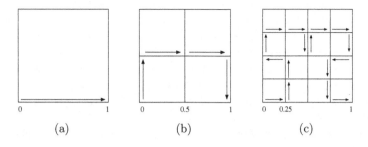

Fig. 2. Example of Hilbert curve generation.

includes sweep curve, Z-order curve [28] and Hilbert curve [14], etc. The space-filling properties make them be extensively used in databases and GIS, and its fractal feature also makes it applicable to parallel implementation. Similarly, such properties can be used to reduce the dimension of signals. In point cloud analysis, space filling curve usually appears with tree structure. For example, an early point cloud indexing work [41] used OCTree + 3D Hilbert curve to compress 3D point cloud information. Similarly, C-Flow [30] also describes point cloud using Hilbert curve. While O-CNN [42] uses OCTree + z-order curve to complete point cloud analysis with relatively low cost. Different space filling curves have different characteristics, and in this paper, we adopt the Hilbert curve because of its good locality preserving property.

Multi-View Fusion Based Point Cloud Analysis. Point cloud can be naturally represented via point based, 2D image based and 3D voxel based methods [7,15,58,62]. The cooperation of different view representation might absorb the complementary advantages from each other and lead to a success to the high-performance point cloud analysis. For example, PVCNN [24] and Cylinder3D [60, 63] adopt the voxel + point method (i.e. 1D and 3D combination) to balance the cost and accuracy. Image2Point [51], Volumetric MCVNN [32] adopt image-based method and voxel based method to perform the 2D and 3D view fusion. Different from previous work, in our proposed method, we use 1D sequence and 2D image as input, so as to incorporate the merit of multi-view fusion and obtain more friendly computational overhead and faster inference speed.

3 Methodologies

3.1 Hilbert Curve Preliminaries

Hilbert curve is a space filling curve that can link all elements in a space (as shown in Fig. 1), which often acts as a fractal function [35]. The formation of a 2D Hilbert curve is shown as follow. Firstly, we define $\mathfrak{I}$ and $\mathfrak{Q}$ as the interval of 1D space [0,1] and the starting point of Hilbert curve in 2D space $[0,1] \times [0,1]$ respectively. As shown in Fig. 2(a), for $z \in \mathbb{C}$, we first shrink z by $\frac{1}{2}$ along the origin, obtaining $z' = \frac{1}{2}z$. Then, we multiply a complex number i to rotate z' by 90°, obtaining $z'' = \frac{1}{2}zi$. Finally, we get the imaginary part of it: $z''' = -\bar{z}''$.

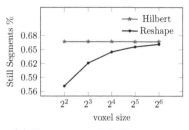
(a) Percentage of *Still* segments

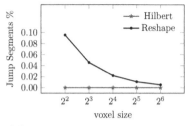
(b) Percentage of *Jump* segments

Fig. 3. Locality analysis of Hilbert curve and reshape function. Here we increase N from 2^2 to 2^6 and choose $D = 3$.

We combine the three transformations and name them as $\mathfrak{N}_0$. The lower-left part of Fig. 2(b) is obtained by $\mathfrak{N}_0 z = \frac{1}{2}\bar{z}i$. Similarly, we shrink z by $\frac{1}{2}$ along starting point $\mathfrak{Q}$ and move it upward, obtaining upper-left part of Fig. 2(b), the operation is $\mathfrak{N}_1 z = \frac{1}{2}z + \frac{i}{2}$. Next, we move upper-left by $\frac{1}{2}$ to get upper-right part of Fig. 2(a), the operation is $\mathfrak{N}_2 z = \frac{1}{2}z + \frac{i}{2} + \frac{1}{2}$. Finally, $\mathfrak{N}_3 z = -\frac{1}{2}\bar{z}i + 1 + \frac{i}{2}$ is obtained by rotating upper-left by $-90°$ and move forward by 1. Because of the characteristics of Hilbert curve, it is more convenient to express it in quaternary form. Assuming $s \in \mathfrak{J}$, then: $s = 0.q_1 q_2 q_3...$ and $q_j = 0, 1, 2, 3$. The Hilbert curve is shown as the infinite combination of these transformations:

$$\mathcal{H}(s) = \begin{pmatrix} \mathcal{Re} \\ \mathcal{Im} \end{pmatrix} \lim_{n \to \infty} \mathfrak{N}_{q_1} \mathfrak{N}_{q_2} \mathfrak{N}_{q_3} ... \mathfrak{N}_{q_n} \mathfrak{Q}. \tag{1}$$

Here n is the order of Hilbert curve. In real application, finite n-th order approximation is often used, which has the formation:

$$\mathcal{H}_n(s) = \mathcal{H}(0.q_1 q_2 q_3 ... q_n) = \begin{pmatrix} \mathcal{Re} \\ \mathcal{Im} \end{pmatrix} \sum_{j=1}^{n} \left(\frac{1}{2^j}\right) H_{q_0} H_{q_1} H_{q_2} ... H_{q_{j-1}} h_{q_j};$$

$$H_0 z = \bar{z}i, H_1 z = z, H_2 z = z, H_3 z = -\bar{z}i; h_0 = 0, h_1 = i, h_2 = 1 + i, h_3 = 2 + i. \tag{2}$$

3.2   Advantages of Hilbert Curve

We claim Hilbert curve is more suitable for data flattening compared with PyTorch "reshape" function (as shown in Fig. 1) and we demonstrate this point in the perspective of locality preserving and structural similarity between flattened and original structure.

Advantage 1: Locality Preserving.
The locality of a space filling curve can be measured using the segments it contains [27]. The better locality, the better feature clustering property.

Definition 1 (Segments). *In space filling curve, the "line" that links two consecutive points is regarded as a segment. For a space filling curve, $N^D - 1$ segments appear to link N^D elements in a D-dimensional space with grid size N.*

Definition 2 (Jump Segments). *For two consecutive points P_i and P_{i+1} in a N-dimensional space, if the distance between them is larger than 1: $abs(P_{i+1} - P_i) > 1$. The segment that links P_i and P_{i+1} is regarded as Jump segment. Jump segment measures the number of jump connections.*

Definition 3 (Still Segments). *For two consecutive points P_i and P_{i+1} in a N-dimensional space, if the distance between P_i and P_{i+1} is equal to 0 in dimension k: $P_{i+1} = P_i$. The segment that links P_i and P_{i+1} is regarded as Still segment in dimension k. Still segment measures the extent that one space filling curve should move in one dimension to move in another dimension.*

The most appealing characteristic of the Hilbert curve is its good locality preserving property, which leads to better feature clustering property. In Fig. 1, we intuitively show its merit compared to reshape function. In the following, a theoretical explanation is given. The locality of a space filling curve can be measured using the percentage of *Jump* and *Still* segments. Smaller *Jump* segments mean smaller number of jump connections, and higher *Still* segments represent higher dimensional consistency. Both of them denote a better locality. The percentage of them are calculated using Eq. (3).

$$J_R = (\frac{N^D - 1}{N - 1} - D) \cdot \frac{1}{D(N^D - 1)},$$

$$S_R = (DN^D - N\frac{N^D - 1}{N - 1}) \cdot \frac{1}{D(N^D - 1)}, \tag{3}$$

$$J_H = 0, \quad S_H = (D - 1)(N^D - 1) \cdot \frac{1}{D(N^D - 1)},$$

where J_R and S_R represent the *Jump* and *Still* segments of reshape function, and J_H and S_H represent the *Jump* and *Still* segments of Hilbert curve, respectively. N and D represent grid size and dimension. The comparison between reshape and Hilbert curve can be found in Fig. 3. It demonstrates that with the increasing of N, the percentage of *Still* segments of Hilbert curve is consistently larger than Reshape and the *Jump* segments of Hilbert curve are always zero. In this way, Hilbert curve is incorporated into our framework to perform the dimension reduction with good locality preserving.

Advantage 2: Lower Space to Linear Ratio
Besides the locality, the similarity between the original stricture and the flattened structure is also an important factor since flattening operations will inevitably alter the original structure which makes some continuous points (in original structure) distinct from each other after flattening. *space to linear ratio* (SLR) is then proposed to describe the similarity between the original structure and its flattened shape.

Definition 4 (Space to Linear Ratio). *If mapping a pair of points $p(t)$ and $p(\tau)$ in the 2D coordination in $[0,1] \times [0,1]$ to two points t and τ in 1D sequence* *in [0,1] using a space filling curve p, namely p:[0,1]→[0,1]×[0,1], the ratio*

$$\frac{|p(t) - p(\tau)|^2}{|t - \tau|} \tag{4}$$

is called space to linear ratio of the two points.

The upper bound of Eq. (4) is called the space to linear ratio of the curve p. Obviously, the lower SLR, the more similarity between original structure and flattened structure, which also leads to better spatial locality.

Theorem 1. *The square-to-linear ratio of the Hilbert curve is equal to 6.*

The details of proof can be found in [3]. While for some consecutive points in PyTorch reshape function, the SLR is $4^n - 2^{n+1} + 2$ [59], where n is the curve order as defined before. It is obvious that Hilbert curve has lower SLR and therefore the flattened structure of Hilbert curve is closer to original one than PyTorch reshape function.

3.3   Pre-processing

All data are pre-processed via Voxelization and Hilbert Flattening Module (VHFM) before sending into neural network. Specifically, we first perform the uniform voxel partition [26,32,60], generating 3D data with size (R, R, R) and then these volumetric representations are flattened rapidly by applying Hilbert curve. Specifically, given a 3D feature $\mathcal{V}^{\in(C,R,R,R)}$ with channel size C, we first separate it into R slices along Z axis, where the slices $\mathcal{V}_{s1}, \mathcal{V}_{s2}...\mathcal{V}_{sR} \in (C, R, R, 1)$. Then, 2D n-th order Hilbert curve $\mathcal{H}_n(s)$ is used to encode each slice, obtaining R sequences with length R^2 as shown in Eq. (5).

$$\mathcal{V}^{\in R \times R \times R} \rightarrow \begin{bmatrix} \mathcal{V}_{s1} \\ \mathcal{V}_{s2} \\ \vdots \\ \mathcal{V}_{sR} \end{bmatrix} \xrightarrow{\mathcal{H}_n(s)} \begin{bmatrix} s_1 \\ s_2 \\ \vdots \\ s_R \end{bmatrix} = \mathcal{I}. \tag{5}$$

The sequences $s_1, s_2...s_R \in (C, R^2)$ and $\mathcal{H}_n(s_k) = \mathcal{V}_{sk}, k = 1, 2...R$. After that we concatenate these sequences in Z axis order, obtaining 2D feature $\mathcal{I}^{\in(C,R^2,R)}$. Additional to the voxelization and Hilbert flattening, data augmentation such as rotation, flip and random jitting are applied to increase input diversity.

3.4   HilbertNet

Unlike previous point-voxel fusion based methods [24,60], in our design, the voxels are flattened into 2D features for representing multi-view data. With the help of Hilbert curve, our method will not only lower the computational overhead but also preserve the 3D spatial locality. As shown in Fig. 4, HilbertNet acts as

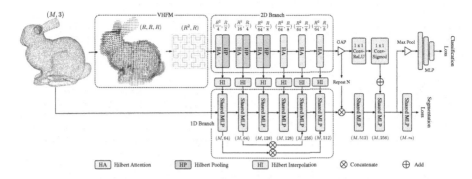

Fig. 4. The main framework of our model. Voxelization and Hilbert flattening module (VHFM) is the data processing part, where Hilbert curve is employed to perform the dimension reduction. Then a two-branch based network, HilbertNet, is designed to fuse 1D points and 2D slices representation to get final results. We employ global average pooling (GAP) and channel attention, which is comprehensively used in 2D tasks [16,46].

a two-branch network, to process 2D and 1D representation and perform the multi-view fusion. In the following, we will present every part of our method including Hilbert interpolation, Hilbert pooling, Hilbert attention in detail.

Feature Gathering. In our model, the 2D branch feature will be gathered in the form of point feature which is similar to the "devoxelization" process (*e.g.* linear interpolation [24], attention-weighted gathering [54]) proposed in previous works. Here we propose *Hilbert interpolation* for 2D feature gathering. To better demonstrate our advantage, we first introduce linear interpolation, a classical feature gathering method.

Linear Interpolation. Linear interpolation is a classical benchmark of voxel grid feature gathering method. Given a 3D feature $\mathcal{V}^{\in(C,R,R,R)}$, it is performed as:

$$O = \text{Reshape}(\mathcal{V}) * F_{linear}, \tag{6}$$

where $O^{\in(M,C)}$ is the point representation with M sampling points and F_{linear} is the linear interpolation kernel (could be Bilinear or Trilinear), $*$ is convolution operation. Although it is widely used, linear interpolation has two problems. Firstly, due to the sparsity of the grid data, if applying linear interpolation, the addition of empty grids with non-empty grids will weaken the output non-empty part of feature. Secondly, the $Reshape(\cdot)$ function is not locality preserving, which also reduces the effectiveness of feature gathering.

Hilbert Interpolation. Given a 2D feature $\mathcal{I}^{\in(C,R^2,R)}$ that flattened by 3D feature and the target point cloud feature $O^{\in(M,C)}$, The proposed Hilbert interpolation $\mathfrak{L}(\cdot)$ is performed as follow:

$$O = \mathfrak{L}(\mathcal{I}), \text{where}$$

$$\mathcal{H}_{\lceil M \rceil}(O) = \begin{cases} (\mathcal{I} \cdot \mathcal{W}_h) * F_{linear}, & M \leq R^3; \\ \mathcal{I} * F_{linear}, & M > R^3. \end{cases} \tag{7}$$

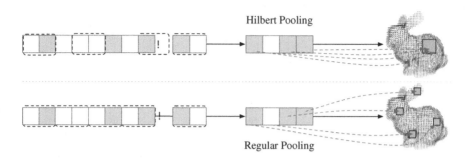

Fig. 5. Hilbert pooling and regular max pooling

Specifically, if the target size M is larger than the 2D feature size, we simply apply linear interpolation then reform the feature into O using Hilbert curve $\mathcal{H}_{\lceil M \rceil}(\cdot)$. $\lceil M \rceil$ represents the closest curve order that the corresponding Hilbert curve has at least M points. If $M \leq R^3$, $\mathcal{I}$ will multiply an adaptive weight $\mathcal{W}_h$, which is designed to emphasize the non-empty part in $\mathcal{I}$. Intuitively, $\mathcal{W}_h$ is the number of empty grids that fall in the linear interpolation kernel, the more empty grids, the larger compensation. To calculate $\mathcal{W}_h$, we first binarize featuremap $\mathcal{I}$ along channel C, obtaining $\mathcal{I}_B$. Then we apply sum filter to $\mathcal{I}_B$, obtaining $\mathcal{W}_B$:

$$\mathcal{W}_B = \mathcal{I}_B * \boldsymbol{F}_{sum}. \tag{8}$$

The kernel size of $\boldsymbol{F}_{sum}$ depends on the size of $\boldsymbol{F}_{linear}$ (marked as K_F) while the size of $\mathcal{W}_B$ is determined by the interpolation scale. Obviously, each element in $\mathcal{W}_B$ represents the number of non-empty grid that falls in the corresponding linear interpolation kernel. Finally, $\mathcal{W}_h^{\in(C,R^2,R)}$ is obtained by nearest expansion $\mathcal{N}(\cdot)$ of $\mathcal{W}_B$:

$$\mathcal{W}_h = K_F - \mathcal{N}(\mathcal{W}_B) + 1. \tag{9}$$

$\mathfrak{L}(\cdot)$ gathers 2D features using adaptive interpolation and Hilbert curve flattening, which overcomes the two problems in traditional linear interpolation. In the real implementation, we choose Bilinear interpolation kernel for $\mathfrak{L}(\cdot)$. After Hilbert interpolation, the gathered point feature O will merge with the 1D branch via additive fusion. The final output is formulated as:

$$\boldsymbol{Y} = \alpha(\boldsymbol{X}) + \boldsymbol{O}, \tag{10}$$

where $\boldsymbol{X}$ is point feature from 1D branch, $\alpha(\cdot)$ means shared MLP.

Hilbert Pooling. Different from previous 2D tasks, the 2D feature $\mathcal{I}$ in our model is obtained by the Hilbert curve, which means, if applying regular max pooling, the gathered feature follows the line of Hilbert curve instead of the original 3D structure. Therefore, the feature-to-be-pool may come from different parts of the original shape (See Fig. 5). Due to the specialty of $\mathcal{I}$, we design a novel pooling technique to harvest spatial information named Hilbert pooling

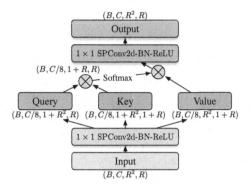

Fig. 6. Hilbert attention. It consists of 2D convolutions and matrix multiplications. Query and Key are generated using **4×1** convolution and **1×4** convolution respectively while Value features are extracted using **4×4** convolution. The shapes of *Query*, *Key*, *Value* are asymmetric because of padding. Sparse convolution [11] is applied during experiments for lower GPU memory cost and faster inference speed.

$\mathfrak{P}(\cdot)$, specifically:

$$\text{MaxPool3D}(\mathcal{H}_n^{-1}(\mathcal{I})) \xrightarrow{\mathcal{H}_{n-1}(s)} = \mathcal{I}' = \mathfrak{P}(\mathcal{I}), \tag{11}$$

where $\mathcal{H}_n^{-1}(\mathcal{I})$ is the inverse operation of Eq. (5), which transform 2D feature into 3D. Then a 3D max pooling is applied to extract context information. After that, we apply $n-1$ order Hilbert curve $\mathcal{H}_{n-1}(s)$ to transform the resultant feature into 2D structure $\mathcal{I}'^{\in(C,\frac{R^2}{4},\frac{R}{2})}$ (similar to Eq. (5)). It is noted that $\mathcal{H}_n(s) \approx \mathcal{H}_{n-1}(s)$ because Hilbert curve is a *fractal* structure also, it has small SLR and good locality. These characteristics guarantee the distribution of features that before and after pooling are similar.

Hilbert Attention. In order to get the richer spatial feature in 2D branch, we introduce Self-attention [5,44,55], a powerful tool for global feature collection. Specifically, we propose Hilbert attention that focuses on space connection, which contains spatial information of all voxel grids. Hilbert attention is formed with 3 feature correlations: intra-slice correlation, inter-slice correlation, and mixed correlation. The detailed workflow is illustrated in Fig. 6.

Intra-Slice Correlation. VHFM module (see Eq. (5)) transforms each slice $\mathcal{V}_{sk}$ into sequence s_k, $k \in [1, R]$. Then, similar to [57] a pointwise linear projection $\sigma(\cdot)$ with weight w_{key} (marked as *Key* in Fig. 6):

$$\sigma(\mathcal{I}) = \sum_{e_k \in s_k} w_{key} e_k \tag{12}$$

is applied along s_k for intra-slice level feature extraction, which collects pointwise feature **along** Hilbert curve.

Inter-Slice Correlation. To collect pointwise features between s_k, we introduce inter-slice correlation. Specifically, the linear projection $\phi(\cdot)$ (marked as

Query in Fig. 6) is used:

$$\phi(\mathcal{I}) = \sigma(\mathcal{I}^\top), \tag{13}$$

where $\phi(\cdot)$ collects pointwise feature **across** Hilbert curve.

Mixed Correlation. Mixed Correlation $\gamma(\mathcal{I})$ considers spatial feature along and across Hilbert curve, which acts as a 4×4 convolution since the spatial neighbors in the 3D voxel is 8, the kernel size of convolution can be set as 4 to cover all neighbors. Finally, Hilbert attention is gathered by considering the importance between inter-slice and intra-slice feature: $HA = \text{Softmax}(\phi(\mathcal{I})\sigma(\mathcal{I}))\gamma(\mathcal{I})$, where HA represents Hilbert attention.

4   Experiments

4.1   Implementation Details

Experimental Setting. HilbertNet is implemented based on PyTorch [29] framework and tested in the point cloud classification and part-segmentation task. For most of the experiments, we set Hilbert curve order $n = 6$, which means the chosen voxel size is 64^3. Adam optimizer [17] is applied during experiments with learning rate $lr = 0.001$ and batch size=16 for both tasks. The learning rate is reduced by half after every 50 epochs and the number of epoch is 200 for both part-segmentation and classification tasks.

Additionally, we conduct a large scale point cloud segmentation experiment on S3DIS [1] dataset with voxel size 128^3, the batch size in this experiment is set to 8 with 80 epochs for training, lr will be reduced by half after every 20 epochs. Other details are identical to the former tasks.

Classification Dataset. We evaluate the performance of our proposed model using ModelNet40 [49] dataset, which contains 9843 objects from 40 categories for training and 2468 objects for testing. Following the settings of previous work [19], we uniformly sampled 1024 points respectively during experiments.

Part-Segmentation Dataset. We use ShapeNetPart segmentation dataset [4] during experiments for part-segmentation tasks. It has 16 categories and 16881 objects in total. Each object in the dataset has 2 to 6 parts. Following previous works [24], we sample 2048 point clouds during experiments.

Large Scale Segmentation Dataset. S3DIS dataset [1] is used to test the performance of HilbertNet in large scale scene parsing task. S3DIS collects data from 271 rooms in 3 different building. Each point in the dataset is classified into 13 categories. Following a common procedure [54,57], we apply Area 5 experiments.

4.2   Experimental Results

ModelNet40. For the ModelNet40 classification task, we add additional 3 FC layers after the network. The results of ModelNet40 can be found in Table 1. Our

Table 2. Comparison of methods

Table 1. Results on ModelNet40 & ShapeNetPart datasets

Method	Voxel size	Inference time	mIoU
3D-UNet [26]	64^3	347ms	84.2
PVCNN [24]	32^3	62.5ms	86.0
HilbertNet-L	64^3	**42.1ms**	85.8
HilbertNet-M	64^3	59.2ms	86.4
HilbertNet	64^3	91.6ms	**87.1**

ModelNet40		ShapeNetPart	
Method	Acc	Method	mIoU
VoxNet [61]	85.9	Kd-Net [18]	82.3
Subvolume [33]	89.2	PointNet [31]	83.7
PointNet [31]	89.2	SO-Net [19]	84.9
DGCNN [45]	92.9	3D-GCN [23]	85.1
PointASNL [53]	92.9	DGCNN [45]	85.2
Grid-GCN [52]	93.1	PointCNN [21]	86.1
PCT [12]	93.2	PVCNN [24]	86.2
SO-Net [19]	93.4	KPConv [40]	86.4
CurveNet [50]	93.8	CurveNet [50]	86.6
Ours	**94.1**	Ours	**87.1**

Table 3. Computational cost and GPU Memory of different methods. The tested voxel resolution is 32^3. (FLOPs: floating point operations)

Method	FLOPs	GPU Memory
3D Convolution	18.86G	162M
2D Convolution	4.45G	148.7M
Sparse 2D Convolution	1.47G	49.6M
NonLocal	0.34G	4G
Hilbert Attention	**0.32G**	**47.8M**

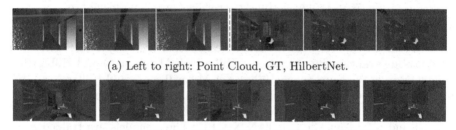

(a) Left to right: Point Cloud, GT, HilbertNet.

(b) Left to right: Point Cloud, GT, PointNet [31], KPConv [40], HilbertNet.

Fig. 7. (a) Visualized results on S3DIS Area 5 dataset; (b) Quantitative comparison.

proposed model reaches SOTA performance with 1024 sample points similar to previous works [20,31,50]. Since our model aggregates 3D voxel information and 1D point information, the performance of our model is better than voxel-only methods and point-only methods such as VoxelNet [61] and PointNet [31].

ShapeNetPart. The overall performance of our model can be found in the right part of Table 1. Our model has the highest mIoU compared with previous works. With the rich location information from volumetric data, our model easily outperforms the point-only models such as PointNet [31], SO-Net [19]. Also, our model gets better results compared with other methods that use 2D or 3D features such as 3D-GCN [23].

S3DIS. We conduct S3DIS [1] Area 5 experiment to show that HilbertNet is qualified for large scale point cloud segmentation and results can be found in Table 4. Due to the successful combination of grid and point data, HilbertNet

Table 4. Results of S3DIS Area 5

	PointNet [31]	PointCNN [21]	PCCN [43]	MinkowskiNet [6]	KPConv [40]	PointTransformer [57]	HilbertNet
ceiling	88.8	92.3	92.3	91.8	92.8	94	**94.6**
floor	97.3	98.2	96.2	**98.7**	97.3	98.5	97.8
wall	69.8	79.4	75.9	86.2	82.4	86.3	**88.9**
beam	0.1	**0.3**	0	0	0	0	0
column	3.9	17.6	6	34.1	23.9	**38**	37.6
window	46.3	22.8	**69.5**	48.9	58	63.4	64.1
door	10.8	62.1	63.5	62.4	69	**74.3**	73.8
table	59	74.4	66.9	81.6	81.5	**89.1**	88.4
chair	52.6	80.6	65.6	89.8	91	82.4	85.4
sofa	5.9	31.7	47.3	47.2	**75.4**	74.3	73.5
bookcase	40.3	66.7	68.9	74.9	75.3	80.2	**82.7**
board	26.4	62.1	59.1	74.4	66.7	**76**	74.7
clutter	33.2	56.7	46.2	58.6	58.9	59.3	**60.1**
mIoU	41.1	57.3	58.3	65.4	67.1	70.4	**70.9**

performs better than point-only [31], convolution-based [21] and transformer-based [57] methods. Some visualized results are posted in Fig. 7(a) while the visualized quantitative comparison between HilbertNet and other methods can be found in Fig. 7(b), in which HilbertNet shows better performance.

Inference Speed. Since our model is trained using both 3D and 1D data, we compare our model with a similar design such as PVCNN [24] for a fair comparison. Additionally, we propose HilbertNet-M (median) and HilbertNet-L(light) during the experiment. HilbertNet-M has $0.5 \times C$ and HilbertNet-L has $0.25 \times C$, where C is the channel number of the features in HilbertNet. We also adopt a pure 3D model 3D-UNet [26] as the baseline and all the models are trained and tested on GTX TITAN X GPU. These models are trained using the identical setting as shown in their paper and ShapeNetPart is applied as our benchmark. The inference speed comparisons are listed in Table 2. It can be found that our model has a higher mIoU than PVCNN with comparable inference speed.

Next, we compare Hilbert attention with 3D convolution, 2D convolution, sparse 2D convolution and non-local attention in the perspective of FLOPs and GPU Memory usage. For a fair comparison, the kernel size for 2D and 3D convolution is set to 4 with 2 paddings. The result can be found in Table 3. It shows that Hilbert attention is more light-weighted than 3D convolution and also faster than 2D convolution and sparse 2D convolution. Moreover, Hilbert attention is much memory-saving than NonLocal attention.

4.3 Ablation Study

In this part, we conduct a set of ablation studies in the perspective of the flattening method, gathering method, pooling method, and convolution method to evaluate the influence of each module in our model. The ModelNet40 dataset is used during the ablation study.

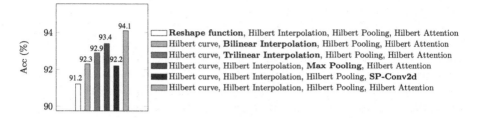

Fig. 8. Ablation study results of HilbertNet. The label refers to: **Flattening Method, Gathering Method, Pooling Method, Convolution Method**.

Hilbert Curve vs. Reshape Function. Our design is based on the Hilbert curve, due to its better locality preserving property compared with other space filling curves such as reshape function. As shown in column 1 and column 6 in Fig. 8, we make a comparison to evaluate different flattening methods. Here we simply replace all the Hilbert curve $\mathcal{H}_n(s)$ in HilbertNet with reshape function including Hilbert interpolation, Hilbert pooling, and Hilbert attention. It can be found that the Hilbert curve achieves the higher accuracy (94.1% vs. 91.2 %), which further illustrates its advantage over reshape function.

Hilbert Interpolation vs. Linear Interpolation. In this experiment, we conduct Bilinear interpolation, Trilinear interpolation (see Eq. (6)) and Hilbert interpolation to test the performance of these voxel feature gathering methods. The results in columns 2, 3, 6 of Fig. 8 show that Hilbert interpolation has an obvious advantage over the other methods. This is because Hilbert interpolation not only applies Hilbert curve, which has a better locality but also enhances the non-empty part in grid data.

Hilbert Pooling vs. 2D Max Pooling. Max pooling is a common technique for 2D feature downsizing and it has been widely used in 2D convolutional networks [13,37,39]. However, the 2D featuremap $\mathcal{I}$ in our design is obtained via 3D flattening, which makes 2D max pooling not feasible for HilbertNet. Therefore we design Hilbert pooling and we compare the performance of it with regular max pooling. The results in columns 4 and 6 of Fig. 8 demonstrate that our proposed Hilbert pooling module is more suitable for handling data that is flattened by Hilbert curve.

Hilbert Attention vs. 2D Convolution. In this part, We simply replace the Hilbert attention with 4×4 sparse 2D convolution. The result can be found in columns 5 and 6 of Fig. 8. This result demonstrates that Hilbert attention plays a crucial role in exploring spatial information across 2D flattened voxels.

5   Conclusion

In this paper, we propose a novel framework for efficient and effective point cloud analysis, that is, introducing Hilbert curve to reduce the dimension of volumetric data, preserving spatial locality and topology, and using 2D convolutions for processing, bypassing the cumbersome 3D convolutions. Based on the proposed Hilbert curve flattening methods, we design the two-branch based HilbertNet, which copes with 1D sequences and 2D slices respectively, and fuses these two views together. Additionally, we propose two useful local feature harvesting modules and one light-weighted attention for exploring the cross-slice context information. Our proposed method is proved to be efficient and effective in point cloud classification and segmentation tasks.

References

1. Armeni, I., Sener, O., Zamir, A.R., Jiang, H., Brilakis, I., Fischer, M., Savarese, S.: 3D semantic parsing of large-scale indoor spaces. In: Proceedings of the IEEE Conference on Computer vision and Pattern Recognition, pp. 1534–1543 (2016)
2. Balkić, Z., Šoštarić, D., Horvat, G.: GeoHash and UUID identifier for multi-agent systems. In: Jezic, G., Kusek, M., Nguyen, N.-T., Howlett, R.J., Jain, L.C. (eds.) KES-AMSTA 2012. LNCS (LNAI), vol. 7327, pp. 290–298. Springer, Heidelberg (2012). https://doi.org/10.1007/978-3-642-30947-2_33
3. Bauman, K.E.: The dilation factor of the peano-hilbert curve. Math. Notes **80**(5), 609–620 (2006)
4. Chang, A.X., et al.: Shapenet: an information-rich 3d model repository. arXiv preprint arXiv:1512.03012 (2015)
5. Chen, Y., Kalantidis, Y., Li, J., Yan, S., Feng, J.: A 2 Nets: double attention networks. In: Proceedings of the NIPS, pp. 352–361 (2018)
6. Choy, C., Gwak, J., Savarese, S.: 4d spatio-temporal convnets: Minkowski convolutional neural networks. In: Proceedings of the IEEE/CVF Conference on Computer Vision and Pattern Recognition, pp. 3075–3084 (2019)
7. Cong, P., Zhu, X., Ma, Y.: Input-output balanced framework for long-tailed lidar semantic segmentation. In: 2021 IEEE International Conference on Multimedia and Expo (ICME), pp. 1–6 (2021)
8. Esteves, C., Xu, Y., Allen-Blanchette, C., Daniilidis, K.: Equivariant multi-view networks. In: Proceedings of the IEEE/CVF International Conference on Computer Vision, pp. 1568–1577 (2019)
9. Faloutsos, C.: Multiattribute hashing using gray codes. In: Proceedings of the 1986 ACM SIGMOD International Conference on Management of Data, pp. 227–238 (1986)
10. Feng, Y., Zhang, Z., Zhao, X., Ji, R., Gao, Y.: GVCNN: group-view convolutional neural networks for 3D shape recognition. In: Proceedings of the IEEE Conference on Computer Vision and Pattern Recognition, pp. 264–272 (2018)
11. Graham, B., van der Maaten, L.: Submanifold sparse convolutional networks. arXiv preprint arXiv:1706.01307 (2017)
12. Guo, M.H., Cai, J.X., Liu, Z.N., Mu, T.J., Martin, R.R., Hu, S.M.: PCT: point cloud transformer. arXiv preprint arXiv:2012.09688 (2020)
13. He, K., Zhang, X., Ren, S., Sun, J.: Deep residual learning for image recognition. In: Proceedings of the CVPR, pp. 770–778 (2016)
14. Hilbert, D.: Über die stetige abbildung einer linie auf ein flächenstück. In: Dritter Band: Analysis· Grundlagen der Mathematik· Physik Verschiedenes, pp. 1–2. Springer, Heidelberg (1935). https://doi.org/10.1007/978-3-662-38452-7_1

15. Hou, Y., Zhu, X., Ma, Y., Loy, C.C., Li, Y.: Point-to-voxel knowledge distillation for lidar semantic segmentation. ArXiv:abs/2206.02099 (2022)
16. Hu, J., Shen, L., Sun, G.: Squeeze-and-excitation networks. In: Proceedings of the CVPR, pp. 7132–7141 (2018)
17. Kingma, D.P., Ba, J.: Adam: a method for stochastic optimization. In: Proceedings of the ICLR (2015)
18. Klokov, R., Lempitsky, V.: Escape from cells: deep KD-networks for the recognition of 3D point cloud models. In: ICCV, pp. 863–872 (2017)
19. Li, J., Chen, B.M., Lee, G.H.: SO-Net: self-organizing network for point cloud analysis. In: Proceedings of the CVPR (2018)
20. Li, J., Chen, B.M., Lee, G.H.: So-net: self-organizing network for point cloud analysis. In: CVPR, pp. 9397–9406 (2018)
21. Li, Y., Bu, R., Sun, M., Wu, W., Di, X., Chen, B.: PointCNN: convolution on X-transformed points. In: Proceedings of the NIPS, pp. 820–830 (2018)
22. Liang, J.Y., Chen, C.S., Huang, C.H., Liu, L.: Lossless compression of medical images using hilbert space-filling curves. Comput. Med. Imaging Graph. **32**(3), 174–182 (2008)
23. Lin, Z.H., Huang, S.Y., Wang, Y.C.F.: Convolution in the cloud: learning deformable kernels in 3D graph convolution networks for point cloud analysis. In: CVPR, pp. 1800–1809 (2020)
24. Liu, Z., Tang, H., Lin, Y., Han, S.: Point-voxel CNN for efficient 3D deep learning. arXiv preprint arXiv:1907.03739 (2019)
25. Milioto, A., Vizzo, I., Behley, J., Stachniss, C.: Rangenet++: fast and accurate lidar semantic segmentation. In: IROS, pp. 4213–4220. IEEE (2019)
26. Milletari, F., Navab, N., Ahmadi, S.A.: V-net: fully convolutional neural networks for volumetric medical image segmentation. In: 2016 Fourth International Conference on 3D Vision (3DV), pp. 565–571. IEEE (2016)
27. Mokbel, M.F., Aref, W.G., Kamel, I.: Analysis of multi-dimensional space-filling curves. GeoInformatica **7**(3), 179–209 (2003)
28. Orenstein, J.A.: Spatial query processing in an object-oriented database system. In: Proceedings of the 1986 ACM SIGMOD International Conference on Management of Data, pp. 326–336 (1986)
29. Paszke, A., et al.: Automatic differentiation in PyTorch. In: NIPS Workshop (2017)
30. Pumarola, A., Popov, S., Moreno-Noguer, F., Ferrari, V.: C-flow: conditional generative flow models for images and 3D point clouds. In: CVPR, pp. 7949–7958 (2020)
31. Qi, C.R., Su, H., Mo, K., Guibas, L.J.: Pointnet: deep learning on point sets for 3D classification and segmentation. In: CVPR, pp. 652–660 (2017)
32. Qi, C.R., Su, H., Nießner, M., Dai, A., Yan, M., Guibas, L.J.: Volumetric and multi-view CNNs for object classification on 3D data. In: Proceedings of the IEEE Conference on Computer Vision and Pattern Recognition, pp. 5648–5656 (2016)
33. Qi, C.R., Su, H., Nießner, M., Dai, A., Yan, M., Guibas, L.J.: Volumetric and multi-view CNNs for object classification on 3D data. In: CVPR, pp. 5648–5656 (2016)
34. Qi, C.R., Yi, L., Su, H., Guibas, L.J.: Pointnet++: deep hierarchical feature learning on point sets in a metric space. arXiv preprint arXiv:1706.02413 (2017)
35. Sagan, H.: Space-Filling Curves. Springer, New York (2012)
36. Samet, H.: Applications of spatial data structures: computer graphics, image processing, and GIS. Addison-Wesley Longman Publishing Co., Inc. (1990)
37. Simonyan, K., Zisserman, A.: Very deep convolutional networks for large-scale image recognition. In: Proceedings of the ICLR, pp. 1–14 (2015)

38. Su, H., Maji, S., Kalogerakis, E., Learned-Miller, E.: Multi-view convolutional neural networks for 3D shape recognition. In: ICCV, pp. 945–953 (2015)
39. Szegedy, C., et al.: Going deeper with convolutions. In: Proceedings of the CVPR, pp. 1–9 (2015)
40. Thomas, H., Qi, C.R., Deschaud, J.E., Marcotegui, B., Goulette, F., Guibas, L.J.: KPConv: flexible and deformable convolution for point clouds. In: ICCV, pp. 6411–6420 (2019)
41. Wang, J., Shan, J.: Space filling curve based point clouds index. In: Proceedings of the 8th International Conference on GeoComputation, pp. 551–562. Citeseer (2005)
42. Wang, P.S., Liu, Y., Guo, Y.X., Sun, C.Y., Tong, X.: O-CNN: octree-based convolutional neural networks for 3d shape analysis. ACM Trans. Graphics (TOG) **36**(4), 1–11 (2017)
43. Wang, S., Suo, S., Ma, W.C., Pokrovsky, A., Urtasun, R.: Deep parametric continuous convolutional neural networks. In: Proceedings of the IEEE Conference on Computer Vision and Pattern Recognition, pp. 2589–2597 (2018)
44. Wang, X., Girshick, R., Gupta, A., He, K.: Non-local neural networks. In: Proceedings of the CVPR, pp. 7794–7803 (2018)
45. Wang, Y., Sun, Y., Liu, Z., Sarma, S.E., Bronstein, M.M., Solomon, J.M.: Dynamic graph CNN for learning on point clouds. TOG **38**(5), 1–12 (2019)
46. Woo, S., Park, J., Lee, J.-Y., Kweon, I.S.: CBAM: convolutional block attention module. In: Ferrari, V., Hebert, M., Sminchisescu, C., Weiss, Y. (eds.) ECCV 2018. LNCS, vol. 11211, pp. 3–19. Springer, Cham (2018). https://doi.org/10.1007/978-3-030-01234-2_1
47. Wu, B., Wan, A., Yue, X., Keutzer, K.: SqueezeSeg: convolutional neural nets with recurrent CRF for real-time road-object segmentation from 3D lidar point cloud. In: ICRA, pp. 1887–1893. IEEE (2018)
48. Wu, W., Qi, Z., Fuxin, L.: Pointconv: deep convolutional networks on 3D point clouds. In: CVPR, pp. 9621–9630 (2019)
49. Wu, Z., et al.: 3D shapenets: a deep representation for volumetric shapes. In: CVPR, pp. 1912–1920 (2015)
50. Xiang, T., Zhang, C., Song, Y., Yu, J., Cai, W.: Walk in the cloud: learning curves for point clouds shape analysis. arXiv preprint arXiv:2105.01288 (2021)
51. Xu, C., et al.: Image2point: 3D point-cloud understanding with pretrained 2D convnets. arXiv preprint arXiv:2106.04180 (2021)
52. Xu, Q., Sun, X., Wu, C.Y., Wang, P., Neumann, U.: Grid-GCN for fast and scalable point cloud learning. In: CVPR, pp. 5661–5670 (2020)
53. Yan, X., Zheng, C., Li, Z., Wang, S., Cui, S.: PointASNL: robust point clouds processing using nonlocal neural networks with adaptive sampling. In: CVPR, pp. 5589–5598 (2020)
54. Ye, M., Xu, S., Cao, T., Chen, Q.: DRINet: a dual-representation iterative learning network for point cloud segmentation. In: Proceedings of the IEEE/CVF International Conference on Computer Vision, pp. 7447–7456 (2021)
55. Zhang, S., He, X., Yan, S.: LatentGNN: learning efficient non-local relations for visual recognition. In: Proceedings of the ICML, pp. 7374–7383 (2019)
56. Zhang, Y., et al.: PolarNet: an improved grid representation for online lidar point clouds semantic segmentation. In: CVPR, pp. 9601–9610 (2020)
57. Zhao, H., Jiang, L., Jia, J., Torr, P.H., Koltun, V.: Point transformer. In: Proceedings of the IEEE/CVF International Conference on Computer Vision, pp. 16259–16268 (2021)

58. Zhao, L., Zhou, H., Zhu, X., Song, X., Li, H., Tao, W.: Lif-seg: lidar and camera image fusion for 3D lidar semantic segmentation. ArXiv abs/2108.07511 (2021)

59. Zhao, Q., et al.: Rethinking the zigzag flattening for image reading. arXiv preprint arXiv:2202.10240 (2022)

60. Zhou, H., et al.: Cylinder3D: an effective 3d framework for driving-scene lidar semantic segmentation. arXiv preprint arXiv:2008.01550 (2020)

61. Zhou, Y., Tuzel, O.: VoxelNet: end-to-end learning for point cloud based 3d object detection. In: CVPR, pp. 4490–4499 (2018)

62. Zhu, X., et al.: Cylindrical and asymmetrical 3D convolution networks for lidar-based perception. IEEE Trans. Pattern Anal. Mach. Intell. **44**, 6807–6822 (2021)

63. Zhu, X., et al.: Cylindrical and asymmetrical 3D convolution networks for lidar segmentation. In: CVPR, pp. 9934–9943 (2021)

Author Index

Printed in the United States
by Baker & Taylor Publisher Services